T0180299

Lecture Notes in Computer Science 9909

Commenced Publication in 1973
Founding and Former Series Editors:
Gerhard Goos, Juris Hartmanis, and Jan van Leeuwen

More information about this series at http://www.springer.com/series/7412

Bastian Leibe · Jiri Matas
Nicu Sebe · Max Welling (Eds.)

Computer Vision – ECCV 2016

14th European Conference
Amsterdam, The Netherlands, October 11–14, 2016
Proceedings, Part V

 Springer

Editors
Bastian Leibe
RWTH Aachen
Aachen
Germany

Jiri Matas
Czech Technical University
Prague 2
Czech Republic

Nicu Sebe
University of Trento
Povo - Trento
Italy

Max Welling
University of Amsterdam
Amsterdam
The Netherlands

ISSN 0302-9743   ISSN 1611-3349   (electronic)
Lecture Notes in Computer Science
ISBN 978-3-319-46453-4   ISBN 978-3-319-46454-1   (eBook)
DOI 10.1007/978-3-319-46454-1

Library of Congress Control Number: 2016951693

LNCS Sublibrary: SL6 – Image Processing, Computer Vision, Pattern Recognition, and Graphics

Printed on acid-free paper

This Springer imprint is published by Springer Nature
The registered company is Springer International Publishing AG
The registered company address is: Gewerbestrasse 11, 6330 Cham, Switzerland

Foreword

Welcome to the proceedings of the 2016 edition of the European Conference on Computer Vision held in Amsterdam! It is safe to say that the European Conference on Computer Vision is one of the top conferences in computer vision. It is good to reiterate the history of the conference to see the broad base the conference has built in its 13 editions. First held in 1990 in Antibes (France), it was followed by subsequent conferences in Santa Margherita Ligure (Italy) in 1992, Stockholm (Sweden) in 1994, Cambridge (UK) in 1996, Freiburg (Germany) in 1998, Dublin (Ireland) in 2000, Copenhagen (Denmark) in 2002, Prague (Czech Republic) in 2004, Graz (Austria) in 2006, Marseille (France) in 2008, Heraklion (Greece) in 2010, Florence (Italy) in 2012, and Zürich (Switzerland) in 2014.

For the 14th edition, many people worked hard to provide attendees with a most warm welcome while enjoying the best science. The Program Committee, Bastian Leibe, Jiri Matas, Nicu Sebe, and Max Welling, did an excellent job. Apart from the scientific program, the workshops were selected and handled by Hervé Jégou and Gang Hua, and the tutorials by Jacob Verbeek and Rita Cucchiara. Thanks for the great job. The coordination with the subsequent ACM Multimedia offered an opportunity to expand the tutorials with an additional invited session, offered by the University of Amsterdam and organized together with the help of ACM Multimedia.

Of the many people who worked hard as local organizers, we would like to single out Martine de Wit of the UvA Conference Office, who delicately and efficiently organized the main body. Also the local organizers Hamdi Dibeklioglu, Efstratios Gavves, Jan van Gemert, Thomas Mensink, and Mihir Jain had their hands full. As a venue, we chose the Royal Theatre Carré located on the canals of the Amstel River in downtown Amsterdam. Space in Amsterdam is sparse, so it was a little tighter than usual. The university lent us their downtown campuses for the tutorials and the workshops. A relatively new thing was the industry and the sponsors for which Ronald Poppe and Peter de With did a great job, while Andy Bagdanov and John Schavemaker arranged the demos. Michael Wilkinson took care to make Yom Kippur as comfortable as possible for those for whom it is an important day. We thank Marc Pollefeys, Alberto del Bimbo, and Virginie Mes for their advice and help behind the scenes. We thank all the anonymous volunteers for their hard and precise work. We also thank our generous sponsors. Their support is an essential part of the program. It is good to see such a level of industrial interest in what our community is doing!

Amsterdam does not need any introduction. Please emerge yourself but do not drown in it, have a nice time.

October 2016

Theo Gevers
Arnold Smeulders

Preface

Welcome to the proceedings of the 2016 European Conference on Computer Vision (ECCV 2016) held in Amsterdam, The Netherlands. We are delighted to present this volume reflecting a strong and exciting program, the result of an extensive review process. In total, we received 1,561 paper submissions. Of these, 81 violated the ECCV submission guidelines or did not pass the plagiarism test and were rejected without review. We employed the iThenticate software (www.ithenticate.com) for plagiarism detection. Of the remaining papers, 415 were accepted (26.6 %): 342 as posters (22.6 %), 45 as spotlights (2.9 %), and 28 as oral presentations (1.8 %). The spotlights – short, five-minute podium presentations – are novel to ECCV and were introduced after their success at the CVPR 2016 conference. All orals and spotlights are presented as posters as well. The selection process was a combined effort of four program co-chairs (PCs), 74 area chairs (ACs), 1,086 Program Committee members, and 77 additional reviewers.

As PCs, we were primarily responsible for the design and execution of the review process. Beyond administrative rejections, we were involved in acceptance decisions only in the very few cases where the ACs were not able to agree on a decision. PCs, as is customary in the field, were not allowed to co-author a submission. General co-chairs and other co-organizers played no role in the review process, were permitted to submit papers, and were treated as any other author.

Acceptance decisions were made by two independent ACs. There were 74 ACs, selected by the PCs according to their technical expertise, experience, and geographical diversity (41 from European, five from Asian, two from Australian, and 26 from North American institutions). The ACs were aided by 1,086 Program Committee members to whom papers were assigned for reviewing. There were 77 additional reviewers, each supervised by a Program Committee member. The Program Committee was selected from committees of previous ECCV, ICCV, and CVPR conferences and was extended on the basis of suggestions from the ACs and the PCs. Having a large pool of Program Committee members for reviewing allowed us to match expertise while bounding reviewer loads. Typically five papers, but never more than eight, were assigned to a Program Committee member. Graduate students had a maximum of four papers to review.

The ECCV 2016 review process was in principle double-blind. Authors did not know reviewer identities, nor the ACs handling their paper(s). However, anonymity becomes difficult to maintain as more and more submissions appear concurrently on arXiv.org. This was not against the ECCV 2016 double submission rules, which followed the practice of other major computer vision conferences in the recent past. The existence of arXiv publications, mostly not peer-reviewed, raises difficult problems with the assessment of unpublished, concurrent, and prior art, content overlap, plagiarism, and self-plagiarism. Moreover, it undermines the anonymity of submissions. We found that not all cases can be covered by a simple set of rules. Almost all controversies during the review process were related to the arXiv issue. Most of the reviewer inquiries were resolved by giving the benefit of the doubt to ECCV authors. However, the problem will have to be discussed by the community so that consensus is found on how to handle the issues brought by publishing on arXiv.

Particular attention was paid to handling conflicts of interest. Conflicts of interest between ACs, Program Committee members, and papers were identified based on the authorship of ECCV 2016 submissions, on the home institutions, and on previous collaborations of all researchers involved. To find institutional conflicts, all authors, Program Committee members, and ACs were asked to list the Internet domains of their current institutions. To find collaborators, the Researcher.cc database (http://researcher.cc/), funded by the Computer Vision Foundation, was used to find any co-authored papers in the period 2012–2016. We pre-assigned approximately 100 papers to each AC, based on affinity scores from the Toronto Paper Matching System. ACs then bid on these, indicating their level of expertise. Based on these bids, and conflicts of interest, approximately 40 papers were assigned to each AC. The ACs then suggested seven reviewers from the pool of Program Committee members for each paper, in ranked order, from which three were chosen automatically by CMT (Microsofts Academic Conference Management Service), taking load balancing and conflicts of interest into account.

The initial reviewing period was five weeks long, after which reviewers provided reviews with preliminary recommendations. With the generous help of several last-minute reviewers, each paper received three reviews. Submissions with all three reviews suggesting rejection were independently checked by two ACs and if they agreed, the manuscript was rejected at this stage ("early rejects"). In total, 334 manuscripts (22.5 %) were early-rejected, reducing the average AC load to about 30.

Authors of the remaining submissions were then given the opportunity to rebut the reviews, primarily to identify factual errors. Following this, reviewers and ACs discussed papers at length, after which reviewers finalized their reviews and gave a final recommendation to the ACs. Each manuscript was evaluated independently by two ACs who were not aware of each others, identities. In most of the cases, after extensive discussions, the two ACs arrived at a common decision, which was always adhered to by the PCs. In the very few borderline cases where an agreement was not reached, the PCs acted as tie-breakers. Owing to the rapid expansion of the field, which led to an unexpectedly large increase in the number of submissions, the size of the venue became a limiting factor and a hard upper bound on the number of accepted papers had to be imposed. We were able to increase the limit by replacing one oral session by a poster session. Nevertheless, this forced the PCs to reject some borderline papers that could otherwise have been accepted.

We want to thank everyone involved in making the ECCV 2016 possible. First and foremost, the success of ECCV 2016 depended on the quality of papers submitted by the authors, and on the very hard work of the ACs, the Program Committee members, and the additional reviewers. We are particularly grateful to Rene Vidal for his continuous support and sharing experience from organizing ICCV 2015, to Laurent Charlin for the use of the Toronto Paper Matching System, to Ari Kobren for the use of the Researcher.cc tools, to the Computer Vision Foundation (CVF) for facilitating the use of the iThenticate plagiarism detection software, and to Gloria Zen and Radu-Laurentiu Vieriu for setting up CMT and managing the various tools involved. We also owe a debt of gratitude for the support of the Amsterdam local organizers, especially Hamdi Dibeklioglu for keeping the website always up to date. Finally, the preparation of these proceedings would not have been possible without the diligent effort of the publication chairs, Albert Ali Salah and Robby Tan, and of Anna Kramer from Springer.

October 2016

Bastian Leibe
Jiri Matas
Nicu Sebe
Max Welling

Organization

General Chairs

Theo Gevers   University of Amsterdam, The Netherlands
Arnold Smeulders   University of Amsterdam, The Netherlands

Program Committee Co-chairs

Bastian Leibe   RWTH Aachen, Germany
Jiri Matas   Czech Technical University, Czech Republic
Nicu Sebe   University of Trento, Italy
Max Welling   University of Amsterdam, The Netherlands

Honorary Chair

Jan Koenderink   Delft University of Technology, The Netherlands
and KU Leuven, Belgium

Advisory Program Chair

Luc van Gool   ETH Zurich, Switzerland

Advisory Workshop Chair

Josef Kittler   University of Surrey, UK

Advisory Conference Chair

Alberto del Bimbo   University of Florence, Italy

Local Arrangements Chairs

Hamdi Dibeklioglu   Delft University of Technology, The Netherlands
Efstratios Gavves   University of Amsterdam, The Netherlands
Jan van Gemert   Delft University of Technology, The Netherlands
Thomas Mensink   University of Amsterdam, The Netherlands
Michael Wilkinson   University of Groningen, The Netherlands

Workshop Chairs

Hervé Jégou   Facebook AI Research, USA
Gang Hua   Microsoft Research Asia, China

Tutorial Chairs

Jacob Verbeek   Inria Grenoble, France
Rita Cucchiara   University of Modena and Reggio Emilia, Italy

Poster Chairs

Jasper Uijlings   University of Edinburgh, UK
Roberto Valenti   Sightcorp, The Netherlands

Publication Chairs

Albert Ali Salah   Boğaziçi University, Turkey
Robby T. Tan   Yale-NUS College and National University
                               of Singapore, Singapore

Video Chair

Mihir Jain   University of Amsterdam, The Netherlands

Demo Chairs

John Schavemaker   Twnkls, The Netherlands
Andy Bagdanov   University of Florence, Italy

Social Media Chair

Efstratios Gavves   University of Amsterdam, The Netherlands

Industrial Liaison Chairs

Ronald Poppe   Utrecht University, The Netherlands
Peter de With   Eindhoven University of Technology, The Netherlands

Conference Coordinator, Accommodation, and Finance

Conference Office
Martine de Wit   University of Amsterdam, The Netherlands
Melanie Venverloo   University of Amsterdam, The Netherlands
Niels Klein   University of Amsterdam, The Netherlands

Area Chairs

Radhakrishna Achanta	Ecole Polytechnique Fédérale de Lausanne, Switzerland
Antonis Argyros	FORTH and University of Crete, Greece
Michael Bronstein	Universitá della Svizzera Italiana, Switzerland
Gabriel Brostow	University College London, UK
Thomas Brox	University of Freiburg, Germany
Barbara Caputo	Sapienza University of Rome, Italy
Miguel Carreira-Perpinan	University of California, Merced, USA
Ondra Chum	Czech Technical University, Czech Republic
Daniel Cremers	Technical University of Munich, Germany
Rita Cucchiara	University of Modena and Reggio Emilia, Italy
Trevor Darrell	University of California, Berkeley, USA
Andrew Davison	Imperial College London, UK
Fernando de la Torre	Carnegie Mellon University, USA
Piotr Dollar	Facebook AI Research, USA
Vittorio Ferrari	University of Edinburgh, UK
Charless Fowlkes	University of California, Irvine, USA
Jan-Michael Frahm	University of North Carolina at Chapel Hill, USA
Mario Fritz	Max Planck Institute, Germany
Pascal Fua	Ecole Polytechnique Fédérale de Lausanne, Switzerland
Juergen Gall	University of Bonn, Germany
Peter Gehler	University of Tübingen — Max Planck Institute, Germany
Andreas Geiger	Max Planck Institute, Germany
Ross Girshick	Facebook AI Research, USA
Kristen Grauman	University of Texas at Austin, USA
Abhinav Gupta	Carnegie Mellon University, USA
Hervé Jégou	Facebook AI Research, USA
Fredrik Kahl	Lund University, Sweden
Iasonas Kokkinos	Ecole Centrale Paris, France
Philipp Krähenbühl	University of California, Berkeley, USA
Pawan Kumar	University of Oxford, UK
Christoph Lampert	Institute of Science and Technology Austria, Austria
Hugo Larochelle	Université de Sherbrooke, Canada
Neil Lawrence	University of Sheffield, UK
Svetlana Lazebnik	University of Illinois at Urbana-Champaign, USA
Honglak Lee	Stanford University, USA
Kyoung Mu Lee	Seoul National University, Republic of Korea
Vincent Lepetit	Graz University of Technology, Austria
Hongdong Li	Australian National University, Australia
Julien Mairal	Inria, France
Yasuyuki Matsushita	Osaka University, Japan
Nassir Navab	Technical University of Munich, Germany

Sebastian Nowozin	Microsoft Research, Cambridge, UK
Tomas Pajdla	Czech Technical University, Czech Republic
Maja Pantic	Imperial College London, UK
Devi Parikh	Virginia Tech, USA
Thomas Pock	Graz University of Technology, Austria
Elisa Ricci	FBK Technologies of Vision, Italy
Bodo Rosenhahn	Leibniz-University of Hannover, Germany
Stefan Roth	Technical University of Darmstadt, Germany
Carsten Rother	Technical University of Dresden, Germany
Silvio Savarese	Stanford University, USA
Bernt Schiele	Max Planck Institute, Germany
Konrad Schindler	ETH Zürich, Switzerland
Cordelia Schmid	Inria, France
Cristian Sminchisescu	Lund University, Sweden
Noah Snavely	Cornell University, USA
Sabine Süsstrunk	Ecole Polytechnique Fédérale de Lausanne, Switzerland
Qi Tian	University of Texas at San Antonio, USA
Antonio Torralba	Massachusetts Institute of Technology, USA
Zhuowen Tu	University of California, San Diego, USA
Raquel Urtasun	University of Toronto, Canada
Joost van de Weijer	Universitat Autònoma de Barcelona, Spain
Laurens van der Maaten	Facebook AI Research, USA
Nuno Vasconcelos	University of California, San Diego, USA
Andrea Vedaldi	University of Oxford, UK
Xiaogang Wang	Chinese University of Hong Kong, Hong Kong, SAR China
Jingdong Wang	Microsoft Research Asia, China
Lior Wolf	Tel Aviv University, Israel
Ying Wu	Northwestern University, USA
Dong Xu	University of Sydney, Australia
Shuicheng Yan	National University of Singapore, Singapore
MingHsuan Yang	University of California, Merced, USA
Ramin Zabih	Cornell NYC Tech, USA
Larry Zitnick	Facebook AI Research, USA

Technical Program Committee

Austin Abrams	Pulkit Agrawal	Andrea Albarelli
Supreeth Achar	Jorgen Ahlberg	Alexandra Albu
Tameem Adel	Haizhou Ai	Saad Ali
Khurrum Aftab	Zeynep Akata	Daniel Aliaga
Lourdes Agapito	Ijaz Akhter	Marina Alterman
Sameer Agarwal	Karteek Alahari	Hani Altwaijry
Aishwarya Agrawal	Xavier Alameda-Pineda	Jose M. Alvarez

Mitsuru Ambai
Mohamed Amer
Senjian An
Cosmin Ancuti
Juan Andrade-Cetto
Marco Andreetto
Elli Angelopoulou
Relja Arandjelovic
Helder Araujo
Pablo Arbelaez
Chetan Arora
Carlos Arteta
Kalle Astroem
Nikolay Atanasov
Vassilis Athitsos
Mathieu Aubry
Yannis Avrithis
Hossein Azizpour
Artem Babenko
Andrew Bagdanov
Yuval Bahat
Xiang Bai
Lamberto Ballan
Arunava Banerjee
Adrian Barbu
Nick Barnes
Peter Barnum
Jonathan Barron
Adrien Bartoli
Dhruv Batra
Eduardo
    Bayro-Corrochano
Jean-Charles Bazin
Paul Beardsley
Vasileios Belagiannis
Ismail Ben Ayed
Boulbaba Benamor
Abhijit Bendale
Rodrigo Benenson
Fabian Benitez-Quiroz
Ohad Ben-Shahar
Dana Berman
Lucas Beyer
Subhabrata Bhattacharya
Binod Bhattarai
Arnav Bhavsar

Simone Bianco
Hakan Bilen
Horst Bischof
Tom Bishop
Arijit Biswas
Soma Biswas
Marten Bjoerkman
Volker Blanz
Federica Bogo
Xavier Boix
Piotr Bojanowski
Terrance Boult
Katie Bouman
Thierry Bouwmans
Edmond Boyer
Yuri Boykov
Hakan Boyraz
Steven Branson
Mathieu Bredif
Francois Bremond
Stefan Breuers
Michael Brown
Marcus Brubaker
Luc Brun
Andrei Bursuc
Zoya Bylinskii
Daniel Cabrini Hauagge
Deng Cai
Jianfei Cai
Simone Calderara
Neill Campbell
Octavia Camps
Liangliang Cao
Xiaochun Cao
Xun Cao
Gustavo Carneiro
Dan Casas
Tom Cashman
Umberto Castellani
Carlos Castillo
Andrea Cavallaro
Jan Cech
Ayan Chakrabarti
Rudrasis Chakraborty
Krzysztof Chalupka
Tat-Jen Cham

Antoni Chan
Manmohan Chandraker
Sharat Chandran
Hong Chang
Hyun Sung Chang
Jason Chang
Ju Yong Chang
Xiaojun Chang
Yu-Wei Chao
Visesh Chari
Rizwan Chaudhry
Rama Chellappa
Bo Chen
Chao Chen
Chao-Yeh Chen
Chu-Song Chen
Hwann-Tzong Chen
Lin Chen
Mei Chen
Terrence Chen
Xilin Chen
Yunjin Chen
Guang Chen
Qifeng Chen
Xinlei Chen
Jian Cheng
Ming-Ming Cheng
Anoop Cherian
Guilhem Cheron
Dmitry Chetverikov
Liang-Tien Chia
Naoki Chiba
Tat-Jun Chin
Margarita Chli
Minsu Cho
Sunghyun Cho
TaeEun Choe
Jongmoo Choi
Seungjin Choi
Wongun Choi
Wen-Sheng Chu
Yung-Yu Chuang
Albert Chung
Gokberk Cinbis
Arridhana Ciptadi
Javier Civera

James Clark
Brian Clipp
Michael Cogswell
Taco Cohen
Toby Collins
John Collomosse
Camille Couprie
David Crandall
Marco Cristani
James Crowley
Jinshi Cui
Yin Cui
Jifeng Dai
Qieyun Dai
Shengyang Dai
Yuchao Dai
Zhenwen Dai
Dima Damen
Kristin Dana
Kostas Danilidiis
Mohamed Daoudi
Larry Davis
Teofilo de Campos
Marleen de Bruijne
Koichiro Deguchi
Alessio Del Bue
Luca del Pero
Antoine Deleforge
Hervé Delingette
David Demirdjian
Jia Deng
Joachim Denzler
Konstantinos Derpanis
Frederic Devernay
Hamdi Dibeklioglu
Santosh Kumar Divvala
Carl Doersch
Weisheng Dong
Jian Dong
Gianfranco Doretto
Alexey Dosovitskiy
Matthijs Douze
Bruce Draper
Tom Drummond
Shichuan Du
Jean-Luc Dugelay

Enrique Dunn
Zoran Duric
Pinar Duygulu
Alexei Efros
Carl Henrik Ek
Jan-Olof Eklundh
Jayan Eledath
Ehsan Elhamifar
Ian Endres
Aykut Erdem
Anders Eriksson
Sergio Escalera
Victor Escorcia
Francisco Estrada
Bin Fan
Quanfu Fan
Chen Fang
Tian Fang
Masoud Faraki
Ali Farhadi
Giovanni Farinella
Ryan Farrell
Raanan Fattal
Michael Felsberg
Jiashi Feng
Michele Fenzi
Andras Ferencz
Basura Fernando
Sanja Fidler
Mario Figueiredo
Michael Firman
Robert Fisher
John Fisher III
Alexander Fix
Boris Flach
Matt Flagg
Francois Fleuret
Wolfgang Foerstner
David Fofi
Gianluca Foresti
Per-Erik Forssen
David Fouhey
Jean-Sebastien Franco
Friedrich Fraundorfer
Oren Freifeld
Simone Frintrop

Huazhu Fu
Yun Fu
Jan Funke
Brian Funt
Ryo Furukawa
Yasutaka Furukawa
Andrea Fusiello
David Gallup
Chuang Gan
Junbin Gao
Jochen Gast
Stratis Gavves
Xin Geng
Bogdan Georgescu
David Geronimo
Bernard Ghanem
Riccardo Gherardi
Golnaz Ghiasi
Soumya Ghosh
Andrew Gilbert
Ioannis Gkioulekas
Georgia Gkioxari
Guy Godin
Roland Goecke
Boqing Gong
Shaogang Gong
Yunchao Gong
German Gonzalez
Jordi Gonzalez
Paulo Gotardo
Stephen Gould
Venu M. Govindu
Helmut Grabner
Etienne Grossmann
Chunhui Gu
David Gu
Sergio Guadarrama
Li Guan
Matthieu Guillaumin
Jean-Yves Guillemaut
Guodong Guo
Ruiqi Guo
Yanwen Guo
Saurabh Gupta
Pierre Gurdjos
Diego Gutierrez

Abner Guzman Rivera
Christian Haene
Niels Haering
Ralf Haeusler
David Hall
Peter Hall
Onur Hamsici
Dongfeng Han
Mei Han
Xufeng Han
Yahong Han
Ankur Handa
Kenji Hara
Tatsuya Harada
Mehrtash Harandi
Bharath Hariharan
Tal Hassner
Soren Hauberg
Michal Havlena
Tamir Hazan
Junfeng He
Kaiming He
Lei He
Ran He
Xuming He
Zhihai He
Felix Heide
Janne Heikkila
Jared Heinly
Mattias Heinrich
Pierre Hellier
Stephane Herbin
Isabelle Herlin
Alexander Hermans
Anders Heyden
Adrian Hilton
Vaclav Hlavac
Minh Hoai
Judy Hoffman
Steven Hoi
Derek Hoiem
Seunghoon Hong
Byung-Woo Hong
Anthony Hoogs
Yedid Hoshen
Winston Hsu

Changbo Hu
Wenze Hu
Zhe Hu
Gang Hua
Dong Huang
Gary Huang
Heng Huang
Jia-Bin Huang
Kaiqi Huang
Qingming Huang
Rui Huang
Xinyu Huang
Weilin Huang
Zhiwu Huang
Ahmad Humayun
Mohamed Hussein
Wonjun Hwang
Juan Iglesias
Nazli Ikizler-Cinbis
Evren Imre
Eldar Insafutdinov
Catalin Ionescu
Go Irie
Hossam Isack
Phillip Isola
Hamid Izadinia
Nathan Jacobs
Varadarajan Jagannadan
Aastha Jain
Suyog Jain
Varun Jampani
Jeremy Jancsary
C.V. Jawahar
Dinesh Jayaraman
Ian Jermyn
Hueihan Jhuang
Hui Ji
Qiang Ji
Jiaya Jia
Kui Jia
Yangqing Jia
Hao Jiang
Tingting Jiang
Yu-Gang Jiang
Zhuolin Jiang
Alexis Joly

Shantanu Joshi
Frederic Jurie
Achuta Kadambi
Samuel Kadoury
Yannis Kalantidis
Amit Kale
Sebastian Kaltwang
Joni-Kristian Kamarainen
George Kamberov
Chandra Kambhamettu
Martin Kampel
Kenichi Kanatani
Atul Kanaujia
Melih Kandemir
Zhuoliang Kang
Mohan Kankanhalli
Abhishek Kar
Leonid Karlinsky
Andrej Karpathy
Zoltan Kato
Rei Kawakami
Kristian Kersting
Margret Keuper
Nima Khademi Kalantari
Sameh Khamis
Fahad Khan
Aditya Khosla
Hadi Kiapour
Edward Kim
Gunhee Kim
Hansung Kim
Jae-Hak Kim
Kihwan Kim
Seon Joo Kim
Tae Hyun Kim
Tae-Kyun Kim
Vladimir Kim
Benjamin Kimia
Akisato Kimura
Durk Kingma
Thomas Kipf
Kris Kitani
Martin Kleinsteuber
Laurent Kneip
Kevin Koeser
Effrosyni Kokiopoulou

Ajmal Mian
Tomer Michaeli
Ondrej Miksik
Anton Milan
Erik Miller
Gregor Miller
Majid Mirmehdi
Ishan Misra
Anurag Mittal
Daisuke Miyazaki
Hossein Mobahi
Pascal Monasse
Sandino Morales
Vlad Morariu
Philippos Mordohai
Francesc Moreno-Noguer
Greg Mori
Bryan Morse
Roozbeh Mottaghi
Yadong Mu
Yasuhiro Mukaigawa
Lopamudra Mukherjee
Joseph Mundy
Mario Munich
Ana Murillo
Vittorio Murino
Naila Murray
Damien Muselet
Sobhan Naderi Parizi
Hajime Nagahara
Nikhil Naik
P.J. Narayanan
Fabian Nater
Jan Neumann
Ram Nevatia
Shawn Newsam
Bingbing Ni
Juan Carlos Niebles
Jifeng Ning
Ko Nishino
Masashi Nishiyama
Shohei Nobuhara
Ifeoma Nwogu
Peter Ochs
Jean-Marc Odobez
Francesca Odone

Iason Oikonomidis
Takeshi Oishi
Takahiro Okabe
Takayuki Okatani
Carl Olsson
Vicente Ordonez
Ivan Oseledets
Magnus Oskarsson
Martin R. Oswald
Matthew O'Toole
Wanli Ouyang
Andrew Owens
Mustafa Ozuysal
Jason Pacheco
Manohar Paluri
Gang Pan
Jinshan Pan
Yannis Panagakis
Sharath Pankanti
George Papandreou
Hyun Soo Park
In Kyu Park
Jaesik Park
Seyoung Park
Omkar Parkhi
Ioannis Patras
Viorica Patraucean
Genevieve Patterson
Vladimir Pavlovic
Kim Pedersen
Robert Peharz
Shmuel Peleg
Marcello Pelillo
Otavio Penatti
Xavier Pennec
Federico Pernici
Adrian Peter
Stavros Petridis
Vladimir Petrovic
Tomas Pfister
Justus Piater
Pedro Pinheiro
Bernardo Pires
Fiora Pirri
Leonid Pishchulin
Daniel Pizarro

Robert Pless
Tobias Pltz
Yair Poleg
Gerard Pons-Moll
Jordi Pont-Tuset
Ronald Poppe
Andrea Prati
Jan Prokaj
Daniel Prusa
Nicolas Pugeault
Guido Pusiol
Guo-Jun Qi
Gang Qian
Yu Qiao
Novi Quadrianto
Julian Quiroga
Andrew Rabinovich
Rahul Raguram
Srikumar Ramalingam
Deva Ramanan
Narayanan Ramanathan
Vignesh Ramanathan
Sebastian Ramos
Rene Ranftl
Anand Rangarajan
Avinash Ravichandran
Ramin Raziperchikolaei
Carlo Regazzoni
Christian Reinbacher
Michal Reinstein
Emonet Remi
Fabio Remondino
Shaoqing Ren
Zhile Ren
Jerome Revaud
Hayko Riemenschneider
Tobias Ritschel
Mariano Rivera
Patrick Rives
Antonio Robles-Kelly
Jason Rock
Erik Rodner
Emanuele Rodola
Mikel Rodriguez
Antonio
    Rodriguez Sanchez

Gregory Rogez
Marcus Rohrbach
Javier Romero
Matteo Ronchi
German Ros
Charles Rosenberg
Guy Rosman
Arun Ross
Paolo Rota
Samuel Rota Bulò
Peter Roth
Volker Roth
Brandon Rothrock
Anastasios Roussos
Amit Roy-Chowdhury
Ognjen Rudovic
Daniel Rueckert
Christian Rupprecht
Olga Russakovsky
Bryan Russell
Emmanuel Sabu
Fereshteh Sadeghi
Hideo Saito
Babak Saleh
Mathieu Salzmann
Dimitris Samaras
Conrad Sanderson
Enver Sangineto
Aswin Sankaranarayanan
Imari Sato
Yoichi Sato
Shin'ichi Satoh
Torsten Sattler
Bogdan Savchynskyy
Yann Savoye
Arman Savran
Harpreet Sawhney
Davide Scaramuzza
Walter Scheirer
Frank Schmidt
Uwe Schmidt
Dirk Schnieders
Johannes Schönberger
Florian Schroff
Samuel Schulter
William Schwartz

Alexander Schwing
Stan Sclaroff
Nicu Sebe
Ari Seff
Anita Sellent
Giuseppe Serra
Laura Sevilla-Lara
Shishir Shah
Greg Shakhnarovich
Qi Shan
Shiguang Shan
Jing Shao
Ling Shao
Xiaowei Shao
Roman Shapovalov
Nataliya Shapovalova
Ali Sharif Razavian
Gaurav Sharma
Pramod Sharma
Viktoriia Sharmanska
Eli Shechtman
Alexander Shekhovtsov
Evan Shelhamer
Chunhua Shen
Jianbing Shen
Li Shen
Xiaoyong Shen
Wei Shen
Yu Sheng
Jianping Shi
Qinfeng Shi
Yonggang Shi
Baoguang Shi
Kevin Shih
Nobutaka Shimada
Ilan Shimshoni
Koichi Shinoda
Takaaki Shiratori
Jamie Shotton
Matthew Shreve
Abhinav Shrivastava
Nitesh Shroff
Leonid Sigal
Nathan Silberman
Tomas Simon
Edgar Simo-Serra

Dheeraj Singaraju
Gautam Singh
Maneesh Singh
Richa Singh
Saurabh Singh
Vikas Singh
Sudipta Sinha
Josef Sivic
Greg Slabaugh
William Smith
Patrick Snape
Jan Sochman
Kihyuk Sohn
Hyun Oh Song
Jingkuan Song
Qi Song
Shuran Song
Xuan Song
Yale Song
Yi-Zhe Song
Alexander
    Sorkine Hornung
Humberto Sossa
Aristeidis Sotiras
Richard Souvenir
Anuj Srivastava
Nitish Srivastava
Michael Stark
Bjorn Stenger
Rainer Stiefelhagen
Martin Storath
Joerg Stueckler
Hang Su
Hao Su
Jingyong Su
Shuochen Su
Yu Su
Ramanathan Subramanian
Yusuke Sugano
Akihiro Sugimoto
Libin Sun
Min Sun
Qing Sun
Yi Sun
Chen Sun
Deqing Sun

Ganesh Sundaramoorthi
Jinli Suo
Supasorn Suwajanakorn
Tomas Svoboda
Chris Sweeney
Paul Swoboda
Raza Syed Hussain
Christian Szegedy
Yuichi Taguchi
Yu-Wing Tai
Hugues Talbot
Toru Tamaki
Mingkui Tan
Robby Tan
Xiaoyang Tan
Masayuki Tanaka
Meng Tang
Siyu Tang
Ran Tao
Dacheng Tao
Makarand Tapaswi
Jean-Philippe Tarel
Camillo Taylor
Christian Theobalt
Diego Thomas
Rajat Thomas
Xinmei Tian
Yonglong Tian
YingLi Tian
Yonghong Tian
Kinh Tieu
Joseph Tighe
Radu Timofte
Massimo Tistarelli
Sinisa Todorovic
Giorgos Tolias
Federico Tombari
Akihiko Torii
Andrea Torsello
Du Tran
Quoc-Huy Tran
Rudolph Triebel
Roberto Tron
Leonardo Trujillo
Eduard Trulls
Tomasz Trzcinski

Yi-Hsuan Tsai
Gavriil Tsechpenakis
Chourmouzios Tsiotsios
Stavros Tsogkas
Kewei Tu
Shubham Tulsiani
Tony Tung
Pavan Turaga
Matthew Turk
Tinne Tuytelaars
Oncel Tuzel
Georgios Tzimiropoulos
Norimichi Ukita
Osman Ulusoy
Martin Urschler
Arash Vahdat
Michel Valstar
Ernest Valveny
Jan van Gemert
Kiran Varanasi
Mayank Vatsa
Javier Vazquez-Corral
Ramakrishna Vedantam
Ashok Veeraraghavan
Olga Veksler
Jakob Verbeek
Francisco Vicente
Rene Vidal
Jordi Vitria
Max Vladymyrov
Christoph Vogel
Carl Vondrick
Sven Wachsmuth
Toshikazu Wada
Catherine Wah
Jacob Walker
Xiaolong Wang
Wei Wang
Limin Wang
Liang Wang
Hua Wang
Lijun Wang
Naiyan Wang
Xinggang Wang
Yining Wang
Baoyuan Wang

Chaohui Wang
Gang Wang
Heng Wang
Lei Wang
Linwei Wang
Liwei Wang
Ping Wang
Qi Wang
Qian Wang
Shenlong Wang
Song Wang
Tao Wang
Yang Wang
Yu-Chiang Frank Wang
Zhaowen Wang
Simon Warfield
Yichen Wei
Philippe Weinzaepfel
Longyin Wen
Tomas Werner
Aaron Wetzler
Yonatan Wexler
Michael Wilber
Kyle Wilson
Thomas Windheuser
David Wipf
Paul Wohlhart
Christian Wolf
Kwan-Yee Kenneth Wong
John Wright
Jiajun Wu
Jianxin Wu
Tianfu Wu
Yang Wu
Yi Wu
Zheng Wu
Stefanie Wuhrer
Jonas Wulff
Rolf Wurtz
Lu Xia
Tao Xiang
Yu Xiang
Lei Xiao
Yang Xiao
Tong Xiao
Wenxuan Xie

Lingxi Xie	Xianghua Ying	Shiliang Zhang
Pengtao Xie	Kuk-Jin Yoon	Lei Zhang
Saining Xie	Chong You	Xiaoqin Zhang
Yuchen Xie	Aron Yu	Shanshan Zhang
Junliang Xing	Felix Yu	Ting Zhang
Bo Xiong	Fisher Yu	Bin Zhao
Fei Xiong	Lap-Fai Yu	Rui Zhao
Jia Xu	Stella Yu	Yibiao Zhao
Yong Xu	Jing Yuan	Enliang Zheng
Tianfan Xue	Junsong Yuan	Wenming Zheng
Toshihiko Yamasaki	Lu Yuan	Yinqiang Zheng
Takayoshi Yamashita	Xiao-Tong Yuan	Yuanjie Zheng
Junjie Yan	Alan Yuille	Yin Zheng
Rong Yan	Xenophon Zabulis	Wei-Shi Zheng
Yan Yan	Stefanos Zafeiriou	Liang Zheng
Keiji Yanai	Sergey Zagoruyko	Dingfu Zhou
Jian Yang	Amir Zamir	Wengang Zhou
Jianchao Yang	Andrei Zanfir	Tinghui Zhou
Jiaolong Yang	Mihai Zanfir	Bolei Zhou
Jie Yang	Lihi Zelnik-Manor	Feng Zhou
Jimei Yang	Xingyu Zeng	Huiyu Zhou
Michael Ying Yang	Josiane Zerubia	Jun Zhou
Ming Yang	Changshui Zhang	Kevin Zhou
Ruiduo Yang	Cheng Zhang	Kun Zhou
Yi Yang	Guofeng Zhang	Xiaowei Zhou
Angela Yao	Jianguo Zhang	Zihan Zhou
Cong Yao	Junping Zhang	Jun Zhu
Jian Yao	Ning Zhang	Jun-Yan Zhu
Jianhua Yao	Quanshi Zhang	Zhenyao Zhu
Jinwei Ye	Shaoting Zhang	Zeeshan Zia
Shuai Yi	Tianzhu Zhang	Henning Zimmer
Alper Yilmaz	Xiaoqun Zhang	Karel Zimmermann
Lijun Yin	Yinda Zhang	Wangmeng Zuo
Zhaozheng Yin	Yu Zhang	

Additional Reviewers

Felix Achilles	Dan Andrei Calian	Jimmy Chen
Sarah Adel Bargal	Lilian Calvet	Melissa Cote
Hessam Bagherinezhad	Federico Camposeco	Berkan Demirel
Qinxun Bai	Olivier Canevet	Zhiwei Deng
Gedas Bertasius	Anirban Chakraborty	Guy Gilboa
Michal Busta	Yu-Wei Chao	Albert Gordo
Erik Bylow	Sotirios Chatzis	Daniel Gordon
Marinella Cadoni	Tatjana Chavdarova	Ankur Gupta

Kun He
Yang He
Daniel Holtmann-Rice
Xun Huang
Liang Hui
Drew Jaegle
Cijo Jose
Marco Karrer
Mehran Khodabandeh
Anna Khoreva
Hyo-Jin Kim
Theodora Kontogianni
Pengpeng Liang
Shugao Ma
Ludovic Magerand
Francesco Malapelle
Julio Marco
Vlad Morariu

Rajitha Navarathna
Junhyuk Oh
Federico Perazzi
Marcel Piotraschke
Srivignesh Rajendran
Joe Redmon
Helge Rhodin
Anna Rohrbach
Beatrice Rossi
Wolfgang Roth
Pietro Salvagnini
Hosnieh Sattar
Ana Serrano
Zhixin Shu
Sven Sickert
Jakub Simanek
Ramprakash Srinivasan
Oren Tadmor

Xin Tao
Lucas Teixeira
Mårten Wädenback
Qing Wang
Yaser Yacoob
Takayoshi Yamashita
Huiyuan Yang
Ryo Yonetani
Sejong Yoon
Shaodi You
Xu Zhan
Jianming Zhang
Richard Zhang
Xiaoqun Zhang
Xu Zhang
Zheng Zhang

Contents – Part V

Action, Activity and Tracking

Poster Session 6

Poster Session 5 (Continued)

Image Quality Assessment Using Similar Scene as Reference

Yudong Liang, Jinjun Wang$^{(\boxtimes)}$, Xingyu Wan, Yihong Gong,
and Nanning Zheng

Institute of Artificial Intelligence and Robotics,
Xi'an Jiaotong University, Xi'an, China
{liangyudong,wanxingyu}@stu.xjtu.edu.cn,
{jinjun,ygong,nnzheng}@mail.xjtu.edu.cn

Abstract. Most of Image Quality Assessment (IQA) methods require
the reference image to be pixel-wise aligned with the distorted image,
and thus limiting the application of reference image based IQA methods. In this paper, we show that non-aligned image with similar scene
could be well used for reference, using a proposed Dual-path deep Convolutional Neural Network (DCNN). Analysis indicates that the model
captures the scene structural information and non-structural information "naturalness" between the pair for quality assessment. As shown in
the experiments, our proposed DCNN model handles the IQA problem
well. With an aligned reference image, our predictions outperform many
state-of-the-art methods. And in more general case where the reference
image contains the similar scene but is not aligned with the distorted one,
DCNN could still achieve superior consistency with subjective evaluation
than many existing methods that even use aligned reference images.

Keywords: Image Quality Assessment · Similar scene referenced
image · Structural similarity · "Naturalness" · Dual-path Deep Convolution Neural Network

1   Introduction

Assessing the quality of a distorted image would benefit from the availability of a
reference image. As revealed in [1], human are more skilled at comparing images
than making direct judgement of the image quality. Accordingly, human can
evaluate the quality of an image more accurately and consistently when provided
with a high-quality reference image, and meanwhile human may give different
quality scores to the same image if different reference images are presented [2].
The situation is the same for Image Quality Assessment (IQA) algorithms, where
methods that make use of reference images could achieve better consistency with

Electronic supplementary material The online version of this chapter (doi:10.
1007/978-3-319-46454-1_1) contains supplementary material, which is available to
authorized users.

© Springer International Publishing AG 2016
B. Leibe et al. (Eds.): ECCV 2016, Part V, LNCS 9909, pp. 3–18, 2016.
DOI: 10.1007/978-3-319-46454-1_1

Fig. 1. Using non-aligned images with similar scene as quality reference. *Original images (top), distorted images (middle) and reference images (bottom) that are only similar to but is neither aligned with nor related by any geometrical transformation with the distorted images*

subjective assessments than those that do not consider references [3,4]. Based on whether and how reference images are used, existing IQA methods could be broadly categorized into the following three groups: full reference (FR) IQA methods [2,3,5,6], reduced referenced (RR) IQA methods [7,8], and no reference (NR) IQA methods [9,10]. The former two groups, *i.e.*,the FR-IQA and the RR-IQA methods groups, take advantage of complete or partial information of the reference image respectively, while the NR-IQA methods are often designed to extract discriminative features [9,10] or to calculate natural scene statistics to qualify the image quality [11]. As explained above, FR-IQA methods often achieve more consistent assessment as human.

However, one strong assumption with most FR-IQA methods is that, the reference image must be pixel-wise aligned with the distorted image for assessment. The requirement could be satisfied if the task is, *e.g.* to measure the quality of JPEG 2000 (JP2K) compression. Unfortunately, in more general scenario, the imaging process that generates the distorted image and the reference image may not produce aligned pair. For instance, a cell phone camera may capture a photo with hand-shake, and it is difficult to then capture an aligned high-quality image as reference. An image enhancement module on an automatic vehicle can improve a low-quality capture of the road but to assess the performance of the enhancement, it is impossible to put the vehicle at the same position to shot a pixel-aligned picture for reference. In both these common scenarios, only NR-IQA method could be used to assess the quality of the distorted images.

In this paper, we are interested in whether the image quality could be assessed using a reference image with similar scene but is not aligned, as illustrated in Fig. 1. We term the problem as NAR-IQA (Non-aligned Reference IQA).

Studies in Human Visual System (HVS) have shown that, HVS presents different sensitivity to different image signals such as spatial frequency [4], luminance [12], structural information [5], etc. Among all these features, the success of the SSIM [5] metric and its extension [13] indicates that measuring the scene structural information does benefit IQA. In addition, the visual attention property [12,14], or well known as saliency [15], tells that human usually pays attention only to a smaller but representative part of the scene, and therefore it is reasonable to assume that, if the reference image contains the same scene structure as the distorted image, it can still be used to evaluate the quality of the distorted one. Unfortunately, limited literature is available for NAR-IQA approaches. One example is the CW-SSIM [16] method that attempts using reference image with small affine transformation (scale, rotation and translation) to assess the quality of medical and binary images, which performs unsatisfactory for natural images as observed in our experiments.

This has motivated us to design a Dual-path deep Convolutional Neural Network (DCNN) for image quality assessment, using reference image of similar scene but not necessarily aligned. The two paths take the distorted image and the reference image respectively. Through weight sharing between paths, the same kind of features are extracted at the lower stage of the model. At the final stage, the proposed model concatenates features from both paths, and then a regressor is used to predict the image quality score.

Experimental results first validate that, the NAR-IQA problem is solvable where in case a pixel-wise aligned reference image is not available, a non-aligned image with similar scene can be well used as reference. In addition, our proposed model handles the IQA problem well. As explained above, the FR-IQA problem can be regarded as a special case of the NAR-IQA problem where an aligned reference image is given to the model. In this case, our predicted image quality scores are more consistent with subjective evaluations than many state-of-the-art methods. In more general case, i.e.,the NAR-IQA problem, our model could still achieve superior consistency than many existing methods that even use aligned reference images. Hence, while there are previous works that attempted IQA with small geometrical transformation between the reference and the distorted images [16], to the best of our knowledge, our work is the first to support IQA from reference image with similar scene but is not aligned, such that reference images become obtainable for more IQA applications.

2   Related Work

A large body of FR-IQA methods has been proposed to judge the quality of distorted images by considering reference images. Most of the approaches in this line require the reference image to be strictly aligned with the distorted images. Simple error sensitivity metrics such as the Mean Square Error (MSE) or the Peak Signal-to-Noise Ratio (PSNR) compare local pixel difference between the reference image and the distorted image, but in general the evaluation does not correlate well with human assessment. The SSIM [5] method modeled the structural information inspired by HVS for quality judgement and could achieve more consistent evaluation as human. Wang et al.[13] further combined multiscale information to improve the situation. Zhang et al. [3] carefully designed the phase congruency and gradient magnitude as complementary features of FSIM for IQA. Different from FR-IQA methods, the RR-IQA methods [7,8] focus on utilizing only parts of the reference image information to accomplish the assessment. In general, FR-IQA and RR-IQA mimic different sensitivity of HVS to different image signals [2,17], including spatial frequency, luminance [12], structural information [5] etc. to devise metric for IQA. As explained before, most FR or RR-IQA methods are extremely sensitive to small geometrical misalignment between the reference and the distorted images, which severely limits their applications.

It is worth noting that, the CW-SSIM [16] algorithm in the FR-IQA class was designed to handle very small scale, rotation and translation changes between the distorted image and the reference. On the other side, since natural images have more variations in frequency domains, in practice, the CW-SSIM method seems to perform well only for medical and binary images but poor for more general cases such as photos, surveillance footage and natural images.

Since aligned reference images are not always available, NR-IQA methods [9,10] have aroused extensive interests. Focus of most NR-IQA methods is to obtain discriminate features, and nowadays many NR-IQA algorithms are based on set of training data to learn such feature rather than proposing handcrafted ones. e.g., the CORNIA [10] method learned codebooks from local image patches to encode features, and then regressor was trained to predict the quality of a distorted image. Kang et al.utilized CNN, a most popular model in the deep learning domain that has recently show excellent performance on visual feature learning [18], to learn features for NR-IQA [9] and achieved impressive result that approaches the state-of-the-art FR-IQA performance. This has motivated us to also apply deep learning technology for feature learning in the stated NAR-IQA problem. As demonstrated in our experiment, under the FR-IQA scenario, our predicted image quality score is more consistent with subjective evaluation than many state-of-the-art methods, and in the NAR-IQA scenario, our model still achieves superior consistency than many existing FR-IQA methods. The next section depicts our approach.

3   IQA with Non-aligned Reference

The wide availability of images from mobile phones, webcam, camcorder and Internet provides possibility to alleviate the non-existence problem of reference images for IQA. In most cases, however, reference images obtained in this way may or may not pixel aligned with the distorted image, or the two are not related by any geometrical transformation, as illustrated in Fig. 1. Hence in this section we want to propose a model that could make use of such type of reference. The model does not loose the capacity of existing FR-IQA methods but further supports the NAR-IQA problem. The proposed model is presented in the following subsection.

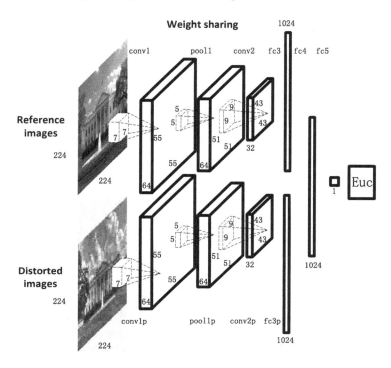

Fig. 2. The proposed Dual-path deep Convolutional Neural Network (DCNN)

3.1   Dual-Path Deep Convolutional Neural Network

We present a Dual-path deep Convolutional Neural Network (DCNN) to accept two channels of inputs and output one image quality score.

To use the proposed DCNN for NAR-IQA, we first decompose the input distorted image and the reference image into multiple standard 224×224 sub-images (Note that since input pair is not aligned, these sub-images are not necessarily aligned), then each pair of sub-images is fed to the model to obtain an quality score, and finally the overall image quality score takes the average score of all pairs of that image. The architecture of our proposed DCNN model is illustrated in Fig. 2. It consists of the convolutional layer, the nonlinear rectified linear unit, the pooling layer, the concat layer and the full connection layer, denoted as *conv#*, *relu#*, *pool#*, *concat#* and *fc#* respectively. The configuration of DCNN is listed in Table 1.

3.2   Layers

The *conv* layers are trained to extract local features. In a recursive fashion, denoting A_i^j as the feature map of path i in the jth layer, W_j and B_j as the weight and bias parameters of the jth layer, then the local information is extracted into deeper layers by Eq. (1), where $*$ denotes the calculation of convolution.

Table 1. Configuration of DCNN for NAR-IQA

Layer name	Padding	Filter size/stride	Output size
$input1$	0		$224 \times 224 \times 3$
$conv1 \ / \ conv1\text{p}$	0	$7 \times 7/4$	$64 \times 55 \times 55$
$relu1 \ / \ relu1\text{p}$			$64 \times 55 \times 55$
$pool1 \ / \ pool1\text{p}$ (MAX)		$5 \times 5/1$	$64 \times 51 \times 51$
$conv2 \ / \ conv2\text{p}$	0	$9 \times 9/1$	$32 \times 43 \times 43$
$relu2 \ / \ relu2\text{p}$			$32 \times 43 \times 43$
$fc3 \ / \ fc3\text{p}$			1024
$concat$	concatenating the features from $fc3$ and $fc3\text{p}$		
$fc4$			1024
$fc5$			1
Euc			1

$$A_i^{j+1} = W_j * A_i^j + B_j, \tag{1}$$

In order to make comparison between the distorted and the reference images, we want to extract the same type of features for the two paths. Thus a weight sharing strategy is applied in the dual paths. Besides, to increases the nonlinear properties and accelerates training, the activation function is selected to be *relu* as follows: $A_i^{j+1} = max(0, A_i^j)$

Another important issue for NAR-IQA is to compensate the offset between similar scene content from the distorted image and the reference image. The *pool* layers are exploited for the purpose by integrating features from a larger local receptive field. Both [9,10] proposed to use max and min pooling over an entire feature map to align the response. Although both works achieved impressive results, these two methods abandoned the structural information which is valuable for IQA problem. Our model considers a rather large sub-image (224×224, Table 1), and we integrate the information from local to global as the network goes deeper. For computational efficiency, max-pooling is applied as Eq. (2), where R is the pooling region of corresponding position.

$$A_i^{j+1} = \max_R A_i^j \tag{2}$$

The *concat* layer concatenates the features from the both paths. Then with the $fc\#$ layer, discriminative features are further combined and mapped to generate image quality assessment in a linear regressor.

Finally, the image quality score is predicted by minimizing the following Euclidean loss,

$$\min_{W,B} \ ||\big(f(I_{ref}, I_{dis}); W, B\big) - Eva||^2 \tag{3}$$

where I_{ref}, I_{dis} and Eva are the input sub reference, distorted images and human evaluations respectively, W, B are the parameters of convolutional and fc layers.

3.3 Preprocessing

Different from traditional IQA methods which need carefully designed hand-crafted features, our proposed DCNN model learns discriminative features from raw data to maximally preserve information from image. Only simple local contrast normalization is needed to ensure numeric stability. The process can also be understood as a data whiten process where the intensity value of pixel $I(x, y)$ is normalized as [9],

$$I(x, y)_N = \frac{I(x, y) - u(x, y)}{\sigma(x, y) + \epsilon}$$

$$u(x, y) = \sum_{a=\frac{-P}{2}}^{a=\frac{P}{2}} \sum_{b=\frac{-Q}{2}}^{b=\frac{Q}{2}} (I(x + a, y + b))$$

$$\sigma(x, y) = \sqrt{\sum_{a=\frac{-P}{2}}^{a=\frac{P}{2}} \sum_{b=\frac{-Q}{2}}^{b=\frac{Q}{2}} (I(x + a, y + b) - u(x, y))^2} \tag{4}$$

where $I(x, y)_N$ denotes values at image location (x, y) normalized by pixels in a neighboring $(P \times Q)$ window, and ϵ is a small positive constant. Although intensity shift and contrast variation sometimes were considered to be distortion, it is highly subjective to judge the image quality for distortion with these type. And we mainly deal with image distortion from degradation. Thus, Eq. (4) was applied for the input.

3.4 Training

DCNN can be trained using stochastic gradient descent with the standard back-propagation [18]. In particular, the weights of the filters of the *conv* or *fc* layer can be updated as Eq. (5)

$$\triangle_{i+1} = m \cdot \triangle_i - \eta \frac{\partial L}{\partial W_i^j}$$

$$W_{i+1}^j = W_i^j + \triangle_{i+1} - \lambda \eta W_i^j \tag{5}$$

where m is the momentum factors, η is the learning rate, j is index of the layer and $\triangle_{i+1}$ is the gradient increment for training iteration i. λ is the weight decay factor. Momentum factor and weight decay factor were fixed in 0.9 and 0.0005 respectively in the following experiments.

3.5 Discussion

The architecture of the proposed model focuses on extracting features and to avoid pixel-wise aligned. This is achievable at deeper layers that integrate information from different receptive fields of earlier layers. The convolution, pooling and other nonlinear operations capture structural information from the local to the global area without explicit pixel-wise alignment, and therefore make the model geometrical robust. Also regarding the final $fc\#$ layers, they behave much more complicated than simple element-wise subtractions. $fc\#$ layers have obtained weights to not only gauge the image distortion from pairs but also ignore the feature disagreement from two paths caused by nonalignment. All the distorted samples have different image contents (such as affine variations) from the reference counterpart, thus image contents are not discriminative.

This has made the architecture and key design strategy of our proposed DCNN model very different from the well-known Siamese [19] model, which has been widely used in face verification [20]. Siamese network use contrastive loss for classification while our dual path CNN (original for IQA problem) is based on Euclidean distance to perform regression. Since our proposed model focus on regression rather than classification, in our DCNN, the mapping from the concatenated features to the image quality score is automatically learned during the training process.

4   Experiment

In this section, we report a series of experiments to validate the effectiveness of the proposed model. The Deep learning toolbox Caffe [21] was applied to built the DCNN model for IQA. Three datasets were adopted in the experiments: The LIVE dataset, the TID2008 dataset and an in-house collected dataset.

Note that since the reference images are aligned with the corresponding distorted images, in order to train and test our proposed DCNN for NAR-IQA, we synthesized the non-aligned reference image by applying affine transform to the original reference image, as nonaligned ref images preserve structures with affine transformation. The scaling factors $s\#$ and rotation θ were randomly ranged from [0.95 1.05] and [$-5°5°$] respectively. As shown in Fig. 3, a pair of training samples are collected as follows: for each reference image that is aligned with the distorted image, first we affine transform it as shown in Fig. 3 left column.

Non-aligned
reference image   Distorted
image

Fig. 3. Nonaligned training samples (Color figure online)

Then from within the border, we randomly sample multiple 224×224 sub-images from both the transformed reference image and the distorted image, cantering at the same coordinates. As can be seen from Fig. 3 middle column, the red box and the blue box correspond to one pair of sub-image for training, and the content in the red box and the blue box are similar but not aligned. Finally we collected hundred thousand pairs of samples for training our proposed DCNN model. A stride of 20 has been applied to extract sub images. The same strategy was applied for both the LIVE and the TID2008 datasets, where 80 % of the data was used for training, and the rest for testing. The performance is comparable when sub images are smaller, *e.g.* 32×32. For succinctness, we omit the experiments with smaller sub images. The next subsection reports the overall performance.

4.1   Overall NAR-IQA Performance

LIVE dataset consists of 779 distorted images with one of the following distortion types: JP2k compression(JP2K), JPEG compression(JPEG), White Gaussian(WN), Gaussian blur(BLUR) and Fast Fading(FF) derived from 29 reference images. The subjective evaluations give the Differential Mean Opinion Scores (DMOS) for each of the distorted images. To compare the performance of different IQA methods, we calculated the correlation of the predicted score with the ground-truth DMOS score, and higher correlation indicates better consistency with human assessment, and thus better performance. Specifically, two widely applied correlation criterions were applied in our experiment: Linear Correlation Coefficient (LCC) and Spearman Rank Order Correlation Coefficient (SROCC). LCC reveals the linear dependence between two quantities, and SROCC measures how well the relationship between two variables can be described using a monotonic function.

The results are listed in Table 2, where we further compared with the following benchmarks: FSIM [3], PSNR and SSIM [5] that are FR-IQA methods, and CNN-NR [9], BRISQUE [11] and CORNIA [10] that are NR-IQA methods. We trained and tested the proposed DCNN with the original reference image (FR-DCNN) and also with the affine transformed reference image (NAR-DCNN). As training the CNN is time and storage consuming, we randomly selected 80 % training images of dataset five times. The results of Tables 2 and 3 appeared in the paper is the median evaluation. We found our architecture was rather robust to data splitting.

Table 2. LCC and SROCC score for the LIVE dataset

	FSIM	PSNR	SSIM	BRISQUE	CNN-NR	CORNIA	FR-DCNN	NAR-DCNN	CNN-NR-d
LCC	0.960	0.856	0.906	0.942	0.953	0.935	**0.977**	0.976	0.968
SROCC	0.964	0.866	0.913	0.940	0.956	0.942	**0.975**	**0.975**	0.967

As can be seen from Table 2, when applying our proposed DCNN for FR-IQA, the obtained LCC and SROCC score both achieved best consistency with subjection evaluation. In the NAR-IQA case, our DCNN model outperformed all the listed benchmark methods, and was only slightly worse than the FR-IQA case.

It is important to also study whether the performance gain comes from the use of deep architecture or through the use of a non-aligned reference image. Hence we used one path of DCNN and add $fc\#$ as well as a regression layer to construct a image quality assessment model. Such model is termed as CNN-NR-d. It applied exactly the same parameters in Table 1. In Tables 2 and 3, we compared the performance of CNN-NR-d to a reported NR-IQA method, the CNN-NR [9] method, as well as our FR-DCNN and NAR-DCNN models. According to the results, we can conclude that, CNN-NR-d did perform better than CNN-NR [9] which shows that DCNN was able to capture more discriminative feature to describe the scene. In addition, the performance of either the FR-DCNN and NAR-DCNN further outperformed CNN-NR-d, which tells that a reference, either aligned or non-aligned, has clearly provided helpful information for IQA.

TID2008 dataset consists of 1700 distorted images derived from 25 reference images. The subjective evaluations give the Mean Opinion Score (MOS) for each of the distorted images. There are 4 types of distortions that are common to the LIVE dataset: JPEG2000, JPEG, WN and GB. These types were considered in our experiments as in many previous works [9,22,23]. Some performances were cited from the published paper, which were tested in a slight different way with an logistic regression. As shown in Table 3, DCNN achieved best consistency with subjection evaluation for the FR-IQA problem, and got comparable performance in the NAR-IQA problem.

Table 3. LCC and SROCC score for the TID2008 dataset

	FSIM	PSNR	SSIM	BRISQUE	CNN-NR	CORNIA	FR-DCNN	NAR-DCNN	CNN-NR-d
LCC	0.926	0.836	0.893	0.892	0.903	0.880	**0.955**	0.941	0.920
SROCC	0.947	0.870	0.902	0.882	0.920	0.890	**0.954**	0.937	0.921

In-house dataset consists of 1050 distorted images derived from 21 high quality images. Each of the 21 image has a reference image that contains similar scene but is not related with the distorted image under any known geometrical transformation. The distorted images deteriorated in the same way that LIVE dataset [24] generated five types of distortion images. Basically, the readme attached with Live dataset was followed. For FF distortion, some adjustments were made as readme of generating FF are difficult to follow. Each distortion type has a same number of distorted images for each reference image on In-house dataset. All the reference and similar reference images were downloaded from Internet with Google or Flickr by searching same keywords, for example "road".

Five of the images are presented in Fig. 1. As can be seen, the scenes between each pair are similar but actually contain different contents. Compared to the previous two datasets that used synthesized non-aligned reference image, the in-house dataset was collected with more realistic setup for the NAR-IQA problem. Specifically, to collect one pair of data, we first collected two high-quality images denoted as I_A and I_B respectively, and then we downgraded I_A to I_A^*. In order to obtain a ground-truth quality score for I_A^*, we used our FR-DCNN method to predict an image quality score for I_A^*, and the score was then regarded as the ground-truth score to evaluate various NAR-IQA and NR-IQA methods. We have also applied the strategy but with the FSIM method to generate another set of ground-truth score. For this strict NAR-IQA setup, we compared with the FSIM method of similar scene reference images, and the results are listed in Table 4. Larger DMOS but smaller FSIM indicates worse image quality, thus the sign of results in Table 4 just indicates anti-correlation or correlation and was ignored. The NAR-DCNN model in Table 2 which were trained with affine transformed image pairs were utilized for experiments of In-house dataset in Tables 4 and 6.

Table 4. LCC and SROCC score for the in-house dataset

GT by FRDCNN	NAR-DCNN	CNN-NR-d	CORNIA	BRISQUE	DIIVINE	NAR-FSIM
LCC	**0.893**	0.880	0.856	0.753	0.737	0.174
SROCC	**0.892**	0.872	0.864	0.756	0.746	0.157
GT by FSIM	NAR-DCNN	CNN-NR-d	CORNIA	BRISQUE	DIIVINE	NAR-FSIM
LCC	0.690	0.684	**0.750**	0.582	0.640	0.234
SROCC	0.835	0.823	**0.907**	0.734	0.754	0.160

It is interesting to see that, first the FSIM algorithm is very sensitive to the mis-alignment between the distorted image and the reference image, and under the NAR-IQA case, FSIM performed very poorly. Second, training on LIVE and testing on new dataset proved great generalization capability of our algorithm.

Third, although NAR-DCNN model were trained on LIVE dataset with random affine transformation, our proposed NAR-DCNN model obtained superior consistency than the benchmark methods, which demonstrates that the presented model can effectively mine the similar scene structural information between the distorted image and the reference image for quality assessment. In fact, as can be seen from Fig. 1, in many cases, although the reference image "looks" similar to the distorted image, they might actually be captured at different locations.

4.2   The Influence of Distortion Type

Which type of distortions could be best modeled in the proposed NAR-IQA setup is an interesting question. Hence we further conducted distortion-specific experiments on LIVE dataset, and the results are listed in Tables 5 and 6. It is clear to see that for most of the stated distortion type, DCNN achieved the best performance under either the FR-IQA problem or the NAR-IQA problem. Interestingly, NAR-DCNN performs less effective for the WN case. We believe it is because that the white noise was added to the image at pixel level. The simulated geometrical transform has spread the white noise, which may break

Table 5. LCC and SROCC score *vs.* Distortion type for the LIVE dataset

LCC	JPEG2k	JPEG	WN	BLUR	FF	SROCC	JPEG2k	JPEG	WN	BLUR	FF
FSIM	0.910	0.985	0.976	0.978	0.912		0.970	**0.981**	0.967	0.972	**0.949**
PSNR	0.873	0.876	0.926	0.779	0.870		0.870	0.885	0.942	0.763	0.874
SSIM	0.921	0.955	0.982	0.893	0.939		0.939	0.946	0.964	0.907	0.941
CNN-NR	0.953	0.981	0.984	0.953	0.933		0.952	0.977	0.978	0.962	0.908
CORNIA	0.951	0.965	**0.987**	0.968	0.917		0.943	0.955	0.976	0.969	0.906
BRISQUE	0.922	0.973	0.985	0.951	0.903		0.914	0.965	**0.979**	0.951	0.877
FR-DCNN	0.972	**0.990**	0.980	**0.990**	**0.975**		0.977	**0.981**	0.950	**0.991**	0.948
NAR-DCNN	**0.981**	0.983	0.964	0.982	0.965		**0.984**	0.976	0.884	0.983	0.918

Table 6. LCC and SROCC score *vs.* Distortion type for in-house dataset

LCC	Ground-truth by FR-DCNN					Ground-truth by FSIM				
	JPEG2k	JPEG	WN	BLUR	FF	JPEG2k	JPEG	WN	BLUR	FF
brisque	0.645	0.733	0.648	0.726	0.486	0.613	0.588	0.744	0.563	0.472
cornia	0.801	0.835	0.594	0.861	0.784	**0.852**	**0.828**	0.638	**0.783**	**0.841**
diivine	0.507	0.718	0.691	0.570	0.534	0.438	0.641	**0.807**	0.501	0.493
CNN-NR-d	**0.911**	**0.944**	0.663	0.726	**0.794**	0.796	0.794	0.781	0.546	0.828
NAR-CNN	0.862	0.909	**0.776**	**0.867**	0.746	0.844	0.768	0.593	0.732	0.746
SROCC	Ground-truth by FR-DCNN					Ground-truth by FSIM				
	JPEG2k	JPEG	WN	BLUR	FF	JPEG2k	JPEG	WN	BLUR	FF
brisque	0.674	0.670	0.556	0.681	0.508	0.677	0.714	0.862	0.631	0.510
cornia	0.616	0.665	0.527	**0.847**	0.770	0.768	0.805	0.673	**0.902**	**0.868**
diivine	0.361	0.533	0.611	0.542	0.449	0.228	0.528	**0.919**	0.567	0.370
CNN-NR-d	**0.812**	**0.921**	0.544	0.700	**0.788**	0.604	0.806	0.826	0.657	0.833
NAR-CNN	0.761	0.852	**0.696**	0.833	0.775	**0.787**	**0.836**	0.644	0.799	0.792

down the structural information. Thus, the proposed DCNN did not discover suitable features for this case. The invariance to image content variation has slightly compromised the discriminating power to the pixel aligned distortion in this case.

4.3 The Influence of Structural Similarity

The Influence of Geometrical Transformation. Since we claim that the proposed DCNN is capable to utilize non-aligned reference image, it is important to analyze the influence of geometrical variation to the NAR-IQA process. Hence we applied rotation, scaling and translation transform individually to the reference image for LIVE dataset and compared their performance. Specifically, for rotation we tested the following values $\pi/18$, $\pi/9$ or $\pi/2$, for scaling we tested shrinking to 0.667 or enlarge to 1.5, and for translation we tested one-tenth (19 pixels) and one-fifth (39 pixels) of sub image size. As Fig. 4 shows, our proposed DCNN is stable to translation, and performance dropped slightly for rotation and scaling. Existing FR-IQA methods cannot handle the NAR-IQA problem well, even performances of CW-SSIM [16] are only around 0.14, while our DCNN could achieve consistency of 0.97+ with human assessment, significantly higher than these existing FR-IQA methods.

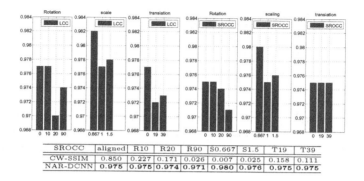

SROCC	aligned	R10	R20	R90	S0.667	S1.5	T19	T39
CW-SSIM	0.850	0.227	0.171	0.026	0.007	0.025	0.158	0.111
NAR-DCNN	0.975	0.975	0.974	0.971	0.980	0.976	0.975	0.975

Fig. 4. The influence of geometrical transformation to LCC and SROCC of the proposed DCNN for NAR-IQA (R, S, T in the table means rotation, scale, translation respectively)

The models were retrained in above different situations, with different geometrical variation images. However, different geometrical variation cases can be handled in our mixture variation cases in Tables 2 and 3. As shown in Fig. 4, our NAR-DCNN were very insensitive to affine transform as it reserve the structure well. Next we will discuss what happened if the structural similarity don't exist.

IQA referenced with different structural similarities. Now, the NAR-DCNN model was fed with distortion images and random selected high quality images. The reference images almost have no structural similarity with distortion images. This experiment is to demonstrate influence of structural similarities in similar reference image selection. The performance of our NAR-DCNN dropped heavily to (**LCC:0.932, SROCC:0.924**), but amazingly, it still better than some existed methods. We believe our NAR-DCNN has also learnt some non-structural feature, "naturalness". Next, reference image same as distorted images were provided to control structural similarity and to explore the "naturalness".

In Fig. 5(a), we listed results in the following setups: both reference and distorted image using same reference images of LIVE dataset (green line), using same distorted images of LIVE dataset (red line), and using randomized 2D matrix (blue line). Since it uses reference image to guide the assessment of image quality, by giving different reference images, the quality score should change accordingly. If reference image is selected to be same as distorted image, then the predicted quality should be very good, because according to the "reference", the distorted image is "perfect". As "naturalness" features worked for our model, statistically, the image assessment Q would be: $Q(I_r, I_r) > Q(I_d, I_d) > Q(I_m, I_m)$, which the experimental results support well. The x axis is the sequence number of the tested distorted image, the higher DMOS value of the distorted images, the larger sequence number it would be. It shows that our DCNN did extract non-structural features, "naturalness" for quality assessment. The quality of the reference image need to be carefully controlled.

Although using 2 different non-aligned reference images may give different scores, they will correlate to each other very well. In fact, as shown in Fig. 5(b), we demonstrate that applying 20 similar scene reference images to NAR-IQA problem for one distorted image of 'whitehouse'. The blue dash line indicates scores predicted by NAR-DCNN(trained with DMOS) referenced with original aligned image, while red '+' demonstrates situation referenced with different similar scenes. The discrepancy between cases referenced with similar scene image and original image was in the range of $[-5, 5]$. Averaging the scores by more reference images could produce more stable results. Algorithms to retrieve very similar images for IQA was also appealing to be exploited. This part will be explored in the future. Different similar reference images and more predicted results will be depicted in the supplementary material.

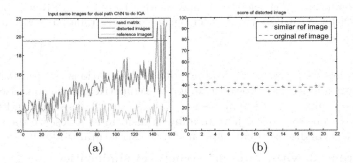

Fig. 5. Comparison of IQA score with different structural similarities: (a)IQA with reference image same as distorted image(b)IQA with different similar reference images (Color figure online)

The selection of similar reference images do have a influence on the performance of NAR-DCNN model. However, the selection of reference image was rather robust with large geometrical variation and image content changing. NAR-DCNN gave state of art performance when these experiments were referenced with random affine transformed reference images of different similarities, large geometrical variation and even content changing images in the paper. These experiments demonstrate that our NAR-DCNN model is very robust to the selection of non-aligned reference images. Although we haven't work out a accurate measurement for IQA similar reference images selection, we believe the selection of structural similarity is not harsh. NAR-DCNN largely benefits from comparison between the nonaligned reference and the distorted images, especially by capturing the structural information.

5   Conclusion and Future Work

This paper presents a Dual-path deep CNN model for image quality assessment using non-aligned reference images with similar scene. The proposed method validates that, the NAR-IQA problem is solvable where an aligned reference image is not available, but a non-aligned image with similar scene can be well used as reference. The proposed DCNN model handles the IQA problem well, and it is observed that DCNN could use non-aligned reference images and achieve superior quality assessment consistency than many existing methods that use aligned reference images.

The next step of the work includes exploring measurement for IQA similar reference images selection, collecting larger non-aligned IQA dataset and building deep model of different architecture to further improve prediction consistency, as well as applying the technique to certain real-world applications.

Acknowledgment. This work is partially supported by National Science Foundation of China under Grant NO. 61473219, and the National Basic Research Program of China (973 Program) under Grant No. 2015CB351705.

References

1. Ponomarenko, N., Lukin, V., Zelensky, A., Egiazarian, K., Carli, M., Battisti, F.: TID 2008-a database for evaluation of full-reference visual quality assessment metrics. Adv. Mod. Radioelectron. **10**(4), 30–45 (2009)
2. Sheikh, H.R., Bovik, A.C.: Image information and visual quality. IEEE Trans. Image Process. **15**(2), 430–444 (2006)
3. Zhang, L., Zhang, L., Mou, X., Zhang, D.: FSIM: a feature similarity index for image quality assessment. IEEE Trans. Image Process. **20**(8), 2378–2386 (2011)
4. Pei, S.C., Chen, L.H.: Image quality assessment using human visual dog model fused with random forest. IEEE Trans. Image Process. **24**(11), 3282–3292 (2015)
5. Wang, Z., Bovik, A.C., Sheikh, H.R., Simoncelli, E.P.: Image quality assessment: from error visibility to structural similarity. IEEE Trans. Image Process. **13**(4), 600–612 (2004)
6. Sheikh, H.R., Bovik, A.C., De Veciana, G.: An information fidelity criterion for image quality assessment using natural scene statistics. IEEE Trans. Image Process. **14**(12), 2117–2128 (2005)
7. Li, Q., Wang, Z.: Reduced-reference image quality assessment using divisive normalization-based image representation. IEEE J. Sel. Top. Sig. Process. **3**(2), 202–211 (2009)
8. Rehman, A., Wang, Z.: Reduced-reference image quality assessment by structural similarity estimation. IEEE Trans. Image Process. **21**(8), 3378–3389 (2012)
9. Kang, L., Ye, P., Li, Y., Doermann, D.: Convolutional neural networks for no-reference image quality assessment. In: 2014 IEEE Conference on Computer Vision and Pattern Recognition (CVPR), pp. 1733–1740. IEEE (2014)
10. Ye, P., Kumar, J., Kang, L., Doermann, D.: Unsupervised feature learning framework for no-reference image quality assessment. In: 2012 IEEE Conference on Computer Vision and Pattern Recognition (CVPR), pp. 1098–1105. IEEE (2012)

11. Mittal, A., Moorthy, A.K., Bovik, A.C.: No-reference image quality assessment in the spatial domain. IEEE Trans. Image Process. **21**(12), 4695–4708 (2012)
12. Gao, X., Lu, W., Tao, D., Li, X.: Image quality assessment and human visual system. In: Visual Communications and Image Processing 2010, International Society for Optics and Photonics, pp. 77440Z–77440Z (2010)
13. Wang, Z., Simoncelli, E.P., Bovik, A.C.: Multiscale structural similarity for image quality assessment. In: Conference Record of the Thirty-Seventh Asilomar Conference on Signals, Systems and Computers, 2004, vol. 2, pp. 1398–1402. IEEE (2003)
14. Posner, M.I., Petersen, S.E.: The attention system of the human brain. Technical report, DTIC Document (1989)
15. Itti, L., Koch, C., Niebur, E.: A model of saliency-based visual attention for rapid scene analysis. IEEE Trans. Pattern Anal. Mach. Intell. **11**, 1254–1259 (1998)
16. Sampat, M.P., Wang, Z., Gupta, S., Bovik, A.C., Markey, M.K.: Complex wavelet structural similarity: a new image similarity index. IEEE Trans. Image Process. **18**(11), 2385–2401 (2009)
17. Damera-Venkata, N., Kite, T.D., Geisler, W.S., Evans, B.L., Bovik, A.C.: Image quality assessment based on a degradation model. IEEE Trans. Image Process. **9**(4), 636–650 (2000)
18. Krizhevsky, A., Sutskever, I., Hinton, G.E.: Imagenet classification with deep convolutional neural networks. In: Advances in Neural Information Processing Systems, pp. 1097–1105 (2012)
19. Bromley, J., Bentz, J.W., Bottou, L., Guyon, I., LeCun, Y., Moore, C., Säckinger, E., Shah, R.: Signature verification using a time delay neural network. Int. J. Pattern Recogn. Artif. Intell. **7**(04), 669–688 (1993)
20. Chopra, S., Hadsell, R., LeCun, Y.: Learning a similarity metric discriminatively, with application to face verification. In: IEEE Computer Society Conference on Computer Vision and Pattern Recognition, CVPR 2005, vol. 1, pp. 539–546. IEEE (2005)
21. Jia, Y., Shelhamer, E., Donahue, J., Karayev, S., Long, J., Girshick, R., Guadarrama, S., Darrell, T.: Caffe: Convolutional architecture for fast feature embedding (2014). arXiv preprint: arXiv:1408.5093
22. Xue, W., Zhang, L., Mou, X.: Learning without human scores for blind image quality assessment. In: Proceedings of the IEEE Conference on Computer Vision and Pattern Recognition, pp. 995–1002 (2013)
23. Moorthy, A.K., Bovik, A.C.: Blind image quality assessment: from natural scene statistics to perceptual quality. IEEE Trans. Image Process. **20**(12), 3350–3364 (2011)
24. Sheikh, H.R., Sabir, M.F., Bovik, A.C.: A statistical evaluation of recent full reference image quality assessment algorithms. IEEE Trans. Image Process. **15**(11), 3440–3451 (2006)

MOON: A Mixed Objective Optimization Network for the Recognition of Facial Attributes

Ethan M. Rudd[✉], Manuel Günther, and Terrance E. Boult

Vision and Security Technology (VAST) Lab,
University of Colorado at Colorado Springs, Colorado Springs, USA
{erudd,mgunther,tboult}@vast.uccs.edu

Abstract. Attribute recognition, particularly facial, extracts many labels for each image. While some multi-task vision problems can be decomposed into separate tasks and stages, e.g., training independent models for each task, for a growing set of problems joint optimization across all tasks has been shown to improve performance. We show that for deep convolutional neural network (DCNN) facial attribute extraction, multi-task optimization is better. Unfortunately, it can be difficult to apply joint optimization to DCNNs when training data is imbalanced, and re-balancing multi-label data directly is structurally infeasible, since adding/removing data to balance one label will change the sampling of the other labels. This paper addresses the multi-label imbalance problem by introducing a novel mixed objective optimization network (MOON) with a loss function that mixes multiple task objectives with domain adaptive re-weighting of propagated loss. Experiments demonstrate that not only does MOON advance the state of the art in facial attribute recognition, but it also outperforms independently trained DCNNs using the same data. When using facial attributes for the LFW face recognition task, we show that our balanced (domain adapted) network outperforms the unbalanced trained network.

Keywords: Facial attributes · Deep neural networks · Multi-task learning · Multi-label learning · Domain adaptation

1 Introduction

Given an input image or video, there are often multiple vision tasks to be accomplished, i.e., multiple objectives to be optimized. Under certain constraints, e.g., when tasks feed into each other, or when there is need to share computed features or representations, then multiple task objectives can benefit from being mixed and jointly optimized. This kind of multi-objective learning has affected many areas of computer vision including scene/object classification and annotation [1–4], tracking [5], facial landmark estimation [6,7], face verification [8], and face detection with head pose estimation [9–11].

Electronic supplementary material The online version of this chapter (doi:10. 1007/978-3-319-46454-1_2) contains supplementary material, which is available to authorized users.

© Springer International Publishing AG 2016
B. Leibe et al. (Eds.): ECCV 2016, Part V, LNCS 9909, pp. 19–35, 2016.
DOI: 10.1007/978-3-319-46454-1_2

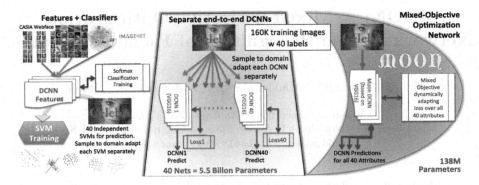

Fig. 1. Three approaches to attribute learning (and other multi-task problems). In the left is a conceptual model of previous state-of-the-art approaches, with features trained for classification problems and then adapted as inputs to independent SVMs for prediction. The middle approach attacks the problem with separately trained deep convolution neural networks (DCNNs). While we demonstrate that this advances the state of the art in attribute accuracy, it is cost prohibitive. This paper shows that for attributes, joint multi-task learning does better. However, for multi-label learning there is no way simply to re-weight or sample inputs to deal with imbalance or domain adaption because each input defines values for all attributes. On the right is our answer, the mixed objective optimization network (MOON) architecture with a domain adaptive multi-task DCNN loss. To adapt, for each input the MOON objective re-weights each part of the loss associated with each attribute. MOON learns to balance its multi-task output predictions with reduced training and storage costs, while producing better accuracy than independently trained DCNNs.

This paper addresses facial attribute recognition, which we hypothesize is well suited to a multi-objective approach because facial attributes have a shared, albeit latent correlation that imposes soft constraints on the space of attributes, e.g., $p(\texttt{Male}|\texttt{Mustache}) \approx 1$. Despite the fact that facial attribute recognition inherently seeks multiple labels for the same image, multi-objective learning has not been widely applied to facial attributes. One potential reason is that balancing the training for the labels is difficult. Prior approaches to facial attribute recognition independently optimize a choice of features and recognition model (Features+Classifiers in Fig. 1). For example, the original approach taken by Kumar et al. [12] used AdaBoost to select a separate feature space for each attribute and independent SVMs to perform classification. Likewise, the current state of the art [13] trains DCNN features with facial identity recognition and localization datasets and then trains independent SVMs in this feature space for attribute classification. In both cases the separation makes it easy to re-balance training per attribute.

In this work, we show that a joint optimization with respect to all attributes offers performance superior to the state-of-the-art Features+Classifiers approach. We also show that joint optimization over all attributes outperforms training a single independent network of similar topology per attribute, in which the feature space is optimized along with the classifier on a per-attribute basis, both in terms of accuracy and storage/processing efficiency. This result suggests that the multi-task approach is far more effective at distilling latent correlations than relying on independent classifiers to learn them implicitly. Thus, not only is a multi-objective approach far more intuitive, it is also far more effective.

It is unlikely that the source distribution of binary facial attributes for the training set will match the target distribution of the test set. We would like facial attribute classifiers trained on a dataset of one demographic to still work well for discrimination on a different demographic; thus some sort of domain adaptation is required. Many approaches to domain adaption exist [14], with input sampling or re-weighting being common. Unfortunately, multi-objective training introduces challenges because balanced training is difficult or impossible via input sampling or weighting. Given a target distribution, domain adaptation is easy for separately trained attribute classifiers, e.g., by re-weighting errors in the cost function in each classifier. However, it is less immediately obvious how to do this in training for a multi-objective classifier. To this end, we introduce the MOON (Mixed-Objective Optimization Network) architecture. MOON is a novel multi-objective neural network architecture, which *mixes* the tasks of multi-label classification and domain adaptation under one unified objective function.

In summary, the contributions of this paper include:

- A mixed objective optimization network (MOON) architecture, which advances face attribute recognition by learning multiple attribute labels simultaneously via a single DCNN that supports domain adaption for multi-task DCNNs.
- A fair evaluation technique which incorporates source and target distributions into the classification measure, leading to the balanced CelebA (CelebAB) evaluation protocol,
- Experiments demonstrating that the MOON architecture significantly advances state-of-the-art attribute recognition on the CelebA dataset, improving both accuracy and efficiency. These experiments also demonstrate that optimizing over all attributes simultaneously offers a noticeable reduction in classification error compared to optimizing single attributes over the same dataset and network topology.
- Experiments showing that domain adaptation on attribute classifiers trained on CelebA enhances the recognition capacity of MOON attributes on LFW, advancing attribute-based face recognition.
- Evaluation of stability of the MOON architecture to fiducial perturbations and data set imbalance.

2   Related Work

Multi-task learning has been applied to several areas that rely on learning fine-grained discriminations or localizations under the constraint of a global correlating structure. In these problems, multiple target labels or objective functions must simultaneously be optimized. In object recognition problems, multiple objects may be present in a training image whose co-occurrences should be explicitly learnt [15]. In text classification problems, joint inference across all characters in a word yields performance gains over independent classification [16]. In multi-label image tagging/retrieval [4,17], representations of the contents of an image across modalities (e.g., textual descriptions, voice descriptions) are jointly inferred from the images. The resulting classifiers can then be used to generate descriptions of novel images (tagging) or to query images based on their descriptions (retrieval). Closer to this work, facial model fitting and landmark estimation [18,19] is another multi-task problem, which requires a fine-grained fit due to tremendous diversity in facial features, poses, lighting conditions, expressions, and many other exogenous factors. Solutions also benefit from global information about the space of face shapes and textures under different conditions. Optimization with respect to local gradients and textures is necessary for a precise fit, while considering the relative locations of all points is important to avoid violating facial topologies.

This paper applies multi-task learning to facial attributes. Applications of facial attributes include searches based on semantically meaningful descriptions (e.g., "Caucasian female with blond hair") [12,20,21], verification systems that explain in a human-comprehensible form *why* verification succeeded or failed [22], relative relations among attributes [23], social relation/sentiment analysis [24], and demographic profiling. Facial attributes also provide information that is more or less independent of that distilled by conventional recognition algorithms, potentially allowing for the creation of more accurate and robust systems, narrowing down search spaces, and increasing efficiency at match time.

The classification of facial attributes was first pioneered by Kumar et al. [22]. Their classifiers depended heavily on face alignment, with respect to a frontal template, with each attribute using AdaBoost-learnt combinations of features from hand-picked facial regions (e.g., cheeks, mouth, etc.). The feature spaces were simplistic by today's standards, consisting of various normalizations and aggregations of color spaces and image gradients. Different features were learnt for each attribute, and a single RBF-SVM per attribute was independently trained for classification. Although novel, the approach was cumbersome due to high dimensional varying length features for each attribute, leading to inefficiencies in feature extraction and classification [25].

In recent years, approaches have been developed to leverage more sophisticated feature spaces. For example, gated CNNs [26] use cross-correlation across an aligned training set to determine which areas of the face are *most relevant* to particular attributes. The outputs of an ensemble of CNNs, one trained for each of the relevant regions, are then joined together into a global feature vector. Final classification is performed via independent binary linear SVMs. Zhang et al. [24] use CNNs to learn facial attributes, with the ultimate goal of using these features as part of an intermediate representation for a Siamese network to infer social relations between pairs of identities within an image. Liu et al. [13]

use three CNNs – a combination of two *localization networks* (LNets), and an *attribute recognition network* (ANet) to first localize faces and then classify facial attributes in the wild. The localization network proposes locations of face images, while the attribute network is trained on face identities and attributes, and is used to extract features, which are fed to independent linear SVMs for final attribute classification. Their approach was the state-of-the-art on the CelebA dataset at the time of the submission of this paper – and serves as a basis of comparison. In contrast to our approach, Liu et al. and many other recent works do not directly use attribute data in learning a feature space representation, but instead use truncated networks trained for other tasks. While research suggests that coarse-grained attribute data (e.g., image-level) can be indirectly embedded into the hidden layers of large-scale identification networks [27], the efficiency of this approach has not been well studied for inferring fine-grained (e.g., facial) attribute representations, and findings from [28] suggest that optimal implicit representations reside across different layers depending on the attribute.

Surprisingly, multi-task learning has not been widely applied to the problem of facial attribute recognition. Only very recently has it been addressed, e.g., Ehrlich et al. [29] developed a Multi-Task Restricted Boltzmann Machine (MT-RBM). In terms of joint inference for facial attributes, it is the first we could find in the literature, but the approach deviates radically from DCNN approaches in many other respects as well: the MT-RBM is generative and non-convolutional and it is unclear what contributed most to their improvement over [13].

While there has been significant prior work in visual domain adaptation [14], including more recent work for CNNs [30], the main problem that we address in this paper – incorporating domain adaptation into the training procedure for multi-objective attribute classifiers – has heretofore not been addressed, either in DCNN multi-task learning or in facial attribute research. For facial attributes in particular, we contend that domain adaptation is essential when building classifiers fit to chosen target demographics. Recently, Wang et al. [31] demonstrated that even throughout New York City, a relatively compact geographic region, differences in demographic profile are so prominent as a function of geolocation that binned geolocation can be used to derive a powerful unsupervised facial attribute feature space representation. In order to leverage attribute data we have for training demographic-specific classifiers, domain adaptation during training is vital to provide a balanced representation and mitigate problems from an over-correlated representation [32].

3 Approach

For multi-task problems, the high level goal is to maximize accuracy over all tasks, where each task has its own objective. In our case, the task is attribute prediction, and we seek to simultaneously maximize prediction accuracy over all attributes.

Formally, let $\mathbb{I}$ be the space of allowable images, and let M be the number of attributes. For a given sample $x \in \mathbb{I}$, let $y_i \in \{-1, +1\}$ be the binary ground truth label for x's ith attribute, where $i \in \{1, \ldots, M\}$ is the attribute index. Let $\mathcal{H}$ be the space of allowable decision functions and $f_i(x; \theta_i) \in \mathcal{H}$ be the decision function, with parameters θ_i, learnt for the ith attribute classifier. Given a set of loss functions $L_i(f_i(x; \theta_i), y_i)$, each of which defines the cost of an error on input x with respect to attribute i, let $\mathbb{E}(f_i(x; \theta_i), y_i)$ be the expected value of that loss over the range of inputs $\mathbb{I}$. Then the idealized problem is to minimize the loss for each attribute, i.e.:

$$\forall i\colon f_i^* = \operatorname*{argmin}_{f_i \in \mathcal{H}} \mathbb{E}(f_i(x; \theta_i), y_i). \tag{1}$$

For input x and attribute i, the classification result $c_i(x)$ and its corresponding error $e_i(x, y_i)$ are obtained by thresholding the associated prediction:

$$c_i(x) = \begin{cases} +1 & \text{if } f_i(x) > 0 \\ -1 & \text{otherwise,} \end{cases} \quad \text{and} \quad e_i(x, y_i) = \begin{cases} 0 & \text{if } y_i c_i(x) > 0 \\ +1 & \text{otherwise.} \end{cases} \tag{2}$$

Intuitively, this appears to lead to M independent optimization problems, for which one should be able to optimize each f_i separately. Accordingly, the most common approach to attribute classification in prior work is to use independent binary classifiers in some characteristic feature space to classify each attribute [13,22]. Both approaches in [22] and [13] learn M independent binary classifiers trained with a hinge-loss objective. The hinge-loss objective function is:

$$\operatorname*{argmin}_{\theta_i} L_i(x, \theta_i, y_i) = max(0, 1 - y_i f_i(x; \theta_i)). \tag{3}$$

When the classifier is a dot product, i.e., $f_i(x) = \theta_i^T (1, x^T)^T$, solving this objective function results in a binary *support vector machine* (SVM) – the hyperplane that separates the two binary classes of data ($+1$ and -1) with maximum softmargin. Given M attributes, this approach leads to M binary classifiers, each of which outputs a decision score. A positive decision score corresponds to the predicted presence of an attribute, while a negative decision score corresponds to its absence.

In order to learn latent correlations, it is also important to use attribute data directly to derive the feature space. Although Liu et al. [13] claim that latent features of attributes are learnt by their feature space representation while optimizing over a dataset for an identification task, the extent to which this is true for attributes that have little to do with identity (e.g., Smiling) is questionable. Rather, intuition suggests the opposite – that networks trained for identification of individuals would learn to ignore such attributes. To uncover such correlations, the network used to learn the feature space should be directly trained on attribute data and the distribution of attributes in training should match the operational or testing distribution.

This leads to the problem of how to appropriately balance the dataset used to learn attribute features. A perfectly balanced dataset can be obtained by collecting separate images for each attribute, but this leads to an enormous dataset, with different identities for different attributes, effectively yielding a relatively small number of training images per attribute in proportion to the size of the dataset [22]. This approach also does not account for label correlations. Using a multi-label dataset, e.g., CelebA [13] allows us to leverage multiple labels in a mixed objective, but the distribution is highly imbalanced for many attributes (cf. Sect. 4). Unfortunately, the attribute distribution of a given target population does not always follow the dataset bias.

In a separate per-class training, balancing the number of positive and negative examples that are input to the classifier is easy, e.g., by weighting or sampling. However, input balancing is nearly impossible for multi-task training. Furthermore, for many tasks, the training frequencies and the operational/test frequencies will not match. Our solution to both problems is to define a mixed objective function including domain adapted weights that incorporate the difference between the source and target distributions. First, we compute the source distribution S_i from the training set for each attribute i by counting the relative number of occurrences of positive S_i^+ and negative samples S_i^-. Given a binary target distribution, T_i^+ and T_i^-, for each attribute i we assign a probability for each class:

$$p(i|+1) = \begin{cases} 1 & \text{if } T_i^+ > S_i^+ \\ \frac{S_i^- T_i^+}{S_i^+ T_i^-} & \text{otherwise} \end{cases} \quad \text{and} \quad p(i|-1) = \begin{cases} 1 & \text{if } T_i^- > S_i^- \\ \frac{S_i^+ T_i^-}{S_i^- T_i^+} & \text{otherwise.} \end{cases} \quad (4)$$

We would like to incorporate this domain adaptation directly into a loss function, but we need a loss function that additionally mixes all attribute predictions and simultaneously infers latent correlations between attribute labels and image data. One approach would be to combine all of the objective functions for each attribute into one joint objective function, e.g.:

$$\operatorname*{argmin}_{\theta} \sum_{i=1}^{M} L_i(x, \theta, y_i), \quad (5)$$

where θ are the parameters of the joint classifier, which for legibility reasons we omit from the following equations. We can then solve that optimization problem via backpropagation using raw attribute images and labels as a training set. While we could use many potential loss functions, in our formulation we optimize a weighted mixed task squared error. Let M be the number of attributes, $\mathbf{X}$ be a data tensor containing N input images, and $\mathbf{Y}$ be a corresponding $N \times M$ matrix of labels. Then our domain-adapted multitask loss function is given by:

$$L(\mathbf{X}, \mathbf{Y}) = \sum_{j=1}^{N} \sum_{i=1}^{M} p(i|Y_{ji}) \, \|f_i(X_j) - Y_{ji}\|^2. \quad (6)$$

Replacing the standard loss layer of a DCNN with a layer implementing Eq. (6) results in the *mixed objective optimization network* (MOON) architecture, which incorporates attribute correlations and can adapt the bias of the training dataset to a target distribution. In our custom implementation we obtain the weights $p(i|Y_{ji})$ via sampling. For each attribute i with target value $Y_{ji} \in \{-1, +1\}$ we only backpropagate the error with the probability $p(i|Y_{ji})$, otherwise we set the gradient for attribute i to 0. The more source and target distributions differ, the more elements in the gradient are reset.

4   Experiments

4.1   Dataset

For comparison with other attribute benchmarks, we conducted our experiments on the CelebA dataset [13]. The dataset consists of batches of 20 images from approximately 10K celebrities, resulting in a total of more than 200K images. Following the standard CelebA evaluation protocol, 8K identities (160K images) are used for training, 1K for validation and 1K for testing. Each image is annotated with 5 key points (both eyes, the mouth corners and the nose tip), as well as binary labels of 40 attributes. These attributes are shown in Fig. 2, which also shows the relative number of images in which the attribute is hand-labeled as present (blue) or absent (tan), respectively. As one can observe, for many of the attributes, there is a strong bias for either of the two classes. This is especially the case for certain attributes, e.g., relatively few images are labeled as `Bald` or `Wearing Hat`, while the majority of the facial images are labeled as `Young`.

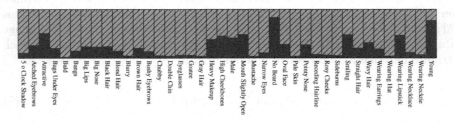

Fig. 2. CelebA Dataset Bias. This figure shows the distribution of the attribute labels throughout the CelebA dataset: presence (blue) or absence (tan). (Color figure online)

The CelebA dataset provides a set of pre-cropped face images, which were aligned using the hand-labeled key points. For our experiments we use these images, but later (cf. Sect. 5.1) we show that the trained classifier can also work with faces which are not perfectly aligned, and we introduce ideas to make our MOON network more robust to mis-alignment.

4.2   Evaluating MOON on CelebA

In order to compare with existing approaches, which do not account for dataset bias, we evaluate MOON on the CelebA dataset, setting the target distribution to the source distribution, i.e., $\forall i \ T_i \equiv S_i$.

Using the CelebA training set, we trained a DCNN to predict attributes under a MOON architecture. As the basic network configuration, we adopted the 16 layer VGG network from [33], where we replaced the final loss layer with the loss in Eq. (6). We also changed the dimension of the RGB image input layer from 224×224 pixels to 178×218 pixels, the resolution of the aligned CelebA images. In opposition to [33], we do not incorporate any dataset augmentation or mirroring, but train the network purely on the aligned images. Due to memory limitations, the batch size was set to 64 images per training iteration and, hence, the training requires approximately 2500 iterations to run a full epoch on the training set. We selected a learning rate of 0.00001, finding empirically that higher learning rates caused the network to learn only the bias of the training set. During training we update the convolution kernel weights using the backpropagation algorithm with an *RMSProp* update rule and an inverse learning rate decay policy.

We ran two types of network training, one training a separate network for each attribute, and one optimizing the combined MOON network. Separately training classifiers is the most common approach taken in the literature. By training one network per individual attribute, each network can concentrate only on the parts of the image it deems relevant to that attribute. During the separate training, we presented each network with all images from the training set, and a single input to the loss layer encoded with labels that denoted the presence $(+1)$ or the absence (-1) of the attribute. Loss was computed according to Eq. (6). As each network required several hours to train on an NVIDIA Titan-X GPU, we chose to train each network for ≈ 2 epochs (5000 iterations). To check if 2 epochs are sufficient to attain convergence to a maximum validation accuracy, we continued training for four attributes. We selected these attributes – `Attractive`, `Chubby`, `Narrow Eyes`, and `Young` – to have varying statistics from the dataset: While `Attractive` is relatively balanced, images with `Chubby` and `Narrow Eyes` are mostly absent from the dataset, whereas `Young` is over-represented. While errors on the training set further decreased, errors on the validation set *increased* after approximately 4–6 epochs, with little improvement over the 2 epochs networks. This leads us to believe that improvements in validation accuracy beyond 2 epochs are negligible.

When training our MOON network, we use a single network with $M = 40$ outputs to learn all attributes simultaneously. Since CelebA has identical source and target distributions, we define the loss layer in (6) to weight all elements equally during backpropagation – which is equivalent to Euclidean loss between the network output and the 40 binary attribute values. We trained the network for 40 epochs since the validation error after 10 epochs was still decreasing. Based on the minimum validation set error, we chose our final MOON network after 24 epochs. While individual classifiers seem to take fewer training iterations than MOON to minimize their validation error, the total training time of the MOON network is still lower than the sum of the separate network training times. We suspect that the additional iterations required for the MOON network

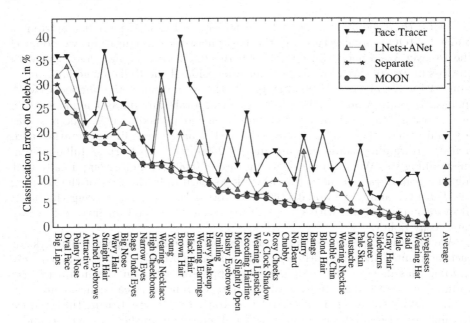

Fig. 3. Error Rates on CelebA. This figure shows the classification errors on the test set of the CelebA dataset for several algorithms, including our Separate networks and MOON. The results of Face Tracer and LNets+ANet are taken from Liu et al. [13]. For a tabular form of these results see the supplement to this paper.

to converge are needed to learn a more sophisticated latent structure than those learnt by the separate networks.

To compare with the results of Liu et al. [13], we measure the success of our training in terms of classification error, i.e., the number of cases, where our classifier f predicted the incorrect label, relative to the total number of test images:

$$E_i(\mathbf{X}, \mathbf{Y}) = \frac{1}{N_{test}} \sum_{j=1}^{N_{test}} e_i(X_j, Y_{ji}). \tag{7}$$

The `Average` classification error is computed by taking the average of the classification errors over all (M) attributes:

$$\overline{E}(\mathbf{X}, \mathbf{Y}) = \frac{1}{M} \sum_{i=1}^{M} E_i(X, Y). \tag{8}$$

Note that this error does not differentiate between positive and negative values. Hence, for very biased attributes, a random classifier which always predicts the dominant class would reach a low classification error, e.g., for `Bald` the random classification error would be as low as 2.24 %!

The classification errors for all the attributes are visually displayed in Fig. 3. There, we also included two results from Liu et al. [13], converting from classification success (reported in [13]) to classification error. The Face Tracer results reflect the best non-DCNN based algorithm that has been evaluated so far on the CelebA dataset. LNets+ANet represent the state-of-the-art results on this dataset obtained by combining three different deep convolutional neural networks with support vector machines.

The average classification errors over all attributes for each classifier are: Face Tracer: 18.88 %, LNets+ANet: 12.70 %, Separate: 9.78 %, and MOON: 9.06 %. Thus, our MOON network achieves a relative reduction of 28.7 % of the error over the state of the art, and a 7.4 % reduction over the separately trained networks. For almost all attributes, the results of our two approaches outperform the LNets+ANet state-of-the-art results, and the MOON network gives a lower error than the Separate networks trained specifically on a single attribute.

Interestingly, for several attributes that are traditionally not considered to be useful in face recognition, such as hair color (e.g. Brown Hair), hair style (e.g. Straight Hair), accessories (e.g. Wearing Necklace), and non face-related attributes (e.g. Blurry), our approach outperforms the LNets+ANet combination by an especially large margin. We suspect that this effect is due to the fact that in [13], the ANet network's feature space was derived from training on a *face recognition* benchmark, and later adapted to the attribute classification task, which offers little direction for inferring the hidden representations of non facial identity related attributes.

4.3   CelebAB: A Balancing Act

As demonstrated in Sect. 4.2, MOON obtains state-of-the-art classification accuracies on the CelebA dataset. However, it is unclear how meaningful these results are for target distributions with different attribute frequencies, e.g., with more realistic distributions of Young or Chubby people.

Since our objective is to learn the network outputs to be +1 or −1 corresponding to presence or absence of attributes, respectively, we plotted the score distributions of the validation set for four of the attributes. From Fig. 2 we observe a strong bias for several attributes in the CelebA dataset, which we can find in the score distribution plots of Fig. 4(a), too. Note that the positive and negative score distributions have been normalized independently, otherwise the positive scores for Narrow Eyes and Chubby would not be visible. For attributes with a balanced number of positive and negative examples, such as Attractive, the distributions of negative (tan) and positive (blue) scores are also balanced. On the other hand, for unbalanced attributes, such as Young, Narrow Eyes or Chubby, the dominant class is well distributed around its desired value, but the other class has not been learnt well. Interestingly, a comparably small bias in the training set (for Young there are 77 % positives and 23 % negatives) can destroy the capability of the network to learn the inferior class.

Intuitively, when having such unbalanced score distributions, one would expect that the threshold of 0 that we use for classification should be adapted. However, given that the validation and test set follow the same bias as the training set, a threshold of 0 works well for the CelebA dataset. Even more astonishingly, a wide range of thresholds around 0 will lead to approximately the same

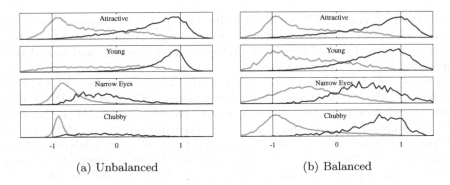

(a) Unbalanced   (b) Balanced

Fig. 4. Score distributions. This figure shows the distributions of the network outputs for four different attributes, when presenting images with present (blue) and absent (tan) attributes. In (a) network outputs after training with unbalanced data are shown, while in (b) the outputs of the network after training with the balancing loss layer are presented. Positive and negative score distributions are normalized independently. (Color figure online)

classification error and, hence, the network has learnt to balance between false positives and false negatives – including the dataset bias.

To obtain balanced score distributions, we chose to have a balanced target distribution, i.e., $T_i^+ = T_i^- = \frac{1}{2}$ for each attribute i. The resulting validation set score distribution for the same four attributes generated by the re-balanced MOON network after 34 training epochs can be seen in Fig. 4(b). Apparently, the score distributions are much more balanced, and the threshold 0 seems to make more sense now. Thus, one would expect that the classification error would be lower, too. However, due to the high dataset bias, which is also present in the validation and test sets, the total average classification error of the balanced network on the (unbalanced) CelebA test set is 13.67 %.

Although this classification error is larger than that obtained by the unbalanced MOON network, *this is an artifact of the significant imbalance in the original test set*; the error measure in Eq. (7) has not been adapted to the target domain. A fair comparison would measure the balanced classification error E_i^B that weights the positive and negative classes according to the target distribution:

$$
E_i^B(\mathbf{X}, \mathbf{Y}) = \sum_{j=1}^{N_{test}} \begin{cases} \frac{e_i(X_j, Y_{ji}) T_i^+}{N_i^+} & \text{if } Y_{ji} = +1 \\ \frac{e_i(X_j, Y_{ji}) T_i^-}{N_i^-} & \text{if } Y_{ji} = -1, \end{cases} \tag{9}
$$

where N_i^+ and N_i^- are the respective numbers of positive and negative examples of attribute i in the test set. With $T_i^+ = T_i^- = \frac{1}{2}$, this error is effectively identical to the *equal error rate* (EER) between errors made with positive and negative target values. When computing classification error of the re-balanced MOON network example with $T_i^+ = T_i^- = \frac{1}{2}$, we obtain an average E_i^B error of 12.98 %.

Note that the unbalanced MOON network, which is not trained to follow the target distribution, obtains an E_i^B error of 21.41 %. This is precisely what we would expect of a domain adaptation system: A classifier adapted to the target distribution does better than a classifier that is not.

5   Discussion

5.1   Handling Mis-aligned Images

In our experiments in Sect. 4, we used aligned images to train and test the networks. To show that MOON is able to deal with badly aligned images, we conducted an additional experiment in which we used perturbed test images. To perturb the images, we applied a random rotation within $\pm 10°$, a random scaling with a scale factor in $[0.9, 1.1]$, and a random translation of up to 10 pixels in either direction to the pre-aligned faces in the CelebA dataset. We selected these parameters to be well outside of the error range of a reasonable (frontal face) eye detector. Alignment errors of these magnitudes have been shown to *highly* influence the performance of many traditional face recognition algorithms [34].

When running this perturbed test set through our (unbalanced) MOON network, which was trained purely on aligned faces, we obtain a classification error of 11.62 %, which is higher than the 9.06 % obtained with aligned test images, but still better than the current state of the art in [13]. We assume that we can improve the network stability against mis-alignment by incorporating augmented (e.g., misaligned perturbations) training data into the training process, since this has shown to improve the performance of DCNNs [35].

Some preliminary experiments seem to verify this claim: When training with mis-aligned and horizontally mirrored images (in total 10 copies for each training image), we were able to decrease the classification error on the mis-aligned test images to 9.50 %. Unfortunately, this also caused a slight performance degradation when evaluating on purely aligned images, causing classification error to increase from the 9.06 % to 9.23 %. Hence, in principle, the MOON architecture is able to work with aligned and mis-aligned images, as long as the conditions during training and testing are similar. These tests further highlight the need to select data augmentation methods appropriate to the respective quality of the actual alignment algorithms used in real end-to-end systems.

5.2   Face Verification on LFW

One application of facial attributes is to enhance other recognition algorithms. In order to evaluate our attribute classifiers on another dataset and to examine the effectiveness of our attributes for a particular application, we conducted the same View 2 LFW verification evaluation as Kumar et al. in [22], using the 40 attributes extracted from MOON under both balanced and unbalanced networks. We also tested the extracted attributes with respect to the features of Face Tracer (we downloaded the attribute vectors from [22] provided on the LFW web page http://vis-www.cs.umass.edu/lfw), using the approach detailed in [22]. After optimizing RBF SVM parameters for each feature type separately using View 1 protocol of the labeled faces in the wild (LFW) dataset, the final classification accuracies that we obtained were 83.43 % ± 2.22 for Kumar's attributes, and 85.05 % ± 1.57 for the re-balanced MOON network. Hence, our 40 MOON attributes provide better face recognition capabilities than the 73 attributes defined by Kumar et al. [22], though they are far from the current state-of-the-art on LFW. This result, consistent with intuition, suggests that the accuracy of the attribute classification is important to providing noticeably better recognition results. With 84.73 % ± 1.99, the verification accuracy for the unbalanced MOON network is only slightly lower than that of the re-balanced MOON network, but the stability is decreased. We assume that training on a target distribution that better reflects the distribution of facial attributes in LFW will result in further increased accuracy/stability. See the supplement to this paper for additional qualitative analysis of our LFW evaluation.

6   Conclusion

The MOON architecture achieves an accurate, computationally efficient, and compact representation which advances the state of the art on the CelebA dataset. Unlike competing approaches, our experiments did not rely on any datasets external to CelebA to train our network. We also investigated dataset bias in CelebA and proposed domain adaptation methods for training to a different target distribution without requiring training samples from that population. Combining domain adaptive methods and multiple-task objectives into one mixed objective function, we conducted evaluations on a novel re-balanced version of CelebA (the *CelebAB* dataset) and the LFW dataset that demonstrate the effectiveness of our approach.

   Our work raises a philosophical question about the mathematics of attribute recognition: How *should* the attribute recognition problem be treated? Contrary to previous work, in which attribute labels are independently learnt, our approach implicitly leverages attribute correlations by explicitly forcing hidden layers in the network to incorporate information from multiple labels while simultaneously enforcing specified balance constraints via a domain adaptive loss. While CelebA labels are binary, MOON's weighted Euclidean loss also offers the capacity to learn labels along a continuous range, which is perhaps a more suitable representation for some attributes (e.g., Big Nose, Young). Matching output score distributions to perceptual continuity and incorporating different types of attribute labels are interesting topics which we leave for future research.

Acknowledgments. This research is based upon work supported in part by the Office of the Director of National Intelligence (ODNI), Intelligence Advanced Research Projects Activity (IARPA), via IARPA R&D Contract No. 2014-14071600012. The views and conclusions contained herein are those of the authors and should not be interpreted as necessarily representing the official policies or endorsements, either expressed or implied, of the ODNI, IARPA, or the U.S. Government. The U.S. Government is

References

1. Zhou, Z.H., Zhang, M.L.: Multi-instance multi-label learning with application to
   scene classification. In: Advances in Neural Information Processing Systems, pp.
   1609–1616 (2007)
2. Quattoni, A., Collins, M., Darrell, T.: Transfer learning for image classification with
   sparse prototype representations. In: Computer Vision and Pattern Recognition,
   pp. 1–8. IEEE (2008)
3. Huang, Y., Wang, W., Wang, L., Tan, T.: Multi-task deep neural network for multi-
   label learning. In: International Conference on Image Processing, pp. 2897–2900.
   IEEE (2013)
4. Wu, F., Wang, Z., Zhang, Z., Yang, Y., Luo, J., Zhu, W., Zhuang, Y.: Weakly
   semi-supervised deep learning for multi-label image annotation. Trans. Big Data
   1(3), 109–122 (2015)
5. Zhang, T., Ghanem, B., Liu, S., Ahuja, N.: Robust visual tracking via multi-task
   sparse learning. In: Computer Vision and Pattern Recognition, pp. 2042–2049.
   IEEE (2012)
6. Zhang, Z., Luo, P., Loy, C.C., Tang, X.: Facial landmark detection by deep multi-
   task learning. In: Fleet, D., Pajdla, T., Schiele, B., Tuytelaars, T. (eds.) ECCV
   2014, Part VI. LNCS, vol. 8694, pp. 94–108. Springer, Heidelberg (2014). doi:10.
   1007/978-3-319-10599-4_7
7. Zhang, C., Zhang, Z.: Improving multiview face detection with multi-task deep
   convolutional neural networks. In: Winter Conference on Applications of Computer
   Vision, pp. 1036–1041. IEEE (2014)
8. Wang, X., Zhang, C., Zhang, Z.: Boosted multi-task learning for face verification
   with applications to web image and video search. In: Computer Vision and Pattern
   Recognition, pp. 142–149. IEEE (2009)
9. Yan, Y., Ricci, E., Subramanian, R., Lanz, O., Sebe, N.: No matter where you
   are: flexible graph-guided multi-task learning for multi-view head pose classification under target motion. In: International Conference on Computer Vision, pp.
   1177–1184. IEEE (2013)
10. Ouyang, W., Chu, X., Wang, X.: Multi-source deep learning for human pose esti-
    mation. In: Computer Vision and Pattern Recognition, pp. 2329–2336. IEEE (2014)
11. Yim, J., Jung, H., Yoo, B., Choi, C., Park, D., Kim, J.: Rotating your face using
    multi-task deep neural network. In: Computer Vision and Pattern Recognition, pp.
    676–684. IEEE (2015)
12. Kumar, N., Belhumeur, P., Nayar, S.: FaceTracer: a search engine for large collec-
    tions of images with faces. In: Forsyth, D., Torr, P., Zisserman, A. (eds.) ECCV
    2008, Part IV. LNCS, vol. 5305, pp. 340–353. Springer, Heidelberg (2008). doi:10.
    1007/978-3-540-88693-8_25
13. Liu, Z., Luo, P., Wang, X., Tang, X.: Deep learning face attributes in the wild. In:
    International Conference on Computer Vision, pp. 3730–3738. IEEE (2015)
14. Patel, V.M., Gopalan, R., Li, R., Chellappa, R.: Visual domain adaptation: a survey
    of recent advances. Sig. Process. Mag. **32**(3), 53–69 (2015)
15. Wei, Y., Xia, W., Huang, J., Ni, B., Dong, J., Zhao, Y., Yan, S.: CNN: single-label
    to multi-label (2014). arXiv preprint: arXiv:1406.5726

16. Jaderberg, M., Simonyan, K., Vedaldi, A., Zisserman, A.: Deep structured output learning for unconstrained text recognition. In: International Conference on Learning Representations (2015)
17. Huang, Y., Wang, W., Wang, L.: Unconstrained multimodal multi-label learning. Trans. Multimedia **17**(11), 1923–1935 (2015)
18. Cootes, T.F., Edwards, G.J., Taylor, C.J.: Active appearance models. Trans. Pattern Anal. Mach. Intell. **23**(6), 681–685 (2001)
19. Blanz, V., Vetter, T.: Face recognition based on fitting a 3D morphable model. Trans. Pattern Anal. Mach. Intell. **25**(9), 1063–1074 (2003)
20. Kumar, N., Berg, A.C., Belhumeur, P.N., Nayar, S.K.: Describable visual attributes for face verification and image search. Trans. Pattern Anal. Mach. Intell. **33**(10), 1962–1977 (2011)
21. Scheirer, W.J., Kumar, N., Belhumeur, P.N., Boult, T.E.: Multi-attribute spaces: Calibration for attribute fusion and similarity search. In: Computer Vision and Pattern Recognition, pp. 2933–2940. IEEE (2012)
22. Kumar, N., Berg, A.C., Belhumeur, P.N., Nayar, S.K.: Attribute and simile classifiers for face verification. In: International Conference on Computer Vision, pp. 365–372. IEEE (2009)
23. Parikh, D., Grauman, K.: Interactively building a discriminative vocabulary of nameable attributes. In: Computer Vision and Pattern Recognition, pp. 1681–1688. IEEE (2011)
24. Zhang, Z., Luo, P., Loy, C.C., Tang, X.: Learning social relation traits from face images. In: International Conference on Computer Vision, pp. 3631–3639. IEEE (2015)
25. Wilber, M.J., Rudd, E., Heflin, B., Lui, Y.M., Boult, T.E.: Exemplar codes for facial attributes and tattoo recognition. In: Winter Conference on Applications of Computer Vision, pp. 205–212. IEEE (2014)
26. Kang, S., Lee, D., Yoo, C.D.: Face attribute classification using attribute-aware correlation map and gated convolutional neural networks. In: International Conference on Image Processing, pp. 4922–4926. IEEE (2015)
27. Escorcia, V., Niebles, J.C., Ghanem, B.: On the relationship between visual attributes and convolutional networks. In: Computer Vision and Pattern Recognition, pp. 1256–1264. IEEE (2015)
28. Zhong, Y., Sullivan, J., Li, H.: Leveraging mid-level deep representations for prediction face attributes in the wild. In: International Conference on Image Processing. IEEE (2016)
29. Ehrlich, M., Shields, T.J., Almaev, T., Amer, M.R.: Facial attributes classification using multi-task representation learning. In: Computer Vision and Pattern Recognition Workshops, pp. 47–55 (2016)
30. Tzeng, E., Hoffman, J., Darrell, T., Saenko, K.: Simultaneous deep transfer across domains and tasks. In: International Conference on Computer Vision, pp. 4068–4076. IEEE (2015)
31. Wang, J., Cheng, Y., Feris, R.S.: Walk and learn: Facial attribute representation learning from egocentric video and contextual data. In: Computer Vision and Pattern Recognition. IEEE (2016)
32. Jayaraman, D., Sha, F., Grauman, K.: Decorrelating semantic visual attributes by resisting the urge to share. In: Computer Vision and Pattern Recognition, pp. 1629–1636. IEEE (2014)
33. Parkhi, O.M., Vedaldi, A., Zisserman, A.: Deep face recognition. In: British Machine Vision Conference, vol. 1(3), p. 6 (2015)

34. Dutta, A., Günther, M., El Shafey, L., Marcel, S., Veldhuis, R., Spreeuwers, L.: Impact of eye detection error on face recognition performance. IET Biometrics **4**, 137–150 (2015)
35. Simard, P.Y., Steinkraus, D., Platt, J.C.: Best practices for convolutional neural networks applied to visual document analysis. In: International Conference on Document Analysis and Recognition, pp. 958–963. IEEE (2003)

Degeneracies in Rolling Shutter SfM

Cenek Albl[1], Akihiro Sugimoto[2]([⊠]), and Tomas Pajdla[1]

[1] Czech Technical University in Prague, Prague, Czech Republic
{alblcene,pajdla}@cmp.felk.cvut.cz
[2] National Institute of Informatics, Tokyo, Japan
sugimoto@nii.ac.jp

Abstract. We address the problem of Structure from Motion (SfM) with rolling shutter cameras. We first show that many common camera configurations, e.g. cameras with parallel readout directions, become critical and allow for a large class of ambiguities in multi-view reconstruction. We provide mathematical analysis for one, two and some multi-view cases and verify it by synthetic experiments. Next, we demonstrate that bundle adjustment with rolling shutter cameras, which are close to critical configurations, may still produce drastically deformed reconstructions. Finally, we provide practical recipes how to photograph with rolling shutter cameras to avoid scene deformations in SfM. We evaluate the recipes and provide a quantitative analysis of their performance in real experiments. Our results show how to reconstruct correct 3D models with rolling shutter cameras.

Keywords: Structure from motion · Rolling shutter · Degeneracy · Non-perspective cameras

1 Introduction

Structure from Motion (SfM) reconstructs geometry of scenes from their images while simultaneously estimating camera poses and (some of) their internal parameters [5]. SfM has many practical applications in scene modelling, 3D mapping, and visual odometry [12,16,18]. Typical SfM considers perspective cameras, incrementally performs [16] and includes relative and absolute camera pose computation and bundle adjustment (BA) [17]. Recently, rolling shutter cameras became very important [11] since the rolling shutter is present in vast majority of current CMOS image sensors in consumer cameras and smart-phones. In rolling shutter cameras, images are not captured at once. They are scanned either along image rows or columns [13]. Since different image lines are exposed at different times, camera movement during the exposure produces image distortions. It has been shown that rolling shutter distortion can severely influence SfM computation [6,14] and that special care has to be taken to achieve sensible results.

Authors of [6] addressed the problem of SfM from video sequences and presented specially adapted BA algorithm for rolling shutter videos [7]. In [9] a SfM pipeline for cellphone videos is presented using video sequences and fusion with

© Springer International Publishing AG 2016
B. Leibe et al. (Eds.): ECCV 2016, Part V, LNCS 9909, pp. 36–51, 2016.
DOI: 10.1007/978-3-319-46454-1_3

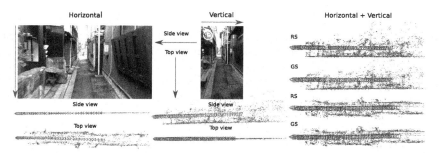

Fig. 1. SfM with rolling shutter model can deliver undesired results. (Left) A reconstruction from forward camera translation with vertical readout direction. (Middle) A reconstruction of the same scene from forward moving camera horizontal readout direction. In both cases, the scene collapses into a plane that is perpendicular to the readout direction. (Right) When both image directions are combined a correct reconstruction is obtained with rolling shutter (RS) projection model, which is close to a reconstruction with global shutter (GS) model.

inertial measurements. These works rely on the fact, that video sequences contain images separated closely in time and space and therefore we can interpolate between camera poses. Authors of [1] presented a technique for simultaneously estimating shape and motion of an object with rolling shutter stereo pair and pointed out a degenerate case.

Recently, techniques for computing absolute camera pose have been presented. In [10] authors estimate the camera pose using global optimization. A general minimal solution viable for incremental SfM is presented in [3]. Another minimal solution for translational movements has been shown in [15]. All of these works present camera models that improve the precision of camera pose estimation under rolling shutter image distortions and which are viable candidates for BA optimization in SfM reconstruction.

1.1 Motivation

Although state-of-the-art algorithms for rolling shutter absolute camera pose and BA have shown promising results, to our best knowledge, no one has yet addressed the task of running a complete RS SfM pipeline on general unordered sets of images. This is an important topic since almost all images taken today, even the still ones, can be affected with rolling shutter distortion. Also video sequences, where rolling shutter is most apparent, are often not desirable to be processed frame by frame, because that is a heavy computational load for longer sequences. The framerate available also could not be high enough for the interpolation used by [7]. Another issue is when combining data from different sources, where it is hard or impossible to enforce relationships between the camera poses and their motion. For these reasons, having SfM pipeline for rolling shutter images with no explicit constraints on the camera movement and temporal displacement is desirable.

Rolling shutter camera models describe the camera motion during image capture by various number of additional parameters. This introduces additional dimensions of freedom to the model. For bundle adjustment, a key component of SfM, this can introduce new and undesired local minimum. We observed in practice that the optimization tends to collapse into a degenerate solution which does not correspond to correct reconstruction in most of the cases (see Fig. 1). Although degenerate solutions have been studied for the case of perspective cameras, there has been no study for any of the rolling shutter camera models used today.

1.2 Contribution

The main purpose of this paper is to show the degeneracies introduced by rolling shutter camera models and to study them. The case of planar degeneracy which occurs most often in practice is explained and the reason why bundle adjustment always prefers this solution is given.

We show that the presence of the degenerate solution is dependent on the relative alignment of the input images. Cases where the scene can collapse into a plane for any number of cameras are shown as well as situations where it is not possible.

Our findings are backed by a number of both synthetic and real experiments that confirm the theory. We suggest a way to capture the images in practice such that the scene is reconstructed without any deformation. Again we verify the method on real data.

1.3 Notation and Concepts

A *similarity* transformation $\mathcal{S}$ is a composition of rotation R, translation $\mathbf{T}$ and uniform scaling s, i.e. $\mathcal{S}(\mathbf{X}) = s\,\mathsf{R}\,\mathbf{X} + \mathbf{T}$, where R is a rotation matrix, $\mathbf{T}$ is a translation vector and s is a scalar. *Image j* is a set of vectors $\mathbf{u}_i^j \in \mathbb{R}^3 \setminus \{\mathbf{0}\}$ with $i = 1, \ldots, n$, $j = 1, \ldots, m$. *Scene* is a set of vectors $\mathbf{X}_i \in \mathbb{R}^3$. We consider only finite scenes for simplicity.

Scene points are projected to image points by cameras as $\alpha_i^j \mathbf{u}_i^j = \pi(\mathsf{P}^j, \mathbf{X}_i)$, where P^j defines a particular camera projection model used and its parameters, and α_j^j are appropriate non-zero scales. For instance, when projecting by internally calibrated perspective cameras, the projection becomes $\alpha_i^j \mathbf{u}_i^j = \mathsf{R}^j \mathbf{X}_i + \mathbf{C}^j$, with rotation R^j and camera center $\mathbf{C}^j$.

A collection $\{\mathbf{X}_i, \mathsf{P}^j, \mathbf{u}_i^j\}$ such that $\alpha_i^j \mathbf{u}_i^j = \pi(\mathsf{P}^j, \mathbf{X}_i)$ for some α_i^j is called a *configuration*. We say that configuration $\{\mathbf{X}_i, \mathsf{P}^j, \mathbf{u}_i^j\}$ *explains* images $\mathbf{u}_i^j$. We say that configuration $\{\mathbf{X}_i, \mathsf{P}^j, \mathbf{u}_i^j\}$ is *related* to configuration $\{\mathbf{Y}_i, \mathsf{Q}^j, \mathbf{u}_i^j\}$ by a similarity transformation when there is a similarity transformation of points $\mathbf{Y}_i = \mathcal{S}(\mathbf{X}_i)$ and camera projection models $\mathsf{Q}^j = \mathcal{S}(\mathsf{P}^j)$ such that $\beta_i^j \mathbf{u}_i^j = \pi(\mathsf{Q}^j, \mathbf{Y}_i)$ for some β_i^j. For instance, for internally calibrated perspective cameras with $\mathsf{P}^j = (\mathsf{R}^j, \mathbf{C}^j)$, $\mathcal{S}(\mathsf{P}^j) = (\mathsf{R}^j \mathsf{R}^\top, s\mathbf{C}^j - \mathsf{R}^j \mathsf{R}^\top \mathbf{T})$ since $\pi(\mathcal{S}(\mathsf{P}^j), \mathcal{S}(\mathbf{X}_i)) = \mathsf{R}^j \mathsf{R}^\top (s\mathsf{R}\mathbf{X}_i + \mathbf{T}) + s\mathbf{C}^j - \mathsf{R}^j \mathsf{R}^\top \mathbf{T} = s\mathsf{R}^j \mathbf{X}_i + s\mathbf{C}^j = s\alpha_i^j \mathbf{u}_i^j$.

The goal of 3D reconstruction is to explain images $\mathbf{u}_i^j$ by a configuration $\{\mathbf{X}_i, \mathtt{P}^j, \mathbf{u}_i^j\}$ with scene points $\mathbf{X}_i$ measured in a Cartesian coordinate system. Different choices of Cartesian coordinate systems and different choices of measurement units produce configurations that are related by similarity transformations. Moreover, it is well-known that internally calibrated perspective images of a generic scene can be explained by a set S of configurations that with every element C of S contains also all configurations related to C by a similarity transformation [5], i.e. scene points can be reconstructed only up to a similarity transformation.

Therefore, every two configurations related by a similarity transformation will be considered equivalent. This equivalence relation partitions the set of all configurations into equivalence classes. Two configurations in one class are related by a similarity while two configurations in different classes are not related by a similarity. The equivalence class containing all configurations with scene points measured in a Cartesian coordinate system will be termed *correct reconstruction*. All other equivalence classes will be termed *incorrect reconstructions*.

We say that images $\mathbf{u}_i^j$ are *critical* if they can be explained by two configurations that are not equivalent, i.e., by at least one configuration that is in the incorrect reconstruction. Notice that our concept of criticality is somewhat different from concepts used in [4,8], where they studied which scenes and cameras produce critical configurations for perspective images. Here we are interested in analyzing when images may be critical when using a rolling shutter models and we therefore modify the concept accordingly for that purpose.

2 Rolling Shutter Camera Model

In this paper, we consider internally calibrated rolling shutter (RS) camera models, which describe RS cameras that are realized as internally calibrated perspective cameras ($\mathtt{K} = \mathtt{I}$) with the row readout speed equal to one. To simplify the exposition, we will, hereafter, drop the adjective "internally calibrated". Therefore, "perspective model" means "internally calibrated perspective model" and "RS model" means "internally calibrated RS model". Calibrated perspective projection can be described by $\alpha_i \mathbf{u}_i = \mathtt{R}\,\mathbf{X}_i + \mathbf{C}$ where $\mathtt{R} \in SO(3)$ and $\mathbf{C} \in \mathbb{R}^3$ is the rotation and the translation transforming a 3D point $\mathbf{X}_i \in \mathbb{R}^3$ from a world coordinate system to the camera coordinate system with $\mathbf{u}_i = [c_i, r_i, 1]^\top$, and $\alpha_i \in \mathbb{R} \setminus \{0\}$.

In the RS [11] model, when the camera is moving during the image capture, every image row or image column is captured at a different time and hence at a different position. Here we assume that image is captured row by row and therefore the rotation $\mathtt{R}$ and the translation $\mathbf{C}$ are functions of the image row r_i: $\alpha_i \mathbf{u}_i = \alpha_i [c_i, r_i, 1]^\top = \mathtt{R}(r_i)\mathbf{X}_i + \mathbf{C}(r_i)$. Various models for $\mathtt{R}(r_i)$ and $\mathbf{C}(r_i)$ have been considered [2,3,7,11]. All of them used a linearized translational motion with constant velocity and direction $\mathbf{C}(r_i) = \mathbf{C}_0 + r_i \mathbf{t}$. This approximation can be justified by the fact that the readout times of one frame are short (tens of milliseconds) and there is not much acceleration over this period of time.

The same justification is used for camera rotational velocity, which is considered constant during the frame capture. Rotation $R(r_i)$ was often modeled as a composition $R(r) = R_r(r_i)R_0$ of a static part R_0 and a motion part $R_r(r_i)$. The motion part $R_r(r_i)$ has been parameterized by SLERP [6,7], Rodriguez formula [2,10] or was linearized by the first order Taylor expansion [2,10,11]. Here we will concentrate on the linearized model of rotation [2,10,11], which approximates rotation $R_r(r_i)$ as

$$R_r(r_i) = \begin{bmatrix} 1 & -r_i\omega_z & r_i\omega_y \\ r_i\omega_z & 1 & -r_i\omega_x \\ -r_i\omega_y & r_i\omega_x & 1 \end{bmatrix}. \tag{1}$$

Putting all the above together, brings us to the following RS camera model

$$\alpha_i\mathbf{u}_i = \alpha_i\left[c_i, r_i, 1\right]^\top = R_r(r_i)R_0\mathbf{X}_i + \mathbf{C}_0 + r_i\mathbf{t} \tag{2}$$

with $P(r) = [R_r(r), R_0, \mathbf{C}_0, \mathbf{t}]$.

3   Bundle Adjustment with Independent RS Models

In this paper we consider Bundle Adjustment (BA) with independent RS models. This is more general than BA developed in [7] for (video) sequences of regularly spaced cameras where the camera motion during the image capture was constrained to be along the global camera trajectory. Our approach is necessary when reconstructing scenes from unorganized RS images.

Bundle adjustment [17] minimizes the sum of squares of reprojection errors which are, in our case, expressed as

$$\mathbf{e}_i^j = \tilde{\mathbf{u}}_i^j - \mu(\pi(P^j(\tilde{r}_i), \mathbf{X}_i)), \tag{3}$$

where $\tilde{\mathbf{u}}_i^j = \left[\tilde{c}_i^j, \tilde{r}_i^j\right]^\top$ is the measured image point, $\mu([x, y, z]^\top) = [x/z, y/z]^\top$ is the perspective division and $P^j(\tilde{r}_i)$ is an RS projection model of the j-th camera.

Non-linear least squares methods are used to find a solution $(P^{j*}, \mathbf{X}_i^*)$ that (locally) minimizes the error over all the visible projections (i, j)

$$(P^{j*}, \mathbf{X}_i^*) = \arg\min \sum_{(i,j)} \|\mathbf{e}_i^j\|^2.$$

When the set of images $\mathbf{u}_i^j$ is critical, it might happen that the bundle adjustment algorithm finds a local minimum producing an incorrect reconstruction. We will see that this indeed often happens.

4   Ambiguities in 3D Reconstruction with RS Camera Models

Ambiguities in 3D reconstruction with the perspective projection model have been extensively studied in [8]. It has been found there that two perspective cameras and any number of scene points on certain ruled quadrics containing the cameras centers are in a critical configuration, as well as that for three perspective cameras, there is always a quartic curve of scene points such that they are in a critical configuration. Hence, there are situations when a set of perspective images become critical. However, the critical perspective images are very special and therefore do not in general pose problems for 3D reconstruction in practical situations with many points in generic scenes.

RS models are more general than the perspective model and therefore we expect to see more critical image sets when reconstructing with RS models. In particular, every perspective image can be explained by an RS model (2) with $\mathbf{t} = \mathbf{0}$ and $R_r(r_i) = I$. Therefore, every set of images that is critical for the perspective projection model is also critical for RS model (2).

RS cameras produce images with large variation of RS effects. Photographing static scenes with static RS cameras produces perspective images while images taken by RS cameras on a fast train exhibit pronounced RS effects. It is therefore desirable to look for RS SfM that can deal with all levels of RS effects. In particular, it is important that any practical RS SfM can handle perspective images.

When RS images are not truly perspective, it is often possible to treat the rolling shutter effect as (perhaps systematic) image error and explain RS images with perspective cameras, distorted scene, and somewhat higher image error. Therefore, it is important to analyze when a set of perspective images become critical w.r.t. RS model (2).

We will next show that, in many practical situations, images taken by perspective cameras become critical when reconstructed with RS model (2) and, even worse, when image noise is present, images can be explained by incorrect reconstructions with smaller error than is the smallest error of a correct reconstruction. Hence, in such situations, BA often prefers incorrect reconstructions.

We will use the RS camera model (2) with the rotation parameterized by the linearized model (1), which was used in [2, 3, 10, 11], since it is simple to show the ambiguities algebraically with this model. The linearized rotation model is an approximation to all the other models used in the literature and therefore images that are critical w.r.t. to model (2) will be close to critical for all other models if a cameras make turns by a small angle during the image capture.. For other models, the derivations we show will not hold exactly but they will be very close for many practical situations. We have observed in experiments that BA converges to incorrect reconstructions for all RS camera models in all the cases we have tested.

4.1   Single Camera

We will start with showing how we can arbitrarily rotate the projection rays of a single RS camera and even collapse them in a single plane.

In order for a 3D point $\mathbf{X}_i$ to project into coordinate $[c_i, r_i, 1]^\top$ in the image, it has to lie on a plane defined by the row r_i and the camera center. All points that lie in such a plane can be therefore described as

$$\mathbf{X}(c, r_i, \alpha) = (\mathtt{R}_r(r_i)\,\mathtt{R}_0)^{-1}\left(\alpha\,[c, r_i, 1]^\top - \mathbf{C}_0 - r_i\mathbf{t}\right).$$

To obtain an equation representing the plane, we need three non-collinear points, e.g.

$$\mathbf{X}(1, r_i, 0) = (\mathtt{R}_r(r_i)\,\mathtt{R}_0)^{-1}\left(-\mathbf{C}_0 - r_i\mathbf{t}\right),$$
$$\mathbf{X}(1, r_i, 1) = (\mathtt{R}_r(r_i)\,\mathtt{R}_0)^{-1}\left([1, r_i, 1]^\top - \mathbf{C}_0 - r_i\mathbf{t}\right),$$
$$\mathbf{X}(0, r_i, 1) = (\mathtt{R}_r(r_i)\,\mathtt{R}_0)^{-1}\left([0, r_i, 1]^\top - \mathbf{C}_0 - r_i\mathbf{t}\right).$$

The plane $\mathbf{n}(r_i)$ determined by these three points is the solution of the following homogeneous equation system:

$$\begin{bmatrix} (-\mathbf{C}_0 - r_i\mathbf{t})^\top\,(\mathtt{R}_r(r_i)\,\mathtt{R}_0)^{-\top} & 1 \\ \left([1, r_i, 1]^\top - \mathbf{C}_0 - r_i\mathbf{t}\right)^\top\,(\mathtt{R}_r(r_i)\,\mathtt{R}_0)^{-\top} & 1 \\ \left([0, r_i, 1]^\top - \mathbf{C}_0 - r_i\mathbf{t}\right)^\top\,(\mathtt{R}_r(r_i)\,\mathtt{R}_0)^{-\top} & 1 \end{bmatrix} \mathbf{n}(r_i) = \mathtt{A}(r_i)\mathbf{n}(r_i) = \mathbf{0} \qquad (4)$$

The solution of this system always spans at least one dimensional space, which is the null-space of $\mathtt{A}(r_i)$, since the rank of $\mathtt{A}(r_i)$ is at most three.

We set $\mathbf{C}_0 = [0, 0, 0]^\top$ and $\mathtt{R}_0 = \mathtt{I}$ for simplicity and disregard the translational motion $\mathbf{t}$. We then set $\omega_y = \omega_z = 0$ to simulate the rotation around the x-axis alone. The 3D point projected on a row r_i is now written as $\mathbf{X}(c, r_i, \alpha) = \alpha\mathtt{R}_r(r_i)^{-1}\,[c, r_i, 1]^\top$. We again choose the triplet $\mathbf{X}(1, r_i, 0)$, $\mathbf{X}(1, r_i, 1)$ and $\mathbf{X}(0, r_i, 1)$ to determine the plane $\mathbf{n}(r_i)$, from which Eq. (4) yields

$$\begin{bmatrix} 0 & 0 & 0 & 1 \\ 1 & 0 & 0 & 0 \\ 0 & \frac{r_i(\omega_x+1)}{r_i^2\omega_x^2+1} & -\frac{r_i^2\omega_x-1}{r_i^2\omega_x^2+1} & 1 \end{bmatrix} \mathbf{n}(r_i) = 0.$$

We see that $\mathbf{n}(r_i)$ below is a solution:

$$\mathbf{n}(r_i) = \left[0, 1, \frac{r_i\,(\omega_x + 1)}{r_i^2\omega_x - 1}, 0\right]^\top.$$

We can see that if we set $\omega_x = -1$ then $\mathbf{n}(r_i)$ becomes the plane $y = 0$ for any r_i. This indicates that there exists a rotational motion (linearized) making all the projected planes $\mathbf{n}(r_i)$ coplanar (see Fig. 2).

We will now extend this example to a camera whose center lies in a plane $y = 0$ and whose corresponding $\mathbf{n}(0)$ is also contained in this plane. Such a camera has $\mathbf{C} = [C_x, 0, C_z]^\top$ and can be rotated around the y-axis by angle ϕ. We will now consider the translational motion $\mathbf{t} = [t_x, t_y, t_z]^\top$ as well. The null-space of the matrix $\mathtt{A}(r_i)$ then changes to

$$\left[-\sin(\phi)(\omega_x + 1), \frac{\omega_x r_i^2 - 1}{r_i}, \cos(\phi)(\omega_x + 1), C_z - t_y + r_i t_z\right]^\top.$$

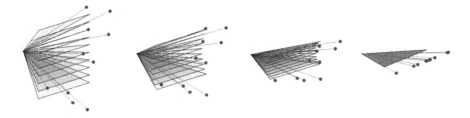

Fig. 2. Changing the rotational velocity ω_x around the x-axis for a rolling shutter camera model changes the alignment of projection rays that correspond to each image row. From left to right there is $\omega_x = 0$, $\omega_x = -0.3$, $\omega_x = -0.6$ and $\omega_x = -1$. For $\omega_x = -1$ all projection rays collapse into a single plane and any image can be explained by 3D points in a plane.

It is clear that by setting $\omega_x = -1$, $t_z = 0$ and $t_y = C_z$, we obtain again the plane $y = 0$ for any r_i. We remark that we need the non-zero t_y which is dependent on the camera position in the plane. The reason for this is that in this camera model we express the camera center in the camera coordinate system, which is changing for each r_i due to ω_x. We show that for the linearized rotation model the rotational velocity $\omega = [\omega_x, 0, 0]^\top$ can be compensated by translational velocity $\mathbf{t} = [0, C_z, 0]^\top$ to fix the camera center in the world coordinate system.

4.2   Two Cameras

Using the findings in the previous section, that arbitrary RS camera can be collapsed in a plane, we will now argue that every two images can be explained by two RS cameras and a planar scene such that the reprojection error (3) is zero.

Since each image can be explained by a camera whose center lies in plane $y = 0$ and this plane also contains all their projection rays, every two rays must intersect at least in one point. We can show this algebraically by using the equations for triangulating 3D points with known camera parameters. We can write the projection matrix parameterized by r_i as

$$\mathsf{P}^j(r_i) = \left[\mathsf{R}^j(r_i^j)\mathsf{R}_0^j \, \mathbf{C}_0^j + \mathbf{C}_r^j(r_i^j) \right] = \left[\mathbf{p}_1^j(r_i^j), \mathbf{p}_2^j(r_i^j), \mathbf{p}_3^j(r_i^j) \right]^\top .$$

Then for a 3D point corresponding to two image measurements $\tilde{\mathbf{u}}_1 = \left[\tilde{c}_i^1, \tilde{r}_i^1 \right]^\top$ and $\tilde{\mathbf{u}}_2 = \left[\tilde{c}_i^2, \tilde{r}_i^2 \right]^\top$ in two cameras having parameters $\mathsf{P}^1(\tilde{r}_i^1)$ and $\mathsf{P}^2(\tilde{r}_i^2)$ the following system of equations must hold with $\lambda (\in \mathbb{R} \setminus \{0\})$

$$\mathsf{M}_i \mathbf{X}_i = \begin{bmatrix} \tilde{c}_i^1 \mathbf{p}_3^1(\tilde{r}_i^1)^\top - \mathbf{p}_1^1(\tilde{r}_i^1)^\top \\ \tilde{r}_i^1 \mathbf{p}_3^1(\tilde{r}_i^1)^\top - \mathbf{p}_2^1(\tilde{r}_i^1)^\top \\ \tilde{c}_i^2 \mathbf{p}_3^2(\tilde{r}_i^2)^\top - \mathbf{p}_1^2(\tilde{r}_i^2)^\top \\ \tilde{r}_i^2 \mathbf{p}_3^2(\tilde{r}_i^2)^\top - \mathbf{p}_2^2(\tilde{r}_i^2)^\top \end{bmatrix} \begin{bmatrix} \lambda x_i \\ \lambda y_i \\ \lambda z_i \\ \lambda \end{bmatrix} = \mathbf{0}. \qquad (5)$$

In order for a 3D point $[x_i, y_i, z_i]^\top$ to exist, the null-space of the 4×4 matrix $\mathtt{M}_i$ has to be at least one-dimensional, i.e., the rank must be at most 3. To calculate the triangulated 3D point coordinates we can compute the null-space. For perspective cameras in general configuration, the null-space will be either zero dimensional for non-intersecting camera rays or one dimensional, corresponding to a single 3D point.

Let us apply Eq. (5) to the above example with two RS cameras whose centers both lie in a plane $y = 0$. The rotation matrices $\mathtt{R}_0^1$ and $\mathtt{R}_0^2$ will be rotations around y axis by angles ϕ^1 and ϕ^2. Camera centers will lie anywhere in $y = 0$: $\mathbf{C}_0^1 = \left[C_x^1, 0, C_z^1\right]^\top$ and $\mathbf{C}_0^2 = \left[C_x^2, 0, C_z^2\right]^\top$. To collapse the projection rays of both cameras we will set, as shown in the previous section, the rotational velocities $\omega_x^1 = -1$ and $\omega_x^2 = -1$ and translational velocities $\mathbf{t}^1 = \left[0, t_y^1, 0\right]^\top$ and $\mathbf{t}^2 = \left[0, t_y^2, 0\right]^\top$. We then obtain the following matrix

$$
\mathtt{M}_i = \begin{bmatrix} -\cos(\phi^1) - \tilde{c}_i^1 \sin(\phi^1) & -\tilde{c}_i^1 \tilde{r}_i^1 & \tilde{c}_i^1 \cos(\phi^1) - \sin(\phi^1) & C_z^1 \tilde{c}_i^1 - C_x^1 \\ 0 & -(\tilde{r}_i^1)^2 - 1 & 0 & 0 \\ -\cos(\phi^2) - \tilde{c}_i^2 \sin(\phi^2) & -\tilde{c}_i^2 \tilde{r}_i^2 & \tilde{c}_i^2 \cos(\phi^2) - \sin(\phi^2) & C_z^2 \tilde{c}_i^2 - C_x^2 \\ 0 & -(\tilde{r}_i^2)^2 - 1 & 0 & 0 \end{bmatrix}.
$$

The rank of $\mathtt{M}_i$ is at most 3 and, therefore, the rays always intersect at least in one point. For any pair of image projections the null-space of $\mathtt{M}_i$ and thus the subspace where the 3D point can lie is $[a, 0, b, 1]^\top$ and therefore all points could be reconstructed in plane $y = 0$.

4.3   Projecting onto a Plane

Before we proceed to analysis of multiple RS cameras we need to explain an important fact, that is, the rotation induced by $\omega = [-1, 0, 0]^\top$ in the linearized RS model is actually a projection onto a plane $y = 0$. Let us see what happens to an arbitrary point on a camera ray. Any 3D point that lies on a camera ray can be expressed in the camera coordinate system as $\alpha \left[c_i, r_i, 1\right]^\top$. For the sake of simplicity we will consider $\mathtt{R}_0 = \mathtt{I}$ and $\mathbf{C}_0 = [0, 0, 0]^\top$ now. We can express the 3D point in a world coordinate system by

$$
\mathbf{X} = \mathtt{R}(r_i)^{-1} \begin{bmatrix} \alpha c_i \\ \alpha r_i \\ \alpha \end{bmatrix} = \begin{bmatrix} 1 & 0 & 0 \\ 0 & \frac{1}{1+r_i^2} & \frac{-r_i}{1+r_i^2} \\ 0 & \frac{r_i}{1+r_i^2} & \frac{1}{1+r_i^2} \end{bmatrix} \begin{bmatrix} \alpha c_i \\ \alpha r_i \\ \alpha \end{bmatrix} = \begin{bmatrix} \alpha c_i \\ 0 \\ \alpha \end{bmatrix},
$$

which shows that the x and z coordinates remain the same while the y coordinate is dropped. An illustration of this is in Fig. 3.

4.4   Multiple Cameras with Parallel y (readout) Directions

We will now use the result from previous subsection to make the following statement.

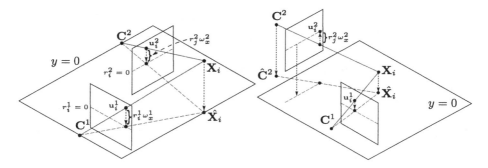

Fig. 3. (Left) Two possible configurations of a scene from image projections u_i^1 and u_i^2. One is represented by two perspective cameras and point $\mathbf{X}_i$ and the other by linearized RS cameras with $\omega_x^1 = \omega_x^2 = -1$ and point $\hat{\mathbf{X}}_i$. This figure illustrates that changing ω_x parameter to -1 equals to a projection into a plane $y = 0$. (Right) This projection is possible even for cameras that do not lie in the plane $y = 0$ but their readout direction is parallel.

Theorem: *Assume any number of images taken by perspective cameras with parallel y (readout) directions in space. Then, if there exists a reconstruction for such cameras using the perspective camera model, then there also exists a reconstruction using the RS camera model (2) with all cameras and 3D points lying in plane $y = 0$.*

This statement can be proven by combining the previous statements. The perspective reconstruction gives a set of 3D points $\mathbf{X}_i = [x_i, y_i, z_i]^\top$ and the cameras whose centers are $\mathbf{C}_0^j = \left[C_x^j, C_y^j, C_z^j\right]^\top$ and whose y axes are aligned with the y axis in the world coordinate system, where j is the index for cameras and i for 3D points. If we project the rays connecting $\mathbf{C}_0^j$ and $\mathbf{X}_i$ onto the plane $y = 0$ we will obtain the rays that pass through $\hat{\mathbf{C}}_0^j = \left[C_x^j, 0, C_z^j\right]^\top$ and $\hat{\mathbf{X}}_i = [x_i, 0, z_i]^\top$ which we have shown that is a configuration that is easily achieved by setting $\omega_x^j = -1$ (see Fig. 3). It follows that if there exists a perspective reconstruction for such images with zero reprojection error, the reconstruction projected to $y = 0$ will also have a zero reprojection error.

4.5   The Effect of Planar Projection in the Presence of Image Noise

The mere existence of the planar representation of the scene is not a reason BA should converge to such a solution. In practice, however, measured image points are affected by noise, and this noise leads to non-zero reprojection error $\mathbf{e}_i^j$ in BA (see Eq. (3)). In this section we show that the planar projection always reduces the reprojection error and therefore it always provides a superior solution in BA.

Suppose measured image points $\tilde{\mathbf{u}}_i^j = \left[\tilde{c}_i^j, \tilde{r}_i^j\right]^\top$ are now affected by noise such that $\mathbf{e}_i^j = \tilde{\mathbf{u}}_i^j - \mu(\mathsf{P}^j(\tilde{r}_i)\mathbf{X}_i)$. For perspective projection, i.e. $\omega^j = [0,0,0]^\top$ and $\mathbf{t}^j = [0,0,0]^\top$ the error can be expressed as

$$\mathbf{e}_i^j = \tilde{\mathbf{u}}_i^j - \mu \left(R_0^j \mathbf{X}_i + \mathbf{C}^j \right) = \begin{bmatrix} \tilde{c}_i^j & - \frac{C_x^j + x\cos(\phi^j) + z\sin(\phi^j)}{C_z^j + z\cos(\phi^j) - x\sin(\phi^j)} \\ \tilde{r}_i^j & - \frac{y}{C_z^j + z\cos(\phi^j) - x\sin(\phi^j)} \end{bmatrix}$$

whereas the reprojection error using the linearized RS camera model with $\omega^j = \left[\omega_x^j, 0, 0\right]^\top$ and $\mathbf{t}^j = \left[0, C_z^j, 0\right]^\top$ is

$$\mathbf{e}_i^j = \begin{bmatrix} e_{ix}^j \\ e_{iy}^j \end{bmatrix} = \tilde{\mathbf{u}}_i^j - \mu \left(R_r^j(\tilde{r}_i^j) R_0^j \mathbf{X}_i + \mathbf{C}^j + \tilde{r}_i^j \mathbf{t}^j \right) = \begin{bmatrix} \tilde{c}_i^j & - \frac{C_x^j + x\cos(\phi^j) + z\sin(\phi^j)}{C_z^j + z\cos(\phi^j) - x\sin(\phi^j)} \\ 0 \end{bmatrix}.$$

The e_{iy}^j component of the reprojection error is eliminated and the e_{ix}^j component remains unchanged by the projection to $y = 0$; therefore the overall error is reduced. This is always true for images taken by the perspective cameras with identical y directions in space.

4.6   What Does It Mean in Practice?

We have shown the reason why the planar projection reduces the reprojection error in the case where all images are captured by perspective cameras with identical y direction in space. This case is in practice hardly achieved exactly, but we can often come very close to this scenario, for example when taking handheld pictures while walking or taking pictures with a camera mounted on a car.

When images are captured with the y directions not parallel, we are still able to reduce e_{iy}^j to zero, but at the cost of increasing the e_{ix}^j component. It follows that BA will try to reduce e_{iy}^j as far as the increase in e_{ix}^j does not exceed the reduction in e_{iy}^j.

The amount of increase in e_{ix}^j depends on camera poses when images are taken and it is complicated to analyze in general. We have, however, practically observed the following fact.

Observation: *For three or more images by perspective cameras with pairwisely different y directions, the deformation of the scene by BA due to using the RS model is directly dependent on the angle between the y axes.*

In synthetic experiments, we show that when the smallest angle between the three pairs of y directions is at least 30 degrees, the reconstruction is recovered correctly. I real experiments, on the other hand, we show that capturing the scene with sufficient amount of images with two distinct y directions that are perpendicular with each other, i.e. taking portrait as well as landscape images provides a correct reconstruction.

5   Experiments

5.1   Synthetic Experiments

In Sect. 4 we have shown that images captured with parallel readout directions used in BA with linearized RS camera model can be explained by a planar scene

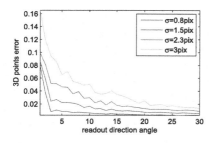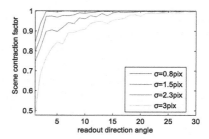

Fig. 4. Experiment with three randomly initialized cameras. The x axis shows the minimal readout direction angle among the three cameras. The figure on the left shows the mean spatial error over all 3D points after the optimization and the figure on the left shows the contraction factor of the scene compared to the ground truth. The lower the contraction factor the more deformation is in the scene. Results are shown for several values of error in the observations, expressed by the variance σ of their zero mean normal distribution.

and that this configuration has lower reprojection error. In synthetic experiments we verified this also for SLERP and Rodriguez parameterization.

Further investigation was aimed at the case when image readout directions were not parallel during capture. We studied the amount of minimal angular difference between the three readout directions needed for the scene to be reconstructed correctly. To express the "correctness" of the reconstruction we introduce a measure which we call the scene contraction factor.

We calculate scene contraction factor as the ratio between the third principal component of the 3D points' coordinates before and after BA. The optimized 3D points after BA are first fitted to the initial 3D points by a similarity transform and then the principal components are calculated. If the scene is deformed, the third principal component will be different. A correctly reconstructed scene will have contraction factor close to 1 whereas completely flat scene will have contraction factor equal to 0.

We sampled three cameras randomly on a sphere with radius of 1 and pointing towards the a cubical scene. We measured the mean distance of initial 3D points from the resulting ones and also the scene contraction factor. Altogether 10,000 samples were generated and we categorized them based on the minimal angle between the three pairs of readout directions.

For each of these samples the same analysis as in previous experiment was done using 1000 different initializations with increasing image noise. We show the results for several values of the image noise in Fig. 4. From these experiments we can predict that if the minimal readout direction angle among the three camera pairs is at least 30 degrees, the reconstruction should be correct.

5.2   Real Data Experiments

To test our hypotheses under real conditions we captured several datasets using smart-phone camera under various angles. In order to have three mutually

distinct RS readout directions we captured the same scene in vertical, horizontal and tilted position of the phone. Images were extracted from short videos
captured handheld while moving around the objects or walking.

An incremental SfM pipeline similar to [16,18] was used to provide a baseline
reconstruction. This pipeline was then adapted to use R6P [3] solver for absolute
camera pose computation and used either linearized camera rotation model,
SLERP or Rodriguez rotation model in bundle adjustment. Since we observed
identical behavior for all rotation models, we present only the results of the
linearized one. This rolling shutter aware version of the pipeline is denoted in
the experiments as RS and the original as global shutter (GS) camera, which is
equivalent with the perspective camera.

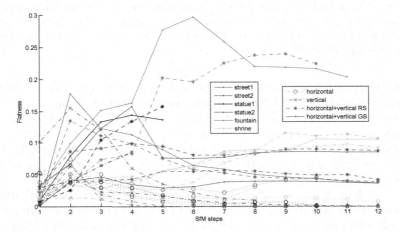

Fig. 5. Analysis of the criticality in real datasets. The degeneracy is shown as flatness of
the scene, where zero means completely flat. For either horizontal or vertical datasets,
the degeneracy is apparent as the scene usually collapses to a plane completely. The
results of the RS pipeline on datasets with both horizontal and vertical images show
the same scene dimensions as the ones with GS pipeline.

For each dataset we ran the two pipelines on several subsets of data – horizontal images, vertical images, horizontal+vertical and horizontal+vertical+tilted.
According to our expectations, for the subsets containing only one readout direction the scene was collapsing to a plane as the RS incremental pipeline was pro-
gressing. We have calculated the flatness of the scene using principal component
analysis (Fig. 5). Note that flatness in Fig. 5 is not the same as scene contraction
factor used in synthetic experiments, value 0 still means the scene is completely
flat, but the maximum is different for each dataset.

It is important to realize that in practice only few iterations of BA are allowed
for the sake of performance and therefore the scene collapses gradually as new
cameras are added and BA step is repeated. For small datasets with only small
number of BA steps (up to 20 cameras) the deformation was not so apparent but

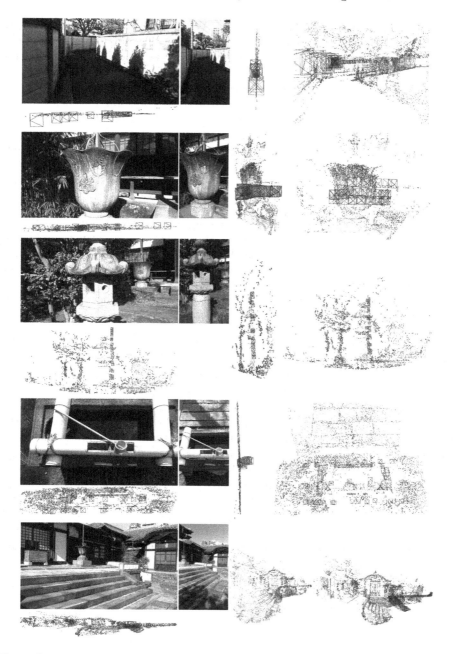

Fig. 6. Reconstructions using SfM pipeline for unorganized RS images. (Left) Horizontal image set sample and its reconstruction below. (Middle) Vertical image set sample and its reconstruction next to it. (Right) Reconstruction from both horizontal and vertical images. Notice the deformations when only one image direction is used. Two perpendicular directions provide correct results.

it was extremely critical in larger datasets. When three distinct image readout directions were present in the dataset, we did not notice any deformation of the model caused by the RS pipeline compared to the GS pipeline, which confirms our predictions.

Even more important, however, are the experiments with two distinct readout directions (horizontal+vertical), which also do not show any deformation compared to the baseline GS reconstruction. This shows that in practice having horizontal as well as vertical images of the scene should be sufficient to successfully reconstruct the scene using RS pipeline. We show the results in (a rather complex) Fig. 6.

6 Conclusion

We tackled the topic of SfM with RS cameras. Recent works have shown that accounting for the camera movement in RS images can greatly improve the result and presented several practical RS camera models. We show that such models when used without constraints on the camera motion lead to incorrect reconstructions.

We analyzed the cases in which incorrect reconstruction arises and the reasons why it is so. We prove that any two perspective images can be explained by the linearized RS camera model and a planar scene. Further we prove that a set of images taken with parallel readout directions that can be explained by perspective cameras can also be explained by RS cameras and a scene all lying in a single plane. Moreover, we prove that the reprojection error is always reduced in such a case and, therefore, BA tends to prefer such solution.

This is a consequence of the linearized rotation being a mere projection on a plane. Since the linearized rotation model is a close approximation to all the other models it is expected that the other models will exert similar effects in BA. We have observed this both in synthetic and real data.

We show that in order to obtain a correct reconstruction using unconstrained RS SfM pipeline the input images should be captured with different readout directions. Synthetic experiments suggest that for 3 or more cameras, the minimal mutual angle between the readout directions should be at least 30 degrees. The experiments on real data confirm our predictions and in addition show that having two image sets with perpendicular readout directions is enough to obtain a correct reconstruction using SfM pipeline with the RS camera model.

Acknowledgment. This research was in part supported by Czech Ministry of Education under Project RVO13000, by Grant Agency of the CTU Prague project SGS16/230/OHK3/3T/13 and by Grant-in-Aid for Scientific Research of the Ministry of Education, Culture, Sports, Science and Technology of Japan.

References

1. Ait-Aider, O., Berry, F.: Structure and kinematics triangulation with a rolling shutter stereo rig. In: IEEE 12th International Conference on Computer Vision, pp. 1835–1840, September 2009

2. Ait-aider, O., Andreff, N., Lavest, J.M., Blaise, U., Ferr, P.C., Cnrs, L.U.: Simultaneous object pose and velocity computation using a single view from a rolling shutter camera. In: Proceedings of the European Conference on Computer Vision, pp. 56–68 (2006)
3. Albl, C., Kukelova, Z., Pajdla, T.: R6p - rolling shutter absolute pose problem. In: 2015 IEEE Conference on Computer Vision and Pattern Recognition (CVPR), pp. 2292–2300, June 2015
4. Hartley, R., Kahl, F.: Critical configurations for projective reconstruction from multiple views. IJCV **71**, 5–47 (2006)
5. Hartley, R., Zisserman, A.: Multiple View Geometry in Computer Vision. Cambridge University Press, New York (2003)
6. Hedborg, J., Ringaby, E., Forssen, P.E., Felsberg, M.: Structure and motion estimation from rolling shutter video. In: 2011 IEEE International Conference on Computer Vision Workshops (ICCV Workshops), pp. 17–23 (2011)
7. Hedborg, J., Forssèn, P.E., Felsberg, M., Ringaby, E.: Rolling shutter bundle adjustment. In: CVPR, pp. 1434–1441 (2012)
8. Kahl, F., Hartley, R.: Critical curves and surfaces for euclidean reconstruction. In: Heyden, A., Sparr, G., Nielsen, M., Johansen, P. (eds.) ECCV 2002. LNCS, vol. 2351, pp. 447–462. Springer, Heidelberg (2002). doi:10.1007/3-540-47967-8_30
9. Klein, G., Murray, D.: Parallel tracking and mapping on a camera phone. In: 8th IEEE International Symposium on Mixed and Augmented Reality, ISMAR 2009, pp. 83–86, October 2009
10. Magerand, L., Bartoli, A., Ait-Aider, O., Pizarro, D.: Global optimization of object pose and motion from a single rolling shutter image with automatic 2D-3D matching. In: Fitzgibbon, A., Lazebnik, S., Perona, P., Sato, Y., Schmid, C. (eds.) ECCV 2012. LNCS, vol. 7572, pp. 456–469. Springer, Heidelberg (2012). doi:10.1007/978-3-642-33718-5_33
11. Meingast, M., Geyer, C., Sastry, S.: Geometric models of rolling-shutter cameras. Comput. Res. Repository (2005)
12. Moulon, P., Monasse, P., Marlet, R.: Global fusion of relative motions for robust, accurate and scalable structure from motion. In: 2013 IEEE International Conference on Computer Vision (ICCV), pp. 3248–3255, December 2013
13. Oth, L., Furgale, P., Kneip, L., Siegwart, R.: Rolling shutter camera calibration. In: 2013 IEEE Conference on Computer Vision and Pattern Recognition (CVPR), pp. 1360–1367, June 2013
14. Saurer, O., Koser, K., Bouguet, J.Y., Pollefeys, M.: Rolling shutter stereo. In: 2013 IEEE International Conference on Computer Vision (ICCV), pp. 465–472, December 2013
15. Saurer, O., Pollefeys, M., Lee, G.H.: A minimal solution to the rolling shutter pose estimation problem. In: 2015 IEEE/RSJ International Conference on Intelligent Robots and Systems (IROS), pp. 1328–1334, September 2015
16. Snavely, N., Seitz, S.M., Szeliski, R.: Photo tourism: exploring photo collections in 3d. In: ACM SIGGRAPH 2006 Papers, pp. 835–846. ACM, New York (2006)
17. Triggs, B., McLauchlan, P.F., Hartley, R.I., Fitzgibbon, A.W.: Bundle adjustment — a modern synthesis. In: Triggs, B., Zisserman, A., Szeliski, R. (eds.) IWVA 1999. LNCS, vol. 1883, pp. 298–372. Springer, Heidelberg (2000). doi:10.1007/3-540-44480-7_21
18. Wu, C.: VisualSFM: A Visual Structure from Motion System (2011)

Deep Deformation Network for Object Landmark Localization

Xiang Yu$^{(\boxtimes)}$, Feng Zhou, and Manmohan Chandraker

Department of Media Analytics, NEC Laboratories America, Cupertino, USA
{xiangyu,manu}@nec-labs.com, zhfe99@gmail.com

Abstract. We propose a novel cascaded framework, namely deep deformation network (DDN), for localizing landmarks in non-rigid objects. The hallmarks of DDN are its incorporation of geometric constraints within a convolutional neural network (CNN) framework, ease and efficiency of training, as well as generality of application. A novel shape basis network (SBN) forms the first stage of the cascade, whereby landmarks are initialized by combining the benefits of CNN features and a learned shape basis to reduce the complexity of the highly nonlinear pose manifold. In the second stage, a point transformer network (PTN) estimates local deformation parameterized as thin-plate spline transformation for a finer refinement. Our framework does not incorporate either handcrafted features or part connectivity, which enables an end-to-end shape prediction pipeline during both training and testing. In contrast to prior cascaded networks for landmark localization that learn a mapping from feature space to landmark locations, we demonstrate that the regularization induced through geometric priors in the DDN makes it easier to train, yet produces superior results. The efficacy and generality of the architecture is demonstrated through state-of-the-art performances on several benchmarks for multiple tasks such as facial landmark localization, human body pose estimation and bird part localization.

Keywords: Landmark localization · Convolutional Neural Network · Non-rigid shape analysis

1 Introduction

Consistent localization of semantically meaningful landmarks or keypoints in images forms a precursor to several important applications in computer vision, such as face recognition, human body pose estimation or 3D visualization. However, it remains a significant challenge due to the need to handle non-rigid shape deformations, appearance variations and occlusions. For instance, facial landmark localization must handle not only coarse variations such as head pose and illumination, but also finer ones such as expressions and skin tones. Human body pose estimation introduces additional challenges in the form of large layout changes of parts due to articulations. Objects such as birds display tremendous variations in both appearance across species, as well as shape within the same

© Springer International Publishing AG 2016
B. Leibe et al. (Eds.): ECCV 2016, Part V, LNCS 9909, pp. 52–70, 2016.
DOI: 10.1007/978-3-319-46454-1_4

species (for example, a perched bird as opposed to a flying one), which renders accurate part localization a largely open problem.

Consequently, there have been a wide range of approaches to solve the problem, starting with those related to PCA-based shape constraints (such as active shape models [1], active appearance models [2] and constrained local models [3]) and pictorial structures (such as DPM [4,5] and poselets [6]). In recent years, the advent of convolutional neural networks (CNNs) has led to significant gains in feature representation [7]. In particular, cascaded regression networks specifically designed for problems such as facial landmark localization [8–10] or human body pose estimation [11] have led to improvements by exploiting problem structure at coarse and fine levels. But challenges for such frameworks have been the need for careful design and initialization, the difficulty of training complex cascades as well as the absence of learned geometric relationships.

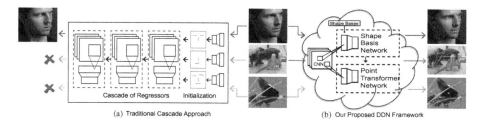

(a) Traditional Cascade Approach   (b) Our Proposed DDN Framework

Fig. 1. (a) Traditional CNN cascades use specialized initializations and directly map the features to landmark locations. This leads to prohibitively expensive training and testing times and frameworks that require complex design of cascade stages for different object types. (b) Our proposed Deep Deformation Network incorporates geometric constraints within the CNN framework. A shape basis network produces rapid global initializations and a point transformer network refines with local non-rigid deformations. The entire framework is trainable end-to-end and results in state-of-the-art accuracy for several object types, while retaining the same network structure.

In this paper, we propose a novel cascaded framework, termed deep deformation network (DDN), that also decomposes landmark localization into coarse and fine localization stages. But in contrast to prior works, we do not train cascaded regressors to learn a mapping between CNN features and landmark locations. Rather, stages in our cascade explicitly account for the geometric structure of the problem within the CNN framework. We postulate that this has three advantages. First, our framework is easier to train and test, in contrast to previous cascaded regressors where proper initialization is required and necessitates training a battery of individual CNNs as sub-problems. Second, incorporation of geometric structures at both the coarse and fine levels regularizes the learning for each stage of the cascade by acting as spatial priors. Third, our cascade structure is general and still results in higher accuracy by learning part geometries and avoiding hard-coded connections of parts. These advantages are illustrated in Fig. 1.

Specifically, in Sect. 3, we propose two distinct mechanisms to inject geometric knowledge into the problem of landmark localization. First, in Sect. 3.2, we propose a shape basis network (SBN) to predict the optimal shape that lies on a low-rank manifold defined by the training samples. Our hypothesis is that shapes or landmarks for each object type reside close to a shape space, for which a low-rank decomposition reduces representation complexity and acts as regularization for learning. Note that unlike DPM, we do not define geometric connections among parts prior to localization, rather these relationships are learned. Further, even cascaded CNN frameworks such as [8] train individual CNNs for pre-defined relative localization of groups of parts within the first level of the cascade, which serves as initialization for later stages. Our SBN avoids such delicate considerations in favor of a learned basis that provides good global initializations. Second, in Sect. 3.3, we propose a point transformer network (PTN) that learns the optimal local deformation in the form of a thin-plate spline (TPS) transformation that maps the initialized landmark to its final position.

A notable feature of our framework is its generality. Prior works explicitly design network structures to handle shape and appearance properties specific to object types such as faces, human bodies or birds. In contrast, our insights are quite general - a shape basis representation is suitable for regularized learning of a global initialization in a CNN framework, following which local deformations through learned TPS transformations can finely localize landmarks. We demonstrate this generality in Sect. 5 with extensive experiments on landmark localization that achieve state-of-the-art in accuracy for three distinct object types, namely faces, human bodies and birds, on several different benchmarks. We use the same CNN architectures for each of these experiments, with identical and novel but straightforward training mechanisms.

To summarize, the main contributions of this paper are:

- A novel cascaded CNN framework, called deep deformation network, for highly accurate landmark localization.
- A shape basis network that learns a low-rank representation for global object shape.
- A point transformer network that learns local non-rigid transformations for fine deformations, using the SBN output as an initialization.
- A demonstration of the ease and generality of deep deformation network through state-of-the-art performance for several object types.

2 Related Work

Facial landmark localization. Facial landmark localization or face alignment is well-studied in computer vision. Models that impose a PCA shape basis have been proposed as Active Shape Models [1] and its variants that account for holistic appearance [2] and local patch appearance [3]. The non-convexity of the problem has been addressed through better optimization strategies that improve modeling for either the shape [12–15] or appearance [16–18]. Exemplar consensus [19,20] and graph matching [21] show high accuracy on localization.

Regression based methods [22–24] that directly learn a mapping from the feature space to predict the landmark coordinates have been shown to perform better. Traditional regression-based methods rely on hand-craft features, for example, shape indexed feature [22], SIFT [24] or local binary feature [25]. Subsequent works such as [26, 27] have also improved efficiency. The recent success of deep networks has inspired cascaded CNNs to jointly optimize over several facial parts [8]. Variants based on coarse-to-fine auto encoders [10, 28] and multi-task deep learning [9, 29] have been proposed to further improve performance. In contrast, cascade stages in our deep deformation networks do not require careful design or initialization and explicitly account for both coarse and fine geometric transformations.

Human body pose estimation. Estimating human pose is more challenging due to greater articulations. Pictorial structures is one of the early influential models for representing human body structure [30]. The deformable part model (DPM) achieved significant progress in human body detection by combining pictorial structures with strong template features and latent-SVM learning [4]. Yang and Ramanan extend the model by incorporating body part patterns [5], while Wang and Li propose a tree-structured learning framework to achieve better performance against handcrafted part connections [31]. Pischulin et al. [32] apply poselets [6] to generate mid-level features regularizing pictorial structures. Chen and Yuille [33] propose dependent pairwise relations with a graphical model for articulated pose estimation. Deep neural network based methods have resulted in better performances in this domain too. Toshev and Szegedy [11] propose cascaded CNN regressors, Tompson et al. [34] propose joint training for a CNN and a graphical model, while Fan et al. [35] propose a dual-source deep network to combine local appearance with a holistic view. In contrast, our DDN also effectively learns part relationships while being easier to train and more efficient to evaluate.

Bird part localization. Birds display significant appearance variations between classes and shape variations within the same class. An early work that incorporates a probabilistic model and user responses to localize bird parts is presented in [36]. Chai et al. [37] apply symbiotic segmentation for part detection. The exemplar-based model of [38], similar to [19], enforces pose and subcategory consistency to localize bird parts. Recently, CNN-based methods, for example, part-based R-CNN [39] and Deep LAC [40] have demonstrated significant performance improvements.

General pose estimation. While the above works focus on a specific object domain, a few methods have been proposed towards pose estimation for general object categories. As a general framework, DPM has also been shown to be effective beyond human bodies for facial landmark localization [41]. A successful example of more general pose estimation is the regression-based framework of [42] and its variants such as [43, 44]. However, such methods are sensitive to initialization, which our framework avoids through an effective shape basis network.

Learning transformations with CNNs. Agrawal et al. use a Siamese network to predict discretized rigid ego-motion transformations formulated as a classification problem [45]. Razavian et al. [46] analyze generating spatial information using CNNs, whereby our SBN and PTN are specific examples of the spatial constraints. Our point transformer network is inspired by the spatial transformer network of [47]. Similar to WarpNet [48], we move beyond the motivation of spatial transformer as an attention mechanism driven by the classification objective, to predict a non-rigid transformation for geometric alignment. In contrast to WarpNet, we exploit both supervised and synthesized landmarks and use the point transformer network only for finer local deformations, while using the earlier stage of the cascade (the shape basis network) for global alignment.

3   Proposed Method

In this section, we present a general deep network to efficiently and accurately localize object landmarks. As shown in Fig. 2, the network is composed of three components:

- A modified VGGNet [7] to extract discriminative features.
- A Shape Basis Network (SBN) that combines a set of shape bases using weights generated from convolutional features to approximately localize the landmark.
- A Point Transformer Network (PTN) for local refinement using a TPS transformation.

The entire network is trained end-to-end. We now introduce each of the above components in detail.

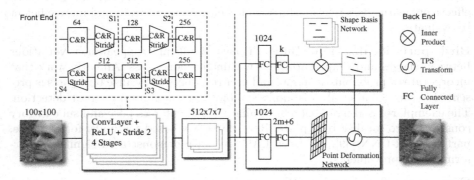

Fig. 2. Overview of the proposed network architecture. Convolutional features are extracted with a 4-stage truncated VGG-16 network [7], denoted as S1 to S4 (C&R stands for convolution and ReLU layers, with stride 2). The $512 \times 7 \times 7$ convolutional maps are sent to the Shape Basis Network and Point Transformer Network as input, where the PTN takes the SBN's output as another input to predict the final landmark positions.

3.1 Convolutional Feature Extraction

For feature extraction, we adopt the VGG-16 network [7] that achieves state-of-the-art performance in various applications [49,50]. The upper left corner in Fig. 2 shows the network structure, where each stage consists of a convolutional layer followed by a ReLU unit. We apply 2 stride across the network. Similar to most localization algorithms, our network takes as input a region of interest cropped by an object detector. We scale input images to 100×100 resolution for facial landmark localization and 200×200 for body and bird pose estimation. Compared to classification and detection tasks, landmark localization requires extracting much finer or low-level image information. Therefore, we remove the last stage from the original 5-stage VGG-16 network of [7]. We also experimented with using just the first three stages, but it performs worse than using four stages. In addition, we remove the pooling layers since we find they harm the localization performance. We hypothesize that shift-invariance achieved by pooling layers is helpful for recognition tasks, but it is beneficial to keep the learned features shift-sensitive for keypoint localization. Given an image at 100×100 resolution, the four-stage convolutional layers generate a 7×7 response map with 512 output channels.

3.2 Shape Basis Network

Let $\mathbf{x} \in \mathbb{R}^d$ denote the features extracted by the convolutional layers. Each training image is annotated with up to n 2D landmarks, denoted $\mathbf{y} = [\mathbf{y}^{1\top}, \cdots, \mathbf{y}^{n\top}]^\top \in \mathbb{R}^{2n}$. To predict landmark locations, previous works such as [8,9] learn a direct mapping between CNN features $\mathbf{x}$ and ground-truth landmarks $\mathbf{y}$. Despite the success of these approaches, learning a vanilla regressor has limitations alluded to in Sect. 1. First, a single linear model is not powerful enough to handle large shape variations. Although cascade regression can largely improve the performance, a proper initialization is required, which is non-trivial. Second, with limited data, training a large-capacity network without regularization from geometric constraints entails a high risk of overfitting.

Both of the above limitations are effectively addressed by our Shape Basis Network (SBN), which predicts optimal object shape that lies in a low-dimensional manifold defined by the training samples. Intuitively, while CNNs allow learning highly descriptive feature representations, frameworks such as active shape models [1] have been historically effective in learning with nonlinear pose manifolds. Our SBN provides an end-to-end trainable framework to combine these complementary advantages. Further, highly articulated structures for challenging shapes such as human bodies cannot be represented by multi-scale autoencoder or detection [10,28]. The complete basis representation of SBN alleviates the problem, while retaining high accuracy and low cost.

More specifically, SBN predicts the shape $\mathbf{y}_s = [\mathbf{y}_s^{1\top}, \cdots, \mathbf{y}_s^{n\top}]^\top \in \mathbb{R}^{2n}$ as,

$$\mathbf{y}_s = \bar{\mathbf{y}} + \mathbf{Q}\mathbf{x}_s \,, \text{ where } \mathbf{x}_s = f(\mathbf{w}_s, \mathbf{x}). \tag{1}$$

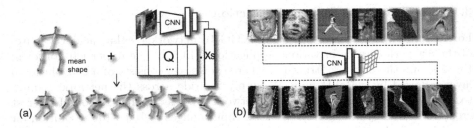

Fig. 3. The workflow illustration of (a) Shape Basis Network and (b) Point Transformer Network. The SBN uses the mean shape and a PCA basis, along with the CNN features, to generate basis weights that compute the initialization for the PTN. The PTN uses the CNN features along with the output of the SBN to estimate non-rigid local deformations parameterized by TPS transformations.

Here $\bar{\mathbf{y}} \in \mathbb{R}^{2n}$ is the mean shape among all training inputs, the columns of $\mathbf{Q} \in \mathbb{R}^{2n \times k}$ store the top-k orthogonal PCA bases and $f(\cdot)$ is a non-linear mapping parameterized by $\mathbf{w}_s$ that takes the CNN feature $\mathbf{x}$ as input to generate the basis weights $\mathbf{x}_s \in \mathbb{R}^k$ as output. We choose k to preserve 99 % of the energy in the covariance matrix of the training inputs, $\sum_{\mathbf{y}} (\mathbf{y} - \bar{\mathbf{y}})(\mathbf{y} - \bar{\mathbf{y}})^\top$. As shown in upper-right corner of Fig. 3a, the mapping $f(\mathbf{w}_s, \mathbf{x})$ is represented by stacking two fully connected layers, where the first layer encodes each input as a 1024-D vector, which is further reduced to k dimension by the second one. Conceptually, we jointly train SBN with other network components in an end-to-end manner. During backward propagation, given the gradient $\nabla \mathbf{y}_s \in \mathbb{R}^{2n}$, the gradient of $\mathbf{x}_s$ is available as $\mathbf{Q}^\top \nabla \mathbf{y}_s \in \mathbb{R}^k$. We then propagate this gradient back to update the parameters $\mathbf{w}_s$ for the fully connected layers as well as the lower convolutional layers.

In practice, we find it advantageous to pre-train the SBN on a simpler task and fine-tune with the later stages of the cascade. This is a shared motivation with curriculum learning [51] and avoids the difficulties of training the whole network from scratch. Given the PCA shape model ($\bar{\mathbf{y}}$ and $\mathbf{Q}$) and the set of training images $\mathbf{x}$, we pre-train SBN to seek the optimal embedding $\mathbf{x}_s = f(\mathbf{w}_s, \mathbf{x})$ such that the Euclidean distance between the prediction and the ground-truth ($\mathbf{y}$) is minimized[1], that is,

$$\min_{\mathbf{w}_s} \quad \mathcal{F} = \|\mathbf{y} - (\bar{\mathbf{y}} + \mathbf{Q}\mathbf{x}_s)\|_2^2 + \lambda \|\mathbf{x}_s\|_2^2, \tag{2}$$

where λ is a regularization factor that penalizes coefficients with large l_2 norm. We set $\lambda = 0.1$ in all experiments. To solve (2), we propagate back the gradient over $\mathbf{x}_s$,

$$\nabla_{\mathbf{x}_s} \mathcal{F} = 2\lambda \mathbf{x}_s - 2\mathbf{Q}^\top (\mathbf{y} - (\bar{\mathbf{y}} + \mathbf{Q}\mathbf{x}_s)), \tag{3}$$

to update the parameters $\mathbf{w}_s$ of the fully connected layers and the lower layers.

---

[1] Strictly speaking, the loss is defined over a mini-batch of images.

Thus, the SBN brings to bear the powerful CNN framework to generate embedding coefficients $\mathbf{x}_s$ that span the highly nonlinear pose manifold. The low-rank truncation inherent in the representation makes SBN clearly insufficient for localization on its own. While simultaneous optimization of the coefficients and PCA bases is possible, preserving basis orthogonality requires further effort. But we remind the reader that the role of SBN is simply to alleviate the difficulty of learning an embedding with large non-linear distortions and to reduce the complexity of shape deformations to be considered by the next stage of the cascade.

3.3   Point Transformer Network

Given the input feature $\mathbf{x}$, SBN generates the object landmark $\mathbf{y}_s$ as a linear combination of pre-defined shape bases. As discussed before, this prediction is limited by its assumption of a linear regression model. To handle more challenging pose variations, this section proposes the Point Transformer Network (PTN) to deform the initialized shape ($\mathbf{y}_s$) using a thin-plate spline (TPS) transformation to best match with ground-truth ($\mathbf{y}$). The refinement is not ideally local as global deformation also exists. Some neural methods place greater emphasis on the local response map [52], while PTN incorporates global transformation into the overall deformation procedure.

A TPS transformation consists of an affine transformation $\mathbf{D} \in \mathbb{R}^{2 \times 3}$ and a non-linear transformation parametrized by m control points $\mathbf{C} = [\mathbf{c}_1, \cdots, \mathbf{c}_m] \in \mathbb{R}^{2 \times m}$ with the corresponding coefficients $\mathbf{U} = [\mathbf{u}_1, \cdots, \mathbf{u}_m] \in \mathbb{R}^{2 \times m}$ [53]. In our experiments, the control points form a 10×10 grid (that is, $m = 100$). The TPS transformation for any 2D point $\mathbf{z} \in \mathbb{R}^2$ is defined as:

$$g(\{\mathbf{D}, \mathbf{U}\}, \mathbf{z}) = \mathbf{D}\tilde{\mathbf{z}} + \sum_{j=1}^{m} \mathbf{u}_j \phi(\|\mathbf{z} - \mathbf{c}_j\|_2), \tag{4}$$

where $\tilde{\mathbf{z}} = \left[\mathbf{z}^\top, 1\right]^\top \in \mathbb{R}^3$ denotes $\mathbf{z}$ in homogeneous form and $\phi(d) = d^2 \log d$ is the radial basis function (RBF).

Given convolutional features $\mathbf{x}$ and landmarks $\mathbf{Y}_s = [\mathbf{y}_s^1, \cdots, \mathbf{y}_s^n] \in \mathbb{R}^{2 \times n}$ initialized by the SBN of Sect. 3.2, the PTN seeks the optimal non-linear TPS mapping $f_p(\mathbf{w}_p, \mathbf{x}) = \{\mathbf{D}, \mathbf{U}\}$ to match the ground-truth $\mathbf{Y} = [\mathbf{y}^1, \cdots, \mathbf{y}^n] \in \mathbb{R}^{2 \times n}$. Similar to SBN, this mapping $f_p(\mathbf{w}_p, \mathbf{x})$ is achieved by concatenating two fully connected layers, which first generate a 1024-D intermediate representation, which is then used to compute $\mathbf{w}_p$. See Fig. 3b for an overview of PTN. Following [53], PTN optimizes:

$$\min_{\mathbf{w}_p} \sum_{i=1}^{n} \|\mathbf{y}^i - g(f_p(\mathbf{w}_p, \mathbf{x}), \mathbf{y}_s^i)\|_2^2 + \gamma \int \|\nabla^2 g\|_2^2 d\mathbf{y}_s^i, \tag{5}$$

where $\nabla^2 g$ is the second-order derivative of transformation g with respect to $\mathbf{y}_s^i$. The weight γ is a trade-off between the transformation error and the bending energy. Substituting (4) into the (5) yields an equivalent objective,

$$\min_{\mathbf{w}_p} \mathcal{E} = \|\mathbf{Y} - \mathbf{D}\tilde{\mathbf{Y}}_s - \mathbf{U}\boldsymbol{\Phi}\|_F^2 + \gamma \mathrm{tr}(\mathbf{U}\boldsymbol{\Phi}\boldsymbol{\Phi}^\top \mathbf{U}^\top), \tag{6}$$

where each element of the RBF kernel $\boldsymbol{\Phi} \in \mathbb{R}^{m \times n}$ computes $\phi_{j,i} = \phi(\|\mathbf{y}_s^i - \mathbf{c}_j\|)$.

It is known that (6) can be optimized over the TPS parameters $\mathbf{D}$ and $\mathbf{U}$ in closed form for a pair of shapes. But in our case, these two parameters are generated by the non-linear mapping $f_p(\mathbf{w}_p, \mathbf{x})$ from image features $\mathbf{x}$ on-the-fly. Thus, instead of computing the optimal solution, we optimize (6) over $\mathbf{w}_p$ using stochastic gradient descent.

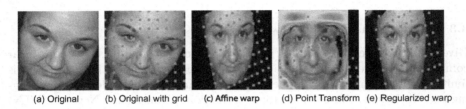

   (a) Original   (b) Original with grid   (c) Affine warp   (d) Point Transform (e) Regularized warp

Fig. 4. Illustration of different transformation models. (a) The input facial image. (b) The input image with uniform grid. (c) The solution of optimizing (6) by replacing $g(\cdot, \cdot)$ with an affine transformation. (d) The solution of point transformation by minimizing (6) without regularization. (e) The solution of regularized point transformation based on (7).

In practice, a key difficulty in training PTN stems from over-fitting of the non-linear mapping $f_p(\mathbf{w}_p, \mathbf{x})$, since the number of parameters in $\mathbf{w}_p$ is larger than the number of labeled point pairs in each mini-batch. For instance, Fig. 4 visualizes the effect of using different spatial transformation to match an example with the mean face. By replacing the TPS in (6) with an affine transformation, PTN may warp the face to a frontal pose only to a limited extent (Fig. 4c) due to out-of-plane head pose variations. Optimizing (6) with $n = 68$ landmarks, PTN is able to more accurately align the landmarks with the mean face. As shown in Fig. 4d, however, the estimated transformation is highly non-linear, which suggests a severe overfitting over the parameters of (6).

To address overfitting, a common solution is to increase the regularization weight γ. However, a large γ reduces the flexibility of the TPS transformation, which runs counter to PTN's purpose of generating highly non-rigid local deformations. Thus, we propose a control point grid regularization method to further constrain the point transformation. For each training image, we estimate the optimal TPS transformation $\{\bar{\mathbf{D}}, \bar{\mathbf{U}}\}$ from the mean shape $\bar{\mathbf{y}}$ to the ground truth $\mathbf{y}$ offline. Then this TPS transformation is applied on the m control points $\mathbf{c}_i$ to obtain their transformed locations $\mathbf{y}_c^i = g(\{\bar{\mathbf{D}}, \bar{\mathbf{U}}\}, \mathbf{c}_i)$. We now obtain m additional synthesized landmarks $\mathbf{Y}_c = [\mathbf{y}_c^1, \cdots, \mathbf{y}_c^m] \in \mathbb{R}^{2 \times m}$ with their original positions $\mathbf{C} = [\mathbf{c}_1, \cdots, \mathbf{c}_m] \in \mathbb{R}^{2 \times m}$. Finally, we define an improved loss incorporating the synthesized control points:

$$\mathcal{E}_c = \mathcal{E} + \varphi \|\mathbf{Y}_c - \mathbf{D}_c \tilde{\mathbf{C}} - \mathbf{U}_c \boldsymbol{\Phi}_c\|_F^2 + \psi \mathrm{tr}(\mathbf{U}_c \boldsymbol{\Phi}_c \boldsymbol{\Phi}_c^\top \mathbf{U}_c^\top), \tag{7}$$

where the terms $\tilde{\mathbf{C}}$, $\mathbf{D}_c$, $\mathbf{U}_c$ and $\mathbf{\Phi}_c$ are defined in a similar way as (6). As shown in Fig. 4e, the new loss $\mathcal{E}_c$ incorporates information from m additional points, which helps to reduce overfitting and produces more stable TPS warps. In our experiments, the values for the involved parameters are $\gamma = 1$ and $\varphi = \psi = 0.4$.

To summarize, PTN forms the refinement stage for our cascade that generates highly non-rigid local deformations for a finer-level localization of landmarks. It is pertinent to note here that unlike the spatial transformer network [47], we directly optimize a geometric criterion rather than a classification objective. Similar to WarpNet [48], we transform point sets rather than the entire image or dense feature maps, but go beyond it in striking a balance between supervised and synthesized landmark points.

4   Implementation Details

We implement DDN using the Caffe platform [54]. The three components of DDN shown in Fig. 2 – the convolutional layers for extracting features $\mathbf{x}$, SBN for computing the intermediate landmarks $\mathbf{y}_s$ and PTN for generating the final position $\mathbf{y}_p$ – can be trained from scratch end-to-end. However, for ease of training, we pre-train SBN and PTN separately, before a joint training. For each task of localizing landmarks on faces, human bodies and birds, we synthetically augment training data by randomly cropping, rotating and flipping images and landmarks. We use the standard hyper-parameters (0.9 for momentum and 0.004 for weight decay) in all experiments.

To pre-train SBN, we minimize (3) without the PTN part. For convolutional layers, we initialize with weights from the original VGG16 model. During the pre-train process, we first fix the convolutional weights and update the fully connected layers of SBN. When the error stops decreasing after 10 epochs, the objective is relaxed to update both the convolutional layers and the fully connected layers. To pre-train PTN, we remove the SBN component from the network and replace the input $\mathbf{y}_s$ with the mean shape $\bar{\mathbf{y}}$. We fix the convolutional weights as the one pre-trained with SBN and train the fully connected layers in PTN only. After 10 epochs, we train both the convolutional and fully connected layers together.

After pre-training, we combine SBN and PTN in a joint network, where the SBN provides shape input $\mathbf{y}_s$ to the PTN. The loss in (7) is evaluated at the end of PTN and is propagated back to update the fully connected and convolutional layers. During the joint training, we first update the weights of PTN by fixing the weights of SBN. Then the weights for SBN are relaxed and the entire network is updated jointly.

5   Experiments

We now evaluate DDN on its accuracy, efficiency and generality. Three landmark localization problems, faces, human bodies and birds are evaluated. The runtime is 1.3 ± 0.5 ms for face landmark localization, 4.3 ± 3.6 ms for human body part localization and 7.6 ± 2.4 ms for bird part localization, on a Tesla K80 GPU with 12G memory, with an Intel 2.4 GHz 8-core CPU machine.

Evaluation metrics. For all the tasks, we use percentage of correctly localized keypoints (PCK) [5] as the metric for evaluating localization accuracy. For the j-th sample in the test set of size N, PCK defines the predicted position of the i-th landmark, $\tilde{\mathbf{y}}_j^i$, to be correct if it falls within a threshold of the ground-truth position $\mathbf{y}_j^i$, that is, if

$$\|\mathbf{y}_j^i - \tilde{\mathbf{y}}_j^i\|_2 \leq \alpha \mathcal{D}, \tag{8}$$

where $\mathcal{D}$ is the reference normalizer, namely, inter-ocular distance for faces and maximum side length of the image bounding box for human bodies and birds. The parameter α controls the threshold for correctness.

5.1   Facial Landmark Localization

To test face alignment in real scenarios, we choose the challenging 300 Faces in-the-Wild Challenge (300-W) [55] as the main benchmark. It contains facial images with large head pose variations, expressions, types of background and occlusions. For instance, the first row of Fig. 6 shows a few test examples from 300-W. The dataset is created from five well-known datasets – LFPW [19], AFW [41], Helen [56], XM2VTS [57] and iBug [55]. Training sets of Helen and LFPW are adopted as the overall training set, random cropping and in-plane rotation as data augmentation. All the datasets use 68 landmark annotation. We report the relative normalized error on the entire 300-W database and further compare the PCK on the proposed component-wise methods.

Table 1. Comparison of accuracy on 300-W dataset.

Dataset	ESR [22]	SDM [24]	ERT [26]	LBF [25]	cGPRT [27]	DDN (Ours)
300-W [55]	7.58	7.52	6.40	6.32	5.71	**5.65**

Table 1 lists the accuracy of five state-of-the-art methods as reported in the corresponding literature– explicit shape regression (ESR) [22], supervised descent method (SDM) [24], ensemble of regression trees (ERT) [26], regression of local binary features (LBF) [25] and cascade of Gaussian process regression tree (cGPRT) [27]. The benefit of the CNN feature representation allows our DDN framework to outperform all the other methods on 300-W. We note that the improvement over cGPRT is moderate. For face alignment, hand-crafted features such as SIFT feature are competitive with CNN features. This indicates that the extent of non-rigid warping in facial images, as opposed to human bodies or birds, is not significant enough to derive full advantage of the power of CNNs, which is also visualized in Fig. 3(b).

To provide further insights into DDN, we also evaluate the independent performances of the two components (SBN and PTN) in Table 2. We note that SBN achieves poor localization compared to PTN. However, the PTN is limited to in-plane transformations. Thus, using SBN as an initialization, the combined DDN framework consistently outperforms the two independent networks.

To illustrate the need for non-rigid TPS transformations, we modify the PTN to use an affine transformation. The network is denoted as a-DDN in Table 2. The performance is worse than DDN, which indicates that the flexibility of representing non-rigid transformations is essential. Visual results in the first row of Fig. 6 show that our method is robust to some degree of illumination changes, head pose variations and partial occlusions. The first failure case in the red box of the first row shows that distortions occur when large parts of the face are completely occluded. Note that in the second failure example, DDN actually adapts well to strong expression change, but is confused by a larger contrast for the teeth than the upper lip.

Table 2. Comparison of the PCK (%) scores on different face datasets. Each component (SBN and PTN) is evaluated, a-DDN and DDN use different transformations (a-DDN for affine transformation and DDN for TPS).

Method	Helen [56]		LFPW [19]		AFW [41]		iBug [55]	
α	0.05	0.10	0.05	0.10	0.05	0.10	0.05	0.10
SBN (Ours)	51.4	87.0	48.1	84.0	36.4	74.0	22.6	57.3
PTN (Ours)	81.4	96.4	63.8	91.3	57.4	90.5	49.1	86.5
a-DDN (Ours)	67.8	93.5	55.5	89.3	44.3	82.9	38.7	79.3
DDN (Ours)	**85.2**	**96.5**	**64.1**	**91.6**	**59.5**	**90.6**	**56.6**	**88.9**

5.2 Human Body Pose Estimation

Compared to facial landmarks, localization of human body parts is more challenging due to the greater degrees of freedom from the articulation of body joints. To evaluate our method, we use the Leeds Sports Pose (LSP) dataset [58], which has been widely used as the benchmark for human pose estimation. The original LSP dataset contains 2,000 images of sportspersons gathered from Flickr, 1000 for training and 1000 for testing. Each image is annotated with 14 joint locations, where left and right joints are consistently labelled from a person-centric viewpoint. To enhance the training procedure, we also use the extended LSP dataset [59], which contains 10,000 images labeled for training, which is the same setup used by most of the baselines in our comparisons.

We compare the proposed DDN with five state-of-the-art methods publicly reported on LSP. Two of them [31,32] are traditional DPM-based methods that model the appearance and shape of body joints in a tree-structure model. The other three [33–35] utilize CNNs for human pose estimation combined with certain canonical frameworks. Our method also uses convolutional features, but proposes two new network structures, SBN and PTN, which can be integrated for end-to-end training and testing. This is in contrast to previous CNN-based methods that include graphical models or pictorial structures that introduce extra inference cost in both training and testing.

Figure 5 compares our method with baselines in terms of PCK scores. In particular, the left two sub-figures show the individual performance for 2 landmarks (Elbow and Wrist), while the right sub-figure contains the overall performance averaged on all 14 joints. Detailed plots for all parts are provided in additional material. Among the baselines, the classical DPM-based methods [31,32] achieve the worst performance due to weaker low-level features. The CNN-based methods of [33–35] improve over those by a large margin. However, the proposed DDN achieves a significant further improvement. PCK numbers for all the landmarks at $\alpha = 0.2$ are listed in Table 3, where DDN performs better across almost all the articulated joints. The mean accuracy over all landmarks is 10.9 % better than the best reported result of [33].

We also report numbers on the version of DDN trained with affine transformations. It is observed that the improvement in accuracy from using TPS

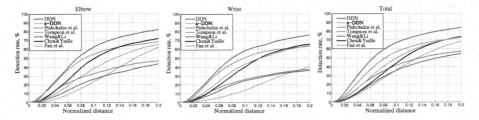

Fig. 5. PCK comparisons on LSP dataset with state-of-the-art methods. The horizontal axis is the normalized distance (α) with respect to the longer dimension of the body bounding box. The vertical axis is the proportion of images in the dataset. The proposed DDN framework (red curve) outperforms previous methods by a significant margin over all $\alpha \in [0, 0.2]$, which shows the utility of an end-to-end CNN framework that incorporates geometric constraints. (Color figure online)

Table 3. Comparison of PCK (%) score at the level of 0.2 on the LSP dataset

Method	Head	Shoulder	Elbow	Wrist	Hip	Knee	Ankle	Mean
Wang & Li [31]	84.7	57.1	43.7	36.7	56.7	52.4	50.8	54.6
Pishchulin et al. [32]	87.2	56.7	46.7	38.0	61.0	57.5	52.7	57.1
Tompson et al. [34]	90.6	79.2	67.9	63.4	69.5	71.0	64.2	72.0
Chen & Yuille [33]	91.8	78.2	71.8	65.5	73.3	70.2	63.4	73.4
Fan et al. [35]	**92.4**	75.2	65.3	64.0	75.7	68.3	70.4	73.0
a-DDN (Ours)	82.3	82.5	62.3	41.2	55.3	77.6	77.1	68.3
DDN (Ours)	87.2	**88.2**	**82.4**	**76.3**	**91.4**	**85.8**	**78.7**	**84.3**

warps as opposed to affine transformations is significantly larger for human body parts than facial landmarks. This reflects the greater non-rigidity inherent in the human body pose estimation problem, which makes our improvement over previous CNN-based methods remarkable.

Table 4. Comparison of PCK (%) score on CUB200-2011. Landmark labels are abbreviated (*e.g.*, "Ba" denotes "Back").

α	Methods	Ba	Be	By	Bt	Cn	Fo	Le	Ll	Lw	Na	Re	Rl	Rw	Ta	Th
0.02	[60]	9.4	12.7	8.2	9.8	12.2	13.2	11.3	**7.8**	6.7	11.5	12.5	7.3	6.2	8.2	11.8
	Ours	**18.8**	**12.8**	**14.2**	**15.9**	**15.9**	**16.2**	**20.3**	7.1	**8.3**	**13.8**	**19.7**	**7.8**	**9.6**	**9.6**	**18.3**
0.05	[60]	46.8	**62.5**	40.7	45.1	59.8	**63.7**	66.3	**33.7**	31.7	**54.3**	63.8	**36.2**	33.3	39.6	56.9
	Ours	**66.4**	49.2	**56.4**	**60.4**	**61.0**	60.0	**66.9**	32.3	**35.8**	53.1	**66.3**	35.0	**37.1**	**40.9**	**65.9**
0.08	[60]	74.8	**89.1**	70.3	74.2	**87.7**	**91.0**	**91.0**	56.6	56.7	**82.9**	88.4	56.4	58.6	65.0	87.2
	Ours	**88.3**	73.1	**83.5**	**85.7**	85.0	84.7	88.3	**57.5**	**58.9**	77.1	**88.7**	**62.1**	**59.1**	**66.6**	**87.4**
0.10	[60]	85.6	**94.9**	81.9	84.5	**94.8**	**96.0**	**95.7**	64.6	67.8	**90.7**	93.8	64.9	**69.3**	74.7	**94.5**
	Ours	**94.0**	82.5	**92.2**	**93.0**	92.2	91.5	93.3	**69.7**	**68.1**	86.0	93.8	**74.2**	68.9	**77.4**	93.4

These results highlight some of the previously discussed advantages of DDN over prior CNN-based frameworks. DDN incorporates geometric structure directly into the network, which makes shape prediction during training and testing end-to-end, while also regularizing the learning. Thus, DDN can learn highly non-linear mappings, which is non-trivial with hand-designed graphical models. Further, we hypothesize that extra modules such as graphical model inference of joint neighborhoods incur additional error. The second row of Fig. 6 shows several qualitative results generated by DDN, which handles a wide range of body poses with good accuracy. The challenging cases within the red box in the second row of Fig. 6 show that our method degrades when the body parts are highly occluded or folded.

5.3 Bird Part Localization

We now evaluate DDN on the well-known CUB200-2011 [61] dataset for bird part localization. The dataset contains 11,788 images of 200 bird species. Each image is annotated with a bounding box and 15 key points. We adopt the standard dataset split, where 5,994 images are used for training and the remaining 5,794 for testing. CUB200-2011 was originally designed for the classification task of fine-grained recognition in the wild, this, it contains very challenging pose variations and severe occlusions. Compared to facial landmark and human body joint, another difficulty is the non-discriminative texture for many bird parts. For instance, the last row of Fig. 6 shows examples where part definitions such as wings or tail might be ambiguous even for humans. The abbreviation in Table 4.

For comparison, we choose the recent work from Zhang et al. [60] as the baseline. We report the PCK numbers at $\alpha = 0.02, 0.05, 0.08, 0.10$ for each of the 15

Fig. 6. Qualitative results of the proposed method for facial landmark localization, human body pose estimation and bird part localization. For bird landmark localization in the last row, the left image in each pair is the ground truth and the right image is our prediction. In each case, we observe that the proposed DDN achieves qualitatively good landmark localization, even with significant non-rigid deformations. Examples in the red boxes show challenging cases, for instance, occlusions around the mouth in face images, limbs in body images or wings in bird images.

landmarks in Table 4. By converting the landmark labels to a dense segmentation mask, Zhang et al. exploit fully convolutional networks [49] for landmark localization. Instead, our DDN directly regresses from the VGG features to the locations of the sparse landmarks, which incurs significantly less computational cost. In addition, Zhang et al. predict each landmark independently without the consideration of geometric relations among landmarks, which are naturally encoded in our SBN. Therefore, our method achieves highly competitive and sometimes better performance than the state-of-the-art, at a significantly lower expense.

6   Conclusion

We propose a cascaded network called Deep Deformation Network (DDN) for object landmark localization. We argue that incorporating geometric constraints in the CNN framework is a better approach than directly regressing from feature maps to landmark locations. This hypothesis is realized by designing a two-stage cascade. The first stage, called the Shape Basis Network, initializes the shape as constrained to lie within a low-rank manifold. This allows a fast initialization that can account for large out-of-plane rotations, while regularizing the estimation. The second stage, called the Point Transformer Network, estimates local deformation in the form of non-rigid thin-plate spline warps. The DDN framework is trainable end-to-end, which combines the power of CNN feature representation with learned geometric transformation. In contrast to prior approaches, DDN avoids complex initializations, large cascades with several CNNs, hand-crafted features or pre-specified part connectivities of DPMs. Our DDN framework consistently achieves state-of-the-art results on three separate tasks, *i.e.*face landmark localization, human pose estimation and bird part localization, which shows the generality of the proposed method.

References

1. Cootes, T., Taylor, C., Cooper, D., Graham, J.: Active shape models-their training and application. CVIU **61**(1), 38–59 (1995)
2. Cootes, T.F., Edwards, G.J., Taylor, C.J.: Active appearance models. In: Burkhardt, H., Neumann, B. (eds.) ECCV 1998. LNCS, vol. 1407, p. 484. Springer, Heidelberg (1998)
3. Cristinacce, D., Cootes, T.: Automatic feature localization with constrained local models. PR **41**(10), 3054–3067 (2007)
4. Felzenszwalb, P., Girshick, R., McAllester, D., Ramanan, D.: Object detection with discriminatively trained part-based models. PAMI **32**(9), 1627–1645 (2010)
5. Yang, Y., Ramanan, D.: Articulated pose estimation with flexible mixtures-of-parts. In: CVPR (2011)
6. Bourdev, L., Maji, S., Brox, T., Malik, J.: Detecting people using mutually consistent poselet activations. In: Daniilidis, K., Maragos, P., Paragios, N. (eds.) ECCV 2010, Part VI. LNCS, vol. 6316, pp. 168–181. Springer, Heidelberg (2010)
7. Simonyan, K., Zisserman, A.: Very deep convolutional networks for large-scale image recognition. In: arXiv preprint (2014)
8. Sun, Y., Wang, X., Tang, X.: Deep convolutional network cascade for facial point detection. In: CVPR (2013)
9. Zhang, Z., Luo, P., Loy, C.C., Tang, X.: Facial landmark detection by deep multi-task learning. In: Fleet, D., Pajdla, T., Schiele, B., Tuytelaars, T. (eds.) ECCV 2014, Part VI. LNCS, vol. 8694, pp. 94–108. Springer, Heidelberg (2014)
10. Zhang, J., Shan, S., Kan, M., Chen, X.: Coarse-to-fine auto-encoder networks (CFAN) for real-time face alignment. In: Fleet, D., Pajdla, T., Schiele, B., Tuytelaars, T. (eds.) ECCV 2014, Part II. LNCS, vol. 8690, pp. 1–16. Springer, Heidelberg (2014)
11. Toshev, A., Szegedy, C.: Deeppose: human pose estimation via deep neural networks. In: CVPR (2014)
12. Saragih, J., Lucey, S., Cohn, J.: Deformable model fitting by regularized landmark mean-shift. IJCV **91**(2), 200–215 (2011)
13. Yu, X., Yang, F., Huang, J., Metaxas, D.: Explicit occlusion detection based deformable fitting for facial landmark localization. In: FG (2013)
14. Pedersoli, M., Timofte, R., Tuytelaars, T., Gool, L.V.: Using a deformation field model for localizing faces and facial points under weak supervisional regression forests. In: CVPR (2014)
15. Yu, X., Huang, J., Zhang, S., Metaxas, D.: Face landmark fitting via optimized part mixtures and cascaded deformable model. PAMI (2015)

16. Matthews, I., Baker, S.: Active appearance models revisited. IJCV **60**(2), 135–164 (2004)
17. Tzimiropoulos, G., Pantic, M.: Optimization problems for fast AAM fitting in-the-wild. In: ICCV (2013)
18. Cheng, X., Sridharan, S., Saragih, J., Lucey, S.: Rank minimization across appearance and shape for AAM ensemble fitting. In: ICCV (2013)
19. Belhumeur, P., Jacobs, D., Kriegman, D., Kumar, N.: Localizing parts of faces using a consensus of exemplars. In: CVPR (2011)
20. Yu, X., Lin, Z., Brandt, J., Metaxas, D.N.: Consensus of regression for occlusion-robust facial feature localization. In: Fleet, D., Pajdla, T., Schiele, B., Tuytelaars, T. (eds.) ECCV 2014, Part IV. LNCS, vol. 8692, pp. 105–118. Springer, Heidelberg (2014)
21. Zhou, F., Brandt, J., Lin, Z.: Exemplar-based graph matching for robust facial landmark localization. In: ICCV (2013)
22. Cao, X., Wei, Y., Wen, F., Sun, J.: Face alignment by explicit shape regression. Int. J. Comput. Vis. **107**(2), 177–190 (2013)
23. Dantone, M., Gall, J., Fanelli, G., Gool, L.V.: Realtime facial feature detection using conditional regression forests. In: CVPR (2012)
24. Xiong, X., la Torre, F.D.: Supervised descent method and its applications to face alignment. In: CVPR (2013)
25. Ren, S., Cao, X., Wei, Y., Sun, J.: Face alignment at 3000 FPS via regressing local binary features. In: CVPR (2014)
26. Kazemi, V., Sullivan, J.: One millisecond face alignment with an ensemble of regression trees. In: CVPR (2014)
27. Lee, D., Park, H., Too, C.: Face alignment using cascade gaussian process regression trees. In: CVPR (2015)
28. Zhu, S., Li, C., Loy, C., Tang, X.: Face alignment by coarse-to-fine shape searching. In: CVPR (2015)
29. Yang, H., Mou, W., Zhang, Y., Patras, I., Gunes, H., Robinson, P.: Face alignment assisted by head pose estimation. In: BMVC (2015)
30. Felzenszwalb, P., Huttenlocher, D.: Pictorial structures for object recognition. IJCV **61**(1), 55–79 (2005)
31. Wang, F., Li, Y.: Beyond physical connections: tree models in human pose estimation. In: CVPR (2013)
32. Pishchulin, L., Andriluka, M., Gehler, P., Schiele, B.: Strong appearance and expressive spatial models for human pose estimation. In: ICCV (2013)
33. Chen, X., Yuille, A.: Articulated pose estimation by a graphical model with image dependent pairwise relations. In: NIPS (2014)
34. Tompson, J., Jain, A., LeCun, Y., Bregler, C.: Joint training of a convolutional network and a graphical model for human pose estimation. In: NIPS (2014)
35. Fan, X., Zheng, K., Lin, Y., Wang, S.: Combining local appearance and holistic view: dual-source deep neural networks for human pose estimation. In: CVPR (2015)
36. Wah, C., Branson, S., Perona, P., Belongie, S.: Multiclass recognition and part localization with humans in the loop. In: ICCV (2011)
37. Chai, Y., Lempitsky, V., Zisserman, A.: Symbiotic segmentation and part localization for fine-grained categorization. In: ICCV (2013)
38. Liu, J., Belhumeur, P.: Bird part localization using exemplar-based models with enforced pose and subcategory consistency. In: ICCV (2013)

39. Zhang, N., Donahue, J., Girshick, R., Darrell, T.: Part-based R-CNNs for fine-grained category detection. In: Fleet, D., Pajdla, T., Schiele, B., Tuytelaars, T. (eds.) ECCV 2014, Part I. LNCS, vol. 8689, pp. 834–849. Springer, Heidelberg (2014)

40. Lin, D., Shen, X., Lu, C., Jia, J.: Deep LAC: deep localization, alignment and classification for fine-grained recognition. In: CVPR (2015)

41. Zhu, X., Ramanan, D.: Face detection, pose estimation and landmark localization in the wild. In: CVPR (2012)

42. Dollar, P., Welder, P., Perona, P.: Cascaded pose regression. In: CVPR (2010)

43. Burgos-Artizzu, X., Perona, P., Dollar, P.: Robust face landmark estimation under occlusion. In: ICCV (2013)

44. Yan, J., Lei, Z., Yang, Y., Li, S.Z.: Stacked deformable part model with shape regression for object part localization. In: Fleet, D., Pajdla, T., Schiele, B., Tuytelaars, T. (eds.) ECCV 2014, Part II. LNCS, vol. 8690, pp. 568–583. Springer, Heidelberg (2014)

45. Agrawal, P., Carreira, J., Malik, J.: Learning to see by moving. In: ICCV (2015)

46. Razavian, A.S., Azizpour, H., Maki, A., Sullivan, J., Ek, C.H., Carlsson, S.: Persistent evidence of local image properties in generic convnets. In: Paulsen, R.R., Pedersen, K.S. (eds.) SCIA 2015. LNCS, vol. 9127, pp. 249–262. Springer, Heidelberg (2015)

47. Jaderberg, M., Simony, K., Zisserman, A., Kavukcuoglu, K.: Spatial transformer networks. In: NIPS (2015)

48. Kanazawa, A., Jacobs, D., Chandraker, M.: Warpnet: weakly supervised matching for single-view reconstruction. In: CVPR (2016)

49. Long, J., Shelhamer, E., Darrell, T.: Fully convolutional networks for semantic segmentation. In: CVPR (2015)

50. Ren, S., He, K., Girshick, R., Sun, J.: Faster R-CNN: Towards real-time object detection with region proposal networks. In: arXiv preprint (2016)

51. Bengio, Y., Louradour, J., Collobert, R., Weston, J.: Curriculum learning. In: ICML (2009)

52. Baltrusaitis, T., Robinson, P., Morency, L.: Constrained local neural fields for robust facial landmark detection in the wild. In: ICCVW (2013)

53. Bookstein, F.L.: Principal warps: thin-plate splines and the decomposition of deformations. PAMI 11(6), 567–585 (1989)

54. Jia, Y., Shelhamer, E., Donahue, J., Karayev, S., Long, J., Girshick, R., Guadarrama, S., Darrell, T.: Caffe: Convolutional architecture for fast feature embedding. arXiv preprint (2014)

55. Sagonas, C., Tzimiropoulos, G., Zafeiriou, S., Pantic, M.: 300 faces in-the-wild challenge: the first facial landmark localization challenge. In: ICCVW (2013)

56. Le, V., Brandt, J., Lin, Z., Bourdev, L., Huang, T.S.: Interactive facial feature localization. In: Fitzgibbon, A., Lazebnik, S., Perona, P., Sato, Y., Schmid, C. (eds.) ECCV 2012, Part III. LNCS, vol. 7574, pp. 679–692. Springer, Heidelberg (2012)

57. Messer, K., Matas, J., Kittler, J., Letting, J., Maitre, G.: XM2VTSDB: the extended M2VTS database. In: Second International Conference on Audio and Video-based Biometric Person Authentication (AVBPA) (1999)

58. Johnson, S., Everingham, M.: Clustered pose and nonlinear appearance models for human pose estimation. In: British Machine Vision Conference (2010)

59. Johnson, S., Everingham, M.: Learning effective human pose estimation from inaccurate annotation. In: CVPR (2011)
60. Zhang, N., Shelhamer, E., Gao, Y., Darrell, T.: Fine-grained pose prediction, normalization and recognition. In: arXiv preprint (2016)
61. Welder, P., Branson, S., Mita, T., Wah, C., Schrod, F., Belong, S., Perona, P.: Caltech-ucsd birds 200. In: CTechnical report CNS-TR-2010-001 (2010)

Learning Visual Storylines with Skipping Recurrent Neural Networks

Gunnar A. Sigurdsson[(✉)], Xinlei Chen, and Abhinav Gupta

Carnegie Mellon University, Pittsburgh, USA
gunnar@cmu.edu
http://www.github.com/gsig/srnn

Abstract. What does a typical visit to Paris look like? Do people first take photos of the Louvre and then the Eiffel Tower? Can we visually model a temporal event like "Paris Vacation" using current frameworks? In this paper, we explore how we can automatically learn the temporal aspects, or storylines of visual concepts from web data. Previous attempts focus on consecutive image-to-image transitions and are unsuccessful at recovering the long-term underlying story. Our novel Skipping Recurrent Neural Network (S-RNN) model does not attempt to predict each and every data point in the sequence, like classic RNNs. Rather, S-RNN uses a framework that skips through the images in the photo stream to explore the space of all ordered subsets of the albums via an efficient sampling procedure. This approach reduces the negative impact of strong short-term correlations, and recovers the latent story more accurately. We show how our learned storylines can be used to analyze, predict, and summarize photo albums from Flickr. Our experimental results provide strong qualitative and quantitative evidence that S-RNN is significantly better than other candidate methods such as LSTMs on learning long-term correlations and recovering latent storylines. Moreover, we show how storylines can help machines better understand and summarize photo streams by inferring a brief personalized story of each individual album.

1 Introduction

In the past few years, there has been a remarkable success in learning visual concepts [1,2] and relationships [1,3] from images and text on the web. In theory, this allows the creation of systems that, given enough time and resources, can grow to know everything there is to learn. However, most of these approaches are still largely centered around single images and focus on learning static semantic relationships such as *is-part-of* [1], *is-eaten-by* [3] *etc*. Moreover, many semantic concepts have not only a visual aspect but also a temporal aspect or even storylines associated with them. For example, a visual representation of *Wedding* would involve guests entering the venue, followed by exchange of rings and finally

Electronic supplementary material The online version of this chapter (doi:10.1007/978-3-319-46454-1_5) contains supplementary material, which is available to authorized users.

© Springer International Publishing AG 2016
B. Leibe et al. (Eds.): ECCV 2016, Part V, LNCS 9909, pp. 71–88, 2016.
DOI: 10.1007/978-3-319-46454-1_5

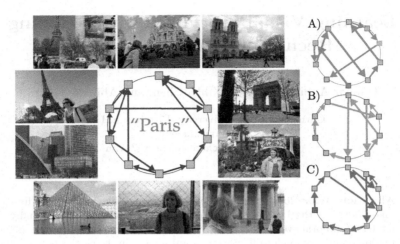

Fig. 1. Given a concept, our algorithm can automatically learn both its visual and temporal aspect (storylines) from the web. To do this, we retrieve related albums from Flickr and apply our S-RNN model to automatically discover long-term temporal patterns. Here is a visualization of the storylines the model learned for the concept *Paris*. For visualization, we distill the top images that a trained S-RNN model prefers by sampling storylines from a *Paris* photo album. Denoting the images as nodes in a graph, we visualize the most common pairwise transitions using arrowed lines. On the right, we sample three probable storylines (A,B,C) that include these 10 images. We can see that the *Eiffel Tower* is prominent early in the story followed by sightseeing of common landmarks (*Arc de Triomphe* and others) and finally visiting the *Lourve*. On a map of Paris, the *Eiffel Tower* and the *Arc de Triomphe* are indeed in close proximity

celebrations in the wedding reception. How can we learn such visual storylines from the web as well?

There are two aspects to these storylines: the visual aspect, often represented by modes in visual appearances, and the temporal aspect, which is the temporal order in which these modes appear. How do we capture both of these aspects from the web data? User photo albums in Flickr are a perfect example of web data that capture both aspects. First, most Flickr images are supplied with sufficiently informative tags, like *Paris* [4]. Second, meta-information like time is usually available. In particular, the photos in each album are taken in ordered sequences, which hypothetically embed common storylines for concepts such as *Paris*. Therefore, we propose to utilize Flickr photo streams across thousands of users and learn underlying visual storylines associated with these concepts. What is the right representation for these storylines and how do we learn it?

Recently, there has been momentous success in using CNN [5] features along with Recurrent Neural Networks [6–11] (RNNs) to represent those temporal dynamics in data [12–19]. We aim to extend that idea to modeling the dynamics in storylines. In theory, RNN can model any sequence, but has limited memory

Fig. 2. Given a concept, such as *Wedding*, our algorithm can retrieve an ordered collection of images to describe that concept (Sect. 4.3). In this figure we show the collections discovered by our model for two concepts. For example, for *Wedding* (first row), it picks images that represent four steps: guests enter; ceremony begins, marriage and celebration. For travel-related concepts like *London*, it prefers iconic landmarks for the story. The subtitles are manually provided for visualization. This is distilled from 1000 photo albums. More examples are provided in the appendix.

in practice, and can only learn short-term relationships due to vanishing gradients [20].

Our Skipping Recurrent Neural Network (S-RNN) skips through the photo sequences to extract the common latent stories, instead of trying to predict each and every item in the sequence. This effectively alleviates the artifacts of short-term correlations[1] (*e.g.* repetition) between consecutive photos in the stream, and focuses the learning effort towards the underlying story. This solution is complementary to, and different from, more complex RNN architectures such as LSTMs [21] that still focus on learning transitions between consecutive images. Similar to clustering, the S-RNN model can be efficiently trained in an *unsupervised* manner to learn a global storyline and infer a private story for each album. Different from most clustering techniques, S-RNN inherits the power of RNNs that can capture the temporal dynamics in the data.

We evaluate the effectiveness of our storyline model by comparing the storylines with baselines. In addition we evaluate the storyline model on two applications: (a) image prediction [22,23]; and (b) photo album summarization [24–27]. Constructing a convincing storyline for a concept of interest requires both visual and temporal aspects. Therefore, algorithms need to retrieve a diverse collection of images, with the right ordering among them. For *image prediction*, we show that our model is particularly suited for discovering the long-term correlations buried under the short-term repetitions in Flickr albums, while other approaches do not. Finally in the *summarization* task, the goal is to take images in a single photo album and select a small summary of those. A typical example is a series

---

[1] In our Flickr dataset, 71.1% of consecutive images are above average (cosine) similarity.

of photos, taken by a family on their visit to *Paris*, visiting all the iconic land-marks, such as the Eiffel Tower. Classically, summarization is approached by collecting a dataset of videos/albums and their associated summaries generated by people [26, 28–31], in order to learn how to make a summary in a supervised way. This process is, however, considerably laborious. In this work, we specifi-cally experiment with the hypothesis that a quality summary of an album can be constructed by exploiting the similarities across thousands of similar albums (*e.g. Paris*). Then a summary of the album is inferred by telling a personalized version of the story.

Contributions. (a) We present a new way of approaching sequence modeling with RNNs, by exploring all ordered subsets of the data to avoid short-term cor-relations between consecutive elements in the sequence. (b) We present the novel S-RNN architecture that efficiently implements this idea on web-scale datasets. (c) We demonstrate that this method can learn visual storylines for a concept (*e.g. Paris*) from the web, by showing state-of-the-art results on selecting repre-sentative images, long-term image prediction, and summarizing photo albums.

Fig. 3. Given an individual photo album, our algorithm can summarize the photo album with a ordered collection of images that capture the album in terms of its underlying concept, by first learning about the concept from thousands of albums. (Sect. 4.5). In this figure we show the summaries generated for three photo albums. One about a *Safari*, the second about *Scuba Diving*, and the third *Snowboarding*. More examples are provided in the appendix.

2   Related Work

Learning storylines. The earliest form of storyline can be traced back to the 1970-80s, where *scripts* [32] (structured representations of events, causation relationships, participants, *etc.*) are used as knowledge backbones for tasks like text summarization and question answering. Unfortunately, these rich knowledge structures require hand construction by the experts, which fundamentally limits their usage in an open domain. This motivates the recent developments of *unsu-pervised* approaches that can learn underlying storylines automatically [33, 34] from text. Inspired by this idea, our work aims to acquire the temporal aspect of a concept automatically from images. Similar work in vision is limited by either the scale of the data [29, 35] or the domain to which the approach is applied [36]. Perhaps the most similar work is [22,23], where the storyline graphs are learned for Flickr albums. However, our work differs in several important aspects. First, while [22] is an important step in learning storylines, it focuses its learning effort on each and every pairwise transition, but our method learns the long-term latent story. In fact, [22] could be extended using this framework, but here we extend a standard RNN model. Second, our method requires no a-priori clustering, feature independence, nor a Markov assumption, and does parameters sharing like RNNs.

Temporal visual summarization. Summarizing video clips is an active area of research [37]. Many approaches have been developed seeking cues ranging from low-level motion and appearances [24,25,38] to high level concepts [26,39] and attentions [40]. This line of research has been recently extended to photo albums, and more external factors are considered for summarization besides the narrative structure. For example, in [41] the authors put forward three criteria: quality, diversity, and coverage. Later, in [42] a system is proposed that considers the social context (*e.g.* characters, aesthetics) into the summarization framework. Sadeghi *et al.* [28] also consider if a photo is memorable or iconic. Moreover, most of these approaches are *supervised*, namely the associated summaries for videos/albums are first collected by crowd-sourcing, then a model is learned to generate good summaries. While performance-wise it may seem best to leverage human supervision and external factors when available, practically it suffers serious issues like scalability and inconsistency in the ground-truth collection process, and generalizablility when applied to other domains. On the other hand, the task of summarization will be less ambiguous if the concept is given, which is exactly what we want to explore in this work.

Sequential learning with RNNs. Recurrent neural networks [6] are a subset of neural networks that can carry information across time steps. Compared to other models for sequential modeling (*e.g.* hidden Markov models, linear dynamic systems), they are better at capturing the long-range and high-order time-dependencies, and have shown superior performance on tasks like language modeling [43] and text generation [44]. In this work we extend the network to model high dimensional trajectories in videos and user albums through the space of continuous visual features. Interestingly, since our network is trained to predict images several steps away, it can be viewed as a simple and effective way to learn long term memories [21] and predict context [45] as well. Fundamentally, LSTM still looks at only the next image and decides if it should be stored it in memory, but S-RNN reasons over all future images, and decides which it should store in memory (greedy vs. global). We outperform multiple LSTM baselines in our results. Furthermore, running LSTMs directly on high-dimensional continuous features is non-trivial, and we present a network that accomplishes that.

3   Learning Visual Storylines

Given hundreds of albums for a concept, our goal is to learn the underlying visual appearances and temporal dynamics simultaneously. Once we have learned this by building upon state-of-the-art tools, we can use it for multiple storyline tasks, and distill the explicit knowledge as needed, such as in Fig. 1. In this section, we explain our novel S-RNN architecture that is trained over all ordered subsets of the data, and show that this can be accomplished with update equations equally efficient to original RNN. The full derivation of these update equations by using the EM-method is presented in the appendix. We formulate the storyline learning problem as learning an S-RNN. To understand S-RNN, we start by introducing the basic RNN model.

3.1   Recurrent Neural Networks

The basic form of RNN [6] models a time sequence by decomposing the probability of a complete sequence into sequentially predicting the next item given the history (in our application, this sequence is images in a temporal order). Given a sequence of T images $\mathbf{x}_{1:T} = \{x_1, \ldots, x_T\}$,[2] the network is trained to maximize the log-likelihood:

$$\mathcal{M}^* = \arg\max_{\mathcal{M}} \log P(\mathbf{x}_{1:T}; \mathcal{M}) - \lambda \mathcal{R}(\mathcal{M})$$

$$\text{where } \log P(\mathbf{x}_{1:T}; \mathcal{M}) = \sum_t \log P(x_{t+1}|\mathbf{x}_{1:t}; \mathcal{M}). \tag{1}$$

Here $\mathcal{M}$ is the set of all model parameters, and $\mathcal{R}(\cdot)$ is the regularizer (*e.g.* ℓ_2). The probability $P(\cdot|\cdot, \cdot)$ is task dependent, *e.g.* for language models it directly compares the soft-max output y_t with the next word x_{t+1} [43]. The standard optimization algorithm for RNNs is Back Propagation Through Time [46,47] (BPTT), a variation of gradient ascent where the gradient is aggregated through time sequences.

The model consists of three layers: input, recurrent, and output. The input layer uses the input x_t to update the hidden recurrent layer h_t using weights $\mathbf{W}_I$. The recurrent layer h_t updates itself via $\mathbf{W}_R$ and predicts the output $\mathbf{y}_t$ via weights $\mathbf{W}_O$. The update function at step t writes as follows:

$$h_t = \sigma(\mathbf{W}_I x_t + \mathbf{W}_R h_{t-1}); \quad y_t = \zeta(\mathbf{W}_O h_t). \tag{2}$$

Here $\sigma(\cdot)$ and $\zeta(\cdot)$ are non-linear activation functions, *e.g.* sigmoid, soft-max, rectified linear units [5], *etc.* All the history in RNN is stored in the memory h_t. This assumes conditional independence of x_{t+1} and $\mathbf{x}_{1:t}$ given h_t.

In practice, the recurrent layer h_t has limited capacity and the error cannot be back propagated effectively (due to vanishing gradients [20]). This can be a

---

[2] For simplicity in notation, we assume a single training sequence, but in our experiments we use multiple albums for one concept to discover *common* latent storylines.

critical issue for modeling sequences like photo streams—due to the high correlation between consecutive images, where the dominant pattern in the short term is *repetition*. For example, people can take multiple pictures of the same object (*e.g.* the Eiffel Tower or family members), or the entire album is about things that are visually similar (*e.g.* artwork in the Louvre or fireworks). This pattern is so salient that if an RNN is directly trained on these albums, the signals of underlying storylines are largely suppressed. How to resolve this issue of learning long-term patterns? One way is to regularize RNN with a diversity term [41]. However, note that if an album is indeed single-themed, we still want visually similar images in the storyline. Furthermore, Flickr tags are not perfect and noise in the album set can easily distract the model.

3.2 Skipping Recurrent Neural Networks

We now build upon the RNN framework to propose a skipping recurrent neural network model. Instead of learning each consecutive transition, S-RNN chooses to learn a "higher-level" version of the story, and focuses its learning effort accordingly. The key underlying idea is to select the storyline nodes by skipping a lot of images in the album and then modeling the transitions between the images selected as nodes.

Formally, let us suppose $\mathbf{x}_{1:T}$ represents the T images in the album, $\mathbf{z}_{1:N}$ is the set of indexes that represent the selected images for the storyline and the constant N is the number of nodes in the storyline. Note that $N \ll T$, $z_n \in \{1, 2, \ldots, T\}$, and $z_n < z_{n+1}$ since $\mathbf{z}$ defines an ordered subset. Our goal is to learn the maximum likelihood model parameters ($\mathcal{M}$) by maximizing the marginal likelihood of the observed data. Therefore, our objective function is:

$$\mathcal{M}^* = \arg \max_{\mathcal{M}} \log \sum_{\mathbf{z}_{1:N}} P(\mathbf{x}_{1:T}, \mathbf{z}_{1:N}; \mathcal{M}) - \lambda \mathcal{R}(\mathcal{M}). \tag{3}$$

We can factorize $P(\mathbf{x}_{1:T}, \mathbf{z}_{1:N}; \mathcal{M})$ as $P(\mathbf{x}_{1:T}|\mathbf{z}_{1:N}; \mathcal{M})P(\mathbf{z}_{1:N})$ where $P(\mathbf{z}_{1:N})$ is a prior on $\mathbf{z}$. As described above, we use a simple prior on $\mathbf{z}$ that it is an ordered subset. In this work, we make an assumption that the likelihood of a whole album is proportional to the likelihood of the selected sub-sequence of images $\mathbf{x_z}$ (that is, we assume $P(\mathbf{x}_{1:T}|\mathbf{z}; \mathcal{M}) \propto P(\mathbf{x_z}; \mathcal{M})$). Factorizing, and inserting this assumption into Eq. 3 we have:

$$\mathcal{M}^* = \arg \max_{\mathcal{M}} \log \sum_{\mathbf{z}_{1:N}} \left(\prod_n P\left(\mathbf{x}_{z_{n+1}}|\mathbf{x}_{\mathbf{z}_{1:n}}; \mathcal{M}\right) \right) P(\mathbf{z}_{1:N}) - \lambda \mathcal{R}(\mathcal{M}). \tag{4}$$

We observe that this equation is starting to look similar to standard RNN (Eq. 1).

Maximizing the S-RNN Objective. Maximizing the marginal likelihood over all possible subsets of $\mathbf{z}$ is computationally intractable. Therefore, we make use of the Expectation Maximization (EM) algorithm, and then sequentially factor the update equations. More details of the EM derivation are given in the

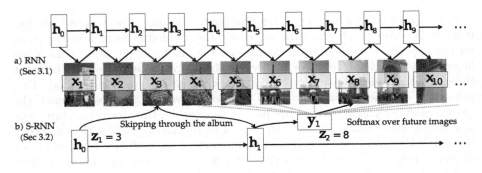

Fig. 4. Our S-RNN model (unrolled in time). Instead of trying to predicting each and every photo in the sequence (as in the basic RNN model), latent variables $\mathbf{z}_n$ are introduced into our model to skip through the photo sequences, which is an effective strategy to address the local repetition issue (multiple pictures are taken for a single object like the Eiffel Tower) and can help extract common latent stories in the entire set of albums related to a concept (*e.g. Paris*). To overcome the high-dimensional regression problem, the loss is an softmax loss over future images

appendix. During the E-step, we sample $\mathbf{z}$ given the current model, and use that to train the model in the M-step, as we would an RNN. We initialize the EM-algorithm by setting $\mathbf{z}$ based on a randomly ordered subsets of images.

S-RNN Implementation Details. Now that we know how to optimize the objective, the only design choice left is the loss $P\left(\mathbf{x}_{z_{n+1}}|\mathbf{x}_{z_{1:n}};\mathcal{M}\right)$ (the data likelihood in Eq. 4). While Gaussian likelihood is often used for real-valued regression, we recognize that the space of allowed future images is not infinite, but simply images after x_{z_n}, defined as $\mathcal{X}_n$. Thus the likelihood is defined as a *softmax likelihood over the future images*:

$$P\left(x_{z_{n+1}}|\mathbf{x}_{\mathbf{z}_{1:n}};\mathcal{M}\right) = \frac{\exp(\mathbf{y}_n^T x_{z_{n+1}})}{\sum_{x\in\mathcal{X}_n}\exp(\mathbf{y}_n^T x)} \tag{5}$$

where $\mathbf{y}_n$ is the output of the network after step n. Effectively, this avoids modeling the negative world as "everything except the ground truth" and instead models the negative world as "other possible choices". This significantly helps with high-dimensional data ($fc7$ features), since the possible image choices in an album are usually only few hundred, but visual features few thousand.

In summary, during training and testing, $\mathbf{z}$ is sequentially sampled using the current model (which skips through the sequence), and during training those samples used to sequentially update the network with BPTT to maximize the objective. A visualization of the idea can be found in Fig. 4. A full implementation of is available.

4 Experiments

Since there has been so little done in the area of learning storyline models and their applications, there are no established datasets, evaluation methodologies, or even much in terms of relevant previous work to compare against. Therefore, we will present our evaluation in two parts: (a) first, in Sect. 4.3, we directly evaluate how "good" our learned storyline model is. Specifically, we ask the Amazon Mechanical Turk (AMT) users how good our storyline model is compared to a baseline in terms of the representativeness and the diversity of image nodes in the storyline model; (b) next, in Sects. 4.4 and 4.5, we evaluate our storyline model for two applications: long-term prediction and album summarization. For these tasks, we show qualitative, quantitative, and user studies to demonstrate the effectiveness of S-RNN based storyline model. We begin by describing our data collection process and the baselines.

4.1 Flickr Albums Dataset

We gather collections of photo albums by querying Flickr through the YFCC100M dataset [48], a recently released public subset of the Flickr corpus containing 99.3 million images with all the meta-information like tags and time stamps. This dataset is an unrefined subset of images on Flickr, making it a reproducible way of working with web data. The selection process gathers at most 1000 photo albums for a single concept (*e.g. Paris*), with an average size of 150 images. Each album is sorted based on a photo's date taken. We experimented with seven concepts: *Christmas, London, Paris, Wedding, Safari, Scuba-diving,* and *Snowboarding* with a total number of 700k images. Examples from the dataset are provided in the appendix. This subset will be made available.

4.2 Implementation Details

We compare our S-RNN model with several approaches to demonstrate its effectiveness in learning visual storylines. For fairness, all the methods used the same *fc7* features from AlexNet [5] pre-trained on ImageNet.

For **S-RNN**, the *fc7* features are directly fed into the model. The network is trained with BPTT, which unrolls the network, and uses gradient ascent with a momentum of 0.9. We set the starting learning rate as 0.05, and gradually reduce it when the likelihood on the validation set no longer increases. The input size of the layer is set to 4096 (size of *fc7*), and the hidden recurrent layer size 50. We keep $N = 10$ for all the concepts as a good compromise between content and brevity (The appendix contains analysis of different sizes of N). We choose ℓ_2 regularization and set weight decay λ to be 10^{-7}. Training takes approximately 2–3 h on a single CPU. Each story was generated by sampling from the model 500 times, and picking the sampled sequence with the highest likelihood. The code is available at github.com/gsig/srnn.

Below we list the main baselines, and note that additional baselines will be added for individual experiments when necessary.

Sample. We uniformly sample from the data distribution.

K-Means. To take advantage of the global storylines shared in a concept, we apply K-Means to all the albums (similar to the first step of [22] except with different features).

Graph. We adapted the original code for [22] to use $fc7$ features. Then a storyline is generated with the forward-backward algorithm as described in [22].

RNN. This architecture is similar to a language model [43] except it predicts the cluster (as in *K-Means*) of the next image. We sample without replacement to generate the story. This is a standard application of RNN to the problem.

LSTM. We train an LSTM network [49], similar to the RNN baseline.

LSTMsub. LSTM trained as before, but when generating the summary, we first generate a longer sequence ($N = 100$) and then sub-sample that sequence to the desired summary length 10. Intuitively, if LSTM was indeed able to learn the long-term correlations regardless of the repetitions, this should perform well.

S-RNN-. For ablation analysis, we also provide a baseline where we use the network without skipping, but with the softmax loss over future images. All the hyper-parameters for training are kept identical to our model except the network predicts each and every item in the sequence. This is similar to RNN, but benefits from our improved loss.

D-RNN. Similar to S-RNN-, except trained on a diverse subset of each album using the k-means++ algorithm [50]. This was significantly better than other variants, including training on random subsets, fixed interval subsets, or a random diverse subset.

4.3   Evaluating Storylines

In the first experiment, we directly evaluate how "good" the learned storyline model is for a given concept. We define the goodness of a storyline model in terms of how representative and diverse the selected images are for a given concept. Two qualitative examples for *Wedding* and *London* are shown in Fig. 2. Figure 5 shows more examples of learned storylines for different concepts. Our storyline model captures the essence of scuba-diving, snowboarding, etc., by capturing representative and diverse images (e.g., beer, fun and snowboarding during day).

Setup. For each concept, we have each method select only 10 images from 50 photo albums (thousands of photos) that best describe the concept, and AMT workers select which one they prefer. Each algorithm has access to the full training data to train the model. For Graph and RNN-based baselines, we sample multiple times from each album and use the highest ranked collection in terms of likelihood. Sample and K-Means are simply applied on all images, and in K-Means we assign the closest image to each cluster center. The appendix contains more qualitative examples.

Table 1. *Evaluating Storylines.* Fraction of the time our S-RNN storylines are preferred against competing baselines. 50 % is equal preference. Our method significantly outperforms the baselines, being preferred 60% of the time against the strongest baseline. See Sect. 4.3 for details

	K-Means	Sample	Graph	LSTM	LSTMsub	D-RNN	RNN	S-RNN-
S-RNN	71.2 %	68.3 %	79.8 %	84.3 %	70.9 %	60.0 %	85.1 %	75.5 %

Safari

Scuba Diving

Snowboarding

Fig. 5. *Evaluating Storylines.* Images selected by S-RNN for three storylines from thousands of images for the concepts *Safari*, *Scuba Diving*, and *Snowboarding*

Results. Table 1 summarizes the results. Each comparison was given to 15 separate AMT workers. We can see that S-RNN is preferred **60 % of the time against the strongest baseline** across all the concepts. Different baselines fail in different ways. For example, Sample and K-Means can capture a diverse set of images to represent the concept, but are prone to the inherent noise in the Flickr albums. On the other hand, Graph and LSTM overfit to the short-term correlations in the data and select repetitive images. Finally, S-RNN outperforms D-RNN since S-RNN is not restricted to a single specific diversity method as in D-RNN.

4.4 Task1: Prediction

Next, we evaluate our storyline models for two applications. The first application we consider is the *prediction* task. There are two possible prediction goals: short-term prediction and long-term prediction. Short-term prediction can be considered as prediction of the next image in the album. This was the task used in [22,23]. In the case of long-term prediction, we predict the next representative event. In the case of *Paris* vacation, if the current event is Eiffel tower, the next likely event would be visiting the Trocadero. In the case of *Wedding*, if the current event is the ring ceremony, then the next representative event is the kiss of the newlyweds.

Setup. For the short-term prediction, the ground-truth is the next image in the album. But how do we collect ground-truth for long-term prediction? We ask experts to summarize the albums (hoping that album summaries will suppress short-term correlations and capture only representative events). Now we can reformulate long-term prediction as predicting the next image in the human-generated *summary* of the album. We collected 10 ground truth summaries on average for each concept from volunteers familiar with the concepts (such as *Paris*, and *London*). Each summary consists of 10 images from a photo album that capture what the album was about. This was used as ground truth only for evaluation. Two settings are compared, the first one (labeled *"long-term"*) predicts the next image in a *summary* ($N = 198$ over 10 folds each); and the second one (labeled *"short-term"*) predicts the next image in the original photo album ($N = 1742$). The problem is posed as a classification task choosing from the true image, and four other images selected uniformly at random from the same album. Here we also consider **NN** that simply picks the nearest neighbor, and **FI** that picks the furthest image from the given image, both in cosine distance of *fc7* features. K-Means is not suitable for this task since it does not include temporal information. All methods were trained in an unsupervised manner for each concept as before.

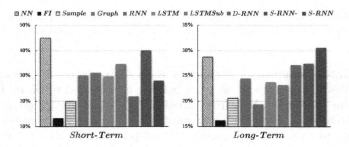

Fig. 6. *Predicting the next image.* S-RNN is best at capturing long-term correlations, and nearest-neighbors is best at capturing short-term correlations, as expected

Results. In Fig. 6 we present results for the prediction of the next image. When we consider long-term interactions between images, S-RNN successfully predicts the next image in the storyline **31** % of the time, significantly higher than baselines. On the other hand, we can see that when we simply want to predict consecutive images, NN is the best. To further visualize the results for *"long-term"* correlations, we also give example comparisons with baseline methods in Fig. 7.

4.5   Task2: Photo Album Summarization

In the final experiment, we evaluate on the task of album summarization. In particular, we focus on summarizing an individual album based on the concept (*e.g.* a *Paris* album), rather than heuristics such as image quality or presence of faces [28,41,42]. This experiment addresses the question whether storylines can help to summarize an album.

Human Generated Summaries. Photo album summarization is inherently a subjective and difficult task. To get a sense of the difficulty, we first compared

Given Image   S-RNN   LSTM   NN   Graph   GT

Fig. 7. *Long-term prediction.* Examples of the images predicted by our method compared to baselines. The image is chosen from a line-up of five images from the same album (generated by experts as summaries). We see our method captures *Santa→Tree* and *Closed Presents→Open Presents* while the baselines focus on similar images

the human summaries (used in Sect. 4.4) to baselines with a separate AMT preference study. We had two findings. First, for some concepts, such as *Wedding*, the albums are frequently already summaries by professional photographers, and thus generating summaries is trivial. Specifically, there is no significant difference between human generated summaries and uniformly sampling from the data distribution (Sample). We thus only evaluate on concepts where there is significant difference between human generated summaries and ones generated by baselines. Second, we found human generated summaries are only preferred **59.5 %** of the time against the strongest baseline.

Setup. The photo albums for a given concept are randomly divided into a training set and a validation set with a ratio of 9:1, and no ground truth summaries were provided. We additionally consider the baseline **Local** where K-Means clustering is used for summarization by applying clustering on $fc7$ features for each individual album. As before, we assign the closest image to the cluster center for clustering-based methods. While it is not required for S-RNN, we sort the selected photos in temporal order as a post-processing step for all the baselines when necessary for fair comparison.

Qualitative Results. The results for a few concepts are presented in Fig. 8. We can see that S-RNN captures a set of relevant images without losing diversity. In contrast, Local captures only diversity, and LSTM that tries to learn short-term correlations between consecutive images, and as result often prefers similar images in a row. Additional summaries by S-RNN are presented in Fig. 3.

Quantitative Evaluation. To directly compare the quality of the generated summaries, another AMT preference study was conducted. For S-RNN and each baseline, 200 random pairwise comparisons were generated. Each question was given to 5 separate workers for consistency. We used a consensus approach where a comparison gets a score of 1 if there is a tie, or a score of 2 if there is consensus.

Fig. 8. Examples of summaries generated by our method and two representative base-lines for *Scuba-diving* and *Snowboarding*. In the *Scuba-diving* example Local aims to capture diversity, and thus our method is more relevant. In *Snowboarding*, LSTM focuses on short-term correlations, and chooses many similar images, while our method effectively captures the album

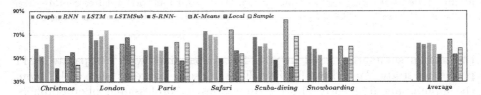

Fig. 9. Photo album summarization. AMT pairwise preference between our method and multiple baselines. 70 % means that summaries by our method were preferred 70 % of the time. It is important to keep in mind that compared to the strongest baseline, a human generated summary was on average only preferred 59.5 % of the time. Section 4.5 contains a detailed explanation of the experiment setup and analysis of the results

In Fig. 9 we present comparison with the baselines. We can see that on average our method is preferred over all the baselines. To provide a more detailed analysis, we divide the baseline methods into two groups: the *Storyline* group (filled with pure colors) that captures the latent temporal information in the data, and the Non-Storyline group (filled with patterns) that do not. The *Storyline* group includes Graph, RNN, LSTM, LSTMSub, and S-RNN- (Our method also falls into this group), while the *Non-Storyline* group has K-Means, Local and Sample. There are few interesting points:

1. S-RNN performs relatively better on travel-related albums (*Paris, London*) suggesting it is easier to latch onto landmarks than high-level concepts like in *Christmas*.
2. For concepts like *Christmas*, methods that learn short-term correlations from the data distribution are still preferred by the users. The fact that S-RNN- outperforms LSTMs and RNNs, can be interpreted as follows. RNNs suffer from the curse of dimensionality if naively applied to storyline learning, but the S-RNN loss reduces the dimensionality of the output space by an order of magnitude (4096 to 100s).

3. While simple as they seem, Local and Sample are very competitive baselines. We believe the reason is that Local aims to provide a diverse set of images from each album, and Sample is representative of the underlying data. Therefore, with the post-processing step that re-arranges the selected images in temporal order, these methods can do well on good albums. However, they do poorly when the album is noisy, as illustrated in Fig. 8 first example.

Does Time Information Help Summarization? For further analysis, we compared the described S-RNN with S-RNN trained on shuffled data (ordering discarded) with a preference study on AMT. S-RNN using the time information was preferred 68.4 % over S-RNN without time information, demonstrating that the time information significantly helps to generate a summary liked by people.

Transferring storyline knowledge. Each album can have different stories and themes. In Fig. 10 we present two different summaries of two photo albums. The first album is a *Scuba Diving* album, and the first summary from that album is generated with the model trained on *Scuba Diving* albums. In the second row, the same album is summarized using a model trained on *Wedding* albums. We can see that this emphasizes scenic beach pictures reminiscent of a beach resort wedding. The second album is a *Paris* album, and the first summary is generated using *Paris* model. The second summary however, is generated using a *Christmas* model, and we can see that this emphasizes pictures of churches and sparkling lights at night.

Fig. 10. The first two rows show a *Scuba Diving* album summarized with a *Scuba* model and a *Wedding* model, and the last two show a *Paris* album summarized with a *Paris* model and a *Christmas* model. The *Wedding* story emphasizes the beach resort images of the *Scuba* album, and the *Christmas* story emphasizes the churches and sparkling lights images in the *Paris* album

5   Conclusion

We have presented an approach to learn visual storylines for concepts automatically from the web. Specifically, we use Flickr albums and train an S-RNN model to capture the long-term temporal dynamics for a concept of interest. The model is designed to overcome the challenges posed by high correlations between consecutive photos in the album if sequence predictors are directly applied. We evaluate our model on learning storylines, image prediction and album summarization, and show both qualitatively and quantitatively that our method excels at both extracting salient visual signals for the concept, and learning long-term storylines to capture the temporal dynamics.

Acknowledgements. This research was supported by the Yahoo-CMU InMind program, ONR MURI N000014-16-1-2007, and a hardware grant from Nvidia. The authors would like to thank Olga Russakovsky and Christoph Dann for invaluable suggestions and advice, and all the anonymous reviewers for helpful advice on improving the manuscript.

References

1. Chen, X., Shrivastava, A., Gupta, A.: NEIL: extracting visual knowledge from web data. In: ICCV (2013)
2. Divvala, S.K., Farhadi, A., Guestrin, C.: Learning everything about anything: webly-supervised visual concept learning. In: CVPR (2014)
3. Sadeghi, F., Divvala, S.K., Farhadi, A.: VisKE: visual knowledge extraction and question answering by visual verification of relation phrases. In: CVPR (2015)
4. Izadinia, H., Farhadi, A., Hertzmann, A., Hoffman, M.D.: Image classification and retrieval from user-supplied tags (2014). arXiv preprint: arXiv:1411.6909
5. Krizhevsky, A., Sutskever, I., Hinton, G.E.: Imagenet classification with deep convolutional neural networks. In: NIPS (2012)
6. Elman, J.L.: Finding structure in time. Cogn. Sci. **14**(2), 179–211 (1990)
7. Malinowski, M., Rohrbach, M., Fritz, M.: Ask your neurons: a neural-based approach to answering questions about images. In: ICCV, pp. 1–9 (2015)
8. Shih, K.J., Singh, S., Hoiem, D.: Where to look: focus regions for visual question answering (2015). arXiv preprint: arXiv:1511.07394
9. Yang, Z., He, X., Gao, J., Deng, L., Smola, A.: Stacked attention networks for image question answering (2015). arXiv preprint: arXiv:1511.02274
10. Zhu, Y., Groth, O., Bernstein, M., Fei-Fei, L.: Visual7w: grounded question answering in images (2015). arXiv preprint: arXiv:1511.03416
11. Xiong, C., Merity, S., Socher, R.: Dynamic memory networks for visual and textual question answering (2016). arXiv preprint: arXiv:1603.01417
12. Karpathy, A., Li, F.: Deep visual-semantic alignments for generating image descriptions (2014). arXiv preprint: arXiv:1412.2306
13. Donahue, J., Hendricks, L.A., Guadarrama, S., Rohrbach, M., Venugopalan, S., Saenko, K., Darrell, T.: Long-term recurrent convolutional networks for visual recognition and description. In: CVPR (2015)
14. Vinyals, O., Toshev, A., Bengio, S., Erhan, D.: Show and tell: a neural image caption generator. In: CVPR (2015)
15. Venugopalan, S., Rohrbach, M., Donahue, J., Mooney, R.J., Darrell, T., Saenko, K.: Sequence to sequence - video to text (2015). arXiv preprint: arXiv:1505.00487
16. Xu, K., Ba, J., Kiros, R., Courville, A., Salakhutdinov, R., Zemel, R., Bengio, Y.: Show, attend and tell: neural image caption generation with visual attention (2015). arXiv preprint: arXiv:1502.03044

17. Gregor, K., Danihelka, I., Graves, A., Wierstra, D.: Draw: a recurrent neural network for image generation (2015). arXiv preprint: arXiv:1502.04623
18. Zhu, Y., Kiros, R., Zemel, R., Salakhutdinov, R., Urtasun, R., Torralba, A., Fidler, S.: Aligning books and movies: towards story-like visual explanations by watching movies and reading books (2015). arXiv preprint: arXiv:1506.06724
19. Chen, X., Zitnick, C.L.: Learning a recurrent visual representation for image caption generation. In: CVPR (2015)
20. Bengio, Y., Simard, P., Frasconi, P.: Learning long-term dependencies with gradient descent is difficult. TNN **5**(2), 157–166 (1994)
21. Hochreiter, S., Schmidhuber, J.: Long short-term memory. Neural Comput. **9**(8), 1735–1780 (1997)
22. Kim, G., Xing, E.P.: Reconstructing storyline graphs for image recommendation from web community photos. In: CVPR (2014)
23. Kim, G., Sigal, L., Xing, E.P.: Joint summarization of large-scale collections of web images and videos for storyline reconstruction. In: CVPR (2014)
24. DeMenthon, D., Kobla, V., Doermann, D.: Video summarization by curve simplification. In: ACM MM, pp. 211–218. ACM (1998)
25. Ngo, C.W., Ma, Y.F., Zhang, H.J.: Video summarization and scene detection by graph modeling. TCSVT **15**(2), 296–305 (2005)
26. Khosla, A., Hamid, R., Lin, C.J., Sundaresan, N.: Large-scale video summarization using web-image priors. In: CVPR (2013)
27. Martin-Brualla, R., He, Y., Russell, B.C., Seitz, S.M.: The 3D jigsaw puzzle: mapping large indoor spaces. In: Fleet, D., Pajdla, T., Schiele, B., Tuytelaars, T. (eds.) ECCV 2014, Part III. LNCS, vol. 8691, pp. 1–16. Springer, Heidelberg (2014)
28. Sadeghi, F., Tena, J.R., Farhadi Ali, S.L.: Learning to select and order vacation photographs. In: WACV (2015)
29. Xiong, B., Kim, G., Sigal, L.: Storyline representation of egocentric videos with an applications to story-based search. In: ICCV, pp. 4525–4533 (2015)
30. Kim, G., Moon, S., Sigal, L.: Joint photo stream and blog post summarization and exploration. In: CVPR, pp. 3081–3089. IEEE (2015)
31. Chu, W.S., Song, Y., Jaimes, A.: Video co-summarization: video summarization by visual co-occurrence. In: CVPR, pp. 3584–3592 (2015)
32. Shank, R., Abelson, R.: Scripts, plans, goals and understanding (1977)
33. Chambers, N., Jurafsky, D.: Unsupervised learning of narrative event chains. In: ACL (2008)
34. McIntyre, N., Lapata, M.: Learning to tell tales: a data-driven approach to story generation. In: ACL (2009)
35. Wang, D., Li, T., Ogihara, M.: Generating pictorial storylines via minimum-weight connected dominating set approximation in multi-view graphs. In: AAAI (2012)
36. Gupta, A., Srinivasan, P., Shi, J., Davis, L.S.: Understanding videos, constructing plots learning a visually grounded storyline model from annotated videos. In: CVPR (2009)
37. Truong, B.T., Venkatesh, S.: Video abstraction: a systematic review and classification. TOMCCAP **3**(1), 3 (2007)
38. Cernekova, Z., Pitas, I., Nikou, C.: Information theory-based shot cut/fade detection and video summarization. TCSVT **16**(1), 82–91 (2006)
39. Lee, Y.J., Ghosh, J., Grauman, K.: Discovering important people and objects for egocentric video summarization. In: CVPR (2012)
40. Ma, Y.F., Lu, L., Zhang, H.J., Li, M.: A user attention model for video summarization. In: ACM MM (2002)

41. Sinha, P., Mehrotra, S., Jain, R.: Summarization of personal photologs using multidimensional content and context. In: ICMR (2011)
42. Obrador, P., De Oliveira, R., Oliver, N.: Supporting personal photo storytelling for social albums. In: ACM MM, pp. 561–570. ACM (2010)
43. Mikolov, T.: Recurrent neural network based language model. In: INTERSPEECH (2010)
44. Sutskever, I., Martens, J., Hinton, G.E.: Generating text with recurrent neural networks. In: ICML (2011)
45. Mikolov, T., Sutskever, I., Chen, K., Corrado, G.S., Dean, J.: Distributed representations of words and phrases and their compositionality. In: NIPS (2013)
46. Williams, R.J., Zipser, D.: Gradient-based learning algorithms for recurrent networks and their computational complexity. In: Back-Propagation: Theory, Architectures and Applications, pp. 433–486 (1995)
47. Werbos, P.J.: Generalization of backpropagation with application to a recurrent gas market model. Neural Netw. 1(4), 339–356 (1988)
48. Thomee, B., Shamma, D.A., Friedland, G., Elizalde, B., Ni, K., Poland, D., Borth, D., Li, L.J.: The new data and new challenges in multimedia research (2015). arXiv preprint: arXiv:1503.01817
49. Karpathy, A., Johnson, J., Li, F.: Visualizing and understanding recurrent networks (2015). arXiv preprint: arXiv:1506.02078
50. Arthur, D., Vassilvitskii, S.: k-means++: the advantages of careful seeding. In: Proceedings of the Eighteenth Annual ACM-SIAM Symposium on Discrete Algorithms, Society for Industrial and Applied Mathematics, pp. 1027–1035 (2007)

Towards Large-Scale City Reconstruction from Satellites

Liuyun Duan and Florent Lafarge(⊠)

Inria, Sophia Antipolis, France
{liuyun.duan,florent.lafarge}@inria.fr

Abstract. Automatic city modeling from satellite imagery is one of the biggest challenges in urban reconstruction. Existing methods produce at best rough and dense Digital Surface Models. Inspired by recent works on semantic 3D reconstruction and region-based stereovision, we propose a method for producing compact, semantic-aware and geometrically accurate 3D city models from stereo pair of satellite images. Our approach relies on two key ingredients. First, geometry and semantics are retrieved simultaneously bringing robustness to occlusions and to low image quality. Second, we operate at the scale of geometric atomic region which allows the shape of urban objects to be well preserved, and a gain in scalability and efficiency. We demonstrate the potential of our algorithm by reconstructing different cities around the world in a few minutes.

Keywords: 3D reconstruction · City modeling · Satellite imagery · Urban scenes

1 Introduction

Automatic city modeling has received an increasing interest during the last decade. In applicative fields such as urban planning, telecommunications and disaster control, producing compact and accurate 3D models is crucial. Aerial acquisitions with Lidar scanning or multi-view imagery constitute the best way so far to automatically create 3D models on large-scale urban scenes [1]. Because of high acquisition costs and authorization constraints, aerial acquisitions are, however, restricted to some spotlighted cities in the world. In particular, Geographic Information System (GIS) companies propose catalogs with typically a few hundred cities in the world. Satellite imagery exhibits higher potential with lower costs, a worldwide coverage and a high acquisition frequency. Satellites have however several technical restrictions that prevent GIS practitioners from producing compact city models in an automatic way [2].

Inspired by recent works on semantic 3D reconstruction and region-based stereovision, we propose a method for producing compact, semantic-aware and

Electronic supplementary material The online version of this chapter (doi:10.1007/978-3-319-46454-1_6) contains supplementary material, which is available to authorized users.

B. Leibe et al. (Eds.): ECCV 2016, Part V, LNCS 9909, pp. 89–104, 2016.
DOI: 10.1007/978-3-319-46454-1_6

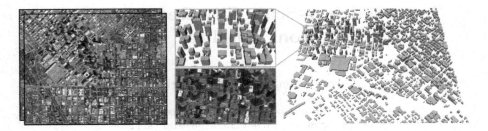

Fig. 1. Reconstruction of Denver downtown. Starting from a stereo pair of satellite images (left), our algorithm produces a compact and semantic-aware 3D model (right) in a few minutes

geometrically accurate 3D city models from stereo pairs of satellite images. Our approach relies on two key ingredients. First, geometry and semantics are retrieved simultaneously bringing robustness to occlusions and to low image quality. Second, contrary to pixel-based methods, we operate at the scale of geometric atomic region: it allows the shape of urban objects to be better preserved, and also a gain in scalability and efficiency. Figure 1 illustrates our goal.

2   Related Works

Our review of previous work covers three main facets of our problem: urban reconstruction, region-based stereo matching, and object polygonalization.

Urban reconstruction. Reconstruction of urban objects and scenes has been deeply explored in vision, with a quest towards full automation, quality and scalability, and robustness to acquisition constraints [1]. In this field, geometry and semantics are closely related. The most traditional strategy consists in retrieving semantics before geometry. In many city modeling methods [3–5], data are first classified so that the subsequent 3D reconstruction can be adapted to the nature of urban objects. Buildings are the most common reconstructed objects, either from multiview imagery [6–8] or airborne Lidar [4,9]. Recent works [10–12] demonstrate that the simultaneous extraction of geometry and semantics, also known as semantic 3D reconstruction, outclasses multiple step strategies in terms of output quality. However, these works typically suffer from a low scalability and often produce 3D models without structural consideration. Semantic 3D reconstruction remains a challenge at the scale of satellite images.

Region-based stereo matching. Numerous works have been proposed in stereo matching [13]. While well-established methods as the Semi-Global Matching (SGM) algorithm [14] reason at the scale of the pixel, some works focus on matching image regions to more accurately preserve object boundaries [15,16]. Beyond boundary accuracy, region-based stereo matching methods can offer high scalability and time-efficiency [17]. Some works [18,19] also combine object segmentation or classification with stereo matching in unified frameworks. Inference for these models is, however, a complex task that requires time-consuming optimization procedures. Overall, most of these methods are not adapted to satellite images whose wide baselines typically produce severe occlusion problems that are not specifically handled. The additional use of geometric primitives as line-segments usually helps to better interpret occluded parts of images [20].

Object polygonalization. Capturing objects by polygonal shapes provides a compact and structure-aware representation of the object contours. It is particularly adapted at representing regular objects as roofs from images. Object polygonalization methods typically depart from the detection of line-segments which are then assembled into polygons. This second step can be done, for instance, by searching for cycles in a graph of line-segments [21], or by connecting line-segments with a gap filling strategy [22]. Grouping atomic regions [23] is also a possible approach, especially when the number of objects is high, and the input image is big. It requires, however, a post-processing step to vectorize chains of pixels into polygons with typically a loss of accuracy.

3 Positioning and Contributions

Satellite context imposes a set of technical constraints with respect to traditional aerial acquisitions, in particular (i) a lower pixel resolution, typically $\geq$0.5 meter, (ii) a lower signal-to-noise-ratio impacting the image quality, and (iii) a wider baseline to guarantee a reasonable depth accuracy. Although these constraints have a low impact on some applications as change detection [24] or generation of dense Digital Surface Models [25], they challenge the automatic reconstruction of compact and semantic-aware city models (Fig. 2).

Fig. 2. Satellite context. A wide baseline is a necessity to reach reasonable depth accuracy, but brings severe occlusion problems. A facade side is typically visible only in one image (see closeups). Note also the high proportion of shadow and the time-varying objects as cars

We propose an automatic city modeling method from satellite imagery whose output approaches the quality of 3D-models delivered by airborne-based methods. We consider as input a calibrated stereo pair of satellite images. Our output city model is a compact mesh composed of ground and building objects. Buildings are represented with a Level Of Detail 1 (LOD1) of the CityGML formalism [26], *ie* piecewise planar buildings with flat roofs and vertical facades. Our method proceeds with three main steps illustrated on Fig. 3.

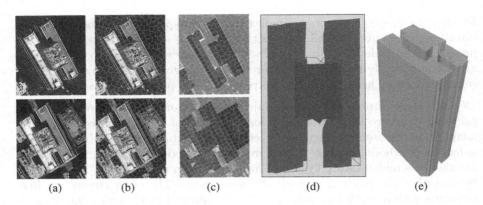

(a)   (b)   (c)   (d)   (e)

Fig. 3. Overview. Input stereo images (a) are first decomposed into atomic convex polygons (b) using existing works (Sect. 4). In a second step detailed in Sect. 5, the semantic class and the elevation of each polygon are simultaneously retrieved in the two partitions (c). The last step (Sect. 6) consists in unifying the two partitions enriched by semantic classes and elevation values into a planimetric elevation representation (d) that allows the generation of the output 3D model (e)

Our main contributions are (i) a full pipeline for producing compact and semantic-aware city models from satellite images, (ii) a time-efficient and scalable approach based on geometric atomic regions, and able to reconstruct big cities in a few minutes, and (iii) a joint classification and reconstruction process that brings robustness to the low quality of input images.

4   Polygonal Partitioning

Reasoning at the scale of pixel on big satellite images tends to produce non-scalable algorithms that poorly capture geometric information at higher scales [2]. We rather analyze satellite images at the scale of atomic regions, whose efficiency has been demonstrated in shape extraction [23] or stereo matching [17]. Instead of using traditional superpixel methods, we rely on a geometric algorithm that decomposes images into atomic convex polygons [27]. This algorithm is applied independently on both stereo images with a polygon size fixed to 5 pixels (average distance to polygon centroids to its edges) in our experiments. As illustrated on Fig. 4, it captures geometric regularities in images by aligning contours of atomic polygons with linear structures as roof edges. Note that the line-segments embedded into the polygonal partitions will be used further in our approach.

The polygons are enriched with an *elevation estimate* which corresponds to the altimetric distance between the observed surface captured in the polygon and the ground. For each polygon, we define its elevation estimate as the difference between the mean of the pixel depths contained inside the polygon (computed by Semi-Global Matching [14] with double checking), and the depth of the ground (computed by a standard Digital Terrain Model (DTM) estimation method [28]).

Fig. 4. Polygonal partitioning and elevation estimates. Left and right polygonal partitions capture linear structures contained in input images, and in particular building edges. Elevation estimates sparsely cover the polygonal partitions (see colored polygons). Each roof contains at least a few elevation estimates

Because of the wide baseline of our stereo pairs, polygons without elevation estimates are frequent, especially when associated to facade elements as illustrated in Fig. 4. In return, elevation estimates are relatively accurate and present on a very large majority of roofs. Our strategy is thus to couple these elevation estimates with the geometric information contained in the polygonal partitions to retrieve building contours even for partially occluded roofs.

We denote by $\mathcal{P}_l$ and $\mathcal{P}_r$ the polygonal partitions produced by [27] for the left and the right images respectively. $\mathcal{P}_l^\star \subset \mathcal{P}_l$ represents the set of polygons in $\mathcal{P}_l$ with elevation estimates. A polygon $i \in \mathcal{P}_l \cup \mathcal{P}_r$ associated with an elevation estimate d_i is projected in 3D using the traditional Rational Polynomial Coefficients (RPC) model [29]. Two polygons $i \in \mathcal{P}_l$ and $j \in \mathcal{P}_r$ with respective elevation estimates d_i and d_j are said to be *imbricate* if the orthographic projections into the horizontal plane of the 3D polygons overlap. In this case, we

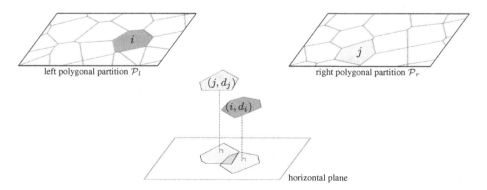

Fig. 5. Orthographic projection of polygons. Polygons i and j with respective elevation estimates d_i and d_j are projected in 3D using the RPC model. These two polygons are imbricate as their orthographic projections into the horizontal plane overlap (see yellow area). (Color figure online)

denote by $\tau_{ij} \in [0,1]$ the overlapping ratio of the orthographic projections, i.e. the intersection area to union area ratio. These notations are illustrated in Fig. 5.

5   Joint Classification and Elevation Recovery

Starting from the two polygonal partitions and sparsely distributed elevation estimates, our goal is now to retrieve simultaneously the semantic class and the elevation of each polygon of the partitions.

Two semantic classes of interest are considered: *roof* and *other*. Class *other* mainly refers to ground and facade elements. Because of the wide baseline, most of these elements are only visible in one image. As our main objective is to reconstruct buildings, considering only these two classes is sufficient under the assumption that facades are vertical. Contrary to class *other*, class *roof* is associated with an elevation value. By considering the classification problem as a labeling formulation, the set of possible labels can then be defined as $L = \{z_1, ..., z_n, other\}$ where $z_1, ..., z_n$ are the n possible elevation values of a roof. To set $z_1, ..., z_n$, we cluster the set of elevation estimates by Kmeans with $K = n+1$, and associate the n highest centroids to them. As the ground falls into the class *other*, the centroid with the lowest value is reset to zero. We denote by $\sigma(z_k)$ the standard deviation of the kth cluster.

The quality of a configuration of labels $l \in L^{card(\mathcal{P})}$ is measured through an energy U of the form:

$$U(l) = \sum_{i \in \mathcal{P}} D_{data}(l_i) + \beta_1 \sum_{(i,j) \in \mathcal{E}_s} V_{smoothness}(l_i, l_j) + \beta_2 \sum_{(i,j) \in \mathcal{E}_c} V_{coupling}(l_i, l_j)$$

(1)

where D_{data} is the unary data term, and $V_{smoothness}$ and $V_{coupling}$ are pairwise potentials favoring respectively label smoothness and label coherence between left and right partitions. $\mathcal{E}_s$ and $\mathcal{E}_c$ correspond to two sets of pairs of adjacent polygons. β_1 and β_2 are parameters weighting the three terms of the energy.

Polygon adjacency. The two adjacency sets $\mathcal{E}_s$ and $\mathcal{E}_c$ impose spatial dependencies between polygons, either within the same polygonal partition for the former or in between the polygonal partitions for the later, as illustrated on Fig. 6.

$\mathcal{E}_s$ contains pairs of polygons who share a common edge which is not supported by one of the line-segments embedded into the polygonal partitions. As illustrated in Fig. 6-right, this condition on line-segments is particularly efficient for stopping label propagation when meeting building edges.

$\mathcal{E}_c$ is defined as the set of imbricate polygons, *ie* the pairs of polygons $i \in \mathcal{P}_l^\star$ and $j \in \mathcal{P}_r^\star$ so that $\tau_{ij} > 0$.

Data term. It measures the coherence between the elevation estimate of a polygon and its proposed label. For polygons without an elevation estimate, we favor the occurrence of the label *other* as a polygon without a depth estimate is most

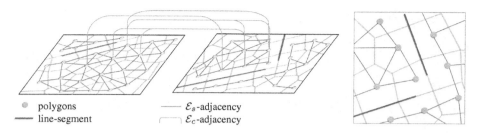

Fig. 6. Polygon adjacency. Two types of pairwise interactions between polygons are taken into account in the labeling formulation: within the same partition and in between partitions (left). Line-segments embedded into the partitions prevent neighboring polygons from interacting (right)

likely to capture an element visible only in one image such as facade and, to a lesser extent, ground. The data term is expressed as

$$D_{data}(l_i) = \begin{cases} 1 - e^{\frac{-(l_i - d_i)^2}{2\sigma(l_i)^2}} & \text{if } i \in \mathcal{P}^\star \\ \alpha \cdot \mathbb{1}_{\{l_i \neq other\}} & \text{otherwise} \end{cases} \tag{2}$$

where d_i is the depth estimate of polygon i, $\mathbb{1}_{\{.\}}$ is the characteristic function, and α is the penalty weight for not choosing *other*. When label *other* is attributed to polygon $i \in \mathcal{P}^\star$, we set l_i to 0.

Smoothness. The smoothness term penalizes $\mathcal{E}_s$-adjacent polygons with different labels using a generalized Potts model:

$$V_{smoothness}(l_i, l_j) = w_{ij} \cdot \mathbb{1}_{\{l_i \neq l_j\}} \tag{3}$$

where the weight w_{ij} reduces the penalty of having different labels when the radiometry of pixels inside the two polygons is not similar. In practice, w_{ij} is chosen as one minus the normalized histogram distance in norm L_2.

Coupling. Similarly to the smoothness potential, the coupling term is defined by a generalized Potts model, here, between imbricate polygons.

$$V_{coupling}(l_i, l_j) = \tau_{ij} \cdot \mathbb{1}_{\{l_i \neq l_j\}} \tag{4}$$

where τ_{ij} allows polygons with different labels to be penalized proportionally to their overlapping ratio.

Optimization. An approximation of the global minimum of the energy is found using the α-β swap algorithm [30]. Figure 7 shows the impact of the different terms of the energy. In the sequel, we call *enriched* partition, a polygonal partition whose polygons have received a class and eventually an elevation value by this energy minimization.

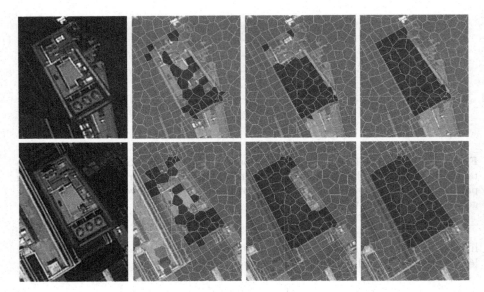

Fig. 7. Impact of the different energy terms. Roofs are sparsely labeled using the data term only ($\beta_1 = \beta_2 = 0$, 2nd column). Adding the smoothness potential propagates roof labels while preserving building edges ($\beta_2 = 0$, 3rd column). The labeling coherence between the left and right partitions is enforced considering the complete energy formulation (right column)

6   Fusion of Enriched Partitions

The projection in 3D of left and right enriched partitions gives two different interpretations of the shape of objects as (i) some roof parts are frequently occluded between the two images, (ii) the shapes of polygons between left and right partitions do not necessarily correspond, and (iii) the coupling term of Eq. 1 is a soft constraint that does not guarantee that imbricate polygons have the same elevation. To unify the two interpretations into a unique 3D model, we project all 3D polygons into the horizontal plane, and relabel elevations inside the new induced horizontal partition.

Orthographic projection. Each polygon $i \in \mathcal{P}$ whose class is not *other* is projected into the horizontal plane. The superposition of projected polygons from left and right partitions produces a decomposition of the horizontal plane into new polygons that we call *cells*. Note that the cells are not necessarily convex. We denote by $\mathcal{C}$ the set of cells. Each cell inherits the elevations of the polygons that overlap with it. We denote by Z_k, the set of elevations inherited by cell $i \in \mathcal{C}$. Different types of cells can be distinguished:

- **Coherent cells** are cells that inherit two identical elevations, one from the left partition and one from the right. The elevation value of these cells is not modified further.

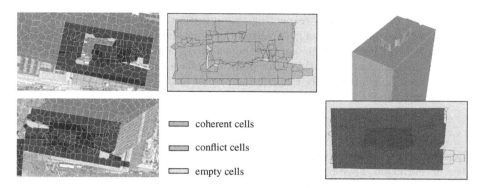

Fig. 8. Fusion of enriched partitions. Projecting the enriched partitions (left) into the horizontal plane produces a cell decomposition in which three groups of cells can be distinguished (middle). The relabeling of the elevation of conflict and empty cells gives a unified 3D model (right)

- **Conflict cells** are cells that inherit at least one elevation, and that are not coherent cells.
- **Empty cells** are cells without inherited elevation. Theses cells, which typically fill in the holes in the cell decomposition, mainly corresponds to ground or small roof parts.

We denote by $\mathcal{C}_{coherent}$, $\mathcal{C}_{conflict}$ and $\mathcal{C}_{empty}$ these three sets of cells respectively, illustrated in Fig. 8.

Cell relabeling. For fusing enriched partitions, each conflict or empty cell must be associated with a unique elevation. We relabel those cells using an energy formulation with a standard form:

$$E(x) = \sum_{k \in \mathcal{C}^\star} A_k \cdot E_d(x_k) + \lambda \sum_{(k,k') \in \mathcal{N}} L_{kk'} \cdot E_r(x_k, x_{k'}) \tag{5}$$

where $\mathcal{C}^\star = \mathcal{C}_{conflict} \cup \mathcal{C}_{empty}$, the label x_k of cell k is an elevation value in $Z = \{0, z_1, ... z_n\}$, and $\mathcal{N}$ is the set of pairs of adjacent cells in $\mathcal{C}$ that have at least one cell belonging to $\mathcal{C}^\star$. E_d, E_r and λ are respectively the unary data term, the pairwise potential and the weighting parameter between the two terms. A_k and $L_{kk'}$ are respectively the area of cell k, and the length of the common edge between cells k and k': they are introduced to normalize the energy with respect to the size of cells.

The intuition behind the data term is that (i) an empty cell is more likely to be ground with an elevation value of 0, and (ii) a conflict cell is more likely to be roof with an elevation value as close as possible to its inherited elevations:

$$E_d(x_k) = \begin{cases} 0 & \text{if } k \in \mathcal{C}_{empty} \text{ and } x_k = 0 \\ \min\{|x_k - z|_{z \in Z_k}\} & \text{else if } k \in \mathcal{C}_{conflict} \text{ and } x_k \neq 0 \\ \gamma & \text{otherwise} \end{cases} \tag{6}$$

where γ is a penalty for not respecting this intuition.

The pairwise potential is a generalized Potts model that increases the penalty between two cells when their common edges projected in 3D back-project well into the images. As we consider the pairs of cells with different elevations x_k and $x_{k'}$, each pair has exactly two common edges in 3D: one at elevation x_k, the other at elevation $x_{k'}$. The pairwise term is expressed by

$$E_r(x_k, x_{k'}) = min(G^l(x_k) + G^l(x_{k'}), G^r(x_k) + G^r(x_{k'})) \cdot \mathbb{1}_{\{x_k \neq x'_k\}} \qquad (7)$$

where $G^l(x_k)$ (respectively $G^r(x_k)$) is a back-projection measure of the common edge at elevation x_k into the left (resp. right) image. In practice, the back-projection measure is defined as the absolute value of one minus the scalar product between the image gradients and the gradients of the back-projected edge.

Optimization. For efficiency reasons, the energy minimization is spatially decomposed into independent subproblems. We regroup the connected conflict and coherent cells into clusters while allowing empty cells to be inside. Each cluster intuitively corresponds to a building or a building block. The α-β swap algorithm [30] is then operated over the set of conflict and empty cells of each cluster. Note that, for each cluster, we restrict the label set Z to the inherited elevations of its cells. Optionally, the optimization can be performed in parallel on each cluster.

Compact city model. The ground is represented in 3D by a mesh surface triangulated from the altitude estimates [28]. From the optimal label configuration, roofs are inserted by simply elevated cells to their elevation label from the ground. The facade components are finally added by creating vertical facets between the adjacent cells with different labels.

7   Experiments

We experimented our method with stereo pairs from QuickBird2, WorldView2 and Pleiades satellite images with pixel resolution at 0.6, 0.5 and 0.5 m respectively. All the experiments have been done on a single computer with Intel Core i7 processor clocked at 2 GHz.

Implementation details. Our algorithm is implemented in C++ using the Computational Geometry Algorithms Library (CGAL) [31] for manipulating geometric data structures in 2D and 3D, and the Geospatial Data Abstraction Library (GDAL) [32] for processing basic operations with satellite images. The cell decomposition in Sect. 6 is computed using a constrained Delaunay triangulation whose constrained edges correspond to the orthographic projection into the horizontal plane of the polygon edges of both partitions. The number of parameters is large, *i.e.* 6, but this is the price to pay for a full pipeline combining semantic and geometric considerations in an unsupervised manner. In all our experiments except Fig. 7, we fixed the weights of the two energies to $\beta_1 = 0.2$, $\beta_2 = 10$ and $\lambda = 2.5$, and the penalties to $\alpha = 0.05$ and $\gamma = 2$. The number of

Fig. 9. Reconstruction of buildings. On simple buildings (top examples), left and right enriched partitions (left columns) are relatively similar. For more complex buildings (bottom examples), enriched partitions are more different: their fusion allows us to find a consensual 3D output model. With freeform architectural structures (middle example), curved roofs are roughly approximated by a step-like geometry. The back-projection into the input images of the roof edges from the output 3D model shows a good accuracy of both building elevations and contours (see red lines in right columns)

possible roof elevations is set to $n = 50$, except for US cities where skyscrapers requires increasing its value to 100.

Robustness. Our output models provide a faithful LOD1 representation of build-ings, as illustrated in Fig. 9. With the current satellite resolutions, a more detailed building representation such as LOD2 is not realistic. Cases that chal-lenge our algorithm are the small buildings, typically houses in residential areas, and the textureless and reflective objects which, generally speaking, constitute an important challenge in stereovision. Our method can handle buildings with some parts are visible only in one image. However, large occluded parts can generally not be recovered.

Scalability. Our algorithm has been tested on several cities presenting different urban landscapes, as shown on Figs. 3 and 10. Dense downtowns in antique cities such as Alexandria, Egypt, are particularly challenging with narrow streets and

Seoul, South Korea

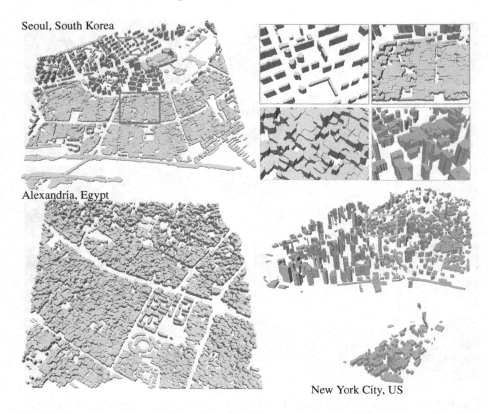

Alexandria, Egypt

New York City, US

Fig. 10. Reconstruction of cities. Our algorithm performs on different types of urban landscapes, including dense downtown (top left), antique city (bottom left), and US downtown (bottom right). Each model was obtained from one stereo pair of satellite images

small buildings massively connected. Our algorithm sometimes fails separating blocks in between these narrow streets as their width can be smaller than the size of our polygons. Business districts of US cities as Denver or New York is the opposite landscape: buildings are large, tall and fairly separated from each other. Our algorithm typically performs better on such areas. In terms of classification, buildings are globally well detected. One of the main reasons is because we do not rely on a radiometric description of buildings. At the scale of big cities, the radiometric variability of buildings is too high to draw likelihoods. Buildings can be missed when there are not enough elevation estimates. This situation is relatively marginal in practice: a visual comparison between our output 3D model of Denver and the building footprints of a cadastral map give us less than 5 % of missed buildings and 14 % of invalid buildings, i.e. buildings with at least 20 % of their footprints missed or over-detected.

Table 1. Running times and output complexity. The output complexity refers to the number of triangular facets in the output 3D model. Note that the fusion step has been optimized sequentially on each building cluster

	New Yory City, US	Denvers, US	Seoul, Korea Korea	Alexandria, Egypt
Polygonal partitioning	0.5 min	1.0 min	0.8 min	0.5 min
Joint classification	2.8 min	4.7 min	3.4 min	2.5 min
Fusion	1.5 min	2.8 min	13.7 min	29.2 min
Total time	4.8 min	8.5 min	17.9 min	32.2 min
Output complexity	0.23 M	0.35 M	0.89 M	1.35 M

Performance. Timings and complexity of output 3D models are given for different cities in Table 1. Input satellite images have typically around 30Mpixels. Each of the three steps of our method takes a few minutes from a typical stereo pair of satellite images. For very dense cities, fusion is the most time-consuming step as the high density of buildings generates complex cell decompositions. For cities with more space in between the buildings such as New York or Denver, fusion is quite fast. Running times for joint classification and elevation recovery, and polygonal partitioning do not depend on the urban landscape, but on the input image size. Overall, the use of compact and efficient geometric data structures allow us to have very competitive timings with respect to airborne-based methods.

Comparisons. While there is no automatic algorithm producing compact and semantic-aware city models from satellite images, we compared our output models to traditional Digital Surface Models generated from stereo matching, fol-

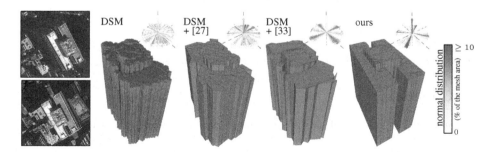

Fig. 11. Comparisons with Digital Surface Models. Traditional DSM derived from stereo matching [14] at the pixel scale gives dense and structure-free 3D models. By postprocessing a DSM with Voronoi clustering [27] or with structure-aware mesh simplification [33], we obtain more compact meshes, but the building structure cannot be not restored. Our output model is both compact and structure-aware (see the low number of principal directions in the distribution of output normals)

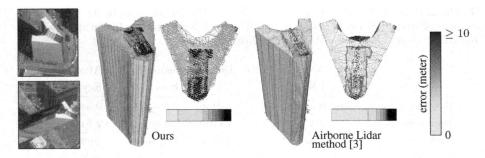

Fig. 12. Geometric accuracy. Airborne Lidar scans constitute precise measurements that can be used as Ground Truth to evaluate the geometric accuracy of our outputs (see the distribution of errors on the horizontal histogram). While a state-of-the-art airborne Lidar method [3] produces more accurate results with a lower mean error to Lidar points ($0.9\,m$ vs $1.7\,m$), the gap is relatively low given the difference of quality between the two types of inputs

lowing by structure recovery algorithms. As shown in Fig. 11, our output model better preserves the building structure while being semantic-aware and compact. We also measure in Fig. 12 the geometric accuracy of our method, and compares it with accuracy of an airborne Lidar based algorithm. Although our output is less accurate, the gap is relatively low given the contrast of data accuracy between airborne Lidar and satellite imagery.

Limitations. Our algorithm has several limitations. First, our output 3D models only contain three semantic labels (ground, roof and facade). The design of our algorithm is, however, flexible enough to account for new urban classes in future works. Second, the limited quality of satellite images makes difficult the reconstruction of small buildings, typically houses in residential areas. Third, our system is robust to occlusions of facades, ground and piece of roofs, but cannot handle severe roof occlusions where a roof is only visible in one image. Our LOD1 representation is also less accurate with freeform architectural roofs as domes or peaky structures. In such cases, roofs are approximated by a step-like geometry whose accuracy depends on the amount of elevation estimates.

8   Conclusion

We proposed a full pipeline for producing compact and semantic-aware city models from satellite images. Big cities such as Denver are reconstructed in a few minutes. Our method relies on two key ingredients. First, we reason at the scale of atomic polygons to capture geometry of urban structures while insuring a fast and scalable process. Second, semantics and 3D geometry are retrieved simultaneously to be robust to low resolution and occlusion problems of satellite images. Whereas the quality of our output models is not as accurate as airborne Lidar solutions, our solution outclasses traditional DSM representations, and offers new perspectives in city modeling.

As future work we wish to include more semantic classes into the pipeline, in particular roads and high vegetation. We also would like to investigate the use of geometric regularities at the scale of a district or an entire city as a way to consolidate input data and reinforce the structure-awareness of the models of buildings.

Acknowledgments. This work was supported by Luxcarta. The authors thank Qian-Yi Zhou, Lionel Laurore, Justin Hyland, Véronique Poujade and Frédéric Trastour for datasets and technical discussions.

References

1. Musialski, P., Wonka, P., Aliaga, D., Wimmer, M., Van Gool, L., Purgathofer, W.: A survey of urban reconstruction. Comput. Graph. Forum **32**(6), 146–177 (2013)
2. Poli, D., Caravaggi, I.: 3D modeling of large urban areas with stereo VHR satellite imagery: lessons learned. Nat. Hazards **68**(1), 52–78 (2013)
3. Lafarge, F., Mallet, C.: Building large urban environments from unstructured point data. In: ICCV (2011)
4. Poullis, C., You, S.: Automatic reconstruction of cities from remote sensor data. In: CVPR (2009)
5. Zhou, Q., Neumann, U.: A streaming framework for seamless building reconstruction from large-scale aerial lidar data. In: CVPR (2009)
6. Zebedin, L., Bauer, J., Karner, K., Bischof, H.: Fusion of feature- and area-based information for urban buildings modeling from aerial imagery. In: Forsyth, D., Torr, P., Zisserman, A. (eds.) ECCV 2008. LNCS, vol. 5305, pp. 873–886. Springer, Heidelberg (2008). doi:10.1007/978-3-540-88693-8_64
7. Vanegas, C., Aliaga, D., Benes, B.: Building reconstruction using Manhattan-world grammars. In: CVPR (2010)
8. Verdie, Y., Lafarge, F., Alliez, P.: LOD generation for urban scenes. ACM Trans. Graph. **34**(3), 30:1–30:14 (2015)
9. Zhou, Q.Y., Neumann, U.: 2.5d building modeling by discovering global regularities. In: CVPR (2012)
10. Haene, C., Zach, C., Cohen, A., Angst, R., Pollefeys, M.: Joint 3D scene reconstruction and class segmentation. In: CVPR (2013)
11. Lin, H., Gao, J., Zhou, Y., Lu, G., Ye, M., Zhang, C., Liu, L., Yang, R.: Semantic decomposition and reconstruction of residential scenes from lidar data. ACM Trans. Graph. **32**(4), 66 (2013)
12. Cabezas, R., Straub, J., Fisher, J.: Semantically-aware aerial reconstruction from multi-modal data. In: ICCV (2015)
13. Scharstein, D., Szeliski, R.: A taxonomy and evaluation of dense two-frame stereo correspondence algorithms. IJCV **47**(1–3), 7–42 (2002)
14. Hirschmuller, H.: Stereo processing by semiglobal matching and mutual information. PAMI **30**(2), 328–341 (2008)
15. Zitnick, C., Kang, S.: Stereo for image-based rendering using image over-segmentation. IJCV **75**(1), 49–65 (2007)
16. Taguchi, Y., Wilburn, B., Zitnick, C.: Stereo reconstruction with mixed pixels using adaptive over-segmentation. In: CVPR (2008)
17. Bodis-Szomoru, A., Riemenschneider, H., Van Gool, L.: Fast, approximate piecewise-planar modeling based on sparse structure-from-motion and superpixels. In: CVPR (2014)

18. Bleyer, M., Rother, C., Kohli, P., Scharstein, D., Sinha, S.: Object stereo - joint stereo matching and object segmentation. In: CVPR (2011)
19. Ladicky, L., Sturgess, P., Russell, C., Sengupta, S., Bastanlar, Y., Clocksin, W., Torr, P.: Joint optimization for object class segmentation and dense stereo reconstruction. IJCV **100**(2), 122–133 (2012)
20. Bay, H., Ferrari, V., Van Gool, L.: Wide-baseline stereo matching with line segments. In: CVPR (2005)
21. Zhang, Z., Fidler, S., Waggoner, J., Cao, Y., Dickinson, S., Siskind, J., Wang, S.: Superedge grouping for object localization by combining appearance and shape information. In: CVPR (2012)
22. Sun, X., Christoudias, C.M., Fua, P.: Free-shape polygonal object localization. In: Fleet, D., Pajdla, T., Schiele, B., Tuytelaars, T. (eds.) ECCV 2014. LNCS, vol. 8694, pp. 317–332. Springer, Heidelberg (2014). doi:10.1007/978-3-319-10599-4_21
23. Levinshtein, A., Sminchisescu, C., Dickinson, S.: Optimal contour closure by superpixel grouping. In: Daniilidis, K., Maragos, P., Paragios, N. (eds.) ECCV 2010. LNCS, vol. 6312, pp. 480–493. Springer, Heidelberg (2010). doi:10.1007/978-3-642-15552-9_35
24. Gueguen, L., Hamid, R.: Large-scale damage detection using satellite imagery. In: CVPR (2015)
25. Zheng, E., Wang, K., Dunn, E., Frahm, J.M.: Minimal solvers for 3D geometry from satellite imagery. In: ICCV (2015)
26. Groger, G., Plumer, L.: Citygml interoperable semantic 3D city models. J. Photogrammetry Remote Sens. **71**, 12–33 (2012)
27. Duan, L., Lafarge, F.: Image partitioning into convex polygons. In: CVPR (2015)
28. Briese, C., Pfeifer, N., Dorninger, P.: Applications of the robust interpolation for DTTM determination. In: Photogrammetric Computer Vision (2002)
29. Hartley, R., Saxena, T.: The cubic rational polynomial camera model. In: Image Understanding Workshop, vol. 649 (1997)
30. Boykov, Y., Kolmogorov, V.: An experimental comparison of min-cut/max-flow algorithms for energy minimization in vision. PAMI **26**(9), 1124–1137 (2004)
31. CGAL. Computational Geometry Algorithms Library. http://www.cgal.org/
32. GDAL. Geospatial Data Abstraction Library. http://www.gdal.org/
33. Salinas, D., Lafarge, F., Alliez, P.: Structure-aware mesh decimation. Comput. Graph. Forum **34**(6), 211–227 (2015)

Weakly Supervised Object Localization Using Size Estimates

Miaojing Shi[(⊠)] and Vittorio Ferrari

University of Edinburgh, Edinburgh, Scotland, UK
{miaojing.shi,vittorio.ferrari}@ed.ac.uk

Abstract. We present a technique for weakly supervised object localization (WSOL), building on the observation that WSOL algorithms usually work better on images with bigger objects. Instead of training the object detector on the entire training set at the same time, we propose a curriculum learning strategy to feed training images into the WSOL learning loop in an order from images containing bigger objects down to smaller ones. To automatically determine the order, we train a regressor to estimate the size of the object given the whole image as input. Furthermore, we use these size estimates to further improve the re-localization step of WSOL by assigning weights to object proposals according to how close their size matches the estimated object size. We demonstrate the effectiveness of using size order and size weighting on the challenging PASCAL VOC 2007 dataset, where we achieve a significant improvement over existing state-of-the-art WSOL techniques.

1 Introduction

Object class detection has been intensively studied during recent years [1–9]. The goal is to place a bounding box around every instance of a given object class. Given an input image, typically modern object detectors first extract object proposals [7,10,11] and then score them with a classifier to determine their probabilities of containing an instance of certain class [12,13]. Manually annotated bounding boxes are typically required for training the classifier.

Annotating bounding boxes is usually tedious and time consuming. In order to reduce the annotation cost, a commonly used strategy is to learn the detector in a weakly supervised manner: we are given a set of images known to contain instances of a certain object class, but we do not know the object locations in these images. This weakly supervised object localization (WSOL) bypasses the need for bounding box annotation and therefore substantially reduces annotation time. WSOL is typically conducted in two iterative steps [13–20]: (1) re-localizing object instances in the images using the current object detector, and (2) re-training the object detector given the current selection of instances.

WSOL algorithms typically apply both the re-training and re-localization steps on the entire training set at the same time. However, WSOL works better on images with bigger objects. For instance, [16] observed that the performance of several WSOL algorithms consistently decays from easy dataset with many

© Springer International Publishing AG 2016
B. Leibe et al. (Eds.): ECCV 2016, Part V, LNCS 9909, pp. 105–121, 2016.
DOI: 10.1007/978-3-319-46454-1_7

RE-TRAINING

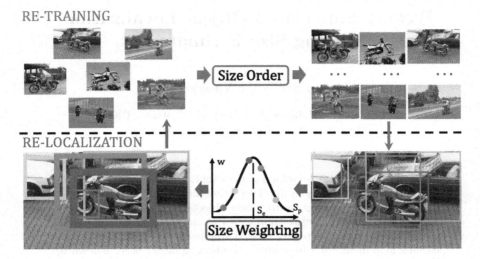

Fig. 1. Overview of our method. We use size estimates to determine the order in which images are fed to a WSOL loop, so that the object detector is re-trained progressively from images with bigger objects down to smaller ones. We also improve the re-localization step, by weighting object proposals according to how close their size (s_p) matches the estimated object size (s_e)

big objects (Caltech4 [21]) to hard dataset with many small objects (PASCAL VOC 07 [2]). In this paper, we propose to feed images into the WSOL learning loop in an order from images containing bigger objects down to smaller ones (Fig. 1, top half). This forms a curriculum learning [22] strategy where the learner progressively sees more and more training samples, starting from easy ones (big objects) and gradually adding harder ones (smaller objects). To understand why this might work better than standard orderless WSOL, let's compare the two. The standard approach re-trains the model from *all* images at each iteration. These include many incorrect localizations which corrupt the model re-training, and result in bad localizations in the next re-localization step, particularly for small objects (Fig. 2). In our approach instead, WSOL learns a decent model from images of big objects in the first few iterations. This initial model then better localizes objects in images of mid-size objects, which in turn leads to an even better model in the next re-training step, as it has now more data, and so on. By the time the process reaches images of small objects, it already has a good detector, which improve the chances of localizing them correctly (Fig. 2).

Our easy-to-hard strategy needs to determine the sequence of images automatically. For this we train a regressor to estimate the size of the object given the whole image as input. In addition to establishing a curriculum, we use these size estimates to improve the re-localization step. We weight object proposals according to how close their size matches the estimated object size (Fig. 1, bottom half). These weights are higher for proposals of size similar to the estimate, and decrease as their size difference increases. This weighting scheme reduces the uncertainty in the proposal distribution, making the re-localization step more likely to pick a proposals correctly covering the object. Figure 3 shows an example of how size weighting changes the proposal score distribution induced by the current object detector, leading to more accurate localization.

In extensive experiments on the popular PASCAL VOC 2007 dataset, we show that: (1) using our curriculum learning strategy based on object size gives a 7 % improvement in CorLoc compared to the orderless WSOL; (2) by further adding size weighting into the re-localization step, we get another 10 % CorLoc improvement; (3) finally, we employ a deep Neural Network to re-train the model and achieve our best performance, significantly outperforming the state-of-the-art in WSOL [13,15,23].

Compared to standard WSOL, our scheme needs additional data to train the size regressor. This consists of a single scalar value indicating the size of the object, for each image in an external dataset. We do not need bounding-box annotation. Moreover, in Sect. 4.5 we show that we can use a size regressor generic across classes, by training it on different classes than those used during WSOL.

2 Related Work

Weakly-Supervised Object Localization (WSOL). In WSOL the training images are known to contain instances of a certain object class but their locations are unknown. The task is both to localize the objects in the training images and to learn an detector for the class. WSOL is often conceptualised as Multiple Instance Learning (MIL) [12,14,16,18–20,24,25]. Images are treated as bags of object proposals [7,10,11] (instances). A negative image contains only negative instances. A positive image contains at least one positive instance, mixed in with a majority of negative ones. The goal is to find the true positives instances from which to learn a classifier for the object class.

Due to the use of strong CNN features [5,26], recent works on WSOL [12, 14,15,19,20,23] have shown remarkable progress. Moreover, researchers also tried to incorporate various advanced cues into the WSOL process, e.g. objectness [13,16,18,27,28], co-occurrence between multiple classes in the same training images [25], and even appearance models from related classes learned from bounding-box annotations [29–31]. In this work, we propose to estimate the size of the object in an image and inject it as a new cue into WSOL. We use it both to determine the sequence of training images in a curriculum learning scheme, and to weight the score function used during the re-localization step.

Curriculum Learning (CL). The curriculum learning paradigm was proposed by Bengio et al. [22], in which the model was learnt gradually from easy to hard samples so as to increase the entropy of training. A strong assumption in [22] is that the curriculum is provided by a human teacher. In this sense, determining what constitute an easy sample is subjective and needs to be manually provided. To alleviate this issue, Kumar and Koller [32] formulated CL as a regularization term into the learning objective and proposed a self-paced learning scheme.

The concept of learning in an easy-to-hard order was visited also in computer vision [33–37]. These works focus on a key question: what makes an image easy or hard? The works differ by how they re-interpret "easiness" in different scenarios. Lee and Grauman [33] consider the task of discovering object classes in an unordered image collection. They relate easiness to "objectness" and "context-awareness". Their context-awareness model is initialized with regions of "stuff" categories, and is then used to support discovering "things" categories in unlabelled images. The model is updated by identifying the easy object categories first and progressively expands to harder categories. Sharmanska *et al.* [35] use some privileged information to distinguish between easy and hard examples in an image classification task. The privileged information are additional cues available at training time, but not at test time. They employ several additional cues, such as object bounding boxes, image tags and rationales to define their concept of easiness [36]. Pentina *et al.* [34] consider learning the visual attributes of objects. They let a human decide whether an object is easy or hard to recognize. The human annotator provides a difficulty score for each image, ranging from easy to hard. In this paper, we use CL in a WSOL setting and propose object size as an "easiness" measure. The most related work to ours is the very recent [37], which learns to predict human response times as a measure of difficulty, and shows an example application to WSOL.

3   Method

In this section we first describe a basic MIL framework, which we use as our baseline (Sect. 3.1); then we show how to use object size estimates to improve the basic framework by introducing a sequence during re-training (Sect. 3.2) and a weighting during re-localization (Sect. 3.3). Finally, we explain how to obtain size estimates automatically in Sect. 3.4.

3.1   Basic Multiple Instance Learning Framework

We represent each image in the input set $\mathcal{I}$ as a bag of proposals extracted using the state of the art object proposal method [11]. It returns about 2000 proposals per image, likely to cover all objects. Following [5,14,19,20,23], we describe the proposals by the output of the second-last layer of the CNN model proposed by Krizhevsky *et al.* [26]. The CNN model is pre-trained for whole-image classification on ILSVRC [38], using the Caffe implementation [39]. This produces a 4096-dimensional feature vector for each proposal. Based on this feature representation, we iteratively build an SVM appearance model A (object detector) in two alternating steps: (1) re-localization: in each positive image, we select the highest scoring proposal by the SVM. This produces the set $\mathcal{S}$ which contains the current selection of one instance from each positive image. (2) re-training: we train the SVM using $\mathcal{S}$ as positive training samples, and all proposals from the negative images as negative samples.

As commonly done in [12,13,17,40–42] we initialize the process by training the appearance model using complete images as training samples. Each image in

Fig. 2. Illustration of the estimated size order for class *bicycle*, for three batches (one per row). We show the ground-truth object bounding-boxes (blue), objects localized by our WSOL scheme using size order (red), and objects localized by the basic MIL framework (green). In the first, third and last examples of the first row the green and red boxes are identical (Color figure online)

$\mathcal{I}$ provides a training sample. Intuitively, this is a good initialization when the object covers most of the image, which is true only for some images.

3.2   Size Order

Assume we have a way to automatically estimate the size of the object in all input images $\mathcal{I}$ (Sect. 3.4). Based on their object size order, we re-organize MIL on a curriculum, as detailed in Alg. 1.

We split the images into K batches according to their estimated object size (Fig. 2). We start by running MIL on the first batch $\mathcal{I}_1$, containing the largest objects. The whole-image initialization works well on them, leading to a reasonable first appearance model A_1 (though trained from fewer images). We continue running MIL on the first batch $\mathcal{I}_1$ for M iterations to get a solid A_1. The process then moves on to the second batch $\mathcal{I}_2$, which contains mid-size objects, *adding* all its images into the current working set $\mathcal{I}_1 \cup \mathcal{I}_2$, and run the MIL iterations again. Instead of starting from scratch, we use A_1 from the first batch MIL iterations. This model is likely to do a better job at localizing objects in batch $\mathcal{I}_2$ than the whole-image initialization of basic MIL (Fig. 2, second row). Hence, the model trains from better samples in the re-training step. Moreover, the model A_2 output by MIL on $\mathcal{I}_1 \cup \mathcal{I}_2$ will be better than A_1, as it is trained from more samples. Finally, during MIL on $\mathcal{I}_1 \cup \mathcal{I}_2$, the localization of objects in I_1 will also improve (Fig. 2, first row).

The process iteratively moves on to the next batch $k + 1$, every time starting from appearance model A_k and running MIL's re-training/re-localization iterations on the image set $\cup_{i=1}^{k+1}\mathcal{I}_i$. As the image set continuously grows, the process does not jump from batch to batch. This helps stabilizing the learning

---

Alg. 1. Multiple instance learning with size order and size weighting

---
Initialization:
1) split the input set $\mathcal{I}$ into K batches according to the estimated object size order
2) initialize the positive and negative examples as the entire images in first batch $\mathcal{I}_1$
3) train an appearance model A_1 on the initial training set
for batch $k = 1 : K$ **do**
    for iteration $m = 1 : M$ **do**
        i) **re-localize** the object instances in images $\cup_{i=1}^{k}\mathcal{I}_i$ using current appearance
model A_k^m and size weighting of object proposals;
        ii) add new negative proposals by hard negative mining;
        iii) **re-train** the appearance model A_k^m given current selection of instances in
images $\cup_{i=1}^{k}\mathcal{I}_i$;
    end for
end for
Return final detector and selected object instances in $\mathcal{I}$

---

process and properly training the appearance model from more and more training samples. By the time the process reaches batches with small objects, the appearance model will already be very good and will do a much better job than the whole-image initialization of basic MIL on them (Fig. 2, third row). Figure 2 shows some examples of applying our curriculum learning strategy compared to basic MIL. In all our work, we set $K = 3$ and $M = 3$.

3.3 Size Weighting

In addition to establishing a curriculum, we use the size estimates to refine the re-localization step of MIL. A naive way would be to filter out all proposals with size different from the estimate. However, this is likely to fail as neither the size estimator nor the proposals are perfectly accurate, and therefore even a good proposal covering the object tightly will not exactly match the estimated size.

Instead, we use the size estimate as indicative of the *range* of the real object size. Assuming the error distribution of the estimated size w.r.t the real size is normal, according to the three-sigma rule of thumb [43], the real object size is very likely to lie in this range $[s_e - 3\sigma, s_e + 3\sigma]$ (with 99.7 % probability), where s_e is the estimated size and σ is the standard deviation of the error. We explain in Sect. 3.4 how we obtain σ.

We assign a continuous weight to each proposal p so that it gives a relatively high weight for the size s_p of the proposal falling inside the 3σ interval of the estimated object size s_e, and a very low weight for s_p outside the interval:

$$W(p; s_e, \sigma, \delta) = \min\left(\frac{1}{1 + e^{\delta \cdot (s_e - 3\sigma - s_p)}}, \frac{1}{1 + e^{\delta \cdot (s_p - s_e - 3\sigma)}}\right). \tag{1}$$

This function decreases with the difference between s_p and s_e (Fig. 3); δ is a scalar parameter that controls how rapidly the function decreases, particularly outside the three sigma range $[s_l, s_r]$. The model is not sensitive to the exact

Fig. 3. Illustration of size weighting. Left: behaviour of the size weighting function W. Example sizes are shown by boxes of the appropriate area centered at the ground truth (GT) object; s_e denotes the estimated object size. The size weight W of each box is written in its bottom left corner. Right: detection result using size weighting (red) compared to basic MIL framework (green) (Color figure online)

choice of δ (we set $\delta = 3$ in all experiments). Weights for proposals falling out of the interval $[s_l, s_r]$ quickly go to zero. Thereby this weight W represents the likelihood of proposal p covering the object, according to the size estimate s_e.

We now combine the size weighting W of a proposal with the score given by the SVM appearance model A. First we transform the output of the SVM into a probability using platt-scaling [44]. Assuming that the two score functions are independent, we combine them by multiplication, yielding the final score of a proposal p: $A(p) \cdot W(p; s_e, \sigma, \delta)$. This score is used in the re-localization step of MIL (Sect. 3.1), making it more likely to pick a proposal correctly covering the object. Figure 4 gives some example results of using this size weighting model.

3.4   Size Estimator

In Subsects. 3.2 and 3.3, we assumed the availability of an automatic estimator of the size of objects in images. In this subsection we explain how we do it.

We use Kernel Ridge Regressor (KRR) [45] to estimate the size of the object given the whole image as input. We train it beforehand on an external set $\mathcal{R}$, disjoint from the set $\mathcal{I}$ on which MIL operates (Sect. 3.1). We train a separate size regressor for each object class. For each class, the training set $\mathcal{R}$ contains images annotated with the size s_t of the largest object of that class in it. The training set can be small, as we demonstrate in Sect. 4.4. The input image is represented by a 4096-dimensional CNN feature vector covering the whole image, output of the second-last layer of the AlexNet CNN architecture [26]. The object size is represented by its area normalized by the image area. As area differences grow rapidly, learning to directly regress to area puts more weight on estimation errors on large objects rather than on smaller objects. To alleviate this bias, we apply a r-th root operation on the regression target values $s_t \leftarrow \sqrt[r]{s_t}$. Empirically, we choose $r = 3$, but the regression performance over different r is very close.

We train the KRR by minimizing the squared error on the training set $\mathcal{R}$ and obtain the regressor along with the standard deviation σ of its error by cross-validation on $\mathcal{R}$. We then use this size regressor to automatically estimate the object size on images in the WSOL input set $\mathcal{I}$.

4   Experiments

4.1   Dataset and Settings

Size Estimator Training. We train the size estimator on the trainval set $\mathcal{R}$ of PASCAL VOC 2012 [2] (PASCAL 12 for short). This has 20 classes, a total of 11540 images, and 834 images per class on average.

WSOL. We perform WSOL on the trainval set $\mathcal{I}$ of PASCAL 07 [2], which has different images of the same 20 classes in $\mathcal{R}$ (5011 images in total). While several WSOL works remove images containing only truncated and difficult objects [12, 13,16,17], we use the complete set $\mathcal{I}$.

We apply the size estimator on $\mathcal{I}$ and evaluate its performance on it in Sect. 4.2. Then, we use the estimated object sizes to improve the basic MIL approach of Sect. 3.1, as described in Sects. 3.2 and 3.3. Finally, we apply the detectors learned on $\mathcal{I}$ to the test set $\mathcal{X}$ of PASCAL 07, which contains 4952 images in total. We evaluate our method and compare to standard orderless MIL in Sect. 4.3.

CNN. We use AlexNet as CNN architecture [26] to extract features for both size estimation and MIL (Sects. 3.1 and 3.4). As customary [13,15,20,23], we pre-train it for whole-image classification on ILSVRC [38], but we do *not* do any fine-tuning on bounding-boxes.

4.2   Size Estimation

Evaluation Protocol. We train the regressor on set $\mathcal{R}$. We adopt 7-fold cross-validation to obtain the best regressor and the corresponding σ. In order to test the generalization ability of the regressor, we gradually reduce the number of training images from an average of 834 per class to 100, 50, 40, 30 per class.

The regression performance on $\mathcal{I}$ is measured via the mean square error (MSE) between the estimated size and the ground-truth size (both in r^{th} root, see Sect. 3.4), and the Kendall's τ rank correlation coefficient [46] between the estimated size order and the ground-truth size order.

Results. Table 1 presents the results. We tried different r^{th} root of the size value during training. While $r = 3$ gives highest performance, it is not sensitive to exact choice of r, as long as $r > 1$. The table also shows the effect of reducing the number of training images N to 100, 50, 40, and 30 per class. Although performance decreases when training with fewer samples, even using as few as 30 samples per class still delivers good results.

We set $r = 3$ and use all training samples in $\mathcal{R}$ by default in the following experiments. We will also present an in-depth analysis of the impact of varying N on WSOL in Sect. 4.4.

Table 1. Size estimation result on set $\mathcal{I}$ with different r and number N of training images per class. r refers to the rth root on size value applied; 'ALL' indicates using the complete $\mathcal{R}$ set, which has 834 images per class on average

r^{th} root	Kendall's τ	N	Kendall's τ	MSE
	N		$r = 3$	
1	0.604	**ALL**	**0.614**	**0.013**
2	0.612	100	0.561	0.016
3	**0.614**	50	0.542	0.018
4	0.612	40	0.530	0.019
5	0.610	30	0.527	0.020

4.3 Weakly Supervised Object Localization (WSOL)

Evaluation Protocol. In standard MIL, given the training set $\mathcal{I}$ with image-level labels, our goal is to localize the object instances in this set and to train good object detectors for the test set $\mathcal{X}$. We quantify localization performance in the training set with the Correct Localization (CorLoc) measure [12,13,15,16,23,47]. CorLoc is the percentage of images in which the bounding-box returned by the algorithm correctly localizes an object of the target class (intersection-over-union ≥ 0.5 [2]). We quantify object detection performance on the test set $\mathcal{X}$ using mean average precision (mAP), as standard in PASCAL VOC.

As in most previous WSOL methods [12–20,23], our scheme returns exactly one bounding-box per class per training image. This enables clean comparisons to previous work in terms of CorLoc on the training set $\mathcal{I}$. Note that at test time the object detector is capable of localizing multiple objects of the same class in the same image (and this is captured in the mAP measure).

Baseline. We use EdgeBoxes [11] as object proposals and follow the basic MIL framework of Sect. 3.1. For the baseline, we randomly split the training set $\mathcal{I}$ into three batches ($K = 3$), then train an SVM appearance model sequentially batch by batch. We apply three MIL iterations ($M = 3$) within each batch, and use hard negative mining for the SVM [12].

Like in [13,16,18,23,25,27,29,48,49], we combine the SVN score with a general measure of "objectness" [10], which measures how likely it is that a proposal tightly encloses an object of any class (*e.g.* bird, car, sheep), as opposed to background (*e.g.* sky, water, grass). For this we use the objectness measure produced by the proposal generator [11]. Using this additional cue makes the basic MIL start from a higher baseline.

Table 2 shows the result: CorLoc 39.1 on the training set $\mathcal{I}$ and mAP 20.1 on the test set $\mathcal{X}$. Examples are in Fig. 4 first row. In the following, we incorporate our ideas (size order and size weighting) into this baseline (Alg. 1).

Size Order. We use the same settings as the baseline ($K = 3$ and $M = 3$), but now the training set $\mathcal{I}$ is split into batches according to the size estimates.

Table 2. Comparison between the baseline MIL scheme, various versions of our scheme, and the state-of-the-art on PASCAL 07. 'Deep' indicates using additional MIL iterations with Fast R-CNN as detector

Method	Size order	Size weight	Deep	CorLoc	mAP
				-	-
Baseline				39.1	20.1
Our scheme	✓			46.3	24.9
	✓	✓		55.8	28.0
	✓	✓	✓	**60.9**	**36.0**
Baseline			✓	43.2	24.7
Cinbis *et al.* [13]				54.2	28.6
Wang *et al.* [23]				48.5	31.6
Bilen *et al.* [15]				43.7	27.7
Shi *et al.* [47]				38.3	-
Song *et al.* [20]				-	24.6

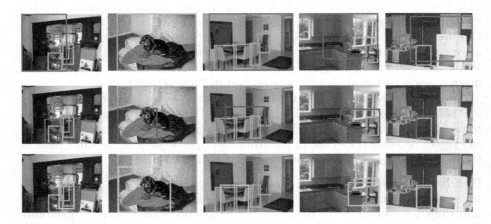

Fig. 4. Example localizations by different WSOL schemes on class *chair*. First row: localizations by the MIL baseline (green, see Sect. 4.3: Baseline setting). Second row: localizations by our method, which adds size order to the baseline (purple, see Sect. 4.3: Size order). Third row: localizations by our method with both size order and weighting (red, see Sect. 4.3: Size weighting). Ground-truth bounding-boxes are shown in blue (Color figure online)

As Table 2 shows, by performing curriculum learning based on size order, we improve CorLoc to 46.3 and mAP to 24.9. Examples are in Fig. 4 second row.

Size Weighting. Significant improvement of CorLoc can be further achieved by adding size weighting on top of size order. Table 2 illustrates this effect: the CorLoc using size order and size weighting goes to 55.8. Compared the baseline

39.1, this is a +16.7 improvement. Furthermore, the mAP improves to 28.0 (+7.9 over the baseline). Examples are in Fig. 4 third row.

Deep Net. So far, we have used an SVM on top of fixed deep features as the appearance model. Now we change the model to a deeper one, which trains all layers during the re-training step of MIL (Sect. 3.1). We take the best detection result we obtained so far (using both size order and size weighting) as an initialization for three additional MIL iterations. During these iterations, we use Fast R-CNN [4] as appearance model. We use the entire set at once (no batches) during the re-training and re-localization steps, and omit bounding-box regression in the re-training step [4], for simplicity. We only carry out three iterations as the system quickly converges after the first iteration.

As Table 2 shows, using this deeper model raises CorLoc to 60.9 and mAP to 36.0, which is a visible improvement. It is interesting to apply these deep MIL iterations also on top of the detections produced by the baseline. This yields a +4.1 higher CorLoc and +4.6 mAP (reaching 43.2 CorLoc and 24.7 mAP). In comparison, the effect of our proposed size order and size weighting is greater (+16.7 CorLoc and +7.9 mAP over the baseline, when both use SVM appearance models). Moreover, size order and weighting have an even greater effect when used in conjunction with the deep appearance model (+17.7 CorLoc and +11.3 mAP, when both the baseline and our method use Fast R-CNN).

Comparison to the State-of-the-Art. Table 2 also compares our method to state-of-the-art WSOL works [13,15,20,23,47]. We compare both the CorLoc on the trainval set $\mathcal{I}$ and mAP on the test set $\mathcal{X}$. We list the best results reported in each paper. Note [13] removes training images with only truncated and difficult object instances, which makes the WSOL problem easier, whereas we train from all images. As the table shows, our method outperforms all these works both in terms of CorLoc and mAP. All methods we compare to, except [47] use AlexNet, pretrained on ILSVRC classification data, as we do.

4.4   Impact of Size of Training Set for Size Regressor

The size estimator we used so far is trained on the complete set $\mathcal{R}$. What if we only have limited training samples with object size annotations? As shown in Sect. 4.2, when we reduce the number of training samples N per class, the accuracy of size estimation decreases moderately. However, we argue that neither Kendall's τ nor MSE are suitable for measuring the impact of the size estimates on MIL, when these are used to establish an order as we do in Sect. 3.2. As $\mathcal{I}$ is split into batches according to the size estimates, only the inter-batch size order matters, the order of images within one batch does not make any difference.

To measure the correlation of inter-batch size order between the ground-truth size sequence Q_{GT} and the estimated size sequence Q_{ES}, we count how many samples in Q_{GT}^k have been successfully retrieved in Q_{ES}^k, where Q^k indicates the set of images in batches 1 through k:

$$\text{recall} = \frac{|Q_{GT}^k \cap Q_{ES}^k|}{|Q_{GT}^k|}, \tag{2}$$

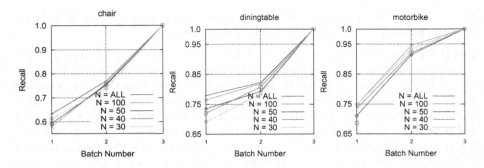

Fig. 5. Correlation between inter-batch size order based on the ground-truth size sequence and the estimated sequence, on class *chair*, *diningtable*, and *motorbike* of $\mathcal{I}$ set; recall is computed as in (2)

$|\cdot|$ denotes number of elements. Figure 5 shows recall curves on set $\mathcal{I}$, with varying N. The curves are quite close to each other, showing that reducing N does not affect the inter-batch order very much.

In Fig. 6 we conduct the WSOL experiment of Sect. 4.3, incorporating size order into the basic MIL framework on $\mathcal{I}$, using different size estimators trained with varying N. The 'baseline + size order' result in Fig. 6a shows little variation: even $N = 30$ leads to CorLoc within 2 % of using the full set $N = $ ALL. This is due to the fact shown above, that a less accurate size estimator does not affect the inter-batch size order much.

We also propose to use the size estimate to help MIL with size weighting (Sect. 3.3). Table 1 shows that MSE gets larger when N becomes smaller, which means the estimated object size gets father from the real value. This lower accuracy estimate affects size weighting and, in turn, can affect the performance of MIL. To validate this, we add size weighting on top of size order into MIL in Fig. 6. This time, the CorLoc improvement brought by size weighting varies significantly with N. Nevertheless, even with just $N = 30$ training samples per class, we still get an improvement. We believe this is due to the three-sigma rule we adopted in the weighting function (1). The real object size is very likely to fall into the 3σ range, and so it gets a relatively high weighting compared to the proposals with size outside the range.

Finally, we apply the additional deep MIL iterations presented in Sect. 4.3, 'Deep net' paragraph. Figure 6 shows a consistent trend of improvement across different N and our proposed size order and weighting schemes, on both CorLoc and mAP.

4.5 Further Analysis

Deep v.s. Deeper. So far we used AlexNet [26] during deep re-training (Sect. 4.3, 'Deep net' paragraph). Here we use an even deeper CNN architecture,

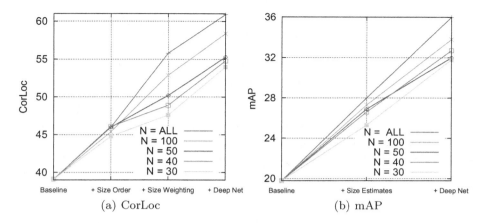

(a) CorLoc   (b) mAP

Fig. 6. WSOL performance on PASCAL 07 when varying N. Size order and weighting are gradually added into the baseline MIL framework, and eventually fed into the deep net. We use 'size estimates' in (b) to denote using both size order and size weighting

Table 3. WSOL results using AlexNet or VGG16 in Fast R-CNN. We report CorLoc on the trainval set $\mathcal{I}$ and mAP on the test set $\mathcal{X}$ of PASCAL 07

CNN architecture	AlexNet [26]	VGG16 [50]
CorLoc (trainval)	60.9	64.7
mAP (test)	36.0	37.2

VGG16 [50]. The result in Table 3 shows the benefits by going deeper, as get to a final CorLoc 64.7 and mAP 37.2.

Class-Specific, Class-Generic and Across-Class. So far we used an object size estimator trained separately for each class. Here we test the class-generalization ability of proposed size order and size weighting ideas. We perform two experiments. In the first, we use the entire $\mathcal{R}$ to train a single size estimator over all 20 classes, and use it on every image in $\mathcal{I}$, regardless of class. We call this estimator *class-generic* as it has to work regardless of the class it is applied to, within the range of classes it has seen during training. In the second experiment, we separate the 20 classes into two groups: (i) bicycle, bottle, car, chair, dining table, dog, horse, motorbike, person, TV monitor; (ii) airplane, bird, boat, bus, cat, cow, potted plant, sheep, sofa, train. We train two size estimators separately, one on each group. When doing WSOL on a class in $\mathcal{I}$, we use the estimator trained on the group not containing that class. We call this estimator *across-class*, as it has to generalize to new classes not seen during training.

Table 4 shows the results of WSOL, in terms of CorLoc on the trainval set $\mathcal{I}$ and the mAP on the test set $\mathcal{X}$ of PASCAL 07. Thanks to our robust batch-by-batch design in curriculum learning, the CorLoc using the size order is about the same for all size estimators. This shows that it is always beneficial to incorporate our proposed size order into WSOL, even when applied to new classes. When incorporating also size weighting into MIL, the benefits gradually diminish when going from the class-specific to the across-class estimators, as they predict object size less accurately. Nonetheless, we still get about +3 CorLoc when using the class-generic estimator and about +1 when using the across-class one.

The last column of Table 4, reports mAP on the test set, with deep re-training. The class-generic estimator leads to mAP 32.2, and the across-class one to 30.0. They are still substantially better than the baseline (24.7 when using deep re-training, see Table 2). Interestingly, the across-class result is only moderately worse than the class-generic one, which was trained on all 20 classes. This shows our method generalizes well to new classes.

Table 4. WSOL results using different size estimators. The first four columns show CorLoc on the trainval set $\mathcal{I}$; the last row shows mAP on the test set $\mathcal{X}$. The baseline does not use size estimates and is reported for reference

Size estimator	Baseline	+ Size order	+ Size weighting	+ Deep net	mAP on test $\mathcal{X}$
Class-specific	39.1	46.3	55.8	60.9	36.0
Class-generic	39.1	45.6	48.4	54.4	32.2
Across-class	39.1	45.0	45.8	51.1	30.0

5   Conclusions

We proposed to use object size estimates to help weakly supervised object localization (WSOL). We introduced a curriculum learning strategy to feed training images into WSOL in an order from images containing bigger objects down to smaller ones. We also proposed to use the size estimates to help the re-localization step of WSOL, by weighting object proposals according to how close their size matches the estimated object size. We demonstrated the effectiveness of both ideas on top of a standard multiple instance learning WSOL scheme.

Currently we use the output of the MIL framework with size order and size weighting as the starting point for additional iterations that re-train the whole deep net. However, the training set is not batched any more during deep re-training. A promising direction for future work is to embed the size estimates into an MIL loop where the whole deep net is updated. Another interesting direction is to go towards a continuous ordering, *i.e.* where the batch size goes towards 1; efficiently updating the model in that setting is another challenge.

Acknowledgments. Work supported by the ERC Starting Grant VisCul.

References

1. Dalal, N., Triggs, B.: Histogram of oriented gradients for human detection. In: CVPR (2005)
2. Everingham, M., Van Gool, L., Williams, C.K.I., Winn, J., Zisserman, A.: The PASCAL visual object classes (VOC) challenge. IJCV **88**, 303–338 (2010)
3. Felzenszwalb, P., Girshick, R., McAllester, D., Ramanan, D.: Object detection with discriminatively trained part based models. IEEE Trans. PAMI **32**(9), 1627–1645 (2010)
4. Girshick, R.: Fast R-CNN. In: ICCV (2015)
5. Girshick, R., Donahue, J., Darrell, T., Malik, J.: Rich feature hierarchies for accurate object detection and semantic segmentation. In: CVPR (2014)
6. Malisiewicz, T., Gupta, A., Efros, A.: Ensemble of exemplar-SVMs for object detection and beyond. In: ICCV (2011)
7. Uijlings, J.R.R., van de Sande, K.E.A., Gevers, T., Smeulders, A.W.M.: Selective search for object recognition. IJCV **104**, 154–171 (2013)
8. Viola, P.A., Platt, J., Zhang, C.: Multiple instance boosting for object detection. In: NIPS (2005)
9. Wang, X., Yang, M., Zhu, S., Lin, Y.: Regionlets for generic object detection. In: ICCV, pp. 17–24. IEEE (2013)
10. Alexe, B., Deselaers, T., Ferrari, V.: What is an object? In: CVPR (2010)
11. Zitnick, C.L., Dollár, P.: Edge boxes: locating object proposals from edges. In: Fleet, D., Pajdla, T., Schiele, B., Tuytelaars, T. (eds.) ECCV 2014. LNCS, vol. 8693, pp. 391–405. Springer, Heidelberg (2014). doi:10.1007/978-3-319-10602-1_26
12. Cinbis, R., Verbeek, J., Schmid, C.: Multi-fold mil training for weakly supervised object localization. In: CVPR (2014)
13. Cinbis, R., Verbeek, J., Schmid, C.: Weakly supervised object localization with multi-fold multiple instance learning. IEEE Trans. PAMI (2016)
14. Bilen, H., Pedersoli, M., Tuytelaars, T.: Weakly supervised object detection with posterior regularization. In: BMVC (2014)
15. Bilen, H., Pedersoli, M., Tuytelaars, T.: Weakly supervised object detection with convex clustering. In: CVPR (2015)
16. Deselaers, T., Alexe, B., Ferrari, V.: Localizing objects while learning their appearance. In: Daniilidis, K., Maragos, P., Paragios, N. (eds.) ECCV 2010. LNCS, vol. 6314, pp. 452–466. Springer, Heidelberg (2010). doi:10.1007/978-3-642-15561-1_33
17. Russakovsky, O., Lin, Y., Yu, K., Fei-Fei, L.: Object-centric spatial pooling for image classification. In: Fitzgibbon, A., Lazebnik, S., Perona, P., Sato, Y., Schmid, C. (eds.) ECCV 2012, Part II. LNCS, vol. 7573, pp. 1–15. Springer, Heidelberg (2012)
18. Siva, P., Xiang, T.: Weakly supervised object detector learning with model drift detection. In: ICCV (2011)
19. Song, H., Girshick, R., Jegelka, S., Mairal, J., Harchaoui, Z., Darell, T.: On learning to localize objects with minimal supervision. In: ICML (2014)
20. Song, H., Lee, Y., Jegelka, S., Darell, T.: Weakly-supervised discovery of visual pattern configurations. In: NIPS (2014)
21. Fergus, R., Perona, P., Zisserman, A.: Object class recognition by unsupervised scale-invariant learning. In: CVPR (2003)
22. Bengio, J., Louradour, J., Collobert, R., Weston, J.: Curriculum learning. In: ICML (2009)

23. Wang, C., Ren, W., Zhang, J., Huang, K., Maybank, S.: Large-scale weakly supervised object localization via latent category learning. IEEE Trans. Image Process. **24**(4), 1371–1385 (2015)
24. Dietterich, T.G., Lathrop, R.H., Lozano-Perez, T.: Solving the multiple instance problem with axis-parallel rectangles. Artif. Intell. **89**(1–2), 31–71 (1997)
25. Shi, Z., Siva, P., Xiang, T.: Transfer learning by ranking for weakly supervised object annotation. In: BMVC (2012)
26. Krizhevsky, A., Sutskever, I., Hinton, G.E.: Imagenet classification with deep convolutional neural networks. In: NIPS (2012)
27. Tang, K., Joulin, A., Li, L.J., Fei-Fei, L.: Co-localization in real-world images. In: CVPR (2014)
28. Alexe, B., Deselaers, T., Ferrari, V.: Measuring the objectness of image windows. IEEE Trans. PAMI **34**, 2189–2202 (2012)
29. Guillaumin, M., Ferrari, V.: Large-scale knowledge transfer for object localization in imagenet. In: CVPR (2012)
30. Rochan, M., Wang, Y.: Weakly supervised localization of novel objects using appearance transfer. In: CVPR (2015)
31. Hoffman, J., Guadarrama, S., Tzeng, E., Hu, R., Donahue, J.: LSDA: Large scale detection through adaptation. In: NIPS (2014)
32. Kumar, M.P., Packer, B., Koller, D.: Self-paced learning for latent variable models. In: NIPS (2010)
33. Lee, Y.J., Grauman, K.: Learning the easy things first: Self-paced visual category discovery. In: CVPR (2011)
34. Pentina, A., Sharmanska, V., Lampert, C.H.: Curriculum learning of multiple tasks. In: CVPR (2015)
35. Sharmanska, V., Quadrianto, N., Lampert, C.: Learning to rank using privileged information. In: CVPR (2013)
36. Lapin, M., Hein, M., Schiele, B.: Learning using privileged information: Svm+ and weighted svm. Neural Netw. **53**, 95–108 (2014)
37. Ionescu, R.T., Alexe, B., Leordeanu, M., Popescu, M., Papadopoulos, D.P., Ferrari, V.: How hard can it be? Estimating the difficulty of visual search in an image. In: CVPR (2016)
38. Russakovsky, O., Deng, J., Su, H., Krause, J., Satheesh, S., Ma, S., Huang, Z., Karpathy, A., Khosla, A., Bernstein, M., Berg, A., Fei-Fei, L.: ImageNet large scale visual recognition challenge. IJCV **115**, 211–252 (2015)
39. Jia, Y.: Caffe: an open source convolutional architecture for fast feature embedding (2013). http://caffe.berkeleyvision.org/
40. Pandey, M., Lazebnik, S.: Scene recognition and weakly supervised object localization with deformable part-based models. In: ICCV (2011)
41. Nguyen, M., Torresani, L., de la Torre, F., Rother, C.: Weakly supervised discriminative localization and classification: a joint learning process. In: ICCV (2009)
42. Kim, G., Torralba, A.: Unsupervised detection of regions of interest using iterative link analysis. In: NIPS (2009)
43. Wheeler, D.J., Chambers, D.S., et al.: Understanding Statistical Process Control. SPC Press, Knoxville (1992)
44. Platt, J.: Probabilistic outputs for support vector machines and comparisons to regularized likelihood methods. In: Advances in Large Margin Classifiers (1999)
45. Shawe-Taylor, J., Cristianini, N.: Kernel Methods for Pattern Analysis. Cambridge University Press, Cambridge (2004)
46. Kendall, M., Stuart, A.: The Advanced Theory of Statistics. Charles Griffin and Company, London (1983)

47. Shi, Z., Hospedales, T., Xiang, T.: Bayesian joint modelling for object localisation in weakly labelled images. IEEE Trans. PAMI. **37**, 1959–1972 (2015)
48. Prest, A., Leistner, C., Civera, J., Schmid, C., Ferrari, V.: Learning object class detectors from weakly annotated video. In: CVPR (2012)
49. Shapovalova, N., Vahdat, A., Cannons, K., Lan, T., Mori, G.: Similarity constrained latent support vector machine: an application to weakly supervised action classification. In: Fitzgibbon, A., Lazebnik, S., Perona, P., Sato, Y., Schmid, C. (eds.) ECCV 2012. LNCS, vol. 7578, pp. 55–68. Springer, Heidelberg (2012). doi:10. 1007/978-3-642-33786-4_5
50. Simonyan, K., Zisserman, A.: Very deep convolutional networks for large-scale image recognition. In: ICLR (2015)

Supervised Transformer Network for Efficient Face Detection

Dong Chen$^{(\boxtimes)}$, Gang Hua, Fang Wen, and Jian Sun

Microsoft Research, Bejing, China
{doch,ganghua,fangwen,jiansun}@microsoft.com

Abstract. Large pose variations remain to be a challenge that confronts real-word face detection. We propose a new cascaded Convolutional Neural Network, dubbed the name Supervised Transformer Network, to address this challenge. The first stage is a multi-task Region Proposal Network (RPN), which simultaneously predicts candidate face regions along with associated facial landmarks. The candidate regions are then warped by mapping the detected facial landmarks to their canonical positions to better normalize the face patterns. The second stage, which is a RCNN, then verifies if the warped candidate regions are valid faces or not. We conduct end-to-end learning of the cascaded network, including optimizing the canonical positions of the facial landmarks. This supervised learning of the transformations automatically selects the best scale to differentiate face/non-face patterns. By combining feature maps from both stages of the network, we achieve state-of-the-art detection accuracies on several public benchmarks. For real-time performance, we run the cascaded network only on regions of interests produced from a boosting cascade face detector. Our detector runs at 30 FPS on a single CPU core for a VGA-resolution image.

1 Introduction

Among the various factors that confront real-world face detection, large pose variations remain to be a big challenge. For example, the seminal Viola-Jones [1] detector works well for near-frontal faces, but become much less effective for faces in poses that are far from frontal views, due to the weakness of the Haar features on non-frontal faces.

There were abundant works attempted to tackle with large pose variations under the regime of the boosting cascade advocated by Viola and Jones [1]. Most of them adopt a divide-and-conquer strategy to build a multi-view face detector. Some works [2–4] proposed to train a detector cascade for each view and combine their results of all detectors at the test time. Some other works [5–7] proposed to first estimate the face pose and then run the cascade of the corresponding face pose to verify the detection. The complexity of the former approach increases

Electronic supplementary material The online version of this chapter (doi:10. 1007/978-3-319-46454-1_8) contains supplementary material, which is available to authorized users.

© Springer International Publishing AG 2016
B. Leibe et al. (Eds.): ECCV 2016, Part V, LNCS 9909, pp. 122–138, 2016.
DOI: 10.1007/978-3-319-46454-1_8

with the number of pose categories, while the accuracy of the latter is prone to the mistakes of pose estimation.

Part-based model offers an alternative solution [8–10]. These detectors are flexible and robust to both pose variation and partial occlusion, since they can reliably detect the faces based on some confident part detections. However, these methods always require the target face to be large and clear, which is essential to reliably model the parts.

Other works approach to this issue by using more sophisticated invariant features other than Haar wavelets, e.g., HOG [8], SIFT [9], multiple channel features [11], and high-level CNN features [12]. Besides these model-based methods, Shen et al. [13] proposed to use an exemplar-based method to detect faces by image retrieval, which achieved state-of-the-art detection accuracy.

It has been shown in recent years that a face detector trained end-to-end using DNN can significantly outperforms previous methods [10,14]. However, to effectively handle the different variations, especially pose variations, it often requires a DNN with lots of parameters, inducing high computational cost. To address the conflicting challenge, Li et al. [15] proposed a cascade DNN architecture at multiple resolutions. It quickly rejects the background regions in the low resolution stages, and carefully evaluates the challenging candidates in the high resolution stage.

However, the set of DNNs in Li et al. [15] are trained sequentially, instead of end-to-end, which may not be desirable. In contrast, we propose a new cascade Convolutional Neural Network that is trained end-to-end. The first stage is a *multi-task* Region Proposal Network (RPN), which simultaneously proposes candidate face regions along with associated facial landmarks. Inspired by Chen et al. [16], we jointly conduct face detection and face alignment, since face alignment is helpful to distinguish faces/non-faces patterns.

Different from Li et al. [15], this network is calculated on the original resolution to better leverage more discriminative information. The alignment step warps each candidate face region to a canonical pose, which maps the facial landmarks into a set of canonical positions. The aligned candidate face region is then fed into the second-stage network, a RCNN [17], for further verification. Note we only keep the K face candidate regions with top responses in a local neighborhood from the RPN. In other words, those Non-top K regions are suppressed. This helps increase detection recall.

Inspired by previous work [18], which revealed that joint features from different spatial resolutions or scales will improve accuracy. We concatenate the feature maps from the two cascaded networks together to form an architecture that is trained end-to-end, as shown in Fig. 1. Note in the learning process, we treat the set of canonical positions also as parameters, which are learnt in the end-to-end learning process.

Note that the canonical positions of the facial landmarks in the aligned face image and the predicted facial landmarks in the candidate face region jointly defines the transform from the candidate face region. In the end-to-end training, the training of the first-stage RPN to predict facial landmarks is also supervised by annotated facial landmarks in each true face regions. We hence call

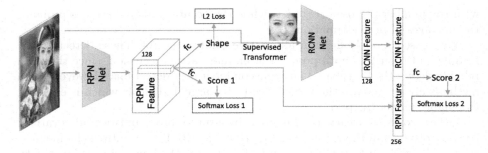

Fig. 1. Illustration of the structure of our Supervised Transformer Network.

our network a Supervised Transformer Network. These two characteristics differentiate our model from the Spatial Transformer Network [19] because (a) the Spatial Transformer Network conducts regression on the transformation parameters directly, and (b) it is only supervised by the final recognition objective.

The proposed Supervised Transformer Network can efficiently run on the GPU. However, in practice, the CPU is still the only choice in most situations. Therefore, we propose a region-of-interest (ROI) convolution scheme to make the run-time of the Supervised Transformer Network to be more efficient. It first uses a conventional boosting cascade to obtain a set of face candidate areas. Then, we combine these regions into irregular binary ROI mask. All DNN operations (including convolution, ReLU, pooling, and concatenation) are all processed inside the ROI mask, and hence significantly reduce the computation.

Our contributions are: (1) we proposed a new cascaded network named Supervised Transformer Network trained end-to-end for efficient face detection; (2) we introduced the supervised transformer layer, which enables to learn the optimal canonical pose to best differentiate face/non-face patterns; (3) we introduced a Non-top K suppression scheme, which can achieve better recall without sacrificing precision; (4) we introduced a ROI convolution scheme. It speeds up our detector 3x on CPU with little recall drop.

Our face detector outperformed the current best performing algorithms on several public benchmarks we evaluated, with real-time performance at 30 FPS with VGA resolution.

2   Network Architecture

2.1   Overview

In this section, we will introduce the architecture of our proposed cascade network. As illustrated in Fig. 1, the whole architecture consists of two stages. The first stage is a multi-task Region Proposal Network (RPN). It produces a set of candidate face regions along with associated facial landmarks. We conduct Non-top K suppression to only keep the candidate face regions with responses ranked in the top K in a local neighborhood.

The second stage starts with a Supervised Transformer layer, and then a RCNN to further verify if a face region is a true face or not. The transformer layer takes the facial landmarks and the candidate face regions, then warp the face regions into a canonical pose by mapping the detected facial landmarks into a set of canonical positions. This explicitly eliminates the effect of rotation and scale variation according to the facial points.

To make this clear, the geometric transformation are uniquely determined by the facial landmarks and the canonical positions. In our cascade network, both the prediction of the facial landmarks and the canonical positions are learned in the end-to-end training process. We call it a Supervised Transformer layer, as it receives supervision from two aspects. On one hand, the learning of the prediction model of the facial landmarks are supervised by the annotated ground-truth facial landmarks. On the other hand, the learning of both the canonical positions and the prediction model of the facial landmarks both are supervised by the final classification objective.

To make a final decision, we concatenate the fine-grained feature from the second-stage RCNN network and the global feature from the first-stage RPN network. The concatenated features are then put into a fully connected layer to make the final face/non-face arbitration. This concludes the whole architecture of our proposed cascade network.

2.2 Multi-task RPN

The design of the multi-task RPN is inspired by the JDA detector [16], which validated that face alignment is helpful to distinguish faces/non-faces. Our method is very straight forward. We use a RPN to simultaneous detect faces and associated facial landmarks. Our method is very similar to the work [20], except that our regression target is facial landmark locations, instead of bounding box parameters.

2.3 The Supervised Transformer Layer

In this section, we describe the detail of the supervised transformer layer. As we know, similarity transformation was widely used in face detection and face recognition task to eliminate scale and rotation variation. The common practice is to train a prediction model to detect the facial landmarks, and then warp the face image to a canonical pose by mapping the facial landmarks to a set of manually specified canonical locations.

This process at least has two drawbacks: (1) one needs to manually set the canonical locations. Since the canonical locations determines the scale and offset of rectified face images, it often takes many try-and-errors to find a relatively good setting. This is not only time-consuming, but also suboptimal. (2) The learning of the prediction model for the facial landmark is supervised by the ground-truth facial landmark points. However, labeling ground-truth facial landmarks is a highly subjective process and hence prone to introducing noise.

We propose to learn both the canonical positions and the prediction of the facial landmarks end-to-end from the network with additional supervision information from the classification objective of the RCNN using end-to-end back propagation. Specifically, we use the following formula to define a similarity transformation, $i.e.$,

$$
\begin{bmatrix} \bar{x}_i - m_{\bar{x}} \\ \bar{y}_i - m_{\bar{y}} \end{bmatrix} = \begin{bmatrix} a & b \\ -b & a \end{bmatrix} \begin{bmatrix} x_i - m_x \\ y_i - m_y \end{bmatrix},
\tag{1}
$$

where x_i, y_i are the detected facial landmarks, $\bar{x}_i, \bar{y}_i$ are the canonical positions, m_* is the mean value of the corresponding variables, $e.g.$, $m_x = \frac{1}{N} \sum x_i$, N is the number of facial landmarks, a and b are parameters of similarity transforms.

We found that this two parameters model is equivalent to the traditional four parameters, but much simpler in derivation and avoid problems of numerical calculation. After some straightforward mathematical derivation, we can obtain the least squares solution of the parameters, $i.e.$,

$$
\begin{aligned}
a &= \frac{c_1}{c_3} \\
b &= \frac{c_2}{c_3}.
\end{aligned}
\tag{2}
$$

where

$$
\begin{aligned}
c_1 &= \sum \left((\bar{x}_i - m_{\bar{x}})(x_i - m_x) + (\bar{y}_i - m_{\bar{y}})(y_i - m_y) \right) \\
c_2 &= \sum \left((\bar{x}_i - m_{\bar{x}})(y_i - m_y) - (\bar{y}_i - m_{\bar{y}})(x_i - m_x) \right) \\
c_3 &= \sum \left((x_i - m_x)^2 + (y_i - m_y)^2 \right).
\end{aligned}
\tag{3}
$$

After obtaining the similarity transformation parameters, we can obtain the rectified image $\bar{I}$ given the original image I, using $\bar{I}(\bar{x}, \bar{y}) = I(x, y)$. Each point $(\bar{x}, \bar{y})$ in the rectified image can be mapped back to the original image space (x, y) by

$$
\begin{aligned}
x &= \frac{a}{a^2 + b^2}(\bar{x} - m_{\bar{x}}) - \frac{b}{a^2 + b^2}(\bar{y} - m_{\bar{y}}) + m_x \\
y &= \frac{b}{a^2 + b^2}(\bar{x} - m_{\bar{x}}) + \frac{a}{a^2 + b^2}(\bar{y} - m_{\bar{y}}) + m_y.
\end{aligned}
\tag{4}
$$

Since x and y may not be integers, bilinear interpolation is always used to obtain the value of $I(x, y)$. Therefore, we can calculate the derivative by the chain rule

$$
\begin{aligned}
\frac{\partial L}{\partial a} &= \sum_{\{\bar{x}, \bar{y}\}} \frac{\partial L}{\partial \bar{I}(\bar{x}, \bar{y})} \frac{\partial \bar{I}(\bar{x}, \bar{y})}{\partial a} = \sum_{\{\bar{x}, \bar{y}\}} \frac{\partial L}{\partial \bar{I}(\bar{x}, \bar{y})} \frac{\partial I(x, y)}{\partial a} \\
&= \sum_{\{\bar{x}, \bar{y}\}} \frac{\partial L}{\partial \bar{I}(\bar{x}, \bar{y})} \left(\frac{\partial I(x, y)}{\partial x} \frac{\partial x}{\partial a} + \frac{\partial I(x, y)}{\partial y} \frac{\partial y}{\partial a} \right) \\
&= \sum_{\{\bar{x}, \bar{y}\}} \frac{\partial L}{\partial \bar{I}(\bar{x}, \bar{y})} \left(I_x \frac{\partial x}{\partial a} + I_y \frac{\partial y}{\partial a} \right)
\end{aligned}
\tag{5}
$$

where L is the final classification loss and $\frac{\partial L}{\partial I(\bar{x},\bar{y})}$ is the gradient signals back propagated from the RCNN network. The I_x and I_y are horizontal and vertical gradient of the original image

$$I_x = \beta_y(I(x_r, y_b) - I(x_l, y_b)) + (1 - \beta_y)(I(x_r, y_t) - I(x_l, y_t))$$
$$I_y = \beta_x(I(x_r, y_b) - I(x_r, y_t)) + (1 - \beta_x)(I(x_l, y_b) - I(x_l, y_t)). \tag{6}$$

Here we use a bilinear interpolation, $\beta_x = x - \lfloor x \rfloor$ and $\beta_y = y - \lfloor y \rfloor$. $x_l = \lfloor x \rfloor, x_r = x_l + 1, y_t = \lfloor y \rfloor, y_b = y_t + 1$ are the left, right, top, bottom integer boundary of point (x, y). Similarly, we can obtain the derivative of other parameters. Finally, we can obtain the gradient of the canonical positions of the facial landmarks, i.e., $\frac{\partial L}{\partial \bar{x}_i}$ and $\frac{\partial L}{\partial \bar{y}_i}$. And the gradient with respect to the detected facial landmarks: $\frac{\partial L}{\partial x_i}$ and $\frac{\partial L}{\partial y_i}$. Please refer to the supplementary material for more detail.

The proposed Supervised Transformer layer is put between of the RPN and RCNN networks. In the end-to-end training, it automatically adjusts the canonical positions and guiding the detection of the facial landmarks such that the rectified image is more suitable for face/non-face classification. We will further illustrate this in the experiments.

2.4 Non-top K Suppression

In RCNN [17,20] based object detection, after the region proposals, non-maximum suppression (NMS) is always adopted to reduce the region candidate number for efficiency. However, the candidate with highest confidence score may be rejected by the later stage RCNN. Decreasing the NMS overlap threshold will bring in lots of useless candidates. This will make subsequent RCNN slow. Our idea is to keep K candidate regions with highest confidence for each potential face, since these samples are more promising for RCNN classifier. In the experiments part we will demonstrate that we can effectively improve the recall with the proposed Non-top K Suppression.

2.5 Multi-granularity Feature Combination

Some works have revealed that joint features from different spatial resolutions or scales will improve accuracy [18]. The most straight-forward way may be combining several RCNN networks with different input scales. However, this approach will obviously increase the computation complexity significantly.

In our end-to-end network, the details of the RPN network structure is shown in Table 1. There are 3 convolution and 2 inception layers in our RPN network. Therefore, we can calculate that its receptive field size is 85. While the target face size is 36~72 pixels. Therefore, our RPN takes advantage of the surrounding contextual information around face regions. On the other hand, the RCNN network focuses more on the rotation and scale variation fine grained detail in the inner face region. So we concatenate these two features in an end-to-end training architecture, which makes the two parts more complementary. Experiments demonstrate that this kind of joint feature can significantly improve the face detection accuracy. Besides, the proposed method is much more efficient.

Table 1. RPN network structure

Type	Receptive field relationship	Receptive field size
Conv1 $(7 \times 7, 2)$	$2\,k + 5$	85
Max pool $(2 \times 2, 2)$	$2\,k$	40
Conv 2a $(1 \times 1, 1)$	k	20
Conv 2b $(3 \times 3, 1)$	$k + 2$	20
Max pool $(2 \times 2, 2)$	$2\,k$	18
Inception 3a	$k + 4$	9
Inception 3b	$k + 4$	5

3   The ROI Convolution

3.1   Motivation

As a practical face detection algorithm, real-time performance is very important. However, the heavy computation incurred at test phase using DNN-based models often make them impractical in real-world systems. That is the reason why current DNN-based models heavily rely on a high-end GPU to increase the runtime performance. However, high-end GPU is not often available in commodity computing system, so most often, we still need to run the DNN model with a CPU. However, even using a high-end CPU with highly optimized code, it is still about 4 times slower than the runtime speed on a GPU [21]. More importantly, for portable devices, such as phones and tablets, mostly have low-end CPUs only, it is necessary to accelerate the test-phase performance of DNNs.

In a typical DNN, the convolutional layers are the most computationally expensive and often take up about more than 90 % of the time in runtime. There were some works attempted to reduce the computational complexity of convolution layer. For example, Jaderberg *et al.* [22] applied a sparse decomposition to reconstruct the convolutional filters. Some other works [23,24] assume that the convolutional filters are approximately low-rank along certain dimensions, and can be approximately decomposed into a series of smaller filters. Our detector may also benefit from these model compression techniques.

Nevertheless, we propose a more practical approach to accelerate the runtime speed of our proposed Supervised Transformer Network for face detection. Our main idea is to use a conventional cascade based face detector to quickly reject non-face regions and obtain a *binary ROI mask*. The ROI mask has the same size as the input. The background area is represented by 0 and the face area is represented by 1. The DNN convolution is only computed within the region marked as 1, ignoring all other regions. Because most regions did not participate in the calculation, we can greatly reduce the amount of computation in the convolution layers.

We want to emphasize that our method is different to those RCNN based algorithm [17,25] which treated each candidate region independently. In those

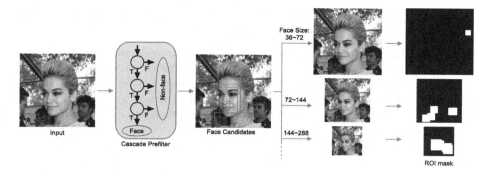

Fig. 2. Illustration of the ROI mask

models, features in the overlap subregions will be calculated repeatedly. Instead, we use the ROI masks, so that different samples can share the feature in the overlapping area. It effectively reduces the computational cost by further avoiding repeated operations. Meanwhile, in the following section, we will introduce the implementation details of our ROI convolution. Similar to Caffe [26], we also take advantage of the matrix multiplication in the BLAS library to obtain almost a linear speedup.

3.2 Implementation Details

Cascade Pre-filter. As shown in Fig. 2, we use a cascade detector as a pre-filter. It is basically a variant of the Volia-Jones's detector [1], but it has more weak classifiers and is trained with more data. Our boosted classifier is consisted of 1000 weak classifiers. Different form [1], we adopted a boosted fern [27] as the weaker classifier, since a fern is more powerful than using a single Haar feature based decision stump, and more efficient than boosted tree on CPUs. For completeness, we briefly describe our implementation.

Each fern contains 8 binary nodes. The splitting function is to compare the difference of two image pixel values in two different locations with a threshold, *i.e.*,

$$s_i = \begin{cases} 1 & p(x_{1_i}, y_{1_i}) - p(x_{2_i}, y_{2_i}) < \theta_i \\ 0 & otherwise \end{cases} \tag{7}$$

where p is the image patch. The patch size is fixed to 32 in our experiments. The $(x_{1_i}, y_{1_i}, x_{2_i}, y_{2_i}, \theta_i)$ are fern parameters learned from training data. Each fern splits the data space into $2^8 = 256$ partitions. We use a Real-Boost algorithm for the cascade classification learning. In each space partition, the classification score is computed as

$$\frac{1}{2} \log \left(\frac{\sum_{\{i \in piece \bigcap y_i = 1\}} w_i}{\sum_{\{i \in piece \bigcap y_i = 0\}} w_i} \right), \tag{8}$$

where the enumerator and denominator are the sum of the weights of positive and negative samples in the space partition, respectively.

The ROI Mask. After we obtain some candidate face regions, we will group them according to their sizes. The maximum size is twice larger than the minimum size in each group. Since the smallest face size can be detected by the proposed DNN based face detector is 36×36 pixels, the first group contains the face size between 36 to 72 pixels. While the second ground contains the face size between 72 to 144, and so on (as shown in Fig. 2).

It should be noted that, beginning from the second group, we need to down-sample the image, such that the candidate face size in the image is always maintained between 36 to 72 pixels. Besides, in order to retain some of the background information, we will double the side length of each candidate. But the side length will not exceed the receptive field size (85) of the following DNN face detector. Finally, we set the ROI mask according to the sizes and positions of the candidate boxes in each group.

We use this grouping strategy for two reasons. First, when there is a face almost filling the whole image, we do not have to deal with the full original image size. Instead, it will be down-sampled to a quite small resolution, so we can more effectively reduce the computation cost. Secondly, since the following DNN detector only need to handle twice the scale variation, this is induces a great advantage when compared with the RPN in [20], which needs to handle all scale changes. This advantage allows us to use a relatively cheaper network for the DNN-based detection.

Besides, such a sparse pyramid structure will only increase about 33 % ($\frac{1}{2^2} + \frac{1}{4^2} + \frac{1}{8^2} \cdots \approx \frac{1}{3}$) computation cost when compared with the computational cost at the base scale.

Details of the ROI Convolution. There are several ways to implement the convolutions efficiently. Currently, the most popular method is to transform the convolutions into a matrix multiplication. As described in [28] and implemented in Caffe [26], this can be done by firstly reshaping the filter tensor into a matrix F with dimensions $CK^2 \times N$, where C and N are input and output channel numbers, and K is the filter width/height.

We can subsequently gather a data matrix by duplicating the original input data into a matrix D with dimensions $WH \times CK^2$, W and H are output width and height. The computation can then be performed with a single matrix multiplication to form an output matrix $O = DF$ with dimension $WH \times N$. This matrix multiplication can be efficiently calculated with optimized linear algebra libraries such as BLAS.

Our main idea in ROI convolution is to only calculate the area marked as 1 (*a.k.a*, the ROI regions), while skipping other regions. According to the ROI mask, we only duplicate the input patches whose centers are marked as 1. So the input data become a matrix D' with dimensions $M \times CK^2$, where M is the number of non-zero entries in the ROI mask. Similarly, we can then use matrix multiplication to obtain the output $O' = D'F$ with dimension $M \times CK^2$. Finally, we put each row of O' to the corresponding channel of the output.

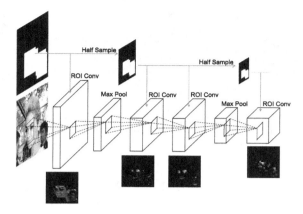

Fig. 3. Illustration of the ROI convolution.

The computation complexity of ROI convolution is MCK^2N. Therefore, we can linearly decrease the computation cost according to the mask sparsity.

As illustrated in Fig. 3, we only apply the ROI convolution in the test phase. We replace all convolution layers into ROI convolution layers. After a max pooling, the size of the input will be halved. So we also half sample the ROI mask, such that their size can be matched. The original DNN detector can run at 50 FPS on GPU and 10 FPS on CPU for a VGA image. With ROI convolution, it can speed up to 30 FPS on CPU with little accuracy loss.

4 Experiments

In this section, we will experimentally validate the proposed method. We collected about 400 K face images from the web with various variations as positive training samples. These images are exclusive from FDDB [29], AFW [8] and PASCAL [30] datasets. We labeled all faces with 5 facial points (two eyes center, nose tip, and two mouth corners). For the negative training samples, we use the Coco database [31]. This dataset has pixel level annotations of various objects, including people. Therefore, we covered all person areas with random color blocks, and ensure that no samples are drawn from those colored regions in these images. We use more than 120 K images (including 2014 training and validation data) for the training. Some sample images are shown in Fig. 4.

We use GoogleNet in both the RPN and RCNN networks. The network structure is similar to that in FaceNet [32], but we cut all the convolution kernel number in half for efficiency. Moreover, we only include two inception layers in RPN network (as shown in Table 1) and the input size of RCNN network is 64.

In order to avoid the initialization problem and improve the convergence speed, we first train the RPN network from random without the RCNN network. After the predicted facial landmarks are largely correct, we add the RCNN network and perform end-to-end training together. For evaluation, we use three

Fig. 4. Illustration of our negative training sample. We covered all person area with random color blocks in Coco [31] dataset and ensured that no positive training samples are drawn from these regions in these images. (Color figure online)

challenging public datasets, *i.e.*, FDDB [29], AFW [8] and PASCAL faces [30]. All these three datasets are widely used as face detection benchmark. We employ the Intersection over Union (IoU) as the evaluation metric and fix the IoU threshold to 0.5.

4.1   Learning Canonical Position

In this part, we verify the effect of the Supervised Transformation in finding the best canonical position. We intentionally initialize the Supervised Transformation with three inappropriate canonical positions according to three settings, respectively, *i.e.*, too large, too small, or with offset. Then we perform the end-to-end training and record the canonical points position after 10 K, 100 K, 500 K iterations.

As shown in Fig. 5, each row shows the canonical positions movement for one kind of initializations. We also place the image warp result besides its corresponding canonical points. We can observe that, for these three different kinds of initializations, they all eventually converge to a very close position setting after 500 K iterations. It demonstrated that the proposed Supervised Transformer module is robust to the initialization. It automatically adjusts the canonical positions such that the rectified image is more suitable for face/non-face classification.

4.2   Ablative Evaluation of Various Network Components

As discussed in Sect. 2, our end-to-end cascade network is consisted of four notable parts, *i.e.*, the multi-task RPN, the Supervised Transformer, the multi-granularity feature combination, and non-top K suppression. The former three will affect the network structure of training, while the last one only appear in the test phase.

In order to separately study the effect of each part, we conduct an ablative study by removing one or more parts from our network structure and evaluate the new network with the same training and testing data. When removing the multi-task RPN, it means that we directly regress the face rectangle similar to [20], instead of facial points. Without the Supervised Transformer layer, we simply replace it with a standard similarity transformation without training with

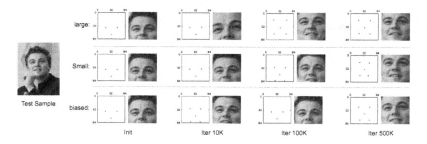

Fig. 5. Results of learning canonical positions.

Table 2. Evaluation of the effect of three parts in training architecture.

Multi-task RPN	N	N	Y	Y	Y	Y
Supervised transformer	/	/	N	Y	N	Y
Feature combination	N	Y	N	N	Y	Y
Recall rate	85.6 %	88.0 %	87.1 %	88.3 %	88.8 %	89.6 %

back propagation. Without the feature combination component means that we directly use the output of the RCNN features to make the finial decision. In the case that we removed multi-task RPN, there will be no facial points for Supervised Transformation or conventional similarity transformation. In this situation, we directly resize the face patch into 64×64 and fed it into a RCNN network.

There are 6 different ablative settings in total. We perform end-to-end training with the same training samples for all settings, and evaluate the recall rate on the FDDB dataset when the *false alarm* number is 10. We manually review the face detection results and add 67 unlabeled faces in the FDDB dataset to make sure all the false alarms are true. As shown in Table 2, multi-task RPN, Supervised Transformer, and feature combination will bring about 1 %, 1 %, and 2 % recall improvement respectively. Besides, these three parts are complementary, remove any one part will cause a recall drop.

In the training phase, in order to increase the variation of training samples, we randomly select K positive/negative samples from each image for the RCNN network. However, in the test phase, we need to balance the recall rate with efficiency. Next, we will compare the proposed non-top K suppression with NMS in the testing phase,

We present a sample visual result of RPN, NMS and non-top K suppression in Fig. 6. We keep the same number of candidates for both NMS and Non-top K suppression ($K = 3$ in the visual result). We found that NMS tend to include too much noisy low confidence candidates. We also compare the PR curves of using all candidates, NMS, and non-top K suppression. Our non-top K suppression is very close to using all candidates, and achieved consistently better results than NMS under the same number of candidates.

RPN   NMS   Non-top K Suppression

Fig. 6. Comparison of NMS and Non-Top K Suppression

4.3   The Effect of ROI Convolution

In this section, we will validate the acceleration performance of the proposed ROI convolution algorithm. We train the Cascade pre-filter with the same training data. By adjusting the classification threshold of the Cascade re-filter, we can obtain the ROI masks in different areas. Therefore, we can strike for the right balance between speed and accuracy.

We conduct the experiments on the FDDB database. We resized all images to 1.5 times of the original size, the resulting average photos resolution is approximately 640 × 480. We evaluate the ROI mask sparsity, run-time speed [1] of each part, and the recall rate when the false alarm number is 10 under different pre-filter threshold. We also compare with the standard network without ROI convolution. Non-top K ($K = 3$) suppression is adopted in all settings to make RCNN network more efficiency.

Table 3 shows the average ROI mask sparsity, testing speed of each part, and recall rate of each setting. Comparing the second row with the fourth row, it proves that we can linearly decrease the computation cost according to the mask sparsity. The last two rows show the recall rate and average test time of different settings. The original DNN detector can run at 10 FPS on CPU for a VGA image. With ROI convolution, it can speed up to 30 FPS on CPU. We can achieve about 3 times speed up with only 0.6 % recall rate drop.

Table 3. Various results demonstrating the effects of ROI convolution.

Pre-filter threshold	N/A	0	1	2	3
ROI Mask sparsity	N/A	31.3 %	27.1 %	10.6 %	5.7 %
Pre-filter time (ms)	0	12.1	12.0	12.0	11.9
RPN time (ms)	98.2 (100 %)	33.9 (34.5 %)	24.2 (24.6 %)	11.0 (11.2 %)	8.1 (8.2 %)
RCNN time (ms)	9.0	9.3	8.7	9.1	9.3
Total time (ms)	107.2	55.3	44.8	32.1	29.3
Recall rate	89.3 %	89.2 %	89.0 %	88.7 %	88.1 %

---

[1] All experiments use a single thread on an Intel i7-4770K CPU.

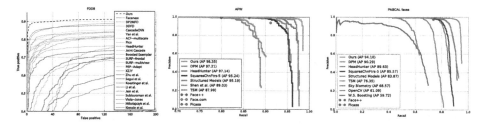

Fig. 7. Comparison with state-of-the-arts on the FDDB [29], AFW [8] and PASCAL faces [30] datasets.

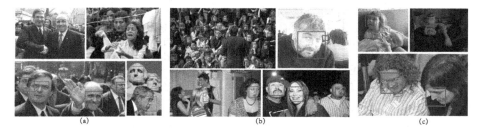

(a)   (b)   (c)

Fig. 8. Qualitative face detection results on (a) FDDB [29], (b) AFW [8], (c) PASCAL faces [30] datasets.

4.4 Comparing with State-of-the-art

We conduct face detection experiments on three benchmark datasets. On the FDDB dataset, we compare with all public methods [8–10, 33–35, 35–42]. We regress the annotation ellipses with 5 facial points and ignore 67 unlabeled faces to make sure all false alarms are true. On the AFW and PASCAL faces datasets, we compare with (1) deformable part based methods, *e.g.* structure model [30] and Tree Parts Model (TSM) [8]; (2) cascade-based methods, *e.g.* Headhunter [4]; (3) commercial system, *e.g.* face.com, Face++ and Picasa. We learn a global regression from 5 facial points to face rectangles to match the annotation for each dataset, and use toolbox from [4] for the evaluation. Figure 8 shows that our method outperforms all previous methods by a considerable margin.

5 Conclusion and Future Work

In this paper, we proposed a new Supervised Transformer Network for face detection. The superior performance on three challenge datasets shows its ability to learn the optimal canonical positions to best distinguish face/non-face patterns. We also introduced a ROI convolution, which speeds up our detector 3x on CPU with little recall drop. Our future work will explore how to enhance the ROI convolution so that it does not incur additional drops in recall.

References

1. Viola, P., Jones, M.: Rapid object detection using a boosted cascade of simple features. In: Proceedings of the 2001 IEEE Computer Society Conference on Computer Vision and Pattern Recognition, 2001, CVPR 2001, vol. 1, pp. 511–518. IEEE (2001)
2. Li, S.Z., Zhu, L., Zhang, Z.Q., Blake, A., Zhang, H.J., Shum, H.: Statistical learning of multi-view face detection. In: Heyden, A., Sparr, G., Nielsen, M., Johansen, P. (eds.) ECCV 2002. LNCS, vol. 2353, pp. 67–81. Springer, Heidelberg (2002). doi:10.1007/3-540-47979-1_5
3. Wu, B., Ai, H., Huang, C., Lao, S.: Fast rotation invariant multi-view face detection based on real adaboost. In: Automatic Face and Gesture Recognition, pp. 79–84 (2004)
4. Mathias, M., Benenson, R., Pedersoli, M., Gool, L.: Face detection without bells and whistles. In: Fleet, D., Pajdla, T., Schiele, B., Tuytelaars, T. (eds.) ECCV 2014. LNCS, vol. 8692, pp. 720–735. Springer, Heidelberg (2014). doi:10.1007/978-3-319-10593-2_47
5. Viola, M., Jones, M.J., Viola, P.: Fast multi-view face detection. In: TR2003-96 (2003)
6. Huang, C., Ai, H., Li, Y., Lao, S.: Vector boosting for rotation invariant multi-view face detection. In: Tenth IEEE International Conference on Computer Vision, 2005, ICCV 2005, vol. 1, pp. 446–453, October 2005
7. Huang, C., Ai, H., Li, Y., Lao, S.: High-performance rotation invariant multiview face detection. IEEE Trans. Pattern Anal. Mach. Intell. 29(4), 671–686 (2007)
8. Zhu, X., Ramanan, D.: Face detection, pose estimation, and landmark localization in the wild. In: 2012 IEEE Conference on Computer Vision and Pattern Recognition (CVPR), pp. 2879–2886. IEEE (2012)
9. Li, H., Hua, G., Lin, Z., Brandt, J., Yang, J.: Probabilistic elastic part model for unsupervised face detector adaptation. In: The IEEE International Conference on Computer Vision (ICCV) (2013)
10. Yang, S., Luo, P., Loy, C.C., Tang, X.: From facial parts responses to face detection: a deep learning approach. In: Proceedings of the IEEE International Conference on Computer Vision, pp. 3676–3684 (2015)
11. Dollar, P., Appel, R., Belongie, S., Perona, P.: Fast feature pyramids for object detection. IEEE Trans. Pattern Anal. Mach. Intell. 36(8), 1532–1545 (2014)
12. Yang, B., Yan, J., Lei, Z., Li, S.Z.: Convolutional channel features for pedestrian, face and edge detection. CoRR abs/1504.07339 (2015)
13. Shen, X., Lin, Z., Brandt, J., Wu, Y.: Detecting and aligning faces by image retrieval. In: 2013 IEEE Conference on Computer Vision and Pattern Recognition (CVPR), pp. 3460–3467, June 2013
14. Farfade, S.S., Saberian, M.J., Li, L.J.: Multi-view face detection using deep convolutional neural networks. In: Proceedings of the 5th ACM on International Conference on Multimedia Retrieval, ICMR 2015, pp. 643–650. ACM, New York (2015)
15. Li, H., Lin, Z., Shen, X., Brandt, J., Hua, G.: A convolutional neural network cascade for face detection. In: 2015 IEEE Conference on Computer Vision and Pattern Recognition (CVPR), pp. 5325–5334, June 2015
16. Chen, D., Ren, S., Wei, Y., Cao, X., Sun, J.: Joint cascade face detection and alignment. In: Fleet, D., Pajdla, T., Schiele, B., Tuytelaars, T. (eds.) ECCV 2014, Part VI. LNCS, vol. 8694, pp. 109–122. Springer, Heidelberg (2014)

17. Girshick, R., Donahue, J., Darrell, T., Malik, J.: Rich feature hierarchies for accurate object detection and semantic segmentation. In: 2014 IEEE Conference on Computer Vision and Pattern Recognition (CVPR), pp. 580–587, June 2014
18. Bell, S., Zitnick, C.L., Bala, K., Girshick, R.: Inside-outside net: detecting objects in context with skip pooling and recurrent neural networks. arXiv preprint (2015). arXiv:1512.04143
19. Jaderberg, M., Simonyan, K., Zisserman, A., et al.: Spatial transformer networks. In: Advances in Neural Information Processing Systems, pp. 2008–2016 (2015)
20. Ren, S., He, K., Girshick, R., Sun, J.: Faster R-CNN: Towards real-time object detection with region proposal networks. In: Advances in Neural Information Processing Systems, pp. 91–99 (2015)
21. Vanhoucke, V., Senior, A., Mao, M.Z.: Improving the speed of neural networks on CPUs. In: Deep Learning and Unsupervised Feature Learning Workshop, NIPS 2011 (2011)
22. Liu, B., Wang, M., Foroosh, H., Tappen, M., Penksy, M.: Sparse convolutional neural networks. In: 2015 IEEE Conference on Computer Vision and Pattern Recognition (CVPR), pp. 806–814, June 2015
23. Jaderberg, M., Vedaldi, A., Zisserman, A.: Speeding up convolutional neural networks with low rank expansions. In: Proceedings of the British Machine Vision Conference. BMVA Press (2014)
24. Zhang, X., Zou, J., Ming, X., He, K., Sun, J.: Efficient and accurate approximations of nonlinear convolutional networks. In: 2015 IEEE Conference on Computer Vision and Pattern Recognition (CVPR), pp. 1984–1992, June 2015
25. Zhang, C., Zhang, Z.: Improving multiview face detection with multi-task deep convolutional neural networks. In: 2014 IEEE Winter Conference on Applications of Computer Vision (WACV), pp. 1036–1041, March 2014
26. Jia, Y., Shelhamer, E., Donahue, J., Karayev, S., Long, J., Girshick, R., Guadarrama, S., Darrell, T.: Caffe: Convolutional architecture for fast feature embedding. In: Proceedings of the ACM International Conference on Multimedia, pp. 675–678. ACM (2014)
27. Ozuysal, M., Fua, P., Lepetit, V.: Fast keypoint recognition in ten lines of code. In: IEEE Conference on Computer Vision and Pattern Recognition, 2007, CVPR 2007, pp. 1–8. IEEE (2007)
28. Chellapilla, K., Puri, S., Simard, P.: High performance convolutional neural networks for document processing. In: Tenth International Workshop on Frontiers in Handwriting Recognition. Suvisoft (2006)
29. Jain, V., Learned-Miller, E.: Fddb: A benchmark for face detection in unconstrained settings. Technical Report UM-CS-2010-009, University of Massachusetts, Amherst (2010)
30. Yan, J., Zhang, X., Lei, Z., Li, S.Z.: Face detection by structural models. Image Vis. Comput. **32**(10), 790–799 (2014)
31. Lin, T.-Y., Maire, M., Belongie, S., Hays, J., Perona, P., Ramanan, D., Dollár, P., Zitnick, C.L.: Microsoft COCO: common objects in context. In: Fleet, D., Pajdla, T., Schiele, B., Tuytelaars, T. (eds.) ECCV 2014, Part V. LNCS, vol. 8693, pp. 740–755. Springer, Heidelberg (2014)
32. Schroff, F., Kalenichenko, D., Philbin, J.: Facenet: a unified embedding for face recognition and clustering. In: Proceedings of the IEEE Conference on Computer Vision and Pattern Recognition, pp. 815–823 (2015)
33. Wu, B., Ai, H., Huang, C., Lao, S.: Fast rotation invariant multi-view face detection based on real adaboost. In: Sixth IEEE International Conference on Automatic Face and Gesture Recognition, 2004. Proceedings, pp. 79–84, May 2004

34. Shen, X., Lin, Z., Brandt, J., Wu, Y.: Detecting and aligning faces by image retrieval. In: 2013 IEEE Conference on Computer Vision and Pattern Recognition (CVPR), pp. 3460–3467, June 2013

35. Li, H., Lin, Z., Brandt, J., Shen, X., Hua, G.: Efficient boosted exemplar-based face detection. In: 2014 IEEE Conference on Computer Vision and Pattern Recognition (CVPR), pp. 1843–1850, June 2014

36. Li, J., Zhang, Y.: Learning surf cascade for fast and accurate object detection. In: 2013 IEEE Conference on Computer Vision and Pattern Recognition (CVPR), pp. 3468–3475, June 2013

37. Jain, V., Learned-Miller, E.: Online domain adaptation of a pre-trained cascade of classifiers. In: 2011 IEEE Conference on Computer Vision and Pattern Recognition (CVPR), pp. 577–584. IEEE (2011)

38. Subburaman, V.B., Marcel, S.: Fast bounding box estimation based face detection. In: ECCV, Workshop on Face Detection: Where We Are, and What Next? (2010)

39. Mikolajczyk, K., Schmid, C., Zisserman, A.: Human detection based on a probabilistic assembly of robust part detectors. In: Pajdla, T., Matas, J.G. (eds.) ECCV 2004. LNCS, vol. 3021, pp. 69–82. Springer, Heidelberg (2004)

40. Yan, J., Lei, Z., Wen, L., Li, S.: The fastest deformable part model for object detection. In: 2014 IEEE Conference on Computer Vision and Pattern Recognition (CVPR), pp. 2497–2504, June 2014

41. Ranjan, R., Patel, V.M., Chellappa, R.: A deep pyramid deformable part model for face detection. In: 2015 IEEE 7th International Conference on Biometrics Theory, Applications and Systems (BTAS), pp. 1–8. IEEE (2015)

42. Farfade, S.S., Saberian, M.J., Li, L.J.: Multi-view face detection using deep convolutional neural networks. In: Proceedings of the 5th ACM on International Conference on Multimedia Retrieval, pp. 643–650. ACM (2015)

A Geometric Approach to Image Labeling

Freddie Åström[1,3](✉), Stefania Petra[1,2], Bernhard Schmitzer[4],
and Christoph Schnörr[1,3]

[1] HCI, Heidelberg University, Heidelberg, Germany
   `freddie.astroem@iwr.uni-heidelberg.de`
[2] MIG, Heidelberg University, Heidelberg, Germany
[3] IPA, Heidelberg University, Heidelberg, Germany
[4] CEREMADE, University Paris-Dauphine, Paris, France

Abstract. We introduce a smooth non-convex approach in a novel geometric framework which complements established convex and non-convex approaches to image labeling. The major underlying concept is a smooth manifold of probabilistic assignments of a prespecified set of prior data (the "labels") to given image data. The Riemannian gradient flow with respect to a corresponding objective function evolves on the manifold and terminates, for any $\delta > 0$, within a δ-neighborhood of an unique assignment (labeling). As a consequence, unlike with convex outer relaxation approaches to (non-submodular) image labeling problems, no post-processing step is needed for the rounding of fractional solutions. Our approach is numerically implemented with sparse, highly-parallel interior-point updates that efficiently converge, largely independent from the number of labels. Experiments with noisy labeling and inpainting problems demonstrate competitive performance.

Keywords: Image labeling · Assignment manifold · Fisher-Rao metric · Riemannian gradient flow

1 Introduction

Image *labeling* is the process of assigning a finite set of labels to given image data and constitutes a key problem of low-level computer vision. This task is typically formulated as Maximum A-Posterior (MAP) problem based on a discrete Markov Random Field (MRF) model. We refer to [1] for a recent survey and to [2] for a comprehensive evaluation of various inference methods. Because the labeling problem is NP-hard (ignoring a subset of problems which can be reformulated as a maximum-flow problem), problem *relaxations* are necessary in order to compute efficiently approximate solutions. The prevailing *convex* approach is based on the linear programming relaxation [3] with the so-called local polytope as feasible set [4]. A major obstacle to speeding up the convergence rate is the inherent non-smoothness of the polyhedral relaxation, e.g. in terms of a dual objective function after a problem decomposition into exactly solvable subproblems. Because the convex approach constitutes an *outer* relaxation, fractional

© Springer International Publishing AG 2016
B. Leibe et al. (Eds.): ECCV 2016, Part V, LNCS 9909, pp. 139–154, 2016.
DOI: 10.1007/978-3-319-46454-1_9

solutions are obtained in general, and a subsequent rounding step is needed to obtain a unique label assignment. *Non-convex* relaxations are e.g. based on the mean-field approach [4, Sect. 5]. They constitute *inner* relaxations of the combinatorially complex feasible set (the so-called marginal polytope) and hence do not require a post-processing step for rounding. However, as for non-convex optimization problems in general, inference suffers from the local-minima problem, and auxiliary parameters introduced for alleviating this difficulty, e.g. by deterministic annealing, can only be heuristically tuned. Variational methods in connection with the labeling problem have been addressed before e.g. [5,6].

Contribution. We introduce a novel approach to the image labeling problem based on a *geometric* formulation. Figure 1 illustrates the major components of the approach and their interplay. *Labeling* denotes the tasks to assign prior features, which are elements of the prior set $\mathcal{P}_\mathcal{F}$, to given features f in any metric space (raw data just constitute a basic specific example). The mapping $\exp_W$ lifts the distance matrix D to the assignment manifold $\mathcal{W}$. The assignment is determined by solving a Riemannian gradient flow with respect to an appropriate objective function $J(W)$, where W is called the assignment matrix, which evolves on the assignment manifold. The latter key concept encompasses the set of all strictly positive stochastic matrices equipped with a Fisher-Rao product metric. This furnishes a proper geometry for computing local Riemannian means, described by the similarity matrix $S(W)$ of the likelihood matrix $L(W)$. This achieves spatially coherent labelings and suppress the influence of noise. The Riemannian metric also determines the gradient flow and leads to efficient, sparse interior-point updates that converge in few dozens of outer iterations. Even larger numbers of labels do not significantly slow down the convergence rate. We show that the local Riemannien means can be accurately approximated by closed-form expressions which eliminates inner iterations and hence further speeds up the numerical implementation. For any specified $\delta > 0$, the iterates terminate within a δ-neighborhood of *unique* assignments, which finally determines the labeling.

Our approach is non-convex and *smooth*. Regarding the non-convexity, *no* parameter tuning is needed to escape from poor local minima: For any problem instance, the flow is naturally initialized at the barycenter of the assignment manifold, from which it smoothly evolves and terminates at a labeling.

Organization. We formally detail the components of our approach in Sects. 2 and 3. The objective function and the optimization approach are described in Sects. 4 and 5. Few academical experiments are reported in Sect. 6 which illustrate properties of our approach and contrast it with the prevailing convex relaxation approach.

Our main objective is to introduce and announce a *novel approach* to the image labeling problem of computer vision. Elaboration of any specific application is beyond the scope of this paper. Due to lack of space, we omitted all proofs and refer the reader to the report [7] which also provides a more comprehensive discussion of the literature.

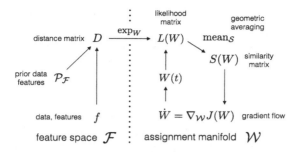

Fig. 1. Geometric labeling approach and its components. The feature space $\mathcal{F}$ with a distance function $d_{\mathcal{F}}$, along with observed data and prior data to be assigned, constitute the application specific part. A labeling of the data is determined by a Riemannian gradient flow on the manifold of probabilistic assignments, which terminates at a unique assignment, i.e. a labeling of the given data. Sections 2–5 detail all depicted components of the approach and their interplay.

Basic Notation. We set $[n] = \{1, 2, \ldots, n\}$ and $\mathbb{1} = (1, 1, \ldots, 1)^\top$. $\langle u, v \rangle = \sum_{i \in [n]} u_i v_i$ denotes the Euclidean inner product and for matrices $\langle A, B \rangle := \mathrm{tr}(A^\top B)$. For strictly positive vectors we often write pointwise operations more efficiently in vector form. For example, for $0 < p \in \mathbb{R}^n$ and $u \in \mathbb{R}^n$, the expression $\frac{u}{\sqrt{p}}$ denotes the vector $(u_1/\sqrt{p_1}, \ldots, u_n/\sqrt{p_n})^\top$.

2   The Assignment Manifold

In this section, we define the feasible set for representing and computating image labelings in terms of assignment matrices $W \in \mathcal{W}$, the assignment manifold $\mathcal{W}$. The basic building block is the open probability simplex $\mathcal{S}$ equipped with the Fisher-Rao metric. We refer to [8,9] for background reading.

2.1   Geometry of the Probability Simplex

The relative interior $\mathcal{S} = \mathring{\Delta}_{n-1}$ of the probability simplex $\Delta_{n-1} = \{p \in \mathbb{R}^n_+ : \langle \mathbb{1}, p \rangle = 1\}$ becomes a differentiable Riemannian manifold when endowed with the Fisher-Rao metric, which in this particular case reads

$$\langle u, v \rangle_p := \left\langle \frac{u}{\sqrt{p}}, \frac{v}{\sqrt{p}} \right\rangle, \ \forall u, v \in T_p\mathcal{S}, \quad T_p\mathcal{S} = \{v \in \mathbb{R}^n : \langle \mathbb{1}, v \rangle = 0\}, \ p \in \mathcal{S}, \quad (1)$$

with tangent spaces denotes by $T_p\mathcal{S}$. The *Riemannian gradient* $\nabla_{\mathcal{S}} f(p) \in T_p\mathcal{S}$ of a smooth function $f \colon \mathcal{S} \to \mathbb{R}$ at $p \in \mathcal{S}$ is the tangent vector given by

$$\nabla_{\mathcal{S}} f(p) = p\big(\nabla f(p) - \langle p, \nabla f(p) \rangle \mathbb{1}\big). \quad (2)$$

We also regard the scaled sphere $\mathcal{N} = 2\mathcal{S}^{n-1}$ as manifold with Riemannian metric induced by the Euclidean inner product of $\mathbb{R}^n$. The following diffeomorphism ψ between $\mathcal{S}$ and the open subset $\psi(\mathcal{S}) \subset \mathcal{N}$, henceforth called *sphere-map*, was suggested e.g. by [10, Sect. 2.1] and [8, Sect. 2.5]

$$\psi : \mathcal{S} \to \mathcal{N}, \qquad p \mapsto s = \psi(p) := 2\sqrt{p}. \tag{3}$$

The sphere-map enables to compute the geometry of $\mathcal{S}$ from the geometry of the 2-sphere. The sphere-map ψ (3) is an isometry, i.e. the Riemannian metric is preserved. Consequently, lenghts of tangent vectors and curves are preserved as well. In particular, geodesics as critical points of length functionals are mapped by ψ to geodesics. We denote by

$$d_{\mathcal{S}}(p, q) \qquad \text{and} \qquad \gamma_v(t), \tag{4}$$

respectively, the *Riemannian distance* on $\mathcal{S}$ between two points $p, q \in \mathcal{S}$, and the *geodesic* on $\mathcal{S}$ emanating from $p = \gamma_v(0)$ in the direction $v = \dot{\gamma}_v(0) \in T_p\mathcal{S}$. The *exponential mapping* for $\mathcal{S}$ is denoted by

$$\mathrm{Exp}_p : V_p \to \mathcal{S}, \quad v \mapsto \mathrm{Exp}_p(v) = \gamma_v(1), \quad V_p = \{v \in T_p\mathcal{S} : \gamma_v(t) \in \mathcal{S}, \, t \in [0, 1]\}. \tag{5}$$

The *Riemannian mean* $\mathrm{mean}_{\mathcal{S}}(\mathcal{P})$ of a set of points $\mathcal{P} = \{p^i\}_{i \in [N]} \subset \mathcal{S}$ with corresponding weights $w \in \Delta_{N-1}$ minimizes the objective function

$$\mathrm{mean}_{\mathcal{S}}(\mathcal{P}) = \arg\min_{p \in \mathcal{S}} \frac{1}{2} \sum_{i \in [N]} w_i d_{\mathcal{S}}^2(p, p^i). \tag{6}$$

We use uniform weights $w = \frac{1}{N}\mathbb{1}_N$ in this paper. The following fact is not obvious due to the non-negative curvature of the manifold $\mathcal{S}$. It follows from [11, Theorem 1.2] and the radius of the geodesic ball containing $\psi(\mathcal{S}) \subset \mathcal{N}$.

Lemma 1. *The Riemannian mean* (6) *is unique for any data* $\mathcal{P} = \{p^i\}_{i \in [n]} \subset \mathcal{S}$ *and weights* $w \in \Delta_{n-1}$.

We call the computation of Riemannian means *geometric averaging* (cf. Fig. 1).

2.2   Assignment Matrices and Manifold

A natural question is how to extend the geometry of $\mathcal{S}$ to the stochastic assignment matrices $W \in \mathbb{R}^{m \times n}$, with rows $W_i \in \mathcal{S}$, $i \in [m]$ consisting of discrete probability distributions where m is the number of features and n is the number of labels, so as to preserve the information-theoretic properties induced by this metric (that we do not discuss here – cf. [8,12]).

This problem was recently studied by [13]. The authors suggested three natural definitions of manifolds. It turned out that all of them are slight variations of taking the product of $\mathcal{S}$, differing only by the scaling of the resulting product metric. As a consequence, we make the following

Definition 1 (Assignment Manifold). *The manifold of assignment matrices, called assignment manifold, is the set*

$$\mathcal{W} = \{W \in \mathbb{R}^{m \times n} : W_i \in \mathcal{S}, \; i \in [m]\}. \tag{7}$$

According to this product structure and based on (1), the Riemannian metric is given by

$$\langle U, V \rangle_W := \sum_{i \in [m]} \langle U_i, V_i \rangle_{W_i}, \qquad U, V \in T_W \mathcal{W}. \tag{8}$$

Note that $V \in T_W \mathcal{W}$ means $V_i \in T_{W_i} \mathcal{S}, \; i \in [m]$.

Remark 1. We call stochastic matrices contained in $\mathcal{W}$ *assignment matrices*, due to their role in the variational approach described next.

3   Features, Distance Function, Assignment

We refer the reader to Fig. 1 for an overview of the following definitions. Let $f : \mathcal{V} \to \mathcal{F}, \; i \mapsto f_i$ and $i \in \mathcal{V} = [m]$ denote any given data, either raw image data or features extracted from the data in a preprocessing step. In any case, we call f *feature*. At this point, we do not make any assumption about the *feature space* $\mathcal{F}$ except that a *distance function* $d_{\mathcal{F}} : \mathcal{F} \times \mathcal{F} \to \mathbb{R}$, is specified. We assume that a finite subset of $\mathcal{F}$

$$\mathcal{P}_{\mathcal{F}} := \{f_j^*\}_{j \in [n]}, \tag{9}$$

additionally is given, called *prior set*. We are interested in the assignment of the prior set to the data in terms of an *assignment matrix* $W \in \mathcal{W} \subset \mathbb{R}^{m \times n}$, with the manifold $\mathcal{W}$ defined by (7). Thus, by definition, every row vector $0 < W_i \in \mathcal{S}$ is a discrete distribution with full support $\operatorname{supp}(W_i) = [n]$. The element

$$W_{ij} = \Pr(f_j^* | f_i), \qquad i \in [m], \quad j \in [n], \tag{10}$$

quantifies the assignment of prior item f_j^* to the observed data point f_i. We may think of this number as the *posterior probability* that f_j^* generated the observation f_i.

The *assignment task* asks for determining an optimal assignment W^*, considered as "explanation" of the data based on the prior data $\mathcal{P}_{\mathcal{F}}$. We discuss next the ingredients of the objective function that will be used to solve assignment tasks (see also Fig. 1).

Distance Matrix. Given $\mathcal{F}, d_{\mathcal{F}}$ and $\mathcal{P}_{\mathcal{F}}$, we compute the *distance matrix*

$$D \in \mathbb{R}^{m \times n}, \; D_i \in \mathbb{R}^n, \quad D_{ij} = \frac{1}{\rho} d_{\mathcal{F}}(f_i, f_j^*), \quad \rho > 0, \quad i \in [m], \quad j \in [n], \tag{11}$$

where ρ is the first (from two) *user parameters* to be set. This parameter serves two purposes. It accounts for the unknown scale of the data f that depends on the application and hence cannot be known beforehand. Furthermore, its value determines what subset of the prior features f_j^*, $j \in [n]$ effectively affects the process of determining the assignment matrix W. We call ρ *selectivity parameter*.

Furthermore, we set

$$W = W(0), \qquad W_i(0) := \frac{1}{n}\mathbb{1}_n, \quad i \in [m]. \tag{12}$$

That is, W is initialized with the uninformative *uniform assignment* that is not biased towards a solution in any way.

Likelihood Matrix. The next processing step is based on the following

Definition 2 (Lifting Map (Manifolds $\mathcal{S}, \mathcal{W}$)). *The lifting mapping is defined by*

$$\exp: T\mathcal{S} \to \mathcal{S}, \qquad (p, u) \mapsto \exp_p(u) = \frac{pe^u}{\langle p, e^u \rangle}, \tag{13a}$$

$$\exp: T\mathcal{W} \to \mathcal{W}, \qquad (W, U) \mapsto \exp_W(U) = \begin{pmatrix} \exp_{W_1}(U_1) \\ \ldots \\ \exp_{W_m}(U_m) \end{pmatrix}, \tag{13b}$$

where $U_i, W_i, i \in [m]$ index the row vectors of the matrices U, W, and where the argument decides which of the two mappings $\exp$ applies.

Remark 2. The lifting mapping generalizes the well-known softmax function through the dependency on the base point p. In addition, it approximates geodesics and accordingly the exponential mapping Exp, as stated next. We therefore use the symbol $\exp$ as mnemomic. Unlike Exp_p in (5), the mapping $\exp_p$ is defined on the entire tangent space, which is convenient for numerical computations.

Proposition 1. *Let*

$$v = \left(\mathrm{Diag}(p) - pp^\top \right)u, \qquad v \in T_p\mathcal{S}. \tag{14}$$

Then $\exp_p(ut)$ given by (13a) solves

$$\dot{p}(t) = p(t)u - \langle p(t), u \rangle p(t), \qquad p(0) = p, \tag{15}$$

and provides a first-order approximation of the geodesic $\gamma_v(t)$ from (4), (5).

$$\exp_p(ut) \approx p + vt, \qquad \|\gamma_v(t) - \exp_p(ut)\| = \mathcal{O}(t^2). \tag{16}$$

Given D and W, we lift the vector field D to the manifold $\mathcal{W}$ by

$$L = L(W) := \exp_W(-U) \in \mathcal{W}, \qquad U_i = D_i - \frac{1}{n}\langle \mathbb{1}, D_i \rangle \mathbb{1}, \quad i \in [m], \tag{17}$$

with $\exp_W$ defined by (13b). We call L *likelihood matrix* because the row vectors are discrete probability distributions which separately represent the similarity of each observation f_i to the prior data $\mathcal{P}_{\mathcal{F}}$, as measured by the distance $d_{\mathcal{F}}$ in (11). Note that the operation (17) depends on the assignment matrix $W \in \mathcal{W}$.

Similarity Matrix. Based on the likelihood matrix L, we define the *similarity matrix*

$$S = S(W) \in \mathcal{W}, \qquad S_i = \text{mean}_{\mathcal{S}}\{L_j\}_{j \in \tilde{\mathcal{N}}_{\mathcal{E}}(i)}, \qquad i \in [m], \qquad (18)$$

where each row is the Riemannian mean (6) of the likelihood vectors, indexed by the neighborhoods as specified by the underying graph $\mathcal{G} = (\mathcal{V}, \mathcal{E})$, such that the local neighborhood $\tilde{\mathcal{N}}_{\mathcal{E}}(i) = \{i\} \cup \mathcal{N}_{\mathcal{E}}(i)$ with $\mathcal{N}_{\mathcal{E}}(i) = \{j \in \mathcal{V} \colon ij \in \mathcal{E}\}$ is augmented by the center pixel. Note that S depends on W because L does so by (17). The *size* of the neighbourhoods $|\tilde{\mathcal{N}}_{\mathcal{E}}(i)|$ is the *second user parameter*, besides the selectivity parameter ρ for scaling the distance matrix (11). Typically, each $\tilde{\mathcal{N}}_{\mathcal{E}}(i)$ indexes the same local "window" around pixel location i. We then call the window size $|\tilde{\mathcal{N}}_{\mathcal{E}}(i)|$ *scale parameter*. In basic applications, the distance matrix D will not change once the features and the feature distance $d_{\mathcal{F}}$ are determined. On the other hand, the likelihood matrix $L(W)$ and the similarity matrix $S(W)$ have to be recomputed as the assignment W evolves, as part of any numerical algorithm used to compute an optimal assignment W^*. We point out, however, that more general scenarios are conceivable – without essentially changing the overall approach – where $D = D(W)$ depends on the assignment as well and hence has to be updated too, as part of the optimization process.

4   Objective Function, Optimization

We specify next the objective function as criterion for assignments and the gradient flow on the assignment manifold, to compute an optimal assignment W^*. Finally, based on W^*, the so-called assignment mapping is defined.

Objective Function. Getting back to the interpretation from Sect. 3 of the assignment matrix $W \in \mathcal{W}$ as *posterior probabilities*,

$$W_{ij} = \Pr(f_j^* | f_i), \qquad (19)$$

of assigning prior feature f_j^* to the observed feature f_i, a natural *objective function* to be maximized is

$$\max_{W \in \mathcal{W}} J(W), \qquad J(W) := \langle S(W), W \rangle. \qquad (20)$$

The functional J together with the feasible set $\mathcal{W}$ formalizes the following objectives:

1. Assignments W should *maximally correlate* with the feature-induced similarities $S = S(W)$, as measured by the inner product which defines the objective function $J(W)$.

2. Assignments of prior data to observations should be done in a *spatially coherent* way. This is accomplished by *geometric averaging* of likelihood vectors over local spatial neighborhoods, which turns the likelihood matrix $L(W)$ into the similarity matrix $S(W)$, *depending* on W.

3. Maximizers W^* should define *image labelings* in terms of rows $\overline{W}_i^* = e^{k_i} \in \{0,1\}^n$, $i, k_i \in [m]$, that are indicator vectors. While the latter matrices are not contained in the assignment manifold $\mathcal{W}$, which we notationally indicate by the overbar, we compute in practice assignments $W^* \approx \overline{W}^*$ arbitrarily close to such points. It will turn out below that the *geometry enforces* this approximation.

As a consequence of 3 and in view of (19), such points W^* *maximize posterior probabilities* akin to the interpretation of MAP-inference with discrete graphical models by minimizing corresponding energy functionals. The mathematical structure of the optimization task of our approach, however, and the way of fusing data and prior information, are quite different. The following Lemma states point 3 above more precisely.

Lemma 2. *Let $\overline{\mathcal{W}}$ denote the closure of $\mathcal{W}$. We have*

$$\sup_{W \in \mathcal{W}} J(W) = m, \tag{21}$$

and the supremum is attained at the extreme points

$$\overline{\mathcal{W}}^* := \{ \overline{W}^* \in \{0,1\}^{m \times n} : \overline{W}_i^* = e^{k_i}, \, i \in [m], \, k_1, \ldots, k_m \in [n] \} \subset \overline{\mathcal{W}}, \tag{22}$$

corresponding to matrices with unit vectors as row vectors.

Assignment Mapping. Regarding the feature space $\mathcal{F}$, no assumptions were made so far, except for specifying a distance function $d_{\mathcal{F}}$. We have to be more specific about $\mathcal{F}$ only if we wish to *synthesize* the approximation to the given data f, in terms of an assignment W^* that optimizes (20) and the prior data $\mathcal{P}_{\mathcal{F}}$. We denote the corresponding approximation by

$$u \colon \mathcal{W} \to \mathcal{F}^{|\mathcal{V}|}, \qquad W \mapsto u(W), \qquad u^* := u(W^*), \tag{23}$$

and call it *assignment mapping*.

A simple example of such a mapping concerns cases where prototypical feature vectors f^{*j}, $j \in [n]$ are assigned to data vectors f^i, $i \in [m]$: the mapping $u(W^*)$ then simply replaces each data vector by the convex combination of prior vectors assigned to it,

$$u^{*i} = \sum_{j \in [n]} W_{ij}^* f^{*j}, \qquad i \in [m]. \tag{24}$$

And if W^* approximates a global maximum $\overline{W}^*$ as characterized by Lemma 2, then each f_i is uniquely replaced ("labelled") by some $u^{*k_i} = f^{*k_i}$.

Optimization Approach. The optimization task (20) does not admit a closed-form solution. We therefore compute the assignment by the *Riemannian gradient ascent flow* on the manifold $\mathcal{W}$,

$$\dot{W}_{ij} = \left(\nabla_{\mathcal{W}} J(W)\right)_{ij} = W_{ij}\left(\left(\nabla_i J(W)\right)_j - \langle W_i, \nabla_i J(W)\rangle\right), \quad j \in [n], \quad (25a)$$

using the initialization (12) with

$$\nabla_i J(W) := \frac{\partial}{\partial W_i} J(W) = \left(\frac{\partial}{\partial W_{i1}} J(W), \ldots, \frac{\partial}{\partial W_{in}} J(W)\right), \quad i \in [m], \quad (25b)$$

which results from applying (2) to the objective (20). The flows 25a, b for $i \in [m]$, are *not* independent as the product structure of $\mathcal{W}$ (cf. Sect. 2.2) might suggest. Rather, they are coupled through the gradient $\nabla J(W)$ which reflects the interaction of the distributions W_i, $i \in [m]$, due to the geometric averaging which results in the similarity matrix (18).

5   Algorithm, Implementation

We discuss in this section specific aspects of the implementation of the variational approach.

Assignment Normalization. Because each vector W_i approaches some vertex $\overline{W}^* \in \overline{\mathcal{W}}^*$ by construction, and because the numerical computations are designed to evolve on $\mathcal{W}$, we avoid numerical issues by checking for each $i \in [m]$ every entry W_{ij}, $j \in [n]$, after each iteration of the algorithm (30) below. Whenever an entry drops below $\eta = 10^{-10}$, we rectify W_i by

$$W_i \quad \leftarrow \quad \frac{1}{\langle \mathbb{1}, \tilde{W}_i\rangle}\tilde{W}_i, \qquad \tilde{W}_i = W_i - \min_{j\in[n]} W_{ij} + \eta, \qquad \eta = 10^{-10}. \quad (26)$$

In other words, the number η plays the role of 0 in our impementation. Our numerical experiments show that this operation removes any numerical issues without affecting convergence in terms of the termination criterion specified at the end of this section.

Computing Riemannian Means. Computation of the similarity matrix $S(W)$ due to Eq. (18) involves the computation of Riemannian means. Although a corresponding fixed-point iteration (that we omit here) converges quickly, carrying out such iterations as a subroutine, at each pixel and iterative step of the outer iteration (30) below, increases runtime (of non-parallel implementations) noticeably. In view of the approximation of the exponential map $\text{Exp}_p(v) = \gamma_v(1)$ by (16), it is natural to approximate the Riemannian mean as well.

Lemma 3. *Replacing in the optimality condition of the Riemannian mean (6) (see, e.g. [9, Lemma 4.8.4]) the inverse exponential mapping Exp_p^{-1} by the inverse $\exp_p^{-1}$ of the lifting map (13a), yields the closed-form expression*

$$\frac{\text{mean}_g(\mathcal{P})}{\langle \mathbb{1}, \text{mean}_g(\mathcal{P})\rangle}, \qquad \text{mean}_g(\mathcal{P}) := \left(\prod_{i\in[N]} p^i\right)^{\frac{1}{N}} \quad (27)$$

as approximation of the Riemannian mean $\text{mean}_{\mathcal{S}}(\mathcal{P})$, *with the geometric mean* $\text{mean}_g(\mathcal{P})$ *applied componentwise to the vectors in* $\mathcal{P}$.

Optimization Algorithm. A thorough analysis of various discrete schemes for numerically integrating the gradient flow 25a, b, including stability estimates, is beyond the scope of this paper. Here, we merely adopt the following basic strategy from [14], that has been widely applied in the literature (in different contexts) and performed remarkably well in our experiments. Approximating the flow 25a, b for each vector W_i, $i \in [m]$, and $W_i^{(k)} := W_i(t_i^{(k)})$, by the time-discrete scheme

$$\frac{W_i^{(k+1)} - W_i^{(k)}}{t_i^{(k+1)} - t_i^{(k)}} = W_i^{(k)}\big(\nabla_i J(W^{(k)}) - \langle W_i^{(k)}, \nabla_i J(W^{(k)})\rangle\mathbb{1}\big), \qquad (28)$$

and choosing the adaptive step-sizes $t_i^{(k+1)} - t_i^{(k)} = \frac{1}{\langle W_i^{(k)}, \nabla_i J(W^{(k)})\rangle}$, yields the multiplicative updates

$$W_i^{(k+1)} = \frac{W_i^{(k)}\big(\nabla_i J(W^{(k)})\big)}{\langle W_i^{(k)}, \nabla_i J(W^{(k)})\rangle}, \qquad i \in [m]. \qquad (29)$$

We further simplify this update in view of the explicit expression of the gradient of the objective function with components $\partial_{W_{ij}} J(W) = \langle T^{ij}(W), W\rangle + S_{ij}(W)$, that comprise two terms. The first one in terms of a matrix T^{ij} (that we do not further specify here) contributes the derivative of $S(W)$ with respect to W_i, which is significantly smaller than the second term $S_{ij}(W)$, because $S_i(W)$ results from *averaging* (18) the likelihood vectors $L_j(W_j)$ over spatial neighborhoods and hence changes slowly, consequently, we simply drop this first term.

Thus, for computing the numerical results reported in this paper, we used the fixed-point iteration

$$W_i^{(k+1)} = \frac{W_i^{(k)}\big(S_i(W^{(k)})\big)}{\langle W_i^{(k)}, S_i(W^{(k)})\rangle}, \qquad W_i^{(0)} = \frac{1}{n}\mathbb{1}, \qquad i \in [m] \qquad (30)$$

together with the approximation due to Lemma 3 for computing Riemannian means, which define by (18) the similarity matrices $S(W^{(k)})$. Note that this requires to recompute the likelihood matrices (17) as well, at each iteration k.

Termination Criterion. Algorithm (30) was terminated if the average entropy

$$-\frac{1}{m} \sum_{i \in [m]} \sum_{j \in [n]} W_{ij}^{(k)} \log W_{ij}^{(k)} \qquad (31)$$

dropped below a threshold. For example, a threshold value 10^{-4} means in practice that, up to a tiny fraction of indices $i \subset [m]$ that should not matter for a subsequent further analysis, all vectors W_i are very close to unit vectors, thus indicating an almost unique assignment of prior items f_j^*, $j \in [n]$ to the data f_i, $i \in [m]$. This termination criterion was adopted for all experiments.

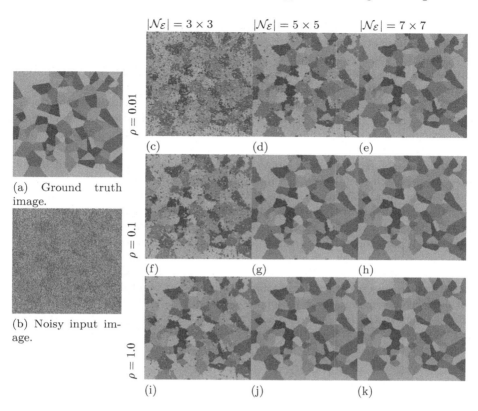

Fig. 2. Parameter influence on labeling. Panels (a) and (b) show a ground-truth image and noisy input data. Panels (c)–(k) show the assignments $u(W^*)$ for various parameter values where W^* maximizes the objective function (20). The spatial scale $|\mathcal{N}_\mathcal{E}|$ increases from left to right. The results illustrate the compromise between sensitivity to noise and to the geometry of signal transitions.

6   Experiments

In this section, we show results on empirical convergence rate and the influence of the fix-point iteration (30). Additionally, we show results on a multi-class labeling problem of inpainting by labeling.

6.1   Parameters, Empirical Convergence Rate

The color images in Fig. 2 comprise of 31 color vectors forming the prior data set $\mathcal{P}_\mathcal{F} = \{f^{1*}, \ldots, f^{31*}\}$ and are used to illustrate the labeling problem. The labeling task is to assign these vectors in a spatially coherent way to the input data so as to recover the ground truth image. Every color vector was encoded by the vertices of the simplex Δ_{30}, that is by the unit vectors $\{e^1, \ldots, e^{31}\} \subset \{0,1\}^{31}$. Choosing the distance $d_\mathcal{F}(f^i, f^j) := \|f^i - f^j\|_1$, this results in unit distances between all pairs of data points and hence enables to assess most clearly the impact of geometric spatial averaging and the influence of the two parameters ρ and $|\mathcal{N}_\varepsilon|$, introduced in Sect. 3. All results were computed using the assignment mapping (24) *without* rounding. This shows that the termination criterion of Sect. 5, illustrated by Fig. 3 leads to (almost) unique assignments.

In Fig. 2, the selectivity parameter ρ increases from top to bottom. If ρ is chosen too small, then there is a tendency to noise-induced oversegmentation, in particular at small spatial scales $|\mathcal{N}_\varepsilon|$. The reader familiar with total variation based denoising [15], where a *single* parameter is only used to control the influence of regularization, may ask why *two* parameters are used in the present approach and if they are necessary. Note, however, that depending on the application, the ability to separate the physical and the spatial scale in order to recognize outliers with small spatial support, while performing diffusion at a larger spatial scale as in panels (c),(d),(f),(i), may be beneficial. We point out that this separation of the physical and spatial scales (image range vs. image domain) is not possible with total variation based regularization where these scales are coupled through the co-area formula. As a consequence, a single parameter is only needed in total variation. On the other hand, larger values of the total variation regularization parameter lead to the well-known loss-of-contrast effect, which in the present approach can be avoided by properly choosing the parameters $\rho, |\mathcal{N}_\varepsilon|$ corresponding to these two scales.

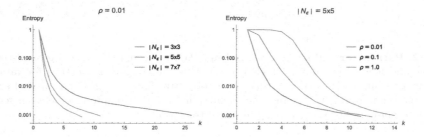

Fig. 3. Parameter values and convergence rate. Average entropy of the assignment vectors $W_i^{(k)}$ as a function of the iteration counter k and the two parameters ρ and $|\mathcal{N}_\varepsilon|$, for the labeling task illustrated by Fig. 2. The left panel shows that despite high selectivity in terms of a small value of ρ, small spatial scales necessitate to resolve more conflicting assignments through propagating information by geometric spatial averaging. As a consequence, more iterations are needed to achieve convergence and a labeling. The right panel, shows that at a fixed spatial scale $|\mathcal{N}_\varepsilon|$ higher selectivity leads to faster convergence, because outliers are simply removed from the averaging process, low selectivity leads to an assignment (labeling) taking all data into account.

6.2   Inpainting by Labeling

Inpainting represents the problem of filling in a known region with the missing data. We set the feature metric as in the previous example, but with the difference of defining the distance between the unknown feature vectors to priors to be large, i.e., we do not bias the final assignment to any of the prior features.

Note that our geometrical approach is significantly different from traditional graphical models where unitary and pair-wise terms are used for labeling. Therefore, the evaluation of an objective function's "energy", as done in [2], is not an applicable criteria. We instead report the more objective ratio of correctly assigned labels. Terminology and abbreviations are adopted from [2] and all competing methods were evaluated using OpenGM 2 [16]. The methods we include in this study are **TRWS**, a polyhedral method stemming from linear programming and block-coordinate-ascent [17]. The popular message passing algorithms **BPS** (sequential) and **LBP** (parallel) of loopy belief propagation [18]. We also include iterative refinement by partitioning the label space via the α-β-**SWAP** algorithm and the α expansion algorithm α-**Exp** algorithms, see [19,20]. For reference, we include the fast primal-dual algorithm **FastPD** [21]. We refer to the respective works for additional details.

Synthetic example. In the synthetic example in Fig. 4, we show the region to be inpainted in black color. This is a labeling problem consisting of 3 uniformly distributed color vectors and 1 label representing the background (white). From the result images in the same figure, it is clear that **LBP** performs better than **TRWS**. However, in **LBP** there are discretization artifacts and the intersection point is not center symmetric as for our **Geometric** approach. A center symmetric intersection of the geometric filter is natural due to the filters isotropic interaction with the neighborhood and lack of prior assumptions. Although, our approach still shows few artifacts on the diagonal borders, computing the ratio of correctly assigned labels, we achieve near perfect reconstruction, 99 %, of the missing data with 120° intersection at the circle center.

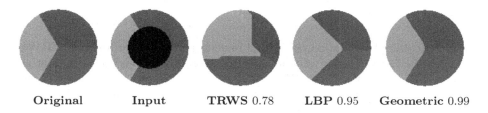

| Original | Input | TRWS 0.78 | LBP 0.95 | Geometric 0.99 |

Fig. 4. Synthetic inpainting example. Here **TRWS** (truncated linear) shows the worst performance with only 78 % correctly assigned labels. The values show ratio of correctly assigned labels and higher is better. **LBP** performs better than **TRWS**, but does not produce an interception of 120° in the circle's center. The update scheme of our geometric filter was terminated at entropy 10^{-4}, with a neighborhood 3×3 and selectivity parameter $\rho = 0.1$ and produces the most accurate labeling.

Inpainting. In this second inpainting problem, where each variable can attain 256 labels, is more challenging for established graphical models with respect

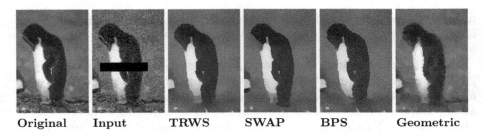

Original   Input   TRWS   SWAP   BPS   Geometric

Fig. 5. Recovery of missing and noisy data. This example is from the *mrf-inpainting* dataset in [2]. The selectivity parameter was set to $\rho = 1$ and the neighborhood size was 3×3. The ratio of correctly assigned labels are shown in Fig. 6. It is evident our geometric filter adopts better to the underlying image data, while producing a plausible labeling of the inpainting area.

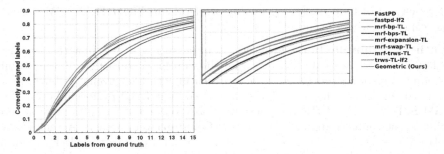

Fig. 6. Ratio of correctly assigned labels for the penguin in Fig. 5 is displayed on the y-axis and the number of labels from the original image are iterated on the x-axis. For label distances 1–6 inference with TRWS shows better agreement with the original image labeling. However, considering larger label distances, our geometric filter shows the most accurate ratio. (TL stands for truncated linear functions and we refer to [2] and respective works for additional details.)

to numerical implementation. Measured in energy of objective function **TRWS** obtained the lowest energy value in the evaluation of [2]. However, as inpainting results, **TRWS**, **SWAP** and **BPS** all show poor performance as much of the image details are not represented by the labeling. In our geometric approach, the labeling retains more image details. In Fig. 6 we show the ratio of correctly assigned labels for the penguin (size 122×179 pixels) in Fig. 5. We again refer to [2] for details on the methods implementations. All methods shows similar accuracy in labeling, and our geometric filter is only challenged by **TRWS** for label distances smaller than 6 from the original image. Considering label distances larger than 6, our approach shows the best ratio. We further remark that our framework is computationally efficient as it only require few dozens of massively parallel outer iterations. Our non-optimized Matlab implementation reaches the termination criteria ($\delta = 10^{-4}$) after 194 iterations in 2 min and 59 s on an Intel i5 CPU at 3.5 GHz.

7   Conclusion

We presented a novel approach to image labeling, formulated in a smooth geometric setting. The approach contrasts with etablished convex and non-convex relaxations of the image labeling problem through smoothness and geometric averaging. The numerics boil down to parallel sparse updates, that maximize the objective along an interior path in the feasible set of assignments and finally return a labeling. Although an elementary first-order approximation of the gradient flow was only used, the convergence rate seems competitive. In particular, a large number of labels does not slow down convergence as is the case of convex relaxations. All aspects specific to an application domain are represented by a distance matrix D and a user parameter ρ. This flexibility and the absence of ad-hoc tuning parameters should promote applications of the approach to various image labeling problems.

Acknowledgments. FÅ, SP and CS thank the German Research Foundation (DFG) for support via grant GRK 1653. BS was supported by the European Research Council (project SIGMA-Vision).

References

1. Wang, C., Komodakis, N., Paragios, N.: Markov random field modeling, inference & learning in computer vision & image understanding: a survey. Comput. Vis. Image Underst. **117**(11), 1610–1627 (2013)
2. Kappes, J., Andres, B., Hamprecht, F., Schnörr, C., Nowozin, S., Batra, D., Kim, S., Kausler, B., Kröger, T., Lellmann, J., Komodakis, N., Savchynskyy, B., Rother, C.: A comparative study of modern inference techniques for structured discrete energy minimization problems. Int. J. Comp. Vis. **115**(2), 155–184 (2015)
3. Werner, T.: A linear programming approach to max-sum problem: a review. IEEE Trans. Patt. Anal. Mach. Intell. **29**(7), 1165–1179 (2007)
4. Wainwright, M., Jordan, M.: Graphical models, exponential families, and variational inference. Found. Trends Mach. Learn. **1**(1–2), 1–305 (2008)
5. Sundaramoorthi, G., Hong, B.W.: Fast label: easy and efficient solution of joint multi-label and estimation problems. In: 2014 CVPR, pp. 3126–3133, June 2014
6. Jung, M., Chung, G., Sundaramoorthi, G., Vese, L.A., Yuille, A.L.: Sobolev gradients and joint variational image segmentation, denoising, and deblurring. In: Proceedings of the SPIE, vol. 7246, pp. 72460I–72460I-13 (2009)
7. Åström, F., Petra, S., Schmitzer, B., Schnörr, C.: Image Labeling by Assignment 16 March 2016, preprint: http://arxiv.org/abs/1603.05285
8. Amari, S.I., Nagaoka, H.: Methods of Information Geometry. Amer. Math. Soc. and Oxford University Press (2000)
9. Jost, J.: Riemannian Geometry and Geometric Analysis, 4th edn. Springer, Heidelberg (2005)
10. Kass, R.: The geometry of asymptotic inference. Statist. Sci. **4**(3), 188–234 (1989)
11. Karcher, H.: Riemannian center of mass and mollifier smoothing. Comm. Pure Appl. Math. **30**, 509–541 (1977)
12. Čencov, N.: Statistical Decision Rules and Optimal Inference. Amer. Math. Soc. (1982)

13. Montúfar, G., Rauh, J., Ay, N.: On the fisher metric of conditional probability polytopes. Entropy **16**(6), 3207–3233 (2014)
14. Losert, V., Alin, E.: Dynamics of games and genes: discrete versus continuous time. J. Math. Biol. **17**(2), 241–251 (1983)
15. Rudin, L.I., Osher, S., Fatemi, E.: Nonlinear total variation based noise removal algorithms. Phys. D **60**(1–4), 259–268 (1992)
16. Andres, B., Beier, T., Kappes, J.: OpenGM: A C++ library for discrete graphical models. CoRR abs/1206.0111 (2012)
17. Kolmogorov, V.: Convergent tree-reweighted message passing for energy minimization. IEEE Trans. Pattern Anal. Mach. Intell. **28**(10), 1568–1583 (2006)
18. Szeliski, R., Zabih, R., Scharstein, D., Veksler, O., Kolmogorov, V., Agarwala, A., Tappen, M., Rother, C.: A comparative study of energy minimization methods for markov random fields with smoothness-based priors. IEEE Trans. Pattern Anal. Mach. Intell. **30**(6), 1068–1080 (2008)
19. Boykov, Y., Veksler, O., Zabih, R.: Fast approximate energy minimization via graph cuts. IEEE Trans. Pattern Anal. Mach. Intell. **23**(11), 1222–1239 (2001)
20. Kolmogorov, V., Zabin, R.: What energy functions can be minimized via graph cuts? IEEE PAMI **26**(2), 147–159 (2004)
21. Komodakis, N., Tziritas, G.: Approximate labeling via graph cuts based on linear programming. IEEE Trans. Pattern Anal. Mach. Intell. **29**(8), 1436–1453 (2007)

ActionSnapping: Motion-Based Video Synchronization

Jean-Charles Bazin$^{(\boxtimes)}$ and Alexander Sorkine-Hornung

Disney Research, Zurich, Switzerland
{jean-charles.bazin,alexander}@disneyresearch.com

Abstract. Video synchronization is a fundamental step for many applications in computer vision, ranging from video morphing to motion analysis. We present a novel method for synchronizing action videos where a similar action is performed by different people at different times and different locations with different local speed changes, e.g., as in sports like weightlifting, baseball pitch, or dance. Our approach extends the popular "snapping" tool of video editing software and allows users to automatically snap action videos together in a timeline based on their content. Since the action can take place at different locations, existing appearance-based methods are not appropriate. Our approach leverages motion information, and computes a nonlinear synchronization of the input videos to establish frame-to-frame temporal correspondences. We demonstrate our approach can be applied for video synchronization, video annotation, and action snapshots. Our approach has been successfully evaluated with ground truth data and a user study.

1 Introduction

Video synchronization aims to temporally align a set of input videos. It is at the core of a wide range of applications such as 3D reconstruction from multiple cameras [20], video morphing [27], facial performance manipulation [6,10], and spatial compositing [44]. When several cameras are simultaneously used to acquire multiple viewpoint shots of a scene, synchronization can be trivially achieved using timecode information or camera triggers. However this approach is usually only available in professional settings. Alternatively, videos can be synchronized by computing a (fixed) time offset from the recorded audio signals [20]. The videos can also be synchronized by manual alignment, for example by finding video frame correspondences and computing the required time offset. These techniques can be extended to also finding a (fixed) speed factor (linear synchronization), for example when using cameras recording at different frame rates. However, the required manual alignment is usually tedious and time consuming: using video editing software, the user needs to manually drag the videos in the timelines in such a way that the frame correspondences are temporally aligned. The popular "snapping" tool can help the user align videos at pre-specified markers (e.g., frame correspondences) but these markers need to be provided manually and the synchronization is limited to a global time offset.

© Springer International Publishing AG 2016
B. Leibe et al. (Eds.): ECCV 2016, Part V, LNCS 9909, pp. 155–169, 2016.
DOI: 10.1007/978-3-319-46454-1_10

Some techniques have been proposed to automatically compute the synchronization, for example using appearance information such as SIFT features [44]. These methods are appropriate to synchronize videos showing the same scene.

In contrast, our goal is to synchronize videos of a similar action performed by different people at different times and locations (see Fig. 1), i.e., with different appearances. Examples of application include video manipulation [6], sport video analysis (e.g., to compare athletes' performances), video morphing [27] and action recognition. Our approach enhances the "snapping" tool of video editing software and allows the user to automatically snap action videos together in a timeline based on their content. Some methods are dedicated to particular setups (e.g., facial performance [6]) or using other data (e.g., skeleton data from a Kinect [44]). Instead, our approach can be applied to general actions and does not rely on appearance information but rather leverages motion information. We obtain motion information from the input videos by taking advantage of the recent work on dense trajectory extraction [43]. Given a set of input videos, our approach computes a nonlinear synchronization path in a frame-to-frame motion similarity matrix that can handle local speed variations of the recorded actions. This synchronization path can then be used to create a synchronized version of the input videos where the action occurs at the same time in both videos.

Our contributions are the following. First, we propose a novel algorithm that allows the nonlinear synchronization of videos of a similar action performed by different people at different times and different locations. Our approach uses point trajectories [43], does not require challenging silhouette or skeleton extraction, and runs in a fully automatic manner. Second, we develop a multi-temporal scale method to deal with videos of large speed differences. Third, we show the applications of our method for different tasks, including video synchronization, video annotation and action snapshots. Finally, we demonstrate the validity of our approach with qualitative and quantitative evaluation.

Fig. 1. Given a set of input videos of a similar action (here, snake arms dance in (a) and (b)) performed by different people at different times and different locations, our approach automatically computes a nonlinear synchronization of these videos from motion cues. Our synchronization results are shown overlaid in (c). While the appearance of the scenes looks very different, our approach successfully manages to synchronize the snake arms in (c).

2   Related Work

Our work is related to synchronization, temporal ordering and temporal correspondences. Below we discuss the most related methods in these areas.

Simultaneous acquisition. When a scene is simultaneously captured by several cameras, camera triggers can be used to start the acquisition of all the cameras at the same time, and therefore the captured videos are directly synchronized. In the absence of camera triggers, the cameras might start the acquisition at different times. In such case, typical synchronization solutions are limited to a fixed temporal offset, or a fixed speed scalar for cameras recording at different frame rates. If the acquisition time of the cameras is stored with synchronized timecode, then the time offset can be easily obtained by the time difference of the timecodes. However, such hardware is usually only available in professional settings. An alternative for casual use cases is to use the recorded audio and compute the time offset that temporally aligns the audio signals, for example for 3D reconstruction from multiple cameras [4, 20].

In our case, actions are performed at different time instances, e.g., by different people and/or at different places. Therefore these videos cannot be captured simultaneously. As a consequence, camera triggers, timecode information and audio signals cannot be used for synchronization. Moreover, such actions cannot be related by a fixed temporal linear relation, i.e., fixed temporal offset and fixed global speed factor, as the local speed might vary along the action. To cope with the local speed change variation, we need to perform a nonlinear synchronization.

Video-based synchronization. Some techniques exist for synchronizing video sequences acquired at different time instances [9, 11, 13, 33, 44]. However, these methods estimate temporal correspondences from appearance-based descriptors such as SIFT. Therefore they work best with camera ego-motion and large-scale scene changes. While these assumptions are reasonable for videos recorded at the same location, they cannot cope with actions performed at different locations with different appearances and/or cannot capture the subtle change of motion since the global appearance might be the same. Note also that some of these methods, such as [9], search for a temporal linear relation which cannot deal with local speed variations.

To represent the status of an action in each video frame, silhouette information is one of the possible options, as for example used by Zhou and De la Torre [49, 50] for human action synchronization, and by Xu et al. [46] for animating animal motion from still images. However, in practice, extracting the silhouette in an automatic way is a challenging task. For example it could be performed by background subtraction [49, 50], but this requires a foreground-background model and/or a clean plate in a controlled environment. An alternative is manual segmentation [46], for example with GrabCut [32], which can be time consuming. Instead we aim for an automatic approach.

Another technique to represent the status of an action is to extract the human body pose and skeleton, for example from a single image [42, 48], video [15, 40] or depth data [18,37]. However despite the recent advances, retrieving an accurate skeleton from a monocular video is still ongoing research due to the difficulty and ambiguity of the task as well as the large variation of human poses. Moreover, while using skeleton information would be appropriate for human actions, we aim for a general method without any priors on shapes, poses and actions, i.e., a method that can be applied on actions of humans and non-humans for example.

Shechtman et al. [35] present a descriptor which captures internal geometric layouts of local self-similarities within images. By applying this technique in space-time, they can detect segments of similar actions in videos. In contrast, our goal is to compute a dense frame-to-frame temporal alignment. In the context of video morphing, Liao et al. [28] establish temporal correspondences between videos using manually given point correspondences. In contrast, we aim for a fully automatic method.

Some existing methods are dedicated to the synchronization of facial performance videos. They are based on facial landmarks [6,10] or the expression coefficients of a morphable face model [47]. While these methods have demonstrated impressive results, they are specifically designed for facial performances.

Additional modalities. Additional modalities can also be used to facilitate the synchronization of actions. For example, Hsu et al. [21] use human motion capture data acquired in a motion capture lab. Zhou and De la Torre [49,50] can align different subjects with different sensors such as video, motion capture and accelerometers. In contrast, our only input data is a set of monocular videos.

Image sequence ordering. Synchronization can also be seen as temporal ordering of a collection of images. Given a set of pictures of a dynamic scene acquired roughly from the same viewpoint and location, Basha et al. [5] compute a temporal order of these pictures using point correspondences. In contrast, we aim for synchronizing videos of actions performed by different people and at different locations.

Images or video frames can also be re-ordered to create new visual contents. For example Bregler et al. [8] re-order mouth sequences from training data to generate a new video sequence according to a given audio track. Kemelmacher-Shlizerman et al. [23] puppeteer a person by finding relevant images from a large image database of the same person and spatially aligning them. Garrido et al. [17] generalize this technique for face reenactment from video sources. Averbuch-Elor et al. [3] compute a spatial ordering (i.e., relative position) of photos of a temporal event. They assume a nearly instantaneous event, such as a particular time instance of a performance. In contrast to these applications, our goal is to synchronize videos, that is establishing dense frame-to-frame temporal correspondences between the input videos.

Action recognition. Since we are working on videos of actions, our work is in part related to the literature of action recognition. Reviewing works of this active research area is beyond the scope of this paper, and we refer the readers to survey papers [1,31]. In contrast to methods for action recognition, our goal is not to explicitly recognize or classify actions. We assume our input videos represent a similar but arbitrary action and we aim to temporally align these videos. The existing methods for action recognition could be applied in pre-processing in order to automatically identify videos of the same action among a large video collection that can then be processed by our method.

3 Overview of Our Approach

Our goal is to synchronize action videos, that is establishing temporal correspondences between the frames of the action videos. Our synchronization algorithm consists of the following three main steps. First, for each input video, we extract motion information of the action by taking advantage of the recent work on dense trajectory extraction [43]. The motion is obtained in the form of point trajectories by tracking and we then represent these trajectories by multi-temporal scale motion descriptors. Secondly, the difference of motions between each pair of frames of the input videos is computed and stored in a cost matrix. Finally, we obtain a nonlinear synchronization path as the lowest-cost path in this cost matrix. Given two input videos, the synchronization path indicates which frame of a video corresponds to which frame of the other video.

Many of the references cited above also compute synchronization as a low cost path [6,44], or by related techniques like dynamic time warping [10,49,50]. However, as discussed, their features (e.g., silhouette, appearance and facial coefficients) are not applicable for our general video settings (background, pose, humans, animals) with different appearances [44] (e.g., see background of Fig. 1) and might require manual segmentation [46]. In contrast, we use general motion features based on point trajectories and apply a multi-temporal scale approach, which allow us to automatically and robustly synchronize general videos of similar action performed by different people at different locations, even with different appearances and speeds.

4 Proposed Approach

Our input is a set of videos showing a similar action. One of these videos is considered the reference video, and the goal is to synchronize the other videos to this reference video. Without lack of generality, we consider two input videos. In the case of multiple input videos, each video is independently synchronized to the reference video.

Let v_1 and v_2 be two input videos, and $v_i(j)$ be the j-th frame of video v_i. Formally, the synchronization is defined as a mapping $p : \mathbb{R} \to \mathbb{R}^2$, where $p(t) = (p_1(t), p_2(t))$ associates a global time t with two corresponding video frames $v_1(p_1(t))$ and $v_2(p_2(t))$. As discussed, a linear time mapping is not applicable for our videos due to the local speed change variations. Instead we are searching for a nonlinear temporal mapping that we compute as the low cost path in a cost matrix using Dijkstra's algorithm [12]. In the following, we describe the details of our algorithm.

4.1   Features

Point trajectories. Several techniques to extract and represent motion information from videos have been proposed, especially for camera motion estimation and action recognition. Some of the most popular options include KLT [36], optical flow [7,22], STIP [25] and SIFT flow [30], among many others. We opted for the dense point trajectory extraction technique of Wang et al. [43] since they demonstrated superior results for action recognition. Other point trajectories like [34] could also be used.

Wang et al. sample feature points on a grid spaced by 5 pixels, and each point is tracked to the next frame by median filtering on a dense optical flow field [14]. The camera motion is computed by homography and RANSAC [19], and canceled out from the optical flow. The point tracks consistent with the homography are considered as due to the camera motion and thus removed. We compensate the positions of the remaining tracks by the camera motion, such that these tracks correspond to the actual motion of the action even for videos acquired by hand-held cameras. To avoid tracking drifting, we track points only over $L = 30$ frames. Given a starting frame at time t, the point $P_t = (x_t, y_t)$ is tracked over the next L frames, and the resulting trajectory is composed of the points $(P_t, P_{t+1}, \ldots, P_L)$. Representative examples of trajectories are shown in Fig. 2.

Fig. 2. Representative examples of point trajectories for our video synchronization approach. For a better visualization, only a subset of the trajectories is displayed.

Trajectory representation. To compare the trajectories, we need an appropriate representation. Given a trajectory, a simple concatenation of the points positions would be sensitive to the location of the action in the image. To be location invariant, we instead use the displacement vectors, i.e., the change of x and y coordinates. We obtain a trajectory representation $S = (\Delta P_t, \ldots, \Delta P_{t+L-1})$ where $\Delta P_t = (x_{t+1} - x_t, y_{t+1} - y_t)$. Finally we normalize the trajectory representation vector by its norm. This normalization permits to handle videos where the action is performed at different distances from the camera and videos with different amounts of zoom.

This approach provides satisfying results when the speed of the actions is not too different, typically up to 1.5 times. Beyond this speed ratio, the descriptors of a same trajectory motion but executed at different speeds would be too different to still have a meaningful correlation. To deal with videos where action is performed at different speeds (in our case up to 10 times), we use a multiple temporal scale approach. For efficiency reason, we do not re-track trajectories over different temporal windows. Instead, we use the trajectories already tracked and compute their multi-temporal scale representation. Concretely, given a trajectory tracked over L frames, we consider the point at mid-time, and compute the trajectory descriptors S over different temporal windows $W = (3, \ldots, 30)$ centered at that mid-time. We write the multi-temporal descriptors of the trajectory as $(S_3, \ldots, S_{30})$.

To handle speed ratios above 10 times, two options could be envisaged. First, a shorter temporal window could be used but the information might get unreliable. Second, points could be tracked over more frames. In practice, capping the speed ratio to 10 worked correctly for all the videos we tested.

4.2   Synchronization

Frame motion representation. From the previous steps, we have the set of trajectories of the input videos and their descriptors. We now would like to represent the motion present in each frame of the input videos from these trajectories. This motion representation will then be used to compare the motion between two different frames of the input videos. First of all, we consider a trajectory is "T-visible" in a frame $v_i(t)$ if at least a part of this trajectory is continuously tracked between $t - T/2$ and $t + T/2$ in v_i. To represent the motion of each video frame, we apply a bag-of-features approach [26]. For this, we first compute a codebook of all the trajectory descriptors of the input videos. To compute the vocabulary words, we apply k-means, with $k = 100$ by default, and for efficiency reason, we run it on a subset of $50,000$ randomly selected trajectories. Then given a frame $v_i(t)$, we collect all the trajectories that are T-visible in that frame. Each of these trajectories is assigned to its closest vocabulary word. By doing so for all the trajectories of $v_i(t)$, we obtain a histogram of word occurrences that we use as a motion descriptor of the frame $v_i(t)$. We note $h_i^T(t)$ the resulting histogram of frame $v_i(t)$ over a temporal window T. By applying this procedure for each temporal window $T \in W$, we obtain a multi-temporal descriptor of the motion of the frame $v_i(t)$.

Motion comparison. We now use the above motion representation to compare the motion between two frames. First, since different frames and different videos might have a different number of trajectories, the number of entries in the histogram bins might vary, and therefore it is needed to normalize the histograms. For normalization, we apply RootSIFT [2].

We compare the motions of two frames of the input video pair by measuring the distance $d()$ between their histograms using χ^2 distance [41]. For the multi-temporal histograms, we conduct a temporal scale selection. Concretely, given the multi-temporal histogram of frames $v_1(t)$ and $v_2(t')$, respectively the multiple $h_1^T(t)$ and $h_2^T(t')$ with each $T \in W$, we select the temporal scale pair (T, T') leading to the lowest histogram distance:

$$c(t, t') = \min_{(T,T') \in W \times W} d(h_1^T(t), h_2^{T'}(t')). \tag{1}$$

The cost $c(t, t')$ represents the cost of the motion difference between the frames $v_1(t)$ and $v_2(t')$, taking into account potential speed differences.

Cost matrix and synchronization path. We compute the costs $c(t, t')$ for each pair of frames $v_1(t)$ and $v_2(t')$ and store them in a 2D cost matrix C of size $N_1 \times N_2$ where N_i refers to the number of frames of video v_i. Representative results of cost matrices computed by our approach are shown in Fig. 3.

Finally, given the cost matrix C, we compute the synchronization path as the lowest cost path in C using Dijkstra's algorithm [12], see the white paths in Fig. 3. This synchronization path p is a nonlinear mapping that establishes frame-to-frame temporal correspondences between the two videos v_1 and v_2. Therefore, by navigating along the path, we can create synchronized versions of the input videos.

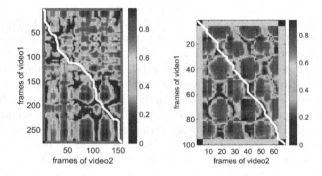

Fig. 3. Representative examples of the computed cost matrix and the low cost nonlinear synchronization path shown in white. The matrix on the left corresponds to a high kick, and the matrix on the right to repetitive bench press motions.

5   Experiments

5.1   Implementation Details

We processed the videos on a desktop computer equipped with an Intel i7 3.2 GHz and 16 GB RAM. The main program is implemented in Matlab and uses some C++ modules for optical flow and point tracking. Given the trajectories [43] obtained in preprocessing, the total execution time (motion descriptors, multi-temporal scale representation, scale selection and path computation) takes around 2–5 min for a pair of typical 20 s full HD videos, depending on the number of trajectories. The entire synchronization pipeline runs in a fully automatic manner, and the synchronized versions of the videos are also generated automatically.

5.2   Results

In the following we show some representative results obtained by our approach. We kindly invite the readers to refer to our project webpage[1] for the full video results, comparisons and additional results. We apply our approach on various videos, for example from the publicly available UCF101 dataset [38] as well as videos that we captured ourselves. A nonlinear synchronization path is computed from the motion cost matrix. This synchronization path is then used to establish temporal correspondences of video frames. Figure 4 shows some examples of synchronized frames obtained from the cost matrix and synchronization path shown in Fig. 3-right.

Fig. 4. Examples of frame synchronization obtained by our approach from the cost matrix and the nonlinear synchronization path of Fig. 3-right. One can observe that the barbell is at the same position in the synchronized frames, which indicates that the synchronization result is correct.

Our approach can be applied on multiple input videos. One of these videos is considered the reference video, and the other videos are then synchronized with respect to this reference video. Figure 5 shows a representative synchronization result of multiple input videos of the weightlifting exercise called *clean and jerk*. Our method can be seamlessly applied to scenes of similar (rows 1 and 2) and different appearances (rows 1, 3 and 4). For example, one can note how the backgrounds, athletes morphologies and clothes look different. Moreover the videos at rows 3 and 4 are acquired by a hand-held camera and thus contain camera motion. The videos at rows 1 and 2 contain tilt and zoom changes. The video at row 4 contains overlayed text (see "140k" in the second column). Despite these challenges, our approach successfully manages to synchronize these videos.

In addition to synchronization, we show that our method can be applied for video labelling. Here we manually annotated the steps of the clean and jerk in the reference video (see text in gray boxes at row 1 of Fig. 5). Thanks to our

---

[1] http://www.disneyresearch.com/publication/ActionSnapping.

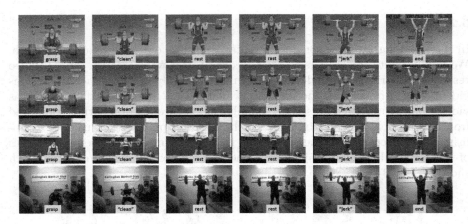

Fig. 5. Automatic synchronization of multiple input videos showing the weightlifting exercise called *clean and jerk*. Our synchronization result can then be used for automatic label propagation for video annotation (see text in gray boxes).

synchronization path, we know which frame of the reference video corresponds to which frame of each other video. Therefore the labels can be automatically propagated from the reference video to the other videos (see gray boxes at rows 2, 3 and 4). Labelling of every single frame of the videos could be achieved manually, but it would be tedious and time consuming, especially for a large set of videos. An alternative strategy could be to explicitly detect the different steps of an action in the context of action recognition [1, 31], for example using machine learning techniques and a large training dataset composed of numerous videos with manual annotations. In contrast, our approach only needs one labelled video and then automatically propagates the labels to the other videos.

5.3   Action Snapshots

Our video synchronization approach allows the creation of action snapshots. In contrast to methods using a single video [24, 39], we can generate action snapshots from different videos of different people by simply sampling the frames of the synchronized videos. It is also possible to choose the number of frames of each input video. A result from 7 input videos using 1 frame per video is shown in Fig. 6.

Fig. 6. Action snapshots of a baseball pitch from 7 input videos of different people.

5.4   Interaction

Our method aims to synchronize the motion visible in the video. If several motions are visible, then we allow the user to specify which motions or which part of the video he/she wants to synchronize in an interactive and intuitive manner, by simply painting over the action of interest. For example, in Fig. 1, the professional dancer had a hip motion that the beginner dancer did not replicate. To indicate that the arms motions should be used for synchronization and not the hip motion, the user can simply draw one rough rectangle over the location of the arms.

5.5   Evaluation

Comparison to ground truth. To evaluate the accuracy of our synchronization path, we create pairs of videos with ground truth speed difference. Given a video, we create its sped up version. To avoid introducing in-between frame interpolation artifacts, we consider high frame rate videos and create sped up versions by simply skipping frames. If the speed is k times faster, then the ground truth synchronization path should be a line of slope k. We do not constrain the computation of our synchronization path to be a straight line. We compare the ground truth path and our computed path as follows: for each point on our path, we measure the distance to the nearest point on the ground truth path. We apply this procedure on 5 different high frame rate videos acquired by a GoPro camera. For each of them, we generate the video versions with a speed up of each $k \in (1, \ldots, 10)$, and compute the path distance. A comparison of the computed path and the ground truth path for one video pair is shown in Fig. 7. The average error is slightly below 3 frames and the maximum error is 15 frames. While this value might sound relatively high, it has to be noted that the computed path has a "feasibility range". For example, in the extreme case where the input videos have no motion at all, then any synchronization path would lead to visually perfect results. To study this further, we conducted a user study.

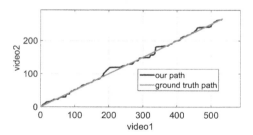

Fig. 7. Evaluation: comparison of our synchronization path to the ground truth path.

User study. We conducted a user study on the results obtained by our synchronization approach on pairs of videos from the UCF101 dataset [38]. We did not consider videos with camera cuts and extreme view point differences (e.g., front vs. side views). Examples of categories include baseball pitch, bench press, and clean and jerk. Instead of conducting the user study on the videos themselves, we conducted it on a set of frames uniformly sampled from each video pair. The key advantage is that it provides a fine measurement at the frame level. 12 people participated and we tested 15 pairs of videos with 10 uniformly sampled frames per video pair, which represents a total of 1800 votes. The participants were asked to respond to the statement "This pair of images corresponds to the same time instance along the course of the action" by choosing a response from a five-point Likert scale: strongly agree (5), agree (4), neither agree not disagree (3), disagree (2) or strongly disagree (1).

The distribution of the scores is available in Fig. 8. The participants strongly agreed in 66.1 % of the experiments, and a total of 87.2 % had a score equal to or higher than 4 (agree). This demonstrates our approach can achieve an accurate frame-to-frame temporal correspondence.

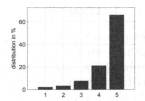

Fig. 8. Distribution of the grades of the user study.

Examples of image pairs with a low score are shown in Fig. 9. In Fig. 9(a), the temporal misalignment is small (around 5 frames, i.e., 0.2 s) but still visible because the baseball pitch of the professional athlete on the right was particularly fast and the video is recorded at 25 fps. A participant graded Fig. 9(b) with 1 because "the athlete on the left is pulling up the bar, while the athlete on the right seems to be at rest". Our method did not manage to synchronize Fig. 9(c) because the motions are horizontally symmetric: the left player threw the ball to the left, while the right player threw the ball to the right. We tested this hypothesis by mirroring one of the videos, and obtained a successful synchronization.

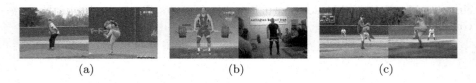

| (a) | (b) | (c) |

Fig. 9. Examples of three image pairs with a low score from the user study.

5.6   Limitations

Our approach computes a continuous synchronization path. Therefore it cannot deal with actions performed in a different order, for example walking then jumping in a video, and jumping then walking in another video. This use case would require a method that allows the computation of a non-continuous path, for example reshuffling of video segments.

While our approach has been shown to be effective, it still depends on the availability of reliable motion information. Difficult cases where tracking is unreliable include fast motion, highly blurred images, and uniform textures.

In the case of hand-held cameras, the current implementation compensates the camera motion from the extracted flow information with a homography model, which assumes the background scene is rather planar or relatively far away. For general scenes, more sophisticated camera motion estimation techniques should be employed [45].

In some particular cases, one of the videos might need to be paused for a long duration. For example, in some clean and jerk sequences (see supplementary material), the athlete of the reference video is at rest for a relatively long time before the final push up, while the athlete of the second video completes the full motion quickly. Therefore this second video needs to be paused over the rest duration. While this is not an issue for many applications (such as motion analysis, morphing and video annotation), this pause artifact needs to be avoided for generating realistic retimed videos. An interesting research direction is how to "pause" a video without a freezing effect, for example by adding artificial movement [16] or with optimized frame looping [29].

6   Conclusion

We have presented a novel approach for synchronizing videos of a similar action performed by different people at different times and different locations. Our approach computes a nonlinear synchronization path between the input videos using motion information. Our multi-temporal scale technique allows to handle videos with large speed differences. Our method is general: since it does not assume any priors on motions, shapes or poses, it can be applied to a wide range of videos with cluttered backgrounds, various actions as well as continuous and repetitive motions. Qualitative and quantitative evaluations demonstrated the validity of our approach.

Our approach runs in a fully automatic manner and obtains satisfying results on different kinds of videos. Therefore we believe it will facilitate and enable several applications that can benefit from video synchronization but currently require tedious manual synchronization, such as video morphing, video analysis and video annotation.

Acknowledgements. We are very grateful to World Dance New York for giving us the permission to use their YouTube videos.

References

1. Aggarwal, J.K., Ryoo, M.S.: Human activity analysis: a review. ACM Comput. Surv. **43**, 16 (2011)
2. Arandjelovic, R., Zisserman, A.: Three things everyone should know to improve object retrieval. In: CVPR (2012)
3. Averbuch-Elor, H., Cohen-Or, D.: RingIt: ring-ordering casual photos of a temporal event. TOG **34**, 33 (2015)

4. Ballan, L., Brostow, G.J., Puwein, J., Pollefeys, M.: Unstructured video-based rendering: interactive exploration of casually captured videos. TOG (SIGGRAPH) **29**, 87 (2010)
5. Basha, T.D., Moses, Y., Avidan, S.: Photo sequencing. IJCV **110**(3), 275–289 (2014)
6. Bazin, J.C., Malleson, C., Wang, O., Bradley, D., Beeler, T., Hilton, A., Sorkine-Hornung, A.: FaceDirector: continuous control of facial performance in video. In: ICCV (2015)
7. Beauchemin, S.S., Barron, J.L.: The computation of optical flow. ACM Comput. Surv. **27**, 433–466 (1995)
8. Bregler, C., Covell, M., Slaney, M.: Video rewrite: driving visual speech with audio. In: SIGGRAPH (1997)
9. Caspi, Y., Irani, M.: Spatio-temporal alignment of sequences. TPAMI **24**, 1409–1424 (2002)
10. Dale, K., Sunkavalli, K., Johnson, M.K., Vlasic, D., Matusik, W., Pfister, H.: Video face replacement. TOG (SIGGRAPH Asia) **30**(6) (2011)
11. Diego, F., Serrat, J., López, A.M.: Joint spatio-temporal alignment of sequences. Trans. Multimedia **15**, 1377–1387 (2013)
12. Dijkstra, E.W.: A note on two problems in connexion with graphs. Numer. Math. **1**, 269–271 (1959)
13. Evangelidis, G.D., Bauckhage, C.: Efficient subframe video alignment using short descriptors. TPAMI **35**, 2371–2386 (2013)
14. Farnebäck, G.: Two-frame motion estimation based on polynomial expansion. In: Scandinavian Conference on Image Analysis (2003)
15. Fossati, A., Dimitrijevic, M., Lepetit, V., Fua, P.: From canonical poses to 3D motion capture using a single camera. TPAMI **32**, 1165–1181 (2010)
16. Freeman, W.T., Adelson, E.H., Heeger, D.J.: Motion without movement. In: SIGGRAPH (1991)
17. Garrido, P., Valgaerts, L., Rehmsen, O., Thormaehlen, T., Perez, P., Theobalt, C.: Automatic face reenactment. In: CVPR (2014)
18. Girshick, R.B., Shotton, J., Kohli, P., Criminisi, A., Fitzgibbon, A.W.: Efficient regression of general-activity human poses from depth images. In: ICCV (2011)
19. Hartley, R.I., Zisserman, A.: Multiple View Geometry in Computer Vision. Cambridge University Press, Cambridge (2004)
20. Hasler, N., Rosenhahn, B., Thormählen, T., Wand, M., Gall, J., Seidel, H.: Markerless motion capture with unsynchronized moving cameras. In: CVPR (2009)
21. Hsu, E., Pulli, K., Popovic, J.: Style translation for human motion. TOG (SIGGRAPH) **24**, 1082–1089 (2005)
22. Jain, M., Jegou, H., Bouthemy, P.: Better exploiting motion for better action recognition. In: CVPR (2013)
23. Kemelmacher-Shlizerman, I., Sankar, A., Shechtman, E., Seitz, S.M.: Being John Malkovich. In: ECCV (2010)
24. Klose, F., Wang, O., Bazin, J.C., Magnor, M.A., Sorkine-Hornung, A.: Sampling based scene-space video processing. TOG (SIGGRAPH) **34**, 67 (2015)
25. Laptev, I.: On space-time interest points. IJCV **64**, 107–123 (2005)
26. Li, F., Perona, P.: A bayesian hierarchical model for learning natural scene categories. In: CVPR (2005)
27. Liao, J., Lima, R.S., Nehab, D., Hoppe, H., Sander, P.V.: Semi-automated video morphing. In: CGF (Eurographics Symposium on Rendering) (2014)
28. Liao, J., Lima, R.S., Nehab, D., Hoppe, H., Sander, P.V., Yu, J.: Automating image morphing using structural similarity on a halfway domain. TOG **33**, 168 (2014)

29. Liao, Z., Joshi, N., Hoppe, H.: Automated video looping with progressive dynamism. TOG (SIGGRAPH) **32**, 4 (2013)
30. Liu, C., Yuen, J., Torralba, A.: SIFT flow: dense correspondence across scenes and its applications. TPAMI (2011)
31. Poppe, R.: A survey on vision-based human action recognition. Image Vis. Comput. **28**, 976–990 (2010)
32. Rother, C., Kolmogorov, V., Blake, A.: "GrabCut": interactive foreground extraction using iterated graph cuts. TOG (SIGGRAPH) **23**, 309–314 (2004)
33. Sand, P., Teller, S.J.: Video matching. TOG (SIGGRAPH) **23**(3), 592–599 (2004)
34. Sand, P., Teller, S.J.: Particle video: Long-range motion estimation using point trajectories. IJCV **80**, 72–91 (2008)
35. Shechtman, E., Irani, M.: Matching local self-similarities across images and videos. In: CVPR (2007)
36. Shi, J., Tomasi, C.: Good features to track. In: CVPR (1994)
37. Shotton, J., Fitzgibbon, A.W., Cook, M., Sharp, T., Finocchio, M., Moore, R., Kipman, A., Blake, A.: Real-time human pose recognition in parts from single depth images. In: CVPR (2011)
38. Soomro, K., Zamir, A.R., Shah, M.: UCF101: A dataset of 101 human actions classes from videos in the wild. Technical Report CRCV-TR-12-01 (2012)
39. Sunkavalli, K., Joshi, N., Kang, S.B., Cohen, M.F., Pfister, H.: Video snapshots: creating high-quality images from video clips. TVCG **18**, 1868–1879 (2012)
40. Urtasun, R., Fleet, D.J., Fua, P.: Temporal motion models for monocular and multiview 3D human body tracking. CVIU **104**, 157–177 (2006)
41. Vedaldi, A., Zisserman, A.: Efficient additive kernels via explicit feature maps. TPAMI **34**, 480–492 (2012)
42. Wang, C., Wang, Y., Lin, Z., Yuille, A.L., Gao, W.: Robust estimation of 3D human poses from a single image. In: CVPR (2014)
43. Wang, H., Schmid, C.: Action recognition with improved trajectories. In: ICCV (2013)
44. Wang, O., Schroers, C., Zimmer, H., Gross, M., Sorkine-Hornung, A.: VideoSnapping: interactive synchronization of multiple videos. TOG (SIGGRAPH) **33**, 77 (2014)
45. Wu, C.: Towards linear-time incremental structure from motion. In: International Conference on 3D Vision (3DV) (2013)
46. Xu, X., Wan, L., Liu, X., Wong, T., Wang, L., Leung, C.: Animating animal motion from still. TOG (SIGGRAPH Asia) **27**, 117 (2008)
47. Yang, F., Bourdev, L.D., Shechtman, E., Wang, J., Metaxas, D.N.: Facial expression editing in video using a temporally-smooth factorization. In: CVPR (2012)
48. Yang, Y., Ramanan, D.: Articulated human detection with flexible mixtures of parts. TPAMI **35**, 2878–2890 (2013)
49. Zhou, F., De la Torre, F.: Canonical time warping for alignment of human behavior. In: NIPS (2009)
50. Zhou, F., De la Torre, F.: Generalized time warping for multi-modal alignment of human motion. In: CVPR (2012)

A Minimal Solution for Non-perspective Pose Estimation from Line Correspondences

Gim Hee Lee$^{(\boxtimes)}$

National University of Singapore, Singapore, Singapore
gimhee.lee@nus.edu.sg

Abstract. In this paper, we study and propose solutions to the relatively un-investigated non-perspective pose estimation problem from line correspondences. Specifically, we represent the 2D and 3D line correspondences as Plücker lines and derive the minimal solution for the minimal problem of three line correspondences with Gröbner basis. Our minimal 3-Line algorithm that gives up to eight solutions is well-suited for robust estimation with RANSAC. We show that our algorithm works as a least-squares that takes in more than three line correspondences without any reformulation. In addition, our algorithm does not require initialization in both the minimal 3-Line and least-squares n-Line cases. Furthermore, our algorithm works without a need for reformulation under the special case of perspective pose estimation when all line correspondences are observed from one single camera. We verify our algorithms with both simulated and real-world data.

Keywords: Pose estimation · Plücker lines · Non-perspective · Gröbner basis · Line correspondences

1 Introduction

Pose estimation is a well-known problem in Computer Vision. It refers to the problem of finding the rigid transformation between a camera frame and a fixed world frame, given a set of 3D structures expressed in the world frame, and its corresponding 2D projections on the camera image. The 2D image projection to 3D structure correspondences can be either points or lines, or less commonly a combination of both. A minimum of three 2D-3D correspondences is needed to solve for the camera pose. Solutions to the pose estimation problem have significant importance in many real-world applications such as robotics localization, visual Simultaneous Localization and Mapping (vSLAM)/Structure-from-Motion (SfM), and augmented reality etc.

The pose estimation problem for a single camera from point or line correspondences is a very well-studied problem, and a huge literature of robust and efficient solutions had been proposed [2,6,9,20,21,23,24,28] since the 1850s. This problem is also commonly known as the perspective pose estimation problem. In the recent years, due to the increasing popularity of multi-camera systems

© Springer International Publishing AG 2016
B. Leibe et al. (Eds.): ECCV 2016, Part V, LNCS 9909, pp. 170–185, 2016.
DOI: 10.1007/978-3-319-46454-1_11

for robotics applications such as self-driving cars [7,15,16,19] and Micro-Aerial Vehicles [10,11], many researchers turned their attentions to the so-called non-perspective pose estimation problem [4,13,17,18,22] from point correspondences. The main difference between the perspective and non-perspective pose estimation problem is that for the latter, light rays casted from the 3D points do not meet at a single point, i.e. there is no single camera center. Consequently, many new algorithms [4,13,17,18,22] for the non-perspective pose estimation problem from point correspondences were proposed.

Despite the fact that the perspective pose estimation problem from point and line correspondences, and non-perspective pose estimation problem from point correspondences are well-studied, the non-perspective pose estimation problem from line correspondences remains relatively un-investigated. The increasingly wide-spread of multi-camera applications, availability of 3D models from line reconstructions [12], and line detector/descriptor algorithms [8,27] made the non-perspective pose estimation problem from line correspondences imperatively relevant.

In this paper, we study and propose solutions to the non-perspective pose estimation problem from line correspondences. Specifically, we represent the 2D and 3D line correspondences as Plücker lines and derive the minimal solution for the minimal problem of three line correspondences with Gröbner basis. Our minimal 3-Line algorithm that gives up to eight solutions is well-suited for robust estimation with RANSAC [1]. We show that our algorithm works as a least-squares that takes in more than three line correspondences without any reformulation. In addition, our algorithm does not require initialization in both the minimal 3-Line and least-squares n-Line cases. Furthermore, our algorithm works without a need for reformulation under the special case of perspective pose estimation when all line correspondences are observed from one single camera. We verify our algorithms with both simulated and real-world data.

2   Related Works

It was mentioned in the previous section that to the best of our knowledge no prior work on the non-perspective pose estimation problem from line correspondences exist. Nonetheless, we will discuss some of the relevant existing works on the perspective pose estimation problem from line correspondences in this section.

One of the earliest work on perspective pose estimation from line correspondences was presented by Dhome et al. [6]. They solve the perspective pose estimation problem as a minimal problem that uses three line correspondences. A major disadvantage of their algorithm is that it does not work with more than three line correspondence, which makes it difficult for least-squares estimation in the presence of noise. The fact that their algorithm requires a line to be collinear with the x-axis, and another line to be parallel to the xy-plane made it impossible to extend their work to the non-perspective case.

Ansar and Daniilidis [2] proposed a linear formulation for the perspective pose estimation problem from line correspondences. Their formulation works for four or more line correspondences, but an addition step of Singular Value Decomposition (SVD) is needed for the case of four line correspondences. A problem with [2] is that it resulted in a linear system of equations with 46 variables. The high number of variables compromises the accuracy of the solution [3]. We did not adopt Ansar's formulation although it is possible to extend the algorithm for the non-perspective pose estimation problem. This is because similar to the perspective case, it results in a linear system of equations with high number of variables. Moreover, the formulation is not minimal, thus not ideal for robust estimation with RANSAC [1].

More recently, Mirzaei et al. [20] proposed an algorithm for perspective pose estimation from three or more line correspondences. They formulated the problem as non-linear least-squares, and solve it as an eigenvalue problem using the Macaulay matrix without a need for initialization. The algorithm yields 27 solutions, and this makes it difficult to identify the correct solution. We do not choose Mirzaei's formulation despite the fact that it is possible to extend the algorithm for non-perspective pose estimation because of the high number of solutions.

In [28], Zhang et al. proposed an algorithm for perspective pose estimation with three or more line correspondences. In contrast to Mirzaei et al. [20], the algorithm proposed by Zhang et al. is more practical since it yields up to only eight solutions. However, the requirement to align one of the 3D lines with the z-axis of the camera frame made it impossible to extend the algorithm for non-perspective pose estimation.

The most recent work on perspective pose estimation from line correspondences is presented by Přibyl et al. [23]. They represent the 2D-3D line correspondences as, and proposed a linear algorithm that works with nine or more correspondences. Unfortunately, their algorithm uses high number of correspondences, i.e. nine or more, thus is unsuitable for RANSAC. We adopt their representation of line correspondences as Plücker lines and extend their work to non-perspective pose estimation. Furthermore, we derive the minimal solution for the 3-Line minimal problem that is suitable for RANSAC, and show that our algorithm works without a need for reformulation under the special case of perspective pose estimation when all line correspondences are observed from the same camera.

3   Problem Definition

Figure 1 shows an example of a minimal case multi-camera non-perspective pose estimation problem from line correspondences. We are given three 3D lines $L_{W_1}, L_{W_2}, L_{W_3}$ defined in a fixed world frame F_W, and its corresponding 2D image projections $l_{c_1}, l_{c_2}, l_{c_3}$ seen respectively by three cameras $F_{C_1}, F_{C_2}, F_{C_3}$. These three cameras are rigidly fixed together, and F_G is the reference frame. We made the assumption that the cameras are fully calibrated, i.e. the camera intrinsics K_i and extrinsics $T_{C_i}^G$ for $i = 1, 2, 3$ are known. Here, $T_{C_i}^G$ is the 4×4 homogeneous transformation matrix that brings a point defined in F_{C_i} to F_G. Note that in general, the minimal case for non-perspective pose estimation can

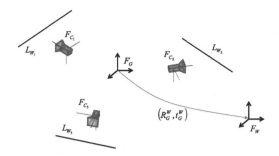

Fig. 1. An example of the non-perspective pose estimation problem from line correspondences.

be three 2D-3D line correspondences from a multi-camera system made up of either two or three cameras.

Definition 1. The non-perspective pose estimation problem seeks to find the pose of the multi-camera system with respect to the fixed world frame, i.e. relative transformation

$$T_G^W = \begin{pmatrix} R_G^W & t_G^W \\ 0_{3\times 3} & 1 \end{pmatrix} \tag{1}$$

that brings a point defined in the multi-camera reference frame F_G to the fixed world frame F_W from the 2D-3D line correspondences $L_{W_j} \leftrightarrow l_{c_j}$, where j is the line correspondence index. We refer to the problem as the Non-Perspective 3-Line (NP3L) or Non-Perspective n-Line problems (NPnL) depending on the number of 2D-3D line correspondences that are used.

4   NP3L: 3-Line Minimal Solution

We represent the 2D-3D line correspondence as a 6-vector Plücker line in our formulation for the non-perspective pose estimation problem. Let us denote $P_a^W = [P_{ax}^W \ P_{ay}^W \ P_{az}^W \ 1]^T$ and $P_b^W = [P_{bx}^W \ P_{by}^W \ P_{bz}^W \ 1]^T$ as the homogeneous coordinates expressed in the world frame F_W that represent the two end points of the 3D line segment L_W. The 6-vector Plücker line of the 3D line segment is given by $L_W = [U_W^T \ V_W^T]^T$, where

$$V_W = \frac{P_b^W - P_a^W}{\|P_b^W - P_a^W\|}, \quad U_W = P_a^W \times V_W. \tag{2}$$

Geometrically, V_W is the unit direction vector of the 3D line segment, and U_W is the vector that represents the moment of the first 3D line segment end point P_a^W and the unit direction vector V_W as illustrated by Fig. 2. Note that for simplicity, we only show the illustration for one camera and one 2D-3D line correspondence in Fig. 2, and we drop the camera and line indices for brevity. $L_W = [U_W^T \ V_W^T]^T$

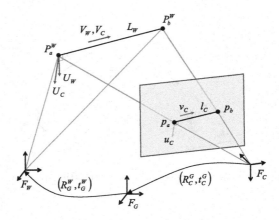

Fig. 2. A 2D-3D line correspondence represented as Plücker lines.

is known in the non-perspective pose estimation problem and it is expressed in the coordinate frame of the fixed world frame F_W.

The Plücker line L_W can be expressed in the camera reference frame F_C as follows:

$$L_C = \mathcal{T}_W^C L_W = \begin{pmatrix} R_W^C & \lfloor t_W^C \rfloor_\times R_W^C \\ 0_{3\times3} & R_W^C \end{pmatrix} L_W, \tag{3}$$

where $\mathcal{T}_W^C$ is the transformation matrix that brings a Plücker line defined in the fixed world frame F_W to the camera reference frame F_C. R_W^C and t_W^C are the 3×3 rotation matrix and 3×1 translation vector. Specifically,

$$\mathcal{T}_W^C = \begin{pmatrix} R_W^C & t_W^C \\ 0_{1\times3} & 1 \end{pmatrix} = \begin{pmatrix} R_G^C & t_G^C \\ 0_{1\times3} & 1 \end{pmatrix} \begin{pmatrix} R_W^G & t_W^G \\ 0_{1\times3} & 1 \end{pmatrix} = \begin{pmatrix} R_G^C R_W^G & R_G^C t_W^G + t_G^C \\ 0_{1\times3} & 1 \end{pmatrix}, \tag{4}$$

where (R_G^C, t_G^C) is the known camera extrinsics, and (R_W^G, t_W^G) is the unknown pose of the multi-camera system defined in the previous section. Since $L_C = [U_C^T \ V_C^T]^T$,

$$U_C = \left(R_W^C \ \lfloor t_W^C \rfloor_\times R_W^C \right) \begin{pmatrix} U_W \\ V_W \end{pmatrix} \tag{5}$$

is a vector defined in F_C that is perpendicular to the plane formed by the projection of the 3D line onto the camera image as shown in Fig. 2, and

$$V_C = R_W^C V_W \tag{6}$$

is the unit direction vector of the 3D line in the camera reference frame F_C.

In addition to the end points P_a^W and P_b^W of the 3D line segment L_W, we are also given the image coordinates of the end points $p_a = [p_{ax} \ p_{ay} \ 1]^T$ and $p_b = [p_{bx} \ p_{by} \ 1]^T$ from the 2D image line correspondence l_C of the 3D line. Similar to L_W, we can also represent l_C as a Plücker line $[u_C^T \ v_C^T]^T$, where

$$v_C = \frac{\hat{p}_b - \hat{p}_a}{\|\hat{p}_b - \hat{p}_a\|}, \quad u_C = \hat{p}_a \times v_C. \tag{7}$$

$\hat{p}_a = [\hat{p}_{ax}\ \hat{p}_{ay}\ 1]^T = K^{-1}p_a$ and $\hat{p}_b = [\hat{p}_{bx}\ \hat{p}_{by}\ 1]^T = K^{-1}p_b$ are the camera matrix normalized image coordinates. v_C is the unit direction vector of the 2D image line segment, and it is parallel to V_C from Eq. 6. The third element of v_C is always zero since l_C lies on the image plane that is parallel to the xy-plane of F_C. u_C is the vector that represents the moment of the first camera matrix normalized 2D image line segment end point $\hat{p}_a$ and the unit direction vector v_C as shown in Fig. 2, and it is parallel to U_C from Eq. 5.

4.1   Solving for R_W^G

It is important to note that the moment vector U is always perpendicular to the unit direction vector V in any Plücker line $[U^T\ V^T]^T$, i.e. the dot product of U and V must be zero. As a result, we get the following constraint from Eq. 6:

$$U_C^T R_W^C V_W = 0. \tag{8}$$

Since we know that u_C is parallel to U_C, and $R_W^C = R_G^C R_W^G$, we can rewrite Eq. 8 as

$$u_C^T R_G^C R_W^G V_W = 0, \tag{9}$$

where the only unknown is R_W^G. Equation 9 can be rearranged into the form of a homogeneous linear equation $ar = 0$, where a is a 1×9 matrix made up of the known variables u_C^T, R_G^C and V_W, and $r = [r_{11}\ r_{12}\ r_{13}\ r_{21}\ r_{22}\ r_{23}\ r_{31}\ r_{32}\ r_{33}]^T$ is a 9-vector made up the nine entries of the unknown rotation matrix R_W^G. Given three 2D-3D line correspondences in the minimal case, we obtain a homogeneous linear equation

$$Ar = 0, \tag{10}$$

where A is a 3×9 matrix made up of a_j for $j = 1, 2, 3$. Taking the Singular Value Decomposition (SVD) of the matrix A gives us six vectors denoted by $b_1, b_2, b_3, b_4, b_5, b_6$ that span the right null-space of A. Hence, r is given by

$$r = \beta_1 b_1 + \beta_2 b_2 + \beta_3 b_3 + \beta_4 b_4 + \beta_5 b_5 + \beta_6 b_6. \tag{11}$$

$\beta_1, \beta_2, \beta_3, \beta_4, \beta_5, \beta_6$ are any scalar values that made up the family of solutions for r. Setting $\beta_6 = 1$, we can solve for $\beta_1, \beta_2, \beta_3, \beta_4, \beta_5$ using the additional constraints from the orthogonality of the rotation matrix R_W^G. Following [25], enforcing the orthogonality constraint on the rotation matrix R_W^G gives us 10 constraints:

$$||\mathbf{r_1}||^2 - ||\mathbf{r_2}||^2 = 0, \quad ||\mathbf{r_1}||^2 - ||\mathbf{r_3}||^2 = 0, \tag{12a}$$

$$||\mathbf{c_1}||^2 - ||\mathbf{c_2}||^2 = 0, \quad ||\mathbf{c_1}||^2 - ||\mathbf{c_3}||^2 = 0, \tag{12b}$$

$$\mathbf{r_1 r_2}^T = 0, \quad \mathbf{r_1 r_3}^T = 0, \quad \mathbf{r_2 r_3}^T = 0, \tag{12c}$$

$$\mathbf{c_1}^T \mathbf{c_2} = 0, \quad \mathbf{c_1}^T \mathbf{c_3} = 0, \quad \mathbf{c_2}^T \mathbf{c_3} = 0. \tag{12d}$$

Here, $\mathbf{r_j}$ for $j = 1, 2, 3$ and $\mathbf{c_j}$ for $j = 1, 2, 3$ are the rows and columns of the rotation matrix R_W^G. Putting r from Eq. 11 into the 10 orthogonality constraints in Eq. 12, we get a system of 10 polynomial equations in terms of $\beta_1, \beta_2, \beta_3, \beta_4, \beta_5$, i.e.

$$f_j(\beta_1, \beta_2, \beta_3, \beta_4, \beta_5) = 0, \quad j = 1, 2...10. \tag{13}$$

We use the automatic generator provided by Kukelova et al. [14] to generate the solver for the system of polynomials in Eq. 13. A maximum of up to eight solutions can be obtained. $\beta_1, \beta_2, \beta_3, \beta_4, \beta_5$ are substituted back into Eq. 11 to get the solutions for r that makes up the rotation matrix R_W^G. For each of the solutions, we divide R_W^G by the norm of its first row $||\mathbf{r_1}||$ to enforce the orthonormal constraint for a rotation matrix. Furthermore, we ensure that R_W^G follows a right-handed coordinate system by multiplying it with -1 if $det(R_W^G) = -1$.

4.2 Solving for t_W^G

It was mentioned earlier that u_C is the vector that represents the moment of the first camera matrix normalized 2D image line segment end point $\hat{p}_a$ and the unit direction vector v_C as shown in Fig. 2, and it is parallel to U_C from Eq. 4. This means that we can write

$$\lambda u_C = U_C, \tag{14}$$

where λ is a scalar value. Substituting Eq. 14 into Eq. 5, we get

$$\lambda u_C = \left(R_W^C \ \lfloor t_W^C \rfloor_\times R_W^C \right) \begin{pmatrix} U_W \\ V_W \end{pmatrix}. \tag{15}$$

$[R_W^C \ \lfloor t_W^C \rfloor_\times R_W^C]$ can be seen as a 3×6 projection matrix that projects a 3D Plücker line $[U_W^T \ V_W^T]^T$ onto a 2D image. It can be easily seen from Fig. 2 that λu_C is the normal vector of the plane formed by the projection of the 3D Plücker line $[U_W^T \ V_W^T]^T$ onto the image plane.

Taking the cross product of u_C on both sides of Eq. 15 to get rid of the unknown λ, we get

$$\lfloor u_C \rfloor_\times \left(R_W^C \ \lfloor t_W^C \rfloor_\times R_W^C \right) \begin{pmatrix} U_W \\ V_W \end{pmatrix} = 0. \tag{16}$$

We substitute the known camera extrinsics (R_G^C, t_G^C) and rotation matrix R_W^G that we solved in Sect. 4.1 into Eq. 16 to get two constraints with the unknown translation t_W^G for each 2D-3D line correspondence $u_C \leftrightarrow [U_W^T \ V_W^T]^T$:

$$\lfloor u_C \rfloor_\times \left(R_G^C R_W^G \ \lfloor R_G^C t_W^G + t_G^C \rfloor_\times R_G^C R_W^G \right) \begin{pmatrix} U_W \\ V_W \end{pmatrix} = 0. \tag{17}$$

Equation 17 can be rearranged into a homogeneous linear equation $bt = 0$, where b is a 2×4 matrix made up of all the known variables $R_G^C, t_G^C, R_W^G, u_C, U_W$ and

V_W, and $t = [t_x \ t_y \ t_z \ 1]^T$ is a 4-vector made up of the three entries of the unknown translation vector t_W^G. Given three 2D-3D line correspondences in the minimal case, we obtain a overdetermined homogeneous linear equation

$$Bt = 0. \tag{18}$$

B is a 6×4 matrix made up of b_j for $j = 1, 2, 3$. We solve for t by taking the 4-vector that spans the right null-space of B. The final solution is obtained by dividing the 4-vector with its last element since $t = [t_x \ t_y \ t_z \ 1]^T$. Finally, t_W^G is the first three elements of t.

We get up to eight solutions for the unknown pose (R_W^G, t_W^G) of the world frame F_W to the multi-camera system F_G. We use each of the solution to transform the end points P_a^W and P_b^W from each of the 3D line into the camera frame F_C, and retain the solutions that give the most number of lines with at least one end point from each line that appears in front of the camera, i.e. $P_{az}^C > 0$ or $P_{bz}^C > 0$. Finally, the correct solution can be identified from the reprojection errors (see Sect. 6 for the details of reprojection errors) for all the other 2D-3D line correspondences. A 2D-3D line correspondence is chosen as an inlier if the reprojection error is lesser than a pre-defined threshold, and the correct solution is chosen as the one that yields the most number of inliers.

5   NPnL: ≥ 3 Line Correspondences

In general, the solution steps remain unchanged for $n \geq 3$ 2D-3D line correspondences. The system of homogeneous linear equations $Ar = 0$ from Eq. 10 is valid for $n \geq 3$ 2D-3D line correspondences, i.e. A is a $n \times 9$ matrix where $n \geq 3$. Similar to the minimal case, we can find six vectors $b_1, b_2, b_3, b_4, b_5, b_6$ that spans the right null-space of A using SVD, where b_6 is set to 1. The solution for R_W^G is obtained by enforcing the orthogonality constraints in Eq. 12. We get up to eight solutions for R_W^G. For each solution of R_W^G, we solve for t_W^G following the steps described in Sect. 4.2. $Bt = 0$ from Eq. 18 is now a $2n \times 4$ matrix, where $n \geq 3$. Solutions that give the most number of lines with at least one end point from each line that appears in front of the camera are retained. The final solution for (R_W^G, t_W^G) is chosen to be the one with the highest number of inliers.

6   Reprojection Error for RANSAC

Figure 3 shows an illustration of the reprojection error that we use to reject outliers within RANSAC, and to determine the correct solution for the pose of the multi-camera system. For each estimated pose (R_W^G, t_W^G), we transform the 3D end points (P_a^W, P_b^W) defined in the world frame F_W into the camera frame F_C as follows:

$$P_k^C = \begin{pmatrix} R_G^C R_W^G & R_G^C t_W^G + t_G^C \\ 0_{1 \times 3} & 1 \end{pmatrix} P_k^W, \quad k = a, b, \tag{19}$$

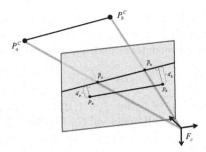

Fig. 3. An illustration of reprojection error from a 2D-3D line correspondence.

where (R_G^C, t_G^C) is the known camera extrinsics. Next, we compute the reprojection of P_a^C and P_b^C onto the image:

$$\tilde{p}_k = KP_k^C, \quad \tilde{p}_k = \frac{\tilde{p}_k}{\tilde{p}_{kz}}, \quad k = a, b, \tag{20}$$

where K is the camera intrinsics. Note that the division by $\tilde{p}_{kz}$ is to ensure that $\tilde{p}_a$ and $\tilde{p}_b$ are homogeneous coordinates. The reprojection error e is then computed as the mean of the shortest distances d_a and d_b from the camera matrix normalized 2D line end points $\hat{p}_a$ and $\hat{p}_b$ to the infinite line formed by the camera matrix normalized reprojected correspondence line end points $K^{-1}\tilde{p}_a$ and $K^{-1}\tilde{p}_b$. We remove the influence from the length of the line segment by normalizing the reprojection error with the distance between $\hat{p}_a$ and $\hat{p}_b$. Specifically,

$$e = \frac{d_a + d_b}{2(\|\hat{p}_b - \hat{p}_a\|)}. \tag{21}$$

Any 2D-3D line correspondence with $e \geq \alpha$, where α is a pre-defined threshold is rejected as an outlier.

7   Special Cases

One Camera: The problem becomes the perspective pose estimation problem with line correspondences when all correspondences are seen by only one camera. Here the camera extrinsics (R_G^C, t_G^C) from Eq. 4 vanishes, and we directly solve for the camera orientation R_W^C from Eq. 8 without the need to decompose the orientation into $R_G^C R_W^G$. Similarly, we can solve for the camera translation t_W^C directly from Eq. 16. The steps for solving the single camera pose from ≥ 3 line correspondences remain the same as described in Sect. 5.

Parallel 3D Lines: This is the minimal case where two or all the three 3D lines are parallel. Since the unit directions V_W from Eq. 8 are the same for parallel lines, the rank of matrix A from Eq. 10 drops below 3. Consequently, R_W^G from Sect. 4.1 cannot be solved. Fortunately, we can easily prevent this degenerate case by omitting parallel lines.

8   Results

We validate our non-perspective pose estimation algorithm with line correspondences from both simulated and real-world datasets. Our algorithm is implemented on Matlab and takes $\sim 0.07\,\mathrm{s}$ to solve for the solution. Note that due to the absence of prior methods for non-perspective pose estimation from line correspondences as comparisons, we focus our evaluations on the stability and accuracy of our algorithm based on different configurations of the multi-camera system. In addition, we also do a comparison of our algorithm under the special case of one camera with the existing methods from Zhang $et\ al.$ [28] and Mirzaei $et\ al.$ [20].

8.1   Simulations

One Line Per Camera: We first evaluate the accuracy of our algorithm for different number of cameras in the multi-camera system. We randomly generate 500 different multi-camera poses T_G^W uniformly drawn from a range of $[-5,5]\,\mathrm{m}$ and $[-1,1]$ rad for all x, y, z axes, and roll, pitch and yaw angles. For each of these multi-camera pose, we randomly generate the extrinsics $T_{C_i}^G$, for $i = 3, 10, 50, 100$ cameras. All the cameras all generated to lie on a sphere centered on the multi-camera frame F_G with their z-axis pointing outwards. Hence, the extrinsics $T_{C_i}^G$ are uniformly drawn from a sphere radius range of $[1,5]\,\mathrm{m}$ with the xy-plane orientation on the sphere uniformly drawn from a range of $[-\pi, \pi]$ rad. We randomly generate one 2D line for each camera, where the line end points are uniformly drawn within the range of the image width and height. We fixed the image size at 1280×1024. Only 2D lines with length more than 30 pixels are accepted. The depths that correspond to the end points of the 2D image lines are uniformly drawn from a range of $[5, 10]\,\mathrm{m}$.

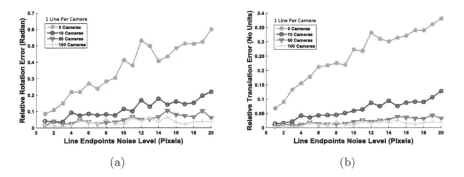

(a)   (b)

Fig. 4. Comparisons of the average relative (a) rotational and (b) translational errors for 3, 10, 50 and 100 cameras with 1 line correspondence per camera. Note that the configuration with 3 cameras is the minimal case. (Color figure online)

Figure 4 shows the plots of the average relative rotational and translational errors for $3, 10, 50, 100$ cameras with one line per camera, where the end points of the 2D image lines are corrupted by noise that follows an uniform distribution with variance of 1 to 20 pixels at a step size of 1 pixel centered around the original end point values. Following [24], the relative translational error is computed as $\frac{2(\|\tilde{t}-t\|)}{\|\tilde{t}\|+\|t\|}$, where $\tilde{t}$ and t is the ground truth and estimated translations. The relative rotational error is computed as the norm of the Euler angles from $\tilde{R}^T R$, where $\tilde{R}$ and R are the ground truth and estimated rotation matrices. We can observe from Fig. 4 that the rotational and translational errors is the highest for the minimal case (shown in green) and decreases with increasing number of cameras. We can also see that the errors remain small with increasing noise.

Ten Cameras: Figure 5 shows the comparisons of the average relative rotational and translational errors for 500 randomly generated multi-camera system with 10 cameras, where each camera sees 1, 10, 50, 100 lines with the end points corrupted with noise from 1 to 20 pixels at a step size of 1 pixel. We can see that the errors for the 1 line per camera case (shown in green) is the highest, and decrease gradually for the 10, 50, 100 lines per camera cases. Overall, the errors increase but remain small with increasing pixel noise.

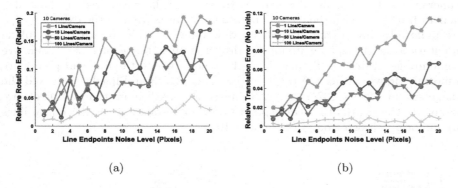

(a)   (b)

Fig. 5. Comparisons of the average relative (a) rotational and (b) translational errors for 1, 10, 50 and 100 lines per camera with 10 cameras. (Color figure online)

One Camera: Figure 6 shows the comparisons of the average rotational and translational errors from our algorithm, [20,28] for 500 randomly generated single cameras, where the end points of the 2D image lines are corrupted with noise from 1 to 20 pixels at a step size of 1 pixel. The number of lines seen by the camera vary from 3 (our), 4 [20,28], 10, 50 and 100. It is the minimal case when the number of lines is 3. Note that no results from the minimal case are shown for [20,28] since the open-source Matlab codes are implemented for ≥ 4 line correspondences. Despite the fact the our algorithm is formulated for non-perspective pose estimation, it can be observed from Fig. 6 that our algorithm shows similar accuracy as [20,28] under the influence of noise for perspective pose estimation without a need for reformulation.

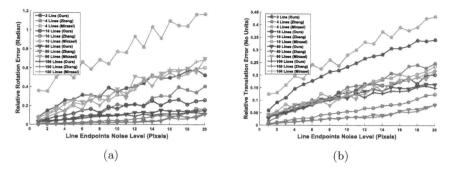

| (a) | (b) |

Fig. 6. Comparisons of the average relative (a) rotational and (b) translational errors from our algorithm, [20, 28] for 3 (our), 4 [20, 28], 10, 50 and 100 lines in one camera. Note that the configuration with 3 lines in one camera is the minimal case for our algorithm.

8.2   Real-World Data

We test the accuracy of our non-perspective pose estimation algorithm with the 3D line models shown in Figs. 7 and 8. The 3D line models are reconstructed from 113 (Dataset 01) and 229 (Dataset 02) images respectively. We first do a 3D reconstruction with [26] to get the camera poses (shown in red) and sparse 3D points of the structures. Next, we discard the 3D points and use the camera poses to compute the 3D lines of the structures (shown in blue) using [12]. In our experiments, we emulate a multi-camera system by randomly selecting ≥ 3 cameras from the cameras in the 3D models. One of the selected cameras is chosen to be the reference frame of the multi-camera system. The ground truth pose of the multi-camera system, i.e. pose of the reference frame, and the extrinsics of the other cameras in the multi-camera system are computed with the known poses from the 3D reconstruction. The camera poses shown in green from Figs. 7 and 8 are examples of the emulated multi-camera system. The images shown on the left of the 3D line models are the images seen by the selected multi-camera system shown in green. For each emulated multi-camera system, we remove the cameras from the 3D model, find the 2D-3D line correspondences, and compute the pose of the multi-camera system with our non-perspective pose estimation algorithm. The estimated pose is then compared with the ground truth, i.e. pose of the reference frame for evaluation.

Table 1 shows the comparisons of the average relative rotational and translational errors from our non-perspective pose estimation algorithm with multi-camera systems that are made up of 3, 5, 10, 20, 25 cameras from both Dataset 01 and 02 respectively. For each multi-camera system, the average rotational and translational errors are computed from 80 sets of randomly selected cameras. We can see that the average errors for both datasets remain low and stable for the different number of cameras in the multi-camera system.

Table 2 shows the comparisons of the average relative rotational and translational errors from our algorithm, [20, 28] for the special case of one camera.

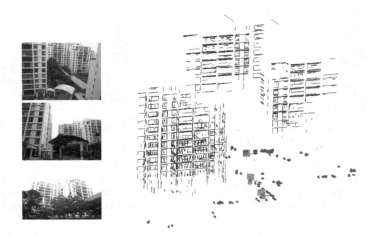

Fig. 7. 3D Line model from Dataset 01 (113 images) for testing our non-perspective pose estimation algorithm. (Color figure online)

Fig. 8. 3D Line model from Dataset 02 [5] (229 images) for testing our non-perspective pose estimation algorithm. (Color figure online)

Table 1. Average relative rotational (R Error, Radian) and translational (t Error, No Units) errors for multi-camera systems emulated with 3, 5, 10, 20 and 25 cameras from datasets 01 and 02 respectively.

Dataset	# of Cameras				
	3	5	10	20	25
01 (R Error)	0.0119	0.0051	0.0041	0.0032	0.0034
02 (R Error)	0.0562	0.1600	0.1381	0.2166	0.2778
01 (t Error)	0.0886	0.0465	0.0256	0.0289	0.0262
02 (t Error)	0.0380	0.0459	0.0700	0.0747	0.0900

Table 2. Comparisons of the average relative rotational (R Error, Radian) and translational (t Error, No Units) errors from our algorithm, and [20,28] for one camera.

Dataset	[28]		[20]		Ours	
	R Error	t Error	R Error	t Error	R Error	t Error
01	0.3016	0.1988	0.3733	0.2015	0.0155	0.0195
02	0.0698	0.0407	0.0186	0.0229	0.0369	0.2549

The average relative rotational and translational errors are computed from 80 randomly selected cameras. We can see that the average errors from our algorithm are small and comparable to [20,28]. Note that RANSAC is used to eliminate outliers for all the algorithms.

9   Conclusions

We derived the minimal solution for the relatively un-investigated minimal problem of non-perspective pose estimation from line correspondences. We showed that our minimal 3-Line algorithm gives up to eight solutions, and is well-suited for robust estimation with RANSAC. Our algorithm works as a least-squares that takes in more than three line correspondences without any reformulation. In addition, our algorithm does not require initialization in both the minimal 3-Line and least-squares n-Line cases. We further showed that our algorithm works without any need for reformulation under the special case of perspective pose estimation when all line correspondences are observed from one single camera. We verified our algorithms with both simulated and real-world data.

Acknowledgement. The work is funded by a start-up grant #R-265-000-548-133 from the Faculty of Engineering at the National University of Singapore, and a Singapore's Ministry of Education (MOE) Tier 1 grant #R-265-000-555-112.

References

1. Fischler, M.A., Bolles, R.C.: Random sample consensus: a paradigm for model fitting with applications to image analysis and automated cartography. Commun. ACM **24**, 381–395 (1981)
2. Ansar, A., Daniilidis, K.: Linear pose estimation from points or lines. IEEE Trans. Pattern Anal. Mach. Intell. (TPAMI) **25**, 578–589 (2003)
3. Burger, M., Repiský, J.: Problems of linear least square regression and approaches to handle them. In: Advanced Research in Scientific Areas (ARSA) (2012)
4. Chen, C.S., Chang, W.Y.: On pose recovery for generalized visual sensors. IEEE Trans. Pattern Anal. Mach. Intell. (TPAMI) **26**, 848–861 (2004)
5. Cohen, A., Zach, C., Sinha, S., Pollefeys, M.: Discovering and exploiting 3d symmetries in structure from motion. In: IEEE Conference on Computer Vision and Pattern Recognition (CVPR) (2012)

6. Dhome, M., Richetin, M., Lapreste, J.T., Rives, G.: Determination of the attitude of 3d objects from a single perspective view. IEEE Trans. Pattern Anal. Mach. Intell. (TPAMI) **11**, 1265–1278 (1989)
7. Furgale, P., Schwesinger, U., Rufli, M., Derendarz, W., Grimmett, H., Muehlfellner, P., Wonneberger, S., Timpner, J., Rottmann, S., Li, B., Schmidt, B., Nguyen, T.N., Cardarelli, E., Cattani, S., Brning, S., Horstmann, S., Stellmacher, M., Mielenz, H., Köser, K., Beermann, M., Häne, C., Heng, L., Lee, G.H., Fraundorfer, F., Iser, R., Triebel, R., Posner, I., Newman, P., Wolf, L., Pollefeys, M., Brosig, S., Effertz, J., Pradalier, C., Siegwart, R.: Toward automated driving in cities using close-to-market sensors, an overview of the v-charge project. In: IEEE Intelligent Vehicle Symposium (IV) (2013)
8. von Gioi, R.G., Jakubowicz, J., Morel, J.M., Randall, G.: LSD: A fast line segment detector with a false detection control. Trans. Pattern Anal. Mach. Intell. (TPAMI) **32**(4), 722–732 (2010)
9. Haralick, R., Lee, D., Ottenburg, K., Nolle, M.: Analysis and solutions of the three point perspective pose estimation problem. In: Computer Vision and Pattern Recognition (CVPR) (1991)
10. Heng, L., Lee, G.H., Pollefeys, M.: Self-calibration and visual slam with a multi-camera system on a micro aerial vehicle. In: Robotics: Science and Systems (RSS) (2014)
11. Heng, L., Lee, G.H., Pollefeys, M.: Self-calibration and visual SLAM with a multi-camera system on a micro aerial vehicle. Autonom. Rob. (AURO) **39**(3), 259–277 (2015)
12. Hofer, M., Donoser, M., Bischof, H.: Semi-global 3d line modeling for incremental structure-from-motion. In: British Machine Vision Conference (BMVC) (2014)
13. Kneip, L., Furgale, P., Siegwart, R.: Using multi-camera systems in robotics: efficient solutions to the NPnP problem. In: International Conference on Robotics and Automation (ICRA) (2013)
14. Kukelova, Z., Bujnak, M., Pajdla, T.: Automatic generator of minimal problem solvers. In: Forsyth, D., Torr, P., Zisserman, A. (eds.) ECCV 2008, Part III. LNCS, vol. 5304, pp. 302–315. Springer, Heidelberg (2008)
15. Lee, G.H., Fraundorfer, F., Pollefeys, M.: Motion estimation for a self-driving car with a generalized camera. In: IEEE Conference on Computer Vision and Pattern Recognition (CVPR) (2013)
16. Lee, G.H., Fraundorfer, F., Pollefeys, M.: Structureless pose-graph loop-closure with a multi-camera system on a self-driving car. In: IEEE/RSJ International Conference on Intelligent Robots and Systems (IROS) (2013)
17. Lee, G.H., Li, B., Pollefeys, M., Fraundorfer, F.: Minimal solutions for pose estimation of a multi-camera system. In: International Symposium on Robotics Research (ISRR) (2013)
18. Lee, G.H., Li, B., Pollefeys, M., Fraundorfer, F.: Minimal solutions for the multi-camera pose estimation problem. Int. J. Rob. Res. (IJRR) **34**(7), 837–848 (2015)
19. Lee, G.H., Pollefeys, M., Fraundorfer, F.: Relative pose estimation for a multi-camera system with known vertical direction. In: IEEE Conference on Computer Vision and Pattern Recognition (CVPR) (2014)
20. Mirzaei, F.M., Roumeliotis, S.I.: Globally optimal pose estimation from line correspondences. In: IEEE International Conference on Robotics and Automation (ICRA) (2011)
21. Moreno-Noguer, F., Lepetit, V., Fua, P.: Accurate non-iterative o(n) solution to the PNP problem. In: International Conference on Computer Vision (ICCV) (2007)

22. Nistér, D.: A minimal solution to the generalised 3-point pose problem. In: IEEE Conference on Computer Vision and Pattern Recognition (CVPR), vol. 1, pp. 560–567 (2004)

23. Přibyl, B., Zemčik, P., ČadíK, M.: Camera pose estimation from lines using plücker coordinates. In: British Machine Vision Conference (BMVC) (2015)

24. Quan, L., Lan, Z.D.: Linear n-point camera pose determination. Trans. Pattern Anal. Mach. Intell. (TPAMI) **21**, 774–780 (1999)

25. Ventura, J., Arth, C., Reitmayr, G., Schmalstieg, D.: A minimal solution to the generalized pose-and-scale problem. In: IEEE Conference on Computer Vision and Pattern Recognition (CVPR) (2014)

26. Wu, C.: VisualSFM: A visual structure from motion system (2014). http://ccwu. me/vsfm/index.html

27. Zhang, L., Koch, R.: An efficient and robust line segment matching approach based on LBD descriptor and pairwise geometric consistency. J. Vis. Commun. Image Represent. **24**(7), 794–805 (2013)

28. Zhang, L., Xu, C., Lee, K.-M., Koch, R.: Robust and efficient pose estimation from line correspondences. In: Lee, K.M., Matsushita, Y., Rehg, J.M., Hu, Z. (eds.) ACCV 2012, Part III. LNCS, vol. 7726, pp. 217–230. Springer, Heidelberg (2013)

Natural Image Stitching with the Global Similarity Prior

Yu-Sheng Chen[(✉)] and Yung-Yu Chuang

Department of Computer Science and Information Engineering,
National Taiwan University, Taipei, Taiwan
{nothinglo,cyy}@cmlab.csie.ntu.edu.tw

Abstract. This paper proposes a method for stitching multiple images together so that the stitched image looks as natural as possible. Our method adopts the local warp model and guides the warping of each image with a grid mesh. An objective function is designed for specifying the desired characteristics of the warps. In addition to good alignment and minimal local distortion, we add a global similarity prior in the objective function. This prior constrains the warp of each image so that it resembles a similarity transformation as a whole. The selection of the similarity transformation is crucial to the naturalness of the results. We propose methods for selecting the proper scale and rotation for each image. The warps of all images are solved together for minimizing the distortion globally. A comprehensive evaluation shows that the proposed method consistently outperforms several state-of-the-art methods, including AutoStitch, APAP, SPHP and ANNAP.

Keywords: Image stitching · Panoramas · Image warping

1 Introduction

Image stitching is a process of combining multiple images into a larger image with a wider field of view [17]. Early methods focus on improving alignment accuracy for seamless stitching, such as finding global parametric warps to bring images into alignment. Global warps are robust but often not flexible enough. For addressing the model inadequacy of global warps and improving alignment quality, several local warp models have been proposed, such as the smoothly varying affine (SVA) warp [12] and the as-projective-as-possible (APAP) warp [20].

This work was supported by Ministry of Science and Technology (MOST) and MediaTek Inc. under grants MOST 104-2622-8-002-002 and MOST 104-2628-E-002-003-MY3.

Electronic supplementary material The online version of this chapter (doi:10. 1007/978-3-319-46454-1_12) contains supplementary material, which is available to authorized users.

© Springer International Publishing AG 2016
B. Leibe et al. (Eds.): ECCV 2016, Part V, LNCS 9909, pp. 186–201, 2016.
DOI: 10.1007/978-3-319-46454-1_12

These methods adopt multiple local parametric warps for better alignment accuracy. Projective (affine) regularization is used for smoothly extrapolating warps beyond the image overlap and resembling a global transformation as a whole. The stitched images are essentially single-perspective. Thus, they suffer from the problem of shape/area distortion and parts of the stitched image could be stretched severely and non-uniformly. The problem is even aggravated when stitching multiple images into a very wide angle of view. In such a case, the distortion accumulates and the images further away from the based image are often significantly stretched. Therefore, the field of view for the stitched image often has a limit. Cylindrical and spherical warps address the problem with a fairly narrow view of the perspective warp by projecting images onto a cylinder or a sphere. Unfortunately, these warps often curve straight lines and are only valid if all images are captured at the same camera center.

Recently, several methods attempt to address the issues with distortion and limited field of view in the stitched image while keeping good alignment quality. Since a single-perspective image with a wide field of view inevitably introduces severe shape/size distortion, these methods provide a multi-perspective stitched image. Chang et al. proposed the shape-preserving half-projective (SPHP) warp which is a spatial combination of a projective transformation and a similarity transformation [4]. SPHP smoothly extrapolates the projective transformation of the overlapping region into the similarity transformation of the non-overlapping region. The projective transformation maintains good alignment in the overlapping region while the similarity transformation of the non-overlapping region keeps the original perspective of the image and reduces distortion. In addition to projective transformations, SPHP can also be combined with APAP for better alignment quality. However, the SPHP warp has several problems. (1) The SPHP warp is formed by analyzing the homography between two images. It inherits the limitations of homography and suffers from the problem of a limited field of view. Thus, it often fails when stitching many images. (2) SPHP handles distortion better if the spatial relations among images are 1D. When the spatial relations are 2D, SPHP could still suffer from distortions (Fig. 5 as an example). (3) As pointed out by Lin et al. [11], SPHP derives the similarity transformation from the homography. If using the global homography, the derived similarity transformation could exhibit unnatural rotation (Fig. 4(e) as an example). They proposed the adaptive as-natural-as-possible (AANAP) warp for addressing the problem with the unnatural rotation. The AANAP warp linearizes the homography and slowly changes it to the estimated global similarity transformation that represents the camera motion. AANAP still suffers from a couple of problems. First, there are still distortions locally when stitching multiple images (Figs. 4(f), 5 and 6). Second, the estimation of the global similarity transformation is not robust and there could still exist unnatural rotation and scaling (Figs. 1(b), 3 and 5).

We propose an image stitching method for addressing these problems and robustly synthesizing natural stitched images. Our method adopts the local warp model. The warping of each image is guided by a grid mesh. An objective

(a) APAP+BA

(b) AANAP

(c) Ours (3D method)

(d) Ours with a specified horizon line

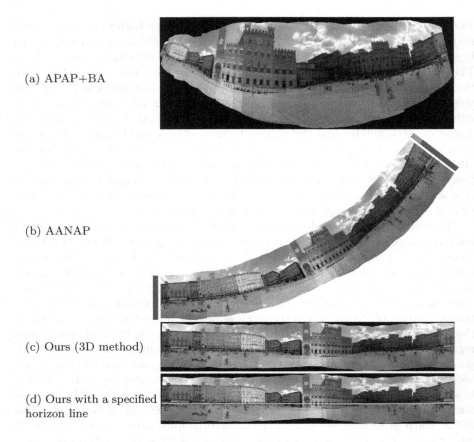

Fig. 1. Image stitching of 18 images.

function is designed for specifying the desired characteristics of the warps. The warps of all images are solved together for an optimal solution. The optimization leads to a sparse linear system and can be solved efficiently. The key idea is to add a global similarity term for requiring that the warp of each image resembles a similarity transformation as a whole. Previous methods have shown that similarity transformations are effective for reducing distortions [4,11], but they are often imposed locally. In contrast, we propose a global similarity prior for each image, in which proper selection of the scale and the rotation is crucial to the naturalness of the stitched image. From our observation, rotation selection is essential to the naturalness. Few paid attention to the rotation selection problem for image stitching. AutoStitch assumes that users rarely twist the camera relative to the horizon and can straighten wavy panoramas by computing the up vector [2]. AANAP uses feature matches for determining the best similarity transformation [11]. These heuristics are however not robust enough. We propose robust methods for selecting the proper scale and rotation for each image.

Our method has the following advantages. First, it does not have the problem with a limited field of view, a problem shared by APAP and SPHP. Second, by solving warps for all images together, our approach minimizes the distortion globally. Finally, it assigns the proper scale and rotation to each image so that the stitched image looks more natural than previous methods. In brief, our method achieves the following goals: accurate alignment, reduced shape distortion, naturalness and without a limit on the field of view. We evaluated the proposed method on 42 sets of images and the proposed method outperforms AutoStitch, APAP, SPHP and AANAP consistently. Figure 1 showcases common problems of previous methods. In Fig. 1(a), APAP+BA (Bundle Adjustment) [21] overcomes the problem with limited field of view by projecting images onto a cylinder. It however uses the wrong scale and rotation and the result exhibits non-uniform distortions over the image. AANAP does not select the rotations and scales properly. The errors accumulate and curve the stitching result significantly in Fig. 1(b). Our result (Fig. 1(c)) looks more natural as it selects the scales and the rotations properly. Our method can also incorporate horizon detection and the result can be further improved (Fig. 1(d)).

2   Related Work

Szeliski has a comprehensive survey on image stitching [17]. Image stitching techniques often utilize parametric transformations to align images either globally or locally. Early methods used global parametric warps, such as similarity, affine and projective transformations. Some assumed that camera motion contains only 3D rotations. A projection is performed to map the viewing sphere to an image plane for obtaining a 2D composite image. A noted example is the AutoStitch method proposed by Brown et al. [1]. Gao et al. proposed the dual-homography warping to specifically deal with scenes containing two dominant planes [5]. The warping function is defined by a linear combination of two homographies with spatially varying weights. Since their warp is based on projective transformations, the resulting image suffers from projective distortion (which stretches and enlarges regions).

Local warp models adopt multiple local parametric warps for better alignment accuracy. Lin et al. prioneered the local warp model for image stitching by using a smoothly varying affine stitching field [12]. Their warp is globally affine while allowing local deformations. Zaragoza et al. proposed the as-projective-as-possible warp which is globally projective while allowing local deviations for better alignment [20].

Instead of focusing on alignment quality, several methods address the problem with distortion in the stitched images. Chang et al. proposed the shape-preserving half-projective warp which is a spatial combination of a projective transformation and a similarity transformation [4]. The projective transformation maintains good alignment in the overlapping region while the similarity transformation of the non-overlapping region keeps the original perspective of the image and reduces distortion. This approach could lead to unnatural rotations at times. Lin et al. proposed the adaptive as-natural-as-possible (AANAP) warp for addressing the problem with the unnatural rotation [11].

A few projection models have been proposed for reducing the induced visual distortion due to projection. Zelnik-Manor et al. used a multi-plane projection as an alternative to the cylindrical projection [22]. Kopf et al. proposed the locally adapted projection which is globally cylindrical while locally perspective [9]. Carroll et al. proposed the content-preserving projection for reducing distortions of wide-angle images [3]. When the underlying assumptions of these models are not met, misalignment occurs and post processing methods (e.g., deghosting and blending) can be used to hide it.

3   Method

Our method adopts the local warp model and consists of the following steps:

1. Feature detection and matching
2. Image match graph verification [2]
3. Matching point generation by APAP [20]
4. Focal length and 3D rotation estimation
5. Scale and rotation selection
6. Mesh optimization
7. Result synthesis by texture mapping

The input is a set of N images, $I_1, I_2, \ldots, I_N$. Without loss of generality, we use I_0 as the reference image. We first detect features and their matches in each image by SIFT [13]. Step 2 determines the adjacency between images. In terms of the quality of pairwise alignment, APAP performs the best. Thus, step 3 applies APAP for each pair of adjacent images and uses the alignment results for generating matching points. Details will be given in Sect. 3.1. Our method stitches images by mesh deformation. Section 3.2 describes our design of the energy function. To make the stitching as natural as possible, we add a global similarity term which requires each deformed image undergo a similarity transform. To determine the similarity transform for each image, our method estimates the focal length and 3D rotation for each image (step 4) and then selects the best scale and rotation (step 5). Section 4 describes the details of these two steps. Finally, the result is synthesize by steps 6 and 7.

3.1   Matching Point Generation by APAP

Let $\mathbf{J}$ denote the set of adjacent image pairs detected by step 2. For a pair of adjacent images I_i and I_j in $\mathbf{J}$, we apply APAP to align them using features and matches from step 1. Note that APAP is a mesh-based method and each image has a mesh for alignment. We collect I_i's mesh vertices in the overlap of I_i and I_j as the set of matching points, $\mathbf{M}^{ij}$. For each matching point in $\mathbf{M}^{ij}$, we know

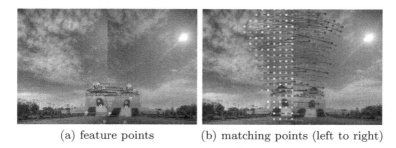

(a) feature points   (b) matching points (left to right)

Fig. 2. Feature points versus matching points. (a) feature points and their matches. (b) matching points and their matches.

its correspondence in I_j since I_i and I_j have been aligned by APAP. Similarly, we have a set of matching points $\mathbf{M}^{ji}$ for I_j.

Figure 2 gives an example of matching points. Given the features and matches in Fig. 2(a), we use APAP to align two images. After alignment, for the left image, we have a set of matching points which are simply the grid points in the overlap regions after APAP alignment. For these matching points, we have their correspondences in the right image. In further steps, we use matching points in place of feature points because matching points are distributed more uniformly.

3.2 Stitching by Mesh Deformation

Our stitching method is based on mesh-based image warping. For each image, we use a grid mesh to guide the image deformation. Let $\mathbf{V}_i$ and $\mathbf{E}_i$ denote the set of vertices and edges in the grid mesh for the image I_i. $\mathbf{V}$ denotes the set of all vertices. Our stitching algorithm attempts to find a set of deformed vertex positions $\tilde{\mathbf{V}}$ such that the energy function $\Psi(\mathbf{V})$ is minimized. The criteria for good stitching could be different from applications to applications. In our case, we stitch multiple images onto a global plane and would like to have the stitched image look as natural as the original images. About the definition of naturalness, we assume that the original images are natural to users. Thus, locally, our method preserves the original perspective of each image as much as possible. At the same time, globally, it attempts to maintain a good structure by finding proper scales and rotations for images. Both contributes to the naturalness of the stitching. Thus, our energy function consists of three terms: the alignment term Ψ_a, the local similarity term Ψ_l and the global similarity term Ψ_g.

Alignment term Ψ_a. This term ensures the alignment quality after deformation by keeping matching points aligned with their correspondences. It is defined as

$$\Psi_a(\mathbf{V}) = \sum_{i=1}^{N} \sum_{(i,j) \in \mathbf{J}} \sum_{p_k^{ij} \in \mathbf{M}^{ij}} \|\tilde{v}(p_k^{ij}) - \tilde{v}(\Phi(p_k^{ij}))\|^2, \tag{1}$$

where $\Phi(p)$ returns the correspondence for a given matching point p. The function $\tilde{v}(p)$ expresses p's position as a linear combination of four vertex positions, $\sum_{i=1}^{4} \alpha_i \tilde{v}_i$ where $\tilde{v}_i$ denote the four corners of the quad that p sits in and α_i are the corresponding bilinear weights.

Local similarity term Ψ_l. This term serves for regularization and propagates alignment constraints from the overlap regions to the non-overlap ones. Our choice for this term is to ensure that each quad undergoes a similarity transform so that the shape will not be distorted too much.

$$\Psi_l(\mathbf{V}) = \sum_{i=1}^{N} \sum_{(j,k) \in \mathbf{E}_i} \|(\tilde{v}_k^i - \tilde{v}_j^i) - \mathbf{S}_{jk}^i (v_k^i - v_j^i)\|^2, \qquad (2)$$

where v_j^i is the position for an original vertex and $\tilde{v}_j^i$ represents the position of the vertex after deformation. $\mathbf{S}_{jk}^i$ is a similarity transformation for the edge (j, k) which can be represented as

$$\mathbf{S}_{jk}^i = \begin{bmatrix} c(e_{jk}^i) & s(e_{jk}^i) \\ -s(e_{jk}^i) & c(e_{jk}^i) \end{bmatrix}. \qquad (3)$$

The coefficients $c(e_{jk}^i)$ and $s(e_{jk}^i)$ can be expressed as linear combinations of vertex variables. Details can be found in [8].

Global similarity term Ψ_g. This term requires each deformed image undergo a similarity transform as much as possible. It is essential to the naturalness of the stitched image. In brief, without this term, the results could be oblique and non-uniformly deformed as exhibited by AANAP and SPHP (Figs. 4 and 5). In addition, it eliminates the trivial solution, $v_j^i = 0$. The procedure for determining the proper scale and rotation is described in Sect. 4. Assume that we have determined the desired scale s_i and rotation angle θ_i for the image I_i. The global similarity term is defined as

$$\Psi_g(\mathbf{V}) = \sum_{i=1}^{N} \sum_{e_j^i \in \mathbf{E}_i} w(e_j^i)^2 \left[(c(e_j^i) - s_i \cos \theta_i)^2 + (s(e_j^i) - s_i \sin \theta_i)^2 \right], \qquad (4)$$

which requires the similarity transform for each edge e_j^i in I_i resembles the similarity transform we have determined for I_i. The functions $c(e)$ and $s(e)$ return the expressions for the coefficients of the input edge e's similarity transform as described in Eq. 3. The weight function $w(e_j^i)$ assigns more weight to the edges further away from the overlapped region. For quads in the overlap region, alignment plays a more important role. On the other hand, for edges away from the overlap region, the similarity prior is more important as there is no alignment constraint. Specifically, it is defined as

$$w(e_j^i) = \beta + \frac{\gamma}{|Q(e_j^i)|} \sum_{q_k \in Q(e_j^i)} \frac{d(q_k, \mathbf{M}^i)}{\sqrt{R_i^2 + C_i^2}}, \qquad (5)$$

where β and γ are constants controlling the importance of the term; $Q(e_j^i)$ is the set of guads which share the edge e_j^i (1 or 2 quads depending on whether the edge is on the border of the mesh); $\mathbf{M}^i$ denotes the set of quads in the overlap region of I_i; the function $d(q_k, \mathbf{M}^i)$ returns the distance of the quad q_k to the quads in the overlap regions in the grid space; R_i and C_i denote the numbers of rows and columns in the grid mesh for I_i. At a high level, an edge's weight is proportional to the normalized distance of the edge to the overlap regions in the grid space.

The optimal deformation of meshes is determined by the following:

$$\tilde{\mathbf{V}} = \arg\min_{\mathbf{V}} \Psi_a(\mathbf{V}) + \lambda_l \Psi_l(\mathbf{V}) + \Psi_g(\mathbf{V}). \tag{6}$$

Note that there are two parameters, β and γ, in Ψ_g, controlling the relative importance of the global similarity term. In all of our experiments, we set $\lambda_l = 0.56$, $\beta = 6$ and $\gamma = 20$. Empirically, we found the parameters are quite stable because there is not severe conflict between terms. The optimization can be efficiently solved by a sparse linear solver.

4   Scale and Rotation Selection

This section describes how to determine the best scale s_i and rotation θ_i for each image I_i, which is the key to the naturalness of the stitched result.

4.1   Estimation of the Focal Length and 3D Rotation

We estimate the focal length and 3D rotation for each image by improving the bundle adjustment method proposed by AutoStitch [2]. We improve their method in two ways: better initialization and better point matches. Better initialization improves convergence of the method.

From a homography between two images, we can estimate the focal lengths of the two images [16–18]. After performing APAP, we have a homography for each quad of a mesh. Thus, each quad gives us an estimation of the focal length of the image. We take the median of these estimations as the initialization of the focal length and form the initial intrinsic matrix $\mathbf{K}_i$ for I_i. Once we have $\mathbf{K}_i$, we obtain the initial guess for 3D rotation $\mathbf{R}_{ij}$ between I_i and I_j by minimizing the following projection error:

$$\mathbf{R}_{ij} = \arg\min_{\mathbf{R}} \sum_{p_k^{ij} \in \mathbf{M}^{ij}} \| \mathbf{K}_j \mathbf{R} \mathbf{K}_i^{-1} p_k^{ij} - \Phi(p_k^{ij}) \|^2. \tag{7}$$

It can be solved by SVD. Note that AutoStich uses features and their matches for estimating the 3D rotation between two images. The problem with features is that they are not uniformly distributed in the image space and it could have adverse influence. We use matching points instead of feature points for estimating 3D rotation.

With the better initialization of $\mathbf{K}_i$ and $\mathbf{R}_{ij}$, bundle adjustment is performed for obtaining the focal length f_i and the 3D rotation $\mathbf{R}_i$ for each image I_i. The scale s_i for I_i in Eq. 4 can be set as

$$s_i = f_0/f_i. \tag{8}$$

4.2 Rotation Selection

As mentioned in Sect. 1, although the selection of rotation is crucial to the naturalness, few paid attention to it. AutoStitch assumes that users rarely twist the camera relative to the horizon and can straighten wavy panoramas by computing the up vector [2]. AANAP uses feature matches for determining the best similarity transformation [11]. The heuristic is not robust enough as illustrated in Fig. 3.

(a) AANAP   (b) Ours (3D method)

Fig. 3. AANAP does not select the right rotation (a). Our method does a better job and generates a more natural result.

The goal of rotation selection is to assign a rotation angle θ_i for each image I_i. We propose a couple of methods for determining the rotation, a 2D method and a 3D method. Before describing these methods, we define several terms first.

Relative rotation range. Given a pair of adjacent images I_i and I_j, each pair of their matching points uniquely determines a relative rotation. Assume that the k-th pair of matching points gives us the relative rotation angle θ_k^{ij}. We define the relative rotation range Θ^{ij} between I_i and I_j as

$$\Theta^{ij} = [\theta_{min}^{ij}, \theta_{max}^{ij}], \tag{9}$$

where $\theta_{min}^{ij} = \min_k \theta_k^{ij}$ and $\theta_{max}^{ij} = \max_k \theta_k^{ij}$.

Minimum Line Distortion Rotation (MLDR). Human is more sensitive to lines. Thus, we propose a procedure for finding the best relative rotation between two adjacent images with respect to line alignment. We first detect lines using the LSD detector [6]. Through the alignment given by APAP, we can find the correspondences of lines between two adjacent images, I_i and I_j. Each pair of corresponding lines uniquely determines a relative rotation. We use RANSAC as a robust voting mechanism to determine the relative rotation between I_i and I_j. The voting power of each line depends on the product of its length and width. The final relative rotation is taken as the average of all inliers' rotation angles. We denote ϕ^{ij} as the relative rotation angle between I_i and I_j determined by MLDR.

Given all relative rotation angles ϕ^{ij} estimated by MLDR, we can find a set of rotation angles $\{\theta_i\}$ to satisfy the MLDR pairwise rotation relationship as much as possible. We represent θ_i as a unit 2D vector (u_i, v_i) and formulate the following energy function:

$$\mathbf{E}_{MLDR} = \sum_{(i,j)\in \mathbf{J}} \left\| R(\phi^{ij}) \begin{bmatrix} u_i \\ v_i \end{bmatrix} - \begin{bmatrix} u_j \\ v_j \end{bmatrix} \right\|^2, \tag{10}$$

where $R(\phi^{ij})$ is the 2D rotation matrix specified by ϕ^{ij}. By minimizing $\mathbf{E}_{MLDR}$, we find a set of rotation angles θ_i to satisfy the MLDR pairwise rotation constraints as much as possible. To avoid the trivial solution, we need at least one more constraint for solving Eq. 10. We propose two methods for obtaining the additional constraints.

Rotation selection (2D method). In this method, we make a similar assumption with Brown et al. [2] by assuming that users rarely twist the camera relative to the horizon. That is, we prefer that $\theta_i = 0°$ if possible. First, we need to determine the rotation angle for one image. Without loss of generality, let the angle of the reference image be $0°$, i.e., $\theta_0 = 0°$. Once we have the rotation angle θ_i for some image I_i, we can determine the rotation range of the image I_j adjacent to I_i by $\Theta_j = \Theta^{ij} + \theta_i$. If $0°$ is within the range Θ_j, it means that zero rotation is a reasonable one and we should set $\theta_j = 0$. By propagating the rotation ranges using BFS along the adjacency graph, we can find a set of images with $0°$ rotation. The pseudo code of the detailed process is given in the supplementary material. Let $\mathbf{\Omega}$ be the set of images whose rotation angles equal $0°$. We find θ_i by minimizing

$$\mathbf{E}_{MLDR} + \lambda_z \mathbf{E}_{ZERO}, \text{ where} \tag{11}$$

$$\mathbf{E}_{ZERO} = \sum_{i\in\mathbf{\Omega}} \left\| \begin{bmatrix} u_i \\ v_i \end{bmatrix} - \begin{bmatrix} 1 \\ 0 \end{bmatrix} \right\|^2 \tag{12}$$

and $\lambda_z = 1000$ so that the images in $\mathbf{\Omega}$ are likely assigned zero rotation, i.e., keeping their original orientations.

Rotation selection (3D method). In this method, we utilize the 3D rotation matrix $\mathbf{R}_i$ estimated at the beginning of this section. We first decompose the 3D rotation matrix $\mathbf{R}_i$ to obtain the rotation angle α_i with respect to the z axis. The relative rotation between two adjacent images I_i and I_j can be determined as $\alpha^{ij} = \alpha_j - \alpha_i$. If $\alpha^{ij} \in \Theta^{ij}$, it means the estimation is reasonable and can be used. Otherwise, we should use the relative rotation ϕ^{ij} by MLDR. Let Ω be the set of pairs which use ϕ^{ij} and $\bar{\Omega} = \mathbf{J} - \Omega$ for others. The rotation angles are determined by minimizing

$$\sum_{(i,j)\in\Omega} \left\| R(\phi^{ij}) \begin{bmatrix} u_i \\ v_i \end{bmatrix} - \begin{bmatrix} u_j \\ v_j \end{bmatrix} \right\|^2 + \lambda_r \sum_{(i,j)\in\bar{\Omega}} \left\| R(\alpha^{ij}) \begin{bmatrix} u_i \\ v_i \end{bmatrix} - \begin{bmatrix} u_j \\ v_j \end{bmatrix} \right\|^2. \quad (13)$$

We set $\lambda_r = 10$ to give 3D rotation more weights.

5   Experiments and Results

We compare our methods (2D and 3D versions) with four methods, AutoStitch [2], APAP [20], SPHP [4] and AANAP [11]. The experiments were performed on a MacBook Pro with 2.8 GHz CPU and 16 GB RAM. SIFT features were extracted using VLFeat [19]. The grid size is 40×40 for mesh-based methods. We tested the six methods on 42 sets of images (3 from [11], 6 from [4], 4 from [20], 7 from [14], 3 from [5] and 19 collected by ourselves). All comparisons can be found in supplementary material. The numbers of images range from 2 to 35. The test sets collected by us are more challenging than existing ones. We will release all our code and data for facilitating further comparisons.[1] Not account for feature detection and matching, for the resolution of 800×600, our method takes 0.1 s for stitching two images (Fig. 4) and 8 s for 35 images (Fig. 6).

Figure 4 compares all methods on stitching two images. Figure 4(a) shows the result of AutoStitch. Note that there is obvious misalignment. Our method can be used to empower other methods with APAP's alignment capability. Figure 4(b) shows the result in which the misalignment has been largely removed. Although with good alignment quality, APAP suffers from the problem with perspective distortion (Fig. 4(c)). One could change APAP's perspective model to similarity model as ASAP which is similar to the method by Schaefer et al. [15]. Figure 4(d) shows the result of ASAP. Although similarity performs well on reducing distortion, it is not effective for good alignment (closeup). In addition, the results would exhibit artifacts with obliqueness and non-uniform deformation. SPHP has the problem with unnatural rotation (Fig. 4(e)). AANAP gives a reasonable result in this example (Fig. 4(f)), but the lines on the floor are slightly distorted as shown more clearly in the closeup. Our method has the best stitching quality in this example (Fig. 4(g)).

Figure 1 presents an example for obtaining a panorama by stitching 18 images. SPHP failed on this example because of its limited field of view. APAP+BA overcomes the problem by projecting images onto a cylinder [21].

---

[1] The project website: http://www.cmlab.csie.ntu.edu.tw/project/stitching-wGSP/.

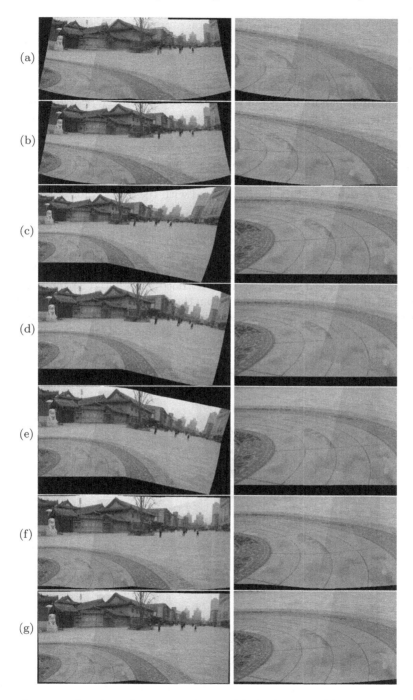

Fig. 4. An example of stitching two images. (a) AutoStitch, (b) AutoStitch+ours, (c) APAP, (d) ASAP, (e) SPHP+APAP, (f) AANAP, (g) Ours (3D method).

However, due to incorrect scale and rotation estimation, the result exhibits non-uniform distortions over the image (Fig. 1(a)). AANAP does not select the rotations and scales properly. The errors accumulate and curve the stitching result significantly as shown in Fig. 1(b). Note that the problem cannot be fixed by the rectangling panorama method [7] because it would maintain the original orientation of the input panorama as much as possible without referring to the original images. The panorama could become rectangular but the scene would remain curved. Our result (Fig. 1(c)) looks more natural as it selects the scales and the rotations properly. Our method is flexible and can be extended to comply with some additional constraints. In this example, we use a vanishing point detection method [10] for detecting the horizon for one image. With this additional constraint, the stitched image is better aligned with the horizon for a more natural result (Fig. 1(d)).

In the example of stitching six images in Fig. 5, AutoStitch introduces obvious distortion because of its spherical projection (top left). SPHP cannot handle 2D topology between images and suffers from distortion (bottom left). AANAP's result exhibits unnatural rotation and shape distortion (top right). Our result looks the most natural among all results (bottom right). The input of Fig. 6 contains 35 images. AutoStitch suffers from the distortion caused by the spherical projection (top left). AANAP has distortions all over the image (top right). Both of our methods give more natural results. The 2D method keeps the perspective

Fig. 5. An example of stitching six images. (top left) AutoStitch, (bottom left) SPHP+APAP, (top right) AANAP, (bottom right) Ours (2D method).

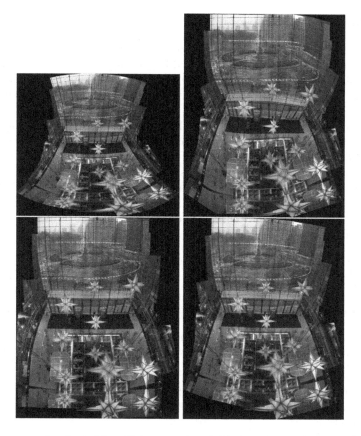

Fig. 6. An example of stitching 35 images. (top left) AutoStitch, (top right) AANAP, (bottom left) Our 2D method, (bottom right) Our 3D method.

of each image better (bottom left) while the 3D method keeps a better 3D perspective of the original scene (bottom right).

In sum, although ASAP, AANAP, SPHP and our method all use similarity, our method gives much better results. The differences come from how similarity is utilized. SPHP attempts to reduce the perspective distortion but it fails when the field of view is wide (Fig. 1) and the spatial relations among images are 2D (Fig. 5). AANAP attempts to address the unnatural rotation but it is not robust enough and fails frequently (Figs. 1(b), 3 and 5). In addition, AANAP does not optimize for shape distortion and it only stitches two images at a time. There could exist distortions locally when stitching multiple images (Figs. 4(f), 5 and 6). Our method addresses all these problems better than previous methods.

6   Conclusions

This paper proposes an image stitching method for synthesizing natural results. Our method adopts the local warp model. By adding the global similarity prior, our method can reduce distortion while keeping good alignment. More importantly, with our scale and rotation selection methods, the global similarity prior leads to a more natural stitched image.

This paper presents two main contributions. First, it presents a method for combining APAP's alignment accuracy and similarity's less distortion. Although individual components could have been explored, we utilize them in a different way. The method also naturally handles alignment of multiple images. Second, it presents methods for robustly estimating proper similarity transformations for images. They serve as two purposes: further enforcing similarity locally and imposing a good global structure. Experiments confirm the effectiveness and robustness of the proposed method.

References

1. Brown, M., Lowe, D.G.: Recognising panoramas. In: Proceedings of the Ninth IEEE International Conference on Computer Vision, ICCV 2003, vol. 2, pp. 1218–1225 (2003)
2. Brown, M., Lowe, D.G.: Automatic panoramic image stitching using invariant features. Int. J. Comput. Vis. **74**(1), 59–73 (2007)
3. Carroll, R., Agrawal, M., Agarwala, A.: Optimizing content-preserving projections for wide-angle images. Int. J. Comput. Vis. **28**(3), 43 (2009)
4. Chang, C.H., Sato, Y., Chuang, Y.Y.: Shape-preserving half-projective warps for image stitching. In: Proceedings of the 2014 IEEE Conference on Computer Vision and Pattern Recognition, CVPR 2014, pp. 3254–3261 (2014)
5. Gao, J., Kim, S.J., Brown, M.S.: Constructing image panoramas using dual-homography warping. In: Proceedings of the 2011 IEEE Conference on Computer Vision and Pattern Recognition, CVPR 2011, pp. 49–56 (2011)
6. Grompone von Gioi, R., Jakubowicz, J., Morel, J.M., Randall, G.: LSD: a line segment detector. Image Process. On Line **2**, 35–55 (2012)
7. He, K., Chang, H., Sun, J.: Rectangling panoramic images via warping. ACM Trans. Graph. **32**(4), 79:1–79:10 (2013)
8. Igarashi, T., Igarashi, Y.: Implementing as-rigid-as-possible shape manipulation and surface flattening. J. Graph., GPU, & Game Tools **14**(1), 17–30 (2009)
9. Kopf, J., Lischinski, D., Deussen, O., Cohen-Or, D., Cohen, M.: Locally adapted projections to reduce panorama distortions. Int. J. Comput. Vis. **28**(4), 1083–1089 (2009)
10. Lezama, J., Grompone von Gioi, R., Randall, G., Morel, J.M.: Finding vanishing points via point alignments in image primal and dual domains. In: The IEEE Conference on Computer Vision and Pattern Recognition (CVPR), June 2014
11. Lin, C., Pankanti, S., Ramamurthy, K.N., Aravkin, A.Y.: Adaptive as-natural-as-possible image stitching. In: IEEE Conference on Computer Vision and Pattern Recognition, CVPR 2015, Boston, MA, USA, 7–12 June 2015, pp. 1155–1163 (2015)
12. Lin, W.Y., Liu, S., Matsushita, Y., Ng, T.T., Cheong, L.F.: Smoothly varying affine stitching. In: Proceedings of the 2011 IEEE Conference on Computer Vision and Pattern Recognition, CVPR 2011, pp. 345–352 (2011)

13. Lowe, D.: Distinctive image features from scale-invariant keypoints. Int. J. Comput. Vis. **60**, 91–110 (2004)
14. Nomura, Y., Zhang, L., Nayar, S.K.: Scene collages and flexible camera arrays. In: Proceedings of the 18th Eurographics Conference on Rendering Techniques, EGSR 2007, pp. 127–138 (2007)
15. Schaefer, S., McPhail, T., Warren, J.: Image deformation using moving least squares. In: ACM SIGGRAPH 2006 Papers, SIGGRAPH 2006, pp. 533–540 (2006)
16. Shum, H.Y., Szeliski, R.: Panoramic image mosaics. Technical Report MSR-TR-97-23, Microsoft Research, September
17. Szeliski, R.: Image alignment and stitching: a tutorial. Int. J. Comput. Vis. **2**(1), 1–104 (2006)
18. Szeliski, R., Shum, H.Y.: Creating full view panoramic image mosaics and environment maps. In: Proceedings of the 24th Annual Conference on Computer Graphics and Interactive Techniques, SIGGRAPH 1997, pp. 251–258 (1997)
19. Vedaldi, A., Fulkerson, B.: Vlfeat: An open and portable library of computer vision algorithms. In: Proceedings of the 18th ACM International Conference on Multimedia, MM 2010, pp. 1469–1472 (2010)
20. Zaragoza, J., Chin, T.J., Brown, M.S., Suter, D.: As-projective-as-possible image stitching with moving DLT. In: Proceedings of the 2013 IEEE Conference on Computer Vision and Pattern Recognition, CVPR 2013, pp. 2339–2346 (2013)
21. Zaragoza, J., Chin, T.J., Tran, Q.H., Brown, M.S., Suter, D.: As-projective-as-possible image stitching with moving DLT. IEEE Trans. Pattern Anal. Mach. Intell. **36**(7), 1285–1298 (2014)
22. Zelnik-Manor, L., Peters, G., Perona, P.: Squaring the circle in panoramas. In: Proceedings of ICCV 2005, vol. 2, pp. 1292–1299 (2005)

Minimal Solvers for Generalized Pose and Scale Estimation from Two Rays and One Point

Federico Camposeco[1][(✉)], Torsten Sattler[1], and Marc Pollefeys[1,2]

[1] Department of Computer Science, ETH Zurich, Zurich, Switzerland
{federico.camposeco,torsten.sattler,marc.pollefeys}@inf.ethz.ch
[2] Microsoft, Redmond, USA

Abstract. Estimating the poses of a moving camera with respect to a known 3D map is a key problem in robotics and Augmented Reality applications. Instead of solving for each pose individually, the trajectory can be considered as a generalized camera. Thus, all poses can be jointly estimated by solving a generalized PnP (gPnP) problem. In this paper, we show that the gPnP problem for camera trajectories permits an extremely efficient minimal solution when exploiting the fact that pose tracking allows us to locally triangulate 3D points. We present a problem formulation based on one point-point and two point-ray correspondences that encompasses both the case where the scale of the trajectory is known and where it is unknown. Our formulation leads to closed-form solutions that are orders of magnitude faster to compute than the current state-of-the-art, while resulting in a similar or better pose accuracy.

Keywords: Absolute camera pose · Pose solver · Generalized cameras

1 Introduction

Estimating the absolute pose of a camera, i.e., the position and orientation from which an image was taken, with respect to a given 3D map is a fundamental building block in many 3D computer vision applications such as Structure-from-Motion (SfM) [27], simultaneous localization and mapping (SLAM) [5], image-based localization [18,26,29,35], Augmented Reality (AR) [21,22], and visual navigation for autonomous vehicles [34]. Traditionally, research on camera pose estimation has mainly focused on individual cameras [8], potentially estimating the extrinsic parameters of the camera pose together with the parameters of its intrinsic calibration [2,10]. In the context of robotics applications such as autonomous drones and vehicles, it is desirable to use multi-camera systems that cover the full field-of-view around the robots. Multi-camera systems can be modelled as a generalized camera [25], i.e., a camera for which not all viewing rays intersect in a single center of projection. Accordingly, camera pose estimation for generalized cameras has started to receive attention lately [3,11,15,17,24,30,33].

Electronic supplementary material The online version of this chapter (doi:10.1007/978-3-319-46454-1_13) contains supplementary material, which is available to authorized users.

© Springer International Publishing AG 2016
B. Leibe et al. (Eds.): ECCV 2016, Part V, LNCS 9909, pp. 202–218, 2016.
DOI: 10.1007/978-3-319-46454-1_13

In this paper, we consider a problem typically arising in AR or video registration against SfM models [14], where visual-inertial odometry (VIO) [9] or visual odometry (VO) [23] is used to track the pose of the camera over time while registering the trajectory against a previously build 3D map acting as a reference coordinate system for the virtual objects [21]. In this scenario, both the local pose tracking and the pose estimation with respect to the map need to be highly accurate. Instead of estimating the absolute pose w.r.t. the map for each image in the trajectory, the movement of the camera defines a generalized camera that can be used to obtain a more accurate and reliable pose estimate due to its larger field-of-view [1]. VIO, VO and SfM compute the trajectory by tracking features across views, which naturally leads to estimates of the corresponding 3D point coordinates in the local coordinate system of the trajectory.

The fact that 3D point positions are available for some features in the images has not been widely used—except for point registration techniques—by pose solvers for generalized cameras. Instead, state-of-the-art methods estimate the pose from three or more standard 2D-3D matches between 3D points in the map and corresponding 2D image features. In this paper, we show that using one known local 3D point coordinate significantly simplifies the pose estimation problem and leads to more efficient minimal solvers with a similar or better pose accuracy.

The above scenario leads to two variants of the generalized absolute pose problem: The scale of the local trajectory w.r.t. the map is either known or unknown. The former variant arises when the absolute scale can be estimated accurately, e.g., from inertial data in a VIO system. The latter variant is most relevant for purely visual odometry (VO) [5, 6, 23] systems, or for SfM methods that rely on building sub-reconstructions and merging them afterwards [31].

In this paper, we show that knowing the local 3D point position for one of the 2D-3D matches leads to a formulation that covers both problem variants, i.e., the know-scale variant is a special case and permits an even more efficient solution. In detail, this paper makes the following contributions. (i) we derive a joint formulation of the generalized absolute pose problem based on a known 3D point position and two matches between 3D points in the map and image observations. (ii) we develop two novel pose solvers for both cases; known and unknown scale. Whereas state-of-the-art approaches need to solve polynomials of degree 8 or higher, both our methods are solvable by radicals, requiring us to only solve polynomials of degree 2 or a polynomial of degree 4, respectively. As a result, both our solvers are significantly more efficient and also generate fewer solutions. (iii) we show through extensive experiments on both synthetic and real data that our solver is not only more efficient to compute, but also at least as stable and accurate as the current state-of-the-art.

The remainder of the paper is structured as follows. Section 2 reviews related work. Section 3 discusses the geometry of the absolute pose problem for generalized cameras with and without known scale. Section 4 derives our solvers, which are then evaluated in Sect. 5.

2   Related Work

The problem of estimating the pose of a calibrated camera from n known 2D-3D correspondences is known as the n-Point-Pose or Perspective n Point (PnP) problem. The problem is typically solved by relating 3D map points to the viewing rays of their corresponding image measurements, i.e., the pose is estimated from *point-ray* correspondences. A computationally inexpensive, numerically stable and minimal solver is very desirable for RANSAC schemes, since it allows for a solution to be found fast and accurately. The P3P problem is the minimal case of the PnP problem, where only three point-ray correspondences are used to solve for the pose of the camera [8]. The solutions by Fischler and Bolles [7] and by Kneip *et al.* [13] are notable solvers of the P3P problem, where a quartic equation needs to be solved as part of the algorithm. Quartic equations can be solved by radicals non-iteratively, resulting in fast solvers that only require a 2 to 4 μs on a modern PC.

Solutions to the PnP problem only cover cameras whose viewing rays intersect in a single center of projection. The *generalized* PnP (gPnP) problem is the corresponding pose estimation problem for generalized cameras, i.e., cameras whose viewing rays do not intersect in a single center of projection. Minimal solvers for this problem require three point-ray correspondences (gP3P) and have been proposed by Níster and Stéwenius [24], Kneip *et al.* [11] and Lee *et al.* [17]. The resulting solvers are noticeably more complex and require solving an octic polynomial, which cannot be solved non-iteratively by radicals. Consequently, gP3P solvers are significantly slower than P3P solvers. An iterative approach was proposed by Chen and Chang [3] as a special case of their gPnP solution.

Little work exists on the gPnP problem with *unknown scale*, referred to as the gPnP+s problem. The solver proposed by Ventura *et al.* [33] requires at least four point-ray correspondences (gP4P+s) and again leads to an octic polynomial. While mainly used as a minimal solver inside a RANSAC framework [7], their method can also use more correspondences to obtain a least squares solution. Kukelova *et al.* [15] recently proposed a gP4P+s solver that finds the coefficient to the octic very efficiently by circumventing any Gröbner basis computation. Compared to Ventura *et al.*, Kukelova's *et al.* speedup is 18.5, while ours is 47. Also, Kukelova's *et al.* method has a slightly worse accuracy than Ventura's *et al.*, while our solver has better accuracy w.r.t. Ventura's *et al.* Finally, in [30,31] Sweeney *et al.* proposed a more efficient scalable solution for n points that can also handle the so-called minimal case[1]. This is an $O(n)$ solution to the gPnP+s problem, minimizing an approximation of the reprojection error. While providing more accurate poses than [33], the solver from Sweeney *et al.* is also significantly slower.

In this work, we use two point-ray correspondences and one point-point match (obtained by triangulating points in the local frame of the camera trajectory) to simplify both the gPnP and the gPnP+s problem. Similar approaches have

---

[1] Estimating a similarity transformation with 7° of freedom (DOF) provides a solution to the gPnP+s problem while four point-ray correspondences provide 8 constraints.

been proposed in the context of *relative* generalized pose solvers [28], since the complexity of such problem is very high (64-degree polynomial). For example, Lee *et al.* [16] use the Ackermann motion constraint and shared observations between the cameras in a multi-camera system to reduce the problem to a six-degree polynomial. More related to our approach, Clipp *et al.* [4] simplify the relative generalized motion problem by triangulating one 4-view point, deriving a solution which requires the solution of 16-th degree polynomial. In contrast, our solver requires triangulating a point from two or more views and results in quadratic and quartic equations for the gPnP and gPnP+s problems.

3   Problem Statement

Consider the following problem: Given a 3D model, e.g., generated from SfM or SLAM, a trajectory of poses for a single camera or a multi-camera system, and n point-ray matches between features found in images from the trajectory and 3D points in the model, compute the position and orientation of the trajectory in the coordinate system of the model. The cameras in the trajectory form a generalized camera [25] and so this is an instance of the gPnP problem.

As mentioned in Sect. 2, a variant of the gPnP problem is the gPnP+s problem, where the internal scale of the generalized camera does not match the scale of the world points. In such cases it is required that the scale of the trajectory is estimated together with the pose. In this paper, we are interested in developing efficient minimal solvers for both problems, i.e., algorithms that compute a solution for the problems where the number of constraints *matches* the number of degrees of freedom (DOF) or unknowns. Such solvers are typically employed inside a RANSAC [7] loop, where using a minimal solver maximizes the probability of picking an all-inlier sample and thus reduces the number of necessary iterations. For solving the gPnP and gPnP+s problems, we assume that a 3D point position is known for at least one feature in the n-point sample drawn in each RANSAC step. Notice that this assumption is not restrictive: We are considering a camera trajectory generated from tracking features. These feature tracks can be triangulated to obtain 3D point positions in the local coordinate system of the trajectory. Triangulatable points are also easily available in multi-camera systems with visual overlap, where our solvers may be used even if there is no trajectory available.

In the following we discuss a mathematical representation of a generalized camera, and then describe the two versions of the generalized absolute pose problem.

3.1   Generalized Cameras

In its most general definition, a generalized camera is a set of viewing rays which do not necessarily intersect in a single center of projection. Given a base frame $\{B\}$ for the generalized camera with origin $\mathbf{0} \in \mathbb{R}^3$, all viewing rays can be expressed using Plücker line coordinates [25] defined in the base frame.

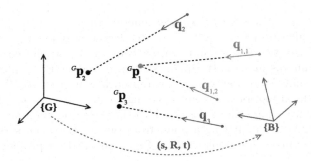

Fig. 1. The pose and scale problem for a generalized camera system. The origin of all rays $\mathbf{q}_i$ defined in base frame $\{B\}$. Notice that the point $^G\mathbf{p}_1$ can be triangulated from $\mathbf{q}_{1,1}$ and $\mathbf{q}_{1,2}$, highlighted in *green*. Note that for the known-scale scenario $s = 1$. (Color figure online)

A Plücker line is a pair of 3-vectors $\mathbf{q}$ and $\mathbf{q}'$, where $\mathbf{q}$ is a vector of any magnitude that points in the direction of the line and $\mathbf{q}' = \mathbf{q} \times \mathbf{p}$, where $\mathbf{p}$ is any point on the line (cf. Fig. 1). This definition implies that $\mathbf{q} \cdot \mathbf{q}' = 0$. Furthermore we enforce that $\mathbf{q} \cdot \mathbf{q} = 1$, which simplifies the terms that appear in our derivations. A 3D point $^B\mathbf{p}_i$ in the base frame $\{B\}$ of the generalized camera can be written as

$$^B\mathbf{p}_i = \mathbf{q}_i \times \mathbf{q}'_i + \lambda_i \mathbf{q}_i, \tag{1}$$

where $\mathbf{q}_i$ is the (unit-length) ray defined in $\{B\}$ that points towards $^B\mathbf{p}_i$ and $\lambda_i \in \mathbb{R}_{>0}$ is the depth of the point along the Plücker line.

3.2   Generalized Pose Estimation with Unknown Scale (gPnP+s)

In the more general case, we aim to compute the similarity transform (pose and scale) between a generalized camera defined in the base frame $\{B\}$ and the global frame of reference $\{G\}$ based on n point-ray matches. This scenario arises more often in vision-only pipelines, e.g., during loop-closure or localization of a local SLAM or SfM trajectory—modeled as a generalized camera—against a known map of 3D landmarks [31]. As illustrated in Fig. 1, the transformation $(s, \mathbf{R}, \mathbf{t})$ maps the i-th point $^G\mathbf{p}_i$ from the global frame $\{G\}$ into the base frame via

$$s\mathbf{R}^G\mathbf{p}_i + \mathbf{t} = {}^B\mathbf{p}_i = \mathbf{q}_i \times \mathbf{q}'_i + \lambda_i \mathbf{q}_i, \tag{2}$$

where $\mathbf{q}_i$ is the (unit-length) ray defined in $\{B\}$ that points towards $^B\mathbf{p}_i$ and λ_i is the depth of the point along the Plücker line.

If we directly use Eq. (2) to solve for the similarity transformation, at least 4 point-ray correspondences are required to find a solution [30, 33]. However, this yields an overdetermined solution since 4 point-ray correspondences provide 8 constraints, while a similarity transformation has only $7°$ of freedom (DOF). This results in having to find the roots of an 8-th degree polynomial and obtaining up to 8 solutions.

Thus, we aim to derive a minimal solution to reduce the complexity of an overdetermined, least-square solution. If we instead consider the case where two of the 4 rays intersect in space, i.e., if we can triangulate the 3D position of *one* point in the base frame $\{B\}$, the gPnP+s problem can be solved by determining the similarity transformation from one point-point correspondence (fixing the three DOF of the translation) and two point-ray correspondences (fixing the remaining 4 DOF). Thus the DOF of the transformation match the number of constraints exactly. We will show in Sect. 4 that this minimal parametrization of the problem can be solved by finding the roots of a quartic, which can be obtained non-iteratively by radicals and yields up to 4 solutions. As a result, our solver is less computationally expensive as state-of-the-art solvers [30,33] and also exhibits fewer solutions. Notice that, in practice, the point we triangulate for the solution might already be known as part of a SLAM trajectory or a local SfM solution. In the case of multi-camera pose estimation however, we might need to explicitly triangulate for this point (e.g. using observations $\mathbf{q}_{1,1}$ and $\mathbf{q}_{1,2}$ as shown in Fig. 1). If so, we employ the method by [19], which is a very efficient (88 floating point operations) approximation to the L_2-optimal triangulation.

3.3 Generalized Pose Estimation with Known Scale (gPnP)

The second scenario assumes that the scale of the preexisting map and the internal scale of the generalized camera are consistent, a situation that usually arises with multi-camera setups and VIO systems, where the scale of the map and the trajectory can be recovered. In this problem variant, the alignment from points in $\{B\}$ to points in $\{G\}$ is defined by a 6 DOF Euclidean transformation. Mathematically, this case is defined similar to Eq. (2), setting $s = 1$ instead of allowing an arbitrary scaling factor.

As discussed in Sect. 2, in the minimal instance this is known as the Generalized P3P problem, or gP3P [11], as we need at least 3 point-ray correspondences to get a finite number of solutions. Compared to the unknown-scale scenario, this has received more attention recently [3,11,12,17,24] due to its applicability in robotic systems, such as VIO trajectories and pre-calibrated multi-camera rigs. The gP3P problem has up to 8 solutions and can be solved by finding the roots of an 8-th degree polynomial.

In our setup, we assume a geometric situation similar to the general scenario (cf. Fig. 1), where one point is known in the base frame, and we aim to find the location of the two remaining points along their Plücker lines. In this case our solution is an overdetermined one—solving a 6 DOF problem with 7 constraints—and our solution is minimal only in the number of points used. Still, our solution to the gPnP problem is highly relevant for practical applications since it can be computed extremely efficiently by finding the roots of two quadratics. At the same time, our approach can outperform the minimal solutions in terms of accuracy and efficiency in the cases where the triangulation is accurate—which can easily be gauged by looking at the subtended angle of the two viewing rays.

4   Solution Methodology

Here we present our two solvers to address the problems presented in the previous section. For both solvers, we use the fact that we know the location of *one* point in the base frame of the generalized camera $\{B\}$, let us denote this point as $^B\mathbf{p}_1$. To simplify the expressions that will appear in both solvers, we translate the base frame $\{B\}$ to coincide with $^B\mathbf{p}_1$, such that in the new intermediate frame $\{B'\}$ points become $^{B'}\mathbf{p}_i = {}^B\mathbf{p}_i - {}^B\mathbf{p}_1$, $i = 1, 2, 3$.

For each problem we now have *one* point-point correspondence and *two* point-ray correspondences

$$
\begin{aligned}
^{B'}\mathbf{p}_1 &= s\mathbf{R}^G\mathbf{p}_1 + \mathbf{t} \\
\mathbf{q}_i \times \mathbf{q}_i' + \lambda_i \mathbf{q}_i &= s\mathbf{R}^G\mathbf{p}_i + \mathbf{t} \text{ for } i = 2, 3.
\end{aligned}
\tag{3}
$$

For the pose and scale case, gPnP+s, we chose a scale-invariant constraint to get a set of equations that do not depend explicitly on s. If we regard the triplet of points in $\{B'\}$ and their counterparts in $\{G\}$ as triangles, we may use the notion of triangular similarity, which states that two triangles are similar if two of their angles are congruent or they have the same *side-length ratio* (cf. Fig. 2a). If the scale of the points is known (gP3P) then our correspondences in Eq. (3) are simplified by setting $s = 1$. In this case there is no need to use the ratio of lengths, instead we can directly enforce that the distances between points in $\{B'\}$ match the known distances in $\{G\}$ (cf. Fig. 2b).

For both problems we end up with a system of equations in λ_2 and λ_3, which when solved give us the location of the remaining points in $\{B'\}$. For each of these solutions we revert the translation offset from the triangulated point to obtain $^B\mathbf{p}_i = {}^{B'}\mathbf{p}_i + {}^B\mathbf{p}_1$, $i = 1, 2, 3$. We may then use this points to compute the rigid transformation between $\{B\}$ and $\{G\}$, for which we use the algorithm proposed in [32].

4.1   Minimal Solution for gP4P+s

Using the above notation, triangular similarity for our three correspondences may be written as

$$
\triangle({}^{B'}\mathbf{p}_1, {}^{B'}\mathbf{p}_2, {}^{B'}\mathbf{p}_3) \sim \triangle({}^G\mathbf{p}_1, {}^G\mathbf{p}_2, {}^G\mathbf{p}_3),
\tag{4}
$$

which allows us to use either angular or length-ratio preservation between the two triangles as constraints. Using the ratio of the lengths we may write

$$
\frac{\left\| {}^{B'}\mathbf{p}_2 - {}^{B'}\mathbf{p}_1 \right\|^2}{\left\| {}^{B'}\mathbf{p}_3 - {}^{B'}\mathbf{p}_1 \right\|^2} = \frac{s^2 \left\| {}^G\mathbf{p}_2 - {}^G\mathbf{p}_1 \right\|^2}{s^2 \left\| {}^G\mathbf{p}_3 - {}^G\mathbf{p}_1 \right\|^2} = \frac{D_{2,1}}{D_{3,1}} \text{ and}
\tag{5a}
$$

$$
\frac{\left\| {}^{B'}\mathbf{p}_3 - {}^{B'}\mathbf{p}_2 \right\|^2}{\left\| {}^{B'}\mathbf{p}_2 - {}^{B'}\mathbf{p}_1 \right\|^2} = \frac{s^2 \left\| {}^G\mathbf{p}_3 - {}^G\mathbf{p}_2 \right\|^2}{s^2 \left\| {}^G\mathbf{p}_2 - {}^G\mathbf{p}_1 \right\|^2} = \frac{D_{3,2}}{D_{2,1}}
\tag{5b}
$$

where $D_{i,j}$ is the known squared distance between points $^G\mathbf{p}_i$ and point $^G\mathbf{p}_j$. Using this results in a very succinct equation system since $^{B'}\mathbf{p}_1 = \mathbf{0}$:

$$\left\| {}^{B'}\mathbf{p}_i - {}^{B'}\mathbf{p}_1 \right\|^2 = \left\| {}^{B'}\mathbf{p}_i \right\| \text{ for } i = 2, 3. \tag{6}$$

Consequently, Eq. (5a) may be then simplified to

$$\left\| \mathbf{q}_2 \times \mathbf{q}_2' + \lambda_2 \mathbf{q}_2 \right\|^2 - \tfrac{D_{2,1}}{D_{3,1}} \left\| \mathbf{q}_3 \times \mathbf{q}_3' + \lambda_3 \mathbf{q}_3 \right\|^2 = 0, \tag{7}$$

and since $(\mathbf{q}_i \times \mathbf{q}_i') \cdot \mathbf{q}_i = 0$, we arrive at

$$\lambda_2^2 - \tfrac{D_{2,1}}{D_{3,1}} \lambda_3^2 + \left\| \mathbf{q}_2 \times \mathbf{q}_2' \right\|^2 - \tfrac{D_{2,1}}{D_{3,1}} \left\| \mathbf{q}_3 \times \mathbf{q}_3' \right\|^2 = 0. \tag{8}$$

The constraint from Eq. (5b) has a more general form, and no simplification occurs. With this, we may write our constraints as

$$\lambda_2^2 + k_1 \lambda_3^2 + k_2 = 0 \tag{9a}$$
$$\lambda_2^2 + k_3 \lambda_2 \lambda_3 + k_4 \lambda_3^2 + k_5 \lambda_2 + k_6 \lambda_3 + k_7 = 0, \tag{9b}$$

where k_i, $i = 1, .., 7$ depends only on the measurements and the known locations of the points in $\{G\}$.

Equations (9) are two quadratic equations with real coefficients (i.e. conic sections) on λ_2 and λ_3, which in general can be solved using a *quartic* univariate polynomial. In fact, the system is small enough that we can generate a Gröbner basis w.r.t. the lexicographic order symbolically. This yields a triangular system where we can get λ_3 as the solution to a quartic and λ_2 linearly afterwards,

$$\left(k_1^2 + k_3^2 k_1 - 2 k_4 k_1 + k_4^2 \right) \lambda_3^4 + 2 \left(k_1 k_3 k_5 - k_1 k_6 + k_4 k_6 \right) \lambda_3^3 +$$
$$\left(k_2 k_3^2 + k_1 k_5^2 + k_6^2 + 2 k_1 k_2 - 2 k_2 k_4 - 2 k_1 k_7 + 2 k_4 k_7 \right) \lambda_3^2 +$$
$$\left(2 k_2 k_3 k_5 - 2 k_2 k_6 + 2 k_6 k_7 \right) \lambda_3 + k_2^2 + k_2 k_5^2 + k_7^2 - 2 k_2 k_7 = 0 \tag{10a}$$
$$\left(k_4 - k_1 \right) \lambda_3^2 + k_6 \lambda_3 + \lambda_2 \left(k_3 \lambda_3 + k_5 \right) - k_2 + k_7 = 0. \tag{10b}$$

4.2 Solution for gP3P

Solving for the known-scale scenario is, as noted in Sect. 3.3, an overdetermined problem. In fact, one can solve for each depth, λ_2 and λ_3 independently. Since the scale is known, we can directly enforce that the distance of the known point $^{B'}\mathbf{p}_1$ to either point $^{B'}\mathbf{p}_i$ with $i = 2, 3$, be preserved by the Euclidean transformation. This results in the constraints

$$f_i(\lambda_i) \triangleq \left\| {}^{B'}\mathbf{p}_i - {}^{B'}\mathbf{p}_1 \right\|^2 = \left\| {}^G\mathbf{p}_i - {}^G\mathbf{p}_1 \right\|^2 = D_{i,1} \text{ with } i = 2, 3, \tag{11}$$

where we have defined f_i as the squared distance from point i to the known point. The constraints from Eq. (11) can be visualized as the intersection of a ray in space parametrized by λ_i, and a sphere centered around $^{B'}\mathbf{p}_1$ with radius $\sqrt{D_{i,1}}$, for $i = 2, 3$ (cf. Fig. 2). However, for some cases the ray will not intersect the sphere because of noise in the image. If this happens, both solutions to Eq. (11) will be complex and we will have no solutions. Instead we *minimize* the error of the ray to the surface of the sphere. The distance to the sphere surface is

$$d_i\left(\lambda_i\right) = \left(f_i\left(\lambda_i\right) - D_{i,1}\right)^2, \tag{12}$$

and we may find its critical points by finding λ_i such that

$$\frac{\partial\, d_i'\left(\lambda_i\right)}{\partial \lambda_i} = 0, \text{ for } i = 2, 3. \tag{13}$$

The constraints in Eq. (13) are univariate cubic equations in λ_2 and λ_3. However, it can be shown that they are reducible to

$$\lambda_i\left(\lambda_i^2 + \left\|\mathbf{q}_i \times \mathbf{q}'_i\right\|^2 - D_{i,1}\right) = 0 \text{ for } i = 2, 3, \tag{14}$$

which can be solved using only *one* square root. If the solution of the square root is real, then the ray intersects the sphere in two places. Otherwise, the closest point to the sphere is at $\lambda_i = 0$. This results in up to 4 real solutions, however, we do not need to output all solutions. In order to discard as many (λ_2, λ_3) pairs as possible, we use the remaining distance of the point triplet, $D_{3,2}$. We discard all solutions for which the distance $\left(\left\|f_3\left(\lambda_3\right) - f_2\left(\lambda_2\right)\right\| - \left\|^G\mathbf{p}_3 - {}^G\mathbf{p}_2\right\|\right)^2$ is larger than a threshold ($0.1D_{3,2}$ in our real-world experiments), leaving out all but one solution in practically all cases.

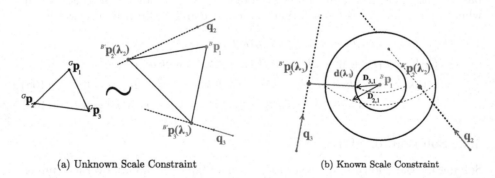

(a) Unknown Scale Constraint   (b) Known Scale Constraint

Fig. 2. Illustration of the geometry of the constraints. In (a) we intend to find the values λ_2 and λ_3 for which the triangle that we form becomes *similar* to the triangle formed by $(^{B'}\mathbf{p}_1, {}^{B'}\mathbf{p}_2, {}^{B'}\mathbf{p}_3)$. In (b), for the given point in the base frame, $^{B'}\mathbf{p}_1$, our goal is to find the depth along the direction $\mathbf{q}_i$ such that the distance from that point along the ray to the sphere centered at $^{B'}\mathbf{p}_1$ with radius $\sqrt{D_{i,1}}$ is minimized. Notice that $\mathbf{q}_3$ has a direction which cannot intersect the sphere and so our results is the closest point to the sphere (the point where $d(\lambda_3)$ is smallest).

5   Evaluation

To evaluate our methods, we use synthetic data to evaluate their numerical stability, sensitivity to measurement noise and to triangulation accuracy. Additionally, our methods' accuracy was evaluated using 11 sequences of real-world data [33], where a SLAM camera trajectory is registered to an SfM model. For both of these evaluation modes, we compared against the following methods:

Absolute Orientation. This method [32] registers two 3D point sets via a similarity transform. The method is very simple and requires only linear operations and returns only one solution, however, it needs at least three points in the $\{B\}$ frame, so at least six point-ray correspondences are needed.

gP+s. Solves the GP4P+s problem as proposed by Ventura in [33] by finding the roots of an octic polynomial and returns up to 8 solutions.

gDLS. Scalable n point method for the GPnP+s problem proposed in [30]. It is designed to handle cases with several point-ray correspondences and minimizes the reprojection error globally, returning up to 27 solutions. For our evaluations, we used it with only 4 point-ray correspondences.

gP3P Chen. Chen's method [3] is the earliest solution to the gP3P problem. This solver is iterative in nature and may return up to 16 solutions.

gP3P Lee. One of the latest methods to tackle the GPnP problem presented in [17]. Similar to ours, this method represents ray-point correspondences as Plücker lines and solves for points along those lines. It includes a closed-form minimal solution the the absolute orientation problem, needed for the last step of aligning points in $\{B\}$ and $\{G\}$. The solution requires finding the roots of an octic and may return up to 8 feasible configurations.

gP3P Kneip. A minimal method from [11] that notably solves for the rotation of $\{B\}$ directly, and thus requires no last step that aligns two points sets. Similarly, it requires to solve an octic and returns up to 8 solutions as well.

g1P2R+s. Our Generalized 1 Point, 2 Rays plus scale solver (cf. Sect. 4.1). For our solver we need to find the roots of a quartic and we return up to four solutions.

g1P2R. Our Generalized 1 Point, 2 Rays solver (cf. Sect. 4.2). For this solver we need to compute two square roots and we return only one solution.

5.1   Synthetic Data Evaluation

For our synthetic data evaluation we first generate four cameras randomly placed in the cube $[-1, 1] \times [-1, 1] \times [-1, 1]$ around the origin. Then, 3D points in $\{B\}$ are sampled randomly from the volume $[-1, 1] \times [-1, 1] \times [2, 6]$. The point-ray correspondences are then generated by projecting all points to all cameras. Each method, however, is given the exact amount of correspondences it requires, e.g. gP3P only gets the first three point-ray correspondences. After this, a random rotation and translation is then applied to cameras and observations. Finally, if evaluating an unknown scale solver, a random scale between 0.5 and 20 is applied to the world points. The experiments were executed several thousand times (the exact number depends on the evaluation mode) in order to obtain a meaningful statistic of the accuracy under varying conditions as explained next.

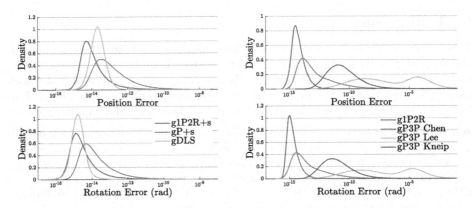

Fig. 3. Kernel-smoothed histograms of the numerical stability of the algorithms tested, gPnP+s algorithms on the *left* and gPnP on the *right*. Each algorithm was ran 10^5 times under noiseless conditions. Because of the lower computational complexity of our methods (*blue lines*), we achieve a very high numerical stability. (Color figure online)

Numerical Stability. One of the benefits of having a less complex solution to a particular problem is that there is less opportunity for numerical errors and instabilities to accumulate. This is specially true for the solvers presented in this paper, since they are both in closed-form. To evaluate this, the point-ray correspondences are left uncorrupted with noise. As seen in Fig. 3, the numerical errors are very small, and most often outperform the stability of other methods in their category. A 32-bit floating point implementation might even prove accurate enough and might increase performance even further.

Measurement Noise Resilience. To compare the accuracy of our solutions in the presence of measurement noise, we add Gaussian pixel noise using a focal length of 800 and an image size of 640 × 480. After each method is executed, we compare their rotational and translational accuracy with ground-truth. Figure 4 shows the median error of all trials for increasing pixel noise. For the unknown scale scenario, our method outperforms gP+s in rotational and translational precision. However, g1P2R+s is not as accurate as gDLS for any noise level. We emphasize here that gDLS optimizes the reprojection error over all four correspondences, and has a vastly larger computational cost (cf. Table 1). gDLS is better suited as a refinement step and is compared here as a baseline for accuracy. In the case of g1P2R, we manage to get precisions comparable to other state-of-the-art methods. Notably, we outperform Kneip's gP3P in most metrics. This might be due to the fact that other solvers absorb some of the errors in the point-ray correspondences when they align the obtained points to the world points as a post-processing step, whereas Kneip's solver computes the pose directly.

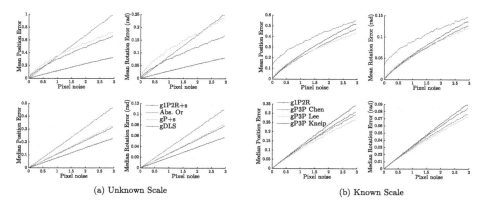

(a) Unknown Scale   (b) Known Scale

Fig. 4. Average (*top rows*) and median (*bottom rows*) translational and rotational errors from 10^5 trials per pixel noise level. The median subtended angle of the triangulated point for our algorithms was of $14.5°$. Notice that our unknown-scale solver (*blue line*) performs better than gP+s for all noise levels. Our known-scale algorithm (*blue line*) is not as resilient to noise as other minimal solvers, however it performs comparably and under higher subtended angles (cf. Fig. 5) it even outperforms them. (Color figure online)

Sensitivity to the Quality of Triangulation. The main concern with the algorithms presented here might be their dependency on the quality of the triangulated point in the base frame. To address this and find the point in which the reliability of our methods might decay due to triangulation errors, we exhaustively tested a wide range of subtended angles for the triangulated point that is used as a part of our solvers. It is known that the accuracy with which a triangulated point can be obtained largely depends on the subtended angle. Note, however, that in many of our target applications triangulated points in the local base frame are already available as part of the VIO/VO/SfM trajectory and one can safely assume that they will have enough accuracy (this assumption is validated with real-world data in Sect. 5.2). Figure 5 shows the accuracy of each method for a constant value of pixel noise (1 pixel standard deviation) while we vary the point configuration such that the subtended angle of the triangulated point changes. Using this, we can see that after approximately $30°$, our solvers are likely to yield comparable or better results than other state-of-the-art methods, while taking only a fraction of the time to compute as it will be shown next. Notice that, since triangulation errors impact Absolute Orientation more dramatically, its performance does not become reliable until a very high subtended angle.

Runtime Analysis. To give an estimate of the computational cost of our algorithms compared to its alternatives, we generated the same random instances of synthetic scenes with fixed pixel noise of 1 pixel standard deviation. We compared against those methods which have available C++ implementations, adding

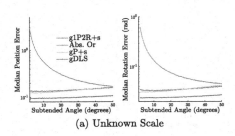
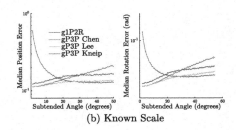

(a) Unknown Scale   (b) Known Scale

Fig. 5. Median rotational and translational errors for a pixel noise of 1. For each of the 10^6 trials, the subtended angle of the triangulated point was varied. The accuracy of our pose and scale solver is comparable to gP+s [33] throughout. However, g1P2R has an acceptable accuracy only after the triangulated point has a subtended angle of more than $15°$. After $30°$, it tends to outperform all other methods.

to those our own C++ implementations of [33] and of [17]. Since our solutions are solvable by radicals, we vastly outperform all other competing methods by at least one order of magnitude (cf. Table 1).

Table 1. Runtime comparison of the algorithms used for our evaluations. Notice that both of our solvers are at least one order of magnitude faster than their counterparts. Timings are reported for C++ implementations running on an Intel i7 at 2.5 GHz.

Method	gDLS	gP+s	gP3P Kneip	g1P2R+s	g1P2R
Microseconds	432.78	98.31	41.01	2.07	0.86

5.2 Real Data Comparison

To validate the performance of our method in real-world scenarios, we used the dataset from [33]. The dataset consists of 12 SLAM sequences of a scene with local poses of cameras in a trajectory and ground-truth obtained from an ART-2 optical tracker, from which the first 11 sequences were used. Additionally, the dataset includes a full SfM reconstruction of the scene. This allows us to register each SLAM sequence against the SfM data via a similarity transform. SIFT [20] keypoints were used to get a set of putative matches between all frames in a sequence and the 3D map using exhaustive search and Lowe's ratio test.

All algorithms we compared against were used within RANSAC. The resulting similarity transform from RANSAC with the highest number of inliers was directly used to transform all the SLAM poses in the sequence. Using these corrected poses, positional accuracy against ground-truth from the tracker was extracted (cf. Fig. 6). To get a robust measure of accuracy, we executed RANSAC 1000 times and took the median positional error for all methods. In order to also evaluate all the known-scale methods, we computed the true scale using the provided ground-truth SLAM poses and scaled each trajectory accordingly. Notice that for our solvers we do not have a simple inlier/outlier partition. Our methods use two modes of data points, one triangulated point and two point-ray observations. In order to accommodate this, our RANSAC stopping criteria needs to be modified, for which we follow the method proposed in [4]. We keep track of *two* inlier ratios; one for point-point correspondence ϵ_p and one four point-ray correspondences ϵ_r. The number of samples used as a stopping criterion becomes

$$k = \log\left(1 - \eta\right) / \log\left(1 - \epsilon_p \epsilon_r^2\right) \tag{15}$$

where η is the confidence that we pick one outlier-free sample.

Our known-scale solver, g1P2R, outperforms all other minimal methods in 6 occasions (cf. Fig. 6). However, it is the least accurate for two trajectories. Our unknown-scale solver performs very well against the tested methods, outperforming even gDLS in two sequences and always outperforming gP+s.

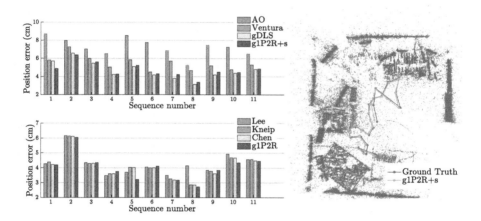

Fig. 6. *Left:* Comparison of position error (in centimeters) for the unknown-scale (*top-left*) and known-scale (*bottom-left*) algorithms. *Right:* Top-down view of the SfM used to register each sequence against. Shown in *orange* is the ground-truth positions given by the ART-2 tracker, and in *yellow* our solution. (Color figure online)

6   Conclusion

In this paper, we have considered the generalized PnP problem for a moving camera. We have derived closed-form solutions based on one point-point and two point-ray correspondences for both the known and unknown-scale cases. The resulting minimal solvers are extremely efficient, resulting in run-times that are orders of magnitude faster than current state-of-the-art methods that purely rely on point-ray correspondences. At the same time, our solvers achieve a similar or even better pose accuracy. Our formulation vastly simplifies the pose estimation problem, and our results show that—contrary to what one might expect—this does not come at the price of reduced accuracy.

Acknowledgements. This research was funded by Google's Tango.

References

1. Arth, C., Klopschitz, M., Reitmayr, G., Schmalstieg, D.: Real-time self-localization from panoramic images on mobile devices. In: International Symposium on Mixed and Augmented Reality (ISMAR) (2011)
2. Bujnak, M., Kukelova, Z., Pajdla, T.: A General solution to the P4P problem for camera with unknown focal length. In: Conference on Computer Vision and Pattern Recognition (CVPR) (2008)
3. Chen, C.S., Chang, W.Y.: On pose recovery for generalized visual sensors. IEEE Trans. Pattern Anal. Mach. Intell. (PAMI) **26**(7), 848–861 (2004)
4. Clipp, B., Zach, C., Frahm, J.M., Pollefeys, M.: A new minimal solution to the relative pose of a calibrated stereo camera with small field of view overlap. In: International Conference on Computer Vision (2009)
5. Davison, A.J., Reid, I.D., Molton, N.D., Stasse, O.: MonoSLAM: real-time single camera SLAM. IEEE Trans. Pattern Anal. Mach. Intell. (PAMI) **29**(6), 1052–1067 (2007)
6. Engel, J., Schöps, T., Cremers, D.: LSD-SLAM: large-scale direct monocular SLAM. In: Fleet, D., Pajdla, T., Schiele, B., Tuytelaars, T. (eds.) ECCV 2014, Part II. LNCS, vol. 8690, pp. 834–849. Springer, Heidelberg (2014)
7. Fischler, M.A., Bolles, R.C.: Random sample consensus: a paradigm for model fitting with applications to image analysis and automated cartography. Commun. ACM (CACM) **24**(6), 381–395 (1981)
8. Haralick, R., Lee, C.N., Ottenberg, K., Nölle, M.: Review and analysis of solutions of the three point perspective pose estimation problem. Int. J. Comput. Vis. (IJCV) **13**(3), 331–356 (1994)
9. Hesch, J.A., Kottas, D.G., Bowman, S.L., Roumeliotis, S.I.: Camera-IMU-based localization: observability analysis and consistency improvement. Int. J. Robot. Res. (IJRR) **33**(1), 182–201 (2014)
10. Josephson, K., Byröd, M.: Pose estimation with radial distortion and unknown focal length. In: Conference on Computer Vision and Pattern Recognition (CVPR) (2009)
11. Kneip, L., Furgale, P., Siegwart, R.: Using multi-camera systems in robotics: efficient solutions to the NPnP problem. In: International Conference on Robotics and Automation (ICRA), pp. 3770–3776. IEEE (2013)
12. Kneip, L., Li, H., Seo, Y.: UPnP: an optimal $O(n)$ solution to the absolute pose problem with universal applicability. In: Fleet, D., Pajdla, T., Schiele, B., Tuytelaars, T. (eds.) ECCV 2014, Part I. LNCS, vol. 8689, pp. 127–142. Springer, Heidelberg (2014). doi:10.1007/978-3-319-10590-1_9
13. Kneip, L., Scaramuzza, D., Siegwart, R.: A novel parametrization of the perspective-three-point problem for a direct computation of absolute camera position and orientation. In: Conference on Computer Vision and Pattern Recognition (CVPR) (2011)

14. Kroeger, T., Van Gool, L.: Video registration to SfM models. In: Fleet, D., Pajdla, T., Schiele, B., Tuytelaars, T. (eds.) ECCV 2014, Part V. LNCS, vol. 8693, pp. 1–16. Springer, Heidelberg (2014)
15. Kukelova, Z., Heller, J., Fitzgibbon, A.: Efficient intersection of three quadrics and applications to computer vision. In: Conference on Computer Vision and Pattern Recognition (CVPR) (2016)
16. Lee, G., Fraundorfer, F., Pollefeys, M.: Motion estimation for self-driving cars with a generalized camera. In: Conference on Computer Vision and Pattern Recognition (CVPR) (2013)
17. Hee Lee, G., Li, B., Pollefeys, M., Fraundorfer, F.: Minimal solutions for pose estimation of a multi-camera system. In: Inaba, M., Corke, P. (eds.) Robotics Research. STAR, vol. 114, pp. 521–538. Springer, Heidelberg (2016). doi:10.1007/978-3-319-28872-7_30
18. Li, Y., Snavely, N., Huttenlocher, D., Fua, P.: Worldwide pose estimation using 3d point clouds. In: Fitzgibbon, A., Lazebnik, S., Perona, P., Sato, Y., Schmid, C. (eds.) ECCV 2012, Part I. LNCS, vol. 7572, pp. 15–29. Springer, Heidelberg (2012)
19. Lindstrom, P.: Triangulation made easy. In: Conference on Computer Vision and Pattern Recognition (CVPR) (2010)
20. Lowe, D.G.: Distinctive image features from scale-invariant keypoints. Int. J. Comput. Vis. (IJCV) 60(2), 91–110 (2004)
21. Lynen, S., Sattler, T., Bosse, M., Hesch, J., Pollefeys, M., Siegwart, R.: Get out of my lab: large-scale, real-time visual-inertial localization. In: Robotics Science and Systems (RSS) (2015)
22. Middelberg, S., Sattler, T., Untzelmann, O., Kobbelt, L.: Scalable 6-DOF localization on mobile devices. In: Fleet, D., Pajdla, T., Schiele, B., Tuytelaars, T. (eds.) ECCV 2014, Part II. LNCS, vol. 8690, pp. 268–283. Springer, Heidelberg (2014)
23. Nister, D., Naroditsky, O., Bergen, J.: Visual odometry. In: Conference on Computer Vision and Pattern Recognition (CVPR) (2004)
24. Nistér, D., Stewénius, H.: A minimal solution to the generalised 3-point pose problem. J. Math. Imaging Vis. 27(1), 67–79 (2007)
25. Pless, R.: Using many cameras as one. In: Conference on Computer Vision and Pattern Recognition (CVPR) (2003)
26. Sattler, T., Havlena, M., Radenovic, F., Schindler, K., Pollefeys, M.: Hyperpoints and fine vocabularies for large-scale location recognition. In: International Conference on Computer Vision (ICCV) (2015)
27. Snavely, N., Seitz, S.M., Szeliski, R.: Photo tourism: exploring photo collections in 3D. In: SIGGRAPH (2006)
28. Stewénius, H., Nistér, D., Oskarsson, M., Åström, K.: Solutions to minimal generalized relative pose problems. In: Workshop on Omnidirectional Vision, Beijing, China (2005)
29. Svärm, L., Enqvist, O., Oskarsson, M., Kahl, F.: Accurate localization and pose estimation for large 3d models. In: Conference on Computer Vision and Pattern Recognition (CVPR) (2014)
30. Sweeney, C., Fragoso, V., Höllerer, T., Turk, M.: gDLS: a scalable solution to the generalized pose and scale problem. In: Fleet, D., Pajdla, T., Schiele, B., Tuytelaars, T. (eds.) ECCV 2014, Part IV. LNCS, vol. 8692, pp. 16–31. Springer, Heidelberg (2014)
31. Sweeney, C., Fragoso, V., Höllerer, T., Turk, M.: Large scale SfM with the distributed camera model (2016). arXiv:1607.03949

32. Umeyama, S.: Least-squares estimation of transformation parameters between two point patterns. IEEE Trans. Pattern Anal. Mach. Intell. (PAMI) **13**(4), 376–380 (1991)
33. Ventura, J., Arth, C., Reitmayr, G., Schmalstieg, D.: A minimal solution to the generalized pose-and-scale problem. In: Conference on Computer Vision and Pattern Recognition (CVPR) (2014)
34. Xu, S., Honegger, D., Pollefeys, M., Heng, L.: Real-time 3d navigation for autonomous vision-guided MAVs. In: Intelligent Robots and Systems (IROS) (2015)
35. Zeisl, B., Sattler, T., Pollefeys, M.: Camera pose voting for large-scale image-based localization. In: International Conference on Computer Vision (ICCV) (2015)

Learning to Hash with Binary Deep Neural Network

Thanh-Toan Do[✉], Anh-Dzung Doan, and Ngai-Man Cheung

Singapore University of Technology and Design, Singapore, Singapore
{thanhtoan_do,dung_doan,ngaiman_cheung}@sutd.edu.sg

Abstract. This work proposes deep network models and learning algorithms for unsupervised and supervised binary hashing. Our novel network design constrains one hidden layer to directly output the binary codes. This addresses a challenging issue in some previous works: optimizing non-smooth objective functions due to binarization. Moreover, we incorporate independence and balance properties in the direct and strict forms in the learning. Furthermore, we include similarity preserving property in our objective function. Our resulting optimization with these binary, independence, and balance constraints is difficult to solve. We propose to attack it with alternating optimization and careful relaxation. Experimental results on three benchmark datasets show that our proposed methods compare favorably with the state of the art.

Keywords: Learning to hash · Neural network · Discrete optimizatization

1 Introduction

We are interested in learning binary hash codes for large scale visual search. Two main difficulties with large scale visual search are efficient storage and fast searching. An attractive approach for handling these difficulties is binary hashing, where each original high dimensional vector $\mathbf{x} \in \mathbb{R}^D$ is mapped to a very compact binary vector $\mathbf{b} \in \{-1, 1\}^L$, where $L \ll D$.

Hashing methods can be divided into two categories: data-independent and data-dependent. Methods in data-independent category [1–4] rely on random projections for constructing hash functions. Methods in data-dependent category use the available training data to learn the hash functions in unsupervised [5–9] or supervised manner [10–15]. The review of data-independent/data-dependent hashing methods can be found in recent surveys [16–18].

One difficult problem in hashing is to deal with the binary constraint on the codes. Specifically, the outputs of the hash functions have to be binary. In general, this binary constraint leads to a NP-hard mixed-integer optimization problem. To handle this difficulty, most aforementioned methods relax the constraint during the learning of hash functions. With this relaxation, the continuous codes are learned first. Then, the codes are binarized (e.g., with thresholding).

© Springer International Publishing AG 2016
B. Leibe et al. (Eds.): ECCV 2016, Part V, LNCS 9909, pp. 219–234, 2016.
DOI: 10.1007/978-3-319-46454-1_14

This relaxation greatly simplifies the original binary constrained problem. However, the solution can be suboptimal, i.e., the binary codes resulting from thresholded continuous codes could be inferior to those that are obtained by including the binary constraint in the learning.

Furthermore, a good hashing method should produce binary codes with the properties [5]: (i) similarity preserving, i.e., (dis)similar inputs should likely have (dis)similar binary codes; (ii) independence, i.e., different bits in the binary codes are independent to each other; (iii) balance, i.e., each bit has a 50 % chance of being 1 or -1. The direct incorporation of the independent and balance properties can complicate the learning. Previous work has used some relaxation to work around the problem [6,19,20], but there may be some performance degradation.

1.1   Related Work

Our work is inspired by a few recent successful hashing methods which define hash functions as a neural network [19,21,22]. We propose an improved design to address their limitations. In Semantic Hashing [21], the model is formed by a stack of Restricted Boltzmann Machine, and a pretraining step is required. This model does not consider the independence and balance of the codes. In Binary Autoencoder [22], a linear autoencoder is used as hash functions. As this model only uses one hidden layer, it may not well capture the information of inputs. Extending [22] with multiple, nonlinear layers is not straight-forward because of the binary constraint. They also do not consider the independence and balance of codes. In Deep Hashing [19], a deep neural network is used as hash functions. However, this model does not fully take into account the similarity preserving. They also apply some relaxation in arriving the independence and balance of codes and this may degrade the performance.

In order to handle the binary constraint, Semantic Hashing [21] first solves the relaxed problem by discarding the constraint and then thresholds the solved continuous solution. In Deep Hashing (DH) [19], the output of the last layer, $\mathbf{H}^n$, is binarized by the *sgn* function. They include a term in the objective function to reduce this binarization loss: $(sgn(\mathbf{H}^n) - \mathbf{H}^n)$. Solving the objective function of DH [19] is difficult because the *sgn* function is non-differentiable. The authors in [19] work around this difficulty by assuming that the *sgn* function is differentiable everywhere. In Binary Autoencoder (BA) [22], the outputs of the hidden layer are passed into a step function to binarize the codes. Incorporating the step function in the learning leads to a non-smooth objective function and the optimization is NP-complete. To handle this difficulty, they use binary SVMs to learn the model parameters in the case when there is only a single hidden layer.

1.2   Contribution

In this work, we first propose a novel deep network model and learning algorithm for unsupervised hashing. In order to achieve binary codes, instead of involving the *sgn* or step function as in [19,22], our proposed network design constrains one layer to directly output the binary codes (hence the network is called as

Table 1. Notations and their corresponding meanings.

Notation	Meaning
$\mathbf{X}$	$\mathbf{X} = \{\mathbf{x}_i\}_{i=1}^m \in \mathbb{R}^{D \times m}$: set of m training samples; each column of $\mathbf{X}$ corresponds to one sample
$\mathbf{B}$	$\mathbf{B} = \{\mathbf{b}_i\}_{i=1}^m \in \{-1, +1\}^{L \times m}$: binary code of $\mathbf{X}$
L	Number of bits in the output binary code to encode a sample
n	Number of layers (including input and output layers)
s_l	Number of units in layer l
$f^{(l)}$	Activation function of layer l
$\mathbf{W}^{(l)}$	$\mathbf{W}^{(l)} \in \mathbb{R}^{s_{l+1} \times s_l}$: weight matrix connecting layer $l+1$ and layer l
$\mathbf{c}^{(l)}$	$\mathbf{c}^{(l)} \in \mathbb{R}^{s_{l+1}}$:bias vector for units in layer $l+1$
$\mathbf{H}^{(l)}$	$\mathbf{H}^{(l)} = f^{(l)}\left(\mathbf{W}^{(l-1)}\mathbf{H}^{(l-1)} + \mathbf{c}^{(l-1)}\mathbf{1}_{1 \times m}\right)$: output values of layer l; convention: $\mathbf{H}^{(1)} = \mathbf{X}$
$\mathbf{1}_{a \times b}$	Matrix has a rows, b columns and all elements equal to 1

Binary Deep Neural Network). Moreover, we propose to directly incorporate the independence and balance properties without relaxing them. Furthermore, we include the similarity preserving in our objective function. The resulting optimization with these binary and direct constraints is NP-hard. We propose to attack this challenging problem with alternating optimization and careful relaxation. To enhance the discriminative power of the binary codes, we then extend our method to supervised hashing by leveraging the label information such that the binary codes preserve the semantic similarity between samples. The solid experiments on three benchmark datasets show the improvement of the proposed methods over state-of-the-art hashing methods.

The remaining of this paper is organized as follows. Section 2 and Sect. 3 present and evaluate the proposed unsupervised hashing method, respectively. Section 4 and Sect. 5 present and evaluate the proposed supervised hashing method, respectively. Section 6 concludes the paper.

2 Unsupervised Hashing with Binary Deep Neural Network (UH-BDNN)

2.1 Formulation of UH-BDNN

We summarize the notations in Table 1. In our work, the hash functions are defined by a deep neural network. In our proposed design, we use different activation functions in different layers. Specifically, we use the sigmoid function as activation function for layers $2, \cdots, n-2$, and the identity function as activation function for layer $n-1$ and layer n. Our idea is to learn the network such that the output values of the *penultimate layer* (layer $n-1$) can be used as the binary codes. We introduce constraints in the learning algorithm such that the output

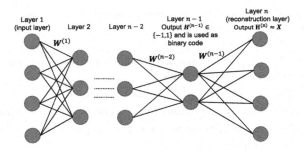

Fig. 1. The illustration of our network ($D = 4, L = 2$). In our proposed network design, the outputs of layer $n-1$ are constrained to $\{-1, 1\}$ and are used as the binary codes. During training, these codes are used to reconstruct the input samples at the final layer.

values at the layer $n-1$ have the following desirable properties: (i) belonging to $\{-1, 1\}$; (ii) similarity preserving; (iii) independent and (iv) balancing. Figure 1 illustrates our network for the case $D = 4, L = 2$.

Let us start with first two properties of the codes, i.e., belonging to $\{-1, 1\}$ and similarity preserving. To achieve the binary codes having these two properties, we propose to optimize the following constrained objective function

$$\min_{\mathbf{W}, \mathbf{c}} J = \frac{1}{2m} \left\| \mathbf{X} - \left(\mathbf{W}^{(n-1)} \mathbf{H}^{(n-1)} + \mathbf{c}^{(n-1)} \mathbf{1}_{1 \times m} \right) \right\|^2 + \frac{\lambda_1}{2} \sum_{l=1}^{n-1} \left\| \mathbf{W}^{(l)} \right\|^2 \quad (1)$$

$$\text{s.t. } \mathbf{H}^{(n-1)} \in \{-1, 1\}^{L \times m} \quad (2)$$

The constraint (2) is to ensure the first property. As the activation function for the last layer is the identity function, the term $\left(\mathbf{W}^{(n-1)} \mathbf{H}^{(n-1)} + \mathbf{c}^{(n-1)} \mathbf{1}_{1 \times m} \right)$ is the output of the last layer. The first term of (1) makes sure that the binary code gives a good reconstruction of $\mathbf{X}$. It is worth noting that the reconstruction criterion has been used as an indirect way for preserving the similarity in state-of-the-art unsupervised hashing methods [6,21,22], i.e., it encourages (dis)similar inputs map to (dis)similar binary codes. The second term is a regularization that tends to decrease the magnitude of the weights, and this helps to prevent overfitting. Note that in our proposed design, we constrain to directly output the binary codes at one layer, and this avoids the difficulties with the sgn/step function such as non-differentiability. On the other hand, our formulation with (1) under the binary constraint (2) is very difficult to solve. It is a mixed-integer problem which is NP-hard. We propose to attack the problem using alternating optimization by introducing an auxiliary variable. Using the auxiliary variable $\mathbf{B}$, we reformulate the objective function (1) under constraint (2) as

$$\min_{\mathbf{W}, \mathbf{c}, \mathbf{B}} J = \frac{1}{2m} \left\| \mathbf{X} - \mathbf{W}^{(n-1)} \mathbf{B} - \mathbf{c}^{(n-1)} \mathbf{1}_{1 \times m} \right\|^2 + \frac{\lambda_1}{2} \sum_{l=1}^{n-1} \left\| \mathbf{W}^{(l)} \right\|^2 \quad (3)$$

$$\text{s.t. } \mathbf{B} = \mathbf{H}^{(n-1)} \tag{4}$$

$$\mathbf{B} \in \{-1, 1\}^{L \times m} \tag{5}$$

The benefit of introducing the auxiliary variable $\mathbf{B}$ is that we can decompose the difficult constrained optimization problem (1) into two sub-optimization problems. Then, we can iteratively solve the optimization by using alternating optimization with respect to $(\mathbf{W}, \mathbf{c})$ and $\mathbf{B}$ while holding the other fixed. We will discuss the details of the alternating optimization in a moment. Using the idea of the quadratic penalty method [23], we relax the equality constraint (4) by solving the following constrained objective function

$$\min_{\mathbf{W}, \mathbf{c}, \mathbf{B}} J = \frac{1}{2m} \left\| \mathbf{X} - \mathbf{W}^{(n-1)} \mathbf{B} - \mathbf{c}^{(n-1)} \mathbf{1}_{1 \times m} \right\|^2$$

$$+ \frac{\lambda_1}{2} \sum_{l=1}^{n-1} \left\| \mathbf{W}^{(l)} \right\|^2 + \frac{\lambda_2}{2m} \left\| \mathbf{H}^{(n-1)} - \mathbf{B} \right\|^2 \tag{6}$$

$$\text{s.t. } \mathbf{B} \in \{-1, 1\}^{L \times m} \tag{7}$$

The third term in (6) measures the (equality) constraint violation. By setting the penalty parameter λ_2 sufficiently large, we penalize the constraint violation severely, thereby forcing the minimizer of the penalty function (6) closer to the feasible region of the original constrained function (3).

Now let us consider the two remaining properties of the codes, i.e., independence and balance. Unlike previous works which use some relaxation or approximation on the independence and balance properties [6,19,20], we propose to encode these properties strictly and directly based on the binary outputs of our layer $n - 1$[1]. Specifically, we encode the independence and balance properties of the codes by having the fourth and the fifth term respectively in the following constrained objective function

$$\min_{\mathbf{W}, \mathbf{c}, \mathbf{B}} J = \frac{1}{2m} \left\| \mathbf{X} - \mathbf{W}^{(n-1)} \mathbf{B} - \mathbf{c}^{(n-1)} \mathbf{1}_{1 \times m} \right\|^2 + \frac{\lambda_1}{2} \sum_{l=1}^{n-1} \left\| \mathbf{W}^{(l)} \right\|^2$$

$$+ \frac{\lambda_2}{2m} \left\| \mathbf{H}^{(n-1)} - \mathbf{B} \right\|^2 + \frac{\lambda_3}{2} \left\| \frac{1}{m} \mathbf{H}^{(n-1)} (\mathbf{H}^{(n-1)})^T - \mathbf{I} \right\|^2 + \frac{\lambda_4}{2m} \left\| \mathbf{H}^{(n-1)} \mathbf{1}_{m \times 1} \right\|^2 \tag{8}$$

$$\text{s.t. } \mathbf{B} \in \{-1, 1\}^{L \times m} \tag{9}$$

(8) under constraint (9) is our final formulation. Before discussing how to solve it, let us present the differences between our work and the recent deep learning based-hashing models Deep Hashing [19] and Binary Autoencoder [22].

The first important difference between our model and Deep Hashing [19] / Binary Autoencoder [22] is the way to achieve the binary codes. Instead of

---

[1] Alternatively, we can constrain the independence and balance on $\mathbf{B}$. This, however, makes the optimization very difficult.

involving the *sgn* or step function as in [19, 22], we constrain the network to directly output the binary codes at one layer. Other differences are presented as follows.

Comparison to Deep Hashing (DH) [19]: the deep model of DH is learned by the following formulation:

$$\min_{\mathbf{W},\mathbf{c}} J = \frac{1}{2} \left\| sgn(\mathbf{H}^{(n)}) - \mathbf{H}^{(n)} \right\|^2 - \frac{\alpha_1}{2m} tr\left(\mathbf{H}^{(n)} (\mathbf{H}^{(n)})^T \right)$$

$$+ \frac{\alpha_2}{2} \sum_{l=1}^{n-1} \left\| \mathbf{W}^{(l)} (\mathbf{W}^{(l)})^T - \mathbf{I} \right\|^2 + \frac{\alpha_3}{2} \sum_{l=1}^{n-1} \left(\left\| \mathbf{W}^{(l)} \right\|^2 + \left\| \mathbf{c}^{(l)} \right\|^2 \right)$$

The DH's model does not have the reconstruction layer. They apply *sgn* function to the outputs at the top layer of the network to obtain the binary codes. The first term aims to minimize quantization loss when applying the *sgn* function to the outputs at the top layer. The balancing and the independent properties are contained in the second and the third terms [19]. It is worth noting that minimizing DH's objective function is difficult due to the non-differentiable of *sgn* function. The authors work around this difficulty by assuming that *sgn* function is differentiable everywhere.

Contrary to DH, we propose a different model design. In particular, our model encourages the similarity preserving by having the reconstruction layer in the network. For the balancing property, they maximize $tr\left(\mathbf{H}^{(n)} (\mathbf{H}^{(n)})^T \right)$. According to [20], maximizing this term is only an approximation in arriving the balancing property. In our objective function, the balancing property is directly enforced on the codes by the term $\left\| \mathbf{H}^{(n-1)} \mathbf{1}_{m \times 1} \right\|^2$. For the independent property, DH uses a relaxed orthogonality constraint $\left\| \mathbf{W}^{(l)} (\mathbf{W}^{(l)})^T - \mathbf{I} \right\|^2$, i.e., constraining on the network weights $\mathbf{W}$. On the contrary, we (once again) directly constrain on the codes using $\left\| \frac{1}{m} \mathbf{H}^{(n-1)} (\mathbf{H}^{(n-1)})^T - \mathbf{I} \right\|^2$. Incorporating the strict constraints can lead to better performance.

Comparison to Binary Autoencoder (BA) [22]: the differences between our model and BA are quite clear. BA as described in [22] is a shallow linear autoencoder network with one hidden layer. The BA's hash function is a linear transformation of the input followed by the step function to obtain the binary codes. In BA, by treating the encoder layer as binary classifiers, they use binary SVMs to learn the weights of the linear transformation. On the contrary, our hash function is defined by multiple, hierarchical layers of nonlinear and linear transformations. It is not clear if the binary SVMs approach in BA can be used to learn the weights in our deep architecture with multiple layers. Instead, we use alternating optimization to derive a backpropagation algorithm to learn the weights in all layers. Another difference is that our model ensures the independence and balance of the binary codes while BA does not. Note that independence and balance properties may not be easily incorporated in their framework, as these would complicate their objective function and the optimization problem may become very difficult to solve.

2.2   Optimization

In order to solve (8) under constraint (9), we propose to use alternating optimization over $(\mathbf{W}, \mathbf{c})$ and $\mathbf{B}$.

$(\mathbf{W}, \mathbf{c})$ **step.** When fixing $\mathbf{B}$, the problem becomes unconstrained optimization. We use *L-BFGS* [24] optimizer with backpropagation for solving. The gradient of the objective function J (8) w.r.t. different parameters are computed as follows.
At $l = n - 1$, we have

$$\frac{\partial J}{\partial \mathbf{W}^{(n-1)}} = \frac{-1}{m}(\mathbf{X} - \mathbf{W}^{(n-1)}\mathbf{B} - \mathbf{c}^{(n-1)}\mathbf{1}_{1\times m})\mathbf{B}^T + \lambda_1 \mathbf{W}^{(n-1)} \qquad (10)$$

$$\frac{\partial J}{\partial \mathbf{c}^{(n-1)}} = \frac{-1}{m}\left((\mathbf{X} - \mathbf{W}^{(n-1)}\mathbf{B})\mathbf{1}_{m\times 1} - m\mathbf{c}^{(n-1)}\right) \qquad (11)$$

For other layers, let us define

$$\Delta^{(n-1)} = \left[\frac{\lambda_2}{m}\left(\mathbf{H}^{(n-1)} - \mathbf{B}\right) + \frac{2\lambda_3}{m}\left(\frac{1}{m}\mathbf{H}^{(n-1)}(\mathbf{H}^{(n-1)})^T - \mathbf{I}\right)\mathbf{H}^{(n-1)}\right.$$
$$\left. + \frac{\lambda_4}{m}\left(\mathbf{H}^{(n-1)}\mathbf{1}_{m\times m}\right)\right] \odot f^{(n-1)\prime}(\mathbf{Z}^{(n-1)}) \qquad (12)$$

$$\Delta^{(l)} = \left((\mathbf{W}^{(l)})^T \Delta^{(l+1)}\right) \odot f^{(l)\prime}(\mathbf{Z}^{(l)}), \forall l = n - 2, \cdots, 2 \qquad (13)$$

where $\odot$ denotes Hadamard product; $\mathbf{Z}^{(l)} = \mathbf{W}^{(l-1)}\mathbf{H}^{(l-1)} + \mathbf{c}^{(l-1)}\mathbf{1}_{1\times m}$, $l = 2, \cdots, n$.
Then, $\forall l = n - 2, \cdots, 1$, we have

$$\frac{\partial J}{\partial \mathbf{W}^{(l)}} = \Delta^{(l+1)}(\mathbf{H}^{(l)})^T + \lambda_1 \mathbf{W}^{(l)} \qquad (14)$$

$$\frac{\partial J}{\partial \mathbf{c}^{(l)}} = \Delta^{(l+1)}\mathbf{1}_{m\times 1} \qquad (15)$$

$\mathbf{B}$ **step.** When fixing $(\mathbf{W}, \mathbf{c})$, we can rewrite problem (8) as

$$\min_{\mathbf{B}} J = \left\|\mathbf{X} - \mathbf{W}^{(n-1)}\mathbf{B} - \mathbf{c}^{(n-1)}\mathbf{1}_{1\times m}\right\|^2 + \lambda_2 \left\|\mathbf{H}^{(n-1)} - \mathbf{B}\right\|^2 \qquad (16)$$

$$\text{s.t. } \mathbf{B} \in \{-1, 1\}^{L\times m} \qquad (17)$$

We adaptively use the recent method *discrete cyclic coordinate descent* [15] to iteratively solve $\mathbf{B}$, i.e., row by row. The advantage of this method is that if we fix $L - 1$ rows of $\mathbf{B}$ and only solve for the remaining row, we can achieve a closed-form solution for that row.

Let $\mathbf{V} = \mathbf{X} - \mathbf{c}^{(n-1)}\mathbf{1}_{1\times m}$; $\mathbf{Q} = (\mathbf{W}^{(n-1)})^T\mathbf{V} + \lambda_2 \mathbf{H}^{(n-1)}$. For $k = 1, \cdots L$, let $\mathbf{w}_k$ be k^{th} column of $\mathbf{W}^{(n-1)}$; $\mathbf{W}_1$ be matrix $\mathbf{W}^{(n-1)}$ excluding $\mathbf{w}_k$; $\mathbf{q}_k$ be k^{th} column of $\mathbf{Q}^T$; $\mathbf{b}_k^T$ be k^{th} row of $\mathbf{B}$; $\mathbf{B}_1$ be matrix of $\mathbf{B}$ excluding $\mathbf{b}_k^T$. We have closed-form for $\mathbf{b}_k^T$ as

$$\mathbf{b}_k^T = sgn(\mathbf{q}^T - \mathbf{w}_k^T\mathbf{W}_1\mathbf{B}_1) \qquad (18)$$

The proposed UH-BDNN method is summarized in Algorithm 1. In the Algorithm 1, $\mathbf{B}_{(t)}$ and $(\mathbf{W}, \mathbf{c})_{(t)}$ are values of $\mathbf{B}$ and $\{\mathbf{W}^{(l)}, \mathbf{c}^{(l)}\}_{l=1}^{n-1}$ at iteration t.

Algorithm 1. Unsupervised Hashing with Binary Deep Neural Network (UH-BDNN)

Input:
   $\mathbf{X} = \{\mathbf{x}_i\}_{i=1}^{m} \in \mathbb{R}^{D \times m}$: training data; L: code length; T: maximum iteration number; n: number of layers; $\{s_l\}_{l=2}^{n}$: number of units of layers $2 \to n$ (note: $s_{n-1} = L$, $s_n = D$); $\lambda_1, \lambda_2, \lambda_3, \lambda_4$.
Output:
   Parameters $\{\mathbf{W}^{(l)}, \mathbf{c}^{(l)}\}_{l=1}^{n-1}$

1: Initialize $\mathbf{B}_{(0)} \in \{-1, 1\}^{L \times m}$ using ITQ [6]
2: Initialize $\{\mathbf{c}^{(l)}\}_{l=1}^{n-1} = \mathbf{0}_{s_{l+1} \times 1}$. Initialize $\{\mathbf{W}^{(l)}\}_{l=1}^{n-2}$ by getting the top s_{l+1} eigenvectors from the covariance matrix of $\mathbf{H}^{(l)}$. Initialize $\mathbf{W}^{(n-1)} = \mathbf{I}_{D \times L}$
3: Fix $\mathbf{B}_{(0)}$, compute $(\mathbf{W}, \mathbf{c})_{(0)}$ with $(\mathbf{W}, \mathbf{c})$ step using initialized $\{\mathbf{W}^{(l)}, \mathbf{c}^{(l)}\}_{l=1}^{n-1}$ (line 2) as starting point for L-BFGS.
4: **for** $t = 1 \to T$ **do**
5:     Fix $(\mathbf{W}, \mathbf{c})_{(t-1)}$, compute $\mathbf{B}_{(t)}$ with $\mathbf{B}$ step
6:     Fix $\mathbf{B}_{(t)}$, compute $(\mathbf{W}, \mathbf{c})_{(t)}$ with $(\mathbf{W}, \mathbf{c})$ step using $(\mathbf{W}, \mathbf{c})_{(t-1)}$ as starting point for L-BFGS.
7: **end for**
8: Return $(\mathbf{W}, \mathbf{c})_{(T)}$

---

3   Evaluation of Unsupervised Hashing with Binary Deep Neural Network (UH-BDNN)

This section evaluates the proposed UH-BDNN and compares it to the following state-of-the-art unsupervised hashing methods: Spectral Hashing (SH) [5], Iterative Quantization (ITQ) [6], Binary Autoencoder (BA) [22], Spherical Hashing (SPH) [8], K-means Hashing (KMH) [7]. For all compared methods, we use the implementations and the suggested parameters provided by the authors.

3.1   Dataset, Evaluation Protocol, and Implementation Note

Dataset. CIFAR10 [25] dataset consists of 60,000 images of 10 classes. The training set (also used as database for retrieval) contains 50,000 images. The query set contains 10,000 images. Each image is represented by a 800-dimensional feature vector extracted by PCA from 4096-dimensional CNN feature produced by AlexNet [26].

MNIST [27] dataset consists of 70,000 handwritten digit images of 10 classes. The training set (also used as database for retrieval) contains 60,000 images. The query set contains 10,000 images. Each image is represented by a 784 dimensional gray-scale feature vector by using its intensity.

SIFT1M [28] dataset contains 128 dimensional SIFT vectors [29]. There are M vectors used as database for retrieval; 100K vectors for training (separated from retrieval database) and 10 K vectors for query.

Evaluation protocol. We follow the standard setting in unsupervised hashing [6–8, 22] using Euclidean nearest neighbors as the ground truths for queries. Number of ground truths are set as in [22], i.e., for CIFAR10 and MNIST datasets, for each query, we use 50 its Euclidean nearest neighbors as ground truths; for large scale dataset SIFT1M, for each query, we use 10, 000 its Euclidean nearest neighbors as ground truths. We use the following evaluation metrics

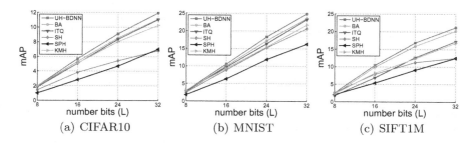

Fig. 2. mAP comparison between UH-BDNN and state-of-the-art unsupervised hashing methods on CIFAR10, MNIST, and SIFT1M.

Table 2. Precision at Hamming distance $r = 2$ comparison between UH-BDNN and state-of-the-art unsupervised hashing methods on CIFAR10, MNIST, and SIFT1M.

L	CIFAR10				MNIST				SIFT1M			
	8	16	24	32	8	16	24	32	8	16	24	32
UH-BDNN	0.55	5.79	22.14	18.35	0.53	6.80	29.38	38.50	4.80	25.20	62.20	80.55
BA [22]	0.55	5.65	20.23	17.00	0.51	6.44	27.65	35.29	3.85	23.19	61.35	77.15
ITQ [6]	0.54	5.05	18.82	17.76	0.51	5.87	23.92	36.35	3.19	14.07	35.80	58.69
SH [5]	0.39	4.23	14.60	15.22	0.43	6.50	27.08	36.69	4.67	24.82	60.25	72.40
SPH [8]	0.43	3.45	13.47	13.67	0.44	5.02	22.24	30.80	4.25	20.98	47.09	66.42
KMH [7]	0.53	5.49	19.55	15.90	0.50	6.36	25.68	36.24	3.74	20.74	48.86	76.04

which have been used in state of the art [6,19,22] to measure the performance of methods. (1) mean Average Precision (mAP); (2) precision of Hamming radius 2 (precision@2) which measures precision on retrieved images having Hamming distance to query ≤ 2 (if no images satisfy, we report zero precision). Note that as computing mAP is slow on large dataset SIFT1M, we consider top $10,000$ returned neighbors when computing mAP.

Implementation note. In our deep model, we use $n = 5$ layers. The parameters $\lambda_1, \lambda_2, \lambda_3$ and λ_4 are empirically set by cross validation as $10^{-5}, 5 \times 10^{-2}, 10^{-2}$ and 10^{-6}, respectively. The max iteration number T is empirically set to 10. The number of units in hidden layers $2, 3, 4$ are empirically set as $[90 \rightarrow 20 \rightarrow 8]$, $[90 \rightarrow 30 \rightarrow 16]$, $[100 \rightarrow 40 \rightarrow 24]$ and $[120 \rightarrow 50 \rightarrow 32]$ for the 8, 16, 24 and 32 bits, respectively.

3.2 Retrieval Results

Figure 2 and Table 2 show comparative mAP and precision of Hamming radius 2 (precision@2), respectively. We find the following observations are consistent for all three datasets. In term of mAP, the proposed UH-BDNN comparable or outperforms other methods at all code lengths. The improvement is more clear at high code length, i.e., $L = 24, 32$. The mAP of UH-BDNN consistently outperforms that of binary autoencoder (BA) [22], which is the current state-of-the-art unsupervised hashing method. In term of precision@2, UH-BDNN is comparable to other methods at low L, i.e., $L = 8, 16$. At $L = 24, 32$, UH-BDNN significantly outperforms other methods.

Comparison with Deep Hashing (DH): [19] As the implementation of DH is not available, we set up the experiments on CIFAR10 and MNIST similar to [19] to make a fair comparison. For each dataset, we randomly sample 1,000 images, 100 per class, as query set; the remaining images are used as training/database set. Follow [19], for CIFAR10, each image is represented by 512-D GIST descriptor [30]. The ground truths of queries are based on their class labels. Similar to [19], we report comparative results in term of mAP and the precision of Hamming radius $r = 2$. The comparative results are presented in the Table 3. It is clearly showed in Table 3 that the proposed UH-BDNN outperforms DH [19] at all code lengths, in both mAP and precision of Hamming radius.

Table 3. Comparison with Deep Hashing (DH) [19]. The results of DH are cited from [19].

L	CIFAR10				MNIST			
	mAP		precision@2		mAP		precision@2	
	16	32	16	32	16	32	16	32
DH [19]	16.17	16.62	23.33	15.77	43.14	44.97	66.10	73.29
UH-BDNN	17.83	18.52	24.97	18.85	45.38	47.21	69.13	75.26

4   Supervised Hashing with Binary Deep Neural Network (SH-BDNN)

In order to enhance the discriminative power of the binary codes, we extend UH-BDNN to supervised hashing by leveraging the label information. There are several approaches proposed to leverage the label information, leading to different criteria on binary codes. In [10,31], binary codes are learned such that they minimize the Hamming distance among within-class samples, while maximizing the Hamming distance among between-class samples. In [15], the binary codes are learned such that they are optimal for linear classification.

In this work, in order to leverage the label information, we follow the approach proposed in Kernel-based Supervised Hashing (KSH) [11]. The benefit of this approach is that it directly encourages the Hamming distances between binary codes of within-class samples equal to 0, and the Hamming distances between binary codes of between-class samples equal to L. In the other words, it tries to perfectly preserve the semantic similarity. To achieve this goal, it enforces that the Hamming distance between learned binary codes has to highly correlate with the pre-computed pairwise label matrix.

In general, the network structure of SH-BDNN is similar to UH-BDNN, excepting that the last layer preserving reconstruction of UH-BDNN is removed.

The layer $n-1$ in UH-BDNN becomes the last layer in SH-BDNN. All desirable properties, i.e. semantic similarity preserving, independence, and balance, in SH-BDNN are constrained on the outputs of its last layer.

4.1   Formulation of SH-BDNN

We define the pairwise label matrix $\mathbf{S}$ as

$$\mathbf{S}_{ij} = \begin{cases} 1 & \text{if } \mathbf{x}_i \text{ and } \mathbf{x}_j \text{ are same class} \\ -1 & \text{if } \mathbf{x}_i \text{ and } \mathbf{x}_j \text{ are not same class} \end{cases} \tag{19}$$

To achieve the semantic similarity preserving property, we learn the binary codes such that the Hamming distance between learned binary codes highly correlates with the matrix $\mathbf{S}$, i.e., we want to minimize the quantity $\left\| \frac{1}{L}(\mathbf{H}^{(n)})^T\mathbf{H}^{(n)} - \mathbf{S} \right\|^2$. In addition, to achieve the independence and balance properties of codes, we want to minimize the quantities $\left\| \frac{1}{m}\mathbf{H}^{(n)}(\mathbf{H}^{(n)})^T - \mathbf{I} \right\|^2$ and $\left\| \mathbf{H}^{(n)}\mathbf{1}_{m \times 1} \right\|^2$.

Follow the same reformulation and relaxation as UH-BDNN (Sect. 2.1), we solve the following constrained optimization which ensures the binary constraint, the semantic similarity preserving, the independence, and the balance properties of codes

$$\min_{\mathbf{W,c,B}} J = \frac{1}{2m} \left\| \frac{1}{L}(\mathbf{H}^{(n)})^T\mathbf{H}^{(n)} - \mathbf{S} \right\|^2 + \frac{\lambda_1}{2}\sum_{l=1}^{n-1}\left\| \mathbf{W}^{(l)} \right\|^2 + \frac{\lambda_2}{2m}\left\| \mathbf{H}^{(n)} - \mathbf{B} \right\|^2$$

$$+ \frac{\lambda_3}{2}\left\| \frac{1}{m}\mathbf{H}^{(n)}(\mathbf{H}^{(n)})^T - \mathbf{I} \right\|^2 + \frac{\lambda_4}{2m}\left\| \mathbf{H}^{(n)}\mathbf{1}_{m \times 1} \right\|^2 \tag{20}$$

$$\text{s.t. } \mathbf{B} \in \{-1,1\}^{L \times m} \tag{21}$$

(20) under constraint (21) is our formulation for supervised hashing. The main difference in formulation between UH-BDNN (8) and SH-BDNN (20) is that the reconstruction term preserving the neighbor similarity in UH-BDNN (8) is replaced by the term preserving the label similarity in SH-BDNN (20).

4.2   Optimization

In order to solve (20) under constraint (21), we alternating optimize over $(\mathbf{W},\mathbf{c})$ and $\mathbf{B}$.

$(\mathbf{W},\mathbf{c})$ **step.** When fixing $\mathbf{B}$, (20) becomes unconstrained optimization. We used *L-BFGS* [24] optimizer with backpropagation for solving. The gradient of objective function J (20) w.r.t. different parameters are computed as follows.

Let us define

$$\Delta^{(n)} = \left[\frac{1}{mL}\mathbf{H}^{(n)}\left(\mathbf{V} + \mathbf{V}^T\right) + \frac{\lambda_2}{m}\left(\mathbf{H}^{(n)} - \mathbf{B}\right) + \frac{2\lambda_3}{m}\left(\frac{1}{m}\mathbf{H}^{(n)}(\mathbf{H}^{(n)})^T - \mathbf{I}\right)\mathbf{H}^{(n)}$$

$$+ \frac{\lambda_4}{m}\left(\mathbf{H}^{(n)}\mathbf{1}_{m \times m}\right) \right] \odot f^{(n)'}(\mathbf{Z}^{(n)}) \tag{22}$$

Algorithm 2. Supervised Hashing with Binary Deep Neural Network (SH-BDNN)

Input:
  $\mathbf{X} = \{\mathbf{x}_i\}_{i=1}^m \in \mathbb{R}^{D \times m}$: training data; $\mathbf{Y} \in R^{m \times 1}$: training label vector; L: code length; T: maximum iteration number; n: number of layers; $\{s_l\}_{l=2}^n$: number of units of layers $2 \to n$ (note: $s_n = L$); $\lambda_1, \lambda_2, \lambda_3, \lambda_4$.
Output:
  Parameters $\{\mathbf{W}^{(l)}, \mathbf{c}^{(l)}\}_{l=1}^{n-1}$

1: Compute pairwise label matrix $\mathbf{S}$ using (19).
2: Initialize $\mathbf{B}_{(0)} \in \{-1, 1\}^{L \times m}$ using ITQ [6]
3: Initialize $\{\mathbf{c}^{(l)}\}_{l=1}^{n-1} = \mathbf{0}_{s_{l+1} \times 1}$. Initialize $\{\mathbf{W}^{(l)}\}_{l=1}^{n-1}$ by getting the top s_{l+1} eigenvectors from the covariance matrix of $\mathbf{H}^{(l)}$.
4: Fix $\mathbf{B}_{(0)}$, compute $(\mathbf{W}, \mathbf{c})_{(0)}$ with $(\mathbf{W}, \mathbf{c})$ step using initialized $\{\mathbf{W}^{(l)}, \mathbf{c}^{(l)}\}_{l=1}^{n-1}$ (line 3) as starting point for L-BFGS.
5: **for** $t = 1 \to T$ **do**
6:    Fix $(\mathbf{W}, \mathbf{c})_{(t-1)}$, compute $\mathbf{B}_{(t)}$ with $\mathbf{B}$ step
7:    Fix $\mathbf{B}_{(t)}$, compute $(\mathbf{W}, \mathbf{c})_{(t)}$ with $(\mathbf{W}, \mathbf{c})$ step using $(\mathbf{W}, \mathbf{c})_{(t-1)}$ as starting point for L-BFGS.
8: **end for**
9: Return $(\mathbf{W}, \mathbf{c})_{(T)}$

---

where $\mathbf{V} = \frac{1}{L}(\mathbf{H}^{(n)})^T \mathbf{H}^{(n)} - \mathbf{S}$.

$$\Delta^{(l)} = \left((\mathbf{W}^{(l)})^T \Delta^{(l+1)} \right) \odot f^{(l)'}(\mathbf{Z}^{(l)}), \forall l = n - 1, \cdots, 2 \qquad (23)$$

where $\odot$ denotes Hadamard product; $\mathbf{Z}^{(l)} = \mathbf{W}^{(l-1)} \mathbf{H}^{(l-1)} + \mathbf{c}^{(l-1)} \mathbf{1}_{1 \times m}$, $l = 2, \cdots, n$.

Then $\forall l = n - 1, \cdots, 1$, we have

$$\frac{\partial J}{\partial \mathbf{W}^{(l)}} = \Delta^{(l+1)}(\mathbf{H}^{(l)})^T + \lambda_1 \mathbf{W}^{(l)} \qquad (24)$$

$$\frac{\partial J}{\partial \mathbf{c}^{(l)}} = \Delta^{(l+1)} \mathbf{1}_{m \times 1} \qquad (25)$$

B step When fixing $(\mathbf{W}, \mathbf{c})$, we can rewrite problem (20) as

$$\min_{\mathbf{B}} J = \left\| \mathbf{H}^{(n)} - \mathbf{B} \right\|^2 \qquad (26)$$

$$\text{s.t. } \mathbf{B} \in \{-1, 1\}^{L \times m} \qquad (27)$$

It is easy to see that the optimal solution for (26) under constraint (27) is $\mathbf{B} = sgn(\mathbf{H}^{(n)})$.

The proposed SH-BDNN method is summarized in Algorithm 2. In the Algorithm, $\mathbf{B}_{(t)}$ and $(\mathbf{W}, \mathbf{c})_{(t)}$ are values of $\mathbf{B}$ and $\{\mathbf{W}^{(l)}, \mathbf{c}^{(l)}\}_{l=1}^{n-1}$ at iteration t.

5   Evaluation of Supervised Hashing with Binary Deep Neural Network (SH-BDNN)

This section evaluates the proposed SH-BDNN and compares it to state-of-the-art supervised hashing methods: Supervised Discrete Hashing (SDH) [15], ITQ-CCA [6], Kernel-based Supervised Hashing (KSH) [11], Binary Reconstructive

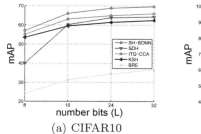
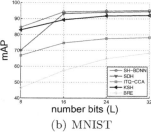

(a) CIFAR10 (b) MNIST

Fig. 3. mAP comparison between SH-BDNN and state-of-the-art supervised hashing methods on CIFAR10 and MNIST.

Table 4. Precision at Hamming distance $r = 2$ comparison between SH-BDNN and state-of-the-art supervised hashing methods on CIFAR10 and MNIST.

L	CIFAR10				MNIST			
	8	16	24	32	8	16	24	32
SH-BDNN	54.12	67.32	69.36	69.62	84.26	94.67	94.69	95.51
SDH [15]	31.60	62.23	67.65	67.63	36.49	93.00	93.98	94.43
ITQ-CCA [6]	49.14	65.68	67.47	67.19	54.35	79.99	84.12	84.57
KSH [11]	44.81	64.08	67.01	65.76	68.07	90.79	92.86	92.41
BRE [14]	23.84	41.11	47.98	44.89	37.67	69.80	83.24	84.61

Embedding (BRE) [14]. For all compared methods, we use the implementation and the suggested parameters provided by the authors.

5.1 Dataset, Evaluation Protocol, and Implementation Note

Dataset We evaluate and compare methods on CIFAR-10 and MNIST datasets. The descriptions of these datasets are presented in Sect. 3.1.

Evaluation protocol. Follow the literature [6,11,15], we report the retrieval results in two metrics: (1) mean Average Precision (mAP) and (2) precision of Hamming radius 2 (precision@2).

Implementation note. The network configuration is same as UH-BDNN excepting the final layer is removed. The values of parameters λ_1, λ_2, λ_3 and λ_4 are empirically set using cross validation as 10^{-3}, 5, 1 and 10^{-4}, respectively. The max iteration number T is empirically set to 5.

Follow the settings in ITQ-CCA [6], SDH [15], all training samples are used in the learning for these two methods. For SH-BDNN, KSH [11] and BRE [14] where label information is leveraged by the pairwise label matrix, we randomly select 3,000 training samples from each class and use them for learning. The ground truths of queries are defined by the class labels from the datasets.

Table 5. Comparison between SH-BDNN and CNN-based hashing DSRH [32], DRSCH [33] on CIFAR10. The results of DSRH and DRSCH are cited from [33].

L	mAP				precison@2			
	16	24	32	48	16	24	32	48
SH-BDNN	64.30	65.21	66.22	66.53	56.87	58.67	58.80	58.42
DRSCH [33]	61.46	62.19	62.87	63.05	52.34	53.07	52.31	52.03
DSRH [32]	60.84	61.08	61.74	61.77	50.36	52.45	50.37	49.38

5.2   Retrieval Results

On CIFAR10 dataset, Fig. 3(a) and Table 4 clearly show the proposed SH-BDNN outperforms all compared methods by a fair margin at all code lengths in both mAP and precision@2.

On MNIST dataset, Fig. 3(b) and Table 4 show the proposed SH-BDNN significantly outperforms the current state-of-the-art SDH at low code length, i.e., $L = 8$. When L increases, SH-BDNN and SDH [15] achieve similar performance. In comparison to remaining methods, i.e., KSH [11], ITQ-CCA [6], BRE [14], SH-BDNN outperforms these methods by a large margin in both mAP and precision@2.

Comparison with CNN-based hashing methods [32,33]: We compare our proposed SH-BDNN to the recent CNN-based supervised hashing methods: Deep Semantic Ranking Hashing (DSRH) [32] and Deep Regularized Similarity Comparison Hashing (DRSCH) [33]. Note that the focus of [32,33] are different from ours: in [32,33], the authors focus on a framework in which the image features and hash codes are *jointly* learned by combining CNN layers (image feature extraction) and binary mapping layer into a single model. On the other hand, our work focuses on only the binary mapping layer given some image feature. In [32,33], their binary mapping layer only applies a simple operation, i.e., an approximation of *sgn* function (i.e., *logistic* [32], *tanh* [33]), on CNN features for achieving the approximated binary codes. Our SH-BDNN advances [32,33] in the way to map the image features to the binary codes (which is our main focus). Given the image features (i.e., pre-trained CNN features), we apply multiple transformations on these features; we constrain one layer to directly output the binary code, without involving *sgn* function. Furthermore, our learned codes ensure good properties, i.e. independence and balance, while DRSCH [33] does not consider such properties, and DSRH [32] only considers the balance of codes.

We follow strictly the comparison setting in [32,33]. In [32,33], when comparing their CNN-based hashing to other non CNN-based hashing methods, the authors use pre-trained CNN features (e.g. AlexNet [26], DeCAF [34]) as input for other methods. Follow that setting, we use AlexNet features [26] as input for SH-BDNN. We set up the experiments on CIFAR10 similar to [33], i.e., the query set contains 10 K images (1 K images per class) randomly sampled from the dataset; the rest 50 K image are used as the training set; in the testing step, each query image is searched within the query set itself by applying the leave-one-out procedure.

The comparative results between the proposed SH-BDNN and DSRH [32], DRSCH [33], presented in Table 5, clearly show that at the same code length, the proposed SH-BDNN outperforms [32,33] in both mAP and precision@2.

6   Conclusion

We propose UH-BDNN and SH-BDNN for unsupervised and supervised hashing. Our network designs constrain to directly produce binary codes at one layer. Our models ensure good properties for codes: similarity preserving, independence and balance. Solid experimental results on three benchmark datasets show that the proposed methods compare favorably with the state of the art.

References

1. Gionis, A., Indyk, P., Motwani, R.: Similarity search in high dimensions via hashing. In: VLDB (1999)
2. Kulis, B., Grauman, K.: Kernelized locality-sensitive hashing for scalable image search. In: ICCV (2009)
3. Raginsky, M., Lazebnik, S.: Locality-sensitive binary codes from shift-invariant kernels. In: NIPS (2009)
4. Kulis, B., Jain, P., Grauman, K.: Fast similarity search for learned metrics. PAMI **31**(2), 2143–2157 (2009)
5. Weiss, Y., Torralba, A., Fergus, R.: Spectral hashing. In: NIPS (2008)
6. Gong, Y., Lazebnik, S.: Iterative quantization: a procrustean approach to learning binary codes. In: CVPR (2011)
7. He, K., Wen, F., Sun, J.: K-means hashing: an affinity-preserving quantization method for learning binary compact codes. In: CVPR (2013)
8. Heo, J.P., Lee, Y., He, J., Chang, S.F. Yoon, S.E.: Spherical hashing. In: CVPR (2012)
9. Kong, W., Li, W.J.: Isotropic hashing. In: NIPS (2012)
10. Strecha, C., Bronstein, A.M., Bronstein, M.M., Fua, P.: LDAHash: improved matching with smaller descriptors. PAMI **34**(1), 66–78 (2012)
11. Liu, W., Wang, J., Ji, R., Jiang, Y.G., Chang, S.F.: Supervised hashing with kernels. In: CVPR (2012)
12. Norouzi, M., Fleet, D.J., Salakhutdinov, R.: Hamming distance metric learning. In: NIPS (2012)
13. Lin, G., Shen, C., Shi, Q., van den Hengel, A., Suter, D.: Fast supervised hashing with decision trees for high-dimensional data. In: CVPR (2014)
14. Kulis, B., Darrell, T.: Learning to hash with binary reconstructive embeddings. In: NIPS (2009)
15. Shen, F., Shen, C., Liu, W., Tao Shen, H.: Supervised discrete hashing. In: CVPR (2015)
16. Wang, J., Liu, W., Kumar, S., Chang, S.: Learning to hash for indexing big data - a survey. CoRR (2015)
17. Wang, J., Shen, H.T., Song, J., Ji, J.: Hashing for similarity search: a survey. CoRR (2014)

18. Grauman, K., Fergus, R.: Learning binary hash codes for large-scale image search. In: Cipolla, R., Battiato, S., Farinella, G.M. (eds.) Machine Learning for Computer Vision. SCI, vol. 411, pp. 55–93. Springer, Heidelberg (2013)

19. Erin Liong, V., Lu, J., Wang, G., Moulin, P., Zhou, J.: Deep hashing for compact binary codes learning. In: CVPR (2015)

20. Wang, J., Kumar, S., Chang, S.: Semi-supervised hashing for large-scale search. PAMI **34**(12), 2393–2406 (2012)

21. Salakhutdinov, R., Hinton, G.E.: Semantic hashing. Int. J. Approximate Reasoning **50**(7), 969–978 (2009)

22. Carreira-Perpinan, M.A., Raziperchikolaei, R.: Hashing with binary autoencoders. In: CVPR (2015)

23. Nocedal, J., Wright, S.J.: Numerical Optimization, 2nd edn. World Scientific, New York (2006). Chap. 17

24. Liu, D.C., Nocedal, J.: On the limited memory BFGS method for large scale optimization. Math. Program. **45**, 503–528 (1989)

25. Krizhevsky, A.: Learning multiple layers of features from tiny images. Technical report, University of Toronto (2009)

26. Jia, Y., Shelhamer, E., Donahue, J., Karayev, S., Long, J., Girshick, R., Guadarrama, S., Darrell, T.: Caffe: Convolutional architecture for fast feature embedding (2014). arXiv preprint: arXiv:1408.5093

27. Lecun, Y., Cortes, C.: The MNIST database of handwritten digits. http://yann.lecun.com/exdb/mnist/

28. Jégou, H., Douze, M., Schmid, C.: Product quantization for nearest neighbor search. PAMI **33**(1), 117–128 (2011)

29. Lowe, D.G.: Distinctive image features from scale-invariant keypoints. IJCV **60**(2), 91–110 (2004)

30. Oliva, A., Torralba, A.: Modeling the shape of the scene: a holistic representation of the spatial envelope. IJCV **42**(3), 145–175 (2001)

31. Nguyen, V.A., Lu, J., Do, M.N.: Supervised discriminative hashing for compact binary codes. In: ACM MM (2014)

32. Zhao, F., Huang, Y., Wang, L., Tan, T.: Deep semantic ranking based hashing for multi-label image retrieval. In: CVPR (2015)

33. Zhang, R., Lin, L., Zhang, R., Zuo, W., Zhang, L.: Bit-scalable deep hashing with regularized similarity learning for image retrieval and person re-identification. IEEE Trans. Image Process. **24**(12), 4766–4779 (2015)

34. Donahue, J., Jia, Y., Vinyals, O., Hoffman, J., Zhang, N., Tzeng, E., Darrell, T.: DeCAF: a deep convolutional activation feature for generic visual recognition. In: ICML (2014)

Automatically Selecting Inference Algorithms for Discrete Energy Minimisation

Paul Henderson$^{(\boxtimes)}$ and Vittorio Ferrari

School of Informatics, University of Edinburgh, Edinburgh, Scotland, UK
{p.m.henderson,vittorio.ferrari}@ed.ac.uk

Abstract. Minimisation of discrete energies defined over factors is an important problem in computer vision, and a vast number of MAP inference algorithms have been proposed. Different inference algorithms perform better on factor graph models (GMs) from different underlying problem classes, and in general it is difficult to know which algorithm will yield the lowest energy for a given GM. To mitigate this difficulty, survey papers [1–3] advise the practitioner on what algorithms perform well on what classes of models. We take the next step forward, and present a technique to automatically select the best inference algorithm for an input GM. We validate our method experimentally on an extended version of the OpenGM2 benchmark [3], containing a diverse set of vision problems. On average, our method selects an inference algorithm yielding labellings with 96 % of variables the same as the best available algorithm.

1 Introduction

Minimisation of discrete energies defined over factors is an important problem in computer vision and other fields such as bioinformatics, with many algorithms proposed in the literature to solve such problems [3]. These models arise from many different underlying *problem classes*; in vision, typical examples are stereo matching, semantic segmentation, and texture reconstruction, each of which yields models with very different characteristics, making different choices of minimisation algorithm preferable.

We consider factor graph models (GMs) defined by sets V and F of variables and factors respectively. Each variable takes values in some discrete label-space, and each factor is a real-valued function on some subset of V, its clique, yielding an additive contribution to a global energy. In this paper, we focus on algorithms to find the labelling of variables that minimises this global energy, the so-called *MAP inference* problem. Different problem classes give rise to problem instances with different characteristics, such as size of cliques and number of variables, affecting which inference algorithms are best suited to them.

The space of published inference algorithms is vast, with methods ranging from highly specialised to very general. For example, message passing [4] is widely applicable, but takes exponential time for large cliques, and may not converge. Dual-space variants such as TRW-S [5] do guarantee convergence, but not necessarily to a global optimum. α-expansion [6] and graph-cuts [7] are better suited

© Springer International Publishing AG 2016
B. Leibe et al. (Eds.): ECCV 2016, Part V, LNCS 9909, pp. 235–252, 2016.
DOI: 10.1007/978-3-319-46454-1_15

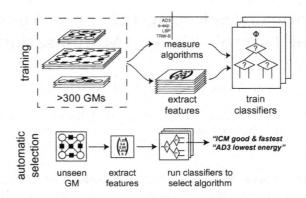

Fig. 1. Our pipeline for automatic algorithm selection

to models with dense connectivity, but require factors to take certain restricted forms, while QPBO [8] only works for binary models and may leave some variables unlabelled. Algorithms solving the Wolfe dual [9–11] such as [12,13] are applicable to models with arbitrary factors and labels, but existing implementations for this generic setting tend to run more slowly.

Thus, when developing a new model, it may be difficult to decide what algorithm to use for inference. Selecting a good algorithm for a given model requires extensive expertise about the landscape of existing algorithms and typically involves understanding the operational details of many of them. Moreover, even for an expert who can choose which algorithm is best overall on a particular problem class, it may not be clear which is best for a particular *instance*—certain problem classes are heterogeneous enough that different instances within them may be best solved by different algorithms (Sect. 3). An alternative solution would be to run many algorithms on each input model and see which one performs best empirically. However, this would be computationally very expensive.

Recently studies appeared that evaluate a number of algorithms on various problems, comparing their performance [1–3,14,15]. These are intended to provide a 'field guide' for the practitioner, suggesting which techniques are suited for which models. In this paper, we take the next step forward and propose a technique to *automatically* select which inference algorithm to run on an input problem instance (Sect. 4). We do so without requiring the user to have any knowledge of the applicability of different inference methods, and without the computational expense of running many algorithms. Thus, our method is particularly suited for the vision practitioner with limited knowledge of inference, but who wishes to apply it to real-world problems.

Our method uses features extracted from the problem instance itself, to select inference algorithms according to two criteria relevant for the practitioner: (1) the fastest algorithm reaching the lowest energy for that instance; or (2) the fastest algorithm delivering a very similar labelling to the lowest energy one (Fig. 1). The features are designed to capture characteristics of the instance that affect algorithm applicability or performance, such as the clique sizes and connectivity structure (Sect. 4.1). We train our selection models without human supervision, based on the results of running many algorithms over a large dataset of training problem instances.

We perform experiments (Sect. 5) on an extended version of the OpenGM2 benchmark [3], containing 344 problem instances drawn from 32 diverse classes (Sect. 2), and consider a pool of 15 inference algorithms drawn from the most prominent approaches (Sect. 3). The results show that on 69 % of problem instances our method selects the best algorithm. On average, the labels of 96 % of variables match that returned by the algorithm achieving the lowest energy. Our automatic selector achieves these results over 88× faster than the obvious alternative of running all algorithms and retaining the best solution.

1.1 Related Work

MAP inference. MAP inference algorithms can be split into several broad categories. Graph-cuts [7] is very efficient, but restricted to pairwise binary GMs with submodular factors. It can be extended to more general models, such as by the move-making methods α-expansion and $\alpha\beta$-swap [6], wherein a subset of variables change label at each iteration, or by transformations introducing auxiliary variables [16–18]. Alternatively, inference is naturally formulated as an integer linear program, which can be solved directly and optimally using off-the-shelf polyhedral solvers for small problems [3]. It can also be relaxed to a non-integer linear program (LP), which can be solved faster. However, it requires rounding the solution, which does not always yield the global optimum of the original problem. Message-passing algorithms [4,19] have each variable/factor iteratively send to its neighbours messages encoding its current belief about each neighbour's min-marginals. Tree-reweighted methods [5,20] use a message-passing formulation, but actually solve a Lagrangian dual of the LP, and can provide a certificate of optimality where relevant. Other dual-decomposition methods [12,13,21] directly solve the Wolfe dual [10,11] to the LP, but by iteratively finding the MAP state of each clique (or other tractable subgraphs) instead of passing messages. Our focus in this paper is not to introduce another inference algorithm, but to consider the meta-problem of learning to select what existing inference algorithm to apply to an input model; as such, we use many of the above algorithms in our framework (Sect. 3).

Inferning. Our work is a form of *inferning* [22], as it considers interactions between inference and learning. A few such methods use learning to guide the inference process. Unlike the hard-wired algorithms mentioned above, these approaches learn to adapt to the characteristics of a particular problem class. Some operate by pruning the model during inference, by learning classifiers to remove labels from some variables [23,24], or to remove certain factors from the model [25,26]. Others learn an optimal sequence of operations to perform during message-passing inference [27]. Our work operates at a higher level than these approaches. Instead of incorporating learning into an algorithm to allow adaptation to a problem class, we instead learn to predict which of a fixed set of hard-wired algorithms is best to apply to a given problem instance.

Surveys on inference. The survey papers [1–3,14,15] evaluate a number of algorithms on various problems, comparing their performance. [1] focuses on stereo matching and considers highly-connected grid models defined on pixels with unary and pairwise factors only. It evaluates three inference algorithms (graph-cuts, TRW-S, and belief propagation). [2] considers a wider selection of problems—stereo matching, image reconstruction, photomontaging, and binary segmentation—but with 4-connectivity only, and applies a wider range of algorithms, adding ICM and α-expansion to the above. Recently, [3,14] substantially widened the scope of such analysis, by considering also models with higher-order potentials, regular graphs with denser connectivity, models based on superpixels with smaller number of variables, and partitioning problems without unary terms. They compare the performance of many different types of algorithms on these models, including some specialised to particular problem classes. These surveys help to understand the space of existing algorithms and provide a guide to which algorithms are suited for which models. Our work takes a natural step forward, with a technique to automatically select the best algorithm to run on an input problem instance.

Automatic algorithm selection. Automatic algorithm selection was pioneered by [28], which considered algorithms for quadrature and process scheduling. More recently, machine learning techniques have been used to select algorithms for constraint-satisfaction [29], and other combinatorial search problems [30]. However, none of these works consider selecting MAP inference algorithms.

2   Dataset of Models

OpenGM2 [3]. The OpenGM2 dataset contains GMs drawn from 28 problem classes, including pairwise and higher-order models from computer vision and bioinformatics; it is the largest dataset of GMs currently available. We briefly summarize here the main kinds of problems and refer to [3] for details.

- low-level vision problems such as stereo matching [2], inpainting [31,32], and montaging [2]. These are all locally-connected graphs with variables corresponding to pixels, and with pairwise factors only; label counts vary widely between classes, from 2–256.
- small semantic segmentation problems with up to eight classes, with labels corresponding to surface types [33] and geometric descriptions [34]. These are irregular, sparse graphs over superpixels; [33] uses pairwise factors only, while [34] has general third-order terms.
- partitioning (unsupervised segmentation by clustering) based on patch similarity, operating on superpixels and with as many labels as variables, in both 2D [35–37] and 3D [38]. Potts or generalised Potts factors are used in all cases; [35] has very large cliques with up to 300 variables, while the other classes are pairwise or third-order, just one class having dense connectivity.

– two problem classes from bioinformatics: protein side-chain prediction [39], and protein folding [40]; both are defined over irregular graphs, with [39] having only two labels but general third-order factors, while [40] has up to 503 labels and dense pairwise connectivity.

Below we complement the OpenGM2 dataset with four additional, interesting problem classes which arise in modern computer vision applications (Fig. 2).

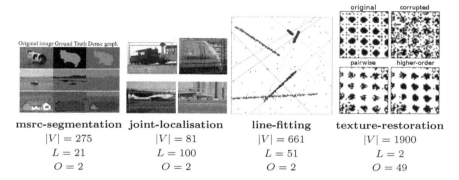

	msrc-segmentation	joint-localisation	line-fitting	texture-restoration
	$|V| = 275$	$|V| = 81$	$|V| = 661$	$|V| = 1900$
	$L = 21$	$L = 100$	$L = 51$	$L = 2$
	$O = 2$	$O = 2$	$O = 2$	$O = 49$

Fig. 2. Our four added GM classes. Variable count $|V|$ is a mean over all instances; L is mean label count, and order O is largest factor clique size

Semantic segmentation with context [23]. Semantic segmentation on the MSRC-21 dataset [41] with relative position factors. Variables correspond to superpixels and labels to 21 object/background classes (*e.g.* car, road, sky). Unary factors are given by appearance classifiers on features of a superpixel, while pairwise factors encode relative location in the image, to favour labellings showing classes in the expected spatial relation to one another (*e.g.* sky above road). The model is fully connected, *i.e.* there is a pairwise factor between every two superpixels in the image.

Joint localisation [23]. Joint object localisation across images on the PASCAL VOC 2007 dataset [42]. The set of images containing a certain object class form a problem instance. Variables correspond to images and labels to object proposals [43] in the images. Unary factors are given by the objectness probability of a proposal [43], while pairwise factors measure the appearance similarity between two proposals in different images. Inference on this model will select one proposal per image, so that they are likely to contain objects and to be visually similar over the images.

Line fitting [44]. Fitting of multiple lines to a set of points in $\mathbb{R}^2$. This an alternative to RANSAC [45] for fitting an unknown number of geometric models to a dataset. Variables correspond to points and labels to candidate lines from a fixed pool (sampled from the point set in a preprocessing stage). Unary factors favour labelling a point with a nearby line, while pairwise factors promote local smoothness of the labelling (*i.e.* nearby points should take the same label).

Texture restoration [46]. Binary texture restoration with pattern potentials. Given a binary image corrupted by noise, the task is to reconstruct the original noise-free image, while preserving the underlying texture regularity. Variables correspond to pixels and labels to 'on' or 'off'. Unary factors penalise deviations from the input noisy image, while pairwise factors prefer pixels at certain offsets taking certain pairs of values (learned on a training image showing a noise-free texture). Higher-order factors reward image patches for taking joint labellings which occur frequently in the training image (patterns). The pairwise and higher-order factors capture low and high order texture properties, respectively.

Data diversity. From each problem class we take all instances up to a maximum of 20. This results in a diverse dataset of 344 problem instances drawn from the 32 classes; 224 of these instances are pairwise and 120 higher-order. 21 of the problem classes have small label-spaces (<20 labels), while the remainder vary greatly up to a maximum of 17074. Variable counts similarly cover a wide range, from 19 to 2356620, with a median of 10148. Amongst the higher-order problems, 58 % of instances have arbitrary dense factor tables, while the remainder have Potts potentials [6] or generalised versions thereof [47,48]. The problem classes also differ greatly in the degrees of homogeneity of their instances. For example, instances in the *line-fitting* class vary by an order of magnitude in variable and label counts, whereas all instances in the *inclusion* class have identical characteristics but for the factor energies themselves.

3   Inference Algorithms and Performance

Inference algorithms. A vast number of MAP inference algorithms have been proposed in the literature, with differing approaches, degrees of generality, and performance characteristics. We selected 15 to use in our experiments (Table 1), including representative algorithms from most prominent approaches, *e.g.* move-making, message-passing, dual-decomposition, combinatorial, etc. This covers many of the most commonly used algorithms in computer vision, such as TRW-S [5], QPBO [8], and α-expansion [6]. Note however that we do not aim to form an exhaustive pool of all good algorithms; our automated selection method is agnostic to the pool of algorithms it is trained to select from, and explicitly avoids making prior assumptions on their applicability.

We also include a simple method, dubbed *unary-modes (UM)*, which labels each variable by minimizing its unary factors only; this should perform poorly on genuinely hard structured prediction problems, where the non-unary factors have a decisive impact on the MAP labelling.

Protocol for inference. We used the original authors' implementation of each algorithm where available, and the implementations in [3] otherwise. Every algorithm was run on every problem instance in our dataset, with limits of 60 min

Table 1. Algorithms used in this study, including the GM orders they are applicable to (pw = pairwise), number of parameter settings included if more than one (#p), full name or description, and reference to the original work

alias	order	#p	name / description	ref.
A*	*all*		implicitly convert to shortest-path problem and apply A*	[49]
AD^3	*all*		alternating directions dual decomposition with branch and bound	[13]
α-exp	*pw*		alpha-expansion	[6]
BPS	*all*	4	sequential loopy belief propagation, implementation of [3]	[4]
DDS	*all*	2	dual decomposition with subgradient descent	[12]
FPD	*pw*	3	fast primal/dual (FastPD)	[50]
ICM	*all*		iterated conditional modes	[51]
ILP	*all*		solve as integer programming problem with Gurobi	[3]
KL	*pw*		Kernighan-Lin method for 2nd order partitioning problems	[52]
LBP	*all*	4	parallel loopy belief propagation, implementation of [3]	[4]
LP	*all*		solve linear programming relaxation with Gurobi	[3]
MPLP	*all*		max-product linear programming with cutting plane relaxation tightening	[21,53]
QPBO	*pw*		quadratic pseudo-boolean optimisation	[8]
TRW-S	*pw*	3	sequential tree-reweighted message-passing	[5]
UM	*all*		take lowest-energy label according to unary factors only	-

CPU time and 4 GB RAM imposed for inference on one instance. For each successful run, we recorded the MAP labelling and time taken.

Many of the algorithms have free parameters that must be defined by the user. While it was not practical to evaluate every possible combination of parameters, for several of the algorithms we included multiple parameterisations where this affects their results significantly. For example, we ran four versions of loopy belief propagation, with damping set to 0.0 and 0.75, and maximum iteration counts of 50 and 250. In such cases, the different parameterisations are combined to create a meta-algorithm, which simulates the user running every parameterisation, then taking the results from that yielding lowest energy on the problem instance.

Several incompatible combinations of algorithms and GMs were included. When possible, we still ran the algorithm to obtain an approximate solution:

- higher-order factors are omitted when passing GMs to pairwise algorithms. However, when evaluating the algorithm's performance, the energy of the output labelling is still computed on the full model including all factors.
- non-metric pairwise factors passed to α-expansion are handled as if they were metric, sacrificing the usual correctness and optimality guarantees [6].

When it was not possible to run the algorithm, we counted this as a failure:

- QPBO aborts when presented with a GM having non-binary variables.
- FastPD aborts when presented with a GM whose pairwise factors are not all proportional to some uniform distance function on labels.
- Kernighan-Lin aborts when presented with a GM having factors that are not pairwise Potts

Table 2. Aggregate performance of each inference algorithm on our dataset; mean time is over instances for which the algorithm successfully returns a result

	% instances for which...			mean time /s
	completes	best-&-fastest	good-&-fastest	
A*	4	0	0	0.1
AD^3	52	7	1	390.2
α-exp	98	5	7	23.4
BPS	72	4	2	158.3
DDS	80	0	0	296.6
FPD	31	9	22	7.2
ILP	48	1	0	96.3
LP	52	2	1	76.8
ICM	100	30	31	60.7
KL	12	10	10	142.2
LBP	73	6	4	193.5
MPLP	56	1	1	1116.3
QPBO	12	0	2	0.1
TRW-S	94	19	10	236.4
UM	100	0	3	0.1

Performance measures. We measured three aspects of the performance of each algorithm:

- *completes:* whether the algorithm runs to completion, *i.e.* returns a solution within 60 min, regardless of the energy of that solution.
- *best-and-fastest:* whether the algorithm reaches the lowest energy among all algorithms, faster than any other one that does so. This is relevant for a user requiring the solution with lowest possible energy, even at high computational cost.

– *good-and-fastest:* whether the algorithm is the fastest to reach a solution with 98 % of variables matching the lowest energy labelling. This is highly relevant in practice, as minor deviations from that labelling may not matter to the user, while achieving it would require a significantly slower algorithm.

Table 2 shows the performance of the algorithms with respect to these measures.

Algorithm diversity. We see that the distributions of both best-and-fastest and good-and-fastest algorithms over instances have high entropy—many different algorithms are best-and-fastest or good-and-fastest for a significant fraction of GMs. 11 of the 15 algorithms are able to return a solution for at least one instance on more than half of the problem classes; the other four are particularly restricted, such as QPBO (which only operates on binary problems). All the algorithms other than A* and DDS are the best-and-fastest for at least one problem instance. TRW-S and FastPD perform particularly well on pairwise problems, with TRW-S generally reaching slightly lower energies, but FastPD being much quicker. Kernighan-Lin outperforms all algorithms on pairwise partitioning problems. AD^3 gives low energies for high-order problems, but often takes longer than other algorithms. Only ICM and unary-modes are able to return a solution for all problem instances. Although they are fast and widely-applicable, these naïve methods are unable to return the best solution in the majority of cases. All these observations show how our goal of learning to select the best inferencer is much harder than simply picking any algorithm that runs to completion.

4   Learning to Select an Algorithm

We now consider how to automatically select the best MAP inference algorithm for an input problem instance. This is the main contribution of this paper. We define two tasks: (1) predicting the best-and-fastest algorithm; and (2) predicting the good-and-fastest algorithm. To address these tasks, we design selection models that take a GM as input, and select an algorithm as output (Sect. 4.2). The selection models operate on features extracted from the GMs themselves (Sect. 4.1). This is different from the typical approach in computer vision of extracting features from images and using these to build a GM.

4.1   GM Features

We extract the following three groups of features from each problem instance (Fig. 3).

Instance size. The number of variables, $|V|$, and of factors, $|F|$, are used to indicate the overall size of the problem instance, hence whether slower algorithms are likely to be applicable. We also include the minimum, maximum and mean label count over all variables. See Fig. 3b.

Structural features. We extract more sophisticated features based on the model structure, *i.e.* which do not depend on the factor values themselves. Firstly, we take a histogram and statistics (minimum, maximum, mean) of both:

- variable orders (*i.e.* for each variable, number of connected factors, Fig. 3c)
- factor orders (*i.e.* for each factor, number of variables in its clique, Fig. 3c)

Secondly, we measure factor densities—for each factor order $M \geq 2$, the number of factors of order M divided by the binomial coefficient $\binom{|V|}{M} = \frac{|V|!}{M!(|V|-M)!}$. Intuitively, this is the number of possible M-cliques that actually have an associated factor. In Fig. 3, this is 1 for third order, as there is only one possible triplet, but 2/3 for second order, as only two of the possible three pairs of variables have a pairwise factor: (x, y) and (x, z) but not (z, y)

Energy features. Our final group of features depend on the values of the factors themselves, *e.g.* the blue values in Fig. 3a. To determine the influence of different orders of factors, we compute means and deviations over values they take, defined as follows:

- for each factor $f \in F$, let μ_f be the mean and σ_f the standard deviation of all unique values taken by f
- then, for each factor order $M \geq 2$, compute for factors F_M of that order, the ratio of each of the following to the same quantity for $M = 1$:
  (i) $\sum_{f \in F_M} \mu_f$ (ii) $\sum_{f \in F_M} \mu_f / |F_M|$ (iii) $\sum_{f \in F_M} \sigma_f / |F_M|$.

Intuitively, these capture how much influence each order of factor has on the final energy, *i.e.* how much changing the labelling will change the values of factors of each order. On pairwise GMs, a large influence of the pairwise (as opposed to unary) factors makes inference harder; on higher-order GMs, pairwise algorithms should perform relatively well only when the influence of higher-order factors is small. We also count the fraction of pairwise factors f having each of the following characteristics for all labels a, b, c:
  (i) $f(a, b) = 0$ iff $a = b$ (ii) $f(a, b) \geq 0$
  (iii) $f(a, b) = f(b, a)$ (iv) $f(a, b) + f(b, c) \geq f(a, c)$

Together, these are the conditions for a factor to be metric; without (iv), to be semi-metric—respectively requirements for the α-expansion and $\alpha\beta$-swap algorithms to fulfill their correctness guarantees [6]. Finally, we measure the fraction of pairwise factors which are submodular; in general pairwise submodular problems are easier to solve by LP-based methods, as their LP relaxation is tight.

4.2 Algorithm Selection Models and Their Training

Selection models. We propose two algorithm selection models. Each is a 1-of-N classifier implemented as a random forest [54], taking the features described in Sect. 4.1 as input. Model BF is trained to predict the best-and-fastest algorithm; model GF is trained to predict the good-and-fastest algorithm. The random forests are trained recursively by selecting the best split from a randomly-generated pool at each step, using information gain (*i.e.* entropy decrease) as the criterion, and with outputs modelled by categorical distributions [54].

Data. We train the selection models on a subset of our dataset (Sect. 2). A training sample consists of features extracted from a problem instance and a target

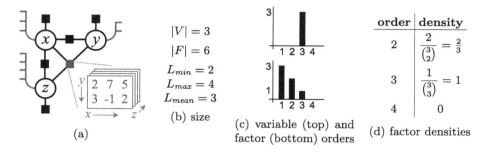

Fig. 3. Example GM structure (a) and associated features (b-d). Circles correspond to variables, and squares to factors; the label space of each variable is shown as purple dashes. Part of the value table for the third-order factor (blue) is also shown (Color figure online)

output label denoting which algorithm works best on it. It is important to note that these training labels are automatically generated by running all algorithms on the training instances, as in Sect. 3. No human annotation is required. At test time, we run the selection models on a separate subset of the dataset. The evaluation compares the algorithm selected by our model to the one known to perform best (Sect. 5). Again, this test label is produced automatically.

5   Experiments

Tasks and baselines. We report results on the two tasks defined in Sect. 4: (i) predicting the good-and-fastest inference algorithm for an input GM; and (ii) predicting the best-and-fastest algorithm. Task (i) is addressed by the selection model GF, and task (ii) by model BF (Sect. 4.2). For both tasks, we also analyse the performance of two baseline methods that select an algorithm without looking at features of the input instance. The first baseline *NB* always selects the algorithm that is most often best over the full training set. This mimics the behaviour of a naïve user who simply chooses one commonly good algorithm to use. For the second, stronger baseline *SB*, we assign each of the problem classes to one of three superclasses:

1. pairwise—many algorithms are designed for pairwise problems only;
2. higher-order—there exist algorithms designed explicitly to handle higher-order factors, but which may be slow for pairwise instances;
3. partitioning—these are a special class which is hard for general algorithms (due to having a large label space, and being invariant to label permutations) but certain methods can exploit this structure to solve them efficiently; most partitioning problems in our dataset are pairwise, but some are third-order.

Then, at test time, each problem instance is assigned the algorithm that is most often best for training problems of its superclass. This strong baseline mimics the behaviour of a user with good working knowledge of inference—enough to recognise how her problem fits in these superclasses, and to know which algorithm will be best for each.

Experimental setup. We select half the problem instances at random to train on, and the remainder are used for testing. As discussed in Sect. 3, the ground-truth labels marking which inference algorithms perform best on a problem instance are obtained automatically by running all algorithms on all instances. No human annotation is necessary for training or testing.

When training and evaluating selection models, the underlying problem classes are always treated as unknown—they are not provided as input data. We want the selection models to freely learn the optimal association between GM features and good algorithms to run. The GM features we propose are designed to enable the selection models to reason upon various properties of GMs, which can be used to characterize problem classes (*e.g.* connectivity structure and distributions of energy values in the factors). So, we might expect the selection models to learn at least some of the problem class structures, given that this often correlates with the best algorithms (Sect. 3).

Table 3. Performance of our model GF and baselines NB and SB for selecting the good-and-fastest algorithm (first three columns), and performance of our model FG and baselines for selecting the best-and-fastest algorithm (last three columns).

algorithm selected by...	good-and-fastest			best-and-fastest		
	GF	NB	SB	BF	NB	SB
% instances correctly classified	69	31	28	62	30	36
mean % matching variables	96.4	75.3	87.5	97.1	75.4	95.6

Evaluation measures. Our algorithm selection models are evaluated on the test set with the following measures (Table 3):

- percentage of instances with the correct algorithm (best-and-fastest or good-and-fastest) selected. This is the measure for which we trained our selection models.
- mean (over instances) of fraction of variables matching the labelling returned by the best-and-fastest algorithm. This is particularly relevant in practice, as users typically care about the quality of the labelling output, by an algorithm, especially in terms of how close it is to the lowest-energy labelling that could have been returned.

6   Analysis

Predicting the good-and-fastest algorithm. Model GF correctly chooses the good-and-fastest algorithm for 69 % of instances, with 96.4 % of variables taking the same label as in the true best labelling on average. This compares favourably to the naïve baseline NB, which correctly selects only on 31 % of the instances and returns labellings that are considerably worse (75.3 % correctly-labelled variables on average). Indeed, our model also substantially outperforms the strong baseline, which only achieves an average of 87.5 % of correctly-labelled variables.

These results show that our selection model successfully generalises to new problem instances not seen during training. It is able to select an algorithm much better than even the strong baseline of a user who knows which algorithm performs best for similar problems in the training set.

Predicting the best-and-fastest algorithm. Model BF correctly selects the best-and-fastest algorithm on 62 % of instances, exceeding the naïve baseline (32 %). This results in 97.1 % of variables taking the same label as in the true lowest-energy solution, greatly exceeding the naïve baseline of 75.4 %. Our model performs well against even the strong baseline, which only classifies 36 % of instances correctly and has a slightly lower fraction of correct variables at 95.6 %.

Table 4. Mean times and speed-ups from using our method, versus exhaustively applying all algorithms. *matching var's* is fraction of variables whose labels match true best result; *speed-up* is ratio of time to that for exhaustive testing

mean...	time /s	speed-up	matching var's
exhaustive	13046.8	1.0×	100 %
good-and-fastest	221.3	88.1×	96.4 %
best-and-fastest	312.5	46.8×	97.1 %

Efficiency. As noted in Sect. 1, a simple alternative to our selection method is to run every algorithm on the test problem instance, and select the lowest-energy solution. However, this is computationally very expensive. To evaluate the speed-up made by our method, for each problem instance we also measured (i) the total time to run every inference algorithm; (ii) the time to predict the best-and-fastest algorithm with model BF then run it; and, (iii) the time to predict the good-and-fastest algorithm with model GF then run it. As we see in Table 4, our method results in an average speed-up of 46.8× using model BF, and 88.1× using model GF, with 97.1 % and 96.4 % of variables correctly labelled respectively. Thus, automated selection achieves labellings very similar to running every algorithm, but at a small fraction the computational expense. Model GF yields a significantly faster-running algorithm on average than model BF, with only a small drop (<1 %) in variables correctly labelled.

Algorithms selected by the strong baseline. As described in Sect. 5, our strong baseline chooses the algorithm that is most often best-and-fastest or good-and-fastest over the training set, for problems in the same superclass as the test instance. For predicting the best-and-fastest algorithm, Kernighan-Lin is selected

Table 5. Confusion matrix showing true (rows) and predicted (columns) good-and-fastest algorithms for pairwise problems. The table only includes those algorithms that are the true good-and-fastest for at least one problem instance.

	AD³	α-exp	BPS	FPD	ICM	KL	LBP	QPBO	TRW-S	UM
AD³	0	0	0	0	2	0	0	0	0	0
α-exp	0	5	1	1	0	0	0	0	2	0
BPS	0	0	1	0	2	0	1	0	1	0
FPD	0	0	1	19	0	0	0	0	0	0
ICM	0	0	0	0	16	1	0	0	3	0
KL	0	0	0	0	0	24	0	0	0	0
LBP	0	0	0	0	3	0	4	0	0	1
QPBO	0	0	3	0	0	0	0	3	0	0
TRW-S	0	1	0	6	1	0	1	0	6	0
UM	0	1	0	1	0	0	0	1	0	0

for partitioning problems, TRW-S for other pairwise instances, and AD³ for other (higher order) instances. However, for the good-and-fastest algorithm, FastPD is selected instead of TRW-S for pairwise instances, and ICM for higher order instances, indicating that these often label 98 % or more of variables correctly, while being faster to run.

Algorithms selected by our method. At a coarse level, for the task of selecting the best-and-fastest algorithm, we find that our model BF most often chooses pairwise-specific algorithms for pairwise problems, and AD³ for higher-order problems. This agrees with intuition—pairwise algorithms are specifically designed to be faster for pairwise instances, while AD³ is a good general-purpose algorithm for higher-order instances. Interestingly, for the good-and-fastest task, model GF correctly learns to choose ICM or a good pairwise method for higher-order problems in place of AD³—for many instances, these provide solutions close in labelling to the lowest-energy, and do so much faster than AD³.

To explore whether our method can also draw more subtle distinctions, we now examine the distribution of algorithms it selects for pairwise problems. 10 of the algorithms we consider are useful for these, in the sense of being good-and-fastest for at least one instance. Table 5 shows the confusion matrix for true and predicted good-and-fastest algorithms amongst these 10. Certain groups of problems can be distinguished based on structural properties, such as partitioning problems to be solved with KL, or very large instances that only run to completion with ICM. Our model correctly makes these distinctions. Other distinctions are even more subtle—such as whether to use α-expansion, TRW-S, or FastPD for a pairwise problem of moderate size. Our model is able to select between these three algorithms, making the correct choice for 75 % of instances.

LOCO regime. We also tested our models and baselines in an even harder 'leave one class out' (LOCO) regime, where for each problem class C in turn, we train on all instances from classes other than C, and test on those in C; the final

Table 6. Performance of algorithm selection methods selecting good-and-fastest and best-and-fastest algorithms in the LOCO regime; see Table 3 for details.

algorithm selected by...	good-and-fastest			best-and-fastest		
	GF	NB	SB	BF	NB	SB
% instances correctly classified	40	26	11	28	25	23
mean % matching variables	89.8	73.3	71.7	85.5	73.3	86.2

performance is given by a weighted mean over classes. This tests generalisation to classes absent from the training set, which is relevant when the user does not wish to train our model on her classes. The results are presented in Table 6.

For selecting the good-and-fastest algorithm, model GF still performs well in LOCO regime, selecting algorithms labelling 89.8 % of variables correctly, and exceeding both naïve and strong baselines by over 15 %. Moreover, we correctly choose the good-and-fastest algorithm 14 % more often than the baselines.

For the best-and-fastest task, model BF results in 85.5 % of variables being correctly labelled, significantly exceeding the naïve baseline at 73.3 % and comparable with the strong baseline at 86.2 %. These results demonstrate that our selection models are strong enough to generalise *across* the hidden problem classes, going beyond discovering and recalling distinguishing features of these.

7 Conclusions

We have presented a method to automatically choose the best inference algorithm to apply to an input problem instance. It selects an inference algorithm that labels 96 % of variables the same as the best available algorithm for that instance. Our method is over 88× faster than exhaustively trying all algorithms. The experiments show that our automated selection methods successfully generalise across problem instances and importantly, even across problem classes.

References

1. Kolmogorov, V., Rother, C.: Comparison of energy minimization algorithms for highly connected graphs. In: Leonardis, A., Bischof, H., Pinz, A. (eds.) ECCV 2006. LNCS, vol. 3952, pp. 1–15. Springer, Heidelberg (2006)
2. Szeliski, R., Zabih, R., Scharstein, D., Veksler, O., Kolmogorov, V., Agarwala, A., Tappen, M., Rother, C.: A comparative study of energy minimization methods for markov random fields with smoothness-based priors. IEEE Trans. on PAMI **30**(6), 1068–1080 (2008)
3. Kappes, J., Andres, B., Hamprecht, F., Schnörr, C., Nowozin, S., Batra, D., Kim, S., Kausler, B., Kröger, T., Lellmann, J., Komodakis, N., Savchynskyy, B., Rother, C.: A comparative study of modern inference techniques for structured discrete energy minimization problems. IJCV **115**, 1–30 (2015)
4. Bishop, C.: Pattern Recognition and Machine Learning. Springer, New York (2006)

5. Kolmogorov, V.: Convergent tree-reweighted message passing for energy minimization. IEEE Trans. PAMI **28**(10), 1568–1583 (2006)
6. Boykov, Y., Veksler, O., Zabih, R.: Fast approximate energy minimization via graph cuts. IEEE Trans. PAMI **23**(11), 1222–1239 (2001)
7. Greig, D.M., Porteous, B.T., Seheult, A.H.: Exact maximum a posteriori estimation for binary images. J. Roy. Stat. Soc. **51**(2), 271–279 (1989)
8. Rother, C., Kolmogorov, V., Lempitsky, V., Szummer, M.: Optimizing binary MRFs via extended roof duality. In: CVPR (2007)
9. Storvik, G., Dahl, G.: Lagrangian-based methods for finding MAP solutions for MRF models. IEEE Trans. Image Process. **9**, 469–479 (2000)
10. Guignard, M., Kim, S.: Lagrangean decomposition: a model yielding stronger Lagrangean bounds. Math. Prog. **39**, 215–228 (1987)
11. Komodakis, N., Paragios, N., Tziritas, G.: MRF optimization via dual decomposition: message-passing revisited. In: ICCV, pp. 1–8 (2007)
12. Kappes, J., Savchynskyy, B., Schnörr, C.: A bundle approach to efficient MAP-inference by lagrangian relaxation. In: CVPR (2012)
13. Martins, A.F.T., Figueiredo, M.A.T., Aguiar, P.M.Q., Smith, N.A., Xing, E.P.: AD3: alternating directions dual decomposition for MAP inference in graphical models. JMLR **16**, 495–545 (2015)
14. Andres, B., Kappes, J.H., Köthe, U., Schnörr, C., Hamprecht, F.A.: An empirical comparison of inference algorithms for graphical models with higher order factors using openGM. In: Goesele, M., Roth, S., Kuijper, A., Schiele, B., Schindler, K. (eds.) Pattern Recognition. LNCS, vol. 6376, pp. 353–362. Springer, Heidelberg (2010)
15. Alahari, K., Kohli, P., Torr, P.: Dynamic hybrid algorithms for discrete map MRF inference. IEEE Trans. PAMI **32**(10), 1846–1857 (2010)
16. Ishikawa, H.: Higher-order clique reduction in binary graph cut. In: CVPR, pp. 2993–3000 (2009)
17. Ishikawa, H.: Transformation of general binary MRF minimization to the first order case. IEEE Trans. PAMI **33**(6), 1234–1249 (2011)
18. Fix, A., Gruber, A., Boros, E., Zabih, R.: A graph cut algorithm for higher-order markov random fields. In: ICCV (2011)
19. Kschischang, F.R., Frey, B.J.: Factor graphs and the sum-product algorithm. IEEE Trans. Inf. Theor. **47**(2), 498–519 (2001)
20. Wainwright, M.J., Jaakkola, T.S., Willsky, A.S.: MAP estimation via agreement on (hyper)trees: message-passing and linear-programming approaches. IEEE Trans. Inf. Theor. **51**(11), 3697–3717 (2005)
21. Sontag, D., Meltzer, T., Globerson, A., Weiss, Y., Jaakkola, T.: Tightening LP relaxations for MAP using message-passing. In: Proceedings of UAI, pp. 503–510 (2008)
22. Doppa, J.R., Kumar, P., Wick, M., Singh, S., Salakhutdinov, R.: ICML 2013 workshop on inferning (2013). http://inferning.cs.umass.edu/
23. Guillaumin, M., Van Gool, L., Ferrari, V.: Fast energy minimization using learned state filters. In: CVPR (2013)
24. Conejo, B., Komodakis, N., Leprince, S., Avouac, J.P.: Inference by learning: speeding-up graphical model optimization via a coarse-to-fine cascade of pruning classifiers. In: NIPS, pp. 1–9 (2014)
25. Stoyanov, V., Eisner, J.: Fast and accurate prediction via evidence-specific MRF structure. In: ICML Workshop on Inferning (2012)

26. Roig, G., Boix, X., De Nijs, R., Ramos, S., Kuhnlenz, K., Van Gool, L.: Active map inference in CRFS for efficient semantic segmentation. In: ICCV, pp. 2312–2319 (2013)
27. Jiang, J., Moon, T., Daumé III., H., Eisner, J.: Prioritized asynchronous belief propagation. In: ICML Workshop on Inferning (2013)
28. Rice, J.R.: The algorithm selection problem. Adv. Comps. **15**, 65–118 (1976)
29. Xu, L., Hutter, F., Hoos, H.H., Leyton-Brown, K.: SATzilla: portfolio-based algorithm selection for SAT. J. Artif. Intel. Res. **32**, 565–606 (2008)
30. Kotthoff, L., Gent, I.P., Miguel, I.: A preliminary evaluation of machine learning in algorithm selection for search problems. In: Symposium on Combinatorial Search (2011)
31. Lellmann, J., Schnörr, C.: Continuous multiclass labeling approaches and algorithms. SIAM J. Im. Sci. **4**(4), 1049–1096 (2011)
32. Nowozin, S., Rother, C., Bagon, S., Sharp, T., Yao, B., Kohli, P.: Decision tree fields. In: ICCV (2011)
33. Gould, S., Fulton, R., Koller, D.: Decomposing a scene into geometric and semantically consistent regions. In: ICCV (2009)
34. Hoiem, D., Efros, A.A., Hebert, M.: Recovering occlusion boundaries from an image. IJCV **91**(3), 328–346 (2011)
35. Kim, S., Nowozin, S., Kohli, P., Yoo, C.D.: Higher-order correlation clustering for image segmentation. In: NIPS (2011)
36. Andres, B., Kappes, J.H., Beier, T., Köthe, U., Hamprecht, F.A.: Probabilistic image segmentation with closedness constraints. In: ICCV (2011)
37. Brandes, U., Delling, D., Gaertler, M., Görke, R., Hoefer, M., Nikoloski, Z., Wagner, D.: On modularity clustering. IEEE Trans. KDE **2**(2), 172–188 (2008)
38. Andres, B., Kroeger, T., Briggman, K.L., Denk, W., Korogod, N., Knott, G., Koethe, U., Hamprecht, F.A.: Globally optimal closed-surface segmentation for connectomics. In: Fitzgibbon, A., Lazebnik, S., Perona, P., Sato, Y., Schmid, C. (eds.) ECCV 2012, Part III. LNCS, vol. 7574, pp. 778–791. Springer, Heidelberg (2012)
39. Jaimovich, A., Elidan, G., Margalit, H., Friedman, N.: Towards an integrated protein-protein interaction network: a relational Markov network approach. J. Comp. Biol. **13**(2), 145–164 (2006)
40. Yanover, C., Schueler-Furman, O., Weiss, Y.: Minimizing and learning energy functions for side-chain prediction. J. Comp. Biol. **15**(7), 899–911 (2008)
41. Shotton, J., Winn, J., Rother, C., Criminisi, A.: TextonBoost for image understanding: multi-class object recognition and segmentation by jointly modeling appearance, shape and context. IJCV **81**(1), 2–23 (2009)
42. Everingham, M., Van Gool, L., Williams, C.K.I., Winn, J., Zisserman, A.: The PASCAL Visual Object Classes Challenge 2007 (VOC 2007) Results (2007). http://www.pascal-network.org/challenges/VOC/voc2007/workshop/index.html
43. Alexe, B., Deselaers, T., Ferrari, V.: What is an object? In: CVPR (2010)
44. Isack, H., Boykov, Y.: Energy-based geometric multi-model fitting. IJCV **97**(2), 123–147 (2012)
45. Fischler, M.A., Bolles, R.C.: Random sample consensus: a paradigm for model fitting with applications to image analysis and automated cartography. Comm. ACM **24**(6), 381–395 (1981)
46. Rother, C., Kohli, P., Feng, W., Jia, J.: Minimizing sparse higher order energy functions of discrete variables. In: CVPR (2009)
47. Kohli, P., Kumar, M., Torr, P.: P3 & beyond: solving energies with higher order cliques. In: CVPR (2007)

48. Kohli, P., Ladicky, L., Torr, P.: Robust higher order potentials for enforcing label consistency. In: CVPR (2008)
49. Bergtholdt, M., Kappes, J.H., Schnörr, C.: Learning of graphical models and efficient inference for object class recognition. In: Franke, K., Müller, K.-R., Nickolay, B., Schäfer, R. (eds.) DAGM 2006. LNCS, vol. 4174, pp. 273–283. Springer, Heidelberg (2006). doi:10.1007/11861898_28
50. Komodakis, N., Tziritas, G., Paragios, N.: Performance vs computational efficiency for optimizing single and dynamic MRFs: setting the state of the art with primal-dual strategies. CVIU **112**(1), 14–29 (2008)
51. Besag, J.: On the statistical analysis of dirty pictures. J. Roy. Stat. Soc. **48**(3), 48–259 (1986)
52. Kernighan, B.W., Lin, S.: An efficient heuristic procedure for partitioning graphs. Bell Sys. Tech. J. **49**(2), 291–307 (1970)
53. Sontag, D., Choe, D.K., Li, Y.: Efficiently searching for frustrated cycles in MAP inference. In: Proceedings of UAI, pp. 795–804 (2012)
54. Criminisi, A., Shotton, J., Konukoglu, E.: Decision forests for classification, regression, density estimation, manifold learning and semi-supervised learning. Microsoft Research Cambridge, Technical report MSRTR-2011-114 (2011)

Ego2Top: Matching Viewers in Egocentric and Top-View Videos

Shervin Ardeshir[✉] and Ali Borji

Center for Research in Computer Vision, University of Central Florida, Orlando, USA
ardeshir@cs.ucf.edu, aborji@crcv.ucf.edu

Abstract. Egocentric cameras are becoming increasingly popular and provide us with large amounts of videos, captured from the first person perspective. At the same time, surveillance cameras and drones offer an abundance of visual information, often captured from top-view. Although these two sources of information have been separately studied in the past, they have not been collectively studied and related. Having a set of egocentric cameras and a top-view camera capturing the same area, we propose a framework to identify the egocentric viewers in the top-view video. We utilize two types of features for our assignment procedure. Unary features encode what a viewer (seen from top-view or recording an egocentric video) visually experiences over time. Pairwise features encode the relationship between the visual content of a pair of viewers. Modeling each view (egocentric or top) by a graph, the assignment process is formulated as spectral graph matching. Evaluating our method over a dataset of 50 top-view and 188 egocentric videos taken in different scenarios demonstrates the efficiency of the proposed approach in assigning egocentric viewers to identities present in top-view camera. We also study the effect of different parameters such as the number of egocentric viewers and visual features.

Keywords: Egocentric vision · Surveillance · Spectral graph matching · Gist · Cross-domain image understanding

1 Introduction

The availability of large amounts of egocentric videos captured by cellphones and wearable devices such as GoPro cameras and Google Glass has opened the door to a lot of interesting research in computer vision [1–3]. At the same time, videos captured with top-down static cameras such as surveillance cameras in airports and subways, unmanned aerial vehicles (UAVs) and drones, provide us with a lot of invaluable information about activities and events taking place at different locations and environments. Relating these two complementary, but drastically different sources of visual information can provide us with rich analytical power, and help us explore what can not be inferred from each of these sources taken separately. Establishing such a relationship can have several applications. For example, athletes can be equipped with body-worn cameras, and their egocentric

© Springer International Publishing AG 2016
B. Leibe et al. (Eds.): ECCV 2016, Part V, LNCS 9909, pp. 253–268, 2016.
DOI: 10.1007/978-3-319-46454-1_16

videos together with the top-view videos can offer new data useful for better technical and tactical sport analysis. Moreover, due to the use of wearable devices and cameras by law enforcement officers, finding the person behind an egocentric camera in a surveillance network could be a useful application. Furthermore, fusing these two types of information can result in better 3D reconstruction of an environment by combining the top-view information with first person views.

The first necessary step to utilize information from these two sources, is to establish correspondences between the two views. In other words, a matching between egocentric cameras and the people present in the top-view camera is needed. In this effort, we attempt to address this problem. More specifically, our goal is to localize people recording egocentric videos, in a top-view reference camera. To the best of our knowledge, such an effort has not been done so far. In order to evaluate our method, we designed the following setup. A dataset containing several test cases is collected. In each test case, multiple people were asked to move freely in a certain environment and record egocentric videos. We refer to these people as ego-centric *viewers*. At the same time, a top-view camera was recording the entire scene/area including all the egocentric viewers and possibly other intruders. An example case is illustrated in Fig. 1.

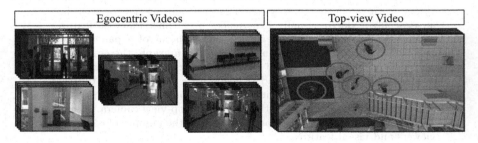

Fig. 1. Left shows a set of 5 egocentric videos. Right shows a top-view video capturing the whole scene. The viewers are highlighted using red circles in the top-view video. We aim to answer the two following questions: (1) Does this set of egocentric videos belong to the viewers visible in the top-view video? (2) Assuming they do, which viewer is capturing which egocentric video? (Color figure online)

Given a set of egocentric videos and a top-view surveillance video, we try to answer the following two questions: (1) Does this set of egocentric videos belong to the viewers visible in the top-view camera? (2) If yes, then which viewer is capturing which egocentric video? To answer these questions, we need to compare a set of egocentric videos to a set of viewers visible in a single top-view video. To find a matching, each set is represented by a graph and the two graphs are compared using a spectral graph matching technique [4]. In general, this problem can be very challenging due to the nature of egocentric cameras. Since the camera-holder is not visible in his own egocentric video leaving us with no cues about his visual appearance.

In what follows we briefly mention some challenges concerning this problem and sketch the layout of our approach.

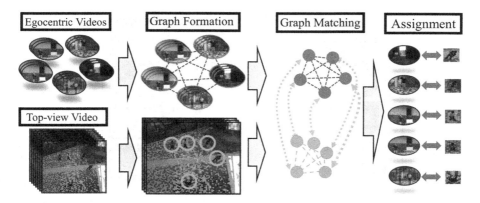

Fig. 2. The input to our framework is a set of egocentric videos (in this case 5 videos), and one top-view video. The goal is defined as assigning the egocentric videos to the people recording them. A graph is formed on the set of egocentric videos (each node being one of the egocentric videos), and the other graph is formed on the top-view video (each node being one of the targets present in the video). Using spectral graph matching, a soft assignment is found between the two graphs, and using a soft-to-hard assignment, each egocentric video is assigned to one of the viewers in the top-view video. This assignment is our answer to the second question in 1.

In order to have an understanding of the behavior of each individual in the top-view video, we use a multiple object tracking method [5] to extract the viewer's trajectory in the top-view video. Note that an egocentric video captures a person's field of view rather than his spatial location. Therefore, the content of a viewer's egocentric video, a 2D scene, corresponds to the content of the viewer's field of view in the top-view camera. For the sake of brevity, we refer to a viwer's top-view field of view as Top-FOV in what follows. Since trajectories computed by multiple object tracking do not provide us with the orientation of the egocentric cameras in the top-view video, we employ the assumption that for the most part humans tend to look straight ahead and therefore shoot videos from the visual content in front of them. Note that this is not a restrictive assumption as most ego-centric cameras are body worn (Please see Fig. 4). Having an estimate of a viewer's orientation and Top-FOV, we then encode the changes in his Top-FOV over time and use it as a descriptor. We show that this feature correlates with the change in the global visual content (or Gist) of the scene observed in his corresponding egocentric video (Fig. 3).

We also define pairwise features to capture the relationship between two egocentric videos, and also the relationship between two viewers in the top-view camera. Intuitively, if an egocentric viewer observes a certain scene and another egocentric viewer comes across the same scene later, this could hint as a relationship between the two cameras. If we match a top-view viewer to one of the two egocentric videos, we are likely to be able to find the other viewer using the mentioned relationship. As we experimentally show, this pairwise relationship significantly

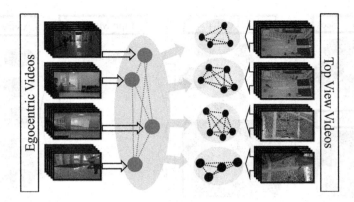

Fig. 3. Adapting our method for evaluating top-view videos. We compare the graph formed on the set of egocentric videos to the ones built on each top-view video. The top-view videos are then ranked based on the graph matching similarity. The performance of this ranking gives us insight on our first question.

improves our assignment accuracy. This assignment will lead to defining a score measuring the similarity between the two graphs. Our experiments demonstrate that the graph matching score could be used for verifying if the top-view video is in fact, capturing the egocentric viewers (See the diagram shown in Fig. 7a).

The rest of this work is as follows. In Sect. 2, we mention related works to our study. In Sect. 3, we describe the details of our framework. Section 4 presents our experimental results followed by discussions and conclusions in Sect. 5.

2 Related Work

Visual analysis of egocentric videos has recently became a hot topic in computer vision [6,7], from recognizing daily activities [1,2] to object detection [8], video summarization [9], and predicting gaze behavior [10–12]. In the following, we review some previous work related to ours spanning *Relating static and egocentric*, *Social interactions among egocentric viewers*, and *Person identification and localization*.

Relating Static and Egocentric Cameras: Some studies have addressed relationships between moving and static cameras. Interesting works reported in [13,14] have studied the relationship between mobile and static cameras for the purpose of improving object detection accuracy. [15] fuses information from egocentric and exocentric vision (other cameras in the environment) and laser depth range data to improve depth perception in 3D reconstruction. [16] predicts gaze behavior in social scenes using first-person and third-person cameras.

Social Interactions among Egocentric Viewers: To explore the relationship among multiple egocentric viewers, [17] combines several egocentric videos to achieve a more complete video with less quality degradation by estimating the importance of different scene regions and incorporating the consensus among several egocentric videos. Fathi et al., [18] detect and recognize the type of social interactions such as dialogue, monologue, and discussion by detecting human faces and estimating their body and head orientations. [19] proposes a multi-task clustering framework, which searches for coherent clusters of daily actions using the notion that people tend to perform similar actions in certain environments such as workplace or kitchen. [20] proposes a framework that discovers static and movable objects used by a set of egocentric users.

Person Identification and Localization: Perhaps, the most similar computer vision task to ours is person re-identification [21–23]. The objective here is to find the person present in one static camera, in another overlapping or non-overlapping static camera. However, the main cue in human re-identification is visual appearance of humans, which is absent in egocentric videos. Tasks such as human-identification and localization in egocentric cameras have been studied in the past. [24] uses the head motion of an egocentric viewer as a biometric signature for determine which videos have been captured by the same person. [25] identifies egocentric observers in other egocentric videos, using their head motion. Relating geo-spatial location to user shared visual content has also been explored. [3] localizes the field of view of an egocentric camera by matching it against a reference dataset of videos or images (such as Google street view), and [26] refines the geo-location of images by matching them against user shared images. Landmarks and map symbols are used in [27] to perform self localization on the map. [28] use semantic cues for spatial localization, and [29] uses location information to infer semantic information.

3   Framework

The block diagram in Fig. 2 illustrates different steps of our approach. First, each view (ego-centric or top-down) is represented by a graph which defines the relationship among the viewers present in the scene. These two graphs may not have the same number of nodes as some the egocentric videos might not be available, or some individuals present in the top-view video might not be capturing videos. Each graph consists of a set of nodes, each of which represents one viewer (egocentric or top-view), and the edges of the graph encode pairwise relationships between pairs of viewers.

We represent each viewer in top-view by describing his expected Top-FOV, and in egocentric view by the visual content of his video over time. This description is encoded in the nodes of the graphs. We also define pairwise relationships between pairs of viewers, which is encoded as the edge features of the graph (i.e., how two viewers' visual experience relate to each other).

Second, we use spectral graph matching to compute a score measuring the similarity between the two graphs, alongside with an assignment from the nodes of the egocentric graph to the nodes of the top-view graph.

Our experiments show that the graph matching score can be used as a measure of similarity between the egocentric graph and the top-view graph.

Therefore, it can be used as a measure for verifying if a set of egocentric videos have been shot in the same environment captured by the top-view camera. In other words, we can evaluate the capability of our method in terms of answering our first question. In addition, the assignment obtained by the graph matching suggests an answer to our second question. We organize this section by going over the graph formation process for each of the views, and then describing the details of the matching procedure.

3.1 Graph Representation

Each view (egocentric or top-view) is described using a single graph. The set of egocentric videos is represented using a graph in which each node represents one of the egocentric videos, and an edge captures the pairwise relationship between the content of the two videos.

In the top-view graph, each node represents the visual experience of a viewer being tracked (in the top-view camera), and an edge captures the pairwise relationship between the two. By visual experience we mean what a viewer is expected to observe during the course of his recording seen from the top view.

3.1.1 Modeling the Top-View Graph

In order to model the visual experience of a viewer in a top-view camera, we need to have knowledge about his spatial location (trajectory) throughout the video. We employ the multiple object tracking method presented in [5] and extract a set of trajectories, each corresponding to one of the viewers in the scene. Similar to [5], we use annotated bounding boxes, and provide their centers as an input to the multiple object tracker. Our tracking results are nearly perfect due to several reasons: the high quality of videos, high video frame rate, and lack of challenges such as occlusion in the top-view videos.

Each node represents one of the individuals being tracked. Employing the general assumption that people often tend to look straight ahead, we use a person's speed vector as the direction of his camera at time t (denoted as θ_t). Further, assuming a fixed angle (θ_d), we expect the content of the person's egocentric video to be consistent with the content included in a 2D cone formed by the two rays emanating from the viewer's location and with angles $\theta - \theta_d$ and $\theta + \theta_d$. Figure 4 illustrates the expected Top-FOV for three different individuals present in a frame. In our experiments, we set θ_d to 30 degrees. In theory, angle θ_d can be estimated more accurately by knowing intrinsic camera parameters such as focal length and sensor size of the corresponding egocentric camera. However, since we do not know the corresponding egocentric camera, we set it to a default value.

Top-FOVs are not directly comparable to viewers' egocentric views. The area in the Top-FOV in a top-view video mostly contains the ground floor which is not what an ego-centric viewer usually observes in front of him. However, what can be used to compare the two views is the relative change in the Top-FOV of a viewer over time. This change should correlate with the change in the content

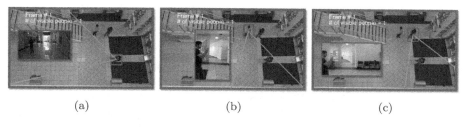

(a)   (b)   (c)

Fig. 4. Expected field of view for three different viewers in the top-view video along-side with their corresponding egocentric frames. The short dark blue line shows the estimated orientation of the camera. The Top-FOV shown in (b) and (c) have a high overlap, therefore we expect their egocentric videos to have relatively similar visual content compared to the pairs (a,b) or (a,c) at this specific time. (Color figure online)

of the egocentric video. Intuitively, if a viewer is looking straight ahead while walking on a straight line, his Top-FOV is not going to have drastic changes. Therefore, we expect the viewer's egocentric view to have a stable visual content.

Node Features: We extract two unary features for each node, one captures the changes in the content covered by his FOV, and the other is the number of visible people in the content of the Top-FOV.

To encode the relative change in the visual content of viewer i visible in the top-view camera, we form the $T \times T$ matrix (T denotes the number of frames in the top-view video) U_i^{IOU} whose elements $U_i^{IOU}(f_p, f_q)$ indicate the IOU (intersection over union) of the Top-FOV of person i in frames f_p and f_q. For example, if the viewer's Top-FOV in frame 10 has high overlap with his FOV in frame 30 (thus $U_i^{IOU}(10, 30)$ has a high value), we expect to see a high visual similarity between frames 10 and 30 in the egocentric video. Examples shown in the middle column of Fig. 5(a).

Having the Top-FOV of viewer i estimated, we then count the number of people within his Top-FOV at each time frame and store it in a $1 \times T$ vector U_i^n. To count the number of people, we used annotated bounding boxes. Figure 4 illustrates three viewers who have one human in their Top-FOV. Examples shown in the top row of Fig. 6.

Edge Features: Pairwise features are designed to capture the relationship among two different individuals. In the top-view videos, similar to the unary matrix U_i^{IOU}, we can form a $T \times T$ matrix B_{ij}^{IOU} to describe the relationship between a pair of viewers (viewers/nodes i and j), in which $B_{ij}^{IOU}(f_p, f_q)$ is defined as the intersection over union of the Top-FOVs of person i in frame f_p and person j in frame f_q. Intuitively, if there is a high similarity between the Top-FOVs of person i in frame 10 and person j in frame 30, we would expect the 30th frame of viewer j's egocentric video to be similar to the 10th frame of viewer i's egocentric video. Two examples of such features are illustrated in the middle column of Fig. 5(b).

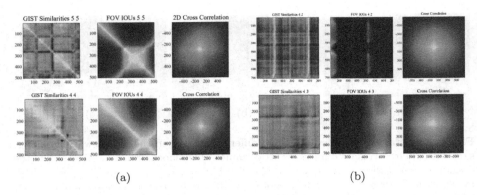

(a)   (b)

Fig. 5. (a) shows two different examples of the 2D features extracted from the **nodes** of the graphs (values color-coded). Left column shows the 2D matrices extracted from the pairwise similarities of the visual descriptors U^{GIST}, middle shows the 2D matrices computed by intersection over union of the FOV in the top-view camera U^{IOU}, and the rightmost column shows the result of the 2D cross correlation between the two. (b) shows the same concept, but between two **edges**. Again, the leftmost figure shows the pairwise similarity between GIST descriptors of one egocentric camera to another B^{GIST}. Middle, shows the pairwise intersection over union of the FOVs of the pair of viewers B^{IOU}, and the rightmost column illustrates their 2D cross correlation. The similarities between the GIST and FOV matrices capture the affinity of two nodes/edges in the two graphs.

3.1.2   Modeling the Egocentric View Graph

As in the top-view graph, we also construct a graph on the set of egocentric videos. Each node of this graph represents one egocentric video. Edges between the nodes capture the relationship between two egocentric videos.

Node Features: Similar to the top-view graph, each node is represented using two features. First, we compute pairwise similarity between GIST features [30] of all video frames (for one viewer) and store the pairwise similarities in the matrix $U_{E_i}^{GIST}$, in which the element $U_{E_i}^{GIST}(f_p, f_q)$ is the GIST similarity between frame f_p and f_q of egocentric video i. Two examples of such features are illustrated in the left column of Fig. 5(a). The GIST similarity is a function of the euclidean distance of the GIST feature vectors.

$$U_{E_i}^{GIST}(f_1, f_2) = e^{-\gamma |g_{f_p}^{E_i} - g_{f_q}^{E_i}|}. \tag{1}$$

In which $g_{f_p}^{E_i}$ and $g_{f_q}^{E_i}$ are the GIST descriptors of frame f_p and f_q of egocentric video i, and γ is a constant which we empirically set to 0.5.

The second feature is a time series counting the number of seen people in each frame. In order to have an estimate of the number of people, we run a pre-trained human detector using deformable part model [31] on each egocentric frame. In order to make sure that our method is not including humans in far distances (which are not likely to be present in top-view), we exclude bounding

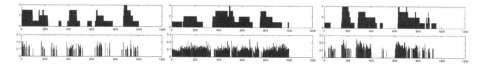

Fig. 6. Examples of the 1D features capturing the number of visible humans time-series. Top row shows the number of visible people in each viewer's Top-FOV over time. Bottom row shows the summation of the detection scores at every frame in an egocentric video.

boxes whose sizes are smaller than a certain threshold (determined considering an average human height of 1.7 m and distance of the radius of the area being covered in the top view video.). Each of the remaining bouding boxes, has a detection score (rescaled into the interval [0 1]) which has the notion of the probability of that bounding box containing a person. Scores of all detections in a frame are added and used as a count of people in that frame. Therefore, similar to the top-view feature, we can represent the node E_i of egocentric video i with a $1 \times T_{E_i}$ vector $U_{E_i}^n$ (Examples shown in the bottom row of Fig. 6.).

Edge Features: To capture the pairwise relationship between egocentric camera i (containing T_{E_i} frames) and egocentric camera j (containing T_{E_j} frames), we extract GIST features from all of the frames of both videos and form a $T_{E_i} \times T_{E_j}$ matrix B_{ij}^{GIST} in which $B_{ij}^{GIST}(f_p, f_q)$ represents the GIST similarity between frame f_p of video i and frame f_q of video j (Examples shown in the left column of Fig. 5(b).).

$$B_{ij}^{GIST}(f_p, f_q) = e^{-\gamma |g_{f_p}^{E_i} - g_{f_q}^{E_j}|}. \tag{2}$$

3.2 Graph Matching

The goal is to find a binary assignment matrix $x_{N^e \times N^t}$ (N^e being the number of egocentric videos and N^t being the number of people in the top-view video). $x(i, j)$ being 1 means egocentric video i is matched to viewer j in top-view. To capture the similarities between the elements of the two graphs, we define the affinity matrix $A_{N^e N^t \times N^e N^t}$. $a_{ik,jl}$ is the affinity of edge ij in the egocentric graph with edge kl in the top-view graph. Reshaping matrix x as a vector $x_{N^e N^t \times 1} \in \{0, 1\}^{N^e N^t}$, the assignment problem is defined as the following:

$$\underset{x}{\mathrm{argmax}} \ x^T A x. \tag{3}$$

We compute $a_{ik,jl}$ based on the similarity between the feature descriptor of edge ij in the egocentric graph B_{ij}^{GIST} and the feature descriptor for edge kl in the top-view graph B_{kl}^{IOU}.

As described in the previous section, each of these features is a 2D matrix. B_{ij}^{GIST} is a $T_{E_i} \times T_{E_j}$ matrix, T_{E_i} and T_{E_j} being the number of frames in egocentric videos i and j, respectively. On the other hand, B_{kl}^{IOU} is a $T_t \times T_t$

matrix, T_t being the number of frames in the top-view video. B_{ij}^{GIST} and B_{kl}^{IOU} are not directly comparable due to two reasons. First, the two matrices are not of the same size (the videos do not necessarily have the same length). Second, the absolute time in the videos do not correspond to each other (videos are not time-synchronized). For example, the relationship between viewers i and j in the 100th frame of the top-view video does not correspond to frame number 100 of the egocentric videos. Instead, we expect to see a correlation between the GIST similarity of frame $100 + d_i$ of egocentric video i and frame $100 + d_j$ of egocentric video j, and the intersection over union of in Top-FOVs of viewers k and l in frame 100. d_i and d_j are the time delays of egocentric videos i and j with respect to the top-view video.

To able to handle this misalignment, we define the affinity between the two 2D matrices as the maximum value of their 2D cross correlation. Hence, if egocentric videos i and j have d_i and d_j delays with respect to the top-view video, the cross correlation between B_{ij}^{GIST} and B_{kl}^{IOU} should be maximum when B_{ij}^{GIST} is shifted d_i units in the first, and d_j units in the second dimension.

$$A_{ikjl} = \max(B_{ij}^{GIST} * B_{kl}^{IOU}). \tag{4}$$

where $*$ denotes cross correlation. For the elements of A for which $i = j$ and $k = l$, the affinity captures the compatibility of node i in the egocentric graph, to node k in the top-view graph. The compatibility between the two nodes is computed using 2D cross correlation between U_k^{IOU} and $U_{E_i}^{GIST}$ and 1D cross correlation between U_k^n and $U_{E_i}^n$. The overall compatibility of the two nodes is a weighted linear combination of the two:

$$A_{ikik} = \alpha\max(U_{E_i}^{GIST} * U_k^{IOU}) + (1 - \alpha)\max(U_{E_i}^n * U_k^n), \tag{5}$$

where α is a constant between 0 and 1 specifying the contribution of each term. In our experiments, we set α to 0.9. Figure 5 illustrates the features extracted from some of the nodes and edges in the two graphs.

Soft Assignment. We employ the spectral graph matching method introduced in [4] to compute a soft assignment between the set of egocentric viewers and top-view viewers. In [4], assuming that the affinity matrix is an empirical estimation of the pairwise assignment probability, and the assignment probabilities are statistically independent, A is represented using it's rank one estimation which is computed by $\underset{p}{\mathrm{argmin}} \, |A - pp^T|$. In fact, the rank one estimation of A is no different than it's leading eigenvector. Therefore, p can be computed either using eigen decompositon, or estimated iteratively using power iteration. Considering vector p as the assignment probablities, we can reshape $p_{N^eN^t \times 1}$ into a $N^e \times N^t$ soft assignment matrix P, for which after row normalization $P(i, j)$ represents the probability of matching egocentric viewer i to viewer j in the top-view video.

Hard Assignment. Any soft to hard assignment method can be used to convert the soft assignment result (generated by spectral matching) to the hard binary assignment between the nodes of the graphs. We used the well known Munkres (also known as Hungarian) algorithm to obtain the final binary assignment.

4   Experimental Results

In this section, we will mention details of our experimental setup and collected dataset, the measures we used to evaluate the performance of our method, and the performance of our proposed method alongside with some baselines.

4.1   Dataset

We collected a dataset containing 50 test cases of videos shot in different indoor and outdoor conditions. Each test case, contains one top-view video and several egocentric videos captured by the people visible in the top-view camera. Depending on the subset of egocentric cameras that we include, we can generate up to 2,862 instances of our assignment problem (will be explained in more detail in Sect. 4.2.4). Overall, our dataset contains more than 225,000 frames. Number of people visible in the top-view cameras varies from 3 to 10, number of egocentric cameras varies from 1 to 6, and the ratio of number of available egocentric cameras to the number of visible people in the top-view camera varies from 0.16 to 1. Lengths of the videos vary from 320 frames (10.6 s) up to 3132 frames (110 s).

4.2   Evaluation

We evaluate our method in terms of answering the two questions we asked. First, given a top-view video and a set of egocentric videos, can we verify if the top-view video is capturing the egocentric viewers? We analyze the capability of our method in answering this question in Sect. 4.2.1.

Second, knowing that a top-view video contains the viewers recording a set of egocentric videos, can we determine which viewer has recorded which video? We answer this question in Sects. 4.2.2 and 4.2.3.

4.2.1   Ranking Top-View Videos

We design an experiment to evaluate if our graph matching score is a good measure for the similarity between the set of egocentric videos and a top-view video. Having a set of egocentric videos from the same test case (recorded in the same environment), and 50 different top-view videos (from different test cases), we compare the similarity of each of the top-view graphs to the egocentric graph. After computing the hard assignment for each top view video(resulting in the assignment vector x), the score $x^T A x$ is associated to that top-view video. This score is effectively the summation of all the similarities between the corresponding nodes and edges of the two graphs. Using this score rank all the top-view videos. The ranking accuracy is measured by measuring the rank of the ground truth top-view video, and computing the cumulative matching curves shown in Fig. 7(a). The blue curve shows the ranking accuracy when we compute the scores only based on the unary features. The red curve shows the ranking accuracy when we consider both the unary and pairwise features for performing graph matching. The dashed black line shows the accuracy of randomly ranking the top-view videos. It can be observed that both the blue and red curves outperform the random ranking. This shows that our graph matching score is a meaningful measure for estimating the similarity between the two graphs. In addition, the red curve, outperforming the blue curve shows the effectiveness of our pairwise features. In general, this experiment answers the first question. We can in fact use the graph matching score as a cue for narrowing down the search space among the top-view videos, for finding the one corresponding to our set of the egocentric cameras.

4.2.2   Viewer Ranking Accuracy

We evaluate our soft assignment results, in terms of ranking capability. In other words, we can look at our soft assignment as a measure to sort the viewers in the top-view video based on their assignment probability to each egocentric video. Computing the ranks of the correct matches, we can plot the cumulative matching curves to illustrate their performance.

We compare our method with three baselines in Fig. 7(b). First, random ranking (dashed black line), in which for each egocentric video we randomly rank the viewers present in the top-view video. Second, sorting the top-view viewers based on the similarities of their 1D unary features to the 1D unary features of each egocentric camera (i.e., number of visible humans illustrated by the blue curve). Third, sorting the top-view viewers based on their 2D unary feature (GIST vs. FOV, shown by the green curve). Note that here (the blue and green curves), we are ignoring the pairwise relationships (edges) in the graphs. The consistent improvement of our method (red curve) over the baselines, justifies the effectiveness of our representation, and shows the contribution of each stage.

4.2.3   Assignment Accuracy

In order to answer the second question, we need to evaluate the accuracy of our method in terms of node assignment accuracy. Having a set of egocentric videos and a top-view video containing the egocentric viewers, we evaluate the percentage of the egocentric videos which were correctly matched to their corresponding viewer. We evaluate the hard-assignment accuracy of our method and compare it with three baselines in Fig. 7(c). First, random assignment (Rnd), in which we randomly assign each egocentric video to one of the visible viewers in the top-view video. Second, Hungarian bipartite matching only on the 1D unary features denoted as H. Third, Hungarian bipartite matching only on the 2D unary feature (GIST vs. FOV, denoted as G-F), ignoring the pairwise relationships (edges) in the graphs.

The consistent improvement of our method using both unary and pairwise features in graph matching (denoted as GM) over the baselines shows the significant contribution of pairwise features in the assignment accuracy. As a result, the promising accuracy acquired by graph matching answers the second question. Knowing a top-view camera is capturing a set of egocentric viewers, we can

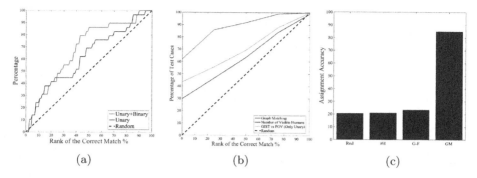

Fig. 7. (a) shows the cumulative matching curve for ranking top-view videos. The blue curve shows the accuracy achieved only using the node similarities. Red is the accuracy considering both node and edge similarities in the graph matching. (b) shows the cumulative matching curve for ranking the viewers in the top-view video. The red, green and blue curves belong to ranking based on spectral graph matching scores, cross correlation between only the 2D, and only the 1D unary scores, respectively. The dashed black line shows random ranking accuracy (c) shows the assignment accuracy based on random assignment, using the number of humans, using unary features, and using spectral graph matching. (Color figure online)

use visual cues in the egocentric videos and the top-view video, to decide which viewer is capturing which egocentric video.

4.2.4 Effect of Number of Egocentric Cameras

In Sects. 4.2.2 and 4.2.3, we evaluated the performance of our method given all the available egocentric videos present in each set as the input to our method. In this experiment, we compare the accuracy of our assignment and ranking framework as a function of the completeness ratio $\left(\frac{n_{Ego}}{n_{Top}}\right)$ of our egocentric set. Each of our sets contain $3 < N^t < 11$ viewers in the top-view camera, and $2 < N^e < 8$ egocentric videos. We evaluated the accuracy of our method and baselines when using different subsets of the egocentric videos. A total of $2^{N^e} - 1$ non-empty subsets of egocentric videos is possible depending on which egocentric video out of N^e are included (all possible non-empty subsets). We evaluate our method on each subset separately.

Figure 8 illustrates the assignment and ranking accuracies versus the ratio of the available egocentric videos to the number of visible people in the top-view camera. It shows that as the completeness ratio increases, the assignment accuracy drastically improves. Intuitively, having more egocentric cameras gives more information about the structure of the graph (by providing more pairwise terms) which leads to improvement in the spectral graph matching and assignment accuracy.

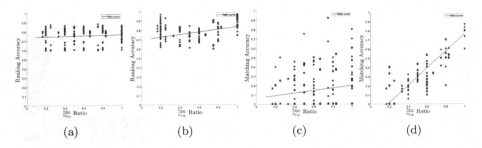

Fig. 8. Effect of the relative number of egocentric cameras referred to as completeness ratio ($\frac{n_{Ego}}{n_{Top}}$). (a) shows the ranking accuracy vs $\frac{n_{Ego}}{n_{Top}}$, only using the unary features. (b) shows the same evaluation using the graph matching output. (c) shows the accuracy of the hard assignment computed based on Hungarian bipartite matching on top of the unary features, and (d) shows the hard-assignment computed based on the spectral graph matching.

5   Conclusion and Discussion

In this work, we studied the problems of matching and assignment between a set of egocentric cameras and a top view video. Our experiments suggest that capturing the pattern of change in the content of the egocentric videos, along with capturing the relationships among them can help to identify the viewers in top-view. To do so, we utilized a spectral graph matching technique. We showed that the graph matching score, is a meaningful criteria for narrowing down the search space in a set of top-view videos. Further, the assignment found by our framework is capable of associating egocentric videos to the viewers in the top-view camera. We conclude that meaningful features can be extracted from single, and pairs of egocentric camera(s) and incorporating the temporal information of the video(s).

References

1. Fathi, A., Farhadi, A., Rehg, J.: Understanding egocentric activities. In: 2011 IEEE International Conference on Computer Vision (ICCV). IEEE (2011)
2. Fathi, A., Li, Y., Rehg, J.M.: Learning to recognize daily actions using gaze. In: Fitzgibbon, A., Lazebnik, S., Perona, P., Sato, Y., Schmid, C. (eds.) ECCV 2012. LNCS, vol. 7572, pp. 314–327. Springer, Heidelberg (2012). doi:10.1007/978-3-642-33718-5_23
3. Bettadapura, V., Essa, I., Pantofaru, C.: Egocentric field-of-view localization using first-person point-of-view devices. In: IEEE Winter Conference on Applications of Computer Vision (WACV) (2015)
4. Egozi, A., Keller, Y., Guterman, H.: A probabilistic approach to spectral graph matching. IEEE Trans. Pattern Anal. Mach. Intell. **35**(1), 18–27 (2013)
5. Dicle, C., Campsm, O., Sznaier., M.: The way they move: tracking multiple targets with similar appearance. In: Proceedings of the IEEE International Conference on Computer Vision (2013)

6. Kanade, T., Hebert, M.: First-person vision. Proc. IEEE **100**(8), 2442–2453 (2012)
7. Betancourt, A., Morerio, P., Regazzoni, C.S., Rauterberg, M.: The evolution of first person vision methods: a survey. IEEE Trans. Circ. Syst. Video Technol. **25**(5), 744–760 (2015)
8. Fathi, A., Ren, X., Rehg, J.M.: Learning to recognize objects in egocentric activities. In: 2011 IEEE Conference on Computer Vision and Pattern Recognition (CVPR) (2011)
9. Lu, Z., Grauman, K.: Story-driven summarization for egocentric video. In: IEEE Conference on Computer Vision and Pattern Recognition (CVPR) (2013)
10. Li, Y., Fathi, A., Rehg, J.: Learning to predict gaze in egocentric video. In: Proceedings of the IEEE International Conference on Computer Vision, pp. 3216–3223 (2013)
11. Polatsek, P., Benesova, W., Paletta, L., Perko, R.: Novelty-based spatiotemporal saliency detection for prediction of gaze in egocentric video. IEEE Sig. Process. Lett. **23**(3), 394–398 (2016)
12. Borji, A., Sihite, D.N., Itti, L.: What/where to look next? modeling top-down visual attention in complex interactive environments. IEEE Trans. Syst., Man Cybern.: Syst. **44**(5), 523–538 (2014)
13. Alahi, A., Bierlaire, M., Kunt, M.: Object detection and matching with mobile cameras collaborating with fixed cameras. In: Workshop on Multi-Camera and Multi-Modal Sensor Fusion Algorithms and Applications-M2SFA2 (2008)
14. Alahi, A., Marimon, D., Bierlaire, M., Kunt, M.: A master-slave approach for object detection and matching with fixed and mobile cameras. In: 15th IEEE International Conference on Image Processing, ICIP 2008 (2008)
15. Ferland, F., Pomerleau, F., Le Dinh, C., Michaud, F.: Egocentric and exocentric teleoperation interface using real-time, 3d video projection. In: 2009 4th ACM/IEEE International Conference on Human-Robot Interaction (HRI) (2009)
16. Park, H., Jain, E., Sheikh, Y.: Predicting primary gaze behavior using social saliency fields. In: Proceedings of the IEEE International Conference on Computer Vision (2013)
17. Hoshen, Y., Ben-Artzi, G., Peleg, S.: Wisdom of the crowd in egocentric video curation. In: Proceedings of the IEEE Conference on Computer Vision and Pattern Recognition Workshops (2014)
18. Fathi, A., Hodgins, J.K., Rehg, J.M.: Social interactions: a first-person perspective. In: IEEE Conference on Computer Vision and Pattern Recognition (CVPR) (2012)
19. Yan, Y., et al.: Egocentric daily activity recognition via multitask clustering. IEEE Trans. Image Process. **24**(10), 2984–2995 (2015)
20. Damen, D., Leelasawassuk, T., Haines, O., Calway, A., Mayol-Cuevas, W.: You-do, i-learn: discovering task relevant objects and their modes of interaction from multi-user egocentric video. In: BMVC (2014)
21. Cheng, D.S., Cristani, M., Stoppa, M., Bazzani, L., Murino, V.: Custom pictorial structures for re-identification. In: BMVC (2011)
22. Bak, S., Corvee, E., Brémond, F., Thonnat, M.: Multiple-shot human re-identification by mean riemannian covariance grid. In: 8th IEEE International Conference on Advanced Video and Signal-Based Surveillance (AVSS) (2011)
23. Bazzani, L., Cristani, M., Murino, V.: Symmetry-driven accumulation of local features for human characterization and re-identification. In: Computer Vision and Image Understanding (2013)
24. Poleg, Y., Arora, C., Peleg, S.: Head motion signatures from egocentric videos. In: Cremers, D., Reid, I., Saito, H., Yang, M.-H. (eds.) ACCV 2014. LNCS, vol. 9005, pp. 315–329. Springer, Heidelberg (2015)

25. Yonetani, R., Kitani, K.M., Sato, Y.: Ego-surfing first person videos. In: 2015 IEEE Conference on Computer Vision and Pattern Recognition (CVPR). IEEE (2015)
26. Zamir, A.R., Ardeshir, S., Shah, M.: Robust refinement of GPS-tags using random walks with an adaptive damping factor. In: IEEE International Conference on Computer Vision and Pattern Recognition (CVPR) (2014)
27. Kiefer, P., Giannopoulos, I., Raubal, M.: Where am i? investigating map matching during selflocalization with mobile eye tracking in an urban environment. Trans. GIS 18(5), 660–686 (2014)
28. Ardeshir, S., Zamir, A.R., Torroella, A., Shah, M.: GIS-assisted object detection and geospatial localization. In: Fleet, D., Pajdla, T., Schiele, B., Tuytelaars, T. (eds.) ECCV 2014, Part VI. LNCS, vol. 8694, pp. 602–617. Springer, Heidelberg (2014)
29. Ardeshir, S., Collins-Sibley, K.M., Shah, M.: Geo-semantic segmentation. In: Proceedings of the IEEE Conference on Computer Vision and Pattern Recognition, CVPR (2015)
30. Torralba, A.: Contextual priming for object detection. Int. J. Comput. Vis. 53(2), 169–191 (2003)
31. Felzenszwalb, P.F., Girshick, R.B., McAllester, D., Ramanan, D.: Object detection with discriminatively trained part based models. IEEE Trans. Pattern Anal. Mach. Intell. 32(9), 1627–1645 (2010)

Online Action Detection

Roeland De Geest[1(✉)], Efstratios Gavves[2], Amir Ghodrati[1], Zhenyang Li[2],
Cees Snoek[2], and Tinne Tuytelaars[1]

[1] ESAT - PSI, KU Leuven, Leuven, Belgium
{roeland.degeest,amir.ghodrati,tinne.tuytelaars}@esat.kuleuven.be
[2] QUVA, University of Amsterdam, Amsterdam, Netherlands
{e.gavves,z.li2,c.g.m.snoek}@uva.n

Abstract. In online action detection, the goal is to detect the start of
an action in a video stream as soon as it happens. For instance, if a child
is chasing a ball, an autonomous car should recognize what is going on
and respond immediately. This is a very challenging problem for four
reasons. First, only partial actions are observed. Second, there is a large
variability in negative data. Third, the start of the action is unknown,
so it is unclear over what time window the information should be integrated. Finally, in real world data, large within-class variability exists.
This problem has been addressed before, but only to some extent. Our
contributions to online action detection are threefold. First, we introduce
a realistic dataset composed of 27 episodes from 6 popular TV series.
The dataset spans over 16 h of footage annotated with 30 action classes,
totaling 6,231 action instances. Second, we analyze and compare various
baseline methods, showing this is a challenging problem for which none
of the methods provides a good solution. Third, we analyze the change
in performance when there is a variation in viewpoint, occlusion, truncation, etc. We introduce an evaluation protocol for fair comparison. The
dataset, the baselines and the models will all be made publicly available
to encourage (much needed) further research on online action detection
on realistic data.

Keywords: Action recognition · Evaluation · Online action detection

1 Introduction

In this paper, we focus on the problem of *online action detection*. Unlike traditional action recognition and action detection as studied in the literature to
date, *e.g.*, [1–6], the goal of online action detection is to detect an action as
it happens and ideally even before the action is fully completed. Being able to

This work was supported by the KU Leuven GOA project *CAMETRON*.

Electronic supplementary material The online version of this chapter (doi:10.
1007/978-3-319-46454-1_17) contains supplementary material, which is available to
authorized users.

© Springer International Publishing AG 2016
B. Leibe et al. (Eds.): ECCV 2016, Part V, LNCS 9909, pp. 269–284, 2016.
DOI: 10.1007/978-3-319-46454-1_17

detect an action at the time of the occurence can be useful in many practical applications - think of a pro-active robot offering a helping hand; a surveillance camera raising an alarm not just after the facts but well in time to allow for intervention; a smart active camera system zooming in on the action scene and recording it from the optimal perspective; or an autonomous car stopping for a child chasing a ball (see Fig. 1).

A similar task coined 'early event detection' has been brought to the attention of the community in the seminal work of Hoai and De la Torre [7,8]. However, they consider only the special case of relatively short video fragments with the category label given as prior information. Hence, it is assumed that it is known beforehand which action is going to take place. As the video is streamed, the system then only needs to indicate, as early as possible but not too early, when the action has started. A further simplified setting, focusing more on classification instead of detection, has been studied in [9–13]. In these works, the video starts with the onset of an action and ends when the action is completed. As the correct temporal segmentation is already provided, the system only needs to choose the most likely action out of a predefined set.

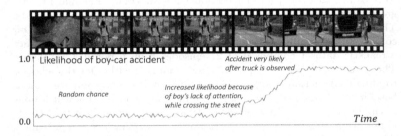

Fig. 1. Illustration of an online action detection prediction.

We claim these simplified setups are not representative for practical applications, where occurrences of any out of possibly many different action categories need to be detected in an online fashion, in (very) long video recordings with widely varying content. As we will show, this is a significantly more challenging task, to which the standard methods proposed in the literature provide only partial answers. Moreover, to date, no realistic benchmark dataset focusing on this problem has been released. In fact, the situation is somewhat reminiscent of the early days of action recognition, with datasets such as KTH [14] or Weizmann [15]. To alleviate this problem, we introduce the *TVSeries* dataset, a new dataset consisting of 27 episodes of 6 popular TV series. The dataset is temporally annotated at the frame level w.r.t. 30 possible actions. Furthermore, metadata is added, containing extra information regarding the action occurrence, *e.g.*, whether the action instance is atypical compared to the rest of the action instances in the same class, occluded, or taken from an unusual viewpoint.

We mark several differences between *online action detection* and 'early event detection'. First, we think the term 'event' should be preserved for longer term activities such as 'baking a cake' or 'changing a tire', as in the TrecVid MED challenge [16], which, by the way, is more a retrieval task than a detection one. Second, for practical applications methods should process the video in an online fashion (as opposed to batch processing), preferably in realtime and with minimal latency. Hence we prefer the term 'online' over 'early'.

Given a streaming video as input, the system should output, ideally in real-time, whether the action is currently taking place (or not). This requires detecting the ongoing action as accurately as possible, no matter what is the stage of the action. Since we focus on longer videos, this task requires in turn discriminating the action from a variety of negative data, including both background frames as well as irrelevant actions. Realistic background frames do not depict prespecified 'neutral' poses as in earlier datasets [8]. Similar to standard action detection, the wide variability and plethora of negative data makes the problem really challenging, although for online action detection the effects are even stronger. For a TV series episode with 20 min of footage, a typical 'standing up' action might not be appearing for more than 10 s in total (less than 1 % of the total number of frames). Only if a method can cope with this data imbalance and the large variability in the negative data, it will be of any practical use. Additionally, given the streaming video as input, the method needs to decide the proper temporal window to pool information from for deriving the frame prediction. This is not trivial in an online setting, since the algorithm does not know starting and ending points bounding the action temporally.

In summary, the challenges of real-world online action detection are the following. First, actions need to be detected as soon as possible, ideally after only part of the action has been observed. Second, actions need to be detected from among a wide variety of irrelevant negative data. Third, starting from long, unsegmented video data, it is unclear what time window to pool information from. Finally, we work with real world data, not artificially created for the purpose of action recognition. By design this results in large within-class variability.

Together with the TVSeries dataset, we propose an evaluation protocol, that allows comparing different solutions in a qualitative and quantitative manner. It is designed to be invariant to the number of instances of an action in the test set and less affected by the flux of negative data present in the videos. Given this protocol we report initial results for a set of state-of-the-art baseline methods on this challenging task. More specifically, we consider Fisher vectors [17] with improved trajectories [1], a deep ConvNet operating on a single frame basis [18] and an LSTM network, recently popular for sequential modelling such as image captioning [19] and action recognition [20], to encode the actions temporally. As it turns out, detecting actions at the time of their occurrence in realistic settings, while keeping the number of false positives under control, is a much harder problem than one might conclude from results reported in the literature under more constrained settings, *e.g.*, offline action detection. With this new dataset and evaluation protocol, we hope to encourage more researchers to look into the challenging yet very practical task of *online action detection*.

In the next section, we discuss related work. In Sect. 3, we describe the TVSeries dataset. Afterwards, we introduce our evaluation protocol. We evaluate several baselines and analyze their performance in Sect. 5 and conclude in Sect. 6.

2 Related Work

Action detection datasets. The current datasets for action detection all have their limitations. In some datasets, *e.g.*, UCF Sports [21], the videos are temporally trimmed: they contain exactly the action, from start to finish. The task here is to find the spatial location of the action. However, in a video stream it is often more important to be able to localize an action in time, rather than in space. In surveillance, for instance, when a guard is alerted that something is happening, he looks at the screen and easily localizes the action.

Some action detection datasets only contain a limited amount of actions. MSRII [22], for example, contains only 54 short video sequences with only three action classes. The actions do not occur concurrently. The MPII Cooking Dataset [23] is larger: it has 44 videos with 65 actions. However, this dataset is recorded with a fixed camera and therefore every video contains only one shot and exactly the same background. Moreover, many actions are location dependent: *e.g.*, 'Taking out of fridge' can only be done near the fridge. Occlusion is rare. Usually, the whole action is recorded and visible, from start to finish.

Recently, some larger and more realistic datasets have been introduced. The Thumos detection challenge [24] contains 24,000 (positive and negative) videos with 20 different actions; a similar dataset is FGA-240 [25]: it has 135,000 videos with 240 categories (85 sports, the rest fine-grained actions of these sports). In these datasets, all actions are sports related, so the background (the playing field) gives strong cues to help detection. The videos are downloaded from YouTube. As they are user created content, they often consist of only one shot: actions do not extend over multiple shots and are the main focus of the videos. Occlusions and partly recorded actions are rare. Another relevant dataset is ActivityNet [26]. ActivityNet is larger and more varied and focuses on more generic categories, not just sports. The videos are downloaded from YouTube as well, so most have a duration between five and ten minutes. Since they are retrieved based on a textual query, it is very unlikely that one video contains multiple actions. Moreover, negative background data is likely class-specific as well. Therefore, action detection on this dataset is easier than the generic problem. Regarding datasets and online action detection, we experimentally make the observation that in realistic data, the negative background frames are by far the hardest obstacle for modeling the actions accurately. Hence, the aforementioned action datasets are not well suited for evaluating *online action detection* reliably.

Early action detection. Hoai and De la Torre [7,8] were the first to present 'early event detection'. They simulate the sequential arrival of training data and train a structured output SVM, with the extra constraint that the output of frame $t + 1$ should be higher than the output of frame t. At test time, they assume every video contains exactly one instance of a given action. As the video is streamed, the system starts detecting the action once a threshold is exceeded. Only at the end of the video, they decide on a specific start and end frame. In [8] they discuss an extended setting where multiple actions per video are processed, however they never evaluate this. In our setting, we do not make any prior assumptions of the content of a video. Moreover, detecting the end of the action in an online fashion, as well as the start, is crucial.

[7] uses three types of video data to test the method: sign language, facial expressions and simple actions from the Weizmann dataset [15]. The videos are all relatively short and look artificial: the person is centered and instructed to perform a specific action. In this work, we use realistic data and introduce a new dataset that is well-suited for online action detection. They also propose to use the ROC curve, AMOC curve and F1-score curve as evaluation metrics. As we will detail later, these metrics are not ideal for online action detection.

In a follow-up work, Huang et al. [27], approach the problem more as classification than detection. They start assuming that every learned action can be happening, as well as a 'non-action'. When more frames of the video are seen, the occurrence of some actions becomes more unlikely and they are discarded. When only one action remains, or no actions are removed for a certain amount of time, a detection happened. In their data, however, the non-action is very simple: a person is just standing. In the real-world data we use, the non-actions have very high variability and it is not easy to learn a model for them.

Offline action detection. In this problem, the whole video is given. The task is to detect whether a given action occurs in this video, and if so, where it starts and ends (see *e.g.* [3,4,28–32]). Often the spatial location is determined as well. In this offline setting, the whole action can be observed first. Moreover, calculation time is not an issue. As a result, the best performing methods are often far too complicated to be used in a real-time setting.

A recent work by Yeung et al. [33] explores action detection based on a limited number of frames. They train a recurrent neural network that takes a representation of a frame as input and selects another frame (at an arbitrary location in the video) to consider next. This way, they look at the most interesting frames only. In online detection, the goal is to detect an action based on a limited number of frames as well. However, the frames considered are always at the beginning of the action, while in [33], that is not necessarily the case: it is assumed the whole video is available and the RNN selects the interesting frames without constraints.

Early action classification. Another simplified setting, focusing on classification instead of detection, has been studied in *e.g.* [9–13]. These works consider segmented actions. The system then only needs to choose one out of a predefined set of actions. A separate classifier is trained for every 10 %, 20 %, ..., 100 % of the video seen. During testing, it is known exactly how much percent of the action has been observed. This is clearly not valid in an online setting.

Table 1. The TVSeries dataset and the specification of the provided metadata.

Dataset	
Source material	27 episodes of TV series: *Breaking Bad, How I Met Your Mother, Mad Men, Modern Family, Sons of Anarchy, 24.*
Size	ca. 16 h
Action classes number	30
Total number of actions	6,231
Metadata	
Atypical	Does the actor perform the action in a way humans would call 'atypical'? Example: 'drinking' upside down.
Multiple persons	Are multiple persons visible during the action?
Small or background	Is the annotated action very small or in the background?
Side viewpoint	Is (part of) the action recorded from the side?
Frontal viewpoint	Is (part of) the action recorded from a frontal viewpoint?
Special viewpoint	Is (part of) the action recorded from a special viewpoint? Example: 'pouring' seen from the bottom of a glass.
Moving camera	Is the camera moving during the action?
Shotcut	Does the action instance extend over a shotcut?
Occlusion	Is the part of the video where the action is (spatially) located occluded at some time during the action?
Spatial truncation	Does part of the action extend beyond the frame borders?
Temporal truncation at the start	Is the start of the action missing?
Temporal truncation at the end	Is the end of the action missing?
Automatically generated Metadata	
Length of action	Actions divided in 4 quartiles based on number of frames
Amount of motion	Actions divided in 4 quartiles based on number of extracted improved trajectories

3   Dataset

In this work, we introduce the TVSeries dataset. The videos in this dataset depict realistic actions as they happen in real life. Similar to the Hollywood2 dataset for action recognition [34], our dataset is composed of professionally recorded videos.

Fig. 2. A characteristic frame for each of the 30 classes in the *TVSeries* dataset.

We annotated the first episodes of six recent TV series[1]. We select the number of episodes such that we have around 150 min of every series: almost 16 hours in total. We divide the episodes over a training, validation and testing set. Every set contains at least one episode of every series: having different series in training and testing set would introduce a domain shift, and online action detection is already difficult enough by itself.

We define 30 actions (see Table 2). Every action occurs at least 50 times in the dataset. Annotations were done manually and afterwards checked by one person. The start of an action is defined as the first frame where one notices something is going to happen; the person is in rest position (or doing something completely different) in the previous frame. The end of an action is defined as the last frame that contains visual evidence of the action. After that, you can no longer tell that action has happened. The actions are only annotated temporally, not spatially.

There is a large variability in this dataset. First, there are multiple actors, and everyone does an action his or her way. Second, different actions can occur at the same time, being performed by the same or multiple actors (as opposed to the easy setting of [8], where actions are separated by a specific non-action). Third, the way the action is recorded can be very different. The viewpoint is not fixed. Part of the action can be occluded. In other cases, the recording only starts after

---

[1] *Breaking Bad* (3 episodes), *How I Met Your Mother* (8), *Mad Men* (3), *Modern Family* (6), *Sons of Anarchy* (3) and *24* (4).

the action has started, or it ends too early. Some of the actions are not crucial for the story in the series, and therefore, the director did not capture the actions clearly. Other actions are performed by bystanders in the background and are very small. Fourth, the camera can be moving. Moreover, there are many shot-cuts. Actions extend over multiple shots: the viewpoint of one action instance can suddenly change. Due to the long video sequences, containing multiple actions and a highly varying background, the shotcuts and the incomplete actions, this dataset is more challenging than the most realistic datasets currently used.

For every action instance, we provide metadata labels that give more information on how the action is performed and captured. In Table 1 we summarize the dataset and the metadata, while in Fig. 2 we present some characteristic frames from different classes. In Fig. 3 we show examples of metadata annotations.

The videos are ripped at a frame rate of 25 fps and have a resolution of 720 by 576 pixels. Some examples can be found in the supplemental material. This dataset will be made publicly available to encourage further research on (online) action detection on realistic data.

Fig. 3. Example frames for some of the metadata annotations. Classes are 'eat', 'smoke', 'stand up', 'drink', 'going up stairway', 'get out of car' and 'use computer'.

4   Evaluation Protocol

Relevant evaluation protocols. Existing evaluation protocols are not suited for the task of online action detection. In *offline detection*, the main goal is to discover the start and end frame of an action, such that the detected action overlaps at least $\alpha\%$ with the ground truth and the label of the detected action is correct [3,4,28,29]. A partial overlap cannot be distinguished from a full overlap, and it is unsure which part of the action is detected. In *early action classification*, temporally segmented actions are classified at points where 10 %, 20 %, ..., 100 % of the action is observed and the accuracies at these percents are measured [9–13]. However, since it is a classification setting, this evaluation protocol cannot handle non-action intervals.

The evaluation metrics used for MMED [7,8] are the area under the ROC curve, the AMOC curve and the F1-score curve. The ROC curve shows, for different thresholds, the number of times a detector fires during the action (true positive rate, TPR) as a function of the number of times the detector fires before the action (false positive rate, FPR). The AMOC curve plots the average normalized time to detection (the percentage of the action that has been seen before the detector fires) as a function of the FPR for different thresholds. The F1-score curve tries to capture how well the method can localize the action. At every frame, the MMED method outputs the most probable start frame if an action ends at that frame. The F1-score is calculated at every *action* frame, and this is plotted from 0–100 % of the action.

These evaluation metrics are not really suited for online action detection. First, having three metrics instead of just one is sub-optimal. Second, every video gives rise to only one TP or FP. The assumption is made that a video contains the action exactly once. In a real-world streaming setting, this is obviously not the case. Finally, in an online action detection setting, methods do not need to label the start of the action in retrospect, after already having seen a sizable part of the action. The evaluation should therefore not consider a retrospective labeling of the action start, as the F1-score curve does.

Proposed evaluation protocol. In online action detection, a decision needs to be made at every frame, for every action: how likely is it that the action is going on in that frame, based on the information available up to that point? Therefore, it is logical to use the average precision over all frames as a metric for the performance of an online action detector. First, the frames are ranked according to their confidence (high to low). The precision of a class at cut-off k in this list is calculated as $Prec(k) = TP(k)/(TP(k) + FP(k))$ with $TP(k)$ the number of true positive frames and $FP(k)$ the number of false positives at the cut-off. The average precision of a class is then defined as $AP = \sum_k Prec(k) * I(k)/P$ with $I(k)$ an indicator function that is equal to 1 if frame k is a true positive, and equal to 0 otherwise. P is the total number of positive frames. The mean of the AP over all classes (mAP) is then the final performance metric of an online action detection method.

This metric has one big disadvantage, though: it is sensitive to changes in the ratio of positive frames versus negative background frames (if the classifiers are not perfect), as discussed by Jeni *et al.* [35]. If there is (relatively speaking) more background data, the probability increases that some background frames are falsely detected with higher confidence than some true positives. So the AP will decrease. This makes it hard to compare the AP of two different classes when they do not have the same positive vs. negative ratio. Likewise, it makes it hard to evaluate performance on subsets of the data (*e.g.*, performance of unoccluded instances vs. occluded ones). To enable an easy, fair comparison, we introduce the *calibrated precision*:

$$cPrec = \frac{TP}{TP + \frac{FP}{w}} = \frac{w * TP}{w * TP + FP} \tag{1}$$

We choose w equal to the ratio between negative frames and positive frames, such that the total weight of the negatives becomes equal to the total weight of the positives. Based on this calibrated precision, we can compute the *calibrated average precision (cAP)*, similar to the AP:

$$cAP = \frac{\sum_k cPrec(k) * I(k)}{P} \tag{2}$$

This way, the average precision is calculated as if there were an equal amount of positive and negative frames: the random score is 50 %. This evaluation metric is inspired by the work of Hoiem *et al.* [36]. They use a normalized average precision to compare object detection scores for different classes. Since in that case the number of negative data cannot be determined, they adjust the average precision as if every class has the same (arbitrary) amount of positive instances. Our calibrated average precision makes use of the number of negative data as well, and therefore, it is more suited for evaluation in our task.

For our dataset, we take the mAP as final performance measure. To compare the effectiveness of the different classifiers and the influence of the metadata labels, we use the cAP instead.

5   Experiments

5.1   Baseline Features

We analyze the difficulty of our dataset with three baseline methods. We opt for these, as they are the backbone of most action detection systems today.

1. Trajectories + FV. In our first approach, we use the improved trajectories of [1], with default parameters. For every trajectory, we calculate the raw trajectory motion, and HOG, HOF and MBH around the trajectory. Based on these descriptors, we calculate Fisher vectors (FV) [17] as in [1]. These FVs are used as input for linear SVM classifiers: one one-vs-all SVM for every action class. As examples for the SVM we use fixed-length windows, obtained as follows. Our positive windows are the ones that are completely in a positive action instance, *i.e.*, intersection of window and ground truth is equal to the length of the window. If the action is shorter than the window size, we take all windows that contain the action completely. As negative windows, we use windows of all other actions as well as background windows, where no action is happening. We train four SVMs for different window lengths: 20, 40, 60 and 80 frames. At test time, the prediction for the current frame is obtained by max-pooling the scores of windows of length 20, 40, 60 and 80 ending in the current frame.

2. CNN. As a second approach, we run a CNN on every frame separately. We choose the VGG-16 architecture [18] which consists of 13 convolutional layers to train the RGB network, including a softmax layer to return class probabilities. Since our training data is relatively small, we first pre-train our model on UCF101 split-1, then we finetune on our dataset. We also do image flipping and multiscale cropping for data augmentation. As CNN relies on single frames only, there is no temporal information encoded.

3. LSTM. Our third approach is based on the recently successful LSTM [20,32]. LSTM is the most popular variant of recurrent neural networks, with a distinct ability of modeling better long and short term temporal patterns in sequence data, making them good candidates for modeling video data. We use a single layer LSTM architecture with 512 hidden units. We directly resize each frame to 224 × 224 pixels (without data augmentation) and use it as input to extract the fc6 features from our CNN. These fc6 features are then fed into the LSTM. For training and testing, each video is split into multiple sequences of 16 frames (stride 1). Our LSTM model takes 16 frames as input at a time, and makes a prediction for the last frame. The LSTM is connected with a softmax, which again returns class probabilities.

5.2 Offline Detection

In offline detection, the goal is to find the start and end frame of any action that occurs in the video. All information of the video is available at once, and calculation time is not an issue. As this is a more widely studied setting, we first report offline detection scores on our new dataset using the methods described above, as a reference.

To this end, the baselines need to be adapted to the offline setting. For baseline 1, we run the SVM classifiers over all windows of lengths 20, 40, 60 and 80. We then use a non-maximum suppression algorithm (as in [3]) to eliminate double detections. For baseline 2 and 3, we take a window around every frame and assign the score of that frame to the whole window. The length of the window is chosen for each class separately as the median of the duration of the instances of that class in the training set. We then use the same non-maximum suppression algorithm.

Evaluation is done in the traditional setting. Intersection over union is calculated between the detected windows and the ground truth. If this value is larger than an overlap ratio and the action class is correctly identified, the detection is considered correct. Then, the average precision is calculated. We obtain a mAP for overlap ratio 0.2 of 4.9 %, 1.1 % and 2.7 % for FV, CNN and LSTM respectively. The results for more overlap ratios and all classes separately can be found in the supplemental material.

In general, FVs are better than LSTM, which is better than CNN. The three methods perform best on different classes. FVs capture motion information, and are therefore best for classes that inherently have a lot of motion, like 'stand up', 'fall' and 'punch', as opposed to actions like 'write' and 'eat'. CNN on the other hand is appearance-based, and therefore needs characteristic poses or context information from objects and scenes ('drive car', 'read' and 'drink' all provide these). The AP is lower than the AP of the FVs: with realistic data, this static information is not sufficient. LSTM uses the CNN features and is able to use their temporal order. This is not the same as having real motion information, but a step in the right direction (reflected by its score in between CNN and FV). It might be a good idea to use motion features (e.g. optical flow) as input for the LSTM, but testing that is beyond the scope of this paper.

The detection scores are quite low, indicating that this is a difficult dataset. For reference: the average classification accuracy of the actions (without taking the background into account), is 15.3 %, 24.7 % and 22.4 % for FV, CNN and LSTM. The FV score is lower than the other ones, likely because some action instances are so short that it is impossible to extract trajectories for them.

5.3   Online Detection

In online detection, we decide at every moment whether a specific action is happening *now*. This decision can not use information of the next frames, since this information is not yet available. We evaluate by reporting the average precision over frames, as discussed in Sect. 4. The mAP is 5.2 %, 1.9 % and 2.7 % for the FV, CNN and LSTM respectively. The values are very low, because the amount of negative data is very high, but still clearly better than the random mAP of 0.7 %. Here too, FVs score higher than LSTM and CNN. However, FVs computed on dense trajectories are slower. Dense trajectories, which occupy most of the computations, have a computational complexity of about $\mathcal{O}(SD^2kf^2 + \mathcal{V})$, for S scales and D average frame width and height, employing k convolutional kernels of size f for smoothing and spatio-temporal gradients used in HOG/HOF/MBH and, $\mathcal{V}$ the computational complexity of the respective optical flow algorithm used. In practice using FVs from the features computed on dense trajectories is hard in a realtime setting. In comparison, CNN have a complexity of $\mathcal{O}(\sum_i^L C_i M_i^2 f_i^2)$ assuming an L-layered network with C_i channels, M_i feature map size (on average considerably smaller than D) and f_i filter size and a thresholding (ReLU) non-linearity, while $\mathcal{O}\left(\sum_i^L C_i M_i^2 f_i^2 + \sum_t \phi(M_t u)\right)$ for LSTMs that receive CNN feature maps as input, considering u memory units and t timesteps and non-linearities with complexity ϕ. Most importantly, because of the recursive nature of matrix multiplications, neural network based models are largely parallelizable in GPU architectures, allowing for much faster computations.

To be able to compare the scores of the different classes, we calculate the cAP (see Table 2). Multiple classifiers perform close to the random value of 50 especially the CNN. The conclusions for offline detection are valid here as well. FVs are best for actions that intrinsically have a lot of motion ('run', 'punch'), while CNN needs context information and characteristic poses for its best classes ('fire weapon', 'get in/out car').

Table 3 shows the mean cAP for frames in every ten-percent interval of actions. FVs need some time to collect information of trajectories in windows. Their performance reaches its maximum near the end of the action. The cAP of the other methods is constant for all frames.

5.4   Metadata Analysis

We do an analysis based on the different metadata provided with the dataset. To be able to derive some meaningful conclusions, we just select those action

Table 2. Calibrated average precision for online action detection. Actions are sorted according to number of instances in the dataset from high to low. For the metadata labels: the difference between the calibrated precision of 'yes' and 'no' is shown. We mark with (−) the entries with less than 5 'yes' and 5 'no' action instances, as results would be unreliable. A: Atypical, B: Multiple persons, C: Small or background, D: Side viewpoint, E: Frontal viewpoint, F: Special viewpoint, G: Moving camera, H: Shotcut, I: Occlusion, J: Spatial truncation, K: Temporal truncation at the start, L: Temporal truncation at the end.

cAP (%)	Overall FV	CNN	LSTM	A FV	CNN	LSTM	B FV	CNN	LSTM	C FV	CNN	LSTM	D FV	CNN	LSTM	E FV	CNN	LSTM	F FV	CNN	LSTM	G FV	CNN	LSTM	H FV	CNN	LSTM	I FV	CNN	LSTM	J FV	CNN	LSTM	K FV	CNN	LSTM	L FV	CNN	LSTM
Pick s/th up	70.0	56.1	68.1	—	—	—	-1.8	-3.2	-12.3	-22.4	-3.4	-26.5	5.1	-5.9	-10.3	-3.7	3.9	9.2	-6.1	5.3	1.6	-2.8	-8.1	8.3	-2.9	-2.2	8.8	-1.7	-0.8	-4.3	-8.9	-13.5	1.2	-11.9	-12.8	-3.1	-10.7	-2.0	-2.3
Point	67.4	53.9	53.1	—	—	—	7.3	-12.3	-3.0	-12.3	9.4	-1.9	-15.9	-16.9	-8.1	17.8	16.9	8.7	—	—	—	1.7	-13.8	-1.3	3.2	-0.4	-9.1	0.5	-9.0	-3.2	-5.5	2.6	-0.9	2.4	-11.9	1.2	11.0	1.5	6.7
Drink	87.7	73.3	79.7	—	—	—	3.6	15.1	17.3	-7.6	9.4	-1.9	3.1	6.5	1.5	-0.9	-5.8	-0.5	—	—	—	-24.0	-11.6	9.1	-6.2	-6.2	-3.1	-6.2	-10.8	-13.7	-4.1	4.8	3.6	-3.2	1.6	-1.2	-5.5	3.1	-0.0
Stand up	81.3	52.9	58.8	-2.6	2.2	—	-5.0	0.9	-0.0	-9.8	-11.4	-21.2	-0.8	-13.2	-7.9	1.8	7.7	11.4	—	—	—	1.5	-1.5	9.3	-1.8	-3.1	-2.5	-7.0	-10.8	-13.7	4.6	7.2	10.8	1.4	3.6	2.6	-8.4	11.5	-15.8
Run	88.2	58.6	72.9	—	—	—	0.9	-2.2	0.9	8.0	10.7	—	-3.1	-6.4	-8.3	0.7	14.8	6.6	2.3	-8.2	9.4	4.4	1.7	-6.9	8.4	-2.5	5.7	1.2	-1.8	7.9	1.7	-4.9	-11.7	-5.1	-14.2	-13.5	-0.5	-8.8	-7.0
Sit down	77.4	45.6	49.1	-12.0	3.8	—	-0.4	-1.4	2.0	-20.3	1.0	-12.0	-1.9	-1.9	-4.8	10.4	4.5	12.3	—	—	—	12.1	2.0	4.2	8.4	0.3	8.2	-8.3	1.2	-0.2	6.1	-3.1	7.3	-5.1	2.1	1.4	-8.0	-1.7	8.7
Read	64.6	60.3	61.8	—	3.7	12.0	5.2	16.7	9.6	7.2	13.2	-0.2	-8.5	-18.0	-13.9	-3.1	14.8	12.3	—	—	—	1.2	4.1	5.9	-2.5	-19.4	-18.6	-1.8	3.5	-5.7	-7.0	-13.2	-15.6	1.0	-2.3	-5.2	5.1	10.9	3.4
Smoke	79.2	66.7	67.1	-0.7	-10.4	7.6	18.4	1.7	6.2	11.5	-4.0	-2.5	3.5	-9.8	-9.6	-3.4	14.2	12.2	—	—	—	1.9	7.6	6.6	—	—	—	10.5	-7.5	-13.7	-7.0	-12.1	-1.1	-6.5	-5.4	-9.9	5.0	-8.6	-9.7
Drive car	91.5	80.7	90.3	—	—	—	18.4	-15.3	1.8	—	—	—	-15.5	5.9	-3.2	4.1	-3.4	7.7	—	—	—	-13.1	34.1	2.3	-13.7	22.6	4.2	10.5	-12.1	-1.1	0.4	14.1	10.0	-12.1	-7.1	-4.1	-0.0	-8.0	2.8
Open door	80.9	51.6	73.1	0.4	24.5	3.6	-9.6	-6.7	-14.3	-24.5	12.3	-11.1	-1.3	-4.5	-8.4	0.1	9.2	6.0	—	—	—	15.9	7.4	1.8	-0.2	1.1	-5.1	5.5	-0.1	-1.7	2.1	5.6	6.7	-6.5	-5.4	-0.6	12.2	8.0	7.2
Give s/th	74.9	53.5	52.2	—	—	—	-4.1	5.6	7.5	—	—	—	-0.6	3.9	-7.1	9.5	4.8	-1.0	—	—	—	-12.6	4.0	-4.8	-6.5	6.4	8.9	4.9	13.8	4.8	2.6	5.8	6.7	-12.1	-7.1	-4.8	-0.0	-8.0	7.2
Use computer	70.2	77.8	83.9	—	—	—	7.8	4.8	2.2	-5.5	33.6	-14.8	1.4	-16.0	-21.1	20.0	6.3	5.0	-4.1	7.1	10.8	-7.4	19.8	2.2	-12.4	1.9	12.9	6.2	9.4	-5.0	-10.2	-6.9	-10.6	15.7	-5.3	-9.9	6.7	-3.3	-10.5
Write	47.2	46.2	62.3	—	—	—	-15.5	-15.3	-17.7	-21.1	-13.8	-18.7	6.6	16.4	12.9	9.5	3.9	9.4	—	—	—	19.8	2.2	—	-6.5	-0.2	4.8	4.9	9.8	4.0	-7.7	-11.6	-6.8	15.7	5.3	-9.9	-1.1	12.3	0.5
Stairway down	83.7	65.2	68.2	—	—	—	-15.5	-15.3	-17.7	-21.1	-13.8	-18.7	2.7	-1.8	-0.7	20.0	6.3	5.0	7.1	10.8	—	10.3	7.0	-7.6	-6.2	-26.6	-28.3	3.1	9.8	4.0	-6.7	-12.0	-6.1	-16.2	-14.0	-6.1	-16.2	-14.0	-15.9
Close door	81.7	54.2	73.7	—	—	—	-4.5	1.1	-0.7	-0.5	8.3	-4.8	2.7	-1.8	-0.7	1.1	10.3	4.7	—	—	—	7.0	3.3	22.6	-7.2	10.4	-0.9	2.6	0.7	16.5	-5.9	0.9	-18.8	-16.4	-12.0	3.4	-3.8	1.5	-18.0
Stairway up	66.1	53.6	69.8	—	—	—	18.0	-6.3	-1.1	-2.6	-1.6	-13.8	6.3	-14.4	-9.0	15.7	-0.7	10.7	—	—	—	-1.7	3.3	22.6	12.6	-5.1	0.1	-16.4	13.3	-11.1	-5.9	0.9	-18.8	-10.6	-0.3	1.6	-10.6	-0.3	1.6
Throw s/th	53.1	55.2	55.2	—	—	—	-10.1	-13.7	-8.7	—	—	—	-3.1	12.3	9.7	-2.2	-5.7	5.7	—	—	—	-8.8	18.7	-3.3	5.5	-0.1	-1.7	9.3	8.7	-9.8	5.1	8.7	9.6	-2.1	11.8	-4.9	-3.8	1.5	1.6
Get in/out car	89.7	84.7	79.0	—	—	—	-16.5	13.6	3.6	—	—	—	3.3	5.9	-8.1	30.7	6.4	10.4	—	—	—	—	—	—	—	—	—	5.1	8.7	9.6	5.1	8.7	9.6	-6.5	18.2	16.7	-6.5	18.2	16.7
Hang up phone	61.5	52.4	47.1	—	—	—	11.4	-29.0	-2.3	—	—	—	-17.3	-18.8	4.0	9.3	8.7	-9.8	—	—	—	—	—	—	-17.3	-18.8	4.0	-17.3	-18.8	4.0	-17.3	-18.8	4.0	22.0	26.0	-4.3	5.0	-8.6	-9.7
Eat	63.7	65.0	52.2	—	—	—	21.1	12.0	7.5	14.6	11.3	13.0	-2.8	1.5	12.2	0.2	-10.1	2.8	—	—	—	-8.2	-27.7	3.1	1.0	-3.5	8.9	0.1	5.8	0.9	-4.1	4.5	-7.2	-2.0	4.5	-7.2	-4.1	11.8	-2.3
Answer phone	57.3	46.4	46.2	—	—	—	-16.5	13.6	3.6	—	—	—	-6.5	5.3	6.9	15.9	-25.7	-19.5	—	—	—	—	—	34.2	—	-3.5	8.9	—	-3.5	8.9	0.1	-0.3	15.4	4.0	2.3	15.4	8.0	5.3	—
Clap	69.7	59.0	79.6	—	—	—	—	—	—	1.7	-13.8	-5.8	-0.4	-15.2	-6.2	—	—	—	—	—	—	13.0	10.1	—	-17.9	7.5	-3.8	7.6	-18.8	0.8	15.0	-0.3	15.4	4.0	2.3	15.4	3.3	5.3	—
Dress up	65.0	45.1	56.3	—	—	—	6.2	-16.6	12.8	—	—	—	-24.7	8.5	-4.5	1.2	-9.8	0.8	—	—	—	—	—	—	-8.8	-16.2	-2.8	-1.4	4.7	-2.8	6.6	15.3	6.4	-11.0	0.1	-17.7	-8.9	3.2	-5.4
Undress	67.8	67.4	55.4	—	—	—	—	—	—	-9.2	-3.3	-8.0	6.0	-3.9	8.3	-1.1	8.9	-4.5	—	—	—	—	—	—	—	—	-4.2	7.1	9.3	-7.3	12.7	-16.5	-3.5	-1.9	3.5	8.6	-1.9	3.5	8.6
Kiss	71.4	51.2	66.3	—	—	—	—	—	—	—	—	—	—	—	—	—	—	—	—	—	—	—	—	—	—	—	—	-8.1	1.0	-7.3	-0.4	-4.1	15.1	—	—	—	—	—	—
Fall/trip	89.6	50.4	70.3	-5.9	3.7	—	—	—	—	—	—	—	9.2	2.2	-12.6	-5.1	-3.8	14.6	—	—	—	—	—	—	2.7	4.2	-19.2	2.7	4.2	-19.2	—	—	—	-6.1	18.2	16.7	7.0	19.7	17.5
Wave	57.9	62.3	55.3	—	37.7	-15.8	-10.1	-13.7	—	—	—	—	6.0	4.8	5.9	-17.6	-13.2	1.0	—	—	—	-17.9	-14.3	22.3	—	—	—	—	—	—	-6.4	37.7	0.3	—	—	—	0.0	-16.9	15.7
Pour	74.4	76.2	68.5	-6.4	37.7	-15.8	—	—	—	—	—	—	12.8	-31.4	12.1	11.9	17.7	-9.1	—	—	—	—	—	—	—	—	-9.0	—	—	—	-6.4	37.7	0.3	-6.1	18.2	16.7	-2.0	-7.5	14.1
Punch	93.7	68.5	46.5	—	—	—	-1.6	-20.4	-23.1	—	—	—	0.6	-0.0	10.0	-5.2	3.2	-7.3	—	—	—	—	—	—	—	—	—	0.5	-0.3	-9.4	-1.2	0.3	-6.4	5.2	0.1	3.6	-4.3	-2.0	4.9
Fire weapon	87.4	90.9	61.8	—	—	—	—	—	—	—	—	—	—	—	—	—	—	—	—	—	—	—	—	—	—	—	—	—	—	—	—	—	—	—	—	—	—	—	—
Mean	**74.3**	**60.8**	**64.1**	**-4.5**	**10.2**	**-1.9**	**2.8**	**-3.2**	**-0.7**	**-5.8**	**3.0**	**-7.8**	**-2.3**	**-3.9**	**-2.7**	**2.9**	**2.4**	**3.4**	**-2.7**	**1.4**	**7.3**	**-0.8**	**1.7**	**5.4**	**-4.0**	**1.0**	**-2.1**	**0.7**	**-0.6**	**-2.9**	**0.4**	**0.4**	**-0.5**	**-3.1**	**-1.8**	**-2.6**	**-1.3**	**0.7**	**0.4**

Table 3. Mean cAP for different baselines when only a part of every action is considered: first 10 % frames of the action, next 10 % ... last 10 %, vs. all frames not containing the considered action.

mean cAP (%)	0–10 %	10–20 %	20–30 %	30–40 %	40–50 %	50–60 %	60–70 %	70–80 %	80–90 %	90–100 %
FV	67.0	68.4	69.9	71.3	73.0	74.0	75.0	76.4	76.5	76.8
CNN	61.0	61.0	61.2	61.1	61.2	61.2	61.3	61.5	61.4	61.5
LSTM	63.3	64.5	64.5	64.3	65.0	64.7	64.4	64.3	64.4	64.3

categories for which we have at least 5 action instances in each of the two splits (*e.g.*, classes that have at least 5 atypical and 5 typical instances). The results are presented in Table 2. The most interesting observations are discussed below.

Multiple persons. When there are multiple persons in the scene, the performance of FV slightly improves. The highest increase occurs with actions like 'throw something' and 'eat', which generally are performed in group. In contrast, actions like 'hang up phone' and 'close door' are recognized less often. For CNN, the average performance decreases when there are more persons present. When one person is present in the image (instead of a group of people), action-specific context is stronger. This explains the reduced performance.

Small or background. The FVs are clearly not capable of capturing the motion of small persons. The trajectories are hard to extract. Moreover, there are few of them, so their contribution to the FVs is relatively limited. CNN relies more on the context that is present in the whole image and is less sensitive to changes in size. In fact, when the action is small, more context may be available.

Side and frontal viewpoint. Analyzing the mean does not make sense here: the definitions of 'frontal' and 'side' depend on the action class. Interesting to note is that the performances of the three classifiers change differently for different actions. When one of them increases, there often is another one that decreases. The classifiers capture different information, and therefore, combining them seems a good idea to obtain better results.

Shotcut. Both temporal methods are negatively affected by shotcuts. Trajectories for FVs are interrupted and discarded, and it takes 15 frames to generate new ones. Therefore, some frames have less information. LSTM combines information from multiple frames. If there is a shotcut, the relation between the frames is not as clear. On the other hand, CNN uses only the current frame, so its accuracy does not change much.

Temporal truncation at start and end. For the temporal methods, the performance is worse when the start of the action is missing. These methods use information from previous frames. If an action is shorter because the beginning is missing, it takes relatively speaking more time before they have constructed a good representation. It does not matter that much whether the end of the action is missing.

6   Conclusion

Online action detection is a difficult problem, that has not been studied in a real-world setting and with realistic data before. There are four main challenges. First, only partial actions are available (as previously stressed in [7,8,27]). Second, the negative data is highly variable and should not give rise to many false positives. Third, the start frame of an action is not known beforehand, so it is unclear over what time window to integrate the information. Fourth, large within-class variability exists in real-world data.

We collected a new dataset and proposed an evaluation protocol to assist the research on online action detection. We tested a few baselines and showed none of the simple methods perform well. A realistic setting is clearly different from the artificial setups that were previously used in an online action detection context. Therefore, online action detection is a novel problem far from being solved, as existing methodologies fall short on delivering reliable results.

References

1. Wang, H., Schmid, C.: Action recognition with improved trajectories. In: ICCV (2013)
2. Laptev, I.: On space-time interest points. IJCV **64**, 107–123 (2005)
3. Gaidon, A., Harchaoui, Z., Schmid, C.: Actom sequence models for efficient action detection. In: CVPR (2011)
4. Jain, M., van Gemert, J., Jegou, H., Bouthemy, P., Snoek, C.: Action localization with tubelets from motion. In: CVPR (2014)
5. Fernando, B., Gavves, E., Oramas, J., Ghodrati, A., Tuytelaars, T.: Rank pooling for action recognition. TPAMI **PP**(99), 1 (2016)
6. Bilen, H., Fernando, B., Gavves, E., Vedaldi, A., Gould, S.: Dynamic image networks for action recognition. In: CVPR (2016)
7. Hoai, M., De la Torre, F.: Max-margin early event detectors. In: CVPR (2012)
8. Hoai, M., Torre, F.: Max-margin early event detectors. IJCV **107**(2), 191–202 (2014)
9. Cao, Y., Barrett, D., Barbu, A., Narayanaswamy, S., Yu, H., Michaux, A., Lin, Y., Dickinson, S., Siskind, J., Wang, S.: Recognize human activities from partially observed videos. In: CVPR (2013)
10. Ryoo, M.: Human activity prediction: early recognition of ongoing activities from streaming videos. In: ICCV (2011)
11. Yu, G., Yuan, J., Liu, Z.: Predicting human activities using spatio-temporal structure of interest points. In: ACM MM (2012)
12. Kong, Y., Kit, D., Fu, Y.: A discriminative model with multiple temporal scales for action prediction. In: Fleet, D., Pajdla, T., Schiele, B., Tuytelaars, T. (eds.) ECCV 2014, Part V. LNCS, vol. 8693, pp. 596–611. Springer, Heidelberg (2014)
13. Lan, T., Chen, T.C., Savarese, S.: A hierarchical representation for future action prediction. In: ECCV
14. Schuldt, C., Laptev, I., Caputo, B.: Recognizing human actions: a local SVM approach. In: ICPR (2004)
15. Blank, M., Gorelick, L., Shechtman, E., Irani, M., Basri, R.: Actions as space-time shapes. In: ICCV (2005)

16. Over, P., Fiscus, J., Sanders, G., Joy, D., Michel, M., Awad, G., Smeaton, A., Kraaij, W., Quénot, G.: Trecvid 2014-an overview of the goals, tasks, data, evaluation mechanisms and metrics. In: Proceedings of TRECVID (2014)
17. Perronnin, F., Sánchez, J., Mensink, T.: Improving the fisher kernel for large-scale image classification. In: Daniilidis, K., Maragos, P., Paragios, N. (eds.) ECCV 2010, Part IV. LNCS, vol. 6314, pp. 143–156. Springer, Heidelberg (2010)
18. Simonyan, K., Zisserman, A.: Very deep convolutional networks for large-scale image recognition. In: ICLR (2015)
19. Jia, X., Gavves, E., Fernando, B., Tuytelaars, T.: Guiding the long-short term memory model for image caption generation. In: ICCV (2015)
20. Donahue, J., Anne Hendricks, L., Guadarrama, S., Rohrbach, M., Venugopalan, S., Saenko, K., Darrell, T.: Long-term recurrent convolutional networks for visual recognition and description. In: CVPR (2015)
21. Rodriguez, M.D., Ahmed, J., Shah, M.: Action mach a spatio-temporal maximum average correlation height filter for action recognition. In: CVPR (2008)
22. Cao, L., Liu, Z., Huang, T.S.: Cross-dataset action detection. In: CVPR (2010)
23. Rohrbach, M., Amin, S., Andriluka, M., Schiele, B.: A database for fine grained activity detection of cooking activities. In: CVPR (2012)
24. Gorban, A., Idrees, H., Jiang, Y.G., Roshan Zamir, A., Laptev, I., Shah, M., Sukthankar, R.: THUMOS challenge: action recognition with a large number of classes (2015). http://www.thumos.info/
25. Sun, C., Shetty, S., Sukthankar, R., Nevatia, R.: Temporal localization of fine-grained actions in videos by domain transfer from web images. In: ACM MM (2015)
26. Heilbron, F., Escorcia, V., Ghanem, B., Niebles, J.: ActivityNet: a large-scale video benchmark for human activity understanding. In: CVPR (2015)
27. Huang, D., Yao, S., Wang, Y., De La Torre, F.: Sequential max-margin event detectors. In: Fleet, D., Pajdla, T., Schiele, B., Tuytelaars, T. (eds.) ECCV 2014, Part III. LNCS, vol. 8691, pp. 410–424. Springer, Heidelberg (2014)
28. Kläser, A., Marszałek, M., Schmid, C., Zisserman, A.: Human focused action localization in video. In: Kutulakos, K.N. (ed.) ECCV 2010 Workshops, Part I. LNCS, vol. 6553, pp. 219–233. Springer, Heidelberg (2012)
29. Tian, Y., Sukthankar, R., Shah, M.: Spatiotemporal deformable part models for action detection. In: CVPR (2013)
30. Wang, Z., Wang, L., Du, W., Qiao, Y.: Exploring fisher vector and deep networks for action spotting. In: CVPR Workshop (2015)
31. Gkioxari, G., Malik, J.: Finding action tubes. In: CVPR (2015)
32. Yeung, S., Russakovsky, O., Jin, N., Andriluka, M., Mori, G., Fei-Fei, L.: Every moment counts: dense detailed labeling of actions in complex videos. arXiv preprint arXiv:1507.05738 (2015)
33. Yeung, S., Russakovsky, O., Mori, G., Fei-Fei, L.: End-to-end learning of action detection from frame glimpses in videos. arXiv preprint arXiv:1511.06984 (2015)
34. Marszałek, M., Laptev, I., Schmid, C.: Actions in context. In: CVPR (2009)
35. Jeni, L.A., Cohn, J.F., De La Torre, F.: Facing imbalanced data-recommendations for the use of performance metrics. In: 2013 Humaine Association Conference on Affective Computing and Intelligent Interaction (ACII), pp. 245–251. IEEE (2013)
36. Hoiem, D., Chodpathumwan, Y., Dai, Q.: Diagnosing error in object detectors. In: Fitzgibbon, A., Lazebnik, S., Perona, P., Sato, Y., Schmid, C. (eds.) ECCV 2012, Part III. LNCS, vol. 7574, pp. 340–353. Springer, Heidelberg (2012)

Cross-Modal Supervision for Learning Active Speaker Detection in Video

Punarjay Chakravarty[(✉)] and Tinne Tuytelaars

ESAT-PSI-iMinds, KU Leuven, Leuven, Belgium
{Punarjay.Chakravarty,Tinne.Tuytelaars}@esat.kuleuven.be

Abstract. In this paper, we show how to use audio to supervise the learning of active speaker detection in video. Voice Activity Detection (VAD) guides the learning of the vision-based classifier in a weakly supervised manner. The classifier uses spatio-temporal features to encode upper body motion - facial expressions and gesticulations associated with speaking. We further improve a generic model for active speaker detection by learning person specific models. Finally, we demonstrate the online adaptation of generic models learnt on one dataset, to previously unseen people in a new dataset, again using audio (VAD) for weak supervision. The use of temporal continuity overcomes the lack of clean training data. We are the first to present an active speaker detection system that learns on one audio-visual dataset and automatically adapts to speakers in a new dataset. This work can be seen as an example of how the availability of multi-modal data allows us to learn a model without the need for supervision, by transferring knowledge from one modality to another.

Keywords: Active speaker detection · Cross-modal supervision · Weakly supervised learning · Online learning

1 Introduction

The problem of detecting active speakers in video is a central one to several applications. In video conferencing, knowing the active speaker allows the application to focus on and transmit the video of one amongst several people at a table. In a Human-Computer-Interaction (HCI) setting, a robot/computer can use active speaker information to address the correct interlocuter. Active speaker detection is also a part of the pipeline in video diarization, the automatic annotation of speakers, their speech and actions in video. Video diarization is useful for movie sub-titling, multimedia retrieval and for video understanding in general.

Traditionally, visual active speaker detection has been done using lip motion detection [1–4]. However, facial expressions and gestures from the upper body,

This work was supported by the KU Leuven GOA project *CAMETRON* and iMinds.

B. Leibe et al. (Eds.): ECCV 2016, Part V, LNCS 9909, pp. 285–301, 2016.
DOI: 10.1007/978-3-319-46454-1_18

movement of the hands, etc., are all cues that can be utilized to assist with this task, as shown in [5], where better detection results are achieved using spatio-temporal features extracted from the entire upper body, compared with just lip motion detection.

Another powerful idea we borrow from [5], is to use audio to supervise the training of a video based active speaker detection system. In that work, a microphone array is used to get directional sound information (assumed to be speech sounds), and based on this input, upper body tracks are associated with speak/non-speak labels. These labels are then used to train an active speaker classifier using video only.

Fig. 1. Audio-based Voice Activity Detection (VAD) is used to weakly supervise the training of a video-based active speaker classifier. VAD tells us that someone in the frame is speaking, but not who. The problem is one of associating the voice activity with one of the people (solid red upper body bounding box) in the frame, and training the classifier at the same time. We use structured output learning to train a latent SVM classifier in the presence of partially observed (latent) inputs. (Color figure online)

However, the presence of reverberation and background noise prevents perfect active speaker identification using directional audio alone, which subsequently affects the training of the video-based classifier. Additionally, in the vast majority of videos, such as the millions of Youtube videos available online, in videos from films and TV series, only a single channel of sound is available, with no directional information. Even in those cases where 2 channels of audio are available, the relative position of the camera and the microphones varies, and no calibration information is available, making it impossible to apply the method of [5].

In the absence of directional information, we propose to use Voice Activity Detection (VAD) [6] to tell us when there is someone speaking in a frame. If there is only one person in the frame, then this can be used to train the video-based classifier directly. However, when this is not the case, the problem becomes one of simultaneously associating the voice activity with one of the people in the frame, and learning the classifier (Fig. 1). That's the challenge we address in this work.

Moreover, there's an additional challenge. Investigating our trained classifier, we find that it has some bias: it works better for some speakers, compared to others. We identify two reasons for this. First, the way people gesticulate while speaking varies a lot from person to person. Indeed, a person-specific model typically outperforms the generic model. Second, there is the domain shift problem: the change of data distribution between training and test data. We address both by extending our previous scheme to an online learning setting that, starting from a generic classifier, gradually adapts to a specific person. To this end, we retrain the model with an incrementally increasing number of training samples coming from a new video of a previously unseen person at each iteration. The online training is also weakly supervised by VAD from audio. The generic classifier is used to label and pick the training samples for each speaker and temporal continuity constraints allow the classification performance to improve in spite of imperfectly labelled training data from the generic classifier.

Our method is completely unsupervised, in the sense that there is no *human* supervision/labelling. We use audio to supervise the learning. This supervision comes "for free" with the video, but is only partial - VAD tells us that one of the persons in the frame is speaking, but not who. As opposed to [5], who use full supervision from directional audio, we use weak supervision from VAD. This work can be seen as an example of how the availability of multi-modal data allows us to learn a model without the need for supervision, by transferring knowledge from one modality to another.

The remainder of the paper is organized as follows. We discuss prior work in this area in Sect. 2. We discuss the use of audio for active speaker detection in Sect. 3, with Subsects. 3.1, 3.2 and 3.3 discussing the weakly supervised learning with Latent SVMs, speaker specific classification and online learning, respectively. Experimental results are discussed in Sect. 4 and concluding remarks and potential for future work in Sect. 5.

2   Related Work

Weakly supervised and multimodal learning. The learning of a classifier in the presence of weak supervision, or partially labelled data, has been studied mostly in the context of object recognition, where labels are available for images, but localization information - bounding boxes around the objects to be classified, are missing [7–11]. Best results in this context are obtained with Structured Output Learning [12], i.e. by learning a classifier that outputs not only the class labels, but also the bounding box coordinates or index. We use the same approach for training a classifier for active speaker detection with only VAD-based supervision, which gives us labels for the images, but not for individual bounding boxes. Audio weakly supervises the training of video. The work of Bojanowski et al. [13] is another example of one mode of information weakly supervising another. They use scripts to weakly supervise the learning of actors and actions in movies. However, scripts are not always available for video data, while audio is.

Dealing with domain shift. In our work, we find that an active speaker classifier trained on a first set of speakers performs less well on previously unseen speakers, while best results are obtained with person-specific classifiers. This is because of the mismatch between the distributions of different speakers. On the one hand, training a generic classifier means that it has seen a larger number of training samples, is less prone to overfitting compared to a person specific classifier, and should generalize well for unseen speakers. However, the generic classifier still suffers from person-specific biases, and gives better classification results for some people over others. The same problem exists for object recognition - a classifier trained on one dataset typically has lower performance when applied to images from another dataset. This is known as the dataset bias problem, and there have been some efforts at reducing this for object recognition [14,15]. One way to deal with person or dataset specific biases is to adapt the source classifier to the target classifier, and this is called Domain Adaptation [16,17]. Transfer Learning [18–20], a related problem, is about using the information available from the source data to aid the learning of the target classifier utilizing only a small number of target training samples. For instance, Aytar et al. [18] use an Adaptive SVM (ASVM) that incrementally adapts an SVM learnt on source data (e.g. motorbike class) to target data (e.g. bicycle class) in the context of object recognition. The source classifier acts as a regularizer for the target classifier in the adaptive SVM framework, and they demonstrate successful adaptation based on a relatively small number of training samples of the target class. This work lies at the basis of our online adaptation to previously unseen persons.

Person-specific models. There has been some work on person specific facial expression recognition and transferring generic to specific models for improving classification performance [21–23]. Chen et al. [21] show that facial expression recognition results improve when using person specific classifiers. They use an Inductive Transfer Learning (ITL) approach, where they learn a source classifier, which is a collection of weak learners in a boosting framework. Subsequently a subset of these are used for training the target classifier with a small number of labeled target samples.

Chu et al. [22] propose a Selective Transfer Machine (STM) approach to re-weight the source samples so that they are closer to the target samples. The algorithm simultaneously learns the parameters of the classifier and the source sample weights that minimize the error between the source and target distributions. They thus personalize a generic classifier to individual, with the resulting personalized classifier improving on the generic classifier on facial action unit detection tasks. However, STM requires the storage of all source samples, with a higher memory requirement than storing just the source classifier, which could be the weights of an SVM.

Zen et al. [23] demonstrate unsupervised adaptation of a generic classifier to a target classifier on single frame expression datasets. They learn a regression function between the "shape" or sample distribution of each user in the labelled source dataset and his/her classifier (source weight vector w_i in the SVM). Applying this function on the unlabelled sample distribution of the target user then gives them the target classifier (target weight vector w_t). They do not require to keep in memory all the samples from the source dataset and outperform the STM method of [22]. However, their approach requires that the relative distribution of positive and negative samples in every user's data is relatively constant and can be learnt using the source users. However, this is not the case in our data. Additionally, we learn the generic source classifier using unlabelled data as well - so our process requires no human supervision from beginning to end.

Online learning is the incremental learning of a classifier with an increasing number of training samples as and when they become available. In our context, we adapt the generic source classifier to the person-specific target classifier with an increasing number of samples from the speaker. This is somewhat similar to the problem of Active Learning, where a new classifier is to be learnt with the minimum budget in terms of time spent in labelling training samples, and the task is one of selecting the most relevant samples to be used for training. Gavves et al. [24] demonstrate Active Transfer Learning, in that the selection of relevant training samples is done with the help of previously learnt classifiers on other datasets. Both [23,24] use the source classifiers as zero-shot priors, giving a baseline performance using only the target classifier, with classification performance gradually increasing with an increasing number of samples from the target dataset. We use this as our inspiration for our online learning problem, except again, our learning is without any manual supervision.

3   Audio Supervised Training

In the original experiment of [5], a 2-mic array was used to associate upper bodies detected in the video, with sound directions. They used a technique proposed by [25] for estimating the number and direction of sound sources. A non-linear function of the Generalized Cross Correlation Phase Transform (GCC-PHAT) between the audio signals is calculated over all the angles of arrival with respect to the microphone array baseline. This is done over short time intervals corresponding to the Time Frequency cells of a Short Term Fourier Transform. This gives an angle of arrival spectrum at each point in time that can be associated with the people detected in the image. In each frame, the sound direction is associated with a speaker's upper body bounding box, and features within that bounding box are used to train the classifier. We use the same data as [5], available on request from the authors, and consider the case when directional information is absent. We simulate the output of VAD by removing the speak/non-speak bounding box labels. We assign a label of speak to the frame if any of the bounding boxes in it are tagged as speaking and non-speak if none of the bounding boxes is speaking. Our problem is one of associating one of the bounding boxes in the image with the sound and training a classifier at the same time. We treat this as a structured output prediction problem [26].

3.1 Classifier Training Under Weak Audio Supervision Using Structured Output Learning

In the absence of information about which upper body bounding box is associated with the active speaker in each frame, the problem can be posed as a structured training problem [7–9,12], in the presence of partially observed training data. In the context of object recognition, there are databases with images labelled with the presence of one or more objects in the scene, but no localization (bounding box) information for the object in the image. [7–9] deal with this by using a Latent SVM formulation, which alternates between the guessing of object bounding boxes, and training a classifier for the object inside the bounding box. They use object proposals [27] to narrow down the search for objects in the image.

Here, we adapt [7–9] to our setting. Our object proposals are the upper body bounding boxes. We know that one of the bounding boxes is an active speaker, but not which one - the speak/non-speak label for the individual bounding boxes are our latent variables. Using structured output prediction, we jointly learn which of the bounding boxes in the image is associated with the active speaker, together with learning the active speaker classifier. Given an image x and upper body bounding box h, let $\phi(x, h)$ denote an image description computed over bounding box h. Given all upper body bounding boxes $h_1, ...h_n$, the algorithm then needs to select the bounding box that contains the active speaker. The labels of the images, speaking/non-speaking, $y = \pm 1$, are obtained from the sound using VAD or, in our experiment, by removing the directional information from the training data. Once the classifier is trained, the best bounding box h is found by

$$h^* = \underset{h}{\mathrm{argmax}} \langle w, \phi(x, h) \rangle \tag{1}$$

where w is the weights vector of the SVM. We define $\Phi(x, y, h) = \phi(x, h)$ if $y = 1$, and 0 otherwise. The learning task is to optimize the following:

$$\hat{w} = \underset{w}{\mathrm{argmin}} \sum_{i=1}^{N} l(w, x^i, y^i) + \frac{C}{2} \|w\|^2 \tag{2}$$

where $l(w, x^i, y^i)$ is the per example loss, $\frac{C}{2}\|w\|^2$ is the regularizer and N is the total number of training data. The max-margin loss function is defined as

$$l_{mm}(w, x^i, y^i) = \underset{y,h}{\max}(\langle w, \Phi(x^i, y, h) \rangle + \Delta(y^i, y)) - \underset{h}{\max}(\langle w, \Phi(x^i, y^i, h) \rangle) \tag{3}$$

where $\Delta(y^i, y)$ is the zero-one error, which is 0 if $y^i = y$ and 1 otherwise.

This loss function tries to maximize the margin between the score of the selected active speaker's bounding box and the non-speaking bounding boxes. Following the work of [8,9], we replace the max-margin loss with a soft-max loss function:

$$l_{sm}(w, x^i, y^i) = \frac{1}{\beta} log \sum_{y,h} exp(\beta \langle w, \Phi(x^i, y, h) \rangle + \beta \Delta(y^i, y))$$

$$- \frac{1}{\beta} log \sum_{h} exp(\beta \langle w, \Phi(x^i, y^i, h) \rangle) \qquad (4)$$

where β controls the sharpness of the distribution. It can be shown that as $\beta \to \infty$, the loss function limits to the standard structured SVM formulation. The softmax loss function allows for multiple active speakers in the same frame. It also makes the optimization function smoother and less prone to local minima. We use the LBFGS solver from minFunc[1] to optimize our cost function and train our classifier.

3.2   Speaker Specific Models

Using the motion of the face and upper body over time assists with active speaker detection. At the same time, it maybe has the disadvantage of making the detector more speaker specific, as different people are likely to have different mannerisms while speaking. We explore this hypothesis by training several person specific Active Speaker classifiers. We do this in two settings: one using the directional audio (i.e., supervised), as a baseline, and subsequently, in the VAD setting, where the learning is weakly supervised by audio, as detailed in the previous section.

In the first case, the learning is straightforward: we have a separate track for each person in the video, and knowledge of the frames in which that track is speaking (from the directional audio).

In the second case, the audio does not tell us which track/person is speaking at any given time, just that one among the multiple tracks in the frame is speaking. For this, we do the training in two steps. We first learn a generic classifier in the weakly supervised case, as detailed previously. Subsequently, we use the generic (source) classifier to guide the selection of the positive samples for the person specific (target) classifier. We run the generic classifier on each "speaking" frame's bounding boxes to get an idea of which track/bounding box is speaking. However, the generic classifier does not always give the highest score to the active speaker in the frame. This is because of the dataset bias and domain shift problem discussed earlier - the generic classifier performs better for some speakers compared to others. So we bring in another cue: temporal continuity.

So far, we have discussed active speaker detection on each frame in isolation. However, people's speech tends to be for periods longer than a single frame. If a person is speaking in one frame, it is more likely than not, that they will be speaking in the next frame as well. We use temporal continuity to reduce the effect of mis-classifications of the generic classifier and guide the sample selection for the speaker specific classifier. The highest scoring sample at each VAD-positive frame is taken to be the positive sample for the associated speaker, and all other samples are selected as negative samples for the other speakers. Both positive

---

[1] http://people.cs.ubc.ca/~schmidtm/Software/minFunc.html.

and negative samples are weighted according to temporal continuity, measured as the number of contiguous neighbouring frames with consistent labels. We use a weighted logistic loss function l_{wll}

$$l_{wll}(w, \Phi(x, y, h^*), \alpha) = \alpha \cdot log\{1 + exp(-\langle w, \Phi(x, y, h^*)\rangle)\} \tag{5}$$

where $\Phi(x, y, h^*)$ is the feature vector from the best scoring bounding box, w is the weights vector of the speaker-specific SVM and α is the temporal continuity weight of the sample.

Note how this integration of temporal continuity directly in the weakly supervised learning framework (as opposed to keeping it as a postprocessing step, as is usually done) reflects again one of the core ideas behind our work, that combining multiple, independent sources of information - be it multiple modalities, or temporal vs. spatial information - allows learning models with less supervision.

3.3   Online Learning

In this section, we deal with the problem of learning the specific model in an online fashion for a speaker who has not been seen earlier during training. This can be the case during a live setting, where we don't have the entire data available to us at any given time, just what we have seen so far. To this end, we use a model inspired by the Tabula Rasa Transfer Learning model of Aytar et al. [18].

The idea is that the generic model is used as a zero-shot prior, and already gives a baseline performance, that can be improved as a new speaker specific model is trained incrementally with every additional batch of samples that trickle in from the new speaker. This allows us to have a model that performs better than the prior, generic model in an iterative fashion, without needing to see all the target samples. The process of online learning of speaker-specific classifiers is again weakly supervised by audio: it assumes that VAD is available for the target speaker data as well.

As in the offline case for training speaker specific models (Subsect. 3.2), we use VAD to detect the frames in which human speech is present. Subsequently, the generic (source) classifier is used to guide the selection of the positive samples for each new speaker (target). We select the highest scoring bounding box in each VAD-positive frame as the positive sample for the speaker associated with it, and the remaining bounding boxes are selected as negative samples for the other speakers. Temporal continuity is used to weigh both the positive and negative samples (Eq. 5). Motivated by [24], we use the prior (source) model, not just for the selection of the target speaker's positive training samples, but also for target prediction. During prediction, the generic model scores are added to the target model scores so that the prediction score from online learning, at each iteration is given as:

$$f^t(\phi(x, h)) = \langle w^{gen}, \phi(x, h)\rangle + \langle w^t, \phi(x, h)\rangle \tag{6}$$

Each time step t has an increasing number of training samples to train the classifier w^t at that iteration. w^{gen} remains constant during online learning. This results in the person-specific target classifier being at least as good as the generic source classifier, and getting progressively better with an increasing number of training samples.

4   Experiments

We use the audio-visual dataset made available by the authors of [5]. It consists of 7 recordings of masters student thesis presentations to a jury of examiners. Each student presents for 25 min, followed by 5 min of questioning by the jury. The microphone array, with its directional sound information in a cone of 180 degrees in front of it is associated with upper body tracks of the jury. We will call this the Masters student dataset in the rest of the paper. An example frame of this data is shown in Fig. 1. [5] used the directional sound information from the microphone array, associated with the bounding boxes of persons in the frame to train their video-based active speaker classifier. We simulate VAD by removing this directional information from the data, leaving only a label of speak/non-speak per frame. Like [5], we only use the 3 people from the jury in the front row of the audience, as others behind them are obscured. The people in all the experiments are the same, and do not change positions. We train the active speaker detection classifier in a Leave-One-Out-Cross-Validation (LOOCV) fashion, where the data from 6 presentations are used for training, and tested on the 7th presentation. This is repeated 7 times.

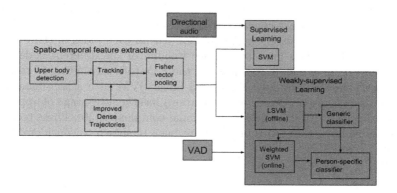

Fig. 2. Experimental setup

Finally, we test the model learnt on the Masters dataset on an entirely new dataset that we present - the Columbia dataset. It is an 87-minute-long video of a panel discussion at Columbia university, available from YouTube[2]. There are 7 speakers on the panel, and the camera focusses on smaller groups of speakers at a time. We only focus on the parts of the video where there is more than

---

[2] https://youtu.be/6GzxbrO0DHM.

one person in the frame, and ignore people on the margins of the video who are not detected by the upper body detector. This gives us sections of video for 5 speakers, with 2–3 speakers visible at any one time. We have annotated the upper body bounding boxes of each speaker with speak/non-speak labels, about 35 min of video in all, which are available at http://www.jaychakravarty.com/?page_id=432. We update the generic classifier learnt on the Masters dataset online, in a completely unsupervised fashion, with the generic classifier adapting to each new speaker in the Columbia dataset, with subsequent improvement in performance.

4.1   Implementation Details

We use the same improved trajectory features (ITF) [28] recommended by [5], for training our active speaker detection classifier. ITF are spatio-temporal features used for state of the art action recognition, and comprise of a concatenation of Histogram of Oriented Gradients (HOG), Histogram of Flow (HoF) and Motion Boundary Histogram (MBH) features. HoG, HoF and MBH features are calculated in the immediate neighbourhood of each point on the grid. We use 15 consecutive frames for calculating the ITF - this corresponds to about 7 s of video in the Masters dataset. The HoG, HoF and MBH features are independently reduced to half their original dimensions using PCA, and feature vectors from within an upper body track are pooled using Fisher vectors (FV) [29]. We apply intra-class L2 normalization, power and a final L2 normalization of the whole FV before classification using a linear SVM. We use a codebook size of 256 for the FV encoding. The FV encoding is done independently for HOG, HoF and MBH, before they are concatenated to a single, 101,376 dimensional vector. Intra-class L2 normalization - normalization within each block of the FV related to a single codeword, is used to balance weights of the different codewords in the FV, and reduces the "burstiness" in the FVs (often resulting from features belonging to the background). Training a linear SVM with a non-linear feature map (obtained using the power normalization) has the advantage of approximating a non-linear SVM at lower computational complexity [30]. These techniques, recommended as best practice in [31], have been to shown to considerably boost performance of FVs.

Table 1. Average AUC (with standard deviations) for active speaker detection fully supervised by directional audio [5], and weakly supervised by VAD, over all experimental folds (Masters dataset).

	Directional audio	VAD
Avg. AUC	$0.69_{\pm 0.07}$	$0.71_{\pm 0.05}$

For upper body detection, we use a detector trained using the Deformable Parts Model from [32]. The tracking is relatively straight-forward, because people don't change positions and there are no crossing tracks. ITF are grouped by their start frame (calculated from the following 15 frames), and a FV is calculated for all the improved trajectories within a bounding box (person) track starting from that frame. A training sample is thus one FV pooling all ITFs from within an upper body track starting in a given frame, with each ITF covering 15 consecutive frames (about 7s of video at 2 fps). The active speaker classifier is sensitive to the frame-rate of the dataset on which it is trained. To have the classifier transfer between datasets, we subsample the Columbia dataset so that its frame-rate matches the frame-rate of the Masters dataset (2 fps). A pipeline of the system is shown in Fig. 2.

4.2 Weak Supervision Using Audio

VAD results in frames with speak/non-speak labels. There are no speak/non-speak labels for individual bounding boxes and the FVs extracted from them. Section 3.1 details the Structured Output SVM classifier that is used for training the active speaker detection classifier in the absence of training labels for individual bounding boxes. Table 1 displays the results of our experiments with the active speaker detection classifier trained using VAD. The results with weak supervision (structured output learning) are comparable with the results from fully supervised learning from directional sound. This shows that the structured output formulation and the soft-max loss function for optimization transfers well from the object localization application of [8,9], to our task of active speaker localization in the absence of bounding box labels for training.

4.3 Speaker Specific Models

Section 3.2 makes the hypothesis that training person specific active speaker detection models will give better results than training a generic model for all speakers. To validate this hypothesis, we perform three experiments:

1. Full directional audio (giving speak/non-speak labels for all bounding boxes in the frame) for training the person specific classifier.
2. VAD audio (speak/non-speak label for the frame, but without information about individual bounding boxes) for training the person-specific classifier. This highest scoring sample using the generic classifier is used to get positive training samples for each person in a VAD-positive frame.
3. Experiment 2, with samples weighted according to temporal continuity (see Eq. 5).

When full directional audio supervision is available (expt. 1), the speaker specific models show better results, a 10 % improvement over the generic classifier of Table 1.

When using VAD for weak supervision with a hard-max posterior (expt. 2), the person-specific classifier performs worse (16 % worse mean average AUC) than the person-specific classifier with full audio supervision (expt. 1), and worse

Table 2. Mean Avg AUC (with standard deviations) for person-specific active speaker detection using (1) directional audio, (2) VAD - no temporal weighting & (3) VAD with temporally weighted samples (All expts. on Masters dataset).

Expt.	Speaker 1	Speaker 2	Speaker 3	Mean Avg. AUC
1	0.79 ±0.08	0.76 ±0.03	0.88 ±0.05	0.81 ±0.07
2	0.60 ±0.10	0.59 ±0.07	0.75 ±0.03	0.65 ±0.10
3	0.79 ±0.10	0.80 ±0.03	0.88 ±0.04	0.82 ±0.07

even than the generic classifier. This confirms the dataset bias problem we discussed in Sect. 2. The generic classifier might be more biased towards one speaker compared to the others and occasionally score the true positive speaker lower than another non-speaker in the same VAD-positive frame. This leads to the use of mis-classified samples for the training of the person-specific classifiers in the weakly supervised case, and their subsequent poor performance.

In experiment 3, a temporal weight is added to each sample - the number of contiguous neighbouring frames in which it has been consistently labelled (see Eq. 5). We use a temporal window of 3 s. This results in a mean average AUC of 0.82, comparable to the fully supervised case (expt. 1). This shows that the temporal weighting of samples correctly guides the sample selection. Thus, it acts as another weak supervisor (apart from the VAD) for the training of the speaker specific classifer. Table 2 presents results for all 3 speaker-specific experiments in the Masters dataset. It should be noted here that for all experiments in this sub-section, the evaluations are performed on individual frames and temporal continuity is exploited as an extra cue during training, not as a postprocessing step to correct results afterwards.

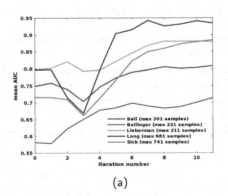

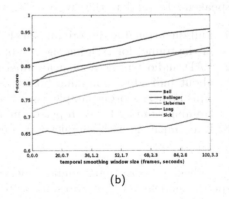

(a)   (b)

Fig. 3. (a) Online Learning: Mean AUC over all speakers in the new Columbia dataset with an increasing number of training samples in each iteration. (b) Temporal smoothing: F-scores for all speakers at the end of online learning, after thresholding and temporal smoothing, with increasing size of temporal window in the Columbia datset.

4.4 Online Learning

Here, we report results of experiments that demonstrate how a generic classifier trained on speakers in the Masters dataset, can be modified online, to specific speakers in the Columbia dataset. We only select sections of video in which there are 2 or more people in the frame at the same time. This is to demonstrate the unsupervised selection of training samples from one among many speakers. The selection of training samples when only 1 speaker is present in the frame is trivial (VAD can be used to detect positive and negative samples for the speaker), and is not considered in this experiment.

The prior classifier is run on each VAD-positive frame in the new dataset and the highest scoring bounding box is taken to be the positive sample for that speaker in the frame, and the remaining bounding boxes are taken to be the negative samples for the other speakers. This assumes that there is only one person speaking at a time in the video, which is actually the case in most target applications. The samples are weighted according to their temporal continuity - a positive sample with a higher number of contiguous positive samples around it gets a higher weight, as was done in number 3 of the speaker specific experiments (Subsect. 4.3). The experiment begins by using the prior classifier to detect active speakers in the new data. Then, with each iteration of online learning, a balanced selection of positive and negative samples are selected from each speaker, and used for training the person-specific classifier. The number of training samples increases with each iteration. Figure 3a displays the mean average AUC results for experiments conducted per speaker over the training iterations. We see that the performance of the iteratively trained person specific target classifier starts out at the performance of the generic source classifier, and gradually improves with increasing number of target training samples. There is an initial dip in the performance of the classifier learnt online for 3 of the 5 people, when there is a small number of training samples. If some of these samples are wrongly selected by the prior classifier, then the classifier's performance will decrease to a level below the generic classifier performance. But, as the speaker speaks for longer, and more correct samples weighted by their temporal continuity are picked, the online learning adapts to the target distribution. We use a maximum of 10 s of video per person for the online learning in the Columbia dataset in our experiments, and see an improvement of about 5–15% over the performance of the prior classifier. Thus, our method of selecting samples weighted by their temporal continuity is resilient against the selection of some wrong samples, and very quickly - within a few seconds - adapts to each new speaker. We use temporal continuity to further improve the performance of the online-learnt classifier during inference as well. The scores from the classifier learnt during the last iteration of online learning are thresholded (at the intersection of the ROC curve with the diagonal) and smoothed over increasing lengths of time (from 0 to about 3 s). Figure 3b shows that the f-scores for all the speakers improve with increasing amounts of temporal smoothing, with plateauing of results at around 3 s. A potential downside of too much smoothing is that if a person speaks for short durations (single, yes/no utterances for example),

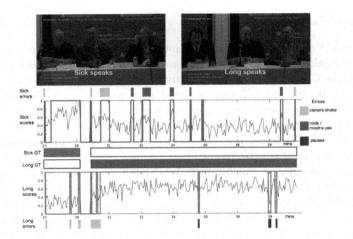

Fig. 4. Normalized raw scores (blue) with the online-learnt classifier and thresholded and temporally smoothed speak/non-speak values for speakers Sick (red) and Long (green), along with Ground Truth (GT, solid colour = speak), in minutes 27:00 to 40:00 in the Columbia dataset. (Color figure online)

then these are not going to be registered. The amount of temporal smoothing applied would depend on the application. For video conferencing, it might not be appropriate to switch focus between speakers for such short utterances, and a smoothing of 3 s (the maximum smoothing applied in our experiments during inference), would probably be adequate.

Figure 4 shows a timeline for Active Speaker Detection in the Columbia dataset, for speakers Sick and Long, during minutes 27:00 to 40:00 in the video. The classifiers for these speakers are learnt online earlier in the video, and the raw scores for these speakers over time are shown in blue. The scores are thresholded and temporally smoothed to obtain speak/non-speak values, shown in red and green for Sick and Long respectively. Ground truth speak/non-speak values for these speakers are also given. It can be seen that the parts of the video where the algorithm apparently makes a mistake can be explained by camera shake, or where a non-active speaker actually nods and mouths yes in response to another active speaker (ground truth does not mark this as speech), or when an active speaker pauses mid-sentence.

5   Conclusions

This paper demonstrates the use of audio for cross-modal supervision of the training of a video-based active speaker detector. The problem is posed in terms of a structured output prediction problem - given information about the presence of an active speaker in a frame from audio-based Voice Activity Detection, find out which particular person is speaking, among the people in the frame, and at the same time, learn the video-based classifier for active speaker detection.

Person-specific classifiers are shown to perform better than generic classifiers, and the learning of the specific classifiers is again weakly supervised by audio. The prior classifier adapts to the specific speaker using samples from just a few seconds of video, with additional improvement in results using temporal smoothing. This shows that the system has the potential to be used in a video conferencing application, and quickly learn the characteristics of new speakers.

In future work, we will close the loop between audio and video. In current work, audio supervises the learning of a video-based person-specific active speaker detector. The learnt video classifier will in turn supervise the learning of person-specific voice models and those voice models will be fed back into the video to further improve active speaker detection. This is expected to be particularly useful in the more challenging data encountered in video diarization: movies and TV series with non-frontal views of people, where the video-only classifier is expected to perform worse than in frontal-view video.

References

1. Khoury, E., Sénac, C., Joly, P.: Audiovisual diarization of people in video content. Multimedia Tools Appl. **68**(3), 747–775 (2014)
2. Everingham, M., Sivic, J., Zisserman, A.: Hello! my name is... buffy"-automatic naming of characters in tv video. In: BMVC, vol. 2, pp. 6 (2006)
3. Everingham, M., Sivic, J., Zisserman, A.: Taking the bite out of automatic naming of characters in TV video. Image Vis. Comput. **27**(5), 545–559 (2009)
4. Haider, F., Al Moubayed, S.: Towards speaker detection using lips movements for humanmachine multiparty dialogue. In: 2012 FONETIK (2012)
5. Chakravarty, P., Mirzaei, S., Tuytelaars, T., Vanhamme, H.: Who's speaking? audio-supervised classification of active speakers in video. In: ACM International Conference on Multimodal Interaction (ICMI) (2015)
6. Germain, F., Sun, D.L., Mysore, G.J.: Speaker and noise independent voice activity detection. In: INTERSPEECH, pp. 732–736 (2013)
7. Bilen, H., Namboodiri, V.P., Gool, L.J.: Object and action classification with latent window parameters. Int. J. Comput. Vis. **106**(3), 237–251 (2014)
8. Bilen, H., Pedersoli, M., Tuytelaars, T.: Weakly supervised object detection with posterior regularization. In: British Machine Vision Conference (2014)
9. Bilen, H., Pedersoli, M., Tuytelaars, T.: Weakly supervised object detection with convex clustering. In: Proceedings of the IEEE Conference on Computer Vision and Pattern Recognition, pp. 1081–1089 (2015)
10. Deselaers, T., Alexe, B., Ferrari, V.: Weakly supervised localization and learning with generic knowledge. Int. J. Comput. Vis. **100**(3), 275–293 (2012)
11. Song, H.O., Girshick, R., Jegelka, S., Mairal, J., Harchaoui, Z., Darrell, T.: On learning to localize objects with minimal supervision. arXiv preprint arXiv:1403.1024 (2014)
12. Nguyen, M.H., Torresani, L., de la Torre, F., Rother, C.: Weakly supervised discriminative localization and classification: a joint learning process. In: 2009 IEEE 12th International Conference on Computer Vision, pp. 1925–1932. IEEE (2009)
13. Bojanowski, P., Bach, F., Laptev, I., Ponce, J., Schmid, C., Sivic, J.: Finding actors and actions in movies. In: 2013 IEEE International Conference on Computer Vision (ICCV), pp. 2280–2287. IEEE (2013)

14. Khosla, A., Zhou, T., Malisiewicz, T., Efros, A.A., Torralba, A.: Undoing the damage of dataset bias. In: Fitzgibbon, A., Lazebnik, S., Perona, P., Sato, Y., Schmid, C. (eds.) ECCV 2012. LNCS, vol. 7572, pp. 158–171. Springer, Heidelberg (2012). doi:10.1007/978-3-642-33718-5_12

15. Tommasi, T., Quadrianto, N., Caputo, B., Lampert, C.H.: Beyond dataset bias: multi-task unaligned shared knowledge transfer. In: Lee, K.M., Matsushita, Y., Rehg, J.M., Hu, Z. (eds.) ACCV 2012, Part I. LNCS, vol. 7724, pp. 1–15. Springer, Heidelberg (2013)

16. Aljundi, R., Emonet, R., Muselet, D., Sebban, M.: Landmarks-based kernelized subspace alignment for unsupervised domain adaptation. In: Computer Vision and Pattern Recognition (CVPR 2015) (2015)

17. Fernando, B., Habrard, A., Sebban, M., Tuytelaars, T.: Unsupervised visual domain adaptation using subspace alignment. In: 2013 IEEE International Conference on Computer Vision (ICCV), pp. 2960–2967. IEEE (2013)

18. Aytar, Y., Zisserman, A.: Tabula rasa: model transfer for object category detection. In: 2011 IEEE International Conference on Computer Vision (ICCV), pp. 2252–2259. IEEE (2011)

19. Tommasi, T., Caputo, B.: The more you know, the less you learn: from knowledge transfer to one-shot learning of object categories. In: BMVC, Number LIDIAP-CONF-2009-049 (2009)

20. Tommasi, T., Orabona, F., Caputo, B.: Safety in numbers: learning categories from few examples with multi model knowledge transfer. In: 2010 IEEE Conference on Computer Vision and Pattern Recognition (CVPR), pp. 3081–3088. IEEE (2010)

21. Chen, J., Liu, X., Tu, P., Aragones, A.: Person-specific expression recognition with transfer learning. In: 2012 19th IEEE International Conference on Image Processing (ICIP), pp. 2621–2624. IEEE (2012)

22. Chu, W.S., De la Torre, F., Cohn, J.F.: Selective transfer machine for personalized facial action unit detection. In: 2013 IEEE Conference on Computer Vision and Pattern Recognition (CVPR), pp. 3515–3522. IEEE (2013)

23. Zen, G., Sangineto, E., Ricci, E., Sebe, N.: Unsupervised domain adaptation for personalized facial emotion recognition. In: Proceedings of the 16th International Conference on Multimodal Interaction, pp. 128–135. ACM (2014)

24. Gavves, E., Mensink, T., Tommasi, T., Snoek, C.G., Tuytelaars, T.: Active transfer learning with zero-shot priors: reusing past datasets for future tasks. arXiv preprint arXiv:1510.01544 (2015)

25. Mirzaei, S., Van hamme, H., Norouzi, Y.: Blind audio source separation of stereo mixtures using bayesian non-negative matrix factorization. In: Signal Processing Conference (EUSIPCO), pp. 621–625, September 2014

26. Pletscher, P., Ong, C.S., Buhmann, J.M.: Entropy and margin maximization for structured output learning. In: Balcázar, J.L., Bonchi, F., Gionis, A., Sebag, M. (eds.) ECML PKDD 2010. LNCS (LNAI), vol. 6323, pp. 83–98. Springer, Heidelberg (2010). doi:10.1007/978-3-642-15939-8_6

27. Uijlings, J.R., Sande, K.E., Gevers, T., Smeulders, A.W.: Selective search for object recognition. Int. J. Comput. Vis. **104**(2), 154–171 (2013)

28. Wang, H., Schmid, C.: Action recognition with improved trajectories. In: ICCV, Sydney, Australia, pp. 3551–3558, December 2013

29. Perronnin, F., Sánchez, J., Mensink, T.: Improving the fisher kernel for large-scale image classification. In: Daniilidis, K., Maragos, P., Paragios, N. (eds.) ECCV 2010, Part IV. LNCS, vol. 6314, pp. 143–156. Springer, Heidelberg (2010)

30. Vedaldi, A., Zisserman, A.: Efficient additive kernels via explicit feature maps. IEEE Trans. Pattern Anal. Mach. Intell. **34**(3), 480–492 (2012)

31. Peng, X., Wang, L., Wang, X., Qiao, Y.: Bag of visual words and fusion methods for action recognition: comprehensive study and good practice. CoRR abs/1405.4506 (2014)

32. Girshick, R.B., Felzenszwalb, P.F., McAllester, D.: Discriminatively trained deformable part models, release 5. http://people.cs.uchicago.edu/rbg/latent-release5/

Recurrent Temporal Deep Field for Semantic Video Labeling

Peng Lei$^{(\boxtimes)}$ and Sinisa Todorovic

School of Electrical Engineering and Computer Science,
Oregon State University, Corvallis, USA
leip@oregonstate.edu, sinisa@eecs.oregonstate.edu

Abstract. This paper specifies a new deep architecture, called Recurrent Temporal Deep Field (RTDF), for semantic video labeling. RTDF is a conditional random field (CRF) that combines a deconvolution neural network (DeconvNet) and a recurrent temporal restricted Boltzmann machine (RTRBM). DeconvNet is grounded onto pixels of a new frame for estimating the unary potential of the CRF. RTRBM estimates a high-order potential of the CRF by capturing long-term spatiotemporal dependencies of pixel labels that RTDF has already predicted in previous frames. We derive a mean-field inference algorithm to jointly predict all latent variables in both RTRBM and CRF. We also conduct end-to-end joint training of all DeconvNet, RTRBM, and CRF parameters. The joint learning and inference integrate the three components into a unified deep model – RTDF. Our evaluation on the benchmark Youtube Face Database (YFDB) and Cambridge-driving Labeled Video Database (Camvid) demonstrates that RTDF outperforms the state of the art both qualitatively and quantitatively.

Keywords: Video labeling · Recurrent Temporal Deep Field · Recurrent Temporal Restricted Boltzmann Machine · Deconvolution · CRF

1 Introduction

This paper presents a new deep architecture for semantic video labeling, where the goal is to assign an object class label to every pixel. Our videos show natural driving scenes, captured by a camera installed on a moving car facing forward, or indoor close-ups of a person's head facing the camera. Both outdoor and indoor videos are recorded in uncontrolled environments with large variations in lighting conditions and camera viewpoints. Also, objects occurring in these videos exhibit a wide variability in appearance, shape, and motion patterns, and are subject to long-term occlusions. To address these challenges, our key idea is to efficiently account for both local and long-range spatiotemporal cues using deep learning.

Our deep architecture, called Recurrent Temporal Deep Field (RTDF), leverages the conditional random field (CRF) [4] for integrating local and contextual

© Springer International Publishing AG 2016
B. Leibe et al. (Eds.): ECCV 2016, Part V, LNCS 9909, pp. 302–317, 2016.
DOI: 10.1007/978-3-319-46454-1_19

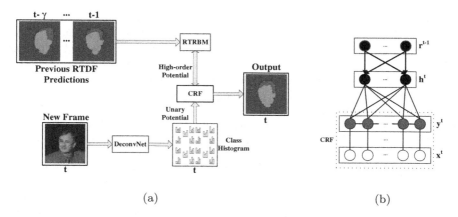

(a)   (b)

Fig. 1. (a) Our semantic labeling for a Youtube Face video [1] using RTDF. Given a frame at time t, RTDF uses a CRF to fuse both local and long-range spatiotemporal cues for labeling pixels in frame t. The local cues (red box) are extracted by DeconvNet [2] using only pixels of frame t. The long-range spatiotemporal cues (blue box) are estimated by RTRBM [3] (precisely, the hidden layer of RTDF) using a sequence of previous RTDF predictions for pixels in frames $t-1, t-2, \ldots, t-\gamma$. (b) An illustration of RTDF with pixel labels $\mathbf{y}^t$ in frame t, unary potentials $\mathbf{x}^t$, and top two layers $\mathbf{r}^{t-1}$ and $\mathbf{h}^t$ belonging to RTRBM. The high-order potential is distributed to all pixels in frame t via the full connectivity of layers $\mathbf{h}^t$ and $\mathbf{y}^t$, and layers $\mathbf{r}^{t-1}$ and $\mathbf{h}^t$. (Color figure online)

visual cues toward semantic pixel labeling, as illustrated in Fig. 1. The energy of RTDF is defined in terms of unary, pairwise, and higher-order potentials.

As the unary potential, we use class predictions of the Deconvolution Neural Network (DeconvNet) [2] for every pixel of a new frame at time t. DeconvNet efficiently computes the unary potential in a feed-forward manner, through a sequence of convolutional and deconvolutional processing of pixels in frame t. Since the unary potential is computed based only on a single video frame, DeconvNet can be viewed as providing local spatial cues to our RTDF. As the pairwise potential, we use the standard spatial smoothness of pixel labels. Finally, as the higher-order potential, we use hidden variables of the Recurrent Temporal Restricted Boltzmann Machine (RTRBM) [3] (see Fig. 1b). This hidden layer of RTRBM is computed from a sequence of previous RTDF predictions for pixels in frames $\{t-1, t-2, \ldots, t-\gamma\}$. RTRBM is aimed at capturing long-range spatiotemporal dependencies among already predicted pixel labels, which is then used to enforce spatiotemporal coherency of pixel labeling in frame t.

We formulate a new mean-field inference algorithm to jointly predict all latent variables in both RTRBM and CRF. We also specify a joint end-to-end learning of CRF, DeconvNet and RTRBM. The joint learning and inference integrate the three components into a unified deep model – RTDF.

The goal of inference is to minimize RTDF energy. Input to RTDF inference at frame t consists of: (a) pixels of frame t, and (b) RTDF predictions for pixels in frames $\{t-1,\ldots,t-\gamma\}$. Given this input, our mean-field inference algorithm *jointly* predicts hidden variables of RTRBM and pixel labels in frame t.

Parameters of CRF, DeconvNet, and RTRBM are *jointly* learned in an end-to-end fashion, which improves our performance over the case when each component of RTDF is independently trained (a.k.a. piece-wise trained).

Our semantic video labeling proceeds frame-by-frame until all frames are labeled. Note that for a few initial frames $t \leq \gamma$, we do not use the high-order potential, but only the unary and pairwise potentials in RTDF inference.

Our contributions are summarized as follows:

1. A new deep architecture, RTDF, capable of efficiently capturing both local and long-range spatiotemporal cues for pixel labeling in video,
2. An efficient mean-field inference algorithm that jointly predicts hidden variables in RTRBM and CRF and labels pixels; as our experiments demonstrate, our mean-field inference yields better accuracy of pixel labeling than an alternative stage-wise inference of each component of RTDF.
3. A new end-to-end joint training of all components of RTDF using loss backpropagation; as our experiments demonstrate, our joint training outperforms the case when each component of RTDF is trained separately.
4. Improved pixel labeling accuracy relative to the state of the art, under comparable runtimes, on the benchmark datasets.

In the following, Sect. 2 reviews closely related work; Sect. 3 specifies RTDF and briefly reviews its basic components: RBM in Sect. 3.1, RTRBM in Sect. 3.2, and DeconvNet in Sect. 3.3; Sect. 4 formulates RTDF inference; Sect. 5 presents our training of RTDF; and Sect. 6 shows our experimental results.

2 Related Work

This section reviews closely related work on semantic video labeling, whereas the literature on unsupervised and semi-supervised video segmentation is beyond our scope. We also discuss our relationship to other related work on semantic image segmentation, and object shape modeling.

Semantic video labeling has been traditionally addressed using hierarchical graphical models (e.g., [5–10]). However, they typically resort to extracting hand-designed video features for capturing context, and compute compatibility terms only over local space-time neighborhoods.

Our RTDF is related to semantic image segmentation using CNNs [11–19]. These approaches typically use multiple stages of training, or iterative component-wise training. Instead, we use a joint training of all components of our deep architecture. For example, a fully convolutional network (FCN) [12] is trained in a stage-wise manner such that a new convolution layer is progressively added to a previously trained network until no performance improvement is obtained. For smoothness, DeepLab [13] uses a fully-connected CRF to post-process CNN predictions, while the CRF and CNN are iteratively trained, one at a time. Also, a deep deconvolution network presented in [20] uses object proposals as a pre-processing step. For efficiency, we instead use DeconvNet [2], as the number of trainable parameters in DeconvNet is significantly smaller in comparison to peer deep networks.

RTDF is also related to prior work on restricted Boltzmann machine (RBM) [21]. For example, RBMs have been used for extracting both local and global features of object shapes [22], and shape Boltzmann machine (SBM) can generate deformable object shapes [25]. Also, RBM has been used to provide a higher-order potential for a CRF in scene labeling [23,24].

The most related model to ours is the shape-time random field (STRF) [26]. STRF combines a CRF with a conditional restricted Boltzmann machine (CRBM) [27] for video labeling. They use CRBM to estimate a higher-order potential of the STRF's energy. While this facilitates modeling long-range shape and motion patterns of objects, input to their CRF consists of hand-designed features. Also, they train CRF and CRBM iteratively, as separate modules, in a piece-wise manner. In contrast, we jointly learn all components of our RTDF in a unified manner via loss backpropagation.

3   Recurrent Temporal Deep Field

Our RTDF is an energy-based model that consists of three components – DeconvNet, CRF, and RTRBM – providing the unary, pairwise, and high-order potentials for predicting class labels $\mathbf{y}^t = \{\mathbf{y}_p^t : \mathbf{y}_p^t \in \{0,1\}^L\}$ for pixels p in video frame t, where $\mathbf{y}_p^t$ has only one non-zero element. Labels $\mathbf{y}^t$ are predicted given: (a) pixels $\mathbf{I}^t$ of frame t, and (b) previous RTDF predictions $\mathbf{y}^{<t} = \{\mathbf{y}^{t-1}, \mathbf{y}^{t-2}, \ldots, \mathbf{y}^{t-\gamma}\}$, as illustrated in Fig. 2.

DeconvNet takes pixels $\mathbf{I}^t$ as input, and outputs the class likelihoods $\mathbf{x}^t = \{\mathbf{x}_p^t : \mathbf{x}_p^t \in [0,1]^L, \sum_{l=1}^L x_{pl}^t = 1\}$, for every pixel p in frame t. A more detailed description of DeconvNet is given in Sect. 3.3. $\mathbf{x}^t$ is then used to define the unary potential of RTDF.

RTRBM takes previous RTDF predictions $\mathbf{y}^{<t}$ as input and estimates values of latent variables $\mathbf{r}^{<t} = \{\mathbf{r}^{t-1}, \ldots, \mathbf{r}^{t-\gamma}\}$ from $\mathbf{y}^{<t}$. The time-unfolded visualization in Fig. 2 shows that $\mathbf{r}^{t-1}$ is affected by previous RTDF predictions $\mathbf{y}^{<t}$ through the full connectivity between two consecutive $\mathbf{r}$ layers and the full connectivity between the corresponding $\mathbf{r}$ and $\mathbf{z}$ layers.

The hidden layer $\mathbf{r}^{t-1}$ is aimed at capturing long-range spatiotemporal dependences of predicted class labels in $\mathbf{y}^{<t}$. Thus, $\mathbf{h}^t$ and $\mathbf{r}^{t-1}$ are used to define the high-order potential of RTDF, which is distributed to all pixels in frame t via the full connectivity between layers $\mathbf{h}^t$ and $\mathbf{z}^t$, as well as between layers $\mathbf{h}^t$ and $\mathbf{r}^{t-1}$ in RTRBM. Specifically, the high-order potential is distributed to each pixel via a deterministic mapping between nodes in $\mathbf{z}^t$ and pixels in $\mathbf{y}^t$. While there are many options for this mapping, in our implementation, we partition frame t into a regular grid of patches. As further explained in Sect. 3.1, each node of $\mathbf{z}^t$ is assigned to a corresponding patch of pixels in $\mathbf{y}^t$.

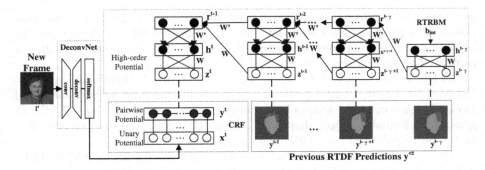

Fig. 2. Our RTDF is an energy-based model that predicts pixel labels $\mathbf{y}^t$ for frame t, given the unary potential $\mathbf{x}^t$ of DeconvNet, the pairwise potential between neighboring pixel labels in frame t, and the high-order potential defined in terms of $\mathbf{z}^t$, $\mathbf{h}^t$ and $\mathbf{r}^{t-1}$ of RTRBM. The figure shows the time-unfolded visualization of computational processes in RTRBM. RTRBM takes as input previous RTDF predictions $\{\mathbf{y}^{t-1}, \ldots, \mathbf{y}^{t-\gamma}\}$ and encodes the long-range and high-order dependencies through latent variables $\mathbf{r}^{t-1}$. The high-order potential is further distributed to all pixels in frame t via a deterministic mapping (vertical dashed lines) between $\mathbf{y}^t$ and $\mathbf{z}^t$.

The energy of RTDF is defined as

$$E_{\mathrm{RTDF}}(\mathbf{y}^t, \mathbf{h}^t | \mathbf{y}^{<t}, \mathbf{I}^t) = -\sum_p \psi_1(\mathbf{x}_p^t, \mathbf{y}_p^t) - \sum_{p,p'} \psi_2(\mathbf{y}_p^t, \mathbf{y}_{p'}^t) + E_{\mathrm{RT}}(\mathbf{y}^t, \mathbf{h}^t | \mathbf{y}^{<t}). \quad (1)$$

In (1), the first two terms denote the unary and pairwise potentials, and the third term represents the high-order potential. As mentioned above, the mapping between $\mathbf{y}^t$ and $\mathbf{z}^t$ is deterministic. Therefore, instead of using $\mathbf{z}^t$ in (1), we can specify E_{RT} directly in terms of $\mathbf{y}^t$. This allows us to conduct *joint* inference of $\mathbf{y}^t$ and $\mathbf{h}^t$, as further explained in Sect. 4.

The unary and pairwise potentials are defined as for standard CRFs:

$$\psi_1(\mathbf{x}_p^t, \mathbf{y}_p^t) = W_{\mathbf{y}_p^t}^1 \cdot \mathbf{x}_p^t, \qquad \psi_2(\mathbf{y}_p^t, \mathbf{y}_{p'}^t) = W_{\mathbf{y}_p^t, \mathbf{y}_{p'}^t}^2 \cdot \exp(-|\mathbf{x}_p^t - \mathbf{x}_{p'}^t|), \quad (2)$$

where $W_{\mathbf{y}}^1 \in \mathbb{R}^L$ is an L-dimensional vector of unary weights for a given class label at pixel p, and $W_{\mathbf{y}, \mathbf{y}'}^2 \in \mathbb{R}^L$ is an L-dimensional vector of pairwise weights for a given pair of class labels at neighboring pixels p and p'.

Before specifying E_{RT}, for clarity, we first review the restricted Boltzmann machine (RBM) and then explain its extension to RTRBM.

3.1 A Brief Review of Restricted Boltzmann Machine

RTRBM can be viewed as a temporal concatenation of RBMs [3]. RBM [21] is an undirected graphical model with one visible layer and one hidden layer. In our approach, the visible layer consists of L-dimensional binary vectors $\mathbf{z} = \{\mathbf{z}_i : \mathbf{z}_i \in \{0,1\}^L\}$ and each $\mathbf{z}_i$ has only one non-zero element representing the class label of the corresponding patch i in a given video frame. The hidden layer consists of binary variables $\mathbf{h} = \{h_j : h_j \in \{0,1\}\}$. RBM defines a joint distribution of the visible layer $\mathbf{z}$ and the hidden layer $\mathbf{h}$, and the energy function between the two layers for a video frame is defined as:

$$E_{\mathrm{RBM}}(\mathbf{z}, \mathbf{h}) = -\sum_j \sum_i \sum_{l=1}^{L} W_{ijl} h_j z_{il} - \sum_i \sum_{l=1}^{L} z_{il} c_{il} - \sum_j b_j h_j \qquad (3)$$

where W is the RBM's weight matrix between $\mathbf{z}$ and $\mathbf{h}$, and $\mathbf{b}$ and $\mathbf{c}$ are the bias vectors for $\mathbf{h}$ and $\mathbf{z}$, respectively. RBM has been successfully used for modeling spatial context of an image or video frame [23,24,26].

Importantly, to reduce the huge number of parameters in RBM (and thus facilitate learning), we follow the pooling approach presented in [26]. Specifically, instead of working directly with pixels in a video frame, our formulation of RBM uses patches i of pixels (8×8 pixels) as corresponding to the visible variables $\mathbf{z}_i$. The patches are obtained by partitioning the frame into a regular grid.

Recall that in our overall RTDF architecture RBM is grounded onto latent pixel labels $\mathbf{y}_p$ through the deterministic mapping of $\mathbf{z}_i$'s to pixels p that fall within patches i (see Fig. 2). When predicted labels $\mathbf{y}^{<t}$ are available for video frames before time t, we use the following mapping $\mathbf{z}_i = 1/|i| \sum_{p \in i} \mathbf{y}_p$, where $|i|$ denotes the number of pixels in patch i. Note that this will give real-valued $\mathbf{z}_i$'s, which we then binarize. Conversely, for frame t, when we want to distribute the high-order potential, we deterministically assign potential of $\mathbf{z}_i$ to every pixel within the patch.

3.2   A Brief Review of RTRBM

RTRBM represents a recurrent temporal extension of an RBM [3], with one visible layer $\mathbf{z}$, and two hidden layers $\mathbf{h}$ and $\mathbf{r}$. As in RBM, $\mathbf{h}$ are binary variables, and $\mathbf{r} = \{r_j : r_j \in [0,1]\}$ represents a set of real-valued hidden variables. In the time-unfolded visualization shown in Fig. 2, RTRBM can be seen as a temporal concatenation of the respective sets of RBM's variables, indexed by time t, $\{\mathbf{z}^t, \mathbf{h}^t, \mathbf{r}^t\}$. This means that each RBM at time t in RTRBM has a dynamic bias input that is affected by the RBMs of previous time instances. This dynamic bias input is formalized as a recurrent neural network [28], where hidden variables $\mathbf{r}^t$ at time t are obtained as

$$\mathbf{r}^t = \sigma(W\mathbf{z}^t + \mathbf{b} + W'\mathbf{r}^{t-1}), \qquad (4)$$

where $\{\mathbf{b}, W, W'\}$ are parameters. Note that $\mathbf{b} + W'\mathbf{r}^{t-1}$ is replaced by $\mathbf{b}_{int}$ for time $t = 1$, $\sigma(\cdot)$ is the element-wise sigmoid function, and W' is the shared weight matrix between $\mathbf{r}^{t-1}$ and $\mathbf{h}^t$ and between $\mathbf{r}^{t-1}$ and $\mathbf{r}^t$. Consequently, the recurrent neural network in RTRBM is designed such that the conditional expectation of $\mathbf{h}^t$, given $\mathbf{z}^t$, is equal to $\mathbf{r}^t$. RTRBM defines an energy of $\mathbf{z}^t$ and $\mathbf{h}^t$ conditioned on the hidden recurrent input $\mathbf{r}^{t-1}$ as

$$E_{\mathrm{RT}}(\mathbf{z}^t, \mathbf{h}^t | \mathbf{r}^{t-1}) = E_{\mathrm{RBM}}(\mathbf{z}^t, \mathbf{h}^t) - \sum_j \sum_k W'_{jk} h_j^t r_k^{t-1}. \qquad (5)$$

From (3), (4) and (5), RTRBM parameters are $\theta_{\mathrm{RT}} = \{\mathbf{b}_{\mathrm{int}}, \mathbf{b}, \mathbf{c}, W, W'\}$. The associated free energy of $\mathbf{z}^t$ is defined as

$$F_{\mathrm{RT}}(\mathbf{z}^t|\mathbf{r}^{t-1}) = -\sum_j \log(1 + \exp(b_j + \sum_{i,l} W_{ijl}z_{il} + \sum_k W'_{jk}r_k^{t-1})) - \sum_{i,l} z_{il}c_{il}. \quad (6)$$

RTRBM can be viewed as capturing long-range and high-order dependencies in both space and time, because it is characterized by the full connectivity between consecutive $\mathbf{r}$ layers, and between the corresponding $\mathbf{r}$, $\mathbf{z}$, and $\mathbf{h}$ layers.

Due to the deterministic mapping between $\mathbf{z}^t$ and $\mathbf{y}^t$ for frame t, we can specify E_{RT} given by (5) in terms of $\mathbf{y}^t$, i.e., as $E_{\mathrm{RT}}(\mathbf{y}^t, \mathbf{h}^t|\mathbf{r}^{t-1})$. We will use this to derive a mean-field inference of $\mathbf{y}^t$, as explained in Sect. 4.

3.3   DeconvNet

As shown in Fig. 2, DeconvNet [2] is used for computing the unary potential of RTDF. We strictly follow the implementation presented in [2]. DeconvNet consists of two networks: one based on VGG16 net to encode the input video frame, and a multilayer deconvolution network to generate feature maps for predicting pixel labels. The convolution network records the pooling indices computed in the pooling layers. Given the output of the convolution network and the pooling indices, the deconvolution network performs a series of unpooling and deconvolution operations for producing the final feature maps. These feature maps are passed through the softmax layer for predicting the likelihoods of class labels of every pixel, $\mathbf{x}_p \in [0, 1]^L$. Before joint training, we pre-train parameters of DeconvNet, θ_{DN}, using the cross entropy loss, as in [2].

4   Inference of RTDF

Pixel labels of the first γ frames of a video are *predicted* using a variant of our model – namely, the jointly trained CRF + DeconvNet, without RTRBM. Then, inference of the full RTDF (i.e., jointly trained CRF + DeconvNet + RTRBM) proceeds to subsequent frames until all the frames have been labeled.

Given a sequence of semantic labelings in the past, $\mathbf{y}^{<t}$, and a new video frame, $\mathbf{I}^t$, the goal of RTDF inference is to predict $\mathbf{y}^t$ as:

$$\hat{\mathbf{y}}^t = \arg\max_{\mathbf{y}^t} \sum_{\mathbf{h}^t} \exp(-E_{\mathrm{RTDF}}(\mathbf{y}^t, \mathbf{h}^t|\mathbf{y}^{<t}, \mathbf{I}^t)). \quad (7)$$

Since the exact inference of RTDF is intractable, we formulate an approximate mean-field inference for jointly predicting both $\hat{\mathbf{y}}^t$ and $\hat{\mathbf{h}}^t$. Its goal is to minimize the KL-divergence between the true posterior distribution, $P(\mathbf{y}^t, \mathbf{h}^t|\mathbf{y}^{<t}, \mathbf{I}^t) = \frac{1}{Z(\theta)}\exp(-E_{\mathrm{RTDF}}(\mathbf{y}^t, \mathbf{h}^t|\mathbf{y}^{<t}, \mathbf{I}^t))$, and the mean-field distribution $Q(\mathbf{y}^t, \mathbf{h}^t) = \prod_p Q(\mathbf{y}_p^t) \prod_j Q(\mathbf{h}_j^t)$ factorized over pixels p for $\mathbf{y}^t$ and hidden nodes j for $\mathbf{h}^t$.

To derive our mean-field inference, we introduce the following two types of variational parameters: (i) $\boldsymbol{\mu} = \{\mu_{pl} : \mu_{pl} = Q(\mathbf{y}_{pl}^t = 1)\}$, where $\sum_{l=1}^L \mu_{pl} = 1$ for

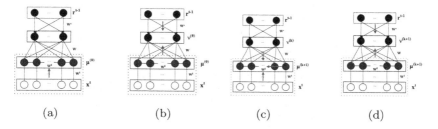

| (a) | (b) | (c) | (d) |

Fig. 3. Key steps of the mean-field inference overlaid over RTDF which is depicted as in Fig. 1b. (a) Initialization of $\boldsymbol{\mu}^{(0)}$. (b) Initialization of $\boldsymbol{\nu}^{(0)}$. (c) Updating of $\boldsymbol{\mu}^{(k+1)}$. (d) Updating of $\boldsymbol{\nu}^{(k+1)}$. The red arrows show the information flow. (Color figure online)

every pixel p; (ii) $\boldsymbol{\nu} = \{\nu_j : \nu_j = Q(\mathbf{h}_j^t = 1)\}$. They allow us to express the mean-field distribution as $Q(\mathbf{y}^t, \mathbf{h}^t) = Q(\boldsymbol{\mu}, \boldsymbol{\nu}) = \prod_p \mu_p \prod_j \nu_j$. It is straightforward to show that minimizing the KL-divergence between P and Q amounts to the following objective

$$\hat{\boldsymbol{\mu}}, \hat{\boldsymbol{\nu}} = \arg\max_{\boldsymbol{\mu}, \boldsymbol{\nu}} \{ \sum_{\mathbf{y}^t, \mathbf{h}^t} Q(\boldsymbol{\mu}, \boldsymbol{\nu}) \ln P(\mathbf{y}^t, \mathbf{h}^t | \mathbf{y}^{<t}, \mathbf{I}^t) + H(Q(\boldsymbol{\mu}, \boldsymbol{\nu})) \}, \quad (8)$$

where $H(Q)$ is the entropy of Q.

Our mean-field inference begins with initialization: $\mu_{pl}^{(0)} = \frac{\exp(W_{\mu_{pl}}^1 \cdot \mathbf{x}_p)}{\sum_{l'} \exp(W_{\mu_{pl'}}^1 \cdot \mathbf{x}_p)}$, $\nu_j^{(0)} = \sigma(\sum_l \sum_i \sum_{p \in i} \frac{1}{|i|} \mu_{pl}^{(0)} W_{ijl} + b_j + \sum_{j'} W'_{jj'} r_{j'}^{t-1})$ and then proceeds by updating $\mu_{pl}^{(k)}$ and $\nu_j^{(k)}$ using the following equations until convergence:

$$\mu_{pl}^{(k+1)} = \frac{\exp(W_{\mu_{pl}^{(k)}}^1 \cdot \mathbf{x}_p + \sum_j W_{ijl} \nu_j^{(k)} + c_{il} + \beta_{p' \to p}^{(k)})}{\sum_{l'} \exp(W_{\mu_{pl'}^{(k)}}^1 \cdot \mathbf{x}_p + \sum_j W_{ijl'} \nu_j^{(k)} + c_{il'} + \beta_{p' \to p}^{(k)})}, \quad (9)$$

$$\nu_j^{(k+1)} = \sigma(\sum_l \sum_i \sum_{p \in i} \frac{1}{|i|} \mu_{pl}^{(k+1)} W_{ijl} + b_j + \sum_{j'} W'_{jj'} r_{j'}^{t-1}), \quad (10)$$

where $\beta_{p' \to p}^{(k)} = \sum_{p'} \sum_{l'} W_{\mu_{pl}^{(k)}, \mu_{p'l'}^{(k)}}^2 \cdot \exp(-|\mathbf{x}_p - \mathbf{x}_{p'}|)$ denotes a pairwise term that accounts for all neighbors p' of p, W^1 and W^2 denote parameters of the unary and pairwise potentials defined in (2), and W_{ijl} and $W'_{jj'}$ are parameters of RTRBM. Also, the second and the third terms in (9) and the first term in (10) use the deterministic mapping between patches i and pixels $p \in i$ (see Sect. 3.1). Figure 3 shows the information flow in our mean-field inference, overlaid over RTDF which is depicted in a similar manner as in Fig. 1b.

After convergence at step K, the variational parameter $\boldsymbol{\mu}^{(k)}$, $k \in \{0, 1, \cdots, K\}$ associated with minimum free energy as defined in (12) is used to predict the label of pixels in frame t. The label at every pixel p is predicted as l for which $\mu_{pl}^{(k)}$, $l \in \{1, 2, \cdots, L\}$ is maximum. This amounts to setting $\hat{y}_{pl}^t = 1$,

---

Algorithm 1. Joint Training of RTDF

---

input : Training set: $\{\mathbf{I}^t, \mathbf{y}^t, t = 1, 2, \cdots\}$, where $\mathbf{y}^t$ is ground truth
output: Parameters of RTDF
repeat
    1. For every training video, conduct the mean-field inference, presented in Sect.4, and calculate the free energy associated with $\mathbf{y}^t$ using (12);
    2. Compute the derivative of $\triangle(\theta)$ given by (11) with respect to:
        2.1. Unary term $\mathbf{x}_p$, using (11) and (2),
        2.2. Pairwise term $\exp(-|\mathbf{x}_p^t - \mathbf{x}_{p'}^t|)$, using (11) and (2);
    3. Update CRF parameters W^1, W^2, using the result of Step 2;
    4. Backpropagate the result of Step 2.1. to DeconvNet using the chain rule in order to update θ_{DN};
    5. Compute $\frac{\partial \triangle}{\partial \theta_{\mathrm{RT}}}$ using (11), (12), (6) and (4) for updating θ_{RT};
until *stopping criteria*;

---

while all other elements of vector $\hat{\mathbf{y}}_p^t$ are set to zero. Also, the value of $\hat{h}_j^t$ is estimated by binarizing the corresponding maximum $\nu_j^{(k)}$.

5   Learning

Parameters of all components of RTDF, $\theta = \{W^1, W^2, \theta_{\mathrm{DN}}, \theta_{\mathrm{RT}}\}$, are trained jointly. For a suitable initialization of RTDF, we first pretrain each component, and then carry out joint training, as summarized in Algorithm 1.

Pretraining. (1) **RTRBM.** The goal of learning RTRBM is to find parameters θ_{RTRBM} that maximize the joint log-likelihood, $\log p(\mathbf{z}^{<t}, \mathbf{z}^t)$. To this end, we closely follow the learning procedure presented in [3], which uses the backpropagation-through-time (BPTT) algorithm [28] for back-propagating the error of patch labeling. As in [3], we use contrastive divergence (CD) [29] to approximate the gradient in training RTRBM. (2) **DeconvNet.** As initial parameters, DeconvNet uses parameters of VGG16 network (without the fully-connected layers) for the deep convolution network, and follows the approach of [2] for the deconvolution network. Then, the two components of DeconvNet are jointly trained using the cross entropy loss defined on pixel label predictions. (3) **CRF.** The CRF is pretrained on the output features from DeconvNet using loopy belief propagation with the LBFGS optimization method.

Joint Training of RTDF. The goal of joint training is to maximize the conditional log-likelihood $\sum_t \log p(\mathbf{y}^t | \mathbf{y}^{<t}, \mathbf{I}^t)$. We use CD-PercLoss algorithm [30] and error back-propagation (EBP) to jointly train parameters of RTDF in an end-to-end fashion. The training objective is to minimize the following generalized perceptron loss [31] with regularization:

$$\triangle(\theta) = \sum_t (F(\mathbf{y}^t | \mathbf{y}^{<t}, \mathbf{I}^t) - \min_{\hat{\mathbf{y}}^t} F(\hat{\mathbf{y}}^t | \mathbf{y}^{<t}, \mathbf{I}^t)) + \lambda \theta^T \theta \qquad (11)$$

where $\lambda > 0$ is a weighting parameter, and $F(\mathbf{y}^t|\mathbf{y}^{<t}, \mathbf{I}^t)$ denotes the free energy of ground truth label $\mathbf{y}^t$ of frame t, and $\hat{\mathbf{y}}^t$ is the predicted label associated with minimum free energy. The free energy of RTDF is defined as

$$F(\mathbf{y}^t|\mathbf{y}^{<t}, \mathbf{I}^t) = -\sum_p \psi_1(\mathbf{x}_p^t, \mathbf{y}_p^t) - \sum_{p,p'} \psi_2(\mathbf{y}_p^t, \mathbf{y}_{p'}^t) + F_{\text{RT}}(\mathbf{y}^t|\mathbf{r}^{t-1}) \qquad (12)$$

where the first two terms denote the unary and pairwise potentials, and the third term is defined in (6). In the prediction pass of training, the pixel label is obtained by the mean-field inference, as explained in Sect. 4. In the updating phase of training, the errors are back-propagated through CRF, DeconvNet and RTRBM in a standard way, resulting in a joint update of θ.

6 Results

Datasets and Metrics: For evaluation, we use the Youtube Face Database (YFDB) [1] and Cambridge-driving Labeled Video Database (CamVid) [32]. Both datasets are recorded in uncontrolled environment, and present challenges in terms of occlusions, and variations of motions, shapes, and lighting. CamVid consists of four long videos showing driving scenes with various object classes, whose frequency of appearance is unbalanced. Unlike other available datasets [33–35], YFDB and CamVid provide sufficient training samples for learning RTRBM. Each YFDB video contains 49 to 889 roughly aligned face images with resolution 256×256. We use the experimental setup of [26] consisting of randomly selected 50 videos from YFDB, with ground-truth labels of hair, skin, and background provided for 11 consecutive frames per each video (i.e., 550 labeled frames), which are then split into 30, 10, and 10 videos for training, validation, and testing, respectively. Each CamVid video contains 3600 to 11000 frames at resolution 360×480. CamVid provides ground-truth pixel labels of 11 object classes for 700 frames, which are split into 367 training and 233 test frames. For fair comparison on CamVid with [2], which uses significantly more training data, we additionally labeled 9 consecutive frames preceding every annotated frame in the training set of CamVid, resulting in 3670 training frames.

For fair comparison, we evaluate our superpixel accuracy on YFDB and pixel accuracy on Camvid. For YFDB, we extract superpixels as in [26] producing 300–400 superpixels per frame. The label of a superpixel is obtained by pixel majority voting. Both overall accuracy and class-specific accuracy are computed as the number of superpixels/pixels classified correctly divided by the total number of superpixels/pixels. Evaluation is done for each RTDF prediction on a test frame after processing 3 and 4 frames preceding that test frame for YFDB and Camvid, respectively.

Implementation Details: We partition video frames using a 32×32 regular grid for YFDB, and a 60×45 regular grid for CamVid. For YFDB, we specify RTRBM with 1000 hidden nodes. For CamVid, there are 1200 hidden nodes in RTRBM. Hyper-parameters of the DeconvNet are specified as in [2]. The

Table 1. Superpixel accuracy on Youtube Face Database [1]. Error reduction in overall superpixel accuracy is calculated w.r.t the CRF. The mean and the standard derivation are given from a 5-fold cross-validation.

Model	Error redu	Overall accu	Hair	Skin	Background	Category avg
CRF [4]	0.0	0.90 ± 0.005	0.63 ± 0.047	0.89 ± 0.025	0.96 ± 0.005	0.83 ± 0.009
GLOC [24]	0.03 ± 0.025	0.91 ± 0.006	0.61 ± 0.038	0.90 ± 0.023	0.96 ± 0.003	0.82 ± 0.008
STRF [26]	0.12 ± 0.025	0.91 ± 0.006	0.72 ± 0.039	0.89 ± 0.025	0.96 ± 0.004	0.86 ± 0.010
RTDF†	0.11 ± 0.027	0.91 ± 0.008	0.70 ± 0.043	0.89 ± 0.024	0.96 ± 0.004	0.85 ± 0.011
RTDF*	0.17 ± 0.028	0.92 ± 0.008	0.76 ± 0.049	0.88 ± 0.025	0.96 ± 0.003	0.87 ± 0.012
RTDF	**0.34 ± 0.031**	**0.93 ± 0.010**	**0.80 ± 0.037**	**0.90 ± 0.026**	**0.97 ± 0.005**	**0.89 ± 0.014**

DeconvNet consists of: (a) Convolution network with 13 convolution layers based on VGG16 network, each followed by a batch normalization operation [41] and a RELU layer; (b) Deconvolution network with 13 deconvolution layers, each followed by the batch normalization; and (c) Soft-max layer producing a $1 \times L$ class distribution for every pixel in the image. We test $\lambda \in [0, 1]$ on the validation set, and report our test results for λ with the best performance on the validation dataset.

Runtimes: We implement RTDF on NVIDIA Tesla K80 GPU accelerator. It takes about 23 h to train RTDF on CamVid. The average runtime for predicting pixel labels in an image with resolution 360×480 is 105.3 ms.

Baselines: We compare RTDF with its variants and related work: (1) RTDF†: RTDF without end-to-end joint training (i.e., piece wise training); (2) RTDF*: jointly trained RTDF without joint inference, i.e., using stage-wise inference where the output of RTRBM is treated as fixed input into the CRF. (3) CRF [4]: spatial CRF inputs with hand-engineered features; (4) GLOC [24]: a jointly trained model that combines spatial CRF and RBM; and (5) STRF [26]: a piecewise trained model that combines spatial CRF, CRBM and temporal potentials between two consecutive frames.

6.1 Quantitative Results

YFDB: Table 1 presents the results of the state of the art, RTDF and its variant baselines on YFDB. As can be seen, RTDF gives the best performance, since RTDF accounts for long-range spatiotemporal dependencies and performs joint training and joint inference. It outperforms STRF [26] which uses local hand-engineered features and piece-wise training. These results suggest that accounting for object interactions across a wide range of spatiotemporal scales is critical for video labeling. We also observe that RTDF† achieves comparable results with STRF [26], while RTDF* outperforms both. This suggests that our end-to-end joint training of all components of RTDF is more critical for accurate video labeling than their joint inference. Also, as RTDF* gives an inferior performance to RTDF, performing joint instead of stage-wise inference gives an additional gain in performance. Finally, we observe that RTDF performance can be slightly increased by using a larger γ. For fair comparison, we use the same γ as in [26].

Table 2. Pixel accuracy on Cambridge-driving Labeled Video Database [32].

Method	Building	Tree	Sky	Car	Sign	Road	Pedestrain	Fence	Col. pole	Sidewalk	Bicycle	Class avg.	Global avg.
Dense Depth Maps [36]	85.3	57.3	95.4	69.2	46.5	**98.5**	23.8	44.3	22.0	38.1	28.7	55.4	82.1
Super Parsing [37]	87.0	67.1	96.9	62.7	30.1	95.9	14.7	17.9	1.7	70.0	19.4	51.2	83.3
High-order CRF [38]	84.5	72.6	**97.5**	72.7	34.1	95.3	34.2	45.7	8.1	77.6	28.5	59.2	83.8
CRF + Detectors [39]	81.5	76.6	96.2	78.7	40.2	93.9	43.0	47.6	14.3	81.5	33.9	62.5	83.8
Neural Decision Forests [40]	N/A											56.1	82.1
Deeplab [13]	82.7	**91.7**	89.5	76.7	33.7	90.8	41.6	35.9	17.9	82.3	45.9	62.6	84.6
CRFasRNN [19]	84.6	91.3	92.4	79.6	43.9	91.6	37.1	36.3	27.4	82.9	33.7	63.7	86.1
SegNet [2]	73.9	90.6	90.1	86.4	**69.8**	94.5	**86.8**	**67.9**	**74.0**	94.7	52.9	80.1	86.7
RTDF[†]	81.8	87.9	91.5	79.2	59.8	90.4	77.1	61.5	66.6	91.2	54.6	76.5	86.5
RTDF[*]	83.6	89.8	92.9	78.5	61.3	92.2	79.6	61.9	67.7	92.8	56.9	77.9	88.1
RTDF	**87.1**	85.2	93.7	**88.3**	64.3	94.6	84.2	64.9	68.8	**95.3**	**58.9**	80.5	**89.9**

CamVid: Table 2 presents the results of the state of the art, RTDF and its variants on CamVid. In comparison to the state of the art and the baselines, RTDF achieves superior performance in terms of both average and weighted accuracy, where weighted accuracy accounts for the class frequency. Unlike RTDF, SegNet [2] treats the label of each pixel independently by using a soft-max classifier, and thus may poorly perform around low-contrast object boundaries. On the other hand, SegNet has an inherent bias to label larger pixel areas with a unique class label [2] (see Fig. 4), which may explain its better performance than RTDF on the following classes: sign-symbol, column-pole, pedestrian and fence. From Table 2, RTDF[†] achieves comparable performance to that of SegNet, while RTDF[*] outperforms RTDF[†]. This is in agreement with our previous observation on YFDB that joint training of all components of RTDF is more critical than their joint inference for accurate video labeling.

6.2 Qualitative Evaluation

Figure 4 illustrates our pixel-level results on frame samples of CamVid. From the figure, we can see that our model is able to produce spatial smoothness pixel labeling. Figure 6 shows superpixel labeling on sample video clips from YFDB. As can be seen, on both sequences, STRF [26] gives inferior video labeling than RTDF in terms of temporal coherency and spatial consistency of pixel labels. Our spatial smoothness and temporal coherency can also be seen in Fig. 5 which shows additional RTDF results on a longer sequence of frames from a sample CamVid video.

Empirically, we find that RTDF poorly handles abrupt scale changes (e.g., dramatic camera zoom-in/zoom-out). Also, in some cases shown in Figs. 4 and 5, RTDF misses tiny, elongated objects like column-poles, due to our deterministic mapping between patches of a regular grid and pixels.

Fig. 4. Frame samples from CamVid. The rows correspond to original images, ground truth, SegNet [2], and RTDF.

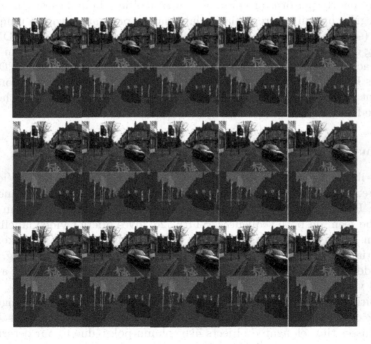

Fig. 5. Sequence of frames from a sample CamVid video. The rows correspond to input frames and RTDF outputs.

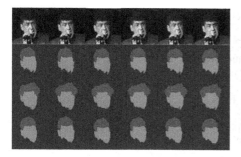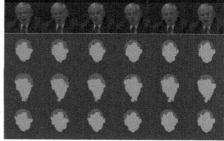

Fig. 6. Frame sequences from two CamVid video clips. The rows correspond to original video frames, ground truth, STRF [26], and RTDF.

7   Conclusion

We have presented a new deep architecture, called Recurrent-Temporal Deep Field (RTDF), for semantic video labeling. RTDF captures long-range and high-order spatiotemporal dependencies of pixel labels in a video by combining conditional random field (CRF), deconvolution neural network (DeconvNet), and recurrent temporal restricted Boltzmann machine (RTRBM) into a unified framework. Specifically, we have derived a mean-field inference algorithm for jointly predicting latent variables in both CRF and RTRBM, and specified an end-to-end joint training of all components of RTDF via backpropagation of the prediction loss. Our empirical evaluation on the benchmark Youtube Face Database (YFDB) [1] and Cambridge-driving Labeled Video Database (CamVid) [32] demonstrates the advantages of performing joint inference and joint training of RTDF, resulting in its superior performance over the state of the art. The results suggest that our end-to-end joint training of all components of RTDF is more critical for accurate video labeling than their joint inference. Also, RTDF performance on a frame can be improved by previously labeling longer sequences of frames preceding that frame. Finally, we have empirically found that RTDF poorly handles abrupt scale changes and labeling of thin, elongated objects.

Acknowledgment. This work was supported in part by grant NSF RI 1302700. The authors would like to thank Sheng Chen for useful discussion and acknowledge Dimitris Trigkakis for helping with the datasets.

References

1. Wolf, L., Hassner, T., Maoz, I.: Face recognition in unconstrained videos with matched background similarity. In: CVPR (2011)
2. Badrinarayanan, V., Kendall, A., Cipolla, R.: Segnet: A deep convolutional encoder-decoder architecture for image segmentation. arXiv preprint arXiv:1511.00561 (2015)

3. Sutskever, I., Hinton, G.E., Taylor, G.W.: The recurrent temporal restricted Boltzmann machine. In: NIPS (2009)
4. Lafferty, J., McCallum, A., Pereira, F.C.: Conditional random fields: probabilistic models for segmenting and labeling sequence data. In: ICML (2001)
5. Galmar, E., Athanasiadis, T., Huet, B., Avrithis, Y.: Spatiotemporal semantic video segmentation. In: MSPW (2008)
6. Grundmann, M., Kwatra, V., Han, M., Essa, I.: Efficient hierarchical graph-based video segmentation. In: CVPR (2010)
7. Jain, A., Chatterjee, S., Vidal, R.: Coarse-to-fine semantic video segmentation using supervoxel trees. In: ICCV (2013)
8. Yi, S., Pavlovic, V.: Multi-cue structure preserving mrf for unconstrained video segmentation. arXiv preprint arXiv:1506.09124 (2015)
9. Zhao, H., Fu, Y.: Semantic single video segmentation with robust graph representation. In: IJCAI (2015)
10. Liu, B., He, X., Gould, S.: Multi-class semantic video segmentation with exemplar-based object reasoning. In: WACV (2015)
11. Farabet, C., Couprie, C., Najman, L., LeCun, Y.: Learning hierarchical features for scene labeling. PAMI $35(8)$, 1915–1929 (2013)
12. Long, J., Shelhamer, E., Darrell, T.: Fully convolutional networks for semantic segmentation. In: CVPR (2015)
13. Chen, L.C., Papandreou, G., Kokkinos, I., Murphy, K., Yuille, A.L.: Semantic image segmentation with deep convolutional nets and fully connected CRFs. In: ICLR (2014)
14. Ciresan, D., Giusti, A., Gambardella, L.M., Schmidhuber, J.: Deep neural networks segment neuronal membranes in electron microscopy images. In: NIPS (2012)
15. Pinheiro, P.H., Collobert, R.: Recurrent convolutional neural networks for scene parsing. In: ICML (2014)
16. Hariharan, B., Arbeláez, P., Girshick, R., Malik, J.: Simultaneous detection and segmentation. In: Fleet, D., Pajdla, T., Schiele, B., Tuytelaars, T. (eds.) ECCV 2014, Part VII. LNCS, vol. 8695, pp. 297–312. Springer, Heidelberg (2014)
17. Gupta, S., Girshick, R., Arbeláez, P., Malik, J.: Learning rich features from RGB-D images for object detection and segmentation. In: Fleet, D., Pajdla, T., Schiele, B., Tuytelaars, T. (eds.) ECCV 2014, Part VII. LNCS, vol. 8695, pp. 345–360. Springer, Heidelberg (2014)
18. Ganin, Y., Lempitsky, V.: N^4-fields: neural network nearest neighbor fields for image transforms. In: Cremers, D., Reid, I., Saito, H., Yang, M.-H. (eds.) ACCV 2014. LNCS, vol. 9004, pp. 536–551. Springer, Heidelberg (2015). doi:10.1007/978-3-319-16808-1_36
19. Zheng, S., Jayasumana, S., Romera-Paredes, B., Vineet, V., Su, Z., Du, D., Huang, C., Torr, P.H.: Conditional random fields as recurrent neural networks. In: ICCV (2015)
20. Noh, H., Hong, S., Han, B.: Learning deconvolution network for semantic segmentation. In: ICCV (2015)
21. Smolensky, P.: Information Processing in Dynamical Systems: Foundations of Harmony Theory. MIT Press Cambridge, Cambridge (1986)
22. He, X., Zemel, R.S., Carreira-Perpiñán, M.Á: Multiscale conditional random fields for image labeling. In: CVPR (2004)
23. Li, Y., Tarlow, D., Zemel, R.: Exploring compositional high order pattern potentials for structured output learning. In: CVPR (2013)
24. Kae, A., Sohn, K., Lee, H., Learned-Miller, E.: Augmenting CRFs with boltzmann machine shape priors for image labeling. In: CVPR (2013)

25. Eslami, S.A., Heess, N., Williams, C.K., Winn, J.: The shape Boltzmann machine: a strong model of object shape. IJCV **107**(2), 155–176 (2014)
26. Kae, A., Marlin, B., Learned-Miller, E.: The shape-time random field for semantic video labeling. In: CVPR (2014)
27. Taylor, G.W., Hinton, G.E., Roweis, S.T.: Modeling human motion using binary latent variables. In: NIPS (2006)
28. Rumelhart, D.E., Hinton, G.E., Williams, R.J.: Learning internal representations by error propagation. Technical report, DTIC Document (1985)
29. Hinton, G.E.: Training products of experts by minimizing contrastive divergence. Neural Comput. **14**(8), 1771–1800 (2002)
30. Mnih, V., Larochelle, H., Hinton, G.E.: Conditional restricted Boltzmann machines for structured output prediction. In: UAI (2011)
31. LeCun, Y., Chopra, S., Hadsell, R., Ranzato, M., Huang, F.: A tutorial on energy-based learning. In: Predicting Structured Data, vol. 1 (2006)
32. Brostow, G.J., Fauqueur, J., Cipolla, R.: Semantic object classes in video: a high-definition ground truth database. PRL **30**(2), 88–97 (2008)
33. Li, F., Kim, T., Humayun, A., Tsai, D., Rehg, J.M.: Video segmentation by tracking many figure-ground segments. In: ICCV (2013)
34. Geiger, A., Lenz, P., Urtasun, R.: Are we ready for autonomous driving? the KITTI vision benchmark suite. In: CVPR (2012)
35. Brox, T., Malik, J.: Object segmentation by long term analysis of point trajectories. In: Daniilidis, K., Maragos, P., Paragios, N. (eds.) ECCV 2010, Part V. LNCS, vol. 6315, pp. 282–295. Springer, Heidelberg (2010)
36. Zhang, C., Wang, L., Yang, R.: Semantic segmentation of urban scenes using dense depth maps. In: Daniilidis, K., Maragos, P., Paragios, N. (eds.) ECCV 2010, Part IV. LNCS, vol. 6314, pp. 708–721. Springer, Heidelberg (2010)
37. Tighe, J., Lazebnik, S.: Superparsing. IJCV **101**(2), 329–349 (2013)
38. Sturgess, P., Alahari, K., Ladicky, L., Torr, P.H.: Combining appearance and structure from motion features for road scene understanding. In: BMVC (2009)
39. Ladický, Ľ., Sturgess, P., Alahari, K., Russell, C., Torr, P.H.S.: What, where and how many? combining object detectors and CRFs. In: Daniilidis, K., Maragos, P., Paragios, N. (eds.) ECCV 2010, Part IV. LNCS, vol. 6314, pp. 424–437. Springer, Heidelberg (2010)
40. Rota Bulo, S., Kontschieder, P.: Neural decision forests for semantic image labelling. In: CVPR (2014)
41. Ioffe, S., Szegedy, C.: Batch normalization: accelerating deep network training by reducing internal covariate shift. In: ICML (2015)

Ultra-Resolving Face Images by Discriminative Generative Networks

Xin Yu$^{(\boxtimes)}$ and Fatih Porikli

Australian National University, Canberra, Australia
{xin.yu,fatih.porikli}@anu.edu.au

Abstract. Conventional face super-resolution methods, also known as face hallucination, are limited up to 2∼4× scaling factors where 4 ∼ 16 additional pixels are estimated for each given pixel. Besides, they become very fragile when the input low-resolution image size is too small that only little information is available in the input image. To address these shortcomings, we present a discriminative generative network that can ultra-resolve a very low resolution face image of size 16 × 16 pixels to its 8× larger version by reconstructing 64 pixels from a single pixel. We introduce a pixel-wise ℓ_2 regularization term to the generative model and exploit the feedback of the discriminative network to make the upsampled face images more similar to real ones. In our framework, the discriminative network learns the essential constituent parts of the faces and the generative network blends these parts in the most accurate fashion to the input image. Since only frontal and ordinary aligned images are used in training, our method can ultra-resolve a wide range of very low-resolution images directly regardless of pose and facial expression variations. Our extensive experimental evaluations demonstrate that the presented ultra-resolution by discriminative generative networks (UR-DGN) achieves more appealing results than the state-of-the-art.

Keywords: Super-resolution · Discriminative Generative Networks · Face

1 Motivation

Face images arguably carry the most interesting and valuable visual information and can be obtained in a non-intrusive manner. Still, for many applications from content enhancement to forensics, face images require significant magnification.

In order to generate high-resolution (HR) face images from low-resolution (LR) inputs, face hallucination [1–12] attracted great interest in the past. These state-of-the-art face hallucination methods can achieve exciting results up to 4× upscaling factors when accurate facial features and landmarks can be found in

---

This work was supported under the Australian Research Council's Discovery Projects funding scheme (project DP150104645).

B. Leibe et al. (Eds.): ECCV 2016, Part V, LNCS 9909, pp. 318–333, 2016.
DOI: 10.1007/978-3-319-46454-1_20

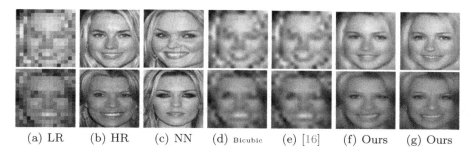

| (a) LR | (b) HR | (c) NN | (d) Bicubic | (e) [16] | (f) Ours | (g) Ours |

Fig. 1. Comparison of our UR-DGN over CNN based super-resolution. (a) 16×16 pixels LR face images [given]. (b) 128×128 original HR images [not given]. (c) The corresponding HR version of the nearest neighbors of (a) in the training set. (d) Upsampling by bicubic interpolation. (e) The results generated by the CNN based super-resolution [16]. This network is *retrained* with face images. (f) Our UR-DGN without the feedback of the discriminative model. (g) Our UR-DGN.

LR images [9,10], manual supervision is provided, suitably similar HR images of the same person are included in the support dataset, and the exemplar HR face images are densely aligned [4–7]. When the input image resolution becomes smaller, landmark based methods fail gravely because of erroneous landmark localization. In other words, their performances highly depend on the input image size. Furthermore, when the appearances of the input LR images are different from the HR images in the dataset due to pose, lighting and expression changes, subspace based methods degrade by producing ghosting artifacts in the outputs.

When ultra-resolving (8× scaling factor) a low-resolution image, almost 98.5 % of the information is missing. This is a severely ill-posed problem. As indicated in [13], when the scaling factor increases to 8×, the performances of existing approaches degrade acutely.

Our intuition is that by better exploring the information available in the natural structure of face images, appearance similarities between individuals, and emerging large-scale face datasets [14,15], it may be possible to derive competent models to reconstruct authentic 8× magnified HR face images. Deep neural networks, in particular convolutional neural networks (CNN), are inherently suitable for learning from large-scale datasets. Very recently, CNN based generic patch super-resolution methods have been proposed [16,17] without focusing on any image class. A straightforward retraining (fine-tuning) of these networks with face image patches cannot capture the global structure of faces. As shown in Fig. 1(e), these networks fail to produce realistic and visually pleasant results. In order to retain the global structure of faces while being able to reconstruct instance specific details, we use whole face images to train our networks.

We are inspired from the generative adversarial network (GAN) [18] that consists of two topologies: a generative network G that is designed to learn the distribution of the training data samples and generate a new sample similar to the training data, and a discriminative network D that estimates the probability that a sample comes from the training dataset rather than G. This work is empowered with a Laplacian pyramid by [19] to progressively generate images due to the higher dimensional nature of the training images. One advantage of GAN is that it generates face images yet sharp images from nothing but noise. However, it has two serious shortcomings: (i) The output faces are totally random. (ii) GAN has fixed output size limitation (32×32 [18] and 64×64 [19]). Therefore, GAN cannot be used for ultra-resolution directly.

Instead of noise, we apply the LR face image l as the input for our discriminative-generative network (DGN) and then generate a HR face image $\hat{h}$. In order to enforce the similarity between the generated HR face image $\hat{h}$ and the exemplar HR image h, we impose a pixel-wise ℓ_2 regularization on the differences between $\hat{h}$ and h in the generative network. This enables us to constrain the affinity between the exemplar HR images and the generated HR images. Hereby, a loss function layer is added to G. Finally, the generative network G produces a HR image consistent with the exemplar HR image. In training DGN, the discriminative network D provides feedback to G to distinguish whether the upsampled face image is considered (classified by the D) as real (sharp) or as generated (smooth). As shown in Fig. 1(f), by directly upsampling images by the generative network G, we are not able to obtain face images with sharp details. In contrast, with the help of the network D, we can generate much sharper HR face images, as shown in Fig. 1(g). Since the discriminative network is designed to distinguish between the real face images and generated ones, the generative network can produce HR face images more similar to real images.

Our method does not make any explicit assumption or require the location of the facial landmarks. Because the convolutional neural network topologies we use provide robustness to translations and deformations, our method does not need densely aligned HR face images or constrain the face images to controlled settings, such as the same pose, lighting and facial expression. Our approach only requires frontal and approximately nearby eye locations in the training images, which can be easily satisfied in most of face datasets. Hence, our UR-DGN method can ultra-resolve $8\times$ a wide range of LR images without taking other information into account.

Overall, the contributions of this paper are mainly in four aspects:

- We present a novel method to ultra-resolve, $8\times$ scaling factor, low-resolution face images. The size of our input low-resolution images is tiny, 16×16 pixels, which makes the magnification task even more challenging as almost all facial details are missing. We reconstruct 64 pixels from only 1 pixel.
- To the best of our knowledge, our method is the first attempt to develop discriminative generative networks for generating authentic face images. We demonstrate that our UR-DGN achieves better visual results than the state-of-the-art.
- We show that by introducing a pixel-wise ℓ_2 regularization term into the network and backpropagating its residual, it is possible to ultra-resolve in any size while GANs can only generate images in fixed and small sizes.

– When training our network, we only require frontal and approximately aligned images, which makes the training datasets more attainable. Our UR-DGN can ultra-resolve regardless of pose, lighting and facial expressions variations.

2 Related Work

Super-resolution can be basically classified into two categories: generic super-resolution methods and class-specific super-resolution methods. When upsampling LR images, generic methods employ priors that ubiquitously exist in natural images without considering any image class information. Class-specific methods, also called face hallucination [1] if the class is face, aim to exploit statistical information of objects in a certain class. Thus, they usually attain better results than generic methods when super-resolving images of a known class.

Generic super-resolution: In general, generic single image super-resolution methods have three types: interpolation based methods, image statistics based methods [20,21] and example (patch)-based methods [7,22–26]. Interpolation based methods such as bicubic upsampling are simple and computationally efficient, but they generate overly smooth edges as the scaling factor increases. Image statistics based methods employ natural image priors to predict HR images, but they are limited to smaller scaling factors [27]. [24,26,28,29] exploit self-similarity of patches in an input image to generate high resolution patches. [22,23] constructs LR and HR patch pairs from a training dataset, and then the nearest neighbor of the input patch is searched in the LR space. The HR output is reconstructed from the corresponding HR patch. [7] proposes a sparse representation formulation by reconstructing corresponding LR and HR dictionaries, while [30] applies convolutional sparse coding instead of patch-based sparse coding. Recently, several deep learning based methods [16,17] have been proposed. Dong *et al.* [16] incorporates convolutional neural networks to learn a mapping function between LR and HR patches from a large-scale dataset. Since many different HR patches may correspond to one LR patch, the output images would suffer from artifacts at the intensity edges. In order to reduce the ambiguity between the LR and HR patches, [31] exploits the statistical information learned from deep convolutional network to reduce ambiguity between LR and HR patches.

Face hallucination: Unlike generic methods, class-specific super-resolution methods [1–6,8–12] further exploit the statistical information in the image categories, thus leading to better performances. In one of the earlier works, [1] builds the relationship between HR and LR patches using Bayesian formulation such that high-frequency details can be transferred from the dataset for face hallucination. It can generate face images with richer details. However, artifacts also appear due to the possible inconsistency of the transferred HR patches.

The work in [4] employs constraints on both LR and HR images, and then hallucinate HR face images by an eigen-transformation. Although it is able to magnify LR images by a large scaling factor, the output HR images suffer from ghosting artifacts as a result of using a subspace. Similarly, [5] enforces linear constraints for HR face images using a subspace learned from the training set via Principle Component Analysis (PCA), and a patch-based Markov Random Field is proposed to reconstruct the high-frequency details in the HR face images. This method works only when the images are precisely aligned at fixed poses and expressions. In other cases, the results usually contain ghosting artifacts due to PCA based holistic appearance model. To mitigate artifacts a blind bilateral filtering is used as a post-processing step. Instead of imposing global constraints, [8] uses multiple local constraints learned from exemplar patches, and [32] reserves to sparse representation on the local structures of faces. [33] uses optimal transport in combination with subspace learning to morph a HR image from the LR input. These subspace based methods require that face images in the dataset are precisely aligned and the test LR image has the same pose and facial expression as the HR face images.

In order to handle various poses and expressions, [9] integrates SIFT flow to align images. This method performs adequately when the training face images are highly similar to the test face image in terms of identity, pose, and expression. Since it uses local features to match image segments, the global structure is not preserved either.

By exploiting local structures of face images, [10] presents a structured face hallucination method. It divides a face image into facial components, and then maintains the structure by matching gradients in the reconstructed output. However, this method relies on accurate facial landmark points that are usually unavailable when the image size is very small. The recent work in [11] proposes a bichannel CNN to hallucinate face images in the wild. Since it needs to extract features from the input images, the smallest input image size is 48 × 48.

Some generative network [18,19,34,35] can generate random face images from nothing but random noise. Among those generative models, generative adversarial networks (GANs) [18,19] can generate face images with much sharper details due to the discriminative network. However, the generated images are only similar in the class domain but different in the appearance domain. In other words, GAN is capable of generating only random faces. Moreover, GAN only uses the cross entropy loss function of discriminative models to optimize the entire network. Hence, the generative models in GAN are difficult to generate images in high resolutions. For instance, [18] only produces images of size 32 × 32 pixels.

3   Proposed Ultra-Resolution Method

A processing pipeline of UR-DGN is shown in Fig. 2. Below, we present the pipeline of UR-DGN and describe the details of training the network. We also discuss the differences between UR-DGN and GAN.

3.1   Model Architecture

Let us first recap the generative model G that takes a noise vector z from a distribution $P_{noise}(z)$ as an input and then outputs an image $\hat{x}$ in [18]. The

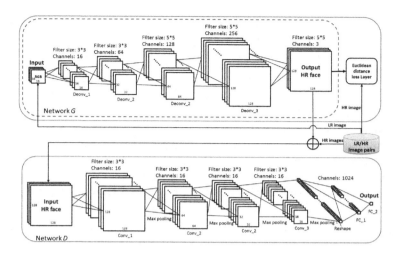

Fig. 2. The pipeline of UR-DGN. In the testing phase, only the generative network in the red dashed block is employed. (Color figure online)

discriminative model D takes an image stochastically chosen from either the generated image $\hat{x}$ or the real image x drawn from the training dataset with a distribution $P_{data}(x)$ as an input. D is trained to output a scalar probability, which is large for real images and small for generated images from G. The generative model G is learned to maximize the probability of D making a mistake. Thus a minmax objective is used to train these two models simultaneously

$$\min_G \max_D \mathbb{E}_{x \sim P_{data}(x)}[\log D(x)] + \mathbb{E}_{z \sim P_{noise}(z)}[\log(1 - D(G(z)))]. \quad (1)$$

This equation encourages G to fit $P_{data}(x)$ so as to fool D with its generated samples $\hat{x}$.

We cannot directly employ Eq. 1 for the ultra-resolution task since GAN takes noise as input to learn the distribution on the training dataset. In UR-DGN, we design a deconvolutional network [36] as the generative model G to ultra-resolve LR inputs, and a convolutional network as the discriminative model D. We construct LR and HR face image pairs $\{l_i, h_i\}$ as the training dataset. Because the generated HR face image $\hat{h}_i$ should be similar to its corresponding HR image h_i, a pixel-wise ℓ_2 regularization term induces the similarity. Thus, the objective function $F(G, D)$ is modeled as follows:

$$\begin{aligned}\min_G \max_D F(G, D) &= \mathbb{E}_{h_i \sim P_H(h)}[\log D(h_i)] + \mathbb{E}_{l_i \sim P_L(l)}[\log(1 - D(G(l_i)))] \\ &\quad + \lambda \mathbb{E}_{(h_i, l_i) \sim P_{HL}(h,l)}[\|\hat{h}_i - h_i\|_F^2] \\ &= \mathbb{E}_{h_i \sim P_H(h)}[\log D(h_i)] + \mathbb{E}_{l_i \sim P_L(l)}[\log(1 - D(G(l_i)))] \\ &\quad + \lambda \mathbb{E}_{(h_i, l_i) \sim P_{HL}(h,l)}[\|G(l_i) - h_i\|_F^2], \end{aligned} \quad (2)$$

where $P_L(l)$ and $P_H(h)$ represent the distributions of LR and HR face images respectively, $P_{HL}(h,l)$ represents the joint distribution of HR and LR face images, and λ is a trade-off weight to balance the cross entropy loss of D and the Euclidean distance loss of G.

3.2 Training of the Network

The parameters of the generative network G and the discriminative network D are updated by backpropagating the loss in Eq. 2 through their respective networks. Specifically, when training G, the loss of the last two terms in Eq. 2 is backpropagated through G to update its parameters. When training D, the loss of the first two terms in Eq. 2 is backpropagated through D to update its parameters.

Training D: Since D is a CNN with a negative cross-entropy loss function, backpropation is used to train the parameters of D. Thus, the derivative of the loss function $F(G, D)$ with respect to D is required when updating the parameters in D. It is formulated as follows:

$$\frac{\partial F(G, D)}{\partial D} = \nabla_{\theta_D} \left(\mathbb{E}_{h_i \sim P_H(h)}[\log D(h_i)] + \mathbb{E}_{l_i \sim P_L(l)}[\log(1 - D(G(l_i)))] \right), \quad (3)$$

where θ_D is the parameters of D, and ∇ is the derivative operator. Specifically, given a batch of LR and HR image pairs $\{l_i, h_i\}, i = 1, \ldots, N$, the stochastic gradient of the discriminator D is written as

$$\frac{\partial F(G, D)}{\partial D} = \nabla_{\theta_D} \left(\frac{1}{N} \sum_{i=1}^{N} \log D(h_i) + \log(1 - D(G(l_i))) \right), \quad (4)$$

where N is the number of LR and HR face image pairs in the batch. Since we need to maximize D, the parameters θ_D are updated by ascending their stochastic gradients. RMSprop [37] is employed to update the parameters θ_D as follows:

$$
\begin{aligned}
\delta^{j+1} &= \alpha\delta^j + (1-\alpha)(\frac{\partial F(G, D)}{\partial D})^2, \\
\theta_D^{j+1} &= \theta_D^j + \eta\frac{\partial F(G, D)}{\partial D}/\sqrt{\delta^{j+1} + \epsilon}.
\end{aligned}
\quad (5)
$$

where η and α represent the learning rate and the decay rate respectively, j indicates the iteration index, ϵ is set to 10^{-8} as a regularizer to avoid division by zero, and δ is an auxiliary variable.

Training G: G is a deconvolutional neural network [36]. It is trained by backpropagation as well. Similar to training D, the derivative of the loss function $F(G, D)$ with respect to G is written as

$$
\begin{aligned}
\frac{\partial F(G, D)}{\partial G} = \nabla_{\theta_G} \Big(\mathbb{E}_{l_i \sim P_L(l)}[\log(1 - D(G(l_i)))] \\
+ \lambda\mathbb{E}_{(h_i,l_i) \sim P_{HL}(h,l)}[\|G(l_i) - h_i\|_F^2] \Big),
\end{aligned}
\quad (6)
$$

Algorithm 1. Minibatch stochastic gradient descent training of UR-DGN

Input: minibatch size N, LR and HR face image pairs $\{l_i, h_i\}$, maximum number of iterations K.

1: **while** iter < K **do**
2:   Choose one minibatch of LR and HR image pairs $\{l_i, h_i\}, i = 1, \ldots, N$.
3:   Generate one minibatch of HR face images $\hat{h}_i$ from $l_i, i = 1, \ldots, N$, where $\hat{h}_i = G(l_i)$.
4:   Update the parameters of the discriminative network D by using Eqs. 4 and 5.
5:   Update the parameters of the generative network G by using Eqs. 7 and 8.
6: **end while**

Output: UR-DGN.

---

where θ_G denotes the parameters of G. Given a batch of LR and HR face image pairs $\{l_i, h_i\}, i = 1, \ldots, N$, the stochastic gradient of the generator G is

$$\frac{\partial F(G, D)}{\partial G} = \nabla_{\theta_G} \left(\frac{1}{N} \sum_{i=1}^{N} \log(1 - D(G(l_i))) + \lambda \|G(l_i) - h_i\|_F^2 \right). \quad (7)$$

Since we will minimize the cost function for G, the parameters θ_G are updated by descending their stochastic gradients as follows:

$$\delta^{j+1} = \alpha \delta^j + (1 - \alpha)(\frac{\partial F(G, D)}{\partial G})^2,$$
$$\theta_G^{j+1} = \theta_G^j - \eta \frac{\partial F(G, D)}{\partial G} / \sqrt{\delta^{j+1} + \epsilon}. \quad (8)$$

In our algorithm, we set the learning rate η to 0.001 and the decay rate to 0.01, and the learning rate is multiplied by 0.99 after each epoch. Since we super-resolve an image rather than generate a face image, we set λ to 100 to constrain the similarity between the generated face image $G(l_i)$ and the exemplar HR face image h_i. The training procedure of our UR-DGN is presented in Algorithm 1.

3.3   Ultra-Resolution of a Given LR Image

The discriminative network D and the pixel-wise ℓ_2 regularization are only required in the training phase. In the ultra-resolution (testing) phase, we take LR face images as the inputs of the generative network G, and the outputs of G are the ultra-resolved face images. This end-to-end mapping is able to keep the global structure of HR face images while reconstructing local details.

3.4   Differences Between GAN and UR-DGN

GAN of [18] consists of fully connected layers, while Denton *et al.* [19] use a fully connected layer and deconvolutional layers. In [19], the noise input is required to be fed into a fully connected layer first before fed into deconvolutional layers.

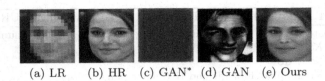

(a) LR   (b) HR   (c) GAN*   (d) GAN   (e) Ours

Fig. 3. Illustration of the differences between GAN and our UR-DGN. (a) Given LR image. (b) Original HR image (not used in training). (c) GAN*: GAN with no fully connected layer. Without a fully connected layer, GAN* cannot rearrange the convolutional layer features (activations) of the input noise to a face image. (d) GAN with fully connected layer. Given the test LR image (not noise!), GAN still outputs a random face image. (e) Result of our UR-DGN.

The fully connected layer can be considered as a nonlinear mapping from the noise to the activations of a feature map. If we remove the fully connected layer while leaving other layers unchanged, GAN will fail to produce face images, as shown in Fig. 3(c). Therefore, fully connected layers are necessary for GAN.

Since deconvolutional layers are able to project low-resolution feature maps back to high-resolution image space, we take a LR face image as a 3-channel feature map, and then project this LR feature map into the HR face image space. However, the fully connected layers are not necessary in our UR-DGN. Because LR face images are highly structured, they can be regarded as feature maps after normalization, which scales the range of intensities between -1.0 and 1.0. Feeding a LR face image into a fully connected layer may destroy the global structure of the feature map, *i.e.* the input LR face image. In other words, UR-DGN does not need a nonlinear mapping from an input LR image to a feature map via a fully connected layer.

Furthermore, since there is no pixel-wise regularization in GAN, it cannot produce HR results faithful to the input LR face images and generate high-quality face images as the output size increases as shown in Fig. 3(d). In conclusion, the original architecture of GAN cannot be employed in the ultra-resolution problem.

4   Experiments

In order to dissect the performance of UR-DGN, we evaluate it qualitatively and quantitatively, and compare with the state-of-the-art methods [5,7,8,10,16]. Liu *et al.*'s method [5] is a subspace based face hallucination method. The work in [7] uses sparse representations to super-resolve HR images by constructing LR and HR dictionaries. Yang *et al.*'s method [10] hallucinates face images by using facial components from exemplar images in the dataset. Dong *et al.* [16] employ CNN to upsample images. Ma *et al.* [8] use position-patches in the dataset to reconstruct HR images.

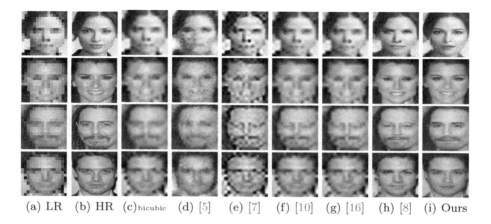

(a) LR   (b) HR   (c)bicubic   (d) [5]   (e) [7]   (f) [10]   (g) [16]   (h) [8]   (i) Ours

Fig. 4. Comparison with the state-of-the-art methods on frontal faces. (a) LR inputs. (b) Original HR images. (c) Bicubic interpolation. (d) Liu *et al.*'s method [5]. (e) Yang *et al.*'s method [7]. (f) Yang *et al.*'s method [10]. (g) Dong *et al.*'s method [16]. (h) Ma *et al.*'s method [8]. (i) UR-DGN. (please zoom-in to see the differences between (f) and (g). In (f), there are artificial facial edges while (g) has jitter artifacts.)

4.1 Datasets

We trained UR-DGN with the celebrity face attributes (CelebA) dataset [15]. There are more than 200K images in this dataset, where Liu *et al.* [15] use similarity transformation to align the locations of eye centers. We use the cropped face images for training. Notice that the images in this dataset cover remarkably large pose variations and facial expressions. We do not classify the face images into different subcategories according to their poses and facial expressions when training UR-DGN.

We randomly draw 16,000 aligned and cropped face images from the CelebA dataset, and then resize them to 128×128. We use 15,000 images for training, 500 images for validation, and 500 images for testing. Thus, our UR-DGN model never sees the test LR images in the training phase.

We downsample the HR face images to 16×16 pixels (without aliasing), and then construct the LR and HR image pairs $\{l_i, h_i\}$. The input of UR-DGN is an image of size 16×16 with 3 RGB channels, and the output is an image of size 128×128 with 3 RGB channels.

4.2 Comparisons with SoA

We do side-by-side comparisons with five state-of-the-art face hallucination methods. In case an approach does not allow $8\times$ scaling factor directly, *i.e.* [7,16], we repeatedly (three times) apply a scaling factor $2\times$ when ultra-resolving a LR image. For a fair comparison, we use the same dataset CelebA for training of all other algorithms. Furthermore, we apply bicubic interpolation to all input LR images as another baseline.

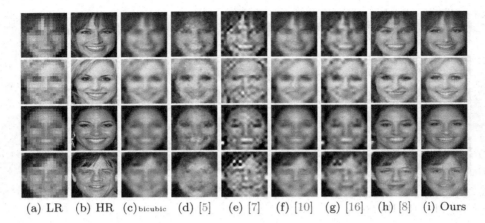

(a) LR   (b) HR   (c) bicubic   (d) [5]   (e) [7]   (f) [10]   (g) [16]   (h) [8]   (i) Ours

Fig. 5. Facial expression: Comparison with the state-of-the-art methods on images with facial expressions. (a) LR inputs. (b) Original HR images. (c) Bicubic interpolation. (d) Liu *et al.*'s method [5]. (e) Yang *et al.*'s method [7]. (f) Yang *et al.*'s method [10]. (g) Dong *et al.*'s method [16]. (h) Ma *et al.*'s method [8]. (i) UR-DGN. (please zoom-in to see the differences between (f) and (g))

Comparison with Liu *et al.*'s method [5]: Since this method requires the face images in the dataset to be precisely aligned, it is difficult for it to learn a representative subspace from the CelebA dataset where face images have large variations. Therefore, the global model of the input LR image cannot be represented by the learned subspace, and its local model impels patchy artifacts on the output. As shown in Figs. 4(d), 5(d) and 6(d), this method cannot recover face details accurately, and suffers from distorted edges and blob-like artifacts.

Comparison with Yang *et al.*'s method [7]: As illustrated in Figs. 4(e), 5(e) and 6(e), Yang *et al.*'s method does not recover high-frequency facial details. Besides, non-smooth over-emphasized edge artifacts appear in their results. As the scaling factor becomes larger, the correspondence between LR and HR patches becomes ambiguous. Therefore, their results suffer exaggerated pixellation pattern of the LR, similar to a contrast enhanced bicubic upsampled results.

Comparison with Yang *et al.*'s method [10]: This method requires landmarks of facial components and building on them, and reconstructs transferred high-resolution facial components over the low-resolution image. In 16×16 input images, it is extremely difficult to localize landmarks. Hence, this method cannot correctly transfer facial components as shown in Figs. 4(f), 5(f) and 6(f). In contrast, UR-DGN does not need landmark localization and still preserve the global structure.

Comparison with Dong *et al.*'s method [16]: It applies convolutional layers to learn a generic patch-based mapping function, and achieves state-of-the-art results on natural images. Even though we retrain their CNN on face images to

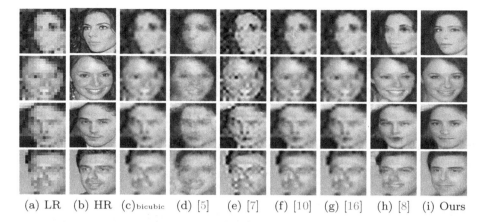

(a) LR   (b) HR   (c)bicubic   (d) [5]   (e) [7]   (f) [10]   (g) [16]   (h) [8]   (i) Ours

Fig. 6. Pose: Comparison with the state-of-the-art methods on face images with different poses. (a) LR inputs. (b) Original HR images. (c) Bicubic interpolation. (d) Liu *et al.*'s method [5]. (e) Yang *et al.*'s method [7]. (f) Yang *et al.*'s method [10]. (g) Dong *et al.*'s method [16]. (h) Ma *et al.*'s method [8]. (i) UR-DGN. (please zoom-in to see the differences between (f) and (g))

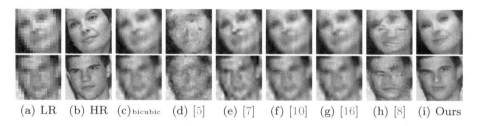

(a) LR   (b) HR   (c)bicubic   (d) [5]   (e) [7]   (f) [10]   (g) [16]   (h) [8]   (i) Ours

Fig. 7. Comparison with the state-of-the-art methods on unaligned faces. (a) LR inputs. (b) Original HR images. (c) Bicubic interpolation. (d) Liu *et al.*'s method [5]. (e) Yang *et al.*'s method [7]. (f) Yang *et al.*'s method [10]. (g) Dong *et al.*'s method [16]. (h) Ma *et al.*'s method [8]. (i) UR-DGN.

suit better for face hallucination, this method cannot generate high-frequency facial details except some noisy spots in the HR images as shown in Figs. 4(g), 5(g) and 6(g).

Comparison with Ma *et al.*'s method [8]: This method employs local constraints learned from positioned exemplar patches to avoid ghosting artifacts caused by a global model such as PCA. However, it requires the exemplar patches to be precisely aligned. As shown in Figs. 4(h), 5(h) and 6(h), this method suffers from obvious blocking artifacts and uneven oversmoothing as a result of the unaligned position patches in the dataset CelebA.

In contrast to the above approaches, our method provides more visually pleasant HR face images that not only contain richer details but also are similar to the original (not given to our method). UR-DGN takes the input LR image as

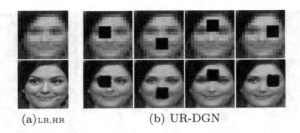

(a)LR,HR   (b) UR-DGN

Fig. 8. Illustrations of influence of occlusions. Top row: the LR inputs, bottom row: the results of UR-DGN. (a) LR and HR images. (b) Results of UR-DGN with occlusions. As seen, occlusions of facial features and landmarks (eyes, mouth, etc.) do not cause any degradation of the unoccluded parts of the faces.

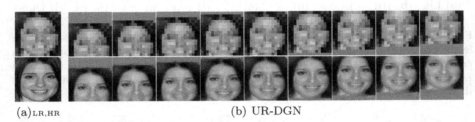

(a)LR,HR   (b) UR-DGN

Fig. 9. Effects of misalignment. Top row: the LR images, bottom row: the results of UR-DGN. (a) LR and HR images. (b) Results with translations. From left to right, the y-axis translations are from -4 to +4 pixels. Notice that, the size of the LR image is 16×16 pixels. As visible, UR-DGN is robust against severe translational misalignments.

a whole and reduces the ambiguity of the correspondence between LR and HR patches. Our method attains much sharper results.

4.3 Quantitative Results

We also assess UR-DGN performance quantitatively by comparing the average PSNR and structural similarity (SSIM) on the entire test dataset. Table 1 shows that our method achieves the best performance. As expected, bicubic interpolation achieves better results than the other baselines since it explicitly builds on pixel-wise intensity values without any hallucination. Notice that bicubic interpolation achieves the second best results, which implies that the high-frequency details reconstructed by the state-of-the-art methods are not authentic. Our

Table 1. Quantitative comparisons on the entire test dataset

Methods	Bicubic	[5]	[7]	[10]	[16]	[8]	Ours
PSNR	23.22	21.60	21.35	23.07	23.11	23.12	**24.82**
SSIM	0.67	0.55	0.60	0.65	0.65	0.64	**0.70**

method on the other hand achieves facial details consistent with real faces as it attains the best PSNR and SSIM results while improving the PSNR an impressive 1.6 dB over the previous best.

5   Limitations

Since we use a generative model to ultra-resolve LR face images, if there are occlusions in the images, our method cannot resolve the occlusions. Still, occlusions of facial features do not adversely affect ultra-resolution of the unoccluded parts as shown in Fig. 8.

Our algorithm alleviates the requirements of exact face alignment. As shown in Figs. 7 and 9, it is robust against translations, but sensitive to rotations. As a future work, we plan to investigate incorporating an affine transformation estimator and adapting the generative network according to estimated transformation parameters.

6   Conclusion

We present a new and very capable discriminative generative network to ultra-resolve very small LR face images. Our algorithm can both increase the input LR image size significantly, $i.e.$ $8\times$, and reconstruct much richer facial details. The larger scaling factors beyond $8\times$ only require larger training datasets (e.g., larger than 128×128 training face images for 16×16 inputs), and it is straightforward to achieve even much extreme ultra resolution results.

By introducing a pixel-wise ℓ_2 regularization on the generated face images into the framework of UR-DGN, our method is able to generate authentic HR faces. Since our method learns an end-to-end mapping between LR and HR face images, it preserves well the global structure of faces. Furthermore, in training, we only assume the locations of eyes to be approximately aligned, which significantly makes the other face datasets more attainable.

References

1. Baker, S., Kanade, T.: Hallucinating faces. In: Proceedings - 4th IEEE International Conference on Automatic Face and Gesture Recognition, FG 2000, pp. 83–88 (2000)
2. Liu, C., Shum, H., Zhang, C.: A two-step approach to hallucinating faces: global parametric model and local nonparametric model. CVPR **1**, 192–198 (2001)
3. Baker, S., Kanade, T.: Limits on super-resolution and how to break them. IEEE Trans. Pattern Anal. Mach. Intell. **24**(9), 1167–1183 (2002)
4. Wang, X., Tang, X.: Hallucinating face by eigen transformation. IEEE Trans. Syst. Man Cybern. Part C Appl. Rev. **35**(3), 425–434 (2005)
5. Liu, C., Shum, H.Y., Freeman, W.T.: Face hallucination: theory and practice. Int. J. Comput. Vis. **75**(1), 115–134 (2007)

6. Jia, K., Gong, S.: Generalized face super-resolution. IEEE Trans. Image Process. **17**(6), 873–886 (2008)
7. Yang, J., Wright, J., Huang, T.S., Ma, Y.: Image super-resolution via sparse representation. IEEE Trans. Image Process. **19**(11), 2861–2873 (2010)
8. Ma, X., Zhang, J., Qi, C.: Hallucinating face by position-patch. Pattern Recogn. **43**(6), 2224–2236 (2010)
9. Tappen, M.F., Liu, C.: A Bayesian approach to alignment-based image hallucination. In: Fitzgibbon, A., Lazebnik, S., Perona, P., Sato, Y., Schmid, C. (eds.) ECCV 2012, Part VII. LNCS, vol. 7578, pp. 236–249. Springer, Heidelberg (2012)
10. Yang, C.Y., Liu, S., Yang, M.H.: Structured face hallucination. In: Proceedings of the IEEE Computer Society Conference on Computer Vision and Pattern Recognition, pp. 1099–1106 (2013)
11. Zhou, E., Fan, H.: Learning face hallucination in the wild. In: Twenty-Ninth AAAI Conference on Artificial Intelligence, pp. 3871–3877 (2015)
12. Wang, N., Tao, D., Gao, X., Li, X., Li, J.: A comprehensive survey to face hallucination. Int. J. Comput. Vis. **106**(1), 9–30 (2014)
13. Yang, C.-Y., Ma, C., Yang, M.-H.: Single-image super-resolution: a benchmark. In: Fleet, D., Pajdla, T., Schiele, B., Tuytelaars, T. (eds.) ECCV 2014. LNCS, vol. 8692, pp. 372–386. Springer, Heidelberg (2014). doi:10.1007/978-3-319-10593-2_25
14. Huang, G.B., Ramesh, M., Berg, T., Learned-Miller, E.: Labeled faces in the wild: a database for studying face recognition in unconstrained environments. Technical report 07–49, University of Massachusetts, Amherst, October 2007
15. Liu, Z., Luo, P., Wang, X., Tang, X.: Deep learning face attributes in the wild. In: Proceedings of International Conference on Computer Vision (ICCV), December 2015
16. Dong, C., Loy, C.C., He, K.: Image super-resolution using deep convolutional networks. IEEE Trans. Pattern Anal. Mach. Intell. **38**(2), 295–307 (2016)
17. Kim, J., Lee, J.K., Lee, K.M.: Accurate image super-resolution using very deep convolutional networks. arXiv:1511.04587 (2015)
18. Goodfellow, I., Pouget-Abadie, J., Mirza, M.: Generative adversarial networks. In: Advances in Neural Information Processing Systems, pp. 2672–2680 (2014)
19. Denton, E., Chintala, S., Szlam, A., Fergus, R.: Deep generative image models using a Laplacian pyramid of adversarial networks. In: Advances In Neural Information Processing Systems, pp. 1486–1494 (2015)
20. Peleg, T., Elad, M.: A statistical prediction model based on sparse representations for single image super-resolution. IEEE Trans. Image Process. **23**(6), 2569–2582 (2014)
21. Yang, C.Y., Yang, M.H.: Fast direct super-resolution by simple functions. In: 2013 IEEE International Conference on Computer Vision (ICCV), pp. 561–568 (2013)
22. Freeman, W.T., Jones, T.R., Pasztor, E.C.: Example-based super-resolution. IEEE Comput. Graph. Appl. **22**(2), 56–65 (2002)
23. Chang, H., Yeung, D-Y., Xiong, Y.: Super-resolution through neighbor embedding. In: CVPR, vol. 1, pp. 275–282 (2004)
24. Glasner, D., Bagon, S., Irani, M.: Super-resolution from a single image. In: ICCV, pp. 349–356 (2009)
25. Schulter, S., Leistner, C.: Fast and accurate image upscaling with super-resolution forests. In: CVPR, pp. 3791–3799 (2015)
26. Huang, J.B., Singh, A., Ahuja, N.: Single image super-resolution from transformed self-exemplars. In: IEEE Conference on Computer Vision and Pattern Recognition, pp. 5197–5206 (2015)

27. Lin, Z., Shum, H.Y.: Response to the comments on fundamental limits of reconstruction-based superresolution algorithms under local translation. IEEE Trans. Pattern Anal. Mach. Intell. **28**(5), 847 (2006)

28. Freedman, G., Fattal, R.: Image and video upscaling from local self-examples. ACM Trans. Graph. **28**(3), 1–10 (2010)

29. Singh, A., Porikli, F., Ahuja, N.: Super-resolving noisy images. In: Proceedings of the IEEE Computer Society Conference on Computer Vision and Pattern Recognition, pp. 2846–2853 (2014)

30. Gu, S., Zuo, W., Xie, Q., Meng, D., Feng, X., Zhang, L.: Convolutional sparse coding for image super-resolution. In: ICCV (2015)

31. Bruna, J., Sprechmann, P., LeCun, Y.: Super-resolution with deep convolutional sufficient statistics. In: ICLR (2016)

32. Li, Y., Cai, C., Qiu, G., Lam, K.M.: Face hallucination based on sparse local-pixel structure. Pattern Recogn. **47**(3), 1261–1270 (2014)

33. Kolouri, S., Rohde, G.K.: Transport-based single frame super resolution of very low resolution face images. In: Proceedings of the IEEE Computer Society Conference on Computer Vision and Pattern Recognition (CVPR) (2015)

34. Kingma, D.P., Welling, M.: Auto-encoding variational Bayes. arXiv:1312.6114 (Ml), pp. 1–14 (2013)

35. Radford, A., Metz, L., Chintala, S.: Unsupervised representation learning with deep convolutional generative adversarial networks, pp. 1–15 (2015). arXiv:1511.06434

36. Zeiler, M.D., Taylor, G.W., Fergus, R.: Adaptive deconvolutional networks for mid and high level feature learning. In: Proceedings of the IEEE International Conference on Computer Vision, pp. 2018–2025 (2011)

37. Hinton, G.: Neural Networks for Machine Learning Lecture 6a: Overview of mini-batch gradient descent Reminder: The error surface for a linear neuron

A Discriminative Framework for Anomaly Detection in Large Videos

Allison Del Giorno[✉], J. Andrew Bagnell, and Martial Hebert

Carnegie Mellon University, Pittsburgh, USA
adelgior@cs.cmu.edu

Abstract. We address an anomaly detection setting in which training sequences are unavailable and anomalies are scored independently of temporal ordering. Current algorithms in anomaly detection are based on the classical density estimation approach of learning high-dimensional models and finding low-probability events. These algorithms are sensitive to the order in which anomalies appear and require either training data or early context assumptions that do not hold for longer, more complex videos. By defining anomalies as examples that can be *distinguished* from other examples in the same video, our definition inspires a shift in approaches from classical density estimation to simple discriminative learning. Our contributions include a novel framework for anomaly detection that is (1) independent of temporal ordering of anomalies, and (2) unsupervised, requiring no separate training sequences. We show that our algorithm can achieve state-of-the-art results even when we adjust the setting by removing training sequences from standard datasets.

Keywords: Anomaly detection · Discriminative · Unsupervised · Context · Surveillance · Temporal invariance

1 Introduction

Anomaly detection is an especially challenging problem because, while its applications are prevalent, it remains ill-defined. Where there have been attempts at definitions, they are often informal and vary across communities and applications. In this paper, we define and propose a solution for a largely neglected subproblem within anomaly detection, where two constraints exist: (1) no additional training sequences are available; (2) the order in which anomalies occur should not affect the algorithm's performance on each instance (Fig. 1). This is an especially challenging setting because we cannot build a model in advance and find deviations from it; much like clustering or outlier detection, the context is defined by the video itself. This setting is prominent in application fields such as robotics, medicine, entertainment, and data mining. For instance:

Electronic supplementary material The online version of this chapter (doi:10.1007/978-3-319-46454-1_21) contains supplementary material, which is available to authorized users.

© Springer International Publishing AG 2016
B. Leibe et al. (Eds.): ECCV 2016, Part V, LNCS 9909, pp. 334–349, 2016.
DOI: 10.1007/978-3-319-46454-1_21

- *First-time data.* A robotics team wants to create a robust set of algorithms. They teleoperate a robot performing a new task or operating in a new environment. The team would like to find out what special cases the robot may have to handle on the perception side, so they ask for a list of the most anomalous instances according to the robot's sensor data relative to that day's conditions and performance.
- *Personalized results: context semantically defined as coming only from the test set.* (a) A father wants to find the most interesting parts of the 4-h home video of his family's Christmas. (b) A healthcare professional wants to review the most anomalous footage of an elderly patient while living under at-home nursing care over the past week.
- *Database sifting.* A consulting analyst is told to find abnormal behavior in a large amount of video from a surveillance camera.

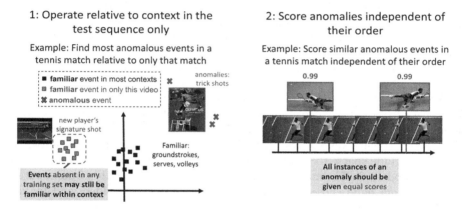

Fig. 1. Characteristics of our anomaly detection setting. **Left: No training sequences.** This setting occurs when we want context to be drawn solely from the test video (e.g. - the player's shot distribution differs for each opponent, and we want anomalies relative to how they played that opponent), or unavailable (a player with a new style debuts at a tournament). **Right: Temporal independence.** Often we want to find the most anomalous frames regardless of the order they appear in.

These illustrate just a few of the practical cases in which it is important to identify all instances of anomalies, regardless of the order in which they appear, and to do so within the context of the testing video. If videos are available for providing context beyond the test video or it is acceptable to ignore later anomalies as long as the first instance is recognized, there are many mature methods that apply (see Sect. 1.1). There are also natural extensions to our method that could incorporate additional context if it were available. Here we consider a challenging setting in which the context must be derived from the test video and the order in which anomalies occur does not affect their score.

In general anomaly detection settings, one cannot use traditional supervised approaches because it is impossible to find a sufficiently representative set of anomalies. In our setting, we are given no context ahead of time; unlike other algorithms, we cannot even build a distribution for a representative set of familiar events. We require the use of approaches that operate solely on the test sequence and adapt to each video's context. This leads us to denote frames as *anomalous* if they are easily distinguished from other frames in the same video, and *familiar* otherwise.

1.1   Previous Approaches

Anomaly detection presents a set of unique challenges beyond those seen in the supervised learning paradigm. The inability to use training data for both classes of data (familiar and anomalous) leads to two possible approaches: (1) Estimate a model distribution of the familiar and then classify sufficiently large deviations as anomalous; or (2) Seek out points that are identifiable in the distribution of all frames and label those anomalous. While these approaches seem similar on the surface, they lead to distinct methodologies that differ in the assumptions and data required as well as the type of anomalies they identify. We show that the latter will satisfy our setting while the former will not, and comes with a few other advantages.

The traditional approach for anomaly detection involves learning a model of familiarity for a given video. Subsequent time points can then be identified as anomalous if they deviate from the model by some distance metric or inverse likelihood. We call this set of approaches "scanning" techniques. Examples in this area include sparse reconstruction [1,2], dynamic textures [3–5], and human behavior models [6]. The methods take a set of training data, either from separate videos or from hand-chosen frames at the beginning of the video, and build a model. Many of these methods update models online, and while some do not need to update the model in temporal order [7], they still need a large amount of training data for initialization. One method in particular achieves reasonable performance with a small number of starting frames [8], but still requires manual identification of these frames for the algorithm. Generative models work well for domains in which the assumed model of normalcy fits the data well. This applies when the model is complex enough to handle a variety of events, or when known context can allow the learner to anticipate a model that will fit the data. These methods generally assume that the features come from a predetermined type of distribution and therefore are likely to fail if the feature distribution changes. For complex models, computational complexity and the amount of 'normal' training data needed to initialize the model becomes a significant bottleneck. Parameter choices also have a larger effect on the ability of the algorithm to fit the data.

Scanning approaches do not satisfy our anomaly detection setting because they violate the two conditions we specified: (1) they require training instances, and (2) they depend on temporal ordering. Building a model in temporal order of the video makes strong assumptions about the way anomalies should be detected. In our setting, we must find the 'most anomalous' events in the video, regardless of their order. By building models with updates in temporal order, events that occur earlier in the video are more likely to be anomalous. For instance, with an event type that occurs only twice in a large video, the first instance will be detected once but the second instance will be ignored. By choosing a discriminative algorithm that acts independently of the ordering of the video, we avoid these assumptions and pitfalls of the scanning techniques.

Our method shares the discriminative spirit of previous works using saliency for anomaly detection [3,5]. However, the saliency methods used require training data to run and only use local context. Our objective is to obtain a fully unsupervised method that uses the context of the entire video and is independent of the ordering in which the anomalies occur. [9] builds a graph and finds anomalies independent of their ordering. However, it is model-based and only designed to work with trajectories; our goal is discriminative and able to operate on any set of features.

The primary challenge in our setting is our inability to assume the form of the underlying distribution. A non-parametric method is preferable so that it can generalize to many domains with few assumptions. Permutation tests are nonparametric methods designed to handle such cases. The general idea is to test the fidelity of a given statistic against a set of other possible statistics from a differently-labeled dataset. We use a similar approach to test the distinctiveness of each frame. In our method, the analogous statistic is the ease with which a given data point can be distinguished from other points sampled from the same video. By testing a frame's distinguishability from different groups of frames, we form a more accurate picture of its global anomaly score.

1.2   Our Approach

Our approach is to directly estimate the discriminability of frames with reference to the context in the video. We do not need a model of every normal event to generate scores for anomalous frames; we can simply attempt to discriminate between anomalous frames and familiar frames to see if there is a difference in the distributions. We present a framework that tests the discriminability of frames. In this framework, we perform change detection on a sequence of data from the video to see which frames are distinguishable from previous frames. Because we want these comparisons to be independent of time, we create *shuffles* of the data by permuting the frames before running each instance of the change detection. Simple classifiers are used to avoid overfitting and so that each frame will be compared against many permutations of other frames. This discriminative framework allows us to perform in a unique setting.

Our contributions are as follows:

- A permutation-based framework for anomaly detection in a setting free from training data and independent of ordering,
- A theory that guides the choice of key parameters and justifies our framework,
- Experimental evaluation demonstrating that this technique achieves performance similar to other techniques that require training data

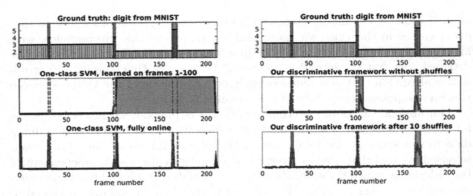

Fig. 2. Detections from one-class SVM and our algorithm on a toy example.
The ground truth represents the digit classes from MNIST that were used to generate
each frame. The red dashes indicate locations of the anomalies. The red shaded region
represents detections made by each algorithm. Our algorithm without shuffling has the
same temporal disadvantages as online one-class SVM. By including shuffling, we do
not trigger false positives on prevalent examples when seen for the first time. We also
detect the full extent of each anomaly and avoid assuming the beginning is familiar.
(Color figure online)

1.3   A Motivating Example

To motivate our method and demonstrate its advantages over scanning techniques, let's walk through a toy example. Suppose we draw four images from
the MNIST dataset, each with a different label (2, 3, 4, or 5). Then we create a 'video' using noisy copies of these images. The order of these images is
shown in Fig. 2. While the first portion of the video contains only instances of
'3', both the 3's and 2's are prevalent. In this case, we would hope that the
algorithm classifies all instances of 4's and 5's as anomalous and considers all
2's and 3's familiar. We use one-class SVM with a RBF kernel as an instance of
scanning techniques. Figure 2 shows scores from a static one-class SVM trained
on the first portion of the video, the same algorithm with an online update, and
our algorithm with and without shuffling. Our algorithm's performance without shuffling is similar to that of the online one-class SVM. When the model
remains static after the first third of the video, all of the 2's are classified as
anomalous. Even with an online model update, the first few 2's are classified
as anomalous. In addition, not all of the 4's and 5's are given equal anomaly
weights within their respective classes. Our algorithm avoids these pitfalls once
shuffling is introduced, classifying only the 4's and 5's as anomalous. By using a
permutation-based framework, we are able to evade assumptions of familiarity
and remove the effects of temporal ordering on anomaly scores.

The issues discussed extend beyond just this toy example. With scanning
methods, anomalies that appear more than once may be missed. In addition, it
is common to see failures due to the assumption that the beginning of the video
represents familiarity, both by anomalies appearing in the beginning and by other

familiar events appearing later in the video. For videos where context changes frequently (imagine a concert light show whose theme changes every song), this can create a dangerously high number of false positives. Also note that while this example uses one-class SVM as an example, all scanning techniques have the same inherent problems. Our method was developed in part to circumvent these previously unavoidable failure cases. In addition, we hope to demonstrate that simple discriminative techniques can match the performance of more complex generative methods while operating in the new setting we have identified.

2   Method

Taking the Direct Approach. Inspired by density ratio estimation for change point detection [10–12], we take a more direct approach to anomaly detection than the popular generative approach. The main objective of density ratio estimation is to avoid doing unnecessary work when deciding from which one of two distributions a data point was generated: rather than model both distributions independently, we can directly compute the ratio of probabilities that a data point is drawn from one or the other. This shortcut is especially helpful in anomaly detection. We are more interested in the *relative* probability that a given frame is anomalous rather than familiar, and are less interested in the distribution of familiar events. The machine learning community has covered several ways to estimate this ratio directly and has enumerated the several cost functions and other paradigms in which this ratio appears [13]. We note that one such way to estimate these ratios directly is simple logistic regression, and therefore we use this standard classifier as a measure of the deviation between two groups of points (see "Larger window sizes decrease the effect of overfitting classifiers" in Sect. 3 for formal justification).

System Overview. The full framework is depicted in Fig. 3. Recall our definition of anomalous frames: those that are easily distinguished from others in the same video. Because this definition avoids domain-specific notions of anomalies, it relies on a robust set of features that can be used to distinguish anomalies in a variety of domains. We assume an appropriate set of features has been computed and forms a descriptor for each frame. Because this is a discriminative method, the choice of features has a smaller impact on the choice of algorithm and parameters than it would for a generative method. The overall proposed framework is agnostic to the feature choice; the user can plug in any relevant or state-of-the-art features based on domain knowledge or novel feature methods. In addition, features can be aggregated within or across frames to obtain different levels of spatial or temporal resolution. Because the framework does not make explicit assumptions about the distribution of the features, these are simply design choices based on the cost of feature computation and the desired resolution of detections.

No Shuffles - Change Detection. If we were to remove permutation from our algorithm, it would perform simple change detection by testing the

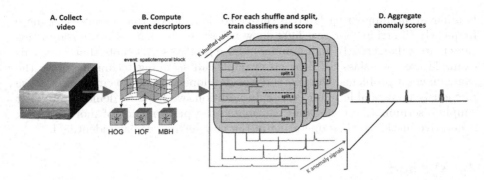

Fig. 3. The proposed anomaly detection framework. (A) Given an input video, (B) a descriptor for each frame is passed into the anomaly detection algorithm, (C) where the descriptors are shuffled K times. For each shuffle, the algorithm evaluates anomaly scores for a sliding window of frames. This score is based on the density ratio compared to frames that came before the sliding window. (D) Finally, the scores are combined with averaging to produce the final output signal. Image depicting dense trajectory features is from Wang et al. [14].

distinguishability of a sliding window of t_w frames, where all frames before it are assumed to be familiar. A conceptual example is shown in Fig. 4.

In the first iteration, a classifier f is learned on the set of $2t_w$ points, where the first t_w points are given the label 0 and the second t_w points are given the label 1. We call this set of labels a 'split' of the data. Each point x that is labeled 1 is then given the score $f(x)$, which is the probability it belongs to class 1 instead of class 0 according to the classifier $f(x)$. In our implementation, $f(x)$ is simply $\frac{1}{1+\exp{(-w^T x)}}$ where w minimizes the $l2$-regularized logistic loss. We say the second set of frames are within a 'sliding time window' or 'sliding window', because in the next iteration these frames are reassigned a label of 0 and the next t_w points are labeled 1[1]. The process repeats until the sliding window reaches the end of the video. As the sliding window reaches the end, events in the window are compared to all events in the past. The higher $f(x)$ for a given point x, the larger the classifier's confidence that it can be distinguished from previous points.

A sliding window is chosen rather than moving point-by-point for several reasons. First of all, it provides inherent regularization for the classifier, since distinguishing any one point the rest can be misleadingly easy even if that point is familiar. In addition, the number of splits the algorithm must compute is inversely proportional to the window size t_w. It may seem that 'polluting' the sliding window with familiars would ruin an anomaly's chance of being accurately scored. However, this is not the case, as anomalies are more easily distinguished

---

[1] For simplicity, we describe the algorithm when the sliding window size and stride equal each other, $t_w = \Delta t_w$. It is just as valid to shorten the stride to increase accuracy. See Algorithm 1.

Algorithm 1. ANOMALY DETECTION Selects the most anomalous frames

---

1 **Parameters**: K (#permutations), t_w (window size), Δt_w (window stride) ;
  Input: $\{x_1, .., x_T\}$ (descriptors for each frame)
  Output: $\{a_1, ..., a_T\}$ (estimates of anomalousness of each frame)
2 Generate a random set of K permutations $\{\sigma_1([1, ..., T]), ..., \sigma_K([1, ..., T])\}$
3 **for** $k = 1, ..., K$ **do**
4   **for** *all sliding windows* $[t_{start}, t_{start} + t_w)$ *until* T **do**
5        $y_{\sigma_k(t)} \leftarrow \begin{cases} 0 & \text{if } t < t_{\text{start}} \\ 1 & \text{if } t_{\text{start}} \leq t < (t_{\text{start}} + t_w) \end{cases}$
6        $w \leftarrow \text{TrainLogisticRegression}(x_{\sigma_k}, y_{\sigma_k})$
7        $p_t^{(k)} \leftarrow P(y_t^{(k)} = 1|x_t, w), \forall(y_t^{(k)} == 1)$
8 $\bar{p}_t \leftarrow \text{mean}(p_t^{(k)})$ across all k
9 $a_t \leftarrow \frac{\bar{p}_t}{(1 - \bar{p}_t)}$
10 **return** $\{a_1, ..., a_T\}$

---

from the rest of the video, and therefore the chance that they fall near the resulting classifier boundary is low, while the probability that a familiar event does is high (see Fig. 4 for intuition).

Adding in Shuffles - Full Anomaly Detection. As we pointed out earlier, the disadvantage of this approach without shuffles is the same as with other scanning techniques: temporal dependencies cause the algorithm to miss events that occur more than once and raise false alarms to events that may be prevalent later in the video but not in the beginning. We therefore shuffle the order of the data and repeat the change detection process described to reduce the effect of the order. Producing a series of distinguishability scores from classifiers learned on different permutations of frames can be thought of as testing a set of hypotheses. If a series of classifiers are all able to easily distinguish a frame labeled "1" from many combinations of those labeled "0", it is likely an anomaly.

Aggregating Scores. Once the scores have been computed for each shuffle, we average the results. The average outperforms other methods of aggregation like the median and maximum. After aggregating over shuffles, log-odds are computed as the final anomaly score. The full overview is explained in Algorithm 1.

3   Supporting Theory

Our method is based on distinguishing two labeled subsets of data. We consider here how to think about the tradeoffs between increasing and decreasing the window size and the number of shuffles given a choice of classifier. We attempt only to provide intuition by considering simple analyses that suggest how one might understand the tradeoffs of parameters and classifier choices.

Overall Objective. In order for the algorithm to work, the classifier needs to have enough capacity to be able to tell anomalies and familiars apart, but simple

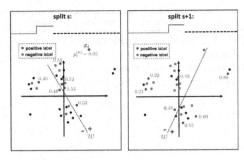

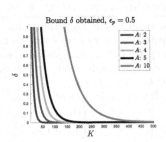

Fig. 4. **Visualizing two consecutive splits.** Points in red and blue have been labeled 1 and 0 respectively. Here the window size $t_w = 7$ (# red points). The values in red are the probability values p_t. Familiars are close to the boundary (p_t close to 0.5) and therefore yield a low log odds score a_t. (Color figure online)

Fig. 5. Upper bound on the probability that any one of A anomalies appears first in fewer than $1/A - \epsilon$ shuffles ($\epsilon = 0.05$). The resulting probability decreases exponentially with the number of shuffles.

enough that it is unable to tell familiars apart from other familiars. This capacity is a function of the classifier complexity, the number of points being compared (related to t_w), and the subset of points being compared (the shuffling).

Classifier Assumptions. We must make basic assumptions about the classifier. We assume that the classifier $f(x)$ is able to correctly distinguish between an anomaly and familiars. In the case of logistic regression, for instance, we assume that f will label an anomaly 1 with relatively high confidence if it is learned on a set of familiars labeled 0 and an anomaly within a set of familiars labeled 1. This means $f(x) = P(y = 1|x, w)$ will be significantly higher than 0.5 if x is an anomaly and close to or below 0.5 if x is a familiar.

Increasing the Number of Shuffles, K, Removes Temporal Dependencies. Here we show that the number of shuffles K needed to remove temporal dependencies scales with the number of anomalies A at $O(A \log A)$.

Suppose a video has A anomalies and a significantly larger number of total frames, $A \ll T$. Consider the worst case scenario for our algorithm, where all A anomalies are identical. Formally, each of these anomalies have identical feature vectors: $x_{n_1} = x_{n_2} = ... = x_{n_A}$. This represents the worst case because if one such anomaly x_{n_i} is labeled 0 while another anomaly x_{n_j} is labeled 1, the score of $f(x_{n_j})$ will be small. In other words, an anomaly in the negative window can negate the score of another in the positive window. Therefore, the best split of the data for a given anomaly instance is when it occurs first in the video.[2] The goal of shuffling is to reorder the anomalies enough times that every anomaly gets the opportunity to be the first instance in the reordered set of frames.

---

[2] Ignoring the rare case when it occurs in the very first negative window.

More formally, let us define random variable F as the event that an anomaly x appears first in a given shuffle. F is a binary variable that occurs with probability $1/A$, so in expectation, the fraction of shuffles in which it appears first is also $\mu = 1/A$. However, we would like to use as few shuffles as possible to ensure that the event F gets close to its mean $1/A$. This means we need a bound on the probability that $\bar{F}_K - \mu$ is less than some ϵ for K shuffles. A relative tolerance $\epsilon = (\epsilon_p/A)$ is required because as the desired fraction $1/A$ gets smaller, the effect of deviations ϵ on the score of an anomaly grows proportionally larger. For instance, $\epsilon_p = 0.25$ requires that every anomaly is first in at least 75 % as many shuffles as it would be on average. To obtain this bound, we apply the Relative Entropy Chernoff Bound [15][3].

The Chernoff bound for Bernoulli random variables states that the average $\bar{F}_K$ of K variables with mean μ falls below $\mu - \epsilon$ for some $\epsilon > 0$ with probability:

$$\Pr\left(\bar{F}_K \leq \mu - \epsilon\right) \leq e^{-K\,\mathrm{KL}(\mu-\epsilon,\mu)}, \tag{1}$$

where $\mathrm{KL}(p_1, p_2)$ is the KL divergence between two Bernoulli distributions with parameters p_1 and p_2. This is a well-known formula, and the KL divergence $\mathrm{KL}(\mu - \epsilon, \mu)$ with $\mu = 1/A$, $\epsilon = \epsilon_p/A$ is:

$$\mathrm{KL}(\mu - \epsilon, \mu) = \frac{1}{A}\left[\log(1 - \epsilon_p)(1 - \epsilon_p) + \log\left(\frac{\epsilon_p}{A - 1}\right)(A - 1 + \epsilon_p)\right] \tag{2}$$

With Eqs. 1 and 2, we have bounded the probability that a single anomaly will not appear first in a large enough fraction of shuffles. To extend this to all A anomalies, we apply the union bound to all events $\bar{F}_K^{(i)}$ to get our final bound:

$$\delta := \Pr\left(\bigcup_{i=1}^{A}\left(\bar{F}_K^{(i)} \leq \mu - \epsilon\right)\right) \leq Ae^{-K\,\mathrm{KL}(\mu-\epsilon,\mu)} \tag{3}$$

The bounding probability δ is defined in terms of A, K, and ϵ_p. Values of this bound for different values of K, δ, and A are depicted in Fig. 5. We are interested in choosing the number of shuffles K for a given δ, A, and ϵ_p, so we solve Eq. 3 for K:

$$K \geq \frac{\log(\frac{A}{\delta})}{\mathrm{KL}(\mu - \epsilon, \mu)} \tag{4}$$

In big O terms, for fixed δ and ϵ_p, we need $O(A \log A)$ shuffles to reorder the anomalies enough times to equally score them.

Larger Window Sizes Decrease the Effect of Overfitting Classifiers. Given a choice K, there is one more parameter in the framework that requires care: the window size t_w. Increasing the window stride decreases the computational load on the system (more splits per shuffle). In terms of performance, it may also seem best to make t_w as small as possible because anomalies

---

[3] Kakade provides a quick summary for those unfamiliar with these bounds [16]:
http://stat.wharton.upenn.edu/~skakade/courses/stat928/lectures/lecture06.pdf.

are easier to distinguish in a smaller window size. In addition, with large window sizes, anomalies of different types can fall within the same window and 'interfere' with each others' scores. However, decreasing the window size beyond a certain point also reduces performance, as the classifier overfits and familiars become distinguishable from other familiars. In other words, we must choose t_w to be able to trade off our ability to distinguish anomalies without being able to distinguish familiars. We consider here a theoretical sketch explicating the relation between the complexity of the classifier and the choice of window size t_w.

Assume we have computed a complexity metric [17] for our chosen classifier f. In this instance, we will work with the Rademacher complexity[4] $\mathcal{R}(m)$, where m is the size of the subset of points being classified [18]. A higher Rademacher complexity indicates the classifier is able to more easily distinguish randomly labeled data. For instance, a highly regularized linear classifier has a much lower Rademacher complexity than a RBF-kernel SVM or complex neural network. This metric is especially convenient because it is measured relative to the data distribution (so it adapts to the video) and can be empirically estimated by simply computing a statistic over randomly labeled subsampled data [18][5].

Given that we have a classifier of complexity $\mathcal{R}$, we can adjust the window size to decrease the probability that familiars can be distinguished from each other. Generalization bounds provide a way to relate the error from overfitting or noisy labels to the classifier complexity and dataset size. In our case, the true error, is the error from classifying anomalous or familiar points incorrectly according to their true labels. The training error is the error when we trained the classifier on our synthetic labels.

While a careful analysis requires understanding errors in the *fixed design* [20] setting, the traditional *i.i.d.* random design provides crude guidance on algorithm behavior and trade-offs. In this setting, the Rademacher complexity provides us a generalization bound [18]. For i.i.d. samples, the difference between the estimated and true error in classifying a set of m datapoints will be err $- \widehat{\text{err}} \le \mathcal{R}(m) + \mathcal{O}\left(\sqrt{\log \frac{1/\delta}{m}}\right)$ with probability $1 - \delta$. This gives a good intuition for how the overfitting of our classifier relates to its complexity and the number of points m that we train on. This bound follows our intuition: (1) as m decreases, the chance of classifying incorrectly increases; (2) as $\mathcal{R}(m)$ increases, the classifier complexity increases and we have a better chance of incorrectly distinguishing familiars from other familiars.

Due to this intuition, we choose a simple classifier, $l2$-regularized logistic regression. Window size t_w is most easily chosen through empirical testing; if the variance in the anomaly signal is large, familiars are too easy to tell apart and the window size t_w should be decreased. When no anomalies are visible, t_w should be increased.

---

[4] The insights that follow generalize to VC dimension and other complexity measures.
[5] For a useful introduction, see [19].

4   Experiments

Dataset. We tested our algorithm on the Avenue Dataset [2][6] as well as the Subway surveillance dataset [21], the Personal Vacation Dataset [11], and the UMN Unusual Activity Dataset [22].

The Avenue dataset contains 16 training videos and 21 testing videos, and locations of anomalies are marked in ground truth pixel-level masks for each frame in the testing videos. The videos include a total of 15324 frames for testing. Our algorithm was permitted to use only the testing videos, and performed anomaly detection with no assumptions on the normality of any section of this video. This is in stark contrast to other methods, which must train a model on a set of frames from the training videos and/or from pre-marked sections of video. There are several other datasets available for anomaly detection, and our algorithm demonstrated reasonable success on all of the ones we tested[7]. We focus on the Avenue Dataset specifically because it was more challenging than staged datasets (such as the UMN Unusual Activity Dataset) and is more recent with more specific labeling than others, such as the Personal Vacation dataset. The dataset is also valuable because the method in [2] has publicly available code and results, so we were able to compare with the same implementation and features as a recent standard in anomaly detection. The UCSD pedestrian anomaly detection dataset [6] is another well-labeled and recent dataset, but nearly half of the frames in each test video contain anomalies, so the provided anomaly labels are not applicable in our unsupervised setting. More precisely, in our setting, no frames would be defined as anomalous since the activities labeled as such in the dataset often compose half of the video.[8]

Implementation. For the Avenue dataset, we follow the same feature generation procedure as Lu [2], courtesy of code they provided upon request. The features computed on the video match their method exactly, resulting in gradient-based features for $10 \times 10 \times 5$ (rows $\times$ columns $\times$ frames) spatiotemporal subunits in the video. After PCA and normalization, each subunit is represented by a 100 dimensional vector. Using the code provided by the authors, we are able to run their algorithm alongside ours on the same set of features. Following their evaluation, we treat each subunit as a 'frame' in our framework, classifying each subunit independently. The results are smoothed with the same filter as [2].

We used liblinear's $l2$-logistic regression for the classifier f in the framework. We experimented with several values of λ across other videos and found that as long as the features are whitened, λ within an order of magnitude of 1 gives reasonable results (see Table 1. We only needed 10 shuffles to get adequate performance, likely because there were few anomalies per video. We display our results

---

[6] http://www.cse.cuhk.edu.hk/leojia/projects/detectabnormal/dataset.html.

[7] See supplementary material for more results, including results on individual videos in the UMN and Avenue datasets.

[8] Other videos are unusable for a similar reason; for instance, 2 of the 8 videos available from [23] contain more than 50 % frames with at least one anomaly, and only 2 contain fewer than 20 % anomalous frames (one of which is the Subway exit sequence).

for a window size of 10. The algorithm is trivially parallelizable across shuffles and splits; we provide a multithreaded version that runs splits simultaneously across all allocated CPUs. This ability to increase accuracy by operating more units in parallel is a significant benefit of this framework. In contrast, scanning techniques that update models in an online fashion must operate serially; their computation cost is dependent on the desired accuracy. An implementation of our method is available online.[9]

Evaluation Metric. We are interested in identifying every instance of an anomaly. We also care about proposing frames for a human to review, meaning we would like to evaluate the fidelity of the anomalousness with a human rating of anomalousness. Consequently, we avoid metrics that score anomaly detections in an event-detection style, where flagging a single frame is counted as a successful detection of adjacent frames. In addition, metrics like Equal Error Rate (EER) can be misleading in the anomaly detection setting.[10] Therefore, we using ROC curves and the corresponding area under the curve (AUC) as the evaluation metric, computed with reference to human-labeled frame and pixel ground truth.

Results. Figure 6 shows example detections and the resulting ROC curves and AUC values for our algorithm and [2] on the Avenue dataset. Note our algorithm operates in a separate setting – it does not (a) use any sequence other than an individual test video, (b) obtain a guiding form for models of familiarity, or (c) assume any partition of the video is familiar. Even with these additional challenges, we are able to obtain near-state-of-the-art performance.

The ROC curve sheds some light on the possible performance bottleneck for these algorithms: the last half of the curves for the two algorithms match closely. This highlights that for difficult anomaly instances, a similar number of false positives seem to be commonly detected by both algorithms. We believe that both are hitting a limitation with the encoding of events in the feature space: either the feature space is not descriptive enough or several other instances appear as anomalous as the true anomalies in feature space. Example detections and per-video analysis (see Supplementary) also shed light on our method's behavior. Since our algorithm is operating only on the test sequence, it exhibits false positives such as the only time someone enters the foreground from the right. This is penalized because the provided ground truth was marked relative to the training data. In addition, by using features that operate on 15-frame chunks of time, we often detect events as early as 15 frames too soon.

In Table 1 we show that our algorithm's robust performance across a range of parameters on the Avenue dataset. These results show that for sub-optimal parameter choices (common in the unsupervised learning setting), shuffles can

---

[9] http://www.cs.cmu.edu/~adelgior/anomalyframework.html.
[10] Consider the case when only 1 % of the video is anomalous: the EER on an algorithm that markes all frames normal would be 1 %, outperforming most modern algorithms. This extreme class imbalance is less prevalent in current standard datasets, but will become an apparent problem as more realistic datasets become prevalent.

improve performance. Imagine an under-regularized classifier (λ too small). The classifier will too easily distinguish normal points from subsets of the data, but this effect is reduced as the number of shuffles increases. A similar argument follows for other sub-optimal parameters. The major benefits of shuffling cannot be seen in the commonly used datasets for anomaly detection because the test sequences are too short to show context changes or multiple instances of the same anomaly that are more commonly found in real-world scenarios.

In addition, we report our AUC values on the Subway dataset (exit: 0.8236; entrance: 0.6913). Results for one of the videos in the Personal Vacation Dataset are shown in Fig. 7. Detailed UMN Dataset results can be found in the supplementary material. Our method outperforms [2] on all but one scene. While the AUC values are good (average = 0.91), the average AUC for both our method and the sparse method is still lower than the sparse and model-based approaches reported in [5]; this indicates that a change in features could make up for the difference in the performance gap.

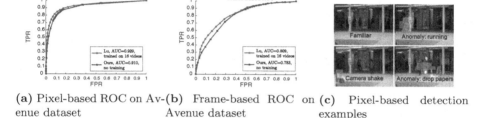

(a) Pixel-based ROC on Avenue dataset (b) Frame-based ROC on Avenue dataset (c) Pixel-based detection examples

Fig. 6. Performance on the Avenue Dataset. ROC curves in (a) and (b) show our performance nearly matches this algorithm, while we require no training data. Detection examples shown in (c) show a correctly classified familiar frame, two detected anomalous frames (running and dropping papers), and a false alarm (camera shake).

Table 1. Frame-based AUC averaged across all 21 test videos of the Avenue dataset. All instances of $K = 10$ outperform their $K = 0$ counterparts.

t_w	$K = 0$			$K = 10$		
	10	100	1000	10	100	1000
$\lambda = 0.01$	0.8697	0.8149	0.7731	0.8950	0.8951	0.8085
$\lambda = 1$	0.8921	0.8736	0.7731	0.8957	0.8954	0.8085
$\lambda = 100$	0.8947	0.8922	0.7751	0.8958	0.8953	0.8088

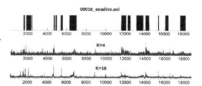

Fig. 7. Results on video 00016 in the Personal Vacation Dataset. As the number of shuffles increases, the signal-to-noise ratio increases.

5 Discussion

We have developed a method for identifying anomalies in videos in a setting that is independent of the order in which anomalies appear and requires no separate training sequences. The permutation-testing methodology requires no assumptions about the content in the descriptors of each frame and the user is able to "plug in" the latest optimal features for their video as long as the anomalous frames are distinguishable in this space. No training data needs to be collected or labeled within the test video. We show that our anomaly detection algorithm is able to perform as well as state of the art on standard datasets, even when we adjust the setting by removing training data. The lack of assumptions on the content or location of familiars is valuable for finding true anomalies that had previously remained unseen.

Acknowledgements. This research was supported through the DoD National Defense Science & Engineering Graduate Fellowship (NDSEG) Program and NSF grant IIS1227495.

References

1. Zhao, B., Fei-Fei, L., Xing, E.: Online detection of unusual events in videos via dynamic sparse coding. In: 2011 IEEE Conference on Computer Vision and Pattern Recognition (CVPR), pp. 3313–3320, June 2011
2. Lu, C., Shi, J., Jia, J.: Abnormal event detection at 150 fps in matlab. In: 2013 IEEE International Conference on Computer Vision (ICCV), pp. 2720–2727. IEEE (2013)
3. Mahadevan, V., Li, W., Bhalodia, V., Vasconcelos, N.: Anomaly detection in crowded scenes. In: 2010 IEEE Conference on Computer Vision and Pattern Recognition (CVPR), pp. 1975–1981. IEEE (2010)
4. Kim, J., Grauman, K.: Observe locally, infer globally: a space-time MRF for detecting abnormal activities with incremental updates. In: IEEE Conference on Computer Vision and Pattern Recognition, 2009, CVPR 2009, pp. 2921–2928. IEEE (2009)
5. Li, W., Mahadevan, V., Vasconcelos, N.: Anomaly detection and localization in crowded scenes. IEEE Trans. Pattern Anal. Mach. Intell. **36**(1), 18–32 (2014)
6. Mehran, R., Oyama, A., Shah, M.: Abnormal crowd behavior detection using social force model. In: IEEE Conference on Computer Vision and Pattern Recognition, 2009, CVPR 2009, pp. 935–942. IEEE (2009)
7. Antić, B., Ommer, B.: Video parsing for abnormality detection. In: 2011 IEEE International Conference on Computer Vision (ICCV), pp. 2415–2422. IEEE (2011)
8. Roshtkhari, M., Levine, M.: Online dominant and anomalous behavior detection in videos. In: Proceedings of the IEEE Conference on Computer Vision and Pattern Recognition, pp. 2611–2618 (2013)
9. Calderara, S., Heinemann, U., Prati, A., Cucchiara, R., Tishby, N.: Detecting anomalies in peoples trajectories using spectral graph analysis. Comput. Vis. Image Underst. **115**(8), 1099–1111 (2011)
10. Liu, S., Yamada, M., Collier, N., Sugiyama, M.: Change-point detection in time-series data by relative density-ratio estimation. Neural Netw. **43**, 72–83 (2013)

11. Ito, Y., Kitani, K.M., Bagnell, J.A., Hebert, M.: Detecting interesting events using unsupervised density ratio estimation. In: Fusiello, A., Murino, V., Cucchiara, R. (eds.) ECCV 2012. LNCS, vol. 7585, pp. 151–161. Springer, Heidelberg (2012). doi:10.1007/978-3-642-33885-4_16
12. Kawahara, Y., Sugiyama, M.: Change-point detection in time-series data by direct density-ratio estimation. In: SDM, vol. 9, pp. 389–400. SIAM (2009)
13. Sugiyama, M., Suzuki, T., Kanamori, T.: Density ratio estimation: a comprehensive review. RIMS Kokyuroku, pp. 10–31 (2010)
14. Wang, H., Kläser, A., Schmid, C., Liu, C.L.: Action recognition by dense trajectories. In: 2011 IEEE Conference on Computer Vision and Pattern Recognition (CVPR), pp. 3169–3176. IEEE (2011)
15. Motwani, R., Raghavan, P.: Randomized algorithms. Chapman & Hall/CRC (2010)
16. Kakade, S.: Hoeffding, Chernoff, Bennet, and Bernstein Bounds. http://stat.wharton.upenn.edu/skakade/courses/stat928/lectures/lecture06.pdf
17. Ben-David, S., Blitzer, J., Crammer, K., Kulesza, A., Pereira, F., Vaughan, J.W.: A theory of learning from different domains. Mach. Learn. **79**(1–2), 151–175 (2010)
18. Bartlett, P.L., Mendelson, S.: Rademacher and gaussian complexities: risk bounds and structural results. J. Mach. Learn. Res. **3**, 463–482 (2003)
19. Balcan, M.F.: Rademacher complexity. http://www.cs.cmu.edu/ninamf/ML11/lect1117.pdf
20. Borenstein, M., Hedges, L.V., Higgins, J., Rothstein, H.R.: A basic introduction to fixed-effect and random-effects models for meta-analysis. Res. Synth. Methods **1**(2), 97–111 (2010)
21. Adam, A., Rivlin, E., Shimshoni, I., Reinitz, D.: Robust real-time unusual event detection using multiple fixed-location monitors. IEEE Trans. Pattern Anal. Mach. Intell. **30**(3), 555–560 (2008)
22. Minnesota, U.: Crowd activity dataset. http://mha.cs.umn.edu/proj_events.shtml
23. Andrei Zaharescu, R.P.W.: Anomalous behavior data set. http://vision.eecs.yorku.ca/research/anomalous-behaviour-data/. Accessed 01 March 2016

ContextLocNet: Context-Aware Deep Network Models for Weakly Supervised Localization

Vadim Kantorov, Maxime Oquab, Minsu Cho, and Ivan Laptev[✉]

WILLOW project team, Inria / ENS / CNRS, Paris, France
{vadim.kantorov,maxime.oquab,minsu.cho,ivan.laptev}@inria.fr

Abstract. We aim to localize objects in images using image-level supervision only. Previous approaches to this problem mainly focus on discriminative object regions and often fail to locate precise object boundaries. We address this problem by introducing two types of context-aware guidance models, *additive* and *contrastive* models, that leverage their surrounding context regions to improve localization. The additive model encourages the predicted object region to be supported by its surrounding context region. The contrastive model encourages the predicted object region to be outstanding from its surrounding context region. Our approach benefits from the recent success of convolutional neural networks for object recognition and extends Fast R-CNN to weakly supervised object localization. Extensive experimental evaluation on the PASCAL VOC 2007 and 2012 benchmarks shows that our context-aware approach significantly improves weakly supervised localization and detection.

Keywords: Object recognition · Object detection · Weakly supervised object localization · Context · Convolutional neural networks

1 Introduction

Weakly supervised object localization and learning (WSL) [1,2] is the problem of localizing spatial extents of target objects and learning their representations from a dataset with only image-level labels. WSL is motivated by two fundamental issues of conventional object recognition. First, the strong supervision in terms of object bounding boxes or segmentation masks is difficult to obtain and prevents scaling-up object localization to thousands of object classes. Second, imprecise and ambiguous manual annotations can introduce subjective biases to the learning. Convolutional neural networks (CNN) [3,4] have recently taken over the state of the art in many computer vision tasks. CNN-based methods for weakly supervised object localization have been explored in [5,6]. Despite this

Electronic supplementary material The online version of this chapter (doi:10.1007/978-3-319-46454-1_22) contains supplementary material, which is available to authorized users.

progress, WSL remains a very challenging problem. The state-of-the-art performance of WSL on standard benchmarks [1,2,6] is considerably lower compared to the strongly supervised counterparts [7–9].

Strongly supervised detection methods often use contextual information from regions around the object or from the whole image [7,9–13]: Indeed, visual context often provides useful information about which image regions are likely to be a target class according to object-background or object-object relations, e.g., a boat in the sea, a bird in the sky, a person on a horse, a table around a chair, etc. However, can a similar effect be achieved for object localization in a weakly supervised setting, where training data does not contain any supervisory information neither about object locations nor about context regions?

The main contribution of this paper is exploring the use of context as a supervisory guidance for WSL with CNNs. In a nutshell, we show that, even without strong supervision, visual context can guide localization in two ways: *additive* and *contrastive* guidances. As the conventional use of contextual information, the additive guidance enforces the predicted object region to be compatible with its surrounding context region. This can be encoded by maximizing the sum of a class score of a candidate region with that of its surrounding context. On the other hand, the contrastive guidance encourages the predicted object region to be outstanding from its surrounding context region. This can be encoded by maximizing the difference between a class score of the object region and that of the surrounding context. For example, let us consider a candidate box for a person and its surrounding region of context in Fig. 1. In additive guidance, appearance of a horse in the surrounding context helps us infer the surrounded region to contain a person. In contrast guidance, the absence of target-specific

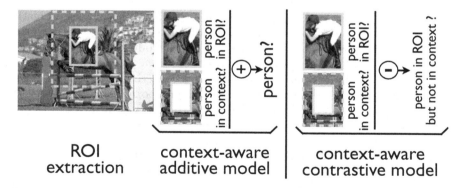

Fig. 1. Context-aware guidance for weakly supervised detection. Given extracted ROIs as localization candidates, our two basic context-aware models, *additive* and *contrastive* models, leverage their surrounding context regions to improve localization. The additive model relies on semantic consistency that aggregates class activations from ROI and context. The contrastive model relies on semantic contrast that computes difference of class activations between ROI and context. For details, see text. (Best viewed in color.) (Color figure online)

(person) features in its surrounding context helps separating the object region from its background.

In this work, we introduce two types of CNN architectures, *additive* and *contrastive* models, corresponding to the two contextual guidances. Building on the efficient region-of-interest (ROI) pooling architecture [8], the proposed models capture effective features among potential context regions to localize objects and learn their representations. In practice we observe that our additive model prevents expansion of detections beyond object boundaries. On the other hand, the contrastive model prevents contraction of detections to small object parts. In experimental evaluation, we show that our models significantly outperform the baselines and demonstrate effectiveness of our models for WSL. The project webpage and the code is available at [42].

2   Related Work

In both computer vision and machine learning, there has been a large body of recent research on WSL [1,2,5,6,14–24]. Such methods typically attempt to localize objects in the form of bounding boxes with visually consistent appearance in the training images, where multiple objects in different viewpoints and configurations appear in cluttered backgrounds. Most of existing approaches to WSL are formulated as or are closely related to multiple instance learning (MIL) [25], where each positive image has at least one true bounding box for a target class, and negative images contain false boxes only. They typically alternate between estimating a discriminative representation of the object and selecting an object box in positive images based on this representation. Since the task consists in a non-convex optimization problem, WSL has focused on robust initialization and effective regularization strategies.

Chum and Zisserman [14] initialize candidate boxes using discriminative visual words, and update localization by maximizing the average pairwise similarity across the positive images. Shi *et al.* [15] introduce the Latent Dirichlet Allocation (LDA) topic model for WSL, and Siva *et al.* [16] propose an effective negative mining approach combined with discriminative saliency measures. Deselaers *et al.* [17] instead initialize candidate boxes using the objectness method [26], and propose a CRF-based model that jointly localizes objects in positive training images. Song *et al.*formulate an initialization strategy for WSL as a discriminative submodular cover problem in a graph-based framework [19], and develop a negative mining technique to increase robustness against incorrectly localized boxes [20]. Bilen *et al.* [21] propose a relaxed version of MIL that softly labels object instances instead of choosing the highest scoring ones. In [22], they also propose a discriminative convex clustering algorithm to jointly learn a discriminative object model and enforce the similarity of the localized object regions. Wang *et al.* [1] propose an iterative latent semantic clustering algorithm based on latent Semantic Analysis (pLSA) that selects the most discriminative cluster for each class in terms of its classification performance. Cinbis *et al.* [2] extend a standard MIL approach and propose a multi-fold strategy that splits the training data to escape bad local optima.

As CNNs have turned out to be surprisingly effective in many vision tasks including classification and detection, recent state-of-the-art WSL approaches also build on CNN architectures [5,6,23,24] or CNN features [1,2]. Cinbis *et al.* [2] combine multi-fold multiple-instance learning with CNN features. Wang *et al.* [1] develop a semantic clustering method on top of pretrained CNN features. While these methods produce promising results, they are not trained end-to-end. Oquab *et al.* [5] propose a CNN architecture with global max pooling on top of its final convolutional layer. Zhou *et al.* [24] apply global average pooling instead to encourage the network to cover the full extent of the object. Rather than directly providing the full extent of the object, however, these pooling-based approaches are limited to a position of a discriminative part or require a separate post-processing step to obtain the final localization. Jaderberg *et al.* [23] propose a CNN architecture with spatial transformer layers that automatically transform spatial feature maps to align objects to a common reference frame. Bilen *et al.* [6] modify a region-based CNN architecture [27] and propose a CNN with two streams, one focusing on recognition and the other one on localization, that performs simultaneously region selection and classification. Our work is related to these CNN-based MIL approaches that perform WSL by end-to-end training from image-level labels. In contrast to the above methods, however, we focus on a context-aware CNN architecture that exploits contextual relation between a candidate region and its surrounding regions.

While contextual information has been widely employed for object detection [7,9,11,12,28], the use of context has received relatively little attention in weakly supervised or unsupervised localization. Russakovsky *et al.* [29] and Cinbis *et al.* [2] use a background descriptor computed over features outside a candidate box, and demonstrate that background modelling can improve WSL as compared to foreground modelling only. Doersch *et al.* [30] align contextual regions of an object patch to gradually discovers a visual object cluster in their method of iterative region prediction and context alignment. Cho *et al.* [31,32] propose a contrast-based contextual score for unsupervised object localization, which measures the contrast of matching scores between a candidate region and its surrounding candidate regions. Our context-aware CNN models are inspired by these previous approaches. We would like to emphasize that while the use of contextual information is not new in itself, we apply it to build a novel CNN architecture for WSL, that is, to the best of our knowledge, unique to our work. We believe that the simplicity of our basic models makes them extendable to a variety of weakly supervised computer vision tasks for more accurate localization and learning.

3   Context-Aware Weakly Supervised Network

In this section we describe our context-aware deep network for WSL. Our network consists of multiple CNN components, each of which builds on previous models [5,6,9,27]. We begin by explaining first its overall architecture, and then detail our guidance models for WSL.

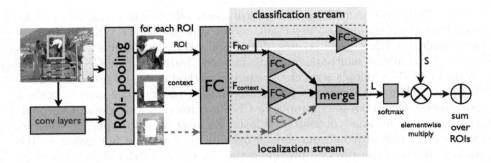

Fig. 2. Our context-aware architecture. Convolutional layers and FC layers (in green) correspond to the VGG-F architecture, pre-trained on ImageNet. The output of FC layers is passed through ReLu to the *classification* and *localization* streams. The classification stream takes features from ROIs, feeds them to a linear layer FC_{cls}, and outputs classification scores S_{ROI}. The localization stream takes features from ROIs and their context regions, processes them through our context-aware guidance models, and outputs localization scores L_{ROI}. The final output is a product of classification and localization scores for each ROI and object class. FC_{cls}, FC_a, FC_b, FC_c (in purple) are fully-connected linear layers trained from scratch. See text for more details. (Color figure online)

3.1 Overview

Following the intuition of Oquab *et al.* [5], our CNN-based approach to WSL learns a network from high-scoring object candidate regions within a classification training setup. In this approach, the visual consistency of classes within the dataset allows the network to localize and learn the underlying objects. The overall network architecture is described in Fig. 2.

Convolutional and ROI Pooling Layers. Our architecture has 5 convolutional layers, followed by a ROI pooling layer that extracts a set of feature maps, corresponding to the ROI (object proposal). The convolutional layers, as our base feature extractor, come from the VGG-F model [33]. Instead of max pooling typically used to process output of the convolutional layers in conventional CNNs for classification [4,5], however, we follow the ROI pooling of Fast R-CNN [27], an efficient region-based CNN for object detection using object proposals [34]. This network first takes the entire image as input and applies a sequence of convolutional layers resulting in feature maps (256 feature maps with the effective stride of 16 pixels). The network then contains a ROI-pooling layer [35], where ROIs (object proposals) extract corresponding features from the final convolutional layer. Given a ROI on the image and the feature maps, the ROI-pooling module projects the ROI on the feature maps, pools corresponding features with a spatially adaptive grid, and then forwards them through subsequent fully-connected layers. This architecture allows us to share computations in convolutional layers for all ROIs in an input image. Following [6],

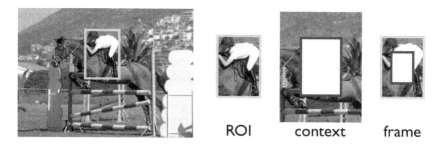

Fig. 3. Region pooling types for our guidance models: ROI pooling, context pooling, and frame pooling. For context and frame, the ratio between the side of the external rectangle and the internal rectangle is fixed as 1.8. Note that context and frame pooling types are designed to produce feature maps of the same shape, *i.e.*, frame-shaped feature maps with zeros in the center.

in this work, we initialize network layers using the weights of ImageNet-pretrained VGG-F model [33], which is then fine-tuned in training.

Feature Pooling for Context-Aware Guidance. For context-aware localization and learning, we extend the ROI pooling by introducing additional pooling types for each ROI, in a similar manner to Gidaris *et al.* [9]. As shown in Fig. 3, we define three types of pooling: ROI pooling, context pooling, and frame pooling. Given a ROI, *i.e.*, an object proposal [34], the *context* is defined as an outer region around the ROI, and the *frame* is an inner region ROI. Note that context pooling and frame pooling produce feature maps of the same shape, *i.e.*, central area of the outputs will have zero values. As will be explained in Sect. 3.3, this property is useful in our contrast model. The extracted feature maps are then independently processed by fully-connected layers (green FC layers in Fig. 2), that outputs a ROI feature vector, a context feature vector, and/or a frame feature vector. The models will be detailed in Sects. 3.2 and 3.3.

Two-Stream Network. To combine the guidance model components with classification, we employ the two-stream architecture of Bilen and Vedaldi [6], which branches a localization stream in parallel with a classification stream, and produces final classification scores by performing element-wise multiplication between them. In this two-stream strategy, the classification score of a ROI is reweighted with its corresponding softmaxed localization score. As illustrated in Fig. 2, the *classification stream* takes the feature vector F_{ROI} as input and feeds it to a linear layer FC_{cls}, that outputs a set of class scores S. Given C classes, processing K ROIs produces a matrix $S \in \mathbb{R}^{K \times C}$. The *localization stream* takes F_{ROI} and F_{context} as inputs, processes them through our guidance models, giving a matrix of localization scores $L \in \mathbb{R}^{K \times C}$. L is then fed to a softmax layer $[\sigma(L)]_{kc} = \frac{\exp(L_{kc})}{\sum_{k'=1}^{K} \exp(L_{k'c})}$ which normalizes the localization scores over the ROIs in the image. The final score for each ROI and class is obtained by element-wise multiplication of the corresponding scores S and $\sigma(L)$.

This procedure is done for each ROI and, as a final step, we sum all the ROI class scores to obtain the image class scores. During training, we use the hinge loss function and train the model for multi-label image classification:

$$L(w) = \frac{1}{C \cdot N} \sum_{c=1}^{C} \sum_{i=1}^{N} \max(0, 1 - y_{ci} \cdot f_c(x_i; w)),$$

where $f_c(x; w)$ is the score of our model evaluated on input image x pararmeterized by w (all weights and biases) for a class c; $y_{ci} = 1$ if i'th image contains a ground truth object of class c, otherwise $y_{ci} = -1$. Note that the loss is normalized by the number of classes C and the number of examples N.

3.2 Additive Model

The additive model, inspired by the conventional use of contextual information [7,9,11,12,28], encourages the network to select a ROI that is semantically compatible with its context. Specifically, we introduce two fully-connected layers FC_{ROI} and $FC_{context}$ as shown in Fig. 4(a), and the localization score for each ROI is obtained by summing outputs of the layers. Note that compared to context-padding [7], this model separates a ROI and its context, and learns the adaptation layers FC_{ROI} and $FC_{context}$ in different branches. This conjunction of separate branches allows us to learn context-aware activations for the ROI in an effective way.

Figure 5(top) illustrates the behavior of the FC_{ROI} and $FC_{context}$ branches of the additive model trained on PASCAL VOC 2007. The scores of the target object (car) vary for different sizes of object proposals. We observe that the $FC_{context}$ branch discourages small detections on the interior of the object as well as large detections outside of object boundaries. $FC_{context}$ is, hence, complementary to FC_{ROI} and can be expected to prevent detections outside of objects.

3.3 Contrastive Model

The contrastive model encourages the network to select a ROI that is outstanding from its context. This model is inspired by Cho et al.'s standout scoring for unsupervised object discovery [31], which measures the maximum contrast of matching scores between a rectangular box and its surrounding boxes. We adapt this idea of semantic contrast to our ROI-based CNN architecture. Specifically, we introduce two fully-connected layers FC_{ROI} and $FC_{context}$ as shown in Fig. 4(b), and the locacalization score for each ROI is obtained by subtracting the output activation of $FC_{context}$ from that of FC_{ROI} for each ROI. Note that in order to make subtraction work properly, all weights of the layers FC_{ROI} and $FC_{context}$ are shared for this model. Without sharing parameters, this model reduces to the additive model.

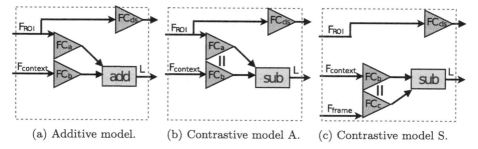

(a) Additive model.   (b) Contrastive model A.   (c) Contrastive model S.

Fig. 4. Context-aware guidance models. The additive model takes outputs of ROI and context pooling, feeds them to independent fully-connected layers, and compute localization scores by adding their outputs. The contrastive models take outputs of ROI (or frame) and context pooling, feed them to a shared fully-connected layer (*i.e.*, two fully-connected layers with all parameter shared), and compute localization scores by subtracting the output of context from the other. For details, see the text.

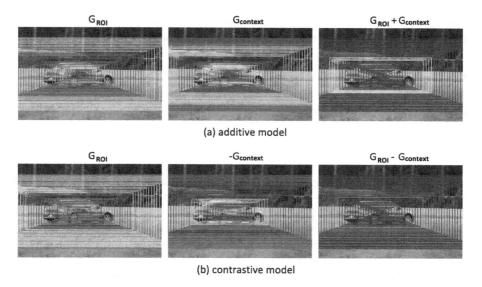

Fig. 5. Visualization of object scores produced by different branches of our models. The scores are computed for the *car* class for bounding boxes of different sizes centered on the target object. Red and blue colors correspond to high and low scores respectively. While the outputs of FC_{ROI} branches for the additive and contrastive models are similar, the $FC_{context}$ branches, corresponding to feature pooling at object boundaries, have notably different behavior. The $FC_{context}$ branch of the additive model discourages detections outside of the object. The $FC_{context}$ branch of the contrastive model, discourages detections on the interior of the object. The combination of the FC_{ROI} and $FC_{context}$ branches results in correct object localization for both models. (Color figure online)

Figure 5(bottom) illustrates the behavior of FC_{ROI} and $FC_{context}$ branches of the contrastive model. We denote by G_{ROI} and $G_{context}$ the outputs of respective layers. The variation of scores for the car object class and different object proposals indicates low responses of $-G_{context}$ on the interior of the object. The combination $G_{ROI} - G_{context}$ compensate each other resulting in correct localization of object boundaries. We expect the contrastive model to prevent incorrect detections on the interior of the object.

One issue in this model is that in the localization stream the shared adaptation layers FC_{ROI} and $FC_{context}$ need to process input feature maps of different shapes F_{ROI} and $F_{context}$, $i.e.$, FC_{ROI} processes features from a whole region (ROI in Fig. 3), whereas $FC_{context}$ processes features from a frame-shaped region ($context$ in Fig. 3). We call this model the asymmetric contrastive model ($contrastive\ A$).

To remove this asymmetry in the localization stream, we replace ROI pooling with $frame$ pooling (Fig. 3) that extracts a feature map from an internal rectangular frame of ROI. This allows the shared adaptation layers in the localization stream to process input feature maps of the same shape F_{frame} and $F_{context}$. We call this model the symmetric contrastive model ($contrastive\ S$). Note that adaptation layer FC_{cls} in the classification stream maintains the original ROI pooling regardless of modification in the localization stream. The advantage of this model will be verified in our experimental section.

4   Experimental Evaluation

4.1   Experimental Setup

Datasets and Evaluation Measures. We evaluate our method on PASCAL VOC 2007 dataset [36], which is a common benchmark in weakly supervised object detection. This dataset contains 2501 training images, 2510 validation images and 4952 test images, with bounding box annotations provided for 20 object classes. We use the standard trainval/test splits. We also evaluate our method on PASCAL VOC 2012 [37]. VOC 2012 contains the same object classes as VOC 2007 and is approximately twice larger in size for both splits.

For evaluation, two performance metrics are used: mAP and CorLoc. Detection mAP is evaluated using the standard intersection-over-union (IoU) criterion defined by [36]. Correct localization (CorLoc) [17] is a standard metric for measuring localization accuracy on a training set, where WSL usually provides one object localization per image for a target class. CorLoc is evaluated per-class, only on positive images for that class, and counts the percentage of images for which the highest-scoring candidate provided by the method overlaps (IoU > 0.5) with a ground truth box. We evaluate this mAP and CorLoc on the test and trainval splits respectively.

Implementation Details. ROIs for VOC 2007 are directly provided by the authors of the Selective Search proposal algorithm [34]. For VOC 2012, we use the Selective Search windows computed by Girshick $et\ al.$ [27]. Our implementation is done using Torch [38], and we use the rectangular frame pooling based on the open-sourced code by Gidaris *et al.* [9, 39][1] which is itself based on Fast R-CNN [27] code. We use the pixel→features map coordinates transform for region proposals from the public implementation of [35][2], with offset parameter set to zero (see the precise procedure in our code online[1]). All of our models, including our reproduction of WSDDN, use the same transform. We use the ratio between the side of the external rectangle and the internal rectangle fixed to 1.8.[3] Our pretrained network is the VGG-F model [33] ported to Torch using the loadcaffe package [40]. We train our networks using cuDNN [41] on an NVidia Titan X GPU. All layers are fine-tuned. Our training parameters are detailed below.

Parameters. For training, we use stochastic gradient descent (SGD) with momentum 0.9, dampening 0.0 on examples using a batch size of 1. In our experiments (both training and testing) we use all ROIs for an image provided by Selective Search [34] that have width and height larger than 20 pixels. The experiments are run for 30 epochs each. The learning rates are set to 10^{-5} for the first ten epochs, then lowered to 10^{-6} until the end of training. We also use jittering over scales. Images are rescaled randomly into one of the five following sizes: $800 \times 608, 656 \times 496, 544 \times 400, 960 \times 720, 1152 \times 864$. Random horizontal flipping is also applied.

At test time, the scores are evaluated on all scales and flips, then averaged. Detections are filtered to have a minimum score of 10^{-4} and then processed by non-maxima suppression with an overlap threshold of 0.4 prior to mAP calculation.

4.2   Results and Discussion

We first evaluate our method on the VOC 2007 benchmark and compare results to the recent methods for weakly-supervised object detecton [1,6] in Table 1. Specifically, we compare to the WSDDN-SSW-S setup of [6] which, similar to our method, uses VGG-F as a base model and Selective Search Windows object proposals. For fair comparison we also compare results to our re-implementation of WSDDN-SSW-S (row (f) in Table 1). The original WSDDN-SSW-S employs an additional softmax in the classification stream and uses binary cross-entropy instead of hinge loss, but we found that these differences to have minor effect on the detection accuracy in our experiments (performance matches up to 1 %, see rows (d) and (f)).

Our best model, contrastive S, reaches 36.3 % mAP and outperforms previous WSL methods using selective search object proposals in rows (a)-(e) of Table 1. Class-specific CorLoc and AP results can be found in Tables 2 and 3, respectively.

---

[1] http://github.com/gidariss/locnet.

[2] http://github.com/ShaoqingRen/SPP_net.

[3] This choice for the frame parameters follows [9,39], and the ratio is kept same for both context and frame pooling types. We have experimented with different ratios, and observed that results of our method change marginally with increasing the ratio, and drop with decreasing the ratio.

Table 1. Comparison of our proposed models on PASCAL VOC 2007 with the state of the art, CorLoc (%) and detection mAP (%)

	Model	CorLoc	mAP
(a)	Cinbis *et al.* [2]	52.0	30.2
(b)	Wang *et al.* [1]	48.5	30.9
(c)	Wang *et al.*+ context [1]		31.6
(d)	WSDDN-SSW-S [6]		31.1
(e)	WSDNN-SSW-ENS [6]	54.2	33.3
(f)	WSDDN-SSW-S*	50.0	30.5
(g)	additive	52.8	33.3
(h)	contrastive A	50.2	32.2
(i)	contrastive S	**55.1**	**36.3**

Bilen *et al.* [6] experiment with alternative options in terms of EdgeBox object proposals, rescaling ROI pooling activations by EdgeBoxes objectness score, a new regularization term and model ensembling. When combined together, these additions improve result in [6] to 39.3 %. Such improvements are orthogonal to our method and we believe our method will benefit from extensions proposed in [6]. We note that our single contrastive S model (36.3 % mAP) outperforms the ensemble of multiple models using SSW in [6] (33.3 % mAP).

Context Branch Helps. The additive model (row (g) in Table 1) improves localization (CorLoc) and detection (mAP) over those of the WSDDN-SSW-S* baseline (row (f)). We also applied a context-padding technique [7] to WSDDN-SSW-S* by enlarging ROI to include context (in the localization branch). Our additive model (mAP 33.3 %) surpasses the context-padding model (mAP 30.9 %). Contrastive A also improves localization and detection, but performs slightly worse than the additive model (Table 1, rows (g) and (h)). These results show that processing the context in a separate branch helps localization in the weakly supervised setup.

Contrastive Model with Frame Pooling. The basic contrastive model above, contrastive A (see Fig. 4), processes different shapes of feature maps (F_{ROI} and $F_{context}$) in the localization branch while sharing weights between FC_{ROI} and $FC_{context}$. To the contrary, contrastive S processes the same shape of feature maps (F_{frame} and $F_{context}$) in the localization branch. As shown in rows (h) and (i) of Table 1, contrastive S greatly improves CorLoc and mAP over contrastive A. Our hypothesis is that, since the weights are shared between the two layers in the the localization branch, these layers may perform better if they process the same shape of feature maps. Contrastive S obtains such a property by using frame pooling. This modification allows us to significantly outperform the baselines (rows (a)–(e) in Table 1). We believe that the model overfits less to the central pixels, achieving better performance. Per-class results are presented in Tables 2 and 3.

Table 2. Per-class comparison of our proposed models on VOC 2007 with the state of the art, detection AP (%)

Model	aer	bik	brd	boa	btl	bus	car	cat	cha	cow	tbl	dog	hrs	mbk	prs	plt	shp	sfa	trn	tv	mAP
Cinbis et al. [2]	39.3	43.0	28.8	20.4	8.0	45.5	47.9	22.1	8.4	33.5	23.6	29.2	38.5	47.9	20.3	20.0	35.8	30.8	41.0	20.1	30.2
Wang et al. [1]	48.8	41.0	23.6	12.1	11.1	42.7	40.9	35.5	11.1	36.6	18.4	35.3	34.8	51.3	17.2	17.4	26.8	32.8	35.1	45.6	30.9
Wang et al.+context [1]	48.9	42.3	26.1	11.3	11.9	41.3	40.9	34.7	10.8	34.7	18.8	34.4	35.4	52.7	19.1	17.4	35.9	33.3	34.8	46.5	31.6
WSDDN-SSW-S*	49.8	50.5	30.1	**12.7**	11.4	54.2	49.2	20.4	1.5	31.2	27.9	18.6	32.2	49.7	**22.9**	15.9	25.6	27.4	38.1	41.3	30.5
additive	48.7	50.7	29.5	12.3	**14.1**	**56.5**	51.7	21.1	**4.0**	30.0	36.5	22.5	42.6	56.2	21.5	**17.5**	**29.5**	27.0	41.3	**52.3**	33.3
contrastive A	52.8	49.6	28.9	6.8	10.9	50.4	52.2	**35.0**	3.2	31.4	37.6	39.7	44.1	53.4	10.7	17.4	24.2	30.9	37.8	26.9	32.2
contrastive S	**57.1**	**52.0**	**31.5**	7.6	11.5	55.0	**53.1**	34.1	1.7	**33.1**	**49.2**	**42.0**	**47.3**	**56.6**	15.3	12.8	24.8	**48.9**	**44.4**	47.8	**36.3**

Table 3. Per-class comparison of our proposed models on VOC 2007 with the state of the art, CorLoc (%)

Model	aer	bik	brd	boa	btl	bus	car	cat	cha	cow	tbl	dog	hrs	mbk	prs	plt	shp	sfa	trn	tv	avg
Conbis et al. [2]	65.3	55.0	52.4	48.3	18.2	66.4	77.8	35.6	26.5	67.0	46.9	48.4	70.5	69.1	35.2	35.2	69.6	43.4	64.6	43.7	52.0
Wang et al. [1]	80.1	63.9	51.5	14.9	21.0	55.7	74.2	43.5	26.2	53.4	16.3	56.7	58.3	69.5	14.1	38.3	58.8	47.2	49.1	60.9	48.5
WSDDN-SSW-S*	80.4	62.4	53.8	**28.2**	26.0	68.0	72.5	45.1	9.3	64.4	38.8	35.6	51.4	77.1	**37.6**	38.1	66.0	31.2	61.6	53.0	50.0
additive	78.8	66.7	52.9	25.0	**26.3**	68.0	73.6	44.8	**14.9**	62.3	45.2	46.3	61.6	82.3	35.3	39.6	**69.1**	30.9	62.0	**69.5**	52.8
contrastive A	78.8	62.7	51.1	20.2	21.8	68.5	71.6	**55.8**	10.3	**67.8**	46.8	53.7	62.2	82.3	26.0	**40.7**	55.7	33.6	55.5	39.4	50.2
contrastive S	**83.3**	**68.6**	54.7	23.4	18.3	**73.6**	**74.1**	54.1	8.6	65.1	**47.1**	**59.5**	**67.0**	**83.5**	35.3	39.9	67.0	**49.7**	**63.5**	65.2	**55.1**

PASCAL VOC 2012 Results. The per-class localization results for the VOC 2012 benchmark using our contrastive model S are summarized in Table 4(detection AP) and Table 5(CorLoc). We are not aware of other weakly supervised localization methods reporting results on VOC 2012.

Observations. We have explored several other options and made the following observations. Training the additive model and the contrastive model in a joint manner (adding the outputs of individual models to compute the localization score that is further processed by softmax) have not improve results in our experiments. Following Gidaris et al. [9], we have tried adding other types of region pooling as input to the localization branch, however, this did not improve our results significantly. It is possible that different types of context pooling

Table 4. Per-class comparison of the contrastive S model on VOC 2012 test set, AP (%)

Model	aer	bik	brd	boa	btl	bus	car	cat	cha	cow	tbl	dog	hrs	mbk	prs	plt	shp	sfa	trn	tv	mAP
contrastive S	64.0	54.9	36.4	8.1	12.6	53.1	40.5	28.4	6.6	35.3	34.4	49.1	42.6	62.4	19.8	15.2	27.0	33.1	33.0	50.0	35.3

Table 5. Per-class comparison of the contrastive S model on VOC 2012 trainval set, CorLoc (%)

Model	aer	bik	brd	boa	btl	bus	car	cat	cha	cow	tbl	dog	hrs	mbk	prs	plt	shp	sfa	trn	tv	Avg.
contrastive S	78.3	70.8	52.5	34.7	36.6	80.0	58.7	38.6	27.7	71.2	32.3	48.7	76.2	77.4	16.0	48.4	69.9	47.5	66.9	62.9	54.8

Fig. 6. The first five rows show localization examples where our method (contrastive S) outperforms WSDDN-SSW-S* baseline. Two next rows show examples where both methods succeed. The last two rows illustrate failure cases for both methods. Our method often suceeds in localizing correct object boundaries on examples where WSDNN-SSW-S* is locked to descriminative object parts such as heads of people and animals. Typical failure cases for both methods include images with multiple objects of the same class.

other than rectangular region pooling can provide improvements. We also found that sharing the weights or replacing the context pooling with the frame pooling in our additive model degrades the performance.

Qualitative Results. We illustrate examples of object detections by our method and WSDDN in Fig. 6. We observe that our method tends to provide more accurate localization results for classes with localized discriminative parts. For example, for person and animal classes our method often finds the whole extent of the objects while previous methods tend to localize head regions. This is consistent with results in Table 2 where, for example, the dog class obtains the highest improvement by our contrastive S model when compared to WSDDN.

Our method still suffers from the second typical failure mode of weakly supervised methods, as shown in the two bottom rows of Fig. 6, which is the multiple-object case: when many objects of the same class are encountered in close vicinity, they tend to be detected as a single object.

5   Conclusions

In this paper, we have presented context-aware deep network models for WSL. Building on recent improvements in region-based CNNs, we designed a novel localization architecture integrating the idea of contrast-based contextual guidance to the weakly-supervised object localization. We studied the localization component of a weakly-supervised detection network and proposed a subnetwork that effectively makes use of visual contextual information that helps refining the boundaries of detected objects. Our results show that the proposed semantic contrast is an effective cue for obtaining more accurate object boundaries. Qualitative results show that our method is less sensitive to the typical failure mode of WSL methods, such as shrinking to discriminative object parts. Our method has been validated on VOC 2007 and 2012 benchmarks demonstrating significant improvements over the baselines.

Given the prohibitive cost of large-scale exhaustive annotation, it is crucial to further develop methods for weakly-supervised visual learning. We believe the proposed approach is complementary to many previously explored ideas and could be combined with other techniques to foster further improvements.

Acknowledgments. We thank Hakan Bilen, Relja Arandjelović, and Soumith Chintala for fruitful discussion and help. This work was supported by the ERC grants VideoWorld and Activia, and the MSR-INRIA laboratory.

References

1. Wang, C., Ren, W., Huang, K., Tan, T.: Weakly supervised object localization with latent category learning. In: Fleet, D., Pajdla, T., Schiele, B., Tuytelaars, T. (eds.) ECCV 2014. LNCS, vol. 8694, pp. 431–445. Springer, Heidelberg (2014). doi:10.1007/978-3-319-10599-4_28
2. Cinbis, R.G., Verbeek, J., Schmid, C.: Weakly supervised object localization with multi-fold multiple instance learning. arXiv preprint (2015). arXiv:1503.00949
3. LeCun, Y., Boser, B., Denker, J.S., Henderson, D., Howard, R.E., Hubbard, W., Jackel, L.D.: Backpropagation applied to handwritten zip code recognition. Neural Comput. **1**(4), 541–551 (1989)
4. Krizhevsky, A., Sutskever, I., Hinton, G.E.: Imagenet classification with deep convolutional neural networks. In: NIPS, pp. 1097–1105 (2012)
5. Oquab, M., Bottou, L., Laptev, I., Sivic, J.: Is object localization for free?-weakly-supervised learning with convolutional neural networks. In: CVPR, pp. 685–694 (2015)
6. Bilen, H., Vedaldi, A.: Weakly supervised deep detection networks. In: CVPR (2016)
7. Girshick, R., Donahue, J., Darrell, T., Malik, J.: Region-based convolutional networks for accurate object detection and segmentation. PAMI **38**(1), 142–158 (2016)
8. Ren, S., He, K., Girshick, R., Sun, J.: Faster R-CNN: towards real-time object detection with region proposal networks. In: NIPS, pp. 91–99 (2015)
9. Gidaris, S., Komodakis, N.: Object detection via a multi-region and semantic segmentation-aware CNN model. In: ICCV, pp. 1134–1142 (2015)
10. Torralba, A., Murphy, K.P., Freeman, W.T., Rubin, M.A.: Context-based vision system for place and object recognition. In: ICCV, pp. 273–280. IEEE (2003)
11. Rabinovich, A., Vedaldi, A., Galleguillos, C., Wiewiora, E., Belongie, S.: Objects in context. In: ICCV, pp. 1–8. IEEE (2007)
12. Felzenszwalb, P.F., Girshick, R.B., McAllester, D., Ramanan, D.: Object detection with discriminatively trained part-based models. PAMI **32**(9), 1627–1645 (2010)
13. Desai, C., Ramanan, D., Fowlkes, C.: Discriminative models for multi-class object layout. In: ICCV, pp. 229–236, September 2009
14. Chum, O., Zisserman, A.: An exemplar model for learning object classes. In: CVPR, pp. 1–8. IEEE (2007)
15. Shi, Z., Siva, P., Xiang, T., Mary, Q.: Transfer learning by ranking for weakly supervised object annotation. In: BMVC, vol. 2, p. 5. Citeseer (2012)
16. Siva, P., Russell, C., Xiang, T.: In defence of negative mining for annotating weakly labelled data. In: Fitzgibbon, A., Lazebnik, S., Perona, P., Sato, Y., Schmid, C. (eds.) ECCV 2012. LNCS, vol. 7574, pp. 594–608. Springer, Heidelberg (2012). doi:10.1007/978-3-642-33712-3_43
17. Deselaers, T., Alexe, B., Ferrari, V.: Weakly supervised localization and learning with generic knowledge. IJCV **100**(3), 275–293 (2012)
18. Siva, P., Russell, C., Xiang, T., Agapito, L.: Looking beyond the image: unsupervised learning for object saliency and detection. In: CVPR, pp. 3238–3245 (2013)
19. Song, H.O., Girshick, R., Jegelka, S., Mairal, J., Harchaoui, Z., Darrell, T.: On learning to localize objects with minimal supervision. arXiv preprint (2014). arXiv:1403.1024
20. Song, H.O., Lee, Y.J., Jegelka, S., Darrell, T.: Weakly-supervised discovery of visual pattern configurations. In: NIPS (2014)

21. Bilen, H., Pedersoli, M., Tuytelaars, T.: Weakly supervised object detection with posterior regularization. In: BMVC (2014)
22. Bilen, H., Pedersoli, M., Tuytelaars, T.: Weakly supervised object detection with convex clustering. In: CVPR, pp. 1081–1089 (2015)
23. Jaderberg, M., Simonyan, K., Zisserman, A., et al.: Spatial transformer networks. In: NIPS, pp. 2008–2016 (2015)
24. Zhou, B., Khosla, A., Lapedriza, A., Oliva, A., Torralba, A.: Learning deep features for discriminative localization. arXiv preprint (2015). arXiv:1512.04150
25. Long, P.M., Tan, L.: PAC learning axis-aligned rectangles with respect to product distributions from multiple-instance examples. Mach. Learn. **30**(1), 7–21 (1998)
26. Alexe, B., Deselaers, T., Ferrari, V.: Measuring the objectness of image windows. PAMI **34**(11), 2189–2202 (2012)
27. Girshick, R.: Fast R-CNN. In: ICCV, pp. 1440–1448 (2015)
28. Oliva, A., Torralba, A.: The role of context in object recognition. Trends in Cogn. Sci. **11**(12), 520–527 (2007)
29. Russakovsky, O., Lin, Y., Yu, K., Fei-Fei, L.: Object-centric spatial pooling for image classification. In: Fitzgibbon, A., Lazebnik, S., Perona, P., Sato, Y., Schmid, C. (eds.) ECCV 2012. LNCS, vol. 7573, pp. 1–15. Springer, Heidelberg (2012)
30. Doersch, C., Gupta, A., Efros, A.A.: Context as supervisory signal: discovering objects with predictable context. In: Fleet, D., Pajdla, T., Schiele, B., Tuytelaars, T. (eds.) ECCV 2014. LNCS, vol. 8691, pp. 362–377. Springer, Heidelberg (2014). doi:10.1007/978-3-319-10578-9_24
31. Cho, M., Kwak, S., Schmid, C., Ponce, J.: Unsupervised object discovery and localization in the wild: part-based matching with bottom-up region proposals. In: CVPR, pp. 1201–1210 (2015)
32. Kwak, S., Cho, M., Laptev, I., Ponce, J., Schmid, C.: Unsupervised object discovery and tracking in video collections. In: ICCV, pp. 3173–3181 (2015)
33. Chatfield, K., Simonyan, K., Vedaldi, A., Zisserman, A.: Return of the devil in the details: delving deep into convolutional nets. In: British Machine Vision Conference (2014)
34. Uijlings, J.R., van de Sande, K.E., Gevers, T., Smeulders, A.W.: Selective search for object recognition. IJCV **104**(2), 154–171 (2013)
35. He, K., Zhang, X., Ren, S., Sun, J.: Spatial pyramid pooling in deep convolutional networks for visual recognition. PAMI **37**(9), 1904–1916 (2015)
36. Everingham, M., Van Gool, L., Williams, C.K., Winn, J., Zisserman, A.: The pascal visual object classes (VOC) challenge. IJCV **88**(2), 303–338 (2010)
37. Everingham, M., Van Gool, L., Williams, C.K.I., Winn, J., Zisserman, A.: The PASCAL Visual Object Classes Challenge 2012 (VOC 2012) Results (2012). http://www.pascal-network.org/challenges/VOC/voc2012/workshop/index.html
38. Collobert, R., Kavukcuoglu, K., Farabet, C.: Torch7: a matlab-like environment for machine learning. In: BigLearn, NIPS Workshop. Number EPFL-CONF-192376 (2011)
39. Gidaris, S., Komodakis, N.: Locnet: Improving localization accuracy for object detection. arXiv preprint (2015). arXiv:1511.07763
40. Zagoruyko, S.: loadcaffe (2015). https://github.com/szagoruyko/loadcaffe
41. Chetlur, S., Woolley, C., Vandermersch, P., Cohen, J., Tran, J., Catanzaro, B., Shelhamer, E.: cuDNN: efficient primitives for deep learning. arXiv preprint (2014). arXiv:1410.0759
42. Project webpage (code/dataset). http://www.di.ens.fr/willow/research/contextlocnet

Network Flow Formulations for Learning Binary Hashing

Lopamudra Mukherjee[1]([⊠]), Jiming Peng[2], Trevor Sigmund[1], and Vikas Singh[3]

[1] University of Wisconsin–Whitewater, Whitewater, USA
{mukherjl,sigmundTJ27}@uww.edu
[2] University of Houston, Houston, USA
jopeng@central.uh.edu
[3] University of Wisconsin–Madison, Madison, USA
vsingh@biostat.wisc.edu

Abstract. The problem of *learning binary hashing* seeks the identification of a binary mapping for a set of n examples such that the corresponding Hamming distances preserve high fidelity with a *given $n \times n$* matrix of distances (or affinities). This formulation has numerous applications in efficient search and retrieval of images (and other high dimensional data) on devices with storage/processing constraints. As a result, the problem has received much attention recently in vision and machine learning and a number of interesting solutions have been proposed. A common feature of most existing solutions is that they adopt continuous iterative optimization schemes which is then followed by a post-hoc rounding process to recover a feasible discrete solution. In this paper, we present a fully combinatorial network-flow based formulation for a relaxed version of this problem. The main maximum flow/minimum cut modules which drive our algorithm can be solved efficiently and can directly learn the binary codes. Despite its simplicity, we show that on most widely used benchmarks, our proposal yields competitive performance relative to a suite of *nine* different state of the art algorithms.

1 Introduction

The need to perform quick indexing and retrieval on large collections of images and videos, both in our personal collections and on the web, has led to a resurgence of interest in efficient methods for hashing.

While the literature on this topic is quite mature, the need to accomplish retrieval tasks on novel mobile architectures has led to numerous interesting variations of the problem. For example, small form factor devices with limited storage capacity as well as the associated power consumption constraints typically involve unique economy/accuracy trade-offs for the algorithm. Separately, when the data correspond to images, notice that it may not be sensible to hash the native image representation expressed as a $\mathbb{R}^D$ vector. Indeed, much of the image may include background clutter as well as other content not directly pertinent to the semantic information of the image. This leads to interesting variations of hashing

© Springer International Publishing AG 2016
B. Leibe et al. (Eds.): ECCV 2016, Part V, LNCS 9909, pp. 366–381, 2016.
DOI: 10.1007/978-3-319-46454-1_23

where each to-be-hashed example may actually correspond to multiple patches (or salient objects) contained within an image.

In vision applications of hashing, it is often the case that rather than represent the image in terms of its components as described above, it is more convenient to compute similarities between pairs of images in the dataset [1,2]. In practice, this is accomplished by running an object detector on each image and assessing whether each pair of images contain similar content. For instance, we may assume that images where detectors find similar objects are likely to be similar. So, for a given corpus of n images, we obtain a $n \times n$ similarity matrix via standard pre-processing. The hashing problem here requires finding a lower dimensional (say, d) mapping for each example in the corpus such that distances (or similarities) in the embedded space are low-distortion, relative to the original similarities. The "binary" version of this problem instead seeks an embedding to a d-dimensional $\{0,1\}$ space — this formulation is called Binary hashing. There is much recent interest in this problem due to two key reasons. First, binary hashing makes the downstream retrieval task extremely easy. For instance, the Hamming distance between a query and an item in the database can now be computed simply via logical operations (e.g., XOR) which leads to efficiency advantages. Second, the storage requirements are modest: even large image datasets such as *ImageNet* can easily be stored on commodity handheld devices without compression.

Deriving a binary embedding which maintains good fidelity with a given similarity matrix is commonly known in the literature as *learning* binary hashing. There is a growing body of work in computer vision and machine learning on various nice approaches to the problem. Note that the core problem is NP-hard (both non-convex and discrete), so most proposed methods involve iterative *continous* optimization schemes or make use of various other spectral relaxations that need solutions to large eigen-value problems [3], coordinate descent [4], Procrustean quantization [5] and concave-convex optimization [6]. These techniques often produce a relaxed solution, which is then 'rounded' based on its sign. These are effective approaches and work well in many cases though approximation ratios may be difficult to obtain. Our goal is to investigate, via an interesting reformulation, the feasibility of (arguably) simpler *discrete* energy minimization algorithms for a relaxed version of this problem and to assess if it can still offer competitive performance. In particular, we seek to derive fully combinatorial algorithms for learning binary hashing. Recall that while combinatorial methods have various benefits and dominate the landscape of image segmentation in vision, one attractive feature is that the primitive operations required (e.g., addition, counting) are simple. This yields substantial efficiency benefits for our main training module and is appropriate in situations where support for more intensive low-level operations is unavailable or otherwise undesirable. We present here a network-flow based formulation that is easy to implement and yields a *provably* partially-optimal solution for each bit of the hash code. To our knowledge, no combinatorial approaches currently exist for learning binary hashing in an unsupervised setup using network flow. Further, our approach extends to any arbitrary $\|.\|_p^p$ norm, though in this paper, for presentation purposes, we restrict our treatment to ℓ_1-norms and sum of squares distances.

Related Work. A well known algorithm for hashing is Locality-Sensitive Hashing (LSH) [7]. LSH creates a hashing scheme where similar items fall in the same bucket with high probability. Such embeddings are obtained via projections on randomly generated hyperplanes, where the query time for a $(1 + \epsilon)$ approximate nearest neighbor can be bounded by $O(n^{\frac{1}{1+\epsilon}})$. An advantage of LSH is that the random projections provably preserve distances in the limit as the number of hash bits increases. But it has been observed that the number of hash bits required may need to be large to faithfully maintain distances. More recent work has focused on better exploiting the structure of the data in specific domains by generating more effective/tailored hash functions. To this [8] end, within vision and machine learning, a number of methods [6] have been proposed including: Semantic Hashing [9,10], Spectral Hashing (SH) [3], Kernelized Spectral Hashing (KLSH) [11], Multi-dimension Spectral Hashing (MDSH) [12], Iterative Quantization (ITQ) [5], BRE [4], Anchor Graph Hashing (AGH) [8,13], NMF based Hashing [14], Self-taught Hashing (STH) [15], and Fast Hash [16]. Other proposals include parameter sensitive hashing [17] and asymmetric hash functions [18]. We briefly review some existing discrete formulations of the hashing problem. Most of these methods focus on the supervised version of the problem. A graph partitioning approach has been used in the supervised case by [19]. For the same problem, [20] employs an approach that solves the NP-hard hashing problem as regularized sub-problems that admits an analytical solution via cyclic coordinate descent. In terms of the unsupervised problem, to the best of our knowledge, [8] is the only approach that uses a discrete optimization based method for graph hashing using the anchor graph method. It proposes a bilevel maximization, one of which can be solved in closed form. It should be noted that the objective and subsequent optimization techniques in [8] are not similar to the network-flow approach proposed in this paper. As we will describe shortly, our proposal is also among a few hashing based approaches such as [21], that uses a simple two stage process for evaluating unseen data: first, we generate classifiers using the training code as labels and later these classifiers are used to predict the hashing code for test examples. Our experiments show that this scheme, though not widely utilized currently, has merit in vision applications.

2   Setting Up the Optimization Model

In this section, we will setup a simple optimization model that expresses the key properties of a desired solution to the learning binary hashing problem. Then, we will describe the details of our proposed algorithm and its analysis.

Notations. We use upper case letters such as Q to denote matrices and bold lower case characters such as $\mathbf{q}$ for vectors. When referring to a set of vectors, the ith vector will be $\mathbf{q}_i$; the jth entry of a vector $\mathbf{q}$ will be denoted as q_i.

Let $Y \in \mathbb{R}^{n \times D}$ be a matrix comprised of n examples in D dimensions as its rows. Let $A \in \mathbb{R}^{n \times n}$ be the matrix of pairwise similarities of examples in Y. Our goal is to find an embedding of Y into a lower dimensional binary space $X \in \{0, 1\}^{n \times d}$, where $D \gg d$. Clearly, the above embedding should preserve the relative distances between the n examples. Since X is binary, we use the Hamming distance between the examples in X. Let $H \in \mathbb{Z}^{n \times n}$ be the matrix of the corresponding pairwise Hamming distances, i.e., each entry H_{ij} computes the Hamming distance between examples i and j in X. The objective is given as

$$\arg \min_X d_f(A - H) \quad \text{s.t.} \quad H = \Gamma(X), \tag{1}$$

where $d_f(\cdot)$ is an appropriate loss function, e.g., capturing the distance between matrices, and the constraint involving $\Gamma(\cdot)$ asks that H must capture the Hamming distances between the examples in the (embedded) binary space.

Let us now define Γ by writing H as a function of X. This can be expressed as $H_{ij} = \sum(\mathbf{x}_{i-} \oplus \mathbf{x}_{j-})$ where $\mathbf{x}_{i-}$ and $\mathbf{x}_{j-}$ are rows of X (i.e., the binary embedding of examples i and j) and $\oplus$ denotes the bitwise XOR operation of two binary vectors. But substituting this format directly into (1) is not very useful. Instead, we can observe that the corresponding XOR operation can be written in quadratic form as

$$H = X(\mathbf{1} - X)^T + (\mathbf{1} - X)X^T, \tag{2}$$

where $\mathbf{1}$ is a matrix of 1s of appropriate size. This formulation, when substituted in (1), unfortunately, does not lead to tractable forms for most choices of $d_f(.)$. But interestingly, as we will see shortly, if the loss function is the *Sum of Square Distances (SSD)* and/or the ℓ_1 distance, then we obtain models with distinct advantages. We focus on these two examples for the loss since they are widely used but our solution extends to arbitrary $\|.\|_p^p$ distances.

3   Minimizing the Sum of Squares Distances

In this section, we first describe how problem (1) can be reformulated as a network flow when the loss function is a sum of squares distance (SSD). After presenting the model, we will give an efficient sequential update strategy.

Let $1_{n \times d}$ denote a matrix of 1s. Let us rewrite (1) to derive an identity for H,

$$H = X(1_{n \times d} - X)^T + (1_{n \times d} - X)X^T \tag{3}$$
$$= -(1_{n \times d} - X)(1_{n \times d} - X)^T - XX^T + d1_{n \times n} = -\bar{X}\bar{X}^T - XX^T + d1_{n \times n}$$

Let $\bar{X}$ denote the term $1_{n \times d} - X$. Immediately, we have that

$$A - H = \bar{X}\bar{X}^T + XX^T - (d1_{n \times n} - A) = \bar{X}\bar{X}^T + XX^T - \bar{A}, \tag{4}$$

where $\bar{A} = d1_{n \times n} - A$. Now, we rewrite problem (1) using the SSD measure,

$$\min_X \|\bar{A} - \bar{X}\bar{X}^T - XX^T\|_2^2 = \min_X \|\bar{A} - \sum_{i=1}^{d}(\mathbf{x}_i \mathbf{x}_i^T + \bar{\mathbf{x}}_i \bar{\mathbf{x}}_i^T)\|_2^2, \tag{5}$$

where $\mathbf{x}_i, \bar{\mathbf{x}}_i$ are the i-th columns of the binary matrices X and $\bar{X}$ respectively. Observe that by definition, we have

$$\mathbf{x}_i + \bar{\mathbf{x}}_i = 1_{n \times 1}, \qquad \mathbf{x}_i^T \bar{\mathbf{x}}_i = 0, \qquad \forall i = 1, \cdots, d. \tag{6}$$

3.1   Bit-by-Bit Network Flow

Solving Problem (5) for all d columns of X concurrently turns out to be difficult. So, we adopt a sequential strategy here — we temporarily fix $d - 1$ columns of the matrix X and update a single column $\mathbf{x}_{\text{iter}}$ at a time. To reduce notational clutter, instead of $\mathbf{x}_{\text{iter}}$, we will drop the subscript and $\mathbf{x}$ will denote the column currently being updated. All other columns will be referred to as $\mathbf{x}_{i|i\neq\text{iter}}$.

To optimize the entries relevant to a single bit iter, we start with (5) and take out terms for all 'frozen' (for this update) entries $i \neq \text{iter}$.

$$\min_{X} \| \bar{A} - \underbrace{\sum_{i=1|i\neq\text{iter}}^{d} (\mathbf{x}_i\mathbf{x}_i^T + \bar{\mathbf{x}}_i\bar{\mathbf{x}}_i^T)}_{G} - (\hat{\mathbf{x}}\hat{\mathbf{x}}^T + \hat{\bar{\mathbf{x}}}\hat{\bar{\mathbf{x}}}^T) \|_2^2.$$

Letting $G = \bar{A} - \sum_{i=1,i\neq\text{iter}}^{d}(\hat{\mathbf{x}}_i\hat{\mathbf{x}}_i^T + \hat{\bar{\mathbf{x}}}_i\hat{\bar{\mathbf{x}}}_i^T)$ is convenient because we can now consider G to be the weight matrix associated with a network (or an undirected graph) of n nodes, i.e., $N = \{v_1, \cdots, v_n\}$ where every entry G_{ij} denotes the weight of the edge from v_i to v_j. Here, we also have that the to-be-updated $\mathbf{x} \in \{0,1\}^n$ and $\bar{\mathbf{x}} = 1_{n\times 1} - \mathbf{x}$. With these definitions, we can formally write down the following subproblem which needs to be solved in any update step,

$$\min \|G - (\mathbf{x}\mathbf{x}^T + \bar{\mathbf{x}}\bar{\mathbf{x}}^T)\|_2^2, \tag{7}$$

A Potential Solution via Minimum Cuts. For given binary $\mathbf{x}$ and $\bar{\mathbf{x}}$, let us define two subsets of nodes as follows.

$$N_1 = \{v_i : x_i = 1\}, \quad \bar{N}_1 = N - N_1 = \{v_i : \bar{x}_i = 1\}.$$

Denote the entry-wise square of the matrix, G as G_{ij}^2. We call $\widehat{G}$ the difference matrix whose elements are defined as $\widehat{G}_{ij} = G_{ij}^2 - (G - 1_{n\times n})_{ij}^2$. By inspection,

$$\mathbf{G}(\mathbf{x}) = \|G - (\mathbf{x}\mathbf{x}^T + \bar{\mathbf{x}}\bar{\mathbf{x}}^T)\|_2^2 \tag{8}$$

$$= \sum_{i,j}(G - 1_{n\times n})_{ij}^2 + 2 \sum_{i\in N_1, j\in \bar{N}_1} \widehat{G}_{ij}. \tag{9}$$

Properties of (9). The identity in (9) has a particularly interesting form. First, note that the first term is constant. Now, if we think of a graph whose edge weights are given by the matrix $\widehat{G}$, then by inspection, we see that the second term precisely minimizes the cut edges of that graph – the resultant partitions induced by the cut are N_1 and $\bar{N}_1$. This means that our objective has reduced to the classic formulation of network flow on graphs. Therefore, solving problem (7) is *equivalent* to finding the minimum cut in a network with a weight matrix $\widehat{G}$ (see footnote). Since the minimum cut problem can be solved effectively in polynomial time [22], we immediately have the following result.

Theorem 1. *Problem* (7) *is poly-time solvable if edge weights are non-negative*[1].

4   Formulating the ℓ_1 Distance Setting

In this section, we will derive an analogous solution scheme when the loss is ℓ_1 distance, natural in various applications. Most steps here will be identical to the SSD setup. However, we will need some additional constraints to derive meaningful solutions for the motivating application, which will require special treatment (to be optimizable combinatorially). Using ℓ_1 loss, analogous to (5),

$$\min_X \|\bar{A} - \bar{X}\bar{X}^T - XX^T\|_1 = \quad \min_X \|\bar{A} - \sum_{i=1}^{d}(\mathbf{x}_i\mathbf{x}_i^T + \bar{\mathbf{x}}_i\bar{\mathbf{x}}_i^T)\|_1, \quad (10)$$

where the constraints in (6) hold, as in the SSD case. As before, to solve problem (10) sequentially, we fix $d-1$ columns of the matrix X and update a single column $\mathbf{x}$ to reduce the objective. Analogous to (7) earlier, this leads to,

$$\min_X \|G - (\mathbf{x}\mathbf{x}^T + \bar{\mathbf{x}}\bar{\mathbf{x}}^T)\|_1, \quad (11)$$

where G is again the weight matrix associated with a network (or an undirected graph) of n nodes ($N = \{v_1, \cdots, v_n\}$), and every entry G_{ij} denotes the weight of the edge from v_i to v_j. Further, $\mathbf{x} \in \{0,1\}^n, \bar{\mathbf{x}} = 1_{n\times 1} - \mathbf{x}$. We next briefly discuss a reformulation as a network flow.

For binary $\mathbf{x}$ and $\bar{\mathbf{x}}$, we define two subsets of nodes as

$$N_1 = \{v_i : x_i = 1\}, \quad \overline{N}_1 = N - N_1 = \{v_i : \bar{x}_i = 1\}.$$

Define $\widetilde{G} = |G| - |G - 1_{n\times n}|$ where $|M|$ denotes the entry-wise absolute value of the matrix. We can easily see that

$$\mathbf{G}(\mathbf{x}) = \|G - (\mathbf{x}\mathbf{x}^T + \bar{\mathbf{x}}\bar{\mathbf{x}}^T)\|_1 \quad = \sum_{i,j} |G - 1_{n\times n}|_{ij} + 2 \sum_{i\in N_1, j\in \overline{N}_1} \widetilde{G}_{ij}. \quad (12)$$

Properties of (12). The properties are analogous to those of (9). Therefore, solving (11) is equivalent to finding the network flow with a weight matrix $\widetilde{G}$. All advantages (and limitations) of the SSD setting extend to the ℓ_1 case as well.

5   Constraints for Balanced Partitions

A network flow formulation for the above model has significant computational benefits. Unfortunately, a disadvantage of the formulation is that it may lead to

---

[1] This requires $G \geq \frac{1}{2}$ entry-wise which can be ensured by a scaling of the input matrix A. However, this scaling is not utilized, since we eventually derive an extended model that generalizes better and needs a QPBO-type solver due to the issues highlighted later in Sect. 5. That formulation is not a min-cut and can handle negative weights.

disproportionate cuts – that is, one partition is small (with only a few nodes), whereas the other partition is large. When the model returns such solutions (for one or more bits), expectedly, it will adversely affect the quality of the resultant hashing. This issue is not specific to our proposal; in minimum cuts based graph partitioning schemes, this behavior has been reported by [23] and others: the so-called "shrinking" bias, i.e., favoring cutting small sets of isolated nodes in the graph. On the other hand, as observed in [3] and other works, a desired property of hashing functions is that ideally each bit has a 50 % chance of being one or zero. This means that, in expectation, our model should return almost size balanced partitions. In other words, we need to regularize our formulation to prefer cuts that are almost size balanced. This is known as the Balanced Cut problem [24]. When formulated via hard constraints, the goal is to ensure that the size of each partition $\geq \beta n$, where $\beta \leq .5$ is a constant and n is a number of nodes in the graph. This problem is NP-hard. While various relaxations exist [25], many are expensive to optimize and difficult to incorporate within our network flow formulation. Our formulation does not have a specific need for a hard size constraint; instead, we ask that the disbalance in the two partition sizes must be penalized as a term in the objective. This leads to a Quadratic Pseudoboolean function (QPB), which can still be solved using network flow.

5.1   Size Regularized Cuts

Let $\mathbf{x} \in \{0, 1\}^n$ be the solution from a bit-level mincut problem. Since there are only two partitions, i.e., $x_i = 0$ or $x_i = 1$, size balance requires that the values of $\sum_{i=1}^n x_i$ and $\sum_{i=1}^n (1 - x_i)$ be close. When normalized, this implies

$$\frac{1}{n}\sum_{i=1}^n x_i \approx \frac{1}{n}\sum_{i=1}^n (1 - x_i) \approx \frac{1}{2}. \tag{13}$$

Let $p = \sum_{i=1}^n x_i$ and $q = \sum_{i=1}^n (1 - x_i)$ where we have $p+q = n$, i.e., each term p (and q) counts the number of nodes in each partition. We can verify that $pq \leq \frac{n^2}{4}$ and this inequality becomes tight only if $p = q$. Therefore, an optimal balance is achieved when pq is maximized or when the value of $p^2 + q^2$ is minimized. This observation yields a reformulated balance regularization term. We see

$$p^2 = \mathbf{x}\mathbf{1}_{n \times n}\mathbf{x}^T, \quad q^2 = (1 - \mathbf{x})\mathbf{1}_{n \times n}(1 - \mathbf{x})^T. \tag{14}$$

So, the size balance regularization can be achieved via minimizing,

$$\mathbf{R}(\mathbf{x}) = \mathbf{x}\mathbf{1}_{n \times n}\mathbf{x}^T + (1 - \mathbf{x})\mathbf{1}_{n \times n}(1 - \mathbf{x})^T$$

Alternatively, via rearranging the above formulation, we can also minimize,

$$\mathbf{R}(\mathbf{x}) = \frac{1}{n^2}\sum_{i=1}^n\sum_{j=1}^n x_i x_j + \frac{1}{n^2}\sum_{i=1}^n\sum_{j=1}^n (1 - x_i)(1 - x_j)$$

$$= \frac{2}{n^2}\sum_{i=1}^n\sum_{j=1}^n x_i x_j - \frac{2}{n}\sum_{i=1}^n x_i + \text{const} \tag{15}$$

5.2   Reparameterization and Graph Construction

Putting together the above expression with the main network flow model, we will solve following model for each bit,

$$\min_{\mathbf{x}} E(\mathbf{x}) = \mathbf{G}(\mathbf{x}) + \alpha \mathbf{R}(\mathbf{x}) \tag{16}$$

where α is the user defined influence of the regularizer.

Properties of (16). The model in (16) is the so-called Quadratic Pseudoboolean form [26–28], which consists of quadratic and linear terms. Functions of this form can be solved as a network flow model on a specially constructed graph. We will shortly discuss the specifics of graph construction for this task. We will represent each variable x_i as a pair of literals, y_i and $\bar{y}_i$ where $\bar{y}_i$ will represent $1 - x_i$. This pair of literals will correspond to a pair of nodes in a to-be-constructed graph $\mathcal{G}$. Edges will be added to $\mathcal{G}$ based on various terms in the corresponding QPB, to be discussed shortly. The partition computed on $\mathcal{G}$ will determine the assignments of variables x_i to 1 (or 0). Depending on how the nodes in $\mathcal{G}$ for a pair of literals y_i and $\bar{y}_i$ are partitioned, we will either get "persistent" integral 0/1 solutions for x_i (provably consistent with the optimal) or have $\frac{1}{2}$ (half integral) values assigned to x_i which will need additional rounding to obtain a $\{0, 1\}$ solution. This is the reason QPB solution are considered *partially optimal* solutions — i.e., entries in the solution which are integral are known to be optimal.

Reparameterization. Before describing the construction of $\mathcal{G}$, we will reparameterize the coefficients in our objective as a vector $\mathbf{\Phi}$. More specifically, we will rewrite the energy by collecting the unary and pairwise costs in (16) as the coefficients of the linear and quadratic variables, denoted by Φ_i and Φ_{ij} respectively. The unary cost is set as $\Phi_i = -\frac{2\alpha}{n}$. Other unary functions can also be included here for stronger guidance. Each pairwise cost can be attributed to one of two possible sources. First, a pair of nodes (x_i and x_j) which if assigned to *different* partitions in a minimum cut will incur a cost based on the relevant entry in $\widehat{G}$ or $\widetilde{G}$ – corresponds to $\mathbf{G}(\mathbf{x})$ in (16). Second, a pair of nodes where both x_i and x_j is equal to 1 will incur a cost $\frac{2\alpha}{n^2}$ – this corresponds to $\mathbf{R}(\mathbf{x})$ in (16).

Therefore, the definition of *pairwise* costs include the following two scenarios:

$$\Phi_{ij} = \begin{cases} \widehat{G}_{ij} \text{ or } \widetilde{G}_{ij} & \text{if } x_i \neq x_j \\ \frac{2\alpha}{n^2} & \text{if } x_i = x_j = 1 \end{cases} \tag{17}$$

Graph Construction. With the reparameterization given as $\mathbf{\Phi} = [\Phi_j \quad \Phi_{ij}]^T$ done, we can now mechanically follow the recipe in [26, 29] to construct a graph $\mathcal{G} = \{V_{\mathcal{G}}, E_{\mathcal{G}}\}$ (briefly summarized below). For each variable x_i, we introduce two nodes, ρ_i and $\bar{\rho}_i$ in $V_{\mathcal{G}}$ (corresponding to literals y_i and $\bar{y}_i$). Hence, the size of the graph is $|V_{\mathcal{G}}| = 2n$. We also have two special nodes s and t which denote the source and sink resp. We connect each node in $V_{\mathcal{G}}$ to the source or the sink based on the unary costs, assuming that the source (and sink) partitions correspond to 1 (and 0). The source is connected to the node ρ_i with weight, $-\frac{1\alpha}{n}$ whereas $\bar{\rho}_i$ is connected to the sink with the same weight.

Edges between node pairs in $V_{\mathcal{G}}$ (except source and sink) give pairwise terms of the energy. These edge weights, also given in Table 1, give all possible relationships of pairwise nodes required.

Table 1. Illustration of edge weights introduced in the graph $\mathcal{G}$

Type of edges in $E_{\mathcal{G}}$	Weight of edge
$(\rho_i \to \rho_j), (\bar{\rho}_j \to \bar{\rho}_i)$	$\frac{1}{2}\widehat{G}_{ij}$ or $\frac{1}{2}\widetilde{G}_{ij}$
$(\rho_j \to \rho_i), (\bar{\rho}_i \to \bar{\rho}_j)$	$\frac{1}{2}\widehat{G}_{ij}$ or $\frac{1}{2}\widetilde{G}_{ij}$
$(\bar{\rho}_j \to \rho_i), (\bar{\rho}_i \to \rho_j)$	$\frac{2\alpha}{n^2}$

A maximum flow/minimum cut procedure on this graph provides a solution to our problem. After the cut is obtained, each node is connected either to the source set or to the sink set. We can obtain a final solution (i.e., 0 or 1 assignment) as,

$$x_j = \begin{cases} 0 \text{ if } v_j \in s, \bar{v}_j \in t \\ 1 \text{ if } v_j \in t, \bar{v}_j \in s \\ \frac{1}{2} \text{ otherwise} \end{cases} \quad (18)$$

The $\frac{1}{2}$ values are then rounded to $\{0, 1\}$.

5.3   Parameter Selection

We now discuss how to choose a suitable α to ensure that the solution to Problem (16) or its associated minimum cut problem is well-balanced. Recall that for every fixed α, Problem (16) is polynomial time solvable. Given an α, let $\mathbf{x}^*(\alpha)$ denote the optimal solution of Problem (16), and let $\phi(\alpha) = \mathbf{R}(\mathbf{x}^*(\alpha))$ be the function value of $\mathbf{R}(\mathbf{x})$ at the optimal solution. We have

Theorem 2. *The function $\phi(\alpha)$ is decreasing in the sense*

$$(\alpha_1 - \alpha_2)(\phi(\alpha_1) - \phi(\alpha_2)) \leq 0, \quad \forall \alpha_1 \neq \alpha_2.$$

Proof. From optimality conditions of Problem (16) we have

$$\mathbf{G}(\mathbf{x}^*(\alpha_1)) + \alpha_1 \mathbf{R}(\mathbf{x}^*(\alpha_1)) \leq \mathbf{G}(\mathbf{x}^*(\alpha_2)) + \alpha_1 \mathbf{R}(\mathbf{x}^*(\alpha_2));$$
$$\mathbf{G}(\mathbf{x}^*(\alpha_2)) + \alpha_2 \mathbf{R}(\mathbf{x}^*(\alpha_2)) \leq \mathbf{G}(\mathbf{x}^*(\alpha_1)) + \alpha_2 \mathbf{R}(\mathbf{x}^*(\alpha_1)).$$

Adding the above two inequalities together, we obtain

$$\alpha_1 \mathbf{R}(\mathbf{x}^*(\alpha_1)) + \alpha_2 \mathbf{R}(\mathbf{x}^*(\alpha_2)) \leq \alpha_1 \mathbf{R}(\mathbf{x}^*(\alpha_2)) + \alpha_2 \mathbf{R}(\mathbf{x}^*(\alpha_1));$$

which implies

$$(\alpha_1 - \alpha_2)(\mathbf{R}(\mathbf{x}^*(\alpha_1)) - \mathbf{R}(\mathbf{x}^*(\alpha_2))) = (\alpha_1 - \alpha_2)(\phi(\alpha_1) - \phi(\alpha_2)) \leq 0.$$

This completes the proof.

The above theorem is interesting in that it suggests that a higher value of α can only improve the balance criteria $\mathbf{R}(\mathbf{x})$. For sufficiently large penalty parameter $\alpha > 0$, the second term $\alpha \mathbf{R}(\mathbf{x})$ in the objective dominates $\mathbf{G}(x)$. Therefore, we can expect that for sufficiently large α, the optimal solution $x^*(\alpha)$ of (16) will be very close to the optimal solution (denoted by $\mathbf{x}^*$) of the following problem $\min \mathbf{R}(\mathbf{x})$ which has a perfect balance. However, for computational purposes, we do not continue optimizing the parameter value α, but are only interested in finding a suitable parameter α such that the solution of (16) meets a pre-specified balance requirement $\mathcal{N}$. This leads us to the simple algorithm in Algorithm 1. The overall algorithm is given in Algorithm 2.

Algorithm 1. Algorithm for $\mathcal{N}$ Balanced Min-Cut

1: **Input:** Graph $\mathcal{G}$, and balance threshold $\mathcal{N}$;
2: Set $k = 0$ and choose a large enough parameter $\alpha_k > 0$;
3: Solve problem (16) with $\alpha = \alpha_k$ and obtain optimal solution $\mathbf{x}(\alpha_k)$;
4: If $R(\mathbf{x}(\alpha_k)) \leq \mathcal{N}$, stop, Output $\mathbf{x}(\alpha_k)$ as final solution.
   Else update $k = k + 1, \alpha_k = 2\alpha_{k-1}$, and go to Step 3.

Algorithm 2. Mincut Hashing

1: **Input:** Similarity matrix A, number of bits d, α
2: Initialize X
3: **for** each node i in $[1, d]$ **do**
4:     Set up $\bar{A}$, G and $\hat{G}$ (or $\tilde{G}$) according to Sec. 3 or 4.
5:     $\mathbf{G} = \hat{G}$ (or $\mathbf{G} = \tilde{G}$)
6:     $\hat{x} = \operatorname{argmin}_x \mathbf{G}(\mathbf{x}) + \alpha \mathbf{R}(\mathbf{x})$ solved as a QPBO (using Alg. 1)
7:     $X(:, i) = \hat{x}$
8: **end for**

5.4   Out of Sample Extensions

When evaluating the hashing scheme on unseen data, we generate d linear classifiers, using the d bits of training code as labels; these classifiers are then used to predict the hash code for the test example. In a departure from existing methods (except [13]), where the separating hyperplanes are learned within the process of hashing itself, our method solves for the code first and then generates the hyperplanes, which are used to determine the codes for unseen test points. Hyperplanes generated in this manner are based on the maximum margin principle, which offers advantages when generating the hash bits for unseen data.

5.5   Time Complexity

The main step in each iteration is to solve the QPBO on a graph with $O(n)$ nodes. This is repeated d times, once for each bit. If the QPBO is solved using a standard algorithm for min-cut/max-flow, the running time is $O(n|E|)$, where E is the number of edges in the graph. However, we use an implementation of QPBO by [29], which was shown to about 700 times faster than other implementations of QPBO [26], even though its worst case time complexity is inferior $(O(n^2|E||C|))$, where $|C|$ is the largest absolute edge capacity in the network. Such implementations of QPBO are routinely used to solve higher order MRF formulations of image segmentation, where the number of nodes in the graphs (number of pixels) are 10^5 or more.

6   Experiments

Baselines and Datasets. We performed a number of experiments to evaluate the efficacy of our proposal, with both loss functions. We compare our methods to nine other approaches for binary hashing, including Locality Sensitive Hashing (LSH) [7], KLSH [11], SH [3], MDSH [12], BRE [4], ITQ [5], Anchor Graph Hashing (1, 2 layer) [13] and Fast Hash [16]. We leave out comparison with DGH [8], since it solves the same problem of partitioning the Laplacian of the Anchor Graph as [13], but uses a different optimization technique. Also, note that Fast Hash can be run both in supervised/unsupervised mode, but since all our comparable methods are unsupervised, we compare only with the unsupervised version. We evaluate the algorithms on a number of machine learning and vision datasets, which vary in size, dimensionality, and number of classes. These include toy datasets where the optimal code is known as well as many other datasets like Nursery, MNIST, Caltech101, LabelMe, PhotoTourism and CIFAR.

Parameters. The distance matrix A is set up as the Euclidean distance between features extracted for pair-wise items in each dataset. For image datasets like CIFAR and Phototourism, we extract HOG features for each image. For machine learning datasets, we use the features provided in the dataset itself. Also, α is set to 0.1 throughout. An initial value of the solution is generated using random hyperplanes similar to LSH.

Design. Broadly, we evaluate two aspects: (i) how well do the set of obtained hash-codes *approximate the original distances*, and (ii) how well do the obtained hash codes *preserve semantic labeling* of the examples. To address the issue of *distance approximation* in (i), we use a two-fold approach: (a) We construct toy datasets, where the ground-truth code (and the optimal objective) is known. So, how well do the eleven algorithms optimize the objective relative to the optimal? (b) We evaluate the goodness of nearest neighbor search in the binary/embedded space. That is, precision of how many neighbors returned by our hash code are "true" neighbors? Next, note that we can quantitatively evaluate the issue in (ii) above because many datasets here have semantic labels for examples, so data points with the same 'labels' are considered "semantic" neighbors as well. For *semantic label experiments*, the data is divided into *training* set which is used to construct the distance matrix on which codes are learned and *test data*, which is used for evaluation only. For datasets where labels are available, we report accuracies of the k nearest Neighbors ($k = 3$) of a given query, w.r.t. the same class labels. This will help us demonstrate whether semantic concepts can be identified using such an approach. These experiments are described next.

6.1 Distance Approximation

Minimization of Objective: We simulate toy datasets where the optimal code is known. To do this, we randomly generate a code(X), and then create a distance matrix A, which is a close estimate (modulo a small error) of the Hamming Distance (H) obtained from X. We repeat this experiment by varying n, d and the magnitude of noise added to the Hamming distance matrix (to obtain A). In some sense, this represents the *ideal* input to the problem (though we may still have multiple binary codes for the same distance matrix). For other comparable methods, which require the affinity matrices, we generate that using the identity

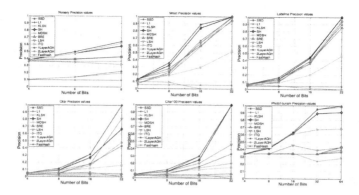

Fig. 1. Precision Values of Nursery, Mnist, Labelme, Cifar, Cifar 100 and Phototourism

Table 2. Ranking results wrt to SSD and ℓ_1 objectives.

Alg on Obj	Rank 1	Rank 2	Rank 3
Alg-ℓ_1 on SSD	85 %	15 %	0
Alg-ℓ_1 on ℓ_1	97 %	3 %	0
Alg-SSD on SSD	60 %	36 %	4 %
Alg-SSD on ℓ_1	57 %	40 %	3 %

$A_{\text{aff}} = \frac{1}{2}(2d\mathbf{1}_{n\times n} - A)$. We run all 11 methods on each of the settings and record rankings of the algorithms in terms of decreasing the objective, for both loss functions. For convenience, below, we will call our actual algorithms Alg-SSD and Alg-ℓ_1 and the distance functions as SSD and ℓ_1 respectively.

Table 2 shows the percentage of times (averaged across 20 realizations), Alg-SSD and Alg-ℓ_1 achieves ranks 1 to 3 (1 being the best, ranks are only shown up to 3 as neither algorithm does worse than third place in any iteration), while minimizing these objectives. The plot shows that Alg-ℓ_1 is the best, minimizing the ℓ_1 objective better than all other algorithms, with a mean weighted rank of 1.1. Alg-SSD is a close second, with a weighted rank of 1.45 across all the runs, compared to other algorithms. These results show that our algorithms do much better than the alternatives in getting close to the global optima.

Generalization to Unseen Data: Instead of looking at faithfully approximating all pair-wise distances, one may attempt to approximate distances of only the nearest neighbors to a query point. To do so, we adopt the following procedure. We divide the data into training and test sets (randomly selected, 1000 points each), and compute distances between training to training and training to test datasets. In order to evaluate how well NN distances are estimated using the hash codes on unseen data, we first define a threshold, such that if the original distance of a pair of points is less than the threshold, they are considered "true neighbors". Given a query and a threshold on the Hamming distance (set to

3), the retrieved items are all examples whose Hamming distance to the query is below this threshold. We compute *precision* as the proportion of retrieved points that are indeed true neighbors. Figure 1 shows the precision as a function of the number of bits for various datasets. In general, our method performs well compared to the baselines.

6.2   Semantic Labels

Datasets such as Nursery, Mnist, Caltech 101 and Cifar (both datasets) have a semantic label associated with each example/image. We present results on these datasets next.

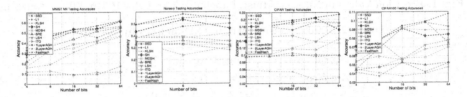

Fig. 2. Semantic Label NN Accuracy for Mnist, Nursery and Cifar, Cifar 100

Generalization to Unseen Data as a Function of Labels: We show several plots of accuracy of k-nearest neighbors having the same label as the query (Fig. 2) for Nursery, Mnist, Cifar and Cifar100 using binary hash codes obtained using a (randomly selected) training set of 2000 and generalized to a much larger testing set (which is typically the rest of the data). Note that some of the datasets (such as Cifar) are harder to classify, therefore the relative percentage accuracy varies depending on the dataset. However, in almost all cases, our models show impressive performance in finding neighbors which have the same class label as the query point.

Effect of Number of Classes in Semantic Label Experiments: We used Caltech101 to evaluate how the number of semantic class labels affect the performance of our algorithm, since the dataset has a large number of classes (up to 101) and a small number of data items per class. Here, we use (the mean of a small set of) pre-computed kernel matrices obtained from UCSD MKL dataset since most of the comparable methods can be run on the kernel matrices (which can be used to define similarities

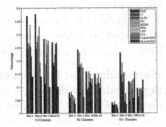

Fig. 3.   UCSD   accuracy results.

also). Whenever actual features were needed for an algorithm, we generated them by implementing the approach in [30]. However, since the features for the test dataset is unavailable, we limit our evaluation to the training dataset only. For the same reason, Fast Hash (which needs features explicitly) could not be applied on this dataset. Figure 3 shows the results on the Caltech 101 dataset, using 10, 50 and 101 classes. The plot shows that in most settings, our methods outperform the other baselines. In addition, increasing the number of classes does affect performance but not drastically.

Running Time: Each iteration of QPBO takes about one second and this is repeated d (number of bits) times. So, given a choice of number of bits, the run time varies from 4 secs to about a minute (when the number of bits is 64). This is comparable to most of the methods tested in this paper, except Spectral Hashing (and MDSH), which do not depend on the number of bits, since their main computational bottleneck is computing the eigen vectors of a matrix once.

7 Discussion

Here we briefly discuss some issues related to our algorithm.

Size of Training Data. We performed limited experiments to see if increasing the size of the training set improves generalization performance but found that in general, the relative improvement saturates pretty quickly. Therefore, a moderate size training set (if chosen randomly) is enough to ensure good generalization. Similar training sizes have also been used in [11].

Rounding of Half Integral Variables in QPBO. In our case, we randomly round the $\frac{1}{2}$ variables to zero or one. Generally, this happens to fewer than 20 % of the variables, so it works fairly well in practice. If in the worst case, a large number of variables have half-integral solutions, there is a mature body of work to deal with this effectively. Roof duality [29, 31, 32] are specifically addresses this issue and can be used though we did not find it necessary.

Existing Literature. In this paper, we discuss 17 other works on binary hashing which are closely related to the ideas presented here. A more comprehensive (but by no means, exhaustive) list can be found in the survey [33].

8 Conclusion

We present a fully combinatorial algorithm for learning hash codes whose Hamming distance closely approximates a target similarity matrix. In a landscape dominated by continous optimization methods for binary hashing, our algorithms provide a different view point — a maximum flow/minimum cut based method in the unsupervised setting. The implementation is simple and the solutions for each hash code bit is provably partially-optimal. Experimentally, we show that these methods exhibit competitive performance, compared against nine state of the methods on seven different datasets.

Acknowledgments. This research is funded by NIH R01 AG040396, NSF CAREER 1252725, NSF CGV 1219016 and NSF CMMI 1359548 and 1537712.

References

1. Mukherjee, L., Singh, V., Peng, J.: Scale invariant cosegmentation for image groups. In: CVPR (2011)
2. Mukherjee, L., Singh, V., Dyer, C.R.: Half-integrality based algorithms for cosegmentation of images. In: CVPR (2009)
3. Weiss, Y., Torralba, A., Fergus, R.: Spectral hashing. In: NIPS (2008)
4. Kulis, B., Darrell, T.: Learning to hash with binary reconstructive embeddings. In: NIPS (2009)
5. Gong, Y., Lazebnik, S.: Iterative quantization: a procrustean approach to learning binary codes. In: CVPR (2011)
6. Norouzi, M., Fleet, D.M.: Minimal loss hashing for compact binary codes. In: Proceedings of the 28th International Conference on Machine Learning (ICML-11) (2011)
7. Indyk, P., Motwani, R.: Approximate nearest neighbors: towards removing the curse of dimensionality. In: Proceedings of the Thirtieth Annual ACM Symposium on Theory of Computing, STOC 1998, pp. 604–613. ACM, New York (1998)
8. Liu, W., Mu, C., Kumar, S., Chang, S.: Discrete graph hashing. In: NIPS (2014)
9. Salakhutdinov, R., Hinton, G.: Semantic hashing. Int. J. Approximate Reasoning 50(7), 969–978 (2009)
10. Krizhevsky, A., Hinton, G.E.: Using very deep autoencoders for content-based image retrieval. In: ESANN (2011)
11. Kulis, B., Grauman, K.: Kernelized locality-sensitive hashing for scalable image search. In: 2009 IEEE 12th International Conference on Computer Vision, pp. 2130–2137. IEEE (2009)
12. Weiss, Y., Fergus, R., Torralba, A.: Multidimensional spectral hashing. In: Fitzgibbon, A., Lazebnik, S., Perona, P., Sato, Y., Schmid, C. (eds.) ECCV 2012. LNCS, vol. 7576, pp. 340–353. Springer, Heidelberg (2012). doi:10.1007/978-3-642-33715-4_25
13. Liu, W., Wang, J., Kumar, S., Chang, S.: Hashing with graphs. In: ICML (2011)
14. Mukherjee, L., Ravi, S.N., Ithapu, V.K., Holmes, T., Singh, V.: An NMF perspective on binary hashing. In: IEEE International Conference on Computer Vision (ICCV), pp. 4184–4192 (2015)
15. Zhang, D., Wang, J., Cai, D., Lu, J.: Self-taught hashing for fast similarity search. In: SIGIR, pp. 18–25 (2010)
16. Lin, G., Shen, C., Suter, D., van den Hengel, A.: A general two-step approach to learning-based hashing. In: ICCV (2013)
17. Shakhnarovich, G., Viola, P., Darrell, T.: Fast pose estimation with parameter-sensitive hashing. In: ICCV (2003)
18. Neyshabur, B., Srebro, N., Salakhutdinov, R., Makarychev, Y., Yadollahpour, P.: The power of asymmetry in binary hashing. In: NIPS (2013)
19. Ge, T., He, K., Sun, J.: Graph cuts for supervised binary coding. In: Fleet, D., Pajdla, T., Schiele, B., Tuytelaars, T. (eds.) ECCV 2014. LNCS, vol. 8695, pp. 250–264. Springer, Heidelberg (2014). doi:10.1007/978-3-319-10584-0_17
20. Shen, F., Shen, C., Liu, W., Shen, H.T.: Supervised discrete hashing. In: CVPR (2015)
21. Li, H., Liu, W., Ji, H.: Two-stage hashing for fast document retrieval. In: ACL (2014)
22. Stoer, M., Wagner, F.: A simple min-cut algorithm. J. ACM 44(4), 585–591 (1997)

23. Wu, Z., Leahy, R.: An optimal graph theoretic approach to data clustering: theory and its application to image segmentation. IEEE Trans. Pattern Anal. Mach. Intell. **15**(11), 1101–1113 (1993)
24. Andreev, K., Racke, H.: Balanced graph partitioning. Theory Comput. Syst. **39**(6), 929–939 (2006)
25. Chen, Y., Zhang, Y., Ji, X.: Size regularized cut for data clustering. In: Advances in Neural Information Processing Systems, pp. 211–218 (2005)
26. Boros, E., Hammer, P.L.: Pseudo-Boolean optimization. Discrete Appl. Math. **123**(1–3), 155–225 (2002)
27. Kolmogorov, V., Rother, C.: Minimizing nonsubmodular functions with graph cuts-a review. IEEE Trans. Pattern Anal. Mach. Intell. **29**(7), 1274–1279 (2007)
28. Rother, C., Kohli, P., Feng, W., Jia, J.: Minimizing sparse higher order energy functions of discrete variables. In: IEEE Conference on Computer Vision and Pattern Recognition, 2009, CVPR 2009, pp. 1382–1389. IEEE (2009)
29. Rother, C., Kolmogorov, V., Lempitsky, V., Szummer, M.: Optimizing binary MRFs via extended roof duality. In: IEEE Conference on Computer Vision and Pattern Recognition, 2007, CVPR 2007, pp. 1–8. IEEE (2007)
30. Balcan, M.F., Blum, A., Vempala, S.: Kernels as features: on kernels, margins, and low-dimensional mappings. Mach. Learn. **65**(1), 79–94 (2006)
31. Kahl, F., Strandmark, P.: Generalized roof duality for pseudo-boolean optimization. In: 2011 IEEE International Conference on Computer Vision (ICCV), pp. 255–262. IEEE (2011)
32. Kolmogorov, V.: Generalized roof duality and bisubmodular functions. In: Advances in Neural Information Processing Systems, pp. 1144–1152 (2010)
33. Wang, J., Shen, H.T., Zhang, T.: A survey on learning to hash. MSRC Technical Report (2014)

SPICE: Semantic Propositional Image Caption Evaluation

Peter Anderson[1]([⊠]), Basura Fernando[1], Mark Johnson[2], and Stephen Gould[1]

[1] The Australian National University, Canberra, Australia
{peter.anderson,basura.fernando,stephen.gould}@anu.edu.au
[2] Macquarie University, Sydney, Australia
mark.johnson@mq.edu.au

Abstract. There is considerable interest in the task of automatically generating image captions. However, evaluation is challenging. Existing automatic evaluation metrics are primarily sensitive to n-gram overlap, which is neither necessary nor sufficient for the task of simulating human judgment. We hypothesize that semantic propositional content is an important component of human caption evaluation, and propose a new automated caption evaluation metric defined over scene graphs coined *SPICE*. Extensive evaluations across a range of models and datasets indicate that SPICE captures human judgments over model-generated captions better than other automatic metrics (e.g., system-level correlation of 0.88 with human judgments on the MS COCO dataset, versus 0.43 for CIDEr and 0.53 for METEOR). Furthermore, SPICE can answer questions such as *which caption-generator best understands colors?* and *can caption-generators count?*

1 Introduction

Recently there has been considerable interest in joint visual and linguistic problems, such as the task of automatically generating image captions [1,2]. Interest has been driven in part by the development of new and larger benchmark datasets such as Flickr 8K [3], Flickr 30K [4] and MS COCO [5]. However, while new datasets often spur considerable innovation—as has been the case with the MS COCO Captioning Challenge [6]—benchmark datasets also require fast, accurate and inexpensive evaluation metrics to encourage rapid progress. Unfortunately, existing metrics have proven to be inadequate substitutes for human judgment in the task of evaluating image captions [3,7,8]. As such, there is an urgent need to develop new automated evaluation metrics for this task [8,9]. In this paper, we present a novel automatic image caption evaluation metric that measures the quality of generated captions by analyzing their semantic content. Our method closely resembles human judgment while offering the additional advantage that the performance of any model can be analyzed in greater detail than with other automated metrics.

One of the problems with using metrics such as Bleu [10], ROUGE [11], CIDEr [12] or METEOR [13] to evaluate captions, is that these metrics are

© Springer International Publishing AG 2016
B. Leibe et al. (Eds.): ECCV 2016, Part V, LNCS 9909, pp. 382–398, 2016.
DOI: 10.1007/978-3-319-46454-1_24

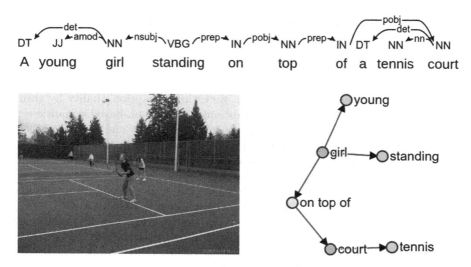

Fig. 1. Illustrates our method's main principle which uses semantic propositional content to assess the quality of image captions. Reference and candidate captions are mapped through dependency parse trees (top) to semantic *scene graphs* (right)— encoding the objects (red), attributes (green), and relations (blue) present. Caption quality is determined using an F-score calculated over tuples in the candidate and reference scene graphs (Color figure online)

primarily sensitive to n-gram overlap. However, *n-gram overlap is neither necessary nor sufficient for two sentences to convey the same meaning* [14].

To illustrate the limitations of n-gram comparisons, consider the following two captions (a,b) from the MS COCO dataset:

(a) A young girl *standing on top of a* tennis court.
(b) A giraffe *standing on top of a* green field.

The captions describe two very different images. However, comparing these captions using any of the previously mentioned n-gram metrics produces a high similarity score due to the presence of the long 5-gram phrase *'standing on top of a'* in both captions. Now consider the captions (c,d) obtained from the same image:

(c) A shiny metal pot filled with some diced veggies.
(d) The pan on the stove has chopped vegetables in it.

These captions convey almost the same meaning, but exhibit low n-gram similarity as they have no words in common.

To overcome the limitations of existing n-gram based automatic evaluation metrics, in this work we hypothesize that *semantic propositional content is an important component of human caption evaluation*. That is, given an image with the caption 'A young girl standing on top of a tennis court', we expect that a human evaluator might consider the truth value of each of the semantic propositions contained therein—such as (1) there is a girl, (2) girl is young, (3) girl is standing, (4) there is a court, (5) court is tennis, and (6) girl is on top of court. If each of these propositions is clearly and obviously supported by the image, we would expect the caption to be considered acceptable, and scored accordingly.

Taking this main idea as motivation, we estimate caption quality by transforming both candidate and reference captions into a graph-based semantic representation called a *scene graph*. The scene graph explicitly encodes the objects, attributes and relationships found in image captions, abstracting away most of the lexical and syntactic idiosyncrasies of natural language in the process. Recent work has demonstrated scene graphs to be a highly effective representation for performing complex image retrieval queries [15,16], and we demonstrate similar advantages when using this representation for caption evaluation.

To parse an image caption into a scene graph, we use a two-stage approach similar to previous works [16–18]. In the first stage, syntactic dependencies between words in the caption are established using a dependency parser [19] pre-trained on a large dataset. An example of the resulting dependency syntax tree, using Universal Dependency relations [20], is shown in Fig. 1 top. In the second stage, we map from dependency trees to scene graphs using a rule-based system [16]. Given candidate and reference scene graphs, our metric computes an F-score defined over the conjunction of logical tuples representing semantic propositions in the scene graph (e.g., Fig. 1 right). We dub this approach SPICE for *Semantic Propositional Image Caption Evaluation*.

Using a range of datasets and human evaluations, we show that SPICE outperforms existing n-gram metrics in terms of agreement with human evaluations of model-generated captions, while offering scope for further improvements to the extent that semantic parsing techniques continue to improve. We make code available from the project page[1]. Our main contributions are:

1. We propose SPICE, a principled metric for automatic image caption evaluation that compares semantic propositional content;
2. We show that SPICE outperforms metrics Bleu, METEOR, ROUGE-L and CIDEr in terms of agreement with human evaluations; and
3. We demonstrate that SPICE performance can be decomposed to answer questions such as 'which caption-generator best understands colors?' and 'can caption generators count?'

2   Background and Related Work

2.1   Caption Evaluation Metrics

There is a considerable amount of work dedicated to the development of metrics that can be used for automatic evaluation of image captions. Typically, these metrics are posed as similarity measures that compare a candidate sentence to

---

[1] http://panderson.me/spice.

a set of reference or ground-truth sentences. Most of the metrics in common use for caption evaluation are based on n-gram matching. Bleu [10] is a modified precision metric with a sentence-brevity penalty, calculated as a weighted geometric mean over different length n-grams. METEOR [13] uses exact, stem, synonym and paraphrase matches between n-grams to align sentences, before computing a weighted F-score with an alignment fragmentation penalty. ROUGE [11] is a package of a measures for automatic evaluation of text summaries using F-measures. CIDEr [12] applies term frequency-inverse document frequency (tf-idf) weights to n-grams in the candidate and reference sentences, which are then compared by summing their cosine similarity across n-grams. With the exception of CIDEr, these methods were originally developed for the evaluation of text summaries or machine translations (MT), and were subsequently adopted for image caption evaluation.

Several studies have analyzed the performance of n-gram metrics when used for image caption evaluation, by measuring correlation with human judgments of caption quality. On the PASCAL 1K dataset, Bleu-1 was found to exhibit weak or no correlation (Pearson's r of -0.17 and 0.05) [7]. Using the Flickr 8K [3] dataset, METEOR exhibited moderate correlation (Spearman's ρ of 0.524) outperforming ROUGE SU-4 (0.435), Bleu-smoothed (0.429) and Bleu-1 (0.345) [8]. Using the PASCAL-50S and ABSTRACT-50S datasets, CIDEr and METEOR were found to have greater agreement with human consensus than Bleu and ROUGE [12].

Within the context of automatic MT evaluation, a number of papers have proposed the use of shallow-semantic information such as semantic role labels (SRLs) [14]. In the MEANT metric [21], SRLs are used to try to capture the basic event structure of sentences – 'who did what to whom, when, where and why' [22]. Using this approach, sentence similarity is calculated by first matching semantic frames across sentences by starting with the verbs at their head. However, this approach does not easily transfer to image caption evaluation, as verbs are frequently absent from image captions or not meaningful – e.g. 'a very tall building with a train *sitting* next to it' – and this can de-rail the matching process. Our work differs from these approaches as we represent sentences using scene graphs, which allow for noun / object matching between captions. Conceptually, the closest work to ours is probably the bag of aggregated semantic tuples (BAST) metric [23] for image captions. However, this work required the collection of a purpose-built dataset in order to learn to identify Semantic Tuples, and the proposed metric was not evaluated against human judgments or existing metrics.

2.2 Semantic Graphs

Scene graphs, or similar semantic structures, have been used in a number of recent works within the context of image and video retrieval systems to improve performance on complex queries [15,16,18]. Several of these papers have demonstrated that semantic graphs can be parsed from natural language descriptions [16,18]. The task of transforming a sentence into its meaning representation has also received considerable attention within the computational linguistics community. Recent work has proposed a common framework for semantic graphs called an abstract meaning representation (AMR) [24], for which a number of parsers [17,25,26] and the Smatch evaluation metric [27] have been developed. However, in initial experiments, we found that AMR representations using Smatch similarity performed poorly as image caption representations. Regardless of the representation used, the use of dependency trees as the starting point for parsing semantic graphs appears to be a common theme [16–18].

3   SPICE Metric

Given a candidate caption c and a set of reference captions $S = \{s_1, \ldots, s_m\}$ associated with an image, our goal is to compute a score that captures the similarity between c and S. For the purposes of caption evaluation the image is disregarded, posing caption evaluation as a purely linguistic task similar to machine translation (MT) evaluation. However, because we exploit the semantic structure of scene descriptions and give primacy to nouns, our approach is better suited to evaluating computer generated image captions.

First, we transform both candidate caption and reference captions into an intermediate representation that encodes semantic propositional content. While we are aware that there are other components of linguistic meaning—such as figure-ground relationships—that are almost certainly relevant to caption quality, in this work we focus exclusively on *semantic meaning*. Our choice of semantic representation is the *scene graph*, a general structure consistent with several existing vision datasets [15,16,28] and the recently released Visual Genome dataset [29]. The scene graph of candidate caption c is denoted by $G(c)$, and the scene graph for the reference captions S is denoted by $G(S)$, formed as the union of scene graphs $G(s_i)$ for each $s_i \in S$ and combining synonymous object nodes. Next we present the semantic parsing step to generate scene graphs from captions.

3.1   Semantic Parsing—Captions to Scene Graphs

We define the subtask of parsing captions to scene graphs as follows. Given a set of object classes C, a set of relation types R, a set of attribute types A, and a caption c, we parse c to a scene graph:

$$G(c) = \langle O(c), E(c), K(c) \rangle \tag{1}$$

where $O(c) \subseteq C$ is the set of object mentions in c, $E(c) \subseteq O(c) \times R \times O(c)$ is the set of hyper-edges representing relations between objects, and $K(c) \subseteq O(c) \times A$ is the set of attributes associated with objects. Note that in practice, C, R and A are *open-world* sets that are expanded as new object, relation and attribute types are identified, placing no restriction on the types of objects, relation and attributes that can be represented, including 'stuff' nouns such as grass, sky, etc. An example of a parsed scene graph is illustrated in Fig. 2.

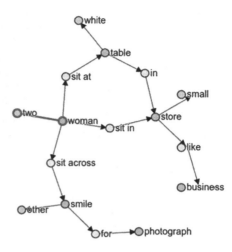

"two women are sitting at a white table"

"two women sit at a table in a small store"

"two women sit across each other at a table smile for the photograph"

"two women sitting in a small store like business"

"two woman are sitting at a table"

Fig. 2. A typical example of a *scene graph* (right) parsed from a set of reference image captions (left)

Our scene graph implementation departs slightly from previous work in image retrieval [15,16], in that we do not represent multiple instances of a single class of object separately in the graph. In previous work, duplication of object instances was necessary to enable scene graphs to be grounded to image regions. In our work, we simply represent object counts as attributes of objects. While this approach does not distinguish collective and distributive readings [16], it simplifies scene graph alignment and ensures that each incorrect numeric modifier is only counted as a single error.

To complete this subtask, we adopt a variant of the rule-based version of the Stanford Scene Graph Parser [16]. A Probabilistic Context-Free Grammar (PCFG) dependency parser [19] is followed by three post-processing steps that simplify quantificational modifiers, resolve pronouns and handle plural nouns. The resulting tree structure is then parsed according to nine simple linguistic rules to extract lemmatized objects, relations and attributes, which together comprise the scene graph. As an example, one of the linguistic rules captures adjectival modifiers, such as the *young* $\xleftarrow{\text{amod}}$ *girl* example from Fig. 1, which results in the object mention 'girl' with attribute 'young'. Full details of the pipeline can be found in the original paper.

SPICE slightly modifies the original parser [16] to better evaluate image captions. First, we drop the plural nouns transformation that duplicates individual nodes of the graph according to the value of their numeric modifier. Instead, numeric modifiers are encoded as object attributes. Second, we add an additional linguistic rule that ensures that nouns will always appear as objects in the scene graph—even if no associated relations can identified—as disconnected graph nodes are easily handled by our semantic proposition F-score calculation.

Notwithstanding the use of the Stanford Scene Graph Parser, our proposed SPICE metric is not tied to this particular parsing pipeline. In fact, it is our hope that ongoing advances in syntactic and semantic parsing will allow SPICE to be further improved in future releases. We also note that since SPICE operates on scene graphs, in principle it could be used to evaluate captions on scene graph datasets [15, 16, 28] that have no reference captions at all. Evaluation of SPICE under these circumstances is left to future work.

3.2 F-Score Calculation

To evaluate the similarity of candidate and reference scene graphs, we view the semantic relations in the scene graph as a conjunction of logical propositions, or tuples. We define the function T that returns logical tuples from a scene graph as:

$$T(G(c)) \triangleq O(c) \cup E(c) \cup K(c) \tag{2}$$

Each tuple contains either one, two or three elements, representing objects, attributes and relations, respectively. For example, the scene graph in Fig. 1 would be represented with the following tuples:

$$\{(girl), (court), (girl, young), (girl, standing)$$
$$(court, tennis), (girl, on\text{-}top\text{-}of, court)\}$$

Viewing the semantic propositions in the scene graph as a set of tuples, we define the binary matching operator $\otimes$ as the function that returns matching tuples in two scene graphs. We then define precision P, recall R, and $SPICE$ as:

$$P(c, S) = \frac{|T(G(c)) \otimes T(G(S))|}{|T(G(c))|} \tag{3}$$

$$R(c, S) = \frac{|T(G(c)) \otimes T(G(S))|}{|T(G(S))|} \tag{4}$$

$$SPICE(c, S) = F_1(c, S) = \frac{2 \cdot P(c, S) \cdot R(c, S)}{P(c, S) + R(c, S)} \tag{5}$$

where for matching tuples, we reuse the wordnet synonym matching approach of METEOR [13], such that tuples are considered to be matched if their lemmatized word forms are equal—allowing terms with different inflectional forms to match—or if they are found in the same wordnet sysnet.

Unlike *Smatch* [27], a recently proposed metric for evaluating AMR parsers that considers multiple alignments of AMR graphs, we make no allowance for partial credit when only one element of a tuple is incorrect. In the domain of image captions, many relations (such as *in* and *on*) are so common they arguably deserve no credit when applied to the wrong objects.

Being an F-score, SPICE is simple to understand, and easily interpretable as it is naturally bounded between 0 and 1. Unlike CIDEr, SPICE does not use cross-dataset statistics—such as corpus word frequencies—and is therefore equally applicable to both small and large datasets.

3.3 Gameability

Whenever the focus of research is reduced to a single benchmark number, there are risks of unintended side-effects [30]. For example, algorithms optimized for performance against a certain metric may produce high scores, while losing sight of the human judgement that the metric was supposed to represent.

SPICE measures how well caption generators recover objects, attributes and the relations between them. A potential concern then, is that the metric could be 'gamed' by generating captions that represent only objects, attributes and relations, while ignoring other important aspects of grammar and syntax. Because SPICE neglects fluency, as with n-gram metrics, it implicitly assuming that captions are well-formed. If this assumption is untrue in a particular application, a fluency metric, such as *surprisal* [31,32], could be included in the evaluation. However, by default we have not included any fluency adjustments as conceptually we favor simpler, more easily interpretable metrics. To model human judgement in a particular task as closely as possible, a carefully tuned ensemble of metrics including SPICE capturing various dimensions of correctness would most likely be the best.

4 Experiments

In this section, we compare SPICE to existing caption evaluation metrics. We study both system-level and caption-level correlation with human judgments. Data for the evaluation is drawn from four datasets collected in previous studies, representing a variety of captioning models. Depending on the dataset, human judgments may consist of either pairwise rankings or graded scores, as described further below.

Our choice of correlation coefficients is consistent with an emerging consensus from the WMT Metrics Shared Task [33,34] for scoring machine translation metrics. To evaluate system-level correlation, we use the Pearson correlation coefficient. Although Pearson's ρ measures linear association, it is smoother than rank-based correlation coefficients when the number of data points is small and systems have scores that are very close together. For caption-level correlation, we evaluate using Kendall's τ rank correlation coefficient, which evaluates the similarity of pairwise rankings. Where human judgments consist of graded scores rather than pairwise rankings, we generate pairwise rankings by comparing scores over all pairs in the dataset. In datasets containing multiple independent judgments over the same caption pairs, we also report inter-human correlation. We include further analysis, including additional results, examples and failure cases on our project page[2].

---

[2] http://panderson.me/spice.

Table 1. System-level Pearson's ρ correlation between evaluation metrics and human judgments for the 15 competition entries plus human captions in the 2015 COCO Captioning Challenge [6]. SPICE more accurately reflects human judgment overall (M1–M2), and across each dimension of quality (M3–M5, representing correctness, detailedness and saliency)

	M1		M2		M3		M4		M5	
	ρ	p-value	ρ	p-value	ρ	p-value	ρ	p-value	ρ	p-value
Bleu-1	0.24	(0.369)	0.29	(0.271)	0.72	(0.002)	−0.54	(0.030)	0.44	(0.091)
Bleu-4	0.05	(0.862)	0.10	(0.703)	0.58	(0.018)	−0.63	(0.010)	0.30	(0.265)
ROUGE-L	0.15	(0.590)	0.20	(0.469)	0.65	(0.006)	−0.55	(0.030)	0.38	(0.142)
METEOR	0.53	(0.036)	0.57	(0.022)	0.86	(0.000)	−0.10	(0.710)	0.74	(0.001)
CIDEr	0.43	(0.097)	0.47	(0.070)	0.81	(0.000)	−0.21	(0.430)	0.65	(0.007)
SPICE-exact	0.84	(0.000)	0.86	(0.000)	0.90	(0.000)	0.39	(0.000)	0.95	(0.000)
SPICE	**0.88**	(0.000)	**0.89**	(0.000)	**0.89**	(0.000)	**0.46**	(0.070)	**0.97**	(0.000)
M1	Percentage of captions evaluated as better or equal to human caption.									
M2	Percentage of captions that pass the Turing Test.									
M3	Average correctness of the captions on a scale 1–5 (incorrect - correct).									
M4	Average detail of the captions from 1–5 (lacking details - very detailed).									
M5	Percentage of captions that are similar to human description.									

4.1 Datasets

Microsoft COCO 2014. The COCO dataset [6] consists of 123,293 images, split into an 82,783 image training set and a 40,504 image validation set. An additional 40,775 images are held out for testing. Images are annotated with five human-generated captions (C5 data), although 5,000 randomly selected test images have 40 captions each (C40 data).

COCO human judgements were collected using Amazon Mechanical Turk (AMT) for the purpose of evaluating submissions to the 2015 COCO Captioning Challenge [6]. A total of 255,000 human judgments were collected, representing three independent answers to five different questions that were posed in relation to the 15 competition entries, plus human and random entries (17 total). The questions capture the dimensions of overall caption quality (M1 - M2), correctness (M3), detailedness (M4), and saliency (M5), as detailed in Table 1. For pairwise rankings (M1, M2 and M5), each entry was evaluated using the same subset of 1000 images from the C40 test set. All AMT evaluators consisted of US located native speakers, white-listed from previous work. Metric scores for competition entries were obtained from the COCO organizers, using our code to calculate SPICE. The SPICE methodology was fixed before evaluating on COCO. At no stage were we given access to the COCO test captions.

Flickr 8K. The Flickr 8K dataset [3] contains 8,092 images annotated with five human-generated reference captions each. The images were manually selected to focus mainly on people and animals performing actions. The dataset also contains graded human quality scores for 5,822 captions, with scores ranging from 1 ('the selected caption is unrelated to the image') to 4 ('the selected caption describes the image without any errors'). Each caption was scored by three expert human evaluators sourced from a pool of native speakers. All evaluated captions were sourced from the dataset, but association to images was performed using an image retrieval system. In our evaluation we exclude 158 correct image-caption pairs where the candidate caption appears in the reference set. This reduces all correlation scores but does not disproportionately impact any metric.

Composite Dataset. We refer to an additional dataset of 11,985 human judgments over Flickr 8K, Flickr 30K [4] and COCO captions as the composite dataset [35]. In this dataset, captions were scored using AMT on a graded correctness scale from 1 ('The description has no relevance to the image') to 5 ('The description relates perfectly to the image'). Candidate captions were sourced from the human reference captions and two recent captioning models [35, 36].

PASCAL-50S. To create the PASCAL-50S dataset [12], 1,000 images from the UIUC PASCAL Sentence Dataset [37]—originally containing five captions per image—were annotated with 50 captions each using AMT. The selected images represent 20 classes including people, animals, vehicles and household objects.

The dataset also includes human judgments over 4,000 candidate sentence pairs. However, unlike in previous studies, AMT workers were not asked to evaluate captions against images. Instead, they were asked to evaluate caption triples by identifying 'Which of the sentences, B or C, is more similar to sentence A?', where sentence A is a reference caption, and B and C are candidates. If reference captions vary in quality, this approach may inject more noise into the evaluation process, however the differences between this approach and the previous approaches to human evaluations have not been studied. For each candidate sentence pair (B,C) evaluations were collected against 48 of the 50 possible reference captions. Candidate sentence pairs were generated from both human and model captions, paired in four ways: human-correct (HC), human-incorrect (HI), human-model (HM), and model-model (MM).

4.2 System-Level Correlation

In Table 1 we report system-level correlations between metrics and human judgments over entries in the 2015 COCO Captioning Challenge [6]. Each entry is evaluated using the same 1000 image subset of the COCO C40 test set. SPICE significantly outperforms existing metrics, reaching a correlation coefficient of 0.88 with human quality judgments (M1), compared to 0.43 for CIDEr and 0.53 for METEOR. As illustrated in Table 1, SPICE more accurately reflects human judgment overall (M1 - M2), and across each dimension of quality (M3 - M5, representing correctness, detailedness and saliency). Interestingly, only SPICE

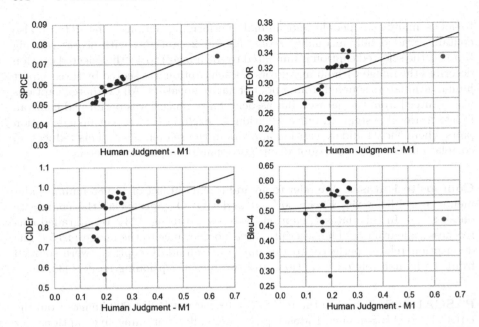

Fig. 3. Evaluation metrics vs. human judgments for the 15 entries in the 2015 COCO Captioning Challenge. Each data point represents a single model with human-generated captions marked in red. Only SPICE scores human-generated captions significantly higher than challenge entries, which is consistent with human judgment (Color figure online)

rewards caption detail (M4). Bleu and ROUGE-L appear to penalize detailed-ness, while the results for CIDEr and METEOR are not statistically significant.

As illustrated in Fig. 3, SPICE is the only metric to correctly rank human-generated captions first—CIDEr and METEOR rank human captions 7th and 4th, respectively. SPICE is also the only metric to correctly select the top-5 non-human entries. To help understand the importance of synonym-matching, we also evaluated SPICE using exact-matching only (SPICE-exact in Table 1). Performance degraded only marginally, although we expect synonym-matching to become more important when fewer reference captions are available.

4.3   Color Perception, Counting and Other Questions

Existing n-gram evaluation metrics have little to offer in terms of understanding the relative strengths and weaknesses, or error modes, of various models. However, SPICE has the useful property that it is defined over tuples that are easy to subdivide into meaningful categories. For example, precision, recall and F-scores can be quantified separately for objects, attributes and relations, or analyzed to any arbitrary level of detail by subdividing tuples even further.

To demonstrate this capability, in Table 2 we review the performance of 2015 COCO Captioning Challenge submissions in terms of *color perception,*

Table 2. F-scores by semantic proposition subcategory. SPICE is comprised of object, relation and attribute tuples. Color, count and size are attribute subcategories. Although the best models outperform the human baseline in their use of object color attributes, none of the models exhibits a convincing ability to count

	SPICE	Object	Relation	Attribute	Color	Count	Size
Human [6]	**0.074**	**0.190**	**0.023**	**0.054**	0.055	**0.095**	**0.026**
MSR [38]	0.064	0.176	0.018	0.039	**0.063**	0.033	0.019
Google [39]	0.063	0.173	0.018	0.039	0.060	0.005	0.009
MSR Captivator [40]	0.062	0.174	0.019	0.032	0.054	0.008	0.009
Berkeley LRCN [1]	0.061	0.170	**0.023**	0.026	0.030	0.015	0.010
Montreal/Toronto [2]	0.061	0.171	**0.023**	0.026	0.023	0.002	0.010
m-RNN [41]	0.060	0.170	0.021	0.026	0.038	0.007	0.004
Nearest Neighbor [42]	0.060	0.168	0.022	0.026	0.027	0.014	0.013
m-RNN [43]	0.059	0.170	0.022	0.022	0.031	0.002	0.005
PicSOM	0.057	0.162	0.018	0.027	0.025	0.000	0.012
MIL	0.054	0.157	0.017	0.023	0.036	0.007	0.009
Brno University [44]	0.053	0.144	0.012	0.036	0.055	0.029	0.025
MLBL [45]	0.052	0.152	0.017	0.021	0.015	0.000	0.004
NeuralTalk [36]	0.051	0.153	0.018	0.016	0.013	0.000	0.007
ACVT	0.051	0.152	0.015	0.021	0.019	0.001	0.008
Tsinghua Bigeye	0.046	0.138	0.013	0.017	0.017	0.000	0.009
Random	0.008	0.029	0.000	0.000	0.000	0.004	0.000

counting ability, and understanding of *size attributes* by using word lists to isolate attribute tuples that contain colors, the numbers from one to ten, and size-related adjectives, respectively. This affords us some insight, for example, into whether caption generators actually understand color, and how good they are at counting.

As shown in Table 2, the MSR entry [38] —incorporating specifically trained visual detectors for nouns, verbs and adjectives—exceeds the human F-score baseline for tuples containing color attributes. However, there is less evidence that any of these models have learned to count objects.

4.4 Caption-Level Correlation

In Table 3 we report caption-level correlations between automated metrics and human judgments on Flickr 8K [3] and the composite dataset [35]. At the caption level, SPICE achieves a rank correlation coefficient of 0.45 with Flickr 8K human scores, compared to 0.44 for CIDEr and 0.42 for METEOR. Relative to the correlation between human scores of 0.73, this represents only a modest improvement over existing metrics. However, as reported in Sect. 4.2, SPICE more closely

Table 3. Caption-level Kendall's τ correlation between evaluation metrics and graded human quality scores. At the caption-level SPICE modestly outperforms existing metrics. All p-values (not shown) are less than 0.001

	Flickr 8K [3]	Composite [35]
Bleu-1	0.32	0.26
Bleu-4	0.14	0.18
ROUGE-L	0.32	0.28
METEOR	0.42	0.35
CIDEr	0.44	0.36
SPICE	**0.45**	**0.39**
Inter-human	0.73	-

Table 4. Caption-level classification accuracy of evaluation metrics at matching human judgment on PASCAL-50S with 5 reference captions. SPICE is best at matching human judgments on pairs of model-generated captions (MM). METEOR is best at differentiating human and model captions (HM) and human captions where one is incorrect (HI). Bleu-1 performs best given two correct human captions (HC)

	HC	HI	HM	MM	All
Bleu-1	**64.9**	95.2	90.7	60.1	77.7
Bleu-2	56.6	93.0	87.2	58.0	73.7
ROUGE-L	61.7	95.3	91.7	60.3	77.3
METEOR	64.0	**98.1**	**94.2**	66.8	**80.8**
CIDEr	61.9	98.0	91.0	64.6	78.9
SPICE	63.3	96.3	87.5	**68.2**	78.8

approximates human judgment when aggregated over more captions. Results are similar on the composite dataset, with SPICE achieving a rank correlation coefficient of 0.39, compared to 0.36 for CIDEr and 0.35 for METEOR. As this dataset only includes one score per image-caption pair, inter-human agreement cannot be established.

For consistency with previous evaluations on the PASCAL-50S dataset [12], instead of reporting rank correlations we evaluate on this dataset using accuracy. A metric is considered accurate if it gives an equal or higher score to the caption in each candidate pair most commonly preferred by human evaluators. To help quantify the impact of reference captions on performance, the number of reference captions available to the metrics is varied from 1 to 48. This approach follows the original work on this dataset [12], although our results differ slightly which may be due to randomness in the choice of reference caption subsets, or differences in metric implementations (we use the MS COCO evaluation code).

On PASCAL-50S, there is little difference in overall performance between SPICE, METEOR and CIDEr, as shown in Fig. 4 left. However, of the four

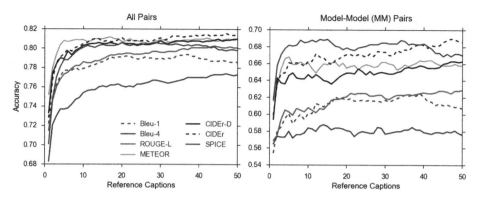

Fig. 4. Pairwise classification accuracy of automated metrics at matching human judgment with 1–50 reference captions

kinds of captions pairs, SPICE performs best in terms of distinguishing between two model-generated captions (MM pairs) as illustrated in Table 4 and Fig. 4 right. This is important as distinguishing better performing algorithms is the primary motivation for this work.

5 Conclusion and Future Work

We introduce SPICE, a novel semantic evaluation metric that measures how effectively image captions recover objects, attributes and the relations between them. Our experiments demonstrate that, on natural image captioning datasets, SPICE captures human judgment over model-generated captions better than existing n-gram metrics such as Bleu, METEOR, ROUGE-L and CIDEr. Nevertheless, we are aware that significant challenges still remain in semantic parsing, and hope that the development of more powerful parsers will underpin further improvements to the metric. In future work we hope to use human annotators to establish an upper bound for how closely SPICE approximates human judgments given perfect semantic parsing. We release our code and hope that our work will help in the development of better captioning models.

Acknowledgements. We are grateful to the COCO Consortium (in particular, Matteo R. Ronchi, Tsung-Yi Lin, Yin Cui and Piotr Dollár) for agreeing to run our SPICE code against entries in the 2015 COCO Captioning Challenge. We would also like to thank Sebastian Schuster for sharing the Stanford Scene Graph Parser code in advance of public release, Ramakrishna Vedantam and Somak Aditya for sharing their human caption judgments, and Kelvin Xu, Jacob Devlin and Qi Wu for providing model-generated captions for evaluation. This work was funded in part by the Australian Centre for Robotic Vision.

References

1. Donahue, J., Hendricks, L.A., Guadarrama, S., Rohrbach, M., Venugopalan, S., Saenko, K., Darrell, T.: Long-term recurrent convolutional networks for visual recognition and description. In: CVPR (2015)
2. Xu, K., Ba, J., Kiros, R., Cho, K., Courville, A.C., Salakhutdinov, R., Zemel, R.S., Bengio, Y.: Show, attend and tell: Neural image caption generation with visual attention (2015). arXiv preprint arXiv:1502.03044
3. Hodosh, M., Young, P., Hockenmaier, J.: Framing image description as a ranking task: data, models and evaluation metrics. JAIR **47**, 853–899 (2013)
4. Young, P., Lai, A., Hodosh, M., Hockenmaier, J.: From image descriptions to visual denotations: new similarity metrics for semantic inference over event descriptions. TACL **2**, 67–78 (2014)
5. Lin, T.-Y., Maire, M., Belongie, S., Hays, J., Perona, P., Ramanan, D., Dollár, P., Zitnick, C.L.: Microsoft COCO: common objects in context. In: Fleet, D., Pajdla, T., Schiele, B., Tuytelaars, T. (eds.) ECCV 2014, Part V. LNCS, vol. 8693, pp. 740–755. Springer, Heidelberg (2014)
6. Chen, X., Fang, H., Lin, T.Y., Vedantam, R., Gupta, S., Dollar, P., Zitnick, C.L.: Microsoft COCO captions: Data collection and evaluation server (2015). arXiv preprint arXiv:1504.00325
7. Kulkarni, G., Premraj, V., Ordonez, V., Dhar, S., Li, S., Choi, Y., Berg, A.C., Berg, T.L.: Babytalk: understanding and generating simple image descriptions. PAMI **35**(12), 2891–2903 (2013)
8. Elliott, D., Keller, F.: Comparing automatic evaluation measures for image description. In: ACL, pp. 452–457 (2014)
9. Bernardi, R., Cakici, R., Elliott, D., Erdem, A., Erdem, E., Ikizler-Cinbis, N., Keller, F., Muscat, A., Plank, B.: Automatic description generation from images: a survey of models, datasets, and evaluation measures. JAIR **55**, 409–442 (2016)
10. Papineni, K., Roukos, S., Ward, T., Zhu, W.: Bleu: a method for automatic evaluation of machine translation. In: ACL (2002)
11. Lin, C.Y.: ROUGE: a package for automatic evaluation of summaries. In: ACL Workshop, pp. 25–26 (2004)
12. Vedantam, R., Zitnick, C.L., Parikh, D.: CIDEr: consensus-based image description evaluation. In: CVPR (2015)
13. Denkowski, M., Lavie, A.: Meteor universal: language specific translation evaluation for any target language. In: EACL 2014 Workshop on Statistical Machine Translation (2014)
14. Giménez, J., Màrquez, L.: Linguistic features for automatic evaluation of heterogenous MT systems. In: ACL Second Workshop on Statistical Machine Translation
15. Johnson, J., Krishna, R., Stark, M., Li, L.J., Shamma, D.A., Bernstein, M.S., Fei-Fei, L.: Image retrieval using scene graphs. In: CVPR (2015)
16. Schuster, S., Krishna, R., Chang, A., Fei-Fei, L., Manning, C.D.: Generating semantically precise scene graphs from textual descriptions for improved image retrieval. In: EMNLP 4th Workshop on Vision and Language (2015)
17. Wang, C., Xue, N., Pradhan, S.: A transition-based algorithm for AMR parsing. In: HLT-NAACL (2015)
18. Lin, D., Fidler, S., Kong, C., Urtasun, R.: Visual semantic search: retrieving videos via complex textual queries. In: CVPR (2014)
19. Klein, D., Manning, C.D.: Accurate unlexicalized parsing. In: ACL (2003)

20. De Marneffe, M.C., Dozat, T., Silveira, N., Haverinen, K., Ginter, F., Nivre, J., Manning, C.D.: Universal stanford dependencies: a cross-linguistic typology. LREC **14**, 4585–4592 (2014)
21. Lo, C.k., Tumuluru, A.K., Wu, D.: Fully automatic semantic MT evaluation. In: ACL Seventh Workshop on Statistical Machine Translation (2012)
22. Pradhan, S.S., Ward, W., Hacioglu, K., Martin, J.H., Jurafsky, D.: Shallow semantic parsing using support vector machines. In: HLT-NAACL, pp. 233–240 (2004)
23. Ellebracht, L., Ramisa, A., Swaroop, P., Cordero, J., Moreno-Noguer, F., Quattoni, A.: Semantic tuples for evaluation of image sentence generation. In: EMNLP 4th Workshop on Vision and Language (2015)
24. Banarescu, L., Bonial, C., Cai, S., Georgescu, M., Griffitt, K., Hermjakob, U., Knight, K., Koehn, P., Palmer, M., Schneider, N.: Abstract meaning representation (AMR) 1.0 specification. In: EMNLP, pp. 1533–1544 (2012)
25. Flanigan, J., Thomson, S., Carbonell, J., Dyer, C., Smith, N.A.: A discriminative graph-based parser for the abstract meaning representation. In: ACL (2014)
26. Werling, K., Angeli, G., Manning, C.: Robust subgraph generation improves abstract meaning representation parsing. In: ACL (2015)
27. Cai, S., Knight, K.: Smatch: an evaluation metric for semantic feature structures. In: ACL (2), pp. 748–752 (2013)
28. Plummer, B.A., Wang, L., Cervantes, C.M., Caicedo, J.C., Hockenmaier, J., Lazebnik, S.: Flickr30k entities: collecting region-to-phrase correspondences for richer image-to-sentence models. In: CVPR, pp. 2641–2649 (2015)
29. Krishna, R., Zhu, Y., Groth, O., Johnson, J., Hata, K., Kravitz, J., Chen, S., Kalantidis, Y., Li, L.J., Shamma, D.A., Bernstein, M., Fei-Fei, L.: Visual genome: Connecting language and vision using crowdsourced dense image annotations (2016). arXiv preprint arXiv:1602.07332
30. Torralba, A., Efros, A.A.: Unbiased look at dataset bias. In: CVPR, June 2011
31. Hale, J.: A probabilistic earley parser as a psycholinguistic model. In: NAACL, pp. 1–8 (2001)
32. Levy, R.: Expectation-based syntactic comprehension. Cognition **106**(3), 1126–1177 (2008)
33. Stanojević, M., Kamran, A., Koehn, P., Bojar, O.: Results of the WMT15 metrics shared task. In: ACL Tenth Workshop on Statistical Machine Translation, pp. 256–273 (2015)
34. Machacek, M., Bojar, O.: Results of the WMT14 metrics shared task. In: ACL Ninth Workshop on Statistical Machine Translation, pp. 293–301 (2014)
35. Aditya, S., Yang, Y., Baral, C., Fermuller, C., Aloimonos, Y.: From images to sentences through scene description graphs using commonsense reasoning and knowledge (2015). arXiv preprint arXiv:1511.03292
36. Karpathy, A., Fei-Fei, L.: Deep visual-semantic alignments for generating image descriptions. In: CVPR (2015)
37. Rashtchian, C., Young, P., Hodosh, M., Hockenmaier, J.: Collecting image annotations using Amazon's Mechanical Turk. In: HLT-NAACL, pp. 139–147 (2010)
38. Fang, H., Gupta, S., Iandola, F.N., Srivastava, R., Deng, L., Dollar, P., Gao, J., He, X., Mitchell, M., Platt, J.C., Zitnick, C.L., Zweig, G.: From captions to visual concepts and back. In: CVPR (2015)
39. Vinyals, O., Toshev, A., Bengio, S., Erhan, D.: Show and tell: a neural image caption generator. In: CVPR (2015)
40. Devlin, J., Cheng, H., Fang, H., Gupta, S., Deng, L., He, X., Zweig, G., Mitchell, M.: Language models for image captioning: The quirks and what works (2015). arXiv preprint arXiv:1505.01809

41. Mao, J., Wei, X., Yang, Y., Wang, J., Huang, Z., Yuille, A.L.: Learning like a child: fast novel visual concept learning from sentence descriptions of images. In: CVPR, pp. 2533–2541 (2015)
42. Devlin, J., Gupta, S., Girshick, R.B., Mitchell, M., Zitnick, C.L.: Exploring nearest neighbor approaches for image captioning (2015). arXiv preprint arXiv:1505.04467
43. Mao, J., Xu, W., Yang, Y., Wang, J., Huang, Z., Yuille, A.: Deep captioning with multimodal recurrent neural networks (m-rnn) (2014). arXiv preprint arXiv:1412.6632
44. Kolár, M., Hradis, M., Zemcík, P.: Technical report: Image captioning with semantically similar images (2015). arXiv preprint arXiv:1506.03995
45. Kiros, R., Salakhutdinov, R., Zemel, R.S.: Multimodal neural language models. ICML **14**, 595–603 (2014)

Transfer Neural Trees for Heterogeneous Domain Adaptation

Wei-Yu Chen[1,2], Tzu-Ming Harry Hsu[2], Yao-Hung Hubert Tsai[3],
Yu-Chiang Frank Wang[2(✉)], and Ming-Syan Chen[1]

[1] Graduate Institute of Electrical Engineering,
National Taiwan University, Taipei, Taiwan
`wyharveychen@gmail.com, mschen@cc.ee.ntu.edu.tw`
[2] Research Center for Information Technology Innovation,
Academia Sinica, Taipei, Taiwan
`harry19930924@gmail.com, ycwang@citi.sinica.edu.tw`
[3] Department of Machine Learning, Carnegie Mellon University, Pittsburgh, USA
`yaohungt@andrew.cmu.edu`

Abstract. Heterogeneous domain adaptation (HDA) addresses the task of associating data not only across dissimilar domains but also described by different types of features. Inspired by the recent advances of neural networks and deep learning, we propose Transfer Neural Trees (TNT) which jointly solves cross-domain feature mapping, adaptation, and classification in a NN-based architecture. As the prediction layer in TNT, we further propose Transfer Neural Decision Forest (Transfer-NDF), which effectively adapts the neurons in TNT for adaptation by stochastic pruning. Moreover, to address semi-supervised HDA, a unique embedding loss term for preserving prediction and structural consistency between target-domain data is introduced into TNT. Experiments on classification tasks across features, datasets, and modalities successfully verify the effectiveness of our TNT.

Keywords: Transfer learning · Domain adaptation · Neural Decision Forest · Neural network

1 Introduction

Domain adaptation (DA) deals with the learning tasks from data across different domains, which aims to adapt the information (e.g., labeled data) observed from different domains so that the instances in the target domain of interest can be properly described/classified [1]. A large number of computer vision and pattern recognition applications (e.g., cross-domain object recognition [2–5] and cross-language text categorization [6,7]) can be viewed as DA problems.

Electronic supplementary material The online version of this chapter (doi:10.1007/978-3-319-46454-1_25) contains supplementary material, which is available to authorized users.

B. Leibe et al. (Eds.): ECCV 2016, Part V, LNCS 9909, pp. 399–414, 2016.
DOI: 10.1007/978-3-319-46454-1_25

Previously, approaches like [8–13] focus on associating cross-domain data described by the same type of features, which is referred to as *homogeneous* domain adaptation task. On the other hand, *heterogeneous* domain adaptation (HDA) particularly address the task of associating data not only across different domains but also in terms of distinct feature representations [14–24]. To solve the challenging HDA problems, existing approaches typically choose to determine a domain-invariant feature space, or derive a proper feature mapping for transforming cross-domain data for adaptation purposes.

Recent advances in neural networks (NN) and deep learning have shown promising results on a variety of real-world applications, including domain adaptation [10,25–28]. However, most NN-based works for DA only consider homogeneous settings [10,25–27]. While a recent work of [28] applied a NN architecture for associating heterogenous data across domains, cross-domain data correspondence information (i.e., co-occurrence data) is required for learning their NN. This requirement would limit its applicability for real-world HDA problems.

In this paper, we propose *Transfer Neural Trees (TNT)* as a novel NN-based architecture, which can be applied for relating and recognizing heterogeneous cross-domain data. In addition to labeled source and target-domain data, our TNT further observes unlabeled target-domain ones during adaptation, and solves semi-supervised HDA problems with improved performance. Our TNT consists of the layers of feature mapping and prediction. Without observing correspondence information across domains, the former layer is able to derive a domain-invariant intermediate representation, while a novel learner of *Transfer Neural Decision Forest (Transfer-NDF)* is obtained as the latter layer for joint adaptation and classification.

The contributions of our TNT are highlighted as follow:

- We are the first to advance neural network architectures for semi-supervised HDA, without the use of data correspondence information across domains during learning and adaptation.
- By introducing stochastic pruning, our proposed Transfer-NDF as the prediction layer in TNT is able to adapt representative neurons for relating cross-domain data.
- We uniquely advocate an embedding loss in the layer of feature mapping, which preserves the prediction and structural consistency between target-domain instances for learning TNT in a semi-supervised fashion.

2   Related Work

Depending on cross-domain data described by the same/distinct types of features, homogeneous/heterogenous domain adaptation (DA) aims at associating data across domains, with the goal of bridging the knowledge between source and target domains for solving the learning tasks. When it comes to the availability of labeled instances in the target domain, one can solve homogeneous DA under *supervised* [8], *semi-supervised* [9,13], or *unsupervised* settings [10–12].

To eliminate the domain difference, existing DA approaches either derive a domain-invariant feature subspace [8–11] for representing cross-domain data, or learn a transformation for mapping such data [12,13]. A variety of pattern recognition tasks like object classification [11–13], text categorization [10], or speech tagging [8,9] benefit from the recent advances of DA.

When cross-domain data are represented by different types of features, the above techniques cannot be easily extended for solving such heterogeneous domain adaptation (HDA) tasks. With the domain mismatch due to differences in terms of both data distributions and feature dimensions, it is necessary for HDA to at least obtain a limited amount of label information in the target domain, so that the adaptation across heterogeneous domains can be realized. Depending on the availability of labeled/unlabeled target-domain data, HDA approaches can be divided into supervised and semi-supervised ones.

For supervised HDA [14–19], only labeled source and (a limited amount of) target-domain data are presented during training. For example, Shi et al. [14] selected a fixed number of source-domain instances to perform heterogeneous spectral mapping (HeMap) for relating cross-domain data. Kulis et al. [15] proposed asymmetric regularized cross-domain transformation (ARC-t), which maximizes similarities on cross-domain data with identical labels. With the goal of preserving label and structure information, Wang and Mahadevan [16] solved HDA by aligning manifolds (DAMA). Inspired by [8], Duan et al. [17] proposed heterogeneous features augmentation (HFA) to perform common-feature-subspace learning, in which SVM classifiers were simultaneously derived. Hoffman et al. [18] presented a max-margin domain transformation (MMDT) to adapt SVM classifiers across domains. Similarly, Zhou et al. [19] considered a sparse heterogeneous feature representation (SHFR) algorithm, in which predictive structures in target domain were sparse represented by the source ones.

In contrast to supervised HDA, semi-supervised HDA [20–24] allows unlabeled target-domain data to be presented for learning and adaptation. For example, Wu et al. [20] proposed an algorithm of heterogeneous transfer discriminant-analysis of canonical correlations (HTDCC), which optimizes the canonical correlations of between the observed data. Li et al. [21] extended HFA [17] to a semi-supervised version (SHFA), with the purpose of exploiting the prediction information of unlabeled target-domain data during the learning process. By demonstrating a semi-supervised kernel matching for domain adaptation (SSKMDA), Xian and Guo [22] matched the cross-domain kernels while jointly preserving the observed data locality information. They also proposed a semi-supervised co-projection (SCP) in [23], with the objective of minimizing the divergence between cross-domain features and their prediction models. Recently, Yao et al. [24] presented the approach of semi-supervised domain adaptation with subspace learning (SDASL), which minimizes the prediction risk while preserving the locality structure and manifold information for HDA.

Recently, a number of researchers focus on advancing the techniques of neural networks and deep learning for solving adaptation tasks. Inspired by [10], Tzeng et al. [25] and Long et al. [29] utilized deep learning frameworks for matching

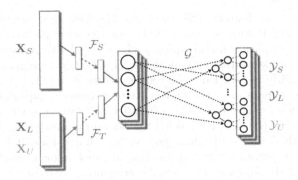

Fig. 1. The architecture of Transfer Neural Trees (TNT), which consists of the layers for feature mappings $\{\mathcal{F}_S, \mathcal{F}_T\}$ and prediction $\mathcal{G}$. To assign the labels $\mathcal{Y}_U$ for unlabeled target-domain data $\mathbf{X}_U$, TNT is learned by source-domain labeled data $\{\mathbf{X}_S, \mathcal{Y}_S\}$, together with labeled data $\{\mathbf{X}_L, \mathcal{Y}_L\}$ and the unlabeled ones $\mathbf{X}_U$ in the target domain.

distributions of cross-doman data. Both Ganin *et al.* [26] and Ajakan *et al.* [27] proposed NN-based architectures which learn classifiers for discriminating data across domains. To further handle heterogeneous cross-domain data, Shu *et al.* [28] presented a deep neural network structure, while co-occurrence cross-domain data are required for training their networks. Based on the above observation, we propose to learn a novel NN-based framework in a semi-supervised HDA setting, without the need of co-occurrence training data pairs.

3   Proposed Method

3.1   Notations and Problem Definition

For the sake of clarity, we first define the notations which will be used in the paper. We have source-domain data $\mathcal{D}_S = \{\mathbf{X}_S, \mathcal{Y}_S\} = \{\mathbf{x}_i^s, y_i^s\}_{i=1}^{n_s}$ in a d_s-dimensional space, where $\mathbf{x}_i^s \in \mathbb{R}^{d_s}$ denotes the ith source-domain instance with the corresponding label $y_i^s \in \{1, ..., C\}$. Note that n_s is the number of source-domain data, and C is the number of classes.

As for the target domain of d_t dimensions, a number n_l of labeled data $\mathcal{D}_L$ can be observed, while the remaining n_u target-domain instances $\mathcal{D}_U$ are unlabeled. Thus, we have $\mathcal{D}_L = \{\mathbf{X}_L, \mathcal{Y}_L\} = \{\mathbf{x}_i^l, y_i^l\}_{i=1}^{n_l}$, $\mathcal{D}_U = \{\mathbf{X}_U, \mathcal{Y}_U\} = \{\mathbf{x}_i^u, y_i^u\}_{i=1}^{n_u}$, and the target domain data is defined as $\mathcal{D}_T = \mathcal{D}_L \cup \mathcal{D}_U$. Note that $\mathbf{x}_i^l, \mathbf{x}_i^u \in \mathbb{R}^{d_t}$ and $y_i^l, y_i^u \in \{1, \ldots, C\}$. For the task of semi-supervised heterogeneous domain adaptation (HDA), the goal is to predict $\mathcal{Y}_U$ by observing $\mathcal{D}_S, \mathcal{D}_L$, and $\mathbf{X}_U$ with $n_l \ll n_u$ and $d_s \neq d_t$.

3.2   Transfer Neural Trees (TNT)

Inspired by the recent advances on neural networks and deep learning [26–28] we propose **Transfer Neural Trees (TNT)**, which can be viewed as a neural network based learning framework for solving semi-supervised HDA problems. As illustrated in Fig. 1, our TNT advocates the learning of source and target-domain mapping $\mathcal{F}_S$ and $\mathcal{F}_T$, respectively, followed by a prediction layer $\mathcal{G}$ for performing joint adaptation and classification.

It is worth noting that, our TNT enforces the mapping $\mathcal{F}_T$ to be updated in a semi-supervised fashion (i.e., $\mathcal{F}_T$ is learned by both labeled and unlabeled target-domain data). And, in order to associate and recognize cross-domain data, we propose **Transfer Neural Decision Forest (Transfer-NDF)** as the prediction layer $\mathcal{G}$ in TNT. The details of each TNT component will be discussed in the following subsections.

(i) Transfer Neural Decision Forest $\mathcal{G}$. As shown in Fig. 1, $\mathcal{G}$ is viewed as a prediction layer in our TNT, which is applied to adapt and recognize cross-domain data. Instead of applying existing techniques like soft-max layers and learning fine-tuned parameters for NN, we propose Transfer Neural Decision Forest (Transfer-NDF) as $\mathcal{G}$ for TNT. Benefiting from the successful developments of random forests and neural networks, our Transfer-NDF is designed to exhibit capabilities in handling and discriminating data with diverse distributions.

We now briefly review Neural Decision Forests (NDF) for the sake of completeness. Viewing decision trees as a special type of NN [30], Kontschieder *et al.* propose NDF and deep NDF (dNDF) for image classification [31,32]. Let dNDF as a forest $\mathbf{F}$ with n_F neural decision trees, and each tree $\mathbf{T}$ in dNDF consists of $\mathcal{N}$ decision nodes and $\mathcal{L}$ leaf nodes (see Fig. 2(a) for example). For an input $\mathbf{x}$ reaching a decision node $n \in \mathcal{N}$ with architecture weight/hyperplane θ_n, probabilities of d_n and $\bar{d}_n = 1 - d_n$ will be output to the subsequent nodes in the following level, i.e.,

$$d_n(\mathbf{x}; \Theta) = \sigma(f_n(\mathbf{x}; \Theta)), \tag{1}$$

with the sigmoid function $\sigma = (1 + e^{-x})^{-1}$ and $f_n(\mathbf{x}; \Theta) = \theta_n^T \mathbf{x}$ (Θ denotes the network parameter). Thus, the probability $\mu_l(\mathbf{x}|\Theta)$ at leaf node $l \in \mathcal{L}$ is:

$$\mu_l(\mathbf{x}|\Theta) = \prod_{n \in \mathcal{N}} d_n(\mathbf{x}; \Theta)^{1_{l \swarrow n}} \bar{d}_n(\mathbf{x}; \Theta)^{1_{l \searrow n}}. \tag{2}$$

Note that $1_{l \swarrow n}$ and $1_{l \searrow n}$ indicate the decision at node n when traversing a path along $\mathbf{T}$ to reach the leaf node l.

In dNDF, each leaf node observes class-label distribution $\boldsymbol{\pi}_l = \{\pi_{l_1}, \ldots, \pi_{l_C}\}$ with each entry denoting the probability of taking the corresponding class. Thus, the prediction from all leaf nodes in $\mathbf{T}$ is computed as:

$$\mathbb{P}_{\mathbf{T}}[y|\mathbf{x}, \Theta, \boldsymbol{\pi}] = \sum_{l \in \mathcal{L}} \pi_{l_y} \mu_l(\mathbf{x}|\Theta). \tag{3}$$

Finally, the overall prediction from the entire forest $\mathbf{F}$ is determined by:

$$\mathbb{P}_{\mathbf{F}}[y|\mathbf{x}, \Theta, \boldsymbol{\pi}] = \frac{1}{n_F} \sum_{\mathbf{T} \in \mathbf{F}} \mathbb{P}_{\mathbf{T}}[y|\mathbf{x}, \Theta, \boldsymbol{\pi}]. \tag{4}$$

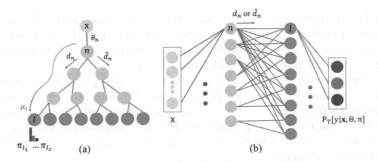

Fig. 2. (a) Illustration of each tree structure in dNDF and (b) visualization of dNDF in terms of a neural network architecture.

As noted in [32], the overall objective function of dNDF is determined by the log-loss term for the training/labeled data, i.e.,

$$L_p(\Theta, \boldsymbol{\pi}; \mathbf{x}, y) = \sum_{\mathbf{T} \in \mathbf{F}} - \log(\mathbb{P}_\mathbf{T}[y|\mathbf{x}, \Theta, \boldsymbol{\pi}]). \tag{5}$$

With stochastic routing and differentiable properties, each decision and leaf node in dNDF can be learned via back propagation, which makes dNDF as an effective alternative to (deep) NN when learning the network parameters.

Despite the above promising properties, dNDF *cannot* be easily extended for domain adaptation tasks. This is because that, not all the leaf nodes learned by source-domain data can generalize to describing target-domain data. More precisely, if a leaf node is seldom updated by source-domain data, the corresponding class-label distribution might not be sufficiently representative for adaptation.

Instead of selecting a threshold to prune such leaf nodes and resulting in a complex neural network in Fig. 2(b), we introduce a novel *stochastic pruning* approach for learning our Transfer-NDF. Given an input $\mathbf{x}$ and network Θ, we choose to learn and update the class-label distribution at a leaf node l by:

$$\pi_{l_y}^{(t+1)} = \frac{1}{Z_l^{(t)}} (p_d + \sum_{(\mathbf{x}, y') \in \mathcal{D}_S} \frac{\mathbf{1}_{y=y'} \pi_{l_y}^{(t)} \mu_l(\mathbf{x}|\Theta)}{\mathbb{P}_\mathbf{T}[y|\mathbf{x}, \Theta, \boldsymbol{\pi}^{(t)}]}). \tag{6}$$

In (6), μ_l is the probability of the input $\mathbf{x}$ reaching leaf node l, $\boldsymbol{\pi}_l^{(t)}$ is the derived class-label distribution at iteration t, and $\mathbb{P}_\mathbf{T}$ denotes the probability of taking class y. Note that $\mathbf{1}$ is the indicator function, and Z_l is a normalizing factor ensuring that $\sum_y \pi_{l_y}^{(t+1)} = 1$. Different from dNDF, we choose to add a small positive p_d in (6) for updating the class-label distributions of *each* leaf node.

We now explain why the use of (6) in our Transfer-NDF can be viewed as a stochastic pruning technique and thus is preferable for domain adaptation. We note that, the second term in (6) (also presented in the original dNDF definition) counts the number of $\mathbf{X}_S$ reaching leaf node l with decision y. If a leaf node is only updated by few source-domain instances, the resulting distribution would

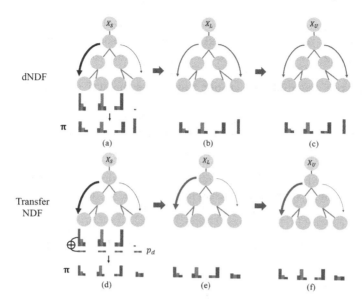

Fig. 3. Comparisons of dNDF [32] and Transfer-NDF as the decision layer $\mathcal{G}$ in TNT. Learning class-label distributions π using $\mathbf{X}_S$, adaptation of $\mathbf{X}_L$, and prediction of $\mathbf{X}_U$ using dNDF are shown in (a), (b), and (c), respectively. The associated processes with Transfer-NDF are shown in (d), (e), and (f).

be sparse and with small π_{l_i} values. However, the normalization process in (6) would amplify their distribution values, as illustrated in the resulting π of the rightmost leaf node in Fig. 3(a). When $\mathbf{X}_L$ are taken as inputs, the prediction loss observed from all leaf nodes would be considered as equally important when updating TNT via back propagation. As a result, prediction of the unlabeled ones $\mathbf{X}_U$ would overfit the outputs from such leaf nodes (see Fig. 3(c)).

With the introduction of p_d in (6), we are able to suppress the above extreme class-label distributions at the leaf nodes with seldom updates. As illustrated in Figs. 3(d), adding p_d in (6) would turn the class-label distributions of such nodes close to uniform distribution after normalization. Thus, as depicted in Figs. 3(e), no strong prediction results can be inferred by $\mathbf{X}_L$ reaching such leaf nodes. This allows the prediction of $\mathbf{X}_U$ to be dominated by the leaf nodes with sufficient representation ability only (see Fig. 3(f)). It is worth repeating that, with this stochastic pruning process for constructing TNT, we do not need to carefully select and disregard particular nodes for adaptation purposes.

(ii) Feature Mapping $\mathcal{F}_S$ and $\mathcal{F}_T$. As illustrated in Fig. 1, $\mathcal{F}_S$ and $\mathcal{F}_T$ in our TNT are neural network based structures which map source and target-domain data for representation learning. Once the domain-invariant feature representation is derived, the prediction layer $\mathcal{G}$ (i.e., Transfer-NDF) will be applied for joint adaptation and classification. While $\mathcal{F}_S$ and $\mathcal{F}_T$ share the same goal of learning cross-domain feature representation, we need to derive these two mappings separately using the observed data in the associated domain. Moreover, when learning $\mathcal{F}_T$, we will utilize both labeled and unlabeled target-domain data for learning our TNT in a semi-supervised setting.

In our work, we apply hyperbolic tangent as the activation function for $\mathcal{F}_S$. When observing the source-domain data as inputs, we have (5) as the objective function with back propagation to update $\mathcal{F}_S$ (and $\mathcal{G}$), with the goal of minimizing the prediction error observed from all the leaf nodes. Similar remarks can be applied to the update of $\mathcal{F}_T$ using labeled target-domain data $\mathbf{X}_L$.

However, due to the lack of label information, we cannot apply (5) for learning $\mathcal{F}_T$ with unlabeled target-domain data $\mathbf{X}_U$. In our work, we advocate to preserve the prediction and structural consistency between $\mathbf{X}_L$ and $\mathbf{X}_U$, and propose to enforce an *embedding loss term* L_e defined as follows:

$$
L_e(\Theta, \boldsymbol{\pi}; \mathbf{x}, \tilde{y}) = \sum_{\mathbf{x} \in \{\mathbf{X}_L, \mathbf{X}_U\}, \mathbf{T} \in \mathbf{F}} -\mathbb{P}_\mathbf{T}[\tilde{y}|\mathbf{x}, \Theta, \boldsymbol{\pi}] \frac{\mathbb{P}_\mathbf{F}[\tilde{y}|\mathbf{x}, \Theta, \boldsymbol{\pi}]}{\mathbb{P}_\mathbf{F}[\tilde{y}|\Theta, \boldsymbol{\pi}]},
$$

$$
\mathbb{P}_\mathbf{F}[\tilde{y}|\Theta, \boldsymbol{\pi}] = \frac{1}{n_l + n_u} \sum_{\mathbf{x} \in \{\mathbf{X}_L, \mathbf{X}_U\}} \mathbb{P}_\mathbf{F}[\tilde{y}|\mathbf{x}, \Theta, \boldsymbol{\pi}].
$$
(7)

In (7), $\tilde{y}$ denotes the output labels of inputs $\mathbf{x} \in \{\mathbf{X}_L, \mathbf{X}_U\}$, and $\mathbb{P}_\mathbf{F}[\tilde{y}|\Theta, \boldsymbol{\pi}]$ is viewed as a normalization term. We can see that, minimizing this embedding loss term L_e is equivalent to maximizing the prediction consistency between the output of each tree $\mathbb{P}_\mathbf{T}[\tilde{y}|\mathbf{x}, \Theta, \boldsymbol{\pi}]$ and that of the decision forests $\mathbb{P}_\mathbf{F}[\tilde{y}|\mathbf{x}, \Theta, \boldsymbol{\pi}]$. By performing adaptation and classification using the prediction layer $\mathcal{G}$ in our TNT, the above process further implies that the structural consistency between $\mathbf{X}_L$ and $\mathbf{X}_U$ can be preserved.

It is worth noting that, when updating $\mathcal{F}_T$, the decision layer $\mathcal{G}$ (i.e., Transfer-NDF) learned from source-domain data is remained fixed. This is to enforce and to adapt $\mathcal{G}$ for recognizing target-domain data. The details of the above learning process will be discussed in the next subsection.

3.3   Learning of TNT

(i) Learning from Source-Domain Data. When observing source-domain data $\mathcal{D}_S = \{\mathbf{X}_S, \mathcal{Y}_S\}$ for learning our TNT, both mapping $\mathcal{F}_S$ and the decision layer $\mathcal{G}$ (i.e., Transfer-NDF) will be updated by:

$$
\min_{\mathcal{F}_S, \mathcal{G}} \sum_{(\mathbf{x}, y) \in \mathcal{D}_S} L_p(\Theta, \boldsymbol{\pi}; \mathbf{x}, y).
$$
(8)

As determined in (5), L_p returns the prediction loss of the input labeled data. We take the derivative of L_p with respect to Θ, and apply back propagation to update the architectures of $\mathcal{F}_S$ and $\mathcal{G}$:

$$
\frac{\partial L_p}{\partial \Theta}(\Theta, \boldsymbol{\pi}; \mathbf{x}, y) = \sum_{n \in \mathcal{N}} \frac{\partial L_p(\Theta, \boldsymbol{\pi}; \mathbf{x}, y)}{\partial f_n(\mathcal{F}(\mathbf{x}), \Theta)} \frac{\partial f_n(\mathcal{F}(\mathbf{x}), \Theta)}{\partial \Theta},
$$
(9)

where $\mathcal{F}$ indicates $\mathcal{F}_S$ or $\mathcal{F}_T$, and we have

$$\frac{\partial f_n(\mathcal{F}(\mathbf{x}), \Theta)}{\partial \Theta} = \frac{\partial \theta_n^T \mathcal{F}(\mathbf{x})}{\partial \Theta} = \mathcal{F}(\mathbf{x}) \text{ and}$$

$$\frac{\partial L_p(\Theta, \boldsymbol{\pi}; \mathbf{x}, y)}{\partial f_n(\mathcal{F}(\mathbf{x}), \Theta)} = \frac{\sum_{l \in \mathcal{L}} \mathbf{1}_{l \searrow n} d_n(\mathbf{x}; \Theta) \boldsymbol{\pi}_{l_y} \mu_l(\mathbf{x}|\Theta) - \mathbf{1}_{l \swarrow n} \bar{d}_n(\mathbf{x}; \Theta) \boldsymbol{\pi}_{l_y} \mu_l(\mathbf{x}|\Theta)}{\mathbb{P}_{\mathbf{T}}[y|\mathbf{x}, \Theta, \boldsymbol{\pi}]}.$$

$$(10)$$

The details of the above derivations can be found in [32].

(ii) Learning from Target-Domain Data. Once $\mathcal{F}_S$ and $\mathcal{G}$ are obtained, we have $\mathbf{X}_L$ and $\mathbf{X}_U$ as the target-domain inputs for deriving $\mathcal{F}_T$. Recall that $\mathcal{G}$ is only updated by source-domain data. Since it is utilized to adapt target-domain data, it would remain fixed when we learn the mapping $\mathcal{F}_T$.

For the mapping $\mathcal{F}_T$, we choose to solve the following optimization task:

$$\min_{\mathcal{F}_T} \sum_{(\mathbf{x}, y) \in \mathcal{D}_L} L_p(\Theta, \boldsymbol{\pi}; \mathbf{x}, y) + \lambda \sum_{\tilde{y}} \sum_{\mathbf{x} \in \{\mathbf{X}_L, \mathbf{X}_U\}} L_e(\Theta, \boldsymbol{\pi}; \mathbf{x}, \tilde{y}). \quad (11)$$

Note that the first term in (11) is in the same formulation as (8), which only calculates the loss observed from the labeled target-domain data $\mathbf{X}_L$. As introduced in Sect. 3.2, the second term L_e is the *embedding loss term* determined in (7) (with $\tilde{y}$ denoting the predicted labels). As discussed earlier, this L_e term enforces prediction/structural consistency between target-domain data, so that semi-supervised HDA can be addressed accordingly.

In (11), we have parameter λ regularizing the embedding loss term. As suggested by[26], we gradually increase the value of λ during iterative updates. This is because that the loss produced by $\mathbf{X}_L$ in early iterations are not sufficiently reliable, and thus we do not emphasize the feedback of L_e in the early stage of our TNT derivation.

To update $\mathcal{F}_T$ via back propagation, we also take the derivatives of L_p and L_e with respect to Θ. While the derivative of L_p is in the same form as (9), that of L_e needs additional efforts to calculate its partial derivative with respect to f_n (see Supplementary for detailed derivations), i.e.,

$$\frac{\partial L_e(\Theta, \boldsymbol{\pi}; \mathbf{x}, \tilde{y})}{\partial f_n(\mathcal{F}(\mathbf{x}); \Theta)} = \frac{\partial L_e(\Theta, \boldsymbol{\pi}; \mathbf{x}, \tilde{y})}{\partial \mathbb{P}_{\mathbf{T}}[\tilde{y}|\mathbf{x}, \Theta, \boldsymbol{\pi}]} \frac{\partial \mathbb{P}_{\mathbf{T}}[\tilde{y}|\mathbf{x}, \Theta, \boldsymbol{\pi}]}{\partial f_n(\mathcal{F}(\mathbf{x}); \Theta)}$$

$$\approx \frac{\mathbb{P}_{\mathbf{F}}[\tilde{y}|\mathbf{x}, \Theta, \boldsymbol{\pi}]}{\mathbb{P}_{\mathbf{F}}[\tilde{y}|\Theta, \boldsymbol{\pi}]} \sum_{l \in \mathcal{L}} \mathbf{1}_{l \searrow n} d_n(\mathbf{x}; \Theta) \boldsymbol{\pi}_{l_y} \mu_l(\mathbf{x}|\Theta) - \mathbf{1}_{l \swarrow n} \bar{d}_n(\mathbf{x}; \Theta) \boldsymbol{\pi}_{l_y} \mu_l(\mathbf{x}|\Theta).$$

$$(12)$$

It is worth noting that, despite the learning of $\mathcal{F}_T$ enforces the prediction consistency between target-domain data, the diversity of all trees in Transfer-NDF $\mathcal{G}$ can be preserved. This is because that the prediction layer $\mathcal{G}$ in TNT is fixed when learning $\mathcal{F}_T$. Thus, the resulting adaptation/recognition performance would not be affected.

Fig. 4. Cross-domain datasets: **Caltech-256**, **Office**, **NUS-WIDE** and **ImageNet**. Note that we apply **Caltech-256** and **Office** for cross-domain object recognition, and we perform translated learning using **NUS-WIDE** and **ImageNet**.

4 Experiment

4.1 Datasets and Settings

We consider cross-domain classification tasks in our experiments. We first address cross-domain object recognition problems using the datasets of **Office** + **Caltech-256** datasets [2,33]. The former is composed of object images of 31 categories, collected from three sources: Amazon (A), Webcam (W) and DSLR (D). On the other hand, **Caltech-256** contains 256 object categories also collected from the Internet. Among these objects, 10 overlapping categories are considered for experiments. For HDA tasks, we consider two type of features: DeCAF$_6$ [34] and SURF [35]. The former is of 4096 dimensions, while the latter is a 100-dimensional bag-of-word feature representation.

In additional to cross-domain object recognition, we further consider the task of associating and recognizing text and image data, also referred to as *translated learning* [6]. While most existing works on this task requires co-occurrence text and image data for learning purposes, we will show that our TNT is able to solve this cross-domain classification problem in a semi-supervised setting without the need of any cross-domain co-occurrence data. Following the setting of [28], we apply NUS-WIDE [36] and ImageNet [37] as the datasets for text and images, respectively. NUS-WIDE contains of tag information of 269,648 Flickr images, while ImageNet is with 5247 synsets and 3.2 million images in total. The selected datasets and their examples images are shown in Fig. 4.

To preprocess the NUS-WIDE tag data, we pre-trained a 5-layer NN with a soft-max layer, and take the 4th hidden layer as the 64-dimensional feature representation. As for the ImageNet data, we follow [38] and extract their DeCAF$_6$ features as representation. For simplicity, we choose 8 overlapping categories of these two datasets: *airplane, birds, buildings, cars, dog, fish, flowers, horses*.

For fair comparisons, we fix our TNT settings for all experiments. Both $\mathcal{F}_S$ and $\mathcal{F}_T$ are single-layer neural networks, which apply hyperbolic tangent as the activation function, with the dimension of the mapping output as 100. Transfer-NDF $\mathcal{G}$ is composed of 20 trees with depth of 7, and each tree randomly samples 20 dimensions from the mapping output (out of 100). And, we have p_d fixed as 0.001, and λ is gradually increased from 0 to 0.1 as noted in Sect. 3.3.

Table 1. Performance comparisons for cross-feature object recognition. Note that $\mathcal{D}_S$ and $\mathcal{D}_T$ denote source (DeCAF$_6$) and target (SURF) domains, respectively.

$\mathcal{D}_S \to \mathcal{D}_T$	SVM$_t$	NN$_t$	MMDT [18]	HFA [21]	SHFR [19]	SCP [23]	TNT
A → A	45.37	45.80	45.47	46.66	44.50	45.47	**50.41**
C → C	37.15	35.02	35.50	36.32	33.39	34.67	**39.03**
W → W	61.51	61.06	61.13	61.89	54.34	60.00	**62.34**

Table 2. Performance comparisons using NN, dNDF, and Transfer-NDF as $\mathcal{G}$ in TNT. Note that Transfer-NDF* denotes dNDF with our stochastic pruning, while our Transfer-NDF observes both labeled and unlabeled target-domain data during adaptation by introducing L_e in (11).

$\mathcal{D}_S \to \mathcal{D}_T$	NN	dNDF	Transfer-NDF*	Transfer-NDF
C → A	42.84	46.57	46.72	**49.50**
C → C	32.31	33.94	34.62	**39.03**
C → W	56.75	60.30	61.36	**62.42**

4.2 Evaluation

When comparing the performance of different HDA approaches, we first consider SVM$_t$ and NN$_t$ as baseline methods, which simply take labeled target-domain data for training SVM and (two-layer) NN, respectively. As for the state-of-the-art HDA ones, we include the results produced by MMDT [18], HFA [21], SCP [23] and SHFR [19] for comparisons.

Object Recognition Across Feature Spaces. For the task of object recognition, we first address the problem of cross-feature image recognition using Office + Caltech-256. DSLR (D) is excluded in the experiments, since only a limited amount of data is available for this subset. For source-domain data, we take images in CNN features (i.e., DeCAF$_6$); as for the target-domain images, we have SURF as the features. In the semi-supervised settings of HDA, we randomly choose 3 images in the target domain as labeled data, while the remaining one in that domain as the images to be recognized.

Table 1 lists the average classification results with 5 random trials. From this table, we see that all the HDA approaches were able to produce improved performance when comparing to SVM$_t$ and NN$_t$. And, our TNT consistently achieves the best results among all cross-feature pairs in this experiment.

Moreover, we further verify the use of our Transfer-NDF in TNT for associating and recognizing cross-domain data. In Table 2, we compare the results of using NN, dNDF and our Transfer-NDF as $\mathcal{G}$ in TNT (with DeCAF$_6$ and SURF describing source and target-domain data, respectively). We can see that, while the use of dNDF exhibited improved adaptation ability than NN, introducing stochastic pruning to dNDF (i.e., Transfer-NDF* in Table 2) further increased

Table 3. Performance comparisons of object recognition across features and datasets. Note that DeCAF$_6$ and SURF describe source and target-domain data, respectively.

$\mathcal{D}_S \rightarrow \mathcal{D}_T$	SVM$_t$	NN$_t$	MMDT [18]	HFA [21]	SHFR [19]	SCP [23]	TNT
C → A	45.37	45.80	45.69	46.44	44.61	41.59	**49.50**
W → A			46.23	46.98	43.86	44.50	**48.45**
A → C	37.15	35.02	35.77	36.32	33.39	35.04	**38.37**
W → C			36.05	36.41	33.21	35.96	**37.75**
A → W	61.51	61.06	61.13	**61.89**	54.34	58.87	60.08
C → W			60.76	62.26	54.34	51.32	**62.42**

Table 4. Comparisons of classification results by adapting text (NUS-WIDE) to image data (ImageNet).

$\mathcal{D}_S \rightarrow \mathcal{D}_T$	SVM$_t$	NN$_t$	MMDT [18]	HFA [21]	SHFR [19]	SCP [23]	TNT
tag → image	63.75	65.65	49.38	62.88	60.38	65.00	**72.22**

the recognition performance. Nevertheless, the full version of Transfer-NDF was able to achieve the best performance.

Object Recognition Across Features and Datasets. We now consider a more challenging object recognition task, in which source and target domains observe distinct features (i.e., DeCAF$_6$ vs. SURF) and from different datasets (i.e., A, C, or W). The average recognition results of different methods are listed in Table 3. From this table, we see that our TNT produced comparable or improved results than baseline and recent HDA approaches did, which confirms that the use of our TNT for cross-domain object recognition is preferable.

Text-to-Image Classification. As noted earlier, we further consider the adaptation and classification of text and image data. With tag information observed in the source domain dataset of NUS-WIDE, our goal is to improve image classification using the ImageNet data. For the semi-supervised setting in the target domain, we randomly select 3 images per category as labeled data, and 100 images for prediction.

Table 4 lists and compares the performances of different approaches with 5 random trials. It can be seen that, without utilizing co-occurrence data across domains for learning, it is not an easy task for solving such cross-domain classification problems. Our TNT was able to achieve a significantly improved result under this semi-supervised setting, and this shows the effectiveness and robustness of our TNT for handling heterogeneous cross-domain data.

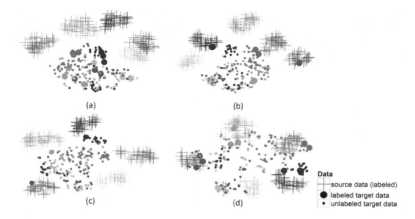

Fig. 5. t-SNE visualization of cross-domain data distributions using NN, dNDF, and Transfer-NDF as $\mathcal{G}$ in TNT: (a) NN, (b) dNDF, (c) Transfer-NDF*, and (d) Transfer-NDF. As noted in Table 2, Transfer-NDF* denotes dNDF with stochastic pruning.

4.3   Analysis and Visualization

Adaptation Ability of Transfer-NDF. Recall that, in Table 2, we compare the performance of the uses of different classifiers as the prediction layer $\mathcal{G}$ in TNT. We now visualize the observed cross-data distributions at the mapping layer output (i.e., the input layer of $\mathcal{G}$), and show the results in Fig. 5.

Comparing Figs. 5(a) and (b), we see the use of NN in TNT over-fitted the target-domain labeled data, and such problems were only slightly alleviated when dNDF was applied as $\mathcal{G}$. While the supervised version of TNT (i.e., Transfer-NDF*) further improved the adaptation ability as depicted in Fig. 5(c), the full version of our Transfer-NDF successfully related cross-domain heterogenous data in this layer and achieved the best recognition performance.

Stochastic Pruning for Transfer-NDF. To confirm that our introduced stochastic pruning for Transfer-NDF would disregard the leaf nodes with insufficient adaptation ability, We plot the observed class-label distributions $\boldsymbol{\pi}$ without and with such pruning (i.e., dNFD and Transfer-NDF) in Figs. 6(a) and (b), respectively. Note that each row in Fig. 6(a) or (b) denotes a tree, in which each entry indicates a leaf node. The color (out of 10 categories) of each entry denotes the dominant class label observed from the associated distribution.

In Fig. 6(a), we see that dNDF (i.e., no stochastic pruning) produced the leaf nodes with different colors. This means that all the leaf nodes were considered equally important for adaptation/prediction, as discussed in Sect. 3.2. With stochastic pruning (i.e., adding a small constant $p_d = 0.001$ for all class labels in (6)), a portion of the leaf nodes were not able to observe dominant distribution values, and thus were shown in black in Fig. 6(b). Note that a cutoff threshold is set as 0.3 in Fig. 6(b) for visualization purposes. Thus, in addition the

Tree  Tree

Leaf node
(a)

Leaf node
(b)

Fig. 6. Class-label distribution π of (a) dNDF and (b) Transfer-NDF on C (DeCAF$_6$) $\rightarrow$ C (SURF). Note that each entry indicates the distribution value of the dominant class (out of 10 categories/colors). (Color figure online)

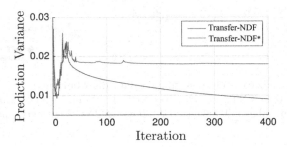

Fig. 7. Prediction variance vs. iteration number on C (DeCAF$_6$) $\rightarrow$ C (SURF). Note that Transfer-NDF* (i.e., dNDF with stochastic pruning) is learned from labeled cross-domain data only.

quantitative evaluation, the above observation further supports our Transfer-NDF for adapting cross-domain data.

Enforcing Embedding Loss L_e. Finally, we verify the effectiveness of introducing L_e in TNT for learning $\mathcal{F}_T$ in a semi-supervised setting. Using Transfer-NDF without and with L_e (i.e., Transfer-NDF* and Transfer-NDF, respectively), we observe the associated variances of the predicted probability outputs of all the target-domain instances, and we plot the results in Fig. 7.

Comparing the two curves in Fig. 7, we see that the use of L_e (i.e., Transfer-NDF) was able to reduce the variance of the prediction probability outputs during the adaptation process. This supports our argument in Sect. 3.3 that, the enforcement of prediction consistency between labeled and unlabeled target-domain data would preserve their structural consistency during adaptation. This is the reason why our TNT is able to handle HDA in a semi-supervised setting.

5   Conclusion

We presented Transfer Neural Trees (TNT) for adapting and recognizing cross-domain heterogeneous data in a semi-supervised setting. With the embedding loss for enforcing prediction and structural consistency between target-domain data, plus the use of our Transfer-NDF with stochastic pruning for adapting representative neurons, our TNT is able to solve feature mapping, adaptation, and classification in a unified NN-based framework. Our experiments confirmed that the proposed TNT performed favorably against state-of-the-art HDA approaches on a variety of classification tasks using data across different feature spaces, collected by different datasets, or in terms of distinct modalities. Among the future research directions, one can extend the feature mapping layers in our TNT architecture. This would further allow the learning and adaptation of cross-domain data with increasing sizes or modalities with more complexities.

References

1. Pan, S.J., Yang, Q.: A survey on transfer learning. IEEE Trans. Knowl. Data Eng. **22**(10), 1345–1359 (2010)
2. Saenko, K., Kulis, B., Fritz, M., Darrell, T.: Adapting visual category models to new domains. In: Daniilidis, K., Maragos, P., Paragios, N. (eds.) ECCV 2010, Part IV. LNCS, vol. 6314, pp. 213–226. Springer, Heidelberg (2010)
3. Zhu, Y., Chen, Y., Lu, Z., Pan, S.J., Xue, G.R., Yu, Y., Yang, Q.: Heterogeneous transfer learning for image classification. In: AAAI (2011)
4. Tzeng, E., Hoffman, J., Darrell, T., Saenko, K.: Simultaneous deep transfer across domains and tasks. In: IEEE ICCV (2015)
5. Chidlovskii, B., Csurka, G., Gangwar, S.: Assembling heterogeneous domain adaptation methods for image classification. In: CLEF (Working Notes) (2014)
6. Dai, W., Chen, Y., Xue, G.R., Yang, Q., Yu, Y.: Translated learning: transfer learning across different feature spaces. In: NIPS (2008)
7. Prettenhofer, P., Stein, B.: Cross-language text classification using structural correspondence learning. In: ACL (2010)
8. Daumé III, H.: Frustratingly easy domain adaptation. In: ACL (2007)
9. Daumé III, H., Kumar, A., Saha, A.: Frustratingly easy semi-supervised domain adaptation. In: Natural Language Processing Workshop (2010)
10. Pan, S.J., Tsang, I.W., Kwok, J.T., Yang, Q.: Domain adaptation via transfer component analysis. IEEE Trans. Neural Networks **22**(2), 199–210 (2011)
11. Gong, B., Shi, Y., Sha, F., Grauman, K.: Geodesic flow kernel for unsupervised domain adaptation. In: IEEE CVPR (2012)
12. Fernando, B., Habrard, A., Sebban, M., Tuytelaars, T.: Unsupervised visual domain adaptation using subspace alignment. In: IEEE ICCV (2013)
13. Donahue, J., Hoffman, J., Rodner, E., Saenko, K., Darrell, T.: Semi-supervised domain adaptation with instance constraints. In: IEEE CVPR (2013)
14. Shi, X., Liu, Q., Fan, W., Yu, P.S., Zhu, R.: Transfer learning on heterogenous feature spaces via spectral transformation. In: IEEE ICDM (2010)
15. Kulis, B., Saenko, K., Darrell, T.: What you saw is not what you get: domain adaptation using asymmetric kernel transforms. In: IEEE CVPR (2011)
16. Wang, C., Mahadevan, S.: Heterogeneous domain adaptation using manifold alignment. In: IJCAI (2011)
17. Duan, L., Xu, D., Tsang, I.: Learning with augmented features for heterogeneous domain adaptation. In: ICML (2012)
18. Hoffman, J., Rodner, E., Donahue, J., Darrell, T., Saenko, K.: Efficient learning of domain-invariant image representations. In: ICLR (2013)
19. Zhou, J.T., Tsang, I.W., Pan, S.J., Tan, M.: Heterogeneous domain adaptation for multiple classes. In: AISTATS (2014)

20. Wu, X., Wang, H., Liu, C., Jia, Y.: Cross-view action recognition over heterogeneous feature spaces. In: IEEE ICCV (2013)
21. Li, W., Duan, L., Xu, D., Tsang, I.W.: Learning with augmented features for supervised and semi-supervised heterogeneous domain adaptation. IEEE T-PAMI **36**(6), 1134–1148 (2014)
22. Xiao, M., Guo, Y.: Feature space independent semi-supervised domain adaptation via kernel matching. IEEE T-PAMI **37**(1), 54–66 (2015)
23. Xiao, M., Guo, Y.: Semi-supervised subspace co-projection for multi-class heterogeneous domain adaptation. In: Appice, A., Rodrigues, P.P., Santos Costa, V., Gama, J., Jorge, A., Soares, C. (eds.) ECML PKDD 2015. LNCS, vol. 9285, pp. 525–540. Springer, Heidelberg (2015)
24. Yao, T., Pan, Y., Ngo, C.W., Li, H., Mei, T.: Semi-supervised domain adaptation with subspace learning for visual recognition. In: IEEE CVPR (2015)
25. Tzeng, E., Hoffman, J., Zhang, N., Saenko, K., Darrell, T.: Deep domain confusion: maximizing for domain invariance. In: CoRR, abs/1412.3474 (2014)
26. Ganin, Y., Lempitsky, V.: Unsupervised domain adaptation by backpropagation. In: ICML (2015)
27. Ajakan, H., Germain, P., Larochelle, H., Laviolette, F., Marchand, M.: Domain-adversarial neural networks. JMLR **17**(59), 1–35 (2014)
28. Shu, X., Qi, G.J., Tang, J., Wang, J.: Weakly-shared deep transfer networks for heterogeneous-domain knowledge propagation. In: ACM Conference on Multimedia Conference (2015)
29. Long, M., Wang, J.: Learning transferable features with deep adaptation networks. In: ICML (2015)
30. Sethi, I.K.: Entropy nets: from decision trees to neural networks. Proc. IEEE (Special Issue on Neural Networks) (1990)
31. Rota Bulo, S., Kontschieder, P.: Neural decision forests for semantic image labelling. In: IEEE CVPR (2014)
32. Kontschieder, P., Fiterau, M., Criminisi, A., Rota Bulo, S.: Deep neural decision forests. In: IEEE ICCV (2015)
33. Griffin, G., Holub, A., Perona, P.: Caltech-256 object category dataset (2007)
34. Donahue, J., Jia, Y., Vinyals, O., Hoffman, J., Zhang, N., Tzeng, E., Darrell, T.: DeCAF: a deep convolutional activation feature for generic visual recognition. In: ICML (2014)
35. Bay, H., Tuytelaars, T., Van Gool, L.: SURF: speeded up robust features. In: Leonardis, A., Bischof, H., Pinz, A. (eds.) ECCV 2006, Part I. LNCS, vol. 3951, pp. 404–417. Springer, Heidelberg (2006)
36. Chua, T.S., Tang, J., Hong, R., Li, H., Luo, Z., Zheng, Y.: NUS-WIDE: a real-world web image database from national university of singapore. In: ACM International Conference on Image and Video Retrieval (2009)
37. Deng, J., Dong, W., Socher, R., Li, L.J., Li, K., Fei-Fei, L.: ImageNet: a large-scale hierarchical image database. In: IEEE CVPR (2009)
38. Tommasi, T., Tuytelaars, T.: A testbed for cross-dataset analysis. In: ECCV Workshops (2014)

Tracking Persons-of-Interest via Adaptive Discriminative Features

Shun Zhang[1], Yihong Gong[1(✉)], Jia-Bin Huang[2], Jongwoo Lim[3],
Jinjun Wang[1], Narendra Ahuja[2], and Ming-Hsuan Yang[4]

[1] Xi'an Jiaotong University, Xi'an, China
[2] University of Illinois, Urbana-Champaign, Champaign, USA
ygong@mail.xjtu.edu.cn
[3] Hanyang University, Seoul, South Korea
[4] University of California, Merced, USA
http://shunzhang.me.pn/papers/eccv2016/

Abstract. Multi-face tracking in unconstrained videos is a challenging problem as faces of one person often appear drastically different in multiple shots due to significant variations in scale, pose, expression, illumination, and make-up. Low-level features used in existing multi-target tracking methods are not effective for identifying faces with such large appearance variations. In this paper, we tackle this problem by learning discriminative, video-specific face features using convolutional neural networks (CNNs). Unlike existing CNN-based approaches that are only trained on large-scale face image datasets offline, we further adapt the pre-trained face CNN to specific videos using automatically discovered training samples from tracklets. Our network directly optimizes the embedding space so that the Euclidean distances correspond to a measure of semantic face similarity. This is technically realized by minimizing an improved triplet loss function. With the learned discriminative features, we apply the Hungarian algorithm to link tracklets within each shot and the hierarchical clustering algorithm to link tracklets across multiple shots to form final trajectories. We extensively evaluate the proposed algorithm on a set of TV sitcoms and music videos and demonstrate significant performance improvement over existing techniques.

1 Introduction

Multi-target tracking (MTT) aims at locating all targets of interest (e.g., faces, players, and cars), and inferring their trajectories in a video sequence over time while maintaining their identities. Multi-face tracking is one important domain of MTT that applies to numerous high-level video understanding tasks such as face recognition, content-based retrieval, surveillance, and group interaction analysis.

The goal of multi-face tracking in unconstrained scenarios is to track faces in videos that are generated from multiple moving cameras with different views or scenes as shown in Fig. 1. Examples include automatic character tracking in

© Springer International Publishing AG 2016
B. Leibe et al. (Eds.): ECCV 2016, Part V, LNCS 9909, pp. 415–433, 2016.
DOI: 10.1007/978-3-319-46454-1_26

Fig. 1. We focus on tracking multiple faces according to their unknown identities in *unconstrained* videos, which consist of many shots from different cameras. The main challenge is to address large face appearance variations from different shots due to changes in pose, view angle, scale, makeup, illumination, camera motion and heavy occlusions.

movies, TV sitcoms, or music videos. It has attracted increased attention in recent years due to the fast growing popularity of such videos on the Internet. Unlike tracking in the *constrained* counterparts (e.g., a video from a single camera that is either fixed or moved slowly) where the main challenge is to deal with occlusions and intersections, multi-face tracking in *unconstrained* videos needs to address the following issues: (1) A video often consists of many shots. The contents of two neighboring shots may be dramatically different; (2) It entails dealing with re-identifying faces of people with large appearance variations due to changes in scale, pose, expression, illumination and make-up in different shots or scenes; and (3) The results of face detection may be unreliable when there are many uncontrolled factors, such as low resolution, occlusion, nonrigid deformation, motion blurring and complex background.

Multi-target tracking has been extensively studied in the literature with a prime focus on humans. The task is often cast as a data association problem [1–5] that integrates several cues such as appearance, position, motion, and size into an affinity model to link detections or tracklets (track fragments) into final trajectories. Such methods are effective when the targets are continuously detected and when the camera is either stationary or slowly moving. However, for unconstrained videos with many shot changes and intermittent appearance of targets, the data association problem becomes difficult because the assumptions such as appearance and size consistency, and continuous motion no longer hold. Therefore, the design of discriminative features plays a critical role in identifying faces *across* shots in unconstrained scenarios.

Existing MTT methods [3–5] generally use combinations of low-level features such as color histograms, Haar-like features, or HOG [6] to construct an appearance model for each target. However, these traditional features often are not sufficiently discriminative to identify faces with large appearance changes. For example, low-level features extracted from faces of two different persons under the same pose (e.g., frontal poses) are likely more similar than those extracted from faces of the same person under different poses (e.g., frontal and profile poses).

Recently, features extracted from a convolutional neural network (CNN) trained on a large-scale object recognition dataset have been successfully applied to a broad range of generic visual recognition tasks [7]. In particular, CNN-based features have shown impressive performance on face recognition and verification tasks [8–11]. These CNNs are often trained using large-scale face recognition datasets in a fully supervised manner and then serve as a feature extractor for unseen face images. Yet, they may not achieve good performance in unconstrained videos as the visual domains of faces in the training set and faces in given videos may be significantly different.

In this paper, we aim to address this domain shift by adapting a pre-trained CNN to the *specific* videos. Due to the lack of manual annotations of target identities, we collect a large number of training samples of faces by exploiting spatio-temporal constraints of tracklets in an unsupervised manner. With these automatically discovered training samples, we adapt the pre-trained CNN with an improved triplet loss function, so the squared Euclidean distance of the learned features reflects the semantic distance of face images. We incorporate these adaptive features into a hierarchical agglomerative clustering algorithm to link tracklets across multiple shots into final trajectories. We demonstrate the effectiveness of the learned features to identify characters in 7 long TV sitcom episodes and singers in 8 challenging music videos.

We make the following four contributions in this work:

- Unlike existing work that uses linear metric learning on hand-crafted features, we address the large appearance variations of faces in videos by learning video-specific features using the deep contrastive and triplet-based metric learning from automatically discovered constraints.
- We propose a triplet loss function (SymTriplet). By visualizing and analyzing the gradient directions, we show that the SymTriplet simultaneously can pull positive pairs closer and pull away negative samples from the positive pairs.
- Unlike prior work that often use face tracks with false positives manually removed, we take raw input video as the input and perform detection, tracking, clustering, and feature adaptation in a fully automatic way.
- We contribute a new dataset with 8 music videos from YouTube. We provide full annotations of 3,845 face tracklets and 117,598 face detections. The new dataset presents a new set of challenges (e.g., frequent shot/scene changes, large appearance variations, and rapid camera motion) that are crucial for developing multi-face tracking algorithms in unconstrained environments.

2   Related Work

Multi-target tracking. Multi-target tracking algorithms typically integrate appearance and motion cues into an affinity model to infer and link detections (or tracklets) into final trajectories [1, 4, 12–14]. However, MTT methods do not work well in unconstrained videos where abrupt changes across different shots/scenes occur as the assumptions of continuous appearance or motion no longer hold.

To identify targets across shots, the features need to be sufficiently discriminative to discern targets in various circumstances. Most existing MTT methods either use simple color histogram features [4,15–18] or hand-crafted features [12,19–22] as the appearance representation of targets. However, all these hand-crafted features are not tailored toward faces, and thus are less effective at handling the large appearance variations of faces in unconstrained scenarios.

Visual constraints in multi-target tracking. Several methods explore visual constraints from tracklets for improving tracking performance. These constraints can then be used implicitly for learning a cast-specific metric [21,23], explicitly for linking clusters [24], or for joint tracklets linking and clustering [18]. Some work [24–26] also exploit the visual constraints from tracklets for face clustering in videos. Note that some other methods use non-visual cues from external sources (e.g., script) [27–29] and exploit the weak supervision for improving face clustering and tracking. In this paper, we exploit visual constraints generated in a manner similar to [24–26]. Our method differs from previous methods in two major aspects. First, existing approaches often rely on hand-crafted features and then learn a linear transformation over the extracted features, which may not be effective to capture the nonlinear manifold where face samples lie on. In this work, we apply a deep nonlinear metric learning method by adapting all layers of the CNN to learn discriminative face feature representations. Second, previous work often use face tracks with false positives manually removed [18,23–26]. In contrast, our approach takes raw input video as the input and perform detection, tracking, clustering, and feature adaptation in a fully automatic way.

CNN-based face representation learning. With advances in deep learning, recent face recognition and verification methods focus on learning identity-preserving feature representations. While the implementation details may differ, in general these CNN-based face representations (e.g., DeepID [8], DeepFace [30], FaceNet [10], VGG-Face [31]) are learned by training CNNs using large-scale face recognition datasets in a fully supervised manner. These CNNs then act as face feature extractors for face recognition, identification, and clustering tasks. Similar to [8,10,30,31], our approach learns feature representation in a purely data-driven manner. The main difference lies in that we further adapt the pre-trained features to a specific video, resulting in improved discriminative ability. Also, we introduce a new triplet-based loss function and demonstrate its effectiveness over the commonly used contrastive loss and triplet loss.

Long-term object tracking. The goal of long-term object tracking [32,33] is to track a specific target over time and re-detect it when the target leaves and re-enters the scene. These trackers perform well on various types of targets, including human faces. However, these online trackers are designed to handle scenes recorded by a stationary or slow-moving camera, and not effective in tracking faces in unconstrained videos because of the following two fundamental limitations. First, they are prone to target drift due to the noisy training samples collected during the online model update process. Second, the features employed by these trackers are rather low-level ones which are not sufficiently discriminative to re-identify faces across different shots/scenes. We tackle the first issue by processing offline, i.e., apply a face detector in every frame and then associate all detections/tracklets in the video. For the second issue, we present to learn discriminative and adaptive features to address face appearance variations.

3 Algorithmic Overview

Our goal is to track multiple faces across many shots in an unconstrained video while maintaining identities of persons. To achieve this, we learn discriminative face appearance features that are adapted to the appearance variations presented in the specific videos. We then use a hierarchical clustering algorithm to link tracklets across shots into final trajectories. We illustrate the four main steps of our algorithm in Fig. 2:

(a) **Pre-training:** We pre-train a CNN model based on the AlexNet [34] using an external face recognition dataset to learn identity-preserving features (Sect. 6.1).

(b) **Automatic training sample discovery:** We detect shot changes and divide the video into non-overlapping shots. Within each shot, we apply a face detector and link adjacent detections into short tracklets. We discover a large collection of face pairs or face triplets from tracklets based on spatio-temporal constraints (Sect. 4.1).

(c) **Adaptive feature learning:** We adapt the pre-trained CNN using the automatically discovered training samples to address large appearance changes of the imaged faces presented in a specific video (Sect. 4.2).

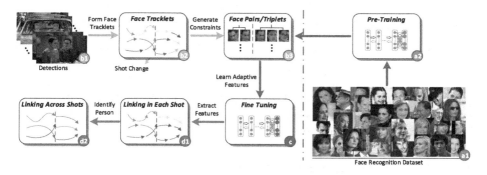

Fig. 2. Our method of tracking faces in unconstrained videos has four main steps. (a) Pre-training a CNN on a large-scale face recognition dataset. (b) Generating face pairs or face triplets from the tracklets in a specific video. (c) Adapting the pre-trained CNN to learn video-specific features. (d) Linking tracklets in each shot and then across shots to form the final face trajectories.

For adapting the CNN, we first introduce two types of loss functions for optimizing the embedding space: the contrastive loss and the triplet loss. Moreover, we present a new triplet loss to improve the discriminative ability of learned features (Sect. 4.3).

(d) **Linking tracklets:** For each shot, we use conventional multi-face tracking methods to link tracklets into short trajectories. We use a hierarchically clustering algorithm to link trajectories across shots. We assign the tracklets in each cluster with the same identity (Sect. 5).

4   Learning Adaptive Discriminative Features

We present the algorithmic details of our unsupervised learning approach of discriminative, video-specific features, including training sample discovery, adaptive feature learning, and the improved triplet loss function.

4.1   Automatic Training Sample Discovery

Shot detection and tracklets linking. We first use a publicly available shot change detection method to divide the input video into non-overlapping shots.[1] We then use an off-the-shelf face detector [35] to locate faces in each frame. Given face detections, we use a two-threshold strategy [16] to generate tracklets within each shot by linking the detected faces in adjacent frames based on their similarities in appearances, positions, and scales of the bounding boxes. Note that the two-threshold strategy for linking detections could be replaced by more sophisticated methods, e.g., tracking using particle filters [13,36]. We discard all tracklets shorter than five frames. Our face tracklets are conservative with limited temporal spans up to the length of each shot.

Spatio-temporal constraints. Given a set of tracklets, we can discover a large collection of positive and negative training sample pairs belonging to the same/different persons: (1) all pairs of faces in one tracklet are from one person and (2) two face tracklets that appear in the same frame contain faces of different persons.

Let $\mathbf{T}^i = \{\mathbf{x}_1^i, \ldots, \mathbf{x}_{n_i}^i\}$ denote the ith face tracklet of length n_i. We generate a set of positive pairs $\mathbf{P}^+$ by collecting all within-tracklet face pairs: $\mathbf{P}^+ = \{(\mathbf{x}_k^i, \mathbf{x}_l^i)\}$, s.t. $\forall k, l = 1, \ldots, n_i,\ k \neq l$. Similarly, if tracklets $\mathbf{T}^i$ and $\mathbf{T}^j$ overlap in some frames, we can generate a set of negative pairs $\mathbf{N}^-$ by collecting all between-tracklet face pairs: $\mathbf{N}^- = \{(\mathbf{x}_k^i, \mathbf{x}_l^j)\}$, s.t. $\forall k = 1, \ldots, n_i,\ \forall l = 1, \ldots, n_j$.

4.2   Adaptive Discriminative Feature Learning

With the automatically discovered training pairs, we aim to optimize the embedding function $\mathbf{f}(\cdot)$ based on the CNN so that the Euclidean distance in the embedding space $D(\mathbf{f}(\mathbf{x}_1), \mathbf{f}(\mathbf{x}_2))$ reflects the semantic similarity of two face images $\mathbf{x}_1$

---

[1] http://sourceforge.net/projects/shot-change/.

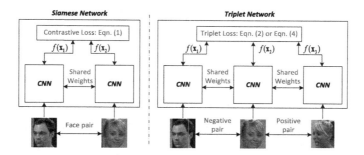

Fig. 3. Illustration of the Siamese network (left) with pairs as inputs and the triplet network (right) with triplets as inputs for Adaptive discriminative feature learning. The Siamese network consists of two CNNs and uses a contrastive loss, while the Triplet network consists of three CNNs and uses a triplet loss. The CNNs in each network share the same architectures and parameters, and are initialized with parameters of the CNN pre-trained on the large-scale face recognition dataset.

and $\mathbf{x}_2$. We set the feature dimension $\mathbf{f}(\cdot)$ as 64 in all our experiments. In what follows, we first describe two commonly used loss functions for optimizing the embedding space: (1) contrastive loss and (2) triplet loss, and then present an improved loss function for feature learning.

Contrastive loss. The Siamese network [37,38] consists of two identical CNNs with shared architecture and parameters as shown in Fig. 3(left). Minimizing the contrastive loss function encourages small distance of two images of the same person and large distance otherwise. Denote $(\mathbf{x}_1, \mathbf{x}_2) \in \{\mathbf{P}^+, \mathbf{N}^-\}$ as a pair of training images generated with the spatio-temporal constraints. Following [37,38], the contrastive loss function is of the form:

$$L_p = \begin{cases} \frac{1}{2}D(\mathbf{f}(\mathbf{x}_1), \mathbf{f}(\mathbf{x}_2)) & \text{if } (\mathbf{x}_1, \mathbf{x}_2) \in \mathbf{P}^+ \\ \frac{1}{2}\max(0, \tau - D(\mathbf{f}(\mathbf{x}_1), \mathbf{f}(\mathbf{x}_2))) & \text{if } (\mathbf{x}_1, \mathbf{x}_2) \in \mathbf{N}^- \end{cases}, \quad (1)$$

where τ ($\tau = 1$ in all our experiments) is the margin. Intuitively, if $\mathbf{x}_1$ and $\mathbf{x}_2$ are from the same person, the loss is $\frac{1}{2}D(\mathbf{f}(\mathbf{x}_1), \mathbf{f}(\mathbf{x}_2))$ and we aim to decrease $D(\mathbf{f}(\mathbf{x}_1), \mathbf{f}(\mathbf{x}_2))$. Otherwise, the loss is $\frac{1}{2}(\max(0, \tau - D(\mathbf{f}(\mathbf{x}_1), \mathbf{f}(\mathbf{x}_2))))$ and we increase $D(\mathbf{f}(\mathbf{x}_1), \mathbf{f}(\mathbf{x}_2))$ until it is larger than the margin τ.

Triplet loss. The Triplet-based network [10] consists of three identical CNNs with shared architecture and parameters as shown in Fig. 3(right). One triplet consists of two face images of one person and one face image from another person. We can generate a set of triplets $\mathbf{S}$ from two tracklets $\mathbf{T}^i$ and $\mathbf{T}^j$ that overlap in some frames: $\mathbf{S} = \{(\mathbf{x}_k^i, \mathbf{x}_l^i, \mathbf{x}_m^j)\}$, s.t. $\forall k, l = 1, ..., n_i, \ k \neq l, \ \forall m = 1, ..., n_j$.

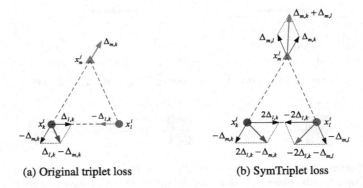

(a) Original triplet loss   (b) SymTriplet loss

Fig. 4. Illustration of the negative partial gradient direction to the triplet sample. (a) the original triplet loss; (b) the SymTriplet loss. The triplet samples $\mathbf{x}_k^i$, $\mathbf{x}_l^i$ and $\mathbf{x}_m^j$ are highlighted with blue, red and magenta, relatively. The circles denote faces from the same person whereas the triangle denotes a different person. The gradient directions are color-coded. (Color figure online)

Here we aim to ensure that the embedded distance of the positive pair $(\mathbf{x}_k^i, \mathbf{x}_l^i)$ is closer than that of the negative pair $(\mathbf{x}_k^i, \mathbf{x}_m^j)$ by a distance margin α ($\alpha = 1$). For one triplet, the triplet loss is of the form:

$$L_t = \frac{1}{2} \max\left(0, D(\mathbf{f}(\mathbf{x}_k^i), \mathbf{f}(\mathbf{x}_l^i)) - D(\mathbf{f}(\mathbf{x}_k^i), \mathbf{f}(\mathbf{x}_m^j)) + \alpha\right). \tag{2}$$

4.3 Improved Triplet Loss

We observe that in one triplet $(\mathbf{x}_k^i, \mathbf{x}_l^i$ and $\mathbf{x}_m^j)$ there are three distances between each pair of samples. The conventional triplet loss in (2), however, takes only two of the three distances into consideration: $D(\mathbf{f}(\mathbf{x}_k^i), \mathbf{f}(\mathbf{x}_l^i))$ and $D(\mathbf{f}(\mathbf{x}_k^i), \mathbf{f}(\mathbf{x}_m^j))$. We illustrate the problem of the original triplet loss by analyzing the gradients of the loss function. We first denote the difference vector between the triplet (k, l, m), e.g., $\Delta_{l,k} = \mathbf{f}(\mathbf{x}_l^i) - \mathbf{f}(\mathbf{x}_k^i)$. If the triplet loss in (2) is non-zero, we can compute the gradients as

$$\frac{\partial L_t}{\partial \mathbf{f}(\mathbf{x}_k^i)} = -(\Delta_{l,k} - \Delta_{m,k}), \quad \frac{\partial L_t}{\partial \mathbf{f}(\mathbf{x}_l^i)} = \Delta_{l,k}, \quad \frac{\partial L_t}{\partial \mathbf{f}(\mathbf{x}_m^j)} = -\Delta_{m,k}. \tag{3}$$

Figure 4(a) visualizes the negative gradient directions for each sample. There are two issues with the original triplet loss. First, the negative point $\mathbf{x}_m^j$ is only pushed away from $\mathbf{x}_k^i$, not both of $\mathbf{x}_k^i$ and $\mathbf{x}_l^i$. Second, the positive pair $(\mathbf{x}_k^i, \mathbf{x}_l^i)$ do not move consistently. For example, $\mathbf{x}_l^i$ only move in the direction between $\mathbf{x}_k^i$ and $\mathbf{x}_l^i$, while $\mathbf{x}_k^i$ would move in the direction with a certain angle.

To address this issue, we propose an improved triplet-based loss function (SymTriplet) by considering all three distances simultaneously. We define the SymTriplet loss as:

$$L_s = \max \left[0, \ D(\mathbf{f}(\mathbf{x}_k^i), \mathbf{f}(\mathbf{x}_l^i)) - \frac{1}{2}(D(\mathbf{f}(\mathbf{x}_k^i), \mathbf{f}(\mathbf{x}_m^j)) + D(\mathbf{f}(\mathbf{x}_l^i), \mathbf{f}(\mathbf{x}_m^j))) + \alpha \right],$$
(4)

where α is the distance margin. The gradients of the SymTriplet loss are

$$\frac{\partial L_s}{\partial \mathbf{f}(\mathbf{x}_k^i)} = -(2\Delta_{l,k} - \Delta_{m,k}), \ \ \frac{\partial L_s}{\partial \mathbf{f}(\mathbf{x}_l^i)} = 2\Delta_{l,k} + \Delta_{m,l}, \ \ \frac{\partial L_s}{\partial \mathbf{f}(\mathbf{x}_m^j)} = -(\Delta_{m,k} + \Delta_{m,l}).$$
(5)

We visualize the negative gradient directions in Fig. 4(b). We show that the proposed SymTriplet loss directly optimize the embedding space so that the positive pair are pulled closer to each other and the negative sample $(\mathbf{x}_m^j)$ is pulled away from the two positive samples $(\mathbf{x}_k^i, \mathbf{x}_l^i)$. This property allows us to improve the discriminative ability of the learned features.

5   Multi-face Tracking via Hierarchical Tracklet Linking

We follow a two-step procedure to associate face tracklets generated in Sect. 4.1 with the learned features: (1) linking the face tracklets within each shot into shot-level tracklets, and (2) merging shot-level tracklets across multiple shots into final trajectories.

Linking tracklets within each shot. We use conventional multi-target tracking algorithms to solve the data association problem of face tracklets within each shot. The appearance of each detection is represented as a feature descriptor extracted from the learned Siamese/Triplet network. The linking probabilities between two tracklets are measured based on temporal, kinematic and appearance information. We then use the Hungarian algorithm to find a global optimum [16,39]. The tracklets with the same label are linked into shot-level tracklets.

Linking tracklets across shots. We use a simple Hierarchical Agglomerative Clustering algorithm with a stopping threshold to link tracklets across shots with the learned appearance features. We explicitly enforce the spatio-temporal constraints by setting the distances between tracklets which have overlapped frames to infinity. We iteratively merge tracklets until the smallest distance is larger than a predefined threshold θ. We present the detailed linking processes in the supplementary material.

6 Experimental Results

In this section, we first describe the implementation details, datasets, and evaluation metrics. We then compare the proposed algorithm with the state-of-the-art methods. More experimental results and videos are available in the supplementary material.

6.1 Implementation Details

Pre-training: We adopt the AlexNet [34] architecture. We replace the original 1,000 node output layer with K nodes where each node corresponds to a specific person. Using the CASIA-WebFace dataset [40], we select $K = 9,427$ persons, 80 % of the images (431,300 images) for training and the rest 20 % (47,140 images) as the validation set. We resize all face images to $227 \times 227 \times 3$ pixels. We use stochastic gradient descent with an initial learning rate of 0.01 that decreases by a factor of 10 for every 20,000 iterations. We use the Caffe [41] framework to train the network.

CNN fine-tuning: We adapt the pre-trained CNN with the Siamese/Triplet network. We replace the classification layer in the pre-trained network with 64 output nodes for feature embedding. As the NVIDIA GT980Ti GPU used in our experiments has only 6GB memory, we find that it does not have sufficient memory to train the VGG-Face model. We set a fixed learning rate to 0.0001 for fine-tuning.

Linking tracklets: For features from the Siamese network, we empirically set the threshold of the HAC algorithm as $\theta = 0.4$. For features from the Triplet network, we use $\theta = 5$ for both the original triplet loss and the improved triplet loss.

6.2 Datasets

We evaluate the proposed algorithm on three types of videos containing multiple persons: (1) a constrained video in a laboratory setting: Frontal [18], (2) TV sitcoms: The Big Bang Theory (BBT) dataset [18,24], and (3) music videos from YouTube.

Frontal video. This is a short video in a constrained scene taken indoors with a fixed camera. Four persons facing the camera move around and occlude each other.

BBT dataset. We select the first 7 episodes from Season 1 of the Big Bang Theory TV Sitcom (referred as BBT01-07). Each video is about 23 min long with the main cast of 5–13 people and is taken mostly indoors. The main difficulty lies in identifying faces of the same person from frequent changes of camera views and scenes, where faces have large appearance variations in viewing angle, pose, scale, and illumination.

Music video dataset. We introduce a new set of 8 music videos from YouTube. These videos present a new set of challenges, e.g., frequent shot/scene changes, large appearance variations, and rapid camera motion. We believe that these challenges are crucial for developing robust multi-face tracking algorithms in unconstrained environments. Three of the sequences (T-ARA, WESTLIFE and PUSSYCAT DOLLS) are live vocal concert recordings from multiple cameras with different views. The other sequences (BRUNO MARS, APINK, HELLO BUBBLE, DARLING and GIRLS ALOUD) are MTV videos. Faces in these videos often undergo large appearance variations due to changes in pose, scale, makeup, illumination, camera motion, and occlusions.

6.3   Evaluation Metrics

We evaluate the proposed method in two aspects. First, to evaluate the effectiveness of the learned video-specific features, we use the bottom-up HAC algorithm to merge pairs of tracklets until all tracklets have been merged into the ideal number of clusters (i.e., the actual number of people in the video). We measure the quality of clustering using the weighted purity: $W = \frac{1}{M} \sum_c m_c \cdot p_c$, where each cluster c contains m_c elements and its purity p_c is measured as a fraction of the largest number of faces from the same person to m_c, and M denotes the total number of faces in the video. Second, we evaluate the method with the metric set commonly used in multi-target tracking [42], including Recall, Precision, F1, FAF, IDS, Frag, MOTA and MOTP.

6.4   Evaluation on Features

We evaluate the proposed adaptive features against several alternatives:

– Ours-SymTriplet: a 64-D feature trained with the SymTriplet loss.
– Ours-Triplet: a 64-D feature trained with the original triplet loss.
– Ours-Siamese: a 64-D feature trained with the contrastive loss.
– HOG: a conventional hand-crafted feature with 4,356 dimensions.
– AlexNet: a generic feature representation with 4,096 dimensions from the AlexNet.
– Pre-trained: a 4,096-dimensional face feature from the AlexNet architecture trained on the WebFace dataset.
– VGG-Face [31]: a publicly available face descriptor with 4,096 dimensions.

We note that our 64-D features are more compact than all other baseline features.

Clustering purity. We quantitatively evaluate the above features on the all videos. Table 1 shows the performance of different features on 7 BBT sequences and 8 music videos. We show that identity-preserving features (Pre-trained and VGG-Face) trained on face datasets offline achieve better performance over generic feature representation (e.g., AlexNet and HOG). Our video-specific features trained with Siamese and Triplet networks achieve superior performance

Table 1. Clustering results on 7 BBT videos and 8 music videos. The weighted purity of each video is measured on the ideal number of clusters.

BBT dataset							
Episodes	BBT01	BBT02	BBT03	BBT04	BBT05	BBT06	BBT07
HOG	0.37	0.32	0.38	0.35	0.29	0.26	0.31
AlexNet	0.47	0.32	0.45	0.35	0.29	0.26	0.45
Pre-trained	0.62	0.72	0.73	0.57	0.52	0.52	0.61
VGG-Face	0.91	0.85	0.83	0.54	0.65	0.46	0.82
Ours-Siamese	**0.94**	**0.95**	0.87	0.74	0.70	0.70	0.89
Ours-Triplet	**0.94**	**0.95**	0.92	0.74	0.68	0.70	0.89
Ours-SymTriplet	**0.94**	**0.95**	**0.92**	**0.78**	**0.85**	**0.75**	**0.91**
Ours-SymTriplet-BBT02	0.90	**0.95**	0.87	0.74	0.79	0.67	0.88

Music dataset							
Videos	T-ara	Pussycat Dolls	Bruno Mars	Hello Bubble	Darling	Apink	Westlife	Girls Aloud
HOG	0.22	0.28	0.36	0.35	0.19	0.20	0.27	0.29
AlexNet	0.25	0.31	0.36	0.31	0.18	0.22	0.37	0.30
Pre-trained	0.31	0.31	0.50	0.34	0.24	0.29	0.37	0.33
VGG-Face	0.23	0.46	0.44	0.29	0.20	0.24	0.27	0.31
Ours-Siamese	**0.69**	0.77	0.88	0.54	0.46	0.48	0.54	0.67
Ours-Triplet	0.68	0.77	0.83	0.60	0.49	0.60	0.52	0.67
Ours-SymTriplet	**0.69**	**0.78**	**0.90**	**0.64**	**0.70**	**0.72**	**0.56**	**0.69**

to other alternatives, highlighting the importance of learning adaptive features. Using the proposed Symmetric Triplet loss function, Ours-SymTriplet achieves the best performance. For example, in the DARING sequence, Ours-SymTriplet achieves the highest weighted purity of 0.70, significantly outperforming other features, e.g., Ours-Siamese: 0.46, Ours-Triplet: 0.49, and VGG-Face: 0.20. Overall, our results are more than twice as accurate as VGG-Face in music videos. For the BBT dataset, Ours-SymTriplet consistently outperform all other alternatives.

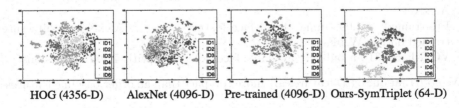

HOG (4356-D)   AlexNet (4096-D)   Pre-trained (4096-D)   Ours-SymTriplet (64-D)

Fig. 5. 2D tSNE visualization of all face features from the proposed fine-tuned CNN for adapting video-specific variations, compared with HOG, AlexNet, and Pre-trained features. T-ARA has 6 main casts. The faces of different people are color coded. (Color figure online)

The t-SNE visualization. In Fig. 5, we extract the features using HOG, AlexNet, Pre-trained and Ours-SymTriplet on the T-ARA video, and visualize them in 2D using the t-SNE algorithm [43]. For HOG there exists no clear cluster structures, faces of the same person are scattered into many different places. It shows that the conventional features are not effective for faces with large appearance variations. Compared to HOG, the AlexNet and Pre-trained features increase inter-person distances, but the clusters of the same person do not group together. Our adaptive features form tighter clusters for the same person and greater separation for different persons.

6.5 Multi-face Tracking

We compare the proposed algorithm with several state-of-the-art MTT trackers, including modified versions of TLD [32], ADMM [44], IHTLS [45], and Wu et al. [18,24]. Note that TLD [32] is a long-term single-target tracker which can re-detect targets of interest when targets leave and re-enter a scene. We implement two multi-face tracking methods with TLD. The first method is called mTLD. On each sequence, we run multiple TLD trackers for all targets, and each TLD tracker is initialized with the ground truth bounding box in the first frame. For the second method, we integrate mTLD into our framework (referred as Ours-mTLD). mTLD is used to generate shot-level trajectories within each shot instead of the two-threshold and Hungarian algorithms. At the beginning of each shot, we initialize TLD trackers with untracked detections, and link the detections in the following frames according to their overlap scores with TLD outputs.

Table 2 shows quantitative results of the proposed algorithm and the mTLD [32], ADMM [44] and IHTLS [45] on the BBT and music video datasets. We also show the tracking results with the Pre-trained features instead of the proposed video-specific features. Note that the results shown in Table 2 are the *overall* evaluation. We leave the results on each individual sequence to the supplementary material.

The mTLD method does not perform well in terms of recall, precision, F1, and MOTA metrics on both datasets. We attribute the poor performance to its tendency to drift and the use of low-level features. The ADMM [44] and IHTLS [45] often produce many identity switches and fragments because they fail to re-identify persons when abrupt camera motions or shot changes occur. The Pre-trained features are not effective to identify faces in different shots, and achieve very low MOTA. Ours-mTLD has more IDS and Frag than Ours-SymTriplet. The main reason is that the shot-level trajectories by mTLD are shorter and noisier than the original trajectories, since TLD trackers sometimes drift or do not output tracking results when there are large appearance changes. Ours-SymTriplet performs better in terms of precision, F1, and MOTA metrics, with significantly fewer identity switches and fragments than the competing algorithms.

Figure 6 shows sample tracking results of our algorithm with Ours-SymTriplet features on all eight music videos and three BBT sequences (BBT01, BBT02,

Fig. 6. Sample tracking results of the proposed algorithm. Shown from the top to bottom are HELLO BUBBLE, APINK, DARLING, T-ARA, BRUNO MARS, GIRLS ALOUD, WESTLIFE, PUSSYCAT DOLLS, BBT01, BBT02 and BBT05. The faces of the different people are color coded. (Color figure online)

Table 2. Quantitative comparison with other state-of-the-art multi-target tracking methods on the BBT and music video datasets. The **best** and <u>second-best</u> values are highlighted with the bold and underline, respectively.

BBT dataset								
Method	Recall↑	Precision↑	F1↑	FAF↓	IDS↓	Frag↓	MOTA↑	MOTP↑
mTLD [32]	1.1%	8.1%	1.9%	**0.18**	**8**	**83**	−11.2%	73.2%
ADMM [44]	**78.3%**	56.8%	65.8%	0.49	2709	4623	39.5%	72.7%
IHTLS [45]	<u>77.7%</u>	63.4%	69.8%	0.49	2648	4496	39.2%	72.7%
Pre-trained	45.0%	76.8%	56.8%	<u>0.19</u>	908	<u>2435</u>	30.0%	**77.9%**
Ours-mTLD	63.7%	78.8%	70.5%	0.24	1224	3487	44.6%	<u>77.6%</u>
Ours-Siamese	74.5%	**81.4%**	77.8%	0.24	884	4051	<u>56.1%</u>	77.4%
Ours-Triplet	76.2%	80.2%	<u>78.1%</u>	0.27	944	4223	55.8%	77.3%
Ours-SymTriplet	76.6%	<u>81.0%</u>	**78.7%**	0.26	<u>846</u>	4261	**57.2%**	77.2%
Music video dataset								
Method	Recall↑	Precision↑	F1↑	FAF↓	IDS↓	Frag↓	MOTA↑	MOTP↑
mTLD [32]	9.7%	36.1%	15.3%	0.39	**280**	**621**	−7.7%	68.4%
ADMM [44]	**75.5%**	61.8%	68.0%	0.50	2382	2959	51.7%	63.7%
IHTLS [45]	**75.5%**	68.0%	71.6%	0.41	2013	2880	56.2%	63.7%
Pre-trained	60.1%	88.8%	71.7%	**0.17**	931	<u>2140</u>	51.5%	<u>79.5%</u>
Ours-mTLD	69.1%	88.1%	77.4%	0.21	1914	2786	57.7%	**80.1%**
Ours-Siamese	71.5%	<u>89.4%</u>	<u>79.5%</u>	<u>0.19</u>	986	2512	<u>62.3%</u>	64.0%
Ours-Triplet	<u>71.8%</u>	88.8%	79.4%	0.20	902	2546	61.8%	64.2%
Ours-SymTriplet	<u>71.8%</u>	**89.7%**	**79.8%**	<u>0.19</u>	<u>699</u>	2563	**62.8%**	64.3%

Fig. 7. Failure cases. Our method incorrectly identifies different persons as the same one across shots on the APINK and DARLING sequences. Numbers and colors of rectangles indicate the *ground truth* identities of persons. The red rectangles show the predicted locations, and are tracked as one person by our method. On the APINK sequence on the left, the three different persons are incorrectly assigned with the same identity. On the DARLING sequence on the right, the middle person is assigned with an incorrect identity. (Color figure online)

and BBT05). The numbers and the colors indicate the inferred identities of the targets. The proposed algorithm is able to track multiple faces well despite large appearance variations in unconstrained videos. For example, there are significant changes in scale and appearance (due to makeup and hairstyle) in the HELLO BUBBLE sequence (first row). In the fourth row, the six singers have similar looks and thus make multi-face tracking particularly challenging within and across shots. Nonetheless, the proposed algorithm is able to distinguish the faces and track them reliably with few id switches. The results in other rows illustrate that our method is able to generate correct identities and trajectories when the same person appears in different shots or different scenes. More results and large images are available in the supplementary material.

6.6   Discussions

While the proposed adaptive feature learning method performs favorably against the state-of-the-art face tracking and clustering methods in handling challenging video sequences, there are three main limitations.

First, as our algorithm takes face detections as inputs, the tracking performance depends on whether faces can be reliably detected. For examples, in the fourth row of Fig. 6, the left-most person was not detected in Frame 419 and adjacent frames due to occlusion, and thus is not tracked. In addition, falsely detected faces could be incorrectly linked as a trajectory, e.g., the Marilyn Monroe image on the T-shirt in Frame 5,704 in the eighth row of Fig. 6.

Second, our method may not perform well on sequences where there are no sufficient training samples. We show in Fig. 7 two failure cases in the DARLING and APINK sequences. In these two sequences, many shots contain only one single person. Our method thus cannot generate negative face pairs for training the Siamese/Triplet network for distinguishing similar faces. Our method incorrectly identifies different persons as the same one. A promising direction would exploit other weak supervision signals (e.g., scripts, voice, contextual information) to generate visual constraints.

Third, the CNN fine-tuning is time-consuming. It takes around 1 hour on a NVIDIA GT980Ti GPU to run 10,000 back-propagation iterations. There are two approaches that may alleviate this issue. First, we may use faster training algorithms [46,47]. Second, for TV Sitcom episodes we can use one or a few videos for feature adaptation and apply the learned features to all other episodes. Note that we only need to adapt features *once* as the main characters are the same. In Table 1, we trained Ours-SymTriplet features on BBT02 (referred to Ours-SymTriplet-BBT02), and tested on other episodes. Although the weight purity of Ours-SymTriplet-BBT02 is slightly inferior than that of Ours-SymTriplet, it still outperforms the pre-trained features and the VGG-Face.

Several other work exploit body descriptors for improving character tracking in TV Sitcom videos [48]. However, these body descriptors may not be helpful for music videos as a person may be in completely different outfits in different scenes, e.g., the first row in Fig. 6. While in this work we investigate the multi-face tracking problem, we believe that our framework based on tracklet information is also applicable to other general unconstrained tracking problem, e.g., crowd analysis for pedestrians or cars in surveillance videos. We leave this for future work.

7   Conclusions

We propose an effective feature learning method for multi-face tracking. We first pre-train a CNN on a large-scale face recognition dataset to learn identity-preserving features. This CNN is adapted with samples automatically discovered from the visual constraints. In addition, we propose the SymTriplet loss function to learn more discriminative features for handling appearance variations of faces presented in a specific video. A hierarchical clustering algorithm is used to link face tracklets across multiple shots. Experimental results show that the proposed algorithm outperforms the state-of-the-art methods in terms of clustering accuracy and tracking performance.

Acknowledgement. The work is partially supported by National Basic Research Program of China (973 Program, 2015CB351705), NSFC (61332018), Office of Naval Research (N0014-16-1-2314), R&D programs by NRF (2014R1A1A2058501) and MSIP/IITP (IITP-2016-H8601-16-1005) of Korea, NSF CAREER (1149783) and gifts from Adobe and NVIDIA.

References

1. Brendel, W., Amer, M., Todorovic, S.: Multiobject tracking as maximum weight independent set. In: CVPR (2011)
2. Collins, R.T.: Multitarget data association with higher-order motion models. In: CVPR (2012)
3. Yang, B., Nevatia, R.: Multi-target tracking by online learning of non-linear motion patterns and robust appearance models. In: CVPR (2012)
4. Zhang, L., Li, Y., Nevatia, R.: Global data association for multi-object tracking using network flows. In: CVPR (2008)
5. Zhao, X., Gong, D., Medioni, G.: Tracking using motion patterns for very crowded scenes. In: Fitzgibbon, A., Lazebnik, S., Perona, P., Sato, Y., Schmid, C. (eds.) ECCV 2012, Part II. LNCS, vol. 7573, pp. 315–328. Springer, Heidelberg (2012)
6. Dalal, N., Triggs, B.: Histograms of oriented gradients for human detection. In: CVPR (2005)
7. Donahue, J., Jia, Y., Vinyals, O., Hoffman, J., Zhang, N., Tzeng, E., Darrell, T.: DeCAF: a deep convolutional activation feature for generic visual recognition. In: ICML (2014)
8. Sun, Y., Wang, X., Tang, X.: Deep learning face representation from predicting 10,000 classes. In: CVPR (2014)
9. Sun, Y., Chen, Y., Wang, X., Tang, X.: Deep learning face representation by joint identification-verification. In: NIPS (2014)
10. Schroff, F., Kalenichenko, D., Philbin, J.: FaceNet: a unified embedding for face recognition and clustering. In: CVPR (2015)
11. Hu, J., Lu, J., Tan, Y.P.: Discriminative deep metric learning for face verification in the wild. In: CVPR (2014)
12. Andriyenko, A., Schindler, K., Roth, S.: Discrete-continuous optimization for multi-target tracking. In: CVPR (2012)
13. Huang, C., Li, Y., Ai, H., et al.: Robust head tracking with particles based on multiple cues. In: ECCVW (2006)
14. Li, Y., Ai, H., Yamashita, T., Lao, S., Kawade, M.: Tracking in low frame rate video: a cascade particle filter with discriminative observers of different lifespans. In: CVPR (2007)
15. Ben Shitrit, H., Berclaz, J., Fleuret, F., Fua, P.: Tracking multiple people under global appearance constraints. In: ICCV (2011)

16. Huang, C., Wu, B., Nevatia, R.: Robust object tracking by hierarchical association of detection responses. In: Forsyth, D., Torr, P., Zisserman, A. (eds.) ECCV 2008, Part II. LNCS, vol. 5303, pp. 788–801. Springer, Heidelberg (2008)

17. Li, Y., Huang, C., Nevatia, R.: Learning to associate: hybridboosted multi-target tracker for crowded scene. In: CVPR (2009)

18. Wu, B., Lyu, S., Hu, B.G., Ji, Q.: Simultaneous clustering and tracklet linking for multi-face tracking in videos. In: ICCV (2013)

19. Andriyenko, A., Schindler, K.: Multi-target tracking by continuous energy minimization. In: CVPR (2011)

20. Roth, M., Bauml, M., Nevatia, R., Stiefelhagen, R.: Robust multi-pose face tracking by multi-stage tracklet association. In: ICPR (2012)

21. Wang, B., Wang, G., Chan, K.L., Wang, L.: Tracklet association with online target-specific metric learning. In: CVPR (2014)

22. Kuo, C.H., Nevatia, R.: How does person identity recognition help multi-person tracking? In: CVPR (2011)

23. Cinbis, R.G., Verbeek, J., Schmid, C.: Unsupervised metric learning for face identification in TV video. In: ICCV (2011)

24. Wu, B., Zhang, Y., Hu, B.G., Ji, Q.: Constrained clustering and its application to face clustering in videos. In: CVPR (2013)

25. Tapaswi, M., Parkhi, O.M., Rahtu, E., Sommerlade, E., Stiefelhagen, R., Zisserman, A.: Total cluster: a person agnostic clustering method for broadcast videos. In: ICVGIP (2014)

26. Xiao, S., Tan, M., Xu, D.: Weighted block-sparse low rank representation for face clustering in videos. In: Fleet, D., Pajdla, T., Schiele, B., Tuytelaars, T. (eds.) ECCV 2014, Part VI. LNCS, vol. 8694, pp. 123–138. Springer, Heidelberg (2014)

27. Bauml, M., Tapaswi, M., Stiefelhagen, R.: Semi-supervised learning with constraints for person identification in multimedia data. In: CVPR (2013)

28. Sivic, J., Everingham, M., Zisserman, A.: "Who are you?" - Learning person specific classifiers from video. In: CVPR (2009)

29. Everingham, M., Sivic, J., Zisserman, A.: "Hello! My name is... Buffy" - automatic naming of characters in TV video. In: BMVC (2006)

30. Taigman, Y., Yang, M., Ranzato, M., Wolf, L.: DeepFace: closing the gap to human-level performance in face verification. In: CVPR (2014)

31. Parkhi, O.M., Vedaldi, A., Zisserman, A.: Deep face recognition. In: BMVC (2015)

32. Kalal, Z., Mikolajczyk, K., Matas, J.: Tracking-learning-detection. TPAMI **34**(7), 1409–1422 (2012)

33. Pernici, F.: FaceHugger: the ALIEN tracker applied to faces. In: Fusiello, A., Murino, V., Cucchiara, R. (eds.) ECCV 2012. LNCS, vol. 7585, pp. 597–601. Springer, Heidelberg (2012). doi:10.1007/978-3-642-33885-4_61

34. Krizhevsky, A., Sutskever, I., Hinton, G.E.: ImageNet classification with deep convolutional neural networks. In: NIPS (2012)

35. Mathias, M., Benenson, R., Pedersoli, M., Van Gool, L.: Face detection without bells and whistles. In: Fleet, D., Pajdla, T., Schiele, B., Tuytelaars, T. (eds.) ECCV 2014, Part IV. LNCS, vol. 8692, pp. 720–735. Springer, Heidelberg (2014)

36. Breitenstein, M.D., Reichlin, F., Leibe, B., Koller-Meier, E., Van Gool, L.: Robust tracking-by-detection using a detector confidence particle filter. In: ICCV (2009)

37. Chopra, S., Hadsell, R., LeCun, Y.: Learning a similarity metric discriminatively, with application to face verification. In: CVPR (2005)

38. Hadsell, R., Chopra, S., LeCun, Y.: Dimensionality reduction by learning an invariant mapping. In: CVPR (2006)

39. Xing, J., Ai, H., Lao, S.: Multi-object tracking through occlusions by local tracklets filtering and global tracklets association with detection responses. In: CVPR (2009)
40. Yi, D., Lei, Z., Liao, S., Li, S.Z.: Learning face representation from scratch. arXiv (2014)
41. Jia, Y., Shelhamer, E., Donahue, J., Karayev, S., Long, J., Girshick, R., Guadarrama, S., Darrell, T.: Caffe: convolutional architecture for fast feature embedding. In: ACM MM (2014)
42. Zhang, S., Wang, J., Wang, Z., Gong, Y., Liu, Y.: Multi-target tracking by learning local-to-global trajectory models. PR **48**(2), 580–590 (2015)
43. Van der Maaten, L., Hinton, G.: JMLR **9**(2579–2605), 85 (2008)
44. Ayazoglu, M., Sznaier, M., Camps, O.I.: Fast algorithms for structured robust principal component analysis. In: CVPR (2012)
45. Dicle, C., Camps, O.I., Sznaier, M.: The way they move: tracking multiple targets with similar appearance. In: ICCV (2013)
46. Lin, Z., Courbariaux, M., Memisevic, R., Bengio, Y.: Neural networks with few multiplications. arXiv (2015)
47. Jaderberg, M., Vedaldi, A., Zisserman, A.: Speeding up convolutional neural networks with low rank expansions. In: BMVC (2014)
48. Tapaswi, M., Bauml, M., Stiefelhagen, R.: Knock! Knock! Who is it? Probabilistic person identification in TV-series. In: CVPR (2012)

Action, Activity and Tracking

Spot On: Action Localization
from Pointly-Supervised Proposals

Pascal Mettes[1(✉)], Jan C. van Gemert[2], and Cees G.M. Snoek[1]

[1] University of Amsterdam, Amsterdam, Netherlands
P.S.M.Mettes@uva.nl
[2] Delft University of Technology, Delft, Netherlands

Abstract. We strive for spatio-temporal localization of actions in videos. The state-of-the-art relies on action proposals at test time and selects the best one with a classifier trained on carefully annotated box annotations. Annotating action boxes in video is cumbersome, tedious, and error prone. Rather than annotating boxes, we propose to annotate actions in video with points on a sparse subset of frames only. We introduce an overlap measure between action proposals and points and incorporate them all into the objective of a non-convex Multiple Instance Learning optimization. Experimental evaluation on the UCF Sports and UCF 101 datasets shows that (i) spatio-temporal proposals can be used to train classifiers while retaining the localization performance, (ii) point annotations yield results comparable to box annotations while being significantly faster to annotate, (iii) with a minimum amount of supervision our approach is competitive to the state-of-the-art. Finally, we introduce spatio-temporal action annotations on the train and test videos of Hollywood2, resulting in *Hollywood2Tubes*, available at http://tinyurl.com/hollywood2tubes.

Keywords: Action localization · Action proposals

1 Introduction

This paper is about spatio-temporal localization of actions like *Driving a car*, *Kissing*, and *Hugging* in videos. Starting from a sliding window legacy [1], the common approach these days is to generate tube-like proposals at test time, encode each of them with a feature embedding and select the most relevant one, *e.g.,* [2–5]. All these works, be it sliding windows or tube proposals, assume that a carefully annotated training set with boxes per frame is available a priori. In this paper, we challenge this assumption. We propose a simple algorithm that leverages proposals at *training* time, with a minimum amount of supervision, to speedup action location annotation.

Electronic supplementary material The online version of this chapter (doi:10.1007/978-3-319-46454-1_27) contains supplementary material, which is available to authorized users.

© Springer International Publishing AG 2016
B. Leibe et al. (Eds.): ECCV 2016, Part V, LNCS 9909, pp. 437–453, 2016.
DOI: 10.1007/978-3-319-46454-1_27

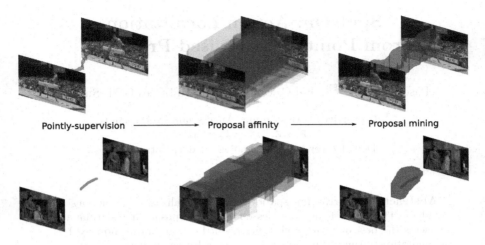

Fig. 1. Overview of our approach for a *Swinging* and *Standing up* action. First, the video is annotated cheaply using point-supervision. Then, action proposals are extracted and scored using our overlap measure. Finally, our proposal mining aims to discover the single one proposal that best represents the action, given the provided points.

We draw inspiration from related work on weakly-supervised object detection, *e.g.*, [6–8]. The goal is to detect an object and its bounding box at test time given only the object class label at train time and no additional supervision. The common tactic in the literature is to model this as a Multiple Instance Learning (MIL) problem [8–10] where positive images contain at least one positive object proposal and negative images contain only negative proposals. During each iteration of MIL, a detector is trained and applied on the train set to re-identify the object proposal most likely to enclose the object of interest. Upon convergence, the final detector is applied on the test set. Methods typically vary in their choice of initial proposals and the multiple instance learning optimization. In the domain of action localization a similar MIL tactic easily extends to action proposals as well but results in poor accuracy as our experiments show. Similar to weakly-supervised object detection, we rely on (action) proposals and MIL, but we include a minimum amount of supervision to retain action localization accuracy competitive with full supervision.

Obvious candidates for the supervision are action class labels and bounding boxes, but other forms of supervision, such as tags and line strokes, are also feasible [11]. In [12], Bearman *et al.* show that human-provided points on the image are valuable annotations for semantic segmentation of objects. By inclusion of an objectness prior in their loss function they report a better efficiency/effectiveness trade off compared to image-level annotations and free-from squiggles. We follow their example in the video domain and leverage point-supervision to aid MIL in finding the best action proposals at training time.

We make three contributions in this work. First, we propose to train action localization classifiers using spatio-temporal proposals as positive examples rather than ground truth tubes. While common in object detection, such an approach is as of yet unconventional in action localization. In fact, we show that using proposals instead of ground truth annotations does not lead to a decrease in action localization accuracy. Second, we introduce an MIL algorithm that is able to mine proposals with a good spatio-temporal fit to actions of interest by including point supervision. It extends the traditional MIL objective with an overlap measure that takes into account the affinity between proposals and points. Finally, with the aid of our proposal mining algorithm, we are able to supplement the complete Hollywood2 dataset by Marszałek *et al.* [13] with action location annotations, resulting in *Hollywood2Tubes*. We summarize our approach in Fig. 1. Experiments on Hollywood2Tubes, as well as the more traditional UCF Sports and UCF 101 collections support our claims. Before detailing our pointly-supervised approach we present related work.

2   Related Work

Action localization is a difficult problem and annotations are avidly used. Single image bounding box annotations allow training a part-based detector [1,14] or a per-frame detector where results are aggregated over time [15,16]. However, since such detectors first have to be trained themselves, they cannot be used when no bounding box annotations are available. Independent training data can be brought in to automatically detect individual persons for action localization [3, 17,18]. A person detector, however, will fail to localize contextual actions such as *Driving* or interactions such as *Shaking hands* or *Kissing*. Recent work using unsupervised action proposals based on supervoxels [2,5,19] or on trajectory clustering [4,20,21], have shown good results for action localization. In this paper we rely on action proposals to aid annotation. Proposals give excellent recall without supervision and are thus well-suited for an unlabeled train set.

Large annotated datasets are slowly coming available in action localization. Open annotations benefit the community, paving the way for new data-driven action localization methods. UCF-Sports [22], HOHA [23] and MSR-II [24] have up to a few hundred actions, while UCF101 [25], Penn-Action [26], and J-HMBD [27] have 1–3 thousand action clips and 3 to 24 action classes. The problem of scaling up to larger sets is not due to sheer dataset size: there are millions of action videos with hundreds of action classes available [25,28–30]. The problem lies with the spatio-temporal annotation effort. In this paper we show how to ease this annotation effort, exemplified by releasing spatio-temporal annotations for all Hollywood2 [13] videos.

Several software tools are developed to lighten the annotation burden. The gain can come from a well-designed user interface to annotate videos with bounding boxes [31,32] or even polygons [33]. We move away from such complex annotations and only require a point. Such point annotations can readily be included in existing annotation tools which would further reduce effort. Other algorithms can reduce annotation effort by intelligently selecting which example to label [34]. Active learning [35] or trained detectors [36] can assist the human annotator. The disadvantage of such methods is the bias towards the used recognition method. We do not bias any algorithm to decide where and what to annotate: by only setting points we can quickly annotate all videos.

Weakly supervised methods predict more information than was annotated. Examples from static images include predicting a bounding box while having only class labels [8,37,38] or even no labels al all [39]. In the video domain, the temporal dimension offers more annotation variation. Semi-supervised learning for video object detection is done with a few bounding boxes [40,41], a few global frame labels [42], only video class labels [43], or no labels at all [44]. For action localization, only the video label is used by [45,46], whereas [47] use no labels. As our experiments show, using no label or just class labels performs well below fully supervised results. Thus, we propose a middle ground: pointing at the action. Compared to annotating full bounding boxes this greatly reduces annotation time while retaining accuracy.

3   Strong Action Localization Using Cheap Annotations

We start from the hypothesis that an action localization proposal may substitute the ground truth on a training set without a significant loss of classification accuracy. Proposal algorithms yield hundreds to thousands of proposals per video with the hope that at least one proposal matches the action well [2,4,5,19–21]. The problem thus becomes how to mine the best proposal out of a large set of candidate proposals with minimal supervision effort.

3.1   Cheap Annotations: Action Class Labels and Pointly-Supervision

A minimum of supervision effort is an action class label for the whole video. For such global video labels, a traditional approach to mining the best proposal is Multiple Instance Learning [10] (MIL). In the context of action localization, each video is interpreted as a bag and the proposals in each video are interpreted as its instances. The goal of MIL is to train a classifier that can be used for proposal mining by using only the global label.

Next to the global action class label we leverage cheap annotations within each video: for a subset of frames we simply point at the action. We refer to such a set of point annotations as *pointly-supervision*. The supervision allows us to easily exclude those proposals that have no overlap with any annotated point. Nevertheless, there are still many proposals that intersect with at least one point. Thus, points do not uniquely identify a single proposal. In the following we will introduce an overlap measure to associate proposals with points. To perform the proposal mining, we will extend MIL's objective to include this measure.

3.2   Measuring Overlap Between Points and Proposals

To explain how we obtain our overlap measure, let us first introduce the following notation. For a video V of N frames, an action localization proposal $A = \{BB_i\}_{i=f}^m$ consists of connected bounding boxes through video frames $(f, ..., m)$ where $1 \leq f \leq m \leq N$. We use $\overline{BB_i}$ to indicate the center of a bounding box i. The pointly-supervision $C = \{(x_i, y_i)\}^K$ is a set of $K \leq N$ subsampled video frames where each frame i has a single annotated point (x_i, y_i). Our overlap measure outputs a score for each proposal depending on how well the proposal matches the points.

Inspired by a mild center-bias in annotators [48], we introduce a term $M(\cdot)$ to represent how close the center of a bounding box proposal is to an annotated point, relative to the bounding box size. Since large proposals have a higher likelihood to contain any annotated point we use a regularization term $S(\cdot)$ on the proposal size. The center-bias term $M(\cdot)$ normalizes the distance to the bounding box center by the distance to the furthest bounding box side. A point $(x_i, y_i) \in C$ outside a bounding box $BB_i \in A$ scores 0 and a point on the bounding box center $\overline{BB_i}$ scores 1. The score decreases linearly with the distance to the center for the point. It is averaged over all annotated points K:

$$M(A, C) = \frac{1}{K} \sum_{i=1}^{K} \max(0, 1 - \frac{||(x_i, y_i) - \overline{BB_{K_i}}||_2}{\max_{(u,v) \in e(BB_{K_i})} ||((u, v) - \overline{BB_{K_i}})||_2}, \quad (1)$$

where $e(BB_{K_i})$ denotes the box edges of box BB_{K_i}.

We furthermore add a regularization on the size of the proposals. The idea behind the regularization is that small spatial proposals can occur anywhere. Large proposals, however, are obstructed by the edges of the video. This biases their middle-point around the center of the video, where the action often happens. The size regularization term $S(\cdot)$ addresses this bias by penalizing proposals with large bounding boxes $|BB_i| \in A$, compared to the size of a video frame $|F_i| \in V$,

$$S(A, V) = \left(\frac{\sum_{i=f}^{m} |BB_i|}{\sum_{j=1}^{N} |F_j|} \right)^2. \quad (2)$$

Using the center-bias term $M(\cdot)$ regularized by $S(\cdot)$, our overlap measure $O(\cdot)$ is defined as

$$O(A, C, V) = M(A, C) - S(A, V). \quad (3)$$

Recall that A are the proposals, C captures the pointly-supervision and V the video. We use $O(\cdot)$ in an iterative proposal mining algorithm over all annotated videos in search for the best proposals.

3.3   Mining Proposals Overlapping with Points

For proposal mining, we start from a set of action videos $\{\mathbf{x}_i, t_i, y_i, C_i\}_{i=1}^N$, where $\mathbf{x}_i \in \mathbb{R}^{A_i \times D}$ is the D-dimensional feature representation of the A_i proposals in video i. Variable $t_i = \{\{BB_j\}_{j=f}^m\}^{A_i}$ denotes the collection of tubes for the A_i proposals. Cheap annotations consist of the class label y_i and the points C_i.

For proposal mining we insert our overlap measure $O(\cdot)$ in a Multiple Instance Learning scheme to train a classification model that can learn the difference between good and bad proposals. Guided by $O(\cdot)$, the classifier becomes increasingly more aware about which proposals are a good representative for an action. We start from a standard MIL-SVM [8,10] and adapt it's objective with the mining score $P(\cdot)$ of each proposal, which incorporates our function $O(\cdot)$ as:

$$\min_{\mathbf{w},b,\xi} \frac{1}{2}||\mathbf{w}||^2 + \lambda \sum_i \xi_i,$$

$$\text{s.t.} \quad \forall_i : y_i \cdot (\mathbf{w} \cdot \operatorname*{argmax}_{\mathbf{z} \in x_i} P(\mathbf{z}|\mathbf{w}, b, t_i, C_i, V_i) + b) \geq 1 - \xi_i, \qquad (4)$$

$$\forall_i : \xi_i \geq 0,$$

where $(\mathbf{w}, b)$ denote the classifier parameters, ξ_i denotes the slack variable and λ denotes the regularization parameter. The proposal with the highest mining score per video is used to train the classifier.

The objective of Eq. 4 is non-convex due to the joint minimization over the classifier parameters $(\mathbf{w}, b)$ and the maximization over the mined proposals $P(\cdot)$. Therefore, we perform iterative block coordinate descent by alternating between clamping one and optimizing the other. For fixed classifier parameters $(\mathbf{w}, b)$, we mine the proposal with the highest Maximum a Posteriori estimate with the classifier as the likelihood and $O(\cdot)$ as the prior:

$$P(\mathbf{z}|\mathbf{w}, b, t_i, C_i, V_i) \propto (<\mathbf{w}, \mathbf{z}> +b) \cdot O(t_i, C_i, V_i). \qquad (5)$$

After a proposal mining step, we fix $P(\cdot)$ and train the classifier parameters $(\mathbf{w}, b)$ with stochastic gradient descent on the mined proposals. We alternate the mining and classifier optimizations for a fixed amount of iterations. After the iterative optimization, we train a final SVM on the best mined proposals and use that classifier for action localization.

4   Experimental Setup

4.1   Datasets

We perform our evaluation on two action localization datasets that have bounding box annotations both for training and test videos.

UCF Sports consists of 150 videos covering 10 action categories [49], such as *Diving*, *Kicking*, and *Skateboarding*. The videos are extracted from sport broadcasts and are trimmed to contain a single action. We employ the train and test data split as suggested in [14].

UCF 101 has 101 actions categories [25] where 24 categories have spatiotemporal action localization annotations. This subset has 3,204 videos, where each video contains a single action category, but might contain multiple instances of the same action. We use the first split of the train and test sets as suggested in [25] with 2,290 videos for training and 914 videos for testing.

4.2   Implementation Details

Proposals. Our proposal mining is agnostic to the underlying proposal algorithm. We have performed experiments using proposals from both APT [4] and Tubelets [2]. We found APT to perform slightly better and report all results using APT.

Features. For each tube we extract Improved Dense Trajectories and compute HOG, HOF, Traj, MBH features [50]. The combined features are reduced to 128 dimensions through PCA and aggregated into a fixed-size representation using Fisher Vectors [51]. We construct a codebook of 128 clusters, resulting in a 54,656-dimensional representation per proposal.

Training. We train the proposal mining optimization for 10 iterations for all our evaluations, similar to Cinbis *et al.* [8]. Following further suggestions by [8], we randomly split the training videos into multiple (3) splits to train and select the instances. While training a classifier for one action, we randomly sample 100 proposals of each video from the other actions as negatives. We set the SVM regularization λ to 100.

Evaluation. During testing we apply the classifier to all proposals of a test video and maintain the top proposals per video. To evaluate the action localization performance, we compute the Intersection-over-Union (IoU) between proposal p and the box annotations of the corresponding test example b as: $\text{iou}(p, b) = \frac{1}{|\Gamma|} \sum_{f \in \Gamma} IoU_{p,b}(f)$, where Γ is the set of frames where at least one of p, b is present [2]. The function IoU states the box overlap for a specified frame. For IoU threshold t, a top selected proposal is deemed a positive detection if $\text{iou}(p, b) \geq t$.

After combining the top proposals from all videos, we compute the Average Precision score using their ranked scores and positive/negative detections. For the comparison to the state-of-the-art on UCF Sports, we additionally report AUC (Area under ROC curve) on the scores and detections.

5   Results

5.1   Training Without Ground Truth Tubes

First we evaluate our starting hypothesis of replacing ground truth tubes with proposals for training action localization classifiers. We compare three approaches: (1) train on ground truth annotated bounding boxes; (2) train on the proposal with the highest IoU overlap for each video; (3) train on the proposal mined based on point annotations and our proposal mining. For the points on both datasets, we take the center of each annotated bounding box.

Training with the best proposal. Figure 2 shows that the localization results for the best proposal are similar to the ground truth tube for both datasets and across all IoU overlap thresholds as defined in Sect. 4.2. This result shows that proposals are sufficient to train classifiers for action localization. The result is somewhat surprising given that the best proposals used to train the classifiers

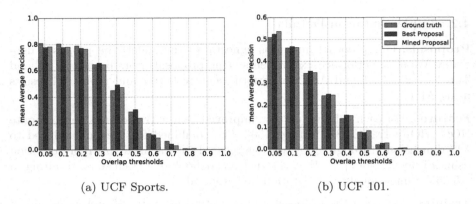

(a) UCF Sports.   (b) UCF 101.

Fig. 2. Training action localization classifiers with proposals vs ground truth tubes on (a) UCF Sports and (b) UCF 101. Across both datasets and thresholds, the best possible proposal yields similar results to using the ground truth. Also note how well our mined proposal matches the ground truth and best possible proposal we could have selected.

have a less than perfect fit with the ground truth action. We computed the fit with the ground truth, and on average the IoU score of the best proposals (the ABO score) is 0.642 on UCF Sports and 0.400 on UCF 101. The best proposals are quite loosely aligned with the ground truth. Yet, training on such non-perfect proposals is not detrimental for results. This means that a perfect fit with the action is not a necessity during training. An explanation for this result is that the action classifier is now trained on the same type of noisy samples that it will encounter at test-time. This better aligns the training with the testing, resulting in slightly improved accuracy.

Training with proposal mining from points. Figure 2 furthermore shows the localization results from training without bounding box annotations using only point annotations. On both data sets, results are competitive to the ground truth tubes across all thresholds. This result shows that when training on proposals, carefully annotated box annotations are not required. Our proposal mining is able to discover the best proposals from cheap point annotations. The discrepancy between the ground truth and our mined proposal for training is shown in Fig. 3 for thee videos. For some videos, *e.g.,* Fig. 3a, the ground truth and the proposal have a high similarity. This does however not hold for all videos, *e.g.,* Fig. 3b, where our mined proposal focuses solely on the lifter (*Lifting*), and Fig. 3c, where our mined proposal includes the horse (*Horse riding*).

Analysis. On UCF 101, where actions are not temporally trimmed, we observe an average temporal overlap of 0.74. The spatial overlap in frames where proposals and ground truth match is 0.38. This result indicates that we are better capable of detecting actions in the temporal domain than the spatial domain. On average, top ranked proposals during testing are 2.67 times larger than their corresponding ground truth. Despite a preference for larger proposals, our results

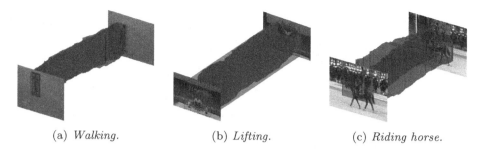

(a) *Walking.*   (b) *Lifting.*   (c) *Riding horse.*

Fig. 3. Training video showing our mined proposal (blue) and the ground truth (red). (a) Mined proposals might have a high similarity to the ground truth. In (b) our mining focuses solely on the person lifting, while in (c) our mining has learned to include part of the horse. An imperfect fit with the ground truth does not imply a bad proposal. (Color figure online)

are comparable to the fully supervised method trained on expensive ground truth bounding box tubes. Finally, we observe that most false positives are proposals from positive test videos with an overlap score below the specified threshold. On average, 26.7 % of the top 10 proposals on UCF 101 are proposals below the overlap threshold of 0.2. Regarding false negatives, on UCF 101 at a 0.2 overlap threshold, 37.2 % of the actions are not among the top selected proposals. This is primarily because the proposal algorithm does not provide a single proposal with enough overlap.

From this experiment we conclude that training directly on proposals does not lead to a reduction in action localization accuracy. Furthermore, using cheap point annotations with our proposal mining yields results competitive to using carefully annotated bounding box annotations.

5.2 Must Go Faster: Lowering the Annotation Frame-Rate

The annotation effort can be significantly reduced by annotating less frames. Here we investigate how a higher annotation frame-rate influences the trade-off between annotation speed-up versus classification performance. We compare higher annotation frame-rates for points and ground-truth bounding boxes.

Setup. For measuring annotation time we randomly selected 100 videos from the UCF Sports and UCF 101 datasets separately and performed the annotations. We manually annotated boxes and points for all evaluated frame-rates $\{1, 2, 5, 10, ...\}$. We obtain the points by simply reducing a bounding box annotation to its center. We report the speed-up in annotation time compared to drawing a bounding box on every frame. Classification results are given for two common IoU overlap thresholds on the test set, namely 0.2 and 0.5.

Results. In Fig. 4 we show the localization performance as a function of the annotation speed-up for UCF Sports and UCF 101. Note that when annotating all frames, a point is roughly 10–15 times faster to annotate than a box.

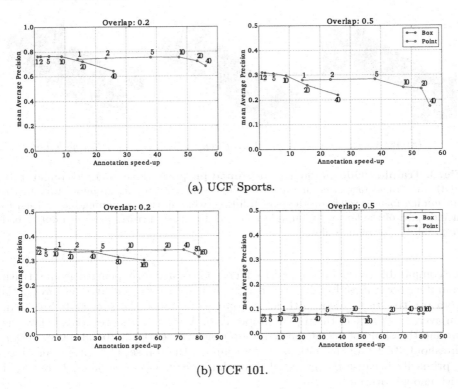

(a) UCF Sports.

(b) UCF 101.

Fig. 4. The annotation speedup versus mean Average Precision scores on (a) UCF Sports and (b) UCF 101 for two overlap thresholds using both box and point annotations. The annotation frame-rates are indicated on the lines. Using points remains competitive to boxes with a 10x to 80x annotation speed-up.

The reason for the reduction in relative speed-up between the higher frame-rates is due to the constant time spent on determining the action label of each video. When analyzing classification performance we note it is not required to annotate all frames. Although the performance generally decreases as less frames are annotated, using a frame rate of 10 (*i.e.,* annotating 10% of the frames) is generally sufficient for retaining localization performance. We can get competitive classification scores with an annotation speedup of 45 times or more.

The results of Fig. 4 show the effectiveness of our proposal mining after the iterative optimization. In Fig. 5, we provide three qualitative training examples, highlighting the mining during the iterations. We show two successful examples, where mining improves the quality of the top proposal, and a failure case, where the proposal mining reverts back to the initially mined proposal.

Based on this experiment, we conclude that points are faster to annotate, while they retain localization performance. We recommend that at least 10% of the frames are annotated with a point to mine the best proposals during training. Doing so results in a 45 times or more annotation time speed-up.

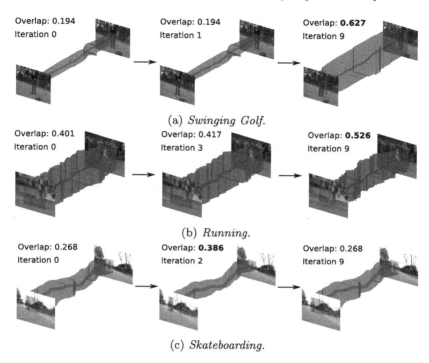

(a) *Swinging Golf.*

(b) *Running.*

(c) *Skateboarding.*

Fig. 5. Qualitative examples of the iterative proposal mining (blue) during training, guided by points (red) on UCF Sports. (a) and (b): the final best proposals have a significantly improved overlap (from 0.194 to 0.627 and from 0.401 to 0.526 IoU). (c): the final best proposal is the same as the initial best proposal, although halfway through the iterations, a better proposal was mined. (Color figure online)

5.3   Hollywood2Tubes: Action Localization for Hollywood2

Based on the results from the first two experiments, we are able to supplement the complete Hollywood2 dataset by Marszałek *et al.* [13] with action location annotations, resulting in *Hollywood2Tubes*. The dataset consists of 12 actions, such as *Answer a Phone, Driving a Car*, and *Sitting up/down*. In total, there are 823 train videos and 884 test videos, where each video contains at least one action. Each video can furthermore have multiple instances of the same action. Following the results of Experiment 2 we have annotated a point on each action instance for every 10 frames per training video. In total, there are 1,026 action instances in the training set; 29,802 frames have been considered and 16,411 points have been annotated. For the test videos, we are still required to annotate bounding boxes to perform the evaluation. We annotate every 10 frames with a bounding box. On both UCF Sports and UCF 101, using 1 in 10 frames yields practically the same IoU score on the proposals. In total, 31,295 frames have been considered, resulting in 15,835 annotated boxes. The annotations, proposals, and localization results are available at http://tinyurl.com/hollywood2tubes.

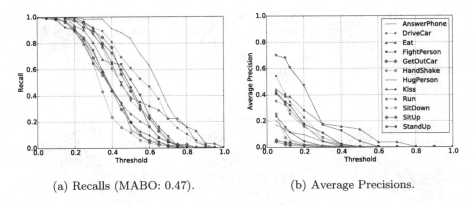

(a) Recalls (MABO: 0.47).   (b) Average Precisions.

Fig. 6. Hollywood2Tubes: Localization results for Hollywood2 actions across all overlap thresholds. The discrepancy between the recall and Average Precision indicates the complexity of the *Hollywood2Tubes* dataset for action localization.

Results. Following the experiments on UCF Sports and UCF 101, we apply proposals [4] on the videos of the Hollywood2 dataset. In Fig. 6a, we report the action localization test recalls based on our annotation efforts. Overall, a MABO of 0.47 is achieved. The recall scores are lowest for actions with a small temporal span, such as *Shaking hands* and *Answer a Phone*. The recall scores are highest for actions such as *Hugging a person* and *Driving a Car*. This is primarily because these actions almost completely fill the frames in the videos and have a long temporal span.

In Fig. 6b, we show the Average Precision scores using our proposal mining with point overlap scores. We observe that a high recall for an action does not necessarily yield a high Average Precision score. For example, the action *Sitting up* yields an above average recall curve, but yields the second lowest Average Precision curve. The reverse holds for the action *Fighting a Person*, which is a top performer in Average Precision. These results provide insight into the complexity of jointly recognizing and localizing the individual actions of *Hollywood2Tubes*. The results of Fig. 6 shows that there is a lot of room for improvement.

In Fig. 7, we highlight a difficult cases for action localization, which are not present in current localization datasets, adding to the complexity of the dataset. In the Supplementary Materials, we outline additional difficult cases, such as cinematographic effects and switching between cameras within the same scene.

5.4   Comparison to the State-of-the-art

In the fourth experiment, we compare our results using the point annotations to the current state-of-the-art on action localization using box annotations on the UCF Sports, UCF 101, and Hollywood2Tubes datasets. In Table 1, we provide a comparison to related work on all datasets. For the UCF 101 and Hollywood2Tubes datasets, we report results with the mean Average Precision.

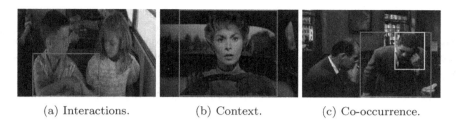

(a) Interactions.   (b) Context.   (c) Co-occurrence.

Fig. 7. Hard scenarios for action localization using Hollywood2Tubes, not present in current localization challenges. Highlighted are actions involving two or more people, actions partially defined by context, and co-occurring actions within the same video.

For UCF Sports, we report results with the Area Under the Curve (AUC) score, as the AUC score is the most used evaluation score on the dataset. All reported scores are for an overlap threshold of 0.2.

We furthermore compare our results to two baselines using other forms of cheap annotations. This first baseline is the method of Jain *et al.* [47] which performs zero-shot localization, *i.e.,* no annotation of the action itself is used, only annotations from other actions. The second baseline is the approach of Cinbis *et al.* [8] using global labels, applied to actions.

UCF Sports. For UCF Sports, we observe that our AUC score is competitive to the current state-of-the-art using full box supervision. Our AUC score of 0.545 is, similar to Experiments 1 and 2, nearly identical to the APT score (0.546) [4]. The score is furthermore close to the current state-of-the-art score of 0.559 [15,16]. The AUC scores for the two baselines without box supervision can not compete with our AUC scores. This result shows that points provide a rich enough source of annotations that are exploited by our proposal mining.

UCF 101. For UCF 101, we again observe similar performance to APT [4] and an improvement over the baseline annotation method. The method of Weinzaepfel *et al.* [16] performs better on this dataset. We attribute this to their strong proposals, which are not unsupervised and require additional annotations.

Hollywood2Tubes. For Hollywood2Tubes, we note that approaches using full box supervision can not be applied, due to the lack of box annotations on the training videos. We can still perform our approach and the baseline method of Cinbis *et al.* [8]. First, observe that the mean Average Precision scores on this dataset are lower than on UCF Sports and UCF 101, highlighting the complexity of the dataset. Second, we observe that the baseline approach using global video labels is outperformed by our approach using points, indicating that points provide a richer source of information for proposal mining than the baselines.

From this experiment, we conclude that our proposal mining using point annotations provides a profitable trade-off between annotation effort and performance for action localization.

Table 1. State-of-the-art localization results on the UCF Sports, UCF 101, and Hollywood2Tubes for an overlap threshold of 0.2. Where * indicates we run the approach of Cinbis *et al.* [8] intended for images on videos. Our approach using point annotations provides a profitable trade-off between annotation effort and performance for action localization.

Method	Supervision	UCF Sports	UCF 101	Hollywood2Tubes
		AUC	mAP	mAP
Lan *et al.* [14]	box	0.380	-	-
Tian *et al.* [1]	box	0.420	-	-
Wang *et al.* [18]	box	0.470	-	-
Jain *et al.* [2]	box	0.489	-	-
Chen *et al.* [20]	box	0.528	-	-
van Gemert *et al.* [4]	box	0.546	0.345	-
Soomro *et al.* [5]	box	0.550	-	-
Gkioxari *et al.* [15]	box	0.559	-	-
Weinzaepfel *et al.* [16]	box	0.559	0.468	-
Jain *et al.* [47]	zero-shot	0.232	-	-
Cinbis *et al.* [8]*	video label	0.278	0.136	0.009
This work	points	0.545	0.348	0.143

6   Conclusions

We conclude that carefully annotated bounding boxes precisely around an action are not needed for action localization. Instead of training on examples defined by expensive bounding box annotations on every frame, we use proposals for training yielding similar results. To determine which proposals are most suitable for training we only require cheap point annotations on the action for a fraction of the frames. Experimental evaluation on the UCF Sports and UCF 101 datasets shows that: (i) the use of proposals over directly using the ground truth does not lead to a loss in localization performance, (ii) action localization using points is comparable to using full box supervision, while being significantly faster to annotate, (iii) our results are competitive to the current state-of-the-art. Based on our approach and experimental results we furthermore introduce *Hollywood2Tubes*, a new action localization dataset with point annotations for train videos. The point of this paper is that valuable annotation time is better spent on clicking in more videos than on drawing precise bounding boxes.

Acknowledgements. This research is supported by the STW STORY project.

References

1. Tian, Y., Sukthankar, R., Shah, M.: Spatiotemporal deformable part models for action detection. In: CVPR (2013)
2. Jain, M., Van Gemert, J., Jégou, H., Bouthemy, P., Snoek, C.G.M.: Action localization with tubelets from motion. In: CVPR (2014)

3. Yu, G., Yuan, J.: Fast action proposals for human action detection and search. In: CVPR (2015)
4. van Gemert, J.C., Jain, M., Gati, E., Snoek, C.G.M.: APT: action localization proposals from dense trajectories. In: BMVC (2015)
5. Soomro, K., Idrees, H., Shah, M.: Action localization in videos through context walk. In: ICCV (2015)
6. Kim, G., Torralba, A.: Unsupervised detection of regions of interest using iterative link analysis. In: NIPS (2009)
7. Russakovsky, O., Lin, Y., Yu, K., Fei-Fei, L.: Object-centric spatial pooling for image classification. In: Fitzgibbon, A., Lazebnik, S., Perona, P., Sato, Y., Schmid, C. (eds.) ECCV 2012, Part II. LNCS, vol. 7573, pp. 1–15. Springer, Heidelberg (2012)
8. Cinbis, R.G., Verbeek, J., Schmid, C.: Multi-fold MIL training for weakly supervised object localization. In: CVPR (2014)
9. Nguyen, M., Torresani, L., de la Torre, F., Rother, C.: Weakly supervised discriminative localization and classification: a joint learning process. In: ICCV (2009)
10. Andrews, S., Tsochantaridis, I., Hofmann, T.: Support vector machines for multiple-instance learning. In: NIPS (2002)
11. Xu, J., Schwing, A.G., Urtasun, R.: Learning to segment under various forms of weak supervision. In: CVPR (2015)
12. Bearman, A., Russakovsky, O., Ferrari, V., Fei-Fei, L.: What's the point: semantic segmentation with point supervision. In: Leibe, B., Matas, J., Sebe, N., Welling, M. (eds.) ECCV 2016, Part VII. LNCS, vol. 9909, pp. 549–565. Springer, Heidelberg (2016)
13. Marszałek, M., Laptev, I., Schmid, C.: Actions in context. In: CVPR (2009)
14. Lan, T., Wang, Y., Mori, G.: Discriminative figure-centric models for joint action localization and recognition. In: ICCV (2011)
15. Gkioxari, G., Malik, J.: Finding action tubes. In: CVPR (2015)
16. Weinzaepfel, P., Harchaoui, Z., Schmid, C.: Learning to track for spatio-temporal action localization. In: ICCV (2015)
17. Lu, J., Xu, R., Corso, J.J.: Human action segmentation with hierarchical supervoxel consistency. In: CVPR (2015)
18. Wang, L., Qiao, Y., Tang, X.: Video action detection with relational dynamic-poselets. In: Fleet, D., Pajdla, T., Schiele, B., Tuytelaars, T. (eds.) ECCV 2014, Part V. LNCS, vol. 8693, pp. 565–580. Springer, Heidelberg (2014)
19. Oneata, D., Revaud, J., Verbeek, J., Schmid, C.: Spatio-temporal object detection proposals. In: Fleet, D., Pajdla, T., Schiele, B., Tuytelaars, T. (eds.) ECCV 2014, Part III. LNCS, vol. 8691, pp. 737–752. Springer, Heidelberg (2014)
20. Chen, W., Corso, J.J.: Action detection by implicit intentional motion clustering. In: ICCV (2015)
21. Marian Puscas, M., Sangineto, E., Culibrk, D., Sebe, N.: Unsupervised tube extraction using transductive learning and dense trajectories. In: ICCV (2015)
22. Soomro, K., Zamir, A.R.: Action recognition in realistic sports videos. In: Moeslund, T.B., Thomas, G., Hilton, A. (eds.) Computer Vision in Sports, pp 181-208. Springer, Heidelberg (2014)
23. Raptis, M., Kokkinos, I., Soatto, S.: Discovering discriminative action parts from mid-level video representations. In: CVPR (2012)
24. Cao, L., Liu, Z., Huang, T.S.: Cross-dataset action detection. In: CVPR (2010)
25. Soomro, K., Zamir, A.R., Shah, M.: Ucf101: A dataset of 101 human actions classes from videos in the wild (2012). arXiv:1212.0402

26. Zhang, W., Zhu, M., Derpanis, K.: From actemes to action: a strongly-supervised representation for detailed action understanding. In: ICCV (2013)
27. Jhuang, H., Gall, J., Zuffi, S., Schmid, C., Black, M.: Towards understanding action recognition. In: ICCV (2013)
28. Gorban, A., Idrees, H., Jiang, Y., Zamir, A.R., Laptev, I., Shah, M., Sukthankar, R.: Thumos challenge: action recognition with a large number of classes. In: CVPR Workshop (2015)
29. Karpathy, A., Toderici, G., Shetty, S., Leung, T., Sukthankar, R., Fei-Fei, L.: Large-scale video classification with convolutional neural networks. In: CVPR (2014)
30. Kuehne, H., Jhuang, H., Garrote, E., Poggio, T., Serre, T.: HMDB: a large video database for human motion recognition. In: ICCV (2011)
31. Mihalcik, D., Doermann, D.: The design and implementation of viper. Technical report (2003)
32. Vondrick, C., Patterson, D., Ramanan, D.: Efficiently scaling up crowdsourced video annotation. IJCV 101(1), 184–204 (2013)
33. Yuen, J., Russell, B., Liu, C., Torralba, A.: Labelme video: building a video database with human annotations. In: ICCV (2009)
34. Settles, B.: Active Learning Literature Survey, vol. 52, pp. 55–66. University of Wisconsin, Madison (2010)
35. Vondrick, C., Ramanan, D.: Video annotation and tracking with active learning. In: NIPS (2011)
36. Bianco, S., Ciocca, G., Napoletano, P., Schettini, R.: An interactive tool for manual, semi-automatic and automatic video annotation. CVIU 131, 88–99 (2015)
37. Bilen, H., Pedersoli, M., Tuytelaars, T.: Weakly supervised object detection with convex clustering. In: CVPR (2015)
38. Oquab, M., Bottou, L., Laptev, I., Sivic, J.: Is object localization for free? - weakly-supervised learning with convolutional neural networks. In: CVPR (2015)
39. Cho, M., Kwak, S., Schmid, C., Ponce, J.: Unsupervised object discovery and localization in the wild: part-based matching with bottom-up region proposals. In: CVPR (2015)
40. Ali, K., Hasler, D., Fleuret, F.: Flowboost - appearance learning from sparsely annotated video. In: CVPR (2011)
41. Misra, I., Shrivastava, A., Hebert, M.: Watch and learn: semi-supervised learning for object detectors from video. In: CVPR (2015)
42. Wang, L., Hua, G., Sukthankar, R., Xue, J., Zheng, N.: Video object discovery and co-segmentation with extremely weak supervision. In: Fleet, D., Pajdla, T., Schiele, B., Tuytelaars, T. (eds.) ECCV 2014, Part IV. LNCS, vol. 8692, pp. 640–655. Springer, Heidelberg (2014)
43. Siva, P., Russell, C., Xiang, T.: In defence of negative mining for annotating weakly labelled data. In: Fitzgibbon, A., Lazebnik, S., Perona, P., Sato, Y., Schmid, C. (eds.) ECCV 2012, Part III. LNCS, vol. 7574, pp. 594–608. Springer, Heidelberg (2012)
44. Kwak, S., Cho, M., Laptev, I., Ponce, J., Schmid, C.: Unsupervised object discovery and tracking in video collections. In: ICCV (2015)
45. Adeli Mosabbeb, E., Cabral, R., De la Torre, F., Fathy, M.: Multi-label discriminative weakly-supervised human activity recognition and localization. In: Cremers, D., Reid, I., Saito, H., Yang, M.-H. (eds.) ACCV 2014. LNCS, vol. 9007, pp. 241–258. Springer, Heidelberg (2015)
46. Siva, P., Xiang, T.: Weakly supervised action detection. In: BMVC (2011)
47. Jain, M., van Gemert, J.C., Mensink, T., Snoek, C.G.M.: Objects2action: Classifying and localizing actions without any video example. In: ICCV (2015)

48. Tseng, P.H., Carmi, R., Cameron, I.G., Munoz, D.P., Itti, L.: Quantifying center bias of observers in free viewing of dynamic natural scenes. JoV **9**(7), 4 (2009)
49. Rodriguez, M.D., Ahmed, J., Shah, M.: Action MACH: a spatio-temporal maximum average correlation height filter for action recognition. In: CVPR (2008)
50. Wang, H., Schmid, C.: Action recognition with improved trajectories. In: ICCV (2013)
51. Sánchez, J., Perronnin, F., Mensink, T., Verbeek, J.: Image classification with the fisher vector: theory and practice. IJCV **105**(3), 222–245 (2013)

Detecting Engagement in Egocentric Video

Yu-Chuan Su$^{(\boxtimes)}$ and Kristen Grauman

The University of Texas at Austin, Austin, USA
`ycsu@cs.utexas.edu`

Abstract. In a wearable camera video, we see what the camera wearer sees. While this makes it easy to know roughly <u>*what*</u> *he chose to look at*, it does not immediately reveal <u>*when*</u> *he was engaged with the environment*. Specifically, at what moments did his focus linger, as he paused to gather more information about something he saw? Knowing this answer would benefit various applications in video summarization and augmented reality, yet prior work focuses solely on the "what" question (estimating saliency, gaze) without considering the "when" (engagement). We propose a learning-based approach that uses long-term egomotion cues to detect engagement, specifically in browsing scenarios where one frequently takes in new visual information (e.g., shopping, touring). We introduce a large, richly annotated dataset for ego-engagement that is the first of its kind. Our approach outperforms a wide array of existing methods. We show engagement can be detected well independent of both scene appearance and the camera wearer's identity.

1 Introduction

Imagine you are walking through a grocery store. You may be mindlessly plowing through the aisles grabbing your usual food staples, when a new product display—or an interesting fellow shopper—captures your interest for a few moments. Similarly, in the museum, as you wander the exhibits, occasionally your attention is heightened and you draw near to examine something more closely.

These examples illustrate the notion of *engagement* in ego-centric activity, where one pauses to inspect something more closely. While engagement happens throughout daily life activity, it occurs frequently and markedly during *"browsing" scenarios* in which one traverses an area with the intent of taking in new information and/or locating certain objects—for example, in a shop, museum, library, city sightseeing, or touring a campus or historic site.

Problem Definition. We explore engagement from the first-person vision perspective. In particular, we ask: Given a video stream captured from a head-mounted camera during a browsing scenario, can we automatically detect those time intervals where the recorder experienced a heightened level of engagement?

Electronic supplementary material The online version of this chapter (doi:10.1007/978-3-319-46454-1_28) contains supplementary material, which is available to authorized users.

B. Leibe et al. (Eds.): ECCV 2016, Part V, LNCS 9909, pp. 454–471, 2016.
DOI: 10.1007/978-3-319-46454-1_28

What cues are indicative of first-person engagement, and how do they differ from traditional saliency metrics? To what extent are engagement cues independent of the particular person wearing the camera (the "recorder"), or the particular environment they are navigating? See Fig. 1.

While engagement is interesting in a variety of daily life settings, for now we restrict our focus to browsing scenarios. This allows us to concentrate on cases where (1) engagement naturally ebbs and flows repeatedly, (2) the environment offers discrete entities (products in the shop, museum paintings, etc.) that may be attention-provoking, which aids objectivity in evaluation, and (3) there is high potential impact for emerging applications.

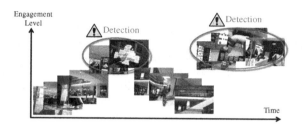

Fig. 1. The goal is to identify time intervals when the camera wearer's engagement is heightened, meaning he interrupts his ongoing activity to gather more information about some object in the environment. Note that this is different than detecting what the camera wearer sees or gazes upon, which comes for "free" with a head-mounted camera and/or eye tracking devices.

Applications. A system that can successfully address the above questions would open up several applications. For example, it could facilitate camera control, allowing the user's attention to trigger automatic recording/zooming. Similarly, it would help construct video summaries. Knowing when a user's engagement is waning would let a system display info on a heads-up display when it is least intrusive. Beyond such "user-centric" applications, third parties would relish the chance to gather data about user attention at scale—for instance, a vendor would like to know when shoppers linger by its new display. Such applications are gaining urgency as wearable cameras become increasingly attractive tools in the law enforcement, healthcare, education, and consumer domains.

Novelty of the Problem. The rich literature on visual saliency—including video saliency [1–8]—does not address this problem. First and foremost, as discussed above, detecting moments of engagement is different than estimating saliency. While a person always sees something, he does not pay attention to everything he sees; knowing *what* a person is looking at does not reveal *when* the person is engaging with the environment. Nearly all prior work studies visual saliency from the *third person* perspective and equates saliency with gaze: salient points are those upon which a viewer would fixate his gaze, when observing a previously recorded image/video on a static screen. In contrast, our problem entails detecting *temporal intervals of engagement as perceived by the person capturing the video as he moves about his environment.* Thus, *recorder engagement* is distinct from *viewer attention.* To predict it from video requires identifying time intervals of engagement as opposed to spatial regions that are salient (gaze worthy) per frame. As such, estimating egocentric gaze [9–11] is also insufficient to predict first-person engagement.

Challenges. Predicting first-person engagement presents a number of challenges. First of all, the motion cues that are significant in third-person video taken with an actively controlled camera (e.g., zoom [4,12–14]) are absent in passive wearable camera data. Instead, first-person data contains both scene motion and unstable body motions, which are difficult to stabilize with traditional methods [15]. Secondly, whereas third-person data is inherently already focused on moments of interest that led the recorder to turn the camera on, a first-person camera is "always on". Thirdly, whereas traditional visual attention metrics operate with instantaneous motion cues [1,2,16,17] and fixed sliding temporal window search strategies, detecting engagement *intervals* requires long-term descriptors and handling intervals of variable length. Finally, it is unclear whether there are sufficient visual cues that transcend user- or scene-specific properties, or if engagement is strongly linked to the specific content a user observes (in which case, an exorbitant amount of data might be necessary to learn a general-purpose detector).

Our Approach. We propose a learning approach to detect time intervals where first-person engagement occurs. In an effort to maintain independence of the camera wearer as well as the details of his environment, we employ motion-based features that span long temporal neighborhoods and integrate out local head motion effects. We develop a search strategy that integrates instantaneous frame-level estimates with temporal interval hypotheses to detect intervals of varying lengths, thereby avoiding a naive sliding window search. To train and evaluate our model, we undertake a large-scale data collection effort.

Contributions. Our main contributions are as follows. First, we precisely define egocentric engagement and systematically evaluate under that definition. Second, we collect a large annotated dataset spanning 14 h of activity explicitly designed for ego-engagement in browsing situations. Third, we propose a learned motion-based model for detecting first-person engagement. Our model shows better accuracy than an array of existing methods. It also generalizes to unseen browsing scenarios, suggesting that some properties of ego-engagement are independent of appearance content.

2   Related Work

Third-Person Image and Video Saliency. Researchers often equate human gaze fixations as the gold standard with which a *saliency* metric ought to correlate [18,19]. There is increasing interest in estimating saliency from video. Initial efforts examine simple motion cues, such as frame-based motion and flicker [8,18,20]. One common approach to extend spatial (image) saliency to the video domain is to sum image saliency scores within a temporal segment, e.g., [21]. Most methods are unsupervised and entail no learning [4–8,18,20]. However, some recent work develops learned measures, using ground truth gaze data as the target output [1–3,16,22].

Our problem setting is quite different than saliency. Saliency aims to *predict viewer attention* in terms of where in the frame a third party is likely to fixate his gaze; it is an image property analyzed independent of the behavior of the person recording the image. In contrast, we aim to *detect recorder engagement* in terms of when (which time intervals) the recorder has paused to examine something in his environment.[1] Accounting for this distinction is crucial, as we will see in results. Furthermore, prior work in video saliency is evaluated on short video clips (e.g., on the order of 10 s [23]), which is sufficient to study gaze movements. In contrast, we evaluate on long sequences—30 min on average per clip, and a total of 14 h—in order to capture the broad context of ego-behavior that affects engagement in browsing scenarios.

Third-Person Video Summarization. In video summarization, the goal is to form a concise representation for a long input video. Motion cues can help detect "important" moments in third-person video [12–14,17,21], including temporal differences [17] and cues from active camera control [12–14]. Whereas prior methods try to extract what will be interesting to a third-party viewer, we aim to capture *recorder* engagement.

First-Person Video Saliency and Gaze. Researchers have long expected that ego-attention detection requires methods distinct from bottom-up saliency [24]. In fact, traditional motion saliency can actually *degrade* gaze prediction for first-person video [11]. Instead, it is valuable to separate out camera motion [10] or use head motion and hand locations to predict gaze [9]. Whereas these methods aim to predict spatial coordinates of a recorder's gaze at every frame, we aim to predict time intervals where his engagement is heightened. Furthermore, whereas they study short sequences in a lab [10] or kitchen [9], we analyze long data in natural environments with substantial scene changes per sequence.

---

[1] Throughout, we will use the term "recorder" to refer to the photographer or the first-person camera-wearer; we use the term "viewer" to refer to a third party who is observing the data captured by some other recorder.

We agree that first-person attention, construed in the most general sense, will inevitably require first-person "user-in-the-loop" feedback to detect [24]; accordingly, our work does not aim to detect arbitrary subjective attention events, but instead to detect moments of engagement to examine an object more closely.

Outside of gaze, there is limited work on attention in terms of head fixation detection [15] and "physical analytics" [25]. In [15], a novel "cumulative displacement curve" motion cue is used to categorize the recorder's activity (walking, sitting, on bus, etc.) and is also shown to reveal periods with fixed head position. They use a limited definition of attention: a period of more than 5 s where the head is still but the recorder is walking. In [25], inertial sensors are used in concert with optical flow magnitude to decide when the recorder is examining a product in a store. Compared to both [15,25], engagement has a broader definition, and we discover its scope from data from the crowd (vs. hand-crafting a definition on visual features). Crucially, the true positives reflect that a person can have heightened engagement yet still be in motion.

First-Person Activity and Summarization. Early methods for egocentric video summarization extract the camera motion and define rules for important moments (e.g., intervals when camera rotation is below a threshold) [26,27], and test qualitatively on short videos. Rather than inject hand-crafted rules, we propose to *learn* what constitutes an engagement interval. Recent methods explore ways to predict the "importance" of spatial regions (objects, people) using cues like hand detection and frame centrality [28,29], detect novelty [30], and infer "social saliency" when multiple cameras capture the same event [31–33]. We tackle engagement, not summarization, though likely our predictions could be another useful input to a summarization system.

In a sense, detecting engagement could be seen as detecting a particular ego-activity. An array of methods for classifying activity in egocentric video exist, e.g., [15,34–40]. However, they do not address our scenario: (1) they learn models specific to the objects [34–37,39,40] or scenes [38] with which the activity takes place (e.g., making tea, snowboarding), whereas engagement is by definition object- and scene-independent, since arbitrary things may capture one's interest; and (2) they typically focus on recognition of trimmed video clips, versus temporal detection in ongoing video.

3   First-Person Engagement: Definition and Data

Next we define first-person engagement. Then we describe our data collection procedure, and quantitatively analyze the consistency of the resulting annotations. We introduce our approach for predicting engagement intervals in Sect. 4.

3.1   Definition of First-Person Engagement

This research direction depends crucially on having (1) a precise definition of engagement, (2) realistic video data captured in natural environments, and (3) a systematic way to annotate the data for both learning and evaluation.

Accordingly, we first formalize our meaning of first-person engagement. There are two major requirements. First, the engagement must be related to external factors, either induced by or causing the change in visual signals the recorder perceives. This ensures predictability from video, excluding high-attention events that are imperceptible (by humans) from visual cues. Second, an engagement interval must reflect the *recorder's* intention, as opposed to the reaction of a third-person viewer of the same video.

Based on these requirements, we **define heightened ego-engagement in a browsing scenario** as follows. A time interval is considered to have a high engagement level if *the recorder is attracted by some object(s), and he interrupts his ongoing flow of activity to purposefully gather more information about the object(s)*. We stress that this definition is scoped specifically for *browsing* scenarios; while the particular objects attracting the recorder will vary widely, we assume the person is traversing some area with the intent of taking in new information and/or locating certain objects.

The definition captures situations where the recorder reaches out to touch or grasp an object of interest (e.g., when closely inspecting a product at the store), as well as scenarios where he examines something from afar (e.g., when he reads a sign beside a painting at the museum). Having an explicit definition allows annotators to consistently identify video clips with high engagement, and it lets us directly evaluate the prediction result of different models.

We stress that ego-engagement differs from gaze and traditional saliency. While a recorder always has a gaze point per frame (and it is correlated with the frame center), periods of engagement are more sparsely distributed across time, occupy variable-length intervals, and are a function of his activity and changing environment. Furthermore, as we will see below, moments where a person is approximately still are *not* equivalent to moments of engagement, making observer motion magnitude [25] an inadequate signal.

3.2   Data Collection

To collect a dataset, we ask multiple recorders to take videos during browsing behavior under a set of *scenarios*, or scene and event types. We aim to gather scenarios with clear distinctions between high and low engagement intervals that will be apparent to a third-party annotator. Based on that criterion, we collect videos under three scenarios: (1) shopping in a market, (2) window shopping in shopping mall, and (3) touring in a museum. All three entail spontaneous stimuli, which ensures that variable levels of engagement will naturally occur.

The videos are recorded using Looxcie LX2 with 640×480 resolution and 15 fps frame rate, which we chose for its long battery life and low profile. We recruited 9 recorders—5 females and 4 males—all students between 20–30 years old. Other than asking them to capture instances of the scenarios above, we did not otherwise instruct the recorders to behave in any way. Among the 9 recorders, 5 of them record videos in all 3 scenarios. The other 4 record videos in 2 scenarios. Altogether, we obtained 27 videos, each averaging 31 minutes, for a total dataset of 14 h. To keep the recorder behavior as natural as possible, we asked the recorders to capture the video when they planned to go to such scenarios anyway; as such, it took about 1.5 months to collect the video.

After collecting the videos, we crowdsource the ground truth annotations on Amazon Mechanical Turk. Importantly, we ask annotators to put themselves in the camera-wearer's shoes. They must precisely mark the start and end points of each engagement interval from the recorder's perspective, and record their confidence.[2] We break the source videos into 3 min overlapping chunks to make each annotation task manageable yet still reveal temporal context for the clip. We estimate the annotations took about 450 worker-hours and cost $3,000. Our collection strategy is congruous with the goals stated above in Sect. 3.1, in that annotators are shown only the visual signal (without audio) and are asked to consider engagement from the point of view of the recorder. See Supp. file.

Table 1. Basic statistics for ground truth intervals.

	Mall	Market	Museum	All
Attention ratio	0.305	0.451	0.580	0.438
#intervals (per min.)	1.19	1.22	1.50	1.30
Length median (sec)	7.5	12.1	13.3	11.3
Length IQR (sec)	11.6	18.2	20.1	17.6

Despite our care in the instructions, there remains room for annotator subjectivity, and the exact interval boundaries can be ambiguous. Thus, we ask 10 Turkers to annotate each video. Positive intervals are those where a majority agree engagement is heightened. To avoid over-segmentation, we ignore intervals shorter than 1 s. For each positive interval, we select the tightest annotation that covers more than half of the interval as the final ground truth.

The resulting dataset contains examples that are diverse in content and duration. The recorders are attracted by a variety of objects: groceries, household items, clothes, paintings, sculptures, other people. In some cases, the attended object is out of the field of view, e.g., a recorder grabs an item without directly looking at it, in which case Turkers infer the engagement from context.

Table 1 summarizes some statistics of the labeled data. On average, the recorder is engaged about 44 % of the time (see "Attention Ratio"), and it increases once to twice per minute. This density reflects the browsing scenarios on which we focus the data. The length of a positive interval varies substantially: the interquartile range (IQR) is 17.6 s, about 50 % longer than the median. Some intervals last as long as 5 min. Also, the different scenarios have different statistics, e.g., Museum scenarios prompt more frequent engagement. All this variability indicates the difficulty of the task.

---

[2] For a portion of the video, we also ask the original recorders to label all frames for their own video; this requires substantial tedious effort, hence to get the full labeled set in a scalable manner we apply crowdsourcing.

The new dataset is the first of its kind to explicitly define and thoroughly annotate ego-engagement. It is also substantially larger than datasets used in related areas—nearly 14 h of video, with test videos over 30 min each. By contrast, clips in third-person saliency datasets are typically 20 s [23] to 2 min [41], since the interest is in gauging instantaneous gaze reactions.

3.3 Evaluating Data Consistency

How consistently do third-party annotators label engagement intervals? We analyze their consistency to verify the predictability and soundness of our definition.

Table 2 shows the analysis. We quantify label agreement in terms of the average F_1 score, whether at the frame or interval level (see Supp.). We consider two aspects of agreement: boundary (how well do annotators agree on the start and end points of a positive interval?) and presence (how well do they agree on the existence of a positive interval?).

First we compare how consistent each of the 10 annotators' labels are with the consensus ground truth (see "Turker vs. Consensus"). They have reasonable agreement on the rough interval locations, which verifies the soundness of our definition. Still, the F_1 score is not perfect, which indicates that the task is non-trivial even for humans. Some discrepancies are due to the fact that even when two annotators agree on the presence of an interval, their annotations will not match exactly in terms of the start and end frame. For example, one annotator might mark the start when the recorder searches for items on the shelf, while another might consider it to be when the recorder grabs the item. Indeed, agreement on the presence criterion (right column) is even higher, 0.914. The "Random vs. Consensus" entry compares a prior-informed random guess to the ground truth.[3] These two extremes give useful bounds of what we can expect from our computational model: a predictor should perform better than random, but will not exceed the inter-human agreement.

Table 2. Analysis of inter-annotator consistency.

			Frame F_1	Interval F_1	
				Boundary	Presence
Turker	vs.	Consensus	0.818	0.837	0.914
	vs	Recorder	0.589	0.626	0.813
Random	vs.	Consensus	0.426	0.339	0.481
	vs	Recorder	0.399	0.344	0.478

Next, we check how well the third-party labels match the experience of the first-person recorder (see "Turker vs. Recorder"). We collect 3 h of self-annotation from 4 of the recorders, and compare them to the Turker annotations.

---

[3] We randomly generate interval predictions 10 times based on the prior of interval length and temporal distribution and report the average.

Similar to above, we see the Turkers are considerably more consistent with the recorder labels compared to the prior-informed random guess, though not perfect. As one might expect, Turker annotations have higher recall, but lower (yet reasonable) precision against the first-person labels. Overall, the 0.813 F_1 score for Turker-Recorder presence agreement indicates our labels are fairly faithful to individuals' subjective interpretation.

4   Approach

We propose to learn the motion patterns in first-person video that indicate engagement. Two key factors motivate our decision to focus on motion. First, camera motion often contains useful information about the recorder's intention [10,12,13]. This is especially true in egocentric video, where the recorder's head and body motion heavily influence the observed motion. Second, motion patterns stand to generalize better across different scenarios, as they are mostly independent of the appearance of the surrounding objects and scene.

Our approach has three main stages. First we compute *frame-wise* predictions (Sect. 4.1). Then we leverage those frame predictions to generate *interval* hypotheses (Sect. 4.2). Finally, we describe each interval as a whole and classify it with an interval-trained model (Sect. 4.3). By departing from traditional frame-based decisions [17,26,27], we capture long-term temporal dependencies. As we will see below, doing so is beneficial for detecting subtle periods of engagement and accounting for their variable length. Figure 2 shows the workflow.

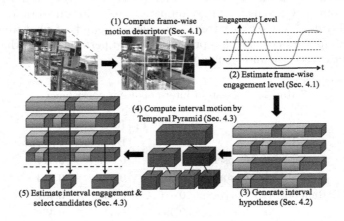

Fig. 2. Workflow for our approach.

4.1   Initial Frame-Wise Estimates

To first compute frame-wise predictions, we construct one motion descriptor per frame. We divide the frame into a grid of 16×12 uniform cells and compute the optical flow vector in each cell. Then we temporally smooth the grid motion with a Gaussian kernel. Since at this stage we want to capture attention within a granularity of a second, we set the width of the kernel to two seconds. As shown in [15], smoothing the flow is valuable to integrate out the regular unstable head bobbles by the recorder; it helps the descriptor focus on prominent scene and camera motion. The frame descriptor consists of the smoothed flow vectors concatenated across cells, together with the mean and standard deviation of all cells in the frame. It captures dominant egomotion and dynamic scene motion—both of which are relevant to first-person engagement.

We use these descriptors, together with the frame-level ground truth (cf. Sect. 3.2), to train an i.i.d. classifier. We use random forest classifiers due to their test-time efficiency and relative insensitivity to hyper-parameters, though of course other classifiers are possible. Given a test video, the confidence (posterior) output by the random forest is used as the initial frame-wise engagement estimate.

4.2   Generating Interval Proposals

After obtaining the preliminary estimate for each frame, we generate multiple hypotheses for engagement *intervals* using a level set method as follows. For a given threshold on the frame-based confidence, we obtain a set of positive intervals, where each positive interval consists of contiguous frames whose confidence exceeds the threshold. By sweeping through all possible thresholds (we use the decile), we generate multiple such sets of candidates. Candidates from all thresholds are pooled together to form a final set of *interval proposals*.

We apply this candidate generation process on both training data and test data. During training, it yields both positive and negative example intervals that we use to train an interval-level classifier (described next). During testing, it yields the hypotheses to which the classifier should be applied. This detection paradigm not only lets us avoid sliding temporal window search, but it also allows us to detect engagement intervals of variable length.

4.3   Describing and Classifying Intervals

For each interval proposal, we generate a motion descriptor that captures both the motion distribution and evolution over time. Motion evolution is important because a recorder usually performs multiple actions within an interval of engagement. For example, the recorder may stop, turn his head to stare at an object, reach out to touch it, then turn back to resume walking. Each action leads to a different motion pattern. Thus, unlike the temporally local frame-based descriptor above, here we aim to capture the statistics of the entire interval. We'd also like the representation to be robust to time-scale variations (i.e., yielding similar descriptors for long and short instances of the same activity).

To this end, we use a temporal pyramid representation. For each level of the pyramid, we divide the interval from the previous level into two equal-length sub-intervals. For each sub-interval, we aggregate the frame motion computed in Sect. 4.1 by taking the dimension-wise mean and variance. So, the top level aggregates the motion of the entire interval, and its descendants aggregate increasingly finer time-scale intervals. The aggregated motion descriptors from all sub-intervals are concatenated to form a temporal pyramid descriptor. We use 3-level pyramids. To provide further context, we augment this descriptor with those of its temporal neighbor intervals (i.e., before and after). This captures the motion *change* from low engagement to high engagement and back.

We train a random forest classifier using this descriptor and the interval proposals from the training data, this time referring to the interval-level ground truth from Sect. 3.2. At test time, we apply this classifier to a test video's interval proposals to score each one. If a frame is covered by multiple interval proposals, we take the highest confidence score as the final prediction per frame.

4.4   Discussion

Our method design is distinct from previous work in video *attention*, which typically operates per frame and uses temporally local measurements of motion [1,2,16,17,26,27]. In contrast, we estimate enagement from interval hypotheses bootstrapped from initial frame estimates, and our representation captures motion changes over time at multiple scales. People often perform multiple actions during an engagement interval, which is well-captured by considering an interval together. For example, it is hard to tell whether the recorder is attracted by an object when we only know he glances at it, but it becomes clear if we know his following action is to turn to the object or to turn away quickly.

Simply flagging periods of low motion [15,25,27] is insufficient to detect all cases of heightened attention, since behaviors during the interval of engagement are often non-static and also exhibit learnable patterns. For example, shoppers move and handle objects they might buy; people sway while inspecting a painting; they look up and sweep their gaze downward when inspecting a skyscraper.

External sensors beyond the video stream could potentially provide cues useful to our task, such as inertial sensors to detect recorder motion and head orientation. However, such sensors are not always available, and they are quite noisy in practice. In fact, recent attempts to detect gazing behavior with inertial sensors alone yield false positive rates of 33 % [25]. Similarly, although gaze could be informative for engagement, it requires greater instrumentation (i.e., eye tracker calibrated for each user) and will limit the applicability to generic egocentric video such as existing data on the web. This argues for the need for visual features for the challenging engagement detection task.

5   Experiments

We validate on two datasets and compare to many existing methods.

Baselines. We compare with 9 existing methods, organized into four types:

Saliency Map: Following [17, 21], we compute the saliency map for each frame and take the average saliency value. We apply the state-of-the-art learned video saliency model [1] and five others that were previously used for video summarization: [6, 7, 17, 19, 20]. We use the original authors' code for [1, 6, 7, 19, 20] and implement [17]. Except [6], all these models use motion.

Motion Magnitude: Following [25, 27], this baseline uses the inverse motion magnitude. Intuitively, the recorder becomes more still during his moments of high engagement as he inspects the object(s). We apply the same flow smoothing as in Sect. 4.1 and take the average.

Learned Appearance (CNN): This baseline predicts engagement based on the video content. We use state-of-the-art convolutional neural net (CNN) image descriptors, and train a random forest with the same frame-based ground truth our method uses. We use Caffe [42] and the provided pre-trained model (BVLC Reference CaffeNet).

Egocentric Important Region: This is the method of [28]. It is a learned metric designed for egocentric video that exploits hand detection, centrality in frame, etc. to predict the importance of regions for summarization. While the objective of "importance" is different than "engagement", it is related and valuable as a comparison, particularly since it also targets egocentric data. We take the max importance per frame using the predictions shared by the authors.

Some of the baselines do not target our task specifically, a likely disadvantage. Nonetheless, their inclusion is useful to see if ego-engagement requires methods beyond existing saliency metrics. Besides, our baselines also include methods specialized for egocentric video [25, 28], and one that targets exactly our task [25].

For the learned methods (ours, CNN and Important Regions), we use the classifier confidences to rate frames by their engagement level. Note that the CNN method has the benefit of training on the exact same data as our method. For the non-learned methods (saliency, motion), we use their magnitude. We evaluate two versions of our method: one with the interval proposals (Ours-interval) and one without (Ours-frame). The boundary agreement is used for interval prediction evaluation to favor methods with better localization of attention.

Datasets. We evaluate on two datasets: our new UT Egocentric Engagement (UT EE) dataset and the public UT Egocentric dataset (UT Ego). We select

Market   Shopping Mall   Museum

Fig. 3. Example engagement intervals detected by our method. Note the intra-interval variation: the recorder either performs multiple actions (Market), looks at an item from multiple views (Mall) or looks at multiple items (Museum). See videos on our website.

Table 3. F_1-score accuracy of all methods on UT EE. (The cross-recorder/scenario distinctions are not relevant to the top block of methods, all of which do no learning.)

		Frame F_1	Interval F_1
GBVS	(Harel 2006 [19])	0.462	0.286
Self Resemblance	(Seo 2009 [20])	0.471	0.398
Bayesian Surprise	(Itti 2009 [7])	0.420	0.373
Salient Object	(Rahtu 2010 [6])	0.504	0.389
Video Attention	(Ejaz 2013 [17])	0.413	0.298
Video Saliency	(Rudoy 2013 [1])	0.435	0.396
Motion Mag	(Rallapalli 2014 [25])	0.553	0.403
Cross Recorder	CNN Appearance	0.685	0.486
	Ours – frame	**0.686**	0.533
	Ours – interval	0.674	**0.572**
	Ours – GT interval	0.822	0.868
Cross Scenario	CNN Appearance	0.656	0.463
	Ours – frame	**0.683**	0.531
	Ours – interval	0.665	**0.553**
	Ours – GT interval	0.830	0.860
Cross Recorder AND Scenario	CNN Appearance	0.655	0.463
	Ours – frame	**0.680**	0.532
	Ours – interval	0.661	**0.544**
	Ours – GT interval	0.823	0.856

all clips from UT Ego that contain browsing scenarios (mall, market), yielding 3 clips with total length of 58 min, and get them annotated with the same procedure in Sect. 3.2.

Implementation Details. We use the code of [43] for optical flow computation. Flow dominates our run-time, about 1.2 s per frame on 48 cores. The default settings are used for this and all the public saliency map codes. Using the scikit-learn package [44] for random forest, we train 2,400 trees in all results and leave all other parameters at default. The sample rate of video frames is 15 fps for optical flow and 1 fps for all other computation, including evaluation.

5.1   UT Egocentric Engagement (UT EE) Dataset

We consider three strategies to form train-test data splits. The first is leave-one-recorder-out, denoted **cross-recorder**, in which we train a predictor for each recorder using exclusively video from *other* recorders. This setting tests the ability to generalize to new recorders (e.g., can we learn from John's video to predict engagement in Mary's video?). The second is leave-one-scenario-out,

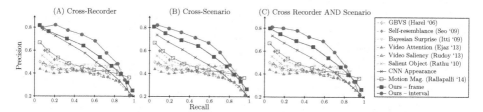

Fig. 4. Precision-recall accuracy on the UT EE dataset. Our approach detects engagement with much greater accuracy than an array of saliency and content-based methods, and our interval proposal idea improves the initial frame-wise predictions.

denoted as **cross-scenario**, in which we train a predictor for each scenario using exclusively video from other scenarios. This setting examines to what extent visual cues of engagement are independent of the specific activity or location the recorder (e.g., can we learn from a museum trip to predict engagement during a shopping trip?). The third strategy is the most stringent, disallowing any overlap in either the recorder or the scenario (**cross recorder AND scenario**).

Figure 4(A)~(C) show the precision-recall curves for all methods and settings on the 14 h UT EE dataset, and we summarize them in Table 3 using the F_1 scores; here we set the confidence threshold for each video such that 43.8 % of its frames are positive, which is the ratio of positives in the entire dataset. Our method significantly outperforms all the existing methods. We also see our interval proposal idea has a clear positive impact on interval detection results. However, when evaluated with the frame classification metric (first column in Table 3), our interval method does not improve over our frame method. This is due to some inaccurate (too coarse) proposals, which may be helped by sampling the level sets more densely. We also show an upper bound for the accuracy with perfect interval hypotheses (see Ours-GT interval), which emphasizes the need to go beyond frame-wise predictions as we propose.

Figure 4 and Table 3 show our method performs similarly in all three train-test settings, meaning it generalizes to both new recorders and new scenarios. This is an interesting finding, since it is not obvious *a priori* that different people exhibit similar motion behavior when they become engaged, or that those behaviors translate between scenes and activities. This is important for applications, as it would be impractical to collect data for all recorders and scenarios.

The CNN baseline, which learns which video content corresponds to engagement, does the best of all the baselines. However, it is noticeably weaker than our motion-based approach. This result surprised us, as we did not expect the *appearance* of objects in the field of view during engagement intervals to be consistent enough to learn at all. However, there are some intra-scenario visual similarities in a subset of clips: four of the Museum videos are at the same museum (though the recorders focus on different parts), and five in the Mall contain long segments in clothing stores (albeit different ones). Overall we find the CNN baseline often fails to generate coherent predictions, and it predicts intervals much shorter than the ground truth. This suggests that appearance alone is a weaker signal than motion for the task.

Motion Magnitude (representative of [25,27]) is the next best baseline. While better than the saliency metrics, its short-term motion and lack of learning lead to substantially worse results than our approach. This also reveals that people often move while they engage with objects they want to learn more about.

Finally, despite their popularity in video summarization, Saliency Map methods [1,6,7,17,19,20] do not predict temporal ego-engagement well. In fact, they are weaker than the simpler motion magnitude baseline. This result accentuates the distinction between predicting gaze (the common saliency objective) and predicting first-person engagement. Clearly, spatial attention does not directly translate to the task. While all the Saliency Map methods (except [6]) incorporate motion cues, their reliance on temporally local motion, like flickers, makes them perform no better than the purely static image methods.

Figure 3 shows example high engagement frames. **Please see the project webpage for video results.**

5.2   UT Egocentric Dataset

Figure 5 shows the results on the UT Ego dataset. The outcomes are consistent with those on UT EE above, and again our method performs the best. Whereas [28] is both trained and tested on UT Ego, our method does not do any training on the UT Ego data; rather, we use our model trained on UT EE. This ensures fairness to the baseline (and some disadvantage to our method).

Our method outperforms the Important Regions [28] method, which is specifically designed for first-person data. This result gives further evidence of our method's cross-scenario generalizability. Important Regions [28] does outperform the Saliency Map methods on the whole, indicating that high-level semantic concepts are useful for detecting engagement, more so than low-level saliency. The CNN baseline does poorly, which reflects that its content-specific nature hinders generalization to a new data domain.

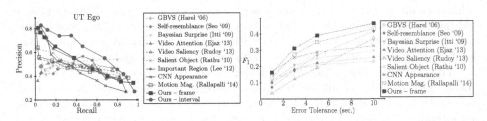

Fig. 5. Precision-recall accuracy on UT Ego dataset.

Fig. 6. Start-point accuracy on UT EE, measuring how well the onset of an engagement interval is detected in a streaming manner.

5.3   Start Point Correctness

Finally, Fig. 6 evaluates start point accuracy on UT EE. This setting is of interest to applications where it is essential to know the onset of engagement, but not necessarily its temporal extent. Here we run our method in a streaming fashion by using its frame-based predictions, without the benefit of hindsight on the entire intervals. Due to space limits, we defer to the Supp. for details.

6   Conclusion

We explore engagement detection in first-person video. By precisely defining the task and collecting a sizeable dataset, we offer the first systematic study of this problem. We introduced a learning-based approach that discovers the connection between first-person motion and engagement, together with an interval proposal approach to capture a recorder's long-term motion. Results on two datasets show our method consistently outperforms a wide array of existing methods for visual attention. Our work provides the foundation for a new aspect of visual attention research. In future work, we will examine the role of external sensors (e.g., audio, gaze trackers, depth) that could assist in ego-engagement detection when they are available.

Acknowledgement. This research is supported in part by ONR YIP N00014-12-1-0754.

References

1. Rudoy, D., Goldman, D., Shechtman, E., Zelnik-Manor, L.: Learning video saliency from human gaze using candidate selection. In: CVPR (2013)
2. Han, J., Sun, L., Hu, X., Han, J., Shao, L.: Spatial and temporal visual attention prediction in videos using eye movement data. Neurocomputing **145**, 140–153 (2014)
3. Lee, W., Huang, T., Yeh, S., Chen, H.: Learning-based prediction of visual attention for video signals. IEEE TIP **20**(11), 3028–3038 (2011)
4. Abdollahian, G., Taskiran, C., Pizlo, Z., Delp, E.: Camera motion-based analysis of user generated video. TMM **12**(1), 28–41 (2010)
5. Mahadevan, V., Vasconcelos, N.: Spatiotemporal saliency in dynamic scenes. TPAMI **32**(1), 171–177 (2010)
6. Rahtu, E., Kannala, J., Salo, M., Heikkilä, J.: Segmenting salient objects from images and videos. In: Daniilidis, K., Maragos, P., Paragios, N. (eds.) ECCV 2010. LNCS, vol. 6315, pp. 366–379. Springer, Heidelberg (2010). doi:10.1007/978-3-642-15555-0_27
7. Itti, L., Baldi, P.: Bayesian surprise attracts human attention. Vision Res. **49**(10), 1295–1306 (2009)
8. Liu, H., Jiang, S., Huang, Q., Xu, C.: A generic virtual content insertion system based on visual attention analysis. In: ACM MM (2008)
9. Li, Y., Fathi, A., Rehg, J.M.: Learning to predict gaze in egocentric video. In: ICCV (2013)

10. Yamada, K., Sugano, Y., Okabe, T., Sato, Y., Sugimoto, A., Hiraki, K.: Attention prediction in egocentric video using motion and visual saliency. In: Ho, Y.-S. (ed.) PSIVT 2011. LNCS, vol. 7087, pp. 277–288. Springer, Heidelberg (2011). doi:10.1007/978-3-642-25367-6_25

11. Yamada, K., Sugano, Y., Okabe, T., Sato, Y., Sugimoto, A., Hiraki, K.: Can saliency map models predict human egocentric visual attention? In: Koch, R., Huang, F. (eds.) ACCV 2010. LNCS, vol. 6468, pp. 420–429. Springer, Heidelberg (2011). doi:10.1007/978-3-642-22822-3_42

12. Kender, J., Yeo, B.L.: On the structure and analysis of home videos. In: ACCV (2000)

13. Li, K., Oh, S., Perera, A., Fu, Y.: A videography analysis framework for video retrieval and summarization. In: BMVC (2012)

14. Gygli, M., Grabner, H., Riemenschneider, H., Gool, L.: Creating summaries from user videos. In: Fleet, D., Pajdla, T., Schiele, B., Tuytelaars, T. (eds.) ECCV 2014. LNCS, vol. 8695, pp. 505–520. Springer, Heidelberg (2014). doi:10.1007/978-3-319-10584-0_33

15. Poleg, Y., Arora, C., Peleg, S.: Temporal segmentation of egocentric videos. In: CVPR (2014)

16. Nguyen, T.V., Xu, M., Gao, G., Kankanhalli, M., Tian, Q., Yan, S.: Static saliency vs. dynamic saliency: a comparative study. In: ACM MM (2013)

17. Ejaz, N., Mehmood, I., Baik, S.: Efficient visual attention based framework for extracting key frames from videos. Image Commun. 28, 34–44 (2013)

18. Itti, L., Dhavale, N., Pighin, F.: Realistic avatar eye and head animation using a neurobiological model of visual attention. In: Proceedings of the SPIE 48th Annual International Symposium on Optical Science and Technology, vol. 5200, pp. 64–78, August 2003

19. Harel, J., Koch, C., Perona, P.: Graph-based visual saliency. In: NIPS (2007)

20. Seo, H., Milanfar, P.: Static and space-time visual saliency detection by self-resemblance. J. Vision 9(7), 1–27 (2009)

21. Ma, Y.F., Lu, L., Zhang, H.J., Li, M.: A user attention model for video summarization. In: ACM MM (2002)

22. Kienzle, W., Schölkopf, B., Wichmann, F.A., Franz, M.O.: How to find interesting locations in video: a spatiotemporal interest point detector learned from human eye movements. In: Hamprecht, F.A., Schnörr, C., Jähne, B. (eds.) DAGM 2007. LNCS, vol. 4713, pp. 405–414. Springer, Heidelberg (2007). doi:10.1007/978-3-540-74936-3_41

23. Dorr, M., Martinetz, T., Gegenfurtner, K.R., Barth, E.: Variability of eye movements when viewing dynamic natural scenes. J. Vision 10(10), 1–17 (2010)

24. Pilu, M.: On the use of attention clues for an autonomous wearable camera. Technical report HPL-2002-195, HP Laboratories Bristol (2003)

25. Rallapalli, S., Ganesan, A., Padmanabhan, V., Chintalapudi, K., Qiu, L.: Enabling physical analytics in retail stores using smart glasses. In: MobiCom (2014)

26. Nakamura, Y., Ohde, J., Ohta, Y.: Structuring personal activity records based on attention-analyzing videos from head mounted camera. In: ICPR (2000)

27. Cheatle, P.: Media content and type selection from always-on wearable video. In: ICPR (2004)

28. Lee, Y.J., Ghosh, J., Grauman, K.: Discovering important people and objects for egocentric video summarization. In: CVPR (2012)

29. Lu, Z., Grauman, K.: Story-driven summarization for egocentric video. In: CVPR (2013)

30. Aghazadeh, O., Sullivan, J., Carlsson, S.: Novelty detection from an egocentric perspective. In: CVPR (2011)
31. Hoshen, Y., Ben-Artzi, G., Peleg, S.: Wisdom of the crowd in egocentric video curation. In: CVPR Workshop (2014)
32. Park, H.S., Jain, E., Sheikh, Y.: 3D gaze concurrences from head-mounted cameras. In: NIPS (2012)
33. Fathi, A., Hodgins, J., Rehg, J.: Social interactions: a first-person perspective. In: CVPR (2012)
34. Fathi, A., Farhadi, A., Rehg, J.: Understanding egocentric activities. In: ICCV (2011)
35. Pirsiavash, H., Ramanan, D.: Detecting activities of daily living in first-person camera views. In: CVPR (2012)
36. Damen, D., Leelasawassuk, T., Haines, O., Calway, A., Mayol-Cuevas, W.: You-do, i-learn: discovering task relevant objects and their modes of interaction from multi-user egocentric video. In: BMVC 2014 (2014)
37. Soran, B., Farhadi, A., Shapiro, L.: Action recognition in the presence of one egocentric and multiple static cameras. In: Cremers, D., Reid, I., Saito, H., Yang, M.-H. (eds.) ACCV 2014. LNCS, vol. 9007, pp. 178–193. Springer, Heidelberg (2015). doi:10.1007/978-3-319-16814-2_12
38. Kitani, K., Okabe, T., Sato, Y., Sugimoto, A.: Fast unsupervised ego-action learning for first-person sports video. In: CVPR (2011)
39. Spriggs, E., la Torre, F.D., Hebert, M.: Temporal segmentation and activity classification from first-person sensing. In: CVPR Workshop on Egocentric Vision (2009)
40. Li, Y., Ye, Z., Rehg, J.: Delving into egocentric actions. In: CVPR (2015)
41. Mital, P.K., Smith, T.J., Hill, R.L., Henderson, J.M.: Clustering of gaze during dynamic scene viewing is predicted by motion. Cogn. Comput. $3(1)$, 5–24 (2011)
42. Jia, Y., Shelhamer, E., Donahue, J., Karayev, S., Long, J., Girshick, R., Guadarrama, S., Darrell, T.: Caffe: convolutional architecture for fast feature embedding. arXiv preprint (2014). arXiv:1408.5093
43. Liu, C.: Beyond Pixels: Exploring New Representations and Applications for Motion Analysis. Ph.D. thesis, Massachusetts Institute of Technology, May 2009
44. Pedregosa, F., Varoquaux, G., Gramfort, A., Michel, V., Thirion, B., Grisel, O., Blondel, M., Prettenhofer, P., Weiss, R., Dubourg, V., Vanderplas, J., Passos, A., Cournapeau, D., Brucher, M., Perrot, M., Duchesnay, E.: Scikit-learn: machine learning in python. JMLR **12**, 2825–2830 (2011)

Beyond Correlation Filters: Learning Continuous Convolution Operators for Visual Tracking

Martin Danelljan$^{(\boxtimes)}$, Andreas Robinson, Fahad Shahbaz Khan, and Michael Felsberg

CVL, Department of Electrical Engineering, Linköping University, Linköping, Sweden
{martin.danelljan,andreas.robinson,fahad.khan,michael.felsberg}@liu.se

Abstract. Discriminative Correlation Filters (DCF) have demonstrated excellent performance for visual object tracking. The key to their success is the ability to efficiently exploit available negative data by including all shifted versions of a training sample. However, the underlying DCF formulation is restricted to single-resolution feature maps, significantly limiting its potential. In this paper, we go beyond the conventional DCF framework and introduce a novel formulation for training *continuous* convolution filters. We employ an implicit interpolation model to pose the learning problem in the continuous spatial domain. Our proposed formulation enables efficient integration of multi-resolution deep feature maps, leading to superior results on three object tracking benchmarks: OTB-2015 (+5.1 % in mean OP), Temple-Color (+4.6 % in mean OP), and VOT2015 (20 % relative reduction in failure rate). Additionally, our approach is capable of sub-pixel localization, crucial for the task of accurate feature point tracking. We also demonstrate the effectiveness of our learning formulation in extensive feature point tracking experiments.

1 Introduction

Visual tracking is the task of estimating the trajectory of a target in a video. It is one of the fundamental problems in computer vision. Tracking of objects or feature points has numerous applications in robotics, structure-from-motion, and visual surveillance. In recent years, Discriminative Correlation Filter (DCF) based approaches have shown outstanding results on object tracking benchmarks [30,46]. DCF methods train a correlation filter for the task of predicting the target classification scores. Unlike other methods, the DCF efficiently utilize all spatial shifts of the training samples by exploiting the discrete Fourier transform.

Deep convolutional neural networks (CNNs) have shown impressive performance for many tasks, and are therefore of interest for DCF-based tracking. A CNN consists of several layers of convolution, normalization and pooling operations. Recently, activations from the last convolutional layers have been successfully employed for image classification. Features from these deep convolutional

Electronic supplementary material The online version of this chapter (doi:10.1007/978-3-319-46454-1_29) contains supplementary material, which is available to authorized users.

B. Leibe et al. (Eds.): ECCV 2016, Part V, LNCS 9909, pp. 472–488, 2016.
DOI: 10.1007/978-3-319-46454-1_29

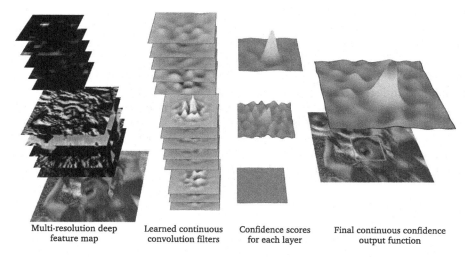

Multi-resolution deep   Learned continuous   Confidence scores   Final continuous confidence
feature map   convolution filters   for each layer   output function

Fig. 1. Visualization of our continuous convolution operator, applied to a multi-resolution deep feature map. The feature map (*left*) consists of the input RGB patch along with the first and last convolutional layer of a pre-trained deep network. The second column visualizes the continuous convolution filters learned by our framework. The resulting continuous convolution outputs for each layer (third column) are combined into the final continuous confidence function (*right*) of the target (green box). (Color figure online)

layers are discriminative while preserving spatial and structural information. Surprisingly, in the context of tracking, recent DCF-based methods [10,35] have demonstrated the importance of shallow convolutional layers. These layers provide higher spatial resolution, which is crucial for accurate target localization. However, fusing multiple layers in a DCF framework is still an open problem.

The conventional DCF formulation is limited to a single-resolution feature map. Therefore, all feature channels must have the same spatial resolution, as in e.g. the HOG descriptor. This limitation prohibits joint fusion of multiple convolutional layers with different spatial resolutions. A straightforward strategy to counter this restriction is to explicitly resample all feature channels to the same common resolution. However, such a resampling strategy is both cumbersome, adds redundant data and introduces artifacts. Instead, a principled approach for integrating multi-resolution feature maps in the learning formulation is preferred.

In this work, we propose a novel formulation for learning a convolution operator in the *continuous* spatial domain. The proposed learning formulation employs an implicit interpolation model of the training samples. Our approach learns a set of convolution filters to produce a *continuous-domain* confidence map of the target. This enables an elegant fusion of multi-resolution feature maps in a joint learning formulation. Figure 1 shows a visualization of our continuous convolution operator, when integrating multi-resolution deep feature maps. We validate the effectiveness of our approach on three object tracking benchmarks:

OTB-2015 [46], Temple-Color [32] and VOT2015 [29]. On the challenging OTB-2015 with 100 videos, our object tracking framework improves the state-of-the-art from 77.3 % to 82.4 % in mean overlap precision.

In addition to multi-resolution fusion, our continuous domain learning formulation enables accurate sub-pixel localization. This is achieved by labeling the training samples with sub-pixel precise continuous confidence maps. Our formulation is therefore also suitable for accurate feature point tracking. Further, our learning-based approach is discriminative and does not require explicit interpolation of the image to achieve sub-pixel accuracy. We demonstrate the accuracy and robustness of our approach by performing extensive feature point tracking experiments on the popular MPI Sintel dataset [7].

2   Related Work

Discriminative Correlation Filters (DCF) [5,11,24] have shown promising results for object tracking. These methods exploit the properties of circular correlation for training a regressor in a sliding-window fashion. Initially, the DCF approaches [5,23] were restricted to a single feature channel. The DCF framework was later extended to multi-channel feature maps [4,13,17]. The multi-channel DCF allows high-dimensional features, such as HOG and Color Names, to be incorporated for improved tracking. In addition to the incorporation of multi-channel features, the DCF framework has been significantly improved lately by, e.g., including scale estimation [9,31], non-linear kernels [23,24], a long-term memory [36], and by alleviating the periodic effects of circular convolution [11,15,18].

With the advent of deep CNNs, fully connected layers of the network have been commonly employed for image representation [38,43]. Recently, the last (deep) convolutional layers were shown to be more beneficial for image classification [8,33]. On the other hand, the first (shallow) convolutional layer was shown to be more suitable for visual tracking, compared to the deeper layers [10]. The deep convolutional layers are discriminative and possess high-level visual information. In contrast, the shallow layers contain low-level features at high spatial resolution, beneficial for localization. Ma et al. [35] employed multiple convolutional layers in a hierarchical ensemble of independent DCF trackers. Instead, we propose a novel continuous formulation to fuse multiple convolutional layers with different spatial resolutions in a *joint* learning framework.

Unlike object tracking, feature point tracking is the task of accurately estimating the motion of distinctive key-points. It is a core component in many vision systems [1,27,39,48]. Most feature point tracking methods are derived from the classic Kanade-Lucas-Tomasi (KLT) tracker [34,44]. The KLT tracker is a generative method, that is based on minimizing the squared sum of differences between two image patches. In the last decades, significant effort has been spent on improving the KLT tracker [2,16]. In contrast, we propose a discriminative learning based approach for feature point tracking.

Our approach: Our main contribution is a theoretical framework for learning discriminative convolution operators in the continuous spatial domain. Our formulation has two major advantages compared to the conventional DCF framework. Firstly, it allows a natural integration of multi-resolution feature maps, e.g. combinations of convolutional layers or multi-resolution HOG and color features. This property is especially desirable for object tracking, detection and action recognition applications. Secondly, our continuous formulation enables accurate sub-pixel localization, crucial in many feature point tracking problems.

3 Learning Continuous Convolution Operators

In this section, we present a theoretical framework for learning continuous convolution operators. Our formulation is generic and can be applied for supervised learning tasks, such as visual tracking and detection.

3.1 Preliminaries and Notation

In this paper, we utilize basic concepts and results in continuous Fourier analysis. For clarity, we first formulate our learning method for data defined in a one-dimensional domain, i.e. for functions of a single spatial variable. We then describe the generalization to higher dimensions, including images, in Sect. 3.5.

We consider the space $L^2(T)$ of complex-valued functions $g : \mathbb{R} \to \mathbb{C}$ that are periodic with period $T > 0$ and square Lebesgue integrable. The space $L^2(T)$ is a Hilbert space equipped with an inner product $\langle \cdot, \cdot \rangle$. For functions $g, h \in L^2(T)$,

$$\langle g, h \rangle = \frac{1}{T} \int_0^T g(t)\overline{h(t)}\, \mathrm{d}t\,, \qquad g * h(t) = \frac{1}{T} \int_0^T g(t-s)h(s)\, \mathrm{d}s. \qquad (1)$$

Here, the bar denotes complex conjugation. In (1) we have also defined the circular convolution operation $* : L^2(T) \times L^2(T) \to L^2(T)$.

In our derivations, we use the complex exponential functions $e_k(t) = e^{i\frac{2\pi}{T}kt}$ since they are eigenfunctions of the convolution operation (1). The set $\{e_k\}_{-\infty}^{\infty}$ further forms an orthonormal basis for $L^2(T)$. We define the Fourier coefficients of $g \in L^2(T)$ as $\hat{g}[k] = \langle g, e_k \rangle$. For clarity, we use square brackets for functions with discrete domains. Any $g \in L^2(T)$ can be expressed in terms of its Fourier series $g = \sum_{-\infty}^{\infty} \hat{g}[k]e_k$. The Fourier coefficients satisfy Parseval's formula $\|g\|^2 = \|\hat{g}\|_{\ell^2}^2$, where $\|g\|^2 = \langle g, g \rangle$ and $\|\hat{g}\|_{\ell^2}^2 = \sum_{-\infty}^{\infty} |\hat{g}[k]|^2$ is the squared ℓ^2-norm. Further, the Fourier coefficients satisfy the two convolution properties $\widehat{g * h} = \hat{g}\hat{h}$ and $\widehat{gh} = \hat{g} * \hat{h}$, where $\hat{g} * \hat{h}[k] := \sum_{l=-\infty}^{\infty} \hat{g}[k-l]\hat{h}[l]$.

3.2 Our Continuous Learning Formulation

Here we formulate our novel learning approach. The aim is to train a continuous convolution operator based on training samples x_j. The samples consist of feature maps extracted from image patches. Each sample x_j contains D feature channels $x_j^1, \ldots, x_j^D$, extracted from the same image patch. Conventional DCF formulations [11,17,24] assume the feature channels to have the same spatial resolution, i.e. have the same number of spatial sample points. Unlike previous works, we eliminate this restriction in our formulation and let N_d denote the number of spatial samples in x_j^d. In our formulation, the feature channel $x_j^d \in \mathbb{R}^{N_d}$ is viewed as a function $x_j^d[n]$ indexed by the discrete spatial variable $n \in \{0, \ldots, N_d - 1\}$. The sample space is expressed as $\mathcal{X} = \mathbb{R}^{N_1} \times \ldots \times \mathbb{R}^{N_D}$.

To pose the learning problem in the continuous spatial domain, we introduce an implicit interpolation model of the training samples. We regard the continuous interval $[0, T) \subset \mathbb{R}$ to be the spatial support of the feature map. Here, the scalar T represents the size of the support region. In practice, however, T is arbitrary since it represents the scaling of the coordinate system. For each feature channel d, we define the interpolation operator $J_d : \mathbb{R}^{N_d} \to L^2(T)$ of the form,

$$J_d\{x^d\}(t) = \sum_{n=0}^{N_d-1} x^d[n] b_d \left(t - \frac{T}{N_d} n \right). \tag{2}$$

The interpolated sample $J_d\{x^d\}(t)$ is constructed as a superposition of shifted versions of an interpolation function $b_d \in L^2(T)$. In (2), the feature values $x^d[n]$ act as weights for each shifted function. Similar to the periodic assumption in the conventional discrete DCF formulation, a periodic extension of the feature map is also performed here in (2).

As discussed earlier, our objective is to learn a linear convolution operator $S_f : \mathcal{X} \to L^2(T)$. This operator maps a sample $x \in \mathcal{X}$ to a target confidence function $s(t) = S_f\{x\}(t)$, defined on the continuous interval $[0, T)$. Here, $s(t) \in \mathbb{R}$ is the confidence score of the target at the location $t \in [0, T)$ in the image. Similar to other discriminative methods, the target is localized by maximizing the confidence scores in an image region. The key difference in our formulation is that the confidences are defined on a continuous spatial domain. Therefore, our formulation can be used to localize the target with higher accuracy.

In our continuous formulation, the operator S_f is parametrized by a set of convolution filters $f = (f^1, \ldots, f^D) \in L^2(T)^D$. Here, $f^d \in L^2(T)$ is the continuous filter for feature channel d. We define the convolution operator as,

$$S_f\{x\} = \sum_{d=1}^{D} f^d * J_d\{x^d\}, \quad x \in \mathcal{X}. \tag{3}$$

Here, each feature channel is first interpolated using (2) and then convolved with its corresponding filter. Note that the convolutions are performed in the continuous domain, as defined in (1). In the last step, the convolution responses from all filters are summed to produce the final confidence function.

In the standard DCF, each training sample is labeled by a discrete function that represents the desired convolution output. In contrast, our samples $x_j \in \mathcal{X}$ are labeled by confidence functions $y_j \in L^2(T)$, defined in the continuous spatial domain. Here, y_j is the desired output of the convolution operator $S_f\{x_j\}$ applied to the training sample x_j. This enables sub-pixel accurate information to be incorporated in the learning. The filter f is trained, given a set of m training sample pairs $\{(x_j, y_j)\}_1^m \subset \mathcal{X} \times L^2(T)$, by minimizing the functional,

$$E(f) = \sum_{j=1}^{m} \alpha_j \left\| S_f\{x_j\} - y_j \right\|^2 + \sum_{d=1}^{D} \left\| wf^d \right\|^2. \tag{4}$$

Here, the weights $\alpha_j \geq 0$ control the impact of each training sample. We additionally include a spatial regularization term, similar to [11], determined by the penalty function w. This regularization enables the filter to be learned on arbitrarily large image regions by controlling the spatial extent of the filter f. Spatial regions typically corresponding to background features are assigned a large penalty in w, while the target region has small penalty values. Thus, w encodes the prior reliability of features depending on their spatial location. Unlike [11], the penalty function w is defined on the whole continuous interval $[0, T)$ and periodically extended to $w \in L^2(T)$. Hence, $\left\| wf^d \right\| < \infty$ is required in (4). This is implied by our later assumption of w having finitely many non-zero Fourier coefficients $\hat{w}[k]$. Next, we derive the procedure to train the continuous filter f, using the proposed formulation (4).

3.3 Training the Continuous Filter

To train the filter f, we minimize the functional (4) in the Fourier domain. By using results from Fourier analysis it can be shown[1] that the Fourier coefficients of the interpolated feature map are given by $\widehat{J_d\{x^d\}}[k] = X^d[k]\hat{b}_d[k]$. Here, $X^d[k] := \sum_{n=0}^{N_d-1} x^d[n]e^{-i\frac{2\pi}{N_d}nk}$, $k \in \mathbb{Z}$ is the discrete Fourier transform (DFT) of x^d. By using linearity and the convolution property in Sect. 3.1, the Fourier coefficients of the output confidence function (3) are derived as

$$\widehat{S_f\{x\}}[k] = \sum_{d=1}^{D} \hat{f}^d[k] X^d[k] \hat{b}_d[k], \quad k \in \mathbb{Z}. \tag{5}$$

By applying Parseval's formula to (4) and using (5), we obtain

$$E(f) = \sum_{j=1}^{m} \alpha_j \left\| \sum_{d=1}^{D} \hat{f}^d X_j^d \hat{b}_d - \hat{y}_j \right\|_{\ell^2}^2 + \sum_{d=1}^{D} \left\| \hat{w} * \hat{f}^d \right\|_{\ell^2}^2. \tag{6}$$

Hence, the functional $E(f)$ can equivalently be minimized with respect to the Fourier coefficients $\hat{f}^d[k]$ for each filter f^d. We exploit the Fourier domain formulation (6) to minimize the original loss (4).

For practical purposes, the filter f needs to be represented by a finite set of parameters. One approach is to employ a parametric model to represent an infinite number of coefficients. In this work, we instead obtain a finite representation by minimizing (6) over the finite–dimensional subspace $V = \text{span}\{e_k\}_{-K_1}^{K_1} \times \ldots \times \text{span}\{e_k\}_{-K_D}^{K_D} \subset L^2(T)^D$. That is, we minimize (6) with respect to the coefficients $\{\hat{f}^d[k]\}_{-K_d}^{K_d}$, while assuming $\hat{f}^d[k] = 0$ for $|k| > K_d$.

---

[1] See the supplementary material for a detailed derivation.

In practice, K_d determines the number of filter coefficients $\hat{f}^d[k]$ to be computed for feature channel d during learning. Increasing K_d leads to a better estimate of the filter f^d at the cost of increased computations and memory consumption. In our experiments, we set $K_d = \lfloor \frac{N_d}{2} \rfloor$ such that the number of stored filter coefficients for channel d equals the spatial resolution N_d of the training sample x^d.

To derive the solution to the minimization problem (6) subject to $f \in V$, we introduce the vector of non-zero Fourier coefficients $\hat{\mathbf{f}}^d = (\hat{f}^d[-K_d] \cdots \hat{f}^d[K_d])^{\mathrm{T}} \in \mathbb{C}^{2K_d+1}$ and define the coefficient vector $\hat{\mathbf{f}} = [(\hat{\mathbf{f}}^1)^{\mathrm{T}} \cdots (\hat{\mathbf{f}}^D)^{\mathrm{T}}]^{\mathrm{T}}$. Further, we define $\hat{\mathbf{y}}_j = (\hat{y}_j[-K] \cdots \hat{y}_j[K])^{\mathrm{T}}$ be the vectorization of the $K := \max_d K_d$ first Fourier coefficients of y_j. To simplify the regularization term in (6), we let L be the number of non-zero coefficients $\hat{w}[k]$, such that $\hat{w}[k] = 0$ for all $|k| > L$. We further define W_d to be the $(2K_d + 2L + 1) \times (2K_d + 1)$ Toeplitz matrix corresponding to the convolution operator $W_d \hat{\mathbf{f}}^d = \mathrm{vec}\, \hat{w} * \hat{f}^d$. Finally, let W be the block-diagonal matrix $W = W_1 \oplus \cdots \oplus W_D$. The minimization of the functional (6) subject to $f \in V$ is equivalent to the following least squares problem,

$$E_V(\hat{\mathbf{f}}) = \sum_{j=1}^{m} \alpha_j \left\| A_j \hat{\mathbf{f}} - \hat{\mathbf{y}}_j \right\|_2^2 + \left\| W \hat{\mathbf{f}} \right\|_2^2. \tag{7}$$

Here, the matrix $A_j = [A_j^1 \cdots A_j^D]$ has $2K + 1$ rows and contains one diagonal block A_j^d per feature channel d with $2K_d + 1$ columns containing the elements $\{X_j^d[k] \hat{b}_d[k]\}_{-K_d}^{K_d}$. In (7), $\|\cdot\|_2$ denotes the standard Euclidian norm in $\mathbb{C}^M$.

To obtain a simple expression of the normal equations, we define the sample matrix $A = [A_1^{\mathrm{T}} \cdots A_m^{\mathrm{T}}]^{\mathrm{T}}$, the diagonal weight matrix $\Gamma = \alpha_1 I \oplus \cdots \oplus \alpha_m I$ and the label vector $\hat{\mathbf{y}} = [\hat{\mathbf{y}}_1^{\mathrm{T}} \cdots \hat{\mathbf{y}}_m^{\mathrm{T}}]^{\mathrm{T}}$. The minimizer of (7) is found by solving the normal equations,

$$\left(A^{\mathrm{H}} \Gamma A + W^{\mathrm{H}} W \right) \hat{\mathbf{f}} = A^{\mathrm{H}} \Gamma \hat{\mathbf{y}}. \tag{8}$$

Here, ^{H} denotes the conjugate-transpose of a matrix. Note that (8) forms a sparse linear equation system if w has a small number of non-zero Fourier coefficients $\hat{w}[k]$. In our object tracking framework, presented in Sect. 4.2, we employ the Conjugate Gradient method to iteratively solve (8). For our feature point tracking approach, presented in Sect. 4.3, we use a single-channel feature map and a constant penalty function w for improved efficiency. This results in a diagonal system (8), which can be efficiently solved by a direct computation.

3.4   Desired Confidence and Interpolation Function

Here, we describe the choice of the desired convolution output y_j and the interpolation function b_d. We construct both y_j and b_d by periodically repeating functions defined on the real line. In general, the T-periodic repetition of a function g is defined as $g_T(t) = \sum_{-\infty}^{\infty} g(t - nT)$. In the derived Fourier domain formulation (6), the functions y_j and b_d are represented by their respective Fourier coefficients. The Fourier coefficients of a periodic repetition g_T can be retrieved from the continuous Fourier transform $\hat{g}(\xi)$ of $g(t)$ as $\hat{g}_T[k] = \frac{1}{T}\hat{g}(\frac{k}{T})$.[2] We use this property to compute the Fourier coefficients of y_j and b_d.

To construct the desired convolution output y_j, we let $u_j \in [0, T)$ denote the estimated location of the target object or feature point in sample x_j. We define y_j as the periodic repetition of the Gaussian function $\exp\left(-\frac{(t-u_j)^2}{2\sigma^2}\right)$ centered at u_j. This provides the following expression for the Fourier coefficients,

$$\hat{y}_j[k] = \frac{\sqrt{2\pi\sigma^2}}{T} \exp\left(-2\sigma^2\left(\frac{\pi k}{T}\right)^2 - i\frac{2\pi}{T}u_j k\right). \tag{9}$$

The variance σ^2 is set to a small value to obtain a sharp peak. Further, this ensures a negligible spatial aliasing. In our work, the functions b_d are constructed based on the cubic spline kernel $b(t)$. The interpolation function b_d is set to the periodic repetition of a scaled and shifted version of the kernel $b\left(\frac{N_d}{T}\left(t - \frac{T}{2N_d}\right)\right)$, to preserve the spatial arrangement of the feature pyramid. The Fourier coefficients of b_d are then obtained as $\hat{b}_d[k] = \frac{1}{N_d}\exp\left(-i\frac{\pi}{N_d}k\right)\hat{b}\left(\frac{k}{N_d}\right)$. (see footnote 2)

3.5   Generalization to Higher Dimensions

The proposed formulation can be extended to domains of arbitrary number of dimensions. For our tracking applications we specifically consider the two-dimensional case, but higher-dimensional spaces can be treated similarly. For images, we use the space $L^2(T_1, T_2)$ of square-integrable periodic functions of two variables $g(t_1, t_2)$. The complex exponentials are then given by $e_{k_1,k_2}(t_1, t_2) = e^{i\frac{2\pi}{T_1}k_1 t_1}e^{i\frac{2\pi}{T_2}k_2 t_2}$. For the desired convolution output y_j, we employ a 2-dimensional Gaussian function. Further, the interpolation functions are obtained as a separable combination of the cubic spline kernel, i.e. $b(t_1, t_2) = b(t_1)b(t_2)$. The derivations presented in Sect. 3.3 also hold for the higher dimensional cases.

4   Our Tracking Frameworks

We apply our continuous learning formulation for two problems: visual object tracking and feature point tracking. We first present the localization procedure, which is based on maximizing the continuous confidence function. This is shared for both the object and feature point tracking frameworks.

4.1   Localization Step

Here, the aim is to localize the tracked target or feature point using the learned filter f. This is performed by first extracting a feature map $x \in \mathcal{X}$ from the region of interest in an image. The Fourier coefficients of the confidence score function

---

[2] Further details are given in the supplementary material.

$s = S_f\{x\}$ are then calculated using (5). We employ a two-step approach for maximizing the score $s(t)$ on the interval $t \in [0, T)$. To find a rough initial estimate, we first perform a *grid search*, where the score function is evaluated at the discrete locations $s\left(\frac{Tn}{2K+1}\right)$ for $n = 0, \ldots, 2K$. This is efficiently implemented as a scaled inverse DFT of the non-zero Fourier coefficients $\hat{s}[k], k = -K, \ldots, K$. The maximizer obtained in the grid search is then used as the initialization for an iterative optimization of the Fourier series expansion $s(t) = \sum_{-K}^{K} \hat{s}[k]e_k(t)$. We employ the standard Newton's method for this purpose. The gradient and Hessian are computed by analytic differentiation of $s(t)$.

4.2 Object Tracking Framework

We first present the object tracking framework based on our continuous learning formulation introduced in Sect. 3.2. We employ multi-resolution feature maps x_j extracted from a pre-trained deep network.[3] Similar to DCF based trackers [11,13,24], we extract a single training sample x_j in each frame. The sample is extracted from an image region centered at the target location and the region size is set to 5^2 times the area of the target box. Its corresponding importance weight is set to $\alpha_j = \frac{\alpha_{j-1}}{1-\lambda}$ using a learning rate parameter $\lambda = 0.0075$. The weights are then normalized such that $\sum_j \alpha_j = 1$. We store a maximum of $m = 400$ samples by replacing the sample with the smallest weight. The Fourier coefficients $\hat{w}$ of the penalty function w are computed as described in [11]. To detect the target, we perform a multi-scale search strategy [11,31] with 5 scales and a relative scale factor 1.02. The extracted confidences are maximized using the grid search followed by five Newton iterations, as described in Sect. 4.1.

The training of our continuous convolution filter f is performed by iteratively solving the normal equations (8). The work of [11] employed the Gauss-Seidel method for this purpose. However, this approach suffers from a quadratic complexity $\mathcal{O}(D^2)$ in the number of feature channels D. Instead, we employ the Conjugate Gradient (CG) [37] method due to its computational efficiency. Our numerical optimization scales linearly $\mathcal{O}(D)$ and is therefore especially suitable for high-dimensional deep features. In the first frame, we use 100 iterations to find an initial estimate of the filter coefficients $\hat{f}$. Subsequently, 5 iterations per frame are sufficient by initializing CG with the current filter (see footnote 2).

4.3 Feature Point Tracking Framework

Here, we describe the feature point tracking framework based on our learning formulation. For computational efficiency, we assume a single-channel feature map ($D = 1$), e.g. a grayscale image, and a constant penalty function $w(t) = \beta$. Under these assumptions, the normal equations (8) form a diagonal system of equations. The filter coefficients are directly obtained as,

$$\hat{f}[k] = \frac{\sum_{j=1}^{M} \alpha_j \overline{X_j[k]\hat{b}[k]}\hat{y}_j[k]}{\sum_{j=1}^{M} \alpha_j \left|X_j[k]\hat{b}[k]\right|^2 + \beta^2}, \quad k = -K, \ldots, K. \qquad (10)$$

---

[3] We use imagenet-vgg-m-2048, available at: http://www.vlfeat.org/matconvnet/.

Here, we have dropped the feature dimension index for the sake of clarity. In this case (single feature channel and constant penalty function), the training equation (10) resembles the original MOSSE filter [5]. However, our continuous formulation has several advantages compared to the original MOSSE. Firstly, our formulation employs an implicit interpolation model, given by $\hat{b}$. Secondly, each sample is labeled by a continuous-domain confidence y_j, that enables sub-pixel information to be incorporated in the learning. Thirdly, our convolution operator outputs continuous confidence functions, allowing accurate sub-pixel localization of the feature point. In our experiments, we show that the advantages of our continuous formulation are crucial for accurate feature point tracking.

5   Experiments

We validate our learning framework for two applications: tracking of objects and feature points. For object tracking, we perform comprehensive experiments on three datasets: OTB-2015 [46], Temple-Color [32], and VOT2015 [29]. For feature point tracking, we perform extensive experiments on the MPI Sintel dataset [7].

Table 1. A baseline comparison when using different combinations of convolutional layers in our object tracking framework. We report the mean OP (%) and AUC (%) on the OTB-2015 dataset. The best results are obtained when combining all three layers in our framework. The results clearly show the importance of multi-resolution deep feature maps for improved object tracking performance.

	Layer 0	Layer 1	Layer 5	Layers 0, 1	Layers 0, 5	Layers 1, 5	Layers 0, 1, 5
Mean OP	58.8	78.0	60.0	77.8	70.7	*81.8*	82.4
AUC	49.9	65.8	51.1	65.7	59.0	*67.8*	68.2

5.1   Baseline Comparison

We first evaluate the impact of fusing multiple convolutional layers from the deep network in our object tracking framework. Table 1 shows the tracking results, in mean overlap precision (OP) and area-under-the-curve (AUC), on the OTB-2015 dataset. OP is defined as the percentage of frames in a video where the intersection-over-union overlap exceeds a threshold of 0.5. AUC is computed from the success plot, where the mean OP over all videos is plotted over the range of thresholds $[0, 1]$. For details about the OTB protocol, we refer to [45].

In our experiments, we investigate the impact of the input RGB image layer (layer 0), the first convolutional layer (layer 1) and the last convolutional layer (layer 5). No significant gain in performance was observed when adding intermediate layers. The shallow layer (layer 1) alone provides superior performance compared to using only the deep convolutional layer (layer 5). Fusing the shallow and deep layers provides a large improvement. The best results are obtained

Table 2. A Comparison with state-of-the-art methods on the OTB-2015 and Temple-Color datasets. We report the mean OP (%) for the top 10 methods on each dataset. Our approach outperforms DeepSRDCF by 5.1 % and 5.0 % respectively.

	DSST	SAMF	TGPR	MEEM	LCT	HCF	Staple	SRDCF	SRDCFdecon	DeepSRDCF	C-COT
OTB-2015	60.6	64.7	54.0	63.4	70.1	65.5	69.9	72.9	76.7	*77.3*	**82.4**
Temple-Color	47.5	56.1	51.6	62.2	52.8	58.2	63.0	62.2	*65.8*	65.4	**70.4**

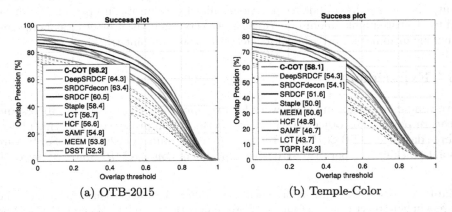

(a) OTB-2015   (b) Temple-Color

Fig. 2. Success plots showing a comparison with state-of-the-art on the OTB-2015 (a) and Temple-Color (b) datasets. Only the top 10 trackers are shown for clarity. Our approach improves the state-of-the-art by a significant margin on both these datasets.

when combining all three convolutional layers in our learning framework. We employ this three-layer combination for all further object tracking experiments.

We also compare our continuous formulation with the discrete DCF formulation by performing explicit resampling of the feature layers to a common resolution. For a fair comparison, all shared parameters are left unchanged. The layers (0, 1 and 5) are resampled with bicubic interpolation such that the data size of the training samples is preserved. On OTB-2015, the discrete DCF with resampling obtains an AUC score of 47.7 %, compared to 68.2 % for our continuous formulation. This dramatic reduction in performance is largely attributed to the reduced resolution in layer 1. To mitigate this effect, we also compare with only resampling layers 0 and 5 to the resolution of layer 1. This improves the result of the discrete DCF to 60.8 % in AUC, but at the cost of a 5-fold increase in data size. Our continuous formulation still outperforms the discrete DCF as it avoids artifacts introduced by explicit resampling.

5.2   OTB-2015 Dataset

We validate our Continuous Convolution Operator Tracker (C-COT) in a comprehensive comparison with 20 state-of-the-art methods: ASLA [25], TLD [26], Struck [21], LSHT [22], EDFT [14], DFT [41], CFLB [18], ACT [13], TGPR [19], KCF [24], DSST [9], SAMF [31], MEEM [47], DAT [40], LCT [36], HCF [35],

Staple [3] and SRDCF [11]. We also compare with SRDCFdecon, which integrates the adaptive decontamination of the training set [12] in SRDCF, and DeepSRDCF [10] employing activations from the first convolutional layer.

State-of-the-art Comparison: Table 2 (first row) shows a comparison with state-of-the-art methods on the OTB-2015 dataset.[4] The results are reported as mean OP over all the 100 videos. The HCF tracker, based on hierarchical convolutional features, obtains a mean OP of 65.5 %. The DeepSRDCF employs the first convolutional layer, similar to our baseline "Layer 1" in Table 1, and obtains a mean OP of 77.3 %. Our approach achieves the best results with a mean OP of 82.4 %, significantly outperforming DeepSRDCF by 5.1 %.

Figure 2a shows the success plot on the OTB-2015 dataset. We report the AUC score for each tracker in the legend. The DCF-based trackers HCF and Staple obtain AUC scores of 56.6 % and 58.4 % respectively. Among the compared methods, the SRDCF and its variants SRDCFdecon and DeepSRDCF provide the best results, all obtaining AUC scores above 60 %. Overall, our tracker achieves the best results, outperforming the second best method by 3.9 %.

Robustness to Initialization: We evaluate the robustness to initializations using the protocol provided by [46]. Each tracker is evaluated using two different initialization strategies: spatial robustness (SRE) and temporal robustness (TRE). The SRE criteria initializes the tracker with perturbed boxes, while the TRE criteria starts the tracker at 20 frames. Figure 3 provides the SRE and TRE success plots. Our approach obtains consistent improvements in both cases.

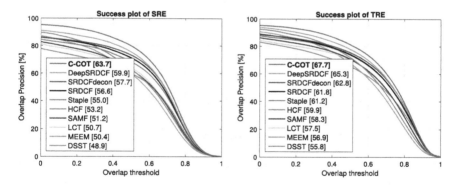

Fig. 3. An evaluation of the spatial (*left*) and temporal (*right*) robustness to initializations on the OTB-2015 dataset. We compare the top 10 trackers. Our approach demonstrates superior robustness compared to state-of-the-art methods.

5.3   Temple-Color Dataset

Here, we evaluate our approach on the Temple-Color dataset [32] containing 128 videos. The second row of Table 2 shows a comparison with state-of-the-art

---

[4] Detailed results are provided in the supplementary material.

methods. The DeepSRDCF tracker provides a mean OP score of 65.4 %. MEEM and SRDCFdecon obtain mean OP scores of 62.2 % and 65.8 % respectively. Different from these methods, our C-COT does not explicitly manage the training set to counter occlusions and drift. Our approach still improves the start-of-the-art by a significant margin, achieving a mean OP score of 70.4 %. A further gain in performance is expected by incorporating the unified learning framework [12] to handle corrupted training samples. In the success plot in Fig. 2b, our method obtains an absolute gain of 3.8 % in AUC compared to the previous best method.

5.4   VOT2015 Dataset

The VOT2015 dataset [29] consists of 60 challenging videos compiled from a set of more than 300 videos. Here, the performance is measured both in terms of accuracy (overlap with the ground-truth) and robustness (failure rate). In VOT2015, a tracker is restarted in the case of a failure. We refer to [29] for details. Table 3 shows the comparison of our approach with the top 10 participants in the challenge according to the VOT2016 rules [28]. Among the compared methods, RAJSSC achieves favorable results in terms of accuracy, at the cost of a higher failure rate. EBT achieves the best robustness among the compared methods. Our approach improves the robustness with a 20 % reduction in failure rate, without any significant degradation in accuracy.

Table 3. Comparison with state-of-the-art methods on the VOT2015 dataset. The results are presented in terms of robustness and accuracy. Our approach provides improved robustness with a significant reduction in failure rate.

	S3Tracker	RAJSSC	Struck	NSAMF	SC-EBT	sPST	LDP	SRDCF	EBT	DeepSRDCF	C-COT
Robustness	1.77	1.63	1.26	1.29	1.86	1.48	1.84	1.24	1.02	1.05	0.82
Accuracy	0.52	0.57	0.47	0.53	0.55	0.55	0.51	0.56	0.47	0.56	0.54

5.5   Feature Point Tracking

We validate our approach for robust and accurate feature point tracking. Here, the task is to track distinctive local image regions. We perform experiments on the MPI Sintel dataset [7], based on the 3D-animated movie "Sintel". The dataset consists of 23 sequences, featuring naturalistic and dynamic scenes with realistic lighting and camera motion blur. The ground-truth dense optical flow and occlusion maps are available for each frame. Evaluation is performed by selecting approximately 2000 feature points in the first frame of each sequence. We use the Good Features to Track (GFTT) [42] feature selector, but discard points at motion boundaries due to their ambiguous motion. The ground-truth tracks are then generated by integrating flow vectors over the sequence. The flow vectors are obtained by a bilinear interpolation of the dense ground-truth flow. We terminate the ground-truth tracks using the provided occlusion maps.

We compare our approach to MOSSE [5] and KLT [34,44]. The OpenCV implementation of KLT, used in our experiments, employs a pyramidal search [6] to accommodate for large translations. For a fair comparison, we adopt a similar pyramid approach for our method and MOSSE, by learning an independent filter for each pyramid level. Further, we use the window size of 31×31 pixels and 3 pyramid levels for all methods. For both our method and MOSSE we use a learning rate of $\lambda = 0.1$ and set the regularization parameter to $\beta = 10^{-4}$. For the KLT we use the default settings in OpenCV. Unlike ours and the MOSSE tracker, the KLT tracks feature points frame-to-frame without memorizing earlier appearances. In addition to our standard tracker, we also evaluate a frame-to-frame version (Ours-FF) of our method by setting the learning rate to $\lambda = 1$.

For quantitative comparisons, we use the endpoint error (EPE), defined as the Euclidian distance between the tracked point and its corresponding ground-truth location. Tracked points with an EPE smaller than 3 pixels are regarded as inliers. Figure 4 (left) shows the distribution of EPE computed over all sequences and tracked points. We also report the average inlier EPE for each method in the legend. Our approach achieves superior accuracy, with an inlier error of 0.449 pixels. We also provide the precision plot (Fig. 4, center), where the fraction of points with an EPE smaller than a threshold is plotted. The legend shows the inlier ratio for each method. Our tracker achieves superior robustness in comparison to the KLT, with an inlier ratio of 0.886. Compared to MOSSE, our method obtains significantly improved precision at sub-pixel thresholds (< 1 pixel). This clearly demonstrates that our continuous formulation enables accurate sub-pixel feature point tracking, while being robust. Unlike the frame-to-frame KLT, our method provides a principled procedure for updating the tracking model, while memorizing old samples. The experiments show that already our frame-to-frame variant (Ours-FF) provides a spectacular improvement compared to the KLT. Hence, our gained performance is due to both the model update *and* the proposed continuous formulation. On a desktop machine, our Matlab code achieves real-time tracking of 300 points at a single scale, utilizing only a single CPU.

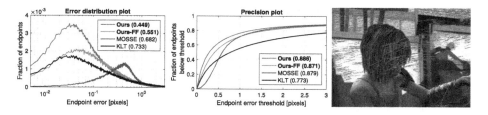

Fig. 4. Feature point tracking results on the MPI Sintel dataset. We report the endpoint error (EPE) distribution (*left*) and precision plot (*center*) over all sequences and points. In the legends, we display the average inlier EPE and the inlier ratio for the error distribution and precision plot respectively. Our approach provides consistent improvements, both in terms of accuracy and robustness, compared to existing methods. The example frame (*right*) from the Sintel dataset visualizes inlier trajectories obtained by our approach (red) along with the ground-truth (green). (Color figure online)

6   Conclusions

We propose a generic framework for learning discriminative convolution operators in the continuous spatial domain. We validate our framework for two problems: object tracking and feature point tracking. Our formulation enables the integration of multi-resolution feature maps. In addition, our approach is capable of accurate sub-pixel localization. Experiments on three object tracking benchmarks demonstrate that our approach achieves superior performance compared to the state-of-the-art. Further, our method obtains substantially improved accuracy and robustness for real-time feature point tracking.

Note that, in this work, we do not use any video data to learn an application specific deep feature representation. This is expected to further improve the performance of our object tracking framework. Another research direction is to incorporate motion-based deep features into our framework, similar to [20].

Acknowledgments. This work has been supported by SSF (CUAS), VR (EMC^2), CENTAURO, the Wallenberg Autonomous Systems Program, NSC and Nvidia.

References

1. Badino, H., Yamamoto, A., Kanade, T.: Visual odometry by multi-frame feature integration. In: ICCV Workshop (2013)
2. Baker, S., Matthews, I.A.: Lucas-kanade 20 years on: a unifying framework. IJCV **56**(3), 221–255 (2004)
3. Bertinetto, L., Valmadre, J., Golodetz, S., Miksik, O., Torr, P.H.S.: Staple: complementary learners for real-time tracking. In: CVPR (2016)
4. Boddeti, V.N., Kanade, T., Kumar, B.: Correlation filters for object alignment. In: CVPR (2013)
5. Bolme, D.S., Beveridge, J.R., Draper, B.A., Lui, Y.M.: Visual object tracking using adaptive correlation filters. In: CVPR (2010)
6. Bouguet, J.Y.: Pyramidal implementation of the lucas kanade feature tracker. Technical report Microprocessor Research Labs, Intel Corporation (2000)
7. Butler, D.J., Wulff, J., Stanley, G.B., Black, M.J.: A naturalistic open source movie for optical flow evaluation. In: Fitzgibbon, A., Lazebnik, S., Perona, P., Sato, Y., Schmid, C. (eds.) ECCV 2012, Part VI. LNCS, vol. 7577, pp. 611–625. Springer, Heidelberg (2012)
8. Cimpoi, M., Maji, S., Vedaldi, A.: Deep filter banks for texture recognition and segmentation. In: CVPR (2015)
9. Danelljan, M., Häger, G., Shahbaz Khan, F., Felsberg, M.: Accurate scale estimation for robust visual tracking. In: BMVC (2014)
10. Danelljan, M., Häger, G., Shahbaz Khan, F., Felsberg, M.: Convolutional features for correlation filter based visual tracking. In: ICCV Workshop (2015)
11. Danelljan, M., Häger, G., Shahbaz Khan, F., Felsberg, M.: Learning spatially regularized correlation filters for visual tracking. In: ICCV (2015)
12. Danelljan, M., Häger, G., Shahbaz Khan, F., Felsberg, M.: Adaptive decontamination of the training set: a unified formulation for discriminative visual tracking. In: CVPR (2016)

13. Danelljan, M., Shahbaz Khan, F., Felsberg, M., van de Weijer, J.: Adaptive color attributes for real-time visual tracking. In: CVPR (2014)
14. Felsberg, M.: Enhanced distribution field tracking using channel representations. In: ICCV Workshop (2013)
15. Fernandez, J.A., Boddeti, V.N., Rodriguez, A., Kumar, B.V.K.V.: Zero-aliasing correlation filters for object recognition. TPAMI **37**(8), 1702–1715 (2015)
16. Fusiello, A., Trucco, E., Tommasini, T., Roberto, V.: Improving feature tracking with robust statistics. Pattern Anal. Appl. **2**(4), 312–320 (1999)
17. Galoogahi, H.K., Sim, T., Lucey, S.: Multi-channel correlation filters. In: ICCV (2013)
18. Galoogahi, H.K., Sim, T., Lucey, S.: Correlation filters with limited boundaries. In: CVPR (2015)
19. Gao, J., Ling, H., Hu, W., Xing, J.: Transfer learning based visual tracking with gaussian processes regression. In: Fleet, D., Pajdla, T., Schiele, B., Tuytelaars, T. (eds.) ECCV 2014. LNCS, vol. 8691, pp. 188–203. Springer, Heidelberg (2014). doi:10.1007/978-3-319-10578-9_13
20. Gladh, S., Danelljan, M., Shahbaz Khan, F., Felsberg, M.: Deep motion features for visual tracking. In: ICPR (2016)
21. Hare, S., Saffari, A., Torr, P.: Struck: structured output tracking with kernels. In: ICCV (2011)
22. He, S., Yang, Q., Lau, R., Wang, J., Yang, M.H.: Visual tracking via locality sensitive histograms. In: CVPR (2013)
23. Henriques, J.F., Caseiro, R., Martins, P., Batista, J.: Exploiting the circulant structure of tracking-by-detection with kernels. In: Fitzgibbon, A., Lazebnik, S., Perona, P., Sato, Y., Schmid, C. (eds.) ECCV 2012, Part IV. LNCS, vol. 7575, pp. 702–715. Springer, Heidelberg (2012)
24. Henriques, J.F., Caseiro, R., Martins, P., Batista, J.: High-speed tracking with kernelized correlation filters. TPAMI **37**(3), 583–596 (2015)
25. Jia, X., Lu, H., Yang, M.H.: Visual tracking via adaptive structural local sparse appearance model. In: CVPR (2012)
26. Kalal, Z., Matas, J., Mikolajczyk, K.: P-N learning: bootstrapping binary classifiers by structural constraints. In: CVPR (2010)
27. Klein, G., Murray, D.: Parallel tracking and mapping for small AR workspaces. In: ISMAR (2007)
28. Kristan, M., Leonardis, A., Matas, J., Felsberg, M., Pflugfelder, R., Čehovin, L., Vojír, T., Häger, G., Lukežič, A., Fernández, G.: The visual object tracking VOT 2016 challenge results. In: ECCV Workshop (2016)
29. Kristan, M., Matas, J., Leonardis, A., Felsberg, M., Čehovin, L., Fernández, G., Vojír, T., Nebehay, G., Pflugfelder, R., Häger, G.: The visual object tracking VOT 2015 challenge results. In: ICCV Workshop (2015)
30. Kristan, M., et al.: The visual object tracking VOT 2014 challenge results. In: Agapito, L., Bronstein, M.M., Rother, C. (eds.) ECCV 2014. LNCS, vol. 8926, pp. 191–217. Springer, Heidelberg (2015). doi:10.1007/978-3-319-16181-5_14
31. Li, Y., Zhu, J.: A scale adaptive kernel correlation filter tracker with feature integration. In: Agapito, L., Bronstein, M.M., Rother, C. (eds.) ECCV 2014. LNCS, vol. 8926, pp. 254–265. Springer, Heidelberg (2015). doi:10.1007/978-3-319-16181-5_18
32. Liang, P., Blasch, E., Ling, H.: Encoding color information for visual tracking: algorithms and benchmark. TIP **24**(12), 5630–5644 (2015)
33. Liu, L., Shen, C., van den Hengel, A.: The treasure beneath convolutional layers: cross-convolutional-layer pooling for image classification. In: CVPR (2015)

34. Lucas, B.D., Kanade, T.: An iterative image registration technique with an application to stereo vision. In: IJCAI (1981)
35. Ma, C., Huang, J.B., Yang, X., Yang, M.H.: Hierarchical convolutional features for visual tracking. In: ICCV (2015)
36. Ma, C., Yang, X., Zhang, C., Yang, M.H.: Long-term correlation tracking. In: CVPR (2015)
37. Nocedal, J., Wright, S.J.: Numerical Optimization, 2nd edn. Springer, New York (2006)
38. Oquab, M., Bottou, L., Laptev, I., Sivic, J.: Learning and transferring mid-level image representations using convolutional neural networks. In: CVPR (2014)
39. Ovren, H., Forssén, P.: Gyroscope-based video stabilisation with auto-calibration. In: ICRA (2015)
40. Possegger, H., Mauthner, T., Bischof, H.: In defense of color-based model-free tracking. In: CVPR (2015)
41. Sevilla-Lara, L., Learned-Miller, E.G.: Distribution fields for tracking. In: CVPR (2012)
42. Shi, J., Tomasi, C.: Good features to track. In: CVPR (1994)
43. Simonyan, K., Zisserman, A.: Very deep convolutional networks for large-scale image recognition. In: ICLR (2015)
44. Tomasi, C., Kanade, T.: Detection and Tracking of Point Features. Technical report (1991)
45. Wu, Y., Lim, J., Yang, M.H.: Online object tracking: a benchmark. In: CVPR (2013)
46. Wu, Y., Lim, J., Yang, M.H.: Object tracking benchmark. TPAMI **37**(9), 1834–1848 (2015)
47. Zhang, J., Ma, S., Sclaroff, S.: MEEM: robust tracking via multiple experts using entropy minimization. In: Fleet, D., Pajdla, T., Schiele, B., Tuytelaars, T. (eds.) ECCV 2014, Part VI. LNCS, vol. 8694, pp. 188–203. Springer, Heidelberg (2014)
48. Zografos, V., Lenz, R., Ringaby, E., Felsberg, M., Nordberg, K.: Fast segmentation of sparse 3D point trajectories using group theoretical invariants. In: Cremers, D., Reid, I., Saito, H., Yang, M.-H. (eds.) ACCV 2014. LNCS, vol. 9006, pp. 675–691. Springer, Heidelberg (2015)

Look-Ahead Before You Leap: End-to-End Active Recognition by Forecasting the Effect of Motion

Dinesh Jayaraman$^{(\boxtimes)}$ and Kristen Grauman

The University of Texas at Austin, Austin, TX, USA
{dineshj,grauman}@cs.utexas.edu

Abstract. Visual recognition systems mounted on autonomous moving agents face the challenge of unconstrained data, but simultaneously have the opportunity to improve their performance by moving to acquire new views of test data. In this work, we first show how a recurrent neural network-based system may be trained to perform end-to-end learning of motion policies suited for this "active recognition" setting. Further, we hypothesize that active vision requires an agent to have the capacity to reason about the effects of its motions on its view of the world. To verify this hypothesis, we attempt to induce this capacity in our active recognition pipeline, by simultaneously learning to forecast the effects of the agent's motions on its internal representation of the environment conditional on all past views. Results across two challenging datasets confirm both that our end-to-end system successfully learns meaningful policies for active category recognition, and that "learning to look ahead" further boosts recognition performance.

1 Introduction

People consistently direct their senses in order to better understand their surroundings. For example, you might swivel around in your armchair to observe a person behind you, rotate a coffee mug on your desk to read an inscription, or walk to a window to observe the rain outside.

In sharp contrast to such scenarios, recent recognition research has been focused almost exclusively on static image recognition: the system takes a single snapshot as input, and produces a category label estimate as output. The ease of collecting large labeled datasets of images has enabled major advances on this task in recent years, as evident for example in the striking gains made on the ImageNet challenge [34]. Yet, despite this recent progress, recognition performance remains low for more complex, unconstrained images [27].

Recognition systems mounted on autonomous moving agents acquire unconstrained visual input which may be difficult to recognize effectively, *one frame*

Electronic supplementary material The online version of this chapter (doi:10. 1007/978-3-319-46454-1_30) contains supplementary material, which is available to authorized users.

© Springer International Publishing AG 2016
B. Leibe et al. (Eds.): ECCV 2016, Part V, LNCS 9909, pp. 489–505, 2016.
DOI: 10.1007/978-3-319-46454-1_30

at a time. However, similar to the human actor in the opening examples above, such systems have the opportunity to improve their performance by moving their camera apparatus or manipulating objects to acquire new information, as shown in Fig. 1. This control of the system over its sensory input has tremendous potential to improve its recognition performance. While such mobile agent settings (mobile robots, autonomous vehicles, etc.) are closer to reality today than ever before, the problem of *learning to actively move* to direct the acquisition of data remains underexplored in modern visual recognition research.

The problem we are describing fits into the realm of *active vision*, which has a rich history in the literature (*e.g.*, [2, 4, 14, 18, 35, 44]). Active vision offers several technical challenges that are unaddressed in today's standard passive scenario. In order to perform active vision, a system must learn to intelligently direct the acquisition of input to be processed by its recognition pipeline. In addition, recognition in an active setting places different demands on a system than in the standard passive scenario. To take one example, "nuisance factors" in still image recognition—such as pose, lighting, and viewpoint changes—become *avoidable* factors in the active vision setting, since in principle, they can often be overcome merely by moving the agent to the right location.

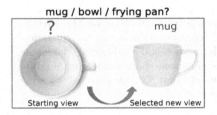 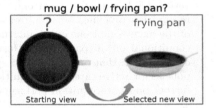

Fig. 1. A schematic illustrating the active categorization of two objects. A moving vision system may not recognize objects after just one view, but may intelligently choose to acquire new views to disambiguate amongst its competing hypotheses.

This calls for a major change of approach. Rather than strive for invariance to nuisance factors as is the standard in static image recognition, an intriguing strategy is to learn to *identify when conditions are non-ideal for recognition* and to *actively select the correct agent motion* that will lead to better conditions. In addition, recognition decisions must be made based on intelligently fusing evidence from multiple observations.

We contend that these three functions of an active vision system—control, per-view recognition, and evidence fusion—are closely intertwined, and must be tailored to work together. In particular, as the first contribution of this paper, we propose to learn all three modules of an active vision system simultaneously and end-to-end. We employ a stochastic neural network to learn intelligent motion policies (control), a standard neural network to process inputs at each timestep (per-view recognition), and a modern recurrent neural network (RNN) to integrate evidence over time (evidence fusion). Given an initial view and a set of possible agent motions, our approach learns how to move in the 3-D environment to produce accurate categorization results.

Additionally, we hypothesize that motion planning for active vision requires an agent to internally "look before it leaps". That is, it ought to simultaneously reason about the effect of its motions on future inputs. To demonstrate this, as a second contribution, we jointly train our active vision system to have the ability to predict *how its internal representation of its environment will evolve* conditioned on its choice of motion. As we will explain below, this may be seen as preferring equivariance *i.e.* predictable feature responses to pose changes, rather than invariance as is standard in passive recognition pipelines.

Through experiments on two datasets, we validate both our key ideas: (1) RNN-based end-to-end active categorization and (2) learning to forecast the effects of self-motion at the same time one learns how to move to solve the recognition task. We study both a scene categorization scenario, where the system chooses how to move around a previously unseen 3-D scene, and an object categorization scenario, where the system chooses how to manipulate a previously unseen object that it holds. Our results establish the advantage of our end-to-end approach over both passive and traditional active methods.

2   Related Work

Active vision. The idea that a subject's actions may play an important role in perception can be traced back almost 150 years [12] in the cognitive psychology literature [4]. "Active perception", the idea of exploiting *intelligent control strategies* (agent motion, object manipulation, camera parameter changes *etc.*) for *goal-directed data acquisition* to improve machine vision, was pioneered by [2,6,7,44]. While most research in this area has targeted low-level vision problems such as segmentation, structure from motion, depth estimation, optical flow estimation [2,7,29], or the "semantic search" task of object localization [3,21,22,38], approaches targeting *active recognition* are most directly related to our work.

Most prior active recognition approaches attempt to identify during training those canonical/"special" views that minimize ambiguity among candidate labels [14,17,18,35,44]. At test time, such systems iteratively estimate the current pose, then select moves that take them to such pre-identified informative viewpoints. These approaches are typically applicable only to *instance* recognition problems, since broader categories can be too diverse in appearance and shape to fix "special viewpoints".

In contrast, our approach handles real world categories. To the best of our knowledge, very little prior work attempts this challenging task of active *category* recognition (as opposed to instance recognition) [10,23,32,46,49]. The increased difficulty is due to the fact that with complex real world categories, it is much harder to anticipate new views conditioned on actions. Since new instances will be seen at test time, it is not sufficient to simply memorize the geometry of individual instances, as many active instance recognition methods effectively do.

Recently, [23, 46] learn to *predict* the next views of *unseen test objects*, and use this to explicitly greedily reason about the most informative "next-best" move. Instead, our approach uses reinforcement learning (RL) in a stochastic recurrent neural network to learn optimal *sequential* movement policies over multiple timesteps. The closest methods to ours in this respect are [31] and [28], both of which employ Q-learning in feedforward neural networks to perform view selection, and target relatively simpler visual tasks compared to this work.

In addition to the above, an important novelty of our approach is in learning the entire system end-to-end. Active recognition approaches must broadly perform three separate functions: action selection, per-instant view processing, and belief updates based on the history of observed views. While previous approaches have explored several choices for action selection, they typically train a "passive" per-instant view recognition module offline and fuse predictions across time using some manually defined heuristic [17, 18, 28, 32, 35]. For example, recently, a deep neural network is trained to learn action policies in [28] after pretraining a per-view classifier and using a simple Naive Bayes update heuristic for label belief fusion. In contrast, we train all three modules jointly within a single active recognition objective.

Saliency and attention. Visual saliency and attention are related to active vision [5, 8, 30, 36, 48]. While active vision systems aim to form policies to acquire *new* data, saliency and attention systems aim to block out "distractors" in *existing* data by identifying portions of input images/video to focus on, often as a faster alternative to sliding window-based methods. Attention systems thus sometimes take a "foveated" approach [13, 30]. In contrast, in our setting, the system never holds a snapshot of the entire environment at once. Rather, its input at each timestep is one portion of its complete physical 3D environment, and it must choose motions leading to more informative—possibly non-overlapping—viewpoints. Another difference between the two settings is that the focus of attention may move in arbitrary jumps (saccades) without continuity, whereas active vision agents may only move continuously.

Sequential attention systems using recurrent neural networks in particular have seen significant interest of late [30], with variants proving successful across several attention-based tasks [5, 36, 48]. We adopt the basic attention architecture of [30] as a starting point for our model, and develop it further to accommodate the active vision setting, instill look-ahead capabilities, and select camera motions surrounding a 3D object that will most facilitate categorization.

Predicting related features. There is recent interest in "visual prediction" problems in various contexts [19, 20, 23, 25, 33, 41, 42, 46], often using convolutional neural networks (CNNs). For example, one can train CNNs [24, 41] or recurrent neural networks (RNNs) to predict future frames based on previously observed frames [33] in an entirely passive setting. These methods do not attempt to reason about *causes* of view transformations *e.g.* camera motions. Closer to our work are methods for view synthesis, such as [19, 25], which allow synthesis of simple synthetic images with specified "factors of variation" (such as pose and lighting). Given surrounding views, high quality unseen views are predicted in [20], effectively learning 3D geometry end-to-end. The methods of [1, 23] model feature responses to a discrete set of observer motions. Different from all the above, we learn to predict the evolution of temporally aggregated features—computed from a complete history of seen views—as a function of observer motion choices. Furthermore, we integrate this idea with the closely tied active recognition problem.

Integrating sensors and actions. Our work is also related to research in sensorimotor feature embeddings [11,15,16,23,26,39,43]. There the idea is to combine (possibly non-visual) sensor streams together with proprioception or other knowledge about the actions of the agent on which the sensors are mounted. Various methods learn features that transform in simple ways in response to an agent's actions [11,16,23] or reflect the geometry of an agent's environment [39]. Neural nets are trained to perform simple robotic tasks in [15,26]. Perhaps conceptually most relevant to our work among these is [43]. Their method learns an image feature space to determine control actions easily from visual inputs, with applications to simulated control tasks. In contrast, we learn embeddings encoding information from complete *histories* of observations and agent actions, with the aim of exposing this information to an active visual recognition controller.

3 Approach

First we define the setting and data flow for active recognition (Sect. 3.1). Then we define our basic system architecture (Sect. 3.2). Finally, we describe our look-ahead module (Sect. 3.3).

3.1 Setting

We first describe our active vision setting at test time, using a 3-D object category recognition scenario as a running example. Our results consider both object and scene category recognition tasks. The active recognition system can issue motor commands to move a camera within a viewing sphere around the 3-D object X of interest. Each point on this viewing sphere is indexed by a corresponding 2-D camera pose vector p indexing elevation and azimuth.

The system is allowed T timesteps to recognize every object instance X. At every timestep $t = 1, 2, \ldots T$:

- The system issues a motor command $\boldsymbol{m}_t$ *e.g.* "increase camera elevation by $20°$, azimuth by $10°$", from a set $\mathcal{M}$ of available camera motions. In our experiments, $\mathcal{M}$ is a discrete set consisting of small camera motions to points on an elevation-azimuth grid centered at the previous camera pose $\boldsymbol{p}_{t-1}$. At time $t = 1$, the "previous" camera pose p_0 is set to some random unknown vector, corresponding to the agent initializing its recognition episode at some arbitrary position with respect to the object.
- Next, the system is presented a new 2-D view $\boldsymbol{x}_t = P(X, \boldsymbol{p}_t)$ of X captured from the new camera pose $\boldsymbol{p}_t = \boldsymbol{p}_{t-1} + \boldsymbol{m}_t$, where $P(., .)$ is a projection function. This new evidence is now available to the system while selecting its next action $\boldsymbol{m}_{t+1}$.

At the final timestep $t = T$, the system must additionally predict a category label $\hat{y}$ for X, *e.g.*, the object category it believes is most probable. In our implementation, the number of timesteps T is fixed, and all valid motor commands have uniform cost. The system is evaluated only on the accuracy of its prediction $\hat{y}$. However, the framework generalizes to the case of variable-length episodes.

3.2   Active Recognition System Architecture

Our basic active recognition system is modeled on the recurrent architecture first proposed in [30] for visual attention. Our system is composed of four basic modules: ACTOR, SENSOR, AGGREGATOR and CLASSIFIER, with weights W_a, W_s, W_r, W_c respectively. At each step t, ACTOR issues a motor command $\boldsymbol{m}_t$, which updates the camera pose vector to $\boldsymbol{p}_t = \boldsymbol{p}_{t-1} + \boldsymbol{m}_t$. Next, a 2-D image $\boldsymbol{x}_t$ captured from this pose is fed into SENSOR together with the motor command $\boldsymbol{m}_t$. SENSOR produces a view-specific feature vector $\boldsymbol{s}_t = \text{SENSOR}(\boldsymbol{x}_t, \boldsymbol{m}_t)$, which is then fed into AGGREGATOR to produce aggregate feature vector $\boldsymbol{a}_t = \text{AGGREGATOR}(\boldsymbol{s}_1, \dots, \boldsymbol{s}_t)$. The cycle is completed when, at the next step $t + 1$, ACTOR processes the aggregate feature from the previous timestep to issue $\boldsymbol{m}_{t+1} = \text{ACTOR}(\boldsymbol{a}_t)$. Finally, after T steps, the category label beliefs are predicted as $\hat{y}(W, X) = \text{CLASSIFIER}(\boldsymbol{a}_t)$, where $W = [W_a, W_s, W_r, W_c]$ is the vector of all learnable weights in the network, and for a C-class classification problem, $\hat{y}$ is a C-dimensional multinomial probability density function representing the likelihoods of the 3-D object X belonging to each of the C classes. See Fig. 2 for a schematic showing how the modules are connected.

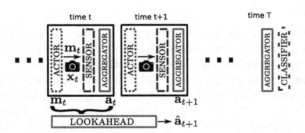

Fig. 2. A schematic of our system architecture depicting the interaction between ACTOR, SENSOR and AGGREGATOR and CLASSIFIER modules, unrolled over timesteps. Information flows from left to right. At training time, the additional LOOKAHEAD acts across two timesteps, learning to predict the evolution of the aggregate feature $\boldsymbol{a}_t$ into $\boldsymbol{a}_{t+1}$ conditional on the selected motion $\boldsymbol{m}_t$. See Sect. 3.2 for details.

In our setup, AGGREGATOR is a recurrent neural network, CLASSIFIER is a simple fully-connected hidden layer followed by a log-softmax and SENSOR separately processes the view $\boldsymbol{x}_t$ and the motor signal $\boldsymbol{m}_t$ in disjoint neural network pipelines before merging them through more layers of processing to produce the per-instance view feature $\boldsymbol{s}_t = \text{SENSOR}(\boldsymbol{x}_t, \boldsymbol{m}_t)$. ACTOR has a non-standard neural net architecture involving stochastic units: at each timestep, it internally produces an $|\mathcal{M}|$-dimensional multinomial density function $\pi(\boldsymbol{m}_t)$ over all candidate camera motions in $\mathcal{M}$, from which it samples one motion. For more details on the internal architectures of these modules, see Supp.

Training. At training time, the network weights W are trained jointly to maximize classifier accuracy at time T. Following [30], training W follows a hybrid procedure involving both standard backpropagation and "connectionist reinforcement learning" [45]. The modules with standard deterministic neural network connections (CLASSIFIER, AGGREGATOR and SENSOR) can be trained directly by backpropagating gradients from a softmax classification loss, while the ACTOR module which contains stochastic units can only be trained using the REINFORCE procedure of [45].

Roughly, REINFORCE treats the ACTOR module as a Partially Observable Markov Decision Process (POMDP), with the pdf $\pi(\boldsymbol{m}_t|\boldsymbol{a}_{t-1}, W)$ representing the policy to be learned. In a reinforcement learning (RL)-style approach, REIN-FORCE iteratively increases weights in the pdf $\pi(\boldsymbol{m})$ on those candidate motions $\boldsymbol{m} \in \mathcal{M}$ that have produced higher "rewards", as defined by a reward function. A simple REINFORCE reward function to promote classification accuracy could be $R_c(\hat{y}) = 1$ when the most likely label in $\hat{y}$ is correct, and 0 when not. To speed up training, we use a variance-reduced version of this loss $R(\hat{y}) = R_c(\hat{y}) - R_c(z)$, where z is set to the most commonly occuring class. Beyond the stochastic units, the REINFORCE algorithm produces gradients that may be propagated to non-stochastic units through standard backpropagation. In our hybrid training approach, these REINFORCE gradients from ACTOR are therefore added to the softmax loss gradients from CLASSIFIER before backpropagation through AGGREGATOR and SENSOR.

More formally, given a training dataset of instance-label pairs $\{(X^i, y^i) : 1 \leq i \leq N\}$, the gradient updates are as follows. Let $W_{\backslash c}$ denote $[W_a, W_s, W_r]$, *i.e.* all the weights in W except the CLASSIFIER weights W_c, and similarly, let $W_{\backslash a}$ denote $[W_c, W_r, W_s]$. Then:

$$\Delta W_{\backslash c}^{RL} \approx \sum_{i=1}^{N} \sum_{t=1}^{T} \nabla_{W_{\backslash c}} \log \pi(m_t^i | \boldsymbol{a}_{t-1}^i; W_{\backslash c}) R^i, \tag{1}$$

$$\Delta W_{\backslash a}^{SM} = - \sum_{i=1}^{N} \nabla_{W_{\backslash a}} L_{\text{softmax}}(\hat{y}^i(W, X), y^i), \tag{2}$$

where indices i in the superscripts denote correspondence to the ith training sample X^i. Eqs. (1) and (2) show the gradients computed from the REINFORCE rewards (RL) and the softmax loss (SM) respectively, for different subsets of weights. The REINFORCE gradients ΔW^{RL} are computed using the approximation proposed in [45]. Final gradients with respect to the weights of each module used in weight updates are given by: $\Delta W_a = \Delta W_a^{RL}$, $\Delta W_s = \Delta W_s^{RL} + \Delta W_s^{SM}$, $\Delta W_r = \Delta W_r^{RL} + \Delta W_r^{SM}$, $\Delta W_c = \Delta W_c^{RL} + \Delta W_c^{SM}$. Training is through standard stochastic gradient descent with early stopping based on a validation set.

3.3   Look-Ahead: Predicting the Effects of Motions

Active recognition systems select the next motion based on some expectation of the next view. Though non-trivial even in the traditional instance recognition setting [14,18,35,44], with instances one can exploit the fact that pose estimation in some canonical pose space is sufficient in itself to estimate properties of future views. In other words, with enough prior experience seeing the object instance, it is largely a 3-D (or implicit 3-D) geometric model formation problem.

In contrast, as discussed in Sect. 2, this problem is much harder in active *categorization* with realistic categories—the domain we target. Predicting subsequent views in this setting is severely under-constrained, and requires reasoning about semantics and geometry together. In other words, next view planning requires some element of learning about how 3-D objects *in general* change in their appearance as a function of observer motion.

We hypothesize that the ability to predict the next view conditional on the next camera motion is closely tied to the ability to select optimal motions. Thus, rather than learn separately the model of view transitions and model of motion policies, we propose a unified approach to learn them jointly. Our idea is that knowledge transfer from a view prediction task will benefit active categorization. In this formulation, we retain the system from Sect. 3.2, but simultaneously learn to predict, at every timestep t, the impact on aggregate features a_{t+1} at the next timestep, given a_t and any choice of motion $m_t \in \mathcal{M}$. In other words, we simultaneously learn how the *accumulated history* of learned features—not only the current view—will evolve as a function of our candidate motions.

For this auxiliary task, we introduce an additional module, LOOKAHEAD, with weights W_l into the setup of Sect. 3.2 at training time. At timestep t, LOOKAHEAD takes as input a_{t-1} and m_{t-1} and predicts $\hat{a}_t = \text{LOOKAHEAD}(a_{t-1}, m_{t-1})$. This module may be thought of as a "predictive auto-encoder" in the space of aggregate features a_t output by AGGREGATOR. A look-ahead error loss is computed at every timestep between the predicted and actual aggregate features: $d(\hat{a}_t, a_t | a_{t-1}, m_{t-1})$. We use the cosine distance to compute this error. This per-timestep look-ahead loss provides a third source of training gradients $\Delta W_{\backslash ca}^{LA}$ for the network weights, as it is backpropagated through AGGREGATOR and SENSOR:

$$\Delta W_{\backslash ca}^{LA} = \sum_{i=1}^{N} \sum_{t=2}^{T} \nabla_{W_{\backslash ca}} d(\hat{a}_t, a_t | a_{t-1}, m_{t-1}), \tag{3}$$

where W now includes W_l and LA denotes lookahead. The LOOKAHEAD module itself is trained solely from this error, so that $\Delta W_l = \Delta W_l^{LA}$. The final gradients used to train SENSOR and AGGREGATOR change to include this new loss: $\Delta W_s = \Delta W_s^{RL} + \Delta W_s^{SM} + \lambda \Delta W_s^{LA}$, $\Delta W_r = \Delta W_r^{RL} + \Delta W_r^{SM} + \lambda \Delta W_r^{LA}$. λ is a new hyperparameter that controls how much the weights in the core network are influenced by the look-ahead error loss.

The look-ahead error loss of Eq. 3 may also be interpreted as an unsupervised regularizer on the classification objective of Eqs. 1 and 2. This regularizer encodes the hypothesis that good features for the active recognition task must respond in learnable, systematic ways to camera motions.

This is related to the role of "equivariant" image features in [23], where we showed that regularizing image features to respond predictably to observer egomotions improves performance on standard static image categorization tasks. This work differs from [23] in several important ways. First, we explore the utility of look-ahead for the active categorization problem, not recognition of individual static images. Second, the proposed look-ahead module is conceptually distinct. In particular, we propose to regularize the aggregate features from a sequence of activity, not simply per-view features. Whereas in [23] the effect of a discrete egomotion on one image is estimated by linear transformations in the embedding space, the proposed look-ahead module takes as input both the history of views and the selected motion when estimating the effects of hypothetical motions.

Proprioceptive knowledge. Another useful feature of our approach is that it allows for easy modeling of proprioceptive knowledge such as the current position p_t of a robotic arm. Since the ACTOR module is trained purely through REINFORCE rewards, all other modules may access its output m_t without having to back-propagate extra gradients from the softmax loss. For instance, while the sensor module is fed m_t as input, it does not directly backpropagate any gradients to train ACTOR. Since p_t is a function solely of $(m_1 \ldots m_t)$, this knowledge is readily available for use in other components of the system without any changes to the training procedure described above. We append appropriate proprioceptive information to the inputs of ACTOR and LOOKAHEAD, detailed in experiments.

Greedy softmax classification loss. We found it beneficial at training time to inject softmax classification gradients after every timestep, rather than only at the end of T timesteps. To achieve this, the CLASSIFIER module is modified to contain a bank of T classification networks with identical architectures (but different weights, since in general, AGGREGATOR outputs a_t at different timesteps may have domain differences). Note that the REINFORCE loss is still computed only at $t = T$. Thus, given that softmax gradients do not pass through the ACTOR module, it remains free to learn non-greedy motion policies.

4   Experiments

We evaluate our approach for object and scene categorization. In both cases, the system must choose how it will move in its 3-D environment such that the full sequence of its actions lead to the most accurate categorization results.

4.1   Datasets and Baselines

While active vision systems have traditionally been tested on custom robotic setups [32] (or simple turn-table-style datasets [35]), we aim to test our system on realistic, off-the-shelf datasets in the interest of benchmarking and reproducibility. We work with two publicly available datasets, SUN360 [47] and GERMS [28].

Our **SUN360** [47] experiments test a scenario where the agent is exploring a 3-D scene and must intelligently turn to see new parts of the scene that will

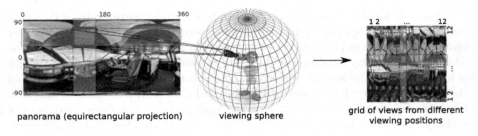

panorama (equirectangular projection)   viewing sphere   grid of views from different
viewing positions

Fig. 3. (Best seen in color) An "airplane interior" class example showing how SUN360 spherical panoramas (equirectangular projection on the left) are converted into 12×12 $45°$ FOV view grid. As an illustration, the view at grid coordinates $x = 4, y = 6$ outlined in green in the view grid on the right corresponds approximately to the overlap region (also outlined in green) on the left (approximate because of panorama distortions—rectangles in the panorama are not rectangles in the rectified views present in the grid). The 5×7 red shaded region in the view grid (right) shows the motions available to ACTOR when starting from the highlighted view. (Color figure online)

enable accurate scene categorization (bedroom, living room, etc.). SUN360 consists of spherical panoramas of various indoor and outdoor scenes together with scene category labels. We use the 26-category subset (8992 panoramic images) used in [47]. Each panorama by itself represents a 3-D scene instance, around which an agent "moves" by rotating its head, as shown in Fig. 3. For our experiments, the agent has a limited field of view ($45°$) at each timestep. We sample discrete views in a 12 elevations (camera pitch) $\times$ 12 azimuths (camera yaw) grid. The pitch and yaw steps are both spaced $30°$ apart ($12 \times 30 = 360$), so that the entire viewing sphere is uniformly sampled on each axis. Starting from a full panorama of size 1024×2048, each $45°$ FOV view is represented first as a 224×224 image, from which 1024-dim. GoogleNet [40] features are extracted from the penultimate layer. At each timestep, the agent can choose to move to viewpoints on a 5×7 grid centered at the current position. We set $T = 5$ timesteps.[1] Proprioceptive knowledge in the form of the current camera elevation angle is fed into ACTOR and LOOKAHEAD. We use a random 80-20 train-test split. Our use of SUN360 to simulate an active agent in a 3D scene is new and offers a realistic scenario that we can benchmark rigorously; note that previous work on the dataset does a different task, *i.e.*, recognition with the full panorama in hand at once [47], and results are therefore not comparable to our setting.

Our **GERMS** [28] experiments consider the scenario where a robot is holding an object and must decide on its next best motion relative to that object, *e.g.*, to gain access to an unseen facet of the object, so as to recognize its instance label. GERMS has 6 videos each (3 train, 3 test) of 136 objects being rotated around different fixed axes, against a television screen displaying moving indoor scenes (see Fig. 4). Each video frame is annotated by the angle at which the robotic arm is holding the object. Each video provides one collection of views that our

---

[1] Episode lengths were set based on learning time for efficient experimentation.

active vision system can traverse at will, for a total of $136 \times 6 = 816$ train/test instances (compared to 8992 on SUN360). While GERMS is small and targets *instance* rather than category recognition, aside from SUN360 it is the most suitable prior dataset facilitating active recognition. Each frame is represented by a 4096-dim. VGG-net feature vector [37], provided by the authors [28]. We set episode lengths to $T = 3$ steps. As proprioceptive knowledge, we feed the current position of the robotic hand into ACTOR and LOOKAHEAD. We use the train-test subsets specified by the dataset authors.

Fig. 4. The GERMS active object instance recognition dataset [28] contains videos of a single-axis robotic hand rotating 136 toys against a moving background.

Baselines: We extensively evaluate our "Look-ahead active RNN" (Sect. 3.3) and simpler "Active RNN" (Sect. 3.2) against six baselines, including passive single-view methods, random view sampling, and traditional prior active vision approaches, upgraded to be competitive in our setting.

- **Single view (neural net):** has access to only one view, like the starting view provided to the active systems. A feed-forward neural network is used for this baseline, composed from the appropriate components of the SENSOR and CLASSIFIER modules of our system. This baseline is entirely pose-agnostic *i.e.*, the same classifier is applied to views from all object poses.
- **Random views (average):** uses the same architecture as "Single view (neural net)", but has access to T views, with successive views being related by randomly selected motions from the same motion set $\mathcal{M}$ available to the active systems. Its output class likelihood at $t = T$ is the average of its independent estimates of class likelihood for each view.
- **Random views (recurrent):** uses the same core architecture as our Active RNN method, except for the ACTOR module. In its place, random motions (from $\mathcal{M}$) are selected. Note that this should be a strong baseline, having nearly all aspects of the proposed approach except for the active view selection module. In particular, it has access to its selected motions in its SENSOR module, and can also learn to intelligently aggregate evidence over views in its AGGREGATOR RNN module.
- **Transinformation:** is closely based on [35], in which views are selected greedily to reduce the information-theoretic uncertainty of the category hypothesis. We make modifications for our setting, such as using 1024-D CNN features in place of the original receptive field histogram features, and using Monte Carlo sampling to approximate information gain. Each view is classified with pose-specific classifiers. When the class hypothesis is identical between consecutive views, it is emitted as output and view selection terminates. Like most

prior approaches, this method relies on a canonical world coordinate space in which all object instances can be registered. Since this is infeasible in the active categorization setting, we treat each instance's coordinates as world coordinates.

- **SeqDP:** is closely based on [17], and extends [35] using a sequential decision process with Bayesian aggregation of information between views. It runs to a fixed number of views.
- **Transinformation + SeqDP:** combines the strengths of [35] and [17]; it uses Bayesian information aggregation across views, and terminates early when the predicted class remains unchanged at consecutive timesteps.

Hyperparameters for all methods were optimized for overall accuracy on a validation set through iterative search over random combinations [9].

4.2   Results

Table 1 shows the recognition accuracy results for scene categorization (SUN360) and object instance recognition (GERMS), and Fig. 5 plots the results as a function of timesteps. Both variants of our method outperform the baselines on both datasets, confirming that our active approach successfully learns intelligent view selection strategies. Passive baselines, representative of the current standard approaches to visual categorization, perform uniformly poorly, highlighting the advantages of the active setting. In addition, our Look-ahead active RNN outperforms our Active RNN variant on both datasets, showing the value in simultaneously learning to predict action-conditional next views at the same time we learn the active vision policy. By "looking before leaping" our look-ahead module facilitates beneficial knowledge transfer for the active vision task.

On SUN360, even though it represents a much harder active *category recognition* problem, the margins between our method and the random view baselines are pronounced. Furthermore, while the traditional active baselines do show significant improvements from observing multiple views, they fall far short of the performance of our method despite upgrading them in order to be competitive, such as by using CNN features, as described above.

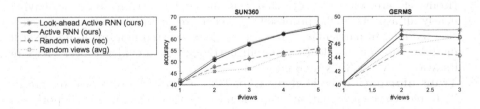

Fig. 5. Evolution of accuracy vs time for various active recognition methods, on SUN360 (left) and GERMS (right).Our methods show steady improvement with additional views, and easily outperform the best baselines. Also see Table 1.

Table 1. Recognition accuracy for both datasets (neural net-based methods' scores are reported as mean and standard error over 5 runs with different initializations)

Method↓/Dataset→		SUN360			GERMS	
Performance measure→		T=2 acc.	T=3 acc.	T=5 acc.	T=2 acc.	T=3 acc.
Passive	Chance	14.08	14.08	14.08	0.74	0.74
approaches	Single view (neural net)	40.12±0.45	40.12±0.45	40.12±0.45	40.31±0.23	40.31±0.23
Random view	Random views (average)	45.71±0.29	50.47±0.37	54.21±0.57	45.71±0.30	46.97±0.43
selection	Random views (recurrent)	47.74±0.27	51.29±0.21	55.64±0.28	44.85±0.40	44.24±0.24
	Transinformation [35]	40.69	40.69	44.86	28.83	31.02
Prior active	SeqDP [17]	42.41	42.91	42.08	28.83	28.10
approaches	Transinformation + SeqDP	44.69	46.91	48.19	29.93	29.56
	Active RNN	50.76±0.41	57.52±0.46	65.32±0.42	47.30±0.73	46.86±0.97
Ours	Look-ahead active RNN	**51.72±0.29**	**58.12±0.43**	**66.01±0.34**	**48.02±0.68**	47.99±0.79
	Look-ahead active RNN+average	49.62±0.43	55.43±0.38	62.61±0.33	47.00±0.45	**48.31±0.72**

On GERMS, our method is once again easily superior to prior active methods. The margins of our gains over random-view baselines are smaller than on SUN360. Upon analysis, it becomes clear that this is due to GERMS being a relatively small dataset. Not only is (1) the number of active recognition instances small compared to SUN360 (816 vs. 8992), but (2) different views of the same object instance are naturally closer to each other than different views from a SUN360 panorama view-grid (see Figs. 3 and 4) so that even single view diversity is low, and (3) there is only a single degree of motion compared to two in SUN360. As a result, the number of possible reinforcement learning episodes is also much smaller. Upon inspection, we found that these factors can lead our end-to-end network to overfit to training data (which we countered with more aggressive regularization). In particular, it is problematic if our method achieves zero training error from just single views, so that the network has no incentive to learn to aggregate information across views well. Our active results are in line with those presented as a benchmark in the paper introducing the dataset [28], and we expect more training data is necessary to move further with end-to-end learning on this challenge. This lack of data affects our prior active method baselines even more since they rely on *pose-specific* instance classifiers, so that each classifier's training set is very small. This explains their poor performance.

As an interesting upshot, we see further improvements on GERMS by averaging the CLASSIFIER modules' outputs *i.e.* class likelihoods estimated from the aggregated features at each timestep $t = 1, .., T$ ("Look-ahead active RNN + average"). Since the above factors make it difficult to learn the optimal AGGREGATOR in an end-to-end system like ours, a second tier of aggregation in the form of averaging over the outputs of our system can yield improvements. In contrast, since SUN offers much more training data, averaging over per-timestep CLASSIFIER outputs significantly *reduces* the performance of the system, compared to directly using the last timestep output. This is exactly as one would hope for a successful end-to-end training. This reasoning is further supported by the fact that "Random views (average)" shows slightly poorer performance than "Random views (recurrent)" on GERMS, but is much better on SUN360 (Table 1).

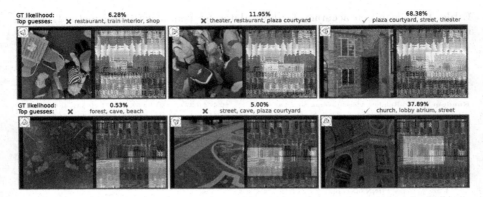

Fig. 6. Views selected using our approach on SUN360. Each row, corresponding to a scene, contains 3 red panels corresponding to the selected views at $t = 1, 2, 3$. Each panel shows the current view (left) and position on view grid (pink highlight is current position). In the top row, given the first view, our method makes reasonable but wrong guesses, but corrects itself within 2 moves, by observing the crowd and following their gaze. (More examples in Supp.)

Indeed, the significant gains of "Random views (recurrent)" over "Random views (average)" on SUN360 points to an important advantage of treating object/scene categorization as a grounded, sequence-based decision process. The ability to intelligently fuse observations over timesteps based on both the views themselves and the camera motions relating them offers substantial rewards. In contrast, the current computer vision literature in visual categorization is largely focused on categorization strategies that process individual images outside the context of any agent motion or sequential data, much like the "Single view" or "Random views (average)" baselines. We see our empirical results as an exciting prompt for future work in this space. They also suggest the need for increased efforts creating large 3-D and video benchmark datasets (in the spirit of SUN360 and GERMS and beyond) to support such vision research, allowing us to systematically study these scenarios outside of robot platforms.

The result on SUN360 in particular is significant since no prior active recognition approach has been shown to successfully handle any comparably complex dataset. While active categorization is technically challenging compared to instance recognition as discussed in Sect. 2, datasets like SUN360, containing complex visual data with ambiguous views may actually be most suited to showing the advantages of the active recognition paradigm.

5   Conclusions

We presented a new end-to-end approach for active visual categorization. Our framework simultaneously learns (1) how the system should move to improve its sequence of observations, and (2) how a sequence of future observations is likely to change conditioned on its possible actions. We show the impact on object and scene recognition, where our active approach makes sizeable strides over single view and passively moving systems. Furthermore, we establish the positive impact in treating all components of the active recognition system simultaneously. All together, the results are encouraging evidence that modern visual recognition algorithms can venture further into unconstrained, sequential data, moving beyond the static image snapshot labeling paradigm.

Acknowledgments. This research is supported in part by ONR PECASE N00014-15-1-2291. We also thank Texas Advanced Computing Center for their generous support, and Mohsen Malmir and Jianxiong Xiao for their assistance sharing GERMS and SUN360 data respectively.

References

1. Agrawal, P., Carreira, J., Malik, J.: Learning to see by moving. In: ICCV (2015)
2. Aloimonos, J., Weiss, I., Bandyopadhyay, A.: Active vision. IJCV **1**, 333–356 (1988)
3. Andreopoulos, A., Tsotsos, J.: A theory of active object localization. In: ICCV (2009)
4. Andreopoulos, A., Tsotsos, J.: 50 years of object recognition: directions forward. CVIU **117**, 827–891 (2013)
5. Ba, J., Mnih, V., Kavukcuoglu, K.: Multiple object recognition with visual attention. In: ICLR (2015)
6. Bajcsy, R.: Active perception. Proc. IEEE **76**, 996–1005 (1988)
7. Ballard, D.: Animate vision. Artif. Intell. **48**, 57–86 (1991)
8. Bazzani, L., et al.: Learning attentional policies for tracking and recognition in video with deep networks. In: ICML (2011)
9. Bergstra, J., Bengio, Y.: Random search for hyper-parameter optimization. JMLR **13**, 281–305 (2012)
10. Borotschnig, H., Paletta, L., Prantl, M., Pinz, A., et al.: Active object recognition in parametric eigenspace. In: BMVC (1998)
11. Bowling, M., Ghodsi, A., Wilkinson, D.: Action respecting embedding. In: ICML (2005)
12. Brentano, F.: Psychologie vom empirischen Standpunkte (1874)
13. Butko, N., Movellan, J.: Optimal scanning for faster object detection. In: CVPR (2009)
14. Callari, F., Ferrie, F.: Active object recognition: looking for differences. IJCV **43**, 189–204 (2001)
15. Chen, C., Seff, A., Kornhauser, A., Xiao, J.: DeepDriving: learning affordance for direct perception in autonomous driving. In: ICCV (2015)
16. Cohen, T.S., Welling, M.: Transformation properties of learned visual representations. arXiv preprint arXiv:1412.7659 (2014)
17. Denzler, J., Brown, C.M.: Information theoretic sensor data selection for active object recognition and state estimation. TPAMI **24**, 145–157 (2002)
18. Dickinson, S., Christensen, H., Tsotsos, J., Olofsson, G.: Active object recognition integrating attention and viewpoint control. CVIU **67**, 239–260 (1997)
19. Ding, W., Taylor, G.W.: Mental rotation by optimizing transforming distance. In: NIPS DL Workshop (2014)

20. Flynn, J., Neulander, I., Philbin, J., Snavely, N.: DeepStereo: Learning to predict new views from the world's imagery. In: CVPR (2016)
21. Garcia, A.G., Vezhnevets, A., Ferrari, V.: An active search strategy for efficient object detection. In: CVPR (2015)
22. Helmer, S., et al.: Semantic robot vision challenge: current state and future directions. In: IJCAI Workshop (2009)
23. Jayaraman, D., Grauman, K.: Learning image representations tied to ego-motion. In: ICCV (2015)
24. Jayaraman, D., Grauman, K.: Slow and steady feature analysis: higher order temporal coherence in video. In: CVPR (2016)
25. Kulkarni, T.D., Whitney, W., Kohli, P., Tenenbaum, J.B.: Deep convolutional inverse graphics network. In: NIPS (2015)
26. Levine, S., Finn, C., Darrell, T., Abbeel, P.: End-to-End training of deep visuomotor policies. In: ICRA (2015)
27. Lin, T.-Y., Maire, M., Belongie, S., Hays, J., Perona, P., Ramanan, D., Dollár, P., Zitnick, C.L.: Microsoft COCO: common objects in context. In: Fleet, D., Pajdla, T., Schiele, B., Tuytelaars, T. (eds.) ECCV 2014, Part V. LNCS, vol. 8693, pp. 740–755. Springer, Heidelberg (2014)
28. Malmir, M., Sikka, K., Forster, D., Movellan, J., Cottrell, G.W.: Deep Q-learning for active recognition of GERMS. In: BMVC (2015)
29. Mishra, A., Aloimonos, Y., Fermuller, C.: Active segmentation for robotics. In: IROS (2009)
30. Mnih, V., Heess, N., Graves, A., Kavukcuoglu, K.: Recurrent models of visual attention. In: NIPS (2014)
31. Paletta, L., Pinz, A.: Active object recognition by view integration and reinforcement learning. In: RAS (2000)
32. Ramanathan, V., Pinz, A.: Active object categorization on a humanoid robot. In: VISAPP (2011)
33. Ranzato, M., Szlam, A., Bruna, J., Mathieu, M., Collobert, R., Chopra, S.: Video (language) modeling: a baseline for generative models of natural videos. arXiv preprint arXiv:1412.6604 (2014)
34. Russakovsky, O., Deng, J., Su, H., Krause, J., Satheesh, S., Ma, S., Huang, Z., Karpathy, A., Khosla, A., Bernstein, M., Berg, A.C., Fei-Fei, L.: ImageNet large scale visual recognition challenge. IJCV 115, 211–252 (2015)
35. Schiele, B., Crowley, J.: Transinformation for active object recognition. In: ICCV (1998)
36. Sermanet, P., Frome, A., Real, E.: Attention for fine-grained categorization. arXiv (2014)
37. Simonyan, K., Zisserman, A.: Very deep convolutional networks for large-scale image recognition. arXiv (2014)
38. Soatto, S.: Actionable information in vision. In: ICCV (2009)
39. Stober, J., Miikkulainen, R., Kuipers, B.: Learning geometry from sensorimotor experience. In: ICDL (2011)
40. Szegedy, C., Liu, W., Jia, Y., Sermanet, P., Reed, S., Anguelov, D., Erhan, D., Vanhoucke, V., Rabinovich, A.: Going deeper with convolutions. In: CVPR (2015)
41. Vondrick, C., Pirsiavash, H., Torralba, A.: Anticipating the future by watching unlabeled video. In: CVPR (2016)
42. Walker, J., Gupta, A., Hebert, M.: Dense optical flow prediction from a static image. In: ICCV (2015)
43. Watter, M., Springenberg, J.T., Boedecker, J., Riedmiller, M.: Embed to control: a locally linear latent dynamics model for control from raw images. In: NIPS (2015)

44. Wilkes, D., Tsotsos, J.: Active object recognition. In: CVPR (1992)
45. Williams, R.: Simple statistical gradient-following algorithms for connectionist reinforcement learning. JMLR **8**, 229–256 (1992)
46. Wu, Z., Song, S., Khosla, A., Yu, F., Zhang, L., Tang, X., Xiao, J.: 3D ShapeNets: a deep representation for volumetric shape modeling. In: CVPR (2015)
47. Xiao, J., Ehinger, K., Oliva, A., Torralba, A., et al.: Recognizing scene viewpoint using panoramic place representation. In: CVPR (2012)
48. Xu, K., Ba, J., Kiros, R., Cho, K., Courville, A., Salakhutdinov, R., Zemel, R., Bengio, Y.: Show, attend and tell: Neural image caption generation with visual attention. In: ICML (2015)
49. Yu, X., Fermuller, C., Teo, C.L., Yang, Y., Aloimonos, Y.: Active scene recognition with vision and language. In: CVPR (2011)

Poster Session 6

Poster Session 6

General Automatic Human Shape and Motion Capture Using Volumetric Contour Cues

Helge Rhodin[1]([✉]), Nadia Robertini[1,2], Dan Casas[1], Christian Richardt[1,2], Hans-Peter Seidel[1], and Christian Theobalt[1]

[1] MPI Informatik, Saarbrücken, Germany
{hrhodin,theobalt}@mpi-inf.mpg.de
[2] Intel Visual Computing Institute, Saarbrücken, Germany

Abstract. Markerless motion capture algorithms require a 3D body with properly personalized skeleton dimension and/or body shape and appearance to successfully track a person. Unfortunately, many tracking methods consider model personalization a different problem and use manual or semi-automatic model initialization, which greatly reduces applicability. In this paper, we propose a fully automatic algorithm that jointly creates a rigged actor model commonly used for animation – skeleton, volumetric shape, appearance, and optionally a body surface – and estimates the actor's motion from multi-view video input only. The approach is rigorously designed to work on footage of general outdoor scenes recorded with very few cameras and without background subtraction. Our method uses a new image formation model with analytic visibility and analytically differentiable alignment energy. For reconstruction, 3D body shape is approximated as a Gaussian density field. For pose and shape estimation, we minimize a new edge-based alignment energy inspired by volume ray casting in an absorbing medium. We further propose a new statistical human body model that represents the body surface, volumetric Gaussian density, and variability in skeleton shape. Given any multi-view sequence, our method jointly optimizes the pose and shape parameters of this model fully automatically in a spatiotemporal way.

1 Introduction

Markerless full-body motion capture techniques refrain from markers used in most commercial solutions, and promise to be an important enabling technique in computer animation and visual effects production, in sports and biomechanics research, and the growing fields of virtual and augmented reality. While early markerless methods were confined to indoor use in more controlled scenes and backgrounds recorded with eight or more cameras [1], recent methods succeed in general outdoor scenes with much fewer cameras [2,3].

Electronic supplementary material The online version of this chapter (doi:10.1007/978-3-319-46454-1_31) contains supplementary material, which is available to authorized users.

B. Leibe et al. (Eds.): ECCV 2016, Part V, LNCS 9909, pp. 509–526, 2016.
DOI: 10.1007/978-3-319-46454-1_31

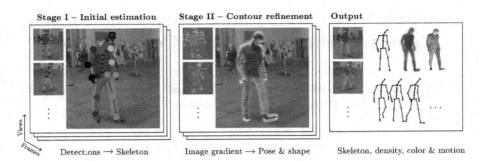

Fig. 1. Method overview. Pose is estimated from detections in Stage I, actor shape and pose is refined through contour alignment in Stage II by space-time optimization. Outputs are the actor skeleton, attached density, mesh and motion.

Before motion capture commences, the 3D body model for tracking needs to be personalized to the captured human. This includes personalization of the bone lengths, but often also of biomechanical shape and surface, including appearance. This essential initialization is, unfortunately, neglected by many methods and solved with an entirely different approach, or with specific and complex manual or semi-automatic initialization steps. For instance, some methods for motion capture in studios with controlled backgrounds rely on static full-body scans [4–6], or personalization on manually segmented initialization poses [7]. Recent outdoor motion capture methods use entirely manual model initialization [3]. When using depth cameras, automatic model initialization was shown [8–12], but RGB-D cameras are less accessible and not usable outdoors. Simultaneous pose and shape estimation from in-studio multi-view footage with background subtraction was also shown [13–15], but not on footage of less constrained setups such as outdoor scenes filmed with very few cameras.

We therefore propose a fully-automatic space-time approach for simultaneous model initialization and motion capture. Our approach is specifically designed to solve this problem automatically for multi-view video footage recorded in general environments (moving background, no background subtraction) and filmed with as few as two cameras. Motions can be arbitrary and unchoreographed. It takes a further step towards making markerless motion capture practical in the aforementioned application areas, and enables motion capture from third-party video footage, where dedicated initialization pose images or the shape model altogether are unavailable. Our approach builds on the following contributions.

First, we introduce a body representation that extends a scene model inspired by light transport in absorbing transparent media [16]. We represent the volumetric body shape by Gaussian density functions attached to a kinematic skeleton. We further define a novel 2D contour-based energy that measures contour alignment with image gradients on the raw RGB images using a new volume raycasting image formation model. We define contour direction and magnitude for each image position, which form a ridge at the model outline, see Fig. 1. No explicit background segmentation is needed. Importantly, our energy features analytic derivatives, including fully-differentiable visibility everywhere.

The second contribution is a new data-driven body model that represents human surface variation, the space of skeleton dimensions, and the space of volumetric density distributions optimally for reconstruction using a low-dimensional parameter space.

Finally, we propose a space-time optimization approach that fully automatically computes both the shape and the 3D skeletal pose of the actor using both contour and ConvNet-based joint detection cues. The final outputs are (1) a rigged character, as commonly used in animation, comprising a personalized skeleton and attached surface, along with the (optionally colored) volumetric human shape representation, and (2) the joint angles for each video frame. We tested our method on eleven sequences, indoor and outdoor, showing reconstructions with fewer cameras and less manual effort compared to the state of the art.

2   Related Work

Our goal is to fully automatically capture a personalized, rigged surface model, as used in animation, *together with* its sequence of skeletal poses from sparse multi-view video of general scenes where background segmentation is hard. Many multi-view markerless motion capture approaches consider model initialization and tracking separate problems [2]. Even in recent methods working outdoors, shape and skeleton dimensions of the tracked model are either initialized manually prior to tracking [3], or estimated from manually segmented initialization poses [7]. In controlled studios, static shape [17,18] or dimensions and pose of simple parametric human models [13,14] can be optimized by matching against chroma-keyed multi-view image silhouettes. Many multi-view performance capture methods [19] deform a static full-body shape template obtained with a full-body scanner [4,5,20,21], or through fitting against the visual hull [22–25] to match scene motion. Again, all these require controlled in-studio footage, an off-line scan, or both. Shape estimation of a naked parametric model in single images using shading and edge cues [26], or monocular pose and shape estimation from video is also feasible [27–29], but require substantial manual intervention (joint labeling, feature/pose correction, background subtraction etc.). For multi-view in-studio setups (3–4 views), where background subtraction works, Bălan et al. [15] estimate shape and pose of the SCAPE parametric body model. Optimization is independent for each frame and requires initialization by a coarse cylindrical shape model. Implicit surface representations yield beneficial properties for pose [30] and surface [31] reconstruction, but do not avoid the dependency on explicit silhouette input. In contrast to all previously mentioned methods, our approach requires no manual interaction, succeeds even with only two camera views, and on scenes recorded outdoors without any background segmentation.

Recently, several methods to capture both shape and pose of a parametric human body model with depth cameras were proposed [9,11,32]; these special cameras are not as easily available and often do not work outdoors. We also build up on the success of parametric body models for surface representation, e.g. [29,33–35], but extend these models to represent the space of volumetric shape models needed for tracking, along with a rigged surface and skeleton.

Our approach is designed to work without explicit background subtraction. In outdoor settings with moving backgrounds and uncontrolled illumination, such segmentation is hard, but progress has been made by multi-view segmentation [36–38], joint segmentation and reconstruction [39–42], and also aided by propagation of a manual initialization [20,43]. However, the obtained segmentations are still noisy, enabling only rather coarse 3D reconstructions [42], and many methods would not work with only two cameras.

Edge cues have been widely used in human shape and motion estimation [1,2,44–47], but we provide a new formulation for their use and make edges in general scenes the primary cue. In contrast, existing shape estimation works use edges are supplemental information, for example to find self-occluding edges in silhouette-based methods and to correct rough silhouette borders [26]. Our new formulation is inspired by the work of Nagel et al., where model contours are directly matched to image edges for rigid object [48] and human pose tracking [49]. Contour edges on tracked meshes are found by a visibility test, and are convolved with a Gaussian kernel. This approach forms piecewise-smooth and differentiable model contours which are optimized to maximize overlap with image gradients. We advance this idea in several ways: our model is volumetric, analytic visibility is incorporated in the model and optimization, occlusion changes are differentiable, the human is represented as a deformable object, allowing for shape estimation, and contour direction is handled separately from contour magnitude.

Our approach follows the generative analysis-by-synthesis approach: contours are formed by a 3D volumetric model and image formation is an extension of the volumetric ray-tracing model proposed by Rhodin et al. [16]. Many discriminative methods for 2D pose estimation were proposed [50–52]; multi-view extensions were also investigated [46,53,54]. Their goal is different to ours, as they find single-shot 2D/3D joint locations, but no 3D rigged body shape and no temporally stable joint angles needed for animation. We thus use a discriminative detector only for initialization. Our work has links to non-rigid structure-from-motion that finds sparse 3D point trajectories (e.g. on the body) from single-view images of a non-rigidly moving scene [55]. Articulation constraints [56] can help to find the sparse scene structure, but the goal is different from our estimation of a fully dense, rigged 3D character and stable skeleton motion.

3   Notation and Overview

Input to our algorithm are RGB image sequences $\mathcal{I}_{c,t}$, recorded with calibrated cameras $c = 1, \ldots, C$ and synchronized to within a frame (see list of datasets in supplemental document). The output of our approach is the configuration of a virtual actor model $\mathcal{K}(\mathbf{p}_t, \mathbf{b}, \boldsymbol{\gamma})$ for each frame $t = 1, \ldots, T$, comprising the per-frame joint angles $\mathbf{p}_t$, the personalized bone lengths $\mathbf{b}$, as well as the personalized volumetric Gaussian representation $\boldsymbol{\gamma}$, including color, of the actor.

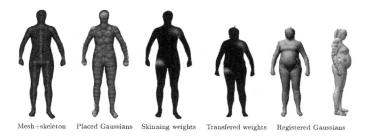

Mesh+skeleton   Placed Gaussians   Skinning weights   Transfered weights   Registered Gaussians

Fig. 2. Registration process of the body shape model. Skeleton and Gaussians are once manually placed into the *reference* mesh, vertex correspondence transfers Gaussian- and joint-neighborhood weights (green and red respectively), to register reference bones and Gaussians to all instance meshes. (Color figure online)

In the following, we first explain the basis of our new image formation model, the Gaussian density scene representation, and our new parametric human shape model building on it (Sect. 4). Subsequently, we detail our space-time optimization approach (Sect. 5) in two stages: (I) using ConvNet-based joint detection constraints (Sect. 5.1); and (II) using a new ray-casting-based volumetric image formation model and a new contour-based alignment energy (Sect. 5.2).

4   Volumetric Statistical Body Shape Model

To model the human in 3D for reconstruction, we build on sum-of-Gaussians representations [7,16] and model the volumetric extent of the actor using a set of 91 isotropic Gaussian density functions distributed in 3D space. Each Gaussian G_q is parametrized by its standard deviation σ_q, mean location $\boldsymbol{\mu}_q$ in 3D, and density c_q, which define the Gaussian shape parameters $\boldsymbol{\gamma} = \{\boldsymbol{\mu}_q, \sigma_q, c_q\}_q$. The combined density field of the Gaussians, $\sum_q c_q G_q$, smoothly describes the volumetric occupancy of the human in 3D space, see Fig. 1. Each Gaussian is rigidly attached to one of the bones of an articulated skeleton with bone lengths $\mathbf{b}$ and 16 joints, whose pose is parameterized with 43 twist pose parameters, i.e. the Gaussian position $\boldsymbol{\mu}_q$ is relative to the attached bone. This representation allows us to formulate a new alignment energy tailored to pose fitting in general scenes, featuring analytic derivatives and fully-differentiable visibility (Sect. 5).

In their original work, Rhodin et al. [16] create 3D density models for tracked shapes by a semi-automatic placement of Gaussians in 3D. Since the shape of humans varies drastically, a different distribution of Gaussians and skeleton dimensions is needed for each individual to ensure optimal tracking. In this paper, we propose a method to automatically find such a skeleton and optimal attached Gaussian distribution, along with a good body surface. Rather than optimizing in the combined high-dimensional space of skeleton dimensions, the number of Gaussians and all their parameters, we build a new specialized, low-dimensional parametric body model.

Traditional statistical human body models represent variations in body surface only across individuals, as well as pose-dependent surface deformations using linear [57,58] or non-linear [28,33] subspaces of the mesh vertex positions. For our task, we build an enriched statistical body model that parameterizes, in addition to the body surface, the optimal volumetric Gaussian density distribution γ for tracking, and the space of skeleton dimensions $\mathbf{b}$, through linear functions $\gamma(\mathbf{s})$, $\mathbf{b}(\mathbf{s})$ of a low-dimensional shape vector $\mathbf{s}$. To build our model, we use an existing database of 228 registered scanned meshes of human bodies in neutral pose [59]. We take one of the scans as *reference* mesh, and place the articulated skeleton inside. The 91 Gaussians are attached to bones, their position is set to uniformly fill the mesh volume, and their standard deviation and density is set such that a density gradient forms at the mesh surface, see Fig. 2 (left). This manual step has to be done only once to obtain Gaussian parameters γ_{ref} for the database reference, and can also be automated by silhouette alignment [16].

The best positions $\{\boldsymbol{\mu}_q\}_q$ and scales $\{\sigma_q\}_q$ of Gaussians γ_i for each remaining database *instance* mesh i are automatically derived by weighted Procrustes alignment. Each Gaussian G_q in the reference has a set of neighboring surface mesh vertices. The set is inferred by weighting vertices proportional to the density of G_q at their position in the reference mesh, see Fig. 2 (right). For each Gaussian G_q, vertices are optimally translated, rotated and scaled to align to the corresponding instance mesh vertices. These similarity transforms are applied on γ_{ref} to obtain γ_i, where scaling multiplies σ_q and translation shifts $\boldsymbol{\mu}_q$.

To infer the adapted skeleton dimensions $\mathbf{b}_i$ for each instance mesh, we follow a similar strategy: we place Gaussians of standard deviation 10 cm at each joint in the reference mesh, which are then scaled and repositioned to fit the target mesh using the same Procrustes strategy as before. This yields properly scaled bone lengths for each target mesh.

Having estimates of volume γ_i and bone lengths $\mathbf{b}_i$ for each database entry i, we now learn a joint body model. We build a PCA model on the data matrix $[(\gamma_1; \mathbf{b}_1), (\gamma_2; \mathbf{b}_2), \ldots]$, where each column vector $(\gamma_i; \mathbf{b}_i)$ is the stack of estimates for entry i. The mean is the average human shape $(\bar{\gamma}; \bar{\mathbf{b}})$, and the PCA basis vectors span the principal shape variations of the database. The PCA coefficients are the elements of our shape model $\mathbf{s}$, and hence define the volume $\gamma(\mathbf{s})$ and bone lengths $\mathbf{b}(\mathbf{s})$. Due to the joined model, bone length and Gaussian parameters are correlated, and optimizing $\mathbf{s}$ for bone length during pose estimation (stage I) thus moves and scales the attached Gaussians accordingly. To reduce dimensionality, we use only the first 50 coefficients in our experiments.

To infer the actor body surface, we introduce a volumetric skinning approach. The reference surface mesh is deformed in a free-form manner along with the Gaussian set under new pose and shape parameters. Similar to linear blend skinning [60], each surface vertex is deformed with the set of 3D transforms of nearby Gaussians, weighted by the density weights used earlier for Procrustes alignment. This coupling of body surfaces to volumetric model is as computationally efficient as using a linear PCA space on mesh vertices [34], while yielding comparable shape generalization and extrapolation qualities to methods using more expensive non-linear reconstruction [33], see supplemental document. Iso-surface reconstruction using Marching Cubes would also be more costly [30].

5   Pose and Shape Estimation

We formulate the estimation of the time-independent 50 shape parameters $\mathbf{s}$ and the time-dependent $43T$ pose parameters $\mathbf{P} = \{\mathbf{p}_1, \ldots, \mathbf{p}_T\}$ as a combined space-time optimization problem over all frames $\mathcal{I}_{c,t}$ and camera viewpoints c of the input sequence of length T:

$$E(\mathbf{P}, \mathbf{s}) = E_{\text{shape}}(\mathbf{s}) + \sum_t \Big(E_{\text{smooth}}(\mathbf{P}, \mathbf{s}, t) + E_{\text{pose}}(\mathbf{p}_t) + \sum_c E_{\text{data}}(c, \mathbf{p}_t, \mathbf{s}) \Big). \quad (1)$$

Our energy uses quadratic prior terms to regularize the solution: E_{shape} penalizes shape parameters that have larger absolute value than any of the database instances, E_{smooth} penalizes joint-angle accelerations to favor smooth motions, and E_{pose} penalizes violation of manually specified anatomical joint-angle limits. The data term E_{data} measures the alignment of the projected model to all video frames. To make the optimization of Eq. 1 succeed in unconstrained scenes with few cameras, we solve in two subsequent stages. In Stage I (Sect. 5.1), we optimize for a coarse skeleton estimate and pose set without the volumetric distribution, but using 2D joint detections as primary constraints. In Stage II (Sect. 5.2), we refine this initial estimate and optimize for all shape and pose parameters using our new contour-based alignment energy. Consequently, the data terms used in the respective stages differ:

$$E_{\text{data}}(c, \mathbf{p}_t, \mathbf{s}) = \begin{cases} E_{\text{detection}}(c, \mathbf{p}_t, \mathbf{s}) & \text{for Stage I (Sect. 5.1)} \\ E_{\text{contour}}(c, \mathbf{p}_t, \mathbf{s}) & \text{for Stage II (Sect. 5.2).} \end{cases} \quad (2)$$

The analytic form of all terms as well as the smoothness in all model parameters allows efficient optimization by gradient descent. In our experiments we apply the conditioned gradient descent method of Stoll et al. [7].

5.1   Stage I – Initial Estimation

We employ the discriminative ConvNet-based body-part detector by Tompson et al. [50] to estimate the approximate 2D skeletal joint positions. The detector is independently applied to each input frame $\mathcal{I}_{c,t}$, and outputs heat maps of joint location probability $\mathcal{D}_{c,t,j}$ for each joint j in frame t seen from camera c. Importantly, the detector discriminates the joints on the left and right side of the body (see Fig. 1). The detections exhibit noticeable spatial and temporal uncertainty, but are nonetheless a valuable cue for an initial space-time optimization solve. The output heat maps are in general multi-modal due to detection ambiguities, but also in the presence of multiple people, e.g. in the background.

   To infer the poses $\mathbf{P}$ and an initial guess for the body shape of the subject, we optimize Eq. 1 with data term $E_{\text{detection}}$. It measures the overlap of the heat maps $\mathcal{D}$ with the projected skeleton joints. Each joint in the model skeleton has an attached joint Gaussian (Sect. 4), and the overlap with the corresponding heat map is maximized using the visibility model of Rhodin et al. [16]. We use a hierarchical approach by first optimizing the torso joints, followed by optimizing the limbs; please see the supplemental document for details. The optimization is initialized with the average human shape $(\bar{\gamma}, \bar{\mathbf{b}})$ in T-pose, at the center of the capture volume. We assume a single person in the capture volume; people in the background are implicitly ignored, as they are typically not visible from all cameras and are dominated by the foreground actor.

Please note that bone lengths $\mathbf{b}(\mathbf{s})$ and volume $\gamma(\mathbf{s})$ are determined through $\mathbf{s}$, hence, Stage I yields a rough estimate of γ. In Stage II, we use more informative image constraints than pure joint locations to better estimate volumetric extent.

5.2   Stage II – Contour-Based Refinement

The pose $\mathbf{P}$ and shape $\mathbf{s}$ found in the previous stage are now refined by using a new density-based contour model in the alignment energy. This model explains the spatial image gradients formed at the edge of the projected model, between actor and background, and thus bypasses the need for silhouette extraction, which is difficult for general scenes. To this end, we extend the ray-casting image formation model of Rhodin et al. [16], as summarized in the following paragraph, and subsequently explain how to use it in the contour data term E_{contour}.

Ray-casting image formation model. Each image pixel spawns a ray that starts at the camera center $\mathbf{o}$ and points in direction $\mathbf{n}$. The visibility of a particular model Gaussian G_q along the ray $(\mathbf{o}, \mathbf{n})$ is defined as

$$\mathcal{V}_q(\mathbf{o}, \mathbf{n}) = \int_0^\infty \exp\left(-\int_0^s \sum_i G_i(\mathbf{o} + t\mathbf{n})\, \mathrm{d}t\right) G_q(\mathbf{o} + s\mathbf{n})\, \mathrm{d}s. \tag{3}$$

This equation models light transport in a heterogeneous translucent medium [61], i.e. $\mathcal{V}_q$ is the fraction of light along the ray that is absorbed by Gaussian G_q. The original paper [16] describes an analytic approximation to Eq. 3 by sampling the outer integral.

Different to their work, we apply this ray casting model to infer the visibility of the background, $\mathcal{B}(\mathbf{o}, \mathbf{n}) = 1 - \sum_q \mathcal{V}_q(\mathbf{o}, \mathbf{n})$. Assuming that the background is infinitely distant, $\mathcal{B}$ is the fraction of light not absorbed by the Gaussian model:

$$\mathcal{B}(\mathbf{o}, \mathbf{n}) = \exp\left(-\int_0^\infty \sum_q G_q(\mathbf{o} + t\mathbf{n})\, \mathrm{d}t\right) = \exp\left(-\sqrt{2\pi} \sum_q \bar{\sigma}_q \bar{c}_q\right). \tag{4}$$

This analytic form is obtained without sampling, but rather it stems from the Gaussian parametrization: the density along ray $(\mathbf{o}, \mathbf{n})$ though 3D Gaussian G_q is a 1D Gaussian with standard deviation $\bar{\sigma}_q = \sigma_q$ and density maximum $\bar{c}_q = c_q \cdot \exp\left(-\frac{(\boldsymbol{\mu}_q - \mathbf{o})^\top (\boldsymbol{\mu}_q - \mathbf{o}) - ((\boldsymbol{\mu}_q - \mathbf{o})^\top \mathbf{n})^2}{2\sigma_q^2}\right)$, and the integral over the Gaussian

Density visibility   Contour   Similarity (per pixel)   Target
Stage I   Stage II   Stage I   Stage II   Stage I   Stage II   gradient image

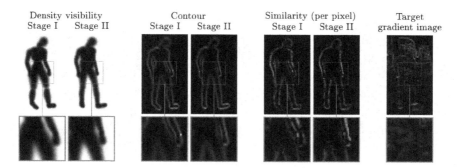

Fig. 3. Contour refinement to image gradients through per-pixel similarity. Contour color indicates direction, green and red energy indicate agreement and disagreement between model and image gradients, respectively. Close-ups highlight the shape optimization: left arm and right leg pose are corrected in Stage II. (Color figure online)

density evaluates to a constant (when the negligible density behind the camera is ignored). A model visibility example is shown in Fig. 3 left.

To extract the contour of our model, we compute the gradient of the background visibility $\nabla \mathcal{B} = (\frac{\partial \mathcal{B}}{\partial u}, \frac{\partial \mathcal{B}}{\partial v})^\top$ with respect to pixel location (u, v):

$$\nabla \mathcal{B} = \mathcal{B}\sqrt{2\pi} \sum_q \frac{\bar{c}_q}{\bar{\sigma}_q} (\boldsymbol{\mu}_q - \mathbf{o})^\top \mathbf{n}(\boldsymbol{\mu}_q - \mathbf{o})^\top \nabla \mathbf{n}. \tag{5}$$

$\nabla \mathcal{B}$ forms a 2D vector field, where the gradient direction points outwards from the model, and the magnitude forms a ridge at the model contour, see Fig. 3 center. In (calibrated pinhole) camera coordinates, the ray direction thus depends on the 2D pixel location (u, v) by $\mathbf{n} = \frac{(u,v,1)^\top}{\|(u,v,1)\|_2}$ and $\nabla \mathbf{n} = (\frac{\partial \mathbf{n}}{\partial u}, \frac{\partial \mathbf{n}}{\partial v})^\top$.

In contrast to Rhodin et al.'s visibility model [16], our model is specific to background visibility, but more accurate and efficient to evaluate. It does not require sampling along the ray to obtain a smooth analytic form, has linear complexity in the number of model Gaussians instead of their quadratic complexity, and improves execution time by an order of magnitude.

Contour energy. To refine the initial pose and shape estimates from Stage I (Sect. 5.1), we optimize Eq. 1 with a new contour data term E_{contour}, to estimate the per-pixel similarity of model and image gradients:

$$E_{\text{contour}}(c, \mathbf{p}_t, \mathbf{s}) = \sum_{(u,v)} E_{\text{sim}}(c, \mathbf{p}_t, \mathbf{s}, u, v) + E_{\text{flat}}(c, \mathbf{p}_t, \mathbf{s}, u, v). \tag{6}$$

In the following, we omit the arguments $(c, \mathbf{p}_t, \mathbf{s}, u, v)$ for better readability. E_{sim} measures the similarity between the gradient magnitude $\|\nabla \mathcal{I}\|_2$ in the input image and the contour magnitude $\|\nabla \mathcal{B}\|_2$ of our model, and penalizes orientation misalignment (contours can be in opposite directions in model and image):

$$E_{\text{sim}} = -\|\nabla \mathcal{B}\|_2 \|\nabla \mathcal{I}\|_2 \cos\big(2\angle(\nabla \mathcal{B}, \nabla \mathcal{I})\big). \tag{7}$$

Input views   Colored density   Actor skeleton and mesh

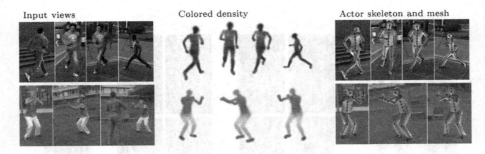

Fig. 4. Reconstruction of challenging outdoor sequences with complex motions from only 3–4 views, showing accurate shape and pose reconstruction.

The term E_{flat} models contours forming in flat regions with gradient magnitude smaller than $\delta_{\text{low}} = 0.1$:

$$E_{\text{flat}} = \|\nabla\mathcal{B}\|_2 \max(0, \delta_{\text{low}} - \|\nabla\mathcal{I}\|_2). \tag{8}$$

We compute spatial image gradients $\nabla\mathcal{I} = (\frac{\partial\mathcal{I}}{\partial u}, \frac{\partial\mathcal{I}}{\partial v})^{\top}$ using the Sobel operator, smoothed with a Gaussian ($\sigma = 1.1\,\text{px}$), summed over the RGB channels and clamped to a maximum of $\delta_{\text{high}} = 0.2$.

Appearance estimation. Our method is versatile: given the shape and pose estimates from Stage II, we can also estimate a color for each Gaussian. This is needed by earlier tracking methods that use similar volume models, but color appearance-based alignment energies [7,16] – we compare against them in our experiments. Direct back-projection of the image color onto the model suffers from occasional reconstruction errors in Stages I and II. Instead, we compute the weighted mean color $\bar{a}_{q,c}$ over all pixels separately for each Gaussian G_q and view c, where the contribution of each pixel is weighted by the Gaussian's visibility $\mathcal{V}_q$ (Eq. 3). Colors $\bar{a}_{q,c}$ are taken as candidates from which outliers are removed by iteratively computing the mean color and removing the largest outlier (in Euclidean distance). In our experiments, removing 50 % of the candidates leads to consistently clean color estimates, as shown in Figs. 4 and 9.

6   Evaluation

We evaluate our method on 11 sequences of publicly available datasets with large variety, both indoor and outdoor, and show comparisons to state-of-the-art methods (see supplementary document for dataset details). The quality of pose and shape reconstruction is best assessed in the supplemental video, where we also apply and compare our reconstructions to tracking with the volumetric Gaussian representations of Rhodin et al. [16] and Stoll et al. [7].

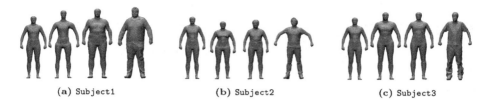

(a) Subject1   (b) Subject2   (c) Subject3

Fig. 5. Visual comparison of estimated body shapes at the different stages. In each subfigure (from left to right): mean PCA $(\bar{\gamma}, \bar{b})$, Stage I, Stage II and ground-truth shape, respectively.

Robustness in general scenes. We validate the robustness of our method on three outdoor sequences. On the `Walk` dataset [3], people move in the background, and background and foreground color are very similar. Our method is nevertheless able to accurately estimate shape and pose across 100 frames from 6 views, see Fig. 1. We also qualitatively compare against the recent the model-free method of Mustafa et al. [42]. On the `Cathedral` sequence of Kim et al. [62], they achieve rough surface reconstruction using 8 cameras without the explicit need for silhouettes; in contrast, 4 views and 20 frames are sufficient for us to reconstruct shape and pose of a quick outdoor run, see Fig. 4 (top) and supplementary material. Furthermore, we demonstrate reconstruction of complex motions on `Subject3` during a two-person volleyball play from only 3 views and 100 frames, see Fig. 4 (bottom). The second player was segmented out during Stage I, but Stage II was executed automatically. Fully automatic model and pose estimation are even possible from only two views as we demonstrate on the `Marker` sequence [3], see Fig. 6.

Shape estimation accuracy. To assess the accuracy of the estimated actor models, we tested our method on a variety of subjects performing general motions such as walking, kicking and gymnastics. Evaluation of estimated shape is performed in two ways: (1) the estimated body shape is compared against ground-truth measurements, and (2) the 3D mesh derived from Stage II is projected from the captured camera viewpoints to compute the overlap with a manually segmented foreground. We introduce two datasets `Subject1` and `Subject2`, in

Table 1. Quantitative evaluation of estimated shapes in different stages and comparison to Guan et al.'s results [26]. We use three body measures (chest, waist and hips, as shown on the right) to evaluate predicted body shapes against the ground truth (GT) captured using a laser scan.

	Chest size [cm]				Waist size [cm]				Hip size [cm]				Height [cm]			
	[26]	Stage I	Stage II	GT	[26]	Stage I	Stage II	GT	[26]	Stage I	Stage II	GT	[26]	Stage I	Stage II	GT
Pose1	92.7	–	92.8	92.6	79.6	–	82.5	80.2	–	–	98.0	–	–	–	183.2	185.0
Pose2	87.4	–	91.3	91.6	78.5	–	82.1	79.4	–	–	98.9	–	–	–	181.9	185.0
Pose3	91.9	–	93.5	91.4	76.9	–	83.2	80.3	–	–	101.3	–	–	–	182.9	185.0
Subject1	–	92.7	132.6	131.3	–	76.7	127.1	132.7	–	108.2	135.4	136.1	–	187.5	194.2	195.0
Subject2	–	92.3	99.3	100.1	–	77.3	90.6	96.5	–	92.5	102.3	99.7	–	168.5	162.5	162.0

Fig. 6. We obtained accurate results even using only two views on the `Marker` sequence.

addition to `Subject3`, with pronounced body proportions and ground-truth laser scans for quantitative evaluation. Please note that shape estimates are constant across the sequence and can be evaluated at sparse frames, while pose varies and is separately evaluated per frame in the sequel.

The shape accuracy is evaluated by measurements of chest, waist and hip circumference. `Subject1` and `Subject2` are captured indoor and are processed using 6 cameras and 40 frames uniformly sampled over 200 frames. `Subject3` is an outdoor sequence and only 3 camera views are used, see Fig. 4. All subjects are reconstructed with high quality in shape, skeleton dimensions and color, despite inaccurately estimated poses in Stage I for some frames. We only observed little variation dependent on the performed motions, i.e. a simple walking motion is sufficient, but bone length estimation degrades if joints are not sufficiently articulated during performance. All estimates are presented quantitatively in Table 1 and qualitatively in Fig. 5. In addition, we compare against Guan et al. [26] on their single-camera and single-frame datasets `Pose1`, `Pose2` and `Pose3`. Stage I requires multi-view input and was not used; instead, we manually initialized the pose roughly, as shown in Fig. 8, and body height is normalized to 185 cm [26]. Our reconstructions are within the same error range, demonstrating that Stage II is well suited even for monocular shape and pose refinement. Our reconstruction is accurate overall, with a mean error of only 2.3 ± 1.9 cm, measured across all sequences with known ground truth.

On top of these sparse measurements (chest, waist and hips), we also evaluate silhouette overlap for sequences `Walk` and `Box` of subject 1 of the publicly available `HumanEva-I` dataset [63], using only 3 cameras. We compute how much the predicted body shape overlaps the actual foreground (*precision*) and how much of the foreground is overlapped by the model (*recall*). Despite the low number of cameras, low-quality images, and without requiring background subtraction, our reconstructions are accurate with 95 % precision and 85 % recall, and improve slightly on the results of Bălan et al. [15]. Results are presented in Fig. 7 and Table 2. Note that Stage II significantly improves shape estimation. The temporal consistency and benefit of the model components are shown in the supplemental video on multiple frames evenly spread along the *HumanEva-I* Box sequence.

Pose estimation accuracy. Pose estimation accuracy is quantitatively evaluated on the public `HumanEva-I` dataset, where ground-truth data is available, see Table 3. We tested the method on the designated validation sequences `Walk` and `Box` of subject `S1`. Reconstruction quality is measured as the average Euclidean

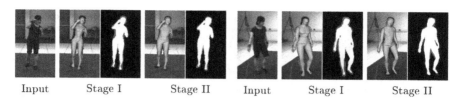

| Input | Stage I | Stage II | Input | Stage I | Stage II |

Fig. 7. Overlap of the estimated shape in Stages I and II for an input frame of `Box` (left) and `Walk` (right) sequences [63]. Note how the white area (correct estimated shape) significantly increases between Stage I and II, while blue (overestimation) and red (underestimation) areas decrease. (Color figure online)

Table 2. Quantitative evaluation of Fig. 7. See Sect. 6 for definitions of *Precision* and *Recall*.

	Precision	Recall
`Walk` Stage I	87.43 %	87.25 %
`Walk` Stage II	95.18 %	86.89 %
`Box` Stage I	93.26 %	81.11 %
`Box` Stage II	95.42 %	85.28 %

distance of estimated and ground-truth joint locations, frames with ground truth inaccuracies are excluded by the provided scripts.

Our pose estimation results are on par with state-of-the-art methods with 6–7 cm average accuracy [3,46,53,54]. In particular, we obtain comparable results to Elhayek et al. [3], which however requires a separately initialized actor model. Please note that Amin et al. [53] specifically trained their model on manually annotated sequences of the same subject in the same room. For best tracking performance, the ideal joint placement and bone lengths of the virtual skeleton may deviate from the real human anatomy, and may generally vary for different tracking approaches. To compensate differences in the skeleton structure, we also report results where the offset between ground truth and estimated joint locations is estimated in the first frame and compensated in the remaining frames, reducing the reconstruction error to 3–5 cm. Datasets without ground-truth data cannot be quantitatively evaluated; however, our shape overlap evaluation results suggest that pose estimation is generally accurate. In summary, pose estimation is reliable, with only occasional failures in Stage I, although the main focus of our work is on the combination with shape estimation.

Runtime. In our experiments, runtime scaled linearly with the number of cameras and frames. Contour-based shape optimization is efficient: it only takes 3 s per view, totaling 15 min for 50 frames and 6 views on a standard desktop machine. Skeleton pose estimation is not the main focus of this work and is not optimized; it takes 10 s per frame and view, totaling 50 min.

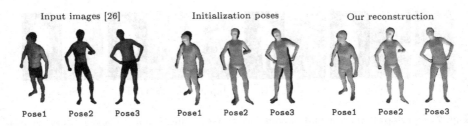

Fig. 8. Monocular reconstruction experiment. Our reconstruction (right) shows high-quality contour alignment, and improved pose and shape estimates.

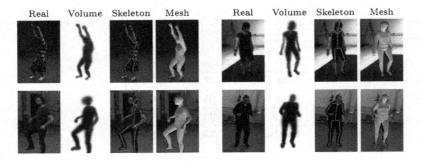

Fig. 9. In-studio reconstruction of several subjects. Our estimates are accurate across diverse body shapes and robust to highly articulated poses.

Table 3. Pose estimation accuracy measured in mm on the HumanEva-I dataset. The standard deviation is reported in parentheses.

Seq	Trained on	Our	Amin et al. [53]	Sigal et al. [46]	Belagiannis et al. [54]	Elhayek et al. [3]
S1, Walk	general	74.9 (21.9)	—	66	68.3	66.5
	HumanEva	54.6 (24.2)	54.5	—	—	—
S2, Box	general	59.7 (15.0)	—	—	62.7	60.0
	HumanEva	35.1 (19.0)	47.7	—	—	—

Limitations and discussion. Even though the body model was learned from tight clothing scans, our approach handles general apparel well, correctly reconstructing the overall shape and body dimensions. We demonstrate that even if not all assumptions are fulfilled, our method produces acceptable results, such as for the dance performance Skirt of Gall et al. [5] in Fig. 9 (top left) that features a skirt. However, our method was not designed to accurately reconstruct fine wrinkles, facial details, hand articulation, or highly non-rigid clothing.

We demonstrate fully automatic reconstructions from as few as two cameras and semi-automatic shape estimation using a single image. Fully automatic pose and shape estimates from a single image remains difficult.

7   Conclusion

We proposed a fully automatic approach for estimating the shape and pose of a rigged actor model from general multi-view video input with just a few cameras. It is the first approach that reasons about contours within sum-of-Gaussians representations and which transfers their beneficial properties, such as analytic form and smoothness, and differentiable visibility [16], to the domain of edge- and silhouette-based shape estimation. This results in an analytic volumetric contour alignment energy that efficiently and fully automatically optimizes the pose and shape parameters. Based on a new statistical body model, our approach reconstructs a personalized kinematic skeleton, a volumetric Gaussian density representation with appearance modeling, a surface mesh, and the time-varying poses of an actor. We demonstrated shape estimation and motion capture results on challenging datasets, indoors and outdoors, captured with very few cameras. This is an important step towards making motion capture more practical.

Acknowledgements. We thank PerceptiveCode, in particular Arjun Jain and Jonathan Tompson, for providing and installing the ConvNet detector, Ahmed Elhayek, Jürgen Gall, Peng Guan, Hansung Kim, Armin Mustafa and Leonid Sigal for providing their data and test sequences, The Foundry for license support, and all our actors. This research was funded by the ERC Starting Grant project CapReal (335545).

References

1. Moeslund, T.B., Hilton, A., Krüger, V.: A survey of advances in vision-based human motion capture and analysis. Comput. Vis. Image Underst. **104**(2), 90–126 (2006)
2. Holte, M.B., Tran, C., Trivedi, M.M., Moeslund, T.B.: Human pose estimation and activity recognition from multi-view videos: comparative explorations of recent developments. IEEE J. Sel. Top. Sign. Proces. **6**(5), 538–552 (2012)
3. Elhayek, A., de Aguiar, E., Jain, A., Tompson, J., Pishchulin, L., Andriluka, M., Bregler, C., Schiele, B., Theobalt, C.: Efficient ConvNet-based marker-less motion capture in general scenes with a low number of cameras. In: CVPR, pp. 3810–3818 (2015)
4. de Aguiar, E., Stoll, C., Theobalt, C., Ahmed, N., Seidel, H.P., Thrun, S.: Performance capture from sparse multi-view video. ACM Trans. Graph. **27**(3), 98 (2008)
5. Gall, J., Stoll, C., de Aguiar, E., Theobalt, C., Rosenhahn, B., Seidel, H.P.: Motion capture using joint skeleton tracking and surface estimation. In: CVPR, pp. 1746–1753 (2009)
6. Zollhöfer, M., Nießner, M., Izadi, S., Rehmann, C., Zach, C., Fisher, M., Wu, C., Fitzgibbon, A., Loop, C., Theobalt, C., Stamminger, M.: Real-time non-rigid reconstruction using an RGB-D camera. ACM Trans. Graph. **33**(4), 156 (2014)
7. Stoll, C., Hasler, N., Gall, J., Seidel, H.P., Theobalt, C.: Fast articulated motion tracking using a sums of Gaussians body model. In: ICCV, pp. 951–958 (2011)
8. Shotton, J., Sharp, T., Kipman, A., Fitzgibbon, A., Finocchio, M., Blake, A., Cook, M., Moore, R.: Real-time human pose recognition in parts from single depth images. Commun. ACM **56**(1), 116–124 (2013)

9. Bogo, F., Black, M.J., Loper, M., Romero, J.: Detailed full-body reconstructions of moving people from monocular RGB-D sequences. In: ICCV, pp. 2300–2308 (2015)
10. Tong, J., Zhou, J., Liu, L., Pan, Z., Yan, H.: Scanning 3D full human bodies using Kinects. IEEE Trans. Vis. Comput. Graph. 18(4), 643–650 (2012)
11. Helten, T., Baak, A., Bharaj, G., Müller, M., Seidel, H.P., Theobalt, C.: Personalization and evaluation of a real-time depth-based full body tracker. In: 3DV, pp. 279–286 (2013)
12. Newcombe, R.A., Fox, D., Seitz, S.M.: DynamicFusion: Reconstruction and tracking of non-rigid scenes in real-time. In: CVPR, pp. 343–352 (2015)
13. Kakadiaris, I.A., Metaxas, D.: Three-dimensional human body model acquisition from multiple views. Int. J. Comput. Vis. 30(3), 191–218 (1998)
14. Ahmed, N., de Aguiar, E., Theobalt, C., Magnor, M., Seidel, H.P.: Automatic generation of personalized human avatars from multi-view video. In: ACM Symposium on Virtual Reality Software and Technology, pp. 257–260 (2005)
15. Bălan, A.O., Sigal, L., Black, M.J., Davis, J.E., Haussecker, H.W.: Detailed human shape and pose from images. In: CVPR (2007)
16. Rhodin, H., Robertini, N., Richardt, C., Seidel, H.P., Theobalt, C.: A versatile scene model with differentiable visibility applied to generative pose estimation. In: ICCV (2015)
17. Hilton, A., Beresford, D., Gentils, T., Smith, R., Sun, W.: Virtual people: capturing human models to populate virtual worlds. In: Computer Animation, pp. 174–185 (1999)
18. Bălan, A.O., Black, M.J.: The naked truth: estimating body shape under clothing. In: Forsyth, D., Torr, P., Zisserman, A. (eds.) ECCV 2008, Part II. LNCS, vol. 5303, pp. 15–29. Springer, Heidelberg (2008)
19. Theobalt, C., de Aguiar, E., Stoll, C., Seidel, H.P., Thrun, S.: Performance capture from multi-view video. In: Ronfard, R., Taubin, G. (eds.) Image and Geometry Processing for 3-D Cinematography. Geometry and Computing, pp. 127–149. Springer, Heidelberg (2010)
20. Wu, C., Stoll, C., Valgaerts, L., Theobalt, C.: On-set performance capture of multiple actors with a stereo camera. ACM Trans. Graph. 32(6), 161 (2013)
21. Wu, C., Varanasi, K., Theobalt, C.: Full body performance capture under uncontrolled and varying illumination: a shading-based approach. In: Fitzgibbon, A., Lazebnik, S., Perona, P., Sato, Y., Schmid, C. (eds.) ECCV 2012, Part IV. LNCS, vol. 7575, pp. 757–770. Springer, Heidelberg (2012)
22. Vlasic, D., Baran, I., Matusik, W., Popović, J.: Articulated mesh animation from multi-view silhouettes. ACM Trans. Graph. 27(3), 97 (2008)
23. Starck, J., Hilton, A.: Model-based multiple view reconstruction of people. In: ICCV, pp. 915–922 (2003)
24. Ballan, L., Cortelazzo, G.M.: Marker-less motion capture of skinned models in a four camera set-up using optical flow and silhouettes. In: 3DPVT (2008)
25. Allain, B., Franco, J.S., Boyer, E.: An efficient volumetric framework for shape tracking. In: CVPR, pp. 268–276 (2015)
26. Guan, P., Weiss, A., Bălan, A.O., Black, M.J.: Estimating human shape and pose from a single image. In: ICCV, pp. 1381–1388 (2009)
27. Guo, Y., Chen, X., Zhou, B., Zhao, Q.: Clothed and naked human shapes estimation from a single image. In: Hu, S.-M., Martin, R.R. (eds.) CVM 2012. LNCS, vol. 7633, pp. 43–50. Springer, Heidelberg (2012)
28. Hasler, N., Ackermann, H., Rosenhahn, B., Thormählen, T., Seidel, H.P.: Multilinear pose and body shape estimation of dressed subjects from image sets. In: CVPR, pp. 1823–1830 (2010)

29. Jain, A., Thormählen, T., Seidel, H.P., Theobalt, C.: MovieReshape: Tracking and reshaping of humans in videos. ACM Trans. Graph. **29**(5) (2010)
30. Plankers, R., Fua, P.: Articulated soft objects for multi-view shape and motion capture. IEEE Trans. Pattern Anal. Mach. Intell. **25**(9), 63–83 (2003)
31. Ilic, S., Fua, P.: Implicit meshes for surface reconstruction. IEEE Trans. Pattern Anal. Mach. Intell. **28**(2), 328–333 (2006)
32. Cui, Y., Chang, W., Nöll, T., Stricker, D.: KinectAvatar: fully automatic body capture using a single Kinect. In: ACCV Workshops, pp. 133–147 (2012)
33. Anguelov, D., Srinivasan, P., Koller, D., Thrun, S., Rodgers, J., Davis, J.: SCAPE: shape completion and animation of people. ACM Trans. Graph. **24**(3), 408–416 (2005)
34. Pishchulin, L., Wuhrer, S., Helten, T., Theobalt, C., Schiele, B.: Building statistical shape spaces for 3D human modeling. arXiv:1503.05860 (2015)
35. Loper, M., Mahmood, N., Black, M.J.: MoSh: Motion and shape capture from sparse markers. ACM Trans. Graph. **33**(6), 220 (2014)
36. Campbell, N.D.F., Vogiatzis, G., Hernández, C., Cipolla, R.: Automatic 3D object segmentation in multiple views using volumetric graph-cuts. In: BMVC, pp. 530–539 (2007)
37. Wang, T., Collomosse, J., Hilton, A.: Wide baseline multi-view video matting using a hybrid Markov random field. In: ICPR, pp. 136–141 (2014)
38. Djelouah, A., Franco, J.S., Boyer, E., Le Clerc, F., Pérez, P.: Sparse multi-view consistency for object segmentation. IEEE Trans. Pattern Anal. Mach. Intell. **37**(9), 1890–1903 (2015)
39. Szeliski, R., Golland, P.: Stereo matching with transparency and matting. In: ICCV, pp. 517–524 (1998)
40. Guillemaut, J.Y., Hilton, A.: Joint multi-layer segmentation and reconstruction for free-viewpoint video applications. Int. J. Comput. Vis. **93**(1), 73–100 (2011)
41. Bray, M., Kohli, P., Torr, P.H.S.: POSECUT: simultaneous segmentation and 3D pose estimation of humans using dynamic graph-cuts. In: Leonardis, A., Bischof, H., Pinz, A. (eds.) ECCV 2006. LNCS, vol. 3952, pp. 642–655. Springer, Heidelberg (2006). doi:10.1007/11744047_49
42. Mustafa, A., Kim, H., Guillemaut, J.Y., Hilton, A.: General dynamic scene reconstruction from multiple view video. In: ICCV (2015)
43. Hasler, N., Rosenhahn, B., Thormahlen, T., Wand, M., Gall, J., Seidel, H.P.: Markerless motion capture with unsynchronized moving cameras. In: CVPR, pp. 224–231 (2009)
44. Deutscher, J., Blake, A., Reid, I.: Articulated body motion capture by annealed particle filtering. In: CVPR, pp. 126–133 (2000)
45. Sidenbladh, H., Black, M.J.: Learning the statistics of people in images and video. Int. J. Comput. Vis. **54**(1–3), 183–209 (2003)
46. Sigal, L., Isard, M., Haussecker, H., Black, M.J.: Loose-limbed people: estimating 3D human pose and motion using non-parametric belief propagation. Int. J. Comput. Vis. **98**(1), 15–48 (2012)
47. Kehl, R., Bray, M., Van Gool, L.: Markerless full body tracking by integrating multiple cues. In: ICCV Workshop on Modeling People and Human Interaction (2005)
48. Kollnig, H., Nagel, H.H.: 3D pose estimation by fitting image gradients directly to polyhedral models. In: ICCV, pp. 569–574 (1995)
49. Wachter, S., Nagel, H.H.: Tracking of persons in monocular image sequences. In: Nonrigid and Articulated Motion Workshop, pp. 2–9 (1997)

50. Tompson, J.J., Jain, A., LeCun, Y., Bregler, C.: Joint training of a convolutional network and a graphical model for human pose estimation. In: NIPS, pp. 1799–1807 (2014)
51. Felzenszwalb, P.F., Huttenlocher, D.P.: Pictorial structures for object recognition. Int. J. Comput. Vis. **61**(1), 55–79 (2005)
52. Andriluka, M., Roth, S., Schiele, B.: Pictorial structures revisited: people detection and articulated pose estimation. In: CVPR, pp. 1014–1021 (2009)
53. Amin, S., Andriluka, M., Rohrbach, M., Schiele, B.: Multi-view pictorial structures for 3D human pose estimation. In: BMVC (2013)
54. Belagiannis, V., Amin, S., Andriluka, M., Schiele, B., Navab, N., Ilic, S.: 3D pictorial structures for multiple human pose estimation. In: CVPR, pp. 1669–1676 (2014)
55. Park, H.S., Shiratori, T., Matthews, I., Sheikh, Y.: 3D trajectory reconstruction under perspective projection. Int. J. Comput. Vis. **115**(2), 115–135 (2015)
56. Fayad, J., Russell, C., Agapito, L.: Automated articulated structure and 3D shape recovery from point correspondences. In: ICCV, pp. 431–438 (2011)
57. Allen, B., Curless, B., Popović, Z.: The space of human body shapes: reconstruction and parameterization from range scans. ACM Trans. Graph. **22**(3), 587–594 (2003)
58. Loper, M., Mahmood, N., Romero, J., Pons-Moll, G., Black, M.J.: SMPL: a skinned multi-person linear model. ACM Trans. Graph. **34**(6), 248 (2015)
59. Hasler, N., Stoll, C., Sunkel, M., Rosenhahn, B., Seidel, H.P.: A statistical model of human pose and body shape. Comput. Graph. Forum **28**(2), 337–346 (2009)
60. Lewis, J.P., Cordner, M., Fong, N.: Pose space deformation: a unified approach to shape interpolation and skeleton-driven deformation. In: SIGGRAPH, pp. 165–172 (2000)
61. Cerezo, E., Pérez, F., Pueyo, X., Seron, F.J., Sillion, F.X.: A survey on participating media rendering techniques. Vis. Comput. **21**(5), 303–328 (2005)
62. Kim, H., Hilton, A.: Influence of colour and feature geometry on multi-modal 3D point clouds data registration. In: 3DV, pp. 202–209 (2014)
63. Sigal, L., Bălan, A.O., Black, M.J.: HumanEva: synchronized video and motion capture dataset and baseline algorithm for evaluation of articulated human motion. Int. J. Comput. Vis. **87**, 4–27 (2010)

Globally Continuous and Non-Markovian Crowd Activity Analysis from Videos

He Wang[1,2(✉)] and Carol O'Sullivan[1,3]

[1] Disney Research Los Angeles, Glendale, USA
[2] University of Leeds, Leeds, UK
realcrane@gmail.com
[3] Trinity College Dublin, Dublin, Ireland
carol.osullivan@scss.tcd.ie

Abstract. Automatically recognizing activities in video is a classic problem in vision and helps to understand behaviors, describe scenes and detect anomalies. We propose an unsupervised method for such purposes. Given video data, we discover recurring activity patterns that appear, peak, wane and disappear over time. By using non-parametric Bayesian methods, we learn coupled spatial and temporal patterns with minimum prior knowledge. To model the temporal changes of patterns, previous works compute Markovian progressions or locally continuous motifs whereas we model time in a globally continuous and non-Markovian way. Visually, the patterns depict flows of major activities. Temporally, each pattern has its own unique appearance-disappearance cycles. To compute compact pattern representations, we also propose a hybrid sampling method. By combining these patterns with detailed environment information, we interpret the semantics of activities and report anomalies. Also, our method fits data better and detects anomalies that were difficult to detect previously.

1 Introduction

Understanding crowd activities from videos has been a goal in many areas [1]. In computer vision, a number of subtopics have been studied extensively, including flow estimation [2], behavior tracking [3] and activity detection [4,5]. The main problem is essentially mining recurrent patterns over time from video data. In this work, we are particularly interested in mining recurrent spatio-temporal activity patterns, i.e., recurrent motions such as pedestrians walking or cars driving. Discovering these patterns can be useful for applications such as scene

---

H. Wang—ORCID ID:orcid.org/0000-0002-2281-5679.
This work is mostly done by the authors when they were with Disney Research Los Angeles.

Electronic supplementary material The online version of this chapter (doi:10.1007/978-3-319-46454-1_32) contains supplementary material, which is available to authorized users.

© Springer International Publishing AG 2016
B. Leibe et al. (Eds.): ECCV 2016, Part V, LNCS 9909, pp. 527–544, 2016.
DOI: 10.1007/978-3-319-46454-1_32

summarization, event counting or unusual activity detection. On a higher level, such patterns could be used to reduce the dimensionality of the scene description for other research questions.

Pattern finding has been previously addressed [4,6,7], but only either for the spatial case, a Markovian progression or local motifs. To consider temporal information in a global non-Markovian fashion, we propose a Spatio-temporal Hierarchical Dirichlet Process (STHDP) model. STHDP leverages the power of Hierarchical Dirichlet Process (HDP) models to cluster location-velocity pairs and time simultaneously by introducing two mutually-influential HDPs. The results are presented as activity patterns and their time-varying presence (e.g. appear, peak, wane and disappear).

Combined with environment information, our approach provides enriched information for activity analysis by automatically answering questions (such as what, where, when and how important/frequent) for each activity, which facilitates activity-level and higher-level analysis. The novelty and contributions of our work are as follows:

1. We present an unsupervised method for activity analysis that requires no prior knowledge about the crowd dynamics, user labeling or predefined pattern numbers.
2. Compared to static HDP variants, we explicitly model the time-varying presence of activity patterns.
3. Complementary to other dynamic HDP variants, we model time in a globally continuous and non-Markovian way, which provides a new perspective for temporal analysis of activities.
4. We also propose a non-trivial split-merge strategy combined with Gibbs sampling to make the patterns more compact.

1.1 Related Work

Activities can be computed from different perspectives. On an individual level, tracking-based methods [8,9] and those with labeled motion features [10,11] have been successful. On a larger scale, flow fields [2,12] can be computed and segmented to extract meaningful crowd flows. However, these methods do not reveal the latent structures of the data at the flow level well where trajectory-based approaches prove to be very useful [5,13–15]. Trajectories can be clustered based on dynamics [5], underlying decision-making processes [14] or the environment [13,15]. However, these works need assumptions or prior knowledge of the crowd dynamics or environment. Another category of trajectory-based approaches is unsupervised clustering to reveal latent structures [4,7,16,17]. This kind of approaches assumes minimal prior knowledge about the environment or cluster number. Our method falls into this category.

Non-parametric Bayesian models have been used for clustering trajectories. Compared to the methods mentioned above, non-parametric Bayesian models have been proven successful due to minimal requirements of prior knowledge such as cluster numbers and have thus been widely used for scene classifications

[18,19], object recognition [20], human action detection [21] and video analysis [7,22]. Initial efforts on using these kinds of models to cluster trajectories mainly focused on the spatial data [7]. Later on, more dynamic models have been proposed [4,16,17]. Wang et al. [16] propose a dynamic Dual-HDP model by assuming a Markovian progression of the activities and manually sliced the data into equal-length intervals. Emonet et al. [4,23] and Varadarajan et al. [17] model time as part of local spatio-temporal patterns, but no pattern progression is modeled. The former requires manual segmentation of the data and assumes the Markovian property, which does not always apply and could adversely affect detecting temporal anomalies. The latter focuses on local continuity in time and cannot learn time activities well when chunks of data are missing.

Inspired by many works in Natural Language Processing and Machine Learning [24–29], we propose a method that is complementary to the methods above in that we model time in a globally continuous and non-Markovian way. We thus avoid manual segmentation and expose the time-varying presence of each activity. We show how our method fits data better and in general more aligned with human judgments. In addition, our method is good at detecting temporal anomalies that could be missed by previous methods.

2 Methodology

2.1 Spatio-Temporal Hierarchical Dirichlet Processes

Given a video, raw trajectories can be automatically estimated by a standard tracker and clustered to show activities, with each activity represented by a trajectory cluster. One has the option of grouping trajectories in an unsupervised fashion where a distance metric needs to be defined, which is difficult due to the ambiguity of the associations between trajectories and activities across different scenarios. Another possibility is to cluster the individual observations of trajectories, such as locations, in every frame. Since observations of the same activity are more likely to co-occur, clustering co-occurring individual observations will eventually cluster their trajectories. This problem is usually converted into a data association problem, where each individual observation is associated with an activity. However, it is hard to know the number of activities in advance, so Dirichlet Processes (DPs) are used to model potentially infinite number of activities. In this way, each observation is associated with an activity and trajectories can be clustered based on a *softmax* scheme (a trajectory is assigned to the activity that gives the best likelihood on its individual observations). During the data association, DPs also automatically compute the ideal number of activities so that the co-occurrences of observations in the whole dataset can be best explained by an finite number of activities. To further capture the commonalities among the activities across different data segments, Hierarchical DPs (HDPs) are used, where one DP captures the activities in one data segment and another DP on a higher level captures all possible activities.

To cluster video data in the scheme explained above, we discretize the camera image into grids, that discretizing a trajectory into locations. We also discretize the velocity into several subdomains based on the orientation so that each location also comes with a velocity component. Finally, we can model activities as Multinomial distributions of time-stamped location-velocity pairs $\{w, t\}$, $w = (p_x,\ p_y,\ p'_x,\ p'_y)$ where $(p_x,\ p_y)$ is the position, $(p'_x,\ p'_y)$ is the velocity and each $\{w, t\}$ is an *observation*. Given multiple data segments consisting of location-velocity pairs, we can use the HDP scheme explained above to cluster trajectories. In addition, our STHDP also has a temporal part. Consider that a time data segment is formed by all the time stamps of the observations associated with one activity, then the distribution of these time stamps reflect the temporal changes of the activity. Since these time stamps might come from different periods (e.g. an activity appears/disappears multiple times), we need a multi-modal model to capture it. Again, since we do not know how many periods there are, we can use a DP to model this unknown too, which can be captured by an infinite mixture of Gaussians over the time stamps. Finally, to compute the time activities across different time data segments, we also use a HDP to model time. The whole scheme is explained by a Bayesian model shown in Fig. 1.

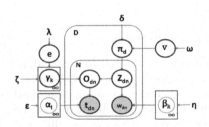

Fig. 1. STHDP model

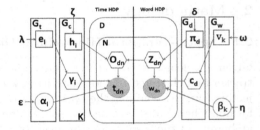

Fig. 2. Model used for sampling

To mathematically explain our model, we first introduce some background and terminologies. In a *stick-breaking* representation [30] of a DP: $G = \sum_{k=1}^{\infty} \sigma_k(v)\beta_k$, where $\sigma_k(v)$ is *iteratively* generated from $\sigma_k(v) = v_k \prod_{j=1}^{k-1}(1 - v_j)$, $\sum_{k=1}^{\infty} \sigma_k(v) = 1$, $v \sim Beta(1, \omega)$ and $\beta_k \sim H(\eta)$. β_k are DP *atoms* drawn from some base distribution H and $\sigma_k(v)$ are *stick proportions*. We refer to the iterative generation of sticks $\sigma_k(v)$ from v as $\sigma \sim GEM(v)$, as in [24]. Following the convention of topics models, we refer to a location-velocity pair as a **word**, its time stamp as a **time word**, activity patterns as **word topics** and time activities as **time topics**. A data segment is called a **document** and a time stamp data segment is called a **time document**. The whole dataset is called a **corpus**. The overall activities and time activities we are aiming for are the corpus-level word topics and time topics.

Figure 1 depicts two HDPs: a word HDP and a time HDP, respectively modeling the spatial and temporal data as described above. The word HDP starts with a DP over corpus-level word topics $v \sim GEM(\omega)$. In each document, there exists a DP $\pi_d \sim DP(v, \sigma)$ governing the document-level topics. For each word, a topic indicator is sampled by $Z_{d_n} \sim \pi_d$ and the word is generated from $w_{dn}|\beta_{Z_{d_n}} \sim Mult(\beta_{Z_{d_n}})$. The time HDP models how word topics evolve. Unlike previous models, it captures two aspects of time: continuity and multi-modality. Continuity is straightforward. Multi-modality means a word topic can appear/disappear several times. Imagine all the time words associated with the words under one word topic. The word topic could peak multiple times which means its time words are mainly aggregated within a number of time intervals. Meanwhile, there can be infinitely many word topics and some of their time words share some time intervals. Finally, there can be infinitely many such shared time intervals or time topics, which are modeled by an infinite mixture of Gaussians, of which each component is a time topic. A global DP $e \sim GEM(\lambda)$ governs all possible time topics. Then, for each corpus-level word topic k, a time DP $\gamma_k \sim DP(\zeta, e)$ is drawn. Finally, when a specific time word is needed, its Z_{d_n} indicates its word topic based on which we draw a time word indicator $O_{d_n} \sim \gamma_{Z_{d_n}}$ and a time word is generated from $t_{dn}|\alpha_{O_{d_n}} \sim Normal(\alpha_{O_{d_n}})$. In this way, each word topic corresponds to a subset of time topics with different weights. Thus a Gaussian Mixture Model (GMM) is naturally used for every word topic. Due to the space limit, the generative process of Fig. 1 is explained in the supplementary material.

2.2   Posterior by Sampling

To compute the word and time topics we need to compute the posterior of STHDP. Both sampling and variational inference have been used for computing the posterior of hierarchical models [24,31]. After our first attempt at variational inference, we found that it suffers from the sub-optimal local minima because of the word-level coupling between HDPs. Naturally, we resort to sampling. Many sampling algorithms have been proposed for such purposes [25,32,33]. However, due to the structure of STHDP, we found that it is difficult to derive a parallel sampling scheme such as the one in [32]. Finally, we employ a hybrid approach that combines Gibbs and Metropolis-Hasting (MH) sampling based on the stick-breaking model shown in Fig. 2, the latter being the split-merge (SM) operation. For Gibbs sampling, we use both Chinese Restaurant Franchise (CRF) [24] and modified Chinese Restaurant Franchise (mCRF) [25]. As there are two HDPs in STHDP, we fix the word HDP when sampling the time HDP which is a standard two-level HDP, so we run CRF sampling [24] on it. For the word HDP, we run mCRF. Please refer to the supplementary material for details.

HDPs suffer from difficulties when two topics are similar, as the sampling needs to go through a low probability area to merge them [34]. This is particular problematic in our case because each observation is pulled by two HDPs. Split-merge (SM) methods have been proposed [34,35] for Dirichlet Processes Mixture Models, but they do not handle HDPs. Wang et al. [26] proposes an SM method for HDP, but only for one HDP, whereas STHDP has two entwined HDPs. We propose a Metropolis-Hasting (MH) sampling scheme to perform SM operations.

Table 1. Variables in CRF

v_w	A word in the vocabulary
V_w	The size of the vocabulary
n_{jik}	The number of words in restaurant j at table i serving dish k
z_{ji}	The table indicator of the ith word in restaurant j
m_{jk}	The number of word tables in restaurant j serving dish k
$m_{j\cdot}$	The number of word tables in restaurant j
K	The number of word dishes

In our version of the CRF metaphor, word topics and time topics are called **word dishes** and **time dishes**. Word documents are called **restaurants** and time documents are called **time restaurants**. Some variables are given in Table 1. Similar to [26], we also only do split-merge on the word dish level. We start with the SM operations for the word HDP. In each operation, we randomly choose two word tables, indexed by i and j. If they serve the same dish, we try to split this dish into two, and otherwise merge these two dishes. Since the merge is just the opposite operation of split, we only explain the split strategy here.

Following [34], the MH sampling acceptance ratio is computed by:

$$a(c^*, c) = min\{1, \frac{q(c|c^*)}{q(c^*|c)} \frac{P(c^*)}{P(c)} \frac{L(c^*|y)}{L(c|y)}\} \tag{1}$$

where c^* and c are states (table and dish indicators) after and before split and $q(c^*|c)$ is the split transition probability. The merge transition probability $q(c|c^*) = 1$ because there is only one way to merge. P is the prior probability, y are the observations, so $L(c^*|y)$ and $L(c|y)$ are the likelihoods of the two states. The split process of MH is: sample a dish, split it into two according to some process, and compute the acceptance probability $a(c^*, c)$. Finally, sample a probability $\phi \sim Uniform(0, 1)$. If $\phi > a(c^*, c)$, it is accepted, and rejected otherwise. The whole process is done only within the sampled dish and two new dishes. All the remaining variables are fixed.

Now we derive every term in Eq. 1. The state c consists of the table and dish indicators. Because the time HDP needs to be considered when sampling the word HDP, the prior of table indicators is:

$$p(\mathbf{z}_j) = \frac{\delta^{m_{j\cdot}} \prod_{t=1}^{m_{j\cdot}} (n_{jt}p(t|\bullet) - 1)!}{\prod_{i=1}^{n_{j\cdot}} (i + \delta - 1)} \tag{2}$$

where $p(t|\bullet)$ represents the marginal likelihood of all time words involved. Similarly, for word dish indicators:

$$p(\mathbf{k}) = \frac{\omega^K \prod_{k=1}^{K} (m_{\cdot k}p(t|\bullet) - 1)!}{\prod_{i=1}^{m_{\cdot\cdot}} (i + \omega - 1)} \tag{3}$$

Now we have the prior for p(c):

$$p(c) = p(\mathbf{k}) \prod_{j=1}^{D} p(\mathbf{z}_j) \tag{4}$$

where D is the number of restaurants; $p(c^*)$ can be similarly computed.

Now we derive $q(c^*|c)$. Assume that tables i and j both serve dish k. We denote S as the set of indices of all tables also serving dish k excluding i and j. In the split state, k is split into k_1 and k_2. We denote S_1 and S_2 as the sets of indices of tables serving dishes k_1 and k_2. We first assign table i to k_1 and j to k_2, then allocate all tables indexed by S into either k_1 or k_2 by *sequential allocation restricted Gibbs sampling* [35]:

$$p(SK = k_j | S_1, S_2) \propto m_{.k_j} f_{k_j}(\mathbf{w}_{SK}) p(\mathbf{t}_{SK}|\bullet) \tag{5}$$

where j = 1 or 2, $SK \in S$, $\mathbf{w}_{SK}$ is all the words at table SK and $m_{.k_j}$ is the total number of tables assigned to k_j. All the tables in S are assigned to either k_1 or k_2. We still approximate $p(\mathbf{t}_{SK}|\bullet)$ by $\hat{p}(\mathbf{t}_{SK}|\bullet)$ as we do for Gibbs sampling (cf. supplementary material). Note that during the process, the sizes of S1 and S2 constantly change. Finally, we compute $q(c^*|c)$ by Eq. 6:

$$q(c^*|c) = \prod_{i \in S} p(k^i = k | S1, S2) \tag{6}$$

Finally, the likelihoods are:

$$\frac{L(c^*|y)}{L(c|y)} = \frac{f_{k_1}^{lik}(\mathbf{w}_{k_1}, \mathbf{t}_{k_1}|c^*) f_{k_2}^{lik}(\mathbf{w}_{k_2}, \mathbf{t}_{k_1}|c^*)}{f_k^{lik}(\mathbf{w}_k, \mathbf{t}_k|c)} \tag{7}$$

where

$$f^{lik}(w, t|c) = \frac{\Gamma(V_w \eta)}{\Gamma(n_{..k} + V_w \eta)} \frac{\prod_{v_w} \Gamma(n_{..k}^{v_w} + \eta)}{\Gamma^{V_w}(\eta)} p(t|\bullet) \tag{8}$$

Γ is the gamma function, $n_{..k}$ is the number of words in topic k, $n_{..k}^{v_w}$ is the number of words v_w assigned to topic k, and $p(t|\bullet)$ is the likelihood of the time words involved.

Now we have fully defined our split-merge operations. Whenever an SM operation is executed, the time HDP needs to be updated. During the experiments, we do one iteration of SM after a certain number of Gibbs sampling iterations.

We found it is unnecessary to do SM on the time HDP for two reasons. First, we already implicitly consider the time HDP here through Eqs. 2–8 and an SM operation on the word HDP will affects the time HDP. Second, we want the word HDP to be the dominating force over the time HDP in SM. A merge operation on the word topics will cause a merge operation on the time HDP, which makes the patterns more compact. The reverse is not ideal because it can merge different word topics. However, this does not mean that the time HDP is always dominated. Its impact in the Gibbs sampling plays a strong role in clustering samples that are temporally close together while separating samples that are not.

3   Experiments

Empirically, we use a standard set of parameters for all our experiments. The prior $Dirichlet(\eta)$ is a symmetric Dirichlet where η is initialized to 0.5. For all GEM weights, we put a vague $Gamma$ prior, $Gamma(0.1, 0.1)$, on their $Beta$ distribution parameters, which are updated in the same way as [24]. The last is the Normal-Inverse-Gamma prior, $NIG(\mu, \lambda, \sigma_1, \sigma_2)$, where μ is the mean, λ is the variance scalar, and σ_1 and σ_2 are the shape and scale. For our datasets, we set μ to the sample mean, $\lambda = 0.01$, $\sigma_1 = 0.3$ and $\sigma_2 = 1$. Because both the Gamma and NIG priors are very vague here, we find that the performance is not much affected by different values, so we fix the NIG parameters. For simplicity, we henceforth refer to all activity Patterns with the letter P.

3.1   Synthetic Data

A straightforward way to show the effectiveness of our method is to use synthetic data where we know the ground truth so that we can compare learned results with the ground truth. Similar to [7], we use grid image data where the ground truth patterns (Fig. 3 P1 and P2) are used to generate synthetic document data. Different from [7], to show the ability of our model in capturing temporal information, we generate data for 4 periods where the two ground truth patterns are combined in different ways for every period. Documents are randomly sampled from the combined pattern for each period. Figure 3 Right shows the learned patterns and their time activities from HDP [24] and STHDP. The time activities for HDP are represented by a GMM over the time words associated with the activity pattern. For STHDP, a GMM naturally arises for each pattern by combining the time patterns and their respective weights.

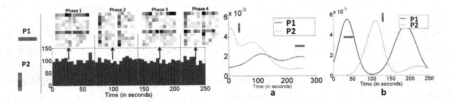

Fig. 3. Left: Two ground truth patterns on a 5 × 5 grid (one distributed over a horizontal bar, the other over a vertical bar) and generated data over four time periods (P1 is used for generating data in phase 1 and phase 3, P2 is used for data in phase 2 and both are used for phase 4. Some document examples and the histogram of observation numbers are shown for each phase). Right: Learned patterns and their time activities by (a) HDP [24] and (b) STHDP. (Color figure online)

Both HDP and STHDP learn the correct spatial patterns. However, HDP assumes exchangeability of all data points thus its time information is not meaningful. In contrast, STHDP not only learns the correct patterns, but also learns a multi-modal representation of its temporal information which reveals three types of information. First, all GMMs are scaled proportionally to the number of associated data samples, so their integrals indicate their relative importance. In Fig. 3 Left, the number of data samples generated from P1 is roughly twice as big as that from P2. This is reflected in Fig. 3 Right (b) (The area under the red curve is roughly twice as big as that under the blue curve). Second, each activity pattern has its own GMM to show its presence over time. The small bump of the blue curve in (b) shows that there is a relatively small number of data samples from P2 beyond the 210th second. It is how we generated data for phase 4. Finally, different activity patterns have different weights across all the time topics. Conversely, at any time, the data can be explained by a weighted combination of all activity patterns. Our method provides an enriched temporal model that can be used for analysis in many ways.

3.2   Real Data

In this section, we test our model on the Edinburgh dataset [36], the MIT Carpark database [16] and New York Central Terminal [13], referred to as **Forum**, **Carpark** and **TrainStation** respectively. They are widely used to test activity analysis methods [7,13,16,37,38]. Each dataset demonstrates different strengths of our method. Forum consists of indoor video data with the environment information available for semantic interpretation of the activities. Carpark is an outdoor scene consisting of periodic video data that serves as a good example to show the multi-modality of our time modeling. TrainStation is a good example of large scenes with complex traffic. All patterns are shown by representative (high probability) trajectories.

Forum Dataset. The forum dataset is recorded by a bird's eye static camera installed on the ceiling above an open area in a school building. 664 trajectories have been extracted as described in [36], starting from 14:19:28 GMT, 24 August 2009 and lasting for 4.68 h. The detailed environment is shown in Fig. 4 (left). We discretize the 640 * 480 camera image into 50×50 pixel grids and the velocity direction into 4 cardinal subdomains and then run a burn-in 50 iterations of Gibbs sampling. For the first 500 iterations, MH sampling is done after every 10 Gibbs sampling iterations. Then we continue to run it for another 1500 iterations.

Nine patterns are shown in Fig. 4, where the semantics can be derived by also considering the environment information in the form of Zones Z1: Stairs, Z2-Z7: Doors, Z8: Conference room, Z9: a floating staircase that blocks the camera view but has no semantic effect here. P3 and P4 are two groups of opposite trajectories connecting Z1 and Z2. We observe many more trajectories in P3 than P4. From the detailed environment information, we know that the side door outside of Z2 is a security door. This door can be opened from the inside, but people need to swipe their cards to open it from outside, which could explain why there are more exiting than entering activities through Z2. P2 is the major flow when people come down the stairs and go to the front entrance. P1 has a

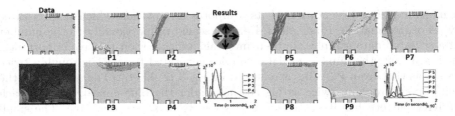

Fig. 4. Top Left: Environment of Edinburgh dataset. Bottom Left: Trajectories overlaid on the environment. Right: Some activities shown by representative trajectories and their respective time activities. Colors indicate orientations described by the legend in the middle. (Color figure online)

relatively small number of trajectories from Z6 to Z7, i.e., leaving through the front entrance. From the temporal point of view, the two major incoming flows can be seen in Fig. 4 P4 and P5, spanning the first half of the data. We also spot a pattern with a high peak at the beginning (around 2:34 pm), shown by Fig. 4 P7, which connects the second part of the area and the conference room. We therefore speculate that there may have been a big meeting around that time.

Carpark Dataset. The Carpark dataset was recorded by a far-distance static camera over a week and 1000 trajectories were randomly sampled as shown in Fig. 5 Left. Since this dataset is periodic, it demonstrates the multi-modality of our time modeling. We run the sampling in the same way as in the Forum experiment.

Four top activity patterns and their respective time presence are shown in Fig. 5. P1 is the major flow of in-coming cars, P2 is an out-going flow, and P3 and P4 are two opposite flows. Unfortunately, we do not have detailed environment information as we do from Forum for further semantic interpretations. The temporal information shows how all peaks are captured by our method, but different patterns have different weights in different periods.

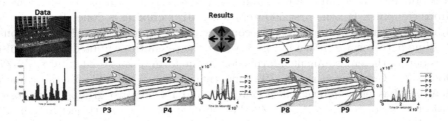

Fig. 5. Top Left: Environment of the car park. Bottom Left: Observation numbers over time. Right: Some activities shown by representative trajectories and their respective time activities. Colors indicate orientations described by the legend in the middle. (Color figure online)

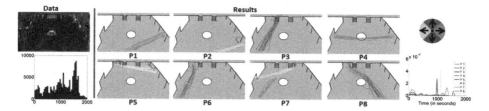

Fig. 6. Top Left: Environment of the New York Central Terminal. Bottom Left: Observation numbers over time. Right: Some activities shown by representative trajectories and their respective time activities. Colors indicate orientations described by the legend on the right. (Color figure online)

TrainStation Dataset. The TrainStation dataset was recorded from a large environment and 1000 trajectories were randomly selected for the experiment. The data and activities are shown in Fig. 6.

3.3 Split and Merge

We test the effectiveness of split-merge (SM) by the per-word log likelihood by:

$$
\begin{aligned}
P_{per-word} &= \frac{\sum_{n=1}^{N} P(w_n, t_n | \beta, v, \alpha, e)}{N} \\
&= \frac{\sum_{n=1}^{N} (\sum_{k=1}^{K} P(w_n | \beta_k, v_k) \sum_{l=1}^{L} P(t_n | \alpha_l, e_l, \bullet))}{N}
\end{aligned}
\tag{9}
$$

where N, K and L are the number of observations, learned spatial activities and time activities respectively. β and v are the spatial activities and their weights, α and e are the time activities and their weights, $\bullet$ represents all the other factors. In general, we found that SM increases the likelihood thus improves the model fitness on the data. Also, we found that MH sampling is more likely to pick a merge operation than a split. One reason is the time HDP tends to separate data samples that are temporally far away from each other, thus causing similar patterns to appear at different times. A merge on those patterns has higher probability, thus is more likely to be chosen. Merging such spatially similar patterns makes each final activity unique. It is very important because not only does it make the activities more compact, it also makes sure that all the time activities for a particular spatial activity can be summarized under one pattern.

3.4 Anomaly Detection

For anomaly detection, Fig. 7 shows the top outliers (i.e., unusual activities) in three datasets: (g) and (l) show trajectories crossing the lawn, which is rare in our sampled data; (i) shows a trajectory of leaving the lot then returning. In the latter case, the trajectory exited in the upper lane, whereas most activities involve entering in the upper lane and exiting in the bottom lane. The

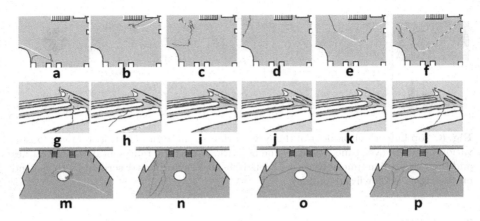

Fig. 7. Top: Outliers in Forum. Middle: Outliers in Carpark. Bottom: Outliers in Train-Station.

outliers in the Forum are also interesting. Figure 7 (a) shows a person entering through the front entrance, checking with the reception then going to the conference room; (b) shows a person entering through Z2 then leaving again; (d) is unexpected because visually it should be in Fig. 4 (P7), but we found that the pattern peaks around 2:34 pm and falls off quickly to a low probability area before 2:27:30 pm whereas Fig. 7 (c) occurs between 2:26:48 pm–2:26:53 pm. This example also demonstrates that our model identifies outliers not only on the spatial domain but also on the time domain. We also found similar cases in Fig. 7 (k), (l) and (o) that are normal when only looking at the spatial activities but become anomalies when the timing is also considered.

3.5   Comparison

Qualitative Comparison. Our model is complementary to dynamic non-parametric models such as DHDP [16] and MOTIF [4]. Theoretically, our time modeling differs in two aspects: continuity and multi-modality. Wang et al. [16] manually segment data into equal-length episodes and Emonet et al. [4] model local spatio-temporal patterns. Our method treats time as a globally continuous variable. Different time modeling affects the clustering differently. All three models are variants of HDP which assumes the *exchangeability* of data samples. This assumption is overly strict when time is involved because it requires any two samples from different time to be exchangeable. The manual segmentation [16] restricts the exchangeability within segment. Enforcing a peak-and-fall-off time prior [4] has similar effects.

For DHDP, we segment both datasets equally into 4 episodes. We run it for 5000 iterations on each episode. For MOTIF, we used the author's implementation [4]. For parameter settings, we use our best effort at picking the same parameters for three models, e.g. the Dirichlet, DP, Gamma and Beta distribution parameters on each level. Other model-specific parameters are empirically set to achieve the best performance. Also, since there is no golden rule regarding when to stop the sampling, we use the time DHDP models takes and run the other two for roughly the same period of time.

Since all three methods learn similar spatial activities, we mainly compare the temporal information. Figure 8 shows one common pattern found by all three methods. The temporal information of DHDP is simply the weight of this activity across different episodes. To get a dense distribution, smaller episodes are needed, but the ideal size is not clear. Therefore, we only plot the temporal information for MOTIF and STHDP. In Fig. 8 Left, (c) is the starting time probability distribution of Fig. 8 Left (b). The distribution is discrete and shows how likely it is that this pattern could start at a certain time instance, which reports quite different information from our pattern. Figure 8 Left (d) shows the time activities of Fig. 4 (P3), which is continuous and shows its appearance, crescendo, multiple peaks, wane and disappearance. An interesting fact is that both methods capture this pattern within the first 8000 s while our model also captures a small bump beyond the first 8000 s. By looking at the data, we find that there are indeed a few trajectories belonging to this pattern beyond the first 8000 s. Figure 8 Right shows a common pattern in the Carpark dataset. Both MOTIF and STHDP capture the periodicity as seen in P3 and P4. They mainly differ at the start in that P3 captures two peaks whereas P4 captures one. Note that the two peaks that P3 captures depict how likely it is that the activity starts at those time instances, while STHDP captures the time span of that activity, which is essentially the same.

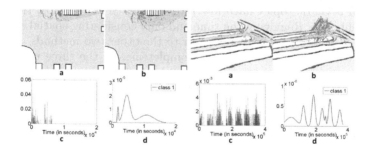

Fig. 8. Left: Forum dataset. (a) A pattern learned by DHDP. (b) A pattern learned by MOTIF. (c) The topic starting time distribution over time from MOTIF. (d) The time activities of Fig. 4 (P3) from STHDP. Right: Carpark dataset. (a) A pattern learned by DHDP. (b) A pattern learned by MOTIF. (c) The topic starting time distribution over time from MOTIF. (d) The time activities of Fig. 5 (1) from STHDP.

Quantitative Comparison. Because all three methods model time differently, it is hard to do a fair quantitative comparison. As a general metric to evaluate a model's ability to predict, we use the per-word log likelihood (Eq. 9). We hold out 10 % of the data as testing data and evaluate the performance of the three models with respect to how well they can predict the testing data. We show the best per-word log likelihood of the methods after the burn-in period in Table 2.

Table 2. Left: Best per-word log likelihoods. Right: $r_{correct}$ and $r_{complete}$ accuracies from 0–1, 1 is the best.

	STHDP	DHDP	MOTIF	$r_{correct}/r_{complete}$	STHDP	DHDP	MOTIF
Forum	-3.84	-9.8	-54.38	Forum	0.92/0.88	0.95/0.63	0.87/0.78
Carpark	-2.8	-7.75	-62.13	Carpark	0.83/0.9	0.89/0.31	0.85/0.42
TrainStation	-3.5	-4.9	-62.2	TrainStation	0.84/0.75	0.72/0.55	0.69/0.58

This experiment favors DHDP and MOTIF. Because DHDP learns topics on different episodes, when computing the likelihood of a testing sample $\{w, t\}$, we only weighted-sum its likelihoods across the topics learned within the corresponding episode. So the likelihood is $p(w|t, \bullet)$ instead of $p(w, t|\bullet)$ where $\bullet$ represents all model parameters and the training data. For MOTIF, the learned results are topics as well as their durations in time. We compute the likelihood of a testing sample by averaging the likelihoods across all topics whose durations contains t, i.e., $p(w, t|\beta_k, t \in rt_k, \bullet)$ where β_k is the topic with duration rt_k. For STHDP, the likelihood is computed across all word topics and all time topics, $p(w, t|\bullet)$, which is much more strict. We found that STHDP outperforms both DHDP and MOTIF, with MOTIF performing more poorly than the other two. We initially found the results surprising given the fact that MOTIF learns similar spatial activities to the other two. Further investigations showed that, since the testing data is randomly selected, this causes gaps in the training data in time. As a consequence of the discrete nature of the time representation in MOTIF, all MOTIF topics have low probabilities in those gaps, thus causing the low likelihoods. Removing the time and only considering spatial activities in this case may help but would not be fair to the other two methods.

Next, we compute the correctness/completeness of the three methods as in [16]. Correctness is the accuracy of trajectories of different activities not clustered together while completeness is the accuracy of trajectories of the same activity clustered together. To get the ground truth data for each dataset, the trajectories were first roughly clustered into activities. Then 2000 pairs of trajectories were randomly selected where each pair comes from the same activity and another 2000 pairs were randomly selected where each pair comes from two different activities. Finally these 4000 pairs of trajectories for each dataset were labeled and compared with the results of our method. We denote the correctness as $r_{correct}$ and the completeness as $r_{complete}$. Because estimating the number of clusters is hard, it was only needed to judge whether a pair of trajectories was from the same activity or not. The correctness/completeness metric indicates that grouping all the trajectories in the same cluster results in 100 % completeness and 0 % correctness while putting every trajectory into a singleton cluster results in 100 % correctness and 0 % completeness. So only an accurate clustering can give good overall accuracies. Table 2 Right shows the accuracies. STHDP outperforms the other two on $r_{complete}$ across all datasets. Its $r_{correct}$ is higher in TrainStation and slightly worse in Forum and Carpark but the difference is small (within 6 %).

Finally, we discuss how different temporal modeling could lead to different temporal anomaly detection. Most of the outliers in Fig. 7 are *spatial* outliers and also detected by DHDP. However, some are not (Fig. 7 (d), (k), (l) and (o)). Figure 7 (d) is a good example. Spatially its probability is high because it is on one major activity shown in Fig. 4 P7. However, if its temporal information is considered, our method gives a low probability because its timing is very different from the observations in Fig. 4 P7. In contrast, DHDP gives a high probability because it first identifies the segment in which this trajectory is, then computes the probability based on the activities computed within the segment and the segments before. Since Fig. 4 P7 and Fig. 7 (d) are in the same segment, a high probability is given. The result is caused by the fact that DHDP models progressions between segments but the temporal information within a segment is not modeled. Meanwhile, MOTIF reports a higher probability on Fig. 7 (d). However, it suffers from the situation explained by the low likelihoods in Table 2 Left. When a continuous chunk of data are missing, there is a void spanning a short period in the training data, which causes low probabilities on any observations in the time span. This kind of temporal information loss leads to false alarms for anomaly detections (all our testing data report low probabilities). In our method, if an activity is seen before and after the void, it will be inferred that there is a probability that the activity also exists in the middle by putting a Gaussian over it. Even if the activity only appears before or after the missing data, the Gaussian there prevents the probability from decreasing as quickly as it does in MOTIF.

4   Limitation and Conclusions

For performance comparison, we tried to run three models and stopped them once satisfactory activities were computed and compared the time. Our method is approximately the same as DHDP and can be slightly slower than MOTIF depending on the dataset. But we did not use larger datasets because although being able to report good likelihoods, sampling is in general slow for largest datasets and it applies to all three models. So we focused on experiments that show the differences between our model and the other two. Also, we find the data is abundant in terms of activities where a random sampling suffices to reveal all activities. Quicker methods for training such as variational inference [39] or parallel sampling can be employed in future.

In summary, we propose a new non-parametric hierarchical Bayesian model with a new hybrid sampling strategy for the posterior estimation for activity analysis. Its unique feature in time modeling provides better likelihoods, correctness/completeness and anomaly detection, which makes it a good alternative to existing models. We have shown its effectiveness on multiple datasets.

References

1. Zhou, S., Chen, D., Cai, W., Luo, L., Low, M.Y.H., Tian, F., Tay, V.S.H., Ong, D.W.S., Hamilton, B.D.: Crowd modeling and simulation technologies. ACM Trans. Model. Comput. Simul. **20**(4), 20:1–20:35 (2010)
2. Ali, S., Shah, M.: Floor fields for tracking in high density crowd scenes. In: Forsyth, D., Torr, P., Zisserman, A. (eds.) ECCV 2008. LNCS, vol. 5303, pp. 1–14. Springer, Heidelberg (2008). doi:10.1007/978-3-540-88688-4_1
3. Antonini, G., Martinez, S.V., Bierlaire, M., Thiran, J.P.: Behavioral priors for detection and tracking of pedestrians in video sequences. Int. J. Comput. Vision **69**(2), 159–180 (2006)
4. Emonet, R., Varadarajan, J., Odobez, J.: Extracting and locating temporal motifs in video scenes using a hierarchical non parametric Bayesian model. In: 2011 IEEE Conference on Computer Vision and Pattern Recognition (CVPR), pp. 3233–3240, June 2011
5. Zhou, B., Tang, X., Wang, X.: Learning collective crowd behaviors with dynamic pedestrian-agents. Int. J. Comput. Vision **111**(1), 50–68 (2014)
6. Wang, X., Ma, K.T., Ng, G.W., Grimson, W.: Trajectory analysis and semantic region modeling using a nonparametric Bayesian model. In: 2008 IEEE Conference on Computer Vision and Pattern Recognition, CVPR 2008, pp. 1–8, June 2008
7. Wang, X., Ma, X., Grimson, W.: Unsupervised activity perception in crowded and complicated scenes using hierarchical Bayesian models. IEEE Trans. Pattern Anal. Mach. Intell. **31**(3), 539–555 (2009)
8. Stauffer, C., Grimson, W.E.L.: Learning patterns of activity using real-time tracking. IEEE Trans. Pattern Anal. Mach. Intell. **22**, 747–757 (2000)
9. Oliver, N., Rosario, B., Pentland, A.: A Bayesian computer vision system for modeling human interactions. IEEE Trans. Pattern Anal. Mach. Intell. **22**(8), 831–843 (2000)
10. Zelnik-Manor, L., Irani, M.: Event-based analysis of video. In: Proceedings of the 2001 IEEE Computer Society Conference on Computer Vision and Pattern Recognition, CVPR 2001, vol. 2, pp. 123–130 (2001)
11. Zhong, H., Shi, J., Visontai, M.: Detecting unusual activity in video. In: Proceedings of the 2004 IEEE Computer Society Conference on Computer Vision and Pattern Recognition, CVPR 2004, vol. 2, pp. II-819–II-826, June 2004
12. Lin, D., Grimson, E., Fisher, J.: Learning visual flows: a lie algebraic approach. In: 2009 IEEE Conference on Computer Vision and Pattern Recognition, CVPR 2009, pp. 747–754, June 2009
13. Yi, S., Li, H., Wang, X.: Understanding pedestrian behaviors from stationary crowd groups. In: 2015 IEEE Conference on Computer Vision and Pattern Recognition (CVPR), pp. 3488–3496, June 2015
14. Kitani, K.M., Ziebart, B.D., Bagnell, J.A., Hebert, M.: Activity forecasting. In: Fitzgibbon, A., Lazebnik, S., Perona, P., Sato, Y., Schmid, C. (eds.) ECCV 2012. LNCS, vol. 7575, pp. 201–214. Springer, Heidelberg (2012). doi:10.1007/978-3-642-33765-9_15
15. Xie, D., Todorovic, S., Zhu, S.C.: Inferring "Dark Matter" and "Dark Energy" from videos. In: 2013 IEEE International Conference on Computer Vision (ICCV), pp. 2224–2231, December 2013
16. Wang, X., Ma, K.T., Ng, G.W., Grimson, W.E.L.: Trajectory analysis and semantic region modeling using nonparametric hierarchical Bayesian models. Int. J. Comput. Vision **95**(3), 287–312 (2011)

17. Varadarajan, J., Emonet, R., Odobez, J.M.: A sequential topic model for mining recurrent activities from long term video logs. Int. J. Comput. Vision **103**(1), 100–126 (2012)
18. Fei-Fei, L., Perona, P.: A Bayesian hierarchical model for learning natural scene categories. In: 2005 IEEE Computer Society Conference on Computer Vision and Pattern Recognition, CVPR 2005, vol. 2, pp. 524–531, June 2005
19. Sudderth, E.B., Torralba, A., Freeman, W.T., Willsky, A.S.: Describing visual scenes using transformed objects and parts. Int. J. Comput. Vision **77**(1–3), 291–330 (2007)
20. Sivic, J., Russell, B.C., Efros, A.A., Zisserman, A., Freeman, W.T.: Discovering object categories in image collections. ICCV 2005 (2005)
21. Niebles, J.C., Wang, H., Fei-Fei, L.: Unsupervised learning of human action categories using spatial-temporal words. Int. J. Comput. Vision **79**(3), 299–318 (2008)
22. Kaufman, L., Rousseeuw, P.J.: Finding Groups in Data: An Introduction to Cluster Analysis. Wiley-Interscience, New York (2005)
23. Emonet, R., Varadarajan, J., Odobez, J.M.: Temporal analysis of motif mixtures using Dirichlet processes. IEEE Trans. Pattern Anal. Mach. Intell. **36**(1), 140–156 (2014)
24. Teh, Y.W., Jordan, M.I., Beal, M.J., Blei, D.M.: Hierarchical Dirichlet processes. J. Am. Stat. Assoc. **101**(476), 1566–1581 (2006)
25. Dubey, A., Hefny, A., Williamson, S., Xing, E.P.: A non-parametric mixture model for topic modeling over time. arXiv: 1208.4411 [stat], August 2012
26. Wang, C., Blei, D.M.: A Split-Merge MCMC Algorithm for the Hierarchical Dirichlet Process. arXiv: 1201.1657 [cs, stat], January 2012
27. Lin, D., Grimson, E., Fisher, J.W.: Construction of dependent Dirichlet processes based on poisson processes. In: Lafferty, J.D., Williams, C.K.I., Shawe-Taylor, J., Zemel, R.S., Culotta, A. (eds.) Advances in Neural Information Processing Systems 23, pp. 1396–1404, Curran Associates, Inc. (2010)
28. Blei, D.M., Frazier, P.I.: Distance dependent Chinese restaurant processes. J. Mach. Learn. Res. **12**, 2461–2488 (2011)
29. Wang, X., McCallum, A.: Topics over time: a non-Markov continuous-time model of topical trends. In: Proceedings of the 12th ACM SIGKDD International Conference on Knowledge Discovery and Data Mining, KDD 2006, pp. 424–433. ACM, New York (2006)
30. Sethuraman, J.: A constructive definition of Dirichlet priors. Statistica Sinica **4**, 639–650 (1994)
31. Hoffman, M.D., Blei, D.M., Wang, C., Paisley, J.: Stochastic variational inference. J. Mach. Learn. Res. **14**(1), 1303–1347 (2013)
32. Chang, J., Fisher III, J.W.: Parallel sampling of HDPs using sub-cluster splits. In: Advances in Neural Information Processing Systems, pp. 235–243 (2014)
33. Hughes, M.C., Fox, E., Sudderth, E.B.: Effective split-merge Monte Carlo methods for nonparametric models of sequential data. In: Advances in Neural Information Processing Systems, pp. 1295–1303 (2012)
34. Jain, S., Neal, R.: A split-merge Markov chain Monte Carlo procedure for the Dirichlet process mixture model. J. Comput. Graph. Stat. **13**, 158–182 (2000)
35. Dahl, D.B.: Sequentially-allocated merge-split sampler for conjugate and nonconjugate Dirichlet process mixture models. J. Comput. Graph. Stat. **11** (2005)
36. Majecka, B.: Statistical models of pedestrian behaviour in the Forum. M.Sc. Dissertation, School of Informatics, University of Edinburgh, Edinburgh (2009)

37. Luber, M., Spinello, L., Silva, J., Arras, K.O.: Socially-aware robot navigation: a learning approach. In: 2012 IEEE/RSJ International Conference on Intelligent Robots and Systems (IROS), pp. 902–907, October 2012
38. Almingol, J., Montesano, L., Lopes, M.: Learning multiple behaviors from unlabeled demonstrations in a latent controller space, 136–144 (2013)
39. Wang, H., Ondřej, J., O'Sullivan, C.: Path patterns: analyzing and comparing real and simulated crowds. In: Proceedings of the 20th ACM SIGGRAPH Symposium on Interactive 3D Graphics and Games. I3D 2016, pp. 49–57. ACM, New York (2016)

Joint Face Alignment and 3D Face Reconstruction

Feng Liu[1], Dan Zeng[1], Qijun Zhao[1(✉)], and Xiaoming Liu[2]

[1] College of Computer Science, Sichuan University, Chengdu, China
qjzhao@scu.edu.cn
[2] Department of Computer Science and Engineering, Michigan State University,
East Lansing, MI, USA

Abstract. We present an approach to simultaneously solve the two problems of face alignment and 3D face reconstruction from an input 2D face image of arbitrary poses and expressions. The proposed method iteratively and alternately applies two sets of cascaded regressors, one for updating 2D landmarks and the other for updating reconstructed pose-expression-normalized (PEN) 3D face shape. The 3D face shape and the landmarks are correlated via a 3D-to-2D mapping matrix. In each iteration, adjustment to the landmarks is firstly estimated via a landmark regressor, and this landmark adjustment is also used to estimate 3D face shape adjustment via a shape regressor. The 3D-to-2D mapping is then computed based on the adjusted 3D face shape and 2D landmarks, and it further refines the 2D landmarks. An effective algorithm is devised to learn these regressors based on a training dataset of pairing annotated 3D face shapes and 2D face images. Compared with existing methods, the proposed method can fully automatically generate PEN 3D face shapes in real time from a single 2D face image and locate both visible and invisible 2D landmarks. Extensive experiments show that the proposed method can achieve the state-of-the-art accuracy in both face alignment and 3D face reconstruction, and benefit face recognition owing to its reconstructed PEN 3D face shapes.

Keywords: Face alignment · 3D face reconstruction · Cascaded regression

1 Introduction

Three-dimensional (3D) face models have recently been employed to assist pose or expression invariant face recognition [3, 14, 42], and the state-of-the-art performance has been achieved. A crucial step in these 3D face-assisted face recognition methods is to reconstruct the 3D face model from a two-dimensional (2D) face image. Besides its applications in face recognition, 3D face reconstruction is also

Electronic supplementary material The online version of this chapter (doi:10.1007/978-3-319-46454-1_33) contains supplementary material, which is available to authorized users.

B. Leibe et al. (Eds.): ECCV 2016, Part V, LNCS 9909, pp. 545–560, 2016.
DOI: 10.1007/978-3-319-46454-1_33

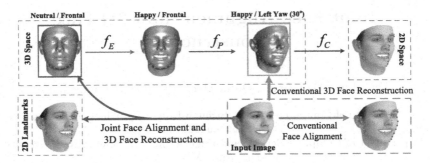

Fig. 1. We view 2D landmarks are generated from a 3D face through 3D expression (f_E) and pose (f_P) deformation, and camera projection (f_C) (top row). While conventional face alignment and 3D face reconstruction are two *separate* tasks and the latter requires the former as the input, this paper performs these two tasks *jointly*, i.e., reconstructing a pose-expression-normalized (PEN) 3D face and estimating visible/invisible landmarks (green/red points) from a 2D face image with arbitrary poses and expressions. (Color figure online)

useful in other face-related tasks, such as facial expression analysis [7,36] and facial animation [4,5]. While many 3D face reconstruction methods are available, they require landmarks on the face image as input, and are difficult to handle large-pose faces that have invisible landmarks due to self-occlusion.

Existing studies tackle the problems of face alignment (or facial landmark localization) and 3D face reconstruction *separately*. However, these two problems are chicken-and-egg problems. On one hand, 2D face images are projections of 3D faces onto the 2D plane. Knowing a 3D face and a 3D-to-2D mapping function, it is easy to compute the visibility and position of 2D landmarks. On the other hand, the landmarks provide rich information about facial geometry, which is the basis of 3D face reconstruction. Figure 1 illustrates the correlation between 2D landmarks and the 3D face. That is, the visibility and position of landmarks in the projected 2D image are determined by three factors: the 3D face shape, 3D deformation due to expression and pose, and camera projection parameters. Let us denote a 3D face shape as S and its 2D landmarks as U. The formation of 2D landmarks from the 3D face can be represented by $U = f_C \circ f_P \circ f_E(S)$, where f_C is camera projection, f_P and f_E are deformation caused by pose and expression, respectively. *Given such a clear correlation between 2D landmarks U and 3D shape S, it is evident that they should ideally be solved jointly, instead of separately as in prior works - indeed this is the core of this work.*

Motivated by the aforementioned observation, this paper proposes to simultaneously solve the two problems of face alignment and 3D face shape reconstruction in one unified framework. To this end, two sets of regressors are jointly learned from a training set of pairing annotated 2D face images and 3D face shapes. These two sets of regressors are alternately applied to locate the landmarks on an input 2D image, and meanwhile reconstruct its pose-expression-normalized (PEN) 3D face shape. Note that most single image-based 3D face reconstruction algorithms aim to assist face recognition. For this purpose, we argue that reconstructing the PEN 3D shape is more useful than reconstructing the 3D shape that has the same pose and expression as the input 2D face [23, 28, 31].

The rest of this paper is organized as follows. Section 2 briefly reviews related work in the literature. Section 3 introduces in detail the proposed joint face alignment and 3D face reconstruction method. Section 4 reports experimental results. Section 5 concludes the paper.

2   Related Work

Face Alignment. Classical face alignment methods, including Active Shape Model (ASM) [9, 11] or Active Appearance Model (AAM) [8, 25], search for landmarks based on global shape models and generative texture models. Constrained Local Model (CLM) [10] also utilizes global shape models to regularize the landmark locations, but it employs discriminative local texture models. Regression based methods [6, 27, 35, 39] have been recently proposed to directly estimate landmark locations by applying cascaded regressors to an input 2D face image. These methods mostly do not consider the visibility of facial landmarks under different view angles. Consequently, their performance degrades substantially for non-frontal faces, and their detected landmarks could be ambiguous because the anatomically correct landmarks might be invisible due to self-occlusion (see Fig. 1).

A few methods focused on large-pose face alignment, which can be roughly divided into two categories: multi-view based and 3D model based. Multi-view based methods [37, 40] define different sets of landmarks as templates, one for each view range. Given an input image, they fit the multi-view templates to it and choose the best fitted one as the final result. These methods are usually complicated to apply, and can not detect invisible self-occluded landmarks. 3D model based methods, in contrast, can better handle self-occluded landmarks with the assistance of 3D face models. Their basic idea is to fit a 3D face model to the input image to recover the 3D landmark locations. Most of these methods [17, 18, 41] use 3D morphable models (3DMM) [2] – either a simplified one with a sparse set of landmarks [18, 41] or a relatively dense one [17]. They estimate the 3DMM parameters by using cascaded regressors with texture features as the input. In [18], the visibility of landmarks is explicitly computed, and the method can cope with face images of yaw angles ranging from $-90°$ to $90°$, whereas the method in [17] does not work properly for faces of yaw angles beyond $60°$. In [33], Tulyakov and Sebe propose to directly estimate the 3D landmark locations via texture-feature-based regressors for faces of yaw angles upto $50°$.

These existing 3D model based methods establish regressions between 2D image features and 3D landmark locations (or indirectly, 3DMM parameters). While our proposed approach is also based on 3D model, unlike existing methods, it carries out regressions both on 2D images and in the 3D space. Regressions on 2D images predict 2D landmarks, while regressions in the 3D space predict 3D landmarks locations. By integrating both regressions, our proposed method can more accurately locate landmarks, and better handle self-occluded landmarks. It thus works well for images of arbitrary view angles in $[-90°, 90°]$.

3D Face Reconstruction. Estimating the 3D face geometry from a single 2D image is an ill-posed problem. Existing methods, such as Shape from Shading (SFS) and 3DMM, thus heavily depend on priors or constraints. SFS based methods [20,31] usually utilize an average 3D face model as a reference, and assume the Lambertian lighting model for the 3D face surface. One limitation of SFS methods lies in its assumed connection between 2D texture clues and 3D shape, which is too weak to discriminate among different individuals. 3DMM [2,3,28] establishes statistical parametric models for both texture and shape, and represents a 3D face as a linear combination of basis shapes and textures. To recover the 3D face from a 2D image, 3DMM-based methods estimate the combination coefficients by minimizing the discrepancy between the input 2D face image and the one rendered from the reconstructed 3D face. They can better cope with 2D face images of varying illuminations and poses. However, they still suffer from invisible facial landmarks when the input face has large pose angles. To deal with extreme poses, Lee et al. [22], Qu et al. [26] and Liu et al. [23] propose to discard the self-occluded landmarks or treat them as missing data. All these existing 3D face reconstruction methods require landmarks as input. Consequently, they either manually mark the landmarks, or employ standalone face alignment methods to automatically locate the landmarks. Moreover, existing methods always generate 3D faces that have the same pose and expression as the input image, which may not be desired in face recognition due to the challenge of matching 3D faces with expressions [12]. In this paper, we improve 3D face reconstruction from two aspects: (i) integrating the face alignment step into the 3D face reconstruction procedure, and (ii) reconstructing PEN 3D faces, which are believed to be useful for face recognition.

3   Proposed Method

3.1   Overview

We denote an n-vertex 3D face shape of neutral expression and frontal pose as,

$$S = \begin{pmatrix} x_1 & x_2 & \cdots & x_n \\ y_1 & y_2 & \cdots & y_n \\ z_1 & z_2 & \cdots & z_n \\ 1 & 1 & \cdots & 1 \end{pmatrix}, \tag{1}$$

and a subset of S with columns corresponding to l landmarks as S_L. The projections of these landmarks on the 2D face image $\mathbf{I}$ are represented by

$$U = \begin{pmatrix} u_1 & u_2 & \cdots & u_l \\ v_1 & v_2 & \cdots & v_l \end{pmatrix} = f_C \circ f_P \circ f_E(S_L) \approx \mathbf{M} \times S_L. \tag{2}$$

Here, we use a 3D-to-2D mapping matrix $\mathbf{M}$ to approximate the composite effect of expression and pose induced deformation and camera projection. Given an input 2D face image $\mathbf{I}$, our goal is to simultaneously locate its

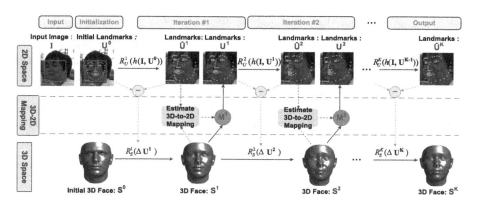

Fig. 2. Flowchart of the proposed joint face alignment and 3D face reconstruction method.

landmarks U and reconstruct its 3D face shape S. Note that, in some context, we also write the 3D face shape and the landmarks as column vectors: $\mathbf{S} = (x_1, y_1, z_1, x_2, y_2, z_2, \cdots, x_n, y_n, z_n)^\mathsf{T}$, and $\mathbf{U} = (u_1, v_1, u_2, v_2, \cdots, u_l, v_l)^\mathsf{T}$, where 'T' is transpose operator.

Figure 2 shows the flowchart of the proposed method. For the input 2D face image $\mathbf{I}$, its 3D face shape $\mathbf{S}$ is initialized as the mean 3D shape of training faces. Its landmarks $\mathbf{U}$ are initialized by fitting the mean landmarks of training frontal faces into the face region specified by a bounding box in $\mathbf{I}$ via similarity transforms. $\mathbf{U}$ and $\mathbf{S}$ are iteratively updated by applying a series of regressors. Each iteration contains three main steps: (i) updating landmarks, (ii) updating 3D face shape, and (iii) refining landmarks.

Updating landmarks. This step updates the landmarks' locations from $\mathbf{U}^{k-1}$ to $\hat{\mathbf{U}}^k$ based on the texture features in the input 2D image. This is similar to the conventional cascaded regressor based 2D face alignment [35]. The adjustment to the landmarks' locations in k^{th} iteration, $\Delta\mathbf{U}^k$ is determined by the local texture features around $\mathbf{U}^{k-1}$ via a regressor,

$$\Delta\mathbf{U}^k = R_U^k(h(\mathbf{I}, \mathbf{U}^{k-1})), \tag{3}$$

where $h(\mathbf{I}, \mathbf{U})$ denotes a texture feature extracted around the landmarks $\mathbf{U}$ in the image $\mathbf{I}$, and R_U^k is a regression function. The landmarks can be then updated by $\hat{\mathbf{U}}^k = \mathbf{U}^{k-1} + \Delta\mathbf{U}^k$. The method for learning these landmark regressors will be introduced in Sect. 3.3.

Updating 3D face shape. In this step, the above-obtained landmark location adjustment is used to estimate the adjustment of the 3D face shape. Specifically, a regression function R_S^k models the correlation between the landmark location adjustment $\Delta\mathbf{U}^k$ and the expected adjustment to the 3D shape $\Delta\mathbf{S}^k$, i.e.,

$$\Delta\mathbf{S}^k = R_S^k(\Delta\mathbf{U}^k). \tag{4}$$

The 3D shape can be then updated by $\mathbf{S}^k = \mathbf{S}^{k-1} + \Delta\mathbf{S}^k$. The method for learning these shape regressors will be given in Sect. 3.4.

Refining landmarks. Once a new estimate of the 3D shape is obtained, the landmarks can be further refined accordingly. For this purpose, the 3D-to-2D mapping matrix is needed. Hence, we estimate $\mathbf{M}^k$ based on $\mathbf{S}^k$ and $\hat{\mathbf{U}}^k$. The refined landmarks $\mathbf{U}^k$ can be then obtained by projecting $\mathbf{S}^k$ onto the image via $\mathbf{M}^k$ according to Eq. (2). During this process, the visibility of the landmarks is also re-computed. Details about this step will be given in Sect. 3.5.

3.2   Training Data Preparation

Before we provide the details about the three steps, we first introduce the training data needed for learning the landmarks and 3D shape regressors. Since the purpose of these regressors is to gradually adjust the estimated landmarks and 3D shape towards their true values, we need a sufficient number of triplet data $\{(\mathbf{I}_i, \mathbf{S}_i^*, \mathbf{U}_i^*) | i = 1, 2, \cdots, N\}$, where $\mathbf{S}_i^*$ and $\mathbf{U}_i^*$ are, respectively, the ground truth 3D shape and landmarks for the image $\mathbf{I}_i$, and N is the total number of training samples. All the 3D face shapes have been established dense correspondences among their vertices; in other words, they have the same number of vertices, and vertices of the same index have the same semantic meaning. Moreover, both visible and invisible landmarks in $\mathbf{I}_i$ have been annotated and included in $\mathbf{U}_i^*$. For invisible landmarks, the annotated positions should be anatomically correct positions (e.g., red points in Fig. 1).

Obviously, to make the regressors robust to expression and pose variations, the training data should contain 2D face images of varying expressions and poses. As for the 3D shape $\mathbf{S}_i^*$ corresponding to the $\mathbf{I}_i$ in the training data, it can either have the same expression and pose as $\mathbf{I}_i$, or just have neutral expression and frontal pose no matter what expression and pose $\mathbf{I}_i$ has. In the former, the learned regressors will output 3D face shapes that have the same expression and pose as the input images; while in the latter, the learned regressors will generate neutral and frontal 3D shapes for any input images. In either case, the dense registration among all 3D shapes $\mathbf{S}_i^*$ is needed for regressor learning. In this paper, we follow the latter for two reasons: (i) dense registration of 3D face shapes with different expressions is difficult, and (ii) the reconstructed PEN 3D shapes are preferred for being used in 3D face recognition.

It is, however, difficult to find in the public domain such data sets of 3D face shapes and corresponding annotated 2D images with various expressions/poses. Thus, we construct two sets of training data by ourselves: one based on BU3DFE [36], and the other based on LFW [16]. BU3DFE database contains 3D face scans of 56 males and 44 females, acquired in neutral plus six basic expressions (happiness, disgust, fear, angry, surprise and sadness). All basic expressions are acquired at four levels of intensity. These 3D face scans have been manually annotated with 84 landmarks (83 landmarks provided by the database and one nose tip marked by ourselves). For each of the 100 subjects, we select one scan of neutral expression as the ground truth 3D shape. For the

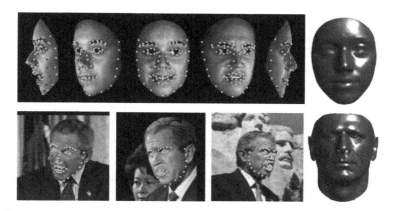

Fig. 3. Example 2D face images with annotated landmarks and corresponding neutral 3D shapes from the BU3DFE and LFW databases.

rest six expressions, we choose the scans of the first level intensity, and project them to 2D images with recorded landmark locations. From each of the seven scans, 19 face images are generated with different poses ($-90°$ to $90°$ yaw with a $10°$ interval). As a result, each 3D shape has 133 images of different poses and expressions. We use the method [13] to establish dense correspondence of BU3DFE neutral scans.

LFW database contains 13,233 images of 5,749 subjects. We select 150 subjects, each having at least 10 images, and use 68 landmarks on these face images that are provided by the work of [41]. From the neutral frontal image of each subject, we employ the method in [23] to reconstruct the 3D shape, which is densely registered. Finally, we obtain 4,149 images of 150 subjects and their corresponding neutral 3D face shapes.

The resultant 3D shapes have $n = 9,677$ for BU3DFE and $n = 53,215$ for LFW. Figure 3 shows some example 2D face images and corresponding 3D faces in the two databases. Obviously, 3D shapes in BU3DFE consist of a sparser set of vertices, and consequently look a little bit blur in Fig. 3.

3.3 Learning Landmark Regressors

According to Eq. (3), landmark regressors estimate the adjustment to $\mathbf{U}^{k-1}$ such that the updated landmarks $\mathbf{U}^k$ get closer to their true positions. In the training phase, the true positions and visibility of the landmarks are given by the ground truth $\mathbf{U}^*$. Therefore, the objective of the landmark regressors R_U^k is to better predict the difference between $\mathbf{U}^k$ and $\mathbf{U}^*$. In this paper, we employ linear regressors as the landmark regressors, and learn them by fulfilling the following optimization:

$$R_U^k = \arg\min_{R_U^k} \sum_{i=1}^{N} \| \left(\mathbf{U}_i^* - \mathbf{U}_i^k \right) - R_U^k(h(\mathbf{I}_i, \mathbf{U}_i^{k-1})) \|_2^2, \qquad (5)$$

which has a close-form least-square solution. Note that other regression schemes, such as CNN [19], can be easily adopted in our framework.

We use 128-dim SIFT descriptors [24] as the local feature. The feature vector of h is a concatenation of the SIFT descriptors at all the l landmarks, i.e., a $128l$-dim vector. If a landmark is invisible, no feature will be extracted, and its corresponding entries in h will be zero. It is worth mentioning that the regressors estimate the semantic positions of all landmarks including invisible landmarks.

3.4   Learning 3D Shape Regressors

The landmark adjustment $\Delta \mathbf{U}^k$ is also used as the input to the 3D shape regressor R_S^k. The objective of R_S^k is to compute an update to the initially estimated 3D shape $\mathbf{S}^{k-1}$ in the kth iteration to minimize the difference between the updated 3D shape and the ground truth. Using similar linear regressors, the 3D shape regressors can be learned by solving the following optimization via least squares:

$$R_S^k = \arg\min_{R_S^k} \sum_{i=1}^{N} \| (\mathbf{S}_i^* - \mathbf{S}_i^k) - R_S^k (\Delta \mathbf{U}_i^k) \|_2^2, \tag{6}$$

with its closed form solution as

$$R_S^k = \Delta \mathbb{S}^k (\Delta \mathbb{U}^k)^{\mathsf{T}} (\Delta \mathbb{U}^k (\Delta \mathbb{U}^k)^{\mathsf{T}})^{-1}, \tag{7}$$

where $\Delta \mathbb{S}^k = \mathbb{S}^* - \mathbb{S}^k$ and $\Delta \mathbb{U}^k$ are, respectively, the 3D shape and landmark adjustment. $\mathbb{S} \in \mathbb{R}^{3n*N}$ and $\mathbb{U} \in \mathbb{R}^{2l*N}$ denote, respectively, the ensemble of 3D face shapes and 2D landmarks of all training samples with each column corresponding to one sample. It can be mathematically shown that N should be larger than $2l$ so that $\Delta \mathbb{U}^k (\Delta \mathbb{U}^k)^{\mathsf{T}}$ is invertible. Fortunately, since the set of used landmarks are usually sparse, this requirement is easy to be satisfied in real-world applications.

3.5   Estimating 3D-to-2D Mapping and Landmark Visibility

In order to refine the landmarks with the updated 3D face shape, we have to project the 3D shape to the 2D image with a 3D-to-2D mapping matrix. In this paper, we dynamically estimate the mapping matrix based on $\mathbf{S}^k$ and $\hat{\mathbf{U}}^k$. As discussed earlier in Sect. 3.1, the mapping matrix is a composite effect of expression and pose induced deformation and camera projection. Here, we assume a weak perspective projection for the camera projection as in prior work [18,38], and further assume that the expression and pose induced deformation can be approximated by a linear transform. As a result, the mapping matrix $\mathbf{M}^k$ is represented by a 2×4 matrix, and can be estimated as a least squares solution to the following fitting problem:

$$\mathbf{M}^k = \arg\min_{\mathbf{M}^k} \| \hat{U}^k - \mathbf{M}^k \times S_L^k \|_2^2 . \tag{8}$$

Once a new mapping matrix is computed, the landmarks can be further refined as $U^k = \mathbf{M}^k \times S_L^k$.

The visibility of the landmarks can be then computed based on the mapping matrix $\mathbf{M}$ using the method in [18]. Suppose the average surface normal around a landmark in the 3D face shape $\mathbf{S}$ is $\overrightarrow{\mathbf{n}}$. Its visibility $\mathbf{v}$ can be measured by

$$\mathbf{v} = \frac{1}{2}\left(1 + sgn\left(\overrightarrow{\mathbf{n}} \cdot \left(\frac{\mathbf{M}_1}{\|\mathbf{M}_1\|} \times \frac{\mathbf{M}_2}{\|\mathbf{M}_2\|}\right)\right)\right), \tag{9}$$

where $sgn()$ is the sign function, '$\cdot$' means dot product and '$\times$' cross-product, and $\mathbf{M}_1$ and $\mathbf{M}_2$ are the left-most three elements at the first and second row of the mapping matrix $\mathbf{M}$. This basically rotates the surface normal and validates if it points toward the camera or not.

The whole process of learning the cascaded coupled landmark and 3D shape regressors is summarized in Algorithm 1.

Algorithm 1. Cascaded Coupled-Regressor Learning.

Input: Training data $\{(\mathbf{I}_i, \mathbf{S}_i^*, \mathbf{U}_i^*)|i = 1, 2, \cdots, N\}$, initial shape $\mathbf{S}_i^0$ & landmarks $\mathbf{U}_i^0$.
Output: Cascaded coupled-regressors $\{R_U^k, R_S^k\}_{k=1}^K$.
 1: **for** $k = 1, ..., K$ **do**
 2:     Estimate R_U^k via Eq. (5), and compute landmark adjustment $\Delta\mathbf{U}_i^k$ via Eq. (3);
 3:     Update landmarks $\hat{\mathbf{U}}_i^k$ for all images: $\hat{\mathbf{U}}_i^k = \mathbf{U}_i^{k-1} + \Delta\mathbf{U}_i^k$;
 4:     Estimate R_S^k via Eq. (6), and compute shape adjustment $\Delta\mathbf{S}_i^k$ via Eq. (4);
 5:     Update 3D face $\mathbf{S}_i^k$: $\mathbf{S}_i^k = \mathbf{S}_i^{k-1} + \Delta\mathbf{S}_i^k$;
 6:     Estimate the 3D-to-2D mapping matrix $\mathbf{M}_i^k$ via Eq. (8);
 7:     Compute the refined landmarks $\mathbf{U}_i^k$ via Eq. (2) and their visibility via Eq. (9).
 8: **end for**

---

4   Experiments

4.1   Protocols

We conduct three sets of experiments to evaluate the proposed method in 3D shape reconstruction, face alignment, and benefits to face recognition.

Datasets. The training data are constructed from two public face databases: BU3DFE and LFW, as detailed in Sect. 3.2. Respectively, two different models are trained using each of the two training sets. Our test sets include BU3DFE and AFW (Annotated Faces in-the-Wild) [40]. To evaluate the 3D shape reconstruction accuracy, a 10-fold cross validation is applied to split the BU3DFE data into training and testing subsets, resulting in 11,970 training samples and 1,330 testing samples. To evaluate the face alignment accuracy, the AFW database [40] is tested using the LFW-trained model. AFW is a widely used benchmark in the face alignment literature. It contains 205 images of 468 faces with different poses within $\pm 90°$. In [30], 337 of these faces have been manually annotated with face bounding boxes and 68 landmarks. We use them in our experiments.

Experiment setup. During training and testing, each image is associated with a bounding box, which specifies the face region in the image. To initialize the landmarks in it, the mean of the landmarks in all neutral frontal training images is fitted to the face region via a similarity transform. In this paper, we set the number of iterations $K = 5$ (discussion of convergence issue is provided in supplemental material). SIFT descriptors are computed on 32×32 local patches around the landmarks, and the implementation by [35] is used in our experiments.

Evaluation metrics. Two metrics are used to evaluate the 3D face shape reconstruction accuracy: Mean Absolute Error (MAE) and Normalized Per-vertex Depth Error (NPDE). MAE is defined as $\texttt{MAE} = \frac{1}{N_T} \sum_{i=1}^{N_T} (\|\mathbf{S}_i^* - \hat{\mathbf{S}}_i\|/n)$, where N_T is the total number of testing samples, $\mathbf{S}_i^*$ and $\hat{\mathbf{S}}_i$ are the ground truth and reconstructed 3D face shape of the ith testing sample. NPDE measures the depth error at the jth vertex in a testing sample as $\texttt{NPDE}(x_j, y_j) = \left(|z_j^* - \hat{z}_j|\right) / \left(z_{max}^* - z_{min}^*\right)$, where z_{max}^* and z_{min}^* are the maximum and minimum depth values in the ground truth 3D shape of the testing sample, and z_j^* and $\hat{z}_j$ are the ground truth and reconstructed depth values at the jth vertex.

The face alignment accuracy is measured by Normalized Mean Error (NME). It is defined as the mean of the normalized estimation error of visible landmarks for all testing samples:

$$\texttt{NME} = \frac{1}{N_T} \sum_{i=1}^{N_T} \left(\frac{1}{d_i} \frac{1}{N_i^{\text{v}}} \sum_{j=1}^{l} \mathbf{v}_{ij} \| (\hat{u}_{ij}, \hat{v}_{ij}) - (u_{ij}^*, v_{ij}^*) \| \right), \tag{10}$$

where d_i is the square root of the face bounding box area of the ith testing sample, N_i^{v} is the number of visible landmarks in it, (u_{ij}^*, v_{ij}^*) and $(\hat{u}_{ij}, \hat{v}_{ij})$ are, respectively, the ground truth and estimated coordinates of its jth landmark.

4.2   3D Face Reconstruction Accuracy

Reconstruction accuracy across poses. Figure 4(a) shows the average MAE of our proposed method under different pose angles of the input 2D images.

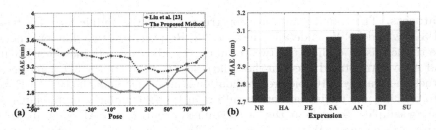

Fig. 4. MAE of the proposed method on BU3DFE (a) under different yaw angles and (b) under different expressions, i.e., neutral (NE), happy (HA), fear (FE), sad (SA), angry (AN), disgust (DI) and surprise (SU).

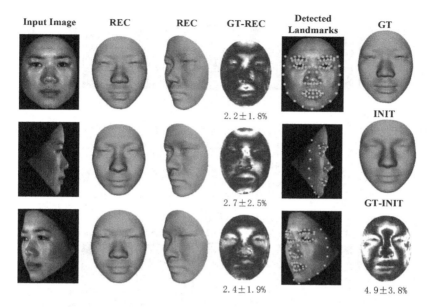

Input Image	REC	REC	GT-REC	Detected Landmarks	GT

2. 2±1. 8%   INIT

2. 7±2. 5%   GT-INIT

2. 4±1.9%   4. 9±3. 8%

Fig. 5. Reconstruction results for a BU3DFE subject at three different pose angles. Column one are input images. Columns 2 and 3 show the reconstructed ('REC') 3D faces from two views. Column 4 are the NPDE between the ground truth ('GT') and REC 3D faces. The detected landmarks are shown in Column 5. The last column shows the GT 3D face of this subject, the initial ('INIT') 3D face, and the NPDE between them. NPDE increases as the color changes from blue to red. The average and the standard deviation are given below each NPDE map. Note that the same INIT 3D face is used for all input images. (Color figure online)

To give a fair comparison with the method in [23], we only compute the reconstruction error of neutral testing images, after rotating the reconstructed 3D faces to frontal view. As can be seen, the average MAE of our method is lower than that of the baseline. Moreover, as the pose angle becomes large, the error does not increase substantially. This proves the effectiveness of the proposed method in handling arbitrary view face images. Figure 5 shows the reconstruction and face alignment results of one subject.

Reconstruction accuracy across expressions. Figure 4(b) shows the average MAE of our proposed method across expressions. Although the error increases as expressions become intensive, the maximum increment (i.e., SU vs. NE) is below 7%. This proves the robustness of the proposed method in normalizing expressions while maintaining model individualities. Figure 6 shows the reconstruction and face alignment results of a subject under seven expressions.

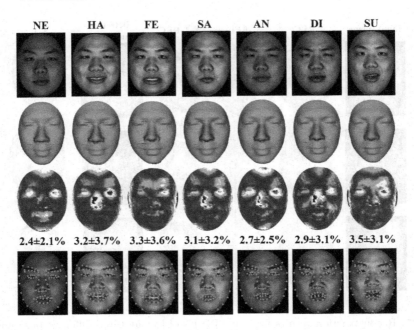

Fig. 6. Face alignment and reconstruction results for a BU3DFE subject with different expressions. Row 1 shows the input images. Row 2 shows the estimated 3D shapes, and Row 3 shows the NPDE maps with the average and standard deviation. The last row shows the detected landmarks.

4.3 Face Alignment Accuracy

As for the face alignment evaluation on AFW, we select two recent works as baseline methods: (1) CDM [37], the first method claimed to perform pose-free face alignment; (2) PIFA [18], a regression-type method that can predict the anatomically correct locations of landmarks for arbitrary view face images. We use the executable code of CDM and PIFA to compute their performance on our test set. The CDM code integrates face detection, and it successfully detects and aligns 268 out of 337 testing images. Therefore, to compare with CDM, we evaluate the NME on the 268 testing images. For PIFA and the proposed method, the face bounding boxes provided by [30] are used. One note is that the CDM detects 66 landmarks and PIFA detects 21 landmarks. For a fair comparison, we evaluate the NME on 18 landmarks that are the *intersection*s of the three landmark sets. As shown in Table 1, our accuracy is better than the two baseline methods. Figure 7 shows some face alignment results.

Table 1. NME of the proposed method and two baseline methods on AFW.

Method	CDM [37]	PIFA [18]	The proposed method
NME	7.52 %	5.60 %	3.15 %

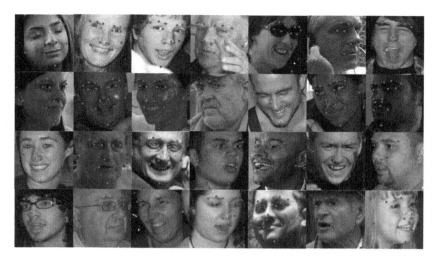

Fig. 7. Detected 18 landmarks for images in AFW by the proposed method.

4.4 Application to Face Recognition

While there are many recent face alignment and reconstruction work [1,15,21, 29,32,34], few work takes one step further to evaluate the contribution of alignment or reconstruction to subsequent tasks. In contrast, we quantitatively evaluate the effect of the reconstructed PEN 3D face shapes on face recognition by performing direct 3D to 3D shape matching and fuse it with conventional 2D face recognition. Specifically, we choose 70 subjects in BU3DFE to train the proposed regressors, and use the rest 30 subjects for testing. The neutral frontal face images of the testing subjects compose the gallery, and their faces under 19 poses and 7 expressions (totally 3,990 images) are the probe images. We use a commercial off-the-shelf (COTS) 2D face matcher[1] as the baseline. The iterative closest points (ICP) algorithm is applied to match the reconstructed normalized 3D face shapes. It aligns the 3D shapes reconstructed from probe and gallery images, and computes the distances between them, which are then converted to similarity scores via subtracting them from the maximum distance. These scores are finally normalized to the range of $[0, 1]$, and fused with the scores of the COTS matcher (which are within $[0, 1]$ also) by using a sum rule. The recognition result for a probe is defined as the subject whose gallery sample has the highest score with it. The recognition rate is then defined as the percentage of correctly recognized subjects. Figure 8 shows the recognition rates. It can be clearly seen that the reconstructed normalized 3D face shapes do help improve the face recognition accuracy, especially for face images of large pose angles and all types of expressions. Interestingly, despite the relatively robust 2D face recognition performance w.r.t. expressions, the fusion with 3D matching

---

[1] http://www.wisesoft.com.cn.

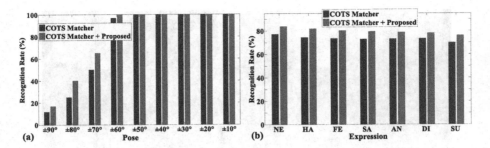

Fig. 8. Face recognition results of a COTS matcher and its fusion with proposed reconstructed 3D face based matcher under varying (a) poses and (b) expressions.

still improves the performance across all expressions – a strong testimony on the discriminative capability of the expression-normalized 3D face shape.

4.5   Computational Efficiency

According to our experiments on a PC with i7-4710 CPU and 8 GB memory, the Matlab implementation of the proposed method runs at ~ 26 FPS ($K = 5$ and $n = 9,677$). Hence, it can detect landmarks and reconstruct 3D face shape in real time.

5   Conclusions

In this paper, we present a novel regression based method for simultaneous face alignment and 3D face reconstruction for 2D images of arbitrary poses and expressions. It utilizes landmarks on a 2D face image as clues for reconstructing 3D shapes, and uses the reconstructed 3D shapes to refine landmarks. By alternately applying cascaded landmark regressors and 3D shape regressors, the proposed method can effectively accomplish the two tasks simultaneously in real time. Unlike existing 3D face reconstruction methods, the proposed method does not require additional face alignment methods, but can fully automatically reconstruct normalized 3D shapes from a single face image of arbitrary poses and expressions. Compared with existing face alignment methods, the proposed method can effectively handle invisible landmarks with the assistance of 3D face models. Extensive experiments with comparison to state-of-the-art methods demonstrate the effectiveness of the proposed method in both face alignment and 3D face shape reconstruction, and in facilitating face recognition as well.

Acknowledgement. All correspondences should be forwarded to Dr. Qijun Zhao via qjzhao@scu.edu.cn. This work is supported by the National Key Scientific Instrument and Equipment Development Projects of China (No. 2013YQ49087904).

References

1. Asthana, A., Zafeiriou, S., Tzimiropoulos, G., Cheng, S., Pantic, M.: From pixels to response maps: discriminative image filtering for face alignment in the wild. IEEE Trans. Pattern Anal. Mach. Intell. **37**(6), 1312–1320 (2015)
2. Blanz, V., Vetter, T.: A morphable model for the synthesis of 3D faces. In: SIGGRAPH, pp. 187–194. ACM Press/Addison-Wesley Publishing Co. (1999)
3. Blanz, V., Vetter, T.: Face recognition based on fitting a 3D morphable model. IEEE Trans. Pattern Anal. Mach. Intell. **25**(9), 1063–1074 (2003)
4. Cao, C., Weng, Y., Lin, S., Zhou, K.: 3D shape regression for real-time facial animation. Trans. Graph. (TOG) **32**(4), 41 (2013)
5. Cao, C., Wu, H., Weng, Y., Shao, T., Zhou, K.: Real-time facial animation with image-based dynamic avatars. ACM Trans. Graph. (TOG) **35**(4), 126 (2016)
6. Cao, X., Wei, Y., Wen, F., Sun, J.: Face alignment by explicit shape regression. Int. J. Comput. Vision **107**(2), 177–190 (2014)
7. Chu, B., Romdhani, S., Chen, L.: 3D-aided face recognition robust to expression and pose variations. In: CVPR, pp. 1907–1914. IEEE (2014)
8. Cootes, T.F., Edwards, G.J., Taylor, C.J.: Active appearance models. IEEE Trans. Pattern Anal. Mach. Intell. **6**, 681–685 (2001)
9. Cootes, T.F., Lanitis, A.: Active shape models: evaluation of a multi-resolution method for improving image search. In: BMVC, pp. 327–338. Citeseer (1994)
10. Cristinacce, D., Cootes, T.: Automatic feature localisation with constrained local models. Pattern Recogn. **41**(10), 3054–3067 (2008)
11. Cristinacce, D., Cootes, T.F.: Boosted regression active shape models. In: BMVC, pp. 1–10 (2007)
12. Drira, H., Ben Amor, B., Srivastava, A., Daoudi, M., Slama, R.: 3D face recognition under expressions, occlusions, and pose variations. IEEE Trans. Pattern Anal. Mach. Intell. **35**(9), 2270–2283 (2013)
13. Gong, X., Wang, G.: An automatic approach for pixel-wise correspondence between 3D faces. Hybrid Inf. Technol. **2**, 198–205 (2006)
14. Han, H., Jain, A.K.: 3D face texture modeling from uncalibrated frontal and profile images. In: BTAS, pp. 223–230. IEEE (2012)
15. Hassner, T.: Viewing real-world faces in 3D. In: ICCV, pp. 3607–3614 (2013)
16. Huang, G.B., Ramesh, M., Berg, T., Learned-Miller, E.: Labeled faces in the wild: A database for studying face recognition in unconstrained environments. Technical Report 07–49, University of Massachusetts, Amherst (2007)
17. Jeni, L.A., Cohn, J.F., Kanade, T.: Dense 3D face alignment from 2D videos in real-time. In: FG. IEEE (2015)
18. Jourabloo, A., Liu, X.: Pose-invariant 3D face alignment. In: ICCV, pp. 3694–3702 (2015)
19. Jourabloo, A., Liu, X.: Large-pose face alignment via CNN-based dense 3D model fitting. In: CVPR, June 2016
20. Kemelmacher-Shlizerman, I., Basri, R.: 3D face reconstruction from a single image using a single reference face shape. IEEE Trans. Pattern Anal. Mach. Intell. **33**(2), 394–405 (2011)
21. Lee, D., Park, H., Yoo, C.D.: Face alignment using cascade Gaussian process regression trees. In: CVPR, pp. 4204–4212. IEEE (2015)
22. Lee, Y.J., Lee, S.J., Park, K.R., Jo, J., Kim, J.: Single view-based 3D face reconstruction robust to self-occlusion. EURASIP J. Adv. Sig. Process. **2012**(1), 1–20 (2012)

23. Liu, F., Zeng, D., Li, J., Zhao, Q.: Cascaded regressor based 3D face reconstruction from a single arbitrary view image. arXiv preprint arXiv:1509.06161 (2015)
24. Lowe, D.G.: Distinctive image features from scale-invariant keypoints. Int. J. Comput. Vision **60**(2), 91–110 (2004)
25. Matthews, I., Baker, S.: Active appearance models revisited. Int. J. Comput. Vision **60**(2), 135–164 (2004)
26. Qu, C., Monari, E., Schuchert, T., Beyerer, J.: Fast, robust and automatic 3D face model reconstruction from videos. In: AVSS, pp. 113–118. IEEE (2014)
27. Ren, S., Cao, X., Wei, Y., Sun, J.: Face alignment at 3000 FPS via regressing local binary features. In: CVPR, pp. 1685–1692. IEEE (2014)
28. Romdhani, S., Vetter, T.: Estimating 3D shape and texture using pixel intensity, edges, specular highlights, texture constraints and a prior. In: CVPR, pp. 986–993. IEEE (2005)
29. Roth, J., Tong, Y., Liu, X.: Adaptive 3D face reconstruction from unconstrained photo collections. In: CVPR, June 2016
30. Sagonas, C., Tzimiropoulos, G., Zafeiriou, S., Pantic, M.: 300 faces in-the-wild challenge: the first facial landmark localization challenge. In: ICCVW, pp. 397–403. IEEE (2013)
31. Suwajanakorn, S., Kemelmacher-Shlizerman, I., Seitz, S.M.: Total moving face reconstruction. In: Fleet, D., Pajdla, T., Schiele, B., Tuytelaars, T. (eds.) ECCV 2014, Part IV. LNCS, vol. 8692, pp. 796–812. Springer, Heidelberg (2014)
32. Suwajanakorn, S., Seitz, S.M., Kemelmacher-Shlizerman, I.: What makes tom hanks look like tom hanks. In: ICCV, pp. 3952–3960 (2015)
33. Tulyakov, S., Sebe, N.: Regressing a 3D face shape from a single image. In: ICCV, pp. 3748–3755. IEEE (2015)
34. Tzimiropoulos, G.: Project-out cascaded regression with an application to face alignment. In: CVPR, pp. 3659–3667. IEEE (2015)
35. Xiong, X., De la Torre, F.: Supervised descent method and its applications to face alignment. In: CVPR, pp. 532–539. IEEE (2013)
36. Yin, L., Wei, X., Sun, Y., Wang, J., Rosato, M.J.: A 3D facial expression database for facial behavior research. In: FG, pp. 211–216. IEEE (2006)
37. Yu, X., Huang, J., Zhang, S., Yan, W., Metaxas, D.N.: Pose-free facial landmark fitting via optimized part mixtures and cascaded deformable shape model. In: ICCV, pp. 1944–1951. IEEE (2013)
38. Zhou, X., Leonardos, S., Hu, X., Daniilidis, K.: 3D shape estimation from 2D landmarks: a convex relaxation approach. In: CVPR, pp. 4447–4455. IEEE (2015)
39. Zhu, S., Li, C., Loy, C.C., Tang, X.: Face alignment by coarse-to-fine shape searching. In: CVPR, pp. 4998–5006 (2015)
40. Zhu, X., Ramanan, D.: Face detection, pose estimation, and landmark localization in the wild. In: CVPR, pp. 2879–2886. IEEE (2012)
41. Zhu, X., Lei, Z., Liu, X., Shi, H., Li, S.Z.: Face alignment across large poses: a 3D solution. In: CVPR, June 2016
42. Zhu, X., Lei, Z., Yan, J., Yi, D., Li, S.Z.: High-fidelity pose and expression normalization for face recognition in the wild. In: CVPR, pp. 787–796. IEEE (2015)

Keep It SMPL: Automatic Estimation of 3D Human Pose and Shape from a Single Image

Federica Bogo[2]([✉]), Angjoo Kanazawa[3], Christoph Lassner[1,4], Peter Gehler[1,4], Javier Romero[1], and Michael J. Black[1]

[1] Max Planck Institute for Intelligent Systems, Tübingen, Germany
{christoph.lassner,pgehler,jromero,black}@tue.mpg.de
[2] Microsoft Research, Cambridge, UK
febogo@microsoft.com
[3] University of Maryland, College Park, USA
kanazawa@umiacs.umd.edu
[4] University of Tübingen, Tübingen, Germany

Abstract. We describe the first method to automatically estimate the 3D pose of the human body as well as its 3D shape from a single unconstrained image. We estimate a full 3D mesh and show that 2D joints alone carry a surprising amount of information about body shape. The problem is challenging because of the complexity of the human body, articulation, occlusion, clothing, lighting, and the inherent ambiguity in inferring 3D from 2D. To solve this, we first use a recently published CNN-based method, DeepCut, to predict (bottom-up) the 2D body joint locations. We then fit (top-down) a recently published statistical body shape model, called SMPL, to the 2D joints. We do so by minimizing an objective function that penalizes the error between the projected 3D model joints and detected 2D joints. Because SMPL captures correlations in human shape across the population, we are able to robustly fit it to very little data. We further leverage the 3D model to prevent solutions that cause interpenetration. We evaluate our method, SMPLify, on the Leeds Sports, HumanEva, and Human3.6M datasets, showing superior pose accuracy with respect to the state of the art.

Keywords: 3D body shape · Human pose · 2D to 3D · CNN

1 Introduction

The estimation of 3D human pose from a single image is a longstanding problem with many applications. Most previous approaches focus only on pose and ignore 3D human shape. Here we provide a solution that is *fully automatic* and estimates a 3D mesh capturing both pose and shape from a 2D image. We solve the problem in two steps. First we estimate 2D joints using a recently proposed convolutional

---

F. Bogo and A. Kanazawa—The first two authors contributed equally to this work. The work was performed at the MPI for Intelligent Systems.

B. Leibe et al. (Eds.): ECCV 2016, Part V, LNCS 9909, pp. 561–578, 2016.
DOI: 10.1007/978-3-319-46454-1_34

neural network (CNN) called DeepCut [36]. So far CNNs have been successful at estimating 2D human pose [20,34–36,51] but not 3D pose and shape from one image. Consequently we add a second step, which estimates 3D pose and shape from the 2D joints using a 3D generative model called SMPL [30]. The overall framework, which we call "SMPLify", fits within a classical paradigm of bottom up estimation (CNN) followed by top down verification (generative model). A few examples are shown in Fig. 1.

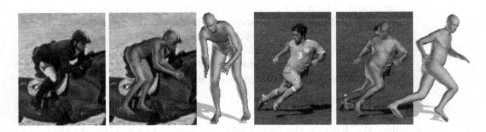

Fig. 1. Example results. 3D pose and shape estimated by our method for two images from the Leeds Sports Pose Dataset [22]. We show the original image (left), our fitted model (middle), and the 3D model rendered from a different viewpoint (right).

There is a long literature on estimating 3D pose from 2D joints. Unlike previous methods, our approach exploits a high-quality 3D human body model that is trained from thousands of 3D scans and hence captures the statistics of shape variation in the population as well as how people deform with pose. Here we use the SMPL body model [30]. The key insight is that such a model can be fit to very little data because it captures so much information of human body shape.

We define an objective function and optimize pose and shape directly, so that the projected joints of the 3D model are close to the 2D joints estimated by the CNN. Remarkably, fitting only 2D joints produces plausible estimates of 3D body *shape*. We perform a quantitative evaluation using synthetic data and find that 2D joint locations contain a surprising amount of 3D shape information.

In addition to capturing shape statistics, there is a second advantage to using a generative 3D model: it enables us to reason about interpenetration. Most previous work in the area has estimated 3D stick figures from 2D joints. With such models, it is easy to find poses that are impossible because the body parts would intersect in 3D. Such solutions are very common when inferring 3D from 2D because the loss of depth information makes the solution ambiguous.

Computing interpenetration of a complex, non-convex, articulated object like the body, however, is expensive. Unlike previous work [14,15], we provide an interpenetration term that is differentiable with respect to body shape and pose. Given a 3D body shape we define a set of "capsules" that approximates the body shape. Crucially, capsule dimensions are linearly regressed from model shape parameters. This representation lets us compute interpenetration efficiently. We show that this term helps to prevent incorrect poses.

SMPL is gender-specific; i.e. it distinguishes the shape space of females and males. To make our method fully automatic, we introduce a gender-neutral model. If we do not know the gender, we fit this model to images. If we know the gender, then we use a gender-specific model for better results.

To deal with pose ambiguity, it is important to have a good pose prior. Many recent methods learn sparse, over-complete dictionaries from the CMU dataset [3] or learn dataset-specific priors. We train a prior over pose from SMPL models that have been fit to the CMU mocap *marker* data [3] using MoSh [29]. This factors shape from pose with pose represented as relative rotations of the body parts. We then learn a generic multi-modal pose prior from this.

We compare the method to recently published methods [4,39,58] using the exact same 2D joints as input. We show the robustness of the approach qualitatively on images from the challenging Leeds Sports Pose Dataset (LSP) [22] (Fig. 1). We quantitatively compare the method on HumanEva-I [41] and Human3.6M [18], finding that our method is more accurate than previous methods.

In summary our contributions are: (1) the first fully automatic method of estimating 3D body shape and pose from 2D joints; (2) an interpenetration term that is differentiable with respect to shape and pose; (3) a novel objective function that matches a 3D body model to 2D joints; (4) for research purposes, we provide the code, 2D joints, and 3D models for all examples in the paper [1].

2 Related Work

The recovery of 3D human pose from 2D is fundamentally ambiguous and all methods deal with this ambiguity in different ways. These include user intervention, using rich image features, improving the optimization methods, and, most commonly, introducing prior knowledge. This prior knowledge typically includes both a "shape" prior that enforces anthropometric constraints on bone lengths and a "pose" prior that favors plausible poses and rules out impossible ones. While there is a large literature on estimating body pose and shape from multi-camera images or video sequences [6,13,19,45], here we focus on static image methods. We also focus on methods that do not require a background image for background subtraction, but rather infer 3D pose from 2D joints.

Most methods formulate the problem as finding a 3D *skeleton* such that its 3D joints project to known or estimated 2D joints. Note that the previous work often refers to this skeleton in a particular posture as a "shape". In this work we take shape to mean the pose-invariant surface of the human body in 3D and distinguish this from pose, which is the articulated posture of the limbs.

3D pose from 2D joints. These methods all assume known correspondence between 2D joints and a 3D skeleton. Methods make different assumptions about the statistics of limb-length variation. Lee and Chen [26] assume known limb lengths of a stick figure while Taylor [48] assumes the ratios of limb lengths are known. Parameswaran and Chellappa [33] assume that limb lengths are isometric across people, varying only in global scaling. Barron and Kakadiaris [7] build

a statistical model of limb-length variation from extremes taken from anthropometric tables. Jiang [21] takes a non-parametric approach, treating poses in the
CMU dataset [3] as exemplars.

Recent methods typically use the CMU dataset and learn a statistical model
of limb lengths and poses from it. For example, both [11,39] learn a dictionary
of poses but use a fairly weak anthropometric model on limb lengths. Akhter
and Black [4] take a similar approach but add a novel pose prior that captures
pose-dependent joint angle limits. Zhou et al. [58] also learn a shape dictionary
but they create a sparse basis that also captures how these poses appear from
different camera views. They show that the resulting optimization problem is
easier to solve. Pons-Moll et al. [37] take a different approach: they estimate
qualitative "posebits" from mocap and relate these to 3D pose.

The above approaches have weak, or non-existent, models of human shape. In
contrast, we argue that a stronger model of body shape, learned from thousands
of people, captures the anthropometric constraints of the population. Such a
model helps reduce ambiguity, making the problem easier. Also, because we
have 3D shape, we can model interpenetration, avoiding impossible poses.

3D pose and shape. There is also work on estimating 3D body shape from
single images. This work often assumes good silhouettes are available. Sigal et
al. [42] assume that silhouettes are given, compute shape features from them,
and then use a mixture of experts to predict 3D body pose and shape from
the features. Like us they view the problem as a combination of a bottom-up
discriminative method and a top-down generative method. In their case the
generative model (SCAPE [5]) is fit to the image silhouettes. Their claim that
the method is fully automatic is only true if silhouettes are available, which is
often not the case. They show a limited set of results using perfect silhouettes
and do not evaluate pose accuracy.

Guan et al. [14,15] take manually marked 2D joints and first estimate the
3D pose of a stick figure using classical methods [26,48]. They use the pose
of this stick figure to pose a SCAPE model, project the model into the image
and use this to segment the image with GrabCut [40]. They then fit the SCAPE
shape and pose to a variety of features including the silhouette, image edges, and
shading cues. They assume the camera focal length is known or approximated,
the lighting is roughly initialized, and that the height of the person is known.
They use an interpenetration term that models each body part by its convex hull.
They then check each of the extremities to see how many other body points fall
inside it and define a penalty function that penalizes interpenetration. This does
not admit easy optimization.

In similar work, Hasler et al. [16] fit a parametric body model to silhouettes.
Typically, they require a known segmentation and a few manually provided correspondences. In cases with simple backgrounds, they use four clicked points
on the hands and feet to establish a rough fit and then use GrabCut to segment the person. They demonstrate this on one image. Zhou et al. [57] also fit
a parametric model of body shape and pose to a cleanly segmented silhouette
using significant manual intervention. Chen et al. [9] fit a parametric model of

body shape and pose to manually extracted silhouettes; they do not evaluate quantitative accuracy.

To our knowledge, no previous method estimates *3D body shape* and pose directly from only *2D joints*. A priori, it may seem impossible, but given a good statistical model, our approach works surprisingly well. This is enabled by our use of SMPL [30], which unlike SCAPE, has explicit 3D joints; we fit their projection directly to 2D joints. SMPL defines how joint locations are related to the 3D surface of the body, enabling inference of shape from joints. Of course this will not be perfect as a person can have the exact same limb lengths with varying weight. SMPL, however, does not represent anatomical joints, rather it represents them as a function of the surface vertices. This couples joints and shape during model training and means that solving for them together is important.

Making it automatic. None of the methods above are automatic, most assume known correspondences, and some involve significant manual intervention. There are, however, a few methods that try to solve the entire problem of inferring 3D pose from a single image.

Simo-Serra et al. [43, 44] take into account that 2D part detections are unreliable and formulate a probabilistic model that estimates the 3D pose and the matches to the 2D image features together. Wang et al. [52] use a weak model of limb lengths [26] but exploit automatically detected joints in the image and match to them robustly using an L1 distance. They use a sparse basis to represent poses as in other methods.

Zhou et al. [56] run a 2D pose detector [54] and then optimize 3D pose, automatically rejecting outliers. Akhter and Black [4] run a different 2D detector [23] and show results for their method on a few images. Both methods are only evaluated qualitatively. Yasin et al. [55] take a non-parametric approach in which the detected 2D joints are used to look up the nearest 3D poses in a mocap dataset. Kostrikov and Gall [24] combine regression forests and a 3D pictorial model to regress 3D joints. Ionescu et al. [17] train a method to predict 3D pose from images by first predicting body part labels; their results on Human3.6M are good but they do not test on complex images where background segmentation is not available. Kulkarni et al. [25] use a generative model of body shape and pose, together with a probabilistic programming framework to estimate body pose from single images. They deal with visually simple images, where the person is well centered and cropped, and do not evaluate 3D pose accuracy.

Recent advances in deep learning are producing methods for estimating 2D joint positions accurately [36, 53]. We use the recent DeepCut method [36], which gives remarkably good 2D detections. Recent work [59] uses a CNN to estimate 2D joint locations and then fit 3D pose to these using a monocular video sequence. They do not show results for single images.

None of these automated methods estimate 3D body shape. Here we demonstrate a complete system that uses 2D joint detections and fits pose and shape to them from a single image.

3   Method

Figure 2 shows an overview of our system. We take a single input image, and use the DeepCut CNN [36] to predict 2D body joints, J_{est}. For each 2D joint i the CNN provides a confidence value, w_i. We then fit a 3D body model such that the projected joints of the model minimize a robust weighted error term. In this work we use a skinned vertex-based model, SMPL [30], and call the system that takes a 2D image and produces a posed 3D mesh, *SMPLify*.

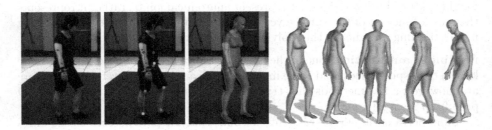

Fig. 2. System overview. Left to right: Given a single image, we use a CNN-based method to predict 2D joint locations (hot colors denote high confidence). We then fit a 3D body model to this, to estimate 3D body shape and pose. Here we show a fit on HumanEva [41], projected into the image and shown from different viewpoints. (Color figure online)

The body model is defined as a function $M(\beta, \theta, \gamma)$, parameterized by shape β, pose θ, and translation γ. The output of the function is a triangulated surface, $\mathcal{M}$, with 6890 vertices. Shape parameters β are coefficients of a low-dimensional shape space, learned from a training set of thousands of registered scans. Here we use one of three shape models: male, female, and gender-neutral. SMPL defines only male and female models. For a fully automatic method, we trained a new gender-neutral model using the approximately 2000 male and 2000 female body shapes used to train the gendered SMPL models. If the gender is known, we use the appropriate model. The model used is indicated by its color: pink for gender-specific and light blue for gender-neutral.

The pose of the body is defined by a skeleton rig with 23 joints; pose parameters θ represent the axis-angle representation of the relative rotation between parts. Let $J(\beta)$ be the function that predicts 3D skeleton joint locations from body shape. In SMPL, joints are a sparse linear combination of surface vertices or, equivalently, a function of the shape coefficients. Joints can be put in arbitrary poses by applying a global rigid transformation. In the following, we denote posed 3D joints as $R_\theta(J(\beta)_i)$, for joint i, where R_θ is the global rigid transformation induced by pose θ. SMPL defines pose-dependent deformations; for the gender-neutral shape model, we use the female deformations, which are general enough in practice. Note that the SMPL model and DeepCut skeleton have slightly different joints. We associate DeepCut joints with the most similar SMPL joints. To project SMPL joints into the image we use a perspective camera model, defined by parameters K.

3.1   Approximating Bodies with Capsules

We find that previous methods produce 3D poses that are impossible due to interpenetration between body parts. An advantage of our 3D shape model is that it allows us to detect and prevent this. Computing interpenetration however is expensive for complex, non-convex, surfaces like the body. In graphics it is common to use proxy geometries to compute collisions efficiently [10,50]. We follow this approach and approximate the body surface as a set of "capsules" (Fig. 3). Each capsule has a radius and an axis length.

We train a regressor from model shape parameters to capsule parameters (axis length and radius), and pose the capsules according to R_θ, the rotation induced by the kinematic chain. Specifically, we first fit 20 capsules, one per body part, excluding fingers and toes, to the body surface of the unposed training body shapes used to learn SMPL [30]. Starting from capsules manually attached to body joints in the template, we perform gradient-based optimization of their radii and axis lengths to minimize the bidirectional distance between capsules and body surface. We then learn a linear regressor from body shape coefficients, $\boldsymbol{\beta}$, to the capsules' radii and axis lengths using cross-validated ridge regression. Once the regressor is trained, the procedure is iterated once more, initializing the capsules with the regressor output. While previous work uses approximations to detect interpenetrations [38,46], we believe this regression from shape parameters is novel.

Fig. 3. Body shape approximation with capsules. Shown for two subjects. Left to right: original shape, shape approximated with capsules, capsules reposed. Yellow point clouds represent actual vertices of the model that is approximated.

3.2   Objective Function

To fit the 3D pose and shape to the CNN-detected 2D joints, we minimize an objective function that is the sum of five error terms: a joint-based data term, three pose priors, and a shape prior; that is $E(\boldsymbol{\beta}, \boldsymbol{\theta}) =$

$$E_J(\boldsymbol{\beta}, \boldsymbol{\theta}; K, J_{\text{est}}) + \lambda_\theta E_\theta(\boldsymbol{\theta}) + \lambda_a E_a(\boldsymbol{\theta}) + \lambda_{sp} E_{sp}(\boldsymbol{\theta}; \boldsymbol{\beta}) + \lambda_\beta E_\beta(\boldsymbol{\beta}) \qquad (1)$$

where K are camera parameters and λ_θ, λ_a, λ_{sp} λ_β are scalar weights.

Our joint-based data term penalizes the weighted 2D distance between estimated joints, J_{est}, and corresponding projected SMPL joints:

$$E_J(\boldsymbol{\beta}, \boldsymbol{\theta}; K, J_{\text{est}}) = \sum_{\text{joint } i} w_i \rho(\Pi_K(R_\theta(J(\boldsymbol{\beta})_i)) - J_{\text{est},i}) \qquad (2)$$

where Π_K is the projection from 3D to 2D induced by a camera with parameters K. We weight the contribution of each joint by the confidence of its estimate, w_i, provided by the CNN. For occluded joints, this value is usually low; pose in this case is driven by our pose priors. To deal with noisy estimates, we use a robust differentiable Geman-McClure penalty function, ρ, [12].

We introduce a pose prior penalizing elbows and knees that bend unnaturally:

$$E_a(\boldsymbol{\theta}) = \sum_i \exp(\boldsymbol{\theta}_i), \qquad (3)$$

where i sums over pose parameters (rotations) corresponding to the bending of knees and elbows. The exponential strongly penalizes rotations violating natural constraints (e.g. elbow and knee hyperextending). Note that when the joint is not bent, θ_i is zero. Negative bending is natural and is not penalized heavily while positive bending is unnatural and is penalized more.

Most methods for 3D pose estimation use some sort of pose prior to favor probable poses over improbable ones. Like many previous methods we train our pose prior using the CMU dataset [3]. Given that poses vary significantly, it is important to represent the multi-modal nature of the data, yet also keep the prior computationally tractable. To build a prior, we use poses obtained by fitting SMPL to the CMU marker data using MoSh [29]. We then fit a mixture of Gaussians to approximately 1 million poses, spanning 100 subjects. Using the mixture model directly in our optimization framework is problematic computationally because we need to optimize the negative logarithm of a sum. As described in [32], we approximate the sum in the mixture of Gaussians by a max operator:

$$E_\theta(\boldsymbol{\theta}) \equiv -\log \sum_j (g_j \mathcal{N}(\boldsymbol{\theta}; \boldsymbol{\mu}_{\theta,j}, \Sigma_{\theta,j})) \approx -\log(\max_j(cg_j\mathcal{N}(\boldsymbol{\theta}; \boldsymbol{\mu}_{\theta,j}, \Sigma_{\theta,j}))) \quad (4)$$

$$= \min_j (-\log(cg_j\mathcal{N}(\boldsymbol{\theta}; \boldsymbol{\mu}_{\theta,j}, \Sigma_{\theta,j}))) \quad (5)$$

where g_j are the mixture model weights of $N = 8$ Gaussians, and c a positive constant required by our solver implementation. Although E_θ is not differentiable at points where the mode with minimum energy changes, we approximate its Jacobian by the Jacobian of the mode with minimum energy in the current optimization step.

We define an interpenetration error term that exploits the capsule approximation introduced in Sect. 3.1. We relate the error term to the intersection volume between "incompatible" capsules (i.e. capsules that do not intersect in natural poses). Since the volume of capsule intersections is not simple to compute, we further simplify our capsules into spheres with centers $C(\boldsymbol{\theta}, \boldsymbol{\beta})$ along the capsule axis and radius $r(\boldsymbol{\beta})$ corresponding to the capsule radius. Our penalty term is inspired by the mixture of 3D Gaussians model in [47]. We consider a 3D isotropic Gaussian with $\sigma(\boldsymbol{\beta}) = \frac{r(\boldsymbol{\beta})}{3}$ for each sphere, and define the penalty as a scaled version of the integral of the product of Gaussians corresponding to "incompatible" parts

$$E_{sp}(\boldsymbol{\theta}; \boldsymbol{\beta}) = \sum_i \sum_{j \in I(i)} \exp \left(\frac{\|C_i(\boldsymbol{\theta}, \boldsymbol{\beta}) - C_j(\boldsymbol{\theta}, \boldsymbol{\beta})\|^2}{\sigma_i^2(\boldsymbol{\beta}) + \sigma_j^2(\boldsymbol{\beta})} \right) \tag{6}$$

where the summation is over all spheres i and $I(i)$ are the spheres incompatible with i. Note that the term penalizes, but does not strictly avoid, interpenetrations. As desired, however, this term is differentiable with respect to pose and shape. Note also that we do not use this term in optimizing shape since this would bias the body shape to be thin to avoid interpenetration.

We use a shape prior $E_\beta(\boldsymbol{\beta})$, defined as

$$E_\beta(\boldsymbol{\beta}) = \boldsymbol{\beta}^T \Sigma_\beta^{-1} \boldsymbol{\beta} \tag{7}$$

where Σ_β^{-1} is a diagonal matrix with the squared singular values estimated via Principal Component Analysis from the shapes in the SMPL training set. Note that the shape coefficients $\boldsymbol{\beta}$ are zero-mean by construction.

3.3   Optimization

We assume that camera translation and body orientation are unknown; we require, however, that the camera focal length or its rough estimate is known. We initialize the camera translation (equivalently $\boldsymbol{\gamma}$) by assuming that the person is standing parallel to the image plane. Specifically, we estimate the depth via the ratio of similar triangles, defined by the torso length of the mean SMPL shape and the predicted 2D joints. Since this assumption is not always true, we further refine this estimate by minimizing E_J over the torso joints alone with respect to camera translation and body orientation; we keep $\boldsymbol{\beta}$ fixed to the mean shape during this optimization. We do not optimize focal length, since the problem is too unconstrained to optimize it together with translation.

After estimating camera translation, we fit our model by minimizing Eq. (1) in a staged approach. We observed that starting with a high value for λ_θ and λ_β and gradually decreasing them in the subsequent optimization stages is effective for avoiding local minima.

When the subject is captured in a side view, assessing in which direction the body is facing might be ambiguous. To address this, we try two initializations when the 2D distance between the CNN-estimated 2D shoulder joints is below a threshold: first with body orientation estimated as above and then with that orientation rotated by 180 degrees. Finally we pick the fit with lowest E_J.

We minimize Eq. (1) using Powell's dogleg method [31], using OpenDR and Chumpy [2,28]. Optimization for a single image takes less than 1 min on a common desktop machine.

4   Evaluation

We evaluate the accuracy of both 3D pose and 3D shape estimation. For quantitative evaluation of 3D pose, we use two publicly available datasets: HumanEva-I [41] and Human3.6M [18]. We compare our approach to three state-of-the-art methods [4,39,58] and also use these data for an ablation analysis. Both of the ground truth datasets have restricted laboratory environments and limited poses. Consequently, we perform a qualitative analysis on more challenging data from the Leeds Sports Dataset (LSP) [22]. Evaluating shape quantitatively is harder since there are few images with ground truth 3D shape. Therefore, we perform a quantitative evaluation using synthetic data to evaluate how well shape can be recovered from 2D joints corrupted by noise. For all experiments, we use 10 body shape coefficients. We tune the λ_i weights in Eq. (1) on the HumanEva training data and use these values for all experiments.

4.1   Quantitative Evaluation: Synthetic Data

We sample synthetic bodies from the SMPL shape and pose space and project their joints into the image with a known camera. We generate 1000 images for male shapes and 1000 for female shapes, at 640×480 resolution.

In the first experiment, we add varying amounts of i.i.d. Gaussian noise (standard deviation (std) from 1 to 5 pixels) to each 2D joint. We solve for pose and shape by minimizing Eq. (1), setting the confidence weights for the joints in Eq. (2) to 1. Figure 4 (left) shows the mean vertex-to-vertex Euclidean error between the estimated and true shape in a canonical pose. Here we fit gender-specific models. The results of shape estimation are more accurate than simply guessing the average shape (red lines in the figure). This shows that joints carry information about body shape that is relatively robust to noise.

In the second experiment, we assume that the pose is known, and try to understand how many joints one needs to accurately estimate body shape. We fit SMPL to ground-truth 2D joints by minimizing Eq. (2) with respect to: the full set of 23 SMPL joints; the subset of 12 joints corresponding to torso and limbs (excluding head, spine, hands and feet); and the 4 joints of the torso. As above, we measure the mean Euclidean error between the estimated and true shape in a canonical pose. Results are shown in Fig. 4 (right). The more joints we have, the better body shape is estimated. To our knowledge, this is the first demonstration of estimating 3D body shape from only 2D joints. Of course some joints may be difficult to estimate reliably; we evaluate on real data below.

4.2   Quantitative Evaluation: Real Data

HumanEva-I. We evaluate pose estimation accuracy on single frames from the HumanEva dataset [41]. Following the standard procedure, we evaluate on the Walking and Box sequences of subjects 1, 2, and 3 from the "validation" set [8,49]. We assume the gender is known and apply the gender-specific SMPL models.

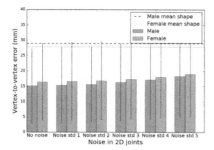 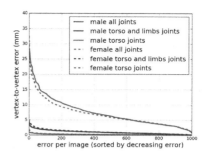

Fig. 4. Evaluation on synthetic data. Left: Mean vertex-to-vertex Euclidean error between the estimated and true shape in a canonical pose, when Gaussian noise is added to 2D joints. Dashed and dotted lines represent the error obtained by guessing the mean shape for males and females, respectively. Right: Error between estimated and true shape when considering only a subset of joints during fitting.

Many methods train sequence-specific pose priors for HumanEva; we do not do this. We do, however, tune our weights on HumanEva training set and learn a mapping from the SMPL joints to the 3D skeletal representation of HumanEva. To that end we fit the SMPL model to the raw mocap marker data in the training set using MoSh to estimate body shape and pose. We then train a linear regressor from body vertices (equivalently shape parameters β) to the HumanEva 3D joints. This is done once on training data for all subjects together and kept fixed. We use the regressed 3D joints as our output for evaluation.

We compare our method against three state-of-the-art methods [4,39,58], which, like us, predict 3D pose from 2D joints. We report the average Euclidean distance between the ground-truth and predicted 3D joint positions. Before computing the error we apply a similarity transform to align the reconstructed 3D joints to a common frame via the Procrustes analysis on every frame. Input to all methods is the same: 2D joints detected by DeepCut [36]. Recall that DeepCut has not been trained on either dataset used for quantitative evaluation. Note that these approaches have different skeletal structures of 3D joints. We evaluate on the subset of 14 joints that semantically correspond across all representations. For this dataset we use the ground truth focal length.

Table 1 shows quantitative results where SMPLify achieves the lowest errors on all sequences. While the recent method of Zhou et al. [58] is very good, we argue that our approach is conceptually simpler and more accurate. We simply fit the body model to the 2D data and let the model constrain the solution. Not only does this "lift" the 2D joints to 3D, but SMPLify also produces a skinned vertex-based model that can be immediately used in a variety of applications.

To gain insight about the method, we perform an ablation study (Table 2) where we evaluate different pose priors and the interpenetration penalty term. First we replace the mixture-model-based pose prior with $E_{\theta'}$, which uses a single Gaussian trained from the same data. This significantly degrades performance. Next we add the interpenetration term, but this does not have a significant

Table 1. HumanEva-I results. 3D joint errors in mm.

Method:	Walking			Boxing			Mean	Median
	S1	S2	S3	S1	S2	S3		
Akhter and Black [4]	186.1	197.8	209.4	165.5	196.5	208.4	194.4	171.2
Ramakrishna et al. [39]	161.8	182.0	188.6	151.0	170.4	158.3	168.4	145.9
Zhou et al. [58]	100.0	98.89	123.1	112.5	118.6	110.0	110.0	98.9
SMPLify	**73.3**	**59.0**	**99.4**	**82.1**	**79.2**	**87.2**	**79.9**	**61.9**

impact on the 3D joint error. However, qualitatively, we find that it makes a difference in more complex datasets with varied poses and viewing angles as illustrated in Fig. 5.

Human3.6M. We perform the same analysis on the Human 3.6M dataset [18], which has a wider range of poses. Following [27,49,59], we report results on sequences of subjects S9 and S11. We evaluate on five different action sequences captured from the frontal camera ("cam3") from trial 1. These sequences consist of 2000 frames on average and we evaluate on all frames *individually.* As above, we use training mocap and MoSh to train a regressor from the SMPL body shape to the 3D joint representation used in the dataset. Other than this we do not use the training set in any manner. We assume that the focal length as well as the

Fig. 5. Interpenetration error term. Examples where the interpenetration term avoids unnatural poses. For each example we show, from left to right, CNN estimated joints, and the result of the optimization *without* and *with* interpenetration error term.

Table 2. HumanEva-I ablation study. 3D joint errors in mm. The first row drops the interpenetration term and replaces the pose prior with a uni-modal prior. The second row keeps the uni-modal pose prior but adds the interpenetration penalty. The third row shows the proposed SMPLify model.

Method:	Walking			Boxing			Mean	Median
	S1	S2	S3	S1	S2	S3		
$E_\beta + E_J + E_{\theta'}$	98.4	79.6	117.8	105.9	98.5	122.5	104.1	82.3
$E_\beta + E_J + E_{\theta'} + E_{sp}$	97.9	79.4	116.0	105.8	98.5	122.3	103.7	82.3
SMPLify	**73.3**	**59.0**	**99.4**	**82.1**	**79.2**	**87.2**	**79.9**	**61.9**

Table 3. Human 3.6M. 3D joint errors in mm.

	Directions	Discussion	Eating	Greeting	Phoning	Photo	Posing	Purchases	Sit
Akhter and Black [4]	199.2	177.6	161.8	197.8	176.2	186.5	195.4	167.3	160.7
Ramakrishna et al. [39]	137.4	149.3	141.6	154.3	157.7	158.9	141.8	158.1	168.6
Zhou et al. [58]	99.7	95.8	87.9	116.8	108.3	107.3	93.5	95.3	109.1
SMPLify	**62.0**	**60.2**	**67.8**	**76.5**	**92.1**	**77.0**	**73.0**	**75.3**	**100.3**
	SitDown	Smoking	Waiting	WalkDog	Walk	WalkTogether		Mean	Median
Akhter and Black [4]	173.7	177.8	181.9	176.2	198.6	192.7		181.1	158.1
Ramakrishna et al. [39]	175.6	160.4	161.7	150.0	174.8	150.2		157.3	136.8
Zhou et al. [58]	137.5	106.0	102.2	106.5	110.4	115.2		106.7	90.0
SMPLify	**137.3**	**83.4**	**77.3**	**79.7**	**86.8**	**81.7**		**82.3**	**69.3**

Fig. 6. Leeds Sports Dataset. Each sub-image shows the original image with the 2D joints fit by the CNN. To the right of that is our estimated 3D pose and shape and the model seen from another view. The top row shows examples using the gender-neutral body model; the bottom row show fits using the gender-specific models.

distortion coefficients are known since the subjects are closer to the borders of the image. Evaluation on Human3.6 M is shown in Table 3 where our method again achieves the lowest average 3D error. While not directly comparable, Ionescu et al. [17] report an error of 92 mm on this dataset.

Fig. 7. LSP Failure cases. Some representative failure cases: misplaced limbs, limbs matched with the limbs of other people, depth ambiguities.

4.3   Qualitative Evaluation

Here we apply SMPLify to images from the Leeds Sports Pose (LSP) dataset [22]. These are much more complex in terms of pose, image resolution, clothing, illumination, and background than HumanEva or Human3.6M. The CNN, however, still does a good job of estimating the 2D poses. We only show results on the LSP test set. Figure 6 shows several representative examples where the system works well. The figure shows results with both gender-neutral and gender-specific SMPL models; the choice has little visual effect on pose. For the gender-specific models, we manually label the images according to gender.

Figure 8 visually compares the results of the different methods on a few images from each of the datasets. The other methods suffer from not having a strong model of how limb lengths are correlated. LSP contains complex poses and these often show the value of the interpenetration term. Figure 5 shows two illustrative examples. Figure 7 shows a few failure cases on LSP. Some of these result from CNN failures where limbs are mis-detected or are matched with those of other people. Other failures are due to challenging depth ambiguities. See Supplementary Material [1] for more results.

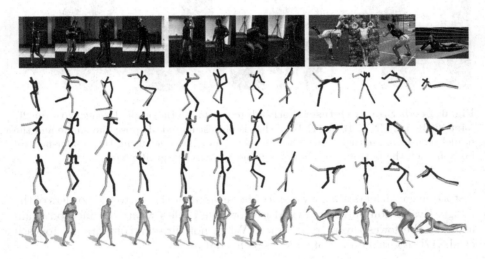

Fig. 8. Qualitative comparison. From top to bottom: Input image. Akhter and Black [4]. Ramakrishna et al. [39]. Zhou et al. [58]. SMPLify.

5   Conclusions

We have presented SMPLify, a fully automated method for estimating 3D body shape and pose from 2D joints in single images. SMPLify uses a CNN to estimate 2D joint locations, and then fits a 3D human body model to these joints. We use the recently proposed SMPL body model, which captures correlations in body shape, highly constraining the fitting process. We exploit this to define an objective function and optimize pose and shape directly by minimizing the error between the projected joints of the model and the estimated 2D joints. This gives a simple, yet very effective, solution to estimate 3D pose and approximate shape.

The resulting model can be immediately posed and animated. We extensively evaluate our method on various datasets and find that SMPLify outperforms state-of-the-art methods.

Our formulation opens many directions for future work. In particular, body shape and pose can benefit from other cues such as silhouettes and we plan to extend the method to use multiple camera views and multiple frames. Additionally a facial pose detector would improve head pose estimation and automatic gender detection would allow the use of the appropriate gender-specific model. It would be useful to train CNNs to predict more than 2D joints, such as features related directly to 3D shape. Our method provides approximate 3D meshes in correspondence with images, which could be useful for such training. The method can be extended to deal with multiple people in an image; having 3D meshes should help with reasoning about occlusion.

Acknowledgements. We thank M. Al Borno for inspiring the capsule representation, N. Mahmood for help with the figures, I. Akhter for helpful discussions.

References

1. http://smplify.is.tue.mpg.de
2. http://chumpy.org
3. http://mocap.cs.cmu.edu
4. Akhter, I., Black, M.J.: Pose-conditioned joint angle limits for 3D human pose reconstruction. In: IEEE Conference on Computer Vision and Pattern Recognition, CVPR, pp. 1446–1455 (2015)
5. Anguelov, D., Srinivasan, P., Koller, D., Thrun, S., Rodgers, J., Davis, J.: SCAPE: shape completion and animation of people. ACM Trans. Graph. (TOG) - Proc. ACM SIGGRAPH **24**(3), 408–416 (2005)
6. Balan, A.O., Sigal, L., Black, M.J., Davis, J.E., Haussecker, H.W.: Detailed human shape and pose from images. In: IEEE Conference on Computer Vision and Pattern Recognition, CVPR, pp. 1–8 (2007)
7. Barron, C., Kakadiaris, I.: Estimating anthropometry and pose from a single uncalibrated image. Comput. Vis. Image Underst. CVIU **81**(3), 269–284 (2001)
8. Bo, L., Sminchisescu, C.: Twin Gaussian processes for structured prediction. Int. J. Comput. Vis. IJCV **87**(1–2), 28–52 (2010)
9. Chen, Y., Kim, T.-K., Cipolla, R.: Inferring 3D shapes and deformations from single views. In: Daniilidis, K., Maragos, P., Paragios, N. (eds.) ECCV 2010. LNCS, vol. 6313, pp. 300–313. Springer, Heidelberg (2010). doi:10.1007/978-3-642-15558-1_22
10. Ericson, C.: Real-Time Collision Detection. The Morgan Kaufmann Series in Interactive 3-D Technology (2004)
11. Fan, X., Zheng, K., Zhou, Y., Wang, S.: Pose locality constrained representation for 3D human pose reconstruction. In: Fleet, D., Pajdla, T., Schiele, B., Tuytelaars, T. (eds.) ECCV 2014. LNCS, vol. 8689, pp. 174–188. Springer, Heidelberg (2014). doi:10.1007/978-3-319-10590-1_12
12. Geman, S., McClure, D.: Statistical methods for tomographic image reconstruction. Bull. Int. Stat. Inst. **52**(4), 5–21 (1987)

13. Grest, D., Koch, R.: Human model fitting from monocular posture images. In: Proceedings of VMV, pp. 665–1344 (2005)
14. Guan, P., Weiss, A., Balan, A., Black, M.J.: Estimating human shape and pose from a single image. In: IEEE International Conference on Computer Vision, ICCV, pp. 1381–1388 (2009)
15. Guan, P.: Virtual human bodies with clothing and hair: From images to animation. Ph.D. thesis, Brown University, Department of Computer Science, December 2012
16. Hasler, N., Ackermann, H., Rosenhahn, B., Thormhlen, T., Seidel, H.P.: Multilinear pose and body shape estimation of dressed subjects from image sets. In: IEEE Conference on Computer Vision and Pattern Recognition, CVPR, pp. 1823–1830 (2010)
17. Ionescu, C., Carreira, J., Sminchisescu, C.: Iterated second-order label sensitive pooling for 3D human pose estimation. In: IEEE Conference on Computer Vision and Pattern Recognition, CVPR, pp. 1661–1668 (2014)
18. Ionescu, C., Papava, D., Olaru, V., Sminchisescu, C.: Human3.6M: large scale datasets and predictive methods for 3D human sensing in natural environments. IEEE Trans. Pattern Anal. Mach. Intell. TPAMI **36**(7), 1325–1339 (2014)
19. Jain, A., Thormählen, T., Seidel, H.P., Theobalt, C.: MovieReshape: tracking and reshaping of humans in videos. ACM Trans. Graph. (TOG) - Proc. ACM SIG-GRAPH **29**(5), 148:1–148:10 (2010)
20. Jain, A., Tompson, J., LeCun, Y., Bregler, C.: MoDeep: a deep learning framework using motion features for human pose estimation. In: Cremers, D., Reid, I., Saito, H., Yang, M.-H. (eds.) ACCV 2014. LNCS, vol. 9004, pp. 302–315. Springer, Heidelberg (2015). doi:10.1007/978-3-319-16808-1_21
21. Jiang, H.: 3D human pose reconstruction using millions of exemplars. In: IEEE Conference on Computer Vision and Pattern Recognition, CVPR, pp. 1674–1677 (2010)
22. Johnson, S., Everingham, M.: Clustered pose and nonlinear appearance models for human pose estimation. In: Proceedings of the British Machine Vision Conference, pp. 12.1-12.11 (2010)
23. Kiefel, M., Gehler, P.V.: Human pose estimation with fields of parts. In: Fleet, D., Pajdla, T., Schiele, B., Tuytelaars, T. (eds.) ECCV 2014. LNCS, vol. 8693, pp. 331–346. Springer, Heidelberg (2014). doi:10.1007/978-3-319-10602-1_22
24. Kostrikov, I., Gall, J.: Depth sweep regression forests for estimating 3D human pose from images. In: Proceedings of the British Machine Vision Conference (2014)
25. Kulkarni, T.D., Kohli, P., Tenenbaum, J.B., Mansinghka, V.: Picture: a probabilistic programming language for scene perception. In: IEEE Conference on Computer Vision and Pattern Recognition, CVPR, pp. 4390–4399 (2015)
26. Lee, H., Chen, Z.: Determination of 3D human body postures from a single view. Comput. Vis. Graph. Image Process. **30**(2), 148–168 (1985)
27. Li, S., Chan, A.B.: 3D human pose estimation from monocular images with deep convolutional neural network. In: Cremers, D., Reid, I., Saito, H., Yang, M.-H. (eds.) ACCV 2014. LNCS, vol. 9004, pp. 332–347. Springer, Heidelberg (2015). doi:10.1007/978-3-319-16808-1_23
28. Loper, M.M., Black, M.J.: OpenDR: an approximate differentiable renderer. In: Fleet, D., Pajdla, T., Schiele, B., Tuytelaars, T. (eds.) ECCV 2014. LNCS, vol. 8695, pp. 154–169. Springer, Heidelberg (2014). doi:10.1007/978-3-319-10584-0_11
29. Loper, M., Mahmood, N., Black, M.J.: MoSh: motion and shape capture from sparse markers. ACM Trans. Graph. (TOG) - Proc. ACM SIGGRAPH Asia **33**(6), 220:1–220:13 (2014)

30. Loper, M., Mahmood, N., Romero, J., Pons-Moll, G., Black, M.J.: SMPL: a skinned multi-person linear model. ACM Trans. Graph. (TOG) - Proc. ACM SIGGRAPH Asia **34**(6), 248: 1–248: 16 (2015)
31. Nocedal, J., Wright, S.: Numerical Optimization. Springer, New York (2006)
32. Olson, E., Agarwal, P.: Inference on networks of mixtures for robust robot mapping. Int. J. Robot. Res. **32**(7), 826–840 (2013)
33. Parameswaran, V., Chellappa, R.: View independent human body pose estimation from a single perspective image. In: IEEE Conference on Computer Vision and Pattern Recognition, CVPR, pp. 16–22 (2004)
34. Pfister, T., Charles, J., Zisserman, A.: Flowing convnets for human pose estimation in videos. In: IEEE International Conference on Computer Vision, ICCV, pp. 1913–1921 (2015)
35. Pfister, T., Simonyan, K., Charles, J., Zisserman, A.: Deep convolutional neural networks for efficient pose estimation in gesture videos. In: Cremers, D., Reid, I., Saito, H., Yang, M.-H. (eds.) ACCV 2014. LNCS, vol. 9003, pp. 538–552. Springer, Heidelberg (2015). doi:10.1007/978-3-319-16865-4_35
36. Pishchulin, L., Insafutdinov, E., Tang, S., Andres, B., Andriluka, M., Gehler, P., Schiele, B.: DeepCut: joint subset partition and labeling for multi person pose estimation. In: IEEE Conference on Computer Vision and Pattern Recognition, CVPR, pp. 4929–4937 (2016)
37. Pons-Moll, G., Fleet, D., Rosenhahn, B.: Posebits for monocular human pose estimation. In: IEEE Conference on Computer Vision and Pattern Recognition, CVPR, pp. 2345–2352 (2014)
38. Pons-Moll, G., Taylor, J., Shotton, J., Hertzmann, A., Fitzgibbon, A.: Metric regression forests for correspondence estimation. Int. J. Comput. Vis. IJCV **113**(3), 1–13 (2015)
39. Ramakrishna, V., Kanade, T., Sheikh, Y.: Reconstructing 3D human pose from 2D image landmarks. In: Fitzgibbon, A., Lazebnik, S., Perona, P., Sato, Y., Schmid, C. (eds.) ECCV 2012. LNCS, vol. 7575, pp. 573–586. Springer, Heidelberg (2012). doi:10.1007/978-3-642-33765-9_41
40. Rother, C., Kolmogorov, V., Blake, A.: Grabcut: interactive foreground extraction using iterated graph cuts. ACM Trans. Graph. (TOG) - Proc. ACM SIGGRAPH **23**(3), 309–314 (2004)
41. Sigal, L., Balan, A., Black, M.J.: HumanEva: synchronized video and motion capture dataset and baseline algorithm for evaluation of articulated human motion. Int. J. Comput. Vis. IJCV **87**(1), 4–27 (2010)
42. Sigal, L., Balan, A., Black, M.J.: Combined discriminative and generative articulated pose and non-rigid shape estimation. In: Advances in Neural Information Processing Systems (NIPS), vol. 20, pp. 1337–1344 (2008)
43. Simo-Serra, E., Quattoni, A., Torras, C., Moreno-Noguer, F.: A joint model for 2D and 3D pose estimation from a single image. In: IEEE Conference on Computer Vision and Pattern Recognition, CVPR, pp. 3634–3641 (2013)
44. Simo-Serra, E., Ramisa, A., Alenya, G., Torras, C., Moreno-Noguer, F.: Single image 3D human pose estimation from noisy observations. In: IEEE Conference on Computer Vision and Pattern Recognition, CVPR, pp. 2673–2680 (2012)
45. Sminchisescu, C., Telea, A.: Human pose estimation from silhouettes, a consistent approach using distance level sets. In: WSCG International Conference for Computer Graphics, Visualization and Computer Vision, pp. 413–420 (2002)
46. Sminchisescu, C., Triggs, B.: Covariance scaled sampling for monocular 3D body tracking. In: IEEE Conference on Computer Vision and Pattern Recognition, CVPR, pp. 447–454 (2001)

47. Sridhar, S., Mueller, F., Oulasvirta, A., Theobalt, C.: Fast and robust hand tracking using detection-guided optimization. In: IEEE Conference on Computer Vision and Pattern Recognition, CVPR, pp. 3121–3221 (2015)

48. Taylor, C.: Reconstruction of articulated objects from point correspondences in single uncalibrated image. Comput. Vis. Image Underst. CVIU **80**(10), 349–363 (2000)

49. Tekin, B., Rozantsev, A., Lepetit, V., Fua, P.: Direct prediction of 3D body poses from motion compensated sequences. In: IEEE Conference on Computer Vision and Pattern Recognition, CVPR, pp. 991–1000 (2016)

50. Thiery, J.M., Guy, E., Boubekeur, T.: Sphere-meshes: shape approximation using spherical quadric error metrics. ACM Trans. Graph. (TOG) - Proc. ACM SIGGRAPH Asia **32**(6), 178:1–178:12 (2013)

51. Toshev, A., Szegedy, C.: DeepPose: human pose estimation via deep neural networks. In: IEEE Conference on Computer Vision and Pattern Recognition, CVPR, pp. 1653–1660 (2014)

52. Wang, C., Wang, Y., Lin, Z., Yuille, A., Gao, W.: Robust estimation of 3D human poses from a single image. In: IEEE Conference on Computer Vision and Pattern Recognition, CVPR, pp. 2369–2376 (2014)

53. Wei, S.E., Ramakrishna, V., Kanade, T., Sheikh, Y.: Convolutional pose machines. In: IEEE Conference on Computer Vision and Pattern Recognition, CVPR, pp. 4724–4732 (2016)

54. Yang, Y., Ramanan, D.: Articulated pose estimation using flexible mixtures of parts. In: IEEE Conference on Computer Vision and Pattern Recognition, CVPR, pp. 3546–3553 (2011)

55. Yasin, H., Iqbal, U., Krüger, B., Weber, A., Gall, J.: A dual-source approach for 3D pose estimation from a single image. In: IEEE Conference on Computer Vision and Pattern Recognition, CVPR, pp. 4948–4956 (2016)

56. Zhou, F., Torre, F.: Spatio-temporal matching for human detection in video. In: Fleet, D., Pajdla, T., Schiele, B., Tuytelaars, T. (eds.) ECCV 2014. LNCS, vol. 8694, pp. 62–77. Springer, Heidelberg (2014). doi:10.1007/978-3-319-10599-4_5

57. Zhou, S., Fu, H., Liu, L., Cohen-Or, D., Han, X.: Parametric reshaping of human bodies in images. ACM Trans. Graph. (TOG) - Proc. ACM SIGGRAPH **29**(4), 126:1–126:10 (2010)

58. Zhou, X., Zhu, M., Leonardos, S., Derpanis, K., Daniilidis, K.: Sparse representation for 3D shape estimation: a convex relaxation approach. In: IEEE Conference on Computer Vision and Pattern Recognition, CVPR, pp. 4447–4455 (2015)

59. Zhou, X., Zhu, M., Leonardos, S., Derpanis, K., Daniilidis, K.: Sparseness meets deepness: 3D human pose estimation from monocular video. In: IEEE Conference on Computer Vision and Pattern Recognition, CVPR, pp. 4447–4455 (2016)

Do We Really Need to Collect Millions of Faces for Effective Face Recognition?

Iacopo Masi[1(✉)], Anh Tuấn Trần[1], Tal Hassner[2,3(✉)], Jatuporn Toy Leksut[1], and Gérard Medioni[1]

[1] Institute for Robotics and Intelligent Systems, USC, Los Angeles, CA, USA
{iacopo.masi,anhttran,leksut,medioni}@usc.edu
[2] Information Sciences Institute, USC, Los Angeles, CA, USA
hassner@isi.edu
[3] The Open University of Israel, Ra'anana, Israel

Abstract. Face recognition capabilities have recently made extraordinary leaps. Though this progress is at least partially due to ballooning training set sizes – huge numbers of face images downloaded and labeled for identity – it is not clear if the formidable task of collecting so many images is truly necessary. We propose a far more accessible means of increasing training data sizes for face recognition systems: *Domain specific* data augmentation. We describe novel methods of enriching an existing dataset with important facial appearance variations by manipulating the faces it contains. This synthesis is also used when matching query images represented by standard convolutional neural networks. The effect of training and testing with synthesized images is tested on the LFW and IJB-A (verification and identification) benchmarks and Janus CS2. The performances obtained by our approach match state of the art results reported by systems trained on millions of downloaded images.

1 Introduction

The recent impact of deep Convolutional Neural Network (CNN) based methods on machine face recognition capabilities has been extraordinary. The conditions under which faces are now recognized and the numbers of faces which systems can now learn to identify improved to the point where some consider machines to be better than humans at this task. This progress is partially due to the introduction of new and improved network designs. However, alongside developments in network architectures, it is also the underlying ability of CNNs to learn from massive training sets that allows these techniques to be so effective.

Realizing that effective CNNs can be made even more effective by increasing their training data, many began focusing efforts on harvesting and labeling large image collections to better train their networks. In [39], a standard CNN was trained by Facebook using 4.4 million labeled faces and shown to achieve what was, at the time, state of the art performance on the Labeled Faces in the

---

I. Masi, A. Tuấn Trần and T. Hassner are equally contributed.

© Springer International Publishing AG 2016
B. Leibe et al. (Eds.): ECCV 2016, Part V, LNCS 9909, pp. 579–596, 2016.
DOI: 10.1007/978-3-319-46454-1_35

Dataset	#ID	#Img	#Img/#ID
CASIA [46]	10,575	494,414	46
Facebook DeepFace [39]	4,030	4.4M	1K
Google FaceNet [33]	8M	200M	25
VGG Face [28]	2,622	2.6M	1K
Facebook Fusion [40]	500M	10M	50
MegaFace [14]	690,572	1.02M	1.5
Aug. pose+shape	10,575	1,977,656	187
Aug. pose+shape+expr	10,575	2,472,070	234

(a) Face set statistics

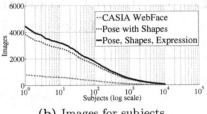

(b) Images for subjects

Fig. 1. (a) Comparison of our augmented dataset with other face datasets along with the average number of images per subject. (b) Our improvement by augmentation (Aug.) in the distribution of per-subject image numbers in order to avoid the long-tail effect of the CASIA set [46] (also shown in the last two rows of (a)).

Wild (LFW) benchmark [13]. Later, [28] proposed the VGG-Face representation, trained on 2.6 million faces, and Face++ proposed its Megvii System [47], trained on 5 million faces. All, however, pale in comparison to the Google FaceNet [33] which used 200 million labeled faces for its training.

Making CNNs better by collecting and labeling huge training sets is unfortunately not easy. The effort required to download, process and label millions of Internet images with reliable subject names is daunting. To emphasize this, the bigger sets, [39,40] and [33], required the efforts of affluent commercial organizations to assemble (Facebook and Google, resp.) and none of these sets was publicly released by its owners. By comparison, the largest publicly available face recognition training set is CASIA WebFaces [46] weighing in at a mere 495K images, several orders of magnitudes smaller than the two bigger commercial sets[1].

But downloading and labeling so many faces is more than just financially hard. Figure 1a provides some statistics for the larger face sets. Evidently, set sizes increase far faster than per-subject image numbers. This may imply that finding many images verified as belonging to the same subjects is hard even when resources are abundant. Regardless of the reason, this is a serious problem: recognition systems must learn to model not just inter-class appearance variations (differences between different people) but also intra-class variations (same person appearance variations) and this appears to remain a challenge for data collection efforts.

In light of these challenges, it is natural to ask: is there no alternative to this labor intensive, data harvesting and labeling approach to pushing recognition performances? Beyond mitigating the challenges of data collection, this question touches a more fundamental issue. Namely, can CNNs benefit from domain specific image preprocessing, and if so, how?

To answer this, we make the following contributions. (1) We propose *synthesizing data* in addition to collecting it. We inflate the size of an existing training

---

[1] MegaFace [14] is larger than CASIA, but was designed as a testing set and so provides few images per subject. It was consequently never used for training CNN systems.

set, the CASIA WebFace collection [46], to several times its size using domain (face) specific image synthesis methods (Fig. 1b). We generate images which introduce new intra-class facial appearance variations, including pose (Sect. 3.1), shape (Sect. 3.2) and expression (Sect. 3.3). **(2)** We describe a novel matching pipeline which uses similar synthesis methods at test time when processing query images. Finally, **(3)**, we test our approach on the LFW [13], IJB-A (verification and identification) and CS2 benchmarks [16]. Our results show that a CNN trained using these generated faces matches state of the art performances reported by systems trained on millions of manually downloaded and labeled faces[2].

Our approach can be considered a novel face data augmentation method (Sect. 2): *Domain specific* data augmentation. Curiously, despite the success of existing generic augmentation methods, we are unaware of previous reports of applying this easily accessible approach to generate new training face images, or indeed training for any other image class.

2   Related Work

Face recognition: Face recognition is one of the central problems in computer vision and, as such, the relevant work is extensive. Face recognition performances greatly improved with the recent introduction of deep learning techniques and in particular CNNs. Though CNNs have been used for face recognition as far back as [19], only when massive amounts of data became available did they achieve state of the art performance. This was originally shown by the Facebook DeepFace system [39], which used an architecture very similar to [19], but with over 4 million images used for training they obtained better results.

Since then, CNN based recognition systems continuously cross performance barriers with some notable examples including the Deep-ID 1-3 systems [36–38]. They and many others since, developed and trained their systems using far fewer training images, at the cost of somewhat more elaborate network architectures.

Though novel network designs can lead to better performance, further improvement can be achieved by collecting more training data. This was shown by Google FaceNet [33], which was trained on 200 million images. Besides improving results, they offered an analysis of the consequences of using more data: apparently, there is a significant diminishing returns effect when training with increasing image numbers. Thus, the performance gained by going from thousands of images to millions is substantial but increasing the numbers further provides smaller and smaller benefits. One way to explain this is that the data they used suffers from a *long tail* phenomenon [46], where most subjects in these sets have very few images for the network to learn intra-subject appearance variations.

These methods were evaluated on LFW, a *standard de facto* for measuring face recognition performances. Many recent LFW results, however, are reaching near-perfect performances, suggesting that LFW is no longer a challenging benchmark for today's systems. Another relevant and popular benchmark is the

---

[2] See www.openu.ac.il/home/hassner/projects/augmented_faces.

YouTube Faces (YTF) set [42]. It contains unconstrained face videos rather than images, but it too is quickly being saturated. Recently, a new benchmark was released, again aiming to push machine face recognition capabilities: the Janus set [16]. Its design offers several novelties compared to existing sets, including template based, rather than image based, recognition and a mix of both images and videos. It is also tougher than previous collections. Not surprisingly, dominating performance on Janus are CNN methods such as [5].

Data augmentation: Data augmentation techniques are transformations applied to training or testing images, without altering their labels. Such methods are well known to improve CNN performances and avoid overfitting [3]. Popular augmentation methods include simple, geometric transformations such as *oversampling* (multiple, translated versions of the input image obtained by cropping at different offsets) [18,20], *mirroring* (horizontal flipping) [3,44], rotating [43] the images as well as various photometric transformations [7,18,34].

Surprisingly, despite being widely recognized as highly beneficial to the training of CNN systems, we are unaware of previous attempts to go beyond these generic image processing transformations as described here. One notable exception is the recent work of [25] which proposes to augment training data for a person re-identification network by replacing image backgrounds. We propose a far more elaborate, yet easily accessible means of data augmentation.

Face synthesis for face recognition: The idea that face images can be synthetically generated in order to aid face recognition is not new. To our knowledge, it was originally proposed in [10] and then effectively used by [8,11,23,39]. Contrary to us, they all produced frontal faces which are presumably better aligned and easier to compare. They did not use other transformations to generate new images (e.g., other poses, facial expressions). More importantly, their images were used to *reduce* appearance variability, whereas we propose the opposite: to dramatically *increase* it to improve training and testing.

3   Domain Specific Data Augmentation for Face Images

We next detail our approach to augmenting a generic face dataset. We use the CASIA WebFace collection [46], enriching it with far greater per-subject appearance variations, without changing existing subject labels or losing meaningful information. Specifically, we propose to generate (synthesize) new face images, by introducing the following face specific appearance variations:

1. **Pose:** Simulating face image appearances across unseen 3D viewpoints.
2. **Shape:** Producing facial appearances using different 3D generic face shapes.
3. **Expression:** Specifically, simulating closed mouth expressions.

As previously mentioned, (1) can be considered an extension of *frontalization* techniques [11] to multiple views. Conceptually, however, they rendered new views to reduce variability for better alignment whereas we do this to increase variability and better capture intra-subject appearance variations. Also noteworthy is that (2) explicitly contradicts previous assumptions on the importance of 3D facial shape in recognizing faces (e.g., [39]): Contrary to their claim that shape carries important subject related information we ignore shape cues by rendering the same face using different underlying shapes. As we later show, this introduces subtle appearance variations at training without changing perceived identities.

3.1 Pose Variations

In order to generate unseen viewpoints given a face image $\mathbf{I}$, we use a technique similar to the frontalization proposed by [11]. We begin by applying the facial landmark detector from [2]. Given these detected landmarks we estimate the six degrees of freedom pose for the face in $\mathbf{I}$ using correspondences between the detected landmarks $\mathbf{p}_i \in \mathbb{R}^2$ and points $\mathbf{P}_i \doteq \mathbf{S}(\mathbf{i}) \in \mathbb{R}^3$, labeled on a 3D generic face model $\mathbf{S}$. Here, i indexes specific facial landmarks in $\mathbf{I}$ and the 3D shape $\mathbf{S}$.

As mentioned earlier, we use CASIA faces for augmentation. These faces are roughly centered in their images, and so detecting face bounding boxes was unnecessary. Instead, we used a fixed bounding box determined once beforehand.

Given the corresponding landmarks $\mathbf{p}_i \leftrightarrow \mathbf{P}_i$ we use PnP [9] to estimate extrinsic camera parameters, assuming the principal point is in the image center and then refining the focal length by minimizing landmark re-projection errors. This process gives us a perspective camera model mapping the generic 3D shape $\mathbf{S}$ on the image such as $\mathbf{p}_i \sim \mathbf{M}\,\mathbf{P}_i$ where $\mathbf{M} = \mathbf{K}\,[\mathbf{R}\,\mathbf{t}]$ is the camera matrix.

Given the estimated pose $\mathbf{M}$, we decompose it to obtain a rotation matrix $\mathbf{R} \in \mathbb{R}^{3\times3}$ containing rotation angles for the 3D head shape with respect to the image. We then create new rotation matrices $\mathbf{R}'_\theta \in \mathbb{R}^{3\times3}$ for unseen (novel) viewpoints by sampling different yaw angles θ. In particular, since CASIA images are biased towards frontal faces, given an image $\mathbf{I}$ we render it at the fixed yaw values $\theta = \{0°, \pm40°, \pm75°\}$. Rendering itself is derived from [11], including soft-symmetry. Figure 2 shows viewpoint (pose) synthesis results for a training subject in CASIA, illustrating the 3D pose estimation process.

Note that in practice, faces are rendered with a uniform black background not shown here (original background from the image was not preserved in rendering).

Fig. 2. Adding pose variations by synthesizing novel viewpoints. Left: original image, detected landmarks, and 3D pose estimation. Right: rendered novel views.

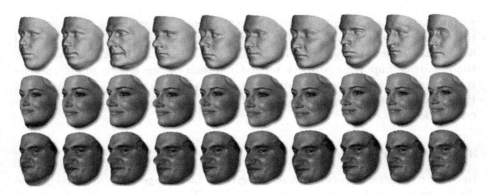

Fig. 3. Top: the ten generic 3D face shapes used for rendering. Bottom: faces rendered with the generic appearing right above them. Different shapes induce subtle appearance variations yet do not change the perceived identity of the face in the image.

3.2 3D Shape Variations

In the past, some argued that to truthfully capture the appearance of a subject's face under different viewpoints, its actual 3D shape must be used. They therefore attempted to estimate 3D face shapes directly from query images prior to frontalization [39]. Because this reconstruction process is unstable, particularly for challenging, unconstrained images, Hassner *et al.* [11] instead used a single generic 3D face to frontalize all faces. We propose the following simple compromise between these two approaches.

Rather than using a single generic 3D shape or estimating it from the image directly, we extend the procedure described in Sect. 3.1 to multiple generic 3D faces. In particular we add the set of generic 3D shapes $\mathcal{S} = \{\mathbf{S}_j\}_{j=1}^{10}$. We then simply repeat the pose synthesis procedure with these ten shapes rather than using only a single one.

We used generic 3D faces from the publicly available Basel set [29]. It provides ten high quality 3D face scans of different people representing different genders, ages, and weights. These scans are well aligned to one another. Hence, 3D landmarks need only be selected once, on one of these scans, and then directly transferred to the other nine. Figure 3 shows these ten generic models, along with images rendered to near profile view using each shape. Clearly, subjects in these images remain identifiable, despite the different underlying 3D shape, meeting the augmentation requirement of not changing subject labels. Yet each image is slightly but noticeably different from the rest, introducing appearance variations to this subject's image set.

3.3 Expression Variations

In addition to pose and shape, we also synthesize expression variations, specifically reducing deformations around the mouth. Given a face image $\mathbf{I}$ and its

Fig. 4. Expression synthesis examples. Top: example face images from the CASIA WebFace dataset. Bottom: synthesized images with closed mouths.

2D detected landmarks $\mathbf{p}_i$, and following pose estimation (Sect. 3.1) we estimate facial expression by fitting a 3D expression *Blendshape*, similarly to [21]. This is a linear combination of 3D generic face models with various basis expressions, including *mouth-closed, mouth-opened* and *smile*. Following alignment of the 3D face model and the 2D face image in both pose and expression, we perform image-based texture mapping to register the face texture onto the model. This is useful to quickly assign texture to our face model given that only one image is available. To synthesize expression, we manipulate the 3D textured face model to exhibit new expressions and render it back to the original image. This technique allows us to render a normalized expression where other image details, including hair and background, remain unchanged. In our experiments we do this to produce images with closed mouths. Some example synthesis results are provided in Fig. 4. Though slight artifacts are sometimes introduced by this process (some can be seen in Fig. 4) these typically do not alter the general facial appearances and are less pronounced than the noise often present in unconstrained images.

4 Face Recognition Pipeline

Data augmentation techniques are not restricted to training and are often also applied at test time. Our augmentations provide opportunities to modify the matching process by using different augmented versions of the input image. We next describe our recognition pipeline including these and other novel aspects.

4.1 CNN Training with Our Augmented Data

Augmented training data: Our pipeline employs a single CNN trained on both real and augmented data generated as described in Sect. 3. Specifically, training data is produced from original CASIA images. It consists of the following image types: (i) original CASIA images aligned by a simple similarity transform to two coordinate systems: roughly frontal facing faces (face yaw estimates in $[-30° \dots 30°]$) are aligned using nine landmarks on an ideal frontal template, while profile images (all other yaw angles) are aligned using the visible eye and the tip of the nose. (ii) Each image in CASIA is rendered from three novel views in yaw angles $\{0°, \pm40°, \pm75°\}$, as described in Sect. 3.1. (iii) Synthesized views are produced by randomly selecting a 3D generic face model from $\mathcal{S}$ as the underlying face shape (see Sect. 3.2), thereby adding shape variations. (iv) Finally, a mouth neutralized version of each image is also added to the training (Sect. 3.3). This process raises the total number of training images from 494,414 in the original CASIA WebFace set to 2,472,070 images in our complete (pose+shape+expression) augmented dataset. Note that this process leaves the number of CASIA WebFace subjects unchanged, inflating only the number of images per subject (Fig. 1b).

CNN fine-tuning: We use the very deep VGGNet [34] CNN with 19 layers, trained on the large scale image recognition benchmark (ILSVRC) [30]. We fine tune this network using our augmented data. To this end, we keep all layers $\{\mathbf{W}_k, \mathbf{b}_k\}_{k=1}^{19}$ of VGGNet except for the last linear layer (FC8) which we train from scratch. This layer produces a mapping from the embedded feature $\mathbf{x} \in \mathbb{R}^D$ (FC7) to the subject labels $N = 10,575$ of the augmented dataset. It computes $\mathbf{y} = \mathbf{W}_{19}\mathbf{x} + \mathbf{b}_{19}$, where $\mathbf{y} \in \mathbb{R}^N$ is the linear response of FC8. Fine-tuning is performed by minimizing the soft-max loss:

$$\mathcal{L}(\{\mathbf{W}_k, \mathbf{b}_k\}) = -\sum_t \log \left(\frac{e^{\mathbf{y}_l}}{\sum_{g=1}^{N} e^{\mathbf{y}_g}} \right) \tag{1}$$

where l is the ground-truth index over N subjects and t indexes all training images. Equation (1) is optimized using Stochastic Gradient Descent (SGC) with standard L2 norm over the learned weights. When performing back-propagation, we learn FC8 faster since it is trained from scratch while other network weights are updated with a learning rate an order of magnitude lower than FC8.

Specifically, we initialize FC8 with parameters drawn from a Gaussian distribution with zero mean and standard deviation 0.01. Bias is initialized with zero. The overall learning rate μ for the entire CNN is set to 0.001, except FC8 which uses learning rate of $\mu \times 10$. We decrease learning rate by an order of magnitude once validation accuracy for the fine tuned network saturates. Meanwhile, biases are learned twice as fast as the other weights. For all the other parameter settings we use the same values as originally described in [18].

4.2   Face Recognition with Synthesized Faces

General matching process: After training the CNN, we use the embedded feature vector $\mathbf{x} = f(\mathbf{I}; \{\mathbf{W}_k, \mathbf{b}_k\})$ from each image $\mathbf{I}$ as a face representation. Given two input images $\mathbf{I}_p$ and $\mathbf{I}_q$, their similarity, $s(\mathbf{x}_p, \mathbf{x}_q)$ is simply the normalized cross correlation (NCC) of their feature vectors.

The value $s(\mathbf{x}_p, \mathbf{x}_q)$ is the recognition score at the image level. In some cases a subject is represented by multiple images (e.g., a *template*, as in the Janus benchmark [16]). This plurality of images can be exploited to improve recognition at test time. In such cases, image sets are defined by $\mathcal{P} = \{\mathbf{x}_1, ..., \mathbf{x}_P\}$ and $\mathcal{Q} = \{\mathbf{x}_1, ..., \mathbf{x}_Q\}$ and a similarity score is defined between them: $s(\mathcal{P}, \mathcal{Q})$.

Specifically, we compute the pair-wise image similarity scores, $s(\mathbf{x}_p, \mathbf{x}_q)$, for all $\mathbf{x}_p \in \mathcal{P}$ and $\mathbf{x}_q \in \mathcal{Q}$, and pool these scores using a SoftMax operator, $s_\beta(\mathcal{P}, \mathcal{Q})$ (Eq. (2), below). Though our use of SoftMax is inspired by the SoftMax loss often used by CNNs, our aim is to get a robust score regression instead of a distribution over the subjects. SoftMax for set fusion can be seen as a weighted average in which the weight depends on the score when performing recognition. It is interesting to note that the SoftMax hyper-parameter β controls the trade-off between averaging the scores or taking the max. (or min.). That is:

$$s_\beta(\cdot, \cdot) = \begin{cases} \max(\cdot) & \text{if } \beta \to \infty \\ \text{avg}(\cdot) & \text{if } \beta = 0 \\ \min(\cdot) & \text{if } \beta \to -\infty \end{cases} \quad \text{and } s_\beta(\mathcal{P}, \mathcal{Q}) = \frac{\sum_{p \in \mathcal{P}, q \in \mathcal{Q}} s(\mathbf{x}_p, \mathbf{x}_q) e^{\beta\, s(\mathbf{x}_p, \mathbf{x}_q)}}{\sum_{p \in \mathcal{P}, q \in \mathcal{Q}} e^{\beta\, s(\mathbf{x}_p, \mathbf{x}_q)}}.$$

$$(2)$$

Pair-wise scores are pooled using Eq. (2) and we finally average the SoftMax responses over multiple values of $\beta = [0...20]$ to get the final similarity score:

$$s(\mathcal{P}, \mathcal{Q}) = \frac{1}{21} \sum_{\beta=0}^{20} s_\beta(\mathcal{P}, \mathcal{Q}).$$

$$(3)$$

The use of β positive values is due to our use of a score for recognition, so the higher the value, the better. In our experiments we found that the SoftMax operator reaches a remarkable trade-off between averaging the scores and taking the maximum. The improvement given by the proposed SoftMax fusion is shown in Table 1: we can see how the proposed method largely outperforms standard fusion techniques on IJB-A, in which subjects are described by templates.

Table 1. SoftMax template fusion for score pooling vs. other standard fusion techniques on the IJB-A benchmark for verification (ROC) and identification (CMC) resp.

Fusion↓	IJB-A Ver. (TAR)		IJB-A Id. (Rec. Rate)		
Metrics →	FAR0.01	FAR0.001	Rank-1	Rank-5	Rank-10
Min	26.3	11.2	33.1	56.1	66.8
Max	77.6	46.4	84.8	93.3	95.6
Mean	79.9	53.0	84.6	94.7	96.6
SoftMax	**86.6**	**63.6**	**87.2**	**94.9**	**96.9**

Exploiting pose augmentation at test time: The Achilles heel of many face recognition systems is cross pose face matching; particularly when one of the two images is viewed at an extreme, near profile angle [6,22,45]. Directly matching two images viewed from extremely different viewpoints often leads to poor accuracy as the difference in viewpoints affects the similarity more than subject identities. To mitigate this problem, we suggest rendering both images from the same view: one that is close enough to the viewpoint of both images.

To this end, we leverage our pose synthesis method of Sect. 3.1 to produce images in poses better suited for recognition and matching.

Cross pose rendering can, however, come at a price: Synthesizing novel views for faces runs the risk of producing meaningless images whenever facial land-marks are not accurately localized and the pose estimate is wrong. Even if pose was correctly estimated, warping images across poses involves interpolating intensities, which leads to smoothing artifacts and information loss. Though this may affect training, it is far more serious at test time where we have few images to compare and ruining one or both can directly affect recognition accuracy.

Rather than commit to pose synthesis or its standard alternative, simple yet robust in-plane alignment, we use both: We found that pose synthesis and in-plane alignment are complimentary and by combining the two, recognition performance improves. For an image pair $(\mathbf{I}_p, \mathbf{I}_q)$ we compute two similarity scores: one using in-plane aligned images and the other using images rendered to a mutually convenient view. This view is determined as follows: If the two images are near frontal then we frontalize them [11], if they are both near profile we render to $75°$, otherwise we render to $40°$.

When matching templates, $(\mathcal{P}, \mathcal{Q})$, scores computed for in-plane aligned image pairs and pose synthesized pairs are pooled separately using Eq. (2). This is equivalent to comparing the sets $\mathcal{P}$ and $\mathcal{Q}$ twice, once with each alignment. The two similarities are then averaged for a final template level score.

5   Experiments

We tested our approach extensively on the IARPA Janus benchmarks [16] and LFW [13]. We perform a minimum of database specific training, using the train-ing images prescribed by each benchmark protocol. Specifically, we perform Prin-cipal Component Analysis (PCA) on the training images of the target dataset with the features $\mathbf{x}$ extracted from the CNN trained on augmented data. This did not include dimensionality reduction; we did not cut any component after PCA projection. Following this, we apply root normalization to the new projected fea-ture, i.e., $\mathbf{x} \rightarrow \text{sign}(\mathbf{x}) |\mathbf{x}|^c$, as previously proposed for the Fisher Vector encoding in [31]. We found that a value of $c = 0.65$ provides a good baseline across all the experiments. For each dataset we report the contribution of our augmentations compared with state-of-the-art methods which use millions of training images.

5.1   Results on the IJB-A Benchmarks

IJB-A is a new publicly available benchmark released by NIST to raise the chal-lenges of unconstrained face identification and verification methods. Both IJB-A and the Janus CS2 benchmark share the same subject identities, represented by images viewed in extreme conditions, including pose, expression and illu-mination variations, with IJB-A splits generally considered more difficult than those in CS2. The IJB-A benchmarks consist of face verification (1:1) and face identification (1:N) tests. Contrary to LFW, Janus subjects are described using templates containing mixtures of still-images and video frames.

It is important to note that the Janus set has some overlap with the images in the CASIA WebFace collection. In order to provide fair comparisons, our CNNs were fine tuned on CASIA subjects that are *not* included in Janus (Sect. 4.1).

Face detection: Our pipeline uses the face landmark detector of [2] for head pose estimation and alignment. Although we found this detector quite robust, it failed to detect landmarks on some of the more challenging Janus faces. Whenever the detector failed on all the images in the same template, we use the images cropped to their facial bounding boxes as provided in the Janus data.

Video pooling: Whenever face templates include multiple frames from a single video we pool together CNN features extracted from the same video: this, by simple element wise average over all the features extracted from that video's frames (i.e., features are not pooled across videos but only within each video). Similar pooling techniques were very recently demonstrated to provide substantial performance enhancements (e.g., [35]). We refer to this technique as *video pooling* and report its influence on our system, and, whenever possible, for our baselines. This process does not change the general matching process explained in Sect. 4.2: When performing video-pooling an entire video is represented as a single pooled feature vector and treated as a single image.

In all our IJB-A and Janus CS2 results this method provided noticeable performance boosts: we compare video pooling to pair-wise single image comparisons (referred as *without video pooling* in our results).

Ablation Study: We analyze the contribution of each augmentation technique on the IJB-A dataset. Clearly, the biggest gain is given by pose augmentation (red curve) over the baseline (blue curve) in Fig. 5a. The improvement is especially noticeable in the rank-1 recognition rate for identification. The effect of video pooling along with each data augmentation method is provided in Table 2.

We next evaluate the effect of pose synthesis at test time combined with the standard in-plane alignment (Sect. 4.2), in Table 3 and in Fig. 5b. Evidently, these methods combined contribute to achieving state-of-the-art performance on the IJB-A benchmark. We conjecture that this is mainly due to three contributions:

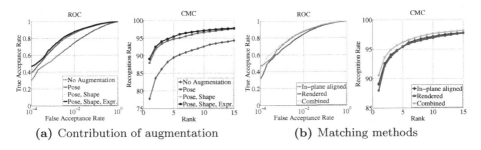

(a) Contribution of augmentation   **(b)** Matching methods

Fig. 5. Ablation study of our data synthesis and test time matching methods on IJB-A.

Table 2. Effect of each augmentation on IJB-A performance on verification (ROC) and identification (CMC), resp. Only in-plane aligned images used in these tests.

	Without Video pooling					With Video pooling				
	IJB-A Ver. (TAR)		IJB-A Id. (Rec. Rate)			IJB-A Ver. (TAR)		IJB-A Id. (Rec. Rate)		
Augmentation ↓ Metrics →	FAR0.01	FAR0.001	Rank-1	Rank-5	Rank-10	FAR0.01	FAR0.001	Rank-1	Rank-5	Rank-10
No Augmentation	74.5±1.88	54.3±2.81	77.1±1.21	89.0±1.02	92.3±0.89	75.0±2.11	55.0±2.55	77.8±1.32	89.5±0.99	92.6±0.69
Pose	84.9±1.56	62.3±6.53	86.3±0.97	94.5±0.61	96.5±0.55	86.3±1.81	67.9±5.37	88.0±1.18	94.7±0.80	96.6±0.59
Pose, Shapes	86.3±1.66	62.0±6.21	87.0±0.81	94.8±0.69	**96.9±0.48**	87.8±1.46	69.2±4.80	88.9±0.96	**95.6±0.69**	97.1±0.52
Pose, Shapes, Expr.	**86.6±1.27**	**63.6±6.00**	**87.2±0.96**	**94.9±0.77**	96.9±0.58	**88.1±1.42**	**71.0±5.24**	**89.1±1.04**	95.4±0.88	**97.2±0.59**

Table 3. Effect of in-plane alignment and pose synthesis at test-time (matching) on IJB-A dataset respectively for verification (ROC) and identification (CMC).

	Without Video pooling					With Video pooling				
	IJB-A Ver. (TAR)		IJB-A Id. (Rec. Rate)			IJB-A Ver. (TAR)		IJB-A Id. (Rec. Rate)		
Image type ↓ Metrics →	FAR0.01	FAR0.001	Rank-1	Rank-5	Rank-10	FAR0.01	FAR0.001	Rank-1	Rank-5	Rank-10
In-plane aligned	86.6±1.27	63.6±6.00	87.2±0.96	94.9±0.77	96.9±0.58	88.1±1.42	71.0±5.24	89.1±1.04	95.4±0.88	97.2±0.59
Rendered	84.7±1.50	64.6±4.40	87.3±1.21	95.0±0.59	96.8±0.69	84.8±1.38	66.4±4.88	88.0±1.15	95.5±0.69	96.9±0.58
Combined	**87.8±1.22**	**67.4±4.32**	**89.5±1.16**	**95.8±0.59**	**97.4±0.39**	**88.6±1.65**	**72.5±4.41**	**90.6±1.27**	**96.2±0.65**	**97.7±0.42**

domain-specific augmentation when training the CNN, combination of SoftMax operator, video pooling and finally pose synthesis at test time.

Comparison with the state-of-the-art: Our proposed method achieves state of the art results in the IJB-A benchmark and Janus CS2 dataset (see Tab. 4). In particular, it largely improves over the off the shelf commercial systems COTS and GOTS [16] and Fisher Vector encoding using frontalization [4]. This gap can be explained by the use of deep learning alone. Even compared with deep learning based methods, however, our approach achieves superior performance and with very wide margins. This is true even comparing our results to [41], who use seven networks and fuse their output with the COTS system. Moreover, our method improves in IJB-A verification over [41] in 15 % TAR at FAR = 0.01 and ~20 % TAR at FAR = 0.001, also showing a better rank-1 recognition rate.

It is interesting to compare our results to those reported by [5,32]. Both fine tuned their deep networks on the ten training splits of each benchmark, at substantial computational costs. Some idea of the impact this fine tuning can have on performance is available by considering the huge performance gap between results reported before and after fine tuning in [5]. Our own results, obtained by training our CNN once on augmented data, far outperform those of [32] also largely outperforming those reported by [5]. We conjecture that by training the CNN with augmented data we avoid further specializing all the parameters of the network on the target dataset. Tuning deep models on in-domain data is computationally expensive and thus, avoiding overfitting the network at training time is preferable.

Table 4. Comparative performance analysis on JANUS CS2 and IJB-A respectively for verification (ROC) and identification (CMC). f.t. denotes fine tuning a deep network multiple times for each training split. A network trained once with our augmented data achieves mostly superior results, without this effort.

Methods ↓ Metrics →	CS2 Ver. (TAR)		CS2 Id. (Rec. Rate)			IJB-A Ver. (TAR)		IJB-A Id. (Rec. Rate)		
	FAR0.01	FAR0.001	Rank-1	Rank-5	Rank-10	FAR0.01	FAR0.001	Rank-1	Rank-5	Rank-10
COTS [16]	58.1±5.4	37	55.1±3.0	69.4±1.7	74.1±1.7	–	–	–	–	–
GOTS [16]	46.7±6.6	25	41.3±2.2	57.1±1.7	62.4±1.8	40.6±1.4	19.8±0.8	44.3±2.1	59.5±2.0	–
OpenBR [17]	–	–	–	–	–	23.6±0.9	10.4±1.4	24.6±1.1	37.5±0.8	–
Fisher Vector [4]	41.1±8.1	25.0	38.1±1.8	55.9±2.1	63.7±2.5	–	–	–	–	–
Wang et al. [41]	–	–	–	–	–	73.3±3.4	51.4±6.0	82.0±2.4	92.9±1.3	–
Chen et al. [5]	64.9±1.5	45	69.4±1.2	80.9±1.1	85.0±0.9	57.3±2.0	–	72.6±3.4	84.0±2.3	88.4±2.5
Pooling Faces [12]	87.8	74.5	82.6	91.8	94.0	81.9	63.1	84.6	93.3	95.1
Deep Multi-Pose [1]	89.7	–	86.5	93.4	94.9	78.7	–	84.6	92.7	94.7
PAMs [24]	89.5±0.6	78.0±1.4	86.2±0.9	93.1±0.5	94.9±0.6	82.6±1.8	65.2±3.7	84.0±1.2	92.5±0.8	94.6±0.7
Chen et al. [5] (f.t.)	92.1±1.3	78	89.1±1.0	**95.7±0.7**	**97.2±0.5**	83.8±4.2	–	90.3±1.2	**96.5±0.8**	**97.7±0.7**
Swami S. et al. [32] (f.t.)	–	–	–	–	–	79±3.0	59±5.0	88±1.0	95±0.7	–
Ours	**92.6±0.61**	**82.4±1.52**	**89.8±0.97**	**95.6±0.58**	**96.9±0.60**	**88.6±1.65**	**72.5±4.41**	**90.6±1.27**	**96.2±0.65**	**97.7±0.42**

5.2   Results on Labeled Faces in the Wild

For many years LFW [13] was the standard benchmark for unconstrained face verification. Recent methods dominating LFW scores use millions of images collected and labeled by hand in order to obtain their remarkable performances. To test our approach, we follow the standard protocol for unrestricted, labeled outside data and report the mean classification accuracy as well as the 100 % - EER (Equal Error Rate). We prefer to use 100 % - EER in general because it is not dependent on the selected classification threshold but we still report verification accuracy to be comparable with the other methods.

Improvement for each augmentation: Figure 6a provides ROC curves for each augmentation technique used in our approach. The green curve represents our baseline, that is the CNN trained on in-plane aligned images with respect to a frontal template. The ROC improves by a good margin when we inject unseen rendered images across poses into each subject. Indeed the 100 % - EER improves by +1.67 %. Moreover, by adding both shapes and expressions, performance improves even more, reaching 100 % - EER rate of 98.00 % (red curve). See Fig. 6b for a comparison with methods trained on millions of downloaded images.

5.3   Summary of Results and Discussion

The results in this section clearly show that synthesizing training images using domain tools leads to dramatic increase in recognition accuracy. This may be attributed to the potential of domain specific augmentation to infuse training data with important intra-subject appearance variations; the very variations that seem hardest to obtain by simply downloading more images. We believe that the extent to which this domain specific data augmentation affects performance depends on the data set used as seed for the augmentation (in this paper, CASIA): Different sets have their own appearance biases and so would benefit differently from the introduction of different synthesized appearance variations.

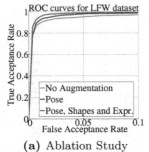

Method	Real	Synth	Net	Acc. (%)	100% - EER
Fisher Vector Faces [27]	–	–	–	93.0	93.1
DeepFace [39]	4M	–	3	97.35	–
Fusion [40]	500M	–	5	98.37	–
FaceNet [33]	200M	–	1	98.87	–
FaceNet + Alignment [33]	200M	–	1	99.63	–
VGG Face [28]	2.6M	–	1	–	97.27
VGG Face (triplet loss) [28]	2.6M	–	1	98.95	99.13
Us, no aug.	495K	–	1	95.31	95.26
Us, aug. pose	495K	2M	1	97.01	96.93
Us, aug. pose, shape, expr.	495K	2.4M	1	98.06	98.00

(a) Ablation Study   (b) Results for methods trained on millions of images

Fig. 6. LFW verification results. (a) Break-down of the influence of different training data augmentation methods. (b) Performance comparison with state of the art methods, showing the numbers of real (original) and synthesized training images, number of CNNs used by each system, accuracy and 100 %-EER

We caution that despite the ability to simulate novel face samples, our system still relies on a deep-learned model and alone, a generative model which synthesizes gallery images to match the probe is still insufficient. The learned model currently handles appearance variations such as occlusions, image quality and other confounding factors, all of which may affect the final face representation and are not handled by our augmentation process. Discriminative deep-learned models are therefore required to accurately compare these representations.

Finally, a comparison of our results on LFW to those reported by methods trained on millions of images [28,33,39,40], shows that with the initial set of less than 500K publicly available images, our method surpasses [39] and [28] (without their metric learning, not applied here), falling only slightly behind the rest.

6   Conclusions

This paper makes several important contributions. First, we show how domain specific data augmentation can be used to generate (synthesize) valuable additional data to train effective face recognition systems, as an alternative to expensive data collection and labeling. Second, we describe a face recognition pipeline with several novel details. In particular, its use of our data augmentation for matching across poses in a natural manner. Finally, *in answer to the question in the title*, our extensive analysis shows that though there is certainly a benefit to downloading increasingly larger training sets, much of this effort can be substituted by simply synthesizing more face images.

There are several compelling directions of extending our work. Primarily, additional face specific data augmentation methods can be used to provide additional intra subject appearance variations. Appealing potential augmentation techniques, not used here, are facial age synthesis [15] or facial hair manipulations [26]. Finally, beyond faces there may be other domains where such approach is relevant and where the introduction of synthetically generated training data can help mitigate the many problems of data collection for CNN training.

Acknowledgments. The authors wish to thank Jongmoo Choi for all his help in this project. This research is based upon work supported in part by the Office of the Director of National Intelligence (ODNI), Intelligence Advanced Research Projects Activity (IARPA), via IARPA 2014-14071600011. The views and conclusions contained herein are those of the authors and should not be interpreted as necessarily representing the official policies or endorsements, either expressed or implied, of ODNI, IARPA, or the U.S. Government. The U.S. Government is authorized to reproduce and distribute reprints for Governmental purpose notwithstanding any copyright annotation thereon. Moreover, we gratefully acknowledge the support of NVIDIA with the donation of a Titan X.

References

1. AbdAlmageed, W., Wu, Y., Rawls, S., Harel, S., Hassner, T., Masi, I., Choi, J., Leksut, J., Kim, J., Natarajan, P., Nevatia, R., Medioni, G.: Face recognition using deep multi-pose representations. In: Winter Conference on Applications of Computer Vision (2016)

2. Baltrusaitis, T., Robinson, P., Morency, L.P.: Constrained local neural fields for robust facial landmark detection in the wild. In: Proceedings of the International Conference on Computer Vision Workshops (2013)

3. Chatfield, K., Simonyan, K., Vedaldi, A., Zisserman, A.: Return of the devil in the details: Delving deep into convolutional nets. In: Proceedings of the British Machine Vision Conference (2014)

4. Chen, J.C., Sankaranarayanan, S., Patel, V.M., Chellappa, R.: Unconstrained face verification using fisher vectors computed from frontalized faces. In: International Conference on Biometrics: Theory, Applications and Systems (2015)

5. Chen, J.C., Patel, V.M., Chellappa, R.: Unconstrained face verification using deep cnn features. In: Winter Conference on Applications of Computer Vision (2016)

6. Ding, C., Xu, C., Tao, D.: Multi-task pose-invariant face recognition. Trans. Image Process. **24**(3), 980–993 (2015)

7. Eigen, D., Fergus, R.: Predicting depth, surface normals and semantic labels with a common multi-scale convolutional architecture. In: Proceedings of the International Conference on Computer Vision, pp. 2650–2658 (2015)

8. Ferrari, C., Lisanti, G., Berretti, S., Del Bimbo, A.: Dictionary learning based 3D morphable model construction for face recognition with varying expression and pose. In: 3DV (2015)

9. Hartley, R., Zisserman, A.: Multiple View Geometry in Computer Vision. Cambridge University Press, Cambridge (2003)

10. Hassner, T.: Viewing real-world faces in 3d. In: Proceedings of the International Conference on Computer Vision, pp. 3607–3614 (2013)

11. Hassner, T., Harel, S., Paz, E., Enbar, R.: Effective face frontalization in unconstrained images. In: Proceedings of the International Conference on Computer Vision Pattern Recognition (2015)

12. Hassner, T., Masi, I., Kim, J., Choi, J., Harel, S., Natarajan, P., Medioni, G.: Pooling faces: template based face recognition with pooled face images. In: Proceedings of the International Conference on Computer Vision Pattern Recognition Workshops, June 2016

13. Huang, G.B., Ramesh, M., Berg, T., Learned-Miller, E.: Labeled faces in the wild: a database for studying face recognition in unconstrained environments. Technical report 07-49, UMass, Amherst, October 2007

14. Kemelmacher-Shlizerman, I., Seitz, S.M., Miller, D., Brossard, E.: The MegaFace benchmark: 1 million faces for recognition at scale. In: Proceedings of the International Conference on Computer Vision Pattern Recognition (2016)

15. Kemelmacher-Shlizerman, I., Suwajanakorn, S., Seitz, S.M.: Illumination-aware age progression. In: Proceedings of the International Conference on Computer Vision Pattern Recognition, pp. 3334–3341. IEEE (2014)

16. Klare, B.F., Klein, B., Taborsky, E., Blanton, A., Cheney, J., Allen, K., Grother, P., Mah, A., Burge, M., Jain, A.K.: Pushing the frontiers of unconstrained face detection and recognition: IARPA Janus benchmark A. In: Proceedings of the International Conference on Computer Vision Pattern Recognition, pp. 1931–1939 (2015)

17. Klontz, J., Klare, B., Klum, S., Taborsky, E., Burge, M., Jain, A.K.: Open source biometric recognition. In: International Conference on Biometrics: Theory, Applications and Systems (2013)

18. Krizhevsky, A., Sutskever, I., Hinton, G.E.: Imagenet classification with deep convolutional neural networks. In: Neural Information Processing Systems, pp. 1097–1105 (2012)

19. Lawrence, S., Giles, C.L., Tsoi, A.C., Back, A.D.: Face recognition: a convolutional neural-network approach. Trans. Neural Netw. **8**(1), 98–113 (1997)
20. Levi, G., Hassner, T.: Age and gender classification using convolutional neural networks. In: Proceedings of the International Conference on Computer Vision Pattern Recognition Workshops, June 2015. http://www.openu.ac.il/home/hassner/projects/cnn_agegender
21. Lewis, J.P., Anjyo, K., Rhee, T., Zhang, M., Pighin, F., Deng, Z.: Practice and theory of blendshape facial models. In: Eurographics 2014 (2014)
22. Li, H., Hua, G., Lin, Z., Brandt, J., Yang, J.: Probabilistic elastic matching for pose variant face verification. In: Proceedings of the IEEE Conference on Computer Vision and Pattern Recognition, pp. 3499–3506 (2013)
23. Masi, I., Ferrari, C., Del Bimbo, A., Medioni, G.: Pose independent face recognition by localizing local binary patterns via deformation components. In: International Conference on Pattern Recognition (2014)
24. Masi, I., Rawls, S., Medioni, G., Natarajan, P.: Pose-aware face recognition in the wild. In: Proceedings of the International Conference on Computer Vision and Pattern Recognition (2016)
25. McLaughlin, N., Martinez Del Rincon, J., Miller, P.: Data-augmentation for reducing dataset bias in person re-identification. In: International Conference on Advanced Video and Signal Based Surveillance. IEEE (2015)
26. Nguyen, M.H., Lalonde, J.F., Efros, A.A., De la Torre, F.: Image-based shaving. Comput. Graph. Forum **27**(2), 627–635 (2008)
27. Parkhi, O.M., Simonyan, K., Vedaldi, A., Zisserman, A.: A compact and discriminative face track descriptor. In: Proceedings of the International Conference on Computer Vision and Pattern Recognition (2014)
28. Parkhi, O.M., Vedaldi, A., Zisserman, A.: Deep face recognition. In: Proceedings of the British Machine Vision Conference (2015)
29. Paysan, P., Knothe, R., Amberg, B., Romdhani, S., Vetter, T.: A 3d face model for pose and illumination invariant face recognition. In: Sixth IEEE International Conference on Advanced Video and Signal Based Surveillance, AVSS 2009, pp. 296–301, September 2009
30. Russakovsky, O., Deng, J., Su, H., Krause, J., Satheesh, S., Ma, S., Huang, Z., Karpathy, A., Khosla, A., Bernstein, M., et al.: Imagenet large scale visual recognition challenge. Int. J. Comput. Vis. **115**(3), 211–252 (2015)
31. Sánchez, J., Perronnin, F., Mensink, T., Verbeek, J.: Image classification with the fisher vector: theory and practice. Int. J. Comput. Vis. **105**(3), 222–245 (2013)
32. Sankaranarayanan, S., Alavi, A., Chellappa, R.: Triplet similarity embedding for face verification (2016). arXiv preprint: arXiv:1602.03418
33. Schroff, F., Kalenichenko, D., Philbin, J.: Facenet: a unified embedding for face recognition and clustering. In: Proceedings of the International Conference on Computer Vision and Pattern Recognition, pp. 815–823 (2015)
34. Simonyan, K., Zisserman, A.: Very deep convolutional networks for large-scale image recognition. In: International Conference on Learning Representations (2015)
35. Su, H., Maji, S., Kalogerakis, E., Learned-Miller, E.: Multi-view convolutional neural networks for 3d shape recognition. In: Proceedings of the International Conference on Computer Vision, pp. 945–953 (2015)
36. Sun, Y., Chen, Y., Wang, X., Tang, X.: Deep learning face representation by joint identification-verification. In: Neural Information Processing System, pp. 1988–1996 (2014)

37. Sun, Y., Liang, D., Wang, X., Tang, X.: Deepid3: face recognition with very deep neural networks (2015). arXiv preprint: arXiv:1502.00873
38. Sun, Y., Wang, X., Tang, X.: Deep learning face representation from predicting 10,000 classes. In: Proceedings of the International Conference on Computer Vision Pattern Recognition. IEEE (2014)
39. Taigman, Y., Yang, M., Ranzato, M., Wolf, L.: Deepface: Closing the gap to human-level performance in face verification. In: Proceedings of the International Conference on Computer Vision and Pattern Recognition, pp. 1701–1708. IEEE (2014)
40. Taigman, Y., Yang, M., Ranzato, M., Wolf, L.: Web-scale training for face identification. In: Proceedings of the International Conference on Computer Vision and Pattern Recognition (2015)
41. Wang, D., Otto, C., Jain, A.K.: Face search at scale: 80 million gallery (2015). arXiv preprint: arXiv:1507.07242
42. Wolf, L., Hassner, T., Maoz, I.: Face recognition in unconstrained videos with matched background similarity. In: Proceedings of the International Conference on Computer Vision Pattern Recognition, pp. 529–534. IEEE (2011)
43. Xie, S., Tu, Z.: Holistically-nested edge detection. In: Proceedings of the International Conference on Computer Vision (2015)
44. Yang, H., Patras, I.: Mirror, mirror on the wall, tell me, is the error small? In: Proceedings of the International Conference on Computer Vision Pattern Recognition (2015)
45. Yi, D., Lei, Z., Li, S.: Towards pose robust face recognition. In: Proceedings of the International Conference on Computer Vision Pattern Recognition, pp. 3539–3545 (2013)
46. Yi, D., Lei, Z., Liao, S., Li, S.Z.: Learning face representation from scratch (2014). arXiv preprint: arXiv:1411.7923, http://www.cbsr.ia.ac.cn/english/CASIA-WebFace-Database.html
47. Zhou, E., Cao, Z., Yin, Q.: Naive-deep face recognition: touching the limit of LFW benchmark or not? (2015). arXiv preprint: arXiv:1501.04690

Generative Visual Manipulation on the Natural Image Manifold

Jun-Yan Zhu[1($\boxtimes$)], Philipp Krähenbühl[1], Eli Shechtman[2], and Alexei A. Efros[1]

[1] University of California, Berkeley, USA
{junyanz,philkr,efros}@eecs.berkeley.edu
[2] Adobe Research, San Jose, USA
elishe@adobe.com

Abstract. Realistic image manipulation is challenging because it requires modifying the image appearance in a user-controlled way, while preserving the realism of the result. Unless the user has considerable artistic skill, it is easy to "fall off" the manifold of natural images while editing. In this paper, we propose to learn the natural image manifold directly from data using a generative adversarial neural network. We then define a class of image editing operations, and constrain their output to lie on that learned manifold at all times. The model automatically adjusts the output keeping all edits as realistic as possible. All our manipulations are expressed in terms of constrained optimization and are applied in near-real time. We evaluate our algorithm on the task of realistic photo manipulation of shape and color. The presented method can further be used for changing one image to look like the other, as well as generating novel imagery from scratch based on user's scribbles.

1 Introduction

Today, visual communication is sadly one-sided. We all perceive information in the visual form (through photographs, paintings, sculpture, etc.), but only a chosen few are talented enough to effectively express themselves visually. This imbalance manifests itself even in the most mundane tasks. Consider an online shopping scenario: a user looking for shoes has found a pair that mostly suits her but she would like them to be a little taller, or wider, or in a different color. How can she communicate her preference to the shopping website? If the user is also an artist, then a few minutes with an image editing program will allow her to transform the shoe into what she wants, and then use image-based search to find it. However, for most of us, even a simple image manipulation in Photoshop presents insurmountable difficulties. One reason is the lack of "safety wheels" in image editing: any less-than-perfect edit immediately makes the image look completely unrealistic. To put another way, classic visual manipulation paradigm does not prevent the user from "falling off" the manifold of natural images.

Understanding and modeling the natural image manifold has been a long-standing open research problem. But in the last two years, there has been rapid

B. Leibe et al. (Eds.): ECCV 2016, Part V, LNCS 9909, pp. 597–613, 2016.
DOI: 10.1007/978-3-319-46454-1_36

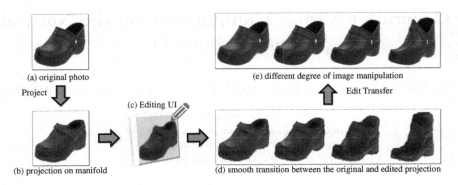

Fig. 1. We use generative adversarial networks (GAN) [1,2] to perform image editing on the natural image manifold. We first project an original photo (a) onto a low-dimensional latent vector representation (b) by regenerating it using GAN. We then modify the color and shape of the generated image (d) using various brush tools (c) (for example, dragging the top of the shoe). Finally, we apply the same amount of geometric and color changes to the original photo to achieve the final result (e). **See interactive image editing video on our website.**

advancement, fueled largely by the development of the generative adversarial networks [1]. In particular, several recent papers [1–5] have shown visually impressive results sampling random images drawn from the natural image manifold. However, there are two reasons preventing these advances from being useful in practical applications at this time. First, the generated images, while good, are still not quite photo-realistic (plus there are practical issues in making them high resolution). Second, these generative models are setup to produce images by sampling a latent vector-space, typically at random. So, these methods are not able to create and/or manipulate visual content in a user-controlled fashion.

In this paper, we use the generative adversarial neural network to learn the manifold of natural images, but we do not actually employ it for image generation. Instead, we use it as a constraint on the output of various image manipulation operations, to make sure the results lie on the learned manifold at all times. This enables us to reformulate several editing operations, specifically color and shape manipulations, in a natural and data-driven way. The model automatically adjusts the output keeping all edits as realistic as possible (Fig. 1).

We show three applications based on our system: (1) Manipulating an existing photo based on an underlying generative model to achieve a different look (shape and color); (2) "Generative transformation" of one image to look more like another; (3) Generate a new image from scratch based on user's scribbles and warping UI.

All manipulations are performed in a straightforward manner through gradient-based optimization, resulting in a simple and fast image editing tool. We hope that this work inspires further research in data-driven generative image editing, and thus release the code and data at our website.

2   Prior Work

Image editing and user interaction: Image editing is a well established area in computer graphics where an input image is manipulated to achieve a certain goal specified by the user. Examples of basic editing include changing the color properties of an image either globally [6] or locally [7]. More advanced editing methods such as image warping [8,9] or structured image editing [10] intelligently reshuffle the pixels in an image following user's edits. While achieving impressive results in the hands of an expert, when these types of methods fail, they produce results that look nothing like a real image. Common artifacts include unrealistic colors, exaggerated stretching, obvious repetitions and over-smoothing. This is because they rely on low-level principles (e.g., similarity of color, gradients or patches) and do not capture higher-level information about natural images.

Image morphing: There are a number of techniques for producing a smooth visual transition between two input images. Traditional morphing methods [11] combine an intensity blend with a geometric warp that requires a dense correspondence. In Regenerative Morphing [12] the output sequence is regenerated from small patches sampled from the source images. Thus, each frame is constrained to look similar to the two sources. Exploring Photobios [13] presented an alternative way to transition between images, by finding a shortest path in a large image collection based on pairwise image distances. Here we extend this idea and produce a morph that is both close to the two sources and stays on, or close to, the natural image manifold.

Natural image statistics: Generative models of local image statistics have long been used as a prior for image restoration problems such as image denoising and deblurring. A common strategy is to learn local filter or patch models, such as Principal Components, Independent Components, Mixture of Gaussians or wavelet bases [14–16]. Some methods attempt to capture full-image likelihoods [17] through dense patch overlap, though the basic building block is still small patches that do not capture global image structures and long range relations. Zhu et al. [18] recently showed that discriminative deep neural networks learn a much stronger prior that captures both low-level statistics, as well as higher order semantic or color-balance clues. This deep prior can be directly used for a limited set of editing operations (e.g. compositing). However it does not extend to the diversity of editing operations considered in this work.

Neural generative models: There is a large body of work on neural network based models for image generation. Early classes of probabilistic models of images include restricted Boltzmann machines (e.g., [19]) and their deep variants [20], auto-encoders [19,21] and more recently, stochastic neural networks [3,22,23] and deterministic networks [24]. Generative adversarial networks (GAN), proposed by Goodfellow et al. [1], learn a generative network jointly with a second discriminative adversarial network in a mini-max objective. The discriminator tries to distinguish between the generated samples and natural image samples, while the generator tries to *fool* the discriminator producing highly realistic looking images.

Fig. 2. GAN as a manifold approximation. (a) Randomly generated examples from a GAN, trained on the shirts dataset; (b) random jittering: each row shows a random sample from a GAN (the first one at the left), and its variants produced by adding Gaussian noise to z in the latent space; (c) interpolation: each row shows two randomly generated images (first and last), and their smooth interpolations in the latent space.

Unfortunately in practice, GAN does not yield a stable training objective, so several modifications have been proposed recently, such as a multi-scale generation [4] and a convolution-deconvolution architecture with batch normalization [2]. While the above methods attempt to generate an image starting from a random vector, they do not provide tools to change the generation process with intuitive user controls. In this paper we try to remedy this by learning a generative model that can be easily controlled via a few intuitive user edits.

3   Learning the Natural Image Manifold

Let us assume that all natural images lie on an ideal low-dimensional manifold $\mathbb{M}$ with a distance function $S(x_1, x_2)$ that measures the perceptual similarity between two images $x_1, x_2 \in \mathbb{M}$. Directly modeling this ideal manifold $\mathbb{M}$ is extremely challenging, as it involves training a generative model in a highly structured and complex million dimensional space. Following the recent success of deep generative networks in generating natural looking images, we approximate the image manifold by learning a model using generative adversarial networks (GAN) [1,2] from a large-scale image collection. Beside the high quality results, GAN has a few other useful properties for our task we will discuss next.

Generative Adversarial Networks: A GAN model consists of two neural networks: (1) a generative network $G(z; \theta_g)$ that generates an image $x \in \mathbb{R}^{H \times W \times C}$ given a random vector $z \in \mathbb{Z}$, where $\mathbb{Z}$ denotes a d-dimensional latent space, and (2) a discriminative network $D(x; \theta_d)$ that predicts a probability of a photo being real ($D = 1$) or generated ($D = 0$). For simplicity, we denote $G(z; \theta_G)$ and $D(x; \theta_D)$ as $G(z)$ and $D(x)$ in later sections. One common choice of $\mathbb{Z}$ is a multivariate uniform distribution $Unif[-1, 1]^d$. D and G are learned using a min-max objective [1]. GAN works well when trained on images of a certain class. We formally define $\tilde{\mathbb{M}} = \{G(z) | z \in \mathbb{Z}\}$ and use it as an approximation to the ideal manifold $\mathbb{M}$ (i.e. $\tilde{\mathbb{M}} \approx \mathbb{M}$). We also approximate the distance function of two generated images as an Euclidean distance between their corresponding latent vectors, i.e., $S(G(z_1), G(z_2)) \approx \|z_1 - z_2\|^2$.

GAN as a manifold approximation: We use GAN to approximate an ideal manifold for two reasons: first, it produces high-quality samples (see Fig. 2(a) for example). Though lacking visual details sometimes, the model can synthesize appealing samples with a plausible overall structure. Second, the Euclidean distance in the latent space often corresponds to a perceptually meaningful visual similarity (see Fig. 2(b) for examples). We therefore argue that GAN is a powerful generative model for modeling the image manifold.

Traversing the manifold: Given two images on the manifold $G(z_0), G(z_N)) \in \tilde{\mathbb{M}}$, one would like to seek a sequence of $N + 1$ images $[G(z_0), G(z_1), \ldots G(z_N)]$ with a smooth transition. This is often done by constructing an image graph with images as nodes, and pairwise distance function as the edge, and computing a shortest path between the starting image and end image [13]. In our case, we minimize $\sum_{t=0}^{N-1} S(G(z_t), G(z_{t+1}))$ where S is the distance function. In our case $S(G(z_1), G(z_2)) \approx \|z_1 - z_2\|^2$, so a simple linear interpolation $\left[(1 - \frac{t}{N}) \cdot z_0 + \frac{t}{N} \cdot z_N\right]_{t=0}^{N}$ is the shortest path. Figure 2(c) shows a smooth and meaningful image sequence generated by interpolating between two points in the latent space. We will now use this approximation of the manifold of natural images for realistic photo editing.

4   Approach

Figure 1 illustrates the overview of our approach. Given a real photo, we first project it onto our approximation of the image manifold by finding the closest latent feature vector z of the GAN to the original image. Then, we present a real-time method for gradually and smoothly updating the latent vector z so that it generates a desired image that both satisfies the user's edits (e.g. a scribble or a warp; more details in Sect. 5) and stays close to the natural image manifold. Unfortunately, in this transformation the generative model usually looses some of the important low-level details of the input image. We therefore propose a dense correspondence method that estimates both per-pixel color and shape changes from the edits applied to the generative model. We then transfer these changes to the original photo using an edge-aware interpolation technique and produce the final manipulated result.

4.1   Projecting an Image onto the Manifold

A real photo x^R lies, by definition, on the ideal image manifold $\mathbb{M}$. However for an approximate manifold $\tilde{\mathbb{M}}$, our goal here is to find a generated image $x^* \in \tilde{\mathbb{M}}$ close to x^R in some distance metric $\mathcal{L}(x_1, x_2)$ as

$$x^* = \arg\min_{x \in \tilde{\mathbb{M}}} \mathcal{L}(x, x^R). \tag{1}$$

For the GAN manifold $\tilde{\mathbb{M}}$ we can rewrite the above equation as follows:

$$z^* = \arg\min_{z \in \tilde{\mathbb{Z}}} \mathcal{L}(G(z), x^R). \tag{2}$$

Our goal is to reconstruct the original photo x^R using the generative model G by minimizing the reconstruction error, where $\mathcal{L}(x_1, x_2) = \|\mathcal{C}(x_1) - \mathcal{C}(x_2)\|^2$ in some differentiable feature space $\mathcal{C}$. If $\mathcal{C}(x) = x$, then the reconstruction error is simply pixel-wise Euclidean error. Previous work [5,25] suggests that using deep neural network activations leads to a reconstruction of perceptually meaningful details. We found that a weighted combination of raw pixels and *conv4* features ($\times 0.002$) extracted from AlexNet [26] trained on ImageNet [27] to perform best.

Projection via optimization: As both the feature extractor $\mathcal{C}$ and the generative model G are differentiable, we can directly optimize the above objective using L-BFGS-B [28]. However, the cascade of $\mathcal{C}(G(z))$ makes the problem highly non-convex, and as a result, the reconstruction quality strongly relies on a good initialization of z. We can start from multiple random initializations and output the solution with the minimal cost. However the number of random initializations required to obtain a stable reconstruction is prohibitively large (more than 100), which makes real-time processing impossible. We instead train a deep neural network to minimize Eq. 2 directly.

Projection via a feedforward network: We train a feedforward neural network $P(x; \theta_P)$ that directly predicts the latent vector z from a x. The training objective for the predictive model P is written as follows:

$$\theta_P^* = \arg\min_{\theta_P} \sum_n \mathcal{L}(G(P(x_n^R; \theta_P)), x_n^R), \tag{3}$$

where x_n^R denotes the n-th image in the dataset. The architecture of the model P is equivalent to the discriminator D of the adversarial networks, and only varies in the final number of network outputs. Objective 3 is reminiscent of an auto-encoder pipeline, with a encoder P and decoder G. However, the decoder G is fixed throughout the training. While the optimization problem 2 is exactly the same as the learning objective 3, the learning based approach often performs better and does not fall into local optima. We attribute this behavior to the regularity in the projection problem and the limited capacity of the network P. Projections of similar images will share similar network parameters and produce a similar result. In some sense the loss for one image provides information for many more images that share a similar appearance [29]. However, the learned inversion is not always perfect, and can often be improved further by a few additional steps of optimization.

A hybrid method: The hybrid method takes advantage of both approaches above. Given a real photo x^R, we first predict $P(x^R; \theta_P)$ and then use it as the initialization for the optimization objective (Eq. 2). So the predictive model we have trained serves as a fast bottom-up initialization method for a non-convex optimization problem. Figure 3 shows a comparison of these three methods. See Sect. 7.4 for a more quantitative evaluation.

Fig. 3. Projecting real photos onto the image manifold using GAN. Top row: original photos (from handbag dataset); 2nd row: reconstruction using optimization-based method; 3rd row: reconstruction via learned deep encoder P; bottom row: reconstruction using the hybrid method (ours). We show the reconstruction loss below each image.

4.2   Manipulating the Latent Vector

With the image x_0^R projected onto the manifold $\tilde{\mathbb{M}}$ as $x_0 = G(z_0)$ via the projection methods just described, we can start modifying the image on that manifold. We update the initial projection x_0 by simultaneously matching the user intentions while staying on the manifold, close to the original image x_0.

Each editing operation is formulated as a constraint $f_g(x) = v_g$ on a local part of the output image x. The editing operations g include color, shape and warping constraints, and are further described in Sect. 5.1. Given an initial projection x_0, we find a new image $x \in \mathbb{M}$ close to x_0 trying to satisfy as many constraints as possible

$$x^* = \arg\min_{x \in \mathbb{M}}\Big\{ \underbrace{\sum_g \|f_g(x) - v_g\|^2}_{\text{data term}} + \underbrace{\lambda_s \cdot S(x, x_0)}_{\substack{\text{manifold} \\ \text{smoothness}}} \Big\}, \tag{4}$$

where the data term measures deviation from the constraint and the smoothness term enforces moving in small steps on the manifold, so that the image content is not altered too much. We set $\lambda_s = 5$ in our experiments.

The above equation simplifies to the following on the approximate GAN manifold $\tilde{\mathbb{M}}$:

$$z^* = \arg\min_{z \in \mathbb{Z}}\Big\{ \underbrace{\sum_g \|f_g(G(z)) - v_g\|^2}_{\text{data term}} + \underbrace{\lambda_s \cdot \|z - z_0\|^2}_{\substack{\text{manifold} \\ \text{smoothness}}} + E_D \Big\}. \tag{5}$$

Here the last term $E_D = \lambda_D \cdot \log(1 - D(G(z)))$ optionally captures the visual realism of the generated output as judged by the GAN discriminator D.

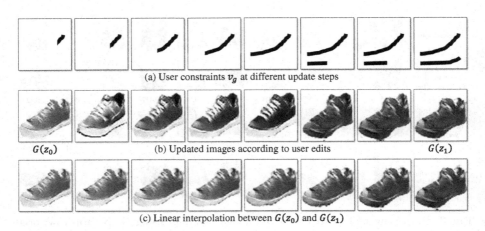

(a) User constraints v_g at different update steps

$G(z_0)$ (b) Updated images according to user edits $G(z_1)$

(c) Linear interpolation between $G(z_0)$ and $G(z_1)$

Fig. 4. Updating latent vector given user edits. (a) Evolving user constraint v_g (black color strokes) at each update step; (b) intermediate results at each update step ($G(z_0)$ at leftmost, and $G(z_1)$ at rightmost); (c) a smooth linear interpolation in latent space between $G(z_0)$ and $G(z_1)$.

This further pushes the image towards the manifold of natural images, and slightly improves the visual quality of the result. By default, we turn off this term to increase frame rates.

Gradient descent update: For most constraints Eq. 5 is non-convex. We solve it using gradient descent, which allows us to provide the user with a real-time feedback as she manipulates the image. As a result, the objective 5 evolves in real-time as well. For computational reasons, we only perform a few gradient descent updates after changing the constraints v_g. Each update step takes 50–100 ms, which ensures an interactive feedback. Figure 4 shows one example of the update of z. Given an initial red shoe as shown in Fig. 4, the user gradually scribbles a black color stroke (i.e. specifies a region is black) on the shoe image (Fig. 4a). Then our update method smoothly changes the image appearance (Fig. 4b) by adding more and more of the user constraints. Once the final result $G(z_1)$ is computed, a user can see the interpolation sequence between the initial point z_0 and z_1 (Fig. 4c), and select any intermediate result as the new starting point. Please see supplemental video for more details.

While this editing framework allows us to modify any generated image on the approximate natural image manifold $\tilde{\mathbb{M}}$, it does not directly provide us a way to modify the original high resolution image x_0^R. In the next section we show how edits on the approximate manifold can be transferred to the original image.

4.3   Edit Transfer

Give the original photo x_0^R (e.g. a black shoe) and its projection on the manifold $G(z_0)$, and a user modification $G(z_1)$ by our method (e.g. the generated red shoe).

The generated image $G(z_1)$ captures the roughly change we want, albeit the quality is degraded w.r.t the original image.

Can we instead adjust the original photo and produce a more photo-realistic result x_1^R that exhibits the changes in the generated image? A straightforward way is to transfer directly the pixel changes (i.e. $x_1^R = x_0^R + (G(z_1) - G(z_0))$). We have tried this approach and it introduces new artifacts due to the misalignment of the two images. To address this issue, we develop a dense correspondence algorithm to estimate both the geometric and color changes induced by the editing process.

Specifically, given two generated images $G(z_0)$ and $G(z_1)$, we can generate any number of intermediate frames $\left[G((1-\frac{t}{N})\cdot z_0 + \frac{t}{N}\cdot z_1)\right]_{t=0}^{N}$, where consecutive frames only exhibit minor visual variations.

Motion+Color flow algorithm: We then estimate the color and geometric changes by generalizing the brightness constancy assumption in traditional optical flow methods [30,31]. This results in the following motion+color flow objective[1]:

$$\iint \underbrace{\|I(x,y,t) - A\cdot I(x+u, y+v, t+1)\|^2}_{\text{data term}} + \underbrace{\sigma_s(\|\nabla u\|^2 + \|\nabla v\|^2)}_{\text{spatial reg}} + \underbrace{\sigma_c\|\nabla A\|^2}_{\text{color reg}} dxdy, \quad (6)$$

where $I(x,y,t)$ denotes the RGB values $(r,g,b,1)^T$ of pixel (x,y) in the generated image $G((1 - \frac{t}{N})\cdot z_0 + \frac{t}{N}\cdot z_1)$. (u,v) is the flow vector with respect to the change of t, and A denotes a 3×4 color affine transformation matrix. The data term relaxes the color constancy assumption by introducing a locally affine color transfer model A [32] while the spatial and color regularization terms encourage smoothness in both the motion and color change. We solve the objective by iteratively estimating the flow (u,v) using a traditional optical flow algorithm, and computing the color change A by solving a system of linear equations [32]. We iterate 3 times. We produce 8 intermediate frames (i.e. $N = 7$).

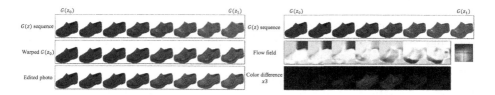

Fig. 5. Edit transfer via Motion+Color Flow. Following user edits on the left shoe $G(z_0)$ we obtain an interpolation sequence in the generated latent space $G(z)$ (top right). We then compute the motion and color flows (right middle and bottom) between neighboring images in $G(z)$. These flows are concatenated and, as a validation, can be applied on $G(z_0)$ to obtain a close reconstruction of $G(z)$ (left middle). The bottom left row shows how the edit is transferred to the original shoe using the same concatenated flow, to obtain a sequence of edited shoes.

---

[1] For simplicity, we omit the pixel subscript (x, y) for all the variables.

We estimate the changes between nearby frames, and concatenate these changes frame by frame to obtain long-range changes between any two frames along the interpolation sequence $z_0 \rightarrow z_1$. Figure 5 shows a warping sequence after we apply the flow to the initial projection $G(z_0)$.

Transfer edits to the original photo: After estimating the color and shape changes in the generated image sequence, we apply them to the original photo and produce an interesting transition sequence of photo-realistic images as shown in Fig. 5. As the resolution of the flow and color fields are limited to the resolution of the generated image (i.e. 64×64), we upsample those edits using a guided image filter [33].

5   User Interface

The user interface consists of a main window showing the current edited photo, a display showing thumbnails of all the candidate results, and a slider bar to explore the interpolation sequence between the original photo and the final result. Please see our supplemental video for more details.

Candidate results: Given the objective (Eq. 5) derived with the user guidance, we generate multiple different results by initializing z as random perturbations of z_0. We generate 64 examples and show the best 9 results sorted by the objective cost (Eq. 5).

Relative edits: Once a user finishes one edit, she can drag a slider to see all the intermediate results interpolated between the original and the final manipulated photo. We call this "relative edits" as it allows a user to explore more alternatives with a single edit. Similar to relative attributes [34], a user can express ideas like changing the handle of the handbag to be more red, or making the heel of the shoes slightly higher, without committing to a specific final state.

5.1   Editing Constraints

Our system provides three constraints to edit the photo in different aspects: coloring, sketching and warping. All constraints are expressed as brush tools. In the following, we explain the usage of each brush, and the corresponding constraints.

Coloring brush: The coloring brush allows the user to change the color of a specific region. The user selects a color from a palette and can adjust the brush size. For each pixel marked with this brush we constrain the color $f_g(I) = I_p = v_g$ of a pixel p to the selected values v_g.

Sketching brush: The sketching brush allows the user to outline the shape or add fine details. We constrain $f_g(I) = HOG(I)_p$ a differentiable HOG descriptor [35] at a certain location p in the image to be close to the user stroke (i.e. $v_g = HOG(stroke)_p$). We chose the HOG feature extractor because it is binned, which makes it robust to sketching inaccuracies.

Warping brush: The warping brush allows the user to modify the shape more explicitly. The user first selects a local region (a window with adjustable size), and then drag it to another location. We then place both a color and sketching constraint on the displaced pixels encouraging the target patch to mimic the appearance of the dragged region.

Figure 8 shows a few examples where the coloring and sketching brushed were used in the context of interactive image generation. Figure 1 shows the result of the warping brush that was used to pull the topline of the shoe up. Figure 6 shows a few more examples.

6   Implementation Details

Network architecture: We follow the same architecture of deep convolutional generative adversarial networks (DCGAN) [2]. DCGAN mainly builds on multiple convolution, deconvolution and ReLU layers, and eases the min-max training via batch normalization [36]. We train the generator G to produce a $64 \times 64 \times 3$ image given a 100-dimensional random vector. Notice that our method can also use other generative models (e.g. variational auto-encoder [3] or future improvements in this area) to approximate the natural image manifold.

Computational time: We run our system on a Titan X GPU. Each update of the vector z takes $50 \sim 100$ ms, which allows the real-time image editing and generation. Once an edit is finished, it takes $5 \sim 10$ s for our edit transfer method to produce high-resolution final result.

7   Results

We first introduce the statistics of our dataset. We then show three main applications: realistic image manipulation, generative image transformation, and generating a photo from scratch using our brush tools. Finally, we evaluate our image reconstruction methods, and perform a human perception study to understand the realism of generated results. Please refer to the supplementary material for more results and comparisons.

Datasets: We experiment with multiple photo collections from various sources as follows: "shoes" dataset [37], which has 50 K shoes collected from Zappos.com (the shoes are roughly centered but not well aligned, and roughly facing left, with frontal to side view); "church outdoor" dataset (126 K images) from the LSUN challenge [38]; "outdoor natural" images (150 K) from the MIT Places dataset [39]; and two query-based product collections downloaded from Amazon, including "handbags" (138 K) and "shirts" (137 K). The downloaded handbags and shirts are roughly centered but no further alignment has been performed.

7.1   Image Manipulation

Our main application is photo-realistic image manipulation using the brush interactions described in Sect. 5.1. See Fig. 6 for a few examples where the brush edits
are depicted on the left (dashed line for the sketch tool, color scribble for the color
brush and a red square with arrow for the warp tool). See the supplementary
video for more interactive manipulation demos.

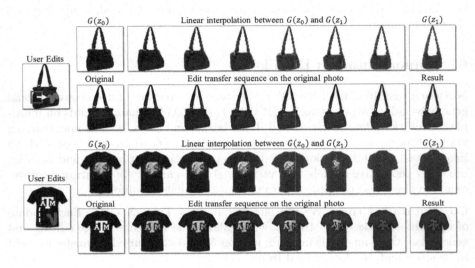

Fig. 6. Image manipulation examples: for each example, we show the original photo
and user edits on the left. The top row on the right shows the generated sequence and
the bottom row shows the edit transfer sequence on the original image. (Color figure
online)

7.2   Generative Image Transformation

An interesting outcome of the editing process is the sequence of intermediate
generated images that can be seen as a new kind of image morphing [11,12,40].
We call it "generative transformation". We use this sequence to transform
the shape and color of one image to look like another image automatically,
i.e., *without* any user edits. This is done by applying the motion+color flow on
either of the sources. Figure 7 shows a few "generative transform" examples.

7.3   Interactive Image Generation

Another byproduct of our method is that if there is no image to begin with and
all we have are the user brush strokes, the method would generate a natural
image that best satisfies the user constraints. This could be useful for dataset
exploration and browsing. The difference with previous sketch-to-image retrieval
methods [41] or AverageExplorer [42], is that due to potentially contradicting

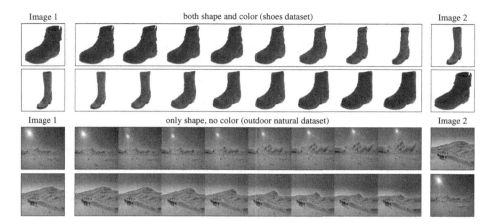

Fig. 7. Generative image transformation. In both rows, the source on the left is transformed to have the shape and color (or just shape in the 2nd example) of the one on the right.

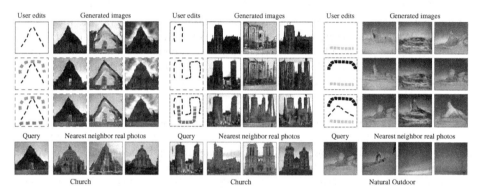

Fig. 8. Interactive image generation. The user uses the brush tools to generate an image from scratch (top row) and then keeps adding more scribbles to refine the result (2nd and 3rd rows). In the last row, we show the most similar real images to the generated images. (dashed line for the sketch tool, and color scribble for the color brush)

user constraints, the result may look very different than any single image from the dataset or an average of such images, and more of a realistic hybrid image [43]. See some examples in Fig. 8.

7.4   Evaluation

Image reconstruction evaluation: We evaluate three image reconstruction methods described in Sect. 4.1: optimization-based, network-based and our hybrid approach that combines the last two. We run these on 500 test images per

Table 1. Average per-dataset image reconstruction error measured by $\mathcal{L}(x, x^R)$.

	Shoes	Church outdoor	Outdoor natural	Handbags	Shirts
Optimization-based	0.155	0.319	0.176	0.299	0.284
Network-based	0.210	0.338	0.198	0.302	0.265
Hybrid (ours)	**0.140**	**0.250**	**0.145**	**0.242**	**0.184**

category, and evaluate them by the reconstruction error $\mathcal{L}(x, x^R)$ defined in Eq. 1. Table 1 shows the mean reconstruction error of these three methods on 5 different datasets. We can see the optimization-based and neural network-based methods perform comparably, where their combination yields better results. See Figure 3 for a qualitative comparison. We include PSNR (in dB) results in the supplementary material.

Class-specific model: So far, we have trained the generative model on a particular class of images. As a comparison, we train a cross-class model on three datasets altogether (i.e. shoes, handbags, and shirts), and observe that the model achieves worse reconstruction error compared to class-specific models (by $\sim 10\,\%$). We also have tried to use a class-specific model to reconstruct images from a different class. The mean cross-category reconstruction errors are much worse: shoes model used for shoes: 0.140 vs. shoes model for handbags: 0.398, and for shirts: 0.451. However, we expect a model trained on many categories (e.g. $1,000$) to generalize better to novel objects.

Perception study: We perform a small perception study to compare the photo realism of four types of images: real photos, generated samples produced by GAN, our method (shape only), and our method (shape+color). We collect 20 annotations for 400 images by asking Amazon Mechanical Turk workers if the image look realistic or not. Real photos: 91.5 %, DCGAN: 14.3 %, ours (shape+color): 25.9 %; ours (shape only): 48.7 %. DCGAN model alone produces less photo-realistic images, but when combined with our edit transfer, the realism significantly improves.

Additional evaluation: In the supplemental material, we evaluate our motion+color flow method, and compare our results against popular alignment methods that are designed to handle large displacement between two images [44, 45].

8   Discussion and Limitations

We presented a step towards image editing with a direct constraint to stay close to the manifold of real images. We approximate this manifold using the state-of-the-art in deep generative models (DCGAN). We show how to make interactive edits to the generated images and transfer the resulting changes in shape and color back to the original image. Thus, the quality of the generated results (low resolution, missing texture and details) and the types of data DCGAN is applicable to (works well on structured datasets such as product images and worse on more general imagery), limits how far we can get with this editing approach. However our method is not tied to a particular generative method and will improve with the advancement of this field. Our current editing brush tools allow rough changes in color and shape but not texture and more complex structure changes. We leave these for future work.

Acknowledgments. This work was supported, in part, by funding from Adobe, eBay and Intel, as well as a hardware grant from NVIDIA. J.-Y. Zhu is supported by Facebook Graduate Fellowship.

References

1. Goodfellow, I., Pouget-Abadie, J., Mirza, M., Xu, B., Warde-Farley, D., Ozair, S., Courville, A., Bengio, Y.: Generative adversarial nets. In: NIPS. 2672–2680. (2014)
2. Radford, A., Metz, L., Chintala, S.: Unsupervised representation learning with deep convolutional generative adversarial networks. In: ICLR (2016)
3. Kingma, D.P., Welling, M.: Auto-encoding variational bayes. In: ICLR (2014)
4. Denton, E.L., Chintala, S., Fergus, R., et al.: Deep generative image models usinga laplacian pyramid of adversarial networks. In: NIPS, pp. 1486–1494 (2015)
5. Dosovitskiy, A., Brox, T.: Generating images with perceptual similarity metrics based on deep networks. arXiv preprint arXiv:1602.02644 (2016)
6. Reinhard, E., Ashikhmin, M., Gooch, B., Shirley, P.: Color transfer between images. IEEE Comput. Graph. Appl. **21**, 34–41 (2001)
7. Levin, A., Lischinski, D., Weiss, Y.: Colorization using optimization. In: SIGGRAPH, SIGGRAPH 2004, pp. 689–694. ACM, New York (2004)
8. Alexa, M., Cohen-Or, D., Levin, D.: As-rigid-as-possible shape interpolation. In: Proceedings of the 27th Annual Conference on Computer Graphics and Interactive Techniques, SIGGRAPH 2000 (2000)
9. Krähenbühl, P., Lang, M., Hornung, A., Gross, M.: A system for retargeting of streaming video. In: ACM Trans. Graph. (TOG), vol. 28. p. 126. ACM (2009)
10. Barnes, C., Shechtman, E., Finkelstein, A., Goldman, D.: Patchmatch: a randomized correspondence algorithm for structural image editing. SIGGRAPH **28**(3), 24 (2009)
11. Wolberg, G.: Digital Image Warping. IEEE Computer Society Press, Los Alamitos (1990)
12. Shechtman, E., Rav-Acha, A., Irani, M., Seitz, S.: Regenerative morphing. In: CVPR, San-Francisco, CA, June 2010
13. Kemelmacher-Shlizerman, I., Shechtman, E., Garg, R., Seitz, S.M.: Exploring photobios. In: SIGGRAPH, vol. 30, p. 61 (2011)
14. Olshausen, B.A., Field, D.J.: Emergence of simple-cell receptive field properties by learning a sparse code for natural images. Nature **381**, 607–609 (1996)
15. Portilla, J., Simoncelli, E.P.: A parametric texture model based on joint statistics of complex wavelet coefficients. IJCV **40**(1), 49–70 (2000)
16. Zoran, D., Weiss, Y.: From learning models of natural image patches to whole image restoration. In: Proceedings of ICCV, pp. 479–486 (2011)
17. Roth, S., Black, M.J.: Fields of experts: a framework for learning image priors. In: CVPR (2005)

18. Zhu, J.Y., Krähenbühl, P., Shechtman, E., Efros, A.A.: Learning a discriminative model for the perception of realism in composite images. In: ICCV (2015)
19. Hinton, G.E., Salakhutdinov, R.R.: Reducing the dimensionality of data with neural networks. Science 313(5786), 504–507 (2006)
20. Salakhutdinov, R., Hinton, G.E.: Deep boltzmann machines. In: AISTATS (2009)
21. Vincent, P., Larochelle, H., Bengio, Y., Manzagol, P.A.: Extracting and composing robust features with denoising autoencoders. In: ICML (2008)
22. Bengio, Y., Laufer, E., Alain, G., Yosinski, J.: Deep generative stochastic networks trainable by backprop. In: ICML, pp. 226–234 (2014)
23. Gregor, K., Danihelka, I., Graves, A., Wierstra, D.: Draw: a recurrent neural network for image generation. In: ICML (2015)
24. Dosovitskiy, A., Tobias Springenberg, J., Brox, T.: Learning to generate chairs with convolutional neural networks. In: CVPR, pp. 1538–1546 (2015)
25. Johnson, J., Alahi, A., Fei-Fei, L.: Perceptual losses for real-time style transfer and super-resolution. arXiv preprint arXiv:1603.08155 (2016)
26. Krizhevsky, A., Sutskever, I., Hinton, G.E.: Imagenet classification with deep convolutional neural networks. In: NIPS, pp. 1097–1105 (2012)
27. Deng, J., Dong, W., Socher, R., Li, L.J., Li, K., Fei-Fei, L.: Imagenet: a large-scale hierarchical image database. In: CVPR, pp. 248–255. IEEE (2009)
28. Byrd, R.H., Lu, P., Nocedal, J., Zhu, C.: A limited memory algorithm for bound constrained optimization. SIAM J. Sci. Comput. 16(5), 1190–1208 (1995)
29. Gershman, S.J., Goodman, N.D.: Amortized inference in probabilistic reasoning. In: Proceedings of the 36th Annual Conference of the Cognitive Science Society (2014)
30. Brox, T., Bruhn, A., Papenberg, N., Weickert, J.: High accuracy optical flow estimation based on a theory for warping. In: Pajdla, T., Matas, J.G. (eds.) ECCV 2004. LNCS, vol. 3024, pp. 25–36. Springer, Heidelberg (2004)
31. Bruhn, A., Weickert, J., Schnörr, C.: Lucas/kanade meets horn/schunck: combining local and global optic flow methods. IJCV 61(3), 211–231 (2005)
32. Shih, Y., Paris, S., Durand, F., Freeman, W.T.: Data-driven hallucination of different times of day from a single outdoor photo. ACM Trans. Graph. (TOG) 32(6), 200 (2013)
33. He, K., Sun, J., Tang, X.: Guided image filtering. In: Daniilidis, K., Maragos, P., Paragios, N. (eds.) ECCV 2010, Part I. LNCS, vol. 6311, pp. 1–14. Springer, Heidelberg (2010)
34. Parikh, D., Grauman, K.: Relative attributes. In: ICCV, pp. 503–510. IEEE (2011)
35. Dalal, N., Triggs, B.: Histograms of oriented gradients for human detection. In: CVPR, vol. 1, pp. 886–893. IEEE (2005)
36. Ioffe, S., Szegedy, C.: Batch normalization: accelerating deep network training by reducing internal covariate shift. ICML 37, 448–456 (2015)
37. Yu, A., Grauman, K.: Fine-grained visual comparisons with local learning. In: CVPR, pp. 192–199 (2014)
38. Yu, F., Zhang, Y., Song, S., Seff, A., Xiao, J.: Construction of a large-scale image dataset using deep learning with humans in the loop. arXiv preprint arXiv:1506.03365 (2015)
39. Zhou, B., Lapedriza, A., Xiao, J., Torralba, A., Oliva, A.: Learning deep features for scene recognition using places database. In: NIPS, pp. 487–495 (2014)
40. Seitz, S.M., Dyer, C.R.: View Morphing, pp. 21–30, New York (1996)
41. Sun, X., Wang, C., Xu, C., Zhang, L.: Indexing billions of images for sketch-based retrieval. In: ACM MM (2013)

42. Zhu, J.Y., Lee, Y.J., Efros, A.A.: Averageexplorer: interactive exploration and alignment of visual data collections. SIGGRAPH **33**(4) (2014)
43. Risser, E., Han, C., Dahyot, R., Grinspun, E.: Synthesizing structured image hybrids. SIGGRAPH **29**(4), 85:1–85:6 (2010)
44. Liu, C., Yuen, J., Torralba, A.: Sift flow: dense correspondence across scenes and its applications. IEEE Trans. Pattern Anal. Mach. Intell. **33**(5), 978–994 (2011)
45. Kim, J., Liu, C., Sha, F., Grauman, K.: Deformable spatial pyramid matching for fast dense correspondences. In: Proceedings of the IEEE Conference on Computer Vision and Pattern Recognition, pp. 2307–2314 (2013)

Deep Cascaded Bi-Network
for Face Hallucination

Shizhan Zhu[1], Sifei Liu[1,2], Chen Change Loy[1,3(✉)], and Xiaoou Tang[1,3]

[1] Department of Information Engineering,
The Chinese University of Hong Kong, Hong Kong, China
{zs014,ccloy,xtang}@ie.cuhk.edu.hk, sliu32@ucmerced.edu
[2] University of California, Merced, Merced, USA
[3] Shenzhen Institutes of Advanced Technology,
Chinese Academy of Sciences, Shenzhen, China

Abstract. We present a novel framework for hallucinating faces of unconstrained poses and with very low resolution (face size as small as 5pxIOD). In contrast to existing studies that mostly ignore or assume pre-aligned face spatial configuration (e.g. facial landmarks localization or dense correspondence field), we alternatingly optimize two complementary tasks, namely face hallucination and dense correspondence field estimation, in a unified framework. In addition, we propose a new gated deep bi-network that contains two functionality-specialized branches to recover different levels of texture details. Extensive experiments demonstrate that such formulation allows exceptional hallucination quality on in-the-wild low-res faces with significant pose and illumination variations.

1 Introduction

Increasing attention is devoted to detection of small faces with an image resolution as low as 10 pixels of height [1]. Meanwhile, facial analysis techniques, such as face alignment [2,3] and verification [4,5], have seen rapid progress. However, the performance of most existing techniques would degrade when given a low resolution facial image, because the input naturally carries less information, and images corrupted with down-sampling and blur would interfere the facial analysis procedure. Face hallucination [6–13], a task that super-resolves facial images, provides a viable means for improving low-res face processing and analysis, e.g. person identification in surveillance videos and facial image enhancement.

Prior on face structure, or face spatial configuration, is pivotal for face hallucination [6,7,12]. The availability of such prior distinguishes the face hallucination task from the general image super-resolution problem [14–21], where the latter lacks of such global prior to facilitate the inference. In this study, we extend the notion of prior to pixel-wise dense face correspondence field. We observe that an informative prior provides a strong semantic guidance that enables face hallucination even from a very low resolution. Here the dense correspondence field is

---

Throughout this paper, we use the inter-ocular distance measured in pixels (denoted as pxIOD), to concisely and unambiguously represent the face size.

© Springer International Publishing AG 2016
B. Leibe et al. (Eds.): ECCV 2016, Part V, LNCS 9909, pp. 614–630, 2016.
DOI: 10.1007/978-3-319-46454-1_37

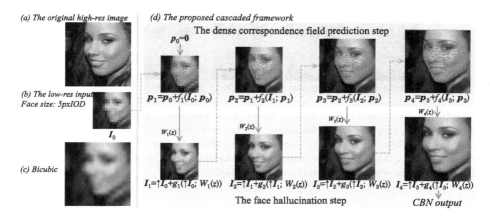

Fig. 1. (a) The original high-res image. (b) The low-res input with a size of 5pxIOD. (c) The result of bicubic interpolation. (d) An overview of the proposed face hallucination framework. The solid arrows indicate the hallucination step that hallucinates the face with spatial cues, i.e. the dense correspondence field. The dashed arrows indicate the spatial prediction step that estimates the dense correspondence field.

necessary for describing the spatial configuration for its pixel-wise (not by facial landmarks) and correspondence (not by face parsing) properties. The importance of dense field will be reflected in Sect. 3.2. An example is shown in Fig. 1 – even an eye is only visible from a few pixels in a low-res image, one can still recover its qualitative details through inferring from the global face structure.

Nevertheless, obtaining an accurate high-res pixel-wise correspondence field is non-trivial given only the low-res input. First, the definition of the high-res dense field is by itself ill-posed because the gray-scale of each pixel is distributed to adjacent pixels on the interpolated image (Fig. 1(c)). Second, the blur causes difficulties for many existing face alignment or parsing algorithms [3, 22–24] because most of them rely on sharp edge information. Consequently, we face a chicken-and-egg problem - face hallucination is better guided by face spatial configuration, while the latter requires a high resolution face. This issue, however, has been mostly ignored or bypassed in previous works (Sect. 2).

In this study, we propose to address the aforementioned problem with a novel *task-alternating cascaded framework*, as shown as Fig. 1(d). The two tasks at hand - the high-level face correspondence estimation and low-level face hallucination are complementary and can be alternatingly refined with the guidance from each other. Specifically, motivated by the fact that both tasks are performed in a cascaded manner [15, 23, 25], they can be naturally and seamlessly integrated into an alternating refinement process. During the cascade iteration, the dense correspondence field is progressively refined with the increasing face resolution, while the image resolution is adaptively upscaled guided by the finer dense correspondence field.

(a) Bicubic   (b) Common   (c) High-Freq.   (d) CBN   (e) Original

Fig. 2. Examples for visualizing the effects of the proposed gated deep bi-network. (a) The bicubic interpolation of the input. (b) Results where only common branches are enabled. (c) Results where only high-frequency branches are enabled. (d) Results of the proposed CBN when both branches are enabled. (e) The original high-res image. Best viewed by zooming in the electronic version.

To better recover different levels of texture details on faces, we propose a new *gated deep bi-network* architecture in the face hallucination step in each cascade. Deep convolutional neural networks have demonstrated state-of-the-art results for image super resolution [14,15,17,18]. In contrast to aforementioned studies, the proposed network consists two functionality-specialized branches, which are trained end-to-end. The first branch, referred as common branch, conservatively recovers texture details that are only detectable from the low-res input, similar to general super resolution. The other branch, referred as high-frequency branch, super-resolves faces with the additional high-frequency prior warped by the estimated face correspondence field in the current cascade. Thanks to the guidance of prior, this branch is capable of recovering and synthesizing un-revealed texture details in the overly low-res input image. A pixel-wise gate network is learned to fuse the results from the two branches. Figure 2 demonstrates the properties of the gated deep bi-network. As can be observed, the two branches are complementary. Although the high-frequency branch synthesizes the facial parts that are occluded (the eyes with sun-glasses), the gate network automatically favours the results from the common branch during fusion.

We refer the proposed framework as *Cascaded Bi-Networks* (CBN) hereafter. We summarize our contribution as follows:

1. While conducting face hallucination or dense face correspondence field is hard on low-res images, we circumvent this problem through a novel task-alternating cascade framework. In comparison to existing approaches, this framework has an appealing property of not assuming pre-aligned inputs or any availability of spatial information (e.g. landmark, parsing map).
2. We propose a gated deep bi-network that can effectively exploit face spatial prior to recover and synthesize texture details that even are not explicitly presented in the low-resolution input.
3. We provide extensive results and discussions to demonstrate and analyze the effectiveness of the proposed approach.

We perform extensive experiments against general super-resolution and face hallucination approaches on various benchmarks. Our method not only achieves high Peak Signal to Noise Ratio (PSNR), but also superior quality perceptually.

Demo codes will be available in our project page http://mmlab.ie.cuhk.edu.hk/projects/CBN.html.

2 Related Work

Face hallucination and spatial cues. There is a rich literature in face hallucination [6–13]. Spatial cues are proven essential in most of previous works, and are utilized in various forms. For example, Liu et al. [7,12] and Jin et al. [6] devised a warping function to connect the face local reconstruction with the high-res faces in the training set. However, a low-res correspondence field[1] may not be sufficient for aiding the high-res face reconstruction process, while obtaining the high-res correspondence field is ill-posed with only a low-res face given. Yang et al. [8] assumed that facial landmarks can be accurately estimated from the low-res face image. This is not correct if the low-res face is rather small (e.g. 5pxIOD), since the gray-scale is severely distributed to the adjacent pixels (Fig. 1(c)). Wang et al. [10] and Kolouri et al. [9] only aligned the input low-res faces with an identical similarity transform (e.g. the same scaling and rotation). Hence these approaches can only handle canonical-view low-res faces. Zhou et al. [26] pointed out the difficulties of predicting the spatial configuration over a low-res input, and did not take any spatial cues into account for hallucination. In contrast to all aforementioned approaches, we adaptively and alternatingly estimate the dense correspondence field as well as hallucinate the faces in a cascaded framework. The two mutual tasks aid each other and hence our estimation of the spatial cues and hallucination can be better refined with each other.

Cascaded prediction. The cascaded framework is privileged both for image super-resolution (SR) [15,25] and facial landmark detection [2,3,22,23,27–30]. For image SR, Wang et al. [15] showed that two rounds of 2× upscaling is better than a single round of 4× upscaling in their framework. For facial landmark detection, the cascaded regression framework has revolutionized the accuracy and has been extended to other areas [31]. The key success of the cascaded regression comes from its coarse-to-fine nature of the residual prediction. As pointed out by Zhang et al. [28], the coarse-to-fine nature can be better achieved by the increasing facial resolution among the cascades. To our knowledge, no existing work has integrated these two related tasks into a unified framework.

The bi-network architecture. The bi-network architecture [32–34] has been explored in various form, such as bilinear networks [35,36] and two-stream convolutional network [37]. In [35], the two factors, namely object identification and localization, are modeled by the two branches respectively. This is different from our model, where the two factors, the low-res face and the prior, are jointly modeled in one branch (the high-frequency branch), while the other branch (the common branch) only models the low-res face. In addition, the two branches are joined via the gate network in our model, different from the outer-production in [35]. In [37], both spatial and temporal information are modeled by the network,

---

[1] We assume that we only correspond from pixel to pixel.

which is different from our model, where no temporal information is incorporated. Our architecture also differs from [26]. In [26], the output is the average weighted by a scalar between the result of one branch and the low-res input. Moreover, neither of the two branches utilizes any spatial cues or prior in [26].

3   Cascaded Bi-Network (CBN)

3.1   Overview

Problem and notation. Given a low-resolution input facial image, our goal is to predict its high-resolution image. We introduce the two main entities involved in our framework:

The *facial image* is denoted as a matrix $\mathbf{I}$. We use $\mathbf{x} \in \mathbb{R}^2$ to denote the (x, y) coordinates of a pixel on $\mathbf{I}$.

The *dense face correspondence field* defines a pixel-wise correspondence mapping from $M \subset \mathbb{R}^2$ (the 2D face region in the mean face template) to the face region in image $\mathbf{I}$. We represent the dense field with a warping function [38], $\mathbf{x} = W(\mathbf{z}) : M \to \mathbb{R}^2$, which maps the coordinates $\mathbf{z} \in M$ from the mean shape template domain to the target coordinates $\mathbf{x} \in \mathbb{R}^2$. See Fig. 3(a,b) for a clear illustration. Following [39], we model the warping residual $W(\mathbf{z}) - \mathbf{z}$ as a linear combination of the dense facial deformation bases, i.e.

$$W(\mathbf{z}) = \mathbf{z} + \mathbf{B}(\mathbf{z})\mathbf{p} \qquad (1)$$

where $\mathbf{p} = [p_1 \ldots p_N]^\top \in \mathbb{R}^{N \times 1}$ denotes the deformation coefficients and $\mathbf{B}(\mathbf{z}) = [\mathbf{b}_1(\mathbf{z}) \ldots \mathbf{b}_N(\mathbf{z})] \in \mathbb{R}^{2 \times N}$ denotes the deformation bases. The N bases are chosen in the AAMs manner [40], that 4 out of N correspond to the similarity transform and the remaining for non-rigid deformations. Note that the bases are pre-defined and shared by all samples. Hence the dense field is actually controlled by the deformation coefficients $\mathbf{p}$ for each sample. When $\mathbf{p} = \mathbf{0}$, the dense field equals to the mean face template.

We use the hat notation (ˆ) to represent ground-truth in the learning step. For example, we denote the high-resolution training image as $\hat{\mathbf{I}}$.

Framework overview. We propose a principled framework to alternatively refine the face resolution and the dense correspondence field. Our framework consists of K iterations (Fig. 1(d)). Each iteration updates the prediction via

$$\mathbf{p}_k = \mathbf{p}_{k-1} + f_k(\mathbf{I}_{k-1};\ \mathbf{p}_{k-1}); W_k(\mathbf{z}) = \mathbf{z} + \mathbf{B}_k(\mathbf{z})\mathbf{p}_k; \qquad (2)$$

$$\mathbf{I}_k = \uparrow\mathbf{I}_{k-1} + g_k(\uparrow\mathbf{I}_{k-1};\ W_k(\mathbf{z})); \qquad (\forall \mathbf{z} \in M_k), \qquad (3)$$

where k iterates from 1 to K. Here, Eq. 2 represents the dense field updating step while Eq. 3 stands for the spatially guided face hallucination step in each cascade. '$\uparrow$' denotes the upscaling process (2× upscaling with bicubic interpolation in our implementation). All the notations are now appended with the index

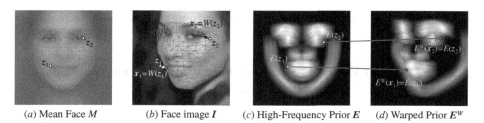

(a) Mean Face M (b) Face image I (c) High-Frequency Prior E (d) Warped Prior E^W

Fig. 3. (a,b) Illustration of the mean face template M and the facial image $\mathbf{I}$. The grid denotes the dense correspondence field $W(\mathbf{z})$. The warping from $\mathbf{z}$ to $\mathbf{x}$ is determined by this warping function $W(\mathbf{z})$. (c,d) Illustration of the high-frequency prior $\mathbf{E}$ and the prior after warping $\mathbf{E}^W$ for the sample image in (b). Note that both $\mathbf{E}$ and $\mathbf{E}^W$ have C channels. Each channel only contains one 'contour line'. For the purpose of visualization, in this figure, we reduce their channel dimension to one channel with max operation. We leave out all indices k for clarity. Best viewed in the electronic version.

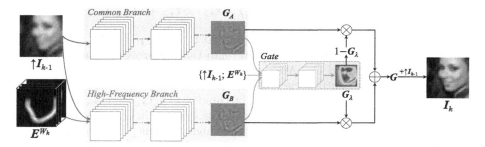

Fig. 4. Architecture of the proposed deep bi-network (for the k-th cascade). It consists of a common branch (blue), a high-frequency branch (red) and the gate network (cyan). (Color figure online)

k to indicate the iteration. A larger k in the notation of $\mathbf{I}_k$, W_k, $\mathbf{B}_k$ and M_k[2] indicates the larger resolution and the same k indicates the same resolution. The framework starts from $\mathbf{I}_0$ and $\mathbf{p}_0$. $\mathbf{I}_0$ denotes the input low-res facial image. $\mathbf{p}_0$ is a zero vector representing the deformation coefficients of the mean face template. The final hallucinated facial image output is $\mathbf{I}_K$.

Model, inference and learning. Our model is composed of functions f_k (dense field estimation) and g_k (face hallucination with spatial cues). The deformation bases $\mathbf{B}_k$ are pre-defined for each cascade and fixed during the whole training and testing procedures. During testing, we repeatedly update the image $\mathbf{I}_k$ and the dense correspondence field $W_k(\mathbf{z})$ (basically the coefficients $\mathbf{p}_k$) with Eqs. 2, 3. The learning procedure works similarly to the inference but incorporating the learning process of the two functions - g_k for hallucination and f_k for predicting

---

[2] We also append the subscript k for M because the mean face template domain M_k do not have the same size in different iteration k.

the dense field coefficients. We present their learning procedures in Sects. 3.2 and 3.3 respectively.

3.2 g_k - Gated Deep Bi-Network: Face Hallucination with Spatial Cues

We propose a gated deep bi-network architecture for face hallucination with the guidance from spatial cues. We train one gated bi-network for each cascade. For the k-th iteration, we take in the input image $\uparrow I_{k-1}$ and the current estimated dense correspondence field $W_k(\mathbf{z})$, to predict the image residual $\mathbf{G} = I_k - \uparrow I_{k-1}$.

As the name indicates, our gated bi-network contains two branches. In contrast to [35] where two branches are joined with outer production, we combine the two branches with a gate network. More precisely, if we denote the output from the common branch (A) and the high-frequency branch (B) as $\mathbf{G}_A$ and $\mathbf{G}_B$ respectively, we combine them with

$$g_k(\uparrow I_{k-1}; W_k(\mathbf{z})) = \mathbf{G} = (1 - \mathbf{G}_\lambda) \otimes \mathbf{G}_A + \mathbf{G}_\lambda \otimes \mathbf{G}_B, \qquad (4)$$

where $\mathbf{G}$ denotes our predicted image residual $I_k - \uparrow I_{k-1}$ (i.e. the result of g_k), and $\mathbf{G}_\lambda$ denotes the pixel-wise soft gate map that controls the combination of the two outputs $\mathbf{G}_A$ and $\mathbf{G}_B$. We use $\otimes$ to denote element-wise multiplication.

Figure 4 provides an overview of the gated bi-network architecture. Three convolutional sub-networks are designed to predict $\mathbf{G}_A$, $\mathbf{G}_B$ and $\mathbf{G}_\lambda$ respectively. The common branch sub-network (blue in Fig. 4) takes in only the interpolated low-res image $\uparrow I_{k-1}$ to predict $\mathbf{G}_A$ while the high-frequency branch sub-network (red in Fig. 4) takes in both $\uparrow I_{k-1}$ and the warped high-frequency prior $\mathbf{E}^{W_k}$ (warped according to the estimated dense correspondence field). All the inputs ($\uparrow I_{k-1}$ and $\mathbf{E}^{W_k}$) as well as $\mathbf{G}_A$ and $\mathbf{G}_B$ are fed into the gate sub-network (cyan in Fig. 4) for predicting $\mathbf{G}_\lambda$ and the final high-res output $\mathbf{G}$.

We now introduce the high-frequency prior and the training procedure of the proposed gated bi-network.

High-frequency prior. We define high-frequency prior as the indication for location with high-frequency details. In this work, we generate high-frequency prior maps to enforce spatial guidance for hallucination. The prior maps are obtained from the mean face template domain. More precisely, for each training image, we compute the residual image between the original image $\hat{I}$ and the bicubic interpolation of I_0, and then warp the residual map into the mean face template domain. We average the magnitude of the warped residual maps over all training images and form the preliminary high-frequency map. To suppress the noise and provide a semantically meaningful prior, we cluster the preliminary high-frequency map into C continuous contours (10 in our implementation). We form a C-channel maps, with each channel carrying one contour. We refer this C-channel maps as our high-frequency prior, and denote it as $E_k(\mathbf{z}) : M_k \to \mathbb{R}^C$. We use $\mathbf{E}_k$ to represent $E_k(\mathbf{z})$ for all $\mathbf{z} \in M_k$. An illustration of the prior is shown in Fig. 3(c).

Learning the gated bi-network. We train the three parts of convolutional neural networks to predict $\mathbf{G}_A$, $\mathbf{G}_B$ and $\mathbf{G}_\lambda$ in our unified bi-network architecture. Each part of the network has a distinct training loss. For training the common branch, we use the following loss over all training samples

$$L_A = \|\hat{\mathbf{I}}_k - \uparrow\mathbf{I}_{k-1} - \mathbf{G}_A\|_F^2. \tag{5}$$

The high-frequency branch has two inputs: $\uparrow\mathbf{I}_{k-1}$ and the *warped* high-frequency prior $\mathbf{E}^{W_k}$ (see Fig. 3(d) for illustration) to predict the output $\mathbf{G}_B$. The two inputs are fused in the channel dimension to form a $(1 + C)$-channel input. We use the following loss over all training samples

$$L_B = \sum_{c=1}^{C} \|(\mathbf{E}^{W_k})_c \otimes (\hat{\mathbf{I}}_k - \uparrow\mathbf{I}_{k-1} - \mathbf{G}_B)\|_F^2, \tag{6}$$

where $(\mathbf{E}^{W_k})_c$ denotes the c-th channel of the warped high-frequency prior maps. Compared to the common branch, we additionally utilize the prior knowledge as input and only penalize over the high-frequency area. Learning to predict the gate map $\mathbf{G}_\lambda$ is supervised by the final loss

$$L = \|\hat{\mathbf{I}}_k - \uparrow\mathbf{I}_{k-1} - \mathbf{G}\|_F^2. \tag{7}$$

We train the proposed gated bi-network with three steps. Step i: We only enable the supervision from L_A (Eq. 5) to pre-train the common branch; Step ii: We only enable L_B (Eq. 6) to pre-train the high-frequency branch; Step iii: We finally fine-tune the whole gated bi-network with the supervision from L (Eq. 7). In the last step, we set the learning rate of the parameters related to the gate map to be 10 times as the parameters in the two branches. Note that we can still use back-propagation to learn the whole bi-network in our last step.

3.3 f_k - Dense Field Deformation Coefficients Prediction

We apply a simple yet effective strategy to update the correspondence field coefficients estimation (f_k). Observing that predicting a sparse set of facial landmarks is more robust and accurate under low resolution, we transfer the facial landmarks deformation coefficients to the dense correspondence field. More precisely, we simultaneously obtain two sets of N deformation bases: $\mathbf{B}_k(\mathbf{z}) \in \mathbb{R}^{2 \times N}$ for the dense field, and $\mathbf{S}_k(l) \in \mathbb{R}^{2 \times N}$ for the landmarks, where l is the landmark index. The bases for the dense field and landmarks are one-to-one related, i.e. both $\mathbf{B}_k(\mathbf{z})$ and $\mathbf{S}_k(l)$ share the same deformation coefficients $\mathbf{p}_k \in \mathbb{R}^N$:

$$W_k(\mathbf{z}) = \mathbf{z} + \mathbf{B}_k(\mathbf{z})\mathbf{p}_k; \quad \mathbf{x}_k(l) = \bar{\mathbf{x}}_k(l) + \mathbf{S}_k(l)\mathbf{p}_k, \tag{8}$$

where $\mathbf{x}_k(l) \in \mathbb{R}^2$ denotes the coordinates of the l-th landmark, and $\bar{\mathbf{x}}_k(l)$ denotes its mean location.

To predict the deformation coefficients $\mathbf{p}_k$ in each cascade k, we utilize the powerful cascaded regression approach [23] for estimation. A Gauss-Newton steepest descent regression matrix $\mathbf{R}_k$ is learned in each iteration k to map the observed appearance to the deformation coefficients update:

$$\mathbf{p}_k = \mathbf{p}_{k-1} + f_k(\mathbf{I}_{k-1}; \mathbf{p}_{k-1}) = \mathbf{p}_{k-1} + \mathbf{R}_k(\phi(\mathbf{I}_{k-1}; \mathbf{x}_{k-1}(l)|_{l=1,...,L}) - \bar{\phi}), \quad (9)$$

where ϕ is the shape-indexed feature [2,27] that concatenates the local appearance from all L landmarks, and $\bar{\phi}$ is its average over all the training samples.

To learn the Gauss-Newton steepest descent regression matrix $\mathbf{R}_k$, we follow [23] to learn the Jacobian $\mathbf{J}_k$ and then obtain $\mathbf{R}_k$ via constructing the project-out Hessian: $\mathbf{R}_k = (\mathbf{J}_k^\top \mathbf{J}_k)^{-1} \mathbf{J}_k^\top$. We refer readers to [23] for more details.

It is worth mentioning that the face flow method [39] that applies a landmark-regularized Lucas-Kanade variational minimization [38] is also a good alternative to our problem. Since we have obtained satisfying results with our previously introduced deformation coefficients transfer strategy, which is purely discriminative and much faster than face flow (8 ms per cascade in our approach v.s. 1.4 s for face flow), we use the coefficients transfer approach in our experiments.

4   Experiments

Datasets. Following [6,8], we choose the following datasets that contain both in-the-wild and lab-constrained faces with various poses and illuminations.

1. *MultiPIE* [41] was originally proposed for face recognition. A total of more than 750,000 faces from 337 identities are collected under lab-constrained environment. We use the same 351 images as used in [8] for evaluation.
2. *BioID* [42] contains 1521 faces also collected in the constrained settings. We use the same 100 faces as used in [6] for evaluation.
3. *PubFig* [43] contains 42461 faces (the evaluation subset) from 140 identities originally for evaluating face verification and later used for evaluating face hallucination [8]. The faces are collected from the web and hence in-the-wild. Due to the existence of invalid URLs, we use a total of 20991 faces for evaluation. Further, following [6], we use *PubFig83* [44], a subset of PubFig with 13838 images, to experiment with input blurred by unknown Gaussian kernel. Similar to [6], we test with the same 100-image-subset of PubFig83.
4. *Helen* [45] contains 2330 in-the-wild faces with high resolution. The mean face size is as large as 275pxIOD. We evaluate with the 330-image test set.

Metric. We follow existing studies [6,8,12,14,15] to adopt PSNR (dB) and only evaluate on the luminance channel of the facial region. The definition of the facial region is the same as used in [6]. Similar to [6], SSIM is not reported for in-the-wild faces due to irregular facial shape.

Implementation details. Our framework consists of $K = 4$ cascades, and each cascade has its specific learned network parameters and Gauss-Newton steepest descent regression matrix. During training, our model requires two parts of training data, one for training the cascaded dense face correspondence field, and the other for training the cascaded gated bi-networks for hallucination. The model is trained by iterating between these two parts of the training data. For the former part, we use the training set from 300 W [46] (the same 2811 images used in [23]) for estimating deformation coefficient and BU4D [47,48] dataset for obtaining dense face correspondence basis (following [39]). For the latter part, as no manual labeling is required, we leverage the existing large face database CelebA [49] for training the gated bi-network.

4.1 Comparison with State-of-the-Art Methods

We compare our approach with two types of methods: (I) general super resolution (SR) approaches and (II) face hallucination approaches. For SR methods, we compare with the recent state-of-the-art approaches [14,15,19,50] based on the original released codes. For face hallucination methods, we report the result of [6,12,51] by directly referring to the literature [6]. We compare with [8,52] by following the implementation of [8]. We re-transform the input face to canonical-view if the method assumes the input must be aligned. Hence, such method would enjoy extra advantages in the comparison. If the method requires exemplars, we feed in the same in-the-wild samples in our training set. We observe that such in-the-wild exemplars improve the exemplar-based baseline methods compared to their original implementation. Codes for [7] is not publicly available. Similar to [6], we provide the qualitative comparison with [7].

We conduct the comparison in two folds: 1. The input is the down-sampled version of the original high-res image as many of the previous SR methods are evaluated on [7,14,15,19,50] (referred as the conventional SR setting, Sect. 4.1); 2. The input is additionally blurred with unknown Gaussian kernel before down-sampling as in [6,8,12] (referred as the Gaussian-blurred setting, Sect. 4.1).

The Conventional SR Evaluation Setting We experiment with two scenarios based on two different types of input face size configuration:

1. *Fixed up-scaling factors* – The input image is generated by resizing the original image with a fixed factor. For MultiPIE, following [8] we choose the fixed factor to be 4. For the in-the-wild datasets (PubFig and Helen), we evaluate for scaling factors of 2, 3 and 4 as in [14,15,19,50] (denoted as $2\times, 3\times, 4\times$ respectively in Table 1). In this case, different inputs might have different face sizes. The proposed CBN is flexible to handle such scenario. Other existing face hallucination approaches [8,12,51,52] cannot handle different input face sizes and their results in this scenario are omitted.

2. *Fixed input face sizes* – Similar to the face hallucination setting, the input image is generated by resizing the original image to ensure the input face size to be fixed (e.g. 5 or 8 pxIOD, denoted as 5/8px in Table 1). Hence, the required up-scaling factor is different for each input. For baseline approaches, [15] can naturally handle any up-scaling requirement. For other approaches, we train a set of models for different up-scaling factors. During testing, we pick up the most suitable model based on the specified up-scaling factor.

Table 1. Results under the conventional SR setting (for Sect. 4.1). Numbers in the parentheses indicate SSIM and the remaining represent PSNR (dB). The first part of the results are from Scenario 1 where each method super-resolves for a fixed factor (2×, 3× or 4×), while the latter part are from Scenario 2 that each method begins from the same face size (5 or 8 pxIOD, i.e. the inter-ocular distance is 5 or 8 pixels). The omitted results (-) are due to their incapability of handling varying input face size.

Dataset	Input size	Bicubic	(I) General super-resolution				(II) Face hallucination			CBN
			A+ [50]	SRCNN [14]	CSCN [15]	NBF [19]	PCA [12,51]	[52]	[8]	
MultiPIE	4×	33.66	34.53	34.75	35.10	34.73	33.98	34.07	34.31	**35.65**
		(.900)	(.910)	(.913)	(.920)	(.912)	(.904)	(.907)	(.903)	**(.926)**
PubFig	2×	34.78	35.89	36.12	36.47	35.98	-	-	-	**36.66**
	3×	31.52	32.02	32.13	32.88	32.09	-	-	-	**33.17**
	4×	29.61	30.02	30.15	30.79	30.16	-	-	-	**31.28**
HELEN	2×	41.96	42.77	42.95	43.37	43.01	-	-	-	**43.51**
	3×	38.52	38.89	39.10	39.57	39.15	-	-	-	**39.78**
	4×	36.59	36.81	36.87	37.61	36.89	-	-	-	**37.94**
MultiPIE	5px	25.39	25.63	25.72	25.93	25.75	25.62	25.83	25.72	**27.14**
		(.752)	(.767)	(.771)	(.773)	(.769)	(.767)	(.774)	(.769)	**(.808)**
PubFig	8px	22.32	22.79	22.98	23.25	23.08	23.37	23.57	23.10	**26.83**
	5px	20.63	20.96	21.07	21.33	21.04	21.42	21.58	21.19	**25.31**
HELEN	8px	21.86	22.24	22.47	22.69	22.53	22.95	23.01	22.62	**26.36**
	5px	20.28	20.50	20.59	20.84	20.57	21.09	21.13	20.64	**25.09**

Table 2. Results under the Gaussian-blur setting (for Sect. 4.1). Numbers in parentheses indicate SSIM and the remaining represent PSNR (dB). Settings adhere to [6]. For a fair comparison, we feed in the same number of *in-the-wild* exemplars from CelebA when evaluating [8], instead of the originally used MultiPIE in the released codes.

Dataset	Bicubic	(I) General super-resolution				(II) Face hallucination				CBN
		A+ [50]	SRCNN [14]	CSCN [15]	NBF [19]	PCA [12,51]	[52]	[8]	[6]	
BioID	19.67	20.47	20.59	20.86	20.60	21.51	21.77	20.01	22.32	**24.55**
	(.670)	(.684)	(.685)	(.695)	(.688)	(.770)	(.776)	(.689)	(.810)	**(.852)**
PubFig83	24.78	25.20	25.22	25.65	25.47	25.72	25.83	25.02	26.17	**29.83**

We need to point out that the latter scenario is more challenging and appropriate for evaluating a face hallucination algorithm, because recovering the details of the face with the size of 5/8pxIOD is more applicable for low-res face processing applications. In the former scenario, the input face is not small enough (as revealed in the bicubic PSNR in Table 1), such that it is more like a facial image enhancement problem rather than the challenging face hallucination task.

We report the results in Table 1, and provide qualitative results in Fig. 5. As can be seen from the results, our proposed CBN outperforms all general SR and face hallucination methods in both scenarios. The improvement is especially significant in the latter scenario because our incorporated face prior is more critical when hallucinating face from very low resolution. We observe that the general SR algorithms did not obtain satisfying results because they take full efforts to recover only the detectable high-frequency details, which obviously contain noise.

Table 3. PSNR results (dB) of in-house comparison of the proposed CBN (for Sect. 4.2).

Dataset	1a. Only common branch i.e. Vanilla cascaded CNN	1b. Only high-freq. branch	2. Fixed correspondence	3. Single cascade	Full Model
PubFig	23.76	24.66	23.85	22.09	**25.31**
HELEN	23.57	24.53	23.77	21.83	**25.09**
PubFig83	28.06	29.31	28.34	26.70	**29.83**

Fig. 5. Qualitative results from PubFig/HELEN with input size 5pxIOD (for Sect. 4.1, detailed results refer Table 1). Best viewed by zooming in the electronic version.

In contrast, our approach recovers the details according to the high-frequency prior as well as the estimated dense correspondence field, thus achieving better performance. The existing face hallucination approaches did not perform well either. In comparison to the evaluation under the constrained or canonical-view condition (e.g. [8]), we found that these algorithms are more likely to fail under in-the-wild setting with substantial shape deformation and appearance variation.

The Gaussian-Blur Evaluation Setting It is also important to explore the capability of handling blurred input images [53]. Our method demonstrates certain degrees of robustness toward unknown Gaussian blur. Specifically, in this section, we still adopt the same model as in Sect. 4.1, with no extra efforts spent in the training to specifically cope with blurring. To compare with [6], we add Gaussian blur to the input facial image in the same way as [6]. The experimental settings are precisely the same as in [6] - the input faces have the same size (around 8pxIOD); the up-scaling factor is set to be 4; and σ for Gaussian blur kernel is set to be 1.6 for *PubFig83* and 2.4 for *BioID*. Additional Gaussian noise with $\eta = 2$ is added in BioID. We note that our approach only uses single frame for inference, unlike multiple frames in [6].

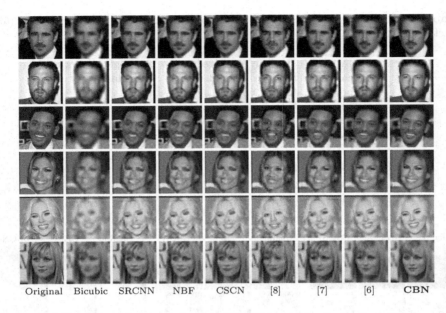

Original Bicubic SRCNN NBF CSCN [8] [7] [6] **CBN**

Fig. 6. Qualitative results from the PubFig83 dataset (for Sect. 4.1, detailed results refer Table 2). The six test samples presented are chosen by strictly following [6].

Bicubic CSCN [6] **CBN**   Bicubic CSCN [6] **CBN**

Fig. 7. Qualitative results for real surveillance videos (for Sect. 4.1). The test samples are directly imported from [6]. Best viewed by zooming in the electronic version.

We summarize the results in Table 2. Qualitative results are shown in Fig. 6. From the results it is observed that again CBN significantly outperforms all the compared approaches. We attribute the robustness toward the unknown Gaussian blur on the spatial guidance provided by the face high-frequency prior.

Taking advantages of such robustness of our approach, we further test the proposed algorithm over the faces from real surveillance videos. In Fig. 7, we compare our result with [6,15]. Note that the presented test cases are directly imported from [6]. Again, our result demonstrates the most appealing visual quality compared to existing state-of-the-art approaches, suggesting the potential of our proposed framework in real-world applications.

Run Time The major time cost of our approach is consumed on the forwarding process of the gated deep bi-networks. On a single core i7-4790 CPU, the face hallucination steps for the four cascades (from 5pxIOD to 80pxIOD) require 0.13 s, 0.17 s, 0.70 s, 2.76 s, respectively. The time cost of the dense field prediction steps is negligible compared to the hallucination step. Our framework totally consumes 3.84 s, which is significantly faster than existing face hallucination approaches, for examples, 15–20 min for [6], 1 min for [8], 8 min for [12], thanks to CBN's purely discriminative inference procedure and the non-exemplar and parametric model structure.

4.2 An Ablation Study

We investigate the effects of three important components in our framework:

1. **Effects of the gated bi-network**. (a) We explore the results if we replace the cascaded gated bi-network with the vanilla cascaded CNN, in which only the common branch (the blue branch in Fig. 4) is remained. In this case, the spatial information, i.e. the dense face correspondence field is not considered or optimized at all. (b) We also explore the case where only the high-frequency branch (the red branch in Fig. 4) is remained.
2. **Effects of the progressively updated dense correspondence field**. In our framework, the pixel-level correspondence field is refined progressively to better facilitate the subsequent hallucination process. We explore the results if we only use the correspondence estimated from the input low-res image[3]. In this case, the spatial configuration estimation is not updated with the growth of the resolution.
3. **Effects of the cascade**. The cascaded alternating framework is the core for our framework. We explore the results if we train one network and directly super resolve the input to the required size. High-frequency prior is still used in this baseline. We observe an even worse result without this prior.

We present the results in Table 3. The experimental setting follows the same setting in Sect. 4.1 - The PubFig and HELEN datasets super-resolve from 5pxIOD while the PubFig83 dataset up-scales 4 times with unknown Gaussian blur. The results suggest that all components are important to our proposed approach.

4.3 Discussion

Despite the effectiveness of our method, we still observe a small set of failure cases. Figure 8 illustrates three typical types of failure: (1) Over-synthesis of occluded facial parts, e.g., the eyes in Fig. 8(a). In this case, the gate network might have been misled by the light-colored sun-glasses and therefore favours the results from the high-frequency branch. (2) Ghosting effect, which is caused by inaccurate spatial prediction under low-res. It is rather challenging to localize

---

[3] As the correspondence estimation is by itself a cascaded process, in this case, we re-order the face corresponding cascades before the super resolution cascades.

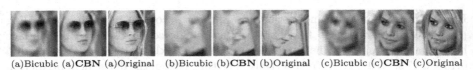

(a)Bicubic (a)**CBN** (a)Original   (b)Bicubic (b)**CBN** (b)Original   (c)Bicubic (c)**CBN** (c)Original

Fig. 8. Three types of representative failure cases of our approach (for Sect. 4.3).

facial parts with very large head pose in the low-res image. (3) Incorrect details such as gaze direction. We found that there is almost no reliable gaze direction information presented in the input. Our method only synthesizes the eyes with the most probable gaze direction. We leave it as future works to address the aforementioned drawbacks.

5   Conclusion

We have presented a novel framework for hallucinating faces under substantial shape deformation and appearance variation. Owing to the specific capability to adaptively refine the dense correspondence field and hallucinate faces in an alternating manner, we obtain state-of-the-art performance and visually appealing qualitative results. Guided by the high-frequency prior, our framework can leverage spatial cues in the hallucination process.

Acknowledgment. This work is partially supported by SenseTime Group Limited and the Hong Kong Innovation and Technology Support Programme.

References

1. Yang, S., Luo, P., Loy, C.C., Tang, X.: Wider face: A face detection benchmark. arXiv preprint arXiv:1511.06523 (2015)
2. Cao, X., Wei, Y., Wen, F., Sun, J.: Face alignment by explicit shape regression. IJCV **107**(2), 177–190 (2014)
3. Xiong, X., De la Torre, F.: Supervised descent method and its applications to face alignment. In: CVPR, pp. 532–539 (2013)
4. Schroff, F., Kalenichenko, D., Philbin, J.: Facenet: a unified embedding for face recognition and clustering. In: CVPR (2015)
5. Taigman, Y., Yang, M., Ranzato, M., Wolf, L.: DeepFace: Closing the gap to human-level performance in face verification. In: CVPR (2014)
6. Jin, Y., Bouganis, C.S.: Robust multi-image based blind face hallucination. In: CVPR (2015)
7. Tappen, M.F., Liu, C.: A bayesian approach to alignment-based image hallucination. In: Fitzgibbon, A., Lazebnik, S., Perona, P., Sato, Y., Schmid, C. (eds.) ECCV 2012, Part VII. LNCS, vol. 7578, pp. 236–249. Springer, Heidelberg (2012)
8. Yang, C.Y., Liu, S., Yang, M.H.: Structured face hallucination. In: CVPR (2013)
9. Kolouri, S., Rohde, G.K.: Transport-based single frame super resolution of very low resolution face images. In: CVPR (2015)

10. Wang, X., Tang, X.: Hallucinating face by eigentransformation. IEEE Trans. Syst. Man Cybern. Part C: Appl. Rev. **35**, 425–434 (2005)
11. Chakrabarti, A., Rajagopalan, A., Chellappa, R.: Super-resolution of face images using kernel PCA-based prior. IEEE Trans. Multimedia **9**(4), 888–892 (2007)
12. Liu, C., Shum, H.Y., Freeman, W.T.: Face hallucination: theory and practice. IJCV **75**, 115–134 (2007)
13. Baker, S., Kanade, T.: Hallucinating faces. In: AFGR (2000)
14. Dong, C., Loy, C.C., He, K., Tang, X.: Image super-resolution using deep convolutional networks. In: PAMI (2015)
15. Wang, Z., Liu, D., Yang, J., Han, W., Huang, T.: Deep networks for image super-resolution with sparse prior. In: ICCV (2015)
16. Huang, J.B., Singh, A., Ahuja, N.: Single image super-resolution from transformed self-exemplars. In: CVPR (2015)
17. Gu, S., Zuo, W., Xie, Q., Meng, D., Feng, X., Zhang, L.: Convolutional sparse coding for image super-resolution. In: ICCV (2015)
18. Bruna, J., Sprechmann, P., LeCun, Y.: Super-resolution with deep convolutional sufficient statistics. In: ICLR (2016)
19. Salvador, J., Perez-Pellitero, E.: Naive bayes super-resolution forest. In: ICCV (2015)
20. Dong, C., Loy, C.C., Tang, X.: Accelerating the super-resolution convolutional neural network. In: Leibe, B., Matas, J., Sebe, N., Welling, M. (eds.) ECCV 2016, PART II. LNCS, vol. 9906, pp. 391–407. Springer, Heidelberg (2016)
21. Hui, T.W., Loy, C.C., Tang, X.: Depth map super resolution by deep multi-scale guidance. In: Leibe, B., Matas, J., Sebe, N., Welling, M. (eds.) ECCV 2016, PART III. LNCS, vol. 9907, pp. 353–369. Springer, Heidelberg (2016)
22. Ren, S., Cao, X., Wei, Y., Sun, J.: Face alignment at 3000 fps via regressing local binary features. In: CVPR (2014)
23. Tzimiropoulos, G.: Project-out cascaded regression with an application to face alignment. In: CVPR (2015)
24. Smith, B.M., Zhang, L., Brandt, J., Lin, Z., Yang, J.: Exemplar-based face parsing. In: CVPR, pp. 3484–3491 (2013)
25. Cui, Z., Chang, H., Shan, S., Zhong, B., Chen, X.: Deep network cascade for image super-resolution. In: Fleet, D., Pajdla, T., Schiele, B., Tuytelaars, T. (eds.) ECCV 2014, Part V. LNCS, vol. 8693, pp. 49–64. Springer, Heidelberg (2014)
26. Zhou, E., Fan, H., Cao, Z., Jiang, Y., Yin, Q.: Learning face hallucination in the wild. In: AAAI (2015)
27. Dollár, P., Welinder, P., Perona, P.: Cascaded pose regression. In: CVPR, pp. 1078–1085 (2010)
28. Zhang, J., Shan, S., Kan, M., Chen, X.: Coarse-to-fine auto-encoder networks (CFAN) for real-time face alignment. In: Fleet, D., Pajdla, T., Schiele, B., Tuytelaars, T. (eds.) ECCV 2014, Part II. LNCS, vol. 8690, pp. 1–16. Springer, Heidelberg (2014)
29. Zhu, S., Li, C., Loy, C.C., Tang, X.: Face alignment by coarse-to-fine shape searching. In: CVPR (2015)
30. Zhu, S., Li, C., Loy, C.C., Tang, X.: Unconstrained face alignment via cascaded compositional learning. In: CVPR (2016)
31. Wang, X., Valstar, M., Martinez, B., Haris Khan, M., Pridmore, T.: Tric-track: tracking by regression with incrementally learned cascades. In: ICCV (2015)
32. Tenenbaum, J.B., Freeman, W.T.: Separating style and content with bilinear models. Neural Comput. **12**, 1247–1283 (2000)

33. Pirsiavash, H., Ramanan, D., Fowlkes, C.C.: Bilinear classifiers for visual recognition. In: NIPS (2009)
34. Xiong, Y., Zhu, K., Lin, D., Tang, X.: Recognize complex events from static images by fusing deep channels. In: CVPR (2015)
35. Lin, T.Y., RoyChowdhury, A., Maji, S.: Bilinear CNN models for fine-grained visual recognition. In: ICCV (2015)
36. Gao, Y., Beijbom, O., Zhang, N., Darrell, T.: Compact bilinear pooling. In: CVPR (2016)
37. Simonyan, K., Zisserman, A.: Two-stream convolutional networks for action recognition in videos. In: NIPS (2014)
38. Alabort-i Medina, J., Zafeiriou, S.: Unifying holistic and parts-based deformable model fitting. In: CVPR (2015)
39. Snape, P., Roussos, A., Panagakis, Y., Zafeiriou, S.: Face flow. In: ICCV (2015)
40. Cootes, T.F., Edwards, G.J., Taylor, C.J.: Active appearance models. TPAMI 23(6), 681–685 (2001)
41. Gross, R., Matthews, I., Cohn, J., Kanade, T., Baker, S.: Multi-pie. Image Vis. Comput. 28(5), 807–813 (2010)
42. Jesorsky, O., Kirchberg, K.J., Frischholz, R.W.: Robust face detection using the Hausdorff distance. In: Bigun, J., Smeraldi, F. (eds.) AVBPA 2001. LNCS, vol. 2091, pp. 90–95. Springer, Heidelberg (2001). doi:10.1007/3-540-45344-X_14
43. Kumar, N., Berg, A.C., Belhumeur, P.N., Nayar, S.K.: Attribute and simile classifiers for face verification. In: CVPR (2009)
44. Pinto, N., Stone, Z., Zickler, T., Cox, D.: Scaling up biologically-inspired computer vision: a case study in unconstrained face recognition on facebook. In: CVPRW (2011)
45. Le, V., Brandt, J., Lin, Z., Bourdev, L., Huang, T.S.: Interactive facial feature localization. In: Fitzgibbon, A., Lazebnik, S., Perona, P., Sato, Y., Schmid, C. (eds.) ECCV 2012, Part III. LNCS, vol. 7574, pp. 679–692. Springer, Heidelberg (2012)
46. Sagonas, C., Tzimiropoulos, G., Zafeiriou, S., Pantic, M.: 300 faces in-the-wild challenge: the first facial landmark localization challenge. In: ICCVW (2013)
47. Zhang, X., Yin, L., Cohn, J.F., Canavan, S., Reale, M., Horowitz, A., Liu, P., Girard, J.M.: BP4D-spontaneous: a high-resolution spontaneous 3d dynamic facial expression database. Image Vis. Comput. 32(10), 692–706 (2014)
48. Zhang, X., Yin, L., Cohn, J.F., Canavan, S., Reale, M., Horowitz, A., Liu, P.: A high-resolution spontaneous 3d dynamic facial expression database. In: 2013 10th IEEE International Conference and Workshops on Automatic Face and Gesture Recognition (FG) (2013)
49. Liu, Z., Luo, P., Wang, X., Tang, X.: Deep learning face attributes in the wild. In: ICCV (2015)
50. Timofte, R., De Smet, V., Van Gool, L.: A+: adjusted anchored neighborhood regression for fast super-resolution. In: Cremers, D., Reid, I., Saito, H., Yang, M.-H. (eds.) ACCV 2014. LNCS, vol. 9006, pp. 111–126. Springer, Heidelberg (2015)
51. Capel, D., Zisserman, A.: Super-resolution from multiple views using learnt image models. In: CVPR (2001)
52. Ma, X., Zhang, J., Qi, C.: Hallucinating face by position-patch. Pattern Recogn. 43(6), 2224–2236 (2010)
53. Efrat, N., Glasner, D., Apartsin, A., Nadler, B., Levin, A.: Accurate blur models vs. image priors in single image super-resolution. In: ICCV (2013)

Cluster Sparsity Field for Hyperspectral Imagery Denoising

Lei Zhang[1], Wei Wei[1(✉)], Yanning Zhang[1], Chunhua Shen[2],
Anton van den Hengel[2], and Qinfeng Shi[2]

[1] School of Computer Science and Engineering,
Northwestern Polytechnical University, Xi'an, China
zhanglei211@mail.nwpu.edu.cn, weiweinwpu@nwpu.edu.cn
[2] School of Computer Science, The University of Adelaide, Adelaide, Australia

Abstract. Hyperspectral images (HSIs) can facilitate extensive computer vision applications with the extra spectra information. However, HSIs often suffer from noise corruption during the practical imaging procedure. Though it has been testified that intrinsic correlation across spectrum and spatial similarity (i.e., local similarity in locally smooth areas and non-local similarity among recurrent patterns) in HSIs are useful for denoising, how to fully exploit them together to obtain a good denoising model is seldom studied. In this study, we present an effective cluster sparsity field based HSIs denoising (CSFHD) method by exploiting those two characteristics simultaneously. Firstly, a novel Markov random field prior, named cluster sparsity field (CSF), is proposed for the sparse representation of an HSI. By grouping pixels into several clusters with spectral similarity, the CSF prior defines both a structured sparsity potential and a graph structure potential on each cluster to model the correlation across spectrum and spatial similarity in the HSI, respectively. Then, the CSF prior learning and the image denoising are unified into a variational framework for optimization, where all unknown variables are learned directly from the noisy observation. This guarantees to learn a data-dependent image model, thus producing satisfying denoising results. Plenty experiments on denoising synthetic and real noisy HSIs validated that the proposed CSFHD outperforms several state-of-the-art methods.

Keywords: Hyperspectral · Denoising · Structured sparsity · Spatial similarity

1 Introduction

Hyperspectral images (HSIs) contain both spectral and spatial information. The spectra represent the reflectance of a real scene across multiple narrow-width

---

L. Zhang's contribution was made when visiting The University of Adelaide.

Electronic supplementary material The online version of this chapter (doi:10. 1007/978-3-319-46454-1_38) contains supplementary material, which is available to authorized users.

© Springer International Publishing AG 2016
B. Leibe et al. (Eds.): ECCV 2016, Part V, LNCS 9909, pp. 631–647, 2016.
DOI: 10.1007/978-3-319-46454-1_38

bands, which can be used to identify and characterize a particular feature of the scene. HSI is thus widely used for extensive applications such as scene classification [1], surveillance [2] and disease diagnosis [3], etc. However, during the imaging process, HSIs are inevitably affected by noise [4]. Since the noise corruption increases the difficulty of applications, e.g., classification, HSIs denoising becomes a crucial step for HSIs based systems [5–7].

Lots of HSIs denoising methods have been proposed, such as wavelet shrinkage based method [8], multi-linear algebra based methods [5,6], etc., among which the following two consensuses have been testified useful to obtain a good denoising result. (1) Since continuous spectrum implies high correlation, exploiting the correlation across spectrum will improve the denoising quality. (2) HSIs especially for natural scene HSIs contain abundant locally smooth areas and recurrent patterns, which result in the local and non-local spatial similarity, respectively, thus exploiting such spatial similarity (i.e., both the local and non-local similarity) in HSIs is also beneficial to denoising.

Based on these two consensuses, many effective methods have been proposed for HSIs denoising. Since spectrum can be sparsely represented in a specific domain, sparse representation model has been widely used to model the correlation across spectrum in HSIs [9, 10]. However, these methods cannot fully exploit the desired correlation, because ℓ_1 norm cannot depict the structure in each sparse signal. To address this problem, Zhang et al. [11] proposed a reweighted Laplace prior to explore the structured sparsity of spectra. Nevertheless, this method models each spectrum independently without considering the spatial similarity in HSIs, which limits its performance in HSIs denoising. To model the spatial similarity in HSIs, Qian et al. [12] and Maggioni et al. [13] adopted small 3D cubes instead of 2D patches in the classical 2D image denosing methods (e.g., NLM [14] and BM3D [15]), to consider the non-local spatial similarity in HSIs. However, they neglected the correlation across spectrum [7]. Considering an HSI as a 3rd tensor, Renard et al. [5] employed the low rank tensor approximation to explore the correlation across spectrum as well as the local spatial similarity. Liu et al. [6] proposed a parallel factor analysis model to further refine the low rank tensor approximation. However, they do not consider the non-local spatial similarity in HSIs. To address this problem, Peng et al. [7] proposed a tensor dictionary learning model to depict the non-local spatial similarity in HSIs. Qian et al. [16] introduced the non-local similarity into spectral-spatial structure based sparse representation model. Nevertheless, none of those two methods explicitly consider the local similarity within the spatially locally smooth areas of HSIs [17]. Recently, Fu et al. [17] further explored the local similarity by learning a spectral-spatial dictionary, however it only fits the uniformly distributed noise across bands. Therefore, how to fully exploit the correlation across spectrum and spatial similarity together for an effective denoising model is still challenging.

In this study, we integrate those two characteristics into a novel cluster sparsity field based HSIs denoising (CSFHD) method. Firstly, a novel Markov random field prior, named cluster sparsity field (CSF), is proposed for the sparse representation of an HSI. By grouping pixels into several spatial clusters with spectral similarity, two different potentials in CSF are defined on each cluster to explore the structures in the HSI. The structured sparsity potential implicitly depicts the correlation over spectrum by exploring the structure within sparse representation, while the graph structure potential adopts the intra-cluster spectral similarity to depict the spatial similarity. Then, proper hyperpriors are employed to regularize the prior parameters, which allow the CSF prior to be suitable for the data-dependent structure as well as to avoid over-fitting in prior learning. Furthermore, we integrate the CSF prior learning and image denoising into a variational optimization framework, where the CSF prior, noise level and the latent clean image are jointly learned from the noisy observation. This guarantees to learn a data-dependent image model and thus producing satisfying denoising results.

In summary, the proposed method has three key benefits: (1) The CSF prior jointly models the correlation across spectrum and spatial similarity of an HSI with the sparse representation model. (2) The CSF prior is data-specific and well regularized. (3) The proposed method can learn the data-dependent structures and outperforms several state-of-the-art methods in extensive experiments.

2   Cluster Sparsity Field (CSF)

To jointly model the correlation across spectrum and spatial similarity into an image prior, we define a novel Markov random field, named cluster sparsity field (CSF), on the sparse representation of an HSI with a given dictionary. Specifically, the 3D HSI is rearranged into a 2D matrix $X = [\mathrm{x}_1, ..., \mathrm{x}_{n_p}] \in \mathbb{R}^{n_b \times n_p}$ for convenience, where n_b indicates the number of bands and n_p is the number of pixels. The 2D image on each band is vectorized as a row of X, while each column x_i of X denotes the spectrum of one pixel. Provided that the imaging scene contains K homogeneous areas, pixels in X thus can be grouped into K spatial clusters based on spectral similarity. Let $X_k \in \mathbb{R}^{n_b \times n_k}$ denote the pixels in the kth cluster, where $k = 1, ..., K$ and n_k is the number of pixels in this cluster. Given a proper spectra dictionary $\Phi \in \mathbb{R}^{n_b \times n_d}$, X_k can be sparsely represented as $X_k = \Phi Y_k$, where $Y_k = [\mathrm{y}_k^1, ..., \mathrm{y}_k^{n_k}] \in \mathbb{R}^{n_d \times n_k}$ is the sparse representation matrix. Given $Y = [Y_1, ..., Y_K]$, $X = \Phi Y$ with a permutation on columns. Let sparse vectors y_k^i be denoted by nodes V in a graph $G = (V, E)$, where E represents edges connecting such nodes. The probability distribution of Y can be characterized by a Gibbs distribution as

$$p(Y) = \frac{1}{Z} \exp \left\{ -\sum_k E_{\mathrm{csf}}(Y_k) \right\}, \quad E_{\mathrm{csf}}(Y_k) = \varphi(Y_k) + \psi(Y_k) \qquad (1)$$

where E_{csf} is the potential function defined on each cluster and Z is a normalization term. In this study, $E_{\mathrm{csf}}(Y_k)$ is defined by tow potentials $\varphi(Y_k)$ and $\psi(Y_k)$, which models the correlation across spectrum and spatial similarity in an HSI, respectively.

2.1   Structured Sparsity Potential

Natural signals (e.g., spectra in HSIs) often produce approximately sparse representation vectors on the given dictionary [18], each of which contains many entries close to but not equal to zero. Moreover, the correlation among signal entries is reflected by the specific structure in each sparse vector [11], e.g., the tree structure of natural signal in wavelet domain. Therefore, it is essential to depict the structured sparsity in Y_k to model the correlation across spectrum in HSIs. Recently developed reweighted Laplace prior [11] specializes in depicting the structure in approximately sparse signals. Hence, we impose the reweighted Laplace prior on each Y_k. First, we define $\varphi(Y_k)$ as

$$\varphi(Y_k) = \frac{1}{2}\|Y_k\|_{\Gamma_k}^2, \quad \Gamma_k = \mathbf{diag}(\boldsymbol{\gamma}_k), \tag{2}$$

where $\|Y_k\|_{\Gamma_k} = \sqrt{\mathbf{tr}(Y_k^T \Gamma_k^{-1} Y_k)}$ denotes a weighted trace norm on Y_k and $\boldsymbol{\gamma}_k = [\gamma_{1k}, ..., \gamma_{n_d k}]^T$. Then, a Gamma distribution is imposed on $\boldsymbol{\gamma}_k$ as

$$p(\boldsymbol{\gamma}_k|\boldsymbol{\varpi}_k) = \prod_j \frac{\varpi_{jk}}{2}\exp\left(-\frac{\varpi_{jk}\gamma_{jk}}{2}\right), \tag{3}$$

where $\boldsymbol{\varpi}_k = [\varpi_{1k}, ..., \varpi_{n_d k}]^T$. When each $\psi(Y_k) = 0$, the CSF prior in Eq. (1) degenerates to a product of K matrix normal distributions. By integrating $\boldsymbol{\gamma}_k$, the hierarchical CSF prior in Eqs. (1), (3) amounts to a joint reweighted Laplace prior for each cluster as

$$p(Y|\{\boldsymbol{\varpi}_k\}_{k=1}^K) \propto \prod_k \prod_i \exp\left(-\|\Omega_k \boldsymbol{y}_k^i\|_1\right), \tag{4}$$

where $\Omega_k = \mathbf{diag}(\hat{\boldsymbol{\varpi}}_k)$ and $\hat{\boldsymbol{\varpi}}_k = [\sqrt{\varpi_{1k}}, ..., \sqrt{\varpi_{n_d k}}]^T$. In contrast to [11] without clustering, the hierarchical CSF prior tries to capture different structures for various clusters. Moreover, the product operation in Eq. (4) forces all clusters to fit their corresponding joint structured sparsity simultaneously.

2.2 Graph Structure Potential

HSIs especially for natural scene HSIs often contain locally smooth areas and recurrent patterns in the spatial domain, which result in abundant spatial similarity in HSIs. Owing to the fact that spatially similar pixels often show similar spectra [19], after spectral similarity based clustering, pixels from locally smooth areas or recurrent patterns fall into the same cluster. Thus, the spatial (i.e., both local and non-local) similarity can be naturally modelled by the intra-cluster spectral similarity. In each cluster, high similarity guarantees that a considered spectrum can be well reconstructed by others. With a given dictionary, such relationship is trivially preserved in the corresponding sparse representation of spectra. Therefore, we introduce a graph structure potential as

$$\psi(Y_k) = \frac{1}{2}\|Y_k - Y_k W_k\|_{\Sigma_k}^2 = \frac{1}{2}\sum_i \|\boldsymbol{y}_k^i - Y_k \boldsymbol{w}_k^i\|_{\Sigma_k}^2, \tag{5}$$

to describe the desired intra-cluster similarity, where each node $\mathbf{y}_k^i$ is linearly represented in terms of other nodes in the same cluster. $\Sigma_k = \mathbf{diag}(\boldsymbol{\eta}_k)$, where $\boldsymbol{\eta}_k = [\eta_{1k}, ..., \eta_{n_k k}]^T$ denotes the variance of the representation error. $W_k = [\boldsymbol{w}_k^1, ..., \boldsymbol{w}_k^{n_k}] \in \mathbb{R}^{n_k \times n_k}$ is the representation weight matrix with $\mathbf{diag}(W_k) = \mathbf{0}$, which implies the node itself is excluded in its representation. Due to the high intra-cluster spectral similarity, representation error $\psi(Y_k)$ could be quite small and sparse. To model the sparse error, a Gamma distribution similar to Eq. (3) is imposed on $\boldsymbol{\eta}_k$ as

$$p(\boldsymbol{\eta}_k | \boldsymbol{\nu}_k) = \prod_j \frac{\nu_{jk}}{2} \exp\left(-\frac{\nu_{jk} \eta_{jk}}{2}\right), \qquad (6)$$

where $\boldsymbol{\nu}_k = [\nu_{1k}, ..., \nu_{n_k k}]^T$. When $\varphi(Y_k) = 0$, this hierarchical prior in Eqs. (1), (6) results in a sparse prior on the representation error as Eq. (4).

The self-expressiveness relation [20] in Eq. (5) implicitly defines a graph structure with W_k. Specifically, each node $\boldsymbol{y}_k^i$ is fully connected with other nodes in Y_k, and the edges are defined by the weight matrix W_k. When entries of W_k exactly equal to zero, the corresponding edges are pruned. In other words, the specific graph structure on Y_k is defined by W_k. To learn the graph structure in each cluster flexibly, the normal distribution is imposed on each weight vector in W_k independently as

$$p(W_k | \epsilon) = \prod_i \mathcal{N}(\boldsymbol{w}_k^i | \mathbf{0}, \epsilon^{-1} \mathbf{I}). \qquad (7)$$

where $\mathbf{I}$ is an identity matrix with proper size and ϵ is a predefined scalar. This ϵ-parametrized normal distribution constrains the ℓ_2 norm of each weight vector $\boldsymbol{w}_k^i$ to avoid over-fitting in graph structure learning.

Substituting those two potentials $\varphi(Y_k)$ and $\psi(Y_k)$ into Eq. (1), we obtain the whole graphic model of Y as

$$p(Y | \{\boldsymbol{\gamma}_k, \boldsymbol{\eta}_k, W_k\}_{k=1}^K) = \frac{1}{Z} \exp\left\{-\frac{1}{2} \sum_k \left(\|Y_k\|_{\Gamma_k}^2 + \|Y_k - Y_k W_k\|_{\Sigma_k}^2\right)\right\}, \qquad (8)$$

where $\varphi(Y_k)$ and $\psi(Y_k)$ act as the unary term and the high-order term, respectively. With those corresponding hyperpriors $p(\boldsymbol{\gamma}_k | \boldsymbol{\varpi}_k)$, $p(\boldsymbol{\eta}_k | \boldsymbol{\nu}_k)$ and $p(W_k | \epsilon)$, the whole hierarchical CSF prior for the sparse representation Y can be written as

$$p_{\mathrm{csf}}(Y | \boldsymbol{\Theta}) = p(Y | \{\boldsymbol{\gamma}_k, \boldsymbol{\eta}_k, W_k\}_{k=1}^K) \prod_k p(\boldsymbol{\gamma}_k | \boldsymbol{\varpi}_k) \prod_k p(\boldsymbol{\eta}_k | \boldsymbol{\nu}_k) \prod_k p(W_k | \epsilon), \quad (9)$$

where $\boldsymbol{\Theta} = \{\boldsymbol{\gamma}_k, \boldsymbol{\varpi}_k, \boldsymbol{\eta}_k, \boldsymbol{\nu}_k, W_k\}_{k=1}^K$. This prior models the spectral correlation and the spatial similarity in HSIs simultaneously by defining the structured sparsity and graph structure based intra-cluster similarity within the sparse representation model.

To employ this prior for HSIs denoising, we have to determine the unknown parameters $\boldsymbol{\Theta}$. Most previous graphic models learn parameters with a set of training examples [21, 22]. However, training examples often show different clustering results, thus learning parameters from training examples is infeasible for the data-specific CSF prior. To address this problem and capture the data-dependent structure of HSIs, we learn the prior parameters directly from the noisy observation in the following section.

3 HSIs Denoising with CSF

Similar as many previous works [5,6], we adopt the noisy observation model for HSIs as $F = X + N$, where $F \in \mathbb{R}^{n_b \times n_p}$ is the noisy observation and $N \in \mathbb{R}^{n_b \times n_p}$ represents the noise. In this study, we mainly focus on the signal-independent noise model, where the noise can be well modelled by Gaussian white noise. In practical hyperspectral imaging, various bands of HSIs often bear different levels of noise [23]. Therefore, we assume noise N comes from a matrix normal distribution $\mathcal{MN}(\mathbf{0}, \Sigma_n, \mathbf{I})$, where $\Sigma_n = \mathbf{diag}(\boldsymbol{\lambda}) \in \mathbb{R}^{n_b \times n_b}$ and $\boldsymbol{\lambda} = [\lambda_1, ..., \lambda_{n_b}]^T$ controls the various noise levels in n_b bands. With a proper spectrum dictionary Φ, we have the following likelihood

$$p(F|Y, \boldsymbol{\lambda}) \propto |\Sigma_n|^{-n_p/2} \exp(-\frac{1}{2} \|\Phi Y - F\|_{\Sigma_n}^2). \tag{10}$$

Given the CSF prior $p_{\mathrm{csf}}(Y|\Theta)$, we can infer Y by the maximum a posteriori (MAP) estimation as

$$Y^{opt} = \arg\max_{Y} p(F|Y, \boldsymbol{\lambda}) p_{\mathrm{csf}}(Y|\Theta). \tag{11}$$

Then, $X^{opt} = \mathrm{Phi} Y^{opt}$. To this end, we learn the parameter Θ and noise level $\boldsymbol{\lambda}$ directly from the noisy observation in advance by solving the following problem

$$\max_{\boldsymbol{\lambda}, \Theta} p(\boldsymbol{\lambda}, \Theta|F) \propto \int p(F|Y, \boldsymbol{\lambda}) p_{\mathrm{csf}}(Y|\Theta) dY. \tag{12}$$

Due to the coupled variables in $p_{\mathrm{csf}}(Y|\Theta)$, it is intractable to solve Eq. (12) directly. To address this issue, we first give an approximation to $p(Y|\{\boldsymbol{\gamma}_k, \boldsymbol{\eta}_k, W_k\}_{k=1}^K)$ in $p_{\mathrm{csf}}(Y|\Theta)$, then simplify this problem to a tractable regularized regression model.

3.1 Approximated CSF and Inference

To approximate $p(Y|\{\boldsymbol{\gamma}_k, \boldsymbol{\eta}_k, W_k\}_{k=1}^K)$, we first replace $Y_k W_k$ in Eq. (8) with $M_k = Y_k' W_k$, where Y_k' is the sparse representation of X_k from the previous iteration. Since the representation error $Y_k - M_k$ and Y_k are almost independent [24], we then approximate $p(Y|\{\boldsymbol{\gamma}_k, \boldsymbol{\eta}_k, W_k\}_{k=1}^K)$ as

$$p(Y|\{\boldsymbol{\gamma}_k, \boldsymbol{\eta}_k, W_k\}_{k=1}^K) \approx \prod_k \mathcal{MN}(Y_k|\mathbf{0}, \Gamma_k, \mathbf{I}) \times \mathcal{MN}(Y_k|M_k, \mathbf{0}, \Sigma_k, \mathbf{I}). \tag{13}$$

When the independence assumption stands and $M_k = Y_k W_k$ (i.e., $Y_k' = Y_k$), the equality of Eq. (13) holds. This approximation simplifies the subsequent optimization and performs well in extensive experiments shown in Sect. 4.

Based on this approximation, the MAP inference in Eq. (11) and prior learning in Eq. (12) can be integrated into a unified regularized regression model as

$$
\min_{Y,\Theta,\boldsymbol{\lambda}} \sum_k \left(\|\Phi Y_k - F_k\|_{\Sigma_n}^2 + \|Y_k\|_{\Gamma_k}^2 + \|Y_k - M_k\|_{\Sigma_k}^2 \right)
$$
$$
+ \sum_k n_k \left(\log|\Sigma_n| - \log|\boldsymbol{\Lambda}_k| + \log|\Sigma_k| + \log|\Gamma_k| \right) \tag{14}
$$
$$
+ \sum_{k,j} \left[\varpi_{jk}\gamma_{jk} + \nu_{jk}\eta_{jk} - 2\log(\varpi_{jk}\nu_{jk}) \right] + \sum_k \epsilon\|W_k\|_F^2.
$$

where F_k is the observation of X_k and $\boldsymbol{\Lambda}_k = (\Gamma_k^{-1} + \Sigma_k^{-1} + \Phi^T\Sigma_n^{-1}\Phi)^{-1}$. $\|\cdot\|_F$ is the Frobenius norm. Equation (14) describes the relation between all unknown variables and the observation. Moreover, we can learn the data-dependent CSF prior, noise level and the desired sparse representation simultaneously by solving Eq. (14).

3.2   Optimization Procedure

In this study, the alternative minimization scheme [11,24] is adopted to optimize Eq. (14). This scheme reduces original problem into several simpler subproblems, which are then alternatively optimized in each iteration until convergence. To start, we conduct K-means[1] on an initialized HSI $\hat{X}$ (the initialization will be illustrated in Sect. 4) to group the pixels of $\hat{X}$ into K clusters based on the spectrum similarity.

A. Graph structure estimation. Given X_k and Φ, we can estimate the weight matrix W_k in the kth cluster from Eq. (14) as[2]

$$
\min_{W_k} \|Y_k W_k - Y_k\|_{\Sigma_n}^2 + \epsilon\|W_k\|_F^2, \quad \text{s.t. } \mathbf{diag}(W_k) = \mathbf{0}, \tag{15}
$$

This least square regression based subspace clustering problem can be effectively solved by the algorithm in [25]. Given W_k and Y_k, M_k can be obtained as $M_k = Y_k W_k$.

B. Sparse representation reconstruction. With the updated M_k for each cluster, the subproblem for Y simplifies to

$$
\min_{Y,\Theta,\boldsymbol{\lambda}} \sum_k \left(\|\Phi Y_k - F_k\|_{\Sigma_n}^2 + \|Y_k\|_{\Gamma_k}^2 + \|Y_k - M_k\|_{\Sigma_k}^2 \right)
$$
$$
+ \sum_k n_k \left(\log|\Sigma_n| - \log|\boldsymbol{\Lambda}_k| + \log|\Sigma_k| + \log|\Gamma_k| \right) \tag{16}
$$
$$
+ \sum_{k,j} \left[\varpi_{jk}\gamma_{jk} + \nu_{jk}\eta_{jk} - 2\log(\varpi_{jk}\nu_{jk}) \right],
$$

---

[1] It should be noted that other clustering methods could also be used instead of the K-means.

[2] Detailed derivation can be found in the supplementary material.

where Θ and λ are the auxiliary variables for optimizing Y. This minimization problem can be divided into three subproblems, namely Y_k-subproblem, Θ-subproblem and λ-subproblem. Firstly, Y_k-subproblem can be written as

$$\min_Y \sum_k \left(\|\Phi Y_k - F_k\|_{\Sigma_n}^2 + \|Y_k\|_{\Gamma_k}^2 + \|Y_k - M_k\|_{\Sigma_k}^2 \right), \tag{17}$$

which gives a closed-form solution as $Y_k = \mathbf{\Lambda}_k(\Phi^T \Sigma_n^{-1} F_k + \Sigma_k^{-1} M_k)$. Then, given Y_k, we can obtain Θ-subproblem as

$$\min_\Theta \sum_k \left(\|Y_k - M_k\|_{\Sigma_k}^2 + \|Y_k\|_{\Gamma_k}^2 - n_k \log |\mathbf{\Lambda}_k| + n_k \log |\Sigma_k| \right)$$
$$+ \sum_k n_k \log |\Gamma_k| + \sum_{k,j} [\varpi_{jk}\gamma_{jk} + \nu_{jk}\eta_{jk} - 2 \log(\varpi_{jk}\nu_{jk})], \tag{18}$$

which can be solved effectively (see footnote 2) by employing alternative minimization on each variable in Θ as [11,26]. Finally, λ-subproblem can be formulated as

$$\min_\lambda \sum_k (\|\Phi Y_k - F_k\|_{\Sigma_n}^2 - n_k \log |\mathbf{\Lambda}_k| + n_k \log |\Sigma_n|), \tag{19}$$

which produces a closed-form solution (see footnote 2) as [11].

C. Dictionary learning and clustering. Currently, the commonly used dictionary is either a universe one (e.g., DCT dictionary) or learned from training examples (e.g., K-SVD [27]). However, they mainly capture the common characteristics over different images rather than the data-dependent characteristics of the desired HSI. To address this problem, we learn a PCA spectra dictionary as Φ from the denoised HSI at each iteration, then K-means (see footnote 1) are conducted to group the pixels in the denoised image into K clusters. At the first iteration, the PCA dictionary is learned from the initialized HSI. Algorithm 1 describes the whole procedure of CSF prior based HSIs denoising. The alternative minimization scheme decreases the cost function at each iteration, thus guaranteeing algorithm converges as [11,26].

Algorithm 1. Cluster Sparsity Filed based HSIs Denoising (CSFHD)

Input: Noisy observation F
Initialization: Parameters λ, γ_k, η_k, ϖ_k and ν_k are initialized by **1** with proper size.
for $t = 1,2,...,T$ **do**

    1. Cluster pixels of the denoised X by K-means and update the PCA dictionary Φ;

    2. Update the graph structure W_k by solving Eq. (15);

    3. Learn the sparse representation Y by solving Eq. (16);

    4. Reconstruct the HSI as $X = \Phi Y$.

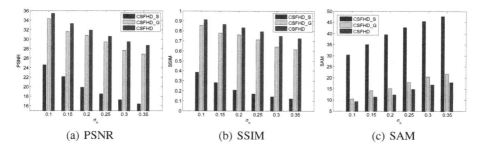

(a) PSNR   (b) SSIM   (c) SAM

Fig. 1. Average performance of CSFHD_S, CSFHD_G and CSFHD on the CAVE dataset with different σ_n. (A) Bar chart of PSNR. (B) Bar chart of SSIM. (C) Bar chart of SAM.

4   Experiments and Analysis

4.1   Experiments on Synthetic Data

In this section, we evaluate CSFHD on the CAVE dataset [28][3]. This dataset consists of 32 HSIs on real-world scenes. Each image contains 512×512 pixels and 31 bands which are captured at a 10 nm wavelength interval in the range from 400 nm to 700 nm. In experiments, we crop subimages of 200×200 pixels from all HSIs as the experimental data and each data is normalized into $[0, 1]$ in advance. To simulate the various levels of noise across bands, n_b levels of Gaussian white noise with standard deviation uniformly sampled in the range of $[\sigma_n - \sigma_n/2, \sigma_n + \sigma_n/2]$ are added into n_b bands of the HSI X to generate the noisy observation F. σ_n denotes the average standard deviation across different bands, which indicates the level of noise corruption on the whole X. Larger σ_n denotes higher level of noise corruption. In experiments, we choose σ_n from 0.1 to 0.35 at a 0.05 interval to simulate different levels of noise corruption on the whole HSI.

In the denoising procedure, to demonstrate the superiority of the proposed method, 5 state-of-the-art hyperspectral denoising methods are employed for comparison, including VBM4D [29], LRTA [5], PARAFAC [6], TDL [7] and TDLNP [7]. Only VBM4D and TDL require σ_n as input parameter. TDLNP is the special version of TDL without given σ_n. To further illustrate the effectiveness of the structured sparsity potential and the graph structure potential in the proposed method, we implemented two special versions of CSFHD, namely CSFHD_S and CSFHD_G. CSFHD_S only considers the structured sparsity in spectral domain, while CSFHD_G only considers the graph structure based spectral similarity in spatial domain. For CSFHD, the denoised result of TDLNP is utilized as the initialization $\hat{X}$. $T = 4$, $K = 30$ are adopted for Algorithm 1. Same parameters are adopted by CSFHD_S and CSFHD_G. Given the noisy F, all methods are conducted to recover the clean HSIs.

To assess the performance of different methods quantitatively, three evaluation measures are adopted in this study, including peak signal-to-noise ratio

---

[3] http://www.cs.columbia.edu/CAVE/databases/multispectral/.

Table 1. Average performance of different methods on CAVE dataset with different σ_n.

Measures	$\sigma_n = 0.1$			$\sigma_n = 0.15$			$\sigma_n = 0.2$		
	PSNR	SSIM	SAM	PSNR	SSIM	SAM	PSNR	SSIM	SAM
VBM4D	34.8906	0.8993	9.4661	32.6669	0.8480	12.0787	30.9966	0.7962	14.1959
LRTA	31.2048	0.7472	15.4954	28.9058	0.6573	18.5854	27.5655	0.6029	20.1945
PARAFAC	32.1217	0.8069	12.9080	29.6105	0.7165	17.1504	27.6266	0.6393	20.6321
TDL	30.5506	0.7492	15.8770	28.1367	0.6412	19.9466	26.4859	0.5618	22.5574
TDLNP	30.3250	0.7429	15.9684	27.8976	0.6339	20.1221	26.3381	0.5560	22.7402
CSFHD_S	24.5822	0.3869	30.3322	22.1135	0.2814	35.0321	19.8914	0.2087	39.4824
CSFHD_G	34.2973	0.8560	10.4724	31.6143	0.7804	14.2423	30.7823	0.7632	15.2192
CSFHD	**35.4313**	**0.9121**	**9.2944**	**33.3121**	**0.8664**	**11.4344**	**31.9040**	**0.8342**	**12.4544**
Measures	$\sigma_n = 0.25$			$\sigma_n = 0.3$			$\sigma_n = 0.35$		
	PSNR	SSIM	SAM	PSNR	SSIM	SAM	PSNR	SSIM	SAM
VBM4D	29.8192	0.7508	16.0144	28.9769	0.7194	17.2004	28.0184	0.6729	18.7588
LRTA	26.0882	0.5388	22.7685	24.7410	0.4767	25.3761	24.0827	0.4454	26.3420
PARAFAC	25.8209	0.5757	23.7778	24.3485	0.5241	26.4290	23.0494	0.4749	29.2837
TDL	24.8031	0.4800	26.0361	23.1180	0.4033	29.4923	22.4145	0.3678	31.0953
TDLNP	24.7219	0.4776	26.0565	23.4305	0.4121	28.8271	22.7176	0.3771	30.3146
CSFHD_S	18.4977	0.1697	42.7583	17.2900	0.1433	45.5512	16.3986	0.1218	47.7250
CSFHD_G	29.4342	0.7150	18.0457	27.7111	0.6448	20.5707	26.8939	0.6178	21.8164
CSFHD	**30.6316**	**0.7941**	**14.8927**	**29.4995**	**0.7502**	**16.9396**	**28.7886**	**0.7271**	**18.0146**

(PSNR), structure similarity (SSIM) and spectral angle map (SAM). PSNR measures the numerical difference between the target image and the reference one, while SSIM calculates their spatial structure similarity. Different with PSNR and SSIM, SAM reflects the performance of spectrum denoising by measuring the average spectrum angles between the spectra from the target image and the reference one. In comparison, larger PSNR, SSIM and smaller SAM denote better performance. For each method, the average results of those three measures are obtained on the whole CAVE dataset.

Effectiveness of different potentials: The comparison of average performance among CSFHD_S, CSFHD_G and CSFHD is shown as the bar charts in Fig. 1, and the detailed numerical comparison is provided in Table 1. We can observe that CSFHD produces significantly superior performance over CSFHD_S. Specifically, when $\sigma_n = 0.2$, compared with CSFHD_S, the PSNR of CSFHD increases by 12 db, SSIM increases by 0.6 and SAM decreases by 27 degree. This demonstrates that only considering the spectral structured sparsity in CSFHD_S is not sufficient. To further clarify this point, the visual comparison on the denoising results of 'Toy' image from the CAVE dataset is provided in Fig. 2, where two areas of interest are zoomed for easy observation. We find that the restored result of CSFHD_S contains a lot of noise and the spatial smoothness in the homogeneous areas are damaged. Similar situations occur on other bands. Therefore, only considering the spectral structured sparsity in CSFHD_S fails to preserve the spatial similarity in HSIs. By contrast,

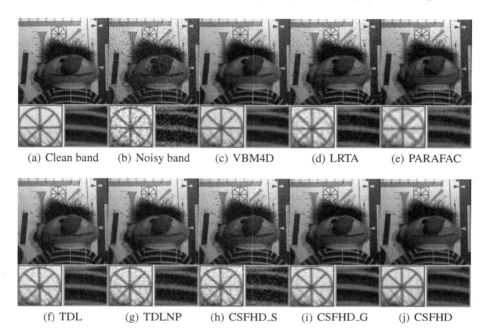

(a) Clean band   (b) Noisy band   (c) VBM4D   (d) LRTA   (e) PARAFAC

(f) TDL   (g) TDLNP   (h) CSFHD_S   (i) CSFHD_G   (j) CSFHD

Fig. 2. Restored results of the 20th band of 'Toy' image in the CAVE dataset from different methods when $\sigma_n = 0.1$.

with introducing the intra-cluster spectral similarity based graph structure potential, CSFHD_G and CSFHD both preserve the spatial similarity well and produces smooth homogeneous areas. Therefore, the proposed graph structure potential is effective in representing the spectral similarity in spatial domain. Additional, CSFHD shows obvious superiority over CSFHD_G for denoising. For example, when $\sigma_n = 0.2$, the PSNR of CSFHD is higher than that of CSFHD_G by 1.2 db, and the SAM reduces by 2.8 degree. Moreover, in the visual comparison on 'Toy' image, CSFHD gives more clear and sharper result than CSFHD_G. This in turn demonstrates the importance of modelling the correlation across spectrum in HSIs with the structured sparsity potential. Based on the above analysis, we can conclude that the structured sparsity potential and the graph structure potential are effective in representing the correlation across spectrum and the spatial similarity, and thus are beneficial to HSIs denoising.

Superiority of the proposed method: The average PSNR, SSIM and SAM of denoised results on the CAVE dataset from different methods are listed in Table 1. Under different levels of noise, CSFHD gives the highest PSNR, while VBM4D is the second best method. When $\sigma_n = 0.2$, the average PNSR of CSFHD is 0.9 db higher than VBM4D and 5.5 db higher than its initialization TDLNP. In addition, CSFHD exhibits superior performance on preserving the spatial structures. With different levels of noise, it always obtains higher SSIM than other methods. When $\sigma_n = 0.1$, only CSFHD gives SSIM larger than

0.9. To make this point more clear, the visual comparison among the denoised results from all methods are given in Fig. 2. Compared with the results from other methods which contain noise corruption or blur at some extent, CSFHD produces more clear and sharper result. In the respect of spectrum, CSFHD produces the smallest SAM among all comparison methods. For example, compared with other methods, the SAM of CSFHD decreases by at least 1.7 degree when $\sigma_n = 0.2$. To further illustrate this point, we plot the spectral reflectance difference curves of all comparison methods in Fig. 3. The curve of each method is interpolated by those discrete spectral reflectance difference across all bands between the denoised HSI and the reference one at a give spatial position. It is clear that CSFHD gives the smallest difference at all three chosen positions. Based on those above results, we can conclude that the proposed CSFHD method shows stable superiority on HSIs denoising over 5 state-of-the-art methods.

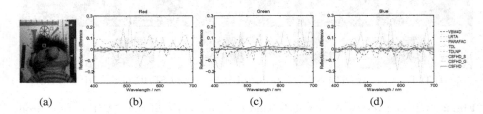

(a)   (b)   (c)   (d)

Fig. 3. Spectral reflectance difference curves of different methods on 'Toy' image under noise corruption with $\sigma_n = 0.25$. (a) 'Toy' image with 3 marked positions. (b)-(d) Spectral reflectance difference curves of different methods at the marked positions.

Effect of the cluster number K: In this part, we conduct experiments to explore the effect of K on the performance of HSIs denoising. For different scenes, the resulted HSIs often have different clustering results. Thus, two images 'Flower' and 'Toy' are selected from the CAVE dataset as the experimental data. Each image is corrupted with two different levels of noise with $\sigma_n = 0.1$ and $\sigma_n = 0.3$ as previous experiments. CSFHD is employed to denoise those two images with different K, which is selected in the range of $[1, 5, 10, 15, ..., 400]$ at a 5 interval. The curves of PSNR, SSIM and SAM versus K are plotted in Fig. 4. First row gives the results on the 'Flower' image and the results on 'Toy' images are provided in the second row. First, we find that there is the best K_{opt} for each image. When $K < K_{opt}$, pixels from different categories are grouped into the same cluster. Spectra difference from different categories cannot guarantee that each node in the cluster is well represented by others with sparse representation error. Furthermore, the uniform structured sparsity potential on one cluster is not appropriate for spectra from different categories. Therefore, the performance decreases. When $K > K_{opt}$, although each node in the cluster can be well represented by the uniform structured sparsity potential, the similar spectra are grouped into different small clusters. Too small amount of similar spectra will reduce the representation precision of each node. For example,

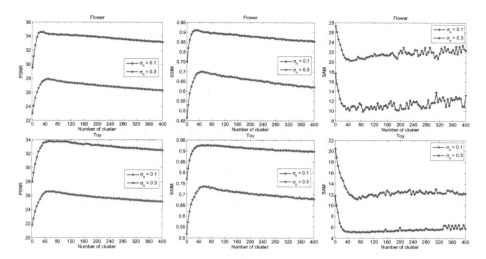

Fig. 4. Effect of the number of cluster K on 'Flower' (top) and 'Toy' (bottom) from CAVE dataset with two different σ_n. Figures from left to right are curves of PSNR, SSIM and SAM versus K.

in the extreme case with $K = n_p$, each pixel is grouped into an individual cluster, which corresponds to ignoring the spectral similarity in spatial domain. Hence, when K is too large, the performance is also reduced. In addition, we find something interesting that the trend of curves and K_{opt} are similar under different levels of noise for the same image. Moreover, K_{opt} varies in different images, e.g., $K_{opt} = 30$ in 'Flower' while $K_{opt} = 50$ in 'Toy'. For simplicity, we set $K = 30$ for the whole CAVE dataset.

Effect of approximation: We investigate the effect of approximation in Eq. (13) by denosing the 'Flower' image from the CAVE dataset when the image is corrupted with band-various noise with the average $\sigma_n = 0.2$ as previous experiments. Since the representation error $Y_k - M_k$ and the sparse signal Y_k are often likely independent [24], we only need to check the difference of sparse representation matrices in two successive iterations as $Y_k' - Y_k$ for all k. For each cluster, we define the error at each node as the ℓ_2 norm of the difference of sparse representation vectors from two successive iteration, which is denoted as $\|\boldsymbol{y}_k'^i - \boldsymbol{y}_k^i\|_2$ ($\boldsymbol{y}_k'^i$ is the corresponding node in Y_k'). After calculating the error at each node defined in the whole image, we can obtain a error map shown as the first row in Fig. 5. From those error maps, we can obviously find that the error is constantly reduced with the increase of iteration, viz., Y_k' is more and more close to Y_k for all k. This implies the approximation in Eq. (13) is more and more accurate and the algorithm converges well, both of which guarantee to produce the constantly refined denoising result shown as the second row in Fig. 5.

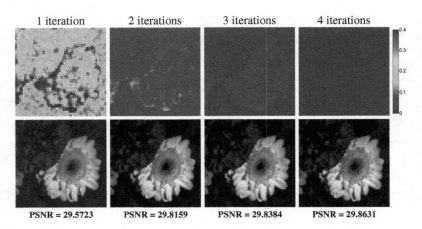

Fig. 5. Effect of approximation on denoising the 'Flower' image from the CAVE dataset. First row includes the error maps with color bar in 4 iterations, and the second row gives the corresponding reconstruction result on the 30th band in each iteration with the PSNR below the image.

4.2　Experiment on Real Data

In this section, we further test the proposed method on the real noisy HSI dataset, INDIANA[4]. This image is of size 145×145 with 10 m spatial resolution and consists of 220 bands covering the wavelength in the range from 400 nm to 2500 nm by 10 nm spectral resolution. Before denoising, we remove the atmospheric and water absorption bands from bands 150–163 from the original HSI [30]. As a result, there are only 206 bands used in the following experiment. This image contains different levels of noise corrupted bands, including heavy noise corruption bands, light noise corruption bands and nearly noise-free bands, respectively. In the denoising procedure, CSFHD is given the same parameters as previous experiments. VBM4D, LRTA, PARAFAC, TDLNP, CSFHD_S and CSFHD_G are employed as the comparison methods. Since the real σ_n is unknown, here we only select the non-parameter version TDLNP of TDL. VBM4D is also tuned to be the noise estimation mode.

To easily observe the superior performance of the proposed method on denoising the real HSI dataset, we provide the denoised 204 band of the INDIANA dataset from all comparison methods in Fig. 6, where two areas of interest are zoomed for easy observation. It is clear that the proposed CSFHD not only appropriately removes the noise corruption but also preserves the spatial structure well. In contrast to CSFHD, VBM4D, PARAFAC and CSFHD_G remove a certain amount of noise corruption but fail to preserve the spatial structure. The edges in their denoising results are blurred, especially in PARAFAC. While the denoising results of LRTA, TDLNP and CSFHD_S still contain obvious noise corruption.

---

[4] http://cobweb.ecn.purdue.edu/~biehl/MultiSpec/.

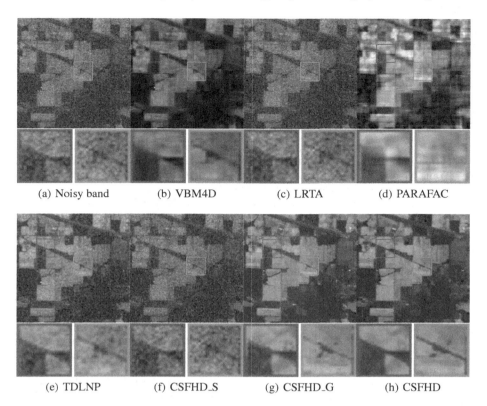

(a) Noisy band   (b) VBM4D   (c) LRTA   (d) PARAFAC

(e) TDLNP   (f) CSFHD_S   (g) CSFHD_G   (h) CSFHD

Fig. 6. Denoising results of the 204th band of INDIANA dataset from different methods.

5   Conclusion

In this study, we present an effective HSIs denoising method, where a novel CSF prior is proposed for the sparse representation of an HSI to better exploit its intrinsic correlation across spectrum and spatial similarity simultaneously. In specific, by grouping the pixels of an HSI into several clusters with spectral similarity, the CSF prior defines two different potentials on each cluster. Among them, the structured sparsity potential models the correlation across spectrum in the HSI by exploring the structure in the sparse representation, while the graph structure potential defines the intra-cluster spectral similarity to model the spatial similarity in the HSI. With a proper approximation, we integrate the CSF prior learning and MAP inference in image denoising into a variational framework for optimization, where the data-dependent structure in the CSF prior can be learned directly from the noisy observation without any training examples. With the learned prior, the correlation across spectrum and spatial similarity are properly preserved in the denoising results. Extensive experiments on synthetic and real noisy HSIs demonstrate the effectiveness of the proposed method in HSIs denoising.

Acknowledgements. This work is in part supported by National Natural Science Foundation of China (No. 61231016, 61301192 and 61571354), Fundamental Research Funds for the Central Universities (No. 3102015JSJ0006), Innovation Foundation for Doctoral Dissertation of Northwestern Polytechnical University (No. CX201521) and Australian Research Council grants (DP140102270, DP160100703, FT120100969).

References

1. Wang, Z., Nasrabadi, N.M., Huang, T.S.: Semisupervised hyperspectral classification using task-driven dictionary learning with Laplacian regularization. IEEE Trans. Geosci. Remote Sens. **53**(3), 1161–1173 (2015)
2. Van Nguyen, H., Banerjee, A., Chellappa, R.: Tracking via object reflectance using a hyperspectral video camera. In: Proceedings of the IEEE Conference on Computer Vision and Pattern Recognition Workshops, pp. 44–51. IEEE (2010)
3. Akbari, H., Kosugi, Y., Kojima, K., Tanaka, N.: Detection and analysis of the intestinal Ischemia using visible and invisible hyperspectral imaging. IEEE Trans. Biomed. Eng. **57**(8), 2011–2017 (2010)
4. Kerekes, J.P., Baum, J.E.: Full-spectrum spectral imaging system analytical model. IEEE Trans. Geosci. Remote Sens. **43**(3), 571–580 (2005)
5. Renard, N., Bourennane, S., Blanc-Talon, J.: Denoising and dimensionality reduction using multilinear tools for hyperspectral images. IEEE Geosci. Remote Sens. Lett. **5**(2), 138–142 (2008)
6. Liu, X., Bourennane, S., Fossati, C.: Denoising of hyperspectral images using the PARAFAC model and statistical performance analysis. IEEE Trans. Geosci. Remote Sens. **50**(10), 3717–3724 (2012)
7. Peng, Y., Meng, D., Xu, Z., Gao, C., Yang, Y., Zhang, B.: Decomposable nonlocal tensor dictionary learning for multispectral image denoising. In: Proceedings of the IEEE Conference on Computer Vision and Pattern Recognition, pp. 2949–2956. IEEE (2014)
8. Othman, H., Qian, S.E.: Noise reduction of hyperspectral imagery using hybrid spatial-spectral derivative-domain wavelet shrinkage. IEEE Trans. Geosci. Remote Sens. **44**(2), 397–408 (2006)
9. Greer, J.B.: Sparse demixing of hyperspectral images. IEEE Trans. Image Process. **21**(1), 219–228 (2012)
10. Rasti, B., Sveinsson, J.R., Ulfarsson, M.O., Benediktsson, J.A.: Hyperspectral image denoising using a new linear model and sparse regularization. In: IEEE International Geoscience and Remote Sensing Symposium, pp. 457–460. IEEE (2013)
11. Zhang, L., Wei, W., Zhang, Y., Tian, C., Li, F.: Reweighted Laplace prior based hyperspectral compressive sensing for unknown sparsity. In: Proceedings of the IEEE Conference on Computer Vision and Pattern Recognition, pp. 2274–2281. IEEE (2015)
12. Qian, Y., Shen, Y., Ye, M., Wang, Q.: 3-D nonlocal means filter with noise estimation for hyperspectral imagery denoising. In: Proceedings of the IEEE International Geoscience and Remote Sensing Symposium, pp. 1345–1348. IEEE (2012)
13. Maggioni, M., Boracchi, G., Foi, A., Egiazarian, K.: Video denoising, deblocking, and enhancement through separable 4-D nonlocal spatiotemporal transforms. IEEE Trans. Image Process. **21**(9), 3952–3966 (2012)
14. Buades, A., Coll, B., Morel, J.M.: A non-local algorithm for image denoising. In: Proceedings of the IEEE Conference on Computer Vision and Pattern Recognition, vol. 2, pp. 60–65. IEEE (2005)

15. Dabov, K., Foi, A., Katkovnik, V., Egiazarian, K.: Image denoising by sparse 3-D transform-domain collaborative filtering. IEEE Trans. Image Process. **16**(8), 2080–2095 (2007)
16. Qian, Y., Ye, M.: Hyperspectral imagery restoration using nonlocal spectral-spatial structured sparse representation with noise estimation. IEEE J. Sel. Top. Appl. Earth Obs. Remote Sens. **6**(2), 499–515 (2013)
17. Fu, Y., Lam, A., Sato, I., Sato, Y.: Adaptive spatial-spectral dictionary learning for hyperspectral image denoising. In: Proceedings of the IEEE Conference on Computer Vision, pp. 343–351 (2015)
18. Baraniuk, R.G., Cevher, V., Wakin, M.B.: Low-dimensional models for dimensionality reduction and signal recovery: a geometric perspective. Proc. IEEE **98**(6), 959–971 (2010)
19. Camps-Valls, G., Tuia, D., Bruzzone, L., Atli Benediktsson, J.: Advances in hyperspectral image classification: earth monitoring with statistical learning methods. IEEE Signal Process. Mag. **31**(1), 45–54 (2014)
20. Li, B., Zhang, Y., Lin, Z., Lu, H., Center, C.M.I.: Subspace clustering by mixture of Gaussian regression. In: Proceedings of the IEEE Conference on Computer Vision and Pattern Recognition, pp. 2094–2102 (2015)
21. Lin, D., Fisher, J.: Manifold guided composite of Markov random fields for image modeling. In: Proceedings of the IEEE Conference on Computer Vision and Pattern Recognition, pp. 2176–2183. IEEE (2012)
22. Schmidt, U., Roth, S.: Shrinkage fields for effective image restoration. In: Proceedings of the IEEE Conference on Computer Vision and Pattern Recognition, pp. 2774–2781. IEEE (2014)
23. Zhang, H., He, W., Zhang, L., Shen, H., Yuan, Q.: Hyperspectral image restoration using low-rank matrix recovery. IEEE Trans. Geosci. Remote Sens. **52**(8), 4729–4743 (2014)
24. Dong, W., Zhang, D., Shi, G.: Centralized sparse representation for image restoration. In: Proceedings of the IEEE Conference on Computer Vision, pp. 1259–1266. IEEE (2011)
25. Lu, C.-Y., Min, H., Zhao, Z.-Q., Zhu, L., Huang, D.-S., Yan, S.: Robust and efficient subspace segmentation via least squares regression. In: Fitzgibbon, A., Lazebnik, S., Perona, P., Sato, Y., Schmid, C. (eds.) ECCV 2012. LNCS, vol. 7578, pp. 347–360. Springer, Heidelberg (2012). doi:10.1007/978-3-642-33786-4_26
26. Wipf, D.P., Rao, B.D., Nagarajan, S.: Latent variable Bayesian models for promoting sparsity. IEEE Trans. Inf. Theory **57**(9), 6236–6255 (2011)
27. Aharon, M., Elad, M., Bruckstein, A.: K-SVD: an algorithm for designing overcomplete dictionaries for sparse representation. IEEE Trans. Signal Process. **54**(11), 4311–4322 (2006)
28. Yasuma, F., Mitsunaga, T., Iso, D., Nayar, S.K.: Generalized assorted pixel camera: postcapture control of resolution, dynamic range, and spectrum. IEEE Trans. Image Process. **19**(9), 2241–2253 (2010)
29. Maggioni, M., Katkovnik, V., Egiazarian, K., Foi, A.: Nonlocal transform-domain filter for volumetric data denoising and reconstruction. IEEE Trans. Image Process. **22**(1), 119–133 (2013)
30. Yuan, Q., Zhang, L., Shen, H.: Hyperspectral image denoising employing a spectral-spatial adaptive total variation model. IEEE Trans. Geosci. Remote Sens. **50**(10), 3660–3677 (2012)

Zoom Better to See Clearer: Human and Object Parsing with Hierarchical Auto-Zoom Net

Fangting Xia$^{(\boxtimes)}$, Peng Wang, Liang-Chieh Chen, and Alan L. Yuille

University of California, Los Angeles, USA
{sukixia,jerrykingpku,lcchen,yuille}@ucla.edu, alan.yuille@jhu.edu

Abstract. Parsing articulated objects, *e.g.* humans and animals, into semantic parts (*e.g.* head, body and arms, *etc.*) from natural images is a challenging and fundamental problem in computer vision. A big difficulty is the large variability of scale and location for objects and their corresponding parts. Even limited mistakes in estimating scale and location will degrade the parsing output and cause errors in boundary details. To tackle this difficulty, we propose a "Hierarchical Auto-Zoom Net" (HAZN) for object part parsing which adapts to the local scales of objects and parts. HAZN is a sequence of two "Auto-Zoom Nets" (AZNs), each employing fully convolutional networks for two tasks: (1) predict the locations and scales of object instances (the first AZN) or their parts (the second AZN); (2) estimate the part scores for predicted object instance or part regions. Our model can adaptively "zoom" (resize) predicted image regions into their proper scales to refine the parsing. We conduct extensive experiments over the PASCAL part datasets on humans, horses, and cows. In all the three categories, our approach significantly outperforms alternative state-of-the-arts by more than 5 % mIOU and is especially better at segmenting small instances and small parts. In summary, our strategy of first zooming into objects and then zooming into parts is very effective. It also enables us to process different regions of the image at different scales adaptively so that we do not need to waste computational resources scaling the entire image.

Keywords: Human parsing · Part segmentation · Multi-scale modeling

1 Introduction

When people look at natural images, they often first locate regions that contain objects, and then perform the more detailed task of object parsing, *i.e.* decomposing each object instance into its semantic parts. In computer vision, object parsing plays a key role in the real understanding of objects in images and helps for many visual tasks, *e.g.* segmentation [9,30], pose estimation [8],

Electronic supplementary material The online version of this chapter (doi:10. 1007/978-3-319-46454-1_39) contains supplementary material, which is available to authorized users.

© Springer International Publishing AG 2016
B. Leibe et al. (Eds.): ECCV 2016, Part V, LNCS 9909, pp. 648–663, 2016.
DOI: 10.1007/978-3-319-46454-1_39

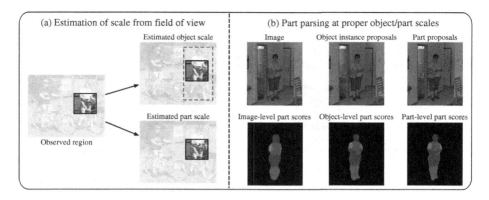

Fig. 1. Intuition of Hierarchical Auto-Zoom Net (HAZN). (a) The scale and location of an object and its parts (the red dashed boxes) can be estimated from the observed field of view (the black solid box) of a neural network. (b) Part parsing can be more accurate by using proper object and part scales. At the top row, we show our estimated object and part scales. In the bottom row, our part parsing results gradually become better by increasingly utilizing the estimated object and part scales. (Color figure online)

and fine-grained recognition [35]. It also has many industrial applications such as robotics and image descriptions for the blind.

There has been a growing literature on the related task of object semantic segmentation due to the availability of benchmarks such as PASCAL VOC [10] and MS-COCO [20]. There has been work on human parsing, *i.e.* segmenting humans into their semantic parts, but this has mainly been studied under constrained conditions which pre-suppose known scale, fairly accurate localization, clear appearances, and/or relatively simple poses [3,8,9,21,34,36]. There are few works done on parsing animals, like cows and horses, yet these also face similar restrictions, *e.g.* roughly known size and location [29,30].

In this paper, we address the task of parsing objects, such as humans and animals, in "the wild" where there are large variations in scale, location, occlusion, and pose. This motivates us to work with PASCAL images [10] because these were chosen for studying multiple visual tasks, do not suffer from dataset design bias [18], and include large variations of objects, particularly of scale. Parsing humans in PASCAL is considerably more difficult than in other datasets like Fashionista [34], which were constructed solely to evaluate human parsing.

Recently, deep learning methods have led to big improvements on object parsing [13,30], with the emergence of fully convolutional nets (FCNs) [23] and the availability of object part annotations on large-scale datasets, *e.g.* PASCAL [6]. However, these methods can still make mistakes on small or large scale objects and, in particular, they have no mechanism to adapt to the size of the object.

In this paper, we present a hierarchical method for object parsing that performs scale estimation and object parsing jointly and is able to adapt its scale to objects and parts. It is partly motivated by the proposal-free end-to-end

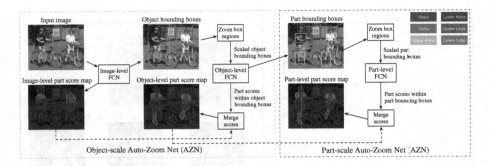

Fig. 2. Testing framework of HAZN. We address object part parsing by adapting to the sizes of objects (object-scale AZN) and parts (part-scale AZN). The part scores are predicted and refined by three FCNs, over three levels of granularity, *i.e.* image-level, object-level, and part-level. At each level, the FCN outputs the part score map for the current level, and estimates the locations and scales for the next level. The details of parts are gradually discovered and improved along the proposed auto-zoom process (*i.e.* location/scale estimation, region zooming, and part score re-estimation).

detection strategies [15,19,26,27], which prove that the scale and location of a target object, and of its corresponding parts, can be estimated accurately from the field-of-view (FOV) window by applying a deep net (Fig. 1(a)). We call our approach "Hierarchical Auto-Zoom Net" (HAZN) which parses the objects at three levels of granularity, namely image-level, object-level, and part-level, gradually giving clearer and better parsing results (see Fig. 1(b)). The HAZN sequentially combines two "Auto-Zoom Nets" (AZNs), each of which predicts the locations and scales for objects (the first AZN) or parts (the second AZN), properly zooms (resizes) the predicted image regions, and refines the object parsing results for those image regions (see Fig. 2). The HAZN uses three FCNs [23] that share the same structure. The first FCN acts directly on the image to estimate a finite set of possible locations and sizes of objects (*e.g.* bounding boxes) with confidence scores, together with a part score map of the image. The part score map is similar to that proposed by previous deep-learned methods. The object bounding boxes are scaled to a fixed size by zooming in or zooming out (as applicable) and the image and part score maps within the boxes are also scaled by bilinear interpolation for zooming in or downsampling for zooming out. Then the second FCN is applied to the scaled object bounding boxes to make proposals (bounding boxes) for the parts, with confidence values, and to re-estimate the part scores within the object bounding boxes. This yields improved part scores. We then apply the third FCN to the scaled part bounding boxes to produce new estimates of the part scores and to combine all of them (for different object and part bounding boxes) to output final part scores, which are our parse of the object. This strategy is modified slightly so that we scale humans differently depending on whether we have detected a complete human or only the upper part of a human, which can be determined from the part score map.

For dealing with scale, the adaptiveness of our approach and the way it combines scale estimation with parsing give novel computational advantages over traditional multi-scale methods. Previous methods mainly select a fixed set of scales and then perform fusion on the outputs of a deep net at different layers. Computational requirements mean that the number of scales must be small and it is impractical to use very fine scales due to memory limitations. Our approach is considerably more flexible because we adaptively estimate scales at different regions in the image which allows us to search over a large range of scales. In particular, we can use very fine scales because we will probably only need to do this within small image regions. For example, our largest zooming ratio is 2.5 (at part level) on PASCAL while that number is 1.5 if we have to zoom the whole image. This is a big advantage when trying to detect small parts, such as the tail of a cow, as is shown by the experiments.

We report extensive experimental results for parsing humans on the challenging PASCAL-Person-Part dataset [6] and for parsing animals on a horse-cow dataset [29]. Our approach outperforms previous state-of-the-arts by a large margin. We are particulary good at detecting small object parts.

2   Background

The study of human part parsing has been largely restricted to constrained environments, where a human instance in an image is well localized and has a relatively simple pose like standing or walking [3, 8, 9, 21, 33, 34, 36]. These shape-based or appearance-based models (with hand-crafted features or bottom-up segments) are limited when applied to parsing human instances in the wild because humans in real-world images are often in various poses, scales, and may be occluded or highly deformed.

Over the past few years, with the powerful deep convolutional neural networks (DCNNs) [17] and big data, researchers have made significant performance improvement for semantic object segmentation in the wild [4, 7, 22, 24, 25, 28, 31], showing that DCNNs can also be applied to segment object parts in the wild. These deep segmentation models work on the whole image, regarding each semantic part as a class label. But this strategy suffers from the large scale variation of objects and parts, and many details can be easily missed. [13] proposed to sequentially perform object detection, object segmentation and part segmentation, in which the object is first localized by a RCNN [12], then the object (in the form of a bounding box) is segmented by a FCN [23] to produce an object mask, and finally part segmentation is performed by partitioning the mask. The process has two potential drawbacks: (1) it is complex to train all components of the model; (2) the error from object masks, *e.g.* local confusion and inaccurate edges, propagates to the part segments. Our model follows this general coarse-to-fine strategy, but is more unified (with all three FCNs employing the same structure) and more importantly, we do not make premature decisions. In order to better discover object details and use object-level context, [30] employed a two-stream FCN to jointly infer object and part segmentations for animals, where the part stream was performed to discover part-level details and the object stream was performed to find object-level context. Although this work discovers object-level context to help part parsing, it only uses a single-scale network for both object and part score prediction, where small-scale objects might be missed at the beginning and the scale variation of parts still remains unsolved.

Many studies in computer vision have addressed the scale issue to improve recognition or segmentation. These include exploiting multiple cues [14], hierarchical region grouping [2,11], and applying general or salient object proposals combined with iterative localization [1,32,37]. However, most of these works either adopted low-level features or only considered constrained scene layouts, making it hard to handle wild scene variations and difficult to unify with DCNNs. Some recent works try to handle the scale issue within a DCNN structure. They commonly use multi-scale features from intermediate layers, and perform late fusion on them [4,13,23] in order to achieve scale invariance. Most recently, [5] proposed a scale attention model, which learns pixel-wise weights for merging the outputs from three fixed scales. These approaches, though developed on powerful DCNNs, are all limited by the number of scales they can select and the possibility that the scales they select may not cover a proper one. Our model avoids the scale selection error by directly regressing the bounding boxes for objects/parts and zooming the regions into proper scales. In addition, this mechanism allows us to explore a broader range of scales, contributing to the discovery of missing objects and the accuracy of part boundaries.

3   The Model

As shown in Fig. 2, our Hierarchical Auto-Zoom model (HAZN) has three levels of granularity for tackling scale variation in object parsing, *i.e.* image-level, object-level, and part-level. At each level, a fully convolutional neural network (FCN) is used to perform scale/location estimation and part parsing simultaneously. The three levels of FCNs are all built on the same network structure, a modified FCN called DeepLab-LargeFOV [4]. This network structure is one of the most effective FCNs in segmentation, so we also treat it as our baseline for final performance comparison.

To handle scale variation in objects and parts, the HAZN concatenates two Auto-Zoom Nets (AZNs), namely object-scale AZN and part-scale AZN, into a unified network. The object-scale AZN refines the image-level part score map with object bounding box proposals while the part-scale AZN further refines the object-level part score map with part bounding box proposals. Each AZN employs an auto-zoom process: first estimates the region of interest (ROI), then properly resizes the predicted regions, and finally refines the part scores within the resized regions.

3.1   Object-Scale Auto-Zoom Net (AZN)

For the task of object part parsing, we are provided with n training examples $\{I_i, L_i\}_{i=1}^{n}$, where I is the given image and L is the pixel-wise semantic part

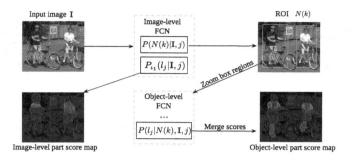

Fig. 3. Object-scale Auto-Zoom Net from a probabilistic view, which predicts ROI region $N(k)$ at object-scale, and then refines part scores based on the properly zoomed region $N(k)$. Details are in Sect. 3.1.

labels. Our target is to learn the posterior distribution $P(l_j|\mathbf{I}, j)$ for each pixel j of an image $\mathbf{I}$, which is approximated by our object-scale AZN (see Fig. 3).

We first use the image-level FCN (see Fig. 2) to produce the image-level part score map $P_{l_1}(l_j|\mathbf{I}, j)$, which gives comparable performance to our baseline method (DeepLab-LargeFOV). This is a normal *part parsing network* that uses the original image as input and outputs the pixel-wise part score map. Our object-scale AZN aims to refine this part score map with consideration of object instance scales. To do so, we add a second component to the image-level FCN, performing regression to estimate the size and location of an object bounding box (or ROI) for each pixel, together with a confidence map indicating the likelihood that the box is an object. This component is called a *scale estimation network* (**SEN**), which shares the first few layers with the part parsing network in the image-level FCN. In math, the SEN corresponds to a probabilistic model $P(b_j|\mathbf{I}, j)$, where b_j is the estimated bounding box for pixel j, and $P(b_j|...)$ is the confidence score of b_j.

After getting $\{b_j|\forall j \in \mathbf{I}\}$, we threshold the confidence map and perform non-maximum suppresion to yield a finite set of object ROIs (typically 5–10 per image, with some overlap): $\{b_k|k \in \mathbf{I}\}$. Each b_k, the bounding box estimated from pixel k, is associated with a confidence score $P(b_k)$. As shown in Fig. 2, a **region zooming** operation is then performed on each b_k, resizing b_k to a standard-sized ROI $N(k)$. Specifically, this zooming operation computes a zooming ratio for bounding box b_k, and then enlarges or shrinks the image within b_k by the zooming ratio. We will discuss how to compute the zooming ratio in Sect. 4.

Now we have a set of zoomed ROI proposals $\{N(k)|k \in \mathbf{I}\}$, each $N(k)$ associated with score $P(b_k)$. We learn another probabilistic model $P(l_j|N(k), \mathbf{I}, j)$, which re-estimates the part label for each pixel j within the zoomed ROI $N(k)$. This probabilistic model corresponds to the part parsing network in the object-level FCN (see Fig. 2), which takes as input the zoomed object bounding boxes and outputs the part scores within those object bounding boxes.

The new part scores for the zoomed ROIs need to be merged to produce the object-level part score map for the whole image. Since there may be multiple

Input image	Object bounding box regression map	Object confidence seeds

Fig. 4. Ground truth regression target for training the scale estimation network (SEN) in the image-level FCN. Details in Sect. 3.3.

ROIs that cover a pixel j, we define the neighbouring region set for pixel j as $\mathcal{Q}(j) = \{N(k)|j \in N(k), k \in \mathbf{I}\}$. Under this definition of $\mathcal{Q}(j)$, the **score merging** process can be expressed as Eq. 1, which essentially computes the weighted sum of part scores for pixel j, from the zoomed ROIs that cover j. For a pixel that is not covered by any zoomed ROI, we simply use its image-level part score as the current part score. Formally, the object-level part score $P_{\iota_2}(l_j|\mathbf{I}, j)$, is computed as,

$$P_{\iota_2}(l_j|\mathbf{I}, j) = \sum_{N(k) \in \mathcal{Q}(j)} P(l_j|N(k), \mathbf{I}, j) P(N(k)|\mathbf{I}, j);$$
$$P(N(k)|\mathbf{I}, j) = P(b_k)/\sum_{k:N(k) \in \mathcal{Q}(j)} P(b_k) \tag{1}$$

3.2 Hierarchical Auto-Zoom Net (HAZN)

The scale of object parts can also vary considerably even if the scale of the object is fixed. This leads to a hierarchical strategy with multiple stages, called the Hierarchical Auto-Zoom Net (HAZN), which applies AZNs to images to find objects and then on objects to find parts, followed by a part score refinement stage. As shown in Fig. 2, we add the part-scale AZN to the end of the object-scale AZN. Specifically, we add a second component (*i.e.* SEN) to the object-level FCN, to estimate the size and location of part bounding boxes, together with confidence maps for every pixel within a zoomed object ROI. Again the confidence map is thresholded, and non-maximal suppresion is applied, to yield a finite set of part ROIs (typically 5–30 per image, with some overlap). Each part ROI is zoomed to a fixed size. Then, we re-estimate the part scores within each zoomed part ROI using the part parsing network in the part-level FCN. The part parsing network is the only component of the part-level FCN, which takes the zoomed part ROI and the zoomed object-level part scores (within the part ROI) as inputs. After getting the part scores within each zoomed Part ROI, the score merging process is the same as in the object-scale AZN.

It's worth mentioning that we can easily extend our HAZN to include more AZNs at finer scale levels if we focus on smaller object parts such as human eyes.

3.3 Training and Testing Phases for Object-Scale AZN

We use **DeepLab-LargeFOV** [4] as the basic network structure for both the scale estimation network (SEN) and the part parsing network. The two networks, serving as components of a multi-tasking FCN, share the first three layers.

Training the SEN. The SEN aims to regress the region of interest (ROI) for each pixel j in the form of a bounding box, b_j. Here we borrow the idea of DenseBox [15] for scale estimation, since it is simple and performs well enough for our task. In detail, at object level, the ROI of pixel j corresponds to the object instance box that pixel j belongs to. For training the SEN, two output label maps are needed as visualized in Fig. 4. The first one is the bounding box regression map $\mathbf{L}_b$, which is a four-channel output for each pixel j to represent its ROI b_j: $\mathbf{l}_{bj} = \{dx_j, dy_j, w_j, h_j\}$. Here (dx_j, dy_j) is the relative position from pixel j to the center of b_j; h_j and w_j are the height and width of b_j. We then re-scale the outputs by dividing them with 400. The other target output map is a binary confidence seed map $\mathbf{L}_c$, in which $\mathbf{l}_{cj} \in \{0, 1\}$ is the ROI selection indicator at pixel j. It indicates the preferred pixels for us to use for ROI prediction, which helps the algorithm prevent many false positives. In practice, we choose the central pixels of each object instance as the confidence seeds, which tend to predict the object bounding boxes more accurately than those pixels at the boundary of an object instance region.

Given the ground-truth label maps of object part parsing, we can easily derive the training examples for the SEN: $\mathcal{H} = \{\mathbf{I}_i, \mathbf{L}_{bi}, \mathbf{L}_{ci}\}_{i=1}^n$, where n is the number of training instances. We minimize the negative log likelihood to learn the weights $\mathbf{W}$ for the SEN, and the loss l_{SEN} is defined in Eq. 2.

$$l_{SEN}(\mathcal{H}|\mathbf{W}) = \frac{1}{n}\sum_i (l_b(\mathbf{I}_i, \mathbf{L}_{bi}|\mathbf{W}) + \lambda l_c(\mathbf{I}_i, \mathbf{L}_{ci}|\mathbf{W}));$$

$$l_c(\mathbf{I}, \mathbf{L}_c|\mathbf{W}) = -\beta \sum_{j:l_{cj}=1} \log P(l_{cj}^* = 1|\mathbf{I}, \mathbf{W}) - (1-\beta)\sum_{j:l_{cj}=0} \log P(l_{cj}^* = 0|\mathbf{I}, \mathbf{W});$$

$$l_b(\mathbf{I}, \mathbf{L}_b|\mathbf{W}) = \frac{1}{|\mathbf{L}_{cj}^+|}\sum_{j:l_{cj}=1} \|\mathbf{l}_{bj} - \mathbf{l}_{bj}^*\|^2 \tag{2}$$

For the confidence seeds, we employ the balanced cross entropy loss, where l_{cj}^* and l_{cj} are the predicted value and ground truth value respectively. The probability is from a sigmoid function performing on the activation of the last layer of the CNN at pixel j. β is defined as the proportion of pixels with $l_{cj} = 0$ in the image, which is used to balance the positive and negative instances. The loss for bounding box regression is the Euclidean distance over the confidence seed points, and $|\mathbf{L}_{cj}^+|$ is the number of pixels with $l_{cj} = 1$.

Testing the SEN. The SEN outputs both the confidence score map $P(l_{cj}^* = 1|\mathbf{I}, \mathbf{W})$ and a four-dimensional bounding box $\mathbf{l}_{bj}^*$ for each pixel j. We regard a pixel j with confidence score higher than 0.5 to be reliable and output its bounding box $b_j = \mathbf{l}_{bj}^*$, associated with confidence score $P(b_j) = P(l_{cj}^* = 1|\mathbf{I}, \mathbf{W})$.

We perform non-maximum suppression (IOU threshold $= 0.4$) based on the confidence scores, yielding several candidate bounding boxes $\{\mathbf{b}_j | j \in \mathbf{I}\}$ with confidence scores $P(\mathbf{b}_j)$. Each b_j is then properly zoomed, becoming $N(j)$.

Training the part parsing. The training of the part parsing network is standard. For the object-level FCN, the part parsing network is trained based on all the zoomed image regions (ROIs), with the ground-truth part label maps $\mathcal{H}_p = \{\mathbf{L}_{pi}\}_{i=1}^n$ within the zoomed ROIs. For the image-level FCN, the part parsing network is trained based on the original training images. We merge the part parsing network with the SEN, yielding the image-level FCN with loss defined in Eq. 3. Here, $l_p(\mathbf{I}, \mathbf{L}_p)$ is the commonly used multinomial logistic regression loss for classification.

$$l_{AZN}(\mathcal{H}, \mathcal{H}_p | \mathbf{W}) = \frac{1}{n} \sum_i l_p(\mathbf{I}_i, \mathbf{L}_{pi}) + l_{SEN}(\mathcal{H} | \mathbf{W}); \qquad (3)$$

Testing the part parsing. For testing the object-scale AZN, we first run the image-level FCN, yielding part score maps at the image level and bounding boxes for the object level. Then we zoom onto the bounding boxes and parse these regions based on the object-level FCN, yielding part score maps at the object level. By merging the part score maps from the two levels, we get better parsing results for the whole image.

4   Experiments

4.1   Implementation Details

Selection of confidence seeds. To train the scale estimation network (SEN), we need to select confidence seeds for object instances or parts. For human instances, we use the human instance masks from the PASCAL-Person-Part Dataset [6] and select the central 7×7 pixels within each instance mask as the confidence seeds. To get the confidence seeds for human parts, we first compute connected part segments from the groundtruth part label map, and then also select the central 7×7 pixels within each part segment. We present the details of our approach for humans because the extension to horses and cows is straightforward.

Zooming ratio of ROIs. The SEN networks in the FCNs provide a set of human/part bounding boxes (ROIs), $\{b_j | j \in \mathbf{I}\}$, which are then zoomed to a proper human/part scale. The zooming ratio of b_j, $f(b_j, L_p^{b_j})$, is decided based on the size of b_j and the previously computed part label map $L_p^{b_j}$ within b_j. We use slightly different strategies to compute the zooming ratio at the human and part levels. For the part level, we simply resize the bounding box to a fixed size, *i.e.* $f_p(b_j) = s_t / max(w_j, h_j)$, where $s_t = 255$ is the target size. Here w_j and h_j are the width and height of b_j. For the human level, we need to consider the frequently occurred truncation case when only the upper half of a human instance is visible. In practice, we use the image-level part label map $L_p^{b_j}$ within the box, and check the existence of legs to decide whether the full body is visible. If the full body is visible, we use the same strategy as parts. Otherwise, we change the target size s_t to 140, yielding relative smaller region than the full body visible case. We select the target size based on a validation set. Finally, we limit all zooming ratio $f_p(b_j)$ within the range $[0.4, 2.5]$ for both human and part bounding boxes to avoid artifacts from up or down sampling of images.

4.2 Experimental Protocol

Dataset. We conduct experiments on humans part parsing using the PASCAL-Person-Part dataset annotated by [6]. The dataset contains detailed part annotations for every person, *e.g.* head, torso, *etc.* We merge the annotations into six clases: Head, Torso, Upper/Lower Arms and Upper/Lower Legs (plus one background class). We only use those images containing humans for training (1716 images in the training set) and testing (1817 images in the validation set), the same as [5]. Note that parsing humans in PASCAL is challenging because it has larger variations in scale and pose than other human parsing datasets. In addtion, we also perform parsing experiments on the horse-cow dataset [29], which contains animal instances in a rough bounding box. In this dataset, we adopt the same experimental setting as in [30].

Training. We train the FCNs using stochastic gradient descent with mini-batches. Each mini-batch contains 30 images. The initial learning rate is 0.001 (0.01 for the final classifier layer) and is decreased by a factor of 0.1 after every 2000 iterations. We set the momentum to be 0.9 and the weight decay to be 0.0005. The initialization model is a modified VGG-16 network pre-trained on ImageNet. Fine-tuning our network on all the reported experiments takes about 30 h on a NVIDIA Tesla K40 GPU. After training, the average inference time for one PASCAL image is 1.3 s/image.

Evaluation metric. The object parsing results is evaluated in terms of mean IOU (mIOU). It is computed as the pixel intersection-over-union (IOU) averaged across classes [10], which is also adopted recently to evaluate parts [5,30]. In the supplementary material, we also evaluate the part parsing performance w.r.t. each object instance in terms of AP_{part}^r as defined in [13].

Network architecture. We use DeepLab-LargeFOV [4] as building blocks for the FCNs in our Hierarchical Auto-Zoom Net (HAZN).

4.3 Experimental Results on Parsing Humans in the Wild

Comparison with state-of-the-arts. As shown in Table 1, we compare our full model (HAZN) with four baselines. The first one is DeepLab-LargeFOV [4]. The second one is DeepLab-LargeFOV-CRF, which adds a post-processing step to DeepLab-LargeFOV by means of a fully-connected Conditional Random Field (CRF) [16]. CRFs are commonly used as postprocessing for object semantic segmentation to refine boundaries [4]. The third one is Multi-Scale Averaging, which feeds the DeepLab-LargeFOV model with images resized to three fixed scales (0.5, 1.0 and 1.5) and then takes the average of the three part score maps to produce the final parsing result. The fourth one is Multi-Scale Attention [5], a most recent work which uses a scale attention model to handle the scale variations in object parsing.

Our HAZN obtains the performance of 57.5 %, which is 5.8 % better than DeepLab-LargeFOV, and 4.5 % better than DeepLab-LargeFOV-CRF. Our model significantly improves the segmentation accuracy in all parts. Note we do not use any CRF for post processing. The CRF, though proven effective in refining boundaries in object segmentation, is not strong enough at recovering details of human parts as well as correcting the errors made by the DeepLab-LargeFOV.

The third baseline (Multi-Scale Averaging) enumerates multi-scale features which is commonly used to handle the scale variations, yet its performance is poorer than ours, indicating the effectiveness of our Auto-Zoom framework.

Our overall mIOU is 1.15 % better than the fourth baseline (Multi-Scale Attention), but we are much better in terms of detailed parts like upper legs (around 3 % improvement). In addition, we further analyze the scale-invariant ability in Table 2, which both methods aim to improve. We can see that our model surpasses Multi-Scale Attention in all instance sizes especially at size XS (9.5 %) and size S (5.5 %).

Importance of object and part scale. Table 1 also shows the effectiveness of the two scales in our HAZN. In practice, we remove either the object-scale AZN or the part-scale AZN from the full HAZN model, yielding two sub-models: (1) **HAZN (no object scale)**, which only handles the scale variation at part level; (2) **HAZN (no part scale)**, which only handles the scale variation at object instance level. Compared with our full model, removing the object-scale AZN causes 2.8 % mIOU degradation while removing the part-scale AZN results in 1 % mIOU degradation. We can see that the object-scale AZN, which handles the scale variation at object instance level, contributes a lot to our final parsing performance. The part-scale AZN further improves the parsing by refining the detailed part predictions, *e.g.* bringing around 3 % improvement on lower arms.

Table 1. Part parsing accuracy (%) on PASCAL-Person-Part in terms of mean IOU.

Method	head	torso	u-arms	l-arms	u-legs	l-legs	bg	Avg.
DeepLab-LargeFOV [4]	78.09	54.02	37.29	36.85	33.73	29.61	92.85	51.78
DeepLab-LargeFOV-CRF	80.13	55.56	36.43	38.72	35.50	30.82	93.52	52.95
Multi-Scale Averaging	79.89	57.40	40.57	41.14	37.66	34.31	93.43	54.91
Multi-Scale Attention [5]	**81.47**	59.06	44.15	42.50	38.28	35.62	93.65	56.39
HAZN (no object scale)	80.25	57.20	42.24	42.02	36.40	31.96	93.42	54.78
HAZN (no part scale)	79.83	59.72	43.84	40.84	40.49	37.23	93.55	56.50
HAZN (full model)	80.76	**60.50**	**45.65**	**43.11**	**41.21**	**37.74**	**93.78**	**57.54**

Part parsing accuracy w.r.t. size of human instance. Since we handle human with various sizes, it is important to check how our model performs w.r.t. the change of human size in images. We categorize all the ground truth human instances into four different sizes according to the bounding box area of each instance s_b (the square root of the bounding box area). Then we compute the mIOU within the bounding box for each of these four scales. The four sizes are defined as follows: (1) Size XS: $s_b \in [0, 80]$, where the human instance is extremely small in the image; (2) Size S: $s_b \in [80, 140]$; (3) Size M: $s_b \in [140, 220]$; (4) Size L: $s_b \in [220, 520]$, which usually corresponds to truncated human instances where the human's head or torso covers the majority of the image.

The results are given in Table 2. The baseline DeepLab-LargeFOV performs badly at size XS or S (usually only the head or the torso can be detected by the baseline), while our HAZN (full model) surpasses it significantly by 14.6 % for size XS and by 10.8 % for size S. This shows that HAZN is particularly good for small objects. For instances in size M and L, our model also significantly improve the baselines by around 5 %. In general, by using HAZN, we achieve much better scale invariant property to object size than a generally used FCN type of model. We also list the results for the other three baselines for reference. In addition, it is also important to jointly perform the two scale AZNs in a sequence. To show this, we additionally list the results from our model without object/part scale AZN in the 5_{th} and the 6_{th} row respectively. By jumping over object scale (HAZN no object scale), the performance becomes significantly worse at size XS, since the model can barely detect the object parts at the image-level when the object is too small. If we remove part scale instead (HAZN no part scale), the performance also dropped in all sizes. This is because using part-scale AZN can recover the part details much better than only using object scale.

Qualitative results. We qualitatively evaluate our model in Fig. 5. The baseline DeepLab-LargeFOV-CRF produces several errors due to lack of object and part scale information, *e.g.* background confusion (1_{st} row), human part confusion (3_{rd} row), important part missing (4_{th} row), *etc.* Our HAZN (no part scale), which only contains object-scale AZN, already successfully relieves the confu-

Table 2. Part parsing accuracy w.r.t. size of human instance (%) on PASCAL-Person-Part in terms of mean IOU.

Method	Size XS	Size S	Size M	Size L
DeepLab-LargeFOV [4]	32.5	44.5	50.7	50.9
DeepLab-LargeFOV-CRF	31.5	44.6	51.5	52.5
Multi-Scale Averaging	33.7	45.9	52.5	54.7
Multi-Scale Attention [5]	37.6	49.8	55.1	55.5
HAZN (no object scale)	38.2	51.0	55.1	53.4
HAZN (no part scale)	45.1	53.1	55.0	55.0
HAZN (full model)	**47.1**	**55.3**	**56.8**	**56.0**

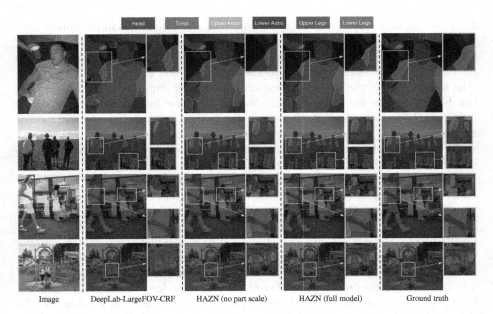

Fig. 5. Qualitative comparison on the PASCAL-Person-Part dataset. We compare with DeepLab-LargeFOV-CRF [4] and HAZN (no part scale). Our proposed HAZN models (the 3_{rd} and 4_{th} columns) attain better visual parsing results, especially for small scale human instances and small parts such as legs and arms.

sions for large scale human instances while recovers the parts for small scale human instances. By further introducing part scale, the part details and boundaries are recovered even more satisfactorily.

Failure cases. Figure 6 shows our typical failure modes. Compared with the baseline DeepLab-LargeFOV-CRF, our models give more reasonable parsing results with less local confusion, but they still suffer from heavy occlusion and unusual poses.

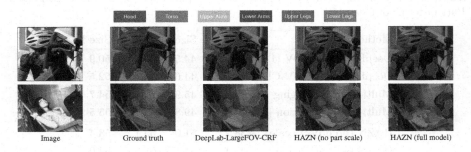

Fig. 6. Failure cases for both the baseline and our models.

Table 3. Mean IOU (mIOU) over the Horse-Cow dataset. We compare with the semantic part segmentation (SPS) [29], the Hypercolumn (HC*) [13] and the joint part and object (JPO) results [30]. We also list the performance of DeepLab-LargeFOV (LargeFOV) [4].

Horse							Cow					
Method	Bkg	head	body	leg	tail	Avg.	Bkg	head	body	leg	tail	Avg.
SPS [29]	79.14	47.64	69.74	38.85	-	-	78.00	40.55	61.65	36.32	-	-
HC* [13]	85.71	57.30	77.88	51.93	37.10	61.98	81.86	55.18	72.75	42.03	11.04	52.57
JPO [30]	87.34	60.02	77.52	58.35	**51.88**	67.02	85.68	58.04	76.04	51.12	15.00	57.18
LargeFOV	87.44	64.45	80.70	54.61	44.03	66.25	86.56	62.76	78.42	48.83	19.97	59.31
HAZN	**90.94**	**70.75**	**84.49**	**63.91**	51.73	**72.36**	**90.71**	**75.18**	**83.33**	**57.42**	**29.37**	**67.20**

4.4 Experiments on the Horse-Cow Dataset

Besides humans, we also applied our method to horses and cows presented in [29]. All the testing procedures are the same as those described above for humans. We copy the baseline numbers from [30], and give the evaluation results in Table 3. It shows that our baseline model, the DeepLab-LargeFOV [4], already achieves competative results with the state-of-the-arts, while our HAZN further provides a big improvement on both horses and cows. The improvement over the state-of-the-art method [30] is roughly 5 % mIOU. It is most noticeable for small parts, *e.g.* the improvement for detecting horse/cow head and cow tails is more than 10 %. This shows that our auto-zoom strategy can be effectively generalized to other objects for part parsing.

5 Conclusions

In this paper, we propose the "Hierarachical Auto-Zoom Net" (HAZN) to parse objects in the wild, yielding per-pixel segmentation of the object parts. It adaptably estimates the scales of objects, and their parts, by a two-stage process of Auto-Zoom Nets. We show that on the challenging PASCAL dataset, HAZN performs significantly better (by 5 % mIOU) than other state-of-the-art methods, when applied to humans, horses, and cows.

In the future, we would love to extend our HAZN to parse more detailed parts, such as human hand and human eyes. Also, the idea of our AZN can be applied to other tasks like pose estimation in the wild, to make further progress.

Acknowledgements. We would like to gratefully acknowledge support from NSF award CCF-1317376, and NSF STC award CCF-1231216. We also thank NVIDIA for providing us with free GPUs that are used to train deep models. Additionally, many thanks to Lingxi Xie, Zhou Ren, and Xianjie Chen for proofreading this paper and giving suggestions.

References

1. Alexe, B., Deselaers, T., Ferrari, V.: Measuring the objectness of image windows. PAMI **34**(11), 2189–2202 (2012)
2. Arbelaez, P., Maire, M., Fowlkes, C., Malik, J.: Contour detection and hierarchical image segmentation. PAMI **33**(5), 898–916 (2011)
3. Bo, Y., Fowlkes, C.C.: Shape-based pedestrian parsing. In: CVPR (2011)
4. Chen, L.C., Papandreou, G., Kokkinos, I., Murphy, K., Yuille, A.L.: Semantic image segmentation with deep convolutional nets and fully connected CRFs. In: ICLR (2015)
5. Chen, L.C., Yang, Y., Wang, J., Xu, W., Yuille, A.L.: Attention to scale: Scale-aware semantic image segmentation. arXiv:1511.03339 (2015)
6. Chen, X., Mottaghi, R., Liu, X., Fidler, S., Urtasun, R., Yuille, A.L.: Detect what you can: Detecting and representing objects using holistic models and body parts. In: CVPR (2014)
7. Dai, J., He, K., Sun, J.: Boxsup: exploiting bounding boxes to supervise convolutional networks for semantic segmentation. In: ICCV (2015)
8. Dong, J., Chen, Q., Shen, X., Yang, J., Yan, S.: Towards unified human parsing and pose estimation. In: CVPR (2014)
9. Eslami, S.M.A., Williams, C.K.I.: A generative model for parts-based object segmentation. In: NIPS (2012)
10. Everingham, M., Eslami, S.A., Gool, L.V., Williams, C.K., Winn, J., Zisserman, A.: The pascal visual object classes challenge: a retrospective. IJCV **111**(1), 98–136 (2014)
11. Florack, L., Romeny, B.T.H., Viergever, M., Koenderink, J.: The gaussian scale-space paradigm and the multiscale local jet. IJCV **18**(1), 61–75 (1996)
12. Girshick, R., Donahue, J., Darrell, T., Malik, J.: Rich feature hierarchies for accurate object detection and semantic segmentation. In: CVPR (2014)
13. Hariharan, B., Arbeláez, P., Girshick, R., Malik, J.: Hypercolumns for object segmentation and fine-grained localization. In: CVPR (2015)
14. Hoiem, D., Efros, A.A., Hebert, M.: Putting objects in perspective. IJCV **80**(1), 3–15 (2008)
15. Huang, L., Yang, Y., Deng, Y., Yu, Y.: Densebox: unifying landmark localization with end to end object detection. arXiv:1509.04874 (2015)
16. Krähenbühl, P., Koltun, V.: Efficient inference in fully connected CRFs with gaussian edge potentials. In: NIPS (2011)
17. LeCun, Y., Bottou, L., Bengio, Y., Haffner, P.: Gradient-based learning applied to document recognition. Proc. IEEE **86**(11), 2278–2324 (1998)
18. Li, Y., Hou, X., Koch, C., Rehg, J., Yuille, A.: The secrets of salient object segmentation. In: Proceedings of the IEEE Conference on Computer Vision and Pattern Recognition, pp. 280–287 (2014)
19. Liang, X., Wei, Y., Shen, X., Yang, J., Lin, L., Yan, S.: Proposal-free network for instance-level object segmentation. CoRR abs/1509.02636 (2015)
20. Lin, T.-Y., Maire, M., Belongie, S., Hays, J., Perona, P., Ramanan, D., Dollár, P., Zitnick, C.L.: Microsoft COCO: common objects in context. In: Fleet, D., Pajdla, T., Schiele, B., Tuytelaars, T. (eds.) ECCV 2014, Part V. LNCS, vol. 8693, pp. 740–755. Springer, Heidelberg (2014)
21. Liu, S., Liang, X., Liu, L., Shen, X., Yang, J., Xu, C., Lin, L., Cao, X., Yan, S.: Matching-CNN meets KNN: quasi-parametric human parsing. In: CVPR (2015)

22. Liu, Z., Li, X., Luo, P., Loy, C.C., Tang, X.: Semantic image segmentation via deep parsing network. In: ICCV (2015)
23. Long, J., Shelhamer, E., Darrell, T.: Fully convolutional networks for semantic segmentation. In: CVPR (2015)
24. Noh, H., Hong, S., Han, B.: Learning deconvolution network for semantic segmentation. arXiv:1505.04366 (2015)
25. Papandreou, G., Chen, L.C., Murphy, K., Yuille, A.L.: Weakly- and semi-supervised learning of a dcnn for semantic image segmentation. In: ICCV (2015)
26. Redmon, J., Divvala, S.K., Girshick, R.B., Farhadi, A.: You only look once: Unified, real-time object detection. CoRR abs/1506.02640 (2015)
27. Ren, S., He, K., Girshick, R., Sun, J.: Faster R-CNN: towards real-time object detection with region proposal networks. arXiv:1506.01497 (2015)
28. Tsogkas, S., Kokkinos, I., Papandreou, G., Vedaldi, A.: Semantic part segmentation with deep learning. arXiv:1505.02438 (2015)
29. Wang, J., Yuille, A.: Semantic part segmentation using compositional model combining shape and appearance. In: CVPR (2015)
30. Wang, P., Shen, X., Lin, Z., Cohen, S., Price, B., Yuille, A.: Joint object and part segmentation using deep learned potentials. In: ICCV (2015)
31. Wang, P., Shen, X., Lin, Z., Cohen, S., Price, B., Yuille, A.L.: Towards unified depth and semantic prediction from a single image. In: CVPR (2015)
32. Wang, P., Wang, J., Zeng, G., Feng, J., Zha, H., Li, S.: Salient object detection for searched web images via global saliency. In: CVPR, pp. 3194–3201 (2012)
33. Xia, F., Zhu, J., Wang, P., Yuille, A.L.: Pose-guided human parsing with deep learned features. AAAI abs/1508.03881 (2016)
34. Yamaguchi, K., Kiapour, M.H., Ortiz, L.E., Berg, T.L.: Parsing clothing in fashion photographs. In: CVPR (2012)
35. Zhang, N., Donahue, J., Girshick, R., Darrell, T.: Part-based R-CNNs for fine-grained category detection. In: Fleet, D., Pajdla, T., Schiele, B., Tuytelaars, T. (eds.) ECCV 2014, Part I. LNCS, vol. 8689, pp. 834–849. Springer, Heidelberg (2014)
36. Zhu, L.L., Chen, Y., Lin, C., Yuille, A.: Max margin learning of hierarchical configural deformable templates (hcdts) for efficient object parsing and pose estimation. IJCV **93**(1), 1–21 (2011)
37. Zhu, Y., Urtasun, R., Salakhutdinov, R., Fidler, S.: segDeepM: exploiting segmentation and context in deep neural networks for object detection. In: CVPR (2015)

Learning Common and Specific Features for RGB-D Semantic Segmentation with Deconvolutional Networks

Jinghua Wang[1], Zhenhua Wang[1], Dacheng Tao[2], Simon See[3],
and Gang Wang[1(✉)]

[1] Nanyang Technological University, Singapore, Singapore
jinghuawng@gmail.com, zhwang.me@gmail.com, wanggang@ntu.edu.sg
[2] University of Technology Sydney (UTS), Ultimo, Australia
dacheng.tao@uts.edu.au
[3] NVIDIA Corporation, Santa Clara, USA
ssee@nvidia.com

Abstract. In this paper, we tackle the problem of RGB-D semantic segmentation of indoor images. We take advantage of deconvolutional networks which can predict pixel-wise class labels, and develop a new structure for deconvolution of multiple modalities. We propose a novel feature transformation network to bridge the convolutional networks and deconvolutional networks. In the feature transformation network, we correlate the two modalities by discovering common features between them, as well as characterize each modality by discovering modality specific features. With the common features, we not only closely correlate the two modalities, but also allow them to borrow features from each other to enhance the representation of shared information. With specific features, we capture the visual patterns that are only visible in one modality. The proposed network achieves competitive segmentation accuracy on NYU depth dataset V1 and V2.

Keywords: Semantic segmentation · Deep learning · Common feature · Specific feature

1 Introduction

Semantic segmentation of scenes is a fundamental task in image understanding. It assigns a class label to each pixel of an image. Previously, most research works focus on outdoor scenarios [1–6]. Recently, the semantic segmentation of indoor images attracts increasing attention [3,7–15]. It is challenging due to many reasons, including randomness of object distribution, poor illumination, occlusion and so on. Figure 1 shows an example of indoor scene segmentation.

Thanks to the Kinect and other low-cost RGB-D cameras, we can obtain not only the color images (Fig. 1(a)), but also the depth maps of indoor scenes (Fig. 1(b)). The additional depth information is independent of illumination,

© Springer International Publishing AG 2016
B. Leibe et al. (Eds.): ECCV 2016, Part V, LNCS 9909, pp. 664–679, 2016.
DOI: 10.1007/978-3-319-46454-1_40

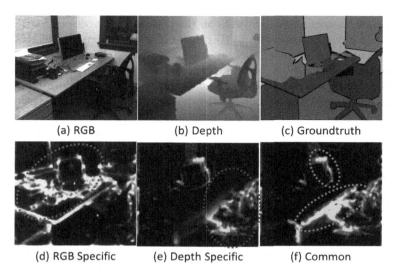

(a) RGB	(b) Depth	(c) Groundtruth
(d) RGB Specific	(e) Depth Specific	(f) Common

Fig. 1. Example images from the NYU Depth Dataset V2 [7]. (a) shows an RGB image captured in a homeoffice. (b) and (c) are the corresponding depth map and groundtruth. (d-f) are the visualized RGB specific feature, depth specific feature, and common feature (The method to obtain these features will be discussed in Sect. 5.2.). RGB specific features encode the texture-rich visual patterns, such as the objects on the desk (the red circle in (d)). The depth specific features encode the visual patterns which are more obvious in the depth map, such as the chair (the green circle in (e)). Common features encode the visual patterns that are visible in both modalities, such as the edges (the yellow circles in (f)) (Color figure online)

which can significantly alleviate the challenges in semantic segmentation. With the availability of RGB-D indoor scene datasets [7,8], many methods [3,9–14,16] are proposed to tackle this problem. These methods can be divided into two categories according to how they learn appropriate features to represent the visual patterns. While the methods [7–10,14] rely on low level or hand-crafted features to produce the label map, the works [3,11,13,17–20] learn deep features based on CNN (convolutional neural networks).

To apply CNN-based method on two modalities (RGB and depth) semantic segmentation, we can train two independent CNN models for RGB images and depth maps, then simply combine them together by decision score fusion. However, this strategy ignores the correlation between these two modalities in feature learning. To capture the correlation between different modalities, the previous methods [3,11,13,18] concatenate the RGB image with the depth map to form a four-channel signal and take them as the input. As pointed out in [21], these methods can only capture the shallow correlations between two modalities. In the learned network structure, most of the hidden units only have strong connections with a single modality. In addition, the modality specific features, which are very useful to characterize one particular modality, are heavily suppressed.

For example, to segment the objects on the desk in Fig. 1, we can learn discriminative features only from the RGB image. If we concatenate the RGB image and depth map, we are more likely to learn the common features that are visible in both modalities, and lose the RGB specific features to encode textures.

To learn informative features from both RGB image and depth map, we propose to correlate these two modalities by discovering their common features while characterize each modality by exploiting its specific features. To achieve this, we introduce a new network structure as an extension of deconvolutional network [6] for RGB-D semantic segmentation. Figure 2 shows the overall structure of the proposed model. The model has a convolutional network and deconvolutional network for each modality, as well as a novel feature transformation network to bridge them. Specifically, the convolutional networks extract features for each modality. The feature transformation network disentangles common features and modality-specific features from the top-layer covolutional features of each modality. The common features (Fig. 1(f)), which represent deep correlations between two modalities, are expected to encode information shared by both modalities. The specific features (Fig. 1(d) and (e)) are expected to encode information that is visible in only one modality. A separate deconvolutional network is used to predict the decision score for each modality, which receives the common and specific features of its corresponding modality and the common features borrowed from the other modality. Finally, the label map is obtained by decision score fusion.

It is worth noting that we explicitly allow one modality to borrow common features learned from other modality to enhance the representation of their shared information. Such a compensation is quite useful especially when the data from one modality is not well captured.

The contribution of this work is mainly twofold. Firstly, we introduce deconvolutional neural network for multimodal semantic segmentation. Secondly, we develop a framework to model common and specific features to enhance the segmentation accuracy. With the learned common feature, the two modalities can help each other to generate robust deconvolutional features.

The rest of this paper is organized as follows. Section 2 reviews the related work. Section 3 presents our network architecture. Section 4 presents our training method. Section 5 shows our experiments. Section 6 concludes this paper.

2   Related Work

Multi-modality feature learning is widely studied these days. Socher et al. [1] introduce recursive neural networks (RNNs) for predicting recursive structure in two different modalities, i.e. the image and the natural language. The proposed RNNs model can not only identify the items inside an image or a sentence but also capture how they interact with each other. Farabet et al. [3] introduce multi-scale convolutional neural networks to learn dense feature extractors. The proposed multi-scale representations successfully capture shape and texture information, as well as the contextual information. However, this method cannot generate cleanly delineated predictions without post-processing.

Ngiam et al. [21] propose bimodal deep auto-encoder to learn more representative shared features from multiple modalities. This work also demonstrates that we can improve the feature learning of one modality if multiple modalities are available at the training time. By introducing a domain classifier, Ganin and Lempitsky [22] learn domain invariant features based on labeled data from source domain and unlabeled data from target domain. In order to generate one modality from the other, Sohn et al. [23] propose to use information variation as the objective function in a multi-modal representation learning framework. To learn transferable features in high layers of the neural network, Long et al. [24] propose a deep adaption network to minimize the maximum mean discrepancy of the features.

Thanks to the low-cost RGB-D camera, we can obtain not only RGB but also depth information to tackle semantic segmentation of indoor images. Koppula et al. [25] use graphical model to capture contextual relations of different features. This method is computationally expensive as it relies on the 3D+RGB point clouds. Ren et al. [9] propose to first model appearance (RGB) and shape (depth) similarities using kernel descriptors, then capture the context using superpixel Markov random field (MRF) and segmentation tree. Couprie et al. [11] extend the multi-scale convolutional neural network [3] to learn multi-modality features for semantic segmentation of indoor scene. Wang et al. [18] propose an unsupervised learning framework that can jointly learn visual patterns from RGB and depth information. Deng et al. [14] introduce mutex constraints in conditional random field (CRF) formulation to eliminate the configurations that violate common sense physics laws.

Long et al. [26] propose fully convolutional networks (FCN) that can produce a label map which has the same size of the input image. FCN is an extension of CNN [27] by interpreting the fully connected layers as convolutional layers with large receptive fields. As FCN can be trained end-to-end, and pixels-to-pixels, it can be directly used for the task of semantic segmentation. However, FCN has two disadvantages: (1) it cannot handle various scales of semantics; (2) it loses many detailed structure of the object. To overcome these limitations, Noh et al. [6] propose to train deconvolutional neural networks based on VGG net for semantic segmentation. Papandreou et al. [28] propose a method to learn deconvolutional neural networks from weakly annotated training data. Hong et al. [4] decouple the tasks of classification and segmentation by modeling them with two different networks and a bridging layer to connect them. Deconvolutional networks can be considered as the reverse process of the convolutional network. It explicitly reconstructs the label map through a series of deconvolutional and unpooling layers. It is suitable for generating dense and precise label maps. Compared with the other CNN-based methods of semantic segmentation, deconvolutional networks [6] are more efficient as they can directly produce the label map.

3   Approach

In the task of RGB-D indoor semantic segmentation, the inputs are the RGB image and the corresponding depth map. The output is the semantic label map, i.e. the class label of every pixel.

Instead of conducting segmentation based on the pixel values, we learn informative representations from regions of these two modalities. The benefit of using multiple modalities is not limited to the fact that one modality can cover the shortage of the other. As stated by Ngiam et al. [21], we can improve the feature extraction procedure of one modality with the help from data of another modality. On one hand, as some visual patterns are visible in both modalities, we expect to extract a set of similar features from the RGB image and the corresponding depth map. On the other hand, as the RGB image mainly captures the appearance information and the depth map mainly captures shape information, we expect to extract some modality-specific features for each of them.

In this work, we explicitly learn common features and modality-specific features for both modalities. By jointly maximizing similarities between shared information and differences between modality-specific information, we learn to disentangle features of each modality into common features and specific features respectively. To achieve robust prediction, we explicitly allow one modality to borrow common features learned from other modality to enhance the representation of their shared information. Such a mechanism is quite useful especially when the data from one modality is not well captured. The final result is obtained by fusing decision scores of the two modalities.

3.1   Network Structure

As shown in Fig. 2, our network has five components: RGB convolutional network, depth convolutional network, feature transformation network, RGB deconvolutional network, and depth deconvolutional network. Both of two convolutional networks are designed based on the VGG16 net [22]. Specifically, each convolutional network has 14 convolutional layers (with corresponding ReLU and pooling layers between them). The two deconvolutional networks are mirrored versions of the convolution networks, each of which has multiple unpooling, deconvolutional and ReLU layers. The feature transformation network lies in-between the convolutional and deconvolutional networks, which consists of several fully connected layers. Table 1 shows the detailed configurations of our network. Note that we only show the networks for RGB modality.

Connecting the convolutional and deconvolutional networks is the feature transformation network, which takes the convolutional features as input and produces the deconvolutional features as output. In Table 1, the convolutional layer conv 6 generates the RGB convolutional features x_{rgb}^{conv}, which are transformed into common feature c_{rgb} by fully connected layers $fc1_{rgb}^c$ and modality specific feature s_{rgb} by layer $fc1_{rgb}^s$.

We expect the common features from two different modalities to be similar to each other while the specific features to be different to each other. Hence, we

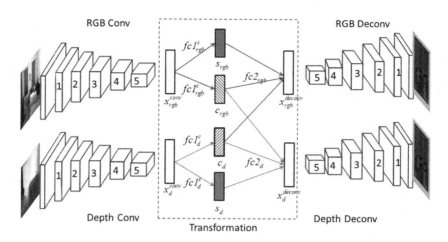

Fig. 2. Overall structure of the proposed network. The RGB and depth convolutional network have the same structure, consisting of 14 convolutional layers and 5 pooling layers. The deconvolutional networks are the mirrored version of the convolutional networks. The last layer of the convolutional network (i.e. conv 6 in Table 1) produce the convolutional features x_{rgb}^{conv} and x_d^{conv}. Based on x_{rgb}^{conv} and x_d^{conv}, our feature transformation network learns to extract common features c_{rgb} (or c_d) by fully connected layer $fc1_{rgb}^c$ (or $fc1_d^c$), and modality specific features s_{rgb} (or s_d) by fully connected layer $fc1_{rgb}^s$ (or $fc1_d^s$). To obtain robust deconvolutional features, the fully connected layer $fc2_{rgb}$ takes three types of feature as input: RGB-based features (c_{rgb} and s_{rgb}), as well as the borrowed common feature (c_d) from depth modality. Similarly, the layer $fc2_d$ also takes three features as input

propose to use multiple kernel maximum mean discrepancy (which will be discussed later in Sect. 3.2) to access these similarities and differences. To obtain robust deconvolutional features, we allow one modality to borrow the common features from the other. As shown in Fig. 2, the fully connected layer $fc2_{rgb}$ produces the RGB deconvolutional features by taking the RGB modality specific feature s_{rgb} and both of the common features (c_{rgb} and c_d) as inputs. Similarly, the layer $fc2_d$ transform s_d, c_d, and c_{rgb} into depth deconvolutional features.

In this framework, the two modalities can boost each other with the learned common features. It is helpful when the data of one modality is poorly captured and loses some key information. As the data from different modalities is captured using different mechanisms, one modality is expected to provide complementary information to the other.

The RGB (depth) deconvolutional network is the mirrored version of the RGB (depth) convolutional network. Each convolutional (pooling) layer in convolutional network has a corresponding deconvolutional (unpooling) layer. The unpooling layers of the RGB (depth) deconvolutional network use the pooling masks learned in RGB (depth) convolutional network. While the pooling layers gradually reduce the size of the feature map, the unpooling layers gradually enlarge the feature maps to obtain precise label map.

Table 1. Detailed configuration of the network. (a) shows the RGB convolutional network. (b) shows the deconvolutional network. (c) shows the feature transformation network. We use *conv (deconv)* to denote convolutional (deconvolutional) layers, and *pool (unpool)* to denote pooling (unpooling) layers. The layer conv 6 produces the convolutional features. The fully connected layers $fc1_{rgb}^{s}$, $fc1_{rgb}^{c}$, $fc2_{rgb}$ respectively produces the RGB modality specific features, RGB common features, and RGB deconvolutional features

(a) Convolutional network

name	kernel	output size
image	-	480×640
conv 1: 1-2	3×3	$480 \times 640 \times 64$
pool 1	2×2	$240 \times 320 \times 64$
conv 2: 1-2	3×3	$240 \times 320 \times 128$
pool 2	2×2	$120 \times 160 \times 128$
conv 3: 1-3	3×3	$120 \times 160 \times 256$
pool 3	2×2	$60 \times 80 \times 256$
conv 4: 1-3	3×3	$60 \times 80 \times 512$
pool 4	2×2	$30 \times 40 \times 512$
conv 5: 1-3	3×3	$30 \times 40 \times 512$
pool 5	2×2	$15 \times 20 \times 512$
conv 6	15×20	$1 \times 1 \times 4096$

(c) Transformation network

name	kernel	output size
$fc1_{rgb}^{s}$	1×1	$1 \times 1 \times 4096$
$fc1_{rgb}^{c}$	1×1	$1 \times 1 \times 4096$
$fc2_{rgb}$	1×1	$1 \times 1 \times 4096$

(b) Deconvolutional network

name	kernel	output size
deconv 6	15×20	$15 \times 20 \times 4096$
unpool 5	2×2	$30 \times 40 \times 512$
deconv 5: 1-3	3×3	$30 \times 40 \times 512$
unpool 4	2×2	$60 \times 80 \times 512$
deconv 4: 1-2	3×3	$60 \times 80 \times 512$
deconv 4: 3	3×3	$60 \times 80 \times 256$
unpool 3	2×2	$120 \times 160 \times 256$
deconv 3: 1-2	3×3	$120 \times 160 \times 256$
deconv 3: 3	3×3	$120 \times 160 \times 512$
unpool 2	2×2	$240 \times 320 \times 128$
deconv 2: 1	3×3	$240 \times 320 \times 128$
deconv 2: 2	3×3	$240 \times 320 \times 64$
unpool 1	2×2	$480 \times 640 \times 64$
deconv 1: 1-2	3×3	$480 \times 640 \times 64$
label map	1×1	$480 \times 640 \times 14$

Unpooling can be considered as a reverse process of pooling. Pooling is a strategy of sub-sampling by selecting the most responsive node in the region of interest. Mathematically, pooling is an irreversible procedure. However, we can record the location of the most responsive node by a mask and use this mask to recover the activation to its right place in the unpooling layer. Note that the RGB and depth deconvolutional network use different pooling masks learned by their corresponding convolutional networks. The unpooling layer can produce a sparse feature map representing the main structure.

Taking a single activation as input, the filters in a deconvolutional layer produce multiple outputs. Based on the sparse un-pooled feature map, deconvolutional layers reconstruct the details of the label map through convolution-like operations but in a reverse manner. A series of deconvolutional layers hierarchically capture different level of the shape information. Higher layer corresponds to more detailed shape structure.

3.2   Multiple Kernel Maximum Mean Discrepancy (MK-MMD)

This section introduces the measurement to assess the similarity between common features and modality specific features. To obtain similar RGB and depth common feature, we may simply minimize their Euclidean distance. However, Euclidean distance is sensitive to outliers which don't share very similar common features. We can overcome this limitation by considering the common (specific) features of two modalities as samples from two distributions and calculating the distance between the distributions. We aim to obtain two similar distributions for common features and different distributions for specific features. If most of RGB common features and depth common features are similar, we may conclude that their distributions are similar, even if they are significantly different for a few noisy outliers.

Hence, we do not expect the common features c_d and c_{rgb} (output of the layer $fc1_d^c$ and $fc1_{rgb}^c$ in Fig. 2) of two different modalities to be the same individually. Instead, we adopt the MK-MMD to assess the similarity between their distributions.

Given a set of independent observations from two distributions p and q, two-sample testing accepts or rejects the null hypothesis $H_0 : p = q$, i.e. the distributions that generate these two sets of observations are the same. The acceptance or rejection is made based a certain test statistic.

There are many existing techniques to calculate the similarity between distributions, such as entropy, mutual information, or KL divergence. However, these information theoretic approaches rely on the density estimation, or sophisticated space-partitioning/bias-correction strategies which are typically infeasible for high-dimensional data.

The kernel embedding allows us to represent a probability distribution as an element of a reproducing kernel Hilbert space. Let the kernel function k define a reproducing kernel Hilbert space F_k in a topological space X. The mean embedding of distribution p in Hilbert space F_k is a unique element $\mu_k(p)$ such that [29]:

$$E_{x \sim p} f(x) = < f(x), \mu_k(p) >_{H_\phi}, \qquad \forall f \in H_k. \tag{1}$$

As stated by Riesz representation theorem, the mean embedding μ_k exists if the kernel function k is Borel-measurable and $E_{x \sim p} k^{1/2}(x, x) < \infty$.

As a popular test statistic in two-sample testing, MMD (maximum mean discrepancy) calculates the norm of the difference between embeddings of two different distributions p and q, as follows

$$MMD(p, q) = \|\mu_k(p) - \mu_k(q)\|_{F_k}^2. \tag{2}$$

In theory, MMD equals to the upper bound of the difference in expectations between two probability distributions, i.e.

$$MMD(p, q) = \sup_{\|f\|_H \leq 1} \|E_p[f(p)] - E_q[f(q)]\|. \tag{3}$$

MMD is heavily dependent on the choice of kernel function k. In other words, we may obtain contradictory results using two different kernel functions. Gretton et al. [30] propose MK-MMD (multiple kernel maximum mean discrepancy) in two-sample testing, which can minimize the Type II error (false accept $p = q$) given an upper bound on Type I error (false reject $p = q$). By generating a kernel function based on a family of kernels, MK-MMD can improve the test power and is successfully applied to domain adaption [24]. The kernel function k in MK-MMD is a linear combination of positive definite functions $\{k_u\}$, i.e.

$$\mathbb{k} := \{k = \sum_{u=1}^{d} \beta_u k_u | \sum_{u=1}^{d} \beta_u = D > 0; \beta_u \geq 0, \forall u\}. \tag{4}$$

The distance between two distributions calculated based on MK-MMD can be formulated as follows

$$d(p, q) = \|\mu_k(p) - \mu_k(q)\|_{F_k}^2 = \sum_{u=1}^{d} \beta_u d_u(p, q). \tag{5}$$

where $d_u(p, q)$ is the MMD for the kernel function k_u.

In the training stage, we use the following function to calculate the unbiased estimation of MK-MMD between the common features

$$d(c_{rgb}, c_d) = \frac{2}{n} \sum_{i=1}^{n/2} \eta(u_i).$$

$$\eta(u_i) = k(c_{rgb}^{2i-1}, c_{rgb}^{2i}) - k(c_{rgb}^{2i-1}, c_d^{2i})$$
$$+ k(c_d^{2i-1}, c_d^{2i}) - k(c_d^{2i-1}, c_{rgb}^{2i}). \tag{6}$$

where n is the batch size, c_{rgb}^i and c_d^i ($1 \leq i \leq n$) are the RGB common feature and depth common feature respectively produced by layer $fc1_{rgb}^c$ and $fc1_d^c$. Also, similar to Eq. 6, we can calculate the similarity between the RGB modality specific feature s_{rgb} (produced by $fc1_{rgb}^s$) and depth specific feature s_d (produced by $fc1_d^s$).

In our framework, the common features c_{rgb} and c_d are expected to be similar to each other as much as possible. The modality specific features s_{rgb} and s_d are expected to different from each other. Thus, we try to minimize $d(c_{rgb}, c_d)$ and simultaneously maximize $d(s_{rgb}, s_d)$. The loss function of our network is as follows

$$L = \alpha_{rgb} l_{rgb} + \alpha_d l_d + \alpha_c d(c_{rgb}, c_d) - \alpha_s d(s_{rgb}, s_d). \tag{7}$$

where l_{rgb} and l_d are the pixel-wise losses between the label map and the outputs of the deconvolutional network. We use the parameters $\alpha_{rgb}, \alpha_d, \alpha_c$, and α_s to balance the four terms. In the back propagation, the gradient of the common and modality specific features are calculated from two different sources: the deconvolutional features and the MK-MMD distances.

4   Training

Following the work [6], we adopt a two-stage method to train our network. In the first stage, we train our network using image patches containing a single object, and learn how to segment an object from its surroundings. In the second stage, we generate patches based on bounding box proposals [31]. The generated patches contain two or more objects. In this stage, we train the network to learn how to segment two or more neighboring objects.

The kernel function in Eq. 6 is a linear combination of d different Gaussian kernels (i.e. $k_u(x,y) = e^{-\|x-y\|^2/\sigma_u}$). In our experiment, we use 11 kernel functions, i.e. $d = 11$ in Eq. 6. The σ_u is set to be $2^{u-6}(u = 1,\ldots,11)$. We observe that 11 kernel functions are sufficient to disentangle common features and specific features in our task. The parameter β in Eq. 5 is learned based on the method proposed in Gretton [30], and the values are [2,3,9,12,14,15,15,14,10,5,1]*1e-2. We learn the four parameters in Eq. 7 by cross-validation.

We implement our network based on caffe [32] and the deconvolutional network [6]. We employ the standard stochastic gradient descent with momentum for optimization. In the training stage, while the convolutional networks are initialized using the VGG 16-layer net [33] pre-trained on ILSVRC dataset [34], the deconvolutional networks are initialized randomly. We set the learning rate, weight decay and momentum respectively to be 0.01, 0.0005 and 0.9.

In this work, we decompose the deconvolutional network into five components based on the size of feature map and train one component after another. Following [35], we train the network by predicting a coarse output for each component. For example, we train the first component (from deconv 6 to deconv 5-3) to predict the downsampled (30 by 40) label map.

5   Experiments

Two popular RGB-D datasets for semantic segmentation of indoor scene images are NYU Depth dataset V1 [8] and NYU Depth dataset V2 [7]. The 2,347 RGB-D images in dataset V1 are captured in 64 different indoor scenes. As in the work [8], we group the 1,518 different names into 13 categories, i.e. *bed, blind, book, cabinet, ceiling, floor, picture, sofa, table, tv, wall, window,others*. The 1,449 RGB-D images in dataset V2 are captured in 464 different indoor scenes. Following [7], we group the 894 different names into 13 categories, i.e. *bed, objects, chair, furniture, ceiling, floor, decorate, sofa, table, wall, window, books, and TV*.

5.1   Baselines

To show the effectiveness of the proposed method, we compare it with five baselines. In the first baseline (B-DN), we train two deconvolutional networks independently, each takes the convolutional features of one modality as the input. The final segmentation results are obtained by decision score fusion. In the second baseline (S-DN), we have two convolutional networks and one deconvolutional network. The deconvolutional features are transformed directly from the concatenation of convolutional features from two modalities. The previous two baselines do not consider the correlations between these two modalities explicitly. By comparing our method with these two baselines, we can prove that learning common features and modality specific features can improve the segmentation accuracy. In the third baseline (C-DN), we train a deconvolutional network that takes the four-channel RGB+depth as the input. By comparing our method with this baseline, we can show that explicitly disentangling the common and specific features can improve the segmentation accuracy. In the fourth baseline (E-DN), we use the proposed network structure and Euclidean distance to assess the similarity between common (or modality specific) features individually. By comparing our method with this baseline, we can prove that MK-MMD is better than Euclidean distance, as a measurement to assess the similarity between feature distributions. The fifth baseline (U-DN) is the unregularized version of our framework. In this baseline, the loss function only has the first two terms of Eq. 7, and the last two terms are removed.

5.2   Testing

For a testing image, we first generate 100 patches or bounding boxes [31], each of them corresponding to a potential object. Then, we segment these patches individually using the learned network. Finally, we combine the segmentation results of these patches by decision score fusion to obtain the final label map.

We first visualize the segmentation results, as well as the learned common and specific features in Fig. 3. In this figure, we also show the segmentation results of FCN and the baseline C-DN (that takes the concatenated RGB-D as input). Both of these comparison methods can not segment the table correctly. However, using in our method, the RGB specific and common features can characterize the table correctly. The second row of Fig. 3 show the feature maps of deconvolutional layers. For visualization of RGB specific features, we only take the s_{rgb} as the input of layer $fc2_{rgb}$ and ignore the common features. The depth specific features are visualized in the similar way. To show the common feature, we drop the specific feature and only take the common features c_{rgb} and c_d as the input of the layer $fc2_{rgb}$. The features in Fig. 3 are the feature maps of layer deconv 2-2. While the RGB specific features mainly characterize the texture-rich regions, the depth specific features characterize the edges of objects.

Table 2 lists the class average accuracies of different methods on the NYU depth dataset V1. We compare our method with five baselines and five different works [8,9,18,36,37]. The methods proposed in [8,9] use hand-craft features. Pei et al. [36] use a one-layer network and Wang et al. [18] use a two-layer network to learn representations. Our deep network can achieve higher accuracy than their methods. It indicates that deep features can perform better than shallow features.

Table 3 lists the accuracies of the proposed method and four baselines, as well as the methods proposed in [11,18] on the dataset NYU V2. We can see from Table 3 that the proposed method outperforms the previous state-of-the-art [18] by 6.3 %. Notably, in the classes of *objects*, *furniture* and *decorate*,

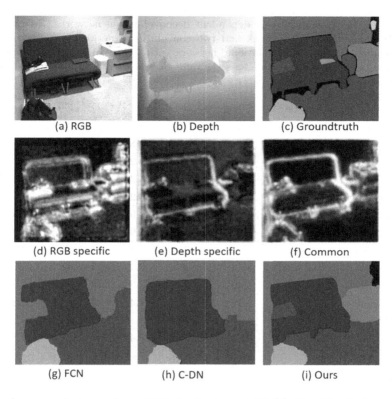

Fig. 3. An example image from NYU depth dataset V2 [7]. The The first row shows
(a) RGB image, (b) depth map, and the (c) ground truth. The second row shows
the learned (d) RGB specific features, (e) depth specific features, and (f) common
features. The third rows shows the segmentation results of two based lines ((g) FCN
and (h) C-DN) and (i) our method

Table 2. The average 13-class segmentation accuracy of different methods on the NYU
depth dataset V1 (KDES represents kernel descriptor)

Method	Acc	Method	Acc
Silberman and Fergus [8]	53.0 %	Pei et al. [36]	50.5 %
Wang et al. [18]	72.9 %	Hermans [37]	59.5 %
KDES-RGB [9]	66.2 %	KDES-depth [9]	63.4 %
KDES RGB-D [9]	71.4 %	KDES Treepath [9]	74.6 %
KDES MRF [9]	74.6 %	KDES Tree+MRF [9]	76.1 %
B-DN	76.5 %	S-DN	72.1 %
C-DN	70.3 %	E-DN	71.4 %
U-DN	69.9 %	Ours	78.8 %

Table 3. The 13-class segmentation accuracy of different methods on NYU depth dataset V2. B-DN trains two independent deconvolutional networks. S-DN contains a single deconvolutional network and two convolutional networks. C-DN trains one convolutional and one deconvolutional network with 4-channel RGBD as input. E-DN uses the Euclidean distance to assess the difference between features in the proposed network

	Couprie [11]	Wang [18]	B-DN	S-DN	C-DN	E-DN	Ours
bed	38.1	47.6	27.4	19.6	19.2	25.3	31.6
objects	8.7	12.4	40.7	43.8	40.1	36.9	61.5
chair	34.1	23.5	43.5	39.2	42.8	39.3	43.6
furniture	42.4	16.7	37.2	36.3	35.7	35.2	49.8
ceiling	62.6	68.1	52.2	56.2	55.9	55.1	58.7
floor	87.3	84.1	82.9	86.5	84.7	90.5	89.0
decorate	40.4	26.4	55.8	56.9	54.6	60.4	68.9
sofa	24.6	39.1	36.7	31.3	28.3	35.7	30.8
table	10.2	35.4	36.4	50.3	50.5	42.7	49.3
wall	86.1	65.9	41.4	32.2	33.3	34.3	44.9
window	15.9	52.2	81.7	87.4	88.9	78.1	83.9
books	13.7	45.0	28.8	23.1	22.5	29.9	39.9
TV	6.0	32.4	53.7	29.4	29.7	35.27	32.8
AVE	36.2	42.2	47.6	45.6	45.1	46.1	52.7

our method significantly outperforms [18]. In Table 4, we compare our method with the previous works on the 4-class, 13-class, and 40-class segmentation task. The proposed method outperforms all of them in segmentation accuracy.

Based on Tables 2 and 3, we can conclude that MK-MMD is a better measurement than Euclidean distance to learn common features and modality specific features in this task. The proposed method outperforms the baseline E-DN by 7.4 % and 6.6 % in dataset V1 and V2, respectively. This is mainly because, the Euclidean distance is heavily effected by the outliers.

In both B-DN and the proposed network, we use a linear combination to conduct decision score fusion. Compared with the baseline B-DN, the proposed network is 2.3 % higher on dataset V1 and 5.1 % higher on dataset V2. It indicates that we should correlate the two modalities in the feature learning stage instead of only fusing them at the decision score level. The baseline B-DN is not robust. Its segmentation accuracy varies a lot as the parameter (for linear combination of decision score fusion) changes. By contrast, our network is much more robust and varies slightly as the parameter changes. In our network, the deconvolutional results from two modalities are much more similar than those in B-DN. The reason is that, by borrowing common features from other modality, our method will produce similar decisions scores for the two modalities, which makes fusing result robust to the linear combination parameter.

Table 4. The per-class accuracy of 4, 13, and 40-class segmentation on NYU depth dataset V2

4-class		13-class		40-class	
Couprie [11]	63.5 %	Couprie [11]	36.2 %	Gupta'13 [10]	28.4 %
Khan [12]	65.6 %	Wang [18]	42.2 %	Gupta'14 [13]	35.1 %
Stuckler [38]	67.0 %	Khan [12]	45.1 %	Long [26]	46.1 %
Muller [39]	71.9 %	Hermans [37]	48.0 %	Eigen [35]	45.1 %
U-DN	71.8 %	U-DN	49.2 %	U-DN	41.7 %
Ours	74.7 %	Ours	52.7 %	Ours	47.3 %

6   Conclusion

In this paper, we propose a new network structure for RGB-D semantic segmentation. The proposed network has a convolutional network and a deconvolutional network for each of the modality. We bridge the convolutional networks and the deconvolutional networks using a feature transformation network. In the feature transformation network, we transform the convolutional features into common features and modality-specific features. Instead of using a one-vs-one strategy to measure the similarity between features, we adopt MK-MMD to calculate the similarity between their distributions. To learn robust deconvolutional features, we allow one modality to borrow the common features from the other modality. Our method achieves competitive performance on NYU depth dataset V1 and V2.

Acknowledgment. The research is supported by Singapore Ministry of Education (MOE) Tier 2 ARC28/14, and Singapore A*STAR Science and Engineering Research Council PSF1321202099. The research is also supported by Australian Research Council Projects DP-140102164, FT-130101457, and LE-140100061.

This work was carried out at the Rapid-Rich Object Search (ROSE) Lab at the Nanyang Technological University, Singapore. The ROSE Lab is supported by a grant from the Singapore National Research Foundation and administered by the Interactive &Digital Media Programme Office at the Media Development Authority.

References

1. Socher, R., Lin, C.C., Ng, A.Y., Manning, C.D.: Parsing natural scenes and natural language with recursive neural networks. In: ICML (2011)
2. Shuai, B., Zuo, Z., Wang, G., Wang, B.: Dag-recurrent neural networks for scene labeling. Comput. Sci. (2015)
3. Farabet, C., Couprie, C., Najman, L., LeCun, Y.: Learning hierarchical features for scene labeling. IEEE Trans. Pattern Anal. Mach. Intell. **35**(8), 1915–1929 (2013)
4. Hong, S., Noh, H., Han, B.: Decoupled deep neural network for semi-supervised semantic segmentation. In: NIPS 2015 (2015)
5. Shuai, B., Zuo, Z., Wang, G., Wang, B.: Scene parsing with integration of parametric and non-parametric models. IEEE Trans. Image Process. **25**(5), 1–1 (2016)

6. Noh, H., Hong, S., Han, B.: Learning deconvolution network for semantic segmentation. arXiv preprint arXiv:1505.04366 (2015)
7. Silberman, N., Hoiem, D., Kohli, P., Fergus, R.: Indoor segmentation and support inference from RGBD images. In: Fitzgibbon, A., Lazebnik, S., Perona, P., Sato, Y., Schmid, C. (eds.) ECCV 2012, Part V. LNCS, vol. 7576, pp. 746–760. Springer, Heidelberg (2012)
8. Silberman, N., Fergus, R.: Indoor scene segmentation using a structured light sensor. In: ICCV Workshops, pp. 601–608 (2011)
9. Ren, X., Bo, L., Fox, D.: RGB-(D) scene labeling: features and algorithms. In: CVPR, pp. 2759–2766 (2012)
10. Gupta, S., Arbelaez, P., Malik, J.: Perceptual organization and recognition of indoor scenes from RGB-D images. In: CVPR, pp. 564–571 (2013)
11. Couprie, C., Farabet, C., Najman, L., LeCun, Y.: Indoor semantic segmentation using depth information. In: International Conference on Learning Representations. Number arXiv preprint arXiv:1301.3572 (2013)
12. Khan, S.H., Bennamoun, M., Sohel, F., Togneri, R.: Geometry driven semantic labeling of indoor scenes. In: Fleet, D., Pajdla, T., Schiele, B., Tuytelaars, T. (eds.) ECCV 2014, Part I. LNCS, vol. 8689, pp. 679–694. Springer, Heidelberg (2014)
13. Gupta, S., Girshick, R., Arbeláez, P., Malik, J.: Learning rich features from RGB-D images for object detection and segmentation. In: Fleet, D., Pajdla, T., Schiele, B., Tuytelaars, T. (eds.) ECCV 2014, Part VII. LNCS, vol. 8695, pp. 345–360. Springer, Heidelberg (2014)
14. Deng, Z., Todorovic, S., Latecki, L.J.: Semantic segmentation of RGBD images with mutex constraints. In: ICCV (2015)
15. Banica, D., Sminchisescu, C.: Second-order constrained parametric proposals and sequential search-based structured prediction for semantic segmentation in RGB-D images. In: Computer Vision and Pattern Recognition (2015)
16. Wang, A., Lu, J., Cai, J., Wang, G., Cham, T.J.: Unsupervised joint feature learning and encoding for RGB-D scene labeling. IEEE Trans. Image Process. A Publication of the IEEE Signal Processing Society 24(11), 4459–4473 (2015)
17. Shuai, B., Wang, G., Zuo, Z., Wang, B., Zhao, L.: Integrating parametric and non-parametric models for scene labeling. In: IEEE Conference on Computer Vision and Pattern Recognition. (2015)
18. Wang, A., Lu, J., Wang, G., Cai, J., Cham, T.-J.: Multi-modal unsupervised feature learning for RGB-D scene labeling. In: Fleet, D., Pajdla, T., Schiele, B., Tuytelaars, T. (eds.) ECCV 2014, Part V. LNCS, vol. 8693, pp. 453–467. Springer, Heidelberg (2014)
19. Wang, A., Cai, J., Lu, J., Cham, T.J.: MMSS: Multi-modal sharable and specific feature learning for RGB-D object recognition. In: IEEE International Conference on Computer Vision, pp. 1125–1133 (2015)
20. Shuai, B., Zuo, Z., Wang, G.: Quaddirectional 2d-recurrent neural networks for image labeling. IEEE Sig. Process. Lett. 22(11), 1 (2015)
21. Ngiam, J., Khosla, A., Kim, M., Nam, J., Lee, H., Ng, A.Y.: Multimodal deep learning. In: ICML 2011, pp. 689–696 (2011)
22. Ganin, Y., Lempitsky, V.: Unsupervised domain adaptation by backpropagation. In: ICML 2015, pp. 1180–1189 (2015)
23. Sohn, K., Shang, W., Lee, H.: Improved multimodal deep learning with variation of information. In: NIPS, pp. 2141–2149 (2014)
24. Long, M., Cao, Y., Wang, J., Jordan, M.: Learning transferable features with deep adaptation networks. In: CML 2015, JMLR Workshop and Conference Proceedings, pp. 97–105 (2015)

25. Koppula, H.S., Anand, A., Joachims, T., Saxena, A.: Semantic labeling of 3d point clouds for indoor scenes. In: NIPS, pp. 244–252 (2011)
26. Long, J., Shelhamer, E., Darrell, T.: Fully convolutional networks for semantic segmentation. In: CVPR 2015 (2015)
27. Krizhevsky, A., Sutskever, I., Hinton, G.E.: Imagenet classification with deep convolutional neural networks. In: Pereira, F., Burges, C., Bottou, L., Weinberger, K. (eds.) NIPS, pp. 1097–1105 (2012)
28. Papandreou, G., Chen, L.C., Murphy, K., Yuille, A.L.: Weakly-and semi-supervised learning of a DCNN for semantic image segmentation. arXiv preprint arXiv:1502.02734 (2015)
29. Berlinet, A., Thomas-Agnan, C.: Reproducing Kernel Hilbert Spaces in Probability and Statistics. Kluwer, Dordrecht (2004)
30. Gretton, A., Sejdinovic, D., Strathmann, H., Balakrishnan, S., Pontil, M., Fukumizu, K., Sriperumbudur, B.K.: Optimal kernel choice for large-scale two-sample tests. In: NIPS, pp. 1205–1213. Curran Associates, Inc. (2012)
31. Zitnick, C.L., Dollár, P.: Edge boxes: locating object proposals from edges. In: Fleet, D., Pajdla, T., Schiele, B., Tuytelaars, T. (eds.) ECCV 2014, Part V. LNCS, vol. 8693, pp. 391–405. Springer, Heidelberg (2014)
32. Jia, Y., Shelhamer, E., Donahue, J., Karayev, S., Long, J., Girshick, R., Guadarrama, S., Darrell, T.: Caffe: Convolutional architecture for fast feature embedding. arXiv preprint arXiv:1408.5093 (2014)
33. Simonyan, K., Zisserman, A.: Very deep convolutional networks for large-scale image recognition. CoRR abs/1409.1556 (2014)
34. Deng, J., Dong, W., Socher, R., Li, L.-J., Li, K., Fei-Fei, L.: Imagenet: a large-scale hierarchical image database. In: CVPR (2009)
35. Eigen, D., Fergus, R.: Predicting depth, surface normals and semantic labels with a common multi-scale convolutional architecture. In: ICCV, pp. 2650–2658 (2015)
36. Pei, D., Liu, H., Liu, Y., Sun, F.: Unsupervised multimodal feature learning for semantic image segmentation. In: IJCNN, pp. 1–6 (2013)
37. Hermans, A., Floros, G., Leibe, B.: Dense 3D semantic mapping of indoor scenes from RGB-D images. In: ICRA (2014)
38. Stückler, J., Waldvogel, B., Schulz, H., Behnke, S.: Dense real-time mapping of object-class semantics from RGB-D video. J. Real-Time Image Process. 10(4), 599–609 (2015)
39. Muller, A.C., Behnke, S.: Learning depth-sensitive conditional random fields for semantic segmentation of RGB-D images. In: ICRA, pp. 6232–6237 (2014)

MADMM: A Generic Algorithm for Non-smooth Optimization on Manifolds

Artiom Kovnatsky[(✉)], Klaus Glashoff, and Michael M. Bronstein

Institute of Computational Science, Faculty of Informatics,
USI Universitá della Svizzera Italiana, Lugano, Switzerland
{artiom.kovnatsky,klaus.glashoff,michael.bronstein}@usi.ch

Abstract. Numerous problems in computer vision, pattern recognition, and machine learning are formulated as optimization with manifold constraints. In this paper, we propose the *Manifold Alternating Directions Method of Multipliers* (MADMM), an extension of the classical ADMM scheme for manifold-constrained non-smooth optimization problems. To our knowledge, MADMM is the first generic non-smooth manifold optimization method. We showcase our method on several challenging problems in dimensionality reduction, non-rigid correspondence, multi-modal clustering, and multidimensional scaling.

1 Introduction

A wide range of problems in machine learning, pattern recognition, computer vision, and signal processing is formulated as optimization problems where the variables are constrained to lie on some Riemannian manifold. For example, optimization on the *Grassman manifold* comes up in multi-view clustering [1] and matrix completion [2]. Optimization on the *Stiefel manifold* arises in eigenvalue-, assignment-, and Procrustes problems, and in 1-bit compressed sensing [3]. Problems involving *products of Stiefel manifolds* include coupled diagonalization with applications to shape correspondence [4] and manifold learning [5], and eigenvector synchronization with applications to sensor localization [6], structural biology [7] and structure from motion recovery [8]. Optimization on the *sphere* is used in principle geodesic analysis [9], a generalization of the classical PCA to non-Euclidean domains. Optimization over the manifold of *fixed-rank matrices* arises in maxcut problems [10], sparse principal component analysis [10], regression [11], matrix completion [12,13], and image classification [14]. *Oblique manifolds* are encountered in problems such as independent component analysis [15], blind source separation [16], and prediction of stock returns [17].

Though some instances of manifold optimization such as eigenvalues problems have been treated extensively in the distant past, the first general purpose algorithms appeared only in the 1990s [18]. With the emergence of numerous applications during the last decade, especially in the machine learning community, there has been an increased interest in general-purpose optimization on different manifolds [19], leading to several manifold optimization algorithms

© Springer International Publishing AG 2016
B. Leibe et al. (Eds.): ECCV 2016, Part V, LNCS 9909, pp. 680–696, 2016.
DOI: 10.1007/978-3-319-46454-1_41

such as conjugate gradients [20], trust regions [21], and Newton [18,22]. Boumal *et al.* [23] released the MATLAB package Manopt, as of today the most complete generic toolbox for smooth optimization on various manifolds.

In this paper, we are interested in manifold-constrained minimization of *non-smooth* functions, such as nuclear, L_1, or $L_{2,1}$ matrix norms. Recent examples of such problems include robust PCA [24], compressed eigenmodes [25,26], robust multidimensional scaling [27], synchronization of rotation matrices [28], and functional correspondence [29,30].

Prior Work. Broadly speaking, optimization methods for non-smooth functions break into three classes of approaches. First, *smoothing* methods replace the non-differentiable objective function with its smooth approximation [31]. Such methods typically suffer from a tradeoff between accuracy (how far is the smooth approximation from the original objective) and convergence speed (less smooth functions are usually harder to optimize). A second class of methods use *subgradients* as a generalization of derivatives of non-differentiable functions. In the context of manifold optimization, several subgradient approaches have been proposed [16,32–34]. The third class of methods are *splitting* approaches, studied mostly for problems involving the minimization of matrix functions with orthogonality constraints. Lai and Osher proposed the method of splitting orthogonal constraints (SOC) based on the Bregman iteration [35]. A similar method was independently developed in [36]. Neumann *et al.* [26] used a different splitting scheme for the same class of problems.

Contributions. In this paper, we propose *Manifold Alternating Direction Method of Multipliers* (MADMM), an extension of the classical ADMM scheme [37] for manifold-constrained non-smooth optimization problems. The core idea is a splitting into a smooth problem with manifold constraints and a non-smooth unconstrained optimization problem. We stress that while very simple, to the best of our knowledge we are the first to employ such a splitting, which leads to a general optimization method. Our method has a number of advantages common to ADMM approaches. First, it is very simple to grasp and implement. Second, it is generic and not limited to a specific manifold, as opposed to e.g. [26,35] developed for the Stiefel manifold, or [16] developed for the oblique manifold. Third, it makes very few assumptions about the properties of the objective function. Fourth, in some settings, our method lends itself to parallelization on distributed computational architectures [38]. Finally, our method demonstrates faster convergence than previous methods in a broad range of applications.

2 Manifold Optimization

The term *manifold-* or *manifold-constrained optimization* refers to a class of problems of the form

$$\min_{X \in \mathcal{M}} f(X), \tag{1}$$

where f is a smooth real-valued function, X is an $m \times n$ real matrix, and $\mathcal{M}$ is some Riemannian submanifold of $\mathbb{R}^{m \times n}$. The manifold is not a vector space and

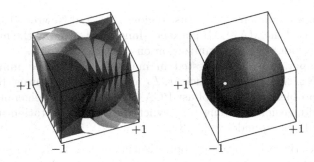

Fig. 1. The minimum eigenvalue problem $\min_{x \in \mathbb{R}^n} x^\top A x$ s.t. $x^\top x = 1$ is a simple example of a manifold optimization problem. Left: level sets of the cost function $x^\top A x$ for a random symmetric 3×3 matrix A. The manifold constraint (unit sphere $\{x \in \mathbb{R}^3 : x^\top x = 1\}$) is shown in grey. Right: values of the cost function on the manifold of feasible solutions. A minimizer (white dot) corresponds to the smallest eigenvector of A. Note that there are two minimizers in this example due to the sign ambiguity of the eigenvectors (the other minimizer is on the back of the sphere).

has no global system of coordinates, however, locally at point X, the manifold is homeomorphic to a Euclidean space referred to as the *tangent space* $T_X \mathcal{M}$.

The main idea of manifold optimization is to treat the objective as a function $f : \mathcal{M} \to \mathbb{R}$ defined on the manifold, and perform descent on the manifold itself rather than in the ambient Euclidean space (see a toy example in Fig. 1). On a manifold, the *intrinsic* (Riemannian) gradient $\nabla_{\mathcal{M}} f(X)$ of f at point X is a vector in the tangent space $T_X \mathcal{M}$ that can be obtained by projecting the standard (Euclidean) gradient $\nabla f(X)$ onto $T_X \mathcal{M}$ by means of a *projection* operator P_X (see an illustration below). A step along the intrinsic gradient direction is performed in the tangent plane. In order to obtain the next iterate, the point in the tangent plane is mapped back to the manifold by means of a *retraction* operator R_X, which is typically an approximation of the *exponential map*. For many manifolds, the projection P and retraction R operators have a closed form expression.

A conceptual gradient descent-like manifold optimization is presented in Algorithm 1. For a comprehensive introduction to manifold optimization, the reader is referred to [19].

3   Manifold ADMM

Let us now consider general problems of the form

$$\min_{X \in \mathcal{M}} f(X) + g(AX), \qquad (2)$$

where f and g are smooth and non-smooth real-valued functions, respectively, A is a $k \times m$ matrix, and the rest of the notation is as in problem (1). Examples of g often used in machine learning applications are nuclear-, L_1-, or $L_{2,1}$-norms.

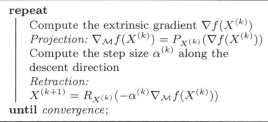

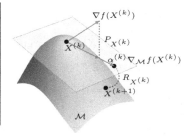

repeat
 Compute the extrinsic gradient $\nabla f(X^{(k)})$
 Projection: $\nabla_{\mathcal{M}} f(X^{(k)}) = P_{X^{(k)}}(\nabla f(X^{(k)}))$
 Compute the step size $\alpha^{(k)}$ along the
 descent direction
 Retraction:
 $X^{(k+1)} = R_{X^{(k)}}(-\alpha^{(k)}\nabla_{\mathcal{M}} f(X^{(k)}))$
until *convergence*;

Algorithm 1. Conceptual algorithm for smooth optimization on manifold $\mathcal{M}$.

Because of non-smoothness of the objective function, Algorithm 1 cannot be used directly to minimize (2).

In this paper, we propose treating this class of problems using the Alternating Directions Method of Multipliers (ADMM). The key idea is that problem (2) can be equivalently formulated as

$$\min_{X \in \mathcal{M}, Z \in \mathbb{R}^{k \times n}} f(X) + g(Z) \quad \text{s.t.} \quad Z = AX \tag{3}$$

by introducing an artificial variable Z and a linear constraint. The method of multipliers [39,40], applied to only the linear constraints in (3), leads to the minimization problem

$$\min_{X \in \mathcal{M}, Z \in \mathbb{R}^{k \times n}} f(X) + g(Z) + \tfrac{\rho}{2}\|AX - Z + U\|_{\mathrm{F}}^2 \tag{4}$$

where $\rho > 0$ and $U \in \mathbb{R}^{k \times n}$ have to be chosen and updated appropriately (see below). This formulation now allows splitting the problem into two optimization sub-problems w.r.t. to X and Z, which are solved in an alternating manner, followed by an updating of U and, if necessary, of ρ. Observe that in the first sub-problem w.r.t. X we minimize a *smooth* function with manifold constraints, and in the second sub-problem w.r.t. Z we minimize a non-smooth function without manifold constraints. Thus, the problem breaks down into two well-known sub-problems. This method, which we call *Manifold Alternating Direction Method of Multipliers* (MADMM), is summarized in Algorithm 2.

Note that MADMM is extremely simple and easy to implement. The X-step is the setting of Algorithm 1 and can be carried out using any standard smooth manifold optimization method. Similarly to common implementation of ADMM algorithms, there is no need to solve the X-step problem *exactly*; instead, only a few iterations of manifold optimization are done. Furthermore, for some manifolds and some functions f, the X-step has a closed-form solution. The implementation of the Z-step depends on the non-smooth function g, and in many cases has a closed-form expression: for example, when g is the L_1-norm, the Z-step boils down to simple shrinkage, and when g is nuclear norm, the Z-step is performed by singular value shrinkage[1]. ρ is the only parameter of

---

[1] More generally, it is a proximity operator of $\tfrac{1}{\rho}g(Z)$ at $AX + U$.

Initialize $k \leftarrow 1$, $Z^{(1)} = AX^{(1)}$, $U^{(1)} = 0$.
repeat

    X-*step:* $X^{(k+1)} = \underset{X \in \mathcal{M}}{\operatorname{argmin}} f(X) + \frac{\rho}{2}\|AX - Z^{(k)} + U^{(k)}\|_{\mathrm{F}}^2$

    Z-*step:* $Z^{(k+1)} = \underset{Z}{\operatorname{argmin}} g(Z) + \frac{\rho}{2}\|AX^{(k+1)} - Z + U^{(k)}\|_{\mathrm{F}}^2$

    $U^{(k+1)} = U^{(k)} + AX^{(k+1)} - Z^{(k+1)}$

    $k \leftarrow k + 1$

until *convergence*;

Algorithm 2. Generic MADMM method for non-smooth optimization on manifold $\mathcal{M}$.

the algorithm and its choice is not critical for convergence. In our experiments, we used a rather arbitrary fixed value of ρ, though in the ADMM literature it is common to adapt ρ at each iteration, e.g. using the strategy described in [38].

Convergence. Our MADMM belongs to the class of multiplier algorithms that can be considered as 'methods with partial elimination of constraints' [41] and as 'augmented Lagrangian methods with general lower-level constraints' [42]. We note that the convergence results of [41,42] do not apply in our case due to non-differentiability of the function g in (2). Furthermore, MADMM is an alternating method and thus is not covered by theoretical results on 'pure' multiplier methods. An avenue for obtaining convergence results for (a regularized version of) MADMM is the recently developed theory by [43], which is applicable to non convex and non-differentiable functions f and g. Attouch et al. [43] show convergence results for the class of *semi algebraic objects*, which includes Stiefel and other matrix manifolds. Wang et al. prove global convergence of ADMM in convex and non-smooth scenarios, however the non-smooth and non-convex parts should belong to a specific class of functions (piecewise linear functions, ℓ_q quasi-norms ($0 \leq q \leq 1$), etc.) [44], which limits the use of their convergence results. We defer a deeper study of convergence properties to future work.

4 Results and Applications

In this section, we show experimental results providing a numerical evaluation of our approach on several challenging applications from the domains of dimensionality reduction, pattern recognition, and manifold learning. All our experiments were implemented in MATLAB; we used the conjugate gradients and trust regions solvers from the Manopt toolbox [23] for the X-step. Time measurements were carried out on a PC with Intel Xeon 2.4 GHz CPU.

4.1 Compressed Modes

Problem Setting. Our first application is the computation of compressed modes, an approach for constructing localized Fourier-like bases [25]. Let us be given a manifold $\mathcal{S}$ with a Laplacian Δ, where in this context, 'manifold' can refer to both continuous or discretized manifolds of any dimension, represented as graphs, triangular meshes, etc., and should not be confused with the matrix manifolds we have discussed so far referring to manifold-constrained optimization problems. Here, we assume that the manifold is sampled at n points and the Laplacian is represented as an $n \times n$ sparse symmetric matrix. In many machine learning applications such as spectral clustering [45], non-linear dimensionality reduction, and manifold learning [46], one is interested in finding the first k eigenvectors of the Laplacian $\Delta\Phi = \Phi\Lambda$, where $\Phi = (\phi_1, \ldots, \phi_k)$ is the $n \times k$ matrix of the first eigenvectors arranged as columns, and $\Lambda = \mathrm{diag}(\lambda_1, \ldots, \lambda_k)$ is the diagonal $k \times k$ matrix of the corresponding eigenvalues.

The first k eigenvectors of the Laplacian can be computed by minimizing the *Dirichlet energy* with orthonormality constraints

$$\min_{\Phi \in \mathbb{R}^{n \times k}} \quad \mathrm{tr}(\Phi^\top \Delta \Phi) \quad \text{s.t.} \quad \Phi^\top \Phi = I. \tag{5}$$

Laplacian eigenfunctions form an orthonormal basis on the Hilbert space $L^2(\mathcal{S})$ with the standard inner product, and are a generalization of the Fourier basis to non-Euclidean domains. The main disadvantage of such bases is that its elements are globally supported. Ozoliņš *et al.* [25] proposed a construction of localized quasi-eigenbases by solving

$$\min_{\Phi \in \mathbb{R}^{n \times k}} \quad \mathrm{tr}(\Phi^\top \Delta \Phi) + \mu\|\Phi\|_1 \quad \text{s.t.} \quad \Phi^\top \Phi = I, \tag{6}$$

where $\mu > 0$ is a parameter. The L_1-norm (inducing sparsity of the resulting basis) together with the Dirichlet energy (imposing smoothness of the basis functions) lead to orthogonal basis functions, referred to as *compressed modes* that are localized and approximately diagonalize Δ.

Lai and Osher [35] and Neumann *et al.* [26] proposed two different splitting methods for solving problem (6). Lai *et al.* [35] solves (6) by the *splitting orthogonality constraint (SOC)*, introducing two additional variables $Q = \Phi$ and $P = \Phi$ so that (6) is equivalent to the following constrained optimization problem,

$$\min_{\Phi, Q, P \in \mathbb{R}^{n \times k}} \quad \mathrm{tr}(\Phi^\top \Delta \Phi) + \mu\|Q\|_1 \quad \text{s.t.} \quad Q = \Phi, \; P = \Phi, \; P^\top P = I, \tag{7}$$

solved by alternating minimization on Φ, P, and Q (Algorithm 3).

Solution. Here, we realize that problem (6) is an instance of manifold optimization on the Stiefel manifold $\mathbb{S}(n, k) = \{X \in \mathbb{R}^{n \times k} : X^\top X = I\}$ and solve it using MADMM, which assumes in this setting the form of Algorithm 4. The X-step involves optimization of a smooth function on the Stiefel manifold and can be carried out using standard manifold optimization algorithms; we use conjugate gradients and trust regions solvers. The Z-step requires the minimization of the sum of L_1- and L_2-norms, a standard problem in signal processing that has an explicit solution by means of thresholding (using the shrinking operator). In all our experiments, we used the parameter $\rho = 2$ for MADMM. For comparison

---

Input $n \times n$ Laplacian matrix Δ, parameter $\mu > 0$
Output $n \times k$ matrix Φ of the first compressed modes of Δ
Initialize $k \leftarrow 1$, $\Phi^{(1)}$, $P^{(1)} = Q^{(1)} = \Phi^{(1)}$, $U^{(1)} = V^{(1)} = 0$
repeat

$\quad \Phi^{(k+1)} = \underset{\Phi}{\operatorname{argmin}} \operatorname{tr}(\Phi^{\top} \Delta \Phi) + \frac{\rho}{2}\|\Phi - Q^{(k)} + U^{(k)}\|_{\mathrm{F}}^2 + \frac{\rho'}{2}\|\Phi - P^{(k)} + V^{(k)}\|_{\mathrm{F}}^2$

$\quad Q^{(k+1)} = \underset{Q}{\operatorname{argmin}} \mu\|Q\|_1 + \frac{\rho}{2}\|\Phi^{(k+1)} - Q + U^{(k)}\|_{\mathrm{F}}^2$

$\quad P^{(k+1)} = \underset{P:P^{\top}P=I}{\operatorname{argmin}} \frac{\rho'}{2}\|\Phi^{(k+1)} - P + V^{(k)}\|_{\mathrm{F}}^2$

$\quad U^{(k+1)} = U^{(k)} + \Phi^{(k+1)} - Q^{(k+1)}$
$\quad V^{(k+1)} = V^{(k)} + \Phi^{(k+1)} - P^{(k+1)}$
$\quad k \leftarrow k + 1$
until *convergence*;

Algorithm 3. SOC method [35] for computing compressed modes.

Input $n \times n$ Laplacian matrix Δ, parameter $\mu > 0$
Output $n \times k$ matrix Φ of the first compressed modes of Δ
Initialize $k \leftarrow 1$, $\Phi^{(1)} \leftarrow$ random orthonormal matrix, $Z^{(1)} = \Phi^{(1)}$, $U^{(1)} = 0$
repeat

$\quad \Phi^{(k+1)} = \underset{\Phi \in \mathbb{S}(n,k)}{\operatorname{argmin}} \operatorname{tr}(\Phi^{\top} \Delta \Phi) + \frac{\rho}{2}\|\Phi - Z^{(k)} + U^{(k)}\|_{\mathrm{F}}^2$

$\quad Z^{(k+1)} = \operatorname{Shrink}_{\frac{\mu}{\rho}}(\Phi^{(k+1)} + U^{(k)})$

$\quad U^{(k+1)} = U^{(k)} + \Phi^{(k+1)} - Z^{(k+1)}$
$\quad k \leftarrow k + 1$
until *convergence*;

Algorithm 4. MADMM method for computing compressed modes. $\operatorname{Shrink}_{\alpha}(x) = \frac{x}{\|x\|} \max\{0, \|x\| - \alpha\}$ is the shrinkage operator.

---

with the method of [35], we used the code provided by the authors, and implemented the method of [26] ourselves. All the methods were initialized by the same random orthonormal $n \times k$ matrix Φ.

Results. To study the behavior of ADMM, we used a simple 1D problem with a Euclidean Laplacian constructed on a line graph with n vertices. Figure 3 (top left) shows the convergence of MADMM with different random initializations. Figure 3 (top right) shows the convergence of MADMM using different solvers and number of iterations in the X-step. We did not observe any significant change in the behavior. Figure 3 (bottom left) studies the scalability of different algorithms, speaking clearly in favor of MADMM compared to the methods of [26,35]. Figure 3 (bottom right) shows the convergence of different methods for the computation of compressed modes on a triangular mesh of a human sampled at 8 K vertices (see examples in Fig. 2). MADMM shows the best performance among the compared methods.

Fig. 2. First six compressed modes computed on a human mesh containing $n = 8\,\mathrm{K}$ points computed using MADMM. Parameter $\mu = 10^{-3}$ and three manifold optimization iterations in the X-step were used in these experiments.

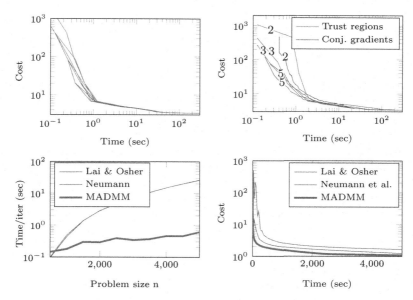

Fig. 3. Compressed modes problem. Top left: convergence of MADMM on a problem of size $n = 500, k = 10$ with different random initialization. Top right: convergence of MADMM using different solvers and number of iterations at X-step on the same problem. Bottom left: scalability of different methods; shown is time/iteration on a problem of different size (fixed $k = 10$ and varying n). Bottom right: comparison of convergence of different splitting methods and MADMM on a problem of size $n = 8\,\mathrm{K}$.

4.2 Functional Correspondence

Problem Setting. Our second problem is coupled diagonalization, which is used for finding functional correspondence between manifolds [47] and multi-view clustering [5]. Let us consider a collection of L manifolds $\{\mathcal{S}_i\}_{i=1}^L$, each discretized at n_i points and equipped with a Laplacian Δ_i represented as an $n_i \times n_i$ matrix. The *functional correspondence* between manifolds $\mathcal{S}_i$ and $\mathcal{S}_j$ is an $n_j \times n_i$ matrix T_{ij} mapping functions from $L^2(\mathcal{S}_i)$ to $L^2(\mathcal{S}_j)$. It can be efficiently approximated using the first k Laplacian eigenvectors as $T_{ij} \approx \Phi_j X_{ij} \Phi_i^\top$, where X_{ij} is the $k \times k$ matrix translating Fourier coefficients from basis Φ_i to basis Φ_j, represented as $n_i \times k$ and $n_j \times k$ matrices, respectively. Imposing a further assumption that T_{ij} is volume-preserving, X_{ij} must be an orthonormal matrix [47], which will be approximated by the product of two orthogonal matrices. For each pair of manifolds $\mathcal{S}_i, \mathcal{S}_j$, we assume to be given a set of q_{ij} functions in $L^2(\mathcal{S}_i)$ arranged as columns of an $n_i \times q_{ij}$ matrix F_{ij} and the corresponding functions in $L^2(\mathcal{S}_j)$ represented by the $n_j \times q_{ij}$ matrix G_{ij}. The correspondence between all the manifolds can be established by solving the problem

$$\min_{X_1,\ldots,X_L} \sum_{i \neq j} \|F_{ij}^\top \Phi_i X_i - G_{ij}^\top \Phi_j X_j\|_{2,1} + \mu \sum_{i=1}^L \mathrm{tr}(X_i^\top \Lambda_i X_i) \quad \text{s.t.} \ X_i^\top X_i = I. \quad (8)$$

The $L_{2,1}$-norm $\|A\|_{2,1} = \sum_j \left(\sum_i a_{ij}^2\right)^{1/2}$ allows to cope with outliers in the correspondence data [28,29]. The problem can be interpreted as simultaneous diagonalization of the Laplacians $\Delta_1, \ldots, \Delta_L$ [5]. As correspondence data F, G, one can use point-wise correspondence between some known 'seeds', or, in computer graphics applications, some shape descriptors [47]. Geometrically, the matrices X_i can be interpreted as rotations of the respective bases, and the problem tries to achieve a coupling between the bases $\hat{\Phi}_i = \Phi_i X_i$ while making sure that they approximately diagonalize the respective Laplacians.

Solution. Here, we consider problem (8) as optimization on a product of L Stiefel manifolds, $(X_1, \ldots, X_L) \in \mathbb{S}^L(k, k)$ and solve it using the MADMM method. The X-step of MADMM was performed using four iterations of the manifold conjugate gradients solver. As in the previous problem, the Z-step boils down to simple shrinkage. We used $\rho = 1$ and initialized all $X_i = I$.

Input $n_i \times q_{ij}$, $n_j \times q_{ij}$ corresponding matrices F_{ij}, G_{ij}, respectively; $n_i \times k$ eigenbases matrices Φ_i, $k \times k$ diagonal matrices Λ_i of corresponding eigenvalues, and parameter $\mu > 0$
Output orthonormal matrices $X_1, \ldots, X_L$ aligning the bases $\Phi_1, \ldots, \Phi_L$ and allowing to express the functional correspondences as
$T_{ij} \approx \Phi_j X_i X_j^\top \Phi_i^\top$
Initialize $k \leftarrow 1$, $X_i^{(1)} \leftarrow I$, $Z_{ij}^{(1)} \leftarrow F_{ij}^\top \Phi_i X_i^{(1)} - G_{ij}^\top \Phi_j X_j^{(1)}$, $U_{ij}^{(1)} \leftarrow I$
repeat
$\quad (X_1^{(k+1)}, \ldots, X_L^{(k+1)}) =$
$\quad \underset{X_i \in \mathbb{S}(k,k)}{\mathrm{argmin}} \sum_i \mathrm{tr}(X_i^\top \Lambda_i X_i) + \frac{\rho}{2} \sum_{i \neq j} \|F_{ij}^\top \Phi_i X_i - G_{ij}^\top \Phi_j X_j - Z_{ij}^{(k)} + U_{ij}^{(k)}\|_F^2$
$\quad Z_{ij}^{(k+1)}(:, l) =$
$\quad \mathrm{Shrink}_{\frac{1}{\mu\rho}} (F_{ij}^\top \Phi_i X_i^{(k+1)}(:, l) - G_{ij}^\top \Phi_j X_j^{(k+1)}(:, l) + U_{ij}^{(k)}(:, l))$
$\quad U_{ij}^{(k+1)} = U_{ij}^{(k)} + F_{ij}^\top \Phi_i X_i^{(k+1)} - G_{ij}^\top \Phi_j X_j^{(k+1)} - Z_{ij}^{(k+1)}$
$\quad k \leftarrow k + 1$
until *convergence*;

Algorithm 5. MADMM method for functional correspondence problem. $X(:, l)$ denotes the lth column of matrix X.

Results. We computed functional correspondences between $L = 6$ human 3D shapes from the TOSCA dataset [48] using $k = 25$ basis functions and $q = 25$

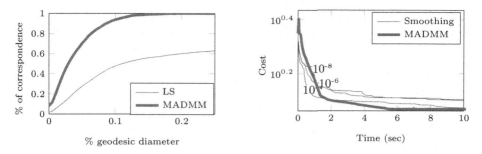

Fig. 4. Functional correspondence problem. Left: evaluation of the functional correspondence obtained using MADMM and least squares. Shown in the percentage of correspondences falling within a geodesic ball of increasing radius w.r.t. the groundtruth correspondence. Right: convergence of MADMM and smoothing method for various values of the smoothing parameter.

Fig. 5. Examples of correspondences obtained with MADMM (top two rows) and least-squares solution (bottom two rows). Rows 1 and 3: similar colors encode corresponding points; rows 2 and 4: color encodes the correspondence error (distance in centimeters to the ground-truth). Leftmost column, 1st row: the reference shape; 2nd row: examples of correspondence between a pair of shapes (outliers are shown in red). (Color figure online)

seeds as correspondence data, contaminated by 16 % outliers. Figure 4 (left) ana-
lyzes the resulting correspondence quality using the Princeton protocol [49], plotting the percentage of correspondences falling within a geodesic ball of increasing radius w.r.t. the groundtruth correspondence. For comparison, we show the
results of a least-squares solution used in [47] (see Fig. 5). Figure 4 (right) shows
the convergence of MADMM in a correspondence problem with $L = 2$ shapes.
For comparison, we show the convergence of a smoothed version of the $L_{2,1}$-
norm $\|A\|_{2,1} \approx \sum_j \left(\sum_i a_{ij}^2 + \epsilon \right)^{1/2}$ in (8) for various values of the smoothing
parameter ϵ.

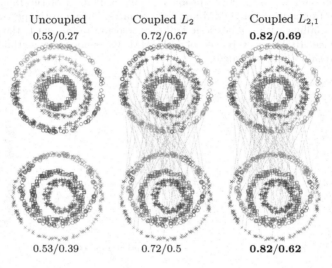

Fig. 6. Clustering of synthetic multimodal datasets *Circles*. Shown is (left to right):
spectral clustering applied to each modality independently; clustering results produced
by coupled diagonalization methods with L_2 and $L_{2,1}$ norms, respectively. Grey lines
depict 10 % of outliers correspondences. Ideally, all markers of each type should have
a single color. Numbers show micro-averaged accuracy [50]/normalized NMI [51] (the
higher the better).

Figure 6 shows the application of our method for multimodal clustering using
the dataset *Circles* from [5], where we introduce 10 % outliers in the correspondence between the modalities data points. Following Eynard *et al.* [5], we use
$\hat{\Phi}_i = \Phi_i X_i$ obtained by solving problem (8) as joint multimodal data embedding,
and perform spectral clustering [52] in this space. Clustering quality was measured using two standard criteria used in the evaluation of clustering algorithms:
the *micro-averaged accuracy* [50] and the *normalized mutual information* (NMI)
[51]. The use of the robust $L_{2,1}$ problem formulation (Fig. 6, right) solved with
our MADMM outperforms the smooth L_2 version (Fig. 6, center).

4.3   Robust Euclidean Embedding

Problem Setting. Our third problem is an L_1 formulation of the multidimensional scaling (MDS) problem treated in [27] under the name *robust Euclidean embedding* (REE). Let us be given an $n \times n$ matrix D of squared distances. The goal is to find a k-dimensional configuration of points $X \in \mathbb{R}^{n \times k}$ such that the Euclidean distances between them are as close as possible to the given ones. The classical MDS approach employs the duality between Euclidean distance matrices and Gram matrices: a squared Euclidean distance matrix D can be converted into a *similarity matrix* by means of double-centering $B = -\frac{1}{2}HDH$, where $H = I - \frac{1}{n}11^\top$. Conversely, the squared distance matrix is obtained from B by $(\mathrm{dist}(B))_{ij} = b_{ii} + b_{jj} - 2b_{ij}$. The similarity matrix corresponding to a Euclidean distance matrix is positive semi-definite and can be represented as a Gram matrix $B = XX^\top$, where X is the desired embedding. In the case when D is not Euclidean, B acts as a low-rank approximation of the similarity matrix (now not necessarily positive semi-definite) associated with D, leading to the problem

$$\min_{X \in \mathbb{R}^{m \times k}} \|HDH - XX^\top\|_{\mathrm{F}}^2 \tag{9}$$

known as *classical MDS* or *classical scaling*, which has a closed form solution by means of eigendecomposition of HDH (Fig 7).

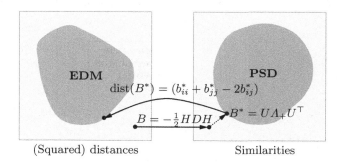

(Squared) distances   Similarities

Fig. 7. Illustration of the classical MDS approach and the equivalence between Euclidean distance matrices (EDM) and positive semi-definite (PSD) similarity matrices.

The main disadvantage of classical MDS is the fact that noise in a single entry of the distance matrix D is spread over entire column/row by the double centering transformation. To cope with this problem, Cayton and Dasgupta [27] proposed an L_1 version of the problem,

$$\min_{B \in \mathbb{R}^{n \times n}} \|D - \mathrm{dist}(B)\|_1 \quad \text{s.t.} \quad B \succeq 0, \ \mathrm{rank}(B) \leq k, \tag{10}$$

where the use of the L_1-norm efficiently rejects outliers. The authors proposed two solutions for problem (10): a semi-definite programming (SDP) formulation and a subgradient descent algorithm (the reader is referred to [27] for a detailed description of both methods).

Solution. Here, we consider (10) as a non-smooth optimization of the form (2) on the manifold of fixed-rank positive semi-definite matrices and solve it using MADMM (Algorithm 6). Note that in this case, we have only the non-smooth function g and $f \equiv 0$. The X-step of the MADMM algorithm is manifold optimization of a quadratic function, carried out using two iterations of manifold conjugate gradients solver. The Z-step is performed by shrinkage. In our experiments, all the compared methods were initialized with the classical MDS solution and the value $\rho = 10$ was used for MADMM. The SDP approach was implemented using MATLAB CVX toolbox [53].

Input squared distance matrix D
Initialize $k \leftarrow 1$, $Z^{(1)} = X^{(1)}$, $U^{(1)} = 0$
repeat
$\quad B^{(k+1)} = \underset{B \in S_+(n,k)}{\mathrm{argmin}} \ \|\mathrm{dist}(B^{(k+1)}) - Z^{(k)} - D + U^{(k)}\|_{\mathrm{F}}^2$
$\quad Z^{(k+1)} = \mathrm{Shrink}_{\frac{1}{\rho}} \left(\mathrm{dist}(B^{(k+1)}) - D + U^{(k)}\right)$
$\quad$ Update $U^{(k+1)} = U^{(k)} + \mathrm{dist}(B^{(k+1)}) - D - Z^{(k+1)}$
$\quad k \leftarrow k + 1$
until *convergence*;

Algorithm 6. MADMM method for robust Euclidean embedding.

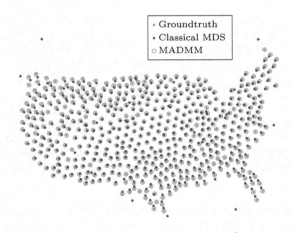

Fig. 8. Embedding of the noisy distances between 500 US cities in the plane using classical MDS (blue) and REE solved using MADMM (red). The distance matrix was contaminated by sparse noise by doubling the distance between some cities. (Color figure online)

Results. Figure 8 shows an example of 2D Euclidean embedding of the distances between 500 US cities, contaminated by sparse noise. The robust embedding is insensitive to such outliers, while the classical MDS result is completely ruined. Figure 9 (right) shows an example of convergence of the proposed MADMM method and the subgradient descent of [27] on the same dataset. We observed that our algorithm outperforms the subgradient method in terms of convergence speed. Furthermore, the subgradient method appears to be very sensitive to the initial step size c; choosing too small a step leads to slower convergence, and if the step is too large the algorithm may fail to converge. Figure 9 (left) studies the scalability of the subgradient-, SDP-, and MADMM-based solutions for the REE problem, plotting the complexity of a single iteration as function of the problem size on random data. Typical number of iterations was of the order of 20 for SDP, 50 for MADMM, and 500 for the subgradient method.

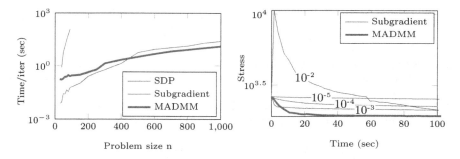

Fig. 9. REE problem. Left: scalability of different algorithms; shown is single iteration complexity as functions of the problem size n using random distance data. SDP did not scale beyond $n = 100$. Right: example of convergence of MADMM and subgradient algorithm of [27] on the US cities problem of size $n = 500$. The subgradient algorithm is very sensitive to the choice of the initial step size c (choosing too large c breaks the convergence, while too small c slows down the convergence).

5   Conclusions

We presented MADMM, a generic algorithm for optimization of non-smooth functions with manifold constraints, and showed that it can be efficiently used in many important problems from the domains of machine learning, computer vision and pattern recognition, and data analysis. Among the key advantages of our method is its remarkable simplicity and lack of parameters to tune - in all our experiments, it worked entirely out-of-the-box. While there exist several solutions for some instances of non-smooth manifold optimization (notably on Stiefel manifolds), MADMM, to the best of our knowledge, is the first generic approach. We believe that MADMM will be very useful in many other applications in the computer vision and pattern recognition community involving manifold optimization. In our experiments, we observed that MADMM converged on par with or better than other methods; a theoretical study of convergence properties is an important future direction. The implementation of the considered problems is at https://github.com/skovnats/madmm.

Acknowledgement. This research was supported by the ERC Starting Grant No. 307047 (COMET).

References

1. Dong, X., Frossard, P., Vandergheynst, P., Nefedov, N.: Clustering on multi-layer graphs via subspace analysis on Grassmann manifolds. Trans. Sig. Process. **62**(4), 905–918 (2014)
2. Keshavan, R.H., Oh, S.: A gradient descent algorithm on the Grassman manifold for matrix completion (2009). arXiv:0910.5260
3. Boufounos, P.T., Baraniuk, R.G.: 1-bit compressive sensing. In: Proceedings of CISS (2008)
4. Kovnatsky, A., Bronstein, M.M., Bronstein, A.M., Glashoff, K., Kimmel, R.: Coupled quasi-harmonic bases. Comput. Graph. Forum **32**(2), 439–448 (2013)
5. Eynard, D., Kovnatsky, A., Bronstein, M.M., Glashoff, K., Bronstein, A.M.: Multimodal manifold analysis using simultaneous diagonalization of Laplacians. Trans. PAMI **37**(12), 2505–2517 (2015)
6. Cucuringu, M., Lipman, Y., Singer, A.: Sensor network localization by eigenvector synchronization over the Euclidean group. ACM Trans. Sensor Netw. **8**(3), 19 (2012)
7. Cucuringu, M., Singer, A., Cowburn, D.: Eigenvector synchronization, graph rigidity and the molecule problem. Inf. Inference **1**(1), 21–67 (2012)
8. Arie-Nachimson, M., Kovalsky, S.Z., Kemelmacher-Shlizerman, I., Singer, A., Basri, R.: Global motion estimation from point matches. In: Proceedings of 3DIM-PVT (2012)
9. Zhang, M., Fletcher, P.T.: Probabilistic principal geodesic analysis. In: Proceedings of NIPS (2013)
10. Journée, M., Bach, F., Absil, P.A., Sepulchre, R.: Low-rank optimization on the cone of positive semidefinite matrices. SIAM J. Optimization **20**(5), 2327–2351 (2010)
11. Meyer, G., Bonnabel, S., Sepulchre, R.: Linear regression under fixed-rank constraints: a Riemannian approach. In: Proceedings of ICML (2011)
12. Boumal, N., Absil, P.A.: RTRMC: A Riemannian trust-region method for low-rank matrix completion. In: Procedings of NIPS, pp. 406–414 (2011)
13. Tan, M., Tsang, I.W., Wang, L., Vandereycken, B., Pan, S.J.: Riemannian pursuit for big matrix recovery. In: Proceedings of ICML (2014)
14. Shalit, U., Weinshall, D., Chechik, G.: Online learning in the manifold of low-rank matrices. In: Proceedings of NIPS (2010)
15. Absil, P.A., Gallivan, K.A.: Joint diagonalization on the oblique manifold for independent component analysis. In: Proceedings of ICASSP (2006)
16. Kleinsteuber, M., Shen, H.: Blind source separation with compressively sensed linear mixtures. Sig. Process. Lett. **19**(2), 107–110 (2012)
17. Higham, N.J.: Computing the nearest correlation matrix - a problem from finance. IMA J. Numer. Anal. **22**(3), 329–343 (2002)

18. Smith, S.T.: Optimization techniques on Riemannian manifolds. Fields Inst. Commun. **3**(3), 113–135 (1994)
19. Absil, P.A., Mahony, R., Sepulchre, R.: Optimization Algorithms on Matrix Manifolds. Princeton University Press, Princeton (2009)
20. Edelman, A., Arias, T.A., Smith, S.T.: The geometry of algorithms with orthogonality constraints. SIAM J. Matrix Anal. Appl. **20**(2), 303–353 (1998)
21. Absil, P.A., Baker, C.G., Gallivan, K.A.: Trust-region methods on Riemannian manifolds. Found. Comput. Math. **7**(3), 303–330 (2007)
22. Alvarez, F., Bolte, J., Munier, J.: A unifying local convergence result for Newton's method in Riemannian manifolds. Found. Comput. Math. **8**(2), 197–226 (2008)
23. Boumal, N., Mishra, B., Absil, P.A., Sepulchre, R.: Manopt, a Matlab toolbox for optimization on manifolds. JMLR **15**(1), 1455–1459 (2014)
24. Candès, E., Li, X., Ma, Y., Wright, J.: Robust principal component analysis? J. ACM **58**(3), 11 (2011)
25. Ozoliņš, V., Lai, R., Caflisch, R., Osher, S.: Compressed modes for variational problems in mathematics and physics. PNAS **110**(46), 18368–18373 (2013)
26. Neumann, T., Varanasi, K., Theobalt, C., Magnor, M., Wacker, M.: Compressed manifold modes for mesh processing. Comput. Graphics Forum **33**(5), 35–44 (2014)
27. Cayton, L., Dasgupta, S.: Robust Euclidean embedding. In: Proceedings of ICML (2006)
28. Wang, L., Singer, A.: Exact and stable recovery of rotations for robust synchronization. Information and Inference (2013)
29. Huang, Q., Wang, F., Guibas, L.: Functional map networks for analyzing and exploring large shape collections. ACM Trans. Graphics **33**(4), 36 (2014)
30. Kovnatsky, A., Bronstein, M.M., Bresson, X., Vandergheynst, P.: Functional correspondence by matrix completion. In: Proceedings of CVPR (2015)
31. Chen, X.: Smoothing methods for nonsmooth, nonconvex minimization. Math. Program. **134**(1), 71–99 (2012)
32. Ferreira, O.P., Oliveira, P.R.: Subgradient algorithm on Riemannian manifolds. J. Optimization Theory Appl. **97**(1), 93–104 (1998)
33. Ledyaev, Y., Zhu, Q.: Nonsmooth analysis on smooth manifolds. Trans. AMS **359**(8), 3687–3732 (2007)
34. Borckmans, P.B., Selvan, S.E., Boumal, N., Absil, P.A.: A Riemannian subgradient algorithm for economic dispatch with valve-point effect. J. Comp. Applied Math. **255**, 848–866 (2014)
35. Lai, R., Osher, S.: A splitting method for orthogonality constrained problems. J. Scientific Comput. **58**(2), 431–449 (2014)
36. Rosman, G., Wang, Y., Tai, X., Kimmel, R., Bruckstein, A.M.: Fast regularization of matrix-valued images. In: Proceedings of Efficient Algorithms for Global Optimization Methods in Computer Vision (2011)
37. Gabay, D., Mercier, B.: A dual algorithm for the solution of nonlinear variational problems via finite element approximation. Comput. Math. Appl. **2**(1), 17–40 (1976)
38. Boyd, S., Parikk, N., Chu, E., Peleato, B., Eckstein, J.: Distributed optimization and statistical learning via the alternating direction method of multipliers. Found. Trends Mach. Learn. **3**, 1–122 (2010)
39. Hestenes, M.R.: Multiplier and gradient methods. J. Optim. Theory Appl. **4**(5), 303–320 (1969)
40. Powell, M.J.D.: A method for nonlinear constraints in minimization problems. In: Optimization. Academic Press, London, New York (1969)

41. Bertsekas, D.P.: Constrained Optimization and Lagrange Multiplier Methods. Academic Press, New York (1982)

42. Andreani, R., Birgin, E.G., Martínez, J.M., Schuverdt, M.L.: On augmented Lagrangian methods with general lower-level constraints. SIAM J. Optimization **18**(4), 1286–1309 (2007)

43. Attouch, H., Bolte, J., Redont, P., Soubeyran, A.: Proximal alternating minimization and projection methods for nonconvex problems: an approach based on the Kurdyka-Lojasiewicz inequality. Math. Oper. Res. **35**(2), 438–457 (2010)

44. Wang, Y., Wotao, Y., Jinshan, Z.: Global Convergence of ADMM in Nonconvex Nonsmooth Optimization (2015). arXiv:1511.06324

45. Ng, A.Y., Jordan, M.I., Weiss, Y.: On spectral clustering: analysis and an algorithm. In: Proceedings of NIPS (2002)

46. Belkin, M., Niyogi, P.: Laplacian eigenmaps and spectral techniques for embedding and clustering. In: Proceedings of NIPS (2001)

47. Ovsjanikov, M., Ben-Chen, M., Solomon, J., Butscher, A., Guibas, L.J.: Functional maps: a flexible representation of maps between shapes. ACM Trans. Graphics **31**(4), 1–11 (2012)

48. Bronstein, A.M., Bronstein, M.M., Kimmel, R.: Numerical Geometry of Non-rigid Shapes. Springer, New York (2008)

49. Kim, V.G., Lipman, Y., Funkhouser, T.: Blended intrinsic maps. Trans. Graphics **30**, 79 (2011)

50. Bekkerman, R., Jeon, J.: Multi-modal clustering for multimedia collections. In: Proceedings of CVPR (2007)

51. Manning, C.D., Raghavan, P., Schütze, H.: Introduction to Information Retrieval. Cambridge University Press, Cambridge (2008)

52. Ng, A.Y., Jordan, M.I., Weiss, Y.: On spectral clustering: analysis and an algorithm. In: Proceedings of NIPS (2001)

53. Grant, M., Boyd, S.: Graph implementations for nonsmooth convex programs. In: Blondel, V., Boyd, S., Kimura, H. (eds.) Recent Advances in Learning and Control. LNCIS, vol. 371, pp. 95–110. Springer, Heidelberg (2008)

Interpreting the Ratio Criterion for Matching SIFT Descriptors

Avi Kaplan[✉], Tamar Avraham, and Michael Lindenbaum

Computer Science Department, Technion - I.I.T., Haifa, Israel
{kavi,tammya,mic}@cs.technion.ac.il

Abstract. Matching keypoints by minimizing the Euclidean distance between their SIFT descriptors is an effective and extremely popular technique. Using the ratio between distances, as suggested by Lowe, is even more effective and leads to excellent matching accuracy. Probabilistic approaches that model the distribution of the distances were found effective as well. This work focuses, for the first time, on analyzing Lowe's ratio criterion using a probabilistic approach. We provide two alternative interpretations of this criterion, which show that it is not only an effective heuristic but can also be formally justified. The first interpretation shows that Lowe's ratio corresponds to a conditional probability that the match is incorrect. The second shows that the ratio corresponds to the Markov bound on this probability. The interpretations make it possible to slightly increase the effectiveness of the ratio criterion, and to obtain matching performance that exceeds all previous (non-learning based) results.

Keywords: SIFT · Matching · *a contrario*

1 Introduction

Matching objects in different images is a fundamental task in computer vision, with applications in object recognition, panorama stitching, and many more. The common practice is to extract a set of distinctive keypoints from each image, compute a descriptor for each keypoint, and then match the keypoints using a similarity measure between the descriptors and possibly also geometric constraints. Many methods for detecting the keypoints and computing their descriptors have been proposed. See the reviews [11,23,25].

The scale invariant feature transform (SIFT) suggested by Lowe [8,9] is arguably the dominant algorithm for both keypoint detection and keypoint description. It specifies feature points and corresponding neighborhoods as maxima in the scale space of the DoG operator. The descriptor itself is a set of histograms of gradient directions calculated in several (16) regions in this neighborhood, concatenated into a 128-dimensional vector. Various normalizations and several filtering stages help to optimize the descriptor. The combination of scale space, gradient direction, and histograms makes the SIFT descriptor robust to scale, rotation, and illumination changes, and yet discriminative. Keypoints are

© Springer International Publishing AG 2016
B. Leibe et al. (Eds.): ECCV 2016, Part V, LNCS 9909, pp. 697–712, 2016.
DOI: 10.1007/978-3-319-46454-1_42

matched by minimizing the Euclidean distance between their SIFT descriptors. However, to rank the matches, it is much more effective to use the distance ratios:

$$\text{ratio}(\mathbf{a}_i, \mathbf{b}_{j(i)}) = \frac{\|\mathbf{a}_i - \mathbf{b}_{j(i)}\|_2}{\|\mathbf{a}_i - \mathbf{b}_{j'(i)}\|_2} \tag{1}$$

and not the distances themselves [8,9]. Here, $\mathbf{a}_i$ denotes a descriptor in one image, and $\mathbf{b}_{j(i)}, \mathbf{b}_{j'(i)}$ correspond to the closest and the second-closest descriptors in the other image.

SIFT has been challenged by many competing descriptors. The variations try to achieve faster runtime (e.g. SURF [2]), robustness to affine transformation (ASIFT [14]), compatibility with color images (CSIFT [1]) or simply represent the neighborhood in a different but related way (PCA-SIFT [7] and GLOH [11]). Performance evaluations [11–13,22] conclude, however, that while various SIFT alternatives may be more accurate under some conditions, the original SIFT generally performs as accurately as the best competing algorithms, and better than the speeded-up versions.

SIFT descriptors are matched based of their dissimilarity, which makes the choice of dissimilarity measure important. The Euclidean distance (L_2) [9] is still the most commonly used. Being concatenations of orientation histograms, SIFT descriptors can naturally and effectively be compared using measures for comparing distributions, such as χ^2 distance [28] and circular variants of the Earth mover's distance. Alternative, probabilistic approaches consider the dissimilarities as random variables. In [10], for instance, the dissimilarities are modeled as Gaussian random variables. The probabilistic *a contrario* theory, which we follow in this work, was effectively applied to matching SIFT-like descriptors [21] (as well as many other computer vision tasks [4]).

This work focuses, for the first time, on using a probabilistic approach for analyzing the ratio criterion. We show that this effective yet nonetheless heuristic criterion may be justified by two alternative interpretations. One shows that the ratio corresponds to a conditional probability that the match is incorrect. The second shows that the ratio corresponds to the Markov bound on this probability. These interpretations hold for every available distribution of dissimilarities between unrelated descriptors, and in particular, for all the distributions suggested later in this paper.

We also consider several dissimilarity measures, including, unusually, a multivalue (vector) one. The distributions of the dissimilarities, corresponding to incorrect matches, are constructed by partitioning the descriptor into parts (following [21]), estimating a rough distribution of the dissimilarities between the corresponding parts, and combining the distributions of the partial dissimilarities into a distribution of the full dissimilarity. These distributions, denoted as *background models* (as in [4]), are estimated, online, only from the matched images, requiring no training phase and making them image adaptive.

Combining these estimated distributions with the conditional probability (the first probabilistic interpretation of the ratio criterion) provides a new criterion, or algorithm, for ranking matches. With this algorithm, we obtain state-of-the-art matching accuracy (for non-learning methods)[1].

In this paper, we make the following contributions:

1. A mathematical explanation of the ratio criterion as a conditional probability, which justifies this effective and popular criterion.
2. A second justification of the ratio criterion using the Markov inequality.
3. New measures of dissimilarity and methods for deriving their distribution.
4. A new matching criterion combining the estimated dissimilarity distribution with the conditional probability interpretation, which obtains excellent results.

Outline: Sect. 2 shows how to use dissimilarity distributions to rank matching hypotheses and, in particular, to justify the ratio criterion as a conditional distribution. Section 3 describes various dissimilarities and the corresponding partition-based background model distributions and summarizes the proposed matching process. Section 4 provides an additional justification of the ratio criterion. Experimental results are described in Sect. 5, and Sect. 6 concludes.

2 Using a Background Model for Matching

2.1 Modeling with Background Models

We would like to generate a set of reliable matches between the feature points of two images A and B, using their corresponding sets of SIFT descriptors, $\mathcal{A} = \{\mathbf{a}_i\}$ and $\mathcal{B} = \{\mathbf{b}_j\}$. Let $a_i \in A$ be a specific feature point and let $\mathbf{a}_i \in \mathcal{A}$ be its corresponding descriptor. Most descriptors in $\mathcal{B}$ (all except possibly one) are unrelated to $\mathbf{a}_i$ in the sense of not corresponding to the same scene point. Our goal is to find the single feature point, if it exists, which matches $\mathbf{a}_i$.

The proposed matching process is based on statistical principles. We model the non-matching descriptors in $\mathcal{B}$ as realizations of a random variable X drawn from some distribution. This distribution is high-dimensional and complex, and we refrain from working with it directly. Instead we consider associated dissimilarity values. Let $\delta(\mathbf{u}, \mathbf{v})$ be some dissimilarity measure between two descriptors $\mathbf{u}$ and $\mathbf{v}$. We shall be interested in the dissimilarities $\delta(\mathbf{a}_i, \mathbf{b}_j)$ between the descriptors in $\mathcal{A}$ and in $\mathcal{B}$. We consider $\mathbf{a}_i$ to be a specific fixed descriptor, and $\mathbf{b}_j$ to be drawn from the distribution of X. Then, the associated dissimilarity $\delta(\mathbf{a}_i, \mathbf{b}_j)$ is an instance of another random variable, which we denote $\mathbf{Y}^{\mathbf{a}_i}$. $\mathbf{Y}^{\mathbf{a}_i}$ is distributed by $F_{\mathbf{Y}^{\mathbf{a}_i}}(y)$, representing the dissimilarity distribution associated with $\mathbf{a}_i$ and non-matches to it. Following the *a contrario* approach, we denote this distribution a *background model*. Note that the dissimilarities associated with different descriptors in $\mathcal{A}$ follow different background models.

---

[1] Recently, learned patch descriptors were introduced as alternatives to SIFT (e.g. [6,27]). We do not compete with their performance, as the focus in this work is to suggest and validate our new explanation to the ratio criterion.

In this section we assume that this distribution is known. In Sect. 3 we consider several dissimilarity measures as well as methods for estimating the corresponding background models. As usual, we consider a scalar dissimilarity. Later, we show that an extension to multi-value (vector) dissimilarity is beneficial.

Given a matching hypothesis by which the two descriptors, $(\mathbf{a}_i, \mathbf{b}_j)$ correspond to the same 3D point, we contrast this hypothesis with the alternative, null hypothesis, by which the descriptor $\mathbf{b}_j$ is drawn from a distribution of false matches. This is a false correspondence, or false alarm event, and we denote its probability (following *a contrario* notations [3]), as the probability of false alarm (PFA). The null background model hypothesis is rejected more strongly if the PFA is lower, and therefore matching hypotheses with lower PFA are preferred. This approach is further developed in the rest of this section.

The PFA replaces the commonly used distance between descriptors with a probabilistic measure. This new matching criterion is mathematically well defined, quantitatively and intuitively meaningful, and possibly image adaptive.

2.2   Ranking Hypothesized Matches by PFA

Let $(\mathbf{a}_i, \mathbf{b}_j)$ be a hypothesized match. To evaluate the null hypothesis we calculate the probability of drawing, from the background model, a value that is as extreme (small) as the dissimilarity of the hypothesized match, $\delta(\mathbf{a}_i, \mathbf{b}_j)$. Let $E^{\mathbf{a}_i}_{1-1}(d)$ denote the event that the value drawn from the distribution of $\mathbf{Y}^{\mathbf{a}_i}$ is smaller or equal to d. Then,

$$PFA_{1-1}(\mathbf{a}_i, \mathbf{b}_j) = \Pr\big(E^{\mathbf{a}_i}_{1-1}(\delta(\mathbf{a}_i, \mathbf{b}_j))\big) = F_{\mathbf{Y}^{\mathbf{a}_i}}(\delta(\mathbf{a}_i, \mathbf{b}_j)). \qquad (2)$$

Thus, PFA_{1-1} is just the one-sided (lower) tail probability of the distribution. A hypothesized match is ranked higher if its PFA_{1-1} is lower, which enables us to reject the null hypothesis with higher confidence. We use this ranking to specify the feature point (and the descriptor) in the image B, corresponding to $\mathbf{a}_i$:

$$\mathbf{b}_{j(i)} = \arg\min\nolimits_{\mathbf{b}_j \in \mathcal{B}} PFA_{1-1}(\mathbf{a}_i, \mathbf{b}_j). \qquad (3)$$

Thus, for every $\mathbf{a}_i \in \mathcal{A}$ we get a single preferred match $(\mathbf{a}_i, \mathbf{b}_{j(i)})$, denoted selected match[2]. Next, we would like to rank these selected matches. To that end, we may use, again, $PFA_{1-1}(\mathbf{a}_i, \mathbf{b}_{j(i)})$, as explained in the next section. Further below (Sect. 2.4), we propose another, more reliable PFA expression.

2.3   Ranking Selected Matches as Complex Events

The selected match, $(\mathbf{a}_i, \mathbf{b}_{j(i)})$, is a false alarm event when at least one of the $|\mathcal{B}|$ random, independently drawn, dissimilarity $\mathbf{Y}^{\mathbf{a}_i}$ values is as extreme as

---

[2] One might think that ranking by the PFA_{1-1} is equivalent to ranking by the dissimilarity measure itself. This is true in the simpler case when the dissimilarity is scalar and the distribution depends directly on this scalar, but not in more complex cases, as we shall see in Sect. 3.

$\delta(\mathbf{a}_i, \mathbf{b}_{j(i)})$. This is a complex event, denoted $E^{\mathbf{a}_i}_{1-|\mathcal{B}|}(\delta(\mathbf{a}_i, \mathbf{b}_{j(i)}))$. Its probability may be calculated as the binomial distribution

$$PFA_{1-|\mathcal{B}|}(\mathbf{a}_i, \mathbf{b}_{j(i)}) = 1 - \left(1 - PFA_{1-1}(\delta(\mathbf{a}_i, \mathbf{b}_{j(i)}))\right)^{|\mathcal{B}|}. \qquad (4)$$

As observed in our experiments, the typical values of $PFA_{1-1}(\delta(\mathbf{a}_i, \mathbf{b}_{j(i)}))$ are small, and usually much smaller than $1/|\mathcal{B}|$. Under this condition,

$$PFA_{1-|\mathcal{B}|}(\mathbf{a}_i, \mathbf{b}_{j(i)}) \approx |\mathcal{B}| \cdot F_{\mathbf{Y}^{\mathbf{a}_i}}(\delta(\mathbf{a}_i, \mathbf{b}_{j(i)})). \qquad (5)$$

We may use this approximation for ranking the selected matches. Note that ranking by PFA_{1-1} is equivalent. We shall also use this approximation below for deriving a more effective, conditional, PFA.

2.4   Ranking Selected Matches by Conditional PFA

Indirect evidence about the dissimilarity values drawn from the background model may improve the estimate of the PFA. Such evidence may be available from small dissimilarity values in $\{\delta(\mathbf{a}_i, \mathbf{b}_j) | j \neq j(i)\}$. These dissimilarities do not correspond to correct matches and come only from the background model. Consider the complex event associated with the second lowest dissimilarity, denoted $\delta(\mathbf{a}_i, \mathbf{b}_{j'(i)})$. Knowing that the event $E^{\mathbf{a}_i}_{1-|\mathcal{B}|}(\delta(\mathbf{a}_i, \mathbf{b}_{j'(i)}))$ occurred allows us to recalculate the probability that the event $E^{\mathbf{a}_i}_{1-|\mathcal{B}|}(\delta(\mathbf{a}_i, \mathbf{b}_{j(i)}))$ occurred as well, as a conditional probability:

$$
\begin{aligned}
PFA_C(\mathbf{a}_i, \mathbf{b}_{j(i)}) &= \Pr\left(E^{\mathbf{a}_i}_{1-|\mathcal{B}|}(\delta(\mathbf{a}_i, \mathbf{b}_{j(i)})) \big| E^{\mathbf{a}_i}_{1-|\mathcal{B}|}(\delta(\mathbf{a}_i, \mathbf{b}_{j'(i)}))\right) \\
&= \frac{\Pr\left(E^{\mathbf{a}_i}_{1-|\mathcal{B}|}(\delta(\mathbf{a}_i, \mathbf{b}_{j(i)})) \cap E^{\mathbf{a}_i}_{1-|\mathcal{B}|}(\delta(\mathbf{a}_i, \mathbf{b}_{j'(i)}))\right)}{\Pr\left(E^{\mathbf{a}_i}_{1-|\mathcal{B}|}(\delta(\mathbf{a}_i, \mathbf{b}_{j'(i)}))\right)} \\
&\leq \frac{\Pr\left(E^{\mathbf{a}_i}_{1-|\mathcal{B}|}(\delta(\mathbf{a}_i, \mathbf{b}_{j(i)}))\right)}{\Pr\left(E^{\mathbf{a}_i}_{1-|\mathcal{B}|}(\delta(\mathbf{a}_i, \mathbf{b}_{j'(i)}))\right)} \approx \frac{|\mathcal{B}| \cdot F_{\mathbf{Y}^{\mathbf{a}_i}}(\delta(\mathbf{a}_i, \mathbf{b}_{j(i)}))}{|\mathcal{B}| \cdot F_{\mathbf{Y}^{\mathbf{a}_i}}(\delta(\mathbf{a}_i, \mathbf{b}_{j'(i)}))}. \quad (6)
\end{aligned}
$$

For scalar dissimilarities, the event $E^{\mathbf{a}_i}_{1-|\mathcal{B}|}(\delta(\mathbf{a}_i, \mathbf{b}_{j(i)}))$ is included in the event $E^{\mathbf{a}_i}_{1-|\mathcal{B}|}(\delta(\mathbf{a}_i, \mathbf{b}_{j'(i)}))$, and the inequality above is actually an equality. For vector dissimilarities (Sect. 3.2) the equality does not strictly hold. We shall use the approximation to the bound as an estimate for PFA_C,

$$PFA_C(\mathbf{a}_i, \mathbf{b}_{j(i)}) \approx \frac{F_{\mathbf{Y}^{\mathbf{a}_i}}(\delta(\mathbf{a}_i, \mathbf{b}_{j(i)}))}{F_{\mathbf{Y}^{\mathbf{a}_i}}(\delta(\mathbf{a}_i, \mathbf{b}_{j'(i)}))}, \qquad (7)$$

and prefer matches with lower PFA_C.

The expression (7) is reminiscent of the ratio of distances (Eq. 1) used by Lowe in the original SIFT paper [9]. We argue, moreover, that the derivation in Sect. 2 mathematically generalizes and justifies the two criteria suggested in [9]. First, (incorrectly) assuming a uniform distribution of the Euclidean distance dissimilarity makes the PFA_{1-1} expression proportional to the Euclidean distance.

Thus, minimizing PFA, as suggested here, is exactly equivalent to minimizing the Euclidean distance (as in [9]). Furthermore, with the uniform distribution assumption, the conditional PFA_C expression (Eq. 7) is simply the distance ratio (Eq. 1). As we show later, replacing the incorrect uniform distribution assumption with a more realistic distribution further improves the matching accuracy.

3   Partition-Based Dissimilarities and Background Models

3.1   Standard Estimation of Dissimilarity Distribution

The various PFA expressions developed in Sect. 2 are valid for any available distribution. To convert these general expressions into a concrete algorithm, we consider several dissimilarity measures, and derive their distributions. We first consider the standard nonparametric distribution estimation method. Then, following the *a contrario* framework, we suggest partition-based methods that overcome some limitations of the standard method.

We may estimate the background distribution from different sources of data; each has pros and cons. One option uses an offline *external* database $\mathcal{F}$ containing many non-matching descriptor pairs, $(\mathbf{u}, \mathbf{v})$, unrelated to $\mathcal{A}, \mathcal{B}$. The distribution, $F(y) = \Pr(\delta(\mathbf{u}, \mathbf{v}) \leq y)$, may be estimated using the formal definition of the empirical distribution function: $\hat{F}(y) = \left|\{(\mathbf{u}, \mathbf{v}) \in \mathcal{F} : \delta(\mathbf{u}, \mathbf{v}) \leq y\}\right|/|\mathcal{F}|$ or more advanced methods, such as kernel density estimation; see [24]. The second option, which is image adapted and denoted *internal*, is to estimate the distribution from all pairs $(\mathbf{a}_i, \mathbf{b}_j)$ related to the specific image. The third option, which is also online, but *point adapted*, is to estimate the distribution using only $\mathcal{F} = \{(\mathbf{a}_i, \mathbf{b}_j) : \mathbf{b}_j \in \mathcal{B}\}$, separately for every descriptor $\mathbf{a}_i$ in $\mathcal{A}$. While more data is available for the two first options, the last option is the one that fits our task. Since $\mathcal{B}$ is relatively small and may contain the descriptor corresponding to the correct match to $\mathbf{a}_i$, more creative methods should be used to estimate the point-adapted distribution. Standard techniques would lead to a coarsely estimated distribution, which is a staircase function with steps of size $1/|\mathcal{B}|$, and $PFA_{1-1}(\mathbf{a}_i, \mathbf{b}_{j(i)})$ will always be $1/|\mathcal{B}|$, regardless of whether the match is correct, which would mean that it is useless for matching. The partition-based approach described below adopts the last option but avoids its problems.

3.2   Partition-Based Dissimilarities

The partition-based approach divides the descriptor vector into K non-overlapping parts: $\mathbf{u} = (\mathbf{u}[1], \ldots, \mathbf{u}[K])$, and calculates the dissimilarity between two (full) descriptors from the dissimilarities between the corresponding parts. Here, we describe the partition and the dissimilarities. In Sect. 3.3 we show how to use this partitioning to estimate the desired distribution. Then we explain why it avoids the problems of the standard approach.

To specify the partition-based dissimilarity, we need to make three choices: how to partition the descriptor, how to measure partial dissimilarities, and how to combine them into the final dissimilarity.

The partitioning - The descriptors may be partitioned in many ways, some of which are more practical and statistically consistent with the independence assumption (made in Sect. 3.3). We tried several finer and coarser options, and ended up with the natural partition of the SIFT vector to its 16 orientation histograms, which gave the best results.

Basis distance - The dissimilarity between parts is denoted $d(\mathbf{u}[j], \mathbf{v}[j])$, and, to distinguish it from the dissimilarity of the full descriptors, is called a *basis distance*. It may be the L_2 metric but may also be some other metric (e.g. L_1) or even a dissimilarity measure which is not a metric (e.g. EMD). In Sect. 5, we experiment with the L_2 distance and two versions of the EMD [19,21].

Dissimilarity measure - There are many ways to combine the part dissimilarities, and we consider three of them:

1. **Sum dissimilarity** - The dissimilarity between two full descriptors, already used and analyzed in [21], is the sum of the basis distances:

$$\delta^{\text{sum}}(\mathbf{u}, \mathbf{v}) = \Sigma_{j=1}^{K} d(\mathbf{u}[j], \mathbf{v}[j]). \tag{8}$$

2. **Max-value dissimilarity** - The dissimilarity between the full descriptors, already used for *a contrario* analysis of shape recognition ([15,17]), is the maximal basis distance.

$$\delta^{\max}(\mathbf{u}, \mathbf{v}) = \max_{j} d(\mathbf{u}[j], \mathbf{v}[j]). \tag{9}$$

3. **Multi-value dissimilarity** - Instead of summarizing all the basis distances associated with the parts with one scalar, we may keep them separate. Then the dissimilarity measure is a vector of K basis distances. This richer, vectorial, dissimilarity has the potential to exploit the non-uniformity in the descriptor's parts and to be more robust.

$$\bar{\delta}^{\text{multi}}(\mathbf{u}, \mathbf{v}) = (d(\mathbf{u}[1], \mathbf{v}[1]), d(\mathbf{u}[2], \mathbf{v}[2]), \ldots, d(\mathbf{u}[K], \mathbf{v}[K]))^{T}. \tag{10}$$

This dissimilarity, being a vector, induces only a partial order. We follow the standard definition and say that one dissimilarity vector is smaller (not larger) than another if each of its components is smaller (not larger) than the corresponding component of the second, or

$$\bar{y}_1 \leq \bar{y}_2 \iff \forall j, (\bar{y}_1)_j \leq (\bar{y}_2)_j. \tag{11}$$

Note that this partial order suffices for defining a distribution because, for every vector $\bar{y}$, the set of all vectors not larger than $\bar{y}$ is well defined.

For brevity, we use $\delta(\mathbf{u}, \mathbf{v})$ as a general notation that, depending on context, may refer to the different types of dissimilarity defined above, and to different basis distances $d(\ )$. Note that $\delta(\mathbf{u}, \mathbf{v})$ may take a vector value. Therefore, we refrain from referring to it as a distance function.

Not all dissimilarities may be represented using the partition-based schemes. Euclidean distance is one example. Note, however, that squared Euclidean distance is representable as a sum of basis distances, and as it is monotonic in the Euclidean distance, they are equivalent with respect to ranking.

3.3   Estimating the Background Models

Different background models are constructed for the three types of partition-based dissimilarities discussed above. Let $\mathbf{Y}^{\mathbf{a}_i}[1], \mathbf{Y}^{\mathbf{a}_i}[2], \dots, \mathbf{Y}^{\mathbf{a}_i}[K]$ be the K random variables corresponding to the K basis distances between the parts of a specific descriptor $\mathbf{a}_i$ and a randomly drawn descriptor from $\mathcal{B}$.

The background models are estimated using the assumption that the set of random variables $\left\{ \mathbf{Y}^{\mathbf{a}_i}[j] \right\}_{j=1}^{K}$, associated with unrelated sub-descriptors, is mutually statistically independent. For SIFT descriptors, this assumption is not completely justified due to the correlation between nearby image regions and because of the common normalization. Yet it seems to be a valid and common approximation. Later we comment on the validity of this assumption, test it empirically, and discuss a model which avoids it.

The background model for multi-value dissimilarity is characterized by the distribution $F_{\mathbf{Y}^{\mathbf{a}_i}}^{\text{multi}}(\bar{y})$. Here $\mathbf{Y}^{\mathbf{a}_i}$ is specified by the partition-based multi-value dissimilarity and is a vector variable. To specify its distribution, we use the partial order between these vectors specified in Eq. (11). Then,

$$F_{\mathbf{Y}^{\mathbf{a}_i}}^{\text{multi}}(\bar{y}) = \Pr\big(\bigcap_{j=1}^{K} \{ \mathbf{Y}[j] \le (\bar{y})_j \} \big). \tag{12}$$

Using the independence assumption, we get

$$F_{\mathbf{Y}^{\mathbf{a}_i}}^{\text{multi}}(\bar{y}) = \prod_{j=1}^{K} \Pr\big(\mathbf{Y}[j] \le (\bar{y})_j \big). \tag{13}$$

Each term is independently estimated as empirical distribution, yielding

$$\hat{F}_{\mathbf{Y}^{\mathbf{a}_i}}^{\text{multi}}(\bar{y}) = \prod_{j=1}^{K} \left(\frac{1}{|\mathcal{F}|} \cdot \big| \{ \mathbf{v} \in \mathcal{F} : d(\mathbf{a}_i[j], \mathbf{v}[j]) \le (\bar{y})_j \} \big| \right). \tag{14}$$

The background model for sum dissimilarity is characterized by the distribution $F_{\mathbf{Y}^{\mathbf{a}_i}}^{\text{sum}}(y)$, which is estimated by convolving the estimated densities of the part dissimilarities; we refer the reader to [21] for details.

The background model for max-value dissimilarity is characterized by the distribution $F_{\mathbf{Y}^{\mathbf{a}_i}}^{\max}(y)$. The max-value dissimilarity is a particular case of the multi-value dissimilarity and is similarly estimated; see also [15, 17].

As before, we use the notation $F_{\mathbf{Y}^{\mathbf{a}_i}}(y)$ for general reference to a dissimilarity distribution that describes the background model.

Partition-based background models have several advantages. First, the quantization of the distribution is fine even for the small descriptor set $\mathcal{B}$, as the multiplication of several distributions reduces the step size exponentially (in the number of parts). Moreover, the presence of a correct match in $\mathcal{B}$ is less harmful

Algorithm 1. Partition-based matching algorithm

Preliminary: Choose a basis distance d, a dissimilarity measure δ, and the type of false alarm probability (conditional or not).

Input: Two sets of descriptors, $\mathcal{A}, \mathcal{B}$, associated with two sets of image points.

Output: A set of matches, one for every descriptor $\mathbf{a}_i \in \mathcal{A}$, with corresponding estimates for probability of false match $\{((\mathbf{a}_i, \mathbf{b}_{j(i)}), PFA(\mathbf{a}_i, \mathbf{b}_{j(i)}))\}$.

Algorithm

1. For each descriptor $\mathbf{a}_i \in \mathcal{A}$,
   (a) For each descriptor part calculate all basis distances $\{d(\mathbf{a}_i, \mathbf{b}_j) : j = 1, 2, \ldots, |\mathcal{B}|\}$ and estimate a one-dimensional empirical distribution.
   (b) Estimate the background model either by taking the convolution of the empirical densities (for sum dissimilarity [21]) or by just keeping them as a set of distributions (for max-value [15, 17] or multi-value dissimilarities (Eq. 14)).
   (c) For each descriptor $\mathbf{b}_j \in \mathcal{B}$, calculate the dissimilarity $\delta(\mathbf{a}_i, \mathbf{b}_j)$ and use the background model to infer the probability of false alarm $PFA_{1-1}(\mathbf{a}_i, \mathbf{b}_j)$.
   (d) Choose the descriptor associated with the lowest PFA_{1-1}: $\mathbf{b}_{j(i)} = arg\,min_{\mathbf{b}_j \in \mathcal{B}} PFA_{1-1}(\mathbf{a}_i, \mathbf{b}_j)$. Let $(\mathbf{a}_i, \mathbf{b}_{j(i)})$ be the resulting match.
   (e) Augment the match $(\mathbf{a}_i, \mathbf{b}_{j(i)})$ with its unconditional PFA (Eq. 2) or the conditional PFA (Eq. 6).

because even if the corresponding descriptor is globally closest to $\mathbf{a}_i$, it doesn't necessarily mean that all its parts are closest to the respective parts $\mathbf{a}_i[j]$ as well.

The proposed matching algorithm, based on the probabilistic interpretation and the distribution estimation, is concisely specified in Algorithm 1.

4   Markov Inequality Based Interpreting

Section 2 describes a method for using a distribution of false dissimilarities for matching. It justifies the ratio criterion [9] as an instance of this approach. Here we propose an alternative explanation of and justification for the ratio criterion.

Consider the set of N_B ordered dissimilarities (e.g. Euclidean distances) $\delta_1, \ldots, \delta_{N_B}$ between a given descriptor $\mathbf{a}_i \in \mathcal{A}$ and all descriptors in $\mathcal{B}$. The hypothesized match $(\mathbf{a}_i, \mathbf{b}_{j(i)})$ corresponds to the smallest dissimilarity δ_1. Our goal, again, is to estimate how likely is it that δ_1 was drawn from the same distribution as the other dissimilarities. To that end, we apply the Markov bound.

We assume that the dissimilarities associated with incorrect matches are independently drawn instances of the random variable Y. Let D, Z be two random variables, related to Y, where D assumes the minimal dissimilarity over a set of N samples, and $Z = 1/D$. Z is nonnegative, and by Markov's inequality, satisfies $\Pr(Z \geq a) \leq \mathrm{E}[Z]/a$, or $\Pr(1/D \geq a) \leq \mathrm{E}[1/D]/a$. Letting $d = 1/a$ and rearranging the inequality, we get

$$\Pr(D \leq d) \leq d \cdot \mathrm{E}[1/D]. \tag{15}$$

Thus, knowing the expected value $E[1/D]$, we could bound the probability that the observed minimal value, δ_1, belongs to the distribution of D. To estimate $E[1/D]$ from a single data set (δ_1 excluded), with a single minimal value, we use bootstrapping. Given a set of N samples, bootstrapping takes multiple samples of length N, drawn uniformly with replacement, and estimates the required statistics from the samples. It is easy to show that, for large $N = N_B$,

$$\hat{E}[1/D] = \sum_{k=2}^{N_B} p_k \frac{1}{\delta_k} \leq \frac{1}{\delta_2}, \tag{16}$$

where $(p_2, p_3, p_4, \dots) \approx (0.63, 0.23, 0.08, \dots)$. Combining Eqs. 15 and 16, we get

$$\Pr(D \leq \delta_1) \leq \delta_1 \cdot E[1/D] \approx \delta_1 \cdot \hat{E}[1/D] \leq \frac{\delta_1}{\delta_2}. \tag{17}$$

We can now justify Lowe's relative criterion by observing that the ratio δ_1/δ_2 approximates a bound over the probability that a randomly drawn dissimilarity associated with incorrect matches is smaller or equal to the observed δ_1. If the bound is small, then so is the probability that δ_1 is associated with an incorrect match. This makes the ratio δ_1/δ_2 a statistically meaningful criterion.

5   Experiments

5.1   Experimental Setup

We experimented with 18 different variations of the proposed matching algorithm, corresponding to combinations of three different basis distances (L_2, circular EMD (CEMD) [20], and thresholded modulo EMD (TMEMD) [19]), the three different dissimilarity measures (sum, max-value, and multi-value), and the unconditional and conditional matching criteria. The variant that uses CEMD distance, sum dissimilarity, and the unconditional criterion corresponds to the algorithm of [21]. We denote by PMV (probabilistic multi-value) and PMV_c (probabilistic multi-value conditional) the variations that use the L_2 basis distance and the multi-value dissimilarity. The probabilistic algorithms are compared to deterministic algorithms which use the same basis distances as dissimilarities between the descriptors (without partition). The deterministic algorithms are implemented in six versions corresponding to the three distance functions and to the two criteria based on distance and distance ratio (two of those variations correspond to [9,19]).

We experimented with the datasets of Mikolajczyk et al. [11] and of Fischer et al. [6]. Both datasets contain 5 image pairs, each composed of an original image and a transformed version of it. We used the evaluation protocol of [11] which relies on finding the homography between the images, for both sets. All the algorithms match SIFT descriptors, extracted using the VLFEAT package [26]. The partition-based algorithms divide the SIFT descriptor into 16 parts, corresponding to the 16 histograms of the standard SIFT. Different partitioning, into 2, 4, 8, and 32 parts, performed less well compared to the 16 part partition.

5.2   Matching Results

The results for the Mikolajczyk et al. [11] dataset are summarized using the mAP (mean average precision) per scene (over the first 4 transformation levels) in Tables 1 and 2, and the mAP per transformation level in Fig. 1. In Table 1 we compare the proposed probabilistic algorithms that use unconditional probability (PFA_{1-1}) to Lowe's first matching criterion, and to the other deterministic algorithms that use CEMD [20] and TMEMD [19]. The algorithms in this set are referred to as *absolute*. Table 2 reports on *relative* algorithms, including the probabilistic algorithms that use the conditional probability of false alarm, PFA_c, and the deterministic versions corresponding to Lowe's distance ratio, as well as to similar ratios of the EMD variants. Figure 1 compares the 4 versions corresponding to PMV, PMV_c, and Lowe's first and second criteria.

The results for the absolute algorithms are clear: PMV obtains the best results on the average. The sum-value based algorithm follows closely. Both algorithms clearly outperform the deterministic algorithms.

The performance obtained by using the unconditional probabilistic criterion is comparable to that obtained by the non-probabilistic distance ratio criterion. This is not surprising because both algorithms rely on the context of other dissimilarities, besides that of the tested descriptor pair; see also [21].

While the three dissimilarities use the same context different results are achieved. The max dissimilarity, for example, performs even worse than the

Table 1. mAP for *absolute* algorithms for the Mikolajczyk et al. [11] dataset. PMV is third from the right.

	Deterministic			sum			max-value			multi-value		
							Probabilistic					
	L2	CEMD	TMEMD	L2	CEMD	TMEMD	L2	CEMD	TMEMD	L2	CEMD	TMEMD
Blur (Bikes)	0.756	0.694	0.737	0.795	0.556	0.795	0.720	0.455	0.706	**0.798**	0.769	0.791
Blur (Trees)	0.513	0.460	0.499	**0.524**	0.483	0.522	0.419	0.318	0.408	0.516	0.481	0.512
Viewpoint (Graffiti)	0.334	0.317	0.337	0.354	0.359	0.373	0.281	0.247	0.277	0.383	0.368	**0.388**
Viewpoint (Wall)	0.686	0.666	0.689	0.697	0.456	0.708	0.587	0.515	0.594	**0.714**	0.688	0.713
Zoom + Rotation (Bark)	0.804	0.750	0.771	0.812	0.622	0.789	0.736	0.665	0.712	**0.823**	0.788	0.812
Zoom + Rotation (Boat)	0.789	0.761	0.783	0.813	0.797	0.815	0.725	0.676	0.714	**0.829**	0.808	0.826
Light (Leuven)	0.861	0.433	0.845	0.899	0.884	0.897	0.855	0.791	0.841	**0.909**	0.886	0.897
JPEG Compression (UBC)	0.874	0.864	0.874	0.878	0.698	**0.882**	0.852	0.447	0.854	0.876	0.874	0.878

Table 2. mAP for *relative* algorithms for the Mikolajczyk et al. [11] dataset. PMV_c is third from the right.

	Deterministic			sum			max-value			multi-value		
							Probabilistic					
	L2	CEMD	TMEMD	L2	CEMD	TMEMD	L2	CEMD	TMEMD	L2	CEMD	TMEMD
Blur (Bikes)	0.812	0.792	0.810	**0.814**	0.383	0.812	0.740	0.649	0.727	0.812	0.776	0.806
Blur (Trees)	0.536	0.499	0.535	**0.539**	0.505	**0.539**	0.430	0.335	0.420	0.533	0.497	0.527
Viewpoint (Graffiti)	0.380	0.381	0.396	0.385	0.161	0.405	0.299	0.270	0.299	0.411	0.398	**0.419**
Viewpoint (Wall)	0.707	0.605	0.713	0.711	0.605	0.718	0.595	0.511	0.603	**0.725**	0.689	0.723
Zoom + Rotation (Bark)	0.816	0.762	0.787	0.816	0.769	0.789	0.739	0.656	0.713	**0.822**	0.787	0.811
Zoom + Rotation (Boat)	0.823	0.799	0.820	0.825	0.623	0.822	0.732	0.684	0.721	**0.834**	0.795	0.825
Light (Leuven)	0.907	0.676	0.908	0.909	0.678	0.909	0.874	0.800	0.862	**0.917**	0.898	0.908
JPEG Compression (UBC)	0.883	0.700	0.886	0.884	0.477	**0.887**	0.855	0.381	0.856	0.881	0.878	0.883

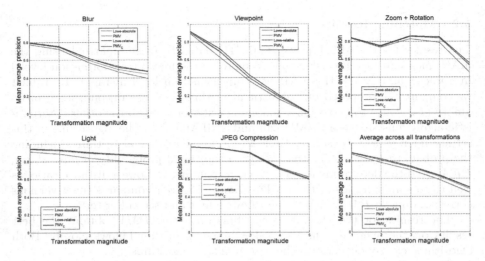

Fig. 1. mAP as a function of the transformation magnitude for PMV, PMV_c, and Lowe's two criteria for the Mikolajczyk et al. [11] dataset.

deterministic approaches. It seems that the multi-value algorithm is able to exploit the cell-dependent variability in the distances between the various SIFT components. This variability could result from the downweighting of the outer cells and the lower variability of their histograms, due to the larger distance of the outer cells from the most likely location of the interest point: the patch's center. We believe that it is also due to the accidental nonuniformity of the distances between the parts, which is averaged by the sum distance, and leads to the poorer performance of the max-value dissimilarity measure, which is based on a uniform dissimilarity threshold.

The differences between the relative algorithms are small. PMV_c is slightly better, especially for viewpoint transformations which is the most common application for matching. We believe that the reason for PMV_c being less successful with the blur and JPEG compression is that these transformations add noise to the image, which has a greater impact on low-dimensional vectors. The results demonstrate the validity of the interpretations proposed in this paper.

Figure 2 summarizes the results obtained for the Fischer et al. dataset [6] (the 3 nonlinear transformations, which do not correspond to a homography, were ignored). The results are consistent, although with only a minor improvement compared to Lowe's ratio criterion. Note that performance differences between Lowe's first criterion and second criterion are not expressed here as well[3].

---

[3] Different matching papers use different evaluation protocols, different feature points (even when using SIFT descriptors), and different criteria for counting recalls and false alarms. As such, the results cannot be directly compared with those reported in some other papers. Nevertheless, we use exactly the same evaluation protocol for all the algorithms tested here.

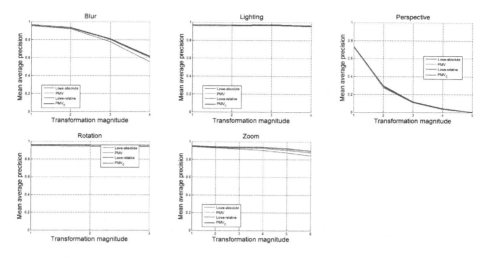

Fig. 2. mAP as a function of the transformation levels for PMV, PMV_c, and Lowe's two criteria, for the Fischer et al. [6] dataset.

The partition-based algorithms are more computationally expensive than the deterministic ones (slower by a factor of 8 to 15, in our current, unoptimized, implementation). As our goal in the implementation was to demonstrate the validity of the probabilistic justification, and to show that the generality of the analysis possibly leads to diverse algorithms, we did not focus on runtime optimizations. Our algorithms can be optimized following common methods of efficient nearest neighbor search [16]. This is left for future work.

5.3   Complementary Experiments

The importance of point-adapted distribution. All the above experiments used *point-adapted* distributions. We experimented also with the *internal* and *external* distributions (defined in Sect. 3.1), using images from the Caltech 101 dataset [5] to compute the external distribution. We found that the algorithms performed best with the point-adapted distribution; see Fig. 3. The external distribution based versions performed worse than Lowe's first distance criterion.

Relaxing the independence assumption. We challenged the statistical independence assumption and found that some substantial correlations between the partial distances exist. Using a more complex distribution model, which relies on a dependence tree (following [18]), did not improve the ranking result.

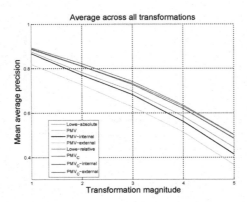

Fig. 3. Comparing external, internal, and point-adaptive distribution estimations (see Sects. 2.1 and 5.3) for the Mikolajczyk et al. [11] dataset.

6   Discussion and Conclusions

The main contributions of this paper are two, independent, probabilistic interpretations of Lowe's ratio criterion. This criterion, used to match SIFT descriptors, is very effective and widely used, yet so far it has only been empirically based. Our interpretations show that, in a probabilistic setting, it corresponds either to a conditional probability that the match is incorrect, or to the Markov bound on this probability. To the best of our knowledge, this is the first rigorous justification of this important tool.

To test the (first) interpretation empirically, we used techniques of the *a contrario* approach to construct a distribution of the dissimilarities associated with false matches. Some dissimilarity functions were considered, including one that, unlike common measures, expresses the dissimilarity by a multi-value (vector) measure and can better capture the variability of the descriptor.

Using a matching criterion based on conditional probability and a multi-value dissimilarity measure led to state-of-the-art matching performance (for non-learning-based algorithms). The improvement over the previous, nonprobabilistic, algorithms is not very large. The experiments nonetheless support the probabilistic interpretation, as they demonstrate that explicit use of it leads to consistent and even better results.

We follow several aspects of the *a contrario* theory [3,4]: we use background models that provide the PFA probability that an event occurs by chance, and the partition-based estimation technique. However, in order to use the probabilistic interpretation of the ratio criterion, and contrary to the *a contrario* approach, we refrain from using the expected number of false alarms (NFA) as the matching criterion and use the probability of false alarm instead.

One promising idea for future work is to combine our method of using only false positive error estimation in the decision-making process with models for false negative errors; see e.g. [10], which focuses on the differences between specific descriptors in different images.

References

1. Abdel-Hakim, A.E., Farag, A.A.: CSIFT: a SIFT descriptor with color invariant characteristics. CVPR **2**, 1978–1983 (2006)
2. Bay, H., Ess, A., Tuytelaars, T., Gool, L.V.: Speeded-up robust features (SURF). Comput. Vis. Image Underst. **110**(3), 346–359 (2008)
3. Desolneux, A., Moisan, L., Morel, J.M.: Meaningful alignments. Int. J. Comput. Vision **40**(1), 7–23 (2000)
4. Desolneux, A., Moisan, L., Morel, J.M.: From Gestalt Theory to Image Analysis: A Probabilistic Approach, vol. 34. Springer Science & Business Media, New York (2007)
5. Fei-Fei, L., Fergus, R., Perona, P.: Learning generative visual models from few training examples: an incremental Bayesian approach tested on 101 object categories. Comput. Vis. Image Underst. **106**(1), 59–70 (2007)
6. Fischer, P., Dosovitskiy, A., Brox, T.: Descriptor matching with convolutional neural networks: a comparison to SIFT. arXiv preprint arXiv:1405.5769 (2014)
7. Ke, Y., Sukthankar, R.: PCA-SIFT: a more distinctive representation for local image descriptors. In: CVPR 2004, vol. 2, p. II-506 (2004)
8. Lowe, D.G.: Object recognition from local scale-invariant features. ICCV **2**, 1150–1157 (1999)
9. Lowe, D.G.: Distinctive image features from scale-invariant keypoints. Int. J. Comput. Vision **60**(2), 91–110 (2004)
10. Mikolajczyk, K., Matas, J.: Improving descriptors for fast tree matching by optimal linear projection. In: ICCV 2007, pp. 1–8 (2007)
11. Mikolajczyk, K., Schmid, C.: A performance evaluation of local descriptors. IEEE Trans. Pattern Anal. Mach. Intell. **27**(10), 1615–1630 (2005)
12. Miksik, O., Mikolajczyk, K.: Evaluation of local detectors and descriptors for fast feature matching. In: ICPR, pp. 2681–2684 (2012)
13. Moreels, P., Perona, P.: Evaluation of features detectors and descriptors based on 3D objects. Int. J. Comput. Vision **73**(3), 263–284 (2007)
14. Morel, J.M., Yu, G.: ASIFT: a new framework for fully affine invariant image comparison. SIAM J. Imaging Sci. **2**(2), 438–469 (2009)
15. Mottalli, M., Tepper, M., Mejail, M.: A contrario detection of false matches in iris recognition. In: Bloch, I., Cesar, R.M. (eds.) CIARP 2010. LNCS, vol. 6419, pp. 442–449. Springer, Heidelberg (2010). doi:10.1007/978-3-642-16687-7_59
16. Muja, M., Lowe, D.G.: Fast approximate nearest neighbors with automatic algorithm configuration. In: VISAPP (1), vol. 2, pp. 331–340, 2 (2009)
17. Musé, P., Sur, F., Cao, F., Gousseau, Y., Morel, J.M.: An a contrario decision method for shape element recognition. Int. J. Comput. Vision **69**(3), 295–315 (2006)
18. Myaskouvskey, A., Gousseau, Y., Lindenbaum, M.: Beyond independence: an extension of the a contrario decision procedure. Int. J. Comput. Vision **101**(1), 22–44 (2013)
19. Pele, O., Werman, M.: A linear time histogram metric for improved SIFT matching. In: Forsyth, D., Torr, P., Zisserman, A. (eds.) ECCV 2008, Part III. LNCS, vol. 5304, pp. 495–508. Springer, Heidelberg (2008). doi:10.1007/978-3-540-88690-7_37
20. Rabin, J., Delon, J., Gousseau, Y.: Circular earth movers distance for the comparison of local features. In: ICPR, pp. 1–4 (2008)
21. Rabin, J., Delon, J., Gousseau, Y.: A contrario matching of SIFT-like descriptors. In: ICPR, pp. 1–4 (2008)

22. Sande, K., Gevers, T., Snoek, C.G.: Evaluating color descriptors for object and scene recognition. IEEE Trans. Pattern Anal. Mach. Intell. **32**(9), 1582–1596 (2010)
23. Schmid, C., Mohr, R., Bauckhage, C.: Evaluation of interest point detectors. Int. J. Comput. Vision **37**(2), 151–172 (2000)
24. Silverman, B.W.: Density Estimation for Statistics and Data Analysis, vol. 26. CRC Press, Boca Raton (1986)
25. Tuytelaars, T., Mikolajczyk, K.: Local invariant feature detectors: a survey. Found. Trends Comput. Graph. Vis. **3**(3), 177–280 (2008)
26. Vedaldi, A., Fulkerson, B.: VLFeat: an open and portable library of computer vision algorithms (2008). http://www.vlfeat.org/
27. Zagoruyko, S., Komodakis, N.: Learning to compare image patches via convolutional neural networks. In: CVPR, pp. 4353–4361 (2015)
28. Zhang, J., Marszałek, M., Lazebnik, S., Schmid, C.: Local features and kernels for classification of texture and object categories: a comprehensive study. Int. J. Comput. Vision **73**(2), 213–238 (2007)

Semi-supervised Learning Based on Joint Diffusion of Graph Functions and Laplacians

Kwang In Kim$^{(\boxtimes)}$

Department of Computer Science, University of Bath, Bath, UK
`k.kim@bath.ac.uk`

Abstract. We observe the distances between estimated function outputs on data points to create an anisotropic graph Laplacian which, through an iterative process, can itself be regularized. Our algorithm is instantiated as a discrete regularizer on a graph's *diffusivity operator*. This idea is grounded in the theory that regularizing the diffusivity operator corresponds to regularizing the metric on Riemannian manifolds, which further corresponds to regularizing the anisotropic Laplace-Beltrami operator. We show that our discrete regularization framework is consistent in the sense that it converges to (continuous) regularization on underlying data generating manifolds. In semi-supervised learning experiments, across ten standard datasets, our diffusion of Laplacian approach has the lowest average error rate of eight different established and state-of-the-art approaches, which shows the promise of our approach.

Keywords: Semi-supervised learning · Graph Laplacian · Diffusion · Regularization

1 Introduction

In semi-supervised learning, we discover a function f which, from a set of data points and partial labels, propagates the labels to an unlabeled subset of data. To achieve this, methods exploit the underlying 'geometry' of or 'relationships' between points in the input space to help learn f. Many times, the underlying relationships between data points can be represented as a graph, or as a set of data points sampled from an underlying manifold. In these cases, the graph Laplacian is useful as it contains the pairwise relations or similarity w_{ij} between data points in the unlabeled space.

Hence, many existing algorithms use the graph Laplacian as a regularizer to directly enforce smoothness over the estimated function f: When a pair of data nodes or points $\mathbf{x}_i$ and $\mathbf{x}_j$ are similar, we can cause their corresponding function evaluations $f(\mathbf{x}_i)$ and $f(\mathbf{x}_j)$ to also be similar by directly trading a training error against a regularization cost. Alternatively, other algorithms use simulations of physical diffusion processes to indirectly promote smoothness on f: At each point $\mathbf{x}$, the evaluated function value $f(\mathbf{x})$ is spread over the neighborhood of $\mathbf{x}$. The strength of this diffusion—the *diffusivity*—between two points $\mathbf{x}_i$ and $\mathbf{x}_j$, is determined by their similarity w_{ij}.

© Springer International Publishing AG 2016
B. Leibe et al. (Eds.): ECCV 2016, Part V, LNCS 9909, pp. 713–729, 2016.
DOI: 10.1007/978-3-319-46454-1_43

For semi-supervised learning, it has been shown that these two approaches are actually equivalent (e.g. [1]): The solution of direct regularization-based approaches that trade training error and regularization cost is also the solution at the limit case of the diffusion process over time. Thus, the graph Laplacian is both the regularizer and the generator of the diffusion process. As such, we will be using the term 'regularization' interchangeably with 'diffusion'.

In general, due to the ill-posed nature of semi-supervised learning, the estimated f evaluations are noisy, and so the constructed new anisotropic graph Laplacian is also noisy. As such, in this paper, we propose to regard the graph Laplacian itself as an object which can be regularized. This is similar to the tradition in learning algorithms where the f estimate is regularized to prevent over-fitting to noisy data.

Our approach builds upon the analysis of learning over continuous spaces, as is commonly assumed in geometry-based semi-supervised algorithms: As the number of sampled data points increases to infinity, the corresponding graph converges to the underlying manifold M which generated those data samples. In this case, the graph Laplacian converges to the Laplace-Beltrami operator on M. Roughly, applying the Laplace-Beltrami operator to a function f measures the first-order variation of f. This operator lets us regularize f by penalizing the first-order f variation.

Our idea of regularizing the graph Laplacian itself extends in the continuous space to regularizing the Laplace-Beltrami operator itself: We measure the variation of the structure that measures the variation of f. As we will show, this structure is prescribed by the metric on M, rendering our framework into metric regularization. In general, regularizing the metric on M is a difficult problem when the manifold M is only observed through sparse data points, as is typical in practical applications. Using recent results on the equivalence of the metric on M and the continuous *diffusivity* operator [2], we develop a regularization framework that enforces the smoothness of the diffusivity operator as a surrogate. Then, discretizing our continuous space formulation into a finite graph G, we construct an efficient regularization framework for the graph Laplacian.

We show that this discrete regularization framework on G converges to the continuous Laplacian regularization on M based on convergence analysis of the graph Laplacian [3,4] and the equivalence of inducing an anisotropic diffusion process with a new metric on M [2]. In experiments, we demonstrate that the resulting algorithms significantly improves upon existing linear/non-linear, and isotropic/anisotropic diffusion-based semi-supervised learning algorithms, as well as other state-of-the-art algorithms.

Related work. Anisotropic diffusion has been known to be particularly effective in processing two-dimensional images [5] and surfaces [6]. Szlam *et al.* [7] extended these algorithms to high-dimensional graph structured data as discrete approximations of smooth manifolds. The resulting semi-supervised learning and denoising algorithms demonstrated significant improvement over existing isotropic diffusion algorithms and isotropic graph Laplacian-based regularization algorithms. Recently Kim *et al.* [2] further extended and improved upon this framework for non-linear diffusion. Our approach extends both the linear diffusion algorithm of Szlam *et al.* [7] and the non-linear diffusion algorithm of Kim *et al.* [2] by introducing the Laplacian as a new object to be diffused/regularized in addition to the classification function f being diffused. As discussed previously and shown in Sect. 2, regularizing the Laplacian is equivalent to regularizing the metric on manifolds, which we take to instantiate our practical algorithms. From this perspective, our approach can be regarded as an instance of tensor regularization [8–10]. Existing tensor regularization approaches rely on known manifold structure (e.g. images or surfaces) [8,9] or they are specialized on specific graph connectivities (e.g. edges focus on orthogonal transform between node data [10]). In contrast, our algorithm is applicable to any graph structured data without having to access the underlying data generating manifold or to introduce restricting assumptions. Accordingly, one of our main contribution is extending existing tensor regularization approaches to graph-based semi-supervised learning.

Our algorithm refines the original graph Laplacian throughout the diffusion process. A single fixed instance of the graph Laplacian can be regarded as a pseudo-inverse of a similarity kernel matrix (Sects. 2 and 4, and [11,12]). In this sense, our algorithm can also be regarded as an instance of spectral kernel design where the kernel matrix (inverse of Laplacian in semi-supervised learning context) is automatically constructed based on the spectral analysis of the kernel matrix itself [11,12]. Section 4 discusses this comparison, and Sect. 5 presents experimental comparisons [11,12]. This perspective also establishes a connection between our approach to graph denoising and link prediction algorithms. In particular, we show that our linear diffusion algorithm corresponds to an iterative solver of existing graph denoising [13] and ensemble ranking [14] algorithms (Sect. 4). In experiments, we demonstrate that adopting our approaches in a linear diffusion algorithm improves semi-supervised learning performance and, furthermore, non-linearly extending them could lead to even further performance improvement.

Overview. To explain our approach, we will first introduce regularization of the Laplace-Beltrami operator on continuous manifolds and show that this is equivalent to regularizing a Riemannian metric on M (Sect. 2). However, regularizing a metric on M is not straightforward, so we show that the goal of regularizing a metric on M (or, equivalently, the Laplace-Beltrami operator) can be achieved by regularizing the diffusivity operator on M as a surrogate in the context of anisotropic diffusion (Sect. 3). As such, we introduce an anisotropic diffusion process on M, and also show that by discretizing this process to sampled data we can achieve a practical metric regularization algorithm which still converges to the solution of the continuous case. Finally, with this, we present a new semi-supervised learning algorithm that jointly diffuses classification functions and the diffusivity operator (Sect. 4).

2 Smoothness of the Laplace-Beltrami Operator

We begin by formally defining regularization of the Laplace-Beltrami operator on continuous manifolds, and show its equivalence to metric regularization.

The Laplace-Beltrami operator (or shortly, Laplacian) $\Delta^g : C^\infty(M) \to C^\infty(M)$ on a Riemannian manifold (M, g) with a metric g is a second order differential operator:

$$\Delta^g f = \nabla^{g*} \nabla^g f, \tag{1}$$

where $\nabla^g : C^\infty(M) \to TM$ and $\nabla^{g*} : TM \to C^\infty(M)$ are the gradient and divergence operators, respectively and TM is the tangent bundle of M.

The typical way to regularize a linear operator (such as Laplacian) is to minimize its operator norm, which corresponds to the largest operator eigenvalue. This finds numerous applications including storage allocation [15] and system stability analysis [16]. Understanding the significance of this approach to semi-supervised learning is not straightforward as, for semi-supervised learning, Zhang and Ando [11] actually suggest exactly the opposite: It has been demonstrated that *maximizing* the largest eigenvalues of the Laplacian corresponds to minimizing the upper bound on the generalization error. More precisely, Zhang and Ando proposed decreasing the smallest eigenvalues of the *kernel* matrix K with the pseudo-inverse of the Laplacian L^+ being a special case of K.

Instead, our regularization approach is based on the analysis of the *spatial* behavior of the Laplacian. First, we will explain our method, but interestingly, we will show that the approach of Zhang and Ando [11] leads to a construction which is similar to our linear diffusion framework Sect. 4.

The Laplacian on the Euclidean space $\mathbb{R}^m$ can be written as [3]:

$$[\Delta^{\mathbb{R}^m} f](x) := \sum_{i=1,\dots,m} \frac{\partial^2}{(\partial x^i)^2} f(x) = \lim_{r \to 0} \frac{1}{C_m r^2} \left([A_B(x)f] - f(x) \right), \tag{2}$$

where

$$[A_B(x)f] = \frac{1}{\text{vol}(B(x,r))} \int_{B(x,r)} f(y) dy, \tag{3}$$

C_m is a constant depending only on m, $B(x, r)$ is a ball of radius r centered at x, and $\text{vol}(B)$ is the volume of B. The equality in Eq. 2 implies that roughly, the Laplacian $\Delta^{\mathbb{R}^m} f$ of a function f evaluated at x measures the deviation of $f(x)$ from its average $[A_B(x)f]$ taken at a local neighborhood. This characterization suggests that the behavior of the Laplacian is determined by the local averaging operator $A_B(x)$. The underlying idea of our approach is to enforce the spatial smoothness of the corresponding averaging operator on M.

As clearly seen from the integral form (Eq. 3), the operator $A_B(x)$ is spatially homogeneous and therefore, its spatial variation is simply zero: Equivalently, the Laplacian is homogeneous in $\mathbb{R}^m$. Now to enforce our underlying idea of spatial smoothness to manifolds, we adopt a generalization of this Laplacian representation to manifolds as proposed by Hein [17], and Coifman and Lafon [18]. Suppose that (M, g) is an n-dimensional submanifold of $\mathbb{R}^m$ with $i : M \to \mathbb{R}^m$ being the corresponding embedding. The local averaging-based Laplacian estimate $\Delta_h^g f$ on (M, g) is defined as

$$[\Delta_h^g f](x) = \frac{1}{h^2}\left(f(x) - \frac{1}{d_h(x)}[A_h^g(x)f]\right), \text{ where } [A_h^g(x)f] = \int_M k_h(x,y)f(y)dV(x),$$
(4)

$d_h(x) = [A_h^g(x)\mathbf{1}]$ with $\mathbf{1}$ being a constant function of ones, and dV is the natural volume element of M $(dV(x) = \sqrt{|\det(\mathbf{g})|}dx$ with $\mathbf{g}$ being the coordinate matrix of g). The kernel k_h is defined based on a Gaussian function on $\mathbb{R}^m$:

$$k_h(x,y) = \begin{cases} \frac{1}{h^m}k(\|i(x) - i(y)\|_{\mathbb{R}^m}^2, h^2) & \text{if } \|i(x) - i(y)\|_{\mathbb{R}^m} \leq h \\ 0 & \text{otherwise,} \end{cases}$$
(5)

with $k(a,b) = \exp(-a/b)$.

It has been shown that when M is compact, Δ_h^g converges uniformly to the Laplacian Δ^g [17] as $h \to 0$.[1] From this convergence result and the definition of the average operator A_h^g (Eq. 4), we can see that the spatial variation of Δ^g is entirely determined by the metric g. This is not surprising as the Laplacian itself is indeed, expressed as a function of the metric g: Writing Eq. 1 in local coordinates $\{x^1, \ldots, x^n\}$ [19],

$$\Delta^g f = \sum_{i,j=1,\ldots,n} -\frac{1}{\sqrt{|\det(\mathbf{g})|}}\partial_j\left([\mathbf{g}^{-1}]_{ij}\sqrt{|\det(\mathbf{g})|}\partial_i f\right)$$

$$= \sum_{i,j=1,\ldots,n} -[\mathbf{g}^{-1}]_{ij}\partial_j\partial_i f + \text{(lower order terms)},$$
(6)

where $\partial_i := [\partial/\partial_{x^i}]$. Furthermore, as the second equality in Eq. 6 shows, by evaluating Δ^g on a function $x^i x^j$, we can reconstruct the metric $\mathbf{g}$. Therefore, defining a new regularization operator $\Delta^{\bar{g}}$ is equivalent to determining a new metric $\bar{g}$. Unfortunately, this equivalence by itself does not make the regularization of Laplacian easier since in general, regularizing a Riemannian metric is a non-trivial problem.[2] However, in the next section we demonstrate that applying this idea to induce an anisotropic diffusion process on a finite graph G that approximates M, regularizing the metric (and equivalently the Laplacian) can be easily instantiated by enforcing the smoothness of the *local diffusivity operator* on G.

3   Anisotropic Diffusion on Graphs and Manifolds

Having defined the Laplacian regularization and established its equivalence to metric regularization, we now present continuous anisotropic diffusion on a

---

[1] Here, we assume for simplicity that the underlying probability distribution p is uniform and M is compact. In general, any compactly supported distribution p can be adopted instead. See [3] for details.

[2] Defining a regularizer on a metric g is not straightforward since, by the construction of the Riemannian connection, $\nabla_X^g g = 0$ for all vector fields X on M. Furthermore, even when the connection (defined on g) is made independent of a new metric $\bar{g}$, evaluating the derivative of a second-order tensor $(\bar{g})$ from finite data points X is a difficult problem in general.

Riemannian manifold (M, g), and its discretization on graphs. We follow the construction of Weickert [5] who applied an anisotropic diffusion process to images as functions on $\mathbb{R}^2$, which has been subsequently extended to functions on manifolds [2, 7].

Anisotropic diffusion of a smooth function $f \in C^\infty(M)$ based on a positive definite *diffusivity operator* $D : TM \to TM$ is described as a partial differential equation:

$$\frac{\partial f}{\partial t} = \nabla^{g*} D \nabla^g f. \tag{7}$$

At each point $x \in M$, D is represented (in coordinates) as a positive definite matrix $\mathbf{D}(x)$ which controls the strength and direction of diffusion. If D is an identity operator, Eq. 7 becomes isotropic diffusion. An important feature of the diffusivity operator D is that it uniquely defines a new metric on M [2]: Anisotropic diffusion on (M, g) generated by the operator $\Delta^D := -\nabla^{g*} D \nabla^g$ is equivalent to an isotropic diffusion on a new manifold $(M, \overline{g})$ with an updated metric $\overline{g}$ which is given in coordinates as

$$\overline{\mathbf{g}}(x) = c(x)\mathbf{g}(x)\mathbf{D}^{-1}(x), \tag{8}$$

where $c \in C^\infty(M)$, and $\mathbf{g}(x)$ and $\overline{\mathbf{g}}(x)$ are the coordinate representations (matrices) of g and $\overline{g}$ at x, respectively. In particular, in Riemannian normal coordinates at x (based on g), g becomes Euclidean (i.e. $[\mathbf{g}]_{ij}(x) = \delta_{ij}(x)$), and therefore, $\mathbf{D}(x)$ can be interpreted as a covariance matrix of a Mahalanobis distance. We will henceforth refer Δ^D as an *anisotropic Laplacian*. This operator will be used to analyze the limit case behavior of the discretization of $\Delta^{\overline{g}}$ (see Proposition 1).

In practical applications, the manifold M is not directly observed and instead, a sampled point cloud X is provided ($X \subset i(M) \subset \mathbb{R}^m$). The remainder of this section focuses on a graph Laplacian-based discretization of Eq. 7.

A weighted graph $G = (X, E, W)$ consists of nodes $X = \{\mathbf{x}_1, ..., \mathbf{x}_u\}$, edges $E \subset X \times X$, and weights assigned for each edge in E:

$$w_{ij} = w(e_{ij}) := k_h(i^{-1}(\mathbf{x}_i), i^{-1}(\mathbf{x}_j)), e_{ij} \in E, w_{ij} \in W. \tag{9}$$

The *graph gradient* operator ∇^G is defined as the collection of node function differences along the edges:

$$[\nabla^G f](e_{ij}) = \sqrt{w_{ij}}(f(\mathbf{x}_j) - f(\mathbf{x}_i)). \tag{10}$$

while the *graph divergence* operator ∇^{G*} measures the variation of functions $\{S : E \to \mathbb{R}\}$ on edges:

$$[\nabla^{G*} S](\mathbf{x}_i) = \frac{1}{2d_i} \sum_{j=1,...,u} \sqrt{w_{ij}}(S(e_{ji}) - S(e_{ij})), \tag{11}$$

where $d_i = \sum_{j=1}^u w_{ij}$. Given the two operators, the (isotropic) graph Laplacian L is defined as

$$[Lf](\mathbf{x}_i) = [\nabla^{G*} \nabla^G f](\mathbf{x}_i). \tag{12}$$

Similarly to the case of continuous anisotropic diffusion (Eq. 7), an anisotropic diffusion process on G can be introduced by *placing* a positive definite diffusivity operator in-between the gradient and divergence operators: The anisotropic graph Laplacian L^D and the corresponding diffusion process are defined as

$$[L^D f](\mathbf{x}_i) := [\nabla^{G^*} D \nabla^G f](\mathbf{x}_i), \frac{\partial}{\partial t} f = [L^D f], \tag{13}$$

where the *graph diffusivity operator* D is represented as

$$[DS](e_{ij}) = q_{ij} \mathbf{b}_{ij} \langle \mathbf{b}_{ij}, S \rangle \tag{14}$$

with the basis function $\mathbf{b}_{ij}$ being the indicator of e_{ij} and the inner-product $\langle S, T \rangle$ of edge functions S and T defined as $\langle S, T \rangle = \sum_{i,j=1}^{u} S(e_{ij}) T(e_{ij})$. It should be noted that by substituting Eq. 14 into Eq. 13, L^D can be constructed by replacing w_{ij} in ∇^G and ∇^{G^*} (Eqs. 10 and 11) with $\overline{w}_{ij} := w_{ij} q_{ij}$ and combining the resulting two operators as in Eq. 12.

As discussed earlier, if X is sampled from (M, g), the graph Laplacian L converges to the Laplace-Beltrami operator Δ^g as $u \to \infty$ [4, 20]. Now we generalize this result to anisotropic graph Laplacian:

Proposition 1 (The convergence of L^D to $\Delta^{\overline{g}}$). *Assume that (M, g) is an n-dimensional Riemannian submanifold of $\mathbb{R}^m$ and $(M, \overline{g})$ is a new manifold with an updated metric $\overline{g}$. Let $X = \{\mathbf{x}_1, \ldots, \mathbf{x}_u\}$ be a sample from a compactly supported, uniform distribution p on M and the coefficients $\{q_{ij}\}$ of the graph diffusivity operator D are given as*

$$h^m q_{ij} = k(\|\mathbf{x}_i - \mathbf{x}_j\|_{\mathbb{R}^m}^2, h^2) + k(-\|i^{-1}(\mathbf{x}_i) - i^{-1}(\mathbf{x}_j)\|_{\overline{g}^2}^2, h^2). \tag{15}$$

Then, L^D converges to $\Delta^{\overline{g}}$ almost surely as $u \to \infty$, $h \to 0$, and $uh^{m+2}/ \log(u) \to \infty$.

Sketch of proof: Equation 15 essentially equates the pairwise distance $\|f(\mathbf{x}_i) - f(\mathbf{x}_j)\|_D$ induced by D at points $\mathbf{x}_i$ and the corresponding distance measured in the resulting metric $\overline{g}$: We represent $\overline{w}_{ij}(= w_{ij} q_{ij})$ as the Gaussian envelop of the new distance $\|\mathbf{x}_j - \mathbf{x}_i\|_{\overline{g}}$: ($\overline{w}_{ij} = \frac{1}{h^m} k\left(\|\mathbf{x}_i - \mathbf{x}_j\|_{\overline{g}}^2, h^2\right)$). The convergence proof is then completed by (1) the equivalence of anisotropic Laplace-Beltrami operator on (M, g) and the isotropic Laplace-Beltrami operator on $(M, \overline{g})$ and (2) the convergence of the isotropic graph Laplacian to Laplace-Beltrami operator (see *Main Result* of [3]).   □

The conditions $h \to 0$ and $uh^{m+2}/\log(u) \to \infty$ in the proposition are required for the convergence of isotropic Laplacian [3]: This implies that the shrink speed of kernel width parameter h has to be controlled in the sense that any ball-shaped region of diameter h contains sufficiently many data points.

This result establishes a connection between the problems of estimating an anisotropic Laplacian L^D on a graph G and a metric $\overline{g}$ on a Riemannian manifold (M, g), and it provides motivation on regularizing the graph diffusivity operator D as a surrogate to $\bar{g}$ in practical estimation problems in general. However, Proposition 1 cannot be used directly in analyzing the behavior our anisotropic diffusion algorithms since, as we shown shortly in Sect. 4, our goal is to *dynamically construct* a new metric depending on the given dataset X and the corresponding labels for a subset of X, rather than restoring a hidden, fixed metric $\bar{g}$. As such, the next section presents the development of a new metric based on the variations of f evaluations.

4   Semi-supervised Learning Based on Non-linear Anisotropic Diffusion on Graphs

Our semi-supervised learning algorithm simultaneously evolves the node-function f as well as the regularizer L^D based on anisotropic diffusion. First, we discuss traditional f-diffusion, and extend it to the diffusion of regularizer L^D. Second, we combine the two diffusion processes (of f and L^D).

Diffusion of f. Suppose that for the first l data points in X, the corresponding labels $Y = \{\mathbf{y}_1, \ldots, \mathbf{y}_l\} \subset \mathbb{R}^c$ are provided where c is the number of classes. Assuming that the class label of the i-th data point is q, $\mathbf{y}_i$ is defined as a row vector of size $1 \times n$ where it has zero everywhere except for the q-th location in which its value is 1. If the regularizer (or diffusion generator) L^D is held fixed, the corresponding (time-discretized) linear diffusion process can be stated as

$$\frac{\mathbf{f}(t + \delta) - \mathbf{f}(t)}{\delta} = -L^D \mathbf{f}(t), \text{ where } \mathbf{f} = [f(\mathbf{x}_1), \ldots, f(\mathbf{x}_u)]^\top. \tag{16}$$

If D is an identity operator, Eq. 16 becomes isotropic diffusion. Otherwise, it is anisotropic. For instance, Szlam et al. [7] proposed tuning the diffusivity based on function evaluations $\mathbf{f}$: On a graph G the diffusivity along the edge e_{ij} becomes stronger or weaker as $\mathbf{f}_i$ and $\mathbf{f}_j$ are similar or different, respectively. This idea can be implemented by directly controlling the diffusivity operator D (Eq. 14):

$$q_{ij} = \exp\left(-\frac{\|\mathbf{f}_i(t_0) - \mathbf{f}_j(t_0)\|_{\mathbb{R}^c}^2}{h'}\right), \tag{17}$$

with a positive number h' being a hyper-parameter. For anisotropic diffusion, Szlam et al. [7] suggested initializing $\mathbf{f}(t_0)$ by running few steps of isotropic diffusion. This has significantly improved the convergence speed in our preliminary experiments. For all anisotropic diffusion algorithms compared in the experiments, we initialized the solutions by executing 20 iterations of isotropic diffusion.

Recently, Kim et al. [2] have demonstrated that extending the linear diffusion process in Eq. 16 to non-linear one can significantly improve the accuracy of the resulting semi-supervised learning algorithm:

$$\mathbf{f}(t + \delta) = (I - \delta L^D(t))\mathbf{f}(t). \tag{18}$$

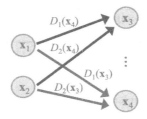

Fig. 1. We regularize the Laplacian on manifolds by enforcing the smoothness of the corresponding diffusivity operator. Instantiating this for graphs, our algorithm enforces the smoothness of the graph diffusivity functions $\{D_1, \ldots, D_u\}$: If $\mathbf{x}_1$ and $\mathbf{x}_2$ are close, the corresponding diffusivity functions $D_1(\cdot)$ and $D_2(\cdot)$ should be *similar*, e.g., $D_1(\mathbf{x}_3) \sim D_2(\mathbf{x}_3)$ and $D_1(\mathbf{x}_4) \sim D_2(\mathbf{x}_4)$.

This process is identical to Eq. 16 except that L^D now depends on t based on Eq. 17.

Diffusion of L^D. Now we apply the diffusion process developed in the previous paragraph to evolve the diffusivity operator D. To facilitate this process, we cast D that originally maps from the spaces of edge functions to itself, to a set of functions on X (Fig. 1): We take inner products of D with basis functions $\{\mathbf{b}_{ij} \otimes \mathbf{b}'_{ij}\}$ (with $\otimes$ and $\mathbf{b}'_{ij}$ being a tensor product and a dual vector of $\mathbf{b}_{ij}$, respectively):

$$D \Rightarrow \{D_1, \ldots, D_u\} \text{ with } D_i(\mathbf{x}_j) := \langle \mathbf{b}_{ij}, [D\mathbf{b}_{ij}] \rangle. \tag{19}$$

Now we can construct a sparse matrix $\mathbf{M} \in \mathbb{R}^{u \times u}$ by combining column-wise the elements of $\{D_i\}$, i.e. $\mathbf{M}_{[:,i]} = [D_i(\mathbf{x}_1), \ldots, D_i(\mathbf{x}_u)]^\top$.[3] Here, the sparsity is induced by adopting the h-neighborhood (Eq. 5) or k-nearest neighborhood (NN) used in constructing the isotropic weight matrix $\{w_{ij}\}$. In the experiments, we use k-NN and regard k as a hyper-parameter. The convergence results of Proposition 1 can be easily modified to k-nearest neighborhood case (e.g. see Sect. 2.4 of [17]).

Using $\mathbf{M}$ as a surrogate, the diffusion of L^D and its time discretization, are stated respectively as:

$$\frac{\partial \mathbf{M}}{\partial t} = -L^D \mathbf{M}, \mathbf{M}(t + \delta) = (I - \delta L^D(t))\mathbf{M}(t). \tag{20}$$

Joint diffusion of f and L^D. The two diffusion processes for $\mathbf{f}$ (Eq. 18) and for L^D (Eq. 20), respectively are both governed by L^D. At the same time, they constantly update L^D. We propose interweaving the two processes: We start with the linear diffusion process of $\mathbf{f}$ (i.e. L^D is fixed at the L). Then, at each N-th iteration of the diffusion, L^D is updated based on Eq. 17 and subsequently by the diffusion process on L^D (Eq. 20). Here we fix N at 20 which provides a moderate tradeoff between the flexibility (non-linearity) of L^D and the computational

---

[3] We adopt Matlab notation where $A_{[:,i]}$ represents the i-th column of matrix A.

Algorithm 1. *AND*: Semi-supervised learning using combined diffusion of function and Laplacian.

Input: Data points $X = \{\mathbf{x}_1, \ldots, \mathbf{x}_u\} \subset \mathbb{R}^d$; labels $Y = \{\mathbf{y}_1, \ldots, \mathbf{y}_l\} \subset \mathbb{R}^c$;
  hyper-parameters T_1, T_2, h', and k (see Sect. 5)
Output: Diffused labels $\mathbf{f}$.

Build an isotropic graph Laplacian L based on Eq. 9
for $t = 1, \ldots, T_1$ **do**
  Update $\mathbf{f}(t)$ based on Eq. 18.
  At each 20-th iteration Update $L^D(t)$ based on Eq. 17;
  for $t' = t, \ldots, t + T_2$ **do**
    | Update $L^D(t')$ based on Eq. 20;
  end
  Assign labels to $\mathbf{f}^t$ and $L^D(t)$;
  Normalize $L^D(t)$;
end

---

complexity. The numbers of diffusion iterations T_1 and T_2 for $\mathbf{f}$ (Eq. 18) and $\mathbf{M}$ (Eq. 20) are taken as hyper-parameters. At each iteration, the Laplacian matrix L^D is normalized (we use *Random-walk* normalization [3]) and parts of $\mathbf{f}$ and $\mathbf{D}$ are updated based on the provided labels: If the i-th data point is labeled, the i-th row of $\mathbf{f}(t + 1)$ is replaced by the corresponding label. Also, if the i-th and j-th data points are labeled, $\mathbf{D}_{ij}$ and $\mathbf{D}_{ji}$ are assigned with 1 (if the class labels of i-th and j-th data points are the same) or 0. Algorithm 1 summarizes the proposed joint diffusion process.

Time complexity. Overall, the time complexity of our algorithm depends on the number u of data points and the size k of the nearest neighborhood. Each f-diffusion iteration requires multiplying the matrix L^D with a vector $\mathbf{f}$ while $\mathbf{M}$-diffusion iteration requires the product of L^D and $\mathbf{M}$. Due to the sparsity of these matrices, this operation can be performed even for relatively large datasets. For the *MNIST* dataset with $60,000$ data points, running 100 iterations of the joint diffusion process takes around 30 s in MATLAB on a 3.6 GHz CPU.

Relations to existing work. The relationship between our algorithm and related existing works presented in Sect. 1 is interesting. Equation 20 is non-linear as the diffusion generator Δ^D depends on the object $\mathbf{M}$ being diffused. If we *linearize* Eq. 20 at t_0, i.e. approximating the generator $\Delta^D(t)$ by the fixed time instance $\Delta^D(t_0)$, we can recover a closed form regularization solution (see Zhou *et al.* [1]):

$$L^{D*} \Leftarrow \mathbf{M}^* = \underset{\mathbf{M} \in \mathbb{R}^{u \times u}}{\arg \min} \|\mathbf{M} - \mathbf{M}(t_0)\|_F^2 + \frac{\delta}{1 - \delta} \mathrm{tr}[\mathbf{M}^\top L^D(t_0)\mathbf{M}], \quad (21)$$

where $\|A\|_F$ and $tr[A]$ are the Frobenius norm and the trace of matrix A, respectively. This type of regularization has been used in few applications including graph denoising and link prediction [13], and ensemble ranking [14]. In addition, this perspective facilitates comparison of our framework with Zhang and Ando's approach [11] where the inverse of the graph Laplacian is regarded as an instance of the (similarity) kernel matrix K. Their analysis on the effect of the largest eigenvalues of L on the expected error bound led to an algorithm that takes powers of the Laplacian: L^p with $p \in \mathbb{Z}^+$ is used as the regularizer instead of L. If we take the graph Laplacian L as the object to be diffused in Eq. 20 instead of the anisotropic diffusivity operator $\mathbf{M}$,[4] the resulting diffusion process is equivalent to regularizing the original weight matrix $\{w_{ij}\}$. Now assigning a specific value 0.5 to δ, and linearizing the resulting diffusion equation, we obtain[5]

$$L(t + \delta) = \delta L^2(t). \tag{22}$$

Therefore, Zhang and Ando's algorithm can be regarded as taking a single step of the linearized diffusion on the original isotropic regularizer L before $\mathbf{f}$ is subsequently optimized. Interestingly, taking powers of the Laplacian can also be regarded as constructing high-order regularizers. Extending the convergence result of the graph Laplacian to Laplace-Beltrami operator on manifolds, we obtain the analogy between high-order regularization and iterated Laplacian. When $f \in C^\infty(M)$ and $u \to \infty$ [21],

$$-\frac{1}{u}C_n \mathbf{f}^\top L^p \mathbf{f} \to \int_M f(x)[(\Delta^g)^p f](x)dV(x)$$

$$= \begin{cases} \int_M \left((\Delta^g)^{\frac{p}{2}} f(x)\right)^2 dV(x) & \text{if } p \text{ is even} \\ \int_M \left\|[\nabla^g(\Delta^g)^{\frac{p-1}{2}} f](x)\right\|_g^2 dV(x) & \text{otherwise,} \end{cases} \tag{23}$$

where C_n is a constant depending on the dimensionality n and the equality is the result of Stokes' theorem. Therefore, $\mathbf{f}^\top L^p \mathbf{f}$ approximates high-order variations of f.[6] Zhou and Belkin [21] demonstrated that using high-order regularizers can significantly improve the semi-supervised learning performance as they help avoiding the degenerate case where the function obtained by minimizing combinations of the training error and the regularization cost is everywhere zero except for the labeled data points. Therefore, the linearization of our diffusion framework can be regarded as adopting high-order regularizers. In particular, the linearized analytical solution in Eq. 21 can be regarded as a variation of adopting an infinite-order variation measure, as the solution corresponds to the limit case of Eq. 20.

Unfortunately, more rigorous comparison between our approach and that of Zhang and Ando's algorithm [11] and equivalently of Zhou and Belkin [21] is not straightforward since (1) in our diffusion algorithms we do not iterate the diffusion process infinite times (i.e. $t \to \infty$) but terminate it at a given time step

---

[4] Essentially L^D and $\mathbf{M}$ contain the same information.

[5] When in general, $\delta \neq 0.5$, iterating p-times, the linearized diffusion generates an operator polynomial. This corresponds to using a (selected) combination of differential operators up to $\lceil p/2 \rceil$-th order.

[6] For simplicity, here we regard that f is a one-dimensional function.

T_1 which is an hyper-parameter taking a similar role as δ in Eq. 21; (2) Furthermore, our diffusion is non-linear where the regularizer itself is dynamically evolved. In this case, the solution cannot be straightforwardly represented in closed-form. In the experiments, we demonstrate that this non-linear diffusion of L^D leads to a significant improvement over the linearized diffusion case and equivalently, over the analytic solution of Eq. 21. Also, an important advantage of the diffusion formulation (Eq. 20) over the analytical solution (Eq. 21) is that, diffusion formulation facilitates a sparse framework: At time 0, the sparsity of $\mathbf{M}$ is controlled by the k-nearest neighbor size. As the diffusion progresses, the matrix $\mathbf{M}$ tends to be denser. In this case, the solution $\mathbf{M}$ can be directly sparsified by assigning selected elements of $\mathbf{M}$ with zero. In our experiments, we sparsified $\mathbf{M}$ by replacing it with $\mathbf{M} \circ (I^w)^2$ where $\circ$ is the Hadamard product and $I_{ij}^w = 1$ if $w_{ij} > 0$ and $I_{ij}^w = 0$ otherwise. In contrast, the analytical solution (Eq. 21) leads to a dense matrix, and therefore it cannot be straightforwardly applied to large-scale problems.

5   Experimental Results

Setup. We evaluate the performance of our Laplacian regularization framework with *AND* (Algorithm 1): the anisotropic non-linear diffusion of the diffusivity operator L^D. To facilitate the comparison of linear and non-linear diffusion processes on L^D, we also implemented *ALD*: the linearization of *AND*, where the evolution of L^D is performed only once at the beginning of the **f**-diffusion and held fixed thereafter. To assess the role of Laplacian diffusion itself, we compared with three different diffusion-based semi-supervised learning algorithms. The isotropic diffusion algorithm (*Iso*) uses a fixed L throughout the optimization, while the linear anisotropic diffusion algorithm (*AL* [7]) constructs an anisotropic Laplacian L^D which is fixed throughout the subsequent **f** optimization. The non-linear anisotropic diffusion algorithm (*AN* [2]) updates L^D during the **f**-optimization but L^D itself is not diffused. For all experiments, the initial graphs were constructed based on k-NNs using a Gaussian weight function (Eq. 5).

We also conduct comparison with existing semi-supervised learning algorithms including Zhou *et al.*'s local and global consistency algorithm (*LGC* [1]), Zhang and Ando's algorithm that takes powers of Laplacian (*p-L* [11]), and Wang and Zhang's linear neighborhood propagation algorithm (*LNP* [22]). *LGC* is equivalent to constructing an analytical solution as the limit case of *Iso* while *p-L* implements the high-order regularization, which is equivalent to Zhou and Belkin's iterated Laplacian-based algorithm [21]. All four anisotropic diffusion-based algorithms compared in the experiments construct L^D based on evaluations of **f**. However, in general, the regularizer can be constructed based on any a priori knowledge available on the problem. *LNP* calculates a new Laplacian by representing each point in X based on a convex combination of its neighbors and assigns the corresponding combination coefficients as edge weights $\{w_{ij}\}$.

All algorithms evaluated in this section requires the nearest neighbor size k which was regarded as a hyper-parameter. Also, all algorithms except for *LNP*,

Table 1. Performances of different semi-supervised learning algorithms: Error rates (standard deviations). The three best results are highlighted with **boldface blue**, *italic green*, and plain orange fonts, respectively. The last row is a percent error difference from the lowest possible error, averaged across all datasets. The intuition is that a technique achieving 100 % would be best performing in all datasets

	LGC [1]		p-L [11]		LNP [22]		Iso		AL [7]		AN [2]		ALD (ours)		AND (ours)	
USPS	7.03	(2.30)	4.07	(1.28)	8.71	(1.82)	7.52	(1.45)	6.00	(2.20)	4.35	(1.38)	4.09	(0.47)	**3.28**	(0.47)
COIL	7.65	(2.56)	9.95	(2.82)	**6.31**	(2.03)	8.24	(1.31)	8.45	(1.24)	7.53	(0.74)	7.63	(0.93)	6.76	(1.61)
COIL 2	1.53	(1.60)	0.80	(0.86)	2.53	(1.18)	0.45	(0.32)	0.79	(0.35)	0.39	(0.29)	0.76	(0.26)	**0.33**	(0.21)
PCMAC	12.48	(1.68)	9.56	(1.04)	13.52	(1.40)	12.34	(1.89)	13.54	(1.14)	13.46	(2.21)	10.98	(0.82)	**8.96**	(2.00)
Text	25.59	(3.44)	**22.33**	(1.89)	36.31	(3.38)	28.72	(2.13)	27.01	(1.51)	26.87	(2.00)	23.89	(2.28)	23.09	(2.07)
ETH	10.92	(1.14)	10.05	(0.93)	13.34	(2.28)	11.62	(1.03)	11.27	(1.18)	10.04	(0.88)	**9.96**	(0.77)	10.11	(0.85)
Cal101	53.41	(0.56)	53.41	(0.56)	65.52	(0.59)	53.22	(0.64)	52.36	(0.71)	**52.23**	(0.87)	52.26	(0.76)	52.26	(0.75)
MNIST	4.50	(0.49)	3.66	(0.16)	5.44	(0.47)	5.08	(0.25)	4.92	(0.24)	3.72	(0.28)	4.72	(0.20)	**3.65**	(0.18)
MPEG7	2.93	(0.27)	2.90	(0.08)	N/A	(N/A)	3.33	(0.56)	3.11	(0.52)	2.87	(0.53)	2.71	(0.19)	**2.69**	(0.12)
SwL	**2.29**	(0.38)	**2.29**	(0.52)	N/A	(N/A)	2.45	(0.47)	2.54	(0.24)	2.45	(0.44)	2.35	(0.21)	2.38	(0.29)
Avg. %	159.72		124.21		231.72		135.11		140.30		115.71		123.82		**101.60**	

requires determining the scale of the input kernel h (Eq. 5). Adopting the experimental convention of Bühler and Hein [23], h was adaptively determined for each point $\mathbf{x}_i \in X$ such that h_i becomes half of the mean distance from $\mathbf{x}_i$ to its k-nearest neighbors. For all diffusion-based algorithms (*Iso, AL, AN, ALD,* and *AND*), the number of iterations T_1 and the time step size δ have to be determined. Our preliminary experiments have demonstrated that the performance of these algorithms are not significantly affected by δ when it is smaller than around 0.2. We fix δ at 0.1 throughout the entire experiments. Except for the linear diffusion *Iso*, all diffusion algorithms also require determining the output kernel scale h' (Eq. 17). In addition, the proposed diffusion of Laplacian algorithms (*ALD* and *AND*) have the number of Laplacian diffusion T_2 as a hyper-parameter. *LGC* has a regularization hyper-parameter which has a similar role to T_1 in the diffusion-based algorithms. *LNP* has a similar hyper-parameter α (See [22]). In addition, *p-L* has the power p as an additional hyper-parameter. Throughout the entire experiments, each training dataset is divided into equally-sized sub-training and validation datasets and the hyper-parameters were tuned based on measuring the validation error. For all experiments with diffusion algorithms, we tune the hyper-parameters of *Iso* first. Then, the parameters of the remaining diffusion algorithms were chosen by restricting the search space of k only at the vicinity of the optimal value (based on the validation error) for *Iso*. Furthermore, the search space of h' for *AN, ALD,* and *AND* were similarly determined based on the optimal value of *AL*. This resulted in the total number of *ALD* and *AND* parameter evaluations being only around three times larger than that of *AL*.

We evaluate the performances of all algorithms on ten different datasets: *USPS, COIL, COIL2,* and *Text* datasets are commonly used in assessing the performances of semi-supervised learning algorithms. These sets are obtained from Chapelle *et al.*'s benchmark datasets repository. See [24] for details of experimental settings. The experiments for *MNIST* [25] and *PCMAC* are prepared in the same way.

The Swedish leaf dataset (*SwL*) consists of 1,125 images of 15 different tree species [26]. Following Ling and Jacobs [27] and Kim *et al.* [2], we use Fourier descriptors to represent each object and use 50 labels per class. We use the code and dataset kindly shared by [26]. The *MPEG7* shape dataset [28] contains 70 different object silhouettes, each of which has 200 instances. Following [29], we used the pairwise distance matrix obtained as the results of shape matching [30] to construct the initial Laplacian *L*. For both *SwL* and *MPEG7*, each data point is not explicitly represented. Instead, only the relationships between data points are presented as pairwise distances. For these datasets, the results for *LNP* are not available as it requires explicit data representation. The *ETH-80* dataset consists of 8 different object classes each of which has 410 instances. Each data point is represented by a histogram of oriented gradients, with 50 labels set following conventions [31]. We use the preprocessed dataset kindly provided by [31]. The Caltech101 dataset (*Cal101*) contains 8,677 images of 101 different object categories. We use a combination of GIST, pyramid of histogram of oriented gradients, and local binary patterns as features, as kindly shared by [32]. For all datasets, the experiments were repeated 5 times with random label selections and the results were averaged.

Results. Table 1 summarizes the results. Overall, the baseline isotropic diffusion algorithm (*Iso*) has been significantly improved by anisotropic diffusion algorithms as well as other state-of-the-art algorithms. The linear neighborhood propagation algorithm (*LNP*) and local and global consistency (*LGC*) are the best on *COIL* and *SwL*, respectively. Except for *SwL*, *p-L* constantly outperformed these algorithms, demonstrating the effectiveness of high-order regularization. The performance of *ALD* is roughly on par with *p-L*. This is in accordance with the observation that *ALD* corresponds to an iterative algorithm that optimizes the criteria adopted by *p-L* (Sect. 4). On the other hand, the significantly improved performance of *AND* over *ALD* demonstrates the effect of non-linear Laplacian diffusion.

The general tendency observed among the four anisotropic diffusion algorithms (*AL*, *AN*, *ALD*, and *AND*) is that non-linear diffusion and Laplacian diffusion improve over both linear diffusion and function-only diffusion, respectively. A notable exception is *Cal101* which highlights the main limitations of non-linear diffusion based approaches. While *AN*, *ALD*, *AND* showed the three best performances, all anisotropic diffusion algorithms did not show any noticeable improvement from the isotropic case (*Iso*). This is because the initial labeling based on isotropic diffusion is very noisy (more than 50 % error rate); hence, refining the graph Laplacian based on it as a starting point did not lead to a better diffusion process. Similarly, the results of *LGC* and *p-L* are only comparable to *Iso* while *LNP* is considerably worse.

For *Text* dataset, *p-L* was the best followed by *ALD* and *AND*. These results are obtained based on automatically tuned hyper-parameters. If we use ground-truth hyper-parameters (i.e. keeping the minimal test error during hyper-parameter search), the performance of *AND* is more than 10 % better than *p-L*. This reveals another main limitation of our algorithm *AND*: When the hyper-parameters are tuned properly, AND can lead to significant improvements over the linear (Laplacian) diffusion algorithms and over the corresponding limit case p-Lap. However, AND has one more hyper-parameter than p-L, and so with limited labeled data this can lead to worse performance through overfitting. Similarly, for $MNIST$ dataset, the performance of AND is only marginally better than p-L, but when using ground-truth hyper-parameters the error rate of AND shows a 14% improvement over p-L.

In general, automatically tuning the hyper-parameters in semi-supervised learning is an open problem especially due to the limited number of labeled data points. Nevertheless, our two algorithms ALD and AND are included in the three best algorithms for most datasets even with automatically tuned parameters. The effectiveness of our algorithms may be improved in interactive scenarios, where users inspect different parameter combinations and chooses ones best-suited to their problem of interest.

6   Conclusions

The success of anisotropic diffusion in semi-supervised learning problems suggests that adaptively tuning the regularizer to the problem and data can be beneficial. However, existing algorithms did not regularize the regularizer itself. We demonstrated that this idea does lead to improved semi-supervised learning performance. Our framework builds upon the equivalence of inducing anisotropic diffusion and metric construction on Riemannian manifolds: Regularizing the regularizer boils down to regularizing the Riemannian metric tensor on manifolds. Instead of directly regularizing the metric tensor (which is a very difficult problem when the manifold itself is not directly available), we regularize the diffusivity operator on a graph. Our analysis shows that the resulting discrete regularizer converges to the analytical regularizer on metric on Riemannian manifolds. The resulting linear and non-linear anisotropic Laplacian diffusion algorithms significantly outperforms classical diffusion-based algorithms as well as the state-of-the-art semi-supervised learning algorithms.

Acknowledgment. We thank James Tompkin for fruitful discussions and comments, and EPSRC for grant EP/M00533X/1.

References

1. Zhou, D., Bousquet, O., Lal, T.N., Weston, J., Schölkopf, B.: Learning with local and global consistency. In: NIPS, pp. 321–328 (2003)
2. Kim, K.I., Tompkin, J., Pfister, H., Theobalt, C.: Context-guided diffusion for label propagation on graphs. In: Proceedings of the IEEE ICCV, pp. 2776–2784 (2015)
3. Hein, M., Audibert, J.Y., von Luxburg, U.: Graph Laplacians and their convergence on random neighborhood graphs. JMLR **8**, 1325–1368 (2007)
4. Belkin, M., Niyogi, P.: Towards a theoretical foundation for Laplacian-based manifold methods. J. Comput. Syst. Sci. **74**(8), 1289–1308 (2005)

5. Weickert, J.: Anisotropic Diffusion in Image Processing. ECMI Series. Teubner-Verlag, Stuttgart (1998)
6. Clarenz, U., Diewald, U., Rumpf, M.: Anisotropic geometric diffusion in surface processing. In: Proceedings of the Visualization, pp. 397–405 (2000)
7. Szlam, A.D., Maggioni, M., Coifman, R.R.: Regularization on graphs with function-adapted diffusion processes. JMLR **9**, 1711–1739 (2008)
8. Tschumperlé, D., Deriche, R.: Diffusion tensor regularization with constraints preservation. In: Proceedings of the IEEE CVPR, pp. I948–I953 (2001)
9. Castaño-Moraga, C.A., Lenglet, C., Deriche, R., Ruiz-Alzola, J.: A Riemannian approach to anisotropic filtering of tensor fields. Sig. Process. **87**(2), 263–276 (2007)
10. Singer, A., Wu, H.T.: Vector diffusion maps and the connection Laplacian. Commun. Pure Appl. Math. **65**(8), 1067–1144 (2012)
11. Zhang, T., Ando, R.: Analysis of spectral kernel design based semi-supervised learning. In: NIPS, pp. 1601–1608 (2006)
12. Johnson, R., Zhang, T.: Graph-based semi-supervised learning and spectral kernel design. IEEE Trans. Inf. Theor. **54**(1), 275–288 (2008)
13. Kim, K.I., Tompkin, J., Theobald, M., Kautz, J., Theobalt, C.: Match graph construction for large image databases. In: Fitzgibbon, A., Lazebnik, S., Perona, P., Sato, Y., Schmid, C. (eds.) ECCV 2012. LNCS, vol. 7572, pp. 272–285. Springer, Heidelberg (2012). doi:10.1007/978-3-642-33718-5_20
14. Szummer, M., Yilmaz, E.: Semi-supervised learning to rank with preference regularization. In: Proceedings of the ACM CIKM, pp. 269–278 (2011)
15. Fan, M.K.H., Nekooie, B.: On minimizing the largest eigenvalue of a symmetric matrix. Linear Algebra Appl. **214**, 225–246 (1995)
16. Boyd, S., Yang, Q.: Structured and simultaneous Lyapunov functions for system stability problems. Int. J. Control **49**(6), 2215–2240 (1989)
17. Hein, M.: Geometrical Aspects of Statistical Learning Theory. Ph.d. thesis, Fachbereich Informatik, Technische Universität Darmstadt, Germany (2005)
18. Coifman, R.R., Lafon, S.: Diffusion maps. Appl. Comput. Harmonic Anal. **21**(1), 5–30 (2006)
19. Rosenberg, S.: The Laplacian on a Riemannian Manifold. Cambridge University Press, Cambridge (1997)
20. Hein, M., Audibert, J.-Y., von Luxburg, U.: From graphs to manifolds – weak and strong pointwise consistency of graph Laplacians. In: Auer, P., Meir, R. (eds.) COLT 2005. LNCS (LNAI), vol. 3559, pp. 470–485. Springer, Heidelberg (2005)
21. Zhou, X., Belkin, M.: Semi-supervised learning by higher order regularization. In: JMLR W&CP (Proceedings of AISTATS), pp. 892–900 (2011)
22. Wang, F., Zhang, C.: Label propagation through linear neighborhoods. In: Proceedings of ICML, pp. 985–992 (2006)
23. Bühler, T., Hein, M.: Spectral clustering based on the graph p-Laplacian. In: Proceedings of ICML, pp. 81–88 (2009)
24. Chapelle, O., Schölkopf, B., Zien, A.: Semi-Supervised Learning. MIT Press, Cambridge (2010). Datasets: http://olivier.chapelle.cc/ssl-book/benchmarks.html
25. LeCun, Y., Bottou, L., Bengio, Y., Haffner, P.: Gradient-based learning applied to document recognition. Proc. IEEE **86**(11), 2278–2324 (1998)
26. Söderkvist, O.: Computer Vision Classification of Leaves from Swedish Trees. Ph.d. thesis, Master thesis, Linköping University, Sweden (2001). Datasets: http://www.dabi.temple.edu/~hbling/code_data.htm
27. Ling, H., Jacobs, D.W.: Shape classification using the inner-distance. IEEE T-PAMI **29**(2), 286–299 (2007)

28. Latecki, L.J., Lakämper, R., Eckhardt, U.: Shape descriptors for non-rigid shapes with a single closed contour. In: Proceedings of the IEEE CVPR, pp. 424–429 (2000)

29. Donoser, M., Bischof, H.: Diffusion processes for retrieval revisited. In: Proceedings of the IEEE CVPR, pp. 1320–1327 (2013)

30. Gopalan, R., Turaga, P., Chellappa, R.: Diffusion processes for retrieval revisited. In: Proceedings of the ECCV, pp. 286–299 (2010). Datasets: http://www.dabi.temple.edu/~hbling/code_data.htm

31. Ebert, S., Fritz, M., Schiele, B.: RALF: a reinforced active learning formulation for object class recognition. In: Proceedings of the IEEE CVPR, pp. 3626–3633 (2012)

32. Dai, D., Gool, L.V.: Ensemble projection for semi-supervised image classification. In: Proceedings of the IEEE ICCV, pp. 2072–2079 (2013). Datasets: http://people.ee.ethz.ch/~daid/EnPro/

Improving Semantic Embedding Consistency by Metric Learning for Zero-Shot Classiffication

Maxime Bucher[1,2(✉)], Stéphane Herbin[1(✉)], and Frédéric Jurie[2(✉)]

[1] ONERA - The French Aerospace Lab, Palaiseau, France
{maxime.bucher,stephane.herbin}@onera.fr
[2] Normandie Univ, UNICAEN, ENSICAEN, CNRS, Caen, France
frederic.jurie@unicaen.fr

Abstract. This paper addresses the task of zero-shot image classification. The key contribution of the proposed approach is to control the semantic embedding of images – one of the main ingredients of zero-shot learning – by formulating it as a metric learning problem. The optimized empirical criterion associates two types of sub-task constraints: metric discriminating capacity and accurate attribute prediction. This results in a novel expression of zero-shot learning not requiring the notion of class in the training phase: only pairs of image/attributes, augmented with a consistency indicator, are given as ground truth. At test time, the learned model can predict the consistency of a test image with a given set of attributes, allowing flexible ways to produce recognition inferences. Despite its simplicity, the proposed approach gives state-of-the-art results on four challenging datasets used for zero-shot recognition evaluation.

Keywords: Zero-shot learning · Attributes · Semantic embedding

1 Introduction

This paper addresses the question of zero-shot learning (ZSL) image classification, i.e., the classification of images belonging to classes not represented by the training examples. This problem has attracted much interest in the last decade because of its clear practical impact: in many applications, having access to annotated data for the categories considered is often difficult, and requires new ways to increase the interpretation capacity of automated recognition systems. The efficiency of ZSL relies on the existence of an intermediate representation level, effortlessly understandable by human designers and sufficiently formal to be the support of algorithmic inferences. Most of the studies have so far considered this representation in the form of *semantic attributes* mainly because it provides an easy way to describe compact yet discriminative descriptions of new classes.

It has also been observed [1,2] that attribute representations as provided by humans may not be the ideal embedding space because it can lack the informational quality necessary to conduct reliable inferences: the structure of the

© Springer International Publishing AG 2016
B. Leibe et al. (Eds.): ECCV 2016, Part V, LNCS 9909, pp. 730–746, 2016.
DOI: 10.1007/978-3-319-46454-1_44

attribute manifold for a given data distribution may be rather complex, redundant, noisy and unevenly organized. Attribute descriptions, although semantically meaningful and useful to introduce a new category, are not necessarily isomorphic to image data or to image processing outputs.

To compensate for the shortcomings induced by attribute representations, the recent trends in ZSL studies are aiming at better controlling the classification inference as well as the attribute prediction in the learning criteria. Indeed, if attribute classifiers are learned independently of the final classification task, as in the Direct Attribute Prediction model [3], they might be optimal at predicting attributes but not necessarily at predicting novel classes.

In the work proposed in this paper, we instead suggest that better controlling the structure of the embedding attribute space is at least as important than constraining the classification inference step. The fundamental idea is to empirically disentangle the attribute distribution by learning a metric able to both select and transform the original data distribution according to informational criteria. This metric is obtained by optimizing an objective function based on pairs of attributes/images without assuming that the training images are assigned to categories; only the semantic annotations are used during training. More specifically, we empirically validated the idea that optimizing jointly the attribute embedding and the classification metric, in a multi-objective framework, is what makes the performance better, even with a simple linear embedding and distance to mean attribute classification.

The approach is experimentally validated on 4 recent datasets for zero-shot recognition, i.e. the 'aPascal&aYahoo', 'Animals with Attributes', 'CUB-200-2011 and 'SUN attribute' datasets for which excellent results are obtained, despite the simplicity of the approach.

The rest of the paper is organized as follows: Sect. 2 presents the related works, Sect. 3 describes the proposed approach while the experimental validation is given in Sect. 4.

2   Related Work

2.1   Visual Features and Semantic Attributes

Image representation – i.e. the set of mechanisms allowing to transform image raw pixel intensities into representations suitable for recognition tasks – plays an important role in image classification. State-of-the art image representations were, a couple of years ago, mainly based on the pooling of hard/soft quantized local descriptors (e.g. SIFT [4]) through the bag-of-words [5] of Fisher vectors [6] models. However, the work of Krizhevsky et al. [7] has opened a new area and most of the state-of-the-art image descriptors nowadays rely on Deep Convolutional Neural Networks (CNN). We follow this trend in our experiments and use the so-called 'VGG-VeryDeep-19' (4096-dim) descriptors of [8].

Two recent papers have exhibited existing links between CNN features and semantic attributes. Ozeki et al. [9] showed that some CNN units can predict some semantic attributes of the 'Animals with Attributes' dataset fairly accurately. One interesting conclusion of their paper is that the visual semantic attributes can be predicted much more accurately than the non-visual ones by the nodes of the CNN. More recently, [10] showed the existence of Attribute Centric Nodes (ACNs) within CNNs trained to recognize objects, collectively encoding information pertinent to visual attributes, unevenly and sparsely distributed across all the layers of the network.

Despite these recent findings could certainly make the performance of our method better, we don't use them in our experiments and stick to the use of standard CNN features, with the intention of making our results directly comparable to the recent zero-shot learning papers (e.g. [11]).

2.2   Describing Images by Semantic and Non-semantic Attributes

Zero-shot learning methods rely on the use of intermediate representations, usually given as *attributes*. This term can, however, encompass different concepts. For Lampert *et al.* [12] it denotes the presence/absence of a given object property, assuming that attributes are *nameable* properties (color or presence or absence of a certain part, etc.). The advantage of so-defined attributes is that they can be used easily to define new classes expressed by a shared semantic vocabulary.

However, finding a discriminative and meaningful set of attributes can sometimes be difficult. [13,14] addressed this issue by proposing an interactive approach that discovers local attributes both discriminative and semantically meaningful, employing a recommender system that selects attributes through human interactions. An alternative for identifying attribute vocabulary without human labeling is to mine existing textual description of images sampled from the Internet, such as proposed by [15]. In the same line of thought, [16] presented a model for classifying unseen categories from their (already existing) textual description. [17] proposed an approach for zero-shot learning where the description of unseen categories comes in the form of typical text such as an encyclopedia entries, without the need to explicitly define attributes.

Another drawback of human generated attributes is that they can be redundant or not adapted to image classification. These issues have been addressed by automatically designing discriminative category-level attributes and using them for tasks of cross-category knowledge transfer, such as in the work of Yu *et al.* [18]. Finally, the attributes can also be structured into hierarchies [19–21] or obtained by text mining or textual descriptions [16,17,21].

Beside these papers which all consider attributes as meaningful for humans, some authors denoted by attributes any latent space providing an intermediate representation between image and hidden descriptions that can be used to transfer information to images from unseen classes. This is typically the case of [22] which jointly learn the attribute classifiers and the attribute vectors, with the intention of obtaining a better attribute-level representation, converting undetectable and redundant attributes into discriminative ones while retaining the useful semantic attributes. [23] has also introduced the concept of *discriminative attributes*, taking the form of random comparisons. The space of class names can also constitute an interesting embedding, such as in the works of [11,24–26] which represent images as mixtures of known classes distributions.

Finally, it worth pointing out that the aforementioned techniques are restricting attributes to categorical labels and dont allow the representation of more general semantic relationships. To counter this limitation, [27] proposed to model relative attributes by learning a ranking function.

2.3 Zero Shot Learning from Semantic and Attribute Embedding

As defined by [28], the problem of zero-shot learning can be seen as the problem of learning a classifier $f : x \rightarrow y$ that can predict novel values of y not available in the training set. Most of existing methods rely on the computation of a similarity or *consistency function* linking image descriptors and the semantic description of the classes. These links are given by learning two embeddings – the first from the image representation to semantic space and the second from the class space to the semantic space – and defining a way to describe the constraints between the class space and the image space, the two being strongly interdependent.

DAP (Direct Attribute Prediction) and Indirect attribute prediction (IAP), first proposed by [3], use the between layer of attributes as variables decoupling the images from the layer of labels. In DAP, independent attribute predictors are used to build the embedding of the image, the similarity between two semantic representations (one predicted from the image representation, one given by the class) being given as the probability of the class attribute knowing the image. In IAP, attributes form a connecting layer between two layers of labels, one for classes that are known at training time and one for classes that are not known. In this case, attributes are predicted from (known) class predictions. Lampert *et al.* [3] concluded that DAP gives much better performance than IAP.

However, as mentioned in the introduction, DAP has two problems: first, it does not model any correlation between attributes, each being predicted independently. Second, the mapping between classes and the attribute space does not weight the relative importance of the attributes nor the correlations between them. Inspired by [29], which learns a linear embedding between image features and annotations, [2,30] tried to overcome this limitation. The work of Akata *et al.* [30] introduced a function measuring the consistency between an image and a label embedding, the parameters of this function is learned to ensure that, given an image, the correct classes rank higher than the incorrect ones. This consistency function has the form of a bilinear relation W associating the image embedding $\theta(x)$ and the label representation $\phi(y)$ as $S(x, y; W) = \theta(x)^t W \phi(y)$. Romera *et al.* [2] proposed a simple closed form solution for W, assuming a specific form of regularization is chosen. In comparison to our work none of the two papers [2,30] use a metric learning framework to control the statistical structure of the attribute embedding space.

The coefficients of the consistency constraint W can be also predicted from a semantic textual description of the image. As an example, the goal of [17] is to predict a classifier for a new category based only on the learned classes and a textual description of this category. They solve this problem as a regression function, learnt from the textual feature domain to the visual classifier domain. [16] builds on these ideas, extending them by using a more expressive regression function based on a deep neural network. They take advantage of the architecture of CNNs and learn features at different layers, rather than just learning an embedding space for both modalities. The proposed model provides means to automatically generate a list of pseudo-attributes for each visual category consisting of words from Wikipedia articles.

In contrast with the aforementioned methods, Hamm et al. [31] introduced the idea of ordinal similarity between classes (eg. d('cat','dog') < d('cat', 'automobile')), claiming that not only this type of similarity may be sufficient for distinguishing cat and truck, but also that it seems a more natural representation since the ordinal similarity is invariant under scaling and monotonic transformation of numerical values. It is also worth mentioning the work of Jayaraman *et al.* [32] which proposed to leverage the statistics about each attribute error tendencies within a random forest approach, allowing to train zero-shot models that explicitly account for the unreliability of attribute predictions.

Wu *et al.* [33] exploit natural language processing technologies to generate event descriptions. They measure their similarity to images by projecting them into a common high-dimensional space using text expansion. The similarity is expressed as the concatenation of L_2 distances of the different modalities considered. Strictly speaking, there is no metric learning involved but a concatenation of L_2 distances. Finally, Frome *et al.* [34] aim at leveraging semantic knowledge learned in the text domain, and transfer it to a model trained for visual object recognition by learning a metric aligning the two modalities. However, in contrast to our work, [33,34] do not explicitly control the quality of the embedding.

2.4   Zero-Shot Learning as Transductive and Semi-supervised Learning

All the previously mentioned approaches consider that the embedding and the consistency function have to be learned from a set of training data of known classes, used in a second time to infer predictions about the images of new classes not available during training. However, a different problem can be addressed when images from the unknown classes are already available at training time and can hence be used to produce a better embedding. In this case, the problem can be cast as a transductive learning problem i.e. the inference of the correct labels for the given unlabeled data only, or a semi-supervised learning problem i.e. the inference of the best embedding using both labeled and unlabeled data.

Wang and Forsyth [35] proposed MIL framework for jointly learning attributes and object classifiers from weakly annotated data. Wang and Mori [22] treated attributes of an object as latent variables and captured the correlations among attributes using an undirected graphical model, allowing to infer object class labels using the information of both the test image and its (latent) attributes. In [1], the class information is incorporated into the attribute classifier to get an attribute-level representation that generalizes well to unseen examples of known classes as well as those of the unseen classes, assuming unlabeled images are available for learning. [36] considered the introduction of unseen classes as a novelty detection problem in a multi-class classification problem. If the image is of a known category, a standard classifier can be used. Otherwise, images are assigned to a class based on the likelihood of being an unseen category. Fu *et al.* [37] rectified the projection domain shift between auxiliary and target datasets by introducing a multi-view semantic space alignment process to correlate different semantic views and the low-level feature view, by projecting them onto a latent embedding space learnt using multi-view Canonical Correlation Analysis. More recently Li *et al.* [38] learned the embedding from the input data in a semi-supervised large-margin learning framework, jointly considering multi-class classification over observed and unseen classes. Finally, [39] formulated a regularized sparse coding framework which used the target domain class label projections in the semantic space to regularize the learnt target domain projection, with the aim of overcoming the projection domain shift problem.

2.5   Zero-Shot Learning as a Metric Learning Problem

Two contributions, [40,41], exploit metric learning to Zero shot class description. Mensink *et al.* [40] learn a metric adapted to measure the similarity of images, in the context of k-nearest neighbor image classification, and apply it in fact to One Shot Learning to show it can generalize well to new classes. They don't use any attribute embedding space nor consider ZSL in their work. Kuznetsova *et al.* [41] learn a metric to infer pose and object class from a single image. They use the expression *zero-shot* to actually denote a (new) transfer learning problem when data are unevenly sampled in the joint pose and class space, and not a Zero-Shot Classification problem where new classes are only known from attribute descriptions.

As far as we know, zero-shot learning has never been addressed explicitly as a metric learning problem in the attribute embedding space, which is one of the key contributions of this paper.

3   Method

3.1   Embedding Consistency Score

Most of the inference problems can be cast into an optimal framework of the form:

$$\mathbf{Y}^* = \arg\min_{\mathbf{Y} \in \mathcal{Y}} S(\mathbf{X}, \mathbf{Y})$$

where $\mathbf{X} \in \mathcal{X}$ is a given sample from some modality, e.g. an image or some features extracted from it, $\mathbf{Y}^*$ is the most consistent association from another modality $\mathcal{Y}$, *e.g.* a vector of attribute indicators or a textual description, and S is a measure able to quantify the joint consistency of two observations from the two modalities. In this formulation, the smaller the score, the more consistent the samples. One can think of this score as a negative likelihood.

When trying to design such a consistency score, one of the difficult aspects is to relate meaningfully the two modalities. One usual approach consists in embedding them into a common representational space $\mathcal{A}$[1] where their heterogeneous nature can be compared. This space can be abstract, i.e. its structure can be obtained from some optimization process, or semantically interpretable e.g. a fixed list of attributes or properties each indexed by a tag referring to some shared knowledge or ontology, leading to a p-dimensional vector space. Let $\hat{\mathbf{A}}_X(\mathbf{X})$ and $\hat{\mathbf{A}}_Y(\mathbf{Y})$ be the two embeddings for each modality X and Y, taking values in $\mathcal{X}$ and $\mathcal{Y}$ and producing outputs in $\mathcal{A}$.

In this work, it is proposed to define the consistency score as a metric on the common embedding space $\mathcal{A}$. More precisely, we use the Mahalanobis like description of a metric parametrized by a linear mapping $\mathbf{W}_A$:

$$d_A(\mathbf{A}_1, \mathbf{A}_2) = \left\| (\mathbf{A}_1 - \mathbf{A}_2)^T \mathbf{W}_A \right\|_2,$$

assuming that the embedding space is a vector space, and define the consistency score as:

$$S(\mathbf{X}, \mathbf{Y}) = d_A(\hat{\mathbf{A}}_X(\mathbf{X}), \hat{\mathbf{A}}_Y(\mathbf{Y})) = \left\| (\hat{\mathbf{A}}_X(\mathbf{X}) - \hat{\mathbf{A}}_Y(\mathbf{Y}))^T \mathbf{W}_A \right\|_2.$$

The Mahalanobis mapping $\mathbf{W}_A$ can be interpreted itself as a linear embedding in an abstract m-dimensional vector space where the natural metric is the Euclidean distance, and acts as a multivariate whitening filter. It is expected that this property will improve empirically the reliability of the consistency score (1) by choosing the appropriate linear mapping.

We are now left with two questions: how to define the embedding? How build the Mahalanobis mapping? We see in the following that these two questions can be solved jointly by optimizing a unique criterion.

3.2   Embedding in the Attribute Space

The main problem addressed in this work is to be able to discriminate a series of new hypotheses that can only be specified using a single modality, the Y one with our notations. In many Zero-Shot Learning studies, this modality is often expressed as the existence or presence of several attributes or properties from a fixed given set. The simplest embedding space one can think of is precisely this attribute space, implying that the Y modality embedding is the identity: $\hat{\mathbf{A}}_Y(\mathbf{Y}) = \mathbf{Y}$ with $\mathcal{A} = \mathcal{Y}$. In this case, the consistency score simplifies as:

$$S(\mathbf{X}, \mathbf{Y}) = \left\| (\hat{\mathbf{A}}_X(\mathbf{X}) - \mathbf{Y})^T \mathbf{W}_A \right\|_2 \tag{1}$$

The next step is to embed the X modality into Y directly. We suggest using a simple linear embedding with matrix $\mathbf{W}_X$ and bias $\mathbf{b}_X$, assuming that X is in a d-dimensional vector space. This can be expressed as:

$$\hat{\mathbf{A}}_X(\mathbf{X}) = \max(0, \mathbf{X}^T \mathbf{W}_X + \mathbf{b}_X). \tag{2}$$

---

[1] We use the letters A and $\mathcal{A}$ in our notations since we will focus on the space of *attribute* descriptions as the embedding space.

We use a reLu-type output normalization to keep the significance of the attribute space as property detectors, negative numbers being difficult to interpret in this context.

In the simple formulation proposed here, we do not question the way new hypotheses are specified in the target modality, nor use any external source of information (e.g. word vectors) to map the attributes into a more semantically organized space such as in [36]. We leave the problem of correcting the original attribute description to the construction of the metric in the common embedding space.

3.3   Metric Learning

The design problem is now reduced to the estimation of three mathematical objects: the linear embedding to the attribute space $\mathbf{W}_X$ of dimensions $d \times p$, a bias $\mathbf{b}_X$ of dimension p, and the Mahalanobis linear mapping $\mathbf{W}_A$ of dimensions $p \times m$, m being a free parameter to choose.

The proposed approach consists in building empirically those objects from a set of examples by appling metric learning techniques. The training set is supposed to contain pairs of data $(\mathbf{X}_i, \mathbf{Y}_i)$ sampling the joint distribution of the two modalities: $\mathbf{X}_i$ is a vector representing an image or some features extracted from it, while $\mathbf{Y}_i$ denotes an attribute-based description. Notice that we do not introduce any class information in this formulation: the link between class and attribute representations is assumed to be specified by the use case considered.

The rationale behind the use of metric learning is to transform the original representational space so that the resulting metric takes into account the statistical structure of the data using pairwise constraints. One usual way to do so is to express the problem as a binary classification on pairs of samples, where the role of the metric is to separate similar and dissimilar samples by thresholding (see [42] for a survey on M.L.). It is easy to build pairs of similar and dissimilar examples from the annotated examples by sampling randomly (uniformly or according to some law) the two modalities $\mathcal{X}$ and $\mathcal{Y}$ and assigning an indicator $Z \in \{-1, 1\}$ stating whether $\mathbf{Y}_i$ is a good attribute description of $\mathbf{X}_i$ ($Z_i = 1$) or not ($Z_i = -1$). Metric learning approaches try to catch a data-dependent way to encode similarity. In general, the data manifold has a smaller intrinsic dimension than the feature space, and is not isotropically distributed.

We are now given a dataset of triplets $\{(\mathbf{X}_i, \mathbf{Y}_i, Z_i)\}_{i=1}^{N}$, the Z indicator stating that the two modalities are similar, i.e. consistent, or not[2]. The next step is to describe an empirical criterion that will be able to learn $\mathbf{W}_X$, $\mathbf{b}_X$ and $\mathbf{W}_A$. The idea is to decompose the problem in three objectives: metric learning, good embedding and regularization.

The metric learning part follows a now standard hinge loss approach [43] taking the following form for each sample:

$$l_H(\mathbf{X}_i, \mathbf{Y}_i, Z_i, \tau) = \max\left(0, 1 - Z_i(\tau - S(\mathbf{X}_i, \mathbf{Y}_i)^2)\right). \tag{3}$$

---

[2] To make notations simpler, we do not rename or re-index from the original dataset the pairs of data for the similar and dissimilar cases.

The extra parameter τ is free and can also be learned from data. Its role is to define the threshold separating similar from dissimilar examples, and should depend on the data distribution.

The embedding criterion is a simple quadratic loss, but only applied to similar data:

$$l_A(\mathbf{X}_i, \mathbf{Y}_i, Z) = \max(0, Z_i). \left\| \mathbf{Y}_i - \hat{\mathbf{A}}_X(\mathbf{X}_i) \right\|_2^2. \tag{4}$$

Its role is to ensure that the attribute prediction is of good quality, so that the difference $\mathbf{Y} - \hat{\mathbf{A}}_X(\mathbf{X})$ reflects dissimilarity due to modality inconsistencies rather than bad representational issues.

The size of the learning problem $(d \times p + p + p \times m)$ can be large and requires regularization to prevent over fitting. We use a quadratic penalization:

$$R(\mathbf{W}_A, \mathbf{W}_X, \mathbf{b}_X) = \|\mathbf{W}_X\|_F^2 + \|\mathbf{b}_X\|_2^2 + \|\mathbf{W}_A\|_F^2 \tag{5}$$

where $\|.\|_F$ is the Frobenius norm.

The overall optimization criterion can now be written as the sum of the previously defined terms:

$$\mathcal{L}(\mathbf{W}_A, \mathbf{W}_X, \mathbf{b}_X, \tau) = \sum_i l_H(\mathbf{X_i}, \mathbf{Y_i}, Z_i, \tau) + \lambda \sum_i l_A(\mathbf{X_i}, \mathbf{Y_i}, Z_i)$$
$$+ \mu R(\mathbf{W}_A, \mathbf{W}_X, \mathbf{b}_X) \tag{6}$$

where λ and μ are hyper-parameters that are chosen using cross-validation. Note that the criterion (6) can also be interpreted as a multi-objective learning approach since it mixes two optimal but dependent issues: attribute embedding and metric on the embedding space.

To solve the optimization problem, we do not follow the approach proposed in [43] since we also learn the attribute embedding part $\mathbf{W}_X$ jointly with the metric embedding $\mathbf{W}_A$. We use instead a global stochastic gradient descent (see Sect. 4 for details).

3.4   Application to Image Recognition and Retrieval

The consistency score (1) is a versatile tool that can be used for several image interpretation problems. Section 4 will evaluate the potential of our approach on three of them.

Zero-Shot Learning. The problem can be defined as finding the most consistent attribute description given the image to classify, and a set of exclusive attribute class descriptors $\{\mathbf{Y}_k^*\}_{k=1}^C$ where k is the index of a class:

$$k^* = \underset{k \in \{1...C\}}{\arg\min} \, S(\mathbf{X}, \mathbf{Y}_k^*) \tag{7}$$

In this formulation, classifying is made equivalent to identifying between the C classes the best attribute description. A variant of this scheme can exploit a voting process to identify the best attribute among a set of k candidates, inspired from a k-nearest neighbor approach.

Few-Shot Learning. Learning a metric in the embedding space can conveniently be used to specialize the consistency score to new data when they are available. We study a simple fine tuning approach using stochastic gradient descent on criterion (6) applied to novel triplets (X, Y, Z) from unseen classes only, starting with the model learned with seen classes. This makes " few-shot learning" possible. The decision framework is identical to the ZSL one.

Zero-Shot Retrieval. The score (1) can also used to retrieve the data from a given database that have at least a consistent level λ with a given query defined in the Y (or A) modality:

$$\text{Retrieve}(\mathbf{A}, \lambda) = \{\mathbf{X} \in \mathcal{X} \, / \, S(\mathbf{X}, \mathbf{A}) < \lambda\}$$

The performance is usually characterized by precision-recall curves.

4   Experiments

This section presents the experimental validation of the proposed method. The section first introduces the 4 datasets evaluated as well as the details of the experimental settings. The method is empirically evaluated on three different tasks as described in Sect. 3: Zero-Shot-Learning (ZSL), Few-Shot Learning (FSL) and Zero-Shot Retrieval (ZSR). The ZSL experiments aim at evaluating the capability of the proposed model to predict unseen classes. This section also evaluates the contribution of the different components of the model to the performance, and makes comparisons with state-of-the-art results. In the FSL experiments, we show how the ZSL model can serve as good prior to learning a classifier when only a few samples of the unknown classes are available. Finally, we evaluate our model on a ZSR task, illustrating the capability of the algorithm to retrieve images using attribute-based queries.

4.1   Datasets and Experimental Settings

The experimental valuation is done on 4 public datasets widely used in the community, allowing to compare our results with those recently proposed in the literature: the aPascal&aYahoo (aP&Y) [23], Animals with Attributes (AwA) [3], CUB-200-2011 (CUB) [44] and SUN attribute (SUN) [45] datasets (see Table 1 for few statistics on their content). Theses datasets exhibit a large number of categories (indoor and outdoor scenes, objects, person, animals, *etc.*) and attributes (shapes, materials, color, parts, *etc.*)

These datasets have been introduced for training and evaluating ZSL methods and contain images annotated with semantic attributes. More specifically, each image of the aP&Y, CUB and SUN datasets has its own attribute description, meaning that two images of the same class can have different attributes. This is not the case for AwA where all the images of a given class share the same attributes. As a consequence, in the ZSL experiments on aP&Y, CUB and SUN,

Table 1. Dataset statistics.

Dataset	#Training classes	#Test classes	#Instances	#Attributes
aPascal & aYahoo [23]	20	12	15,339	64
Animals with Attributes [3]	40	10	30,475	85
CUB 200-2011 [44]	150	50	11,788	312
SUN Attributes [45]	707	10	14,340	102

the attribute representation of unknown classes, required for class prediction, is taken as their mean attribute frequencies.

In order to make comparisons with previous works possible, we use the same training/testing splits as [23] (aP&Y), [3] (AwA), [21] CUB and [32] (SUN).

Regarding the representation of images, we used both the VGG-VeryDeep-19 [8] and AlexNet [7] CNN models, both pre-trained on imageNet – without fine tuning to the attribute datasets – and use the penultimate fully connected layer (*e.g.*, FC7 4096-d layer for VGG-VeryDeep-19) for representing the images. Very deep CNN models act as generic feature extractors and have been demonstrated to work well for object recognition. They have been also used in many recent ZSL experiments and we use exactly the same descriptors as [11,21].

One of the key characteristics of our model is that it requires a set of image/attributes pairs for training. Positive (resp. negative) pairs are obtained by taking the training images associated with their own provided attribute vector (resp. by randomly assigning attributes not present in the image) and are assigned to the class label '1 (resp. -'1). In order to bound the size of the training set we generate only 2 pairs per training image, one positive and one negative.

Our model has three hyper-parameters: the weight λ, the dimensionality of the space in which the distance is computed (m) and the regularization parameters μ. These hyper-parameters are estimated through a grid search validation procedure by randomly keeping 20 % of the training classes for cross-validating the hyper-parameters, and choosing the parameters giving best accuracy for these so-obtained validation classes. The parameter are searched in the following ranges: $m \in [20\%, 120\%]$ of the initial attribute dimension, $\lambda \in [0.05, 1.0]$ and $\mu \in [0.01, 10.0]$. τ is a parameter learned during training.

Once the hyper-parameters are tuned, we take the whole training set to learn the final model and evaluate it on the test set (unseen classes in case of ZSL).

The optimization of $\mathbf{W}_A$ and $\mathbf{W}_X$ is done with stochastic gradient descent, the parameters being initialized randomly with normal distribution. The size of the mini-batch is of 100. As the objective function is non-convex, different initializations can give different parameters. We addressed this issue by doing 5 estimations of the parameters starting from 5 different initializations and selecting the best one on a validation set (we keep a part of the train set for doing this and fine-tune the parameters on the whole train set when the best initialization is known). We use the optimizer provided in the TensorFlow framework [46].

Using the GPU mode with a Nvidia 750 GTX GPU, learning a model ($\mathbf{W}_A$ and $\mathbf{W}_X$) takes 5–10 minutes for a given set of hyper-parameters. Computing image/attribute consistency takes around 4ms per pair.

4.2   Zero-Shot Learning Experiments

The experiments follow the standard ZSL protocol: during training, a set of images from known classes is available for learning the model parameters. At test time, images from unseen classes are processed and the goal is to find the class described by an attribute representation most consistent with the images.

Table 2 gives the performance of our approach on the 4 datasets considered – expressed as multi-class accuracy – and makes comparisons with state-of-the-art approaches. The performances of previous methods are taken from [11,21,47]. Performance is reported with 2 different features i.e. VGG-VeryDeep-19 [8] and AlexNet [7] for fair comparisons. As images of AwA are not public anymore it is only possible to use the features available for download. On the four datasets our model achieves above state-of-the-art performance (note: [47] was published after our submission), with a noticeable improvement of more than 8 % on aP&Y.

Table 2. Zero-shot classification accuracy (mean ± std). We report results both with VGG-verydeep-19 [8] and AlexNet [7] features for fair comparisons, whenever it's possible (AwA images are not public anymore preventing the computation of their AlexNet representations).

Feat	Method	aP&Y	AwA	CUB	SUN
Alex Net [7]	Akata *et al.* [21]	-	61.9	40.3	-
	Ours	46.14±0.91	-	**41.98 ± 0.67**	75.48 ± 0.43
VGG-VeryDeep [8]	Lampert *et al.* [12]	38.16	57.23	-	72.00
	Romera-Paredes *et al.* [2]	24.22 ± 2.89	75.32 ± 2.28	-	82.10 ± 0.32
	Zhang *et al.* [11]	46.23 ± 0.53	76.33 ± 0.83	30.41 ± 0.20	82.50 ± 1.32
	Zhang *et al.* [47]	50.35 ± 2.97	**80.46 ± 0.53**	42.11 ± 0.55	83.83 ± 0.29
	Ours w/o ML	47.25 ± 0.48	73.81 ± 0.13	33.87 ± 0.98	74.91 ± 0.12
	Ours w/o constraint	48.47 ± 1.24	75.69 ± 0.56	38.35 ± 0.49	79.21 ± 0.87
	Ours	**53.15 ± 0.88**	77.32 ± 1.03	**43.29 ± 0.38**	**84.41 ± 0.71**

As explained in the previous section, our model is based on a multi-objective function trying to maximize metric discriminating capacity as well as attribute prediction. It is interesting to observe how the performance degrades when one of the two terms is missing. In Table 2, the 'Ours w/o ML' setting makes use of the Euclidean distance i.e. $\mathbf{W}_A = \mathbb{I}$. The 'Ours w/o constraint' setting is when the attribute prediction term (Eq. 4) is missing in the criterion. This term gives a 4 % improvement, on average.

Figure 1a shows the accuracy as a function of the embedding dimension. This projection maps the original data in a space in which the Euclidean distance is good for the task considered. It can be seen as a way to exploit and select the correlation structure between attributes. We experimented that the best performance is generally obtained when the dimension of this space less than 40 % smaller than the size of the initial attribute space.

4.3 Few-Shot Learning

Few-shot learning corresponds to the situation where 1 (or more) annotated example(s) from unseen classes are available at test time. In this case our model is first trained using only the seen classes (same as with ZSL), and we introduced the examples from unseen class data one by one before fine-tuning the model parameters by doing a few more learning iterations using these new data only.

Figure 1b shows the accuracy evolution, given as a function of the number of additional images from the unseen classes. Please note that for the SUN dataset we have used a maximum of 10 additional examples as unseen classes contain

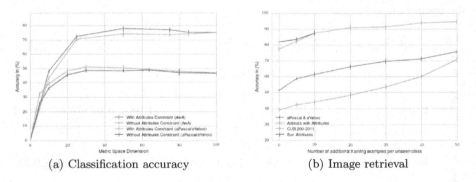

(a) Classification accuracy   (b) Image retrieval

Fig. 1. ZSL accuracy as a function of the dimensionality of the metric space; best results are obtained when the dimension of the metric embedding is less than 40 % of the image space dimension. It also shows the improvement due to the attribute prediction term in the objective function. Few-shot learning: Classification accuracy (%) as a function of the amount of training examples per unseen classes.

Table 3. Zero-Shot Retrieval task: Mean Average Precision (%) on the 4 datasets

	aP&Y	AwA	CUB	SUN	Av
Zhang *et al.* [11]	15.43	46.25	4.69	**58.94**	31.33
Ours (VGG features)	**36.92**	**68.1**	**25.33**	52.68	**45.76**

only 20 images. We observed that knowing even a very few number of annotated examples significantly improves the performance. It is a very encouraging behavior for large-scale applications where annotations for a large number of categories are hard and expensive to get.

4.4   Zero-Shot Retrieval

The task of Zero-Shot image Retrieval consists in searching an image database with attribute-based queries. For doing this, we first train our model as for standard ZSL. We then take the attribute descriptions of unseen classes as queries, and rank the images from the unseen classes based on the similarity with the query. Table 3 reports the mean average precision on the 4 datasets. Our model outperforms the state-of-the-art SEE method [11] by more than 10 % on average.

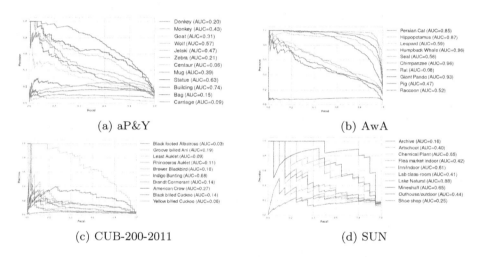

(a) aP&Y   (b) AwA

(c) CUB-200-2011   (d) SUN

Fig. 2. Precision Recall curve for each unseen class by dataset. For CUB dataset we randomly choose 10 classes (best viewed on a computer screen).

Figure 2 shows the average precision for each class of the 4 datasets. In the aP&aYa dataset, the 'donkey', 'centaur' and 'zebra' classes have a very low average precision. This can be explained by the strong visual similarity between these classes which only differ by a few attributes.

5   Conclusion

This paper has presented a novel approach for zero-shot classification exploiting multi-objective metric learning techniques. The proposed formulation has the nice property of not requiring any ground truth at the category level for learning a consistency score between the image and the semantic modalities, but only requiring weak consistency information. The resulting score can be used with versatility on various image interpretation tasks, and shows close or above state-of-the-art performance on four standard benchmarks. The formal simplicity of the approach allows several avenues for future improvement. A first one would be to provide a better embedding on the semantic side of the consistency score $\hat{A}_Y(\mathbf{Y})$. A second one would be to explore more complex functions than the linear mappings tested in this work, and introduce, for instance, deep network architectures.

References

1. Mahajan, D.K., Sellamanickam, S., Nair, V.: A joint learning framework for attribute models and object descriptions. In: IEEE International Conference on Computer Vision (ICCV) (2011)
2. Romera-Paredes, B., Torr, P.H.: An embarrassingly simple approach to zero-shot learning. In: Proceedings of the International Conference on Machine learning. 2152–2161 (2015)
3. Lampert, C.H., Nickisch, H., Harmeling, S.: Learning to detect unseen object classes by between-class attribute transfer. In: IEEE International Conference on Computer Vision and Pattern Recognition (CVPR) (2009)
4. Lowe, D.G.: Distinctive image features from scale-invariant keypoints. Int. J. Comput. Vis. (IJCV) **60**(2), 91–110 (2004)
5. Csurka, G., Dance, C., Fan, L., Willamowski, J., Bray, C.: Visual categorization with bags of keypoints. In: Workshop on statistical learning in computer vision, ECCV, pp. 1–2 (2004)
6. Sánchez, J., Perronnin, F., Mensink, T., Verbeek, J.: Image classification with the Fisher vector: theory and practice. Int. J. Comput. Vis. (IJCV) **105**(3), 222–245 (2013)
7. Krizhevsky, A., Sutskever, I., Hinton, G.E.: ImageNet classification with deep convolutional neural networks. In: Conference on Neural Information Processing Systems (NIPS), pp. 1106–1114 (2012)
8. Simonyan, K., Zisserman, A.: Very deep convolutional networks for large-scale image recognition. In: ICLR (2014)
9. Ozeki, M., Okatani, T.: Understanding convolutional neural networks in terms of category-level attributes. In: Cremers, D., Reid, I., Saito, H., Yang, M.-H. (eds.) ACCV 2014. LNCS, vol. 9004, pp. 362–375. Springer, Heidelberg (2015)
10. Escorcia, V., Niebles, J.C., Ghanem, B.: On the relationship between visual attributes and convolutional networks. In: IEEE International Conference on Computer Vision and Pattern Recognition (CVPR) (2015)
11. Zhang, Z., Saligrama, V.: Zero-shot learning via semantic similarity embedding. In: IEEE International Conference on Computer Vision (ICCV) (2015)
12. Lampert, C.H., Nickisch, H., Harmeling, S.: Attribute-based classification for zero-shot visual object categorization. IEEE Trans. Pattern Anal. Mach. Intell. **36**(3), 453–465 (2014)
13. Parikh, D., Grauman, K.: Interactively building a discriminative vocabulary of nameable attributes. In: IEEE International Conference on Computer Vision and Pattern Recognition (CVPR) (2011)
14. Duan, K., Parikh, D., Crandall, D., Grauman, K.: Discovering localized attributes for fine-grained recognition. In: IEEE International Conference on Computer Vision and Pattern Recognition (CVPR) (2012)

15. Berg, T.L., Berg, A.C., Shih, J.: Automatic attribute discovery and characterization from noisy web data. In: Daniilidis, K., Maragos, P., Paragios, N. (eds.) ECCV 2010, Part I. LNCS, vol. 6311, pp. 663–676. Springer, Heidelberg (2010)
16. Ba, L.J., Swersky, K., Fidler, S., Salakhutdinov, R.: Predicting deep zero-shot convolutional neural networks using textual descriptions. In: 2015 IEEE International Conference on Computer Vision, ICCV 2015, Santiago, Chile, 7–13 December 2015, pp. 4247–4255 (2015)
17. Elhoseiny, M., Saleh, B., Elgammal, A.: Write a classifier: zero-shot learning using purely textual descriptions. In: IEEE International Conference on Computer Vision (ICCV) (2013)
18. Yu, F.X., Cao, L., Feris, R.S., Smith, J.R., Chang, S.F.F.: Designing category-level attributes for discriminative visual recognition. In: IEEE International Conference on Computer Vision (ICCV). IEEE (2013)
19. Verma, N., Mahajan, D., Sellamanickam, S., Nair, V.: Learning hierarchical similarity metrics. In: IEEE International Conference on Computer Vision and Pattern Recognition (CVPR) (2012)
20. Rohrbach, M., Stark, M., Schiele, B.: Evaluating knowledge transfer and zero-shot learning in a large-scale setting. In: IEEE International Conference on Computer Vision and Pattern Recognition (CVPR) (2011)
21. Akata, Z., Reed, S., Walter, D., Lee, H., Schiele, B.: Evaluation of output embeddings for fine-grained image classification. In: IEEE International Conference on Computer Vision and Pattern Recognition (CVPR) (2015)
22. Wang, Y., Mori, G.: A discriminative latent model of object classes and attributes. In: Daniilidis, K., Maragos, P., Paragios, N. (eds.) ECCV 2010, Part V. LNCS, vol. 6315, pp. 155–168. Springer, Heidelberg (2010)
23. Farhadi, A., Endres, I., Hoiem, D., Forsyth, D.: Describing objects by their attributes. In: IEEE International Conference on Computer Vision and Pattern Recognition (CVPR) (2009)
24. Mensink, T., Gavves, E., Snoek, C.G.M.: COSTA: co-occurrence statistics for zero-shot classification. In: IEEE International Conference on Computer Vision and Pattern Recognition (CVPR) (2014)
25. Norouzi, M., Mikolov, T., Bengio, S., Singer, Y., Shlens, J., Frome, A., Corrado, G.S., Dean, J.: Zero-shot learning by convex combination of semantic embeddings. In: International Conference on Learning Representations (ICLR), December 2013
26. Fu, Z., Xiang, T.A., Kodirov, E., Gong, S.: Zero-shot object recognition by semantic manifold distance. In: IEEE International Conference on Computer Vision and Pattern Recognition (CVPR) (2015)
27. Parikh, D., Grauman, K.: Relative attributes. In: IEEE International Conference on Computer Vision (ICCV) (2011)
28. Palatucci, M., Pomerleau, D., Hinton, G.E., Mitchell, T.M.: Zero-shot learning with semantic output codes. In: Conference on Neural Information Processing Systems (NIPS) (2009)
29. Weston, J., Bengio, S., Usunier, N.: WSABIE: scaling up to large vocabulary image annotation. In: IJCAI. 2764–2770. (2011)
30. Akata, Z., Perronnin, F., Harchaoui, Z., Schmid, C.: Label-embedding for image classification. IEEE Trans. Pattern Anal. Mach. Intell. (2015)
31. Hamm, J., Belkin, M.: Probabilistic Zero-shot Classification with Semantic Rankings. arXiv.org, February 2015
32. Jayaraman, D., Grauman, K.: Zero-shot recognition with unreliable attributes. In: Conference on Neural Information Processing Systems (NIPS) (2014)

33. Wu, S., Bondugula, S., Luisier, F., Zhuang, X., Natarajan, P.: Zero-shot event detection using multi-modal fusion of weakly supervised concepts. In: IEEE International Conference on Computer Vision and Pattern Recognition (CVPR) (2014)
34. Frome, A., Corrado, G.S., Shlens, J., Bengio, S., Dean, J., Ranzato, M., Mikolov, T.: DeViSE: a deep visual-semantic embedding model. In: Conference on Neural Information Processing Systems (NIPS) (2013)
35. Wang, G., Forsyth, D.: Joint learning of visual attributes, object classes and visual saliency. In: IEEE International Conference on Computer Vision (ICCV) (2009)
36. Socher, R., Ganjoo, M., Manning, C.D., Ng, A.: Zero-shot learning through cross-modal transfer. In: Conference on Neural Information Processing Systems (NIPS) (2013)
37. Fu, Y., Hospedales, T.M., Xiang, T., Fu, Z., Gong, S.: Transductive multi-view embedding for zero-shot recognition and annotation. In: Fleet, D., Pajdla, T., Schiele, B., Tuytelaars, T. (eds.) ECCV 2014, Part II. LNCS, vol. 8690, pp. 584–599. Springer, Heidelberg (2014)
38. Li, X., Guo, Y., Schuurmans, D.: Semi-supervised zero-shot classification with label representation learning. In: IEEE International Conference on Computer Vision (ICCV) (2015)
39. Kodirov, E., Xiang, T., Fu, Z., Gong, S.: Unsupervised domain adaptation for zero-shot learning. In: IEEE International Conference on Computer Vision (ICCV) (2015)
40. Mensink, T., Verbeek, J., Perronnin, F., Csurka, G.: Metric learning for large scale image classification: generalizing to new classes at near-zero cost. In: Fitzgibbon, A., Lazebnik, S., Perona, P., Sato, Y., Schmid, C. (eds.) ECCV 2012, Part II. LNCS, vol. 7573, pp. 488–501. Springer, Heidelberg (2012)
41. Kuznetsova, A., Hwang, S.J., Rosenhahn, B., Sigal, L.: Exploiting view-specific appearance similarities across classes for zero-shot pose prediction: a metric learning approach. In: Proceedings of the Thirtieth AAAI Conference on Artificial Intelligence, Phoenix, Arizona, USA, 12–17 February 2016, pp. 3523–3529 (2016)
42. Bellet, A., Habrard, A., Sebban, M.: A Survey on Metric Learning for Feature Vectors and Structured Data. Technical report arXiv:1306.6709v4, University of St Etienne (2013)
43. Shalev-Shwartz, S., Singer, Y., Ng, A.Y.: Online and batch learning of pseudo-metrics. In: Proceedings of the International Conference on Machine learning, p. 94. ACM (2004)
44. Wah, C., Branson, S., Welinder, P., Perona, P., Belongie, S.: The Caltech-UCSD Birds-200-2011 Dataset. Technical report, July 2011
45. Patterson, G., Xu, C., Su, H., Hays, J.: The SUN attribute database: beyond categories for deeper scene understanding. Int. J. Comput. Vis. (IJCV) **108**(1–2), 59–81 (2014)
46. Abadi, M., Agarwal, A., Barham, P., Brevdo, E., Chen, Z., Citro, C., Corrado, G.S., Davis, A., Dean, J., Devin, M., Ghemawat, S., Goodfellow, I., Harp, A., Irving, G., Isard, M., Jia, Y., Jozefowicz, R., Kaiser, L., Kudlur, M., Levenberg, J., Mané, D., Monga, R., Moore, S., Murray, D., Olah, C., Schuster, M., Shlens, J., Steiner, B., Sutskever, I., Talwar, K., Tucker, P., Vanhoucke, V., Vasudevan, V., Viégas, F., Vinyals, O., Warden, P., Wattenberg, M., Wicke, M., Yu, Y., Zheng, X.: TensorFlow: Large-scale machine learning on heterogeneous systems Software available from tensorflow.org (2015)
47. Zhang, Z., Saligrama, V.: Zero-shot learning via joint latent similarity embedding. In: IEEE International Conference on Computer Vision and Pattern Recognition (CVPR), pp. 6034–6042 (2016)

A Sequential Approach to 3D Human Pose Estimation: Separation of Localization and Identification of Body Joints

Ho Yub Jung[2], Yumin Suh[1], Gyeongsik Moon[1], and Kyoung Mu Lee[1(✉)]

[1] Department of ECE, ASRI, Seoul National University, Seoul, Korea
{n12345,mks0601,kyoungmu}@snu.ac.kr
[2] Division of CESE, Hankuk University of Foreign Studies, Yongin-si, Korea
jung.ho.yub@gmail.com

Abstract. In this paper, we propose a new approach to 3D human pose estimation from a single depth image. Conventionally, 3D human pose estimation is formulated as a detection problem of the desired list of body joints. Most of the previous methods attempted to simultaneously localize and identify body joints, with the expectation that the accomplishment of one task would facilitate the accomplishment of the other. However, we believe that identification hampers localization; therefore, the two tasks should be solved separately for enhanced pose estimation performance. We propose a two-stage framework that initially estimates all the locations of joints and subsequently identifies the estimated joints for a specific pose. The locations of joints are estimated by regressing K closest joints from every pixel with the use of a random tree. The identification of joints are realized by transferring labels from a retrieved nearest exemplar model. Once the 3D configuration of all the joints is derived, identification becomes much easier than when it is done simultaneously with localization, exploiting the reduced solution space. Our proposed method achieves significant performance gain on pose estimation accuracy, thereby improving both localization and identification. Experimental results show that the proposed method exhibits an accuracy significantly higher than those of previous approaches that simultaneously localize and identify the body parts.

Keywords: Depth camera · Human pose · Regression forest

1 Introduction

Real-time 3D human pose estimation is a core technique for activity recognition. It has diverse applications including human-computer-interface development, teleoperation, health monitoring, and learning by demonstration(LbD) [1]. Conventionally, 3D human pose estimation is formulated as a detection problem of the desired list of body joints. Most of the previous methods simultaneously localize and identify joints, such as localization of left shoulder, with the expectation that the accomplishment of one task would facilitate the accomplishment

© Springer International Publishing AG 2016
B. Leibe et al. (Eds.): ECCV 2016, Part V, LNCS 9909, pp. 747–761, 2016.
DOI: 10.1007/978-3-319-46454-1_45

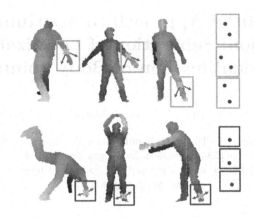

Fig. 1. Similar local depth features are exhibited by different body parts at various poses. Thus, a local depth feature may be insufficiently distinctive to distinguish the identity of parts

of other [2–5]. By contrast, we assert in this paper that identification hampers localization; therefore, the two tasks are treated separately and significant performance boost is obtained.

In depth images, similar local patch patterns are easily observed from different body parts at various poses. For example, in Fig. 1, right arm of the first person, left arm of the second person, and left leg of the third person in the first row shows similar depth map features. Similarly, in the second row, right hand of the first person and left foot of the second and third person also share similar depth features. Therefore, if one tries to localize a particular joint of interest by primarily relying on local depth features, then a confusion between the parts may arise [2,3,5]. On the contrary, for a given 3D configuration of joints and possible pose candidates, people can easily infer the corresponding pose and distinguish which joints are matched to body parts such as head, knees, wrists and etc., as shown in Fig. 2. Thus, the configuration of joints itself without labels already provides us a general idea of the body pose.

Based on the observation, we propose a new two-stage framework that first localize joints and then assign identity to the discovered joint positions. This strategy avoids the possible confusion between parts of similar depth maps in the localization step by postponing the body part label assignment to the identification step, wherein the global configuration of joints can be exploited.

In particular, a regression tree that predicts the relative displacements of the K nearest joints from a given input pixel position is trained in the localization step. During the test, all the joint locations are predicted by aggregating votes cast by the foreground pixels. Considering that each leaf node may contain similar offset vectors from different body parts as well as different poses, it can effectively pin-point joints from rare or unconventional poses, by sharing a prediction model across different parts. As a result, in the experiments, our method shows enhanced accuracy compared to previous methods in particular for wrists, elbows, ankles, and knees.

In the identification step, each joint position is identified for a given 3D configuration of detected body joints. As shown in Fig. 2, a configuration of joints serves as a distinctive representation of a corresponding pose. Therefore, the nearest exemplar is retrieved from the training set based on a simple distance measure between point sets, and joint labels are transferred from this exemplar. This simple strategy works sufficiently well enough to achieve the upper-bound accuracy on the available dataset and effective enough to be applied to a real-time operation.

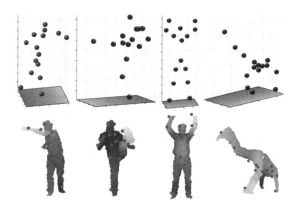

Fig. 2. 3D configuration of joints itself provides a general idea of a pose. People can easily find similar pose from possible candidates (below) and distinguish the joints, even when only a 3D joint configuration is given without body joint labels (above)

In summary, the contributions of this paper are as follows. The 3D body pose estimation problem is formulated into two subsequent problems, namely, localization and identification, and a new two-stage pose estimation algorithm is proposed to solve them. This approach makes both problem easier to solve, thus enabling improvement for both tasks.

2   Related Works

Existing 3D human pose estimation methods can be classified into generative, discriminative and combined approach according to the presence of a body model. Generative approaches [6–10] estimate pose by finding point correspondence between the input depth map and the known body model. These approaches usually require an accurate body model and good initialization to avoid being trapped in a local optimum. Recently, Ye et al. [11] proposed a fast and accurate generative method by representing a body as a Gaussian mixture model. On the contrary, discriminative approaches do not assume a generative model and directly estimate the location of body joints. Random forest [12,13] based approaches have achieved impressive performances in terms of speed and accuracy by formulating 3D body pose estimation as pixel-wise classification [2], offset regression [3], and random walk [5]. These approaches estimate the location of each individual joint independently while, ignoring the spatial dependence between them. To exploit global information, Sun et al. [4] proposed a conditional regression forest that considers dependence between joints through a global latent variable. All of these approaches focus on improving localization accuracy of a given target joint, with the use of various cues including local and global appearances.

Our method is also related to some works on 3D body/hand pose estimation in which the extracted geometric extreme points are used as rough but fast global configurations of body/hand poses. Baak et al. [14] used Dijkstra algorithm to compute geodesic distances and consequently extract extreme points from a point cloud to retrieve the nearest pose exemplar from the database. Liang et al. [15] adapted the same idea to hand pose estimation. Qian et al. [16] also initialized their tracking based hand pose estimation by detecting fingers without identification. The weakness of the approaches using extreme points, however, is apparent when desired parts, such as hands and feet, do not correspond to the extreme points in the depth maps, for example, folded hands. Therefore, all of the previous methods used detected extreme points to estimate coarse global configuration, whereas elaborate localization of joints are conducted simultaneously with identification

Works from Plagemann et al. [17] is related to our approach as they also first extracted interesting points and then classified them into specific parts or background. However, their interest point detector targeted on general interest points rather than body joints. Given that several interesting points could also be detected from the background, they used a classifier based on local features to classify the points, rather than using a global joint configuration. In addition, their method also exhibits the limitation of the aforementioned approaches using extreme points. Agarwal and Triggs [18] detected points by shape descriptor vectors instead of the extreme points, however detected points do not directly corresponds to the location of joints. By contrast, our approach targets directly the detection of body joints, thus enabling the use of the global configuration of joints for identification.

The body joint localization without identification can also be interpreted as semantic saliency detection [19,20]. The idea of limiting the search space by finding the points of interest shares the same motivation behind saliency detection. In our problem, saliency regions or the points of interest are defined by semantically identifiable body joints.

3   Overview

We address the 3D human pose estimation problem from a single depth image. We formulate this problem as two separate sequential problems, namely,

Fig. 3. The offset distributions in leaf nodes are shown for 2-nearest joints($K = 2$). In each pair of images, the left image shows the distribution of offset vectors contained in a leaf node and the right image illustrates the corresponding training images in the leaf node. In both the left and right image, input pixel positions are marked as green circles, and the offsets to the nearest and the second nearest joints are respectively represented by red and blue dots. The average offset vectors for unidentified joint are drawn with arrows. Note that many of leafs contain pixels from different body parts as well as different poses. (Best viewed in color) (Color figure online)

localization and identification. The goal of the localization step is to discover every joint location in the 3D world coordinate system without identifying labels. Our method localizes joints based on a regression forest and k-means clustering. The details of training and inference are explained in Sect. 4. In the identification step, labels are assigned to each of the joint locations discovered in the previous step. Joints are identified by transferring labels from the nearest training sample, whose joint configuration is closest to the estimated configuration. The detailed procedures for exemplar set construction and nearest pose retrieval are described in Sect. 5. Section 6 presents the evaluation of our method on the publicly available dataset and provide the comparison with two existing methods. We also present in Sect. 6 the analyses of the effect of the proposed localization and identification decomposition and that of the system parameters.

4   Body Joint Localization Without Identification

We establish a variant of the Hough forest [21] to localize body joints, following the approach of Girshick et al. [3]. However, in our proposed method, a regression tree is trained to estimates offset vectors to the nearest K joints of any body parts, whereas in [3] the forest was trained to regress offset vectors to the specific body joints. In the test stage, every foreground pixel in the input depth image traverses the regression tree and casts K votes in the 3D world coordinate system. The joints are localized by aggregating the votes cast by the regression tree.

4.1   Training Set Collection

Let us denote a set of body depth images by $\{I^1, I^2, ...\}$ and the corresponding ground truth poses by $\{P^1, P^2, ...\}$. Each pose P is represented by a set of 15 skeletal body joint positions in the world coordinate system: $P = (p_1, p_2, ..., p_{15})$, where $p_j = (x, y, z)$, $j = 1, ..., 15$. The corresponding projected pixel coordinate position of p in the depth image I and its depth are represented by $\tilde{p} = (\tilde{x}, \tilde{y})$ and $d_I(\tilde{p})$, respectively. For a a given depth image, the corresponding points are reconstructed in the world coordinate system using the camera calibration parameters.

For a given position q in a depth image of pose P^n, the location of the closest body joints from q in the world coordinate system is expressed as

$$\alpha_1^n(q) = \arg \min_{p \in P^n} \|p - q\|^2 \tag{1}$$

and the k-th nearest joint from q is found recursively as $\alpha_k^n(q)$. The offset vector from q to the k-th nearest joint $\alpha_k^n(q)$ is denoted by by $\Delta_q^k = \alpha_k^n(q) - q$. A training sample S consists of a body depth image I, a pixel position $\tilde{q}$ in the pixel coordinate system, and offset vectors to K nearest joints from q in the world coordinate system.

$$S = (I^n, \tilde{q}, \Delta_q^1, ..., \Delta_q^K), \tag{2}$$

where K is the number of nearest body joints to consider.

4.2   Training Regression Tree

The goal of training is to find a regression tree that minimizes the sum of the variances of offset vectors Δ_q^k in the leaf nodes. The objective function is formulated as follows,

$$E^{reg}(\mathbf{Q}) = \sum_{Q_s \subset \mathbf{Q}} \sum_{(I^n, q) \in Q_s} \sum_{k=1}^{K} \|\Delta_q^k - \bar{\Delta}_{\alpha_k, s}\|^2, \tag{3}$$

where Q_s is a set of training samples contained in a leaf node s, $\mathbf{Q} = \{Q_s\}$ is a partition of the training samples, and $\bar{\Delta}_{\alpha_k, s} = \frac{1}{|Q_s|} \sum_{(I^n, q) \in Q_s} \Delta_q^k$ is the mean offset vector of all the offsets in Q_s. For notational simplicity, we slightly abused the notation $(I^n, q) \in Q_s$ to represent $S = (I^n, \tilde{q}, \Delta_q^1, ..., \Delta_q^K) \in Q_s$.

The following depth difference comparison features, similar to those in [2], are employed for splitting at the nodes:

$$f_\theta(I, \tilde{q}) = d_I \left(\tilde{q} + \frac{\tilde{t}_1}{d_I(\tilde{q})} \right) - d_I \left(\tilde{q} + \frac{\tilde{t}_2}{d_I(\tilde{q})} \right), \tag{4}$$

Fig. 4. Qualitative results of the proposed method. In each pair of images, the left side visualizes a voting result and the right side shows the estimated joint positions on the input depth image. Estimated locations of joints are indicated by circles

where parameters $\theta = (\tilde{t}_1, \tilde{t}_2)$ are offsets from the current pixel position $\tilde{q}$. Given that $\tilde{t}_1$ and $\tilde{t}_2$ are the values in the pixel coordinate system, they are divided by depth to provide the same relative position in the world coordinate system at different distances from the depth sensor.

The standard greedy decision tree algorithm is used to train a tree structure and to obtain the parameters for node splitting [12]. In each node, samples are iteratively separated into left and right children using a weak binary classifier until the termination conditions are satisfied. A pool of binary tests consisting of $\phi = (\theta, \tau) = (\tilde{t}_1, \tilde{t}_2, \tau)$ with random values of $\tilde{t}_1, \tilde{t}_2, \tau$, where τ is a threshold, is generated to train a weak learner. At each node, all the binary tests in the pool are evaluated and the ϕ^* that minimizes the following objective is selected:

$$\phi^* = \arg\min_{\phi} \sum_{s \in \{l,r\}} \sum_{(I^n, q) \in Q_s} \sum_{k=1}^{K} \| \Delta_q^k - \bar{\Delta}_{\alpha_k, s} \|^2, \tag{5}$$

where Q is a set of training samples reached at the current split node, $Q_l(\phi) = \{S = (I^n, q) \mid f_\theta(I, \tilde{q}) < \tau, S \in Q\}$ and $Q_r(\phi) = Q \setminus Q_l(\phi)$. The objective measures the uncertainty of leaf node prediction models by the sum of offset variations.

For a set of training samples reached at each leaf node, representative values are stored in the leaf node. Each set of offset vectors pointing to k-th nearest joint are cluster them into two clusters by $k = 2$-means clustering. A leaf node s is represented by K pairs of two cluster centers and two corresponding relative cluster sizes as

$$((\frac{|C_{1,1}|}{|Q_s|}, \bar{\Delta}_{\alpha_1, C_{1,1}}, \frac{|C_{1,2}|}{|Q_s|}, \bar{\Delta}_{\alpha_1, C_{1,2}}),$$
$$\cdots,$$
$$(\frac{|C_{K,1}|}{|Q_s|}, \bar{\Delta}_{\alpha_K, C_{K,1}}, \frac{|C_{K,2}|}{|Q_s|}, \bar{\Delta}_{\alpha_K, C_{K,2}})). \tag{6}$$

where $C_{k,1}$ and $C_{k,2}$ are sets of training samples clustered into the first and second cluster, respectively, based on the k-th nearest joints. $\bar{\Delta}_{\alpha_k,C_{k,i}}$ is the average of offset vectors from k-th nearest joints, included in the i-th cluster $C_{k,i}$. Figure 3 shows some examples of leaf nodes and the training samples they represent. The leaf nodes contain offsets for different body parts at different poses. See Fig. 3 for the detailed description.

4.3   Inference

During the test time, each foreground pixel of an input depth image passes through the trained regression tree (Sect. 4.2), until a leaf node s is reached. From each of K pairs in Eq. (6), an element is randomly sampled according to the probability proportional to the weight $|C_{K,i}|/|Q_s|$. Then, pixel casts votes to K positions in the 3D world coordinate where the positions are obtained by adding offset vectors to its own location. There are 15 different body joints, therefore, 15 regions with dense votes are expected to be generated, which correspond to the joint locations. Accordingly, k-means clustering [22] is used to find cluster centers which represent joint locations. Some example results of voting are shown in Fig. 4. To make the clustering more reliable, the outlier votes are excluded, which lies outside of the depth image image when projected to the pixel coordinate, before the clustering. Also, the computation time for k-means clustering is reduced by sub-sampling n_s pixels. The detailed performance for various values of n_s is tested in the Sect. 6.3. Note that there is still a room for further improvement of both speed and accuracy by using an advanced method to find a set of local clusters.

5   Body Joint Identification

Once the joint locations are discovered in the localization step, each joint is labeled in the identification step by retrieving the nearest training sample as an exemplar. Then, the labels from the exemplar is simply transferred. For the exemplar retrieval, the distance between a set of joints $P' = \{p'_1, p'_2, \cdots, p'_{15}\}$ and pose $P = (p_1, p_2, \cdots, p_{15})$ can be measured by rigidly aligning the exemplar pose to the localized points.

$$d(P, P') = \sum_{j=1}^{15} \| s\mathbf{R}(p_j - \Delta c) - (p'_{\sigma(j)} - \Delta c) \|^2. \tag{7}$$

$\sigma(\cdot)$ is the assignment function and Δc is the offset vector between the centers of foreground pixels. Respectively, s and $\mathbf{R}$ are scale factor and rotation matrix that minimizes the sum of squared error between two set of points [23]. We use $\sigma(j) = \arg\min_{j' \in \{1, \cdots, 15\}} \| s\mathbf{R}(p_j - \Delta c) - (p_{j'} - \Delta c) \|^2$ which assigns a nearest discovered joint to each of known joint in an exemplar. The subscript of $\{p'_1, p'_2, \cdots, p'_{15}\}$ is used here only for distinction in the equation, while having

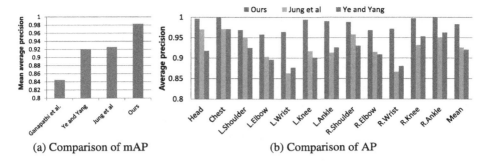

(a) Comparison of mAP   (b) Comparison of AP

Fig. 5. Comparison of body joint detection accuracy on the EVAL dataset

no relation with joint labels. For EVAL [24] dataset, however, only a minor accuracy difference is found between the least squared solution and simple translation invariant point matching solution, and the simpler solution was implemented.

A set of exemplars from a subset of training set is constructed and a nearest exemplar is retrieve. In order to diversify poses contained in the exemplars, well scattered points [25] in the pose space are selected iteratively. In the first iteration, a random sample is selected from the training set. In each subsequent iteration, a sample whose pose is farthest from those of previously selected sample set is selected. For the distance between a set of poses $\mathcal{P}$ and a pose P, the minimum distance is used, $d(\mathcal{P}, P) = \min_{R \in \mathcal{P}} \sum_{i=1}^{15} \|p_i - r_i\|^2$, where $P = (p_1, p_2, \cdots, p_{15})$ and $R = (r_1, r_2, \cdots, r_{15})$.

In our experiments, the simple retrieval strategy almost achieves the upper bound of average precision (AP) with 1000 exemplars on the EVAL dataset (Sect. 6). This performance implies that the intermediate representation of joint configuration is adequately discriminate to find the reliable nearest neighbor. We only used the configuration of joints for the retrieval, without any depth information. We believe incorporating depth information as a feature for each joint label would further increase the accuracy by helping discriminate confusing poses, which will have the same set of joint locations but with different labels. However, we leave this aspect as future extension.

6   Experimental Results

The evaluation of the proposed method consists of three parts. In the first part, we evaluate our method on the EVAL [24] dataset. We compare the performance of our method with two previous 3D pose estimation algorithms, namely, the method of Jung et al. [5] and Ye and Yang [11]. In the second part, we analyze each step of our algorithm; the localization step the and identification step. Finally, we investigate the effect of various system parameters on accuracy.

6.1   Comparison with Existing Methods

We evaluated our method on the publicly available EVAL dataset [24] using leave-one-out cross validation, as done in the previous works [5,11]. The EVAL

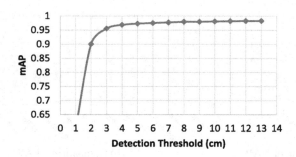

Fig. 6. mAP values for various detection thresholds

dataset consists of 24 sequences, which are obtained from 3 different people performing 8 actions. The sequences from two people are used in the training set, whereas the sequenced from excluded person is used as test set. Final accuracy is averaged over all three people. We used the conventional 10 cm rule as an evaluation measure [5, 11]. If the distance between the estimated and ground truth joint is less than 10 cm, then the estimation is considered to be correct. As pose estimation is considered as the detection problem of every joints, AP is used to quantify the accuracy for each joint, and the mean average precision (mAP) of joints is used as the overall accuracy measure. The runtime is measured on a PC with Intel Core i5-2500 3.3GHz CPU.

The accuracy comparison of our proposed method with those of Jung et al. [5] and Ye and Yang [11] is shown in Fig. 5(a). The proposed method achieved an mAP of 98.3 %, which is 5.7 % and 6.2 % higher compared to 92.6 % and 92.1 % of [5] and [11], respectively. As shown in Fig. 5(b), our method outperforms the previous works in every joint. In particular, our method improves accuracy of second best methods by 8.7 %, 7.1 %, 6.3 % and 5.4 % for wrists, knees, ankles, and elbows, respectively. The accuracy boosts are prominent for the joints with large articulation, whereas AP of other joints, head, chest and shoulder, are 2.6 %, 2.8 %, and 2.4 % higher than the second best method, respectively. Figure 4 shows some qualitative results of our method. Each circle indicates the estimated positions of joints.

We further evaluated our method on the EVAL dataset while varying the detection threshold from 1 cm to 13 cm. The mAP values are shown in Fig. 6. The curve steeply increases, showing 95.6 % mAP at 3 cm threshold. Our approach was able to precisely estimate the joint locations within 3 cm radius for 95.6 % of time. This is higher accuracy percentage even compared to the 10 cm rule of the previous methods.

6.2   Algorithm Analysis

In this section, we evaluate the accuracy of the localization step and that of the identification step separately to investigate the effect of problem decomposition.

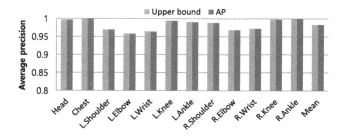

Fig. 7. Comparison of the upper bound and AP for each joint

When the joint localization is considered as a preprocessing step for the joint detection, the upper bound of AP serves as a meaningful indication of localization accuracy. On the other hand, the relative value of AP with respect to the upper bound indicates the accuracy of identification step. Each ground truth joint should be considered correctly detected if at least one of the estimated joints exists within the distance threshold(10 cm) to obtain the upper bound. Upper bound matching allows for multiple corresponding matches for a single joint. Ideally, the upper bound accuracy is achieved if every joint is properly labeled.

Figure 7 shows the upper bound and AP for each joint. In our method, the difference between AP and upper bound is smaller than 0.1 %. The simple exemplar matching method is sufficient to deal with the translation and scale variations in the EVAL set. To deal with drastic view point and pose variations, we should consider a pose tracking approach with temporal prior.

Table 1. Runtime speed comparison

Alg.	Ours	Jung et al. [5]	Ye and Yang [11]
Runtime speed (fps)	37	1262	>30

Table 2. Runtime analysis

Proces	Voting (Sect. 4.3)	Clustering (Sect. 4.3)	Labeling (Sect. 5)	Total
Runtime (ms)	13 (48 %)	10 (37 %)	4 (15 %)	27 (100 %)

The runtime speed comparison is shown in Table 1. Our method performs in real-time (37 fps) under a single-core CPU operation. Ye and Yang achieves real-time with GPU and Jung et al. is extremely fast with its random walk strategy. The computation time used in each process of our method is shown in Table 2. Most of the computation time is spent during the localization step, occupying 85 % of the entire process, where the offset generation from regression tree and k-means clustering take about the same computational resources.

6.3   Effect of the Parameters

In this section, we analyze the effects of different parameters on the performance of our method. We performed the same experiment in Sect. 6.1 on the EVAL dataset while varying the number of training samples, the number of nearest joints, the number of minimum samples allowed at each leaf node, the number of subsampled offset votes, and the number of exemplars.

Figure 8(a) shows the AP values for each joint at varying the number of training samples during regression tree construction. Our method achieves 92.8 % mAP using 500 training images, where each images contains about 8000 foreground pixels. Head, knees, and ankles require a smaller number of training samples while wrists, elbows, and shoulders need a larger number of samples to achieve the same accuracy.

We also evaluated our method at different numbers of K nearest joints used in the localization step. A high K increases the number of votes per joint as well as the computational cost and memory, while making the voting results more stable. However, with large K, the offsets reach farther away joints with higher uncertainty. Each leaf node is also less likely to contain samples from different parts and poses; thus, the effect of sharing different joints is reduced. The result is shown in Fig. 8(b). When two-nearest joints are used, the accuracy is higher for elbows and wrists, but lower for shoulders with respect to the accuracy when three-nearest joints are used. We used $K = 2$ for all other experiments settings.

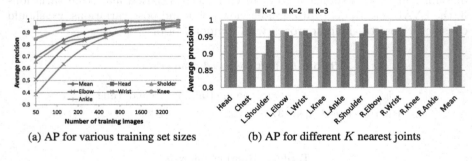

(a) AP for various training set sizes   (b) AP for different K nearest joints

Fig. 8. Effect of various system parameters

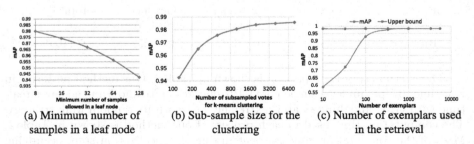

(a) Minimum number of samples in a leaf node   (b) Sub-sample size for the clustering   (c) Number of exemplars used in the retrieval

Fig. 9. Effect of various system parameters

Figure 9(a) shows the effect of the number of minimum samples n_{min} allowed in each leaf node with unlimited tree depth when $K = 2$. Allowing a smaller number of samples increases the memory required for the model while better fitting the training set. As the value of n_{min} varies from 128 to 8, mAP consistently increases. We used $n_{min} = 8$ for all the other experiments.

Figure 9(b) shows the mAP values at varying sub-sample sizes before k-means clustering. As the clustering step consumes approximately 40 % of the total runtime of our method, the sub-sample size directly affects both speed and accuracy. With only 125 votes, our algorithm achieves 94.3 % mAP, which is higher than those of the previous methods. We used sub-sampled 1000 votes for k-means clustering for all the other experiments.

Figure 9(c) shows the mAP values at varying numbers of exemplars used in the identification step. With only 100 templates, our method achieved 93.4 % mAP, which is comparable to those of the state-of-the-art methods. We used 1000 exemplars in all the other experiments.

7   Conclusion

In this paper, we propose a new two-stage framework for 3D human pose estimation from a single depth image. Unlike existing approaches that address localization and identification of body joints as a single task, our proposed method decomposes the problem into two subproblems, namely, localization without identification and identity assignment. These subproblems are then solved sequentially. Our method effectively overcomes the confusion between body parts and joints with large articulation by sharing the offset prediction model across different body parts and poses. The experimental results show that our method exhibits significantly improved performance compared with the previous methods. It achieved high accuracy particularly for wrists, elbows, ankles, and knees, which are usually considered difficult to localized.

There are a number of different implementation improvements we may consider in the future. First, a more advanced offset clustering scheme can be used. We currently use the k-means clustering algorithm which may require large number of iterations and has high dependency on the initial points. There are various advanced cluster and mode seeking methods available for replacing the k-mean algorithm. Second, the simple least squared error point matching algorithm many not be robust to large view point and pose variations. RANSAC like algorithm can be used to deal with large view changes, as well as considering time sequenced pose estimation which uses previous frame's pose estimation as the initial pose of current frame.

Acknowledgments. This work was supported by Hankuk University of Foreign Studies Research Fund of 2016.

References

1. Romero, J., Kjellstrom, H., Kragic, D.: Monocular real-time 3D articulated hand pose estimation. In: Humanoids (2009)
2. Shotton, J., Fitzgibbon, A., Cook, M., Sharp, T., Finocchio, M., Moore, R., Kipman, A., Blake, A.: Real-time human pose recognition in parts from a single depth image. In: CVPR (2011)
3. Girshick, R., Shotton, J., Kohli, P., Criminisi, A., Fitzgibbon, A.: Efficient regression of general-activity human poses from depth images. In: ICCV (2011)
4. Sun, M., Kohli, P., Shotton, J.: Conditional regression forests for human pose estimation. In: CVPR (2012)
5. Yub Jung, H., Lee, S., Seok Heo, Y., Dong Yun, I.: Random tree walk toward instantaneous 3d human pose estimation. In: CVPR (2015)
6. Wei, X., Zhang, P., Chai, J.: Accurate realtime full-body motion capture using a single depth camera. In: SIGGRAPH ASIA (2012)
7. Helten, T., Baak, A., Bharaj, G., Muller, M., Seidel, H., Theobalt, C.: Personalization and evaluation of a real-time depth-based full body tracker. In: 3DV (2014)
8. Gall, J., Stoll, C., de Auiar, E., Theobalt, C., Rosenhahn, B., Seidel, H.P.: Motion capture using joint skeleton tracking and surface estimation. In: CVPR (2009)
9. Grest, D., Krüger, V., Koch, R.: Single view motion tracking by depth and Silhouette information. In: Ersbøll, B.K., Pedersen, K.S. (eds.) SCIA 2007. LNCS, vol. 4522, pp. 719–729. Springer, Heidelberg (2007). doi:10.1007/978-3-540-73040-8_73
10. Ionescu, C., Carreira, J., Sminchisescu, C.: Iterated second-order label sensitive pooling for 3d human pose estimation. In: 2014 IEEE Conference on Computer Vision and Pattern Recognition, pp. 1661–1668 (2014)
11. Ye, M., Yang, R.: Real-time simulataneous pose and shape estimation for articulated objects using a single depth camera. In: CVPR (2014)
12. Criminisi, A., Shotton, J.: Decision forests for computer vision and medical image analysis. Springer Science & Business Media (2013)
13. Breiman, L.: Random forest. Mach. Learn. 45, 5–32 (2001)
14. Baak, A., Müller, M., Bharaj, G., Seidel, H.P., Theobalt, C.: A data-driven approach for real-time full body pose reconstruction from a depth camera. In: ICCV (2011)
15. Liang, H., Yuan, J., Thalmann, D., Zhang, Z.: Model-based hand pose estimation via spatial-temporal hand parsing and 3d fingertip localization. In: The Visual Computer (2013)
16. Qian, C., Sun, X., Wei, Y., Tang, X., Sun, J.: Realtime and robust hand tracking from depth. In: CVPR (2014)
17. Plagemann, C., Ganapathi, V., Koller, D., Thrun, S.: Real-time identification and localization of body parts from depth images. In: ICRA (2010)
18. Agarwal, A., Triggs, B.: 3d human pose from silhouettes by relevance vector regression. In: Proceedings of the IEEE Computer Society Conference on Computer Vision and Pattern Recognition, CVPR 2004, vol. 2, p. II-882. IEEE (2004)
19. Zhang, Z., Liu, Z., Zhang, Z., Zhao, Q.: Semantic saliency driven camera control for personal remote collaboration. In: 2008 IEEE 10th Workshop on Multimedia Signal Processing (2008)
20. Chang, X., Yang, Y., Xing, E., Yu, Y.: Complex event detection using semantic saliency and nearly-isotonic SVM. In: ICML (2015)
21. Gall, J., Lempitsky, V.: Class-specific hough forests for object detection. In: PAMI (2009)

22. Hartigan, J.A., Wong, M.A.: Algorithm as 136: A k-means clustering algorithm. Appl. Stat. **28**(1), 100–108 (1979)
23. Umeyama, S.: Least-squares estimation of transformation parameters between two point patterns. In: Pattern Analysis and Machine Intelligence (1991)
24. Ganapathi, V., Plagemann, C., Koller, D., Thrun, S.: Real-time human pose tracking from range data. In: Fitzgibbon, A., Lazebnik, S., Perona, P., Sato, Y., Schmid, C. (eds.) ECCV 2012. LNCS, vol. 7577, pp. 738–751. Springer, Heidelberg (2012). doi:10.1007/978-3-642-33783-3_53
25. Guha, S., Rastogi, R., Shim, K.: Cure: an efficient clustering algorithm for large databases. In: ACM SIGMOD Record (1998)

A Novel Tiny Object Recognition Algorithm Based on Unit Statistical Curvature Feature

Yimei Kang$^{(\boxtimes)}$ and Xiang Li

College of Software, Beihang University, Beijing, China
{kangyimei,sy1421103}@buaa.edu.cn

Abstract. To recognize tiny objects whose sizes are in the range of 15×15 to 40×40 pixels, a novel image feature descriptor, unit statistical curvature feature (USCF), is proposed based on the statistics of unit curvature distribution. USCF can represent the local general invariant features of the image texture. Due to the curvature features are independent of image sizes, USCF algorithm had high recognition rate for object images in any size including tiny object images. USCF is invariant to rotation and linear illumination variation, and is partially invariant to viewpoint variation. Experimental results showed that the recognition rate of USCF algorithm was the highest for tiny object recognition compared to other nine typical object recognition algorithms under complex test conditions with simultaneous rotation, illumination, viewpoint variation and background interference.

Keywords: Object recognition · Tiny object · Feature descriptor · Unit Statistical Curvature Feature

1 Introduction

Recognition of tiny image objects taken by digital cameras is a key subject in machine vision. Recognizing an object accurately and quickly when it is very small and in a distance provides more time to take appropriate actions for a system that relies on machine vision, such as a robot, an Unmanned Aerial Vehicle (UAV), *etc.* However, automatic recognition gets more and more difficult when the objects are getting smaller, due to the tiny objects have very few pixels and texture information.

There are limited studies focused on this subject. Torralba *et al.* [1] implemented tiny objects classification whose sizes are 32×32 color pixels by using the nearest neighbor matching schemes and image indexing techniques. They showed that the 32×32 color pixel tiny images already seem to contain most of the relevant information needed to support reliable recognition. However, the approach is only used to classify objects but not to distinguish a tiny object from other objects in an image.

Multiple approaches can be used to recognize a big image object whose size is larger than 40×40 pixels by matching the image features, *e.g.* edge features [2–4],

© Springer International Publishing AG 2016
B. Leibe et al. (Eds.): ECCV 2016, Part V, LNCS 9909, pp. 762–777, 2016.
DOI: 10.1007/978-3-319-46454-1_46

invariant features [5–10], statistical features [11–13], *etc.* Tiny object whose size is smaller than 40×40 pixels has vague contours, and the algorithms based on edge features cannot work on tiny object recognition.

Some recognition algorithms based on invariant features are commonly used to recognize objects. SIFT [5] constructed feature descriptors based on histogram of magnitude and direction of gradients to characterize an object. To improve the calculation efficiency of SIFT, SURF [6] built feature descriptors based on sum of Haar wavelet responses. Rani *et al.* [7] found that the number of keypoints detected by using SIFT is more than that of SURF through a set of experiments. Rublee *et al.* prompted an efficient matching method called ORB [8] by combining FAST keypoint detector and BRIEF descriptor. Hauagge *et al.* proposed another kind of invariant feature based on local symmetry feature [9].

The above mentioned invariant feature descriptors are invariant to uniform scaling and orientation variation. SIFT can precisely recognize the images by matching the keypoints which are extremes in a set of three DoG (Different of Gaussian) images. Similarly, SURF recognize the objects by matching keypoints derived from blob structure and ORB uses descriptor derived from corner keypoints in images. However, there are often no suitable keypoints when the image size is very small, such as in the range from 15×15 to 40×40 pixels.

Hu proposed a geometric feature descriptor based on invariant moments [10]. Hu's method is suitable for object recognition by using object shape. There is little information to construct the boundaries for tiny object images. Therefore, Hu's method cannot be used directly to recognize tiny objects. However, the invariant features of Hu's method can represent the tiny objects and can be used to recognize tiny objects.

Statistical features, such as histogram and entropy of an image, can also be used to characterize small objects because they do not rely on the size of the images. However, statistical features are too general and have no position information, therefore, they can hardly be applied to object recognition. In contrary to global entropy, unit entropy has information of position, and it can be used to recognize small objects. Fritz *et al.* [11] used unit entropy to build an entropy-based object model from discriminative local patterns for object representation and recognition.

HoG [12] and GIST [13] algorithms are also based on statistical features. HoG employs a histogram binning on the gradient orientation and extracts feature vector with a grid of overlapping blocks. GIST divides an image into 4×4 grids in which orientation histograms are extracted by using Gabor filters. When we tried to apply existing recognition algorithms to an industrial application to distinguish between tiny objects, unit entropy, HoG and GIST all performed well. Unfortunately, they didn't work when the object rotates.

Some nonlinear method based on machine learning can also be used to recognize objects, *e.g.* the methods using k-nearest neighbor method and semi-supervised learning [14], weight kernels over orientations [15], wavelet neural network [16], two-layer neural network [17], and convolutional neural network [18]. All these algorithms must train sample images before recognizing objects.

In this paper, we proposed a novel image feature descriptor, unit statistical curvature feature (USCF) of the grayscale surface of an image, to characterize tiny objects with 15×15 to 40×40 pixels. The recognition algorithm based on USCF can recognize an object image in any size. Specifically, it had high recognition rate and computation efficiency for tiny objects. USCF is completely invariant to rotation and linear illumination variation. It is also partially invariant to viewpoint variation and background interference. The USCF algorithm is compared with other recognition algorithms including SIFT, SURF, ORB, gray histogram, entropy, unit entropy, GIST, HoG and Hu's moment invariants (Hu's MI) algorithms on the image datasets from ALOI-COL Database [19], COIL-100 Database [20], ETH-80 Database [21], ETHZ another 53 Objects Database and images from two videos, respectively. The experimental results showed that USCF algorithm had best performance in tiny object recognition under real complex environment against rotation, illumination, viewpoint variation and background interference.

2   The Principle of USCF Algorithm

An object image with less than 40×40 pixels often has vague contour and texture. It is difficult for existing recognition algorithms to extract enough features from such tiny objects. Hence, we tried a new way to recognize such tiny objects.

To recognize a tiny object, we need utilize the limited pixel information as much as possible. Firstly, we build a three-dimensional coordinate system $Oxyz$ with the positions and gray values of pixels in an image I. Let (x, y, z) represent a point in $Oxyz$, and let z be the gray value of pixel (x, y) in image I. Then we construct a fitting function $z = f(x, y)$ to convert the discrete points in $Oxyz$ to a curved surface, which outlines the gray value distribution tendency of image I. Figure 1 shows two objects with their fitted curved surfaces under different conditions. As shown in Fig. 1, different objects have different fitted curved surfaces while the shape of the fitted curved surfaces of an object is invariant to object rotation and illumination variation. Therefore, object recognition can be converted to compare the similarity of the fitted curved surfaces.

We constructed image features derived from the curvature to estimate the similarity of the fitted curved surface. Curvature can describe the gray value distribution of an image. Different from gradient, curvature is independent of the object orientation and keeps more object details because second derivative enhances the difference in details. Curvature is invariant to object rotation and linear illumination variation since it only relies on the shape of curved surface. Mean curvature reflects the local shape feature of the curved surface and Gaussian curvature reflects the convexity and concavity feature of the curved surface. Therefore, we combined Gaussian curvature $K(x, y, z)$ and mean curvature $H(x, y, z)$ of each point (x, y, z) in the fitted curved surface of an object to build the invariant feature of the object.

Map $K(x, y, z)$ and $H(x, y, z)$ to a two-dimensional coordinate O_{HK} to generate the curvature feature space of the object as shown in Fig. 2. We used

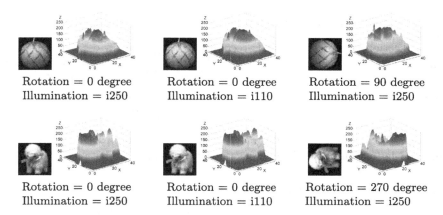

Rotation = 0 degree Illumination = i250	Rotation = 0 degree Illumination = i110	Rotation = 90 degree Illumination = i250
Rotation = 0 degree Illumination = i250	Rotation = 0 degree Illumination = i110	Rotation = 270 degree Illumination = i250

Fig. 1. Images (left) and fitted curved surfaces (right) of two objects in different conditions. The object images and their parameters of illumination condition were selected from ALOI-COL Database

coordinate (H, K) to represent a point in O_{HK}. The curvature feature space reflects the change of object image texture. If the color of a pixel is changed slightly or not changed at all compared to surrounding pixels, the absolute values of $K(x, y, z)$ and $H(x, y, z)$ should both be low. Hence, the smoother the image texture change is, the more points closer to the origin in O_{HK} are. Conversely, when image texture is changed dramatically, more points are away from the origin in O_{HK}. In general, majority of points in O_{HK} are close to origin because smooth area is the majority in an image.

The curvature of a pixel is calculated based on pixels surrounding that pixel, therefore it is sensitive to any changes of neighboring pixels. Any color variation of pixels will have an impact on the value of the curvature. This means the whole map in O_{HK} of an object is also sensitive to gray value fluctuation of each pixel. Hence, we partition the curvature feature space of an object to a number of unit areas and use the statistics of curvature features in each unit to generate a stable curvature feature matrix, *i.e.* unit statistical curvature feature. Then we recognize tiny objects by matching the similarity of their USCF matrices.

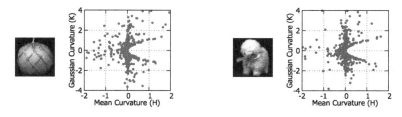

Fig. 2. Mapping of each pixel in two object images to O_{HK} using Gaussian curvature and mean curvature as coordinates

3   Proposed Algorithm

In this section, we present USCF recognition algorithm in details. Firstly, we employ least square method to fit curved surfaces of object images. Secondly, we calculate the Gaussian curvature and mean curvature of each pixel in object images according to the fitted curved surfaces. Thirdly, we build the curvature feature space in O_{HK}, and partition it into a number of unit areas according to the curvature distribution density. Then we count the number of points in each unit area to construct the USCF matrix. Finally, the similarity of the objects is obtained by matching the USCF matrices with Euclidean distance.

3.1   Generate Fitted Curved Surface

Least square method was used in this paper to generate the curved surface fitting function. The reason to use least square method is that it can optimize fitting function globally, and it is simple and converges quickly.

A function which consists of a number of primary functions and an unknown coefficient set is usually used to describe an unknown curved surface. We use polynomial functions as primary functions. Polynomial function can be differentiated arbitrary times, and it is easy to calculate. For X axis, we chose $P + 1$ polynomial functions of x denoted as $\varphi_r(x)$, where $r = 0, 1, \ldots, P$. For Y axis, we chose $Q+1$ polynomial functions of y denoted as $\phi_s(y)$, where $s = 0, 1, \ldots, Q$. Let $\varphi_r(x)\phi_s(y)$ be the primary functions. Denote $\{c_{rs}\}$ as the unknown coefficient set. We can construct a function to represent an unknown curved surface as follows:

$$f(x, y) = \sum_{s=0}^{Q} \sum_{r=0}^{P} c_{rs} \varphi_r(x) \phi_s(y) \tag{1}$$

Assume there are $(m + 1) \times (n + 1)$ points in $Oxyz$ denoted as $S = \{(x_i, y_j, z_{ij})\}$, where $i = 0, 1, \ldots, m$ and $j = 0, 1, \ldots, n$. Fitted curved surface is an approximation to the actual curved surface, therefore, there exist errors between the calculated values from the fitted curved surface function and the actual values. We define the error square as follows:

$$I = \sum_{j=0}^{n} \sum_{i=0}^{m} \left[f(x_i, y_j) - z_{ij} \right]^2$$

$$= \sum_{j=0}^{n} \sum_{i=0}^{m} \left[\sum_{s=0}^{Q} \sum_{r=0}^{P} c_{rs} \varphi_r(x) \phi_s(y) - z_{ij} \right]^2 \tag{2}$$

If there is a coefficient set $\{c_{rs}^*\}$ which minimize I, then $f^*(x, y)$ based on $\{c_{rs}^*\}$ is the fitted curved surface of point set S by using least square fitting method. In this situation, the following equation set must be true:

$$\frac{\partial I}{\partial c_{rs}^*} = 2 \sum_{j=0}^{n} \sum_{i=0}^{m} \left[(f^*(x_i, y_j) - z_{ij}) \varphi_r(x_i) \phi_s(y_j) \right]$$

$$= 0 \quad (r = 0, 1, \ldots, P; s = 0, 1, \ldots, Q) \tag{3}$$

Denoting matrices

$$A = [\varphi_r(x_i)]_{(m+1)\times(P+1)}$$
$$B = [\phi_s(y_j)]_{(n+1)\times(Q+1)}$$
$$Z = [z_{ij}]_{(m+1)\times(n+1)}$$
$$C = [c_{ij}^*]_{(P+1)\times(Q+1)}$$

(4)

We can obtain coefficient values by simplifying Eq. (3) and substituting the matrices in Eq. (4) into the simplified equation.

$$C = (A^T A)^{-1} A^T Z B (B^T B)^{-1}$$

(5)

Correspondingly, we get the fitted curved surface $f^*(x, y)$ of point set S.

3.2   Calculate Curvatures

Once the fitted curved surface is obtained, we can calculate the curvatures of the curved surface. The fitted curved surface function can be rewritten as a vector equation as follows:

$$\vec{t} = (x, y, f^*(x, y))$$

(6)

Denoting f^* as $f^*(x, y)$, we can obtain the first order differential and the second order differential about x and y of $\vec{t}$ as follows:

$$\vec{t}_x = (1, 0, f_x^*), \quad \vec{t}_y = (0, 1, f_y^*)$$
$$\vec{t}_{xx} = (0, 0, f_{xx}^*), \quad \vec{t}_{yy} = (0, 0, f_{yy}^*), \quad \vec{t}_{xy} = (0, 0, f_{xy}^*)$$
$$f_x^* = \frac{\partial f^*}{\partial x}, \quad f_y^* = \frac{\partial f^*}{\partial y}, \quad f_{xx}^* = \frac{\partial^2 f^*}{\partial x^2}, \quad f_{yy}^* = \frac{\partial^2 f^*}{\partial y^2}, \quad f_{xy}^* = \frac{\partial^2 f^*}{\partial x \partial y}$$

(7)

The values of H and K can be obtained through the fundamental form definition of the curved surface as follows:

$$H = \frac{LG - 2MF + NE}{2(EG - F^2)}$$
$$K = \frac{LN - M^2}{EG - F^2}$$

(8)

where E, F, G, L, M, N are parameters of the first fundamental form and the second fundamental form of the curved surface and depend on Eq. (7).

$$E = \vec{t}_x \cdot \vec{t}_x, \quad L = \vec{t}_{xx} \cdot \frac{\vec{t}_x \times \vec{t}_y}{|\vec{t}_x \times \vec{t}_y|}$$

$$F = \vec{t}_x \cdot \vec{t}_y, \quad M = \vec{t}_{xy} \cdot \frac{\vec{t}_x \times \vec{t}_y}{|\vec{t}_x \times \vec{t}_y|}$$

(9)

$$G = \vec{t}_y \cdot \vec{t}_y, \quad N = \vec{t}_{yy} \cdot \frac{\vec{t}_x \times \vec{t}_y}{|\vec{t}_x \times \vec{t}_y|}$$

Replacing parameters in Eq. (8) with the parameters in Eq. (9) and combining with Eq. (7), we can get H and K represented by the differential forms of f^* shown as following:

$$H = \frac{(1 + f_y^{*2})f_{xx}^* + (1 + f_x^{*2})f_{yy}^* - 2f_x^* f_y^* f_{xy}^*}{2(1 + f_x^{*2} + f_y^{*2})^{3/2}}$$

$$K = \frac{f_{xx}^* f_{yy}^* - f_{xy}^{*2}}{(1 + f_x^{*2} + f_y^{*2})^2}$$

(10)

Using Eq. (10), we can get H and K of pixels in an image based on the fitted function of the image.

3.3 Generate USCF Matrix

Once the curvature feature space in O_{HK} is obtained, we partition the curvature feature space into $w \times v$ units. Then we count the number of pixels in each unit to generate the USCF matrix of an image.

The non-uniform distribution of pixels in O_{HK} made it ineffective to uniformly partition the curvature distribution area. Points in O_{HK} are distributed widely but most points are close to the origin. Uniform partition of the curvature feature space will result in non-uniform statistical features, *e.g.* a small number of units will contain most points and most units are empty, which will result in USCF matrices of different objects with no significant difference. Hence, we partition the curvature feature space non-uniformly according to the density to generate distinct USCF matrix with uniform statistical features.

Assume the curvature feature space of the image is $Area$, which is defined as $Area = \{(H, K)|a < H < b, c < K < d\}$. We use delimiters $H_i(i = 0, 1, \ldots, w)$ and $K_j(j = 0, 1, \ldots, v)$ to divide curvature feature space $Area$ into $w \times v$ parts, where $H_{i-1} < H_i$, $H_0 = a$, $H_w = b$ and $K_{j-1} < K_j$, $K_0 = c$, $K_v = d$. We denote a part as $Area_{ji}$, which is defined as follows:

$$Area_{ji} = \{(H, K)|H_{i-1} < H \le H_i, K_{j-1} < K \le K_j\}$$

(11)

where $i = 1, 2, \ldots, w$ and $j = 1, 2, \ldots, v$.

We use $count(Area_{ji})$ to represent the number of pixels whose curvature coordinates (H, K) are located in $Area_{ji}$. Subsequently, we can define the USCF matrix as follows:

$$D = [count(Area_{ji})]_{v \times w}$$

(12)

The USCF matrix D reflects the curvature feature of a curved surface and we use it to represent the image that the curved surface is fitted from.

The recognition ability of USCF algorithm depends on the partition of curvature feature space. The more units curvature feature space is divided into, the more detailed textures of an object are kept. Meanwhile, the recognition result can be easily affected by image change because smaller unit partition weakens general feature and is more sensitive to local feature variation. On the other side, the less parts curvature feature space is divided into, the better image change immunity of USCF algorithm is, with the cost of reducing the recognition precision of USCF algorithm.

3.4   Compare the Similarity of USCF Matrices

We can obtain the similarity of template object image and candidate object image by comparing the similarity of their USCF matrices. Let $D[i, j]$ represent the element located in the ith row and the jth column of matrix D. Let D_T and D_M represent the USCF matrices of template object image and candidate object image, respectively. We define $dist$ as the metric to measure the similarity between D_T and D_M by calculating their Euclidean distance. To normalize $dist$ so that all the values are in $[0, 1]$, every element in the matrix will be divided by the sum of all elements in the matrix.

$$dist = \sum_{i=1}^{v} \sum_{j=1}^{w} \left(D_T[i,j] \Big/ \sum_{p=1}^{v} \sum_{q=1}^{w} D_T[p,q] - D_M[i,j] \Big/ \sum_{p=1}^{v} \sum_{q=1}^{w} D_M[p,q] \right)^2 \quad (13)$$

The value of $dist$ represents the degree of similarity between template and candidate images. If $D_T = D_M$, the value of $dist$ is equal to zero.

4   Experimental Results

All experiments in this section were carried out on a desktop PC with Intel(R) Core(TM) i5-3470 CPU and 8 GB memory space. USCF algorithm was compared with SIFT, SURF, ORB, gray histogram, entropy, unit entropy, GIST, HoG and Hu's moment invariants algorithms on ALOI-COL Database, COIL-100 Database, ETH-80 Database and ETHZ another 53 Objects Database, respectively. SIFT, SURF, ORB, HoG and Hu's moment invariants algorithms were provided by OpenCV 3.0. Other algorithms were programmed in C++ language.

Firstly, we compared the recognition rates of the ten test algorithms on the images against one of the variables, *i.e.* rotation, illumination, or viewpoint variation. Then we compared USCF algorithm with the other nine algorithms under a real complex environment with simultaneous variation of multiple variables including rotation, illumination and viewpoint. These four types of experiments were performed on images with sizes of 15×15, 20×20, 25×25, 30×30, 35×35 and 40×40 pixels, which were shrunk from the images in above image database by using bicubic interpolation, respectively. Finally, we gave comparison of USCF and other nine algorithms on images from two videos.

4.1   Parameter Selection

The selection of fitting parameters affects the results of USCF algorithm. To avoid complex fitting function and get accurate curvature values, we calculated the curvatures of every pixel by using the pixel with 8 surrounding pixels to fit each local small curved surface respectively. To simplify calculation, the primary functions $\varphi_r(x)$ and $\phi_s(y)$ were chosen as follows:

$$\varphi_r(x) = x^r \quad (r = 0, 1, 2)$$
$$\phi_s(y) = y^s \quad (s = 0, 1, 2) \tag{14}$$

After performing a large number of experiments, we found that the distribution area of K and H of most pixels are in the range of (-1000, 1000) and partitioning the distribution area into 17 parts and 11 parts can get a good recognition performance. In this situation, most units are not empty and contain enough points to distinguish tiny objects and eliminate interference. The demarcation points was generated as follows:

$$H_i = [(i - 5.5)/|i - 5.5|] \times 10^{|i-5.5|-2.5} \quad (i = 0, 1, \ldots, 11)$$
$$K_j = [(j - 8.5)/|j - 8.5|] \times 10^{|j-8.5|-5.5} \quad (j = 0, 1, \ldots, 17) \tag{15}$$

In the experiments, FlannBasedMatcher was used as the matching strategy and at least 3 keypoints were required to correctly match the candidate and the template images for SIFT, SURF and ORB algorithms. For entropy algorithm, the absolute value of entropy difference between the template and candidate object images was the matching criterion. For unit entropy and HoG algorithms, we used 5×5 pixels as the size of each unit. We directly applied Hu's moment invariants of the whole image to match the object but did not extract the contour of the object, and the cosine value of its feature vector was the metric to measure the similarity of the template object image and candidate object image. For unit entropy, GIST, HoG and gray histogram, we compared their feature vector similarity by using Euclidean distance.

4.2 Robustness Against Rotation

COIL-100 Database was used to evaluate the anti-rotation performance of USCF and other nine algorithms. The candidate object images were rotated clockwise by 15, 60, 90 and 175°, respectively. Some of the selected experimental images are shown in Fig. 3.

As shown in Fig. 4, the recognition rate of USCF algorithm was from 70 % up to 90 % with the size of the objects from 15×15 to 40×40 pixels. USCF is robust to rotation because USCF is based on curvature, which is independent of the object orientation, and USCF non-uniformly partitions the curvature distribution map according to the curvature distribution density but not directly partitions the original images. The recognition rate of Hu's moment invariants was from 80 % to 90 %. The performance of USCF algorithm was as good as that of Hu's moment invariants algorithm when the size of the object was larger than 35×35 pixels.

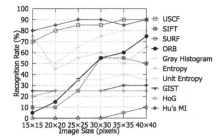

Fig. 3. Examples of selected experimental images. From left to right, the rotation angles of the objects are 0, 15, 60, 90 and 175°, respectively

Fig. 4. Anti-rotation experimental results of USCF and other nine algorithms on the test images with different sizes

Entropy and gray histogram had worse performance than USCF and Hu's moment invariants but had better performance than other algorithms, because they are based on general statistical feature of the images which is insensitive to image rotation. Unit entropy, HoG and GIST performed poorly because they directly partition the original images. SIFT, SURF and

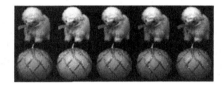

Fig. 5. Examples of selected experimental images from ALOI-COL Database. From left to right, the illumination conditions are i110, i140, i170, i210 and i250, respectively

ORB are robust to rotation, but they cannot obtain enough keypoints for tiny object recognition. The best recognition rate of SURF was only 10 % in the experiments due to its method used to detect keypoints. SIFT and ORB had better performance than SURF. However, the recognition rates for those algorithms increased as the object sizes increased.

4.3   Robustness Against Illumination Variation

ALOI-COL Database was used to evaluate the robustness against illumination variation of the algorithms. We used the object images in the dataset illuminated under condition i250 as template object image and the object images illuminated under conditions i110, i140, i170 and i210 as candidate object images, respectively. Some of the selected test images are shown in Fig. 5.

As shown in Fig. 6, unit entropy, HoG and GIST algorithm recognized tiny object very well under varying illumination because their local statistical features are insensitive to illumination change. The recognition rate of the three algorithms were 100 % almost in all cases except it was 80 % for unit entropy when the object size was 15×15 pixels. USCF algorithm performed better than other six algorithms because USCF is invariant to linear illumination change. When the object size became 40×40 pixels, the recognition rate of USCF algorithm was 100 %. Gray histogram, entropy and Hu's moment invariants algorithms are

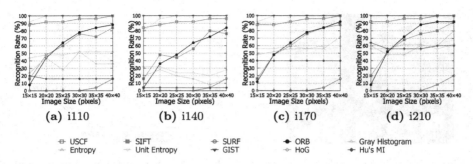

(a) i110   (b) i140   (c) i170   (d) i210

⊟ USCF   ▪ SIFT   ⊖ SURF   ◆ ORB   ⟋ Gray Histogram
⟋ Entropy   ⟋ Unit Entropy ▾ GIST   ◇ HoG   ✦ Hu's MI

Fig. 6. Experimental results of USCF and other nine algorithms under different illumination conditions for different sizes of the images

based on whole gray values which change obviously with illumination varying. Their recognition rates were worse than those of SIFT and ORB. SIFT, SURF and ORB are also invariant to linear illumination change. Their poor performance is mainly due to their limitation to tiny object and the contrast change produced by non-uniform illumination change. However, the recognition rates increased with the object sizes increased. The best recognition rate of SURF was only 20 % while those of SIFT and ORB were 90 %.

4.4 Robustness Against Slight Camera Viewpoint Variation

The COIL-100 Database was used to evaluate the performance of the ten test algorithms under varying viewpoint. The images with the view of 0 degree were used as the template images while the images with views of 5, 10, 15 and 20° were candidate images. Some of the selected test images are shown in Fig. 7.

Fig. 7. Examples of the selected test images from COIL-100 Database. From left to right, the view of camera are 0, 5, 10, 15 and 20° respectively

As shown in Fig. 8, the algorithms based on local statistical information, including HoG, GIST, unit entropy, and USCF, performed much better than other algorithms. Their recognition rates were close to 100 % when viewpoint change was no more than 10°, while the performance reduced with the increasing of viewpoint change. This indicates that HoG, GIST, unit entropy and USCF algorithms are partially invariant to viewpoint variation. Curvature is derived from calculating second derivative of the fitted curved surface, which keeps more image details and is more sensitive to non-uniform change of local gray value than gradient, energy spectra and entropy. Therefore, the recognition rates of USCF were close to those of HoG, GIST, and unit entropy algorithms but lower than them.

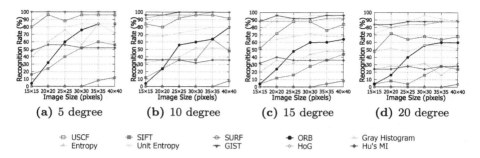

Fig. 8. Experimental results of USCF and other nine algorithms under different viewports for different sizes of images

Slight viewpoint changes have relatively little impact on statistical features. As shown in Fig. 8, the best recognition rates of gray histogram and entropy algorithms were 84 % when the camera view changed by 5°. However, entropy algorithm performed worse than gray histogram. The recognition rates of Hu's moment invariants algorithm were from 50 % down to about 25 % with the viewpoint varied from 5° to 20°. The results shows that Hu's moment invariants algorithm is sensitive to viewpoint variation, because Hu's moment invariants are based on the image centroid which shift as viewpoint changes. ORB performed much better than SIFT, SURF algorithms. The best recognition rate of ORB reached 80 % when the size of the object was 40×40 pixels and the viewpoint changed by 10°. The best performance of SURF was only 12 % when the size of the object was 40×40 pixels and the viewpoint changed by 5°.

4.5   Recognition Rate in Complicated Conditions

In a real-world environment, object recognition is usually carried under a complicated condition with simultaneous variation of multiple variables including variation of rotation, illumination and viewpoint. ETH-80 Database and ETHZ another 53 Objects Database were used to test the recognition ability of the algorithms in complicated conditions. In the two datasets, each object is represented by multiple images with different status such as upside down, rotation, different viewpoint or illumination. Some of the selected test images are shown in Fig. 9.

As shown in Fig. 10, USCF algorithm had the best performance among the ten algorithms in the experiments. The recognition rate of USCF was 90 % when the sizes of tiny objects were from 25×25 to 35×35 pixels. The best recognition rate of USCF algorithm reached 95 % when the object size was 40×40 pixels. Since unit entropy, HoG and GIST algorithms are sensitive to rotation, the best performance of unit entropy algorithm was 75 % when the sizes of tiny object was 35×35 pixels and the recognition rates of HoG and GIST algorithms were no more than 60 % in all sizes. The recognition rates of gray histogram was from 50 % to 63 % with the object sizes from 15×15 to 40×40 pixels. The best recognition rate of Hu's moment invariants was 70 % when the object size was 30×30 pixels. In such a complex environment, entropy, ORB, SIFT and SURF algorithms had poor performance. The best recognition rate of entropy algorithm was 35 % when the object size was 20×20 pixels. The best performance of SIFT and ORB was 40 % and 42 %, respectively, and SUFR algorithm could hardly have effective recognition to any sizes of tiny objects used in the experiments.

The experimental results showed that USCF algorithm had best performance among all algorithms tested in tiny object recognition under real complex environment with simultaneous variation of rotation, illumination and viewpoint.

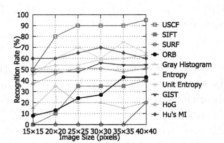

Fig. 9. Examples of selected test images from ETH-80 Database and ETHZ another 53 Objects Database

Fig. 10. Experimental results of USCF and other nine algorithms on the test images with different sizes under complex conditions

4.6   Comparison of the Test Algorithms on Images from Videos

In this section, the ten algorithms were applied on the images from two videos, a toy car video taken by ourselves and a jet flight video taken in an air show, with background interference and random varying in rotation, viewpoint and illumination as shown in Fig. 11. The jet of the flight was great background interference because it is similar to the object. The information of the test images is shown in Table 1. We cut the object image from a frame as the template and used the object image with similar scale in other frames as candidate images. All test images were directly cut from the videos without preprocessing.

From Table. 2, we can see that USCF had the best performance among the test algorithms. The recognition rates of USCF were from 65 % to 100 % while those of HoG and GIST, which performed best among the nine compared algorithms, were from 2 % to 100 % and 4 % to 100 %, respectively. HoG and GIST performed quite poorly when object rotates violently. Algorithms based on simple statistic of gray values, such as entropy, unit entropy and gray histogram, were badly affected by the background whose color is similar to the object color. Such background interference greatly affected Hu's moment invariants as well. SURF could hardly recognize the tiny objects. SIFT and ORB were badly affected by comprehensive condition changes but had relative good performance to the jet background.

Table 1. The information of the test images used in the experiment

Video	Images set (number)	Template size	Range of candidate image size	Rotation	Viewpoint change	Illumination chang
Toy Car	Data1 (60)	40×29	38×27 to 44×33	Slight	Mean	Slight
	Data2 (110)	36×26	32×22 to 38×28	Great	Mean	Slight
	Data3 (26)	26×17	25×14 to 27×18	Slight	Mean	Mean
Jet Flight	Data4 (51)	35×35	23×23 to 38×38	Slight	Slight	Slight
	Data5 (100)	23×23	18×18 to 29×29	Slight	Slight	Slight

Table 2. The performance of the test algorithms on images from the video datasets

Test algorithm	Recognition rate				
	Data1	Data2	Data3	Data4	Data5
USCF	100 %	100 %	65 %	90 %	97 %
SIFT	25 %	0	0	90 %	42 %
SURF	0	0	0	4 %	0
ORB	17 %	5 %	7 %	60 %	23 %
Gray Histogram	50 %	52 %	57 %	16 %	29 %
Entropy	13 %	18 %	4 %	17 %	2 %
Unit Entropy	98 %	77 %	65 %	53 %	13 %
GIST	96 %	4 %	100 %	100 %	100 %
HoG	100 %	2 %	100 %	100 %	100 %
Hu's MI	27 %	26 %	11 %	16 %	5 %

Fig. 11. Some recognition results of USCF applied in recognizing object images from two videos. The template images are on the left top corner. The red boxes show the recognition results (Color figure online)

5 Conclusions

In this paper, we proposed a novel object recognition algorithm, USCF algorithm, based on unit statistical curvature feature. USCF algorithm calculates mean curvature and Gaussian curvature of each pixel in the fitted curved surface of an object image to generate a unit statistical curvature feature matrix to characterize the tiny object. The experimental results showed that USCF algorithm is robust to rotation and illumination variation, and can tolerate slight viewpoint variation. Under complex test conditions with simultaneous rotation, illumination, viewpoint variation and background interference, the recognition rate of USCF was the highest among all ten tested algorithms. USCF cost less than 40 ms on a desktop PC with Intel(R) Core(TM) i5-3470 CPU when the image sizes were smaller than 40×40 pixels, which indicates that USCF can be applied in a real time application for tiny object recognition.

References

1. Torralba, A., Fergus, R., Freeman, W.T.: 80 million tiny images: a large data set for nonparametric object and scene recognition. IEEE Trans. Pattern Anal. Mach. Intell. **30**(11), 1958–1970 (2008)
2. Nguyen, D.T.: A novel chamfer template matching method using variational mean field. In: 2014 IEEE Conference on Computer Vision and Pattern Recognition, pp. 2425–2432. IEEE (2014)
3. Satpathy, A., Jiang, X., Eng, H.L.: LBP-based edge-texture features for object recognition. IEEE Trans. Image Process. **23**(5), 1953–1964 (2014)
4. Xu, Y., Quan, Y., Zhang, Z., Ji, H., Fermüller, C., Nishigaki, M., Dementhon, D.: Contour-based recognition. In: 2012 IEEE Conference on Computer Vision and Pattern Recognition (CVPR), pp. 3402–3409. IEEE (2012)
5. Lowe, D.G.: Distinctive image features from scale-invariant keypoints. Int. J. Comput. Vis. **60**(2), 91–110 (2004)
6. Bay, H., Ess, A., Tuytelaars, T., Van Gool, L.: Speeded-up robust features (SURF). Comput. Vis. Image Underst. **110**(3), 346–359 (2008)
7. Rani, R., Grewal, S.K., Panwar, K.: Object recognition: performance evaluation using SIFT and SURF. Int. J. Comput. Appl. **75**(3), 39–47 (2013)
8. Rublee, E., Rabaud, V., Konolige, K., Bradski, G.: ORB: an efficient alternative to SIFT or SURF. In: 2011 International Conference on Computer Vision, pp. 2564–2571. IEEE (2011)
9. Hauagge, D.C., Snavely, N.: Image matching using local symmetry features. In: 2012 IEEE Conference on Computer Vision and Pattern Recognition (CVPR), pp. 206–213. IEEE (2012)
10. Hu, M.K.: Visual pattern recognition by moment invariants. IRE Trans. Inf. Theor. **8**(2), 179–187 (1962)
11. Fritz, G., Paletta, L., Bischof, H.: Object recognition using local information content. In: Proceedings of the 17th International Conference on Pattern Recognition, ICPR 2004, vol. 2, pp. 15–18. IEEE (2004)
12. Dalal, N., Triggs, B.: Histograms of oriented gradients for human detection. In: 2005 IEEE Computer Society Conference on Computer Vision and Pattern Recognition (CVPR 2005), vol. 1, pp. 886–893. IEEE (2005)
13. Douze, M., Jégou, H., Sandhawalia, H., Amsaleg, L., Schmid, C.: Evaluation of GIST descriptors for web-scale image search. In: Proceedings of the ACM International Conference on Image and Video Retrieval, p. 19. ACM (2009)
14. Ebert, S., Larlus, D., Schiele, B.: Extracting structures in image collections for object recognition. In: Daniilidis, K., Maragos, P., Paragios, N. (eds.) ECCV 2010. LNCS, vol. 6311, pp. 720–733. Springer, Heidelberg (2010). doi:10.1007/978-3-642-15549-9_52
15. Fasel, B., Gatica-Perez, D.: Rotation-invariant neoperceptron. In: 18th International Conference on Pattern Recognition (ICPR 2006), vol. 3, pp. 336–339. IEEE (2006)
16. Pan, H., Xia, L.Z.: Efficient object recognition using boundary representation and wavelet neural network. IEEE Trans. Neural Netw. **19**(12), 2132–2149 (2008)
17. Wang, B., Bai, X., Wang, X., Liu, W., Tu, Z.: Object recognition using junctions. In: Daniilidis, K., Maragos, P., Paragios, N. (eds.) Computer Vision – ECCV 2010. LNCS, vol. 6315, pp. 15–28. Springer, Heidelberg (2010)

18. Agrawal, P., Girshick, R., Malik, J.: Analyzing the performance of multilayer neural networks for object recognition. In: Fleet, D., Pajdla, T., Schiele, B., Tuytelaars, T. (eds.) ECCV 2014. LNCS, vol. 8695, pp. 329–344. Springer, Heidelberg (2014). doi:10.1007/978-3-319-10584-0_22

19. Nene, S.A., Nayar, S.K., Murase, H., et al.: Columbia object image library (coil-20). Technical report, Technical report CUCS-005-96 (1996)

20. Geusebroek, J.M., Burghouts, G.J., Smeulders, A.W.: The amsterdam library of object images. Int. J. Comput. Vis. **61**(1), 103–112 (2005)

21. Leibe, B., Schiele, B.: Analyzing appearance and contour based methods for object categorization. In: Proceedings of the 2003 IEEE Computer Society Conference on Computer Vision and Pattern Recognition, vol. 2, pp. II-409. IEEE (2003)

Fine-Grained Material Classification Using Micro-geometry and Reflectance

Christos Kampouris[1]([✉]), Stefanos Zafeiriou[1], Abhijeet Ghosh[1],
and Sotiris Malassiotis[2]

[1] Department of Computing, Imperial College London, London, UK
{c.kampouris12,s.zafeiriou,ghosh}@imperial.ac.uk
[2] Centre for Research and Technology Hellas (CERTH), Thessaloniki, Greece
malasiot@iti.gr

Abstract. In this paper we focus on an understudied computer vision problem, particularly how the micro-geometry and the reflectance of a surface can be used to infer its material. To this end, we introduce a new, publicly available database for fine-grained material classification, consisting of over 2000 surfaces of fabrics (http://ibug.doc.ic.ac.uk/resources/fabrics.). The database has been collected using a custom-made portable but cheap and easy to assemble photometric stereo sensor. We use the normal map and the albedo of each surface to recognize its material via the use of handcrafted and learned features and various feature encodings. We also perform garment classification using the same approach. We show that the fusion of normals and albedo information outperforms standard methods which rely only on the use of texture information. Our methodologies, both for data collection, as well as for material classification can be applied easily to many real-word scenarios including design of new robots able to sense materials and industrial inspection.

Keywords: Material classification · Micro-geometry · Reflectance · Photometric stereo

1 Introduction

Materials recognition from their visual appearance is an important problem in computer vision having numerous applications spanning from scene analysis to robotics and industrial inspection. Knowledge of the material of an object or surface can provide useful information about its properties. Metallic objects are usually rigid while fabric is deformable and glass is fragile. Humans use daily this kind of information when they interact with the physical world. For example, they are more careful when they hold a glass bottle than a plastic one and they avoid walking on ice or other slippery surfaces. It would be useful in many applications, such as robotic manipulation or autonomous navigation, if a computer vision system had the same ability.

Due to the limited amount of data available the problem of material recognition/classification was not among the most popular computer vision areas [1–7].

© Springer International Publishing AG 2016
B. Leibe et al. (Eds.): ECCV 2016, Part V, LNCS 9909, pp. 778–792, 2016.
DOI: 10.1007/978-3-319-46454-1_47

But with the advent of the Internet and crowd-source annotation, collection and annotation of large databases of materials and textures was made feasible, which in turn brought renewed attention to the problem of material classification [8–12]. Currently the trend is to use materials captured in unconstrained conditions, also referred to as "in-the-wild", and mainly in the large scale [8–11]. In this paper, we take a different direction which has, to the best of our knowledge, has received limited attention. We study the problem of fine-grained material, and particularly fabric, classification in the fine scale introducing the first large database suitable for the task.

Recognizing materials from images is a challenging task because the appearance of a surface depends on a variety of factors such as its shape, its reflectance properties, illumination, viewing direction etc. Material recognition is usually treated as texture classification. Statistical learning techniques have been employed [1–3] on databases of different materials taken under multiple illumination and viewing directions [13–15]. Despite the very high classification rates achieved this way [3], the introduction of data captured "in-the-wild" have recently showed that the problem is extremely challenging in real world conditions.

On the other hand, humans do not rely only on vision to recognize materials. The sense of touch can be really useful to discriminate materials with subtle differences. For example, when someone wants to find out the material a garment is made of, they usually rub it to assess its roughness. This gives us the hint that the micro-geometry of the garment surface provides useful information for its material.

In this paper, we study how the micro-geometry and the reflectance of a surface can be used to infer its material. To recover the micro-geometry we use

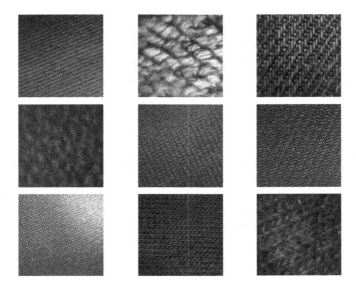

Fig. 1. Samples from our database. From left to right, top to bottom: cotton, terrycloth, denim, fleece, nylon, polyester, silk, viscose, and wool.

photometric stereo, which gives us the normal map and the albedo of the surface by capturing images under different illumination conditions. An advantage of photometric stereo over other techniques, like binocular stereo, is that there is no correspondence problem between images. All images are captured under the same view point and only the illumination is different. That makes photometric stereo a fast and computational efficient technique that suits well the time constraints of a real-world application.

To be able to apply photometric stereo in unconstrained environments, we built a portable photometric stereo sensor using low cost, off-the-shelf components. The sensor recovers the normal map and the albedo of various surfaces fast and accurately and has the ability to capture fine micro-structure details, as we can see in Fig. 1. Using the sensor we collected surface patches of over 2000 garments. Knowing the fabric of a garment can help robots manipulate clothes more robustly and facilitate the automation of household chores like laundry [16] and ironing.

In contrast to most datasets [17,18] where fabrics are treated as one of the material classes, we investigate the problem of classifying 9 different fabric classes - cotton, denim, fleece, nylon, polyester, silk, terrycloth, viscose, and wool. This fine-grained classification problem is much more challenging due to the large intra-class and small inter-class variance that fabrics have. We perform a thorough evaluation of various feature encoding methodologies such as Bag of Visual Words (BoVW) [1], Pyramid Histogram Of visual Words (PHOW) [19], Fisher Vectors [20,21], Vector of Locally-Aggregated Descriptors (VLAD) [22] using both SIFT [23], as well as features from Convolutional Neural Networks (CNNs) [24]. We show that using both normals and albedo the classification accuracy is improved. In summary, our main contributions are:

– The first large, publicly available database of garment surfaces captured under different illumination conditions.
– An evaluation of texture features and encodings which shows that the micro-geometry and reflectance of a fabric can be used to classify its material more accurately than by using its texture.

2   Related Work

At first, texture classification was implemented on 2-D patches from image databases such as Brodatz textures [25]. One of the first efforts to collect a large database suitable for studying appearance of real-world surfaces was made in [13]. The so-called CUReT database contains image textures from around 60 different materials, each observed with over 200 different combinations of viewing and illumination directions. Leung and Malik [1] used the CUReT database for material classification, introducing the concept of 3D textons. They used a filter bank to obtain filter responses for each class of the CUReT database and they clustered them to obtain the 3-D textons. Then, they created a model for every training image by building its texton frequency histogram and they classified each test image by comparing its model with the learned models, introducing what is now known as the BoVW representation. In [1] a set of 48 filters were used for feature extraction (first and second derivatives of Gaussians at 6 orientations and 3 scales making a total of 36, 8 Laplacian of Gaussian filters and 4 Gaussians). A similar approach was followed in [2] using the so-called MR8 filter. The MR8 filter bank consists of 38 filters but only 8 filter responses. To achieve rotation invariance the filter bank contains filters (Gaussian and a Laplacian of Gaussian) at multiple orientations but only the maximum filter response across all orientations is used. Later Varma and Zisserman [3] questioned about the necessity of filter banks by succeeding comparable results using image patch exemplars as small as 3×3 instead of a filter bank. The KTH-TIPS (Textures under varying Illumination, Pose and Scale) image database was created to extend the CUReT database by providing variations in scale [4]. Despite the almost perfect classification rate in CUReT database the results of the same algorithms in KTH-TIPS showed that the performance drops significantly [5].

Sharan et al. created the more challenging material database FMD [18] with images taken from the Flickr website and captured under unknown real-world conditions (10 materials with 100 samples per material). Liu et al. [26] used the FMD and a Bayesian framework to achieve 45 % classification rate while Hu et al. [27] by using the Kernel Descriptor framework improved the accuracy to 54 %. Sharan et al. [7] used perceptually inspired features to further improve the results to 57 %.

Recently, in [10] the authors presented the first database with textures "in-the-wild" with various attributes (including the material of the texture) and in [9] a very large-scale, open dataset of materials in the wild, the so-called Materials in Context Database (MINC) was proposed [9]. Another database (UBO2014) that appeared recently for synthesising training images for material classification appeared in [28] (7 material categories, each consisting of measurements of 12 different material samples, measured in a darkened lab environment with controlled illumination). The above databases are suitable for training and testing generic material classification methodologies from appearance information.

In this paper we study the problem of fine-grained material classification using both the reflectance properties (albedo) and the micro-geometry (surface normals) of a surface. The most closely related work on fusing albedo and normals for material classification is the work on [29] which proposes a rotational invariant classification method. The authors applied successfully their method on real textures but they used only 30 samples belonging to various material classes (fabric, gravel, wood). In contrast, our database contains around 2000 samples and is suitable for fine-grained classification.

Regarding recognition of materials using micro-geometry the only relevant published technology is the tactile GelSight sensor [30,31]. In [30] the authors used the Gelsight sensor to collect a database of 40 material classes with 6 samples per class (the database is not publicly available). The Gelsight sensor is able to provide very high resolution height maps but cannot recover albedo [31] (contrary to our sensor which provides both micro-geometry and albedo).

3   Photometric Stereo Sensor

Photometric stereo [32] is a computer vision method that uses three or more images of a surface from the same viewpoint but under different illumination conditions to estimate the normal vector and albedo at each point. By integrating the normal map the 3-D shape of the surface can be acquired. Photometric stereo has found application in a wide variety of fields, ranging from medicine [33] to security [34] and from robotics [35] to archaeology [36].

We used this method to acquire the micro-geometry and the reflectance properties of garment surfaces. In order to capture a large number of garments, we built a small-sized, portable photometric stereo sensor using low-cost, off-the-shelf components, Fig. 2. The sensor consists of a webcam with adjustable focus, white light emitting diode (LED) arrays and a micro-controller to synchronize the LED arrays with the camera. It features an easy to use USB interface that connects directly to a computer with a standard USB port. All the components are enclosed in a 3-D printed cylindrical case with a diameter of 38 mm and height of 40 mm. The case has also a rectangular base that allows the sensor to be mounted in the gripper of a robot, Fig. 2 (right).

Fig. 2. The photometric stereo sensor on a table (left) and installed in the gripper of an industrial robot (right)

Fig. 3. Bottom view of our photometric stereo sensor having all lights off (left) and with one light on (right)

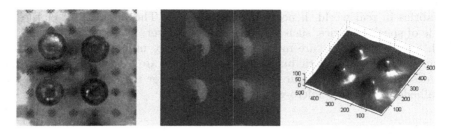

Fig. 4. Albedo, normals, and 3-D shape of our calibration target

The sensor captures 4 RGB images of a small patch of the inspected surface, one for each light source, in less than a second. The working distance of the camera is 3 cm and to achieve focus we had to modify appropriately the camera optics. The sensor resolution is 640×480 pixels but we crop all images to 400×400 pixels to avoid out-of-focus regions at the corners due to the very shallow depth of field. The corresponding field of view is approximately 10 mm × 10 mm, adequate to capture the micro-structure of most fabrics.

We use near-grazing illumination to maximize contrast and eliminate specularities. Because the light sources are close to the inspected surface the lighting field is not uniform. To confront this issue, we have captured with our sensor a flat surface with known albedo and use these images to normalize every new surface we capture.

As can be seen in Fig. 3, we use LED arrays to illuminate uniformly the inspected surface. However in such a close distance the illumination is not directional and we have to know the light vectors in each position to apply photometric stereo. To do so, we used a chrome sphere (2 mm diameter) in different locations to calibrate our lights and by interpolation we found the light vectors for each pixel. Next, we run photometric stereo to get the albedo and the normal map using the method of Barsky and Petrou [37] to deal with shadows and highlights. At the end we integrate the normals to obtain the 3D shape of the surface [38].

We evaluated the accuracy of our sensor by using a calibration target, consisting of a 2 × 2 grid of spheres of diameter of 2 mm. As we can see in Fig. 4 the sensor can accurately reconstruct the shape of the spheres. Since our goal is to capture the geometry of a surface for classification, we didn't further assess the reconstruction accuracy.

4   Dataset

Using the photometric stereo sensor we collected samples of the surface of over 2000 garments and fabrics. We visited many clothes shops with the sensor and a laptop and captured all our images "in the field". For every garment we kept information (attributes) about its material composition from the manufacturer label and its type (pants, shirt, skirt etc.). The dataset reflects the distribution of fabrics in real world, hence it is not balanced. The majority of clothes are made of specific fabrics, such as cotton and polyester, while some other fabrics, such as silk and linen, are more rare. Also, a large number of clothes are not composed of a single fabric but two or more fabrics are used to give the garment the desired properties. Figure 5 presents samples for major classes, along with its albedo and its 3-D micro-geometry.

Fig. 5. The 9 main fabric classes with albedo and 3D shape

4.1   Data Collection

The procedure we followed to capture our fabric dataset is depicted in Fig. 6. The photometric stereo sensor is placed on a flat region of the garment, equal to the field of view (10 mm × 10 mm). Initially the sensor turns on one light source to allow the camera to focus on the surface of the garment. Due to the shallow depth of field, this task is very important. Subsequently we capture 4 images, one for each light source. We normalize the captured images using reference images of a flat surface with known albedo.

Fig. 6. Capturing setup

Figure 6 shows the graphical user interface we use to collect the data. In the top row the 4 captured images are shown, while in the bottom row we visualize the albedo, the normal map (as an RGB image) and the 3-D shape of the surface. On the right side we can select the fabric of the garment (cotton, wool, etc.) as well as its type (t-shirt, pants, etc.).

5   Experiments

In this section we describe the experiments we run on our fabric database for fine-grained material and garment classification. First of all, a very important aspect of every classification system is the selection of features to use. In our case, we want to use features that distinguish fabric classes from one another. We are mostly interested in features that represent the micro-geometry and reflectance of the surface as they are encoded in normals and albedo respectively. To this end we have followed similar steps as [10]. We have used handcrafted, i.e. dense SIFT [23] features[1], as well as features coming from Deep Convolutional Neural Networks (CNN) [24,40]. Deep learning and especially CNNs dominate the field of object and speech recognition. CNNs contain a hierarchical model where we have a succession of convolutions and non-linearities. CNNs can learn very complex relationships, given that exist a large amount of data. In our case we used the VGG-M [40] pre-trained neural network which has 8 layers, 5 convolutional layers plus 3 fully connected. We have applied the non-linear features (dense SIFT and CNNs) to (a) albedo images, (b) the original images under different illuminants, (c) the normals (concatenate the three components, N_x, N_y, N_z, into a single image) and (d) fusing normals and albedo (by creating a larger image consisting of the albedo plus the three components of the normals). The following feature encodings have been applied to the local (dense SIFT) features:

- Feature encoding via the use of BoVW. BoVW uses Vector Quantisation (VQ) [41] of local features (i.e., responses of linear or non-linear filters) by mapping them to the closest visual word in a dictionary. The visual words (vocabulary) are prototypical features, i.e. kind of centroids, and are computed by applying a clustering methodology (e.g., K-means [42]). The BoVW encoding is a vector of occurrence counts the above vocabulary of visual words. BoVW was first proposed in [1] for the purpose of material classification.
- Another popular orderless encoding is the so-called VLAD [22]. VLAD, similar to BoVW, applies VQ to a collection of local features. It differs from the BoVW image descriptor by recording the difference from the cluster center, rather than the number of local features assigned to the cluster. VLAD accumulates first-order descriptor statistics instead of simple occurrences as in BoVW.
- A feature encoding that accumulated first and second order statistics of local features is the FV [21]. FV uses a soft clustering assignment by using a Gaussian Mixture Model (GMM) [43] instead of K-means. The soft-assignments (posterior probability of each GMM component) is used to weight first and second order statistics of local features.

For the case of CNNs features we have used them directly in the classifier or we used FV encoding before performing classification [11]. The classifier we used was a linear 1 versus "all" Support Vector Machine (SVM) [44]. We have performed four fold cross-validation (i.e., using 75 % for training and 25 % for testing in each fold).

In all experiments, we used the VLFeat library [45] to extract the SIFT features and to compute the feature encodings (BoVW, VLAD, FV). For the CNNs we used the MatConvNet library [46].

---

[1] We have tried other features such as Local Binary Patterns (LBPs) [39] and the MR8 filters in [2] but the results were much poorer than dense SIFT, hence are not reported.

5.1   Results

For our classification experiments we didn't use garments with blended fabrics. We kept only those whose composition is 95 % of one material. We also discarded fabric classes with too few samples. So, for our experiments we have chosen a subset of 1266 samples which belong to one of the following fabric classes: cotton, terrycloth, denim, fleece, nylon, polyester, silk, viscose, and wool. The number of samples in each class is shown in Table 1.

Table 1. Number of samples per class for fabric classification

Cotton	Terrycloth	Denim	Fleece	Nylon	Polyester	Silk	Viscose	Wool
588	30	162	33	50	226	50	37	90

Table 2 summarizes the results of our experiments for fabric classification. As we can see, the combination of albedo and normals gives constantly slightly better accuracy. This is true not only for the hand-made features but also for the learned features of CNNs. This provides evidence that using both geometry and texture is useful for fine grained material classification problems.

Table 2. Results for fabric classification

	SIFT			CNN - VGG-M		
Modality	FV	VLAD	BoVW	FV	FC	FC+FV
Images	65.3	58.9	58.4	66.5	44.0	71.7
Albedo	63.5	56.5	56.6	67.9	47.6	71.2
Normals	72.5	57.2	54.3	73.9	41.9	74.1
Alb+Norm	74.7	61.7	60.1	76.1	50.5	79.6

We also run experiments for garment recognition to investigate whether the garment type can be estimated by the microgeometry or albedo. Here we split our dataset in 6 classes: blouses, jackets, jeans, pants, shirts, and t-shirts. Table 3 shows the number of samples per garment class.

Table 3. Number of samples per class for garment classification

Blouses	Jackets	Jeans	Pants	Shirts	T-shirts
294	146	139	205	159	261

We used the same approach with fabric classification testing SIFT features in different encodings as well as CNN features. The results are presented in Table 4.

Table 4. Results for garment classification

	SIFT			CNN - VGG-M		
Modality	FV	VLAD	BoVW	FV	FC	FC+FV
Images	50.1	48.3	44.7	55.7	40.0	61.2
Albedo	49.5	49.7	46.6	57.3	40.6	63.4
Normals	54.9	51.3	53.3	54.2	41.9	64.3
Alb+Norm	55.6	51.6	52.8	57.1	50.5	64.6

It is obvious that this problem is a more difficult and requires more research but also in this case the fusion of albedo and normals gives the best results.

Figure 7 presents the confusion matrix for the combination of albedo and normals using fully-connected deep convolutional features from the VGG-M model and FV pooling. This model achieved 79.6 % average accuracy, surpassing both dense SIFT features with FV pooling and CNN with FV pooling (74.7 % and 76.1 % respectively). As we can see cotton, terrycloth, denim and fleece can be recognized successfully with almost no errors. On the other hand, classes like nylon and viscose are more difficult to classify due to their glossy appearance and the small number of samples in our dataset.

The same combination of local features and pooling encoder (FC-CNN + FV) gives also the best result for the problem of garment classification. Here the accuracy is 64.6 %, while using dense SIFT we get 55.6 % and using CNN + FV, 57.1 %. As we can see by observing the confusion matrix in Fig. 8 only the

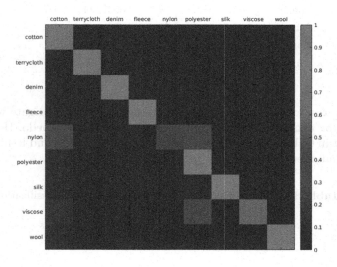

Fig. 7. Confusion matrix of the best fabric classifier (albedo and normals with FC-CNN and FV)

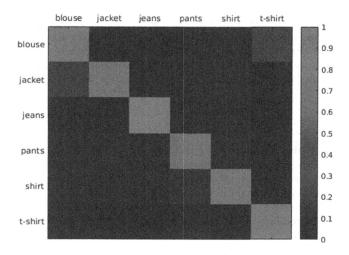

Fig. 8. Confusion matrix of the best garment classifier (albedo and normals with FC-CNN and FV)

classification rate of jeans is high. This is expected since jeans are made by denim fabric and our system can recognize denim accurately (Fig. 7). On the contrary, all other garments can be made of various fabrics and there is no one-to-one correspondence between fabric and garment class.

6   Conclusion

Material classification is important but challenging problem for computer vision. This work focuses on recognizing the material of clothes. Inspired by the fact that humans use their sense of touch to infer the fabric of a garment, we investigated the use of the micro-geometry of garments to recognize their materials. We built a portable photometric stereo sensor and introduced the first large scale dataset of garment surfaces, belonging to 9 different fabric classes. We tested a number of different features for material classification and showed that using both the micro-geometry and the reflectance properties of a fabric can improve the classification rate. Although there is room for improvement, our system is efficient and practical solution for material classification that can be applied in many different scenarios in robotics and industrial inspection.

Acknowledgments. This work has been inspired and initiated by the late Maria Petrou, professor at the department of Electrical and Electronic Engineering, Imperial College London and director of the Informatics Institute of the Centre for Research and Technology Hellas.

The work of Sotiris Malassiotis has been funded by the European Community 7th Framework Programme [FP7/2007-2013] under grant agreement FP7-288553 (CloPeMa). The database collection has taken place while Christos Kampouris was with

CERTH funded by CloPeMA. Experiments were conducted and the paper was written while Christos Kampouris was with Imperial College partially funded by the EPSRC project EP/N006259/1 (Computational Imaging and Analysis of Scene Appearance). The work of Abhijeet Ghosh has been funded by the EPSRC Early Career Fellowship EP/N006259/1 and the Royal Society Wolfson Research Merit Award.

References

1. Leung, T., Malik, J.: Representing and recognizing the visual appearance of materials using three-dimensional textons. Int. J. Comput. Vis. **43**(1), 29–44 (2001)
2. Varma, M., Zisserman, A.: A statistical approach to texture classification from single images. Int. J. Comput. Vis. **62**(1), 61–81 (2005)
3. Varma, M., Zisserman, A.: A statistical approach to material classification using image patch exemplars. IEEE Trans. Pattern Anal. Mach. Intell. **31**(11), 2032–2047 (2009)
4. Caputo, B., Hayman, E., Mallikarjuna, P.: Class-specific material categorisation. In: Tenth IEEE International Conference on Computer Vision, ICCV 2005, vol. 2, pp. 1597–1604. IEEE (2005)
5. Caputo, B., Hayman, E., Fritz, M., Eklundh, J.O.: Classifying materials in the real world. Image Vis. Comput. **28**(1), 150–163 (2010)
6. Varma, M., Zisserman, A.: Classifying images of materials: achieving viewpoint and illumination independence. In: Heyden, A., Sparr, G., Nielsen, M., Johansen, P. (eds.) ECCV 2002, Part III. LNCS, vol. 2352, pp. 255–271. Springer, Heidelberg (2002). doi:10.1007/3-540-47977-5_17
7. Sharan, L., Liu, C., Rosenholtz, R., Adelson, E.: Recognizing materials using perceptually inspired features. Int. J. Comput. Vis. **103**(3), 348–371 (2013)
8. Cimpoi, M., Maji, S., Kokkinos, I., Mohamed, S., Vedaldi, A.: Describing textures in the wild. In: Proceedings of the IEEE Conference on Computer Vision and Pattern Recognition, pp. 3606–3613 (2014)
9. Bell, S., Upchurch, P., Snavely, N., Bala, K.: Material recognition in the wild with the materials in context database. In: Proceedings of the IEEE Conference on Computer Vision and Pattern Recognition, pp. 3479–3487 (2015)
10. Cimpoi, M., Maji, S., Kokkinos, I., Vedaldi, A.: Deep filter banks for texture recognition, description, and segmentation. Int. J. Comput. Vis. **118**, 1–30 (2015)
11. Cimpoi, M., Maji, S., Vedaldi, A.: Deep filter banks for texture recognition and segmentation. In: Proceedings of the IEEE Conference on Computer Vision and Pattern Recognition, pp. 3828–3836 (2015)
12. Bell, S., Upchurch, P., Snavely, N., Bala, K.: Opensurfaces: a richly annotated catalog of surface appearance. ACM Trans. Graph. (TOG) **32**(4), 111 (2013)
13. Dana, K., Van-Ginneken, B., Nayar, S., Koenderink, J.: Reflectance and texture of real world surfaces. ACM Trans. Graph. (TOG) **18**(1), 1–34 (1999)
14. ALOT. www.science.uva.nl/~mark/alot
15. KTH-TIPS2. www.nada.kth.se/cvap/databases/kth-tips
16. Miller, S., van den Berg, J., Fritz, M., Darrell, T., Goldberg, K., Abbeel, P.: A geometric approach to robotic laundry folding. Int. J. Robot. Res. **31**(2), 249–267 (2012)
17. Deng, J., Dong, W., Socher, R., Li, L.J., Li, K., Fei-Fei, L.: Imagenet: a large-scale hierarchical image database. In: IEEE Conference on Computer Vision and Pattern Recognition, CVPR 2009, pp. 248–255, June 2009

18. Sharan, L., Rosenholtz, R., Adelson, E.: Material perception: what can you see in a brief glance? J. Vis. **9**(8), 784 (2009)
19. Bosch, A., Zisserman, A., Munoz, X.: Image classification using random forests and ferns. In: IEEE 11th International Conference on Computer Vision, ICCV 2007, pp. 1–8. IEEE (2007)
20. Jaakkola, T.S., Haussler, D., et al.: Exploiting generative models in discriminative classifiers. In: Advances in Neural Information Processing Systems, pp. 487–493 (1999)
21. Perronnin, F., Dance, C.: Fisher kernels on visual vocabularies for image categorization. In: IEEE Conference on Computer Vision and Pattern Recognition, CVPR 2007, pp. 1–8. IEEE (2007)
22. Jégou, H., Douze, M., Schmid, C., Pérez, P.: Aggregating local descriptors into a compact image representation. In: 2010 IEEE Conference on Computer Vision and Pattern Recognition (CVPR), pp. 3304–3311. IEEE (2010)
23. Lowe, D.: Object recognition from local scale-invariant features. In: The Proceedings of the Seventh IEEE International Conference on Computer Vision, vol. 2, pp. 1150–1157 (1999)
24. Simonyan, K., Zisserman, A.: Very deep convolutional networks for large-scale image recognition (2014). arXiv preprint: arXiv:1409.1556
25. Brodatz, P.: Textures. Dover Publications, New York (1966)
26. Liu, C., Sharan, L., Adelson, E., Rosenholtz, R.: Exploring features in a bayesian framework for material recognition. In: 2010 IEEE Conference on Computer Vision and Pattern Recognition (CVPR), pp. 239–246 (2010)
27. Hu, D., Bo, L., Ren, X.: Toward robust material recognition for everyday objects. In: Proceedings of the British Machine Vision Conference, pp. 48.1–48.11 (2011)
28. Weinmann, M., Gall, J., Klein, R.: Material classification based on training data synthesized using a BTF database. In: Fleet, D., Pajdla, T., Schiele, B., Tuytelaars, T. (eds.) ECCV 2014, Part III. LNCS, vol. 8691, pp. 156–171. Springer, Heidelberg (2014). doi:10.1007/978-3-319-10578-9_11
29. Wu, J., Chantler, M.J.: Combining gradient and albedo data for rotation invariant classification of 3d surface texture. In: Proceedings of the Ninth IEEE International Conference on Computer Vision, pp. 848–855. IEEE (2003)
30. Li, R., Adelson, E.: Sensing and recognizing surface textures using a gelsight sensor. In: Proceedings of the IEEE Conference on Computer Vision and Pattern Recognition, pp. 1241–1247 (2013)
31. Johnson, M.K., Cole, F., Raj, A., Adelson, E.H.: Microgeometry capture using an elastomeric sensor. ACM Trans. Graph. (TOG) **30**, 46 (2011). ACM
32. Woodham, R.: Photometric method for determining surface orientation from multiple images. Opt. Eng. **19**, 139–144 (1980)
33. Smith, L., Smith, M., Farooq, A.R., Sun, J., Ding, Y., Warr, R.: Machine vision 3D skin texture analysis for detection of melanoma. Sens. Rev. **31**(2), 111–119 (2011)
34. Zafeiriou, S., Atkinson, G., Hansen, M., Smith, W., Argyriou, V., Petrou, M., Smith, M., Smith, L.: Face recognition and verification using photometric stereo: the photoface database and a comprehensive evaluation. IEEE Trans. Inf. Forensics Secur. **8**(1), 121–135 (2013)
35. Ikeuchi, K., Nishihara, H.K., Horn, B.K., Sobalvarro, P., Nagata, S.: Determining grasp configurations using photometric stereo and the prism binocular stereo system. Int. J. Robot. Res. **5**(1), 46–65 (1986)
36. Einarsson, P., Hawkins, T., Debevec, P.: Photometric stereo for archeological inscriptions. In: ACM SIGGRAPH 2004 Sketches, p. 81. ACM, New York (2004)

37. Barsky, S., Petrou, M.: The 4-source photometric stereo technique for three-dimensional surfaces in the presence of highlights and shadows. IEEE Trans. Pattern Anal. Mach. Intell. **25**(10), 1239–1252 (2003)
38. Frankot, R., Chellappa, R.: A method for enforcing integrability in shape from shading algorithms. IEEE Trans. Pattern Anal. **10**(4), 439–451 (1988)
39. Ojala, T., Pietikäinen, M., Mäenpää, T.: Multiresolution gray-scale and rotation invariant texture classification with local binary patterns. IEEE Trans. Pattern Anal. Mach. Intell. **24**(7), 971–987 (2002)
40. Chatfield, K., Simonyan, K., Vedaldi, A., Zisserman, A.: Return of the devil in the details: delving deep into convolutional nets. In: British Machine Vision Conference (2014)
41. Gray, R.M.: Vector quantization. IEEE ASSP Mag. **1**(2), 4–29 (1984)
42. Jain, A.K., Dubes, R.C.: Algorithms for Clustering Data. Prentice-Hall, Inc., Upper Saddle River (1988)
43. Fukunaga, K.: Introduction to Statistical Pattern Recognition. Academic Press, Cambridge (2013)
44. Hsu, C.W., Lin, C.J.: A comparison of methods for multiclass support vector machines. IEEE Trans. Neural Netw. **13**(2), 415–425 (2002)
45. Vedaldi, A., Fulkerson, B.: VLFeat: an open and portable library of computer vision algorithms (2008). http://www.vlfeat.org/
46. Vedaldi, A., Lenc, K.: Matconvnet - convolutional neural networks for MATLAB. CoRR abs/1412.4564 (2014)

The Conditional Lucas & Kanade Algorithm

Chen-Hsuan Lin, Rui Zhu, and Simon Lucey[(✉)]

The Robotics Institute, Carnegie Mellon University, Pittsburgh, PA 15213, USA
{chenhsul,rz1}@andrew.cmu.edu, slucey@cs.cmu.edu

Abstract. The Lucas & Kanade (LK) algorithm is the method of choice
for efficient dense image and object alignment. The approach is efficient
as it attempts to model the connection between appearance and geometric displacement through a linear relationship that assumes independence across pixel coordinates. A drawback of the approach, however, is
its generative nature. Specifically, its performance is tightly coupled with
how well the linear model can synthesize appearance from geometric displacement, even though the alignment task itself is associated with the
inverse problem. In this paper, we present a new approach, referred to
as the Conditional LK algorithm, which: (i) directly learns linear models
that predict geometric displacement as a function of appearance, and
(ii) employs a novel strategy for ensuring that the generative pixel independence assumption can still be taken advantage of. We demonstrate
that our approach exhibits superior performance to classical generative
forms of the LK algorithm. Furthermore, we demonstrate its comparable
performance to state-of-the-art methods such as the Supervised Descent
Method with substantially less training examples, as well as the unique
ability to "swap" geometric warp functions without having to retrain
from scratch. Finally, from a theoretical perspective, our approach hints
at possible redundancies that exist in current state-of-the-art methods
for alignment that could be leveraged in vision systems of the future.

Keywords: Image alignment · Lucas & Kanade · Supervised Descent
Method

1   Introduction

The Lucas & Kanade (LK) algorithm [9] has been a popular approach for tackling
dense alignment problems for images and objects. At the heart of the algorithm
is the assumption that an approximate linear relationship exists between pixel
appearance and geometric displacement. Such a relationship is seldom exactly
linear, so a linearization process is typically repeated until convergence. Pixel
intensities are not deterministically differentiable with respect to geometric displacement; instead, the linear relationship must be established stochastically

Electronic supplementary material The online version of this chapter (doi:10.
1007/978-3-319-46454-1_48) contains supplementary material, which is available to
authorized users.

© Springer International Publishing AG 2016
B. Leibe et al. (Eds.): ECCV 2016, Part V, LNCS 9909, pp. 793–808, 2016.
DOI: 10.1007/978-3-319-46454-1_48

through a learning process. One of the most notable properties of the LK algorithm is how efficiently this linear relationship can be estimated. This efficiency stems from the assumption of independence across pixel coordinates - the parameters describing this linear relationship are classically referred to as image gradients. In practice, these image gradients are estimated through finite differencing operations. Numerous extensions and variations upon the LK algorithm have subsequently been explored in literature [3], and recent work has also demonstrated the utility of the LK framework [1,2,4] using classical dense descriptors such as dense SIFT [8], HOG [5], and LBP [12].

A drawback to the LK algorithm and its variants, however, is its generative nature. Specifically, it attempts to synthesize, through a linear model, how appearance changes as a function of geometric displacement, even though its end goal is the inverse problem. Recently, Xiong and De la Torre [14–16] proposed a new approach to image alignment known as the Supervised Descent Method (SDM). SDM shares similar properties with the LK algorithm as it also attempts to establish the relationship between appearance and geometric displacement using a sequence of linear models. One marked difference, however, is that SDM directly learns how geometric displacement changes as a function of appearance. This can be viewed as estimating the conditional likelihood function $p(\mathbf{y}|\mathbf{x})$, where $\mathbf{y}$ and $\mathbf{x}$ are geometric displacement and appearance respectively. As reported in literature [7] (and also confirmed by our own experiments in this paper), this can lead to substantially improved performance over classical LK as the learning algorithm is focused directly on the end goal (i.e. estimating geometric displacement from appearance).

Although it exhibits many favorable properties, SDM also comes with disadvantages. Specifically, due to its non-generative nature, SDM cannot take advantage of the pixel independence assumption enjoyed through classical LK (see Sect. 4 for a full treatment on this asymmetric property). Instead, it needs to model full dependence across all pixels, which requires: (i) a large amount of training data, and (ii) the requirement of adhoc regularization strategies in order to avoid a poorly conditioned linear system. Furthermore, SDM does not utilize prior knowledge of the type of geometric warp function being employed (e.g. similarity, affine, homography, point distribution model, etc.), which further simplifies the learning problem in classical LK.

In this paper, we propose a novel approach which, like SDM, attempts to learn a linear relationship between geometric displacement directly as a function of appearance. However, unlike SDM, we enforce that the pseudo-inverse of this linear relationship enjoys the generative independence assumption across pixels while utilizing prior knowledge of the parametric form of the geometric warp. We refer to our proposed approach as the Conditional LK algorithm. Experiments demonstrate that our approach achieves comparable, and in many cases better, performance to SDM across a myriad of tasks with substantially less training examples. We also show that our approach does not require any adhoc regularization term, and it exhibits a unique property of being able to "swap" the type of warp function being modeled (e.g. replace a homography with an affine warp function) without the need to retrain. Finally, our approach offers some unique theoretical insights into the redundancies that exist when attempting to learn efficient object/image aligners through a conditional paradigm.

Notations. We define our notations throughout the paper as follows: lowercase boldface symbols (*e.g.* $\mathbf{x}$) denote vectors, uppercase boldface symbols (*e.g.* $\mathbf{R}$) denote matrices, and uppercase calligraphic symbols (*e.g.* $\mathcal{I}$) denote functions. We treat images as a function of the warp parameters, and we use the notations $\mathcal{I}(\mathbf{x}) : \mathbb{R}^2 \to \mathbb{R}^K$ to indicate sampling of the K-channel image representation at subpixel location $\mathbf{x} = [x, y]^\top$. Common examples of multi-channel image representations include descriptors such as dense SIFT, HOG and LBP. We assume $K = 1$ when dealing with raw grayscale images.

2   The Lucas & Kanade Algorithm

At its heart, the Lucas & Kanade (LK) algorithm utilizes the assumption that,

$$\mathcal{I}(\mathbf{x} + \Delta\mathbf{x}) \approx \mathcal{I}(\mathbf{x}) + \nabla\mathcal{I}(\mathbf{x})\Delta\mathbf{x}. \tag{1}$$

where $\mathcal{I}(\mathbf{x}) : \mathbb{R}^2 \to \mathbb{R}^K$ is the image function representation and $\nabla\mathcal{I}(\mathbf{x}) : \mathbb{R}^2 \to \mathbb{R}^{K \times 2}$ is the image gradient function at pixel coordinate $\mathbf{x} = [x, y]$. In most instances, a useful image gradient function $\nabla\mathcal{I}(\mathbf{x})$ can be efficiently estimated through finite differencing operations. An alternative strategy is to treat the problem of gradient estimation as a per-pixel linear regression problem, where pixel intensities are samples around a neighborhood in order to "learn" the image gradients [4]. A focus of this paper is to explore this idea further by examining more sophisticated conditional learning objectives for learning image gradients.

For a given geometric warp function $\mathcal{W}\{\mathbf{x}; \mathbf{p}\} : \mathbb{R}^2 \to \mathbb{R}^2$ parameterized by the warp parameters $\mathbf{p} \in \mathbb{R}^P$, one can thus express the classic LK algorithm as minimizing the sum of squared differences (SSD) objective,

$$\min_{\Delta\mathbf{p}} \sum_{d=1}^{D} \left\| \mathcal{I}(\mathcal{W}\{\mathbf{x}_d; \mathbf{p}\}) + \nabla\mathcal{I}(\mathcal{W}\{\mathbf{x}_d; \mathbf{p}\}) \frac{\partial \mathcal{W}(\mathbf{x}_d; \mathbf{p})}{\partial \mathbf{p}^\top} \Delta\mathbf{p} - \mathcal{T}(\mathbf{x}_d) \right\|_2^2, \tag{2}$$

which can be viewed as a quasi-Newton update. The parameter $\mathbf{p}$ is the initial warp estimate, $\Delta\mathbf{p}$ is the warp update being estimated, and $\mathcal{T}$ is the template image we desire to align the source image $\mathcal{I}$ against. The pixel coordinates $\{\mathbf{x}_d\}_{d=1}^{D}$ are taken with respect to the template image's coordinate frame, and $\frac{\partial \mathcal{W}(\mathbf{x}; \mathbf{p})}{\partial \mathbf{p}^\top} : \mathbb{R}^2 \to \mathbb{R}^{2 \times P}$ is the warp Jacobian. After solving Eq. 2, the current warp estimate has the following additive update,

$$\mathbf{p} \leftarrow \mathbf{p} + \Delta\mathbf{p}. \tag{3}$$

As the relationship between appearance and geometric deformation is not solely linear, Eqs. 2 and 3 must be applied iteratively until convergence is achieved.

Inverse Compositional Fitting. The canonical LK formulation presented in the previous section is sometimes referred to as the forwards additive (FA) algorithm [3]. A fundamental problem with the forwards additive approach is that it requires recomputing the image gradient and warp Jacobian in each iteration, greatly impacting computational efficiency. Baker and Matthews [3] devised a computationally efficient extension to forwards additive LK, which they refer to as the inverse compositional (IC) algorithm. The IC-LK algorithm attempts to iteratively solve the objective

$$\min_{\Delta\mathbf{p}} \sum_{d=1}^{D} \left\| \mathcal{I}(\mathcal{W}\{\mathbf{x}_d; \mathbf{p}\}) - \mathcal{T}(\mathbf{x}_d) - \nabla\mathcal{T}(\mathbf{x}_d)\frac{\partial\mathcal{W}(\mathbf{x}_d; \mathbf{0})}{\partial\mathbf{p}^\top}\Delta\mathbf{p} \right\|_2^2, \quad (4)$$

followed by the inverse compositional update

$$\mathbf{p} \leftarrow \mathbf{p} \circ (\Delta\mathbf{p})^{-1}, \quad (5)$$

where we have abbreviated the notation $\circ$ to be the composition of warp functions parametrized by $\mathbf{p}$, and $(\Delta\mathbf{p})^{-1}$ to be the parameters of the inverse warp function parametrized by $\Delta\mathbf{p}$. We can express Eq. 4 in vector form as

$$\min_{\Delta\mathbf{p}} \|\mathcal{I}(\mathbf{p}) - \mathcal{T}(\mathbf{0}) - \mathbf{W}\Delta\mathbf{p}\|_2^2, \quad (6)$$

where,

$$\mathbf{W} = \begin{bmatrix} \nabla\mathcal{T}(\mathbf{x}_1) \cdots & 0 \\ \vdots & \ddots & \vdots \\ 0 & \cdots \nabla\mathcal{T}(\mathbf{x}_D) \end{bmatrix} \begin{bmatrix} \frac{\partial\mathcal{W}(\mathbf{x}_1; \mathbf{0})}{\partial\mathbf{p}^\top} \\ \vdots \\ \frac{\partial\mathcal{W}(\mathbf{x}_D; \mathbf{0})}{\partial\mathbf{p}^\top} \end{bmatrix}$$

and

$$\mathcal{I}(\mathbf{p}) = \begin{bmatrix} \mathcal{I}(\mathcal{W}\{\mathbf{x}_1; \mathbf{p}\}) \\ \vdots \\ \mathcal{I}(\mathcal{W}\{\mathbf{x}_D; \mathbf{p}\}) \end{bmatrix}, \quad \mathcal{T}(\mathbf{0}) = \begin{bmatrix} \mathcal{T}(\mathcal{W}\{\mathbf{x}_1; \mathbf{0}\}) \\ \vdots \\ \mathcal{T}(\mathcal{W}\{\mathbf{x}_D; \mathbf{0}\}) \end{bmatrix}.$$

Here, $\mathbf{p} = \mathbf{0}$ is considered the identity warp (*i.e.* $\mathcal{W}\{\mathbf{x}; \mathbf{0}\} = \mathbf{x}$). It is easy to show that the solution to Eq. 6 is given by

$$\Delta\mathbf{p} = \mathbf{R}[\mathcal{I}(\mathbf{p}) - \mathcal{T}(\mathbf{0})], \quad (7)$$

where $\mathbf{R} = \mathbf{W}^\dagger$. The superscript $\dagger$ denotes the Moore-Penrose pseudo-inverse operator. The IC form of the LK algorithm comes with a great advantage: the gradients $\nabla\mathcal{T}(\mathbf{x})$ and warp Jacobian $\frac{\partial\mathcal{W}(\mathbf{x}; \mathbf{0})}{\partial\mathbf{p}^\top}$ are evaluated at the identity warp $\mathbf{p} = \mathbf{0}$, regardless of the iterations and the current state of $\mathbf{p}$. This means that $\mathbf{R}$ remains constant across all iterations, making it advantageous over other variants in terms of computational complexity. For the rest of this paper, we shall focus on the IC form of the LK algorithm.

3   Supervised Descent Method

Despite exhibiting good performance on many image alignment tasks, the LK algorithm can be problematic to use when there is no specific template image $\mathcal{T}$ to align against. For many applications, one may be given just an ensemble of M ground-truth images and warps $\{\mathcal{I}_m, \mathbf{p}_m\}_{m=1}^M$ of the object of interest. If one has prior knowledge of the distribution of warp displacements to be encountered, one can synthetically generate N examples to form a much larger set $\mathcal{S} = \{\Delta\mathbf{p}_n, \mathcal{I}_n(\mathbf{p}_n \circ \Delta\mathbf{p}_n)\}_{n=1}^N$ to learn from, where $N \gg M$. In these circumstances, a strategy recently put forward known as the Supervised Descent Method (SDM) [14] has exhibited state-of-the-art performance across a number of alignment tasks, most notably facial landmark alignment. The approach attempts to directly learn a regression matrix that minimizes the following SSD objective,

$$\min_{\mathbf{R}} \sum_{n \in \mathcal{S}} \|\Delta\mathbf{p}_n - \mathbf{R}[\mathcal{I}_n(\mathbf{p}_n \circ \Delta\mathbf{p}_n) - \mathcal{T}(\mathbf{0})]\|_2^2 + \Omega(\mathbf{R}). \tag{8}$$

The template image $\mathcal{T}(\mathbf{0})$ can be learned either with $\mathbf{R}$ directly or by taking it to be $\frac{1}{N} \sum_{n \in \mathcal{S}} \mathcal{I}(\mathbf{p}_n)$, the average of ground-truth images [15].

Regularization. Ω is a regularization function used to ensure that the solution to $\mathbf{R}$ is unique. To understand the need for this regularization, one can reform Eq. 8 in matrix form as

$$\min_{\mathbf{R}} \|\mathbf{Y} - \mathbf{R}\mathbf{X}\|_F^2 + \Omega(\mathbf{R}), \tag{9}$$

where

$$\mathbf{Y} = [\Delta\mathbf{p}_1, \dots, \Delta\mathbf{p}_N], \text{ and}$$
$$\mathbf{X} = [\mathcal{I}(\mathbf{p}_1 \circ \Delta\mathbf{p}_1) - \mathcal{T}(\mathbf{0}), \dots, \mathcal{I}(\mathbf{p}_N \circ \Delta\mathbf{p}_N) - \mathcal{T}(\mathbf{0})].$$

Here, $\|\cdot\|_F$ indicates the matrix Frobenius norm. Without the regularization term $\Omega(\mathbf{R})$, the solution to Eq. 9 is $\mathbf{R} = \mathbf{Y}\mathbf{X}^\top(\mathbf{X}\mathbf{X}^\top)^{-1}$. It is understood in literature that raw pixel representations of natural images stem from certain frequency spectrums [13] that leads to an auto-covariance matrix $\mathbf{X}\mathbf{X}^\top$ which is poorly conditioned in nearly all circumstances. It has been demonstrated [13] that this property stems from the fact that image intensities in natural images are highly correlated in close spatial proximity, but this dependence drops off as a function of spatial distance.

In our experiments, we have found that $\mathbf{X}\mathbf{X}^\top$ is always poorly conditioned even when utilizing other image representations such as dense SIFT, HOG, and LBP descriptors. As such, it is clear that some sort of regularization term is crucial for effective SDM performance. As commonly advocated and practiced, we employed a weighted Tikhonov penalty term $\Omega(\mathbf{R}) = \lambda\|\mathbf{R}\|_F^2$, where λ controls the weight of the regularizer. We found this choice to work well in our experiments.

Iteration-Specific Regressors. Unlike the IC-LK approach, which employs a single regressor/template pair $\{\mathbf{R}, \mathcal{T}(\mathbf{0})\}$ to be applied iteratively until convergence, SDM learns a set of regressor/template pairs $\{\mathbf{R}^{(l)}, \mathcal{T}^{(l)}(\mathbf{0})\}_{l=1}^{L}$ for each iteration $l = 1 : L$ (sometimes referred to as layers). On the other hand, like the IC-LK algorithm, these regressors are precomputed in advance and thus are independent of the current image and warp estimate. As a result, SDM is computationally efficient just like IC-LK. The regressor/template pair $\{\mathbf{R}^{(l)}, \mathcal{T}^{(l)}(\mathbf{0})\}$ is learned from the synthetically generated set $\mathcal{S}^{(l)}$ within Eq. 8, which we define to be

$$\mathcal{S}^{(l)} = \{\Delta\mathbf{p}_n^{(l)}, \mathcal{I}(\mathbf{p}_n \circ \Delta\mathbf{p}_n^{(l)})\}_{n=1}^{N}, \tag{10}$$

where

$$\Delta\mathbf{p}^{(l+1)} \leftarrow \mathbf{R}^{(l)} \left[\mathcal{I}\left(\mathbf{p} \circ (\Delta\mathbf{p}^{(l)})^{-1}\right) - \mathcal{T}(\mathbf{0})\right]. \tag{11}$$

For the first iteration ($l = 1$), the warp perturbations are generated from a pre-determined random distribution; for every subsequent iteration, the warp perturbations are re-sampled from the same distribution to ensure each iteration's regressor does not overfit. Once learned, SDM is applied by employing Eq. 11 in practice.

Inverse Compositional Warps. It should be noted that there is nothing in the original treatment [14] on SDM that limits it to compositional warps. In fact, the original work employing facial landmark alignment advocated an additive update strategy. In this paper, however, we have chosen to employ inverse compositional warp updates as: (i) we obtained better results for our experiments with planar warp functions, (ii) we observed almost no difference in performance for non-planar warp functions such as those involved in face alignment, and (iii) it is only through the employment of inverse compositional warps within the LK framework that a firm theoretical motivation for fixed regressors can be entertained. Furthermore, we have found that keeping a close mathematical relationship to the IC-LK algorithm is essential for the motivation of our proposed approach.

4   The Conditional Lucas & Kanade Algorithm

Although enjoying impressive results across a myriad of image alignment tasks, SDM does have disadvantages when compared to IC-LK. First, it requires large amounts of synthetically warped image data. Second, it requires the utilization of an adhoc regularization strategy to ensure good condition of the linear system. Third, the mathematical properties of the warp function parameters being predicted is ignored. Finally, it reveals little about the actual degrees of freedom necessary in the set of regressor matrices being learned through the SDM process.

In this paper, we put forward an alternative strategy for directly learning a set of iteration-specific regressors,

$$\min_{\nabla \mathcal{T}(\mathbf{0})} \sum_{n \in \mathcal{S}} \| \Delta \mathbf{p}_n - \mathbf{R}[\mathcal{I}(\mathbf{p}_n \circ \Delta \mathbf{p}_n) - \mathcal{T}(\mathbf{0})] \|_2^2 \qquad (12)$$

$$\text{s.t.} \quad \mathbf{R} = \left(\begin{bmatrix} \nabla \mathcal{T}(\mathbf{x}_1) \dots & 0 \\ \vdots & \ddots & \vdots \\ 0 & \dots \nabla \mathcal{T}(\mathbf{x}_D) \end{bmatrix} \begin{bmatrix} \frac{\partial \mathcal{W}(\mathbf{x}_1;\mathbf{0})}{\partial \mathbf{p}^\top} \\ \vdots \\ \frac{\partial \mathcal{W}(\mathbf{x}_D;\mathbf{0})}{\partial \mathbf{p}^\top} \end{bmatrix} \right)^\dagger,$$

where

$$\nabla \mathcal{T}(\mathbf{0}) = \begin{bmatrix} \nabla \mathcal{T}(\mathbf{x}_1) \\ \vdots \\ \nabla \mathcal{T}(\mathbf{x}_D) \end{bmatrix}.$$

At first glance, this objective may seem strange, as we are proposing to learn template "image gradients" $\nabla \mathcal{T}(\mathbf{0})$ within a conditional objective. As previously discussed in [4], this idea deviates from the traditional view of what image gradients are - parameters that are derived from heuristic finite differencing operations. In this paper, we prefer to subscribe to the alternate view that image gradients are simply weights that can be, and should be, learned from data. The central motivation for this objective is to enforce the parametric form of the generative IC-LK form through a conditional objective.

An advantage of the Conditional LK approach is the reduced number of model parameters. Comparing the model parameters of Conditional LK ($\nabla \mathcal{T}(\mathbf{0}) \in \mathbb{R}^{KD \times 2}$) against SDM ($\mathbf{R} \in \mathbb{R}^{P \times KD}$), there is a reduction in the degrees of freedom needing to be learned for most warp functions where $P > 2$. More fundamentally, however, is the employment of the generative pixel independence assumption described originally in Eq. 1. This independence assumption is useful as it ensures that a unique $\mathbf{R}$ can be found in Eq. 12 without any extra penalty terms such as Tikhonov regularization. In fact, we propose that the sparse matrix structure of image gradients within the psuedo-inverse of $\mathbf{R}$ acts as a much more principled form of regularization than those commonly employed within the SDM framework.

A further advantage of our approach is that, like the IC-LK framework, it utilizes prior knowledge of the warp Jacobian function $\frac{\partial \mathcal{W}(\mathbf{x};\mathbf{0})}{\partial \mathbf{p}^\top}$ during the estimation of the regression matrix $\mathbf{R}$. Our insight here is that the estimation of the regression matrix $\mathbf{R}$ using a conditional learning objective should be simplified (in terms of the degrees of freedom to learn) if one had prior knowledge of the deterministic form of the geometric warp function.

A drawback to the approach, in comparison to both the SDM and IC-LK frameworks, is the non-linear form of the objective in Eq. 12. This requires us to resort to non-linear optimization methods, which are not as straightforward as linear regression solutions. However, as we discuss in more detail in the experimental portion of this paper, we demonstrate that a Levenberg-Marquardt optimization strategy obtains good results in nearly all circumstances. Furthermore, compared to SDM, we demonstrate good solutions can be obtained with significantly smaller numbers of training samples.

Iteration-Specific Regressors. As with SDM, we assume we have an ensemble of images and ground-truth warps $\{\mathcal{I}_m, \mathbf{p}_m\}_{m=1}^{M}$ from which a much larger set of synthetic examples can be generated $\mathcal{S} = \{\Delta\mathbf{p}_n, \mathcal{I}_n(\mathbf{p}_n \circ \Delta\mathbf{p}_n)\}_{n=1}^{N}$, where $N \gg M$. Like SDM, we attempt to learn a set of regressor/template pairs $\{\mathbf{R}^{(l)}, \mathcal{T}^{(l)}(\mathbf{0})\}_{l=1}^{L}$ for each iteration $l = 1 : L$. The set $\mathcal{S}^{(l)}$ of training samples is derived from Eqs. 10 and 11 for each iteration. Once learned, the application of these iteration-specific regressors is identical to SDM.

Pixel Independence Asymmetry. A major advantage of the IC-LK framework is that it assumes generative independence across pixel coordinates (see Eq. 1). A natural question to ask is: could not one predict geometric displacement (instead of appearance) directly across independent pixel coordinates?

The major drawback to employing such strategy is its ignorance of the well-known "aperture problem" [10] in computer vision (*e.g.* the motion of an image patch containing a sole edge cannot be uniquely determined due to the ambiguity of motion along the edge). As such, it is impossible to ask any predictor (linear or otherwise) to determine the geometric displacement of all pixels within an image while entertaining an independence assumption. The essence of our proposed approach is that it circumvents this issue by enforcing global knowledge of the template's appearance across all pixel coordinates, while entertaining the generative pixel independence assumption that has served the LK algorithm so well over the last three decades.

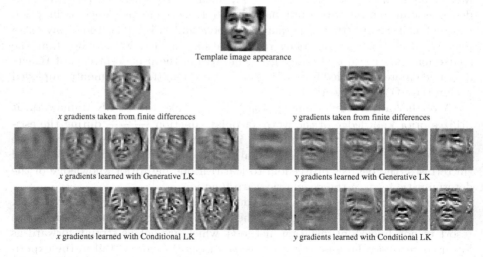

Template image appearance

x gradients taken from finite differences   *y* gradients taken from finite differences

x gradients learned with Generative LK   *y* gradients learned with Generative LK

x gradients learned with Conditional LK   *y* gradients learned with Conditional LK

Fig. 1. Visualization of the learned image gradients for LK from layers 1 (left) to 5 (right).

Generative LK. For completeness, we will also entertain a generative form of our objective in Eq. 12, where we instead learn "image gradients" that predict generative appearance as a function of geometric displacement, formulated as

$$\min_{\nabla \mathcal{T}(0)} \sum_{n \in \mathcal{S}} \|\mathcal{I}(\mathbf{p}_n \circ \Delta \mathbf{p}_n) - \mathcal{T}(0) - \mathbf{W} \Delta \mathbf{p}_n\|_2^2 \tag{13}$$

$$\text{s.t.} \quad \mathbf{W} = \begin{bmatrix} \nabla \mathcal{T}(\mathbf{x}_1) \dots & 0 \\ \vdots & \ddots & \vdots \\ 0 & \dots \nabla \mathcal{T}(\mathbf{x}_D) \end{bmatrix} \begin{bmatrix} \frac{\partial \mathcal{W}(\mathbf{x}_1;0)}{\partial \mathbf{p}^\top} \\ \vdots \\ \frac{\partial \mathcal{W}(\mathbf{x}_D;0)}{\partial \mathbf{p}^\top} \end{bmatrix}.$$

Unlike our proposed Conditional LK, the objective in Eq. 13 is linear and directly solvable. Furthermore, due to the generative pixel independence assumption, the problem can be broken down into D independent sub-problems. The Generative LK approach is trained in an identical way to SDM and Conditional LK, where iteration-specific regressors are learned from a set of synthetic examples $\mathcal{S} = \{\Delta \mathbf{p}_n, \mathcal{I}_n(\mathbf{p}_n \circ \Delta \mathbf{p}_n)\}_{n=1}^N$.

Figure 1 provides an example of visualizing the gradients learned from the Conditional LK and Generative LK approaches. It is worthwhile to note that the Conditional LK gradients get sharper over regression iterations, while it is not necessarily the case for Generative LK. The rationale for including the Generative LK form is to highlight the importance of a conditional learning approach, and to therefore justify the added non-linear complexity of the objective in Eq. 12.

5 Experiments

In this section, we present results for our approach across three diverse tasks: (i) planar image alignment, (ii) planar template tracking, and (iii) facial model fitting. We also investigate the utility of our approach across different image representations such as raw pixel intensities and dense LBP descriptors.

5.1 Planar Image Alignment

Experimental Settings. In this portion of our experiments, we will be utilizing a subsection of the Multi-PIE [6] dataset. For each image, we denote a 20×20 image $\mathcal{I}(\mathbf{p})$ with ground-truth warp $\mathbf{p}$ rotated, scaled and translated around hand-labeled locations. For the IC-LK approach, this image is then employed as the template $\mathcal{T}(0)$. For the SDM, Conditional LK and Generative LK methods, a synthetic set of geometrically perturbed samples $\mathcal{S}$ are generated $\mathcal{S} = \{\Delta \mathbf{p}_n, \mathcal{I}_n(\mathbf{p}_n \circ \Delta \mathbf{p}_n)\}_{n=1}^N$.

We generate the perturbed samples by adding i.i.d. Gaussian noise of standard deviation σ to the four corners of the ground-truth bounding box as well as an additional translational noise from the same distribution, and then finally fitting the perturbed box to the warp parameters $\Delta \mathbf{p}$. In our experiments, we choose $\sigma = 1.2$ pixels. Figure 2 shows an example visualization of the training procedure as well as the generated samples. For SDM, a Tikhonov regularization term is added to the training objective as described in Sect. 3, and the penalty factor λ is chosen by evaluating on a separate validation set; for Conditional LK, we use Levenberg-Marquardt to optimize the non-linear objective where the parameters are initialized through the Generative LK solution.

Frequency of Convergence. We compare the alignment performance of the four types of aligners in our discussion: (i) IC-LK, (ii) SDM, (iii) Generative LK, and (iv) Conditional LK. We state that convergence is reached when the point RMSE of the four corners of the bounding box is less than one pixel.

Fig. 2. Visualization of the perturbed samples $\mathcal{S} = \{\Delta \mathbf{p}_n, \mathcal{I}_n(\mathbf{p}_n \circ \Delta \mathbf{p}_n)\}_{n=1}^N$ used for training the SDM, Conditional LK, and Generative LK methods. Left: the original source image, where the red box is the ground truth and the green boxes are perturbed for training. Right: examples of the synthesized training samples.

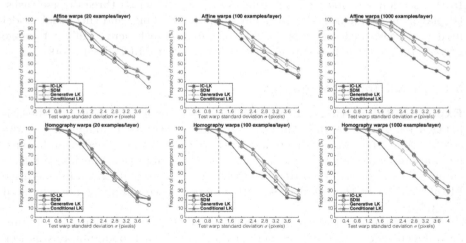

Fig. 3. Frequency of convergence comparison between IC-LK, SDM, Generative LK, and Conditional LK. The vertical dotted line indicates σ that they were trained with.

Figure 3 shows the frequency of convergence tested with both a 2D affine and homography warp function. Irrespective of the planar warping function, our results indicate that Conditional LK has superior convergence properties over the others. This result holds even when the approach is initialized with a warp perturbation that is larger than the distribution it was trained under. The alignment performance of Conditional LK is consistently better in all circumstances, although the advantage of the approach is most noticeable when training with just a few training samples.

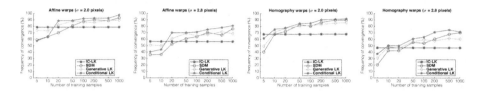

Fig. 4. Frequency of convergence comparison between SDM, Generative LK, and Conditional LK in terms of number of samples trained with.

Figure 4 provides another comparison with respect to the amount of training data learned from. It can be observed that SDM is highly dependent on the amount of training data available, but it is still not able to generalize as well as Conditional LK. This is also empirical proof that incorporating principled priors in Conditional LK is more desirable than adhoc regularizations in SDM.

Convergence Rate. We also provide some analysis on the convergence speed. To make a fair comparison, we take the average of only those test runs where

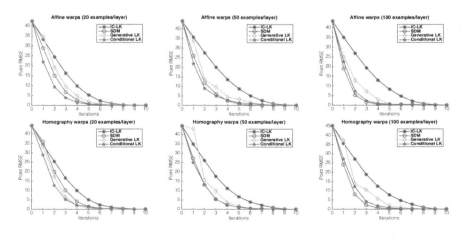

Fig. 5. Convergence rate comparison between IC-LK, SDM, Generative LK, and Conditional LK, averaged from the tests ($\sigma = 2.8$) where all four converged in the end.

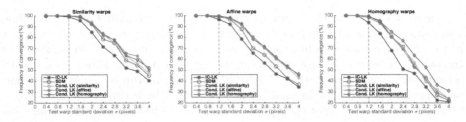

Fig. 6. Frequency of convergence comparison between IC-LK, SDM, and Conditional LK trained with 100 examples per layer and tested with swapped warp functions. The parentheses indicate the type of warp function trained with.

all regressors converged. Figure 5 illustrates the convergence rates of different regressors learned from different amounts of training data. The improvement of Conditional LK in convergence speed is clear, especially when little training data is provided. SDM starts to exhibit faster convergence rate when learned from over 100 examples per layer; however, Conditional LK still surpasses SDM in term of the frequency of final convergence.

Swapping Warp Functions. A unique property of Conditional LK in relation to SDM is its ability to interchange between warp functions after training. Since we are learning image gradients $\nabla \mathcal{T}(\mathbf{0})$ for the Conditional LK algorithm, one can essentially choose which warp Jacobian to be employed before forming the regressor $\mathbf{R}$. Figure 6 illustrates the effect of Conditional LK learning the gradient with one type of warp function and swapping it with another during testing. We see that whichever warp function Conditional LK is learned with, the learned conditional gradients are also effective on the other and still outperforms IC-LK and SDM.

It is interesting to note that when we learn the Conditional LK gradients using either 2D planar similarity warps ($P = 4$) or homography warps ($P = 8$), the performance on 2D planar affine warps ($P = 6$) is as effective. This outcome leads to an important insight: it is possible to learn the conditional gradients with a simple warp function and replace it with a more complex one afterwards; this can be especially useful when certain types of warp functions (*e.g.* 3D warp functions) are harder to come by.

5.2   Planar Tracking with LBP Features

In this section, we show how Conditional LK can be effectively employed with dense multi-channel LBP descriptors where $K = 8$. First we analyze the convergence properties of Conditional LK on the dense LBP descriptors, as we did similarly in the previous section, and then we present an application to robust planar tracking. A full description of the multi-channel LBP descriptors we used in our approach can be found in [1].

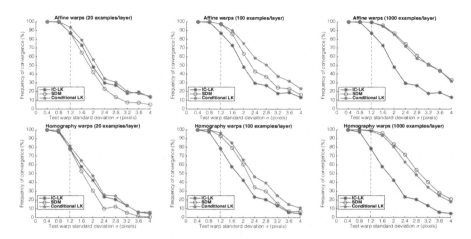

Fig. 7. Frequency of convergence comparison between IC-LK, SDM and Conditional LK with dense binary descriptors. The vertical dotted line indicates σ that they were trained with.

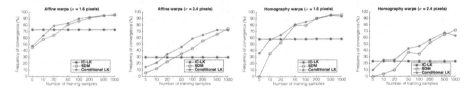

Fig. 8. Frequency of convergence comparison between SDM and Conditional LK with dense binary descriptors in terms of number of samples trained with.

Figure 7 provides a comparison of robustness by evaluating the frequency of convergence with respect to the scale of test warps σ. This suggests that Conditional LK is as effective in the LK framework with multi-channel descriptors: in addition to increasing alignment robustness (which is already a well-understood property of descriptor image alignment), Conditional LK is able to improve upon the sensitivity to initialization with larger warps.

Figure 8 illustrates alignment performance as a function of the number of samples used in training. We can see the Conditional LK only requires as few as 20 examples per layer to train a better multi-channel aligner than IC-LK, whereas SDM needs more than 50 examples per iteration-specific regressor. This result again speaks to the efficiency of learning with Conditional LK.

Low Frame-Rate Template Tracking. In this experiment, we evaluate the advantage of our proposed approach for the task of low frame-rate template tracking. Specifically, we borrow a similar experimental setup to Bit-Planes [1]. LBP-style dense descriptors are ideal for this type of task as their computation is computationally feasible in real-time across a number of computational

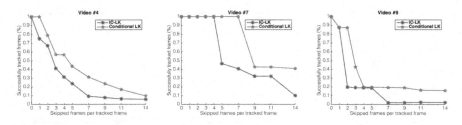

Fig. 9. Tracking performance using IC-LK and Conditional LK with dense LBP descriptors for three videos under low frame-rate conditions, with and without lighting variations.

Fig. 10. Snapshots of tracking results. Blue: IC-LK; yellow: Conditional LK. The second image of each row shows where IC-LK fails but Conditional LK still holds. (Color figure online)

platforms (unlike HOG or dense SIFT). Further computational speedups can be entertained if we start to skip frames to track.

We compare the performance of Conditional LK with IC-LK and run the experiments on the videos collected in [1]. We train the Conditional LK tracker on the first frame with 20 synthetic examples. During tracking, we skip every k frames to simulate low frame-rate videos. Figure 9 illustrates the percentage of successfully tracked frames over the number of skipped frames k. It is clear that the Conditional LK tracker is more stable and tolerant to larger displacements between frames.

Figure 10 shows some snapshots of the video, including the frames where the IC-LK tracker starts to fail but the Conditional LK tracker remains. This further demonstrates that the Conditional LK tracker maintains the same robustness to brightness variations by entertaining dense descriptors, but meanwhile improves upon convergence. Enhanced susceptibility to noises both in motion and brightness also suggests possible extensions to a wide variety of tracking applications.

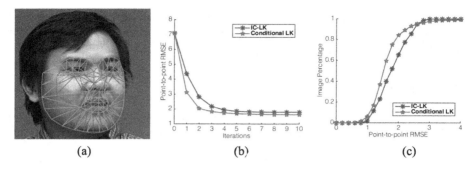

(a)   (b)   (c)

Fig. 11. (a) An example of facial model fitting. The red shape indicates the initialization, and the green shape is the final fitting result. (b) Convergence rate comparison between IC-LK and Conditional LK. (c) Comparison of fitting accuracy. (Color figure online)

5.3 Facial Model Fitting

In this experiment, we show how Conditional LK is applicable not only to 2D planar warps like affine or homography, but also to more complex warps that requires heavier parametrization. Specifically, we investigate the performance of our approach with a point distribution model (PDM) [11] on the IJAGS dataset [11], which contains an assortment of videos with hand-labeled facial landmarks. We utilize a pretrained 2D PDM learned from all labeled data as the warp Jacobian and compare the Conditional LK approach against IC-LK (it has been shown that there is an IC formulation to facial model fitting [11]). For Conditional LK, we learn a series of regressor/template pairs with 5 examples per layer; for IC-LK, the template image is taken by the mean appearance.

Figure 11 shows the results of fitting accuracy and convergence rate of subject-specific alignment measured in terms of the point-to-point RMSE of the facial landmarks; it is clear that Conditional LK outperforms IC-LK in convergence speed and fitting accuracy. This experiment highlights the possibility of extending our proposed Conditional LK to more sophisticated warps. We would like to note that it is possible to take advantage of the Conditional LK warp swapping property to incorporate a 3D PDM as to introduce 3D shape modelling; this is beyond the scope of discussion of this paper.

6   Conclusion

In this paper, we discuss the advantages and drawbacks of the LK algorithm in comparison to SDMs. We argue that by enforcing the pixel independence assumption into a conditional learning strategy we can devise a method that: (i) utilizes substantially less training examples, (ii) offers a principled strategy for regularization, and (iii) offers unique properties for adapting and modifying the warp function after learning. Experimental results demonstrate that the Conditional LK algorithm outperforms both the LK and SDM algorithms in terms of convergence. We also demonstrate that Conditional LK can be integrated with a variety of applications that potentially leads to other exciting avenues for investigation.

References

1. Alismail, H., Browning, B., Lucey, S.: Bit-planes: dense subpixel alignment of binary descriptors. CoRR abs/1602.00307 (2016). http://arxiv.org/abs/1602.00307
2. Antonakos, E., Alabort-i Medina, J., Tzimiropoulos, G., Zafeiriou, S.P.: Feature-based lucas-kanade and active appearance models. IEEE Trans. Image Process. **24**(9), 2617–2632 (2015)
3. Baker, S., Matthews, I.: Lucas-Kanade 20 years on: A unifying framework. Int. J. Comput. Vis. **56**(3), 221–255 (2004)
4. Bristow, H., Lucey, S.: In defense of gradient-based alignment on densely sampled sparse features. In: Hassner, T., Liu, C. (eds.) Dense Correspondences in Computer Vision, pp. 135–152. Springer, Switzerland (2014)
5. Dalal, N., Triggs, B.: Histograms of oriented gradients for human detection. In: IEEE Computer Society Conference on Computer Vision and Pattern Recognition, CVPR 2005, vol. 1, pp. 886–893. IEEE (2005)
6. Gross, R., Matthews, I., Cohn, J., Kanade, T., Baker, S.: Multi-pie. Image Vis. Comput. **28**(5), 807–813 (2010)
7. Jebara, T.: Discriminative, generative and imitative learning. Ph.D. thesis, Massachusetts Institute of Technology (2001)
8. Lowe, D.G.: Distinctive image features from scale-invariant keypoints. Int. J. Comput. Vis. **60**(2), 91–110 (2004)
9. Lucas, B.D., Kanade, T., et al.: An iterative image registration technique with an application to stereo vision. In: IJCAI, vol. 81, pp. 674–679 (1981)
10. Marr, D.: Vision: A Computational Investigation into the Human Representation and Processing of Visual Information. Henry Holt and Co., Inc., New York (1982)
11. Matthews, I., Baker, S.: Active appearance models revisited. Int. J. Comput. Vis. **60**(2), 135–164 (2004)
12. Ojala, T., Pietikäinen, M., Mäenpää, T.: Multiresolution gray-scale and rotation invariant texture classification with local binary patterns. IEEE Trans. Pattern Anal. Mach. Intell. **24**(7), 971–987 (2002)
13. Simoncelli, E.P., Olshausen, B.A.: Natural image statistics and neural representation. Ann. Rev. Neurosci. **24**(1), 1193–1216 (2001)
14. Xiong, X., De la Torre, F.: Supervised descent method and its applications to face alignment. In: 2013 IEEE Conference on Computer Vision and Pattern Recognition (CVPR), pp. 532–539. IEEE (2013)
15. Xiong, X., De la Torre, F.: Global supervised descent method. In: Proceedings of the IEEE Conference on Computer Vision and Pattern Recognition, pp. 2664–2673 (2015)
16. Xiong, X., la Torre, F.D.: Supervised descent method for solving nonlinear least squares problems in computer vision. CoRR abs/1405.0601 (2014). http://arxiv.org/abs/1405.0601

Where Should Saliency Models Look Next?

Zoya Bylinskii[1]([✉]), Adrià Recasens[1], Ali Borji[2], Aude Oliva[1],
Antonio Torralba[1], and Frédo Durand[1]

[1] Computer Science and Artificial Intelligence Laboratory,
Massachusetts Institute of Technology, Cambridge, USA
{zoya,recasens,oliva,torralba,fredo}@mit.edu
[2] Center for Research in Computer Vision,
University of Central Florida, Orlando, USA
aborji@crcv.ucf.edu

Abstract. Recently, large breakthroughs have been observed in saliency modeling. The top scores on saliency benchmarks have become dominated by neural network models of saliency, and some evaluation scores have begun to saturate. Large jumps in performance relative to previous models can be found across datasets, image types, and evaluation metrics. Have saliency models begun to converge on human performance? In this paper, we re-examine the current state-of-the-art using a fine-grained analysis on image types, individual images, and image regions. Using experiments to gather annotations for high-density regions of human eye fixations on images in two established saliency datasets, MIT300 and CAT2000, we quantify up to 60% of the remaining errors of saliency models. We argue that to continue to approach human-level performance, saliency models will need to discover higher-level concepts in images: text, objects of gaze and action, locations of motion, and expected locations of people in images. Moreover, they will need to reason about the relative importance of image regions, such as focusing on the most important person in the room or the most informative sign on the road. More accurately tracking performance will require finer-grained evaluations and metrics. Pushing performance further will require higher-level image understanding.

Keywords: Saliency maps · Saliency estimation · Eye movements · Deep learning · Image understanding

1 Introduction

Where human observers look in images can provide important clues to human image understanding: where the main focus of the image is, where an action or event is happening in an image, and who the main participants are. The collection of human eye movements can help highlight image regions of interest to

Electronic supplementary material The online version of this chapter (doi:10. 1007/978-3-319-46454-1_49) contains supplementary material, which is available to authorized users.

© Springer International Publishing AG 2016
B. Leibe et al. (Eds.): ECCV 2016, Part V, LNCS 9909, pp. 809–824, 2016.
DOI: 10.1007/978-3-319-46454-1_49

Fig. 1. Recent progress in saliency modeling has significantly driven up performance scores on saliency benchmarks. On first glance, model detections of regions of interest in an image appear to approach ground truth human eye fixations (Fig. 3). A finer-grained analysis can reveal where models can still make significant improvements. High-density regions of human fixations are marked in yellow, and show that models continue to miss these semantically-meaningful elements. (Color figure online)

human observers, and models can be designed to make computational predictions. The field of saliency estimation has moved beyond the modeling of low-level visual attention to the prediction of human eye fixations on images. This transition has been driven in part by large datasets and benchmarks of human eye movements (Fig. 1).

For a long while, the prediction scores of saliency models have increased at a stable rate. The recent couple of years have seen tremendous improvements on well-established saliency benchmark datasets [1]. These improvements can be attributed to the resurgence of neural networks in the computer vision community, and the application of deep architectures to saliency estimation. As a result, a large number of neural network based saliency models have emerged in a short period of time, creating a large gap in performance relative to traditional saliency models that are based on hand-crafted features, and learning-based models that integrate low-level features with object detectors and scene context [2–6]. Neural network-based models are trained to predict saliency in a single end-to-end manner, combining feature extraction, feature integration, and saliency value prediction.

These recent advances in the state-of-the-art and the corresponding saturation of some evaluation scores motivate the questions: Have saliency models begun to converge on human performance and is saliency a solved problem? In this paper we provide explanations of what saliency models are still missing, in order to match the key image regions attended to by human observers. We argue that to continue to approach human-level performance, saliency models will need to discover increasingly higher-level concepts in images: text, objects of gaze and action, locations of motion, and expected locations of people in images. Moreover, they will need to reason about the relative importance of image regions, such as focusing on the most important person in the room or the most informative sign on the road. In other words, more accurately predicting where people look in images will require higher-level image understanding. In this paper, we examine the kinds of problems that remain and what will be required to push performance forward.

2   Related Work

Computational modeling of bottom-up attention dates back to the seminal works by Treisman and Gelade [7] (Feature Integration Theory), the computational architecture by Koch and Ullman [8] and the bottom-up model of Itti et al. [9]. Parkhurst and Neibur were the first to measure saliency models against human eye fixations in free-viewing tasks [10]. Followed by this work and the Attention for Information Maximization model of Bruce and Tsotsos [11], a cascade of saliency models emerged, establishing saliency as a subarea in computer vision. Large datasets of human eye movements were constructed to provide training data, object detectors and scene context were added to models, and learning approaches gained traction for discovering the best feature combinations [2–6]. Please refer to [12, 13] for recent reviews of saliency models.

One of the first attempts to leverage deep learning for saliency prediction was Vig et al. [14], using convnet layers as feature maps to classify fixated local regions. Kümmerer et al. [15] introduced the model DeepGaze, built on top of the AlexNet image classification network [16]. Similarly, Liu et al. [17] proposed the Multiresolution-CNN model in which three convnets, each on a different image scale, are combined to obtain the saliency map. In the SALICON model [18], CNNs are applied at two different image scales: fine and coarse. The SALICON dataset, a large-scale crowd-sourced mouse movement dataset, made available to the saliency community for training new deep models [18], has led to the emergence of a number of other neural network models. For instance, DeepFix [19] is a fully convolutional neural network built on top of the VGG network [20] and trained on the SALICON dataset to predict pixel-wise saliency values in an end-to-end manner. DeepFix has additionally been fine-tuned on MIT1003 [3] and CAT2000 [21]. Pan et al. [22] also trained two architectures on SALICON in an end-to-end manner: a shallow convnet trained from scratch, and a deeper one whose first three layers were adapted from the VGG network (SalNet). Other saliency models based on deep learning have been proposed for salient region detection [23–26]. In this paper, we focus on predicting eye fixations rather than detecting and segmenting salient objects in scenes.

While deep learning models have shown impressive performance for saliency prediction, a finer-grained analysis shows that they continue to miss key elements in images. Here we investigate where the next big improvements can come from.

3   Evaluating Progress

We perform our evaluation on two datasets from the well-established MIT Saliency Benchmark [1]. We use the data from this benchmark because it has the most comprehensive set of traditional and deep saliency models evaluated. The **MIT300** dataset [27] is composed of 300 images from Flickr Creative Commons and personal collections. It is a difficult dataset for saliency models, as images are highly varied and natural. Fixations of 39 observers have been collected on this dataset, leading to fairly robust ground-truth to test models against. The **CAT2000** dataset [21] is composed of 2000 images from 20 different categories, varying from natural indoor and outdoor scenes to artificial stimuli like patterns and sketches. Images in this dataset come from search engines and computer vision datasets [28,29]. The test portion of this dataset, used for evaluation, contains the fixations of 24 observers.

As of March 2016, of the top 10 (out of 57) models evaluated on MIT300, neural network models filled 6 spots (and the top 3 ranks) according to many metrics[1]. DeepFix [19] and SALICON [18], both neural network models, hold the top 2 spots. The CAT2000 dataset, a recent addition to the MIT benchmark, has 19 models evaluated to date. DeepFix is the best model on the CAT2000 dataset overall and on all 20 image categories. BMS (Boolean map based saliency) [30] is the best-performing non neural network model across both datasets.

A finer-grained analysis on MIT300 (see Supplemental Material) shows that on a per-image level, DeepFix and SALICON alternate in providing the best prediction for ground-truth fixations. In the rest of the paper, our analyses are carried out on these models. Performances of these models on the MIT benchmark according to the benchmark metrics are provided in Table 1. We supplement

Table 1. Scores of top-performing neural network models (DeepFix, SALICON) and best non-neural network model (BMS) on MIT300 Benchmark. Top scores are bolded. Lower scores for KL and EMD are better. There has been significant progress since the traditional bottom-up IttiKoch model, but a gap remains to reach human-level performance. Chance and human limit values have been taken from [1,32].

Saliency model	AUC ↑	sAUC ↑	NSS ↑	CC ↑	KL ↓	EMD ↓	SIM ↑	IG ↑
Human limit	0.92	0.81	3.29	1	0	0	1	1.80
DeepFix [19]	**0.87**	0.71	**2.26**	**0.78**	0.63	**2.04**	**0.67**	0.67
SALICON [18]	**0.87**	**0.74**	2.12	0.74	**0.54**	2.62	0.60	**0.71**
BMS [30]	0.83	0.65	1.41	0.55	0.81	3.35	0.51	0.22
IttiKoch[a]	0.75	0.63	0.97	0.37	1.03	4.26	0.44	-0.15
Chance	0.50	0.50	0	0	2.09	6.35	0.33	-1.67

[a]Implementation from http://www.vision.caltech.edu/~harel/share/gbvs.php.

---

[1] As of July 2016, 8 of the top 10 (out of 62) models on MIT300 are neural networks.

Fig. 2. Saliency model ranking is preserved when evaluating models on this subset of 10 images as when evaluating them on the whole 300-image benchmark. These images help to accentuate differences in model performance. These images contain people at varying scales, as well as text (small here) amidst distracting textures.

these scores with a measure of Information Gain (IG) as suggested in [31,32]. Definitions and interpretations of these metrics are provided in [32].

To begin to explore where these recent large gains in performance are coming from, we visualize the most representative dataset images in Fig. 2. We define representative images as those that best preserve model rankings when tested on, compared to the whole dataset. Our correlation-based greedy image selection is described in the Supplemental Material. We find that a subset of $k = 10$ images can already rank the saliency models on the MIT benchmark with a Spearman correlation of 0.97 relative to their ranking on all dataset images. These images help to accentuate differences in model performance. By visualizing the predic-

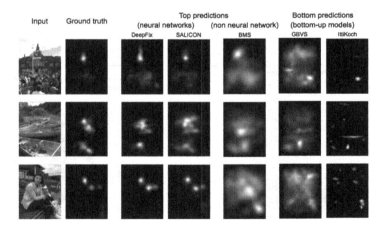

Fig. 3. Some of the best and worst model predictions on a few of the representative images from Fig. 2. Unlike traditional bottom-up models, recent neural network models can discover faces, text, and object-like features in images, prioritizing them over textures and low-level features appropriately, to better approximate human fixations.

tions of some of the top and bottom models on these images (Fig. 3), we can see that driving performance is a model's ability to detect people and text in images in the presence of clutter, texture, and potentially misleading low-level pop-out.

4   Quantifying Where People and Models Look in Images

To understand where models might fail, we must first understand where people look. Our goal is to name all the image regions lying beneath the high-density locations in fixation heatmaps. We computed fixation heatmaps aggregated over all observers on an image (39 observers in the MIT300 dataset, for a robust ground truth). Then we thresholded these ground truth heatmaps at the 95th percentile and collected all the connected components. This produced an average of 1–3 regions per image for a total of 651 regions.

The resulting region outlines were plotted on top of the original images and shown to Amazon Mechanical Turk (MTurk) participants with the task of selecting the labels that most clearly describe the image content that people look at (Fig. 4a). The labels provided for this task were not meant to serve as an exhaustive list of all objects, but to have good coverage of label types, with sufficient instances per label. If an image contained multiple image regions, only one would be displayed to participants at a time. Participants could select out of 15 different label categories as many labels as were appropriate to describe a region. For each image region, we collected labels from a total of 20 participants. Majority vote was used to assign labels to regions. A region could have multiple labels in case of ties. For further analyses, related labels (e.g. "animal face", "part of an animal", etc.) were aggregated to have sufficient instances per label type (see Supplemental Material). Not all regions are easily nameable, and in these cases participants could select the "background" or "other" labels. To account for these image regions to which simple labels could not be assigned, a second question-based MTurk task was deployed, described in the next section.

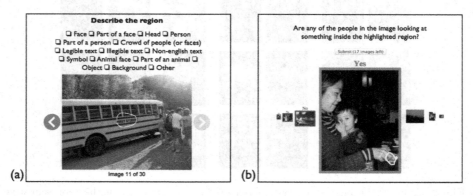

Fig. 4. Two types of Mechanical Turk tasks were used for gathering annotations for the highly-fixated regions in an image. These annotations were then used to quantify where people look in images.

4.1 What Do Models Miss?

Given labels for all the highly-fixated image regions in the MIT300 dataset, we intersected these labeled regions with the saliency maps of different computational models. To determine if saliency models made correct predictions in these regions, we calculated whether the mean saliency in these regions was within the 95-th percentile of the saliency map for the whole image. We then tallied up the types of regions that were most commonly under-predicted by models. In Table 2 we provide the error percentages, by region type, where saliency models assigned a value less than the percentile threshold to the corresponding regions. Our analyses are performed over DeepFix and SALICON models on the MIT300 dataset, and on DeepFix on the CAT2000 dataset (additional analyses in the Supplemental Material). The four categories chosen from the CAT2000 dataset are ones that contain natural images with a variety of objects and settings.

About half the failure modes are due to misdetections of parts of people, faces, animals, and text. Such failure cases can be ameliorated by training models on more instances of faces (partial, blurry, small, non-frontal views, occluded), more instances of text (different sizes and types), and animals. However, the labels "background", "object", and "other" assigned to image regions by MTurk participants originally accounted for about half of model errors on MIT300.

A second MTurk task was designed to better understand the content found in these harder-to-name image regions. Participants were asked to answer binary questions, such as whether or not a highlighted region in an image is an object of gaze or action in the image (see Fig. 4b and Supplemental Material). The results of this task allowed us to further break down model failure modes, and account for 60 % of total mispredictions on MIT300 and 39 %-98 % of mispredictions on four categories of CAT2000. The remaining failure modes (labeled "other") vary from image to image, caused by low-level features, background elements, and other objects or parts of objects that are not the main subjects of the photograph, nor are objects of gaze or action. Later in this paper, the most common failure modes are explored in greater detail. Examples are provided in Fig. 6.

4.2 What Can Models Gain?

With the region annotations obtained from our MTurk tasks, we performed an analysis complementary to the one in Sect. 4.1. Instead of computing model misses across image regions of different types, here we estimate the potential gains models could have if specific image regions were correctly predicted. A region is treated as a binary mask for the image, and a modified saliency map is computed as a combination of the original saliency map and ground truth fixation map. For each region type (e.g. "part of a person", "object of gaze"), we compute modified saliency maps. We replace model predictions in those regions with ground truth values obtained from the human fixation map (e.g., Fig. 5, top row). Figure 5 provides the score improvements of the modified models on the MIT300 benchmark. This analysis is meant to provide a general sense of the possible performance boost if different prediction errors are ameliorated.

Table 2. Labels for under-predicted regions on MIT300 and CAT2000 datasets. Percentages are computed over 681 labels assigned to 651 regions (some regions have multiple labels so percentages do not add up to 100 %). See Fig. 6 for visual examples.

Dataset	MIT300		CAT2000			
Model	DeepFix	SALICON	DeepFix			
Image category	All		Social	Action	Indoor	Outdoor
Part of main subject	31 %	36 %	49 %	68 %	12 %	24 %
Unusual element	18 %	16 %	33 %	63 %	8 %	8 %
Location of action/motion	16 %	16 %	67 %	78 %	8 %	11 %
Text	16 %	13 %	6 %	5 %	8 %	29 %
Part of a person	15 %	14 %	23 %	37 %	8 %	5 %
Possible location for a person	15 %	7 %	6 %	24 %	10 %	11 %
Object of action	14 %	15 %	27 %	51 %	0 %	3 %
Object of gaze	11 %	11 %	50 %	44 %	0 %	0 %
Part of a face	6 %	8 %	46 %	7 %	0 %	0 %
Part of an animal	5 %	5 %	3 %	10 %	0 %	0 %
Other	40 %	40 %	3 %	2 %	61 %	37 %

We include performance boosts of Normalized Scanpath Saliency (NSS) and Information Gain (IG) scores, which follow the distribution of region types in Table 2. The complete set of scores is provided in the Supplemental Material. It is important to note that the Area under ROC Curve (AUC) metrics have either saturated or are close to saturation. The focus of saliency evaluation should turn instead towards metrics that can continue to differentiate between models, and that can measure model performances at a finer-grained level (Sect. 5).

4.3   The Importance of People

A significant part of the regions missed by saliency models involve people (Table 2): people within the salient region, or people acting on or looking at a salient object. In this section we provide a deeper analysis of the images containing people. To expand our analysis, we annotated all the people's faces in the MIT300 images with bounding boxes. This provided a more complete set of annotations than the regions extracted for the MTurk labeling tasks, where only the top 1–3 most highly-fixated regions per image were labeled. In this section we compute the importance of faces in an image following the approach of Jiang et al. [18]: given a bounding box for an object in an image, the maximum saliency value falling within the object's outline is taken as the object's importance score (the maximum is a good choice for such analyses as it does not scale with object size). This will be used to analyze if saliency models are able to capture the relative importance of people in scenes.

Across the images in MIT300 containing only one face (53 images), the face is the most highly fixated region in 66 % of the images, and the DeepFix model

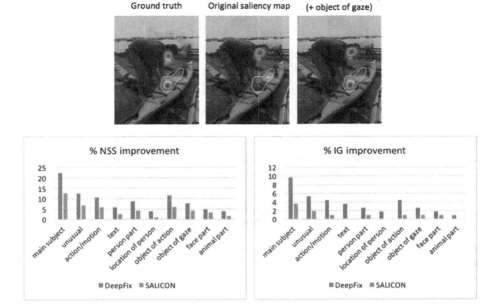

Fig. 5. Improvements of DeepFix and SALICON models on MIT300 if specific regions were accurately predicted. Performance numbers are over all 300 benchmark images, where regions from the ground truth fixation map are substituted into each model's saliency maps to examine the change in performance (top row). The percentage score improvement is computed as a fraction of the score difference between the original model score and the human limit (from Table 1).

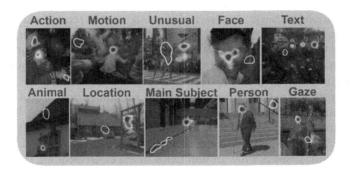

Fig. 6. Regions often fixated by humans but missed by computational models.

correctly predicts this in 77 % of these cases. Out of the 53 images with faces, the saliency of the face is underestimated (by more than 10 % of the range of saliency values) by the DeepFix model in 15 cases, and overestimated in 3 cases. In other words, across these images, the DeepFix model does not assign the

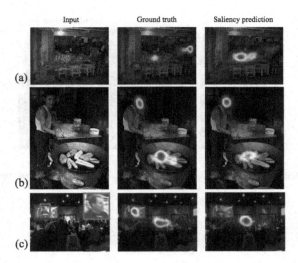

Fig. 7. Saliency prediction failure cases for faces: (a) Face saliency is underestimated when faces are small, non-frontal, or not centered in an image; (b) Sometimes the actions in a scene are more salient to human observers than the participants, but saliency models can overestimate the relative saliency of the faces; (c) Face detection can fail on depictions (such as in posters and photographs within the input images) which often lack the context of a body, or appear at an unusual location in the image.

correct relative importance to the face relative to the rest of the image elements in a third of the total cases. Some of these examples are provided in Fig. 7 and in the Supplemental Material. Note that the importance of faces extends to depictions of faces as well: portraits or posters containing human faces in images. Human attention is drawn to these regions, but models tend to miss these faces, perhaps because they are lacking the necessary context to discover them.

Similarly to the analysis in Sect. 4.2, here we quantify the performance boost of saliency models if the saliency of faces were always correctly predicted. We used the same procedure: to create the modified saliency map for an image we assign the ground truth saliency value to the bounding box region and the predicted output of the model to the remaining part of the image. The DeepFix model's Normalized Scanpath Saliency (NSS) score on the MIT300 benchmark improves by 7.8 % of the total remaining gap between the original model scores and human limit, when adding ground truth in the face bounding boxes. Information Gain (IG) also goes up 1.8 %. A full breakdown of all the scores is provided in the Supplemental Material. Improving the ability of models to detect and assign correct relative importance to faces in images can provide better predictions of human eye fixations.

4.4   Not All People in an Image Are Equally Important

Considering images containing multiple faces, we measure the extent to which the computational prediction of the relative importance of the different faces matches human ground-truth fixations. For all the faces labeled in an image, we use the human fixation maps to compute the importance score for each face, and analogously we use the saliency map to assign a predicted importance score to the same faces. Since both fixation and saliency maps are normalized, each face in an image will receive an importance score ranging from 0 to 1. A score of 1 occurs when the face bounding box overlapped a region of maximum density in the corresponding fixation/saliency map. Interpreted in terms of ground truth, this is the face that received the most fixations.

Across the images with more than one visible face, the average Spearman correlation between the ground truth and predicted face importance values is 0.53. This means that for many images, the relative ordering assigned by the saliency model to people does not match the importance given by human fixations. As depicted in Fig. 8, discovering the most important person in the image is a task that requires higher-level image understanding. Human participants tend to fixate people in an image that are central to a depicted action, a conversation, or an event; people who stand out from the crowd (based on some high-level features like facial expression, age, accessories, etc.).

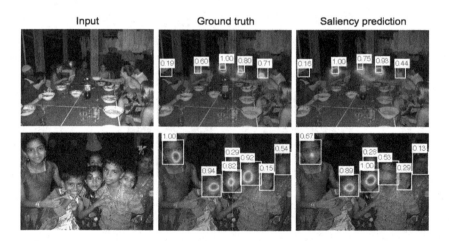

Fig. 8. Although recent saliency models have begun to detect faces in images with high precision, they do not assign the correct relative importance to different faces in an image. This requires an understanding of the interactions in an image: who is participating in an action and who has authority. Facial expressions, accessories/embellishments, facial orientation, and position in a photo also contribute to the importance of individual faces. We assign an importance score to each face in an image using the maximum ground truth (fixation) or predicted (saliency) density in the face bounding box. These importance scores, ranging from 0 to 1, are included above each bounding box.

4.5   The Informativeness of Text

In the MIT300 and CAT2000 datasets, most text, large or small, has attracted many human fixations, with regions containing text accounting for 7 % of all highly-fixated image regions. While text has been previously noted as attracting human visual attention [33], not all text is equal. The informativeness of text in the context of the rest of the image, or the interestingness of the text on its own can affect how long individual observers fixate it, and what proportion of observers look at it. There are thus a number of reasons why the human ground truth might have a high saliency on a particular piece of text, and some of those reasons depend on understanding the text itself - something that computational models currently lack (Fig. 9).

To expand our analysis on text regions, we annotated all instances of text present in the MIT300 dataset with bounding boxes. The DeepFix model's NSS scores improves by 7.8 % of the total remaining gap between the original model scores and human upper bound, when adding ground truth in the text bounding boxes. Its IG score improves by 4.4 %. A full breakdown of all the scores is provided in the Supplemental Material. Overall, an accurate understanding of text is another step towards better predictions of human fixations.

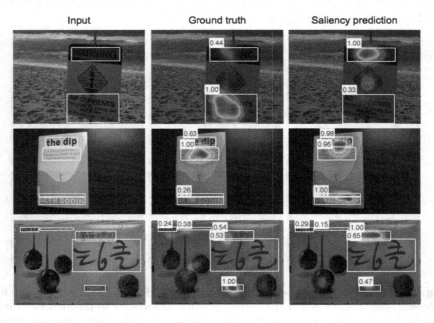

Fig. 9. Example images containing text that receive many fixations by human observers, but whose saliency is under-estimated by computational models. Text labels can be used to give the observer more information. For instance, the description of a warning or a book are more informative to observers than the warning or book title itself. These regions receive more eye fixations. The informativeness of text also depends on the context of the observer: most observers fixated the only piece of English text on the box of chocolates.

4.6   Objects of Gaze and Action

Another common source of missed predictions are objects of gaze and/or action. These are objects or, more generally, regions in an image that are looked at or interacted with by one or more persons in an image. In Fig. 10, we include 4 images from the MIT300 dataset that include objects of gaze missed by both DeepFix and SALICON. In the last column of Fig. 10 we also show the predictions that can be made possible by a computational model specifically trained to predict gaze [34]. For each person in an image, this model predicts the scene saliency from the vantage point of the individual selected (details in Supplemental Material). Training saliency models to explicitly follow gaze can improve their predictive power of modeling the saliency of the entire scene [35].

The gaze-following model only works when gaze information can be extracted from the orientation of the head and, if visible, the location and orientation of the eyes. However, the orientation of the body and location of body parts (specifically the hands) can provide additional clues as to which objects in an image are relevant from the vantage point of different people in the image, even if not fully visible. Detecting such objects of action remains a problem area for saliency models (some failure cases are provided in the Supplemental Material).

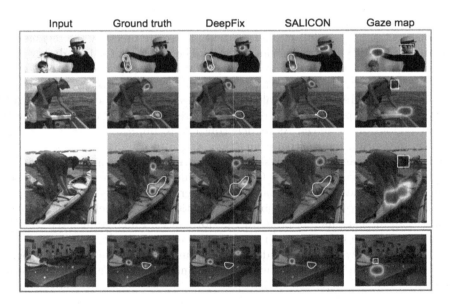

Fig. 10. Both top neural network saliency models perform worse on these images than on any other images in the MIT300 dataset labeled with objects of gaze. The yellow outlines highlight high-density regions in the ground truth fixation map that were labeled by MTurk participants as regions on which the gaze of someone in the image falls. A model that explicitly predicts the gaze of individuals in an image can locate these objects of gaze [34]. The last row is a failure of the gaze-following model, requiring an understanding of actions that is beyond just gaze. (Color figure online)

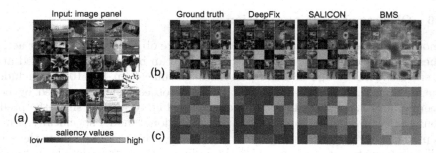

Fig. 11. A finer-grained test for saliency models: determining the relative importance of different sub-images in a panel. (a) A panel image from the MIT300 dataset. (b) The saliency map predictions given the panel as an input image. (c) The maximum response of each saliency model on each subimage is visualized (as an importance matrix).

5   Conclusion

As the number of saliency models grows and score differences between models shrink, evaluation procedures should be adjusted to elucidate differences between models and human eye movements. This calls for finer-grained evaluation metrics, datasets, and prediction tasks. Models continue to under-predict crucial image regions containing people, actions, and text. These are precisely the regions with greatest semantic importance in an image, and become essential for saliency applications like image compression and image captioning. Aggregating model scores over all image regions and large image collections conceals these errors. Moreover, traditionally favored saliency evaluation metrics like the AUC can not distinguish between cases where models predict different relative importance values for different regions of an image. As models continue to improve in detection performance, measuring the relative values they assign to the detected objects is the next step. This can be accomplished with metrics like the Normalized Scanpath Saliency (NSS) and Information Gain (IG), which take into account the range of saliency map values during evaluation [32]. Finer-grained tasks like comparing the relative importance of image regions in a collection or in a panel such as the one in Fig. 11 can further differentiate model performances. Finer-grained datasets like CAT2000 [21] can help measure model performance per image type.

Recent saliency models with deep architectures have shown immense progress on saliency benchmarks, with a wide performance gap relative to previous state-of-the-art. In this paper we demonstrated that a finer-grained analysis of the top-performing models on the MIT Saliency Benchmark can uncover areas for further improvement to narrow the remaining gap to human ground truth.

Acknowledgments. This work has been partly funded by an NSERC PGS-D Fellowship to Z.B., La Caixa Fellowship to A.R., NSF grant #1524817 to A.T., and a Toyota Grant to F.D.

References

1. Bylinskii, Z., Judd, T., Borji, A., Itti, L., Durand, F., Oliva, A., Torralba, A.: MIT saliency benchmark. http://saliency.mit.edu/
2. Kienzle, W., Wichmann, F.A., Franz, M.O., Schölkopf, B.: A nonparametric approach to bottom-up visual saliency. In: Advances in Neural Information Processing Systems, pp. 689–696 (2006)
3. Judd, T., Ehinger, K., Durand, F., Torralba, A.: Learning to predict where humans look. In: IEEE 12th International Conference on Computer Vision, pp. 2106–2113 (2009)
4. Borji, A.: Boosting bottom-up and top-down visual features for saliency estimation. In: IEEE Conference on Computer Vision and Pattern Recognition (CVPR), pp. 438–445 (2012)
5. Xu, J., Jiang, M., Wang, S., Kankanhalli, M.S., Zhao, Q.: Predicting human gaze beyond pixels. J. Vis. **14**(1), 1–20 (2014)
6. Zhao, Q., Koch, C.: Learning a saliency map using fixated locations in natural scenes. J. Vis. **11**(3), 9 (2011)
7. Treisman, A.M., Gelade, G.: A feature-integration theory of attention. Cogn. Psychol. **12**(1), 97–136 (1980)
8. Koch, C., Ullman, S.: Shifts in selective visual attention: towards the underlying neural circuitry. Hum. Neurbiology **4**, 219–227 (1985)
9. Itti, L., Koch, C., Niebur, E.: A model of saliency-based visual attention for rapid scene analysis. IEEE Trans. Pattern Anal. Mach. Intell. **11**, 1254–1259 (1998)
10. Parkhurst, D., Law, K., Niebur, E.: Modeling the role of salience in the allocation of overt visual attention. Vis. Res. **42**(1), 107–123 (2002)
11. Bruce, N., Tsotsos, J.: Attention based on information maximization. J. Vis. **7**(9), 950 (2007)
12. Borji, A., Itti, L.: State-of-the-art in visual attention modeling. IEEE Trans. Pattern Anal. Mach. Intell. **35**(1), 185–207 (2013)
13. Borji, A., Sihite, D.N., Itti, L.: Quantitative analysis of human-model agreement in visual saliency modeling: a comparative study. IEEE Trans. Image Process. **22**(1), 55–69 (2013)
14. Vig, E., Dorr, M., Cox, D.: Large-scale optimization of hierarchical features for saliency prediction in natural images. In: Proceedings of the IEEE Conference on Computer Vision and Pattern Recognition, pp. 2798–2805 (2014)
15. Kümmerer, M., Theis, L., Bethge, M.: Deep Gaze I: Boosting saliency prediction with feature maps trained on ImageNet. arXiv preprint (2014). arXiv:1411.1045
16. Krizhevsky, A., Sutskever, I., Hinton, G.E.: Imagenet classification with deep convolutional neural networks. In: Advances in Neural Information Processing Systems, pp. 1097–1105 (2012)
17. Liu, N., Han, J., Zhang, D., Wen, S., Liu, T.: Predicting eye fixations using convolutional neural networks. In: Proceedings of the IEEE Conference on Computer Vision and Pattern Recognition, pp. 362–370 (2015)
18. Jiang, M., Huang, S., Duan, J., Zhao, Q.: Salicon: saliency in context. In: The IEEE Conference on Computer Vision and Pattern Recognition (CVPR), June 2015
19. Kruthiventi, S.S., Ayush, K., Babu, R.V.: Deepfix: A fully convolutional neural network for predicting human eye fixations. arXiv preprint (2015). arXiv:1510.02927
20. Simonyan, K., Zisserman, A.: Very deep convolutional networks for large-scale image recognition. arXiv preprint (2014). arXiv:1409.1556

21. Borji, A., Itti, L.: Cat2000: A large scale fixation dataset for boosting saliency research. arXiv preprint (2015). arXiv:1505.03581
22. Pan, J., Sayrol, E., Giro-i-Nieto, X., McGuinness, K., O'Connor, N.E.: Shallow and deep convolutional networks for saliency prediction. In: The IEEE Conference on Computer Vision and Pattern Recognition (CVPR), June 2016
23. Zhao, R., Ouyang, W., Li, H., Wang, X.: Saliency detection by multi-context deep learning. In: Proceedings of the IEEE Conference on Computer Vision and Pattern Recognition, pp. 1265–1274 (2015)
24. Li, G., Yu, Y.: Visual saliency based on multiscale deep features. In: Proceedings of the IEEE Conference on Computer Vision and Pattern Recognition, pp. 5455–5463 (2015)
25. Wang, L., Lu, H., Ruan, X., Yang, M.H.: Deep networks for saliency detection via local estimation and global search. In: Proceedings of the IEEE Conference on Computer Vision and Pattern Recognition, pp. 3183–3192 (2015)
26. Li, X., Zhao, L., Wei, L., Yang, M.H., Wu, F., Zhuang, Y., Ling, H., Wang, J.: Deepsaliency: multi-task deep neural network model for salient object detection. IEEE Trans. Image Process. **25**(8), 3919–3930 (2016)
27. Judd, T., Durand, F., Torralba, A.: A benchmark of computational models of saliency to predict human fixations. In: MIT Technical report (2012)
28. Yao, B., Jiang, X., Khosla, A., Lin, A.L., Guibas, L., Fei-Fei, L.: Human action recognition by learning bases of action attributes and parts. In: IEEE International Conference on Computer Vision (ICCV), pp. 1331–1338 (2011)
29. Xiao, J., Hays, J., Ehinger, K.A., Oliva, A., Torralba, A.: Sun database: large-scale scene recognition from abbey to zoo. In: IEEE conference on Computer Vision and Pattern Recognition (CVPR), pp. 3485–3492 (2010)
30. Zhang, J., Sclaroff, S.: Saliency detection: a boolean map approach. In: IEEE International Conference on Computer Vision (2013)
31. Kümmerer, M., Wallis, T.S., Bethge, M.: Information-theoretic model comparison unifies saliency metrics. Proc. Nat. Acad. Sci. **112**(52), 16054–16059 (2015)
32. Bylinskii, Z., Judd, T., Oliva, A., Torralba, A., Durand, F.: What do different evaluation metrics tell us about saliency models? arXiv preprint (2016). arXiv:1604.03605
33. Cerf, M., Frady, E.P., Koch, C.: Faces and text attract gaze independent of the task: experimental data and computer model. J. Vis. **12**(10), 1–15 (2009)
34. Recasens, A., Khosla, A., Vondrick, C., Torralba, A.: Where are they looking? In: Advances in Neural Information Processing Systems, pp. 199–207 (2015)
35. Soo Park, H., Shi, J.: Social saliency prediction. In: Proceedings of the IEEE Conference on Computer Vision and Pattern Recognition, pp. 4777–4785 (2015)

Robust Face Alignment Using a Mixture of Invariant Experts

Oncel Tuzel[1], Tim K. Marks[1(✉)], and Salil Tambe[2]

[1] Mitsubishi Electric Research Labs (MERL), Cambridge, USA
onceltuzel@gmail.com, tmarks@merl.com
[2] Intel Corporation, Santa Clara, USA
salil.tambe@intel.com

Abstract. Face alignment, which is the task of finding the locations of a set of facial landmark points in an image of a face, is useful in widespread application areas. Face alignment is particularly challenging when there are large variations in pose (in-plane and out-of-plane rotations) and facial expression. To address this issue, we propose a cascade in which each stage consists of a mixture of regression experts. Each expert learns a customized regression model that is specialized to a different subset of the joint space of pose and expressions. The system is invariant to a predefined class of transformations (e.g., affine), because the input is transformed to match each expert's prototype shape before the regression is applied. We also present a method to include deformation constraints within the discriminative alignment framework, which makes our algorithm more robust. Our algorithm significantly outperforms previous methods on publicly available face alignment datasets.

1 Introduction

Face alignment refers to finding the pixel locations of a set of predefined facial landmark points (e.g., eye and mouth corners) in an input face image. It is important for many applications such as human-machine interaction, videoconferencing, gaming, and animation, as well as numerous computer vision tasks including face recognition, face tracking, pose estimation, and expression synthesis. Face alignment is difficult due to large variations in factors such as pose, expression, illumination, and occlusion.

1.1 Previous Work

Great strides have been made in the field of face alignment since the Active Shape Model (ASM) [1] and Active Appearance Model (AAM) [2] were first proposed. AAM-based face alignment methods proposed since then include [3–5]. To handle wider variations in pose, multi-view AAM and ASM models [6–8] explicitly

Electronic supplementary material The online version of this chapter (doi:10. 1007/978-3-319-46454-1_50) contains supplementary material, which is available to authorized users.

© Springer International Publishing AG 2016
B. Leibe et al. (Eds.): ECCV 2016, Part V, LNCS 9909, pp. 825–841, 2016.
DOI: 10.1007/978-3-319-46454-1_50

model and predict the head pose, e.g., by learning a different deformable model for each of several specific pose ranges [7,8]. Another line of research involves multi-camera AAMs, in which an AAM is simultaneously fitted to images of a face captured by multiple cameras [9,10]. Like ASMs and AAMs, Constrained Local Models (CLMs) [11–14] have explicit joint constraints on the landmark point locations (e.g., a subspace shape model) that constrain the positions of the landmarks with respect to each other. Building on CLMs, [15] propose the Gauss-Newton Deformable Part Model (GN-DPM), which uses Gauss-Newton optimization to jointly fit an appearance model and a global shape model.

Recently, much of the focus in face alignment research has shifted toward discriminative methods [16–22]. These methods learn an explicit regression that directly maps the features extracted at the facial landmark locations to the face shape (e.g., the locations of the landmarks) [17,18,23–26]. In Project-Out Cascaded Regression (PO-CR) [26], the regression is performed in a subspace orthogonal to facial appearance variation. To cope with inaccurate initialization, [27] begin a regression cascade at multiple initial locations and combine the results. Tree-based regression methods [16,23–25,28] are also gathering interest due to their speed. In [23], a set of local binary features are learned using a random forest regression to jointly learn a linear regression function for the final estimation, while [24] utilize a gradient boosting tree algorithm to learn an ensemble of regression trees. Software libraries such as [29] implement a wide range of face alignment methods.

In the Supervised Descent Method (SDM) [17], a cascade of regression functions operate on extracted SIFT features to iteratively estimate facial landmark locations. An extension of SDM, called Global SDM (GSDM) [30], partitions the parameter space into regions of similar gradient direction, and uses the result from the previous frame of video to determine which region's model to use in the current frame. Unlike our method, which takes individual test images as input, GSDM is a tracking method that requires a video sequence. Other methods that report results only on video input include [31].

A variety of recent face alignment methods incorporate deep neural networks, including deep regression networks [32] and coarse-to-fine neural network approaches [33,34]. A different coarse-to-fine approach is taken by [35]. Other recent variations on face alignment research include methods that are specially designed to handle partially occluded faces [36,37].

1.2 Our Approach

Our method is related to SDM [17] in that we also perform a cascade of regressions on SIFT features that are computed at the currently estimated landmark locations. However, our method improves upon SDM in a number of ways. In SDM, the same linear regression function must work across all possible variations in facial expressions and pose, including both in-plane and out-of-plane head rotations. In addition to requiring a large and varied training dataset, this forces the learned regression functions to be too generic, thereby limiting

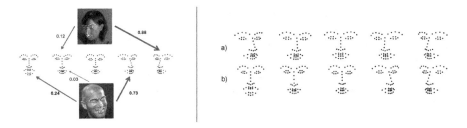

Fig. 1. *Left:* Each expert specializes in a subset of the possible poses and facial expressions. Arrows show the assignment weights of each image's landmark point configuration to the 5 experts. *Right:* Cluster evaluation. (a) Euclidean cluster centers. (b) Affine-invariant cluster centers. Affine-invariant clustering accounts for both the pose variations and the facial expressions.

accuracy. We address this shortcoming in two ways. First, we propose a transformation invariance step at each level of the cascade, prior to the regression step, which makes our method invariant to an entire class of transformations. (Here, we choose the class of 2D affine transformations.) As a result, our regression functions do not need to correct for such global changes in pose and face shape, enabling them to be fine tuned to handle the remaining, smaller variations in landmark locations.

To further improve robustness to variations in pose and expression, at each stage of the cascade we replace the linear regression from SDM by a mixture of experts [38]. In our cascade, each stage is a mixture of experts, where each expert is a regression specialized to handle a subset of the possible face shapes (e.g., a particular region of the joint space of face poses and expressions). As illustrated in Fig. 1 (left), each expert corresponds to a different prototype face shape. This improves alignment significantly, especially when the training dataset is biased towards a certain pose (e.g., frontal).

Unlike alignment methods based on parametric shape models (such as AAM, ASM, and CLM), SDM has no explicit global constraints to jointly limit the locations of multiple landmark points. Our method addresses this limitation simply, by penalizing deviations of landmark locations from each expert's prototype face shape. We accomplish this in the regression framework by extending the feature vector to include the difference between the prototype landmark locations and the currently estimated landmark locations, weighted by a scalar that determines the rigidity of the model. This global regularization of the face shape prevents feature points from drifting apart.

Contributions. In summary, we propose a robust method for real-time face alignment which we call **M**ixture of **I**nvariant E**x**perts (MIX). Novel elements include:

– A transformation invariance step, before each stage of regression, which makes our method invariant to a specified class of transformations. (In this study, we choose the class of 2D affine transformations.)

- A simple extension to the feature vectors that enables our regressions to penalize deviations of feature locations from a prototypical face shape.
- A mixture-of-experts regression at each stage of the cascade, in which each expert regression function is specialized to align a different subset of the input data (e.g., a particular range of expressions and poses).
- A novel affine-invariant clustering algorithm to learn the prototype shapes used in the mixture model.

These novel elements enable our method to achieve precise face alignment on a wide variety of images. We perform exhaustive tests on the 300W [39,40] and AFW [41] datasets, comparing with eight recent methods: Coarse-to-Fine Auto-encoder Networks (CFAN) [34], ensemble of regression trees (TREES) [24], Coarse-to-Fine Shape Searching (CFSS) [35], SDM [17], its incrementally learned adaptation CHEHRA [18], GN-DPM [15], Fast-SIC (an AAM method trained on "in-the-wild" images) [5], and PO-CR [26]. We demonstrate that the proposed method significantly outperforms these previous state-of-the-art approaches.

2   Supervised Descent Method

We now describe the Supervised Descent Method (SDM) [17], which is related to our method, while introducing notation that we will use throughout the paper. Let I be an input face image, and let $\mathbf{x}$ be the $2p \times 1$ vector of p facial landmark locations in image coordinates. At each of the p landmark locations in $\mathbf{x}$, we extract a d-dimensional feature vector. In this paper, we use SIFT features [42] with $d = 128$. Let $\phi(I, \mathbf{x})$ be the $pd \times 1$ consolidated feature vector, which is a concatenation of the p feature descriptors extracted from image I at the landmark locations $\mathbf{x}$.

Given a current estimate, $\mathbf{x}_k$, of the landmark locations in image I, SDM formulates the alignment problem as finding an update vector $\Delta \mathbf{x}$ such that the features computed at the new landmark locations $\mathbf{x}_k + \Delta \mathbf{x}$ better match the features computed at the ground-truth landmark locations $\hat{\mathbf{x}}$ in the face image. The corresponding error can be written as a function of the update vector $\Delta \mathbf{x}$:

$$f(\mathbf{x}_k + \Delta \mathbf{x}) = \left\| \phi(I, \mathbf{x}_k + \Delta \mathbf{x}) - \hat{\phi} \right\|^2, \tag{1}$$

where we define $\hat{\phi} = \phi(I, \hat{\mathbf{x}})$. This function f could be minimized by Newton's method. The Newton step is given by

$$\Delta \mathbf{x} = -\mathbf{H}^{-1} \mathbf{J}_f = -2\mathbf{H}^{-1} \mathbf{J}_\phi \left[\phi_k - \hat{\phi} \right], \tag{2}$$

where $\mathbf{H}$ is the Hessian matrix of f, $\mathbf{J}_f$ and $\mathbf{J}_\phi$ represent the Jacobian with respect to $\mathbf{x}$ of f and ϕ, respectively, and we define $\phi_k = \phi(I, \mathbf{x}_k)$. The Hessian and Jacobian in (2) are evaluated at $\mathbf{x}_k$, but we have omitted the argument $\mathbf{x}_k$ to emphasize the dependence on ϕ_k. In SDM, (2) is approximated by the multivariate linear regression

$$\Delta \mathbf{x} = \mathbf{W}_k \phi_k + \mathbf{b}_k, \tag{3}$$

in which coefficients $\mathbf{W}_k$ and bias $\mathbf{b}_k$ do not depend on $\mathbf{x}_k$.

In SDM [17], a cascade of K linear regressions $\{\mathbf{W}_k, \mathbf{b}_k\}$, where $k = 1, \ldots, K$, are learned using training data. Face alignment is achieved by sequentially applying the learned regressions to features computed at the landmark locations output by the previous stage of the cascade:

$$\mathbf{x}_{k+1} = \mathbf{x}_k + \mathbf{W}_k \boldsymbol{\phi}_k + \mathbf{b}_k. \tag{4}$$

To learn the regressions $\{\mathbf{W}_k, \mathbf{b}_k\}$, the N face images in the training data are augmented by repeating every training image M times, each time perturbing the ground-truth landmark locations by a different random displacement. For each image I_i in this augmented training set ($i = 1, \ldots, MN$), with ground-truth landmark locations $\hat{\mathbf{x}}_i$, we displace the landmarks by random displacement $\Delta \hat{\mathbf{x}}_i$. The first regression function ($k = 1$) is learned by minimizing the L2-loss function

$$\{\mathbf{W}_k, \mathbf{b}_k\} = \arg \min_{\mathbf{W}, \mathbf{b}} \sum_{i=1}^{MN} \| \Delta \hat{\mathbf{x}}_i - \mathbf{W} \phi(I_i, \hat{\mathbf{x}}_i - \Delta \hat{\mathbf{x}}_i) - \mathbf{b} \|^2. \tag{5}$$

For training the later regressions $\{\mathbf{W}_k, \mathbf{b}_k\}_{k=2,\ldots,K}$, rather than using a random perturbation, the target $\Delta \hat{\mathbf{x}}_i$ is the residual after the previous stages of the regression cascade.

3   Mixture of Invariant Experts

In this section, we present our model. Our model significantly improves upon the alignment accuracy and robustness of SDM by introducing three new procedures: a transformation invariance step before each stage of regression, learned deformation constraints on the regressions, and the use of a mixture of expert regressions rather than a single linear regression at each stage of the cascade.

3.1   Transformation Invariance

In order for the regression functions in SDM [17] to learn to align facial landmarks for any face pose and expression, the training data must contain sufficiently many examples of faces covering the entire space of possible variations. Although being able to align faces at any pose is a desired property, learning such a function requires collecting (or synthesizing) training data containing all possible face poses. In addition, the learning is a more difficult task when there are large variations in the training set, and hence either a sufficiently complex regression model (functional form and number of features) is required, or the alignment method will compromise accuracy in order to align all these poses. As a general rule, increased model complexity leads to poorer generalization performance. This suggests that a simpler or more regularized model, which learns to align faces for a limited range of poses, would perform better for those poses than would a general alignment model that has been trained on all poses. As a simple example, consider a regression function that is trained using a single upright face image versus one trained using multiple in-plane rotations of that face image. In the former case, the regression function must have a root for the upright pose, whereas in the latter case, the regression function must have a root for every in-plane rotation.

Algorithm 1. Stage k of Transformation-Invariant SDM (TI-SDM)

Inputs: Prototype shape $\bar{\mathbf{x}}$, Regression $\{\mathbf{W}_k, \mathbf{b}_k\}$,
                   Image I, Initial landmark estimates $\mathbf{x}_k$

1: Use (6) to find transformation $\mathbf{A}_k$ that warps $\mathbf{x}_k$ to $\bar{\mathbf{x}}$
2: Warp to prototype coords: $I' = \mathbf{A}_k(I)$, $\mathbf{x}'_k = \mathbf{A}_k(\mathbf{x}_k)$
3: Extract features: $\phi'_k = \phi(I', \mathbf{x}'_k)$
4: Linear regression: $\mathbf{x}'_{k+1} = \mathbf{x}'_k + \mathbf{W}_k \phi'_k + \mathbf{b}_k$
5: Warp back to image coords: $\mathbf{x}_{k+1} = \mathbf{A}_k^{-1}(\mathbf{x}'_{k+1})$
Output: Landmark locations $\mathbf{x}_{k+1}$

Our goal with transformation invariance is to train each regression on a smaller set of poses, while still being able to align faces in an arbitrary pose. To do so, we apply a transformation invariance step prior to each stage's regression function. We first construct a prototype shape, $\bar{\mathbf{x}}$, which contains the mean location of each landmark point across all of the training data (after uniform scaling and translation transformations have been applied to each training image to make them all share a canonical location and scale).

In this paper, we choose affine transformations as our class of transformations for invariance, although one could also use our method with a different class of transformations. At each stage k of regression, we find the affine transformation $\mathbf{A}_k$ that transforms the landmark locations $\mathbf{x}_k$ that were estimated by the previous stage of regression so as to minimize their sum of squared distances to the prototype landmark locations, $\bar{\mathbf{x}}$:

$$\mathbf{A}_k = \arg\min_{\mathbf{A} \in \mathcal{A}} \|\mathbf{A}(\mathbf{x}_k) - \bar{\mathbf{x}}\|^2, \tag{6}$$

where $\mathcal{A}$ denotes the set of all affine transformations. Next, we use the transformation $\mathbf{A}_k$ to warp the input image I and the landmark locations into the prototype coordinate frame: $I' = \mathbf{A}_k(I)$, and $\mathbf{x}'_k = \mathbf{A}_k(\mathbf{x}_k)$. Note that we slightly abuse notation here by using the same affine transformation operator $\mathbf{A}_k$ to both transform a vector of landmark locations, $\mathbf{A}_k(\mathbf{x}_k)$, and warp an image, $\mathbf{A}_k(I)$. The regression is then performed in the prototype coordinate frame:

$$\mathbf{x}'_{k+1} = \mathbf{x}'_k + \mathbf{W}_k \phi(I', \mathbf{x}'_k) + \mathbf{b}_k. \tag{7}$$

The estimated landmark locations in image coordinates are given by the inverse transformation, $\mathbf{x}_{k+1} = \mathbf{A}_k^{-1}(\mathbf{x}'_{k+1})$.

The resulting algorithm, which we call Transformation-Invariant SDM (TI-SDM), consists of K stages of alignment and regression, illustrated in Fig. 2. Algorithm 1 summarizes what happens at each stage of TI-SDM.

3.2   Learning Deformation Constraints

One of the problems associated with using SDM for tracking landmark locations is that it puts no explicit constraint on the regression behavior of neighboring

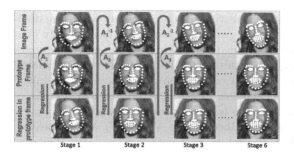

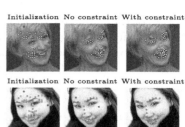

Fig. 2. The Transformation-Invariant SDM (TI-SDM) algorithm. See Sect. 3.1 and Algorithm 1 for details.

Fig. 3. Effect of initial outliers (red) on results *without* vs. *with* deformation constraint. (Color figure online)

points, which makes it possible for the points to drift apart. This would be a straightforward problem to deal with in an optimization setting by introducing explicit constraints or penalties on the free-form deformation of the landmark points. However, rather than utilizing an optimization procedure, which can be slow, we want to maintain the speed advantages of forward prediction using a regression function. To achieve the effect of constraints within a regression framework, we introduce additional features that allow the regression model to learn to constrain landmark points from drifting.

We introduce a soft constraint in the form of an additional cost term $||\mathbf{x} - \bar{\mathbf{x}}||^2$ in Eq. (1):

$$f_c(\mathbf{x}_k + \Delta \mathbf{x}) = \left\| \phi(I, \mathbf{x}_k + \Delta \mathbf{x}) - \hat{\phi} \right\|^2 + \lambda \left\| \mathbf{x}_k + \Delta \mathbf{x} - \bar{\mathbf{x}} \right\|^2. \qquad (8)$$

This enforces a quadratic penalty when the landmark locations drift away from the prototype shape $\bar{\mathbf{x}}$. The weight λ controls the tradeoff between data and the constraint. The Newton step for this constrained f is given by

$$\Delta \mathbf{x} = -2\mathbf{H}^{-1} \left(\mathbf{J}_\phi \ \mathbf{I} \right) \begin{pmatrix} \phi_k - \hat{\phi} \\ \lambda \left(\mathbf{x}_k - \bar{\mathbf{x}} \right) \end{pmatrix}, \qquad (9)$$

where $\mathbf{H}$ is the Hessian matrix of f_c with respect to $\mathbf{x}$, and $\mathbf{J}_\phi$ is the Jacobian of ϕ with respect to $\mathbf{x}$. Just as we approximated (2) by (3), we can approximate this constrained Newton step (9) by a linear regression function of a constrained feature vector, ϕ_k^*:

$$\Delta \mathbf{x} = \mathbf{W}_k \phi_k^* + \mathbf{b}_k, \quad \text{where} \quad \phi_k^* = \begin{pmatrix} \phi_k \\ \lambda \left(\mathbf{x}_k - \bar{\mathbf{x}} \right) \end{pmatrix}. \qquad (10)$$

As in unconstrained SDM, we can learn the regression coefficients $\mathbf{W}_k$ and bias $\mathbf{b}_k$ using training data. The only difference between the constrained (10) and unconstrained (3) regression models is that in the constrained version, we extend the feature vector to include additional features, $\lambda (\mathbf{x}_k - \bar{\mathbf{x}})$, encoding the deviation of the landmark locations from the prototype landmark locations. In general, during our experiments, the constrained regression learns to move landmark locations towards the mean shape by learning negative values for the associated regression coefficients. The learned coefficients' norms are larger for the initial regression stage of the cascade, but smaller in the later stages, which enforces weaker constraints on deformation as the landmark locations approach convergence. Note that it would be possible to incorporate λ into $\mathbf{W}_k$ and $\bar{\mathbf{x}}$ into $\mathbf{b}_k$, and just expand the feature vector ϕ^* with $\mathbf{x}_k$ rather than $\lambda (\mathbf{x}_k - \bar{\mathbf{x}})$. However, we choose to keep the difference vector form as in (10), which becomes important for the regularized training described in Sect. 3.4.

To unify notation, in the rest of this paper we will refer to the expanded feature vector ϕ^* as simply ϕ. That way, Eqs. (3–7) and Algorithm 1 apply to the constrained model without modification. In Fig. 3, we analyze the effect of the deformation constraint. See Sect. 4 for details.

3.3   Mixture-of-Experts Regression

The transformation invariance step described in Sect. 3.1 lets our model learn regression functions that are invariant to affine transformations of the faces. Still, the remaining variations in the data (e.g., due to out-of-plane rotations and facial expressions) are large enough that it is challenging for a single regression function to accurately align all faces. In particular, the training set in our experiments includes many more frontal faces with mild facial expressions than faces with large out-of-plane rotations or extreme expressions. Thus, the prototype (mean) face is close to a frontal face with neutral expression, and the regression function tends to work less well for more extreme poses and expressions.

We propose to use a mixture-of-experts regression model, in which each expert is a regression function that is specialized for a different subset of the possible poses and expressions. Each expert's subset is determined by the expert's prototype shape. We construct L prototype shapes, $\{\bar{\mathbf{x}}^l\}_{l=1,\ldots,L}$, such that the set of ground-truth landmark locations $\hat{\mathbf{x}}_n$ of each of the N faces in the dataset is well aligned with one of the prototype shapes. We write the determination of the prototype shapes as an optimization problem:

$$\{\bar{\mathbf{x}}^l\}_{l=1,\ldots,L} = \underset{\{\dot{\mathbf{x}}^l\}_{l=1,\ldots,L}}{\arg\min} \sum_{n=1}^{N} \underset{\substack{\mathbf{A}\in\mathcal{A}, \\ l\in\{1,\ldots,L\}}}{\min} \left\| \mathbf{A}(\hat{\mathbf{x}}_n) - \dot{\mathbf{x}}^l \right\|^2, \tag{11}$$

where each $\dot{\mathbf{x}}^l$ is a $2p \times 1$ vector representing a possible prototype face shape (i.e., the locations of p landmarks). If the class of transformations, $\mathcal{A}$, only contains the identity transformation, then this problem reduces to Euclidean clustering of training samples based on landmark locations (see Fig. 1a).

When $\mathcal{A}$ is the class of affine transformations, we call this affine-invariant clustering. In this case, (11) is a homogenous optimization problem in which additional constraints on the prototype shapes or the transformations are necessary to avoid the zero solution (which assigns zero to all of the transformations and prototype shapes). Moreover, the objective function is non-convex due to the joint optimization of the shapes and the assignment of training samples to shapes. We decouple this problem into two convex sub-problems, which we solve iteratively. The first sub-problem assigns every training face image n to one of the prototype shapes via the equation

$$l_n = \arg\min_l \left[\min_{\mathbf{A} \in \mathcal{A}} \left\| \mathbf{A}(\hat{\mathbf{x}}_n) - \bar{\mathbf{x}}^l \right\|^2 \right] \tag{12}$$

assuming that the prototype shapes $\bar{\mathbf{x}}^l$ are fixed. This problem can be solved independently for each training face: The optimal assignment is the prototype to which the face's ground-truth landmark locations can be affine-aligned with minimum alignment error. The second sub-problem solves for the prototype shapes. Each prototype shape consists of the landmark locations that minimize the sum of the squared affine alignment errors of the ground-truth locations $\hat{\mathbf{x}}_n$ of the training faces that were assigned to that prototype shape:

$$\bar{\mathbf{x}}^l = \arg\min_{\dot{\mathbf{x}}^l} \sum_{n \text{ s.t. } l_n = l} \min_{\mathbf{A} \in \mathcal{A}} \left\| \mathbf{A}(\hat{\mathbf{x}}_n) - \dot{\mathbf{x}}^l \right\|^2 \quad s.t. \quad \mathbf{C}\dot{\mathbf{x}}^l = \mathbf{m}, \tag{13}$$

where to avoid degeneracy, the matrix $\mathbf{C}$ and vector $\mathbf{m}$ impose linear constraints on the prototype shape such that the mean location of the 5 landmark points of the left eyebrow is fixed, as are the mean location of the 5 right eyebrow points and the mean vertical location of the 16 mouth points. This optimization problem is quadratic with linear constraints, and the optimal solution is computed by solving a linear system. The two optimization sub-problems are alternately solved until the assignments do not change. In our experiments, 20–30 iterations suffice for convergence.

In Fig. 1 (right), we compare Euclidean clustering (a) with the proposed affine-invariant clustering (b). Euclidean clustering only accounts for the pose variations in the dataset. However, some of the out-of-plane poses can be approximately aligned to each other with an affine alignment, enabling the affine-invariant clustering to account for variations in both pose and facial expressions.

Each expert E^l corresponds to one of the L prototype shapes. At each stage of the regression cascade, we learn a separate regression for each expert. Hence, in addition to its prototype shape $\{\bar{\mathbf{x}}^l\}$, each regression expert E^l has a regression function $\{\mathbf{W}_k^l, \mathbf{b}_k^l\}$ for each of the K levels of the cascade:

$$E^l = \left\{ \bar{\mathbf{x}}^l, \ \{\mathbf{W}_k^l, \mathbf{b}_k^l\}_{k=1,\dots,K} \right\}. \tag{14}$$

At each stage, k, of the cascade, each expert E^l performs Algorithm 1 using prototype $\bar{\mathbf{x}}^l$ and regression function $\{\mathbf{W}_k^l, \mathbf{b}_k^l\}$:

$$\mathbf{x}_{k+1}^l = \text{Algorithm 1}(\bar{\mathbf{x}}^l, \{\mathbf{W}_k^l, \mathbf{b}_k^l\}, I, \mathbf{x}_k). \tag{15}$$

Algorithm 2. Mixture of Invariant Experts (MIX)

Inputs: Image I, Initial landmark estimates $\mathbf{x}_1$,
Experts $E^l = \left\{ \bar{\mathbf{x}}^l, \left\{ \mathbf{W}_k^l, \mathbf{b}_k^l \right\}_{k=1,\dots,K} \right\}_{l=1,\dots,L}$

1: **for** $k = 1$ to K **do**
2:   **for** $l = 1$ to L **do**
3:    Compute soft assignment $\alpha^l(\mathbf{x}_k)$ using (16)
4:    Apply one stage of TI-SDM:
      $\mathbf{x}_{k+1}^l = \text{Algorithm 1}\left(\bar{\mathbf{x}}^l, \left\{ \mathbf{W}_k^l, \mathbf{b}_k^l \right\}, I, \mathbf{x}_k\right)$
5:   **end for**
6:   Average over L experts:
      $\mathbf{x}_{k+1} = \sum_{l=1}^{L} \alpha^l(\mathbf{x}_k)\, \mathbf{x}_{k+1}^l$
7: **end for**
Output: Final landmark locations $\mathbf{x}_{K+1}$

The gating function for each regression expert E^l is a soft assignment $\alpha^l(\mathbf{x}_k)$ given by the softmax transformation of the transformation invariance error $\epsilon^l(\mathbf{x}_k)$ between the starting landmark locations $\mathbf{x}_k$ and each prototype shape $\bar{\mathbf{x}}^l$. The soft assignments are computed using

$$\alpha^l(\mathbf{x}) = \frac{e^{-\epsilon^l(\mathbf{x})}}{\sum_{l=1}^{L} e^{-\epsilon^l(\mathbf{x})}}, \quad \text{where} \quad \epsilon^l(\mathbf{x}) = \min_{\mathbf{A} \in \mathcal{A}} \left\| \mathbf{A}(\mathbf{x}) - \bar{\mathbf{x}}^l \right\|^2. \quad (16)$$

Here, as in (6), $\mathcal{A}$ denotes the set of all affine transformations. A high score $\alpha^l(\mathbf{x}_k)$ indicates that the current estimate $\mathbf{x}_k$ is close to the prototype shape of the lth expert, and hence the regression results obtained from E^l would be given a high weight. In Fig. 1 (left), we show the assignment weights of two faces to experts in the model.

At each stage, k, of the cascade, our alignment algorithm applies every expert's regression function to the starting estimate of landmark locations $\mathbf{x}_k$, then averages the outputs according to the gating function $\alpha^l(\mathbf{x}_k)$ to obtain the updated estimate of landmark locations, $\mathbf{x}_{k+1}$:

$$\mathbf{x}_{k+1} = \sum_{l=1}^{L} \alpha^l(\mathbf{x}_k)\, \mathbf{x}_{k+1}^l. \quad (17)$$

Algorithm 2 summarizes our alignment method, which we call **Mixture of Invariant Experts** (MIX).

Note that our mixture-of-experts model is quite different from multi-view models [6–8,43], which explicitly model and predict the head pose (e.g., by learning a different deformable model for each of several specific pose ranges). In contrast, MIX is a discriminative mixture model that discovers a data-dependent partitioning of the shape space (see Fig. 1b) based on facial expressions and other affine-invariant shape variations (including affine-invariant variations due to pose), and learns a different optimization for each partition.

3.4   Training the Experts Model

To learn the regression experts E^l, the N face images in the training data are augmented by repeating every training image M times, each time perturbing the

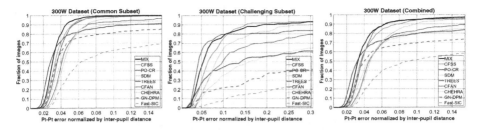

Fig. 4. Comparison of MIX with other state-of-the-art methods on the 300 W dataset.

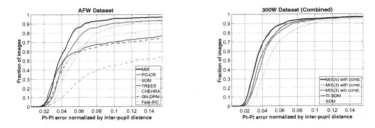

Fig. 5. *Left:* Comparison of MIX with other state-of-the-art methods on the AFW dataset. CFAN and CFSS are not compared, because both included AFW in their training set. *Right:* Comparing variations of proposed method on 300 W (Combined).

ground-truth landmark locations by a different random displacement. For each image I_i in this augmented training set ($i = 1, \ldots, MN$), with ground-truth landmark locations $\hat{\mathbf{x}}_i$, we displace the landmarks by a random displacement $\Delta\hat{\mathbf{x}}_i$. For every expert E^l, we use (16) to compute the soft assignment α_i^l of the ith sample's perturbed landmark locations to the prototype shape $\bar{\mathbf{x}}^l$:

$$\alpha_i^l = \alpha^l \left(\hat{\mathbf{x}}_i + \Delta\hat{\mathbf{x}}_i \right). \tag{18}$$

While computing this soft assignment, let $\mathbf{A}_i^l$ denote the global (affine) transformation from (16) that best aligns the ith sample's perturbed landmark locations to prototype shape $\bar{\mathbf{x}}^l$. Use $\mathbf{A}_i^l$ to transform the ground-truth landmark locations and displacement vectors into the prototype coordinate frame of expert E^l:

$$\hat{\mathbf{x}}_i^l = \mathbf{A}_i^l(\hat{\mathbf{x}}_i), \qquad \Delta\hat{\mathbf{x}}_i^l = \mathbf{A}_i^l(\Delta\hat{\mathbf{x}}_i). \tag{19}$$

The first regression function ($k = 1$) is then learned by minimizing a Tikhonov regularized L2-loss function:

$$\{\mathbf{W}_k^l, \mathbf{b}_k^l\} = \underset{\mathbf{W}, \mathbf{b}}{\arg\min} \sum_{i=1}^{MN} \alpha_i^l \|\Delta\hat{\mathbf{x}}_i^l - \mathbf{W}\phi(I_i, \hat{\mathbf{x}}_i^l - \Delta\hat{\mathbf{x}}_i^l) - \mathbf{b}\|^2 + \gamma \left[\|\mathbf{W}\|_F^2 + \|\mathbf{b}\|_F^2 \right]. \tag{20}$$

For each l and k, the regularizer weight γ is selected via grid search in log space using 2-fold cross validation.

Table 1. Numerical comparison of all tested methods on the 300 W (Combined) dataset.

Method	$NAUC_{0.1}$	$NAUC_{0.2}$	$NAUC_{0.3}$	$NAUC_{0.4}$	$NAUC_{0.5}$
MIX	**0.5945**	**0.7810**	**0.8482**	**0.8828**	**0.9043**
CFSS [35]	0.5528	0.7613	0.8354	0.8733	0.8967
PO-CR [26]	0.5610	0.7568	0.8242	0.8588	0.8798
SDM [17]	0.4475	0.6957	0.7880	0.8362	0.8662
TREES [24]	0.5187	0.6746	0.7406	0.7792	0.8063
CFAN [34]	0.4357	0.6594	0.7487	0.7985	0.8317
CHEHRA [18]	0.4376	0.6390	0.7217	0.7703	0.8038
GN-DPM [15]	0.4274	0.5796	0.6531	0.7000	0.7354
Fast-SIC [5]	0.2490	0.4122	0.4984	0.5644	0.6179

For training the later regressions $\{\mathbf{W}_k, \mathbf{b}_k\}_{k=2,\dots,K}$, rather than using a random perturbation, the target $\Delta\hat{\mathbf{x}}_i$ is the residual of the previous stages of the cascade. In training, the regression function may diverge for a few samples, producing large residuals. To avoid fitting these outliers, at each stage k, we remove 5 % of the samples with the largest residuals from the training set. We choose the number of regression stages K by training until the cross-validation error cannot be reduced further.

The training samples are generated by randomly perturbing the ground-truth facial landmark locations along the major deformation directions of the training set, which are determined via principal component analysis. In addition, we apply random rotation, translation, and anisotropic scaling to the landmark locations, and add i.i.d. Gaussian noise. After learning the cascade model for this training set (usually $K = 3$–4 stages), we learn a second cascade model using a training set consisting of only small amount of i.i.d. Gaussian noise, and append this model to the original model. The second model has 1–2 stages and improves fine alignment.

During testing, the initial landmark locations for regression are given by the mean landmark locations from all of the training data, translated and scaled to fit the given face detector bounding box.

4   Experiments

In the first experiment, we compare our proposed algorithm (MIX) to eight state-of-the-art algorithms: CFAN [34], TREES [24], CFSS [35], SDM [17], CHEHRA [18], GN-DPM (using SIFT features) [15], Fast-SIC [5], and PO-CR [26]. We evaluate performance on the 300 W [39,40] and AFW [41] datasets.

We train our MIX algorithm on the training sets of two standard datasets: LFPW [44] (811 training faces) and Helen [45] (2000 training faces). We augment the training data by horizontally flipping each image, yielding $N = 5,622$

training images. From each image, we sample $M = 15$ training initializations (see Sect. 3.4). We use 3 experts ($L = 3$), because using more ($L = 5$) did not significantly improve performance (see the second experiment, below). For SDM, we use our own implementation, trained on the same training data as MIX.

For the other seven methods, we use their authors' publicly available code. Note that the training set for our algorithm is a smaller subset of the training sets used by CFSS [35] and CFAN [34]. Both CFSS and CFAN include AFW (337 faces) in the training set, but we do not, opting instead to test on AFW.

We test all methods on 300 W using the same test set as [35], which comprises the test sets of LFPW [44] (224 test faces) and Helen [45] (330 test faces)[1] as well as the IBUG dataset (135 test faces). For all test images, we used the bounding box initializations provided on the 300 W website (face detector bounding boxes). To compute errors of results, for all datasets we used the ground-truth locations of 49 landmarks from [39, 40]. As in [35], the 300 W *common subset* contains the test samples from LFPW (224) and HELEN (330), the *challenging subset* is IBUG (135), and *combined* refers to all 689 test images. Figure 4 plots the cumulative distribution of the fraction of images, as a function of error normalized by the inter-pupil distance.

Table 1 presents a numerical comparison of our MIX algorithm with the previous eight methods on the entire (combined) 300 W test set. Rather than measuring mean error, which is extremely sensitive to outliers with large alignment error [46], we instead use a normalized variation of the AUC_α error metric proposed by [46]. The error metric we use, Normalized AUC_α (NAUC_α), measures the area under each cumulative distribution curve (the curves in Fig. 4) up to a threshold normalized error value α, then divides by α (the maximum possible area for that threshold). The resulting NAUC_α error measure, indexed by α, is always between 0 and 1 (where 1 is a perfect score): $\text{NAUC}_\alpha = \frac{1}{\alpha} \int_0^\alpha f(e) de$, where e is the normalized error, $f(e)$ is the cumulative error distribution function, and α is the upper bound that is used to calculate the definite integral.

The results in Fig. 4 and Table 1 show that our method outperforms all of the other recent methods on 300 W. Note that for the next best method, CFSS, we used the code provided by the authors (the more accurate, but slower, version described in [35]), which is not practical for real-time use: the CFSS code required 1.7 s per face on our machine.

The evaluation results on the AFW dataset (Fig. 5, left) show a similar trend, in which our algorithm outperforms the other methods. CFAN and CFSS are not compared on AFW, because both included AFW in their training set.

In the second experiment, we compare several variants of our algorithm and analyze the contribution of each of the novel components described in Sect. 3. The baseline algorithm for this experiment is SDM [17]. MIX(L) refers to our Mixture of Invariant Experts with L experts (Sect. 3.3), and *with* or *without const.* refers to whether or not we use our extended deformation-constraint features (Sect. 3.2). TI-SDM is our Transformation-Invariant SDM (Sect. 3.1),

---

[1] The CFAN [34] algorithm included the 330 test faces from Helen in its training data. Thus when testing CFAN, we had to omit these 330 faces from the 300 W test set.

Fig. 6. Visual results on the challenging subset of 300 W dataset. *First row:* SDM. *Second row:* TI-SDM. *Third row:* Our MIX algorithm. Transformation invariance (TI) significantly improves the accuracy of SDM. Improvement from single models (SDM and TI-SDM) to mixture models (MIX) is apparent particularly for large out-of-plane rotations and unusual facial expressions.

which could also be called MIX(1) w/out const. Figure 5 (right) shows that each element of our algorithm improves its performance. Performance is significantly improved by adding transformation invariance (SDM → TI-SDM), by including the mixture of experts at each stage of the cascade (TI-SDM → MIX(3) w/out const.), and by using the extended deformation constraint features (MIX(3) w/out const. → MIX(3) with const.). Using mixtures of more than 3 regression experts (MIX(3) → MIX(5)) yields very minor improvement. This is because of the limited number of training images, particularly with extreme expressions or large out-of-plane rotations, which leads experts specializing in these less common face shapes to overfit the data (as we observed during cross-validation). In Fig. 6, we visually compare sample results on the challenging subset of 300 W dataset. The improvement from a cascade of single models (SDM and TI-SDM, rows 1–2) to a cascade of mixture models (MIX, row 3) is greatest for large out-of-plane rotations and unusual facial expressions. As shown in Fig. 1, each expert specializes for particular poses and expressions, yielding more precise alignment.

In the third experiment, we illustrate the behavior of deformation constraint features by simulating a case in which a few points are poorly initialized or drift away during any regression stage. As shown in column 1 of Fig. 3, we initialize the alignment algorithm within the detection bounding box as usual, but to simulate drifting points we manually displace the two points shown in red (on the left eyebrow and on the outer corner of the right eye) to outside of the detection box. We then align using two models, one without deformation constraint (column 2) and the other with our extended deformation-constraint features (column 3). The model without deformation constraint fails to correct the outlier points, whereas the deformation constraint features move outlier points towards the prototype shape of the expert, enabling it to obtain the correct landmark locations.

On a single core of an Intel Core i5-6600 3.30 GHz processor, MIX with 3 experts runs at 65 ms, of which SIFT feature computation takes 54 ms and the rest of the algorithm takes 11 ms. With multi-core implementation (3 experts run in parallel), run time is reduced to 30 ms (including SIFT feature computation). Please see the supplementary material for additional results.

5 Conclusion

We proposed a novel face alignment algorithm based on a cascade in which each stage consists of a mixture of transformation-invariant (e.g., affine-invariant) regression experts. Each expert specializes in a different part of the joint space of pose and expressions by (affine) transforming the landmark locations to its prototype shape and learning a customized regression model. We also present a method to include deformation constraints within the discriminative alignment framework. Extensive evaluation on benchmark datasets shows that the proposed method significantly improves upon the state of the art.

References

1. Cootes, T.F., Taylor, C.J., Cooper, D.H., Graham, J.: Active shape models-their training and application. Comput. Vis. Image Understand. **61**(1), 38–59 (1995)
2. Cootes, T.F., Edwards, G.J., Taylor, C.J.: Active appearance models. IEEE Trans. Pattern Anal. Mach. Intell. **23**(6), 681–685 (2001)
3. Sauer, P., Cootes, T.F., Taylor, C.J.: Accurate regression procedures for active appearance models. In: BMVC, pp. 1–11 (2011)
4. Sung, J., Kim, D.: Adaptive active appearance model with incremental learning. Pattern Recogn. Lett. **30**(4), 359–367 (2009)
5. Tzimiropoulos, G., Pantic, M.: Optimization problems for fast AAM fitting in-the-wild. In: Proceedings of IEEE International Conference on Computer Vision (ICCV) (2013)
6. Romdhani, S., Gong, S., Psarrou, A., et al.: A multi-view nonlinear active shape model using kernel PCA. BMVC **10**, 483–492 (1999)
7. Cootes, T.F., Wheeler, G.V., Walker, K.N., Taylor, C.J.: View-based active appearance models. Image Vis. Comput. **20**(9), 657–664 (2002)
8. Asthana, A., Marks, T., Jones, M., Tieu, K., M.V., R.: Fully automatic pose-invariant face recognition via 3d pose normalization. In: IEEE International Conference on Computer Vision (ICCV), pp. 937–944, November 2011
9. Cootes, T.F., Wheeler, G.V., Walker, K.N., Taylor, C.J.: Coupled-view active appearance models. In: BMVC, pp. 52–61 (2000)
10. Hu, C., Xiao, J., Matthews, I., Baker, S., Cohn, J.F., Kanade, T.: Fitting a single active appearance model simultaneously to multiple images. In: BMVC, pp. 1–10 (2004)
11. Cristinacce, D., Cootes, T.F.: Feature detection and tracking with constrained local models. In: BMVC (2006)
12. Cristinacce, D., Cootes, T.F.: Boosted regression active shape models. In: BMVC, pp. 1–10 (2007)
13. Zhou, F., Brandt, J., Lin, Z.: Exemplar-based graph matching for robust facial landmark localization. In: 2013 IEEE International Conference on Computer Vision (ICCV), pp. 1025–1032. IEEE (2013)

14. Smith, B.M., Zhang, L.: Joint face alignment with non-parametric shape models. In: Fitzgibbon, A., Lazebnik, S., Perona, P., Sato, Y., Schmid, C. (eds.) ECCV 2012. LNCS, vol. 7574, pp. 43–56. Springer, Heidelberg (2012). doi:10.1007/978-3-642-33712-3_4

15. Tzimiropoulos, G., Pantic, M.: Gauss-newton deformable part models for face alignment in-the-wild. In: 2014 IEEE Conference on Computer Vision and Pattern Recognition (CVPR), pp. 1851–1858. IEEE (2014)

16. Tuzel, O., Porikli, F., Meer, P.: Learning on lie groups for invariant detection and tracking. In: IEEE Conference on Computer Vision and Pattern Recognition, 2008, CVPR 2008, pp. 1–8. IEEE (2008)

17. Xiong, X., De la Torre, F.: Supervised descent method and its applications to face alignment. In: 2013 IEEE Conference on Computer Vision and Pattern Recognition (CVPR), pp. 532–539. IEEE (2013)

18. Asthana, A., Zafeiriou, S., Cheng, S., Pantic, M.: Incremental face alignment in the wild. In: 2014 IEEE Conference on Computer Vision and Pattern Recognition (CVPR), pp. 1859–1866. IEEE (2014)

19. Liu, X.: Discriminative face alignment. IEEE Trans. Pattern Anal. Machine Intell. 31(11), 1941–1954 (2009)

20. Kazemi, V., Sullivan, J.: Face alignment with part-based modeling. In: Proceedings of the British Machine Vision Conference, p. 27:1. BMVA Press (2011)

21. Saragih, J.M., Lucey, S., Cohn, J.F.: Deformable model fitting by regularized landmark mean-shift. Int. J. Comput. Vis. 91(2), 200–215 (2011)

22. Dollár, P., Welinder, P., Perona, P.: Cascaded pose regression. In: 2010 IEEE Conference on Computer Vision and Pattern Recognition (CVPR), pp. 1078–1085. IEEE (2010)

23. Ren, S., Cao, X., Wei, Y., Sun, J.: Face alignment at 3000 fps via regressing local binary features. In: 2014 IEEE Conference on Computer Vision and Pattern Recognition (CVPR), pp. 1685–1692. IEEE (2014)

24. Kazemi, V., Sullivan, J.: One millisecond face alignment with an ensemble of regression trees. In: 2014 IEEE Conference on Computer Vision and Pattern Recognition (CVPR), pp. 1867–1874. IEEE (2014)

25. Cao, X., Wei, Y., Wen, F., Sun, J.: Face alignment by explicit shape regression. Int. J. Comput. Vis. 107(2), 177–190 (2014)

26. Tzimiropoulos, G.: Project-out cascaded regression with an application to face alignment. In: The IEEE Conference on Computer Vision and Pattern Recognition (CVPR), June 2015

27. Yan, J., Lei, Z., Yi, D., Li, S.Z.: Learn to combine multiple hypotheses for accurate face alignment. In: 2013 IEEE International Conference on Computer Vision Workshops (ICCVW), pp. 392–396. IEEE (2013)

28. Cootes, T.F., Ionita, M.C., Lindner, C., Sauer, P.: Robust and accurate shape model fitting using random forest regression voting. In: Fitzgibbon, A., Lazebnik, S., Perona, P., Sato, Y., Schmid, C. (eds.) ECCV 2012. LNCS, vol. 7578, pp. 278–291. Springer, Heidelberg (2012). doi:10.1007/978-3-642-33786-4_21

29. Alabort-i Medina, J., Antonakos, E., Booth, J., Snape, P., Zafeiriou, S.: Menpo: A comprehensive platform for parametric image alignment and visual deformable models. In: Proceedings of the ACM International Conference on Multimedia, MM 2014, pp. 679–682. ACM, New York (2014)

30. Xiong, X., De la Torre, F.: Global supervised descent method. In: IEEE Conference on Computer Vision and Pattern Recognition (CVPR), June 2015

31. Xiao, S., Yan, S., Kassim, A.A.: Facial landmark detection via progressive initialization. In: The IEEE International Conference on Computer Vision (ICCV) Workshops, December 2015
32. Zhang, J., Kan, M., Shan, S., Chen, X.: Leveraging datasets with varying annotations for face alignment via deep regression network. In: The IEEE International Conference on Computer Vision (ICCV), December 2015
33. Zhou, E., Fan, H., Cao, Z., Jiang, Y., Yin, Q.: Extensive facial landmark localization with coarse-to-fine convolutional network cascade. In: ICCV Workshop (2013)
34. Zhang, J., Shan, S., Kan, M., Chen, X.: Coarse-to-fine auto-encoder networks (CFAN) for real-time face alignment. In: ECCV (2014)
35. Zhu, S., Li, C., Change Loy, C., Tang, X.: Face alignment by coarse-to-fine shape searching. In: CVPR (2015)
36. Burgos-Artizzu, X.P., Perona, P., Dollar, P.: Robust face landmark estimation under occlusion. In: The IEEE International Conference on Computer Vision (ICCV), December 2013
37. Yu, X., Lin, Z., Brandt, J., Metaxas, D.N.: Consensus of regression for occlusion-robust facial feature localization. In: Fleet, D., Pajdla, T., Schiele, B., Tuytelaars, T. (eds.) ECCV 2014. LNCS, vol. 8692, pp. 105–118. Springer, Heidelberg (2014). doi:10.1007/978-3-319-10593-2_8
38. Rao, A., Miller, D., Rose, K., Gersho, A.: Mixture of experts regression modeling by deterministic annealing. IEEE Trans. Sig. Process. **45**(11), 2811–2820 (1997)
39. Sagonas, C., Tzimiropoulos, G., Zafeiriou, S., Pantic, M.: A semi-automatic methodology for facial landmark annotation. In: Proceedings of IEEE Conference on Computer Vision and Pattern Recognition (CVPR-Workshops), 5th Workshop on Analysis and Modeling of Faces and Gestures (AMFG2013), Portland Oregon, USA, June 2013
40. Sagonas, C., Tzimiropoulos, G., Zafeiriou, S., Pantic, M.: 300 faces in-the-wild challenge: the first facial landmark localization challenge. In: Proceedings of IEEE International Conference on Computer Vision (ICCV-Workshops), 300 Faces in-the-Wild Challenge (300-W), Sydney, Australia, December 2013
41. Zhu, X., Ramanan, D.: Face detection, pose estimation, and landmark localization in the wild. In: 2012 IEEE Conference on Computer Vision and Pattern Recognition (CVPR), pp. 2879–2886. IEEE (2012)
42. Lowe, D.G.: Distinctive image features from scale-invariant keypoints. Int. J. Comput. Vis. **60**(2), 91–110 (2004)
43. Čech, J., Franc, V., Uřičář, M., Matas, J.: Multi-view facial landmark detection by using a 3D shape model. Image Vis. Comput. **47**, 60–70 (2016)
44. Belhumeur, P.N., Jacobs, D.W., Kriegman, D., Kumar, N.: Localizing parts of faces using a consensus of exemplars. In: 2011 IEEE Conference on Computer Vision and Pattern Recognition (CVPR), pp. 545–552. IEEE (2011)
45. Le, V., Brandt, J., Lin, Z., Bourdev, L., Huang, T.S.: Interactive facial feature localization. In: Fitzgibbon, A., Lazebnik, S., Perona, P., Sato, Y., Schmid, C. (eds.) ECCV 2012. LNCS, vol. 7574, pp. 679–692. Springer, Heidelberg (2012). doi:10.1007/978-3-642-33712-3_49
46. Yang, H., Jia, X., Loy, C.C., Robinson, P.: An empirical study of recent face alignment methods. CoRR abs/1511.05049 (2015)

Partial Linearization Based Optimization for Multi-class SVM

Pritish Mohapatra[1(✉)], Puneet Kumar Dokania[2], C.V. Jawahar[1], and M. Pawan Kumar[3]

[1] IIIT-Hyderabad, Hyderabad, India
pritish.mohapatra@research.iiit.ac.in
[2] CentraleSupelec and Inria Saclay, Palaiseau, France
[3] University of Oxford, Oxford, UK

Abstract. We propose a novel partial linearization based approach for optimizing the multi-class SVM learning problem. Our method is an intuitive generalization of the Frank-Wolfe and the exponentiated gradient algorithms. In particular, it allows us to combine several of their desirable qualities into one approach: (i) the use of an expectation oracle (which provides the marginals over each output class) in order to estimate an informative descent direction, similar to exponentiated gradient; (ii) analytical computation of the optimal step-size in the descent direction that guarantees an increase in the dual objective, similar to Frank-Wolfe; and (iii) a block coordinate formulation similar to the one proposed for Frank-Wolfe, which allows us to solve large-scale problems. Using the challenging computer vision problems of action classification, object recognition and gesture recognition, we demonstrate the efficacy of our approach on training multi-class SVMs with standard, publicly available, machine learning datasets.

Keywords: Multi-class SVM, Partial linearization, Optimization

1 Introduction

Many tasks in computer vision can be formulated as multi-class classification problems. In other words, given an image or a video, the task is to assign it a label that belongs to a specified finite set. For example, in the case of object recognition from an image, the label can be car, chair or person. Similarly, for action recognition from a video, actions categories like jumping, kicking or clapping can be candidate labels. There has been extensive research in the area of multi-class classification with a plethora of solutions being proposed [2,4,16,18]. In this work, we focus on multi-class SVM (MC-SVM), which is one of the most popular methods for this task. The MC-SVM model provides a linear function that

Electronic supplementary material The online version of this chapter (doi:10. 1007/978-3-319-46454-1_51) contains supplementary material, which is available to authorized users.

© Springer International Publishing AG 2016
B. Leibe et al. (Eds.): ECCV 2016, Part V, LNCS 9909, pp. 842–857, 2016.
DOI: 10.1007/978-3-319-46454-1_51

gives a score for each class. Given a test sample, its class is predicted by maximizing the score. During learning, the MC-SVM objective minimizes an upper bound on the empirical risk of the training data, for which we know the ground-truth labels. The risk is typically measured by the standard 0–1 loss function. However, any other loss function can be easily substituted into the MC-SVM learning framework.

The size of the MC-SVM learning problem rapidly increases with the number of classes and size of the training dataset. In order to enable the use of MC-SVM with large scale problems, several optimization algorithms for minimizing its learning objective have been proposed in the literature. One of the most successful algorithms is a recent adaptation of the Frank-Wolfe algorithm [8]. Briefly, the algorithm solves the dual of the MC-SVM optimization problem iteratively. At each iteration, it obtains a descent direction by minimizing a linear approximation of the dual objective. It was shown in [10] that the computation of the descent direction corresponds to a call to the so-called *max-oracle* for each sample. In other words, for each training sample, we maximize over the set of output classes with respect to the loss-augmented scores. As the max-oracle can be solved efficiently for the MC-SVM, the Frank-Wolfe algorithm can be effectively used to learn such models. There are two main advantages of the Frank-Wolfe algorithm. First, the optimal step-size in the descent direction can be computed analytically, thereby avoiding a tedious line search [10]. Second, it can be suitably modified to a block-coordinate version [14], where the max-oracle is solved for only one training sample at each iteration. The gain in efficiency obtained by this version does not affect the accuracy of the solution.

A key disadvantage of the Frank-Wolfe algorithm is that it only provides a very local approximation of the objective function with the aid of the max-oracle. In other words, it effectively focuses on one constraint (the most violated one) of the primal MC-SVM learning problem. In contrast, the exponentiated gradient algorithm [1] makes use of a more informative *expectation oracle*. To elaborate, instead of maximizing, it computes an expectation over the set of output classes with respect to a distribution parameterized by the loss-augmented scores. However, the exponentiated gradient algorithm suffers from the difficulty of choosing an optimal step-size, for which it has to resort to line search. Furthermore, despite the availability of a stochastic version of the algorithm, its worst-case time complexity is worse than that of the Frank-Wolfe algorithm.

In this paper, we propose a novel algorithm for optimizing the MC-SVM learning problem based on partial linearization [17]. Our algorithm provides a natural generalization to the Frank-Wolfe and the exponentiated gradient algorithms, thereby combining their desirable properties. Specifically, (i) it allows for the use of a potentially more informative descent direction based on the expectation oracle; (ii) it computes the optimal step-size in the descent direction analytically; and (iii) it can also be applied in a block coordinate fashion without losing the accuracy of the solution. We demonstrate the efficacy of our approach on the challenging computer vision problems of action classification, object recognition and gesture recognition using standard publicly available datasets.

In certain cases, our method can also be used for efficient optimization of the more general structured SVM (SSVM) models. Specifically, in case of output spaces that have a low tree-width structure, we can employ efficient max-oracles and expectation-oracles. This in turn means that similar to the Frank-Wolfe [10] and exponentiated gradient algorithms [1], our method can be effectively used for learning an SSVM model. We demonstrate this on the problem of handwritten word recognition using a chain structured output space.

2   Related Work

Several algorithms have been proposed for optimizing multi-class SVMs. Most of the popular methods are iterative algorithms that make use of efficient sub-routines called *oracles* in each iteration [1,10,11,19,23]. The most popular algorithms can be bracketed into two classes depending on the type of oracles they use: ones that use the max-oracle [10,11,19]; and the ones that use the expectation oracle [1,23].

A max-oracle sub-routine maximizes the loss-augmented score over the output space. In other words, given the current estimate of the parameters and a training sample, it returns the output that maximizes the sum of the classifier score and the loss. The sub-gradient descent algorithm [19] calls the max-oracle to compute the sub-gradient of the primal objective and uses it as the update direction in each iteration. The cutting-plane algorithm [11] uses the max-oracle to get the most violating constraint or the cutting plane. It accumulates the cutting planes to generate increasingly accurate approximations to the primal problem that it solves in each iteration. The recent adaptation [10] of the Frank-Wolfe algorithm to the MC-SVM and SSVM learning problems uses the max-oracle to compute the conditional gradient of the dual problem. All three aforementioned algorithms have a complexity of $O(1/\epsilon)$, where ϵ is the user-specified optimization tolerance. However, in practice, the block-coordinate Frank-Wolfe algorithm has been shown to provide faster convergence on a variety of problems [10].

In contrast to the max-oracle, the expectation-oracle computes an expectation over the output space with respect to a distribution parameterized by the loss-augmented scores. In [1], the expectation-oracle is used to make exponentiated gradient updates [12], which guarantees descent in each iteration. The Bregman projection based excessive gap reduction technique presented in [23] also uses the expectation oracle. While this algorithm has a highly competitive complexity of $O(1/\sqrt{\epsilon})$, the method does not work with noisy oracles and hence cannot lend itself to a stochastic or a block-coordinate version.

As will be seen shortly, our approach naturally generalizes over algorithms from both the categories with the use of a temperature hyperparameter. When the temperature is set to 0, the expectation oracle resembles the max-oracle and our method reduces to the Frank-Wolfe algorithm [10]. Importantly, for a non-zero temperature, the use of the expectation-oracle can provide us with a less local approximation of the objective function. Hence, for the multi-class SVM learning problem, it may be beneficial to use the expectation-oracle instead of the max-oracle. Another key aspect of our algorithm is that it chooses an optimal step-size at each iteration. If we instead fix the step-size to 1 in every iteration and use a non-zero value of the temperature hyperparameter, then our method reduces to the exponentiated gradient algorithm [1]. Moreover, unlike the cutting plane [11] and the excessive gap reduction [23] algorithms our approach allows for a block-coordinate version, which leads to faster rate of convergence without affecting the accuracy of the solution.

3 Preliminaries

3.1 The Multi-class SVM Optimization Problem

We provide a brief overview of the multi-class SVM (MC-SVM) optimization problem. Given an input $\mathbf{x} \in \mathcal{X}$ the aim of multi-class classification is to predict the output y that belongs to the output space $\mathcal{Y}$. If the number of classes is denoted by c, the output space $\mathcal{Y} = \{1, \ldots, c\}$. Let the feature representation of sample $\mathbf{x}$ be $\boldsymbol{\varphi}(\mathbf{x})$, then a joint feature map $\Phi(\mathbf{x}, y) : \mathcal{X} \times \mathcal{Y} \to \mathcal{R}^d$ is defined as

$$\Phi(\mathbf{x}, y) = [\boldsymbol{v}_1^\top \ \ldots \ \boldsymbol{v}_j^\top \ \ldots \ \boldsymbol{v}_c^\top]^\top \tag{1}$$

$$where, \ \boldsymbol{v}_j = \begin{cases} \boldsymbol{\varphi}(\mathbf{x}) \text{ if } j = y, \\ \mathbf{0} \quad \text{otherwise.} \end{cases}$$

A multi-class SVM, parameterized by $\mathbf{w}$, provides a linear prediction rule as follows: $h_{\mathbf{w}}(\mathbf{x}) = \operatorname{argmax}_{y \in \mathcal{Y}} \left(\mathbf{w}^\top \Phi(\mathbf{x}, y) \right)$. Given a set of labelled samples $\mathcal{D} = \{(\mathbf{x}_1, y_1), \ldots, (\mathbf{x}_n, y_n)\}$, the parameter vector $\mathbf{w}$ is learnt by solving the following convex optimization problem:

$$\min_{\mathbf{w}, \xi} \ \frac{\lambda}{2} ||\mathbf{w}||^2 + \frac{1}{n} \sum_{i=1}^n \xi_i \tag{2}$$

$$\text{s.t.} \quad \mathbf{w}^\top \Psi_i(y) \geq \Delta(y_i, y) - \xi_i, \forall i \in [n], \forall y \in \mathcal{Y}$$

Here, $\Psi_i(y) = \Phi(\mathbf{x}_i, y_i) - \Phi(\mathbf{x}_i, y)$ and the loss incurred for predicting y, given the ground truth y_i for the sample $\mathbf{x}_i$, is defined as

$$\Delta(y_i, y) = \begin{cases} 0 \text{ if } y = y_i, \\ 1 \text{ otherwise.} \end{cases} \tag{3}$$

We use $[n]$ to denote the set $\{1, 2, \ldots, n\}$ and shall use $\Delta_i(y)$ as a short hand for $\Delta(y, y_i)$. The Lagrangian dual of problem (2) is given by:

$$\min_{\boldsymbol{\alpha} \geq 0} \ T(\boldsymbol{\alpha}) = -\mathbf{b}^\top \boldsymbol{\alpha} + \frac{\lambda}{2} \boldsymbol{\alpha}^\top A^\top A \boldsymbol{\alpha} \tag{4}$$

$$\text{s.t.} \ \sum_{y \in \mathcal{Y}} \boldsymbol{\alpha}_{iy} = 1, \forall i \in [n].$$

Here the dual variable vector $\boldsymbol{\alpha}$ is of size $m = n \times c$; $\mathbf{b} \in \mathcal{R}^m$ is defined as $\mathbf{b} = \{b_{iy} = \frac{1}{n}\Delta_i(y) \mid i \in [n], y \in \mathcal{Y}\}$ and the matrix $A \in \mathcal{R}^{d \times m}$ is defined as $A = \{A_{iy} = \frac{1}{\lambda n}\Psi_i(y) \in \mathcal{R}^d \mid i \in [n], y \in \mathcal{Y}\}$.

It is possible to cheaply evaluate the objective of the primal MC-SVM formulation since the following problem lends itself to efficient optimization. Specifically, in order to compute the MC-SVM objective at a given set of parameters $\mathbf{w}$, we can solve the following problem for each sample i.

$$\bar{y}_i = \operatorname*{argmax}_{y \in \mathcal{Y}} \Delta_i(y) - \mathbf{w}^\top \Psi_i(y). \tag{5}$$

Given $\bar{y}_i$, the value of the slack variable $\xi_i = \Delta_i(\bar{y}_i) - \mathbf{w}^\top \Psi_i(\bar{y}_i)$. We refer to the above problem as the *max-oracle*. Let $P(y)$ denote the probability distribution over the set of output classes, parameterized by the loss augmented scores, that is,

$$P(y) = \frac{\exp\left(\Delta_i(y) - \mathbf{w}^\top \Psi_i(y)\right)}{\sum_{y \in \mathcal{Y}} \exp\left(\Delta_i(y) - \mathbf{w}^\top \Psi_i(y)\right)}. \tag{6}$$

The max-oracle gives the most probable class according to the distribution $P(y)$. It has been shown through several works, including cutting-plane algorithms [11], subgradient descent [19] and Frank-Wolfe [14], that an inexpensive max-oracle is sufficient to minimize problem (2) and/or its Lagrangian dual (4) efficiently.

As we will see shortly, our work exploits the fact that, for multi-class classification problems, a related problem known as the *expectation-oracle* can be solved efficiently as well (with the same time complexity as the max-oracle). While the max-oracle gives the most probable class, the expectation-oracle returns an expectation over the complete output space with respect to the distribution $P(y)$. By cleverly exploiting this observation, we obtain a natural generalization of the Frank-Wolfe algorithm that retains many of its desirable properties such as: guaranteed descent direction, analytically computable optimal step size and guaranteed convergence even in block-coordinate mode. At the same time it also allows the use of the expectation-oracle to find a valid descent direction that can often lead to improved performance in practice.

3.2   Partial Linearization

Let us consider the following optimization problem with a convex and continuously differentiable objective $T(\boldsymbol{\alpha})$ defined over a compact and convex feasible set U: $\min_{\boldsymbol{\alpha} \in U} T(\boldsymbol{\alpha})$. For this problem, Patriksson [17] proposes a framework that unifies several feasible-direction finding methods for non-linear optimization through the concept of partial linearization of the objective function. The idea of partial linearization is to construct a convex approximation to the original objective $T(\boldsymbol{\alpha})$ at each iteration. The approximation involves substituting the original function with a surrogate function. Furthermore, in order to model the difference between the original function and the surrogate function, we add a first order approximation of this difference.

Formally, at each iteration k, we solve the following problem:

$$\min_{\boldsymbol{\alpha} \in U} \; T^k(\boldsymbol{\alpha}) = f(\boldsymbol{\alpha}, \boldsymbol{\alpha}^k) + T(\boldsymbol{\alpha}^k) - f(\boldsymbol{\alpha}^k, \boldsymbol{\alpha}^k) \tag{7}$$
$$+ [\nabla T(\boldsymbol{\alpha}^k) - \nabla_{\boldsymbol{\alpha}} f(\boldsymbol{\alpha}^k, \boldsymbol{\alpha}^k)]^T (\boldsymbol{\alpha} - \boldsymbol{\alpha}^k).$$

The term $f(\boldsymbol{\alpha}, \boldsymbol{\alpha}^k)$ denotes the surrogate function defined at the current solution $\boldsymbol{\alpha}^k$. The term $T(\boldsymbol{\alpha}^k) - f(\boldsymbol{\alpha}^k, \boldsymbol{\alpha}^k) + [\nabla T(\boldsymbol{\alpha}^k) - \nabla_{\boldsymbol{\alpha}} f(\boldsymbol{\alpha}^k, \boldsymbol{\alpha}^k)]^T (\boldsymbol{\alpha} - \boldsymbol{\alpha}^k)$ is the first order Taylor expansion of the actual error term $T(\boldsymbol{\alpha}^k) - f(\boldsymbol{\alpha}, \boldsymbol{\alpha}^k)$ and is used as an approximation for it. Patriksson [17] showed that the approximation proposed in Eq. (7) actually preserves the gradient of the original objective function. This guarrantees that a valid descent direction for the approximate problem (7) is also a valid descent direction for the original problem. The optimal solution $\bar{\boldsymbol{\alpha}}^k$ to problem (7) gives a descent direction. This allows us to update the solution as $\boldsymbol{\alpha}^{k+1} = (1 - \gamma)(\boldsymbol{\alpha}^k) + (\gamma)(\bar{\boldsymbol{\alpha}}^k)$, where γ is the step-size that can be determined via line search in general. Interestingly, in some special cases, including the one considered in this work, the optimal step-size can also be computed analytically, which avoids the tedious line search. For convergence, $f(\mathbf{x}, \mathbf{y})$ has to be convex and continuously differentiable with respect to $\mathbf{x}$ and continuous with respect to $\mathbf{y}$. We adapt the partial linearization method for solving problem (4) in the following section.

4   Partial Linearization for Multi-class SVM Optimization

The dual multi-class SVM problem defined in problem (4) has a compact convex feasible set and has a continuously differentiable convex objective. This allows us to use the partial linearization method to solve the optimization problem. However, as the above description shows, partial linearization is a very general framework. For it to be applied successfully, we need to ensure that we make the right choice for the surrogate function. Specifically, the resulting problem (7) must lend itself to efficient optimization. Furthermore, in our case, we would like to ensure that problem (7) captures the information regarding how much each constraint of the primal multi-class SVM problem is violated, similar to the expectation-oracle. To this end, we define the surrogate function as follows:

$$f(\boldsymbol{\alpha}, \boldsymbol{\alpha}^k) = \frac{\tau}{n} \sum_{i \in [n]} \sum_{y \in \mathcal{Y}} \boldsymbol{\alpha}_{iy} \log(\boldsymbol{\alpha}_{iy}). \tag{8}$$

Here, τ is a non-negative hyperparameter, which we refer to as the temperature. In the following subsection, we show that for the above choice of surrogate function, the partial linearization approach generalizes both the Frank-Wolfe and the exponentiated gradient algorithm.

4.1   Partial Linearization in the Dual Space

When we use the surrogate function defined in Eq. (8) for partial linearization of the dual multi-class SVM problem, the form of the update direction in the resulting optimization algorithm is described by the following proposition.

Proposition 1. *If the surrogate function is defined as*

$$f(\boldsymbol{\alpha}, \boldsymbol{\alpha}^k) = \frac{\tau}{n} \sum_{i \in [n]} \sum_{y \in \mathcal{Y}} \boldsymbol{\alpha}_{iy} \log(\boldsymbol{\alpha}_{iy}),$$

then the update direction $\mathbf{s}^k$ *in iteration* k *for given* i *and* $y \in \mathcal{Y}$ *can be computed as*

$$\mathbf{s}_{iy}^k = \frac{\exp\left(\log(\boldsymbol{\alpha}_{iy}^{k-1}) + \frac{1}{\tau}(\Delta_i(y) - \mathbf{w}^{k-1^\top} \Psi_i(y))\right)}{z_i}. \tag{9}$$

The proof of the above proposition is provided in Appendix 1.1 (supplementary material).

In Eq. 9, for each sample i, $\mathbf{s}_i^k(y)$ forms a probability distribution over the set of classes $\mathcal{Y}$. In the primal setting, this is equivalent to having an expectation over the entire output space as the update direction and is therefore similar to an expectation-oracle. In each iteration of the algorithm, given the update direction, we need to perform a line search to find the optimal step size γ in that direction. Since the dual multi-class SVM problem involves optimizing a quadratic function, it is possible to analytically compute the optimal step-size. The following proposition that gives the form of the optimal step size directly follows from the work of Jaggi *et al.* [14].

Proposition 2. *The optimal step-size along the update direction* $\mathbf{s}^k$ *can be computed to be equal to*

$$\gamma = \frac{< \boldsymbol{\alpha}^{k-1} - \mathbf{s}^k, -\mathbf{b} + A^\top A \boldsymbol{\alpha}^{k-1} >}{\lambda \|A(\boldsymbol{\alpha}^{k-1} - \mathbf{s}^k)\|^2}. \tag{10}$$

Here it should be observed that setting the temperature parameter τ to 0 results in a distribution $\mathbf{s}_i^k$ that has probability 1 for the label

$$\bar{y}_i = \underset{y \in \mathcal{Y}}{\operatorname{argmax}} \left(L_i(y) - \mathbf{w}^{k-1^T} \Psi_i(y)\right)$$

and 0 elsewhere. This results in an update direction that is the same as that of the Frank-Wolfe algorithm and thus reduces the partial linearization method to the Frank-Wolfe algorithm [14]. Moreover, fixing the step-size γ to 1 for all iterations, reduces our approach to the exponentiated-gradient algorithm [1]. Hence, our partial linearization based approach for optimizing the MC-SVM problem generalizes both the Frank-Wolfe as well as the exponentiated-gradient algorithms. Importantly, the descent direction obtained using some $\tau > 0$ can be significantly better than that obtained using $\tau = 0$. This is illustrated in the following example.

In problem 4, let $n = 1$, $\lambda = 1$, $A = [2, 0, 0; 0, 1, 0; 0, 0, 3]$ and $b = [1; 1; 0]$. Assume, after the $(k-1)^{th}$ iteration of the optimization algorithm, the location in the feasible set is $\alpha^{k-1} = [0.125, 0.5, 0.5]^\top$. Now, if we take $\tau = 0$, the descent direction for the kth iteration can be computed to be $\mathbf{s}_{\tau=0}^k = [1, 0, 0]^\top$. Similarly, for $\tau = 1$, the descent direction would be $\mathbf{s}_{\tau=1}^k = [0.199, 0.796, 0.005]^\top$. In each case, we take the optimal step in the descent direction. It can be verified that while the step along $s_{\tau=0}^k$ reduces the objective function by 0.5341, the step along $s_{\tau=1}^k$ reduces the objective function by a bigger value of 1.2550. This is primarily due to the fact that the Frank-Wolfe algorithm ($\tau = 0$) constraints the descent directions to be only towards vertices of the feasible domain polytope. For instance in this example, $\mathbf{s}_{\tau=0}^k$ can only take values from among $\{[1, 0, 0]^\top, [0, 1, 0]^\top, [0, 0, 1]^\top\}$, which prevents it from taking a more direct path towards the optimal solution ($[0.25, 1, 0]^\top$) which lies on one of the facets of the polytope and hence away from the direction of any of the vertices. On the other hand, with $\tau > 0$, our algorithm can explore more direct descent paths towards the solution.

Algorithm 1. *Partial linearization for optimizing multi-class* SVM

1: $\mathcal{D} = (\mathbf{x}_i, y_i), \ldots, (\mathbf{x}_n, y_n)$
2: Initialize $\boldsymbol{\alpha}^0$ such that $\mathbf{w}(\boldsymbol{\alpha}^0) \sim [0]^d$, $k \leftarrow 1$
3: **repeat**
4:    **for all** $i \in [n]$ **do**
5:      $\forall y \in \mathcal{Y}$,
6:      $\mathbf{s}_{iy}^k \leftarrow \dfrac{\exp\left(\log(\boldsymbol{\alpha}_{iy}^{k-1}) + \frac{1}{\tau}(\Delta_i(y) - \mathbf{w}^{k-1^\top}\Psi_i(y))\right)}{z_i}$
7:    **end for**
8:    Optimal step size, $\gamma \leftarrow \dfrac{<\boldsymbol{\alpha}^{k-1} - \mathbf{s}^k, -\mathbf{b} + A^\top A \boldsymbol{\alpha}^{k-1}>}{\lambda ||A(\boldsymbol{\alpha}^{k-1} - \mathbf{s}^k)||^2}$
9:    Update $\boldsymbol{\alpha}$, $\boldsymbol{\alpha}^k \leftarrow (1 - \gamma)\boldsymbol{\alpha}^{k-1} + (\gamma)\mathbf{s}^k$
10:   Update $\mathbf{w}$, $\mathbf{w}^k \leftarrow A\boldsymbol{\alpha}^k$
11:   $k \leftarrow k + 1$
12: **until** Convergence
13: Optimal parameter, $\mathbf{w}$

The partial linearization algorithm for optimizing the dual MC-SVM problem is outlined in Algorithm 1. Step 6 in Algorithm 1 requires us to explicitly compute the update direction corresponding to each dual variable. For the MC-SVM problem, as the number of dual variables is a reasonable (*number of samples*) × (*number of classes*), $\mathbf{s}_{iy}^k$ can be efficiently computed for every sample $\mathbf{x}_i$ as the marginal probability of each class y. Once we have the update direction we take a step in that direction with optimal step-size γ as computed in Step 8. Then the dual and the primal variables are updated to complete an iteration of the algorithm.

4.2 Block-Coordinate Partial Linearization

In many tasks, it is very common to learn classification models using very large datasets. In such scenarios, learning an MC-SVM model using the partial linearization algorithm described in Algorithm 1 can be very slow. This is because,

---

Algorithm 2. *Block-Coordinate Partial linearization for optimizing multi-class* SVM

1: $\mathcal{D} = (\mathbf{x}_i, y_i), \ldots, (\mathbf{x}_n, y_n)$
2: Initialize $\boldsymbol{\alpha}^0$ such that $\mathbf{w}(\boldsymbol{\alpha}^0) \sim [0]^d$, $k \leftarrow 1$
3: Initialize a $(d \times n)$ matrix W such that i^{th} column of W, $\mathbf{w}_i = \mathbf{w}(\boldsymbol{\alpha}_i^0)$
4: **repeat**
5:    Chose a random $i \in [n]$
6:    $\forall y \in \mathcal{Y}$,
7:    $\mathbf{s}_{iy}^k \leftarrow \dfrac{\exp\left(\log(\boldsymbol{\alpha}_{iy}^{k-1}) + \frac{1}{\tau}(\Delta_i(y) - \mathbf{w}^{k-1^\top}\Psi_i(y))\right)}{z_i}$
8:    Optimal step size, $\gamma \leftarrow \dfrac{<\boldsymbol{\alpha}_i^{k-1} - \mathbf{s}_i^k, -\mathbf{b} + A^\top A\boldsymbol{\alpha}_i^{k-1}>}{\lambda||A(\boldsymbol{\alpha}_i^{k-1} - \mathbf{s}_i^k)||^2}$
9:    Update $\boldsymbol{\alpha}_i$, $\boldsymbol{\alpha}_i^k \leftarrow (1 - \gamma)\boldsymbol{\alpha}_i^{k-1} + (\gamma)\mathbf{s}_i^k$
10:   Update $\mathbf{w}_i$, $\mathbf{w}_i^k \leftarrow A\boldsymbol{\alpha}_i^k$
11:   Update $\mathbf{w}$, $\mathbf{w}^k \leftarrow \mathbf{w}^{k-1} - \mathbf{w}_i^{k-1} + \mathbf{w}_i^k$
12:   $k \leftarrow k + 1$
13: **until** Convergence
14: Optimal parameter, $\mathbf{w}$

---

each update iteration of Algorithm 1 requires a pass through the entire dataset. In order to circumvent this expensive step, we present a block-coordinate version of the algorithm, which updates the model parameters after every single sample encounter. Algorithm 2 outlines the details of the block-coordinate partial linearization algorithm. The key difference is that, unlike Algorithm 1, Algorithm 2 does not have to loop through all the samples in the training set before updating the primal variable vector. Instead, we pick a random sample i from the training set (step 5) and compute the marginals just for this sample. Accordingly we update the primal weight vector $\mathbf{w}$ with this new marginal for sample i while the marginals for all other samples remain unchanged. This is similar to the coordinate descent method and is more efficient compared to the batch method as instead of solving n convex optimization problems, we have to solve only one in each iteration. As shown in the following proposition, this improvement in run-time does not affect the accuracy of the solution.

Proposition 3. *The block-coordinate partial linearization algorithm is guaranteed to converge to the global optima of the multi-class* SVM *learning problem.*

The proof of the above proposition is provided in Appendix 1.3 (supplementary material).

4.3 Partial Linearization for Structured SVM Optimization

The multi-class SVM solves a prediction problem in which the output space is a set of classes. However, for many tasks, the output space can have a more complicated structure. The structured SVM (SSVM), which is a generalization of the binary SVM to structured output spaces, can effectively model such structures. Given an input $\mathbf{x} \in \mathcal{X}$, the aim is to predict the output $\mathbf{y}$ that belongs to a structured space $\mathcal{Y}(\mathbf{x})$. Borrowing the notations from Sect. 3.1, a structured SVM, parameterized by $\mathbf{w}$, provides a linear prediction rule as follows: $h_{\mathbf{w}}(\mathbf{x}) = \text{argmax}_{\mathbf{y} \in \mathcal{Y}} (\mathbf{w}^\top \Phi(\mathbf{x}, \mathbf{y}))$. Given a set of labelled samples $\mathcal{D} = \{(\mathbf{x}_1, \mathbf{y}_1), ..., (\mathbf{x}_n, \mathbf{y}_n)\}$, the parameter vector $\mathbf{w}$ is learnt by solving the following convex optimization problem:

$$\min_{\mathbf{w}, \xi} \frac{\lambda}{2}||\mathbf{w}||^2 + \frac{1}{n}\sum_{i=1}^{n} \xi_i, \quad \text{s.t. } \mathbf{w}^\top \Psi_i(\mathbf{y}) \geq \Delta(\mathbf{y}_i, \mathbf{y}) - \xi_i, \forall i \in [n], \forall \mathbf{y} \in \mathcal{Y}_i \quad (11)$$

The key differences from the multi-class SVM formulation are that here we can have any general joint feature map $\Phi(\mathbf{x}, \mathbf{y})$ and loss function $\Delta(\mathbf{y}_i, \mathbf{y})$ designed to effectively model the structure of the output space. The Lagrangian dual of problem (11) is given by:

$$\min_{\boldsymbol{\alpha} \geq 0} T(\boldsymbol{\alpha}) = -\mathbf{b}^\top \boldsymbol{\alpha} + \frac{\lambda}{2}\boldsymbol{\alpha}^\top A^\top A\boldsymbol{\alpha}, \quad \text{s.t. } \sum_{\mathbf{y} \in \mathcal{Y}_i} \boldsymbol{\alpha}_{iy} = 1, \forall i \in [n]. \quad (12)$$

Here the dual variable vector $\boldsymbol{\alpha}$ is of size $m = \sum_{i=1}^{n} |\mathcal{Y}_i|$; $\mathbf{b}$ and A have the same definition as in Sect. 3.1.

In general the size of output space can be exponential in the number of output variables. This would result in exponentially large number of primal constraints and dual variables, which can be hard to deal with. However, these problems can be overcome by making clever use of the structure of the output space. The key observation behind our effective partial linearization based optimization algorithm is that we can efficiently compute the marginals of the output variables. Now, when the output space $\mathcal{Y}_i$ has a low tree-width graph structure, it is possible to efficiently compute the exact marginals of the output variables, by solving the expectation-oracle problem. This can be done using a message passing algorithm over a junction tree corresponding to the underlying graph of the output space [22]. In such a setting, our algorithm can be used for efficient optimization of the SSVM learning problem for low tree-width models. We discuss the partial-linearization algorithm for learning low tree-width SSVM models in detail in the supplementary material. We demonstrate the applicability of such an approach on the task of handwritten word recognition.

5 Experiments

We now demonstrate the efficacy of our algorithm on the challenging multiclass classification tasks of action classification, object recognition and gesture recognition. We also present some preliminary results for tree-structured models on the task of handwritten word recognition.

5.1   Datasets and Tasks

Action Classification

Dataset. We use the PASCAL VOC 2011 [6] action classification dataset for our experiments. This dataset consists of 4846 bounding boxes of persons, each of which is labeled using one of ten action classes. It includes 3347 'trainval' person bounding boxes for which the ground-truth action classes are known.

Modelling and Features. We train a multi-class SVM as an action classifier using 2800 labelled bounding boxes from the 'trainval' set. We use the standard poselet [15] activation features as sample feature for each person bounding box. The feature vector consists of 2400 action poselet activations and 4 object detection scores. We refer the reader to [15] for details regarding the feature vector.

Object Recognition on CIFAR-10 Dataset

Dataset. We use the CIFAR-10 dataset [13] for this set of experiments. It consists of a total of 60,000 images of 10 different object classes with 6,000 images per class. The dataset is divided into a 'trainval' set of 50,000 images and a 'test' set of 10,000 images.

Modelling and Features. We train a multi-class SVM for object recognition on the trainval set. To represent each image, we use a feature representation that is extracted from a trained Convolutional Neural Network. Specifically, we pass the resized image as input to the VGG-NET [20] network and use the activation vector of its penultimate layer as the feature vector. The length of the resulting feature vector is 4096.

Object Recognition on PASCAL VOC Dataset

Dataset. We use the PASCAL VOC 2007 [5] object detection dataset, which consists of a total of 9963 images of which 5011 images are in the 'trainval' set. All the images are labelled to indicate the presence or absence of the instances of 20 different object categories. Each image can have multiple instances of an object and we are provided with tight bounding boxes around each of them.

Modelling and Features. We train a multi-class SVM for object recognition on 12,608 object bounding boxes extracted from the trainval set. For each object bounding box, we use a feature representation extracted from a trained Convolutional Neural Network (CNN). Specifically, we pass the bounding box as input to the CNN and use the activation vector of the penultimate layer of the CNN as the feature vector. Inspired by the work of Girshick *et al.* [9], we use the CNN that is trained on the ImageNet dataset [3], by rescaling each window to a fixed size of 224×224. The length of the resulting feature vector is 4096.

Gesture Recognition

Dataset. We use the MSRC-12 data set [7] which contains 594 sequences of motion capture data obtained using a Kinect sensor. Each sequence corresponds to a person repeatedly performing one out of the 12 gestures represented in the dataset. For each frame of the sequence, we are given the 3D world position of 20 human body joints. In addition to the sequence level gesture annotations, we are also provided with frame level annotations which we ignore in our experiments.

Modelling and Features. We treat each sequence as a single sample and train a multi-class latent-SVM for sequence level gesture recognition. The exact location of the gesture in a sequence is held by a latent variable. We represent a sequence $\mathbf{x}$ using a feature vector $\phi(\mathbf{x}, h)$ which is extracted from the frame in the sequence denoted by the latent variable h. We extract the same 130 dimensional feature vector from a frame as used in [7].

Handwritten Word Recognition

Dataset. We use the OCR dataset [21] for our experiments. The dataset consists of 6251 images of handwritten words. We use 626 images for training and the rest for testing. Each word image is already segmented into individual characters. Each character can be of one of the 26 classes: $\{a, ..., z\}$.

Modelling and Features. The dataset provides the handwritten-word images in binary format. Each segmented character image in the dataset is of size 16×8 pixels. We use binary pixel values of the character images to construct a 128 dimensional feature vector for each character. We use an indicator basis function to represent the correlation between adjacent characters. We also use indicator basis functions to represent location independent bias for each of the characters and additional bias for the first and the last characters of any word. This makes the overall size of the feature vector equal to $(128 \times 26 + 26 \times 26 + 26 + 26 \times 2) = 4082$. The Note that the underlying graph has a 'chain' structure, which enables the computation of exact marginals via sum-product belief propagation [22].

5.2 Methods

For all the tasks, we compare the runtime of our block-coordinate partial linearization (BCPL) approach to those of two baseline algorithms for solving the multi-class SVM or the SSVM optimization problem, namely the block-coordinate Frank-Wolfe algorithm [14] (BCFW) and the online exponentiated gradient (OEG) algorithm [1]. We ran each of the algorithms for 3 different values $(0.1, 0.01, 0.001)$ of the regularization parameter λ. For most practical setups λ is chosen to be very low since large datasets avoid the problem of high generalization error via overfitting. In all the experiments, we used a fixed temperature of $\tau = 0.01$ for our algorithm. For OEG, we repeated the experiments for 8 different values $(100, 10, 1, 0.1, 0.01, 0.001, 0.0001, 10^{-5}, 10^{-10})$ of the temperature

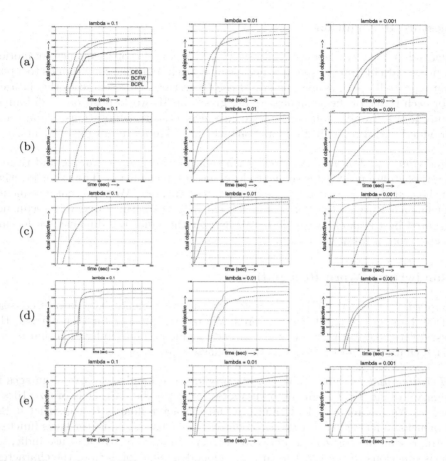

Fig. 1. Comparison of different optimization algorithms in terms of change in the dual objective (negative of the objective of problem (4)) with respect to training time. The results correspond to (a) Action classification (b) Object recognition on CIFAR-10 (c) Object recognition on PASCAL VOC (d) Gesture recognition (e) Hand written word recognition. The figures are zoomed-in along the vertical axis to highlight the differences between the top most competing methods. Note that for $\lambda = 0.01$ and $\lambda = 0.001$, the exponentiated gradient algorithm performs significantly worse than the other two methods, and is therefore not visible in the plots. This figure is best viewed in colour. (Color figure online)

parameter τ and report he results for the best performing value. We initialize all the optimization algorithms in a manner which ensures that the weight parameters are almost equal to 0. In each iteration of training, we sample without repetition from the dataset. For the BCPL and OEG algorithms, in order to avoid getting stuck on a facet of the domain polytope, we truncate the step size γ at each iteration to $1 - \epsilon$. Where, $\epsilon = 2.2204 \times 10^{-16}$ is the machine epsilon.

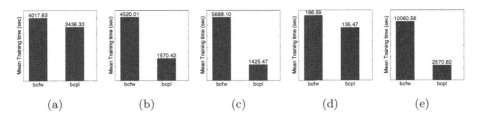

Fig. 2. Comparison of Block-coordinate Frank-Wolfe (BCFW) and Block-coordinate Partial linearization (BCPL) in terms of the mean training time. The results correspond to (a) Action classification (b) Object recognition on CIFAR-10 (c) Object recognition on PASCAL VOC (d) Gesture recognition (e) Hand written word recognition.

5.3   Results

We report the performance of the different methods in terms of the increase in the dual MC-SVM or the SSVM objective function with respect to training time. Figure 1 provides the detailed plots for the experiments for different values of λ. As can be observed from the plots, in most cases, our BCPL algorithm converges faster than BCFW and OEG. It should be noted that the relative difference between the rate of convergence of the two algorithms may seem comparatively small. However, due to the low absolute rate of convergence of both the algorithms in the later stages, this small gap leads to significant saving in terms of iterations and time for our algorithm. The OEG algorithm performs consistently worse than the other 2 algorithms for these set of experiments. For all the tasks, we also report the mean time taken for training by our method and the Frank-Wolfe algorithm. For each task, the training time is averaged over all values of λ. Figure 2 shows that our approach consistently does better than the Frank-Wolfe algorithm. Note that since we solve a convex optimization problem, all the methods are guaranteed to converge to the same or very similar solutions. Hence, we have focused on only a comparison of the run time in the paper.

6   Discussion

We proposed a partial linearization based approach for optimizing multi-class SVM, which naturally generalizes the Frank-Wolfe and the exponentiated gradient algorithms. Our method introduces the key temperature hyperparameter for which we keep a fixed value through out the optimization. This leaves scope for exploring ideas for varying the temperature across iterations for faster convergence. In this work, we discussed our approach only in context of multi-class classification models and structured SVM models that have a tree structure. However, the efficacy of our approach in the context of loopy graphs that require approximate computation of the expectation oracle is still unknown. Another interesting direction for future research would be to explore the applicability of our approach for variations of the SVM optimization problem (such as those that use soft constraints), or for other learning frameworks such as convolutional neural networks.

Acknowledgements. Pritish is supported by the TCS Research Scholar Program.

References

1. Collins, M., Globerson, A., Koo, T., Carreras, X., Bartlett, P.L.: Exponentiated gradient algorithms for conditional random fields and max-margin markov networks. J. Mach. Learn. Res. **9**, 1775–1822 (2008)
2. Crammer, K., Singer, Y.: On the algorithmic implementation of multiclass kernel-based vector machines. J. Mach. Learn. Res. **2**, 265–292 (2001)
3. Deng, J., Dong, W., Socher, R., Li, L.J., Li, K., Fei-Fei, L.: ImageNet: a large-scale hierarchical image database. In: CVPR (2009)
4. Engel, J.: Polytomous logistic regression. Statistica Neerlandica (1988)
5. Everingham, M., Van Gool, L., Williams, C., Winn, J., Zisserman, A.: The PASCAL Visual Object Classes Challenge 2007 (VOC2007) Results. http://www.pascal-network.org/challenges/VOC/voc2007/workshop/index.html
6. Everingham, M., Van Gool, L., Williams, C., Winn, J., Zisserman, A.: The PASCAL visual object classes (VOC) challenge. IJCV **88**, 303–338 (2010)
7. Fothergill, S., Mentis, H., Kohli, P., Nowozin, S.: Instructing people for training gestural interactive systems. In: SIGCHI Conference on Human Factors in Computing Systems (2012)
8. Frank, M., Wolfe, P.: An algorithm for quadratic programming. Naval research logistics quarterly (1956)
9. Girshick, R., Donahue, J., Darrell, T., Malik, J.: Rich feature hierarchies for accurate object detection and semantic segmentation. In: CVPR (2014)
10. Jaggi, M.: Revisiting frank-wolfe: projection-free sparse convex optimization. In: ICML (2013)
11. Joachims, T., Finley, T., Yu, C.J.: Cutting-plane training of structural SVMs. Mach. Learn. **77**, 27–59 (2009). Springer
12. Kivinen, J., Warmuth, M.: Relative loss bounds for multidimensional regression problems. JMLR **45**, 301–329 (2001)
13. Krizhevsky, A., Hinton, G.: Learning multiple layers of features from tiny images (2009)
14. Lacoste-Julien, S., Jaggi, M., Schmidt, M., Pletscher, P.: Block-coordinate frank-wolfe for structural SVMs. In: ICML (2012)
15. Maji, S., Bourdev, L., Malik, J.: Action recognition from a distributed representation of pose and appearance. In: CVPR (2011)
16. Malouf, R.: A comparison of algorithms for maximum entropy parameter estimation. In: Conference on Natural Language Learning (2002)
17. Patriksson, M.: Partial linearization methods in nonlinear programming. J. Optim. Theory Appl. **78**, 227–246 (1993). Springer
18. Quinlan, J.: Classification and regression trees. Programs for Machine Learning (2011)
19. Shalev-Shwartz, S., Singer, Y., Srebro, N., Cotter, A.: Pegasos: primal estimated sub-gradient solver for SVM. Math. Program. **127**, 3–30 (2011). Springer

20. Simonyan, K., Zisserman, A.: Very deep convolutional networks for large-scale image recognition. In: ICLR (2015)
21. Taskar, B., Guestrin, C., Koller, D.: Max-margin markov networks. In: NIPS (2004)
22. Wainwright, M.J., Jordan, M.: Graphical models, exponential families, and variational inference. Foundations and Trends® in Machine Learning (2008)
23. Zhang, X., Saha, A., Vishwanathan, S.: Accelerated training of max-margin markov networks with kernels. Theoret. Comput. Sci. **519**, 88–102 (2014). Elsevier

Search-Based Depth Estimation via Coupled Dictionary Learning with Large-Margin Structure Inference

Yan Zhang[1], Rongrong Ji[2], Xiaopeng Fan[1(✉)], Yan Wang[3], Feng Guo[2], Yue Gao[4], and Debin Zhao[1]

[1] School of Computer Science and Technology,
Harbin Institute of Technology, Harbin, China
{y.zhang,fxp,dbzhao}@hit.edu.cn
[2] School of Information Science and Engineering,
Xiamen University, Xiamen, China
{rrji,betop}@xmu.edu.cn
[3] Microsoft, Redmond, USA
wanyan@microsoft.com
[4] School of Software, Tsinghua University, Beijing, China
gaoyue@tsinghua.edu.cn

Abstract. Depth estimation from a single image is an emerging topic in computer vision and beyond. To this end, the existing works typically train a depth regressor from visual appearance. However, the state-of-the-art performance of these schemes is still far from satisfactory, mainly because of the over-fitting and under-fitting problems in regressor training. In this paper, we offer a different data-driven paradigm of estimating depth from a single image, which formulates depth estimation from a search-based perspective. In particular, we handle the depth estimation of local patches via a novel cross-modality retrieval scheme, which searches for the 3D patches with similar structure/appearance to the 2D query from a dataset with 2D-3D mappings. To that effect, a coupled dictionary learning formulation is proposed to link the 2D query with the 3D patches, on the reconstruction coefficients to capture the cross-modality similarity, to obtain a rough depth estimation locally. In addition, consistency on spatial context is further introduced to refine the local depth estimation using a Conditional Random Field. We demonstrate the efficacy of the proposed method by comparing it with the state-of-the-art approaches on popular public datasets such as Make3D and NYUv2, upon which significant performance gains are reported.

Keywords: Single image depth estimation · Cross-modality retrieval · Coupled dictionary learning · Contextual refinement

1 Introduction

Depth estimation from a single monocular image [24] is a fundamental problem in computer vision, with various applications in stereo vision, robotics, and

© Springer International Publishing AG 2016
B. Leibe et al. (Eds.): ECCV 2016, Part V, LNCS 9909, pp. 858–874, 2016.
DOI: 10.1007/978-3-319-46454-1_52

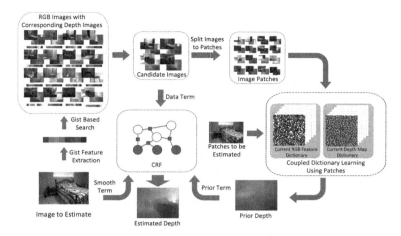

Fig. 1. The framework of our method.

scene understanding [17, 26]. In a typical setting most approaches [1,9,17,25] use a standard regression or classification pipeline to predict the depth fitting, orientation and plane fitting. Such pipeline consists of the calculation of dense or sparse features, followed by an appearance feature representation and regressor training. The responses of a classifier or a regressor are combined in a probabilistic framework, and under very strong geometric priors the most probable scene layout is estimated. Despite promising progress achieved, these methods are still far from practical applications, with the conflict between the model capability and the data scalability, resulting in over-fitting or under-fitting for such learning-based paradigm.

Coming with the proliferation of 3D sensing devices *e.g.* Kinect and matured 3D modeling techniques *e.g.* Structure-from-Motion [5,7] and visual SLAM [21,30], massive-scale 3D data such as point clouds and depth maps are available nowadays, which can provide rich correspondences between 2D visual appearance and 3D depth structures. Therefore, is it possible to take advantage of such rich 2D-3D correspondences towards a search-based paradigm in depth estimation? In this work, we tackle the depth estimation from a different perspective with traditional methods [11–13,16,17,25,26]. In general, we adopt a search-based paradigm that leverages a dictionary-based cross-modality retrieval to robustly and efficiently find best-matches 3D depth given a 2D query patch as the local depth estimator. It is followed by a Taylor formula based contextual refinement to achieve a consistent yet accurate global depth estimation at the image-level.

In particular, unlike the traditional approaches [25,26] that learn a regressor from image to depth indirectly, we first perform joint dictionary learning to bridge the similarity gap between 2D image patches and 3D depth maps to facilitate cross-modal retrieval. Then, given an image patch, we search for the corresponding 3D patches from a large reference set with the depth information between 2D and 3D local patches. This approach provides key advantages in both online efficiency and generalization ability.

The above patch-wised local depth estimation is further integrated with spatial contextual constraints using Conditional Random Field (CRF), as was commonly adopted in existing works [6,11,17,26]. To evaluate the performance of the proposed method, we conduct experiments on the widely-used Make3D and NYUv2 datasets. We compare the proposed method with several existing state-of-the-art ones, including make3D [26], Semantic Labelling [17] and Depth Transfer [11]. We report significant performance gain to demonstrate the advantages of the proposed model. The main contributions of our work are three-fold:

- We propose a novel cross-modality retrieval paradigm that does not rely on training depth regressors to tackle over- and under-fitting issues previously existed;
- A novel coupled dictionary learning is introduced to bridge the similar gap between 2D query and 3D references, with detailed analytical solutions for fast yet accurate parameter learning;
- Adopting contextual refinement with Taylor expansion and CRF inference, which also improves the generalization capability. Compared with traditional methods [11,26], the proposed inference does not require parameter fitting on the training set.

2   Related Work

Previous works [4,26] in depth estimation from a single monocular image typically follow a regression setting. In this setting, the image is first over-segmented into superpixels, and then a pre-trained local depth regressor is applied on each individual superpixel to estimate the corresponding local depth. Subsequently, the Markov Random Field (MRF) or Conditional Random Field (CRF) [4] is frequently employed to impose spatial constraints on the estimated local depth. Such contextual cues usually include 3D location and orientation of the patch [26], as well as the global context [25] among patches. For instance in [17], Liu et al. partitioned depth estimation into two phrases, i.e., semantic segmentation [27] and 3D reconstruction, with the semantic labels guiding the 3D reconstruction. In [20], Liu et al. modeled depth estimation as a discrete-continuous optimization problem, where the continuous variables encode the depth of superpixels in the input image, and the discrete ones represent relationships between neighboring superpixels. Karsch et al. [10,11] inferred the depth map by three stages: candidate images discovery, point-wise alignment and optimization procedure. More recently, deep learning [6] was introduced for single image depth estimation. For instance, Liu et al. [19] combined the Convolutional Neural Network (CNN) and the CRF model for depth estimation, where the CNN learns the geometric priors and the CRF model could further optimize the depth among adjacent superpixels. Similar to [19], the method in [15] also extracted deep CNN features for depth regression, which was combined with the CRF-based post processing. The limitation of the state-of-the-art methods for single image depth estimation is closely tied to the property of perspective geometry, which becomes a bottleneck for the current RGB-D based methods. In contrast, this limitation severely affects methods based on 3D model, since the 3D model can offer all stereo perspectives, which provides a new aspect to conquer this limitation.

Cross-modality retrieval has also attracted vast research focuses in recent years. In [34], Wang *et al.* built a cross-modality probabilistic graphical model to discover mutually consistent semantic information among different modalities. In [23], cross-modal correlations and semantic abstraction were employed to jointly model the text and image components. Zhuang *et al.* [37] proposed a SliM 2 model to formulate the multimodal mapping as a constrained dictionary learning problem, where the label information [3] is employed to discover the shared intra-modality structure. More recently, deep learning methods were further employed in cross-modality retrieval [31,34] for the tasks of text-to-image and image-to-text search. The main disadvantage of the existing cross-modality retrieval methods is that they can not learn the structure information from images and 3D models. However, we can rebuild the structure information of image patches by sharing the reconstruction coefficients with coupled dictionary learning.

Recent works have shown the effectiveness of coupled dictionary learning in exploring inherent correlations between two data channels. Here, we introduce the most relevant works to ours. Wang *et al.* [32] proposed a semi-coupled dictionary learning (SCDL) method to conduct cross-style image synthesis. Yang *et al.* [36] employed neural network to jointly learn dictionaries of different resolutions. To tackle the deblurring problem, Xiang *et al.* [35] trained dictionaries on both clean and blurred images jointly, and Wang *et al.* [33] learned a dictionary on deblurred intermediate results and blurred images jointly. Shekhar *et al.* [28] established the identity of multi-source information by joint sparse representation. And He *et al.* [8] jointly learned overcomplete dictionaries for one single super-resolution image. Note that the above methods suppose that both dictionaries are learned upon data with the same modality, which is very challenging to capture the cross-modality similarity using learned existing coupled dictionary learning methods.

3 Cross-Modality Retrieval for Local Depth Estimation

The first step is to infer local depth from a single image. To this end, we first train dictionaries from different modalities (*i.e.*, 2D image patches and 3D models) synchronously and then conduct cross-modality retrieval for each target patch. Based on the retrieval results, we estimate the depth from the most correlated 3D model directly. Section 3 presents the details of the above process.[1]

3.1 Coupled Dictionary Learning

Our basic assumption is that if an object can be decomposed into a set of 3D objects, its 2D projection should be able to decomposed in the same way, and

---

[1] Contextual refinement will be further introduced in Sect. 4.

vise versa. Therefore, given a set of 2D patches[2] x_{im}^j ($j = 1, \cdots, n$) and the corresponding 3D model x_{depth}^j ($j = 1, \cdots, n$), from a dictionary learning perspective, we aim to obtain a pair of *codes* y_{im}^j for x_{im}^j and y_{depth}^j for x_{depth}^j based on two dictionaries D_{im} and D_{depth}. And these two codes are supposed to be similar after the proper projection. This intuition leads to the following formulation:

$$\min_{D_{\text{im}}, D_{\text{dep}}} \sum_j \left\| x_{\text{im}}^j - D_{\text{im}} \cdot y_{\text{im}}^j \right\|_2^2 + \alpha \left\| x_{\text{dep}}^j - D_{\text{dep}} \cdot y_{\text{dep}}^j \right\|_2^2$$

$$+ \beta \left\| y_{\text{dep}}^j - R \cdot y_{\text{im}}^j \right\|_2^2 \tag{1}$$

$$s.t. \quad R^T \cdot R = I,$$

where y_{dep}^j and y_{im}^j are the reconstruction coefficients. $D_{\text{im}} = [d_{\text{im}}^1, d_{\text{im}}^2, \cdots, d_{\text{im}}^c] \in \Re^{p \times c}$ is the dictionary 2D patches, while $D_{\text{dep}} = \left[d_{\text{dep}}^1, d_{\text{dep}}^2, \cdots, d_{\text{dep}}^c \right] \in \Re^{q \times c}$ is the dictionary of 3D models.. The first term in Eq. 1 is the reconstruction error between the 2D image patches x_{im}^j and their corresponding representation results. The second term is 3D reconstruction error. And the third term is the projection error of coefficient y_{dep}^j and y_{im}^j. Through the projection matrix R, 3D and 2D coefficients are connected to enable cross-modality similarity matching.

However, it is not exactly proper to force projection matrix R to be orthogonal. Although orthogonality can guarantee R to be full rank and make the coefficient spaces equivalent, such strict constraint may leads to a suboptimal result. We therefore relax the constraint and merge the second and third terms in Eq. 2 which is equivalent to Eq. 1, but less restrict.

$$\min_{D_{\text{im}}, D_{\text{dep}}} \| X_{\text{im}} - D_{\text{im}} Y \|_F^2 + \alpha \| X_{\text{dep}} - D_{\text{dep}} Y \|_F^2 . \tag{2}$$

where $Y = [y^1, y^2, \cdots, y^n]$ is the coefficient matrix and $X_{\text{im}} = \{x_{\text{im}}^1, x_{\text{im}}^2, \cdots, x_{\text{im}}^n\}$, $x_{\text{im}}^i \in \Re^{p \times 1}$ is a set of n RGB image patches, whose corresponding depth image patches[3] are $X_{\text{dep}} = \{x_{\text{dep}}^1, x_{\text{dep}}^2, \cdots, x_{\text{dep}}^n\}$, $x_{\text{dep}}^i \in \Re^{q \times 1}$.

To solve Eq. 2, an alternative minimization approach is designed.

1. Fix D to optimize Y

$$\min_Y \| X_{\text{im}} - D_{\text{im}} Y \|_F^2 + \alpha \| X_{\text{dep}} - D_{\text{dep}} Y \|_F^2 , \tag{3}$$

is an unconstrained optimization. And we can give the analytic solution as

$$Y = \left(D_{\text{im}}^T D_{\text{im}} + \alpha D_{\text{dep}}^T D_{\text{dep}} \right)^{-1} \left(D_{\text{im}}^T X_{\text{im}} + \alpha \cdot D_{\text{dep}}^T X_{\text{dep}} \right), \tag{4}$$

2. Fix Y to update D, then Eq. 2 can be reformed as:

$$\min_{D_t} \| X_t - D_t Y \|_F^2 , t \in \{\text{im}, \text{dep}\}, \tag{5}$$

---

[2] We chose training patches by retrieving the most similar images from the database with gist.

[3] Without loss of generality, we take the depth image, the most popular 3D form in single monocular depth estimation, as an example.

Fig. 2. Visualization results of Dictionaries: The left four columns are visualized from Make3D dataset and the right four columns from NYUv2 dataset. The first row consists of test images, the second row and third row consist of RGB feature dictionaries and depth dictionaries,respectively, which are trained by the candidate [22] images.

which can be solved by postmultiplication of Moore-Penrose generalized inverse matrix [2] of $\boldsymbol{Y}^4$ as

$$
\begin{aligned}
\boldsymbol{D}_t &= \boldsymbol{X}_t \text{Inverse}\,(\boldsymbol{Y}) \\
\text{Inverse}\,(\boldsymbol{Y}) &= \boldsymbol{Y}^T \left(\boldsymbol{Y}\boldsymbol{Y}^T + \boldsymbol{I}\epsilon\right)^{-1},
\end{aligned}
\tag{6}
$$

3.2 Cross-Modality Retrieval

So far, we have trained the dictionaries $\boldsymbol{D}_{\text{dep}}$ and $\boldsymbol{D}_{\text{im}}$. Given a set of queries $\boldsymbol{X}_{\text{im}}^{\theta}$ of 2D patches, our goal is to get the corresponding 3D model $\boldsymbol{X}_{\text{dep}}^{\theta}$. The optimal result can be obtained by Eq. 2 as

$$
\min_{\boldsymbol{Y}^{\theta}, \boldsymbol{X}_{\text{dep}}^{\theta}} \left\| \boldsymbol{X}_{\text{im}}^{\theta} - \boldsymbol{D}_{\text{im}} \boldsymbol{Y}^{\theta} \right\|_F^2 + \alpha \left\| \boldsymbol{X}_{\text{dep}}^{\theta} - \boldsymbol{D}_{\text{dep}} \boldsymbol{Y}^{\theta} \right\|_F^2.
\tag{7}
$$

To accelerate the convergence in Eq. 7, we can initialize parameters using

$$
\begin{aligned}
\hat{\boldsymbol{Y}}^{\theta} &= \min_{\boldsymbol{Y}} \left\| \boldsymbol{X}_{\text{im}}^{\theta} - \boldsymbol{D}_{\text{im}} \boldsymbol{Y}^{\theta} \right\|_2^2 + \alpha \left\| \boldsymbol{X}_{\text{dep}}^{\theta} - \boldsymbol{D}_{\text{dep}} \boldsymbol{Y}^{\theta} \right\|_F^2, \\
\hat{\boldsymbol{X}}_{\text{dep}}^{\theta} &= \boldsymbol{D}_{\text{dep}} \hat{\boldsymbol{Y}}^{\theta}.
\end{aligned}
\tag{8}
$$

After obtaining the reconstruction coefficient $\hat{\boldsymbol{Y}}^{\theta}$ and the related 3D model $\hat{\boldsymbol{X}}_{\text{dep}}^{\theta}$ of image patches, we can optimize the entire image by setting initial depth value $\hat{\boldsymbol{X}}_{\text{dep}}^{\theta}$ [5].

---

[4] Generally, Inverse $(\boldsymbol{Y}) = \boldsymbol{G}^H \left(\boldsymbol{G}\boldsymbol{G}^H\right)^{-1} \left(\boldsymbol{M}^H \boldsymbol{M}\right)^{-1} \boldsymbol{M}^H$ takes too much time, and is replaced by Eq. 6. $\boldsymbol{G}$, $\boldsymbol{M}$ are the row and column full rank matrices computed by a full rank decomposition of $\boldsymbol{Y}$,respectively.

[5] Further process will be explained in Sect. 4.

4 Large Margin Structure Inference

We gather the initial depth patches (Sect. 3.2) to form the initial depth of the entire image $\boldsymbol{I}_{\mathrm{dep}}^0$. There are N images $\boldsymbol{I}_{\mathrm{im}}^i$ $(i = 1, \cdots, N)$ from dataset that are similar [22] with the query image $\boldsymbol{I}_{\mathrm{im}}^0$ in RGB space, whose depth images are $\boldsymbol{I}_{\mathrm{dep}}^i$ $(i = 1, \cdots, N)$. And the depth image, we want to infer, is $\widetilde{\boldsymbol{I}}_{\mathrm{dep}}$.

The Algorithm 1. the Proposed Method**

Input
Query Image $\boldsymbol{I}_{\mathrm{im}}^0 \in \Re^{w \times h}$,
Candidate Images $\boldsymbol{I}_{\mathrm{im}}^i \in \Re^{w \times h}$ $(i = 1, \cdots, N)$,
Corresponding Candidate 3D Models $\boldsymbol{I}_{\mathrm{dep}}^i \in \Re^{w \times h}$ $(i = 1, \cdots, N)$.

1. Cross-Modality based Prior Depth Inference

 (a) Extract overlapped image patches $x_{\mathrm{im}}^j \in \Re^{p \times 1}$ $(j = 1, \cdots, n)$ from $\boldsymbol{I}_{\mathrm{im}}^i$, and corresponding depth map patches $x_{\mathrm{dep}}^j \in \Re^{q \times 1}$ $(j = 1, \cdots, n)$ from $\boldsymbol{I}_{\mathrm{dep}}^i$, using Eq. 4 and Eq. 6 to calculate Dictionary $\boldsymbol{D}_{\mathrm{im}} \in \Re^{p \times c}$ and $\boldsymbol{D}_{\mathrm{dep}} \in \Re^{q \times c}$
 (b) Extract non-overlapped image patches $x_{\mathrm{im}}^k \in \Re^{p \times 1}$ $(k = 1, \cdots, m)$ from $\boldsymbol{I}_{\mathrm{im}}^0$, using Eq. 8 to calculate the corresponding initial depth map patches $x_{\mathrm{dep}}^k \in \Re^{p \times 1}$ $(i = 1, \cdots, m)$.

 (c) Obtain the prior depth $\boldsymbol{I}_{\mathrm{dep}}^0$ of the entire image $\boldsymbol{I}_{\mathrm{im}}^0$

2. Large Margin Structure Inference
 To minimize Eq. 16, is equivalent to minimize

$$\ln \Psi_d \left(\widetilde{\boldsymbol{I}}_{\mathrm{dep}}, \boldsymbol{I}_{\mathrm{dep}}^i, \widetilde{\boldsymbol{I}}_{\mathrm{im}}, \boldsymbol{I}_{\mathrm{im}}^i \right) = \ln \Psi_{ds} \left(\widetilde{\boldsymbol{I}}_{\mathrm{dep}} \right) + \ln \Psi_{dp} \left(\boldsymbol{I}_{\mathrm{dep}}^0, \widetilde{\boldsymbol{I}}_{\mathrm{dep}} \right) \\ + \ln \Psi_{dd} \left(\widetilde{\boldsymbol{I}}_{\mathrm{dep}}, \boldsymbol{I}_{\mathrm{dep}}^i, \widetilde{\boldsymbol{I}}_{\mathrm{im}}, \boldsymbol{I}_{\mathrm{im}}^i \right). \tag{9}$$

 Eq. 16 can be transformed into the following format

$$\ln \Psi_d \left(\widetilde{\boldsymbol{I}}_{\mathrm{dep}}, \boldsymbol{I}_{\mathrm{dep}}^i, \widetilde{\boldsymbol{I}}_{\mathrm{im}}, \boldsymbol{I}_{\mathrm{im}}^i \right) = \sum_r \left\| \boldsymbol{A}_r \widetilde{\boldsymbol{I}}_{\mathrm{dep}} - b_r \right\|. \tag{10}$$

 To minimize Eq. 10, we can get the lth iteration solution of $\widetilde{\boldsymbol{I}}_{\mathrm{dep}}$ by gradient descent

$$\widetilde{\boldsymbol{I}}_{\mathrm{dep}}^l = \left(\sum_{r,s} \frac{\boldsymbol{A}_{(r,s)}^T \boldsymbol{A}_{(r,s)}}{\sqrt{\left(\boldsymbol{A}_{(r,s)} \widetilde{\boldsymbol{I}}_{\mathrm{dep}}^{l-1} - b_{(r,s)} \right)^2 + \epsilon}} \right)^{-1} \left(\sum_{r,s} \frac{\boldsymbol{A}_{(r,s)}^T b_{(r,s)}}{\sqrt{\left(\boldsymbol{A}_{(r,s)} \widetilde{\boldsymbol{I}}_{\mathrm{dep}}^{l-1} - b_{(r,s)} \right)^2 + \epsilon}} \right) \tag{11}$$

 where $\boldsymbol{A}_{(r,s)}$ is the sth row of $\boldsymbol{A}_r$, $b_{(r,s)}$ is the sth element of vector b_r and ϵ is 10^{-6}

Output
 The optimized depth map $\widetilde{\boldsymbol{I}}_{\mathrm{dep}}^*$ of image $\boldsymbol{I}_{\mathrm{im}}^0$

---

*The overall time complexity is $O(mn + p^3 + p^2q + N)$, in which m is the average number of patches in a training image, n is the number of images used for dictionary learning, p is the size of the codebook, and N is the size of the database to search, assuming the patch size is $q \times q$.

The Taylor expansion of $\widetilde{I}_{\text{dep}}$ and I_{dep}^i at point (a, b) are

$$
\begin{aligned}
\widetilde{I}_{\text{dep}}(x, y) = {} & \widetilde{I}_{\text{dep}}(a, b) + \nabla_x \widetilde{I}_{\text{dep}}(a, b) \cdot (x - a) + \nabla_y \widetilde{I}_{\text{dep}}(a, b) \cdot (y - b) \\
& + \frac{1}{2} \nabla_x^2 \widetilde{I}_{\text{dep}}(a, b) \cdot (x - a)^2 + \frac{1}{2} \nabla_y^2 \widetilde{I}_{\text{dep}}(a, b) \cdot (y - b)^2 \\
& + \frac{1}{2} \nabla_{x,y} \widetilde{I}_{\text{dep}}(a, b) \cdot (x - a)(y - b) \\
& + \frac{1}{2} \nabla_{y,x} \widetilde{I}_{\text{dep}}(a, b) \cdot (x - a)(y - b) + R_n(x, y)
\end{aligned}
\tag{12}
$$

and

$$
\begin{aligned}
I_{\text{dep}}^i(x, y) = {} & I_{\text{dep}}^i(a, b) + \nabla_x I_{\text{dep}}^i(a, b) \cdot (x - a) + \nabla_y I_{\text{dep}}^i(a, b) \cdot (y - b) \\
& + \frac{1}{2} \nabla_x^2 I_{\text{dep}}^i(a, b) \cdot (x - a)^2 + \frac{1}{2} \nabla_y^2 I_{\text{dep}}^i(a, b) \cdot (y - b)^2 \\
& + \frac{1}{2} \nabla_{x,y} I_{\text{dep}}^i(a, b) \cdot (x - a)(y - b) \\
& + \frac{1}{2} \nabla_{y,x} I_{\text{dep}}^i(a, b) \cdot (x - a)(y - b) + L_n(x, y),
\end{aligned}
\tag{13}
$$

where $R_n(x, y)$ and $L_n(x, y)$ are the higher order infinitesimals. To make $\widetilde{I}_D$ and I_D^i similar, Eqs. 12 and 13 should also be similar. Then we can get the expression of G_{sim} and G_{sel} as

$$
\begin{aligned}
G_{sim} = {} & \sum_{i=1}^{N} \left\| W_i \cdot \left(\widetilde{I}_D - I_D^i \right) \right\| + \alpha \left\| W_i \cdot \left(\nabla_x \widetilde{I}_D - \nabla_x I_D^i \right) \right\| \\
& + \alpha \left\| W_i \cdot \left(\nabla_y \widetilde{I}_D - \nabla_y I_D^i \right) \right\| + \beta \left\| W_i \left(\nabla_x^2 \widetilde{I} - \nabla_x^2 I_D^i \right) \right\| \\
& + \beta \left\| W_i \left(\nabla_y^2 \widetilde{I} - \nabla_y^2 I_D^i \right) \right\| + \beta \left\| W_i \left(\nabla_{x,y} \widetilde{I} - \nabla_{x,y} I_D^i \right) \right\| \\
& + \beta \left\| W_i \left(\nabla_{y,x} \widetilde{I} - \nabla_{y,x} I_D^i \right) \right\|,
\end{aligned}
\tag{14}
$$

and

$$
\begin{aligned}
G_{sel} = {} & \gamma \left\| \widetilde{I}_D - I_D^0 \right\| + \alpha \left(\left\| W_0 \cdot \nabla_x \widetilde{I}_D \right\| + \left\| W_0 \cdot \nabla_y \widetilde{I}_D \right\| \right) \\
& + \beta \left(\left\| W_0 \cdot \nabla_x^2 \widetilde{I} \right\| + \left\| W_0 \cdot \nabla_y^2 \widetilde{I} \right\| + \left\| W_0 \cdot \nabla_{x,y} \widetilde{I} \right\| + \left\| W_0 \cdot \nabla_{y,x} \widetilde{I} \right\| \right).
\end{aligned}
\tag{15}
$$

where G_{sim} is used to calculate similarity between input RGB image and candidate images and G_{sel} is the self control item which guarantees that adjacent points in an image have similar depth value.

Similar to the regular CRF, G_{sim} and G_{sel} can be reformed as traditional MRF *i.e.* the smoothing term $\Psi_{ds}\left(\widetilde{I}_{\text{dep}}\right)$, the data term $\Psi_{dd}\left(\widetilde{I}_{\text{dep}}, I_{\text{dep}}^i, \widetilde{I}_{\text{im}}, I_{\text{im}}^i\right)$ and the prior depth term $\Psi_{dp}\left(I_{\text{dep}}^0, \widetilde{I}_{\text{dep}}\right)$, defined as

$$
\Psi_d\left(\widetilde{I}_{\text{dep}}, I_{\text{dep}}^i, \widetilde{I}_{\text{im}}, I_{\text{im}}^i\right) = \Psi_{ds}\left(\widetilde{I}_{\text{dep}}\right) \Psi_{dd}\left(\widetilde{I}_{\text{dep}}, I_{\text{dep}}^i, \widetilde{I}_{\text{im}}, I_{\text{im}}^i\right) \Psi_{dp}\left(I_{\text{dep}}^0, \widetilde{I}_{\text{dep}}\right).
\tag{16}
$$

Data Term. Depending on our basic assumption that similar image should have similar depth map, we use similar [22] candidate images to infer our depth map $\widetilde{I}_{\text{dep}}$. We claim that this "similarity" should not only happen in the original RGB images, but also in the gradient of RGB images. When comparing with pixels in I_{im}^{0} and I_{im}^{i}, the more similar they are, the less weight they have. Then we give our formulation of $\Psi_{dd}\left(\widetilde{I}_{\text{dep}}, I_{\text{dep}}^{i}, \widetilde{I}_{\text{im}}, I_{\text{im}}^{i}\right)$ as

$$
\begin{aligned}
\Psi_{dd}\left(\widetilde{I}_{\text{dep}}, I_{\text{dep}}^{i}, \widetilde{I}_{\text{im}}, I_{\text{im}}^{i}\right) = \prod_{i=1}^{N} exp(&\left\|W_i\left(\widetilde{I}_{\text{dep}} - I_{\text{dep}}^{i}\right)\right\| + \alpha\left\|W_i\left(\nabla_x\widetilde{I}_{\text{dep}} - \nabla_x I_{\text{dep}}^{i}\right)\right\| \\
&+ \alpha\left\|W_i\left(\nabla_y\widetilde{I}_{\text{dep}} - \nabla_y I_{\text{dep}}^{i}\right)\right\| + \beta\left\|W_i\left(\nabla_x^2\widetilde{I}_{\text{dep}} - \nabla_x^2 I_{\text{dep}}^{i}\right)\right\| \\
&+ \beta\left\|W_i\left(\nabla_y^2\widetilde{I}_{\text{dep}} - \nabla_y^2 I_{\text{dep}}^{i}\right)\right\| + \beta\left\|W_i\left(\nabla_{x,y}\widetilde{I}_{\text{dep}} - \nabla_{x,y} I_{\text{dep}}^{i}\right)\right\| \\
&+ \beta\left\|W_i\left(\nabla_{y,x}\widetilde{I}_{\text{dep}} - \nabla_{y,x} I_{\text{dep}}^{i}\right)\right\|)
\end{aligned}
\tag{17}
$$

where $W_i{}^6$ is the point-wise similarity diagonal matrix.[7]

Smoothing Term. We encourage neighborhood pixels have smooth depth estimations. This is achieved in $\Psi_{ds}\left(\widetilde{I}_{\text{dep}}\right)$ by setting self-adapting coefficient of adjacent pixels smoothing. When the features of adjacent pixels are similar, then the smoothing coefficient of that pixel pair would achieve a low smoothing weight to make the pixel pair very smooth; meanwhile, when the adjacent pixel features are dramatically different, then the smoothing coefficient will be very high, which makes the smoothing term lose their efficacies. We come up with the following design to characterize the above intuitions.

$$
\begin{aligned}
\Psi_{ds}\left(\widetilde{I}_{\text{dep}}\right) = exp(&\alpha\left\|W_0\nabla_x\widetilde{I}_{\text{dep}}\right\| + \alpha\left\|W_0\nabla_y\widetilde{I}_{\text{dep}}\right\| + \beta\left\|W_0\nabla_x^2\widetilde{I}_{\text{dep}}\right\| \\
&+ \beta\left\|W_0\nabla_y^2\widetilde{I}_{\text{dep}}\right\| + \beta\left\|W_0\nabla_{x,y}\widetilde{I}_{\text{dep}}\right\| + \beta\left\|W_0\nabla_{y,x}\widetilde{I}_{\text{dep}}\right\|)
\end{aligned}
\tag{18}
$$

where the first two terms in Eq. 18 are of first-order gradient smooth, which cover the nearest four pixels neighbours; while the other terms in Eq. 18 are second-order gradient smooth, which cover more further area. $\nabla_x, \nabla_y, \nabla_x^2, \nabla_y^2, \nabla_{x,y}, \nabla_{y,x}$, are the gradient operator matrix, $\widetilde{I}_{\text{dep}}$ is a column vector and W_0 is the self-adapting smooth control (diagonal) matrix.

Prior Term. We also claim that the estimated prior should join in the depth consistency potential as

$$
\Psi_{dp}\left(\widetilde{I}_{\text{dep}}, I_{\text{dep}}^{0}\right) = exp\left(\gamma\left\|\widetilde{I}_{\text{dep}} - I_{\text{dep}}^{0}\right\|\right)
\tag{19}
$$

Comparing with traditional methods [11,26], there is no pre-trained parameters in our model, which provides a highly generalization ability. Meanwhile, the

---

[6] $W_i\left(j,j\right) = $ sigmoid $\left(\frac{\left\|F_{\text{im}}^{0}(j)-F_{\text{im}}^{i}(j)\right\|-\mu_i}{\sigma_i}\right)$, F_{im}^{*} is the SIFT [18] feature of image I_{im}^{*}.
    And the elements of W_0 in Eq. 18 are calculated with the same image but adjacent point.

[7] $\|\cdot\|$ is the one-norm.

larger neighbourhood have been considered,[8] without increasing time complexity. We show the proposed algorithm and the entire framework in Algorithm 1 and Fig. 1, respectively.

5   Experiments

In this section, we report our experimental results on single image depth estimation for both outdoor and indoor scenes. We use the Make3D [26] range image data set and the NYUv2 [29] Kinect data set, as they are the largest open data available at present.

5.1   Evaluation Protocols

For quantitative evaluation, we report errors obtained with the following error metrics, which have been extensively used in [11,14,17,26].

- Mean relative error (rel): $\frac{1}{L}\sum_i \frac{|\hat{d}_i - d_i|}{d_i}$;
- Mean $log10$ error $(lg10)$: $\frac{1}{L}\sum_i |log_{10}\hat{d}_i - log_{10}d_i|$;
- Root mean squared error (rms): $\sqrt{\frac{1}{L}\sum_i \left\|\hat{d}_i - d_i\right\|_2^2}$

where d_i is the ground truth depth, $\hat{d}_i$ is the estimated depth, and L denotes the total number of pixels in all the evaluated images.

In the training stage, we select 10 similar [22] images from dataset with the query image, and use the patches(7×7 pixels, 3 pixels overlap) extracted from these similar images to train RGB feature [26] dictionary and depth dictionary simultaneously, whose dimensionality is 1024. And the balance parameter in Eq. 2 is 1. In the testing stage, we extract non-overlapping patches of query image to infer the prior depth image. And to optimize this prior depth image with Eq. 11, we fix the parameter of Eqs. 17, 18 and 19 as γ for 0.5, α for 10 and β for 0.1.

5.2   Performance on Make3D Dataset

The Make3D dataset consists of 534 images with corresponding depth maps. There are 400 training images and 134 testing images. All images are resized to 460×345 pixels. It is worth noting that this data set is published a decade ago, the resolution and distance range of the depth image is rather limited (only 55×305 pixels). Furthermore, it contains noise in the locations of glass window etc. These limitations have some influence on the training stage and the resulting error metrics. Therefore we report errors based on two different criteria in Table 1: (C1) Errors are computed in the regions with ground-truth depth less than 70;

---

[8] First-order derivation covers the nearest 4 points, and second-order derivation effect as a two-level first-order derivation.

Table 1. Result comparisons on the Make3D dataset.(C1) Errors are computed in the regions with ground-truth depth less than 70; (C2) Errors are computed in the entire image

Method	Error(C1) (lower is better)			Error(C2) (lower is better)		
	rel	lg10	rms	rel	lg10	rms
Make3D [26]	-	-	-	0.370	0.187	-
Semantic Labelling [17]	-	-	-	0.379	0.148	-
Depth MRF*[25]	-	-	-	0.530	0.198	16.7
Feedback Cascades*[16]	-	-	-	-	-	15.2
DepthTransfer [11]	0.355	**0.127**	**9.20**	0.361	0.148	15.10
Ours	**0.345**	**0.127**	9.41	**0.337**	**0.137**	**13.70**

*Results reported in DepthTransfer [11].

(C2) Errors are computed in the entire image. We compare our method with the state-of-the-art methods such as Make3D [26], Depth Transfer [11] and Semantic Labelling [17].

In Table 1, we present a quantitative comparison of the depth estimation between our method and these methods on representative images from Make3D data set. Table 1 demonstrates that, in most cases, our method outperforms those competing methods in terms of two evaluation criteria. Also, to make the result visible, we show the depth prediction results achieved by our method in Fig. 3. From Fig. 3, we can observe that the prediction results achieved by our method are very close to the ground truth images, and are much better than those obtained by the Make3D approach. To prove the validity of our methods, we also compare our method with state-of-the-art in the "Prior Depth Inference" and "Depth optimization", respectively (Table 2 and Table 3). At last, we show the influence of parameters in Table 4.

From Table 1, we can see that our method outperforms in most of the metrics. Furthermore, comparing "Error (C2)" criteria with "Error (C1)", our model achieves more gains in far distance objects than the near ones. And comparing with other methods, without pre-trained parameter [25,26] and supplementary information [17], our model can still work well.

We also test our model with state-of-the-art in each stage. In Table 2 we assess the effectiveness of the "Prior Depth Inference" stage, and test our model in learned-dictionary and random dictionary. From the result we can see that, even with a random dictionary our model still outperforms state-of-the-art methods. Compared with Table 4, random dictionary performance is similar to learned-dictionary of 5 pixels patch size. In Table 3, we assess the effectiveness of the "Entire image depth inference" stage with the same prior depth value of [11]. From this table we can see that, our model have lower rms but higher rel which means our method effective but slightly unstable.

In Table 4, we can see that the patch size parameter poses greater influence than the other two. Generally speaking, mapping RGB to depth is an ill-posed

Table 2. Result comparisons on the Make3D dataset without MRF to fine-tune.

Method	Error(C1) (lower is better)			Error(C2) (lower is better)		
	rel	lg10	rms	rel	lg10	rms
Make3D [26]	-	-	14.79	-	-	29.27
DepthTransfer [11]	0.936	0.217	12.01	0.903	0.247	20.49
Ours(with random dictionary)	0.936	0.216	**11.96**	0.862	0.218	16.45
Ours	**0.866**	**0.216**	11.99	**0.801**	**0.217**	**16.41**

Table 3. Result comparisons on the Make3D dataset, with the same prior depth estimation, different MRF to fine-tune.

Method	Error(C1) (lower is better)			Error(C2) (lower is better)		
	rel	lg10	rms	rel	lg10	rms
DepthTransfer [11]	**0.355**	**0.127**	9.20	**0.361**	0.148	15.10
Ours	0.375	**0.127**	**9.18**	0.364	**0.141**	**14.11**

Fig. 3. Examples of depth predictions on the Make3D dataset.

problem that there may be many depth patches for a certain RGB patch. And the larger the patch is, the more details can be learnt. However, due to the lack of adequate images, the range of patch size is also limited. Based on this reason, the dictionary size effects a little, which can also be seen in Fig. 2 that there are lots of reduplicative feature in the trained dictionary.

From Fig. 3 we can see that our method reproduce the depth map well, especially at shape controlling.

5.3 Performance on NYUv2 Dataset

The NYUv2 dataset contains of 1449 images, where 795 images are used as a training set and 654 images are used as a testing set[9]. All images are resized

---

[9] We only compare the result of standard data partition, when the code is not available.

Table 4. Result comparisons on the Make3D dataset with different parameters. Patch-Size is the size of extracted patches for "Coupled Dictionary Learning" and Dictionary-Size is the capacity of Dictionary D_{im} and D_{dep} in Eq. 2.

Parameter	Error(C1) (lower is better)			Error(C2) (lower is better)		
	rel	lg10	rms	rel	lg10	rms
PatchSize = 3	1.470	0.216	12.02	1.332	0.217	16.41
PatchSize = 5	0.936	0.216	11.99	0.862	0.217	16.41
PatchSize = 7	**0.866**	**0.216**	**11.99**	**0.801**	**0.217**	**16.41**
DictionarySize = 256	0.867	0.216	12.03	0.803	0.217	16.41
DictionarySize = 512	0.867	0.216	12.03	0.803	0.217	16.41
DictionarySize = 1024	**0.866**	**0.216**	**11.99**	**0.801**	**0.217**	**16.41**
*$\alpha = 0.1$	0.866	0.216	11.99	0.801	0.217	16.41
$\alpha = 1$	**0.866**	**0.216**	**11.99**	**0.801**	**0.217**	**16.41**
$\alpha = 10$	0.866	0.216	11.99	0.801	0.217	16.41

*α is the balance parameter in Eq. 2

Fig. 4. Examples of depth predictions on the NYUv2 dataset.

to 460×345 pixels in order to preserve the aspect ratio of the original images. In Table 5, we compare our method with state-of-the-art methods, including Make3D [26], Depth Transfer [11] and so on.

As illustrated in Table 5, we present a qualitative comparison of the depth estimation with these methods on representative images from NYUv2 data set, which demonstrates the superior performance of our method. Also, to make the result visible, we show our method in Fig. 4. The set of parameter in our method is the same as in Sect. 5.2. Due to the similar experiment result (Sect. 5.2) and the limitation of pages.

5.4   Comparison with Deep Learning Methods

It is well known that deep learning methods have obtained remarkable achievement in many research areas, due to their greater learning ability than most of traditional methods. The proposed method has no advantage in model capability or complexity, compared to deep learning.

Table 5. Result comparisons on the NYUv2 dataset.

Method	Error (lower is better)		
	rel	lg10	rms
Make3D [26]	0.349	-	1.214
Depth Fusion*[12]	0.368	0.135	1.3
Depth Fusion(no warp)*[13]	0.371	0.137	1.3
DepthTransfer [11]	0.350	0.131	1.2
Ours	**0.342**	**0.130**	**1.18**

*Results reported in DepthTransfer [11].

However deep learning has a critical drawback that the training process usually takes a long time (weeks and even months), despite considerable efforts have been taken to alleviate this problem. Most deep neural networks also heavily rely on parameter tuning, with significant sensitivity on certain parameters such as learning rate. This prevents deep learning approaches from being applied in scenarios that require frequent and agile updating.

On the contrary, the proposed approach requires no traditional training stage and few parameters. This greatly reduces the effort of adapting to a new dataset, making the approach more flexible and reliable. Since these two methods are designed for different scenarios, we do not conduct the experimental comparison.

6   Conclusion

In this paper, we propose a novel cross-modality retrieval method to estimate the object depth value from a given 2D image. To our best knowledge, this is the first method to estimate depth value by cross-modality retrieval. And to solve the cross-modality problem, we propose a novel and effective coupled dictionary learning method. Based on the local depth estimation from the cross-modal retrieval using the dictionary, we further refine the depth of the entire image by solving a convex optimization problem. From the depth estimation result (Figs. 3 and 4), we can see that details are not well reserved in our method. Because our method highly depends on the candidate images. When the images do not describe the same scene as query image does, or the "bad" image win a high similar score on pixel level, our method can not work well. In the future, we plan to combine our model with the deep learning or other methods to improve the robustness in handling real-world image transformation. Furthermore, we plan to augment the performance by integrating the semantic information from the recent development in CNN framework.

Acknowledgement. This work was supported in part by the Major State Basic Research Development Program of China (973 Program) under Grant 2015CB351804, the National Key R&D Program (No. 2016YFB1001503), the National Science Foundation of China (No. 61422210, No.61472101, No. 61373076, No. 61402388), the CCF-

Tencent Open Research Fund, and the Open Projects Program of National Laboratory of Pattern Recognition.

References

1. Barinova, O., Konushin, V., Yakubenko, A., Lee, K.C., Lim, H., Konushin, A.: Fast automatic single-view 3-d reconstruction of urban scenes. In: Forsyth, D., Torr, P., Zisserman, A. (eds.) ECCV 2008. LNCS, vol. 5303, pp. 100–113. Springer, Heidelberg (2008). doi:10.1007/978-3-540-88688-4_8

2. Bellman, R., Bellman, R.E., Bellman, R.E., Bellman, R.E.: Introduction to Matrix Analysis, vol. 960. SIAM (1970)

3. Byeon, W., Breuel, T.M., Raue, F., Liwicki, M.: Scene labeling with lstm recurrent neural networks. In: Computer Vision and Pattern Recognition (CVPR), pp. 3547–3555. IEEE (2015)

4. Chellappa, R., Jain, A. (eds.): Markov Random Fields. Theory and Application. Academic Press, Boston (1993)

5. Dellaert, F., Seitz, S.M., Thorpe, C.E., Thrun, S.: Structure from motion without correspondence. In: Computer Vision and Pattern Recognition (CVPR), vol. 2, pp. 557–564. IEEE (2000)

6. Eigen, D., Puhrsch, C., Fergus, R.: Depth map prediction from a single image using a multi-scale deep network. In: Advances in Neural Information Processing Systems (NIPS), pp. 2366–2374 (2014)

7. Engel, J., Schöps, T., Cremers, D.: LSD-SLAM: large-scale direct monocular SLAM. In: Fleet, D., Pajdla, T., Schiele, B., Tuytelaars, T. (eds.) ECCV 2014. LNCS, vol. 8690, pp. 834–849. Springer, Heidelberg (2014). doi:10.1007/978-3-319-10605-2_54

8. He, L., Qi, H., Zaretzki, R.: Beta process joint dictionary learning for coupled feature spaces with application to single image super-resolution. In: Computer Vision and Pattern Recognition (CVPR), pp. 345–352. IEEE (2013)

9. Hoiem, D., Efros, A.A., Hebert, M.: Geometric context from a single image. In: International Conference on Computer Vision (ICCV), vol. 1, pp. 654–661. IEEE (2005)

10. Karsch, K., Liu, C., Kang, S.B.: Depth extraction from video using non-parametric sampling. In: Fitzgibbon, A., Lazebnik, S., Perona, P., Sato, Y., Schmid, C. (eds.) ECCV 2012. LNCS, vol. 7576, pp. 775–788. Springer, Heidelberg (2012). doi:10.1007/978-3-642-33715-4_56

11. Karsch, K., Liu, C., Kang, S.B.: Depth transfer: Depth extraction from video using non-parametric sampling. IEEE Trans. Pattern Anal. Mach. Intell. (TPAMI) 36(11), 2144–2158 (2014)

12. Konrad, J., Brown, G., Wang, M., Ishwar, P., Wu, C., Mukherjee, D.: Automatic 2d-to-3d image conversion using 3d examples from the internet. In: IS&T/SPIE Electronic Imaging, p. 82880F. International Society for Optics and Photonics (2012)

13. Konrad, J., Wang, M., Ishwar, P.: 2d-to-3d image conversion by learning depth from examples. In: Computer Vision and Pattern Recognition Workshops (CVPRW), pp. 16–22. IEEE (2012)

14. Ladicky, L., Shi, J., Pollefeys, M.: Pulling things out of perspective. In: Computer Vision and Pattern Recognition (CVPR), pp. 89–96. IEEE (2014)

15. Li, B., Shen, C., Dai, Y., van den Hengel, A., He, M.: Depth and surface normal estimation from monocular images using regression on deep features and hierarchical CRFs. In: Computer Vision and Pattern Recognition (CVPR), pp. 1119–1127 (2015)
16. Li, C., Kowdle, A., Saxena, A., Chen, T.: Towards holistic scene understanding: feedback enabled cascaded classification models. In: Advances in Neural Information Processing Systems (NIPS), pp. 1351–1359 (2010)
17. Liu, B., Gould, S., Koller, D.: Single image depth estimation from predicted semantic labels. In: Computer Vision and Pattern Recognition (CVPR), pp. 1253–1260. IEEE (2010)
18. Liu, C., Yuen, J., Torralba, A.: Sift flow: dense correspondence across scenes and its applications. IEEE Trans. Pattern Anal. Mach. Intell. (TPAMI) 33(5), 978–994 (2011)
19. Liu, F., Shen, C., Lin, G.: Deep convolutional neural fields for depth estimation from a single image. In: Computer Vision and Pattern Recognition (CVPR), pp. 5162–5170. IEEE (2015)
20. Liu, M., Salzmann, M., He, X.: Discrete-continuous depth estimation from a single image. In: Computer Vision and Pattern Recognition (CVPR), pp. 716–723. IEEE (2014)
21. Mullane, J., Vo, B.N., Adams, M.D., Vo, B.T.: A random-finite-set approach to Bayesian slam. IEEE Trans. Robot. 27(2), 268–282 (2011)
22. Oliva, A., Torralba, A.: Modeling the shape of the scene: a holistic representation of the spatial envelope. Intl. J. Comput. Vis. (IJCV) 42(3), 145–175 (2001)
23. Rasiwasia, N., Costa Pereira, J., Coviello, E., Doyle, G., Lanckriet, G.R., Levy, R., Vasconcelos, N.: A new approach to cross-modal multimedia retrieval. In: International Conference on Multimedia (MM), pp. 251–260. ACM (2010)
24. Rock, J., Gupta, T., Thorsen, J., Gwak, J., Shin, D., Hoiem, D.: Completing 3d object shape from one depth image. In: Computer Vision and Pattern Recognition (CVPR), pp. 2484–2493. IEEE (2015)
25. Saxena, A., Chung, S.H., Ng, A.Y.: Learning depth from single monocular images. In: Advances in Neural Information Processing Systems (NIPS), pp. 1161–1168 (2005)
26. Saxena, A., Sun, M., Ng, A.Y.: Make3d: learning 3d scene structure from a single still image. IEEE Trans. Pattern Anal. Mach. Intell. (TPAMI) 31(5), 824–840 (2009)
27. Sharma, A., Tuzel, O., Jacobs, D.W.: Deep hierarchical parsing for semantic segmentation (2015)
28. Shekhar, S., Patel, V.M., Nasrabadi, N.M., Chellappa, R.: Joint sparse representation for robust multimodal biometrics recognition. Pattern Anal. Mach. Intell. (TPAMI) 36(1), 113–126 (2014)
29. Silberman, N., Hoiem, D., Kohli, P., Fergus, R.: Indoor segmentation and support inference from RGBD images. In: Fitzgibbon, A., Lazebnik, S., Perona, P., Sato, Y., Schmid, C. (eds.) ECCV 2012. LNCS, vol. 7576, pp. 746–760. Springer, Heidelberg (2012). doi:10.1007/978-3-642-33715-4_54
30. Silveira, G., Malis, E., Rives, P.: An efficient direct approach to visual slam. IEEE Trans. Robot. 24(5), 969–979 (2008)
31. Srivastava, N., Salakhutdinov, R.R.: Multimodal learning with deep boltzmann machines. In: Advances in Neural Information Processing Systems (NIPS), pp. 2222–2230 (2012)

32. Wang, S., Zhang, L., Liang, Y., Pan, Q.: Semi-coupled dictionary learning with applications to image super-resolution and photo-sketch synthesis. In: Computer Vision and Pattern Recognition (CVPR), pp. 2216–2223. IEEE (2012)
33. Wang, Y., Cho, S., Wang, J., Chang, S.-F.: Discriminative indexing for probabilistic image patch priors. In: Fleet, D., Pajdla, T., Schiele, B., Tuytelaars, T. (eds.) ECCV 2014. LNCS, vol. 8692, pp. 200–214. Springer, Heidelberg (2014). doi:10.1007/978-3-319-10593-2_14
34. Wang, Y., Wu, F., Song, J., Li, X., Zhuang, Y.: Multi-modal mutual topic reinforce modeling for cross-media retrieval. In: International Conference on Multimedia (MM), pp. 307–316. ACM (2014)
35. Xiang, S., Meng, G., Wang, Y., Pan, C., Zhang, C.: Image deblurring with coupled dictionary learning. Int. J. Comput. Vis. (IJCV) 1–24 (2014)
36. Yang, J., Wang, Z., Lin, Z., Cohen, S., Huang, T.: Coupled dictionary training for image super-resolution. IEEE Trans. Image Process. (TIP) **21**(8), 3467–3478 (2012)
37. Zhuang, Y.T., Wang, Y.F., Wu, F., Zhang, Y., Lu, W.M.: Supervised coupled dictionary learning with group structures for multi-modal retrieval. In: Twenty-Seventh AAAI Conference on Artificial Intelligence (AAAI) (2013)

Scalable Metric Learning via Weighted Approximate Rank Component Analysis

Cijo Jose$^{(\boxtimes)}$ and François Fleuret

Idiap Research Institute, École Polytechnique Fédérale de Lausanne,
Martigny, Switzerland
{cijo.jose,francois.fleuret}@idiap.ch

Abstract. We are interested in the large-scale learning of Mahalanobis distances, with a particular focus on person re-identification. We propose a metric learning formulation called Weighted Approximate Rank Component Analysis (WARCA). WARCA optimizes the precision at top ranks by combining the WARP loss with a regularizer that favors orthonormal linear mappings and avoids rank-deficient embeddings. Using this new regularizer allows us to adapt the large-scale WSABIE procedure and to leverage the Adam stochastic optimization algorithm, which results in an algorithm that scales gracefully to very large data-sets. Also, we derive a kernelized version which allows to take advantage of state-of-the-art features for re-identification when data-set size permits kernel computation. Benchmarks on recent and standard re-identification datasets show that our method beats existing state-of-the-art techniques both in terms of accuracy and speed. We also provide experimental analysis to shade lights on the properties of the regularizer we use, and how it improves performance.

Keywords: Metric learning · Orthonormal regularizer · Person re-identification

1 Introduction

Metric learning methods aim at learning a parametrized distance function from a labeled set of samples, so that under the learned distance, samples with the same labels are nearby and samples with different labels are far apart [1]. Many fundamental questions in computer vision such as "How to compare two images? and for what information?" boil down to this problem. Among them, person re-identification is the problem of recognizing individuals at different physical locations and times, on images captured by different devices.

It is a challenging problem which recently received a lot of attention because of its importance in various application domains such as video surveillance, biometrics, and behavior analysis [2].

The performance of person re-identification systems relies mainly on the image feature representation and the distance measure used to compare them.

© Springer International Publishing AG 2016
B. Leibe et al. (Eds.): ECCV 2016, Part V, LNCS 9909, pp. 875–890, 2016.
DOI: 10.1007/978-3-319-46454-1_53

Hence the research in the field has focused either on designing features [3,4] or on learning a distance function from a labeled set of images [4–9].

It is difficult to analytically design features that are invariant to the various non-linear transformations that an image undergoes such as illumination, viewpoint, pose changes, and occlusion. Furthermore, even if such features were provided, the standard Euclidean metric would not be adequate as it does not take into account dependencies on the feature representation. This motivates the use of metric learning for person re-identification.

Re-identification models are commonly evaluated by the cumulative match characteristic (CMC) curve [6]. This measure indicates how the matching performance of the algorithm improves as the number of returned image increases. Given a matching algorithm and a labeled test set, each image is compared against all the others, and the position of the first correct match is recorded. The CMC curve indicates for each rank the fraction of test samples which had that rank or better. A perfect CMC curve would reach the value 1 for rank #1, that is the best match is always of the correct identity.

In this paper we are interested in learning a Mahalanobis distance by minimizing a weighted rank loss such that the precision at the top rank positions of the CMC curve is maximized. When learning the metric, we directly learn the low-rank projection matrix instead of the PSD matrix because of the computational efficiency and the scalability to high dimensional datasets (see Sect. 3.1). But naively learning the low-rank projection matrix suffers from the problem of matrix rank degeneration and non-isolated minima [10]. We address this problem by using a simple regularizer which approximately enforces the orthonormality of the learned matrix very efficiently (see Sect. 3.2). We extend the WARP loss [10–12] and combine it with our approximate orthonormal regularizer to derive a metric learning algorithm which approximately minimizes a weighted rank loss efficiently using stochastic gradient descent (see Sect. 3.3).

We extend our model to kernel space to handle distance measures which are more natural for the features we are dealing with (see Sect. 3.4). We also show that in kernel space SGD can be carried out more efficiently by using preconditioning [5,13].

We validate our approach on nine person re-identification datasets: Market-1501 [14], CUHK03 [15], OpeReid [16], CUHK01 [17], VIPeR [18], CAVIAR [3], 3DPeS [19], iLIDS [20] and PRI450s [21], where we outperform other metric learning methods proposed in the literature, both in speed and accuracy.

2   Related Works

Metric learning is a well studied research problem [22]. Most of the existing approaches have been developed in the context of the Mahalanobis distance learning paradigm [1,5,6,23,24]. This consists in learning distances of the form:

$$\mathcal{D}_M^2(x_i, x_j) = (x_i - x_j)^T M (x_i - x_j), \tag{1}$$

where M is a positive semi-definite matrix. Based on the way the problem is formulated the algorithms for learning such distances involve either optimization in the space of positive semi-definite (PSD) matrices, or learning the projection matrix W, in which case $M = W^T W$.

Large margin nearest neighbors [1] (LMNN) is a metric learning algorithm designed to maximize the performance of k-nearest neighbor classification in a large margin framework. Information theoretic metric learning [24] (ITML) exploits the relationship between the Mahalanobis distance and Gaussian distributions to learn the metric. Many researchers have applied LMNN and ITML to re-identification problem with varying degree of success [21].

Pairwise Constrained Component Analysis (PCCA) [5] is a metric learning method that learns the low rank projection matrix W in the kernel space from sparse pairwise constraints. Xiong et al. [8] extended PCCA with a L_2 regularization term and showed that it further improves the performance.

Köstinger et al. [6] proposed the KISS ("Keep It Simple and Straight forward") metric learning abbreviated as KISSME. Their method enjoys very fast training and they show good empirical performance and scaling properties along the number samples. However this method suffers from of the Gaussian assumptions on the model.

Li et al. [7] consider learning a local thresholding rule for metric learning. This method is computationally expensive to train, even with as few as 100 dimensions.

The performance of many kernel-based metric learning methods for person re-identification was evaluated in [8]. In particular the authors evaluated PCCA [5], variants of kernel Fisher discriminant analysis (KFDA) and reported that the KFDA variants consistently out-perform all other methods. The KFDA variants they investigated were Local Fisher Discriminant Analysis (LFDA) and Marginal Fisher Discriminant Analysis (MFA).

Chen et al. [25] attempt to learn a metric in the polynomial feature map exploiting the relationship between Mahalanobis metric and the polynomial features. Ahmed et al. [26] propose a deep learning model which learns the features as well as the metric jointly. Liao et al. [4] propose XQDA exploiting the benefits of Fisher discriminant analysis and KISSME to learn a metric. However like FDA and KISSME, XQDA's modeling power is limited because of the Gaussian assumptions on the data. In another work Liao et al. [9] apply accelerated proximal gradient descent (APGD) to a Mahalanobis metric under a logistic loss similar to the loss of PCCA [5]. The application of APGD makes this model converge fast compared to existing batch metric learning algorithms but still it suffers from scalability issues because all the pairs are required to take one gradient step and the projection step on to the PSD cone is computationally expensive.

None of the above mentioned techniques explicitly models the objective that we are looking for in person re-identification, that is to optimize a weighted rank measure. We show that modeling this in the metric learning objective improves the performance. We address scalability through stochastic gradient descent (SGD) and our model naturally eliminates the need for asymmetric sample weighting as we use triplet based loss function.

There is an extensive body of work on optimizing ranking measures such as AUC, precision at k, F_1 score, etc. Most of this work focuses on learning a linear decision boundary in the original input space, or in the feature space for ranking a list of items based on the chosen performance measure. A well known such model is the structural SVM [27]. In contrast here we are interested in ranking pairs of items by learning a metric. A related work by McFee *et al.* [28] studies metric learning with different rank measures in the structural SVM framework. Wu *et al.* [29] used this framework to do person re-identification by optimizing the mean reciprocal rank criterion. Outside the direct scope of metric learning from a single feature representation, Paisitkriangkrai *et al.* [30] developed an ensemble algorithm to combine different base metrics in the structural SVM framework which leads to excellent performance for re-identification. Such an approach is complementary to ours, as combining heterogeneous feature representations requires a separate additional level of normalization or the combination with a voting scheme.

We use the WARP loss from WSABIE [12], proposed for large-scale image annotation problem, that is a multi-label classification problem. WSABIE learns a low dimensional joint embedding for both images and annotations by optimizing the WARP loss. This work reports excellent empirical results in terms of accuracy, computational efficiency, and memory footprint.

The work that is closely related to us is FRML [10] where they learn a Mahalanobis metric by optimizing the WARP loss function with SGD. However there are some key differences with our approach. FRML is a linear method using L_2 or LMNN regularizer, and relies on an expensive projection step in the SGD. Beside, this projection requires to keep a record of all the gradients in the minibatch, which results in high memory footprint. The rationale for the projection step is to accelerate the SGD because directly optimizing low rank matrix may result in rank deficient matrix and thus result in non-isolated minimizers which might generalize poorly to unseen samples. We propose a computationally cheap solution to this problem by using a regularizer which approximately enforces the rank of the learned matrix efficiently.

Table 1. Notation

N	Number of training samples
D	Dimension of training samples
Q	Number of classes
$(x_i, y_i) \in \mathbb{R}^D \times \{1, \ldots, Q\}$	i-th training sample
$\mathbb{1}_{\text{condition}}$	is equal to 1 if the condition is true, 0 otherwise
S	the pairs of indices of samples of same class
$\mathcal{T}_y$	the indices of samples not of class y
$\mathcal{F}_W$	distance function under the linear map W
$rank_{i,j}(\mathcal{F}_W)$	for i and j of same label, no. of miss-labeled points closer to i than j is
$\mathcal{L}(W)$	the loss we minimize
$L(r)$	rank weighting function

3   Weighted Approximate Rank Component Analysis

This section presents our metric learning algorithm, Weighted Approximate Rank Component Analysis (WARCA). Table 1 summarizes some important notations that we use in the paper.

Let us consider a training set of data point/label pairs:

$$(x_n, y_n) \in \mathbb{R}^D \times \{1, \ldots, Q\}, \ n = 1, \ldots, N. \tag{2}$$

and let $\mathcal{S}$ be the set of pairs of indices of samples of same labels:

$$\mathcal{S} = \left\{ (i,j) \in \{1, \ldots, N\}^2, \ y_i = y_j \right\}. \tag{3}$$

For each label y we define the set $\mathcal{T}_y$ of indices of samples of a class different from y:

$$\mathcal{T}_y = \{k \in \{1, \ldots, N\}, \ y_k \neq y\}. \tag{4}$$

In particular, to each $(i,j) \in \mathcal{S}$ corresponds a set $\mathcal{T}_{y_i}$.

Let W be a linear transformation that maps the data points from $\mathbb{R}^D$ to $\mathbb{R}^{D'}$, with $D' \leq D$. For the ease of notation, we do not distinguish between matrices and their corresponding linear mappings. The distance function under the linear map W is given by:

$$\mathcal{F}_W(x_i, x_j) = \|W(x_i - x_j)\|_2. \tag{5}$$

3.1   Problem Formulation

For a pair of points (i,j) of same label $y_i = y_j$, we define a ranking error function:

$$\forall (i,j) \in \mathcal{S}, \ err(\mathcal{F}_W, i, j) = L\left(rank_{i,j}\left(\mathcal{F}_W\right)\right) \tag{6}$$

where:

$$rank_{i,j}\left(\mathcal{F}_W\right) = \sum_{k \in \mathcal{T}_{y_i}} \mathbb{1}_{\mathcal{F}_W(x_i, x_k) \leq \mathcal{F}_W(x_i, x_j)}. \tag{7}$$

is the number of samples x_k of different labels which are closer to x_i than x_j is.

Formulating our objective that way, following closely the formalism of [12], shows how training a multi-class predictor shares similarities with our metric-learning problem. The former aims at avoiding, for any given sample to have incorrect classes with responses higher than the correct one, while the latter aims at avoiding, for any pair of samples (x_i, x_j) of the same label, to have samples x_k of other classes in between them.

Minimizing directly the rank treats all the rank positions equally, and usually in many problems including person re-identification we are interested in maximizing the correct match within the top few rank positions. This can be achieved by a weighting function $L(\cdot)$ which penalizes more a drop in the rank at the top positions than at the bottom positions. In particular we use the rank weighting function proposed by Usunier et al. [11], of the form:

$$L(r) = \sum_{s=1}^{r} \alpha_s, \ \alpha_1 \geq \alpha_2 \geq \ldots \geq 0. \tag{8}$$

For example, using $\alpha_1 = \alpha_2 = \ldots = \alpha_m$ will treat all rank positions equally, and using higher values of αs in top few rank positions will weight top rank positions more. We use the harmonic weighting, which has such a profile and was also used in [12] as it yielded state-of-the-art results on their application.

Finally, we would like to solve the following optimization problem:

$$\underset{W}{\operatorname{argmin}} \ \frac{1}{|\mathcal{S}|} \sum_{(i,j) \in \mathcal{S}} L\left(rank_{i,j}\left(\mathcal{F}_W\right)\right). \tag{9}$$

3.2   Approximate OrthoNormal (AON) Regularizer

The optimization problem of Eq. 9 may lead to severe over-fitting on small and medium scale datasets. Regularizing penalty terms are central in re-identification for that reason.

The standard way of regularizing a low-rank metric learning objective function is by using a L_2 penalty, such as the Frobenius norm [10]. However, such a regularizer tends to push toward rank-deficient linear mappings, which we observe in practice (see Sect. 4.4, and in particular Fig. 2a).

Lim *et al.* [10] in their FRML algorithm, addresses this problem by using a Riemannian manifold update step in their SGD algorithm, which is computationally expensive and induces a high memory footprint. We propose an alternative approach that maintains the rank of the matrix by pushing toward orthonormal matrices. This is achieved by using as a penalty term the L_2 divergence of WW^T from the identity matrix $\mathbf{I}$:

$$\|WW^T - \mathbf{I}\|^2. \tag{10}$$

This orthonormal regularizer can also be seen as a strategy to mimic the behavior of approaches such as PCA or FDA, which ensure that the learned linear transformation is orthonormal. For such methods, this property emerges from the strong Gaussian prior over the data, which is beneficial on small data-sets but degrades performance on large ones where it leads to under-fitting. Controlling the orthonormality of the learned mapping through a regularizer weighted by a meta-parameter λ allows us to adapt it on each data-set individually through cross-validation.

Finally, with this regularizer the optimization problem of Eq. 9 becomes:

$$\underset{W}{\operatorname{argmin}} \ \frac{\lambda}{2} \|WW^T - \mathbf{I}\|^2 + \frac{1}{|\mathcal{S}|} \sum_{(i,j) \in \mathcal{S}} L\left(rank_{i,j}\left(\mathcal{F}_W\right)\right). \tag{11}$$

3.3   Max-Margin Reformulation

The metric learning problem in Eq. 11 aims at minimizing the 0-1 loss, which is a difficult optimization problem. Applying the reasoning behind the WARP loss to make it tractable, we upper-bound this loss with the hinge one with margin γ. This is equivalent to minimizing the following loss function:

$$\mathcal{L}(W) = \frac{\lambda}{2}\|WW^T - \mathbf{I}\|^2 + \frac{1}{|\mathcal{S}|} \sum_{(i,j)\in\mathcal{S}} \sum_{k\in\mathcal{T}_{y_i}} L(rank_{i,j}^{\gamma}(\mathcal{F}_W)) \frac{|\gamma + \xi_{ijk}|_+}{rank_{i,j}^{\gamma}(\mathcal{F}_W)}, \quad (12)$$

where:

$$\xi_{ijk} = \mathcal{F}_W(x_i, x_j) - \mathcal{F}_W(x_i, x_k) \quad (13)$$

and $rank_{i,j}^{\gamma}(\mathcal{F}_W)$ is the margin penalized rank:

$$rank_{i,j}^{\gamma}(\mathcal{F}_W) = \sum_{k\in\mathcal{T}_{y_i}} \mathbb{1}_{\gamma+\xi_{ijk}>0}. \quad (14)$$

The loss function in Eq. 12 is the WARP loss [10–12]. It was shown by Weston *et al.* [12] that the WARP loss can be efficiently solved by using stochastic gradient descent and we follow the same approach:

1. Sample (i,j) uniformly at random from $\mathcal{S}$.
2. For the selected (i,j) uniformly sample k in $\{k \in \mathcal{T}_{y_i} : \gamma + \xi_{ijk} > 0\}$, *i.e.* from the set of incorrect matches scored higher than the correct match x_j.

The sampled triplet (i,j,k) has a contribution of $L(rank_{i,j}^{\gamma}(\mathcal{F}_W))|\gamma + \xi_{ijk}|_+$ because the probability of drawing a k in step 2 from the violating set is $\frac{1}{rank_{i,j}^{\gamma}(\mathcal{F}_W)}$.

We use the above sampling procedure to solve WARCA efficiently using minibatch stochastic gradient descent (SGD). We use Adam SGD algorithm [31], which is found to converge faster empirically compared to vanilla SGD.

3.4   Kernelization

Most commonly used features in person re-identification are histogram-based such as LBP, SIFT BOW, RGB histograms to name a few. The most natural distance measure for histogram-based features is the χ^2 distance. Most of the standard metric learning methods work on the Euclidean distance with PCCA being a notable exception. To plug any arbitrary metric which is suitable for the features, such as χ^2, one has to resort to explicit feature maps that approximate the χ^2 metric. However, it blows up the dimension and the computational cost. Another way to deal with this problem is to do metric learning in the kernel space, which is the approach we follow.

Let W be spanned by the samples:

$$W = AX^T = A \begin{pmatrix} x_1^T \\ \dots \\ x_N^T \end{pmatrix}. \quad (15)$$

which leads to:

$$\mathcal{F}_A(x_i, x_j) = \|AX^T(x_i - x_j)\|_2, \quad (16)$$
$$= \|A(\kappa_i - \kappa_j)\|_2. \quad (17)$$

Where κ_i is the ith column of the kernel matrix $K = X^T X$. Then the loss function in Eq. 12 becomes:

$$\mathcal{L}(A) = \frac{\lambda}{2}\|AKA^T - \mathbf{I}\|^2 + \frac{1}{|\mathcal{S}|} \sum_{(i,j)\in\mathcal{S}} \sum_{k\in\mathcal{T}_{y_i}} L(rank_{i,j}^\gamma(\mathcal{F}_A)) \frac{|\gamma + \xi_{ijk}|_+}{rank_{i,j}^\gamma(\mathcal{F}_A)}, \quad (18)$$

with:

$$\xi_{ijk} = \mathcal{F}_A(x_i, x_j) - \mathcal{F}_A(x_i, x_k). \quad (19)$$

Apart from being able to do non-linear metric learning, kernelized WARCA can be solved efficiently again by using stochastic sub-gradient descent. If we use the inverse of the kernel matrix as the pre-conditioner of the stochastic sub-gradient, the computation of the update equation, as well the parameter update, can be carried out efficiently. Mignon $et\ al.$ [5] used the same technique to solve their PCCA, and showed that it converges faster than vanilla gradient descent. We use the same technique to derive an efficient update rule for our kernelized WARCA. A stochastic sub-gradient of Eq. 18 with the sampling procedure described in the previous section is given as:

$$\nabla\mathcal{L}(A) \quad = \quad 2\lambda(AKA^T - \mathbf{I})AK + 2L(rank_{i,j}^\gamma(\mathcal{F}_A))A\mathbb{1}_{\gamma+\xi_{ijk}>0}\mathcal{G}_{ijk}, \quad (20)$$

where:

$$\mathcal{G}_{ijk} = \frac{(\kappa_i - \kappa_j)(\kappa_i - \kappa_j)^T}{d_{ij}} - \frac{(\kappa_i - \kappa_k)(\kappa_i - \kappa_k)^T}{d_{ik}}, \quad (21)$$

and:

$$d_{ij} = \mathcal{F}_A(x_i, x_j), \quad d_{ik} = \mathcal{F}_A(x_i, x_k). \quad (22)$$

Multiplying the right hand side of Eq. 20 by K^{-1}:

$$\nabla\mathcal{L}(A)K^{-1} \quad = \quad 2\lambda(AKA^T - \mathbf{I})A + 2L(rank_{i,j}^\gamma(\mathcal{F}_A))AK\mathbb{1}_{\gamma+\xi_{ijk}>0}\mathcal{E}_{ijk}. \quad (23)$$

with:

$$\mathcal{E}_{ijk} = K^{-1}\mathcal{G}_{ijk}K^{-1} = \frac{(e_i-e_j)(e_i-e_j)^T}{d_{ij}} - \frac{(e_i-e_k)(e_i-e_k)^T}{d_{ik}}. \quad (24)$$

where e_l is the lth column of the canonical basis that is the vector whose l^{th} component is one and all others are zero. In the preconditioned stochastic sub-gradient descent we use the updates of the form:

$$A_{t+1} = (\mathbf{I} - 2\lambda\eta(A_t K A_t^T - \mathbf{I}))A_t - 2\eta L(rank_{i,j}^\gamma(\mathcal{F}_A))A_t K\mathbb{1}_{\gamma+\xi_{ijk}>0}\mathcal{E}_{ijk}. \quad (25)$$

Please note that $\mathcal{E}_{ijk}$ is a very sparse matrix with only nine non-zero entries. This makes the update extremely fast. Preconditioning also enjoys faster convergence rates since it exploits second order information through the preconditioning operator, here the inverse of the kernel matrix [13].

4   Experiments

We evaluate our proposed algorithm on nine standard person re-identification datasets. We first describe the datasets and baseline algorithms and then present our results. Our code will be made publicly available.

4.1   Datasets and Baselines

The largest dataset we experimented with is the **Market-1501** dataset [14] which is composed of 32,668 images of 1,501 persons captured from 6 different view points. It uses DPM [32] detected bounding boxes as annotations. **CUHK03** dataset [15] consists of 13,164 images of 1,360 persons and it has both DPM detected and manually annotated bounding boxes. We use the manually annotated bounding boxes here. **OpeReid** dataset [16] consists of 7,413 images of 200 persons. **CUHK01** dataset [17] is composed of 3,884 images of 971 persons, with two pairs of images per person, each pair taken from a different viewpoint. **VIPeR** [18] dataset has 1,264 images of 632 person, with 2 images per person. The **PRID450s** dataset [21] consists of 450 image pairs recorded from two different static surveillance cameras. The **CAVIAR** dataset [3] consists of 1,220 images of 72 individuals from 2 cameras in a shopping mall. The **3DPeS** dataset [19] has 1,011 images of 192 individuals, with 2 to 6 images per person. The dataset is captured from 8 outdoor cameras with horizontal but significantly different viewpoints. Finally the **iLIDS** dataset [20] contains 476 images and 119 persons, with 2 to 8 images per individual.

We compare our method against the current state-of-the-art baselines MLAPG, rPCCA, SVMML, FRML, LFDA and KISSME. A brief overview of these methods is given in Sect. 2. rPCCA, MLAPG, SVMML, FRML are iterative methods whereas LFDA and KISSME are spectral methods on the second order statistics of the data. Since WARCA, rPCCA and LFDA are kernel methods we used both the χ^2 kernel and the linear kernel with them to benchmark the performance. Marginal Fisher discriminant analysis (MFA) is proven to give similar result as that of LFDA so we do not use them as the baseline.

We did not compare against other ranking based metric learning methods such as LORETA [33], OASIS [34] and MLR [28] because all of them are linear methods. In fact we derived a kernelized OASIS but the results were not as good as ours or rPCCA. We also do not compare against LMNN and ITML because many researchers have evaluated them before [5–7] and found out that they do not perform as well as other methods considered here.

4.2   Technical Details

For the Market-1501 dataset we used the experimental protocol and features described in [14]. We used their baseline code and features. As Market-1501 is quite large for kernel methods we do not evaluate them. We also do not evaluate the linear methods such as Linear rPCCA and SVMML because their optimization algorithms were found to be very slow.

Table 2. Table showing the rank 1, rank 5 and AUC performance measure of our method WARCA against other state-of-the-art methods. Bold fields indicate best performing methods. The dashes indicate computation that could not be run in a realistic setting on Market-1501

(a) Rank 1 accuracy

Dataset	WARCA-χ^2	WARCA-L	rPCCA-χ^2	rPCCA-L	MLAPG	FRML	SVMML	LFDA-χ^2	LFDA-L	KISSME
Market-1501	–	**45.16±0.00**	–	–	–	–	–	–	34.65±0.00	42.81±0.00
CUHK03	**78.38±2.44**	62.12±2.07	76.74±2.06	59.22±2.65	44.90±1.57	53.87±2.31	47.89±2.59	69.94±2.21	46.02±1.55	47.88±1.80
CUHK01	**58.34±1.26**	39.30±0.76	48.55±1.12	34.73±1.06	22.92±0.94	33.58±0.69	27.96±0.86	54.25±1.04	33.74±0.73	35.74±0.95
OpeReid	**57.65±1.60**	43.74±1.34	52.89±1.78	43.66±1.45	40.63±1.31	42.27±1.35	30.63±1.51	53.58±1.65	42.84±1.18	41.76±1.36
VIPeR	**37.47±1.70**	20.86±1.04	22.25±1.91	15.91±1.16	19.49±2.26	18.52±0.78	23.28±1.53	36.77±2.10	20.22±1.85	20.89±1.22
PRID450s	**24.58±1.75**	10.33±1.20	16.35±1.30	8.34±1.25	2.13±0.59	7.05±1.60	13.08±1.63	24.31±1.44	3.24±0.95	15.24±1.56
CAVIAR	**43.44±1.82**	39.35±1.98	37.56±2.17	27.26±2.15	36.74±1.96	35.40±2.67	26.82±1.64	41.29±2.25	37.72±2.08	31.99±2.17
3DPeS	**51.89±2.27**	43.57±2.18	46.42±2.25	33.12±1.58	41.17±2.26	39.03±1.85	29.94±2.10	51.44±1.40	43.24±2.57	37.55±1.80
iLIDS	**36.61±2.40**	31.77±2.77	26.57±2.60	23.07±3.07	31.13±1.57	25.68±2.25	21.32±2.89	36.23±1.89	32.70±3.12	28.29±3.59

(b) Rank 5 accuracy

Dataset	WARCA-χ^2	WARCA-L	rPCCA-χ^2	rPCCA-L	MLAPG	FRML	SVMML	LFDA-χ^2	LFDA-L	KISSME
Market-1501	–	**68.23±0.00**	–	–	–	–	–	–	52.76±0.00	62.74±0.00
CUHK03	**94.55±1.31**	86.03±1.62	94.50±1.29	84.52±1.41	71.80±1.52	80.36±1.22	79.97±2.08	90.15±1.27	65.41±1.66	69.29±2.35
CUHK01	**79.76±0.69**	61.84±0.98	73.29±1.32	56.67±1.20	48.48±1.49	55.27±0.83	53.11±0.78	74.60±1.00	49.73±0.91	53.34±0.69
OpeReid	**80.43±1.71**	67.39±1.02	77.95±1.82	67.68±1.25	61.45±1.61	66.08±1.30	60.32±1.31	75.34±1.76	59.70±1.37	61.74±1.55
VIPeR	**70.78±2.43**	50.29±1.61	53.82±2.32	42.71±2.02	46.49±2.23	46.15±1.62	55.28±1.99	69.30±2.23	45.25±1.90	47.73±2.28
PRID450s	**55.52±2.23**	31.73±3.08	43.82±2.18	26.89±2.21	11.29±1.66	24.16±3.04	38.38±1.77	54.58±2.06	12.55±1.41	37.22±1.81
CAVIAR	**74.06±3.13**	68.06±2.44	70.62±2.26	57.44±2.48	65.83±2.73	66.24±3.08	61.53±3.64	69.12±3.02	61.60±2.94	61.17±3.21
3DPeS	**75.64±2.80**	68.26±1.91	73.54±2.26	58.34±2.31	65.06±1.89	65.20±2.15	59.52±2.62	75.36±1.91	65.64±1.91	60.22±2.05
iLIDS	**66.09±2.31**	59.27±3.12	57.07±2.93	51.55±3.59	57.31±3.12	53.42±2.17	51.45±4.30	65.20±2.68	59.66±2.51	54.08±3.63

(c) AUC score

Dataset	WARCA-χ^2	WARCA-L	rPCCA-χ^2	rPCCA-L	MLAPG	FRML	SVMML	LFDA-χ^2	LFDA-L	KISSME
Market-1501	–	**75.41±0.00**	–	–	–	–	–	–	60.53±0.00	70.02±0.00
CUHK03	**93.94±0.76**	89.67±0.80	93.92±0.81	89.17±0.69	82.30±1.01	86.64±0.65	86.64±1.07	91.66±0.68	74.23±1.51	77.68±1.83
CUHK01	**84.99±0.65**	71.88±0.67	81.00±0.88	67.56±0.93	62.84±1.51	66.39±0.76	65.73±1.07	80.84±0.80	58.92±1.08	62.36±0.95
OpeReid	**86.47±1.08**	77.17±0.94	85.25±1.16	77.42±1.01	72.34±1.11	76.51±0.88	73.88±1.04	82.67±1.30	68.96±1.53	71.33±1.14
VIPeR	**81.87±1.07**	67.00±1.11	71.30±1.50	62.40±1.43	64.71±1.15	64.19±1.39	71.04±1.63	81.34±1.21	62.67±1.35	64.74±1.20
PRID450s	**72.13±1.49**	50.07±2.25	63.10±2.16	46.19±1.89	30.81±2.19	42.97±2.84	59.54±1.25	71.55±1.70	28.18±1.22	53.83±1.86
CAVIAR	**85.76±1.48**	83.01±1.44	84.41±1.28	76.57±1.29	81.58±1.50	81.88±1.85	79.38±2.19	81.94±2.32	76.76±1.69	78.85±1.54
3DPeS	**83.89±1.53**	78.07±1.57	82.84±1.44	72.27±1.96	75.98±1.28	76.89±1.44	73.38±1.70	83.49±0.95	75.87±1.49	72.22±1.31
iLIDS	**79.04±1.60**	73.42±1.96	74.10±2.04	69.60±2.44	72.45±1.99	71.26±1.55	70.25±2.09	78.98±1.43	74.26±2.02	70.33±2.90

All other evaluations where carried out in the single-shot experiment setting [2] and our experimental settings are very similar to the one adopted by Xiong *et al.* [8]. Except for Market-1501, we randomly divided all the other datasets into two subsets such that there are p individuals in the test set. We created 10 such random splits. In each partition one image of each person was randomly selected as a probe image, and the rest of the images were used as gallery images and this was repeated 10 times. The position of the correct match was processed to generate the CMC curve. We followed the standard train-validation-test splits for all the other datasets and P was chosen to be 100, 119, 486, 316, 225, 36, 95 and 60 for CUHK03, OpeReid, CUHK01, VIPeR, PRID450s, CAVIAR, 3DPeS and iLIDS respectively.

We used the same set of features for all the datasets except for the Market-1501 and all the features are essentially histogram based. First all the datasets were re-scaled to 128×48 resolution and then 16 bin color histograms on RGB, YUV, and HSV channels, as well as texture histogram based on Local Binary Patterns (LBP) were extracted on 6 non-overlapping horizontal patches. All the histograms are normalized per patch to have unit L_1 norm and concatenated into a single vector of dimension 2,580 [5,8].

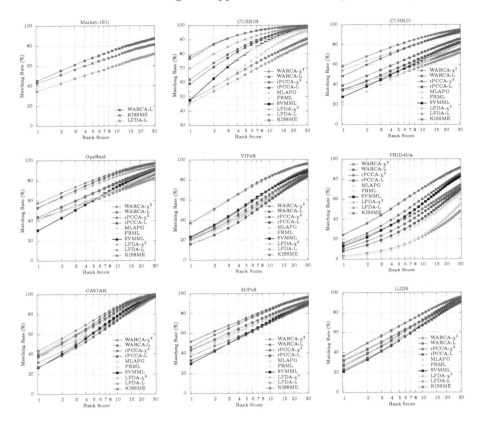

Fig. 1. CMC curves comparing WARCA against state-of-the-art methods on nine re-identification datasets

The source codes for LFDA, KISSME and SVMML are available from their respective authors website, and we used those to reproduce the baseline results [8]. The code for PCCA is not released publicly. A version from Xiong *et al.* [8] is available publicly but the memory footprint of that implementation is very high making it impossible to use with large datasets (e.g. it requires 17 GB of RAM to run on the CAVIAR dataset). Therefore to reproduce the results in [8] we wrote our own implementation, which uses 30 times less memory and can scale to much larger datasets. We also ran sanity checks to make sure that it behaves the same as that of the baseline code. All the implementations were done in Matlab with mex functions for the acceleration of the critical components.

In order to fairly evaluate the algorithms, we set the dimensionality of the projected space to be same for WARCA, rPCCA and LFDA. For the Market-1501 dataset the dimensionality used is 200 and for VIPeR it is 100 and all the other datasets it is 40. We choose the regularization parameter and the learning rate through cross-validation across the data splits using grid search in

$(\lambda, \eta) \in \{10^{-8}, \ldots, 1\} \times \{10^{-3}, \ldots, 1\}$. Margin γ is fixed to 1. Since the size of the parameter matrix scales in $O(D^2)$ for SVMML and KISSME we first reduced the dimension of the original features using PCA keeping 95% of the original variance and then applied these algorithms. In our tables and figures WARCA$-\chi^2$, WARCA-L, rPCCA$-\chi^2$, rPCCA-L, LFDA$-\chi^2$ and LFDA-L denote WARCA with χ^2 kernel, WARCA with linear kernel, rPCCA with χ^2 kernel, rPCCA with linear kernel, and LFDA with χ^2 kernel, LFDA with linear kernel respectively.

For all experiments with WARCA we used harmonic weighting for the rank weighting function of Eq. 8. We also tried uniform weighting which gave poor results compared to the harmonic weighting. For all the datasets we used a mini-batch size of 512 in the SGD algorithm and we ran the SGD for 2000 iterations (A parameter update using the mini-batch is considered as 1 iteration).

Tables 2a and b summarize respectively the rank-1 and rank-5 performance of all the methods, and Table 2c summarizes the Area Under the Curve (AUC) performance score. Figure 1 reports the CMC curves comparing WARCA against the baselines on all the nine datasets. The circle and the star markers denote linear and kernel methods respectively.

WARCA improves over all other methods on all the datasets. On VIPeR, 3DPeS, PRID450s and iLIDS datasets LFDA come very close to the performance of WARCA. The reason for this is that these datasets are too small and consequently simple methods such as LFDA which exploits strong prior assumptions on the data distribution work nearly as well as WARCA.

4.3   Comparison Against State-of-the-Art

We also compare against the state-of-the-art results reported using recent algorithms such as MLAPG on LOMO features [9], MLPOLY [25] and IDEEP [26] on VIPeR, CUHK01 and CUHK03 datasets. The reason for not including these comparisons in the main results is because apart from MLAPG the code for other methods is not available, or the features are different which makes a fair comparison difficult. Our goal is to evaluate experimentally that, given a set of features, which is the best off-the-shelf metric learning algorithm for re-identification.

Table 3. Comparison of WARCA against state-of-the-art results for person re-identification

Dataset	WARCA(Ours)				MLAPG [9]				MLPOLY [25]				IDEEP [26]			
	rank=1	rank=5	rank=10	rank=20	rank=1	rank=5	rank=10	rank=20	rank=1	rank=5	rank=10	rank=20	rank=1	rank=5	rank=10	rank=20
VIPeR	40.22	68.16	80.70	91.14	40.73	69.94	82.34	92.37	36.80	70.40	83.70	91.70	34.81	63.61	75.63	84.49
CUHK01	65.64	85.34	90.48	95.04	64.24	85.41	90.84	94.92	-	-	-	-	47.53	71.60	80.25	87.45
CUHK03	78.38	94.5	97.52	99.11	57.96	87.09	94.74	98.00	-	-	-	-	54.74	86.50	94.02	97.02

In this set of experiments we used the state-of-the-art LOMO features [4] with WARCA for VIPeR and CUHK01 datasets. The results are summarized in the Table 3. We improve the rank-1 performance by 21 % on CUHK03 by 1.40 % on CUHK01 dataset.

4.4   Analysis of the AON Regularizer

Here we present an empirical analysis of the AON regularizer against the standard Frobenius norm regularizer. We used the VIPeR dataset with LOMO features for the experiments shown in the first row of Fig. 2. With very low regularization strength AON and Frobenius behave the same. As the regularization strength increases, Frobenius results in rank deficient mappings (Fig. 2a), which is less discriminant and perform poorly on the test set (Fig. 2b). The AON regularizer on the contrary pushes towards orthonormal mappings, and results in an embedding well conditioned, which generalizes well to the test set. It is also worth noting that training with the AON regularizer is robust over a wide range of the regularization parameter, which is not the case the Frobenius norm. Finally, the AON regularizer was found to be very robust to the choice of the SGD step size η (Fig. 2c) which is a crucial parameter in large-scale learning. A similar behavior was observed by Lim et al. [10] with their orthonormal Riemannian gradient update step in the SGD but it is computationally expensive and not trivial to use with modern SGD algorithms such as Adam [31], and Nesterov's momentum [35].

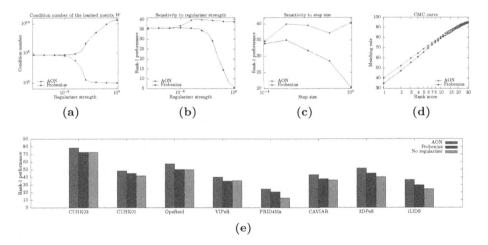

Fig. 2. Comparison of the Approximate OrthoNormal (AON) regularizer we use in our algorithm to the standard Frobenius norm (L_2) regularizer. Graph (a) shows the condition number (ratio between the two extreme eigenvalues of the learned mapping) vs. the weight λ of the regularization term. As expected, the AON regularizer pushes this value to one, as it eventually forces the learning to chose an orthonormal transformation, while the Frobenius regularizer eventually kills the smallest eigenvalues to zero, making the ratio extremely large. Graph (b) shows the Rank-1 performance vs. the regularizer weight λ, graph (c) the Rank-1 performance vs. the SGD step size η, graph (d) CMC curve with the two regularizers and finally graph (e) shows the Rank-1 performance on different datasets

4.5   Analysis of the Training Time

Figure 3 illustrates how the performance in test of WARCA and rPCCA increase as a function of training time on 3 datasets. We implemented both the algorithms entirely in C++ to have a fair comparison of running times. In this set of experiments we used 730 test identities for CUHK03 dataset to have a quick evaluation. Experiments with other datasets follow the same protocol described above. Please note that we do not include spectral methods in this plot because the solutions are found analytically. Linear spectral methods are very fast for low dimensional problems but the training time scales quadratically in the data dimension. In case of kernel spectral methods the training time scales quadratically in the number of data points. We also do not include iterative methods MLAPG and SVMML because they proved to be very slow and not giving good performance.

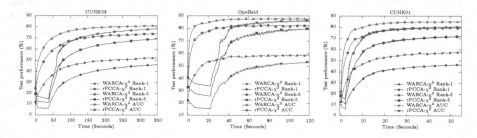

Fig. 3. WARCA performs significantly better than the state-of-the-art rPCCA on large datasets for a given training time budget

5   Conclusion

We have proposed a simple and scalable approach to metric learning that combines a new and simple regularizer to a proxy for a weighted sum of the precision at different ranks. The later can be used for any weighting of the precision-at-k metrics. Experimental results show that it outperforms state-of-the-art methods on standard person re-identification datasets, and that contrary to most of the current state-of-the-art methods, it allows for large-scale learning.

Acknowledgements. This work was supported by the Swiss National Science Foundation under grant number, CRSII2-147693 WILDTRACK.

References

1. Weinberger, K.Q., Saul, L.K.: Distance metric learning for large margin nearest neighbor classification. J. Mach. Learn. Res. **10**, 207–244 (2009)
2. Gong, S., Cristani, M., Yan, S., Loy, C.C. (eds.): Person Re-identification. Advances in Computer Vision and Pattern Recognition. Springer, London (2014)

3. Cheng, D.S., Cristani, M., Stoppa, M., Bazzani, L., Murino, V.: Custom pictorial structures for re-identification. In: British Machine Vision Conference (BMVC) (2011)

4. Liao, S., Hu, Y., Zhu, X., Li, S.Z.: Person re-identification by local maximal occurrence representation and metric learning. In: Proceedings of the IEEE Conference on Computer Vision and Pattern Recognition, pp. 2197–2206 (2015)

5. Mignon, A., Jurie, F.: PCCA: a new approach for distance learning from sparse pairwise constraints. In: 2012 IEEE Conference on Computer Vision and Pattern Recognition (CVPR), pp. 2666–2672. IEEE (2012)

6. Köstinger, M., Hirzer, M., Wohlhart, P., Roth, P.M., Bischof, H.: Large scale metric learning from equivalence constraints. In: 2012 IEEE Conference on Computer Vision and Pattern Recognition (CVPR), pp. 2288–2295. IEEE (2012)

7. Li, Z., Chang, S., Liang, F., Huang, T.S., Cao, L., Smith, J.R.: Learning locally-adaptive decision functions for person verification. In: 2013 IEEE Conference on Computer Vision and Pattern Recognition (CVPR), pp. 3610–3617. IEEE (2013)

8. Xiong, F., Gou, M., Camps, O., Sznaier, M.: Person re-identification using kernel-based metric learning methods. In: Fleet, D., Pajdla, T., Schiele, B., Tuytelaars, T. (eds.) ECCV 2014. LNCS, vol. 8695, pp. 1–16. Springer, Heidelberg (2014). doi:10.1007/978-3-319-10584-0_1

9. Liao, S., Li, S.Z.: Efficient PSD constrained asymmetric metric learning for person re-identification. In: Proceedings of the IEEE International Conference on Computer Vision, pp. 3685–3693 (2015)

10. Lim, D., Lanckriet, G.: Efficient learning of mahalanobis metrics for ranking. In: Proceedings of the 31st International Conference on Machine Learning (ICML 2014), pp. 1980–1988 (2014)

11. Usunier, N., Buffoni, D., Gallinari, P.: Ranking with ordered weighted pairwise classification. In: Proceedings of the 26th Annual International Conference on Machine Learning (ICML 2009), pp. 1057–1064. ACM (2009)

12. Weston, J., Bengio, S., Usunier, N.: WSABIE: scaling up to large vocabulary image annotation. IJCAI 11, 2764–2770 (2011)

13. Chapelle, O.: Training a support vector machine in the primal. Neural Comput. 19(5), 1155–1178 (2007)

14. Zheng, L., Shen, L., Tian, L., Wang, S., Wang, J., Bu, J., Tian, Q.: Scalable person re-identification: a benchmark. In: IEEE International Conference on Computer Vision (2015)

15. Li, W., Zhao, R., Xiao, T., Wang, X.: DeepReID: deep filter pairing neural network for person re-identification. In: 2014 IEEE Conference on Computer Vision and Pattern Recognition (CVPR), pp. 152–159. IEEE (2014)

16. Liao, S., Mo, Z., Hu, Y., Li, S.Z.: Open-set person re-identification. arXiv preprint arXiv:1408.0872 (2014)

17. Li, W., Zhao, R., Wang, X.: Human reidentification with transferred metric learning. In: Lee, K.M., Matsushita, Y., Rehg, J.M., Hu, Z. (eds.) ACCV 2012. LNCS, vol. 7724, pp. 31–44. Springer, Heidelberg (2013). doi:10.1007/978-3-642-37331-2_3

18. Gray, D., Tao, H.: Viewpoint invariant pedestrian recognition with an ensemble of localized features. In: Forsyth, D., Torr, P., Zisserman, A. (eds.) ECCV 2008. LNCS, vol. 5302, pp. 262–275. Springer, Heidelberg (2008). doi:10.1007/978-3-540-88682-2_21

19. Baltieri, D., Vezzani, R., Cucchiara, R.: 3DPeS: 3D people dataset for surveillance and forensics. In: Proceedings of the 2011 Joint ACM Workshop on Human Gesture and Behavior Understanding, pp. 59–64. ACM (2011)

20. Zheng, W.S., Gong, S., Xiang, T.: Associating groups of people. In: British Machine Vision Conference (BMVC), vol. 2, p. 6 (2009)
21. Roth, P.M., Hirzer, M., Köstinger, M., Beleznai, C., Bischof, H.: Mahalanobis distance learning for person re-identification. In: Gong, S., Cristani, M., Yan, S., Loy, C.C. (eds.) Person Re-identification, pp. 247–267. Springer, London (2014)
22. Yang, L., Jin, R.: Distance metric learning: a comprehensive survey, vol. 2. Michigan State Universiy (2006)
23. Xing, E.P., Jordan, M.I., Russell, S., Ng, A.Y.: Distance metric learning with application to clustering with side-information. In: Advances in Neural Information Processing Systems, pp. 505–512 (2002)
24. Davis, J.V., Kulis, B., Jain, P., Sra, S., Dhillon, I.S.: Information-theoretic metric learning. In: Proceedings of the 24th Annual International Conference on Machine Learning (ICML 2007), pp. 209–216. ACM (2007)
25. Chen, D., Yuan, Z., Hua, G., Zheng, N., Wang, J.: Similarity learning on an explicit polynomial kernel feature map for person re-identification. In: Proceedings of the IEEE Conference on Computer Vision and Pattern Recognition, pp. 1565–1573 (2015)
26. Ahmed, E., Jones, M., Marks, T.K.: An improved deep learning architecture for person re-identification. In: Proceedings of the IEEE Conference on Computer Vision and Pattern Recognition, pp. 3908–3916 (2015)
27. Tsochantaridis, I., Hofmann, T., Joachims, T., Altun, Y.: Support vector machine learning for interdependent and structured output spaces. In: Proceedings of the 21st Annual International Conference on Machine Learning (ICML 2004), p. 104. ACM (2004)
28. McFee, B., Lanckriet, G.R.: Metric learning to rank. In: Proceedings of the 27th Annual International Conference on Machine Learning (ICML 2010), pp. 775–782 (2010)
29. Wu, Y., Mukunoki, M., Funatomi, T., Minoh, M., Lao, S.: Optimizing mean reciprocal rank for person re-identification. In: 2011 8th IEEE International Conference on Advanced Video and Signal-Based Surveillance (AVSS), pp. 408–413. IEEE (2011)
30. Paisitkriangkrai, S., Shen, C., van den Hengel, A.: Learning to rank in person re-identification with metric ensembles. In: IEEE Conference on Computer Vision and Pattern Recognition (CVPR) (2015)
31. Kingma, D., Ba, J.: Adam: A method for stochastic optimization. arXiv preprint arXiv:1412.6980 (2014)
32. Felzenszwalb, P., McAllester, D., Ramanan, D.: A discriminatively trained, multi-scale, deformable part model. In: 2008 IEEE Conference on Computer Vision and Pattern Recognition, CVPR 2008, pp. 1–8. IEEE (2008)
33. Shalit, U., Weinshall, D., Chechik, G.: Online learning in the embedded manifold of low-rank matrices. J. Mach. Learn. Res. 13(1), 429–458 (2012)
34. Chechik, G., Sharma, V., Shalit, U., Bengio, S.: Large scale online learning of image similarity through ranking. J. Mach. Learn. Res. 11, 1109–1135 (2010)
35. Sutskever, I.: Training recurrent neural networks. Ph.D. thesis, University of Toronto (2013)

Author Index

Printed in the United States
By Bookmasters